ECONOMICS EXPLAINED

SECOND EDITION

Peter Maunder

*Senior Lecturer in Economics,
Loughborough University;
Joint Chief Examiner for A Level, University of London,
School Examinations Board*

Danny Myers

*Senior Lecturer in Economics,
Faculty of the Built Environment
University of the West of England, Bristol
Assistant Examiner for A Level,
Associated Examination Board*

Nancy Wall

Co-director, Nuffield Economics and Business Project

Roger LeRoy Miller

*Centre for Policy Studies and Department of Economics
Clemson University*

Collins Educational
An imprint of HarperCollins*Publishers*

Published by Collins Educational
77–85 Fulham Palace Road
Hammersmith, London W6 8JB
An imprint of HarperCollins *Publishers*

First published 1987
Second edition 1991, Reprinted 1992, 1993

ISBN 0 00 3274810

PREFACE TO THE SECOND EDITION

This new edition of *Economics Explained* appears nearly four years after the first adaptation of Roger LeRoy Miller's highly successful US textbook *Economics Today* for the UK market. The first edition has been very well received and we have now revised those sections where inevitably the passage of time has left the coverage somewhat dated. In particular we have replaced many of the case studies with new material, and the sections dealing with current economic policy have all been rewritten. Many of the questions have been replaced with examples drawn from recent past papers.

It has been our pleasure to work with many of the original team who helped us in preparing the first edition. Su Spencer has again prepared new drafts from each author into well-presented typescripts. Conan Nicholas has scrutinized the manuscript very carefully and the layout of the material has been in the best possible hands of John Fitzmaurice.

Our whole task has been coordinated throughout by Kate Harris and we owe a particular debt to her. We also wish to acknowledge the input of Graham Bradbury and others at HarperCollins in the production of this new edition.

Peter Maunder
Danny Myers
Nancy Wall

Contents

Part B
Introductory Macroeconomics

Part C
Product Markets

Part D
Factor Markets

Part E
Economic Policies and Issues

Acknowledgements

The authors and publishers wish to acknowledge the following photograph sources: BBC Hulton Picture Library pp. 25, 36, 229; London School of Economics p.201.

The authors and publishers are grateful to the following Boards for permission to reproduce Multiple Choice Questions (MCQs) and Related Essay Questions (REQs) from past examination papers.

The Associated Examining Board
Chapter 1: MCQs 3 (June 86), 5 (June 87), 6 (June 82); REQs 1 (June 82), 2 (Nov. 82) 3 (June 85). Chapter 2: MCQ 1 (Nov. 83). Chapter 4: REQ 3 (Nov. 83). Chapter 5: MCQs (June 84). Chapter 7: MCQ 4 (June 87); REQ 3 (June 85). Chapter 8: MCQ 1 (June 87); REQs 1 (June 82), 2 (June 83). Chapter 9: MCQs 1 (June 89), 2 (June 89), 5 (June 87), 6 (June 89). Chapter 10: MCQs 3 (June 84), 4 (June 84), 5 (June 84), 7 (June 86), REQs 1 (June 84), 5 (Nov. 84). Chapter 11: MCQs 2 (June 89), 3 (June 84); REQ 4 (June 89). Chapter 12: MCQ 5 (June 87); REQ 4 (June 86). Chapter 13: MCQ 2 (June 83). Chapter 15: MCQ 1 (June 85); Chapter 17: MCQ 5 (Nov. 82). Chapter 18: MCQ 5 (June 88); REQs 1 (Nov. 82), 2 (June 88), 6 (June 86). Chapter 19: MCQ 7 (Nov. 85). Chapter 20: MCQ 11 (June 88). Chapter 21: MCQ 9 (June 86). Chapter 23: MCQ 4 (June 88). Chapter 24: Exercise 1 (June 87); MCQ 4 (June 88); REQ 12 (June 88). Chapter 25: MCQs 1 (Nov. 82), 2 (June 87), 6 (June 85). Chapter 27: MCQs 1 (June 85), 3 (June 82); REQ 4 (June 84). Chapter 28: MCQs 1 (June 85), 5 (Nov 86); REQs 1 (June 82), 3 (June 88). Chapter 29: MCQ 5 (Nov. 86); REQ 1 (June 82). Chapter 30: MCQ 6 (89); REQ 7 (84). Chapter 31: MCQs 4 (89), 5 (89), 6 (89); REQ 1 (89). Chapter 32: MCQs 2 (88), 3 (89), 4 (89); REQ 5 (88). Chapter 33: MCQs 1 (June 86), 2 (June 86); REQ 1 (June 82). Chapter 34: MCQs 2 (Nov. 86), 4 (Nov. 85), 5 (Nov. 85); REQ 2 (Nov. 85).

Joint Matriculation Board
Chapter 4: REQs 5 (June 84), 7 (June 86). Chapter 7: REQ 5 (June 80). Chapter 9: MCQs 3 (June 89), 4 (June 89); REQ 4 (June 86). Chapter 10: REQ 6 (June 81). Chapter 11: REQ 5 (June 83). Chapter 15: REQ 2 (June 87). Chapter 17: REQ 7 (June 87). Chapter 20: REQ 8 (June 88). Chapter 21: REQ 4 (June 85). Chapter 25: REQs 4 (June 85), 6 (June 86), 7 (June 86), 8 (June 87). Chapter 27: REQs 5 (June 86), 6 (June 88). Chapter 28: REQ 5 (June 88). Chapter 30: REQ 4 (June 87). Chapter 31: REQ 2 (June 88). Chapter 32: REQ 1 (June 88). Chapter 33: REQs 4 (June 81), 5 (June 82 – Special Paper), 9 (June 87). Chapter 34: REQs 7 (June 84); 8 (June 87). Chapter 35: REQ 3 (June 87).

Northern Ireland GCE Examination Board
Chapter 7: REQ 1 (June 84). Chapter 34: REQ 6 (June 84).

Northern Ireland Schools Examinations Council
Chapter 2: REQ 3 (June 87). Chapter 24: REQs 1 (June 87), 6 (June 88).

Oxford and Cambridge Schools Examination Board
Chapter 2: REQs 1 (July 84), 2 (June 88). Chapter 4: REQ 1 (June 89). Chapter 13: REQs 1 (June 88), 5 (June 83). Chapter 9: REQ 2 (July 80). Chapter 20: REQ 6 (June 88). Chapter 21: REQ 2 (June 88). Chapter 22: REQ 1 (June 87). Chapter 23: REQs 2 (June 88), 3 (June 87). Chapter 24: REQs 2 (June 89), 5 (June 89), 7 (June 88). Chapter 28: REQ 6 (June 89). Chapter 30: REQ 3 (June 85). Chapter 32: REQ 2 (June 87). Chapter 34: REQ 3 (July 82).

Scottish Examining Board
Chapter 29: Exercise 3 (May 87). Chapter 35: REQs 2 (May 88), 5 (May 87).

Southern Universities Joint Board
Chapter 12: REQ 1 (June 79). Chapter 20: REQ 4 (June 85).

Universities of Cambridge Local Examinations Syndicate
Chapter 5: REQ 1 (June 1989). Chapter 10: REQ 4 (June 85). Chapter 11: REQ 1 (Nov. 84). Chapter 12: REQ 2 (Nov. 84). Chapter 17: REQs 2 (June 85), 4 (June 85). Chapter 20: REQs 4 (June 88), 5 (June 87), 8 (June 88). Chapter 21: REQ 3 (June 85). Chapter 22: REQ 3 (June 87). Chapter 23: REQ 1 (Nov. 87). Chapter 24: REQ 4 (June 89). Chapter 25: REQ 2 (June 85). Chapter 27: REQ 2 (June 82). Chapter 28: REQ 2 (June 82). Chapter 29: REQ 1 (Nov. 88). Chapter 30: REQ 5 (June 89). Chapter 34: REQ 5 (Nov. 88).

University of London School Examinations Board
Chapter 1: Exercise 1 (June 77); MCQs 2 (Jan. 83), 5 (Jan. 86), 7 (Jan. 88). Chapter 3: REQ 1 (June 81). Chapter 4: REQs 2 (June 87), 4 (June 85 – Special Paper), 6 (June 86 – Special Paper), 8 (June 87), 9 (Jan. 88), 10 (June 88). Chapter 5: MCQs 1 (June 84), 2 (June 84), 3 (Jan. 84), 6 (Jan. 87). Chapter 6: REQ 1 (June 85). Chapter 7: Study 1 (June 89), 2 (June 85); Exercise 1 (June 86); MCQs 1 (Jan. 87), 2 (Jan. 87), 3 (June 86), 5 (June 83), 6 (Jan. 84); REQ 7 (June 88). Chapter 8: MCQs 2 (Jan. 89), 3 (Jan. 84), 4 (Jan. 83), 7 (June 89), 8 (June 89); REQs 3 (June 86), 4 (Jan. 86), 5 (June 85 – Special Paper), 6 (Jan. 87), 7 (Jan. 87). Chapter 9: REQ 3 (June 85); Cert .Study 2 (June 87) Q5, Cert Study 3 (June 88) Q4. Chapter 10: MCQs 8 (Jan. 85); 10 (Jan. 85); REQs 2 (June 89), 3 (June 86), 4 (June 85). Chapter 11: MCQs 1 (Jan. 83), 6 (June 88); REQs 2 (Jan. 85), 3 (Jan. 89), 6 (June 85). Chapter 12: MCQs 2 (June 86). Chapter 13: MCQ 5 (Jan. 84); REQ 4 (Jan. 86). Chapter 15: MCQ 3 (June 85). Chapter 16: MCQ 3 (June 86). Chapter 17: MCQs 1 (June 85), 2 (June 85), 3 (June 86); 4 (Jan. 86); REQs 1 (Jan. 85), 6 (1989). Chapter 18: MCQs 1 (Jan. 85), 6 (Jan. 89); REQs 3 (Jan. 85), 4 (Jan. 79). Chapter 19: MCQs 6 (June 86), 8 (June 88). Chapter 20: MCQs 1 (Jan. 86), 2 (June 85), 3 (Jan. 88), 4 (June 88), 5 (Jan. 89), 7 (June 85), 8 (June 83); REQs 1 (June 84), 2 (June 82). Chapter 21: MCQs 1 (Jan. 86), 2 (June 85), 4 (Jan. 87), 5 (Jan. 87), 6 (June 89), 7 (June 85), 8 (June 83); REQs 1 (June 84), 2 (June 82). Chapter 22: MCQs 1 (Jan. 88), 2 (June 89), 3 (June 88), 4 (Jan. 89), 5 (Jan. 89), 6 (Jan. 89); REQ 2 (June 87). Chapter 23: Exercise 2 (June 89); MCQs 1 (June 89), 2 (Jan. 89), 3 (June 89); REQs 4 (June 89), 5 (Jan. 89), 6 (June 88). Chapter 24: Exercise 2 (June 88); MCQs 1 (Jan. 89), 2 (Jan. 89), 3 (Jan. 89), 5 (June 89); REQs 3 (Jan. 88), 11 (Jan. 90). Chapter 25: MCQs 3 (June 81), 4 (June 86), 5 (June 85); REQs 1 (June 90), 3 (June 90). Chapter 26: MCQs 1 (Jan. 86), 2 (June 86), 3 (June 81), 4 (June 86), 5 (June 85); REQs 5 (1989). Chapter 27: MCQs 1 (Jan. 86), 2 (June 86), 3 (June 81), 4 (June 81); REQ 3 (Jan. 85). Chapter 28: MCQ 4 (June 81), REQ 4 (June 88). Chapter 29: Exercise 2 (Jan. 90). Chapter 30: MCQs 1 (Jan. 86), 3 (Jan. 86), REQs 6 (1990). Chapter 31: MCQs 2 (1989), 3 (1989), 1 (Jan. 86), 3 (Jan. 86); REQs 3 (June 83 – Special Paper), 5 (Jan. 90). Chapter 32: MCQ 1 (1988); REQ 6 (1988). Chapter 33: 7 (Jan. 89). Chapter 34: MCQ 1 (Jan. 87); REQs 1 (June 85), 9 (Jan. 89). Chapter 35: Exercise 1 (Jan. 90); REQs 1 (June 87), 4 (June 87).

University of Oxford Delegacy of Local Examinations
Chapter 4: REQ 1 (June 84). Chapter 10: REQs 7 (June 89). Chapter 13: REQs 2 (June 89), 3 (June 84). Chapter 14: REQ 1 (June 86). Chapter 17: REQ 5 (June 1988). Chapter 21: REQ 1 (June 87). Chapter 24: REQs 8 (June 88), 9 (June 88), 10 (June 88). Chapter 26: REQs 1 (June 89), 6 (June 87). Chapter 27: REQ 1 (June 85). Chapter 29: REQ 3 (June 88). Chapter 32: REQs 4 (June 88), 7 (June 89). Chapter 33: REQs 6 (June 89), 8 (June 88).

Welsh Joint Education Committee
Chapter 1: Exercise 3 (June 89). Chapter 7: REQ 6 (June 88). Chapter 17: REQ 3 (June 85). Chapter 20: REQ 5 (June 87). Chapter 22: REQ 4 (June 88). Chapter 23: REQ 7 (June 88). Chapter 25: REQ 5 (June 85). Chapter 26: REQs 2 (June 89), 3 (June 88).

The following questions are reproduced by permission from A. Baker (ed.), Multiple Choice Questions in Advanced Level Economics, Cambridge University Press, 1981: Chapter 1: MCQ 1. Chapter 3: MCQ 1. Chapter 8: MCQs 5, 6. Chapter 10: MCQs 1, 2. Chapter 13: MCQ 6. Chapter 15: MCQs 2, 4. Chapter 16: MCQs 1, 2. Chapter 19: MCQs 1, 2, 3, 4, 5. Chapter 22: MCQs 2, 3. Chapter 29: MCQ 3.

MCQs 3 and 4 in Chapter 18 are reproduced by permission from Maile and Jenkins, A Textbook of Questions and Answers in A Level Economics, Bell and Hyman, 1983. MCQs 1-5 in Chapter 6 are reproduced by permission from T. Wilson, Test Bank to R Miller, Economics Today, 3rd edn, Harper and Row, 1979.

Every effort has been made to contact copyright holders, but in some cases this has been impossible. The publishers would be grateful to hear from anyone who has not yet given us permission to reproduce material.

How to Use this Book Effectively

This book has been designed around six key features to help you build towards exam success. These are outlined below as a guide to guarantee your effective use of this established and distinctive book.

Firstly, each chapter has brief summaries every few pages to help you identify and remember the main concepts that have been surveyed. These are numbered and called **Key Points**.

These key points are also picked up in the second feature of the book, namely **Key Points to Review**. Each chapter begins with a list of these, to encourage you to refer back to the relevant sections already covered. This highlights the integrated nature of the subject matter.

Thirdly, each chapter is also preceded by a list of **Questions for Preview**. These are designed to encourage you to scan forwards through the chapter to get the flavour of it before embarking on a serious study of that chapter's content. These questions could be used as homework or for discussion.

Fourthly, each time a new technical term or phrase is introduced it is identified in bold type. These and other essential terms are then gathered at the back with brief definitions to form a **Dictionary of Economics** to help you come to terms with your new subject and its peculiar language. Some important concepts require detailed definitions in the text. These are identified in green type.

Next, as you move towards the close of each chapter you will notice two further important features. Chapters conclude with some **Case Study** material. These have been carefully selected to help you to apply what you have learnt; to appreciate economics in action; to become familiar with the related literature (therefore note the sources) and also to prepare you for any stimulus type question that you may experience in your exam in a year or two from now.

Finally, each chapter closes with an **Exam Preparation** section. This contains a battery of questions selected from past papers of the UK exam boards. The number of multiple-choice and essay questions that follow each chapter will vary according to the nature of the topic. Examiners have a tendency to explore different topics via different exam strategies. Consequently some chapters have half a dozen multiple-choice questions and others half a dozen essays. There are also constructive practical exercises which we have included to set your thoughts on the right tracks.

The Answers to the multiple-choice questions and practical exercises are gathered at the back. Essay questions are a 'free response' (as some exam boards describe them) so it would unfortunately be impossible to standardize the answers.

You may find you want, or need, to have access to additional up-to-date information on the UK economy. For this purpose you will find the *Collins Economics Brief Series* helpful. Each book in the series focuses on an important empirical area of the A level syllabus. These Briefs are regularly updated to take account of the latest developments, trends and statistics.

You may find your Economics course hard work at times but we are sure that once you have mastered the principles you will find it a fascinating and enjoyable subject.

Part A

Introductory Microeconomics

1 What Economics is all about

Questions for Preview

1 The United Kingdom is one of the most developed nations in the world. Do its inhabitants face the problem of scarcity?

2 Fresh air and clean water can often be consumed in the United Kingdom free of charge. Does this mean that these 'goods' are free or costless to society?

3 Why does the scarcity problem force people to consider opportunity costs?

4 What is the difference between positive and normative economics?

5 What does the phrase an 'Economic Model' mean?

6 How can a graph be regarded as portraying an Economic Model?

The reason that we face economic problems individually and as a nation is that none of us can have all that we want – we live in a world of scarcity. Economic problems face you, me, your friends, the nation, and the world. It is impossible to avoid these problems personally or as a nation. They involve choosing a career and where to live, what price to pay for a house, how to solve the problems of unemployment and rising prices, plus thousands of other decisions.

This book is about economics and economic problem-solving. Consequently, it relates to you as an individual who must decide how to earn income and how to spend it. It relates to you as an individual who must vote for political candidates who decide how much of your income to tax and how to spend tax revenues. Finally, it relates to your country and how much it buys from and sells to the rest of the world. We study economics because the economic system that we have helps to determine our political, social, religious, and personal environment.

Scarcity – the Bane of Civilization

Would you like to be able to study more and also to have more time to relax and drink coffee with your friends? Would you like to own an expensive home computer as well as enjoy a skiing holiday? Would you like to have more clothes but not give up any spending on records and video tapes? Your answer to all of these questions is highly likely to be a resounding, *yes*. But why can't we have more of everything? It is because individually and collectively we face a constraint called scarcity. **Scarcity** is the most basic concept in all of economics. Scarcity means that we do not and cannot have enough income or wealth to satisfy our every desire. Note that we are not referring to any *measurable* standard of wants; rather, we are referring to the way people want, need, or desire relative to what is available at any moment. If the world were such that everyone could have as much of everything as desired, without sacrifice, then economics would no longer exist as a meaningful intellectual or practical pursuit. But there is scarcity. And we have not just recently moved into the 'age of scarcity', as many people seem to believe. Scarcity has always been with us and will be with us as long as we cannot get everything we want at a zero or free price, that is one where there is no charge.

It is important to distinguish scarcity from poverty. Scarcity occurs among poor people and among rich people. It applies to everyone because there will never be enough of everything that people want to go round at a zero or free price. And, because there are limits on people's time, even the richest person on earth will still have unfulfilled wants.

Resources (or Factors of Production) are Scarce

The scarcity concept just described arises from the existence of scarce resources. Resources can be defined as the inputs used in the production of those things that we desire. When resources are productive, they are typically called *factors of production*. Indeed, some economists use the terms resources and factors of production synonymously. The total quantity, or stock, of resources that an economy has determines what that economy can produce. Every economy has, in varying degrees of quantities, vast amounts of different resources, or factors of production. Factors of production can be classified in many ways. One common scheme of classification includes natural, human, and manufactured resources.

NATURAL RESOURCES = LAND AND MINERAL DEPOSITS

Basically, **land** with its inherent mineral deposits is the natural resource we think of most often. Some land can grow very large amounts of crops without any addition of fertilizer; other land is incapable of growing anything in its natural state. Today, some economists contend that natural resources are often the least important factors of production in an economy. They believe that what is more important is the transformation of existing natural resources into what is truly usable by man, and that transformation requires the other types of resources – labour and capital. This point becomes understandable if we do not simply think of land as the only natural resource. The resources of the oceans and polar ice-caps are attracting increasing interest. Thus natural resources include water, climate, and vegetation in a global context.

HUMAN RESOURCES = LABOUR

In order to produce the things we desire, a human resource must be used. That human resource consists of the productive contributions of **labour** made by individuals who work – for example, coal-miners, ballet-dancers, and professional soccer players. The contribution of labour to the production process can be increased. Whenever potential labourers obtain schooling and training and whenever actual labourers obtain new skills, labour's contribution to productive output will increase. When there is such an improvement to human resources we say that human capital has been improved.

MANUFACTURED RESOURCES = CAPITAL

When labour is applied to land to grow wheat, for example, something else is used. Usually it is a plough or a tractor. That is to say, land and labour are combined with manufactured resources in order to produce the things that we desire. These manufactured resources are called **capital,** which consists of machines, buildings, and tools. Additionally, capital consists of improvements to natural resources, such as irrigation channels.

ANOTHER HUMAN RESOURCE = ENTREPRENEURSHIP

There is, in effect, a fourth type of input used in production. It is a special type of human resource; it consists of entrepreneurial ability, or **entrepreneurship.** Entrepreneurship is associated with the founding of new businesses, or the introduction of new products and new techniques. But it means more than that: it encompasses taking risks (possibly losing large sums of wealth on new ventures), inventing new methods of making existing goods, and generally experimenting with any type of new thinking that could lead to a monetary benefit.

Without entrepreneurship, virtually no business organizations could operate. Clearly, entrepreneurship as a human resource is scarce: not everyone is willing to take risks or has the ability to undertake successful business decision-making.

We see the classification of resources in Figure 1.1.

Figure 1.1

Resource Classification. We can arbitrarily classify resources or factors of production into those that are natural, human, and manufactured. We have denoted specific names within those three classifications.

Natural resources	*Human resources*	*Manufactured resources*
Land	Labour and entrepreneurship	Capital

Scarce resources produce what are called **economic goods** – the subject of our study throughout this book.

ECONOMIC GOODS

Any good (or service) produced from scarce resources is also scarce and is called an economic good. Because economic goods are scarce, we constantly face decisions about how best to use them. After all, the desired quantity of an economic good, by definition, exceeds the amount that is directly available from nature at a zero or free price.

However, not all goods are economic; some are free.

FREE GOODS

There are, of course, some things that are free. We call them **free goods,** as opposed to economic goods. Not many are left. Economics textbooks used to call air a free good, but that is really no longer true, because in many of the world's cities pollution makes air unpleasant to breathe. In many mountain areas, clean air is still a free good (once you are there); you can have as much as you want at a zero or free price, and so can anybody else who bothers to hike up to where you are. There is no scarcity involved. Who is interested in free goods, then? Certainly not most economists. Perhaps physicists, hydrologists, biologists, and chemists are interested in free air and water, but the economist steps in only when the problem of scarcity arises and people become concerned about how to use the scarce resource. We have seen throughout our history that as population and production increase, many 'free' goods become 'economic' goods, such as land for mining, water and air for industrial uses, and water for hydroelectric power. To the population of native American Indians, tobacco leaves were a free good before the time of Sir Walter Raleigh. The Indians could have all that they wanted. Later, however, tobacco leaves became (and remain) an economic good.

Choice

Scarcity forces us to choose. You have to choose whether to carry on at school or go to work. If you take a job then you have given up taking unemployment pay. You have to choose between going out or studying. Government policy-makers have to choose between using more resources in the production of military goods or using more resources in the production of, say, educational services. In fact, the concept of choice forms the basis of our formal definition of **economics:**

Economics is the social science studying human behaviour, and, in particular, the way in which individuals and societies choose among the alternative uses of scarce resources to satisfy wants.

As we see throughout our study of economics, the choices we make affect not only how we live today, but how we will live in the future. Moreover, the choices that we can make are constrained not only by scarcity, but also by political, legal, traditional, and moral forces. In other words, there are numerous non-economic forces that determine and mould our decision-making processes. In this text, however, we will concentrate on how economic forces affect our choices. We are not, though, denying that the others are important too. (Now read Key Points 1.1.)

The Methodology of Economics

In this introductory chapter we begin to explain what economics is all about. Therefore apart from identifying the central concepts we also need to consider the methods employed by economists – as these too help to specify the nature of our subject.

Is Economics a Science?

Economics is a social science that makes use of the same kinds of methods as other sciences, such as biology, physics, and chemistry. Like these other sciences, economics uses models, or theories. Economic models and theories are simplified representations of the real world that we use to help us to understand, explain, and predict economic phenomena in the real world.

For many centuries, most people thought that the world was flat. Using this model, they predicted that if one sailed to the edge of the world, one would fall off into space. Columbus, however, applied a new model. His model, or theory, postulated that the world was round. He predicted that one could sail round the world without falling off an edge, because there were no edges. He tested his model, or theory, by sailing and sailing and sailing. He did not fall off any edges, and thereby refuted the flat-earth model empirically.

Economic models, or theories, are no different from those presented in other sciences. They may take on various forms such as verbal statements, numerical tables, graphs, mathematical equations. For the most part, the models presented in this text consist of verbal

Key Points 1.1

- **Scarcity exists because we cannot have all that we want from nature without sacrifice.**
- **We use scarce resources, such as land, labour, capital, and entrepreneurship, to produce economic goods.**
- **Economic goods are those that are desired but are not directly obtainable from nature to the extent demanded or desired.**
- **Scarcity requires us to choose, and economics is the study of how we make those choices.**

statements and graphs. Indeed the development of an understanding of graphic analysis is a common aim of most introductory economics courses. Consequently we next review some graphic techniques and note some matters that you should be aware of in their use.

Reading and Working with Graphs

'A picture is worth a thousand words . . .' And so is a graph! It is often easier to communicate an idea by using a picture than by using a lengthy description. A graph performs much the same function as a picture. A graph is a visual representation of the relationship between two or more variables. In this section, we shall stick to just two variables – an **independent variable**, which can change in value freely, and a **dependent variable,** which changes in value according to changes in the value of the independent variable.

Before we present the 'picture', that is, a graph, let us return to the 'thousand words', that is, a table. A table is a 'list' of values showing, the relationship between two variables. Any table can be converted into a graph, which is a visual representation of that list.

Graphs Represent Relationships

Two variables can be related in different ways, some simple, others more complex, for example, a person's weight and height are often related. If we measured the height and weight of thousands of people, we would surely find that taller people tend to weigh more than shorter people. That is, we would discover that there is a **direct relationship** between height and weight. By direct relationship we simply mean that an *increase* in one variable is usually associated with an *increase* in the related variable. This can easily be seen in panel (a) of Figure 1.2.

Let us look at another simple way two variables can be related: much evidence indicates that as price rises for a specific commodity, the amount purchased decreases – there is an **inverse relationship** between the variable's 'price per unit' and 'quantity purchased'. A table listing the data for this relationship would indicate that for higher and higher prices, smaller and smaller quantities would be purchased. We see this relationship in panel (b) of Figure 1.2.

Now for a slightly complicated relationship between two variables: beginning with the average person's first job, earnings increase each year up to a certain age, then beyond that age, earnings decline each year. This is not a surprising economic research finding. Most people are more energetic and productive in the early and middle years of life. In this example, the two variables – earnings and age – would yield a more complex pattern. At earlier ages, these variables are directly related – earnings increase as age increases – and at later ages these variables are inversely related – earnings decline as age increases. We have also implied the concept of *maximum* – that is, there is an age at which annual earnings are at a maximum over the lifetime of annual earnings. We see all this in panel (c) of Figure 1.2

Note that an inverse relationship between two variables shows up on a graph as a line or curve that slopes downwards, that is, from left to right. (You may as well get used to the idea that economists call a straight line on a graph, a curve, even though it may not 'curve' at all. Much of economists' data turns out to be curves, so they refer to everything represented graphically as curves, even straight lines.)

Figure 1.2
Relationships between variables

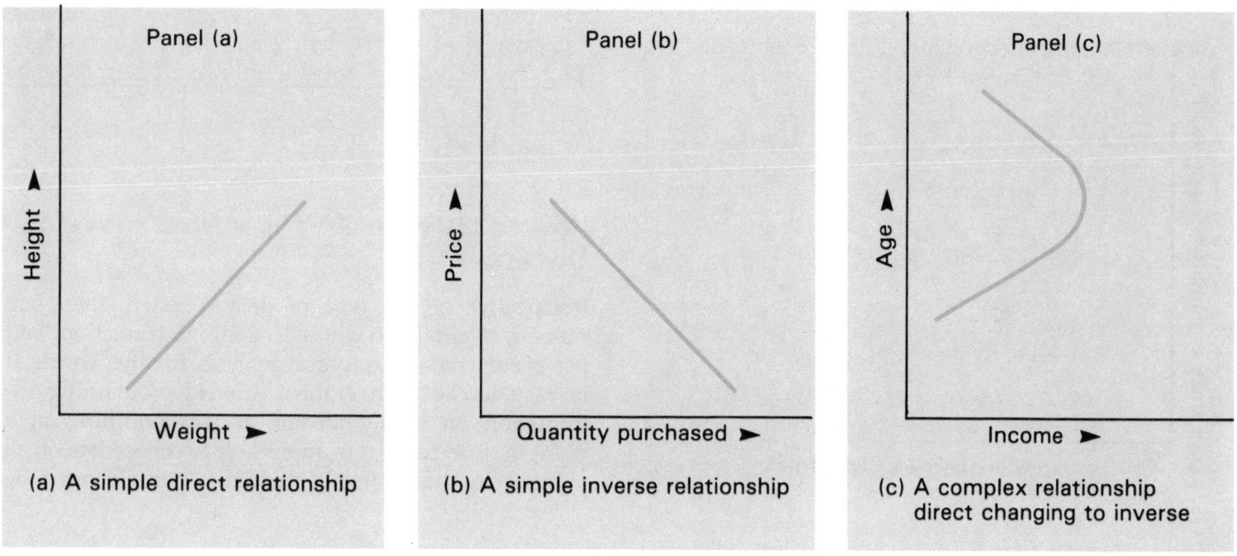

(a) A simple direct relationship

(b) A simple inverse relationship

(c) A complex relationship direct changing to inverse

Constructing Graphs in the Real World

Throughout much of this text, most of the graphs shown will be hypothetical in nature. But economists do quite often examine actual (empirical) relationships between the two economic variables in order to confirm theories about how the world works. (Actually, one never confirms a theory; one simply attempts to reject it by submitting it to real-world evidence.) Consequently, economists gather one of two types of real-world data: **time-series data** and **cross-section data.** Time-series data involve obtaining information on the value of economic variables over time. For example, an economist might collect information on average family income and average family expenditures each year over a 25-year period. These data can then be plotted on a graph to show the relationship, over time, of family income and family expenditures. Alternatively, cross-section data could be gathered at a point in time. Different families with different incomes and their resulting expenditure levels would be used as the observations. A similar graph would show the relationship between family income and family expenditures at a point in time.

Scatter Diagrams

Of course, the economists who make these real-world measurements about economic variables do not usually get nice, neat curves like the ones we draw in our hypothetical examples. Rather, economists typically obtain observations that are scattered 'all over the place', and from these they try to derive trends. To illustrate, say that an economist has collected data on family income and expenditure, as above. Using these data, the economist has plotted the observations on a graph, shown in Figure 1.3. Such a graph is known as a **scatter diagram,** for obvious reasons. Looking at this graph, it is easy to see that a pattern exists. While the relationship is not perfect, it does appear that when income rises, expenditures rise; and when income falls, expenditures fall. There are techniques that can be used to 'fit' a curve which best summarizes all the points in the scatter diagram. Such a curve would be analogous to the nice, neat lines of the hypothetical graphs we have shown so far and the ones we will show throughout the text. It would not perfectly describe the *actual relationship between the two economic variables* (here, family income and expenditure), but it can come close. Of course, when economists fit lines to scatter diagrams, they have to report how well the lines fit, and there are statistics that do just that.

Now consider the scatter diagram in Figure 1.4. Can a line be fitted to best describe these observations? No. Any line would do just as well as any other, which means that no line will do. When an economist gets results such as these, he or she reports that 'no relationship appears to exist'.

Figure 1.3
A Scatter Diagram of Observations on Family Income and Family Expenditures

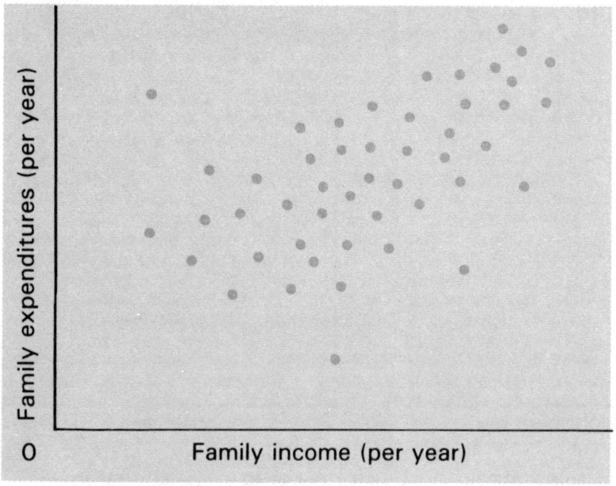

Figure 1.4
A Random Scatter Pattern

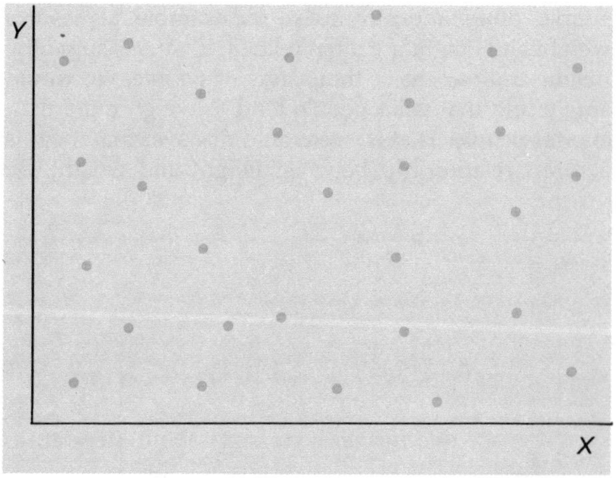

How to Lie with Graphs — What to Watch Out For

Irrespective of the type of data collected, there are numerous pitfalls in the collection, interpretation, and use of such data in graphical analysis. In other words, it is easy to 'lie with graphs'. Consider obtaining information on family income and expenditures at a point in time. Since it is impossible to collect data on all families in the United Kingdom, a sample must be taken. What if the sample is unrepresentative? Then the resulting plotted graphical relationship between family income and expenditures may be quite wrong. Also, the collection of the data could be done improperly – numbers transcribed incorrectly, some families left out, and so on. That means that the researcher must constantly be on the look-out for improper measurement before he or she 'believes' in the resulting plotted graphical relationship.

Consider the time-series example just discussed. What if the time-series data on average family income and expenditure starts during the Great Depression of the 1930s and includes the years 1939–45? The resulting plotted relationship may not be indicative of the average relationship during peacetime and when the UK was not suffering from a serious fall in the state of business activity. The choice of years covered, therefore, can seriously bias a plotted graphical relationship.

Taking Note of the Origin

One aspect of the presentation of data in graphic form deserves a particular comment. It is the way in which a particular change can be given prominence by showing only part of the total values of the relevant variable. Consider the data in Figures 1.5 and 1.6.

Note that the vertical axis in both cases does not begin at the origin or what one can call the baseline. As a result the reduced scale portrays rather dramatic changes both in the numbers of cars imported into the UK and also the quantity of crude oil exported by the UK during 1989. Whilst the fact that there were changes is not in question the graphs do rather exaggerate the *magnitude* of the changes. Thus data as in these figures have to be considered very carefully before an over-hasty interpretation is made. You should look carefully at the vertical scale in any graph to see if the data begins at zero. Has the origin or baseline been shown? If not, is the portrayal of the data in any sense misleading? (See Key Points 1.2.)

Monetary and Real Values

We will make two further comments about the nature of the data used by economists. One is that in the real world we often need to know what difference it makes to those figures which are affected by rising prices. If the price of cassette tapes rises rapidly some people may not buy as many tapes as they would have done had the price remained more stable. It is thus interesting to establish not only whether there is a rise in the *value* of cassette-tape sales but also any changes in the *volume* of tapes sold. In other words the effect of rising prices may mask the changing situation in terms of the number of tapes now bought. Given that the real world is characterized by rising prices – which we later call inflation – economists often use *price indices* which

Figure 1.5

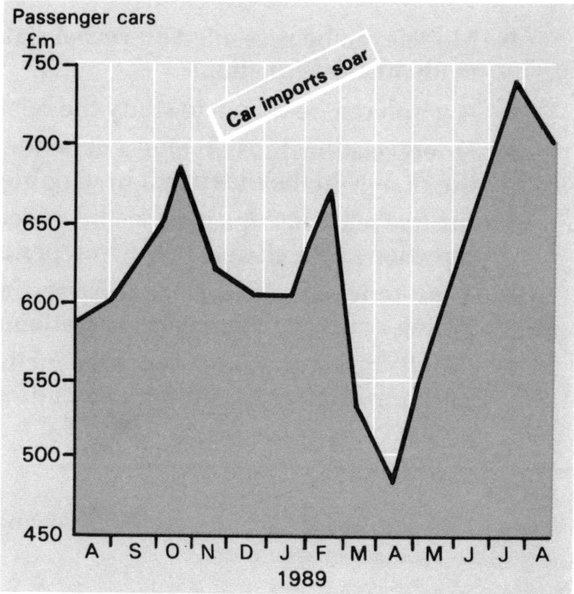

Figure 1.6

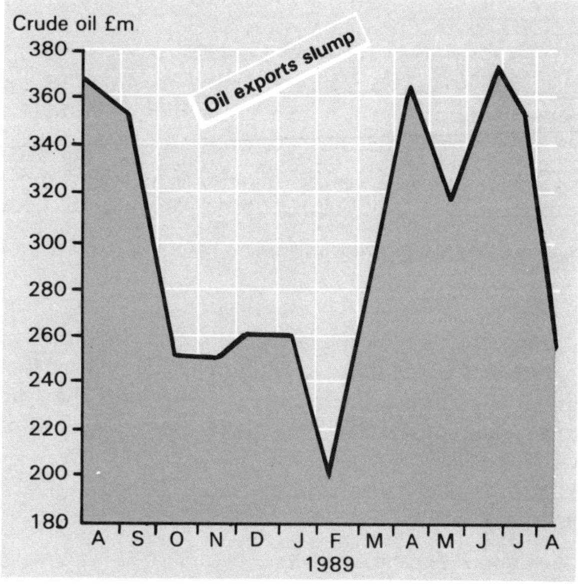

Source: M. Milner and C. Huhne, '£2bn Trade Gap spurs Loan Fears', *Guardian*, 27 Sept. 1989

measure the magnitude of price changes to establish the difference between value and volume measurements. We will discuss indices later in the book and for the moment all we need to concern ourselves with is what use can be made of them. If, for example, we assumed that retail prices had not altered in the UK

Key Points 1.2

- **Models can be presented by verbal statements, numerical tables, graphs, or mathematical equations.**
- **A graph can be drawn to study the relationship between two economic variables.**
- **Direct relationships involve a dependent variable changing in the same direction as the change in the independent variable.**
- **Inverse relationships involve the dependent variable changing in the opposite direction to the change in the independent variable.**
- **Time-series data, as well as cross-section data, can be shown on scatter diagrams. Fitting a curve to these data is an attempt to infer the relationship between them.**
- **Pitfalls to watch out for in graphs include: (a) using improper data; (b) choosing unrepresentative beginning and ending points for time-series data; and (c) the data on the vertical axis may not begin at zero.**

between 1980 and 1988 we can observe the following changes in consumers' expenditure.

Figure 1.7

Consumers' Expenditure in the UK at Constant 1985 Prices

	1980 (£m)	*1988 (£m)*
Household food	30 419	31 911
Cars, motor cycles, and other vehicles	7 623	13 340
Total consumers' expenditure	195 060	257 918

Source: United Kingdom National Accounts 1989, HMSO London.

But now look at the actual situation in terms of consumers' expenditure in Figure 1.8. You will see that these value figures in Figure 1.8 rather blur the way that rising prices had an impact on the quantities purchased.

Figure 1.8

Consumers' Expenditure in the UK at Current Market Prices

	1980 (£m)	*1988 (£m)*
Household food	23 655	36 687
Cars, motor cycles, and other vehicles	6 510	17 437
Total consumers' expenditure	139 016	293 560

Source: United Kingdom National Accounts 1989, HMSO, London.

Household food expenditure increased between 1980 and 1988 but the volume increase was not as significant as the effect of rising prices.

Economists refer to actual values such as those in Figure 1.8 as data in *current prices* or *money terms.* This means the data reflect actual spending, including any rise in prices as compared with previous years. In contrast, Figure 1.7 shows data in *constant prices* or *real terms.* These data 'take out' the impact of rising prices and thus we can observe volume changes and the 'real' scene not disguised by the fact that prices have not been stable. One effective way of identifying trends in data which relate to volume changes is to express the figures in index number form. This is the second comment we will make here about the nature of statistical data. Figure 1.9 shows the spending by households in the UK expressed in index form. What does this reveal? Note the sluggish movement in the volume of food sales between 1976 and 1986. It contrasts with the rapid growth in the purchase of vehicles and in household expenditure abroad. These data show very clearly how different forms of household spending have changed in volume terms.

Models, Graphs, and Realism

We have shown that graphs with their focus on two variables present models that can be used to gain insight into much economic analysis. Right at the outset, however, it must be emphasized that *no* model in any form, in *any* science, and therefore no economic model, is complete in the sense that it captures every detail and interrelationship that exists. Indeed, **a model, by definition, is an abstraction from reality. It should capture only the essential relationships that are sufficient to analyse the particular problem in question.**

It is conceptually impossible to construct a perfectly realistic model. For example, in physics we cannot account for every atom and its position and certainly

Figure 1.9

Household Expenditure in the UK (indices at constant 1985 prices)

	1976	*1981*	*1982*	*1983*	*1984*	*1985*	*1986*	*1987*
Food	96	99	98	100	99	100	103	104
Alcoholic drink	93	95	93	96	98	100	100	103
Tobacco	126	117	108	106	103	100	97	97
Clothing and footwear	68	80	83	88	94	100	107	115
Housing	84	92	93	96	98	100	103	107
Fuel and power	92	96	94	94	93	100	103	102
Household goods and services								
Household durables	82	85	88	95	97	100	106	109
Other	89	90	89	90	94	100	106	113
Transport and communication								
Purchase of vehicles	64	78	80	101	95	100	108	119
Running of vehicles	81	90	93	95	96	100	105	109
Other travel	86	93	90	93	96	100	105	117
Post and telecommunications	61	85	85	91	95	100	108	117
Household expenditure abroad	47	94	94	96	96	100	112	128
Household expenditure	82	90	91	95	97	100	105	111

Source: *Social Trends 19*, 1989, Table 6.2

not for every molecule and subparticle. Not only is such a model impossibly expensive to build, but it would also be impossible to work with. No model of the solar system, for example, could possibly take into account all aspects of the entire solar system. Likewise a graph is simply a model presenting two essential variables in order that specific economic relationships can be studied. (Now read Key Points 1.3.)

Back to Concepts

Unlimited Wants

As pointed out earlier, scarcity exists because there are not enough resources to satisfy our wants. And economics is a science studying how individuals make choices about the use of resources in order to satisfy wants. Does that mean that economists are only interested in how people make choices about what kind of car to buy, how many clothes to purchase, and whether to add a swimming-pool to their house? The answer is certainly, *no*. Of course, wants include material goods, such as houses, cars, stereos, clothes, and computers. But wants also include desires for more love, affection, power, prestige, justice, fairness, equity, charity, friendship, improved health, and peace in the world. Clearly, then, economics is not the study of the 'baser material desires' of men and women. The wants that individuals wish to satisfy are, indeed, unlimited and encompass virtually anything that at least someone believes is 'good' or 'preferred'.

Wants versus Needs

Wants are not the same thing as needs. Indeed, from the economist's point of view, the term 'need' is objectively *un*definable. When someone says, I need some new clothes', there is no way of knowing whether that person is simply stating a wish or a want, or a 'need' in the commonly accepted sense of the word indicating 'absolute necessity'. If the individual making the statement were dying of over-exposure in a

Key Points 1.3

- **Economists make a distinction between current prices (money terms) and constant prices (real terms) to eliminate the problem of rising prices (changing values) over time.**
- **Figures expressed in the form of an index, such as those displayed in Figure 1.9, enable economists to make a careful scrutiny of underlying changes in the economy.**
- **A model is, by its very nature, a simplification of the real world.**

northern country during the winter, we might argue, indeed, that the person *did* need new clothes perhaps, or at least some more warm clothes. Typically, however, the term 'need' is used in a very casual manner in most conversations. What people mean, usually, is that they want or desire something that they do not currently have. That is quite a different statement from one indicating an absolute, life-or-death need for some item. Even when we discuss so-called 'basic' needs – such as food – there is no fixed, absolute minimum. Some individuals in some countries can survive on 50 per cent fewer calories than other individuals 'need' in order to survive in other countries. As it turns out, one person's need may be considered a folly by another person.

Analytically it is necessary to consider the definition of scarcity, carefully; **every individual has competing 'needs' or wants but cannot satisfy all of them given limited resources.** Therefore, a choice must be made. When that choice is made, something that is also desired has to be forgone. In other words, in a world of scarcity, every want that ends up being satisfied results in some other want, or wants, remaining unsatisfied. Also new wants may arise as a result of some wants being satisfied. (See Key Points 1.4.)

Choice and Opportunity Costs

Choosing one thing requires giving up something else. When you sit down to read this book, you are making a choice. You have chosen not to do at least a thousand other things with your time. You could have read another book or you could have watched television. You could have slept, or you could have listened to the cassette player. Thus, the time scarcity that you face requires you to choose between reading this book and doing something that is presumably less valuable. In other words, there is a cost associated with spending time reading these words. Economists call it **opportunity cost.**

Let us assume that of all the other things you could have done instead of reading this book, the thing you most wanted to do, but did not do, was to watch television. If that is the case, then watching television is the opportunity cost of reading this book. **Opportunity cost is defined as the highest valued alternative that had to be sacrificed for the option that was chosen.** Opportunity cost is a powerful concept that allows us to place a value on the resources that are used to produce something.

The Trade-offs Facing You

Whatever you do, you are trading off one use of a resource for one or more alternative uses. The value of these **trade-offs** is represented by the opportunity cost just discussed. We can examine the opportunity cost of reading this book. Let us assume that you have a maximum of 4 hours per week to spend studying just two topics – economics and geography (or whatever other subject is relevant to you). The more you study economics, the higher will be your expected grade; the more you study geography, the higher will be your expected grade in that subject. There is a trade-off, then, between spending one more hour reading this book and spending that hour studying geography. This can be more clearly brought out in a graph that shows the trade-off involved.

Graphical Analysis

In Figure 1.10, we have put the expected grade in geography on the vertical axis and the expected grade in economics on the horizontal axis. In this simplified world, if you spend all your time on economics, you will get a B in the course, but you will fail geography. On the other hand, if you spend all your time on geography you will get a B in that subject and you will fail economics. The trade-off is a special case: one to one. A one-to-one trade-off means that in this case the opportunity cost of receiving one grade higher in economics (for example, improving from a D to a C) is one grade lower in geography (falling from a D to an E in our example).

Key Points 1.4

- **Wants are unlimited; they include all material wants plus all non-material wants, such as love, affection, power, and prestige.**
- **The concept of need is objectively difficult to define for every person; consequently, we simply consider that an individual's wants are unlimited.**
- **Scarcity is a two-sided concept with competing 'needs' or wants on one side set against limited resources on the other.**
- **In a world of scarcity, satisfaction of one want necessarily means the non-satisfaction of one or more other possible wants.**

Figure 1.10

Production Possibilities Curve for Grades in Geography and Economics. On the vertical axis, we measure the expected grade in geography; on the horizontal axis, the expected grade in economics. We assume that there are only 4 hours total time that can be spent per week on studying. If all 4 hours are spent on economics, a B is received in economics and an F in geography. If all 4 hours are spent on geography, a B is received in that subject and an F in economics. There is a one-to-one trade-off. If the student is at point *x*, equal time (2 hours a week) is spent on both courses and equal grades of D will be received. If a higher grade in economics is desired, the student may go to point *y* where 1 hour is spent on geography and 3 hours on economics and receive a C in economics, but an E in geography.

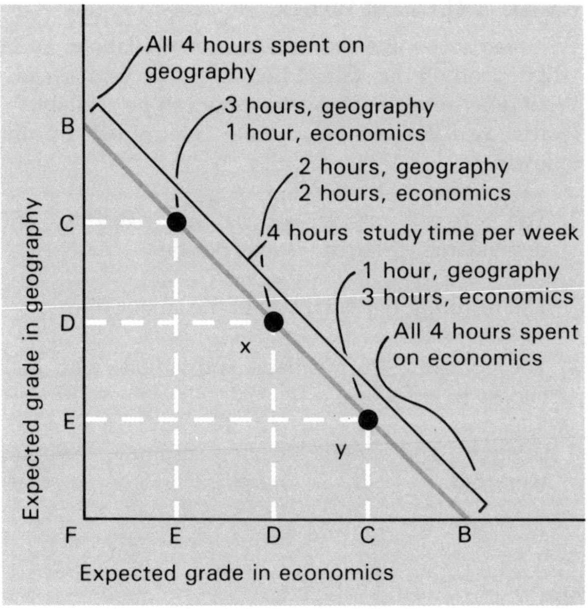

Production Possibilities Curve

The diagram in Figure 1.10 illustrates the relationship between the possible results that can be produced in each of two activities, depending on how much time you choose to put into each activity. Economists call this kind of diagram a **production possibilities curve.***

If you consider that what you are producing is a grade when you study economics and geography then Figure 1.10 can be related to the production possibilities that you face. The line that goes from B on one axis to the B on the other therefore becomes a production possibilities curve. *It is defined as all possible combinations of the maximum amount of any two goods or services that can be produced from a fixed amount of resources.* In the example, your time for studying was limited to 4 hours per week. The two possible outputs were grades in geography and grades in economics. The particular production possibilities curve presented in Figure 1.10 is a graphic representation of the opportunity cost of studying one more hour in one subject. *It is a straight-line production possibilities curve,* which is a special case. (The more general case will be discussed next.) If the student decides to be at point *x* in Figure 1.10, then 2 hours of study time will be spent on geography and 2 hours will be spent on economics. The expected grade in each course will be a D. If the student is more interested in getting a C in economics, then he or she will go to point *y* on the production possibilities curve, spending only 1 hour on geography but 3 hours on economics. The expected grade in geography will then drop from a D to an E. Note that these trade-offs between expected grades in geography and economics are given holding constant total study time as well as all other factors that may influence the student's ability to learn. Quite clearly, if the student wished to spend more total time studying, then it would be possible to have higher grades in both economics and geography! However, then we would no longer be on the specific production possibilities curve illustrated in Figure 1.10. We would have to draw a new curve in order to show the greater total study time and a different set of possible trade-offs. Grade As might then be possible! (Read Key Points 1.5.)

*Other terms used for production possibilities curves are: production possibilities frontier, production possibilities boundary, production possibility curve and transformation curve. We use the word possibilities rather than possibility to emphasize the multiplicity of combinations of output exemplified in this diagram.

Society's Choices

The straight-line production possibilities curve presented in Figure 1.10 can be generalized to demonstrate the related concepts of scarcity, choice, and trade-offs facing an entire nation. You may have already heard the phrase, 'guns or butter'. Implicit in that phrase is that at any point in time a nation can either have more military goods (guns) or civilian goods (butter). Let us restrict our example to the production of military goods and civilian goods. We assume that these are the only two classes of goods that can be produced in the economy. In Figure 1.11(a), there are the hypothetical numerical trade-offs, expressed in terms of units of military goods produced per year. If no civilian goods are produced, all resources will be used in the production of military goods, of which 5 000 units will be produced per year. On the other hand, if no military goods are produced, all resources will be used to produce 6 000 units of civilian goods per year. In between, there are various combinations that are possible. These combinations are plotted as points *A, B, C, D, E, F,* and *G* in Figure 1.11(b) on page 12. If these points are connected with a smooth curve, society's production possibilities curve is shown, and it demonstrates the trade-off between the production of military and civilian goods. These trade-offs occur *on* the production possibilities curve.

Key Points 1.5

- **Any use of a resource involves an opportunity cost because an alternative use, by necessity, was sacrificed.**
- **We look only at the highest-valued alternative to determine opportunity cost.**
- **The graphic representation of trade-offs that must be made is displayed in a production possibilities curve.**

Assumptions Underlying the Production Possibilities Curve

There are a number of assumptions underlying this particular production possibilities curve. The first one relates to the fact that we are referring to the output possible on a *yearly* basis. In other words, we have specified a time-period over which the production takes place.

Second, we are assuming that resources are fixed over this time-period. To understand fully what is meant by a fixed amount of resources, consider that there are (a) factors that influence labour hours available for work and (b) factors that influence *productivity*, or the output per unit of input.

FACTORS INFLUENCING LABOUR HOURS AVAILABLE FOR WORK

We must recognize that the number of labour hours will depend on the state of human resources in society. What determines how much labour can be available? Hours available for work are determined by the following:

1. The size of population, its age structure, and dependants (children, retired persons)
2. The resulting potential size of the labour force
3. The percentage of available individuals who then choose to work
4. Custom and tradition (for example, women working).

Figure 1.11

Society's Trade-off between Military Goods and Civilian Goods. The production of military goods is measured in units per year. The production of civilian goods is measured in units per year also. We look at seven combinations from *A* to *G*. The first one, *A*, involves the production of no civilian goods, which allows us – using all of our resources – to produce 5 000 units of military goods. At the other extreme, combination *G*, society produces no military goods and can therefore use its productive resources to produce 6 000 units of civilian goods per year. These combinations are given in panel (a). The combinations *A* to *G* are plotted on the graph in panel (b). Connecting the points *A* to *G* with a smooth line gives society's production possibilities curve for military goods and civilian goods. Point *R* lies outside the production possibilities curve and is therefore unattainable at the point in time for which the graph is given; point *S* lies inside the production possibilities curve and therefore represents an inefficient use of available resources.

Panel (a)

Combination	*Military goods (units per year)*	*Civilian goods (units per year)*
A	5 000	0
B	4 800	1 000
C	4 500	2 000
D	4 000	3 000
E	3 300	4 000
F	2 250	5 000
G	0	6 000

Panel (b)

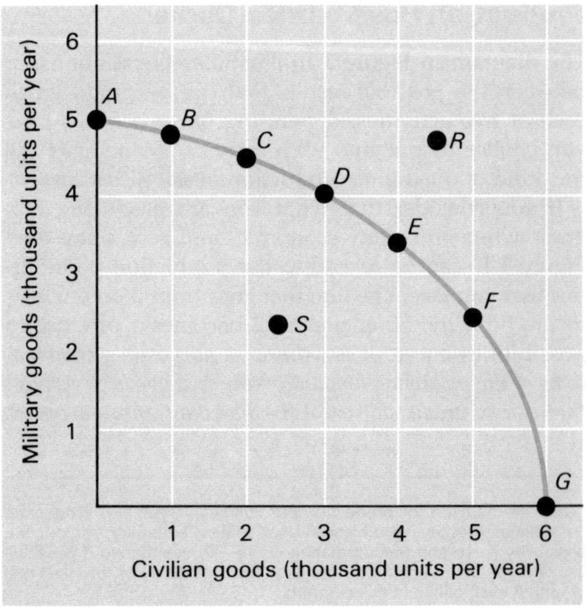

FACTORS INFLUENCING PRODUCTIVITY

There are a number of factors influencing how productive our society can be and if you recall our discussion of the inputs used in production then we can list the following:

1. Quantity and quality of natural resources
2. Quantity and quality of capital
3. Health, education, motivation, and skill levels of the labour force
4. Research and development.

We are assuming that at the present time our society is using all its human, natural and manufactured resources to maximum effect *given the state of knowledge* about how to make military goods and civilian goods. If the state of technology does not change, then our society cannot make more productive use of its resources. Thus we assume when drawing a production possibilities curve that no earth-shaking invention that could reduce significantly the cost of producing either military or civilian goods in our example is possible in the present time-period. We are further assuming that the size of the labour force remains the same during this time-period, that the health, motivation, and skill levels remain the same, and so on. If any one of the factors influencing labour hours or productivity changes, then the production possibilities curve will shift. Any improvement in technology (productivity) will move the entire curve outwards to the right, as in Figure 1.12(a). Any significant reduction in the labour force, all other things held constant, will shift the entire production possibilities curve inwards to the left, as in Figure 1.12(b).

The third and final assumption that we are making when we draw the production possibilities curve is that we are making efficient use of all available resources. (The concept of efficiency will be examined more closely in Chapter 6.) Society cannot for the moment be more productive with the present quantity and quality of its resources.

BEING OFF THE PRODUCTION POSSIBILITIES CURVE

Point *R* lies outside the production possibilities curve in Figure 1.11(b). Any point outside the curve is impossible to achieve during the present time-period. By definition, the possibilities curve relates to a specific unit of time. Additionally, the production possibilities curve is drawn for a given resource base. Under these two constraints, the production possibilities curve therefore indicates, by definition, the maximum quantity of one good available, given some quantity of the other. Point *R*, lying outside the production possibilities curve, occurs because we live in a world of scarcity. Look at point *S* in Figure 1.11(b). It is inside the curve which means that society's resources are not being fully utilized. This could be due to unemployment.

Figure 1.12

Shifting Production Possibilities Curve In panel (a), we see that improved productivity will shift the entire production possibilities curve outwards over time. In panel (b), a reduced amount of labour available to the economy will shift the entire production possibilities curve inwards over time.

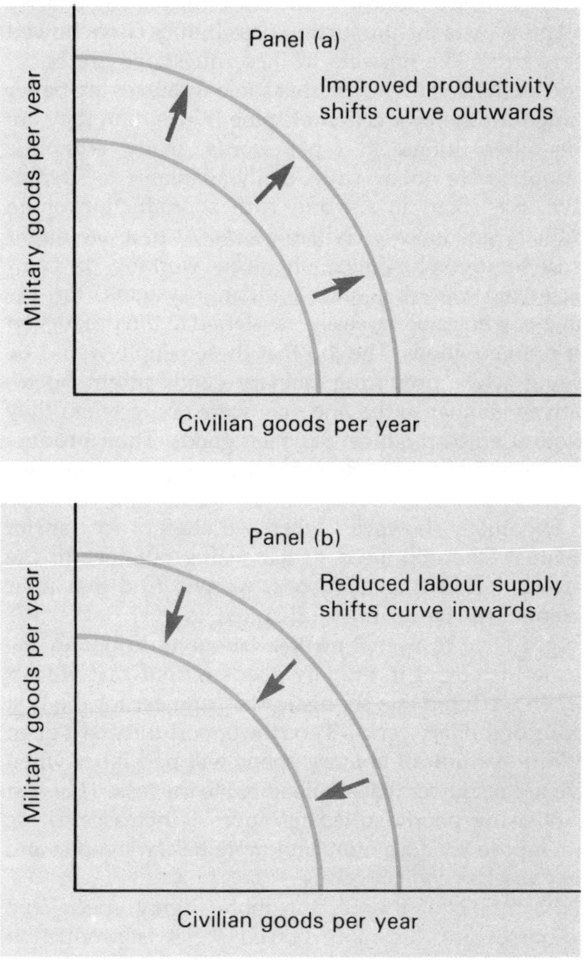

Why the Production Possibilities Curve is Bowed Outward

In the example in Figure 1.10, the trade-off between a grade in geography and a grade in economics was one to one. The trade-off ratio was fixed. That is to say, the production possibilities curve is a straight line, which, as we pointed out before, is a special case. Figure 1.11 is the more general case, showing a bowed production possibilities curve. The opportunity cost of obtaining more and more units of military goods rises. That is to say, each additional unit costs society more in forgone alternatives than the previously produced unit. We can see this more clearly in Figure 1.13. Each increment in military output is the same, but look at what we have to *give up* in civilian goods when we go from the next to last unit of military output to the last unit where the entire economy is producing just military goods. The opportunity cost is very large relative to what an equivalent increase in military goods costs society, when we start with none being produced at all. Figure 1.13 illustrates the **law of increasing relative costs**. As society takes more and more resources and applies them to the production of any specific item, the opportunity cost for each additional unit produced increases at an increasing rate.

Why are we faced with the law of increasing relative costs? Why is the production possibilities curve bowed outwards? The answers to these questions are basic, and are related to the fact that some resources are better suited for the production of some things than they are for other things. In other words, many economic resources are not as a rule easily adaptable to alternative uses. Start in a world with a production of no military goods, only civilian goods. At first, we might find some sophisticated engineers working on computerized watering and fertilizing systems, for example, who could be easily transferred to the production of military goods. The job that these people would be doing while producing military goods might be relatively similar to the one they were doing when they were used in producing civilian goods. Their productivity might be approximately the same as it was prior to the move.

Eventually, however, when we attempt to transfer manual labourers used to harvesting potatoes to the production of military goods, we will find that their talents will be relatively ill-suited to such tasks. We might have to use 50 manual labourers to obtain the same increment in military goods output that we got when we hired one sophisticated engineer for the first units of military goods. Thus the opportunity cost of an additional unit of military goods will be higher when we use resources that are ill-suited to the task. That cost – of using poorly suited resources – increases as we attempt to produce more and more military goods and less and less civilian goods.

As a rule of thumb, the more highly specialized resources are, the more bowed society's production possibilities curve will be. At the other extreme, if all resources were equally suitable for all production purposes, then the curves in Figures 1.11, 1.12, and 1.13 would have simply approached a straight line, as in Figure 1.10. (Now read Key Points 1.6.)

Figure 1.13

The Law of Increasing Costs Consider equal increments in military goods production, as measured on the vertical axis. Thus, all of the vertical arrows – *H–I, J–K, L–M, N–O,* and *P–Q* – are of equal length. What is the cost to society of obtaining the first such increment in military goods production? It is a reduction in civilian goods output, *G–H*. This cost for each additional equal increment in military goods production rises, however. Finally, to get the last increment in military goods production – *P–Q* – society must give up the entire distance *O–P* in civilian goods production. The opportunity cost of each additional increase in military goods production rises.

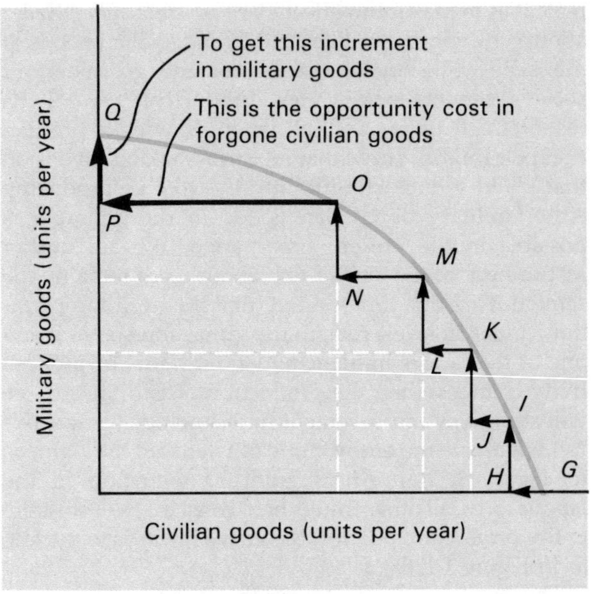

Scarcity Revisited

We have emphasized that productive resources are limited. Thus, we must make choices about how we

Key Points 1.6

- **Trade-offs are represented graphically by a production possibilities curve showing the maximum output combinations obtainable over a one-year period from a given set of resources.**
- **Points outside the production possibilities curve are unattainable; points inside represent an inefficient use or under-utilization of available resources.**
- **Since many resources are better suited for certain productive tasks than for others, society's production possibilities curve is bowed outwards reflecting the law of increasing relative cost.**

use them. We have to decide how much of which goods we will produce with our resources. For our purposes here, there will be only two choices: those goods that we consume directly, called **consumer goods** – food, clothes, cars – and those that we consume indirectly, called **capital goods** – machines and equipment. Everyone acts as a consumer in using consumer goods. On the other hand, capital goods, such as lathes, factories, and engines are used to make the consumer goods to which we just referred.

WHY WE MAKE CAPITAL GOODS

Why would we be willing to use productive resources to make things – capital goods – that we cannot consume directly? One of the reasons we use productive resources to make capital goods is that the latter enable us to produce larger quantities of consumer goods or to produce them more cheaply than we otherwise could. Before fish are produced for the market, fishing-boats and nets are first produced. Now imagine, for example, how expensive it would be to obtain fish for market without using these capital goods. Getting fish with one's hands is not an easy task. The price per fish would be very high if capital were not used.

FORGOING CURRENT CONSUMPTION

Whenever we use productive resources to make capital goods, we are implicitly forgoing current consumption. We are waiting for some time in the future to consume the fruit that will be reaped from the use of capital goods. Indeed, if we were to produce only consumer goods now and no capital goods, then our capacity to produce consumer goods in the future would suffer. Here we see a trade-off situation, one which lends itself to the sort of graphical analysis that we have used already in this chapter.

THE TRADE-OFF BETWEEN CONSUMPTION GOODS AND CAPITAL GOODS

In order to have more consumer goods in the future, we must accept fewer consumer goods today. With the resources that we do not use to produce consumer goods for today, we invest in capital goods that will produce more consumer goods for us later. The trade-off is depicted in Figure 1.14, on page 16. On the left-hand diagram of panel (a), you can see this trade-off depicted as a production possibilities curve between capital goods and consumption goods. If we decide to use all our resources to produce goods and services for consumption today, we can produce £2 million worth per year, which is represented as point *B*. In this extreme case, using all our productive resources for only consumption goods leads to no future growth.

Now assume, however, that we are willing to give up, say, £200 000 worth of consumption today. We will be at point *A* in the left-hand diagram of panel (b). These will allow the economy to grow. We will have more future consumption because we invested in more capital goods today. In the right-hand diagram of panel (b), we see two goods represented – food and recreation. The production possibilities curve will move outwards if we collectively decide to restrict consumption each year and invest in capital goods – that is, if we agree to be at point *A*.

In panel (c), we show the result of our willingness to forgo quite a bit more current consumption. We move to point *C*, where we have many fewer consumer goods today, but produce a lot more capital goods. This leads to more future growth in this simple model, and thus the production possibilities curve in the right-hand side of panel (c) shifts outwards more than it did in the right-hand side of panel (b).

In other words, the more we give up today, the more we can have tomorrow. (Now read Key Points 1.7.)

Other Things Being Equal

Let us again return to our production possibilities curve concerning you as a student in order to develop another important point. We looked at the trade-offs concerning your use of scarce time in studying geography and economics. As a model it illustrated the

Key Points 1.7

- **Consumer goods are used directly by consumers.**
- **Capital goods are the means by which consumer goods are produced and are not directly used by consumers.**
- **The use of capital requires using productive resources to produce capital goods that in turn will later produce consumer goods.**
- **A trade-off is involved between current consumption and capital goods, or alternatively, between current consumption and future consumption, because the more we invest in capital goods today, the greater the amount of consumer goods we can produce in the future.**

Figure 1.14
Capital Goods and Growth

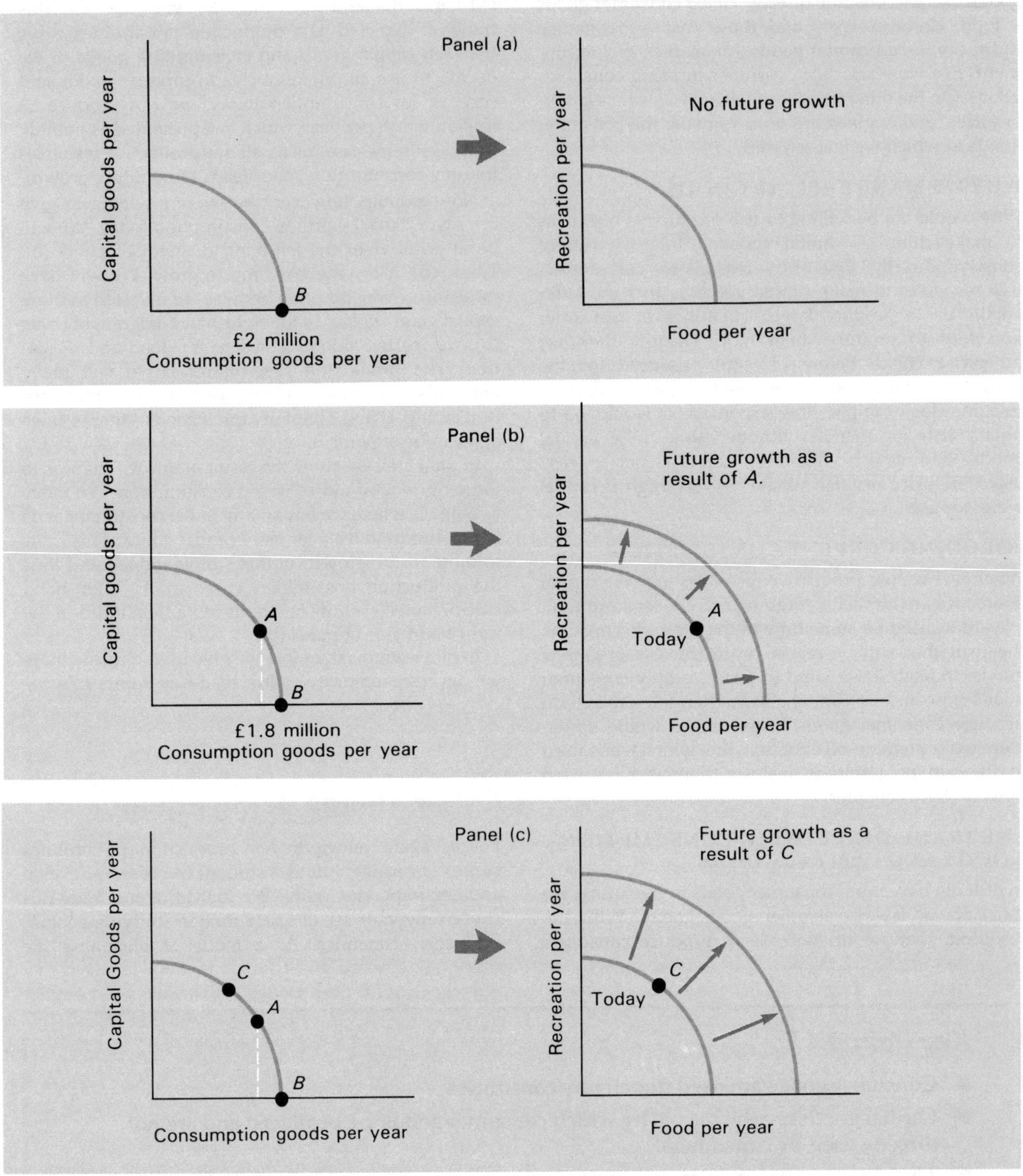

principle of opportunity cost. But you may have thought that various factors were left out of account in this model so let us now recognize these.

Your performance in either geography or economics was assumed to improve by exactly one grade for every hour of study. There was, it seems no particular difficulty in using one hour to raise the standard of your assessed performance. Now you may say that you would find more difficulty in improving your performance in economics than in geography: in other words another 2 or even 3 hours would be necessary to move from a C grade to a B grade and not just one! For some of your fellow students still more hours than this might be needed, but for yet others less than a full hour might be sufficient to achieve a similar result. But on reflection did not our discussion of the production of military and civilian goods recognize the possibility of a production possibility curve that was not a straight line? Figure 1.11 was drawn as a curve not as a line: we could now redraw a curve rather than a line in Figure 1.10. Our model of study of geography and economics can also easily incorporate the principle of increasing relative cost!

If you reread carefully you will note we assumed that not only was the amount of study time held constant but also 'all other factors that may influence the student's ability to learn'. Thus it was implicitly assumed that it is as effective to study during a hot summer afternoon as during a cold winter evening. Or that it makes no difference whether you are studying alone in your own room or in a public library. What particular book you are reading in the hour of study also makes no difference at all. Now you may well wonder whether, in the light of these and other influences on the student's learning situation, our model is not too simplistic.

What we have just recognized is that there are indeed many factors which would influence a student's performance in a subject. But in our model we are assuming that we are *holding all other things constant.* In our model we are showing the relationship between the amount of time devoted to a subject and the assessed performance resulting from the amount of study. In Figure 1.15 we show this relationship.

Of course, there are other influencing variables, but they are not explicitly shown on any graph that has only two variables, such as study time and grade performance. In other words, the relationships shown on our graphs, by their very nature, cannot explicitly include all of the other relationships that are involved in determining the grades of students. We say, therefore, that when we draw a graph showing the relationship between two variables, we are holding all other things constant. The graph shown in Figure 1.15 is therefore holding constant, or fixed, the time of year, place of study, student motivation, and all other influences on the learning situation. This is sometimes referred to as the **ceteris paribus assumption,** where the words 'ceteris paribus' mean 'other things constant'. There is a way to show the effect of changes in 'other things' that are not explicitly depicted in two-dimensional graphs. When some other determining variable changes, it will affect the *position* of the line, or curve, representing the relationship between the two variables on the curve. For example, consider Figure 1.15 showing the relationship between study time and study grade. If the place where one studies affects *grade performance*, and there is a change in study location, that entire line will move somewhere else in the graph when this variable is recognized as a relevant factor in the learning situation.

In sum, then, an economic model cannot be faulted as unrealistic merely because it does not represent every detail of the real world. That same model may be very realistic in terms of elucidating the *central* issue at hand or forces at work. Every theory is an abstraction of reality.

Figure 1.15

The Relationship between Study Time and Performance in Economics. Grade obtained in economics depends on the amount of time devoted to the study of the subject. The relationship is a direct one and assumes there is no influence on the learning situation other than the amount of time devoted to the study of economics.

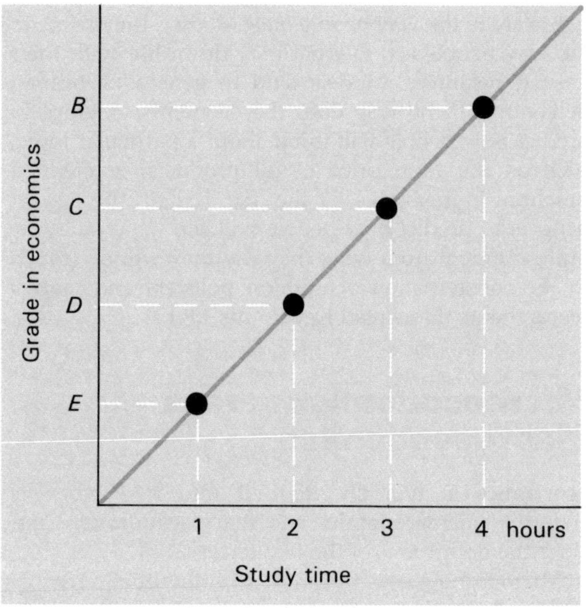

Assumptions

Every model, or theory, must be based on a set of assumptions. Assumptions define the set of circumstances in which our model is most likely to be applicable. When scientists predicted that sailing-ships would fall off the edge of the earth, they used the assumption that the earth was flat. Columbus did not accept the implications of such a model. He tested the predictions of his own model, which was based on the assumption that the world was round. He sailed and did not fall off any 'edge'. The empirical test of his own model refuted the flat-earth model. Indirectly, then, it was a test of the assumption of that model that the earth was flat.

Deciding on the Usefulness of a Model

We generally do not attempt to determine the usefulness of a model or how 'good' it is merely by evaluating how realistic its assumptions are. Rather, we consider that a model is 'good' if it yields usable predictions and implications for the real world. In other words, can we predict what will happen in the world around us with the model? Are there implications in the model of how things will happen in our world?

Once we have determined that the model does predict real-world phenomena, then the scientific approach to analysis of the world around us requires that we consider evidence. Evidence is used to test the usefulness of a model. This is why we call economics an empirical science – empirical meaning that real evidence (data) is looked at to see whether we are right.

Models of Behaviour, not Thought Processes

Take special note of the fact that economists' models do not relate to the way people *think*. Rather, they relate to the way people act, to what they do in life with their limited resources. Models tend to generalize human behaviour. In no way does the economist attempt to predict how people will think about a particular topic, such as the high price of oil products, accelerated inflation, higher taxes, or the like. Rather, the task at hand is to predict how people will act, which may be quite different from what they say they will do (much to the consternation of opinion pollsters and market researchers). (Now read Key Points 1.8.)

Microeconomics versus Macroeconomics

Economics is typically divided into two types of analysis: **microeconomics** and **macroeconomics**. Consider the definitions of the two terms.

Microeconomics is the study of individual decision-making by both individuals and firms.

Macroeconomics is the study of economy-wide phenomena resulting from group decision-making in entire markets. As such, it deals with the economy as a whole.

The best way to understand the distinction between microeconomics and macroeconomics is to consider some examples. Microeconomic analysis would tackle the effects of changes in the price of petrol relative to other energy sources. It would be involved in the examination of the effects of new taxes on a specific product or industry. If price controls were reinstituted in the United Kingdom, how individual firms and consumers would react to such price controls would be in the realm of microeconomics. The raising of wages by an effective union strike would be analysed, using the tools of microeconomics.

On the other hand, questions relating to the rate of inflation, the amount of national unemployment, the growth in production in the whole economy, and numerous other economy-wide subjects all fall into the realm of macroeconomic analysis. In other words, macroeconomics deals with, so-called *aggregates* or totals, such as total output in an economy. It is a study, therefore, of aggregate behaviour rather than individual behaviour.

You should be aware, however, of the blending together of microeconomics and macroeconomics in modern economic theory. Modern economists are increasingly using microeconomic analysis – the study of decision-making by individuals and by firms – as the basis of macroeconomic analysis. They do this because, even though in macroeconomic analysis aggregates are being examined, those aggregates are made up of individuals and firms. Consider an example: some economists believe that reducing income tax rates will lead to greater total output. Why? Because, using microeconomic analysis, they predict that individuals will respond to lower income tax rates by working longer, taking fewer holidays, and taking on second jobs. The task is then to establish whether empirical evidence supports these predictions.

Positive versus Normative Economics – What is versus What ought to be

Economics is a social science; it uses *positive* analysis. This is a scientific term that relates to the value-free nature of the inquiry; no subjective or 'gut' feelings enter into the analysis. Positive analysis relates to basic

Key Points 1.8

- **The phrase *'Ceteris paribus'* is frequently applied in the study of economics and means that all other things have been held constant whilst a relationship between specified variables is being considered.**
- **Every model, or theory, must be based on a set of assumptions. How realistic these assumptions are is not as important as how effective they make the model, or theory.**
- **Models in economics relate to behaviour rather than individuals' thought-processes.**
- **Models enable generalizations to be made.**

statements, such as *if A, then B*. For example, if the price of petrol goes up relative to all other prices, then the amount of it that people will buy will fall. That is a positive economic statement. It is a statement of *what is*. It is not a statement of anyone's value-judgement, or subjective feelings. 'Hard' sciences, such as physics and chemistry, are considered to be virtually value free. After all, how can someone's values enter into a theory of molecular behaviour? But economists face a different problem. They deal with the behaviour of individuals, not molecules. Thus, it is more difficult to stick to what we consider to be value-free or **positive economics** without reference to our feelings.

When our values come into the analysis, we enter the realm of **normative economics,** or normative analysis, which is defined as analysis containing, whether explicity or implicitly, someone's values. A positive economic statement is: 'If the price of books goes up, people will buy less'. If we add to that analysis the statement 'and therefore we *should* not allow the price to go up', we have entered the realm of normative economics; we have expressed a personal opinion or value-judgement. In fact, any time you see the word *should*, you will know that values are entering into the discussion.

The world of value-judgements is the world in which individuals' preferences are at issue. Each of us has a desire for different things: we have different values. When we express a value-judgement, we are simply saying what we prefer, like, or desire. Since individual values are quite diverse, we expect – and indeed observe – people expressing widely varying value-judgements about how the world should or ought to be.

Using Positive Economics in Normative Analysis

Even though this economics textbook, along with virtually all others, contains mostly positive economic analyses, such analyses can be used when one passes into the realm of policy-making in which values play a part. Suppose, for example, that you desire to raise the income of employed teenagers. That is a normative judgement (that is, a value-judgement) that you have made and in which you believe. Assume that you are a policy-maker with many options available to you such as specifying minimum wage-levels. Here is where positive analysis can come to your aid.

Suppose that you construct a model of the teenage labour market. Your examination of real-world evidence tells you that in the past raising the minimum wage has not led to higher incomes for employed teenagers.

In fact you find out that it can even cause increased unemployment among teenagers. Even though your normative goal is to help unemployed teenagers, you may use positive economic analysis to decide that you must seek an alternative policy to raising the minimum wage. Hence, positive economics can be used as the basis for deciding on the appropriate policies to carry out one's goals or the goals of the nation.

A Warning

It is easy to define positive economics. It is quite another matter to catch all unlabelled normative statements in a textbook like this one, even though the authors go over the manuscript many times before it is printed. Therefore, do not get the impression that a textbook author will be able to keep his or her values out of the book. They will slip through. In fact, the choice itself of which topics to include in an introductory textbook involves normative economics. There is no value-free or objective way to decide which ones to use in a textbook. The author's 'gut feelings' ultimately make a difference when choices have to be made. From your own personal standpoint, what you might hope to do is to be able to recognize *when* you are engaging in normative as opposed to positive economic analysis. Reading this text should equip you for that task.

Key Points 1.9

- **Microeconomics involves the study of *individual* decision-making. Macroeconomics involves the study of *aggregates*. Modern economic theory often involves blending these two branches together.**
- **Positive economics indicates what *is*, whereas normative economics considers what *ought to be*.**

CASE STUDY

Costless Opportunities

In the summer of 1975 the 'Fourth People's Free Festival' was held at Watchfield in Oxfordshire. The previous year a similar 'pop music' festival had been held in Windsor Great Park which is in Berkshire, a different rating authority. The police who worked at the Watchfield site were financed by three counties, Berkshire, Buckinghamshire and Oxfordshire. They complained that only a token force of policemen could actually patrol the Festival site; the remainder were outside protecting villagers and their property and keeping the traffic moving. They resented that they had been paid for what they considered to be virtually standing around and doing nothing while drug offences took place on the actual Festival site.

They were all the more aware of this because they too are tax- and rate-payers and the cost to the police was several thousand pounds.

A Festival organizer said that those responsible for the Festival would not have any money left to contribute to the costs of running the Festival. (No admission charges were made.) The rate-payers of Berkshire are paying a bill of over £10 000 for an anti-festival campaign organised by Berkshire County Council. The Crown Estate Commissioners (who manage Windsor Great Park) also paid £10 000 towards the Festival's costs provided that it was held elsewhere.

Source: Based on *Daily Telegraph*, 1 Sept. 1975.

Questions

1. Identify two economic concepts involved in the above text.
2. (a) What term do economists use to describe the cost of something in terms of the next best alternative forgone?
   (b) Illustrate this term to explain the cost of reducing the number of drug offences that took place at the festival.
3. (a) Prices have risen in the UK since 1975. What problem arises when making comparisons of money values in 1975 with those of today?
   (b) How may economists resolve this problem?

Exam Preparation

PRACTICAL EXERCISES

1. An economy has a working population of 800 men who can only produce two goods, X and Y. All other resources are specific to the production of only one of the goods. The potential outputs of each good are as follows:

Good X		*Good Y*	
No. of men	*Weekly output*	*No. of men*	*Weekly output*
100	60	100	25
200	120	200	65
300	190	300	110
400	260	400	160
500	330	500	200
600	380	600	235
700	420	700	260
800	450	800	275

A Present the data in the form of a production possibility curve.

B Comment on the relationship between the change in the number of workers and the change in the weekly output of both good X and good Y.

C What would be the effects of some of the labour force becoming more efficient at the production of good X while the remainder become more efficient at the production of good Y?

D Assume that X is an investment good and Y is a consumption good and that, last year, 260X and 160Y were produced weekly. What would be the consequences if, next year, 330X and 110Y were produced weekly?

2. What does Economics mean? Economics is a word having its roots in the Greek *oikonomos* which is a combination of two other Greek words. The first of these oikos means 'household' and the second *nemein* means 'to manage resources'. Together therefore the Greek origin of the word points to the study of economics referring to the management of the limited resources of a household.

Consider how this definition of the word economics is applicable to:

A you as a student
B your parent(s)
C local government
D central government
E anyone else.

3. The following sets of numbers represent a set of hypothetical production possibilities for a nation in 1986.

Butter	*Guns*
4	0
3	1.6
2	2.4
1	2.8
0	3.0

Plot these points on a piece of graph paper. Does the law of increasing relative costs seem to hold? Why? On the same graph, now plot and draw the production possibilities curve that will represent 10 per cent economic growth.

MULTIPLE CHOICE QUESTIONS

1. The diagram below shows the production possibilities available to a closed economy without foreign trade.
If the economy produces *OK* of good X then it forgoes

A *OJ* of good Y
B *OA* of good Y
C *AJ* of good Y
D *KB* of good X for *OA* of good Y
E *KB* of good X for *AJ* of good Y

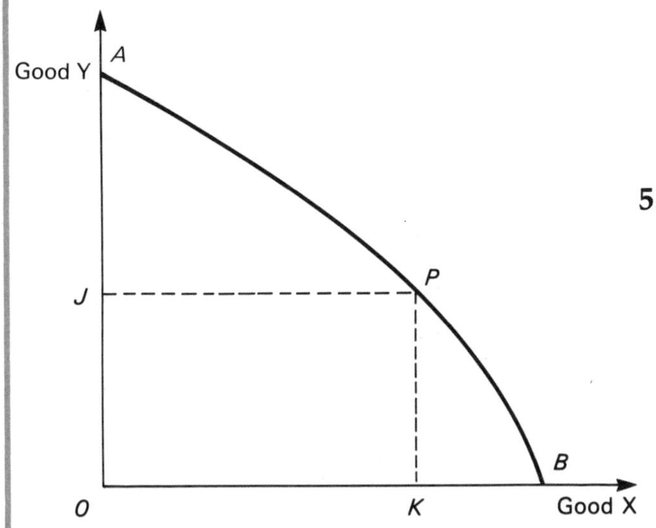

2. The opportunity cost to society of constructing a motorway would be the

A money spent on the road
B goods and services that could otherwise have been produced had the road not been constructed
C the cost of government borrowing to finance the construction of the road
D increased taxation needed to pay the cost of the new road
E goods and services that could otherwise have been produced by the labour employed in constructing the road, had the road not been constructed

3. In the following diagram, XY represents an economy's production possibility curve. Which point (**A**, **B**, **C**, or **D**) would indicate that the country could increase its standard of living without incurring an opportunity cost?

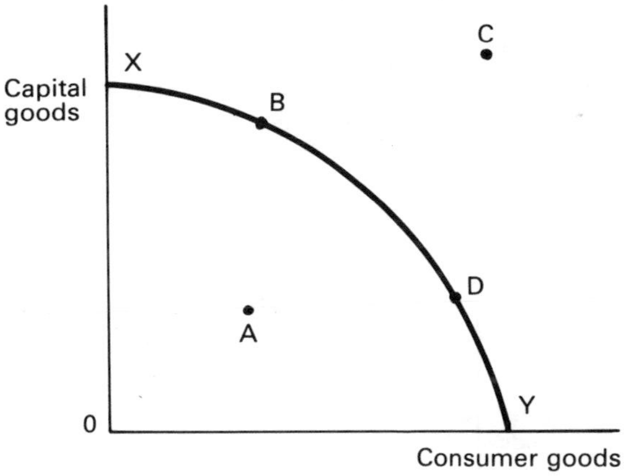

4. Assume you bought a bicycle for £100, but never use it. A similar bicycle would now cost £120 new, but yours would fetch only £40 secondhand. The present opportunity cost of owning the bicycle is

A £20
B £40
C £60
D £100
E £120

5. A farmer can feed any combination of animals within the following range:

Pigs		*Cows*
84	and	12
75	and	15

Given the options available to him, what is the opportunity cost to the farmer of rearing one cow?

A 1 pig
B 3 pigs
C 5 pigs
D 7 pigs
E 9 pigs

One or more of the options given in Questions 6 and 7 may be correct. Select your answer by means of the code set out in the grid:

A	B	C	D
1, 2, 3 all correct	1, 2 only correct	2, 3 only correct	1 only correct

6. A normative statement in economics
   1 is one that it is possible to refute by an appeal to the facts
   2 typically contains the words 'ought' or 'should'
   3 depends on value-judgements

7. The production possibility curve of a given country changes from X to Y as shown in the diagram. From this information it can be inferred that the
   1 country has become more efficient in the production of defence goods
   2 opportunity cost of producing consumer goods has risen in relation to defence goods
   3 country's preference for defence goods has increased

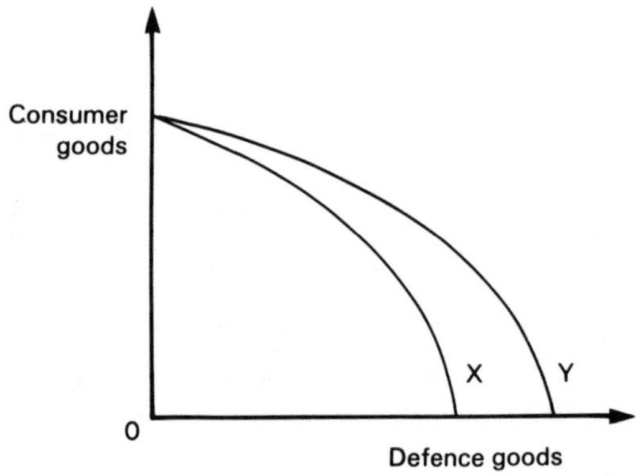

RELATED ESSAY QUESTIONS

1. Define opportunity cost, and explain the importance of the concept.

2. Explain what is meant by a production possibility curve and discuss the circumstances in which such a curve would change its position.

3. Explain what is meant by
   A microeconomics and macroeconomics
   B positive economics and normative economics

Discuss the relevance of each concept to the problem of scarcity and choice.

2 Economic Systems: The Capitalist Economy

Key Points to Review

- Scarcity (1.1, 1.4)
- Opportunity costs, trade-offs (1.5, 1.6)
- Production possibilities curve (1.5, 1.6)
- Consumer goods, capital goods (1.7)

Questions for Preview

1 Capitalist economies are associated with great economic freedoms with regard to ownership and use of private property. Why does all this freedom not lead to chaos and anarchy? What gives *direction* and *regulation* to a capitalist economy?

2 Money economies are more advanced than barter economies. Why?

3 A trade-off exists between present consumption and future consumption. Why?

Economic Systems

We characterize an **economic system** as all the institutional means through which national resources are used to satisfy human wants. By **institutions**, we mean principally the laws of the nation, but also the habits, ethics, and customs of its society. From the outset, you should be aware that all economic systems are artificial in the sense that the institutions in an economy are exactly what human beings have made them. In this chapter we define capitalism as one economic system and examine how it faces up to the fundamental problems facing any society.

An Analysis of Capitalist Ideology

Capitalism is a type of economic system that is typically characterized by limited involvement of government in the economy, coupled with individual ownership of the means of production. We might further add that in a capitalist system individuals can pursue their own self-interest without many constraints. The capitalist system is thus one where decisions are decentralized.

Analysing the Institutions and Assumptions of Capitalist Ideology

Capitalist ideology is based on a set of fundamental assumptions. These assumptions are not, of course, accepted by all, but they must be understood in order to understand what capitalist ideology is all about. The institutions of capitalist ideology are, in many senses, abstract but play an important role in determining the way in which individuals can act in a pure capitalist system.

Our analysis will be limited to a discussion of:

1. The system of private property
2. Free enterprise and free choice
3. Competition and unrestricted markets
4. Self-interest
5. The pricing system in those markets
6. The limited role of government.

THE SYSTEM OF PRIVATE PROPERTY

The ownership of most property under a capitalist system is usually vested in individuals or in groups of individuals. The state is thus not the predominant owner of, for example, productive resources that are important forms of property. In the United Kingdom, the government does own certain property, but in general we live with a system of private property.

Private property is controlled and enforced through the legal framework of laws, courts, and police. Under capitalism, individuals have their *property rights* protected; individuals are usually free to use their private property as they choose, so long as they do not infringe on the legal property rights of others.

FREE ENTERPRISE AND FREE CHOICE

Another attribute of a capitalist system is free enterprise, which is merely an extension of the concept of property rights. **Free enterprise** exists when private individuals are allowed to obtain resources, to organize those resources, and to sell the resulting product in any way the person chooses. In other words, there are no artificial obstacles or restrictions that a government or other producers can put up to block a business person's choice in the matter of purchasing inputs and selling outputs.

Additionally, all members of the economy are free to choose to do whatever they wish. Workers will be free to enter any line of work for which they are qualified and consumers can buy the desired basket of goods and services that they feel is most appropriate for them. The ultimate voter in the capitalist system is the consumer, who votes with pounds and decides which product 'candidates' will survive; that is, there is **consumer sovereignty** in that the ultimate purchaser of products and services determines what, in fact is produced.

COMPETITION AND UNRESTRICTED MARKETS

Competition is rivalry among sellers who wish to attract customers and rivalry among buyers to obtain desired goods. In general, competition exists among buyers and sellers of all resources who wish to obtain the best terms possible when they transact their business.

Competition requires, at a minimum, two things:

(a) A relatively large number of independently acting sellers and buyers, and

(b) The freedom of sellers and buyers to enter or leave a particular industry.

(a) **Many participants.** The presence of a large number of buyers and sellers means that power is diffuse, that no one buyer or one seller can noticeably influence the price that a particular product fetches in the marketplace.

Basically, economic competition – rivalry among buyers and sellers – imposes limits on the self-interest of buyers and sellers. Competition, then, is the regulating force in capitalism.

(b) **Easy entry and exit.** Another thing that makes competition a regulatory force is the ability of individuals to enter an industry that is profitable. Furthermore, those who feel that they could earn more profits in another industry must have the legal ability to leave the industry they are in now. We say, then, that there are *weak barriers to entry and exit* from industries so that competition can prevail throughout.

SELF-INTEREST AND THE INVISIBLE HAND

In 1776, Adam Smith, the author of *The Wealth of Nations*, described a system in which government had a limited role and individuals pursued their own self-interest. Smith reasoned that, in so doing, individuals will be guided as if by an invisible hand to achieve maximum social welfare for the nation. In his own words:

> An individual generally, indeed, neither intends to promote the public interest, nor knows how much he is promoting it . . . he intends only his own gain, and he is in this, as in many other cases, led by an invisible hand to promote an end which was no part of his intention. Nor is it always the worse for the society that it was no part of it. By pursuing his own interest he frequently promotes that of the society more effectually than when he really intends to promote it.*

What does self-interest entail? For the entrepreneur it normally means maximizing profits or minimizing losses. For the consumer, it means maximizing the amount of satisfaction possible from spending a given amount of income. From the worker's point of view, it means obtaining the highest level of income possible for a given amount of work. For the owner of a resource, it means obtaining the highest price possible when that resource is sold, or the greatest rent if it is rented.

Capitalism, therefore, presumes self-interest as the fundamental way that people operate in the system. Self-interest is the guiding light in capitalism.

THE PRICING SYSTEM

Capitalism is a **market economy** defined as one in which buyers and sellers express their opinions through how much they are willing to pay for, or how much they demand of goods and services. A market economy is also called **a price system**. In a price system, or market economy, prices are used to *signal* the *value* of individual resources. Prices are the guideposts to which resource owners, entrepreneurs, and consumers refer when they make their choices as they attempt to improve their lives. In other words, the **market economic system** is the organizing force in our economy. When we refer to **organization**, we mean the co-ordination of individuals, often doing different things, in the furtherance of a common end. This process of co-ordinating economic activity can be considered as being mechanical or machine-like in its mode of

*A. Smith *Wealth of Nations* (1776), Bk. IV, Ch. 11, Everyman Edn (1964).

ADAM SMITH

SCOTTISH ECONOMIST (1723–90)

Of Markets and Men

'I have never known much good done by those who affected to trade for the public good', Adam Smith once remarked. If he put little stock in good intentions, Smith did invest heavily in demonstrating that selfish intentions could lead to public good. In *The Theory of Moral Sentiments* (1759), his first book, Smith tried to show how altruism could come out of self-interest. In his second and more famous book, Smith attempted to reveal how the self-interest of private individuals could be transformed by the sleight of an invisible hand (the unfettered market) into social harmony and public benefit, producing the wealth of the nation in the best of all possible ways. The result of this effort was *An Inquiry into the Nature of Causes of the Wealth of Nations* (1776), perhaps the most influential economics treatise ever written, one that has set the tone for capitalist ideology for the past two centuries.

As the title indicates, Smith attempted to examine the sources of the wealth of nations. He proposed that first on the list of such sources was the division of labour [discussed in Chapter 6]. Smith's pin-factory example showing the dramatic increases in productivity possible through the division of labour has made its mark on virtually every textbook written on the subject since then. He went on to point out that the division of labour does not occur because individuals possess an overall perception of its ultimate benefit to society. Rather, the division of labour occurs simply because it is in each individual's self-interest to specialize and to exchange: 'The natural effort of every individual to better his own condition, when suffered to exert itself with freedom and security, is so powerful a principle, that it is alone, and without any assistance . . . capable of carrying on the society to wealth and prosperity.'

In addition to Smith's famous 'invisible hand' theme, referred to above, the theme of individual economic freedom also was quite strong in the *Wealth of Nations*. He believed that any governmental attempt to guide or to regulate the actions of individuals in the economic marketplace would end up doing more harm than good. Smith was especially harsh on legally protected monopolies.

Smith's critics of today contend that his model may have fit the United Kingdom at the time he wrote his treatise, but it does not fit industrialized Western countries today – where the state plays a large role and large corporations have replaced the shopkeepers. None the less, for many, the *Wealth of Nations* remains a *laissez-faire* Bible, and Smith remains a central figure in the development of economic thought.

working. Hence we can also refer to the market system as using the mechanism of prices to effect changes in resource use. How does the **price mechanism** achieve this?

Resources tend to flow where they yield the highest rate of return, or highest profit. Prices generate the signals for resource movements, they provide information cheaply and quickly, and they affect incentives.

THE LIMITED ROLE OF GOVERNMENT

Even in an 'idealized' capitalistic system there is still a role for government, for someone has to define and enforce private property rights. The government protects the rights of individuals and entrepreneurs to keep private property private and to keep the control of that property vested with the owners. Even Adam Smith, the so-called father of free enterprise, described in detail the role of government in a purely capitalist system. He suggested the need for government in providing national defence and in eliminating monopolies that would restrain trade. Smith further suggested that the functions of government within a capitalist system might include issuing money, prescribing standards of weights and measures, raising funds by taxation and assorted other means for public works, and settling disputes judicially. Government is thus essential to the existence of even a purely capitalist system but operates in a restrained way. The words **laissez-faire** referred to in the biography of Adam Smith indicate that the business community should be left alone by government.

Finally – A Definition of Capitalism

We are now in a position formally to define in more detail what we mean by **capitalism**:

Key Points 2.1

- **An idealized capitalist system works within the institution of private property that is controlled and enforced through the legal framework of laws, courts, and police.**
- **Further, such a system is one of free enterprise, where producers freely choose the resources they use in the products they produce. Consumers have freedom of choice also, as do workers and owners of resources in general.**
- **Individuals and producers express their desires through the market system, where prices are signals about the relative scarcities of different goods, services, and resources.**
- **The role of government is a limited one.**

Capitalism is an economic system in which individuals privately own productive resources and possess the right to use these resources in whatever manner they choose, subject to certain (minimal) legal restrictions.

Notice here that we use the words *productive resources*, rather than capital. This takes into account not only machines and land, but also labour services. (Now read Key Points 2.1.)

Fundamental Problems Facing Any Society

The previous chapter explained the significance of economic goods. We now turn to the three major questions concerning the production and distribution of such goods. These questions are simply put.

1. What goods are to be produced?
2. How should these goods be produced?
3. For whom should these goods be produced?

These three questions have varying 'answers' depending on the nature of the economic system. We must thus now examine how the capitalist economic system faces up to these three questions.

What? How? For Whom? In Pure Capitalism

In pure capitalism, **consumers** ultimately determine what will be produced by their spending – their voting in the market-place – what they are willing to spend their income on. As far as producers are concerned their motivation as to what goods are produced is determined by the search for profit. Only those goods that can be produced profitably will be produced.

Since resources can substitute for one another in the production process, the pure capitalist economy must decide *how* to produce a commodity once society votes for it. Producers will be forced (by the discipline of the market-place) to combine resources in the cheapest way for a particular standard of quality. The cheapest way will depend on relative resource prices. Those firms that combine resources in the most efficient manner will earn the highest profits and force losses on their competitors. Competitors will be driven out of business or forced to combine resources in the same way as the profit-makers.

The *what* and *how* questions are concerned with production. The *for whom* question is concerned with the *distribution* of goods after they are produced. How is the pie divided? In pure capitalism, production and distribution are closely linked, because in the production of goods, incomes are automatically generated. People get paid according to their productivity; that is, a person's income reflects the value that society places on that person's resources. Since income largely determines one's share of the output 'pie' in pure capitalism, what people get out of the economic system is based on what they put into it. Any exception to this situation – for example the welfare provided to those persons in society such as the handicapped and elderly who are not capable of contributing to the productive process – arises only if that society, through its government chooses to make it so. (Now read Key Point 2.2.)

The Use of Money

Figure 2.1 demonstrates the flow of resources and the flow of goods and services within a capitalist system. It is called the **circular flow** model. This model of a monetary economy makes it necessary to explain why we use money.

In a capitalist economic system, money is used as a *medium of exchange*. In other words, we have one standard good that everyone knows everyone else is willing to accept in exchange for all other goods and services. Money also serves many other functions that are described in later chapters.

Key Point 2.2

- **Any economic system must answer the questions: (1) *what* will be produced? (2) *how* will it be produced? and (3) *for whom* will it be produced?**

Using money as a medium of exchange facilitates specialization and exchange among people. In fact, it is necessary that there be a convenient means of exchanging goods and services in order for us to be able to specialize. Consider the alternative to using money – **barter** – where we exchange goods for goods, or services for goods, or services for services.

Bartering has been around for a long time. However, it requires a double coincidence of wants between two individuals or businesses.

Suppose that you make frying-pans and I make shoes. I decide I want a frying-pan. If you, at the same time, want shoes, then we can probably make a barter exchange. Suppose, though, that you want a couple of new hats. I must go and find someone who wants some shoes in exchange for some hats. When I finally get the hats, then perhaps I can exchange them for your frying-pans.

The time involved in this process is tremendous compared to the facility with which exchange takes place when money is used. Money is thus one of the most important inventions of man. It has existed in many forms, such as shells, pieces of metal, cigarettes, and more recently, paper money. The essential characteristic that it must have in order to facilitate exchange is that it must be generally accepted by sellers in exchanges. Whatever fits this definition can be called money.

Our willingness to accept paper money, metal money or any other type of money allows each person and each region to specialize in production despite a non-coincidence of wants. (Read Key Point 2.3)

The Circular Flow of Income

With money being used as a medium of exchange, households sell economic resources to businesses, and in return they are paid money income in the form of wages, interest, rents, and profits. They receive wages for their labour services, interest for the capital services that they provide, rents for the land that they own, and profits for their entrepreneurial abilities. (These money incomes are examined in detail later.) This is shown in the bottom loops in Figure 2.1. Firms, on the other hand, sell finished goods and services to households, for which, in exchange, they are paid money. This is shown in the top loop in Figure 2.1.

The circular flow diagram does offer us a context within which to understand how the three basic questions are faced up to in the capitalist model.

Figure 2.1

The Circular Flow – A Monetary Economy. In this simplified model there are only households and businesses (or firms). Money is used as the medium of exchange. Households sell the services of land, labour, capital, and entrepreneurship that they own, to firms. Firms, in turn, pay households rent, wages, interest, and profits. Firms also sell goods and services to households for which the firms receive payment in the form of consumer expenditure of money income.

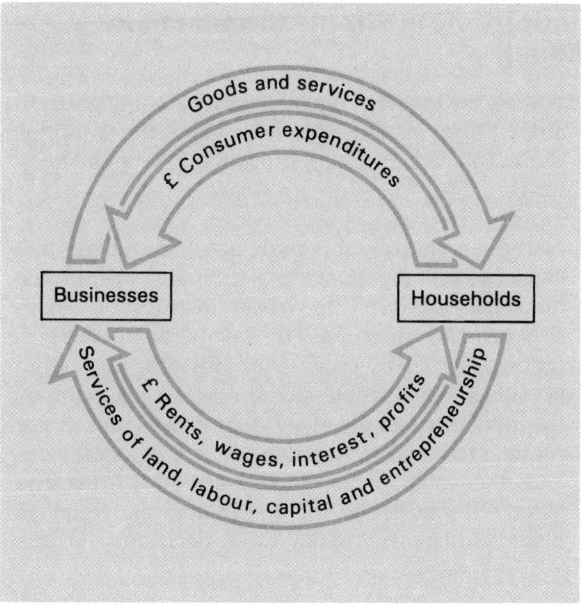

Key Point 2.3

- **Money is any generally accepted medium of exchange. It facilitates exchange and thereby allows for increased specialization.**

What?

1. What goods? *Households 'vote' with money for goods and services desired.*

How?

2. How? *Competitive forces exert pressures on firms to produce goods and services as efficiently as possible. Competition regulates profits which are the driving force for firms.*

For Whom?

3. For whom? *Goods and services are obtained by those with money available.*

Each of these three 'answers' in the pure capitalist model raise many fascinating issues. Is it really true that households possess consumer sovereignty or are they persuaded to buy goods and services that they do not really want as a result of successful advertising by firms? Does the capitalist model really contain such strong competitive pressures to which firms are responsive? How fair is such a system when some households have more money than others? These questions raise some normative questions which we cannot ignore. Before considering these we can note some value-free or positive observations about the circular flow model.

Limitations in Simple Circular Flow Models

Of course, the model of the monetary economy given in Figure 2.1 is an extreme simplification of the workings of capitalism. For example, it has the following shortcomings:

1. Nothing is said about transactions or exchanges that occur within the business sector and within the household sector. The whole distribution chain between manufacturers of intermediate parts is ignored, as is the chain of events that goes from manufacturer to wholesaler to retailer. For example, the model ignores the many steps it takes for a motor car to get to market. It ignores the selling of car tyres and other components to the car assembly firms. The latter sell vehicles to car distributors and retailers before consumers make their decisions on the purchase of a car.
2. The model makes no mention of the economic role of government which does, of course, tax and spend, as well as regulate. In a purely capitalist world, we would have a self-regulated economy in which the government's role would be minor anyway. In a more complete model of our actual economy the role of government cannot be ignored.
3. The model assumes our monetary economy is one that has no dealings with any other economic system. There is no international trade or any other transactions such as tourism. It is a **closed economy** which is clearly not a picture of a real-life capitalist economic system or **open economy**.
4. Nothing is said about how resources and products come into existence and at what prices they are sold. That is the job of supply and demand anlaysis and also requires an explanation of our pricing system, which is explained in a later chapter.
5. There is nothing shown in the model relating to what happens to that part of money income of households which is not spent on goods but in fact is saved.
6. The model does not suggest how firms create and expand their production systems so as to be able to offer goods for sale to consumers.

This is a rather formidable list of simplifying assumptions of the model of capitalism. The first assumption means we are glossing over a great deal of activity that takes place before consumers are involved in paying for goods at the retail level. But once that fact is recognized this assumption is not a serious flaw in our picture of the working of a market economy. It simply minimizes the multiplicity of markets in the capitalist system. The next assumptions are more substantial for the validity of the capitalist model. We need to explain why there is a widely recognized role for government. This role is discussed in Chapter 10. We shall also certainly need to develop a picture of an open economy and this will begin in Chapter 9. How prices are actually determined is explained in Chapter 5 and the role of prices is considered in Chapter 6. The implications of how the sums available to households are allocated – to consumption expenditures or saving – are analysed in Chapter 15. So we will in subsequent chapters relax the extremely simplistic model of the capitalist system. Meanwhile we turn in the next chapter to an alternative model of how economic activity might be organized.

Key Points 2.4

- **The simple closed economy circular flow model does not identify any intermediate economic activity.**
- **This model ignores the role of government and also the significance of saving and investment.**

CASE STUDY

Desert Island Economics

Many years ago, before earth's exploration had got underway, there was a thriving community in the South Seas. The climate was only temperate and the people were energetic. They had become strongly individualistic and great lovers and respecters of personal freedom under the law.

They lived on a series of islands, each island much independent; they had avoided the tribal paternalistic culture.

From time to time they mounted explorations to see what was over the horizon. Their canoes were large and could span great distances.

On one such exploration, they failed to outrun a hurricane. The canoe was wrecked. All but three perished. The trio were washed up on an uninhabited island. They had to make a new life for themselves. The chances of rescue were remote and there was no suitable material to build a new craft. Timber was sparse.

The island was reasonably, but not over fertile. Given hard work, they could manage. They were lucky – Tom was a baker and knew about growing corn; Dick was good with animals and Harry was a cultivator of the vine. With much effort they managed to draw sustenance from the island, respectively providing bread, chickens and eggs, and wine. There was little spare time. This was so especially since periodically their cultivated area was overrun by goat-like creatures causing much damage. They could not catch them and had to spend a good deal of their time in making and building stockades, ditches and the like to keep the creatures out. Even then, occasionally the press of them overwhelmed such protection. Timber supply was limited and much work was needed.

But they thrived. A problem they found irritating, bearing in mind their individual independence, was how to exchange their produce. They used barter. But a chicken was not an easy unit to exchange for bread. Moreover, bartering and haggling took time – especially if you were to enjoy it. But time could not be wasted. They managed, however, in a crude kind of way.

Then, one day, another castaway was washed up from another exploration. John came from a different island. Somewhat more intellectual of mind. Strong, robust, but not a farmer. They all realised they had an extra mouth to feed. John thought the best thing he could do was to take charge of their defences against the goats. So he got to work on the fences, ditches and the like. The others were content, it was like a fair allocation of labour. But it made the problem of exchange more severe. John's work was 'public works'. Hard labour for days on end, slackness at other periods.

And then they had two strokes of luck. The first was when John found a colony of dog-like animals in another part of the island. He befriended a pair and brought them home. Soon he had some dogs he trained as if they were sheep dogs. They protected the cultivation from the roaming goats. Fencing and ditching were things of the past. Timber could be used for preferable purposes. The second piece of good fortune was when they discovered an old chest – left there by Western explorers long before – containing many copper coins. Although their homes had been bereft of much metal, they knew enough to value them both intrinsically (for tools) but, more important, as a medium of exchange. They had a great feast, and with much haggling and giggling, eventually shared out the coins between the four of them. Thereafter they used such coins – they called them dallors – to buy and sell each other their goods or services.

John periodically had some spare time and extended his services. More important, he built a warehouse and offered to buy everyone's product as produced, store it and sell it on demand. This was most useful since weather and yield varied. He could also think things out and advise on problems. He became something of an administrator. Thus a mini-market community became established. The price of produce went up and down (depending on the harvests) but, there being only 1 000 coins originally, there was no inflation. On average each of them worked sufficiently, had sufficient leisure and made sufficient money not to want for goods. They earned on average 20 dallors a day. Sometimes one or other got rather more, sometimes less, depending on weather, anticipation and sheer good luck. After a few years all was in what many centuries later would be called 'equilibrium'.

And then they had some bad luck. Another castaway was washed ashore. Peter came from a different island – he had no skills except one – he was a carpenter. He was an extra mouth to feed and yet had no direct productive capacity himself. As a farmer or such he was hopeless and he wasn't very energetic either. What was to be done?

The four met – John taking the lead. 'Clearly, we can't let Peter die' all agreed (for their individualism, or libertarianism, in no way denied either goodwill or selflessness – they were rather nice people in fact). 'We have two options,' said John. 'First, we could all work harder, produce more and keep him fed and looked after like ourselves.' There was a silence. 'Surely that isn't right,' said Tom. 'We work hard enough in all conscience, this island is not an easy one, we need such rest and leisure as we get.' Dick took a more puritan line, 'We would all be working our hands to the bone to keep him in sloth – that can't be right.' Harry thought it out further, 'That system can't be right – what happens if two more like Peter arrive?' John was at his most

continued overleaf

statesmanlike: 'Quite so; the second option is for us to work as we do now, but to consume less; say 10 per cent less each and give this to Peter. He won't live as well as we do, but he won't starve either. We all agree he can't be ignored, everyone should expect his fellows to have a minimum income. What do you say?' With some grumbling from Dick they all agreed. Each would give John two dallors each day for Peter, who would have eight to purchase produce to his preference. He would have time on his hands. Perhaps he might eventually hit upon a productive contribution he could make.

When they told Peter of their decision, he was aghast. (His island home had been tribal and collectivistic in life-style.) 'You can't do that,' he stormed. 'Why should I live in a lesser style than any of you?' They were taken aback. Said John, 'Surely you see that because of no reason other than luck you cannot contribute.' 'But I can,' said Peter, 'I could build you proper stockades, that is my skill, and I could maintain them and so I could earn my full day's pay.'

'But Peter,' they remonstrated gently, 'just think a moment. We don't need stockades any more. We wouldn't want to buy this service from you since John provides it so much more efficiently. It would not provide any incentive for us to work harder. Whilst we agree to forgo 10 per cent of our earnings for you (what much later became known as a 'transfer payment') this does not use up our resources. Your way would not only require us to use up more resources of our own, it would also use up the island's resources of timber. To proceed in this way would be a heavy resource cost on our community without any material contribution from you.'

'But you'd be saving the eight dallors you give me,' said Peter, 'and make a proper job for me. I wouldn't be idle.'

'You don't need to be idle, even if you cannot yet produce what we wish to buy. You could assist in various ways to ease our life here. But there is no obligation, and we are content to provide you with the eight dallors. But to "make" a job for you would cost us all much more – and to no avail. Your work would not contribute to our community's well-being. There is no demand from any of us for it.' Peter had the innate tolerance of his race. He realised he had to consider the matter in ways new to him. He eventually came to realise that there was no alternative, saving only coercion. Even that would not be practicable since the total produce of the five of them would reduce if any one of them became dominant and could dictate to the others.

He turned to John, 'You have time on your hands occasionally. What do you do then?'

'I try to think of ways of easing our life here,' said John. 'Why don't you do the same?'

During the ensuing months, Peter lived very modestly but realised that perhaps there was something he might learn to do. He explored the rivers and found that he could learn, and did learn, to fish. Using rudimentary spears and traps he eventually became sufficiently good at it not only to augment his limited food purchases, but to create a surplus. Thus a new trade was born. The others enjoyed the new-found delicacy. Peter charged prices accordingly. The 10 per cent donations from the others soon became unnecessary and stopped. Peter got a nest-egg of dallors. He became a fully productive member of the community. A new equilibrium was reached. Five men's goods and services formed the market.

And interestingly, they found the value of each dallor had increased. Not surprisingly – since there were only 1 000 coins on the island, now representing five men's production. Everyone was better off. They lived content and in peace.

(For none of them had thought of printing money, either to pay Peter or to 'make' a non-economic job for him.)

Source: A Goldstein, 'A Desert Island Economic Tale', *Royal Bank of Scotland Review*, Dec. 1987.

Questions

1. Give two examples of scarcity from this tale.
2. Explain with the use of a production possibility curve the constraints on output facing Tom, Dick and Harry when they first arrived on the island.
3. How could the five men further increase their total output?
4. What economic costs and benefits would arise if the three men now find a fourth person – a woman – has been shipwrecked on this island?
5. In what ways does the above article illustrate the operation of a free-enterprise system?
6. In a comment on the above tale one critic suggested that its author had constructed an economic model and it illustrated

   'certain features which are shared by all economic models. In particular it demonstrates the point, which applies to economic models, computer programmes and sewers, that you can only get out of them what you put into them. The conclusions of the parable are, in fact, the assumptions on which the story was based. Moreover, these assumptions are not only economic ones; they are also political and philosophical.'*

   What assumptions are made in the tale?

---

* M. Kelly, 'Mr Goldstein's Desert Island', *Royal Bank of Scotland Review*, Dec. 1988.

CASE STUDY

It's no Fun and Games in Toytown

With less than 50 shopping days to go until Christmas, toy manufacturers worldwide are about to plunge into the most nail-biting season of the year. Only now are they going to learn whether the past months of planning, design, and heavy investment will bring rich profits, or a potentially disastrous drain on funds.

As up to two-thirds of all toys and games are bought in the two months before Christmas the strength of consumer spending this year is being monitored as never before.

The buoyancy of spending in Britain's shops so far this year has made the industry rather more optimistic than usual as the Christmas run-in approaches.

Yet even a 'good' Christmas has in the past not always enabled toy companies to survive, especially in the international arena.

Major US operators such as Coleco Industries and Worlds of Wonder have both discovered that even buoyant sales in the mid-1980s were insufficient to stave off the more fundamental management and marketing problems which eventually forced them into bankruptcy. The lessons of the toy industry in the US – over-production, over-hype and poor cost control – have not been lost on other manufacturers worldwide.

Moreover, US manufacturers' love-affair with high-tech toys – such as Worlds of Wonder's 'interactive' microchip crammed talking-doll Julie – have turned parents and children off, both because of the technology involved as well as the high prices.

Yet, ironically, the US toy industry has potentially the most optimistic outlook of all Western toy markets. While the overall child market in Europe will decline by about 5 per cent over the next 30 years, and the Japanese market by 10 per cent, only the US child population is forecast to increase.

Moreover, some European countries have particular problems with the crucial pre-school toys market in the short term. The number of children aged under 4 years will continue to decline into the middle of the 1990s, with the exception of the UK, Austria, West Germany, Greece and Ireland.

But the US and Europe remain the most important markets in an industry with estimated worldwide sales of $40bn last year.

This Christmas the industry – not only in the UK but in other European and US markets – is having to face up to the fact that there are no real winners as in previous years, such as Cabbage Patch dolls or the board game Trivial Pursuit. These have stimulated enormous excitement and interest in the market.

'Gone are the vast majority of action characters, robots and transforming creatures which filled the shelves last year,' reports the Argos stores chain, one of the largest toy retailers in Britain. 'Back for the 1988 festivities are the familiar dolls, prams, trains and cars.'

This trend first became apparent last Christmas when parents and their children started turning away from heavily advertised toys towards more traditional products. Those retailers which had banked heavily on selling large volumes of such toys at discount prices soon found themselves forced to sell at a loss simply to shift the stock.

What the UK and other markets have rediscovered to their cost in recent years is that consumers – especially children – are fickle. In the early 1980s it seemed that nothing would stop the advance of electronic and video toys and games.

But just as quickly as they embraced these toys, so children forsook them for character toys such as Masters of the Universe. Now they have seemingly lost interest in this genre and are searching for something else, yet to be identified by the industry.

Mr Peter Eio, managing director of Lego in the UK, believes that the industry does not need to be so totally reliant on fashion. 'In the pre-school market, for example, the entire consumer base changes every four to five years and mothers search longingly for the perennial toys that they themselves enjoyed in childhood,' he says.

But the fickleness of fashion is not the only problem for the international toy trade: compression is the latest factor to take into account. This refers to the fact that while the target age group for toys and games used to run up to about 15, the growing sophistication of children means that once they are into their teens children from all countries are more interested in clothes, records and videos than toys and games. The world toy industry may need to do some serious thinking about where its products and markets should be directed in the decades ahead.

Source: D. Churchill, 'All Work and Little Play', *Financial Times*, Survey on Toys and Games, 2 Nov. 1988.

Questions

1. What are the main characteristics of the market for toys?
2. What are your impressions about the nature of competition between toy manufacturers?
3. How do these characteristics of the toy market differ from other markets such as (a) tomatoes; (b) books; (c) funeral services?
4. In what ways does the above article illustrate the operation of a free-enterprise system?
5. The article makes no reference to government intervention in the toy industry. Does this surprise you?

CASE STUDY

Nursing a Fortune

Danny Shamtally, from Mauritius, arrived in Britain at the age of 18 with a place on a student nurse training course at Belmont Hospital, Surrey, and not much else. That was in 1970. He and his Filipino wife, Carmelita, are now well on their way to being millionaires – on paper, at least. They own two private nursing-homes in the county, with a total of more than 40 beds, and are buying a third. They are outstanding examples of the way a nursing background can lead people with an interest in running something of their own into the care-homes business.

They met and married while student nurses, and both eventually qualified as Registered Nurses. Danny worked as an assistant officer and then officer in charge of council-owned residential homes in Sutton and Wallington for 10 years before they opened their first private home in 1983.

They used a Lloyds Bank mortgage to buy a Victorian house in Sutton for £88,000 and opened for business just before the 1984 Registered Homes Act, which was to help bring about a widely expanded national market for residential and nursing-home places. Now, Carmelita is matron there while Danny spends most of his time managing their second home, Chalden Rise, in Merstham.

Looking south from the slopes of the Downs, with a large garden beyond the french windows, Chalden Rise used to be a comfortable, stockbroker belt home. The Shamtallys have turned it into a psycho-geriatric category nursing home at rates of £300 per person a week. With day and night nurses, catering and cleaning staff, they are employing 24 people to look after 20 residents. (Danny drives a minibus for outings.)

He acknowledges that he would not have dared to open such a specialised home without his own background in psychiatric nursing. But, just one year later, he believes he has an efficient and profitable unit running in a style he is confident he can repeat if he acquires a third home.

Such rapid expansion follows the style of go-ahead business people in the care-homes sector who are expanding their businesses by almost the only way open to them – providing more beds. Danny says he has never had an empty bed at either of his homes and there is always a waiting-list for the next room that becomes vacant, despite his fees being in the more expensive segment of the sector. The homes are run with a relaxed, country-house atmosphere and almost every person has an en-suite bathroom.

To buy his second home, he restructured his family and business finances (he and his wife work as a business partnership) with the Bank of Scotland and obtained a £500 000 loan at 3 per cent above base rate over 15 years. Almost all the profits continue to be ploughed back into the business. Competition is growing, but he says: 'Although a lot of homes are being opened now it doesn't frighten us. We still get a call on average at least once a day from someone looking for a bed for a relative or a patient.'

The Shamtallys are well on their way to realising their ambition to manage a group of nursing-homes. Danny has firm ideas about size. 'They can be too big and become mini-institutions,' he says. 'I believe the magical figure for a nursing-home is 20 residents. Below that level, the fees do not cover the overheads unless the owners work full-time in it.'

Source: R. Hodson 'From Penniless Students to Wealthy Entrepreneurs' *Financial Times*, 28 Oct. 1989.

Questions

1. What are the characteristics of the market for nursing care as suggested by this case study?
2. What is the difference between the market for nursing care and the market for toys in respect of entry?
3. What is the nature of competition between suppliers of nursing care?
4. How does the growth in the market for nursing care contrast with the growth in the market for toys?

Exam Preparation

PRACTICAL EXERCISES

1. List the main characteristics of a capitalist economy.
2. Some critics believe and have suggested that consumer sovereignty is non-existent in economies like that of the USA and the UK. List the possible reasons that consumer sovereignty might not exist.

MULTIPLE CHOICE QUESTIONS

1. In most modern societies the price mechanism plays some part in the distribution of resources. This means that
   A prices are always held stable
   B rising prices of some goods encourage production of them, so diverting resources to them, and vice versa
   C prices are entirely determined by the cost of production
   D the price system could not work in societies that did not use some universally recognized form of money
   E prices are bound to rise
2. Which of the following statements is *untrue* about the operation of a wholly capitalist economy?
   A the price mechanism allocates resources
   B households freely decide how to spend on goods and services
   C there is government intervention in price determination
   D consumer sovereignty exists
   E all decisions are assumed to be made in a rational manner
3. The term 'consumer sovereignty' means that in a capitalist economy
   A consumers have a great deal more economic power than do producing firms simply because they are so much greater in number
   B each consumer knows what is good for him or her and they are all fully aware of available consumption possibilities
   C each consumer is like a medieval monarch being able to ensure that he or she gets what they want through being able to purchase an unlimited quantity of a good at the prevailing market price
   D consumers are responsible for determining the nature of economic activity as determined by their demands, as backed by money, on manufacturers and producers
4. The essence of a market economy is that
   A fruit and vegetables are commonly sold in open markets in many large towns
   B manufacturers sell a restricted variety of goods
   C the costs incurred by manufacturers in advertising their goods is not generally considered to be too high
   D resource allocation is affected by a set of signals which link buyers and sellers

RELATED ESSAY QUESTIONS

1. How does a market economy decide what to produce, how to produce, and for whom to produce?
2. What do you understand by 'opportunity cost'? Why is this concept relevant to the allocation of resources of a market economy?

3 Economic Systems: The Command Economy

Key Points to Review

- Capitalism (2.1)
- What, how, for whom to produce? (2.2)
- The trade-off between consumption goods and capital goods (1.7)

Questions for Preview

1 What are the characteristics of a command economy?

2 What is Marxian economics?

3 What problems face command economies?

Capitalism is not the only theoretical model of an economic system that exists. The polar extreme alternative to 'pure' capitalism, from a theoretical point of view, is an economic system of a command economy.

Command Economy

The central issues in a **command economy** again relate to who should have the property rights to all non-labour productive resources, who should make decisions about the use of these goods, and how income should be distributed once it is created. We can once more consider how the three fundamental questions facing any society are resolved in a command economy in direct contrast to the market economy.

What? How? For Whom? In a Command Economy

What?

1. What goods? *In the command economy the decentralized decision-making process is replaced by the collective preferences of the central planners.*

How?

2. How? *The central planners decide on not only quantities of output but also appropriate methods of production. They have to co-ordinate all aspects of productive activity through an organized system of resource allocation.*

For Whom?

3. For whom? *The forces that determine the relative rewards people get from producing are set by the central planners not by the market. Thus market forces are not given full expression to determine wage-rates.*

The Political Dimension

Too often the command economy is seen as synonymous with a socialist or communist system. This is quite wrong as a right-wing dictatorship could also operate a command economy. It is thus misleading to attach a political label to the two contrasting types of economic system. Concern about political control (i.e. how democratic a society is), is, strictly speaking, a separate issue from that of economic control. A socialist system could be a democratic society when the key government officials making decisions about the use of resources are elected in genuine elections, i.e. where there is a choice of candidates facing electors. A socialist system could also come under the political control of a dictator just as in a capitalist system.

Having confronted the political dimension in our discussion we now briefly distinguish between **socialism** and **communism.**

Socialism

In a 'pure' socialist system the state owns the major non-labour productive resources – land and capital goods. Individuals can own consumer goods and consumer durables, but they are not allowed to own factories, machines, and other things that are used to produce what society wants. Second, people are induced to produce by wage differentials. However, taxation of large incomes to redistribute income may reduce some of the incentives to produce as much. Third, the state determines people's wage-rates and who should be paid what in government-owned and -operated factories. Fourth, individuals are allowed to enter only certain areas of activity. They cannot, for example, freely set up their own factories. They cannot become entrepreneurs or capitalists, for the state has this function and controls all enterprises. (Read Key Points 3.1.)

Communism

With 'pure' communism all resources are, in principle, owned in common. What then about the role of the state? Here we turn to Karl Marx (1818–83) who perhaps more than anyone else in the history of economic thought is responsible for the development of the communist movement.

Marx envisaged the fall of capitalism leading to the rise of socialism and eventually to the world of ideal communism. Marx foresaw a final state where the relations of production and distribution would be: 'From each according to his ability, to each according to his needs.' In fact, in the ideal communist world, that Marx predicted would eventually emerge, there would be little or no need for government. Everything would take care of itself, for man's basic human nature would have been changed because the relations of production and distribution would no longer create class conflict and alienation would not occur.

Having now made this summary explanation of socialism and communism we must not lose sight of the important point made earlier. Neither socialism nor communism are theoretically necessary features of a command economy. None the less it is true that in practice socialism is the main political system under which most command economies are administered. This being so we need briefly to examine the case for socialism put forward by critics of the market economy.

Marxian Economics

What was it about the market economy to which Marx objected? Basically he saw a conflict existing between the capitalist class and those they employed as labourers. The capitalists were regarded as exploiting their workers and also possessing considerable market and political power. Marx rejected the notion that the capitalists meekly responded to the wishes of consumers. In their long-term struggle to survive the capitalists were seen by Marx as trying to cut the costs of production by mechanizing production, i.e. reducing employment. Rising unemployment would eventually provoke the development of class consciousness among workers and the capitalist order be overthrown.

The Marxian critique of the market economy is, inevitably, the subject of continuing debate. The revolutionary ideology he offered makes him the subject of much study by social scientists. What can we offer here in a brief but carefully couched response to his picture of capitalism as a historically limited form of economic system?

A first comment is that Marx was essentially a critic of capitalism rather than an architect of the ideal communist world that he thought would ultimately emerge. Because of this he is open to criticism concerning how such an economy should actually be organized. In particular the immense problems facing the central planners in a socialist command economy

Key Points 3.1

- **We can simplify the different types of economic systems by looking at them in terms of decentralization. Pure market capitalism would be on one end of the scale, pure command socialism on the other.**
- **The key attributes of socialism are: (1) The government owns the major productive resources. (2) People are induced to produce by wage differentials, but taxation is often used to redistribute income, thereby reducing some incentive to produce. (3) The rewards for producing are usually set by the state rather than the market. (4) Individuals can enter only certain areas of activity and cannot, for example, freely set up their own factories.**

KARL MARX

GERMAN ECONOMIST (1818–83)

Ghost of Western Economics

Marx was more than an economist. He was a revolutionary who was instrumental in developing the communist movement, a sociologist, and a historian. He marshalled all these talents for his analysis of capitalism and the ways in which this economic system affected social life. According to Marx (and his frequent collaborator Friedrich Engels), history is the struggle for power of competing classes based on their material interests in the production process. Unlike most economists since the time of Adam Smith, Marx saw capitalism as a specific and historically limited form of social organization. The internal dynamics of capitalism, he argued, would eventually create conditions ripe for its overthrow by the working class and the institution of a new form of social organization based on collective ownership.

Marx was a prolific writer, but the culminating work of his career is undoubtedly *Das Kapital*, the first volume of which appeared in 1867. In this gigantic text, Marx set out to do nothing less, he said, than 'to lay bare the economic law of motion of modern society'. Like Adam Smith and David Ricardo, Marx adhered to the labour theory of value – the theory that the value of commodities ultimately depends on the human labour time expended in their production. But to explain how profits could be generated in a society built on equivalent exchanges of commodities and money, Marx added a new concept – *surplus value*. Under capitalism, labour power is treated as a commodity like any other; workers are paid according to the cost of their reproduction and maintenance. But workers in fact can produce an equivalent to their subsistence in only part of a working day. The difference between the labour time workers spend producing for a capitalist and the labour time equivalent to the wages they actually receive Marx called *surplus value*. Here, he argued, was a scientific index of exploitation.

But it was, Marx argued, the workers who would get the last laugh. Capitalists, faced with competition, are continually driven to expand and mechanize production, thus eliminating some labour costs. But since labour is the ultimate source of value, capitalists, in effect, are cutting their own throats. Over the long term, Marx argued, the rate of profit would fall, while at the same time more and more people would be left without jobs. Through a combination of economic crises of increasing severity and the development of class consciousness among workers, capitalism would finally collapse.

The capitalist economic system appeared to break down partially in the 1930s depression, but Marx had not considered the possibility of Keynesian intervention by the state. Furthermore, the rate of profit has not fallen in the way he expected. But if the Marxian vision of capitalist breakdown has not taken place, Marx's analysis of the workings of capitalism contains many insights, some of which have only begun to be appreciated in the non-communist nations.

were played down. The central planners have to make decisions concerning production targets and ensure that the necessary inputs be available in the right place and at the right time to make meeting such targets actually possible. This requires an effective organizational structure or bureaucracy to exist. As regards the labour input, the socialist economy requires some sort of incentive (moral or by way of threat) to exist for people to become fully involved in the economic process. Critics of the socialist economy have thus doubted whether a mixture of patriotic exhortation and brute fear are an effective substitute for the self-interest motivation on which the capitalist system is based.

As in the case of capitalism the extreme form of central planning is a stylized description that has no counterpart in the real world. Even the USSR does not correspond to a pure command economy because in recent years there has been a greater use of market prices and profitability to allocate resources. None the less if we look at the experience of central planning in the USSR it should give us some evidence of how a basically socialist economy has performed.

The Growth of the Soviet Economy after 1917

The most influential disciple of Marxist ideology has been Vladimir Ilyich Lenin. His Bolsheviks came to power in Russia in 1917 soon after the overthrow of the Russian monarchy. Lenin did not immediately get rid of all capitalist institutions in Russia. His New Economic Policy (NEP) allowed small industry and trade to be privately owned. In the agricultural sector, forced requisitions were eliminated – the peasants no longer had to give away any products to the government or the army. The market was once again used. Peasant farmers found it profitable to sow fallow land in order to sell the crops. Only heavy industry, transportation, foreign trade, and banking remained in government hands. In retrospect, the NEP was a success. By 1928, industry and agricultural production surpassed pre-revolutionary war levels. In 1924, however, Lenin had died; Stalin his successor decided to take the 'several steps forward' that Lenin had promised.

Stalin did not like the inability of central authorities to control the direction of the economy, which was the result of Lenin's having allowed so much of the economy to revert to private hands. Stalin felt that there were certain industries that should be treated favourably in order to get the economy growing rapidly. Thus, a course of economic development *in advance* was plotted in **five-year plans**. These plans were called five-year plans because they plotted a coarse of economic activity for the following five years. Special industries were picked for growth, which was to be 'financed' by obtaining more agricultural produce to feed urban industrial workers. In order to obtain more agricultural products, collectivization was to be the key. Between 1928 and 1932, over 15 million peasant households were formed into over 200 000 collective farms. On the collectives, land and livestock were owned in common – that is, they were not private property. Land was also worked in common, since no one person owned it, and a system of wage-payments to collective farmers was introduced. Communist Party control over the peasant was strengthened.

Agricultural collectivization was not an overwhelming success. Peasants slaughtered and then ate, sold, or traded much of their livestock rather than turn it over to the collectives. At the end of the first five-year plan, the number of livestock had fallen by half. Grain output also fell, perhaps because of the reduced incentive to produce but partly because of the problems of instituting collectives at the onset. None the less, at the point of a gun more agricultural products flowed from the country to the city, and that was in fact the major objective of the first five-year plan. Clearly, since agricultural output had fallen with more going to the city, much less was left for the peasants.

Capital Goods and Growth

In Chapter 1 we showed that there was a trade-off between current consumption and future consumption. If you turn back to Figure 1.14 you will see how we showed with the use of the production possibilities curve that the more we invest in capital goods the more likely it is that the economy will grow so as to allow greater consumption by households in the future. The Russian economy after 1928 illustrates this trade-off. There was a marked increase in the proportion of resources devoted to the production of capital goods. Whereas in 1928 investment accounted for about 15 per cent of all output, by 1937 it had doubled. Under the first five-year plan there was a massive development of heavy industry and the output of the coal, steel, and electricity industries increased very rapidly. If one realizes that at that time well over 80 per cent of the Russian population was rural-based, then one can appreciate the massive emphasis placed on rapid industrialization. The second and third five-year plans continued the emphasis on capital goods and since too the Russian leadership developed an enthusiasm for defence expenditure there was a reduced share of resources left available for production of consumption goods. It was indeed machinery and guns rather than butter. Any hope by the Russian peasant of more consumption tomorrow was counteracted by conscious actions by the state to lower current consumption standards. The preference for capital equipment and military goods meant that for many Russians a major improvement in the material standard of living was denied them. The Russian economy indeed grew impressively between 1928 and 1937 but decisions on the quantity, quality, and variety of goods for private consumption were not made by consumers but by the central planners. Thus there is a problem in appraising the 'success' of the Russian approach to development in the inter-war period.

We have looked back to the inter-war period in Russia to consider the decision of the central planners concerning the question *what goods are to be produced?* Our next question, you will recall, was *how are these to be produced?* This makes it necessary to explain what is meant by 'the planners'.

The Soviet Economy Today

Figure 3.1 shows central planning for industry in the Soviet Union. At the top is the Presidium, which is the administrative body of the Soviet government. The Presidium delegates authority to the Council of Ministers, which establishes broad goals for the economy – such as what proportion of available resources should be devoted to consumer goods, what percentage to producer goods, what percentage to military goods. Once these goals have been established, the State Planning Commission (Gosplan) must then decide how the goals are to be achieved. The Gosplan generates production targets for each particular industry and also decides where the output of each industry will go. Next, the planners in each of the fifteen republics within the Soviet Union apply the Gosplan's decisions to their jurisdiction.

Figure 3.1
Central Planning for Industry in the Soviet Union

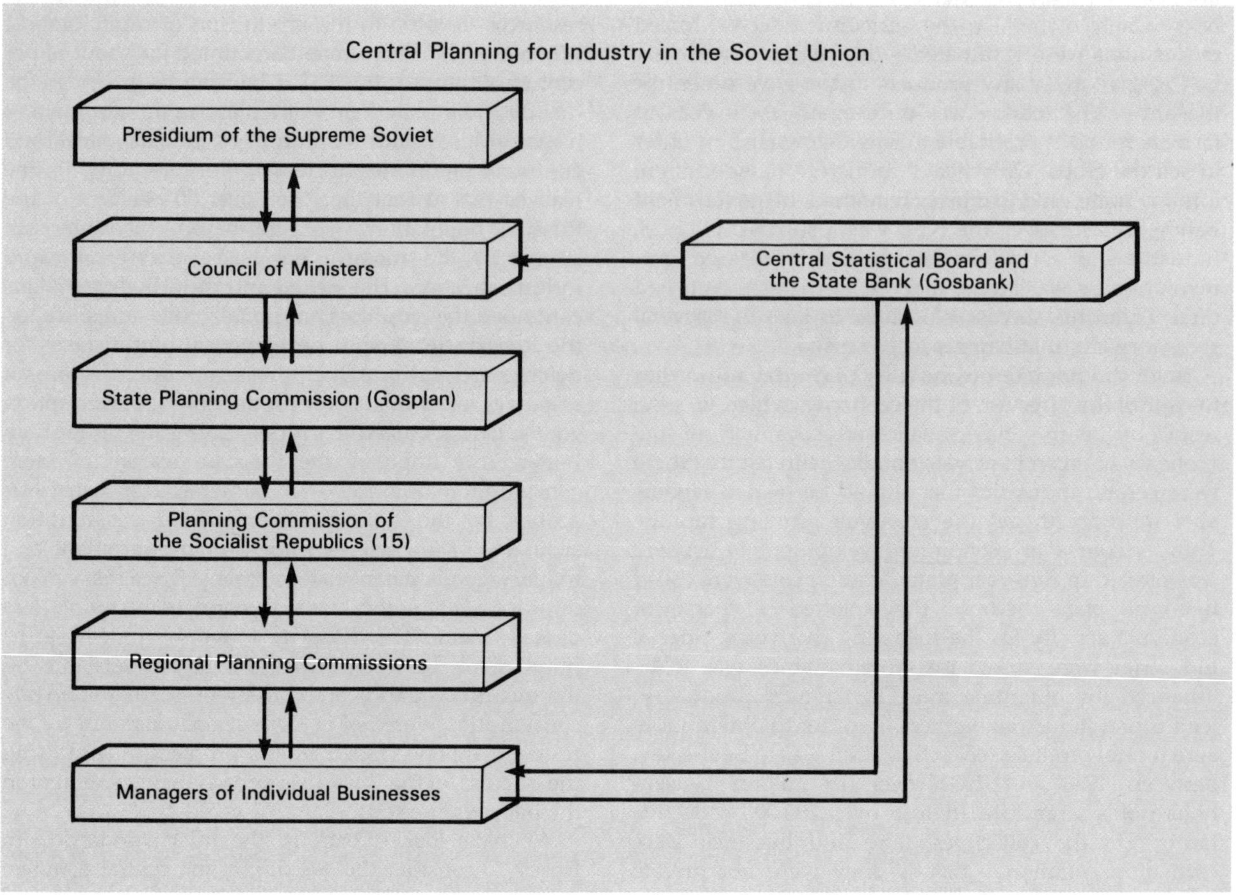

These plans are then forwarded to regional planning councils, who assign production targets and allocate resources to specific industries. The final level in this planning hierarchy are the plant managers. They can affect planning by asking the regional councils for lower or higher production quotas and by demanding greater resources.

This complex planning system does have some checks and balances. Each level is responsible to, and supervised by, the level above it. Gosplan is also the official government banking system so it can verify all receipts and expenditures and discover fraud and corruption.

The central statistical board evaluates businesses in terms of their abilities to meet quotas and reports its findings to the Council of Ministers. Communist Party officials oversee the operation of actual factories. Union officials represent management (the government), not the workers. These unions encourage workers and businesses to meet their quotas and to handle the numerous welfare programmes for workers.

The problem of incentives in a socialist economy has already been mentioned. Soviet experience shows that there are numerous problems in setting quotas for plant managers. Forcing plant managers to meet quotas sometimes contributes to the poor quality of the goals produced. Quotas are typically measured in the number of units produced, or by weight or volume – not by quality. Pressure to meet quotas has also encouraged the rise of a black economy which involves illegal transactions – such as bartering for supplies among plant managers, buying supplies on the black market, and bribing government officials to reduce quotas or change allocations.

Some students of the Soviet system argue that quotas have kept managers from experimenting with new production techniques for fear of not meeting their quotas. This presumed unwillingness to develop and use technology could in principle have caused the Soviet economy to fall further behind Western nations in its ability to produce. Some experts have claimed that the Soviet Union is many years behind in production techniques in many vital industries.

We have seen that a centrally planned economic

system faces several major difficulties in operating successfully. In Chapter 2 we saw that there are also problems in how the capitalist economy operates. It should not surprise you that most countries in reality are neither purely capitalist nor purely of the command type of economic system. We examine the situation in Chapter 4.

Key Points 3.2

- **In Russia after 1928 there was less production of goods to satisfy consumer wants. More production went into capital formation.**
- **Heavy industry grew rapidly. Collectivization of agriculture resulted in lower food production.**
- **In any command economy, there are problems of co-ordination among different sectors. Millions of planning decisions must be made, and they are all interrelated. The Russian planning system is thus, not surprisingly, complex.**

CASE STUDY

Checkmate and Win a Dacha

Anatoly Karpov, the chess star, has a car telephone in his chauffeur-driven limousine.

All members of the élite in the sporting world, the arts, and above all in the Kremlin bureaucracy enjoy carefully graded privileges to which the ordinary Soviet worker can never hope to aspire. Karpov's car telephone puts him in the superstar bracket, but even middle-ranking officials and celebrities can expect to get a Moscow flat larger than the usual cramped allocation of five or six square metres per person (the official figure is nine metres minimum), a place at the head of the long waiting-list for a car, as well as access to top health care and to the best schools and colleges.

They also get a government-provided country home, or *dacha*. All Russians love to retreat to a *dacha* in the beautiful countryside around Moscow, but the definition of a *dacha* can range from a dilapidated garden shed for the lower orders to a magnificent mansion screened by discreet birch trees and security fences for the cultural and political élite.

Karpov, who is judged to have earned his privileged status by conquering the world of chess, is building an £80 000 *dacha* outside the city, and has an Audi 100 for his personal use as well as his official car. One prominent musician recently acquired a palatial country house which formerly belonged to a KGB general and which, like other élite *dachas*, is set in a closed area rarely penetrated by either foreigners or ordinary Russians.

The extraordinary aspect of all this to a Western mind is that working-class Muscovites fighting their way on to crammed buses or standing in long queues in the snow for scarce foodstuffs do not seem to resent this hidden privilege in the least. They are aware that those who govern them, from the President downwards, have access to special shops and even Western goods.

The official Marxist-Leninist ideology, hammered home every day in the press and media, professes egalitarianism and social justice. Yet most Russians seem to accept fatalistically that abuse of power and humiliation by officialdom are inevitable, possibly because this has been so since Tsarist times.

The Tsar's ministers used to drive their carriages at speed down the middle of the city's avenues, scattering the *hoi polloi* to right and left, much as today's Kremlin Zils thunder down the middle lane pushing mere mortals aside.

Although there is no overt resentment of official privilege, condemnation of the abuse of such privilege does occasionally surface in the Soviet press and at party meetings. The late Yuri Andropov's stern drive against official abuses won him widespread popular approval, and the late Konstantin Chernenko continued to attack corruption, noting that it caused 'profound anger' among the masses.

One female lathe-operator from Rostov-on-Don recently wrote to *Komsomolskaya Pravda* to complain that her monthly wage of 200 roubles (£200) had little purchasing power.

'I understand that our society cannot yet afford for everyone to dress well and fashionably' she wrote. 'But the point is that those who deserve them should receive the most benefits, and by that I mean the workers.'

There is little sign, however, of privilege being reduced – if anything the reverse. When, at the local Soviet elections, officials and their well-dressed wives turned up to vote in chauffeur-driven Chaikas, there was not a murmur of protest from the proletariat trudging through the ice and snow to the ballot-box.

The newest development, which again has aroused some public protest but is likely to go ahead anyway with full Kremlin approval, is the establishment of a series of luxury clothing stores for those with spare roubles, regardless of rank or status.

The new shops are to be for those who find the ordinary Soviet stores too drab.

It seems doubtful whether Lenin or Marx would have approved.

Source: R. Owen, 'Letter from Moscow: Lives of Luxury in the Land of Marx', *The Times*, 2 Apr. 1985.

Questions

1. In what ways does the above article suggest that life in Russia differs from the socialist model?
2. Are the departures from an egalitarian system (a) inevitable and (b) desirable?

CASE STUDY

Life in the Russian Heartland

When Mikhail Gorbachev presented his vision to the Communist Party plenum this week of a socialist agriculture revived by tenant farmers, Natalya Sergeyevna was sitting at her oilcloth-covered kitchen table roundly cursing her lot.

'Who the hell does he think is going to take a lease here?' she said. 'We are all pensioners. The young people left years ago. Who is going to do the work?'

Natalya Sergeyevna lives in a miserable little settlement called Popova, a good three hours' drive north of Moscow in the heart of what they call the non-black-earth zone of the Soviet Union. Twenty years ago there were 29 homes in the village, which boasted a school and a shop. Today only seven are still permanently occupied, all by old-age pensioners.

The school and shop are closed, and the nearest civilisation is three miles away at the other end of a pot-holed sea of mud called a rural road, virtually impassable to anything but a tractor.

The conditions in Popova, on the fringes of a giant collective farm called *Iskra* (the Spark), the name of the revolutionary newspaper edited by Vladimir Lenin, are typical of the sorry state of Soviet agriculture, above all in the Russian heartland of the country. There is no running water, erratic electricity supplies where they exist at all, no telephone, no public transport, nor remotely adequate health facilities. In spite of being in the heart of the countryside, the supply of food in the shops is paltry.

'You know what *perestroika* means to us?' Natalya Sergeyevna demanded. 'Sugar is rationed. There is no meat. No butter. No fish. There's nothing.' Yet she still manages to serve slices of a plain cake to her guests, and sugary sweets, with tea and milk. It does not affect rural hospitality.

Her husband Yegor Mikhailovich sits in the corner, too deaf to hear the conversation. He is a war veteran, a labour veteran, once given the title of 'achiever of Communist labour'. 'He applied for a house in Pankova (the main village of the collective). You know what they told him? Get stuffed . . . And he fought in three wars.'

Natalya Sergeyevna's story, and her bitterness, bordering on tears, are just a tiny picture of the depression in the Soviet countryside.

Mr Gorbachev and his fellow Community Party leaders know perfectly well how disastrous the rural situation has become. They also know that the lack of decent food supplies is the single most sensitive political issue right across the country. Mr Yegor Ligachev, now the agriculture supremo, denied that there had been any food riots, or even demonstrations. But he admitted: 'The agriculture problem, the food problem, goes to the heart of every Soviet citizen. It is not easing. It is being aggravated in several areas, and this affects the social situation.'

As for the Soviet leader, he delivered a devastating indictment of the situation in his address to the central committee plenum. He spelt out a record of more than 60 years of Soviet agricultural policy which ranged from outright persecution, through blatant discrimination, to plain neglect of the country's peasant population.

He admitted that millions of peasants had been evicted in Stalin's mass collectivisation programme, many of them condemned to die in labour camps. Yet even when that process ended, 'the disdainful attitude to the conditions of life of rural workers not only did not weaken, but became even more sophisticated'.

He said that wages for collective farmers were a mere 'token'; they had no (internal) passports, so they could not leave their villages without permission. Attempts to tackle rural deprivation foundered on the underlying discrimination in favour of the cities. Prices for industrial goods rose far faster than farm prices, a campaign was launched to wipe out private plots, and a policy was begun to close down 'unpromising villages'.

It was a speech very close to his heart, for Mikhail Gorbachev spent his entire career in agriculture before he reached the Soviet leadership. He was born on a collective farm in the Caucasus, returned to the area from Moscow University to become a Communist Party organiser, and by the age of 31 became party organiser for agriculture in the whole Stavropol region. That was where he made his name.

He cited one attempt after another by the ruling party to reverse the trend, either by introducing new forms of administration, new programmes to open up virgin lands, or new plans to invest in a massive expansion of machinery and modern farming techniques.

And all the time the rural emigration continued at a hectic pace. 'I do not wish to arouse passions,' Mr Gorbachev declared, 'but it ought to be said, nevertheless, that the situation is so grave that in many regions the people are deserting the land, moving out of the villages. Migration of the rural population has reached a critical level.'

This week's meeting of the Communist Party central committee was nothing less than an attempt to reverse that process of rural decay and destruction, and redefine the essence of socialist agricultural policy.

Mr Gorbachev's stated ambition is to make the peasant farmer once more, or possible for the first time, 'master of his land'. The word he uses in Russian – *khozyain* – is a thoroughly unsocialist, pre-revolutionary word for 'boss'.

Its main plank is a system of leasehold tenure, whether for small groups of workers, or for family farmers. But what the Soviet leadership is proposing is also choice, and decentralisation. No one system will be perfect for all areas, Mr Gorbachev said. Indeed, the range of leasehold allowed will also be open-ended: from 5 years to 50, or more.

As such, the debate goes to the heart of the whole debate on *perestroika*, for it concerns the concept of property in a socialist society. 'The restructuring of economic relations in the countryside demands the revision, in theory and in practice, of existing views on socialist ownership,' Mr Gorbachev told the plenum.

At the heart of his vision is a desire to revive the enterprise and independence of the Soviet peasantry, based on a concept of leasehold farming within a socialist framework.

He faces fundamental problems on at least three levels.

First, there is still huge resistance in the Communist Party to any redefinition of ideology which calls into question such a key institution as the collective farm. Whatever Mr Gorbachev may say about preserving the collective and state farm system, the development of widespread tenant-farming must undermine the existing structure of rural bureaucracy.

But second, in attempting to reconcile reform with ideology, he is leaving much of the old structure in place, and with a controlling say in the development of the new. Any prospective tenant-farmer has to negotiate with the collective-farm management, which is usually synonymous with the local Communist Party leadership, on the terms of his new contract.

Third, and perhaps most intractable of all, he has to revive the desire and belief of the Soviet peasant in working for himself. He moved from Tsarist serfdom to enforced collectivisation with barely time to learn the difference. Since then, the interminable shifts in policy and neglect have left the farm-workers sullen and unresponsive to all incentives.

Mr Alexei Durnov, chairman of the Iskra collective farm, says the single most important change he could wish for is 'labour discipline'. His farm-workers have no desire to work, and 'I have no rights to make them'. It is not quite what Mr Gorbachev is talking about, but it shows the problem he is up against.

Source: Q. Peel, 'The Harvest isn't Home yet', *Financial Times*, 18 Mar. 1989.

Questions

1. What does the case study suggest about the quality of life for those working on collective farms in the Soviet Union?
2. What factors appear to have contributed to the growth in rural emigration?
3. Why does the author suggest that in the light of historical experience it is uncertain whether reform of Soviet agricultural policy will be successful?

Exam Preparation

PRACTICAL EXERCISE

Suppose you are an economic planner and you have been told by our country's political leaders that they want to increase car production by 10 per cent over the previous year. What other industries will be affected by this decision?

MULTIPLE CHOICE QUESTIONS

1. Which one of the following statements is necessarily true of any centrally planned economy?

A It cannot overcome the problem of economic scarcity, because it cannot use increases in the money supply to finance government expenditure.
B It cannot overcome the problem of economic scarcity, because it will come up against the constraint of factor limitation.
C It can overcome the problem of economic scarcity by deciding what is to be produced, thus relieving the consumer of the problem of choice.
D It can overcome the problem of economic scarcity by income redistribution from rich to poor.
E It can overcome the problem of scarcity by regulating the price mechanism.

2. Which of the following statements is necessarily incorrect as a feature of a fully centrally planned economy?

A Resources are directed by the price mechanism.
B Workers do not earn equal wages.
C The profit motive is severely constrained.
D There is a bureaucratic structure to take decisions about how the economy is organized.

One or more of the options given in Questions 3, 4, 5, and 6 may be correct. Select your answer by means of the code set out in the grid:

A	B	C	D
1, 2, 3 all correct	1, 2 only correct	2, 3 only correct	1 only correct

3. A command economy is a term to describe an economic system which is

1. state regulated
2. decentralized
3. motivated by self-interest

4. It would be incorrect to suggest that after the Russian Revolution

1. the Russian economy was totally controlled by the state
2. the Russian economy grew very slowly
3. some elements of a market economy were reintroduced

5. In Russia collectivization of agriculture after 1928

1. resulted in a rapid rise in agricultural output
2. led to food shortages in rural areas
3. was a policy favoured by Stalin

6. The Russian economy after 1928 illustrates the fact that

1. there is a trade-off between current consumption and future consumption
2. the central planners preferred capital equipment to consumer goods
3. a complex planning system can experience major difficulties in operation

RELATED ESSAY QUESTIONS

1. Compare and contrast the principal economic characteristics of a free market with those of a planned economy.

2. 'A centrally planned economy has both advantages and disadvantages compared with a free market economy.' Discuss.

4 Economic Systems: The Mixed Economy

Key Points to Review

- Capitalism (2.1)
- Socialism (3.1)

Questions for Preview

1 **How can economic systems be classified?**

2 **How do privately owned firms in the UK mixed economy differ from those of the pure capitalist type?**

3 **Why is the extent of state intervention in Western economies not easy to measure?**

The two previous chapters have discussed two model economic systems – capitalism and the socialist command economy. In practice most countries around the world have an economic system neither purely capitalist nor purely of the socialist command type. They have a mixed economic system – that is a mixture of private decision-making and central organization. Private enterprise responding to market forces operates to a greater or lesser extent with some measure of state control and economic planning. In this chapter we show how the private sector and the state relate in some of the real world's mixed economic systems. We focus on the UK economy but also look at some recent changes in the Soviet economy to show how that has now become less of a true command economy.

Looking at the Spectrum of Systems

One possible way of comparing several economic systems in the world is to look at them according to how decentralized their decision-making processes are. In other words, to what degree do individuals make the decisions about what to produce, how to produce it, how much to produce, and for how much to sell it? In Figure 4.1 we have put on the extreme right-hand side of the scale pure free market capitalism, where all

Figure 4.1

Economic Systems: The scale of Decentralization. On the extreme right-hand side of the diagram we find pure market capitalism, and on the extreme left-hand side is pure command socialism. Albania is a country whose system is extremely centralized and relatively close to pure command socialism. On the other extreme is Hong Kong, which is virtually totally decentralized and relatively close to pure market capitalism. In between are the mixed economies of the world, with varying degrees of government intervention represented by their closeness to the left-hand side of the diagram.

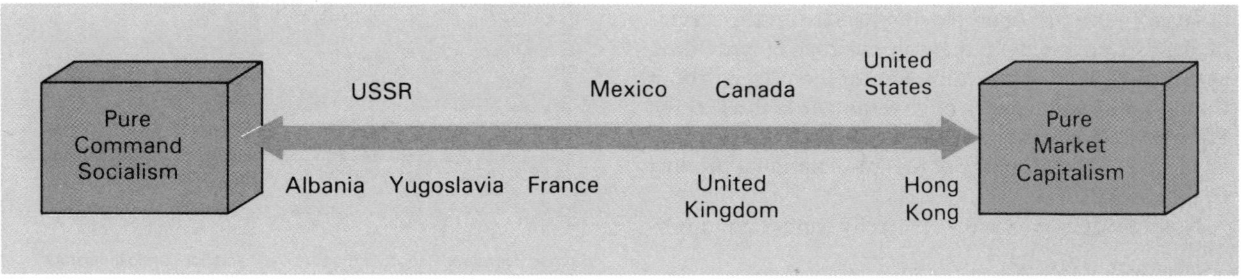

Key Point 4.1

- **In reality all economies are mixed economies or mixed systems since private markets, self-interest, state allocation of resources, income redistribution, and altruism exist to some degree in all societies.**

economic decisions are made by individuals without government intervention. On the extreme left-hand side of the scale, we have put pure command socialism, where economic decisions are made by some central authority such as a group of government planners or even a dictator. Somewhere in between would be the mixed economic systems such as those existing in the United States, France, the USSR, and the United Kingdom. Very broadly speaking the closer we go to a pure capitalist system, the less political centralization there is, and vice versa.

Albania is a country whose system is extremely centralized and relatively close to pure command socialism. On the other extreme is Hong Kong, which is virtually totally decentralized and relatively close to pure market capitalism. In between are the mixed economies of the world, with varying degrees of government intervention and centralization, represented by their closeness to the left-hand side of the diagram. You will note Figure 4.1 has no scale. This is because of the very real problem of actually measuring the absolute differences between the countries shown as regards their overall public/private sector mixture. (Now read Key Point 4.1.)

The United States

If we had to place the US economic system somewhere within the spectrum of economic systems ranging from pure capitalism to pure command socialism it would have to be put closer to the former system than the latter. But it has tended through the years towards a system in which the government plays an ever more influential role. The role of government in the US economic system has expanded greatly, especially since the Second World War. When we speak of government in the US – federal, state, and local – we are referring to the collective total of all individuals who, in one way or another, are paid out of tax revenue and who regulate private transactions. This regulatory activity means that apart from the cost of employing persons in the service of the US government there is the cost of providing appropriate tools and equipment for them to go about their work. The business of government is thus costly. Figure 4.2 shows the growth in government spending in the US as a percentage of the gross national product in the period since 1890.

Not only does government directly control an important share of the US economy, but it has entered into many aspects of hitherto private economic dealings. For example, it has stepped in to help out (subsidize) certain industries, e.g. loan guarantees to Lockheed and Chrysler, or to tax others, e.g. a windfall profits tax on oil companies. As another example, the US government has put many restrictions on the working of the agricultural sector. Additionally, through its many departments and agencies, the government controls numerous aspects of energy, transportation, communication, and commerce in general. In the last several decades, the government has increased its welfare programmes – tax dollars are redistributed to those who are deemed 'needy'. Education has become primarily a government activity but the desirability of state intervention in medical care continues to be a politically contentious issue. The business of modern government in the US is thus complex and much debated. Furthermore, the extent of government involvement in the economy is not simply revealed by the size of government spending as shown in Figure 4.2. Apart from hiring staff and purchasing equipment the US government is also engaged in making **transfer**

Figure 4.2

Government Spending in the US. Here we show government purchases at all levels – federal, state, and local – of goods and services expressed as a percentage of **total national output**, or **gross national product**. The biggest jumps occurred during the First World War and the Second World War; although, proportionally, government spending fell dramatically after the Second World War, it did not remain at previous peacetime levels for long.

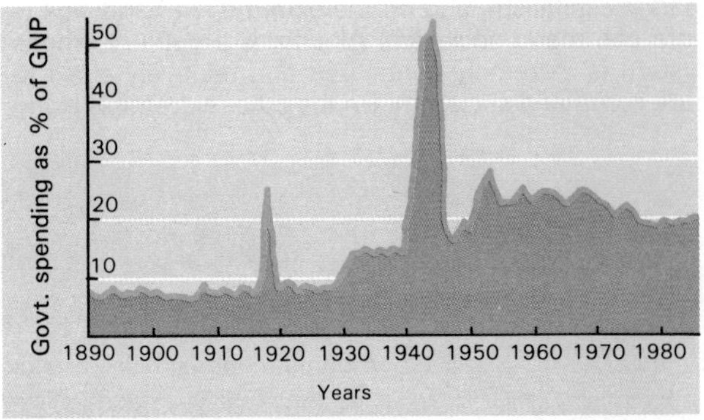

Source: Economic Report of the President and Economic Indicators.

Figure 4.3
General Government Expenditure in the UK (% of GDP)

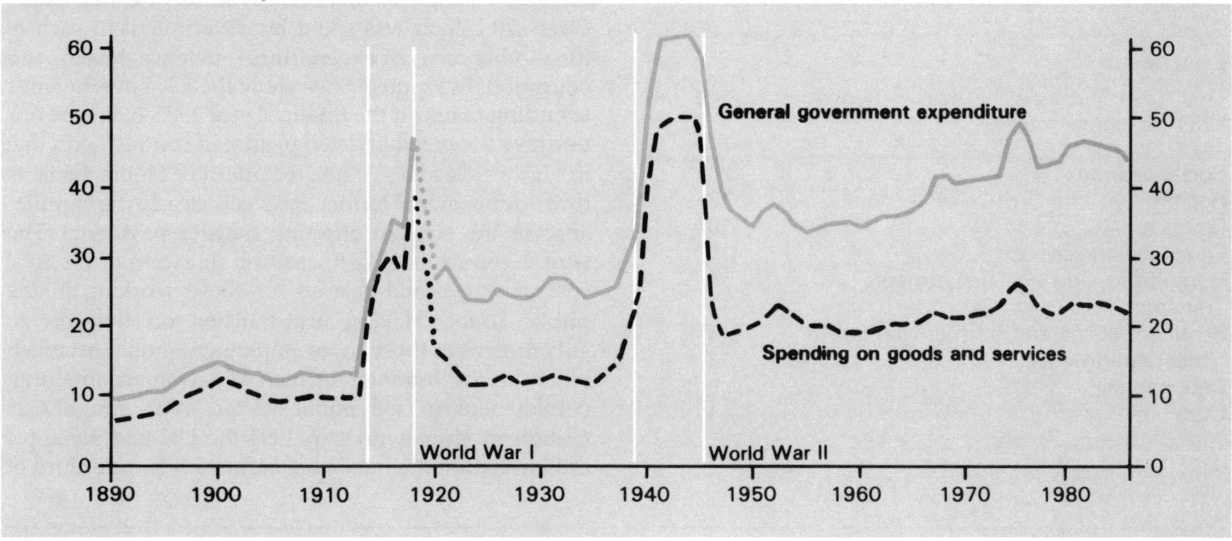

Source: 'Public Expenditure: Long-Term Trends', *Economic Progress Report*, no. 194, Feb. 1988.

payments. Part of government tax revenues are used to make payments to some citizens in the form of cash and other welfare benefits. If these transfer payments are now included as part of all government spending we then find there is an upward trend in the proportion of GNP accounted for by all aspects of government.

The United Kingdom

Broadly speaking there has been a similar growth in the scale of government activity in most other developed economies as in the US economy during the past fifty years. Figure 4.3 shows government spending in the UK as a percentage of output or gross domestic product since 1890.

The extent of this influence of the state would seem to be based on whatever is the size of the **public sector**. As we have shown in the case of the US the public sector can be defined as the part of the economy that falls within the domain of central (or federal) government plus local (or provincial) government.

Figure 4.4 and Figure 4.5 show the size of public expenditure in the UK for 1989–90. However, we must treat the data shown with great caution in viewing them as a measure of the influence of the state because there is a wide range of expenditures by central and local government. Some items reflect *collective* decisions to spend on defence and education. Other items such as social security leave much discretion to individuals. Recipients of unemployment and sickness benefits are, within limits, able to spend these incomes from government as they wish. Thus data such as that in Figures 4.4 and 4.5 cannot be used as an unambiguous measure of 'the state's influence' and by implication, of the weakening of individual freedom of choice. The important point, which is not a subjective matter, is that when governments redistribute money from one section of society to another in the form of transfer payments, they do not add to the sum of expenditures which involve collective decision-making. In other words public expenditure includes both some spending which involves a claim on economic resources available and also other spending which involves government acting as a giant redis-

Figure 4.4
General Government Expenditure Plans, 1989–90, £billion

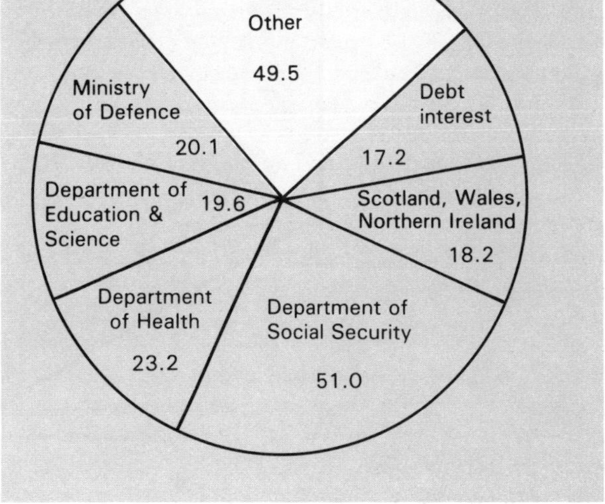

tribution agency. In this latter case resources are *not* diverted from the private sector in favour of the state. This matter is considered further in Chapter 10.

Figure 4.5

The Main Forms of Public Expenditure in the UK 1989–90 (percentages)

Social security	26
Health	12
Defence	10
Education and science	10
Home Office and legal departments	4
Transport	3
Scotland, Wales, and Northern Ireland	9
Other departments	13
Debt interest	9
Other	4
	100

(Read Key Point 4.2.)

We see that in 1989–90 social security accounted for the largest single element in government expenditure. Over £20 billion was spent by government in each of three other areas of expenditure – defence, health, and education. In Figure 4.6 we show the UK government's spending plans for the financial year 1985–6. Whilst this portrays a somewhat dated picture in contrast with that in Figures 4.4 and 4.5 the great merit of Figure 4.6 is its three-dimensional format. It reveals clearly the significance of the state in effecting transfer payments. The sum involved in 1985–6 was well in excess of the total cost of wages and salaries for those working in the public sector. Having just touched on the cost to government of those in its employ we should establish what are the numbers of men and women obtaining employment in the public sector. With roughly 25 million in employment in 1987 the UK had some 6.4 million within the public sector. Just under one-third of

Figure 4.6

Public Spending for 1985–6: Where, Who, and What (percentages) This three-dimensional diagram shows spending by spending authority, programme, and economic category. Central government was the major spending authority and social security accounted for the biggest single programme of spending. The significance of transfer payments as a category of spending is evident being greater than the labour costs of those involved in central and local government.

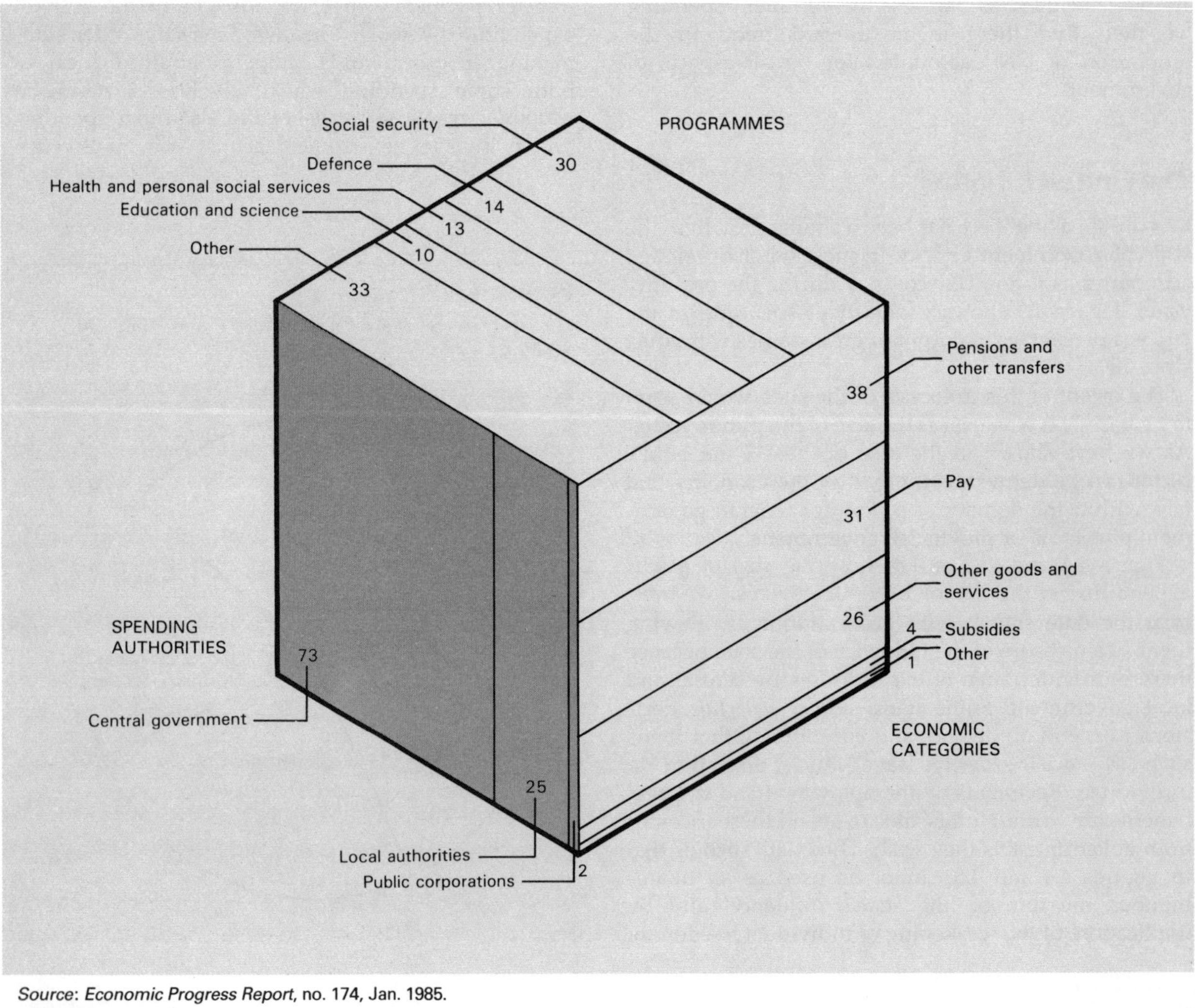

Source: *Economic Progress Report*, no. 174, Jan. 1985.

Key Point 4.2

▶ **Public expenditure by all forms of government in the US and UK exaggerates the influence of the state because the total figure includes spending which does not involve any claims on economic resources. Transfer payments from one section of society to another by government should not be included in a list of public expenditure programmes intended to indicate the extent of the state's interference in a pure market economy.**

these were engaged in market activity, the rest in the production of services, such as the Army where market prices played little or no role in resource allocation. Figure 4.7 shows the changing picture of employment by sector between 1961 and 1987.

Figure 4.7

Workforce in Employment: by Sector, United Kingdom (millions) In mid-1987 73 per cent of the 25 million workforce in employment were in the private sector. The decrease in numbers in public corporations since 1981 is mainly accounted for by privatization of such organizations.

	Public sector			*Private sector*	*Work-related government training programmes*	*Work force in employment*
	General government	*Public corporations*	*Total*			
1961	3.7	2.2	5.9	18.6	-	24.5
1971	4.6	2.0	6.6	17.9	-	24.5
1981	5.3	1.9	7.2	17.2	-	24.3
1987	5.4	1.0	6.4	18.5	0.3	25.3
Male	2.2	0.9	3.1	11.1	0.2	14.5
Female	3.2	0.1	3.3	7.4	0.1	10.8

Source: *Social Trends 19*, 1989.

Political Views

The balance of the public sector–private sector mixture in the UK is one that has varied over time because of the differing philosophies of the main political parties towards state intervention. The desirability of less or more public ownership of industry has long been at the heart of the political divide between the Labour and Conservative parties. The Labour Party has generally aspired to an extension of the public sector in the pursuit of socialist ideals. The Conservative Party has broadly opposed any such extension and indeed tried to reduce the influence of the state.

Nationalization

The fundamental extension of the public sector in the UK took place within the space of five years after the end of the Second World War in 1945. Mr Attlee's newly elected Labour government proceeded to take into full public ownership the Bank of England, the coal-mines, railways, steel, civil aviation, broadcasting, gas, and electricity. Waterways and some road transport also became state-owned. The overwhelming reasons for this remarkable interventionist activity were political. The party's commitment to managing the capitalist system and to injecting a socialist philosophy was paramount. Clause Four of the Labour Party's constitution called (and still does) for 'the public ownership of the means of production, distribution, and exchange'. In practice the party both in 1945–51 and since was content to take over what were regarded as '*the commanding heights*' of the economy. From the list of new state industries above, it can be seen that these commanding heights included at its core the *fuel, power*, and *transport* industries. The influence these state-owned industries could have over the remainder of the economy in private hands should be obvious enough. The supporters of **nationalization** in the early 1950s argued that only the co-ordination resulting from unified (geographical) ownership could produce really efficient industries as in the case of the railways. However, it was not too clear whether it was intended that these state-owned industries should be run on a commercial basis: the 'social service' argument was never far in the background. In other words, was the profitability of railways secondary in importance to the availability of rail services especially in rural areas?

In Chapter 2 we pointed out that in the capitalist model competition between rival suppliers results in pressures to increase efficiency. But it has long been argued that in some industries, by their very nature, only one supplier can exist. This argument holds that costs per unit of output are lowest when just one single firm supplies say electricity, gas, or water to all consumers within a locality. For example, if there is more than one supplier of electricity then duplication in cable systems and generating capacity, the argument runs, results in a waste of scarce economic resources. In these special cases competitive forces are held to be inappropriate as a monopoly supplier minimizes resource use. We shall examine these arguments closely in Chapter 28 but for the moment we just need to be aware of how the **natural monopoly** argument has been one part of the case for an increase in state intervention in many economies and not just in the UK.

In the case of these 'natural monopolies' nationalization was regarded by the Labour government as essential in order to prevent abuse of the consumer. If economic factors pointed to a monopoly situation then it should be publicly rather than privately owned.

In addition to the general arguments just discussed Attlee's administration held that there were sometimes specific reasons for taking industries into public ownership. Thus in the case of the coal-mines there was a strong belief in the need for state ownership as a means of improving both technical methods and industrial relations, since it was judged that industry's record up to 1939 was particularly deficient in these respects. But the steel industry was, in the late 1940s and long afterwards very much at the heart of the political divide. The incoming Conservative government denationalized the industry in 1953 but retained a measure of central control, concerning pricing and investment policies, over the industry. There was a change yet again when in 1967 the Wilson government nationalized the biggest fourteen steel-making firms. This is not the place to assess the economic performance of the nationalized industries (see Chapter 28) but we can offer the non-contentious comment that the post-war relationship between government and state corporation has, for various reasons, been a rather troubled one.

It has not been easy to square autonomy for the managers of these undertakings with the need for both accountability to Parliament and an appropriate measure of Ministerial direction.

Public ownership is, of course, not the only alternative to private enterprise. In the US, for example, a third option has long been used. This is leaving energy and transportation in private hands but leaving price and output decisions to public utility regulatory bodies.

The Private Sector in the UK

The previous section has pointed out that the line drawn between the public and private sector is one at the centre of political debate. It has also indicated the precise difficulty of defining what constitutes the public sector.

At first sight the private sector element in the mixed economy seems to be free of definitional difficulties. Surely we mean firms owned and controlled by individuals independently of the state? In fact there is a rich variety in the forms of private enterprise in an economy like the UK. We have at one end of this spectrum owner-managed businesses, such as corner shops and partnerships. (We formally define types of businesses in the UK in Chapter 21.) At the other end of the spectrum are giant companies like ICI and Shell with operations in more than just one country (multinationals). Some giant companies like BP have shares owned by the government, a fact that illustrates the blurred state-private sector divide! There are many distinctive types of institutions having quite varied objectives and constraints on their operations. These institutions include the building societies, insurance companies, and the co-operative movement. In their various ways they differ from the imagined nineteenth-century concept of the capitalist enterprise somewhat aloof from the legislative powers of government. Thus today the private sector contains a very mixed group of institutions, and they have been increasingly affected by the predisposition of post-war governments to constrain their behaviour through legislation.

Post-war UK governments have legislated freely on many aspects of industry and trade. They have concerned themselves with the location and physical growth of firms through planning controls and regional policies. Governments have shown increasing concern with the quality and condition of goods and services produced (consumer protection measures). The terms and nature of employment practices – wages and safety aspects – have given rise to much legislation. In short, the varied institutions within the private sector are now much more constrained and answerable than was the case of the nineteenth-century capitalist firm. Some parts of the private sector are very dependent on central and local government buying their goods and services – for example, publishers of school books and firms making electrical generating equipment. Similarly government support for research through contracts with companies making technologically advanced goods such as computers and military hardware illustrates how employment in private industry can be sensitive to state patronage.

Modern governments thus affect private enterprise

Key Points 4.3

- **In the UK there has been prolonged debate on the desirability of public ownership or nationalization of the energy and transport sectors of the economy on political and economic grounds.**
- **The problem of natural monopolies – where economic activity tends to be undertaken by a single producer – can be approached by nationalization or public regulatory supervision.**

even with small shifts in public expenditure. This shows how truly mixed the character of economic activity in the UK economy now is. (Read Key Points 4.3.)

Other Western Economies

We have already tried to show that the UK today has a very mixed economy. It is even more difficult to quantify how much more or less mixed is the UK economy as compared with some other European economies because of national variations in the forms of enterprise as found, say, in France or Italy. The extent of state control is not easily inferred from the proportions of capital held by the government. Thus in the case of France a number of government agencies are significant shareholders in industry. Being active participants in the affairs of those companies such institutions have an influence that often exceeds what would be suggested by nominal share *ownership*. Indeed France illustrates the point that actual public ownership is not essential for the state to have much influence on private industry. France has a long history of contractual relationships between the state and private industry and since 1946 there have been five-year plans specifying targets for various industries. These plans have aimed at improving information between those involved in economic activity and have not required compliance from particular firms to fulfil specified levels of output. On the other hand, indirect financial assistance to industry has enabled French governments to exert considerable *control* over institutions not in state ownership.

Public ownership is usually held to be desirable for political reasons but is sometimes justified on historical and essentially pragmatic grounds, such as the need to preserve jobs in what are considered key parts of the economy. As a result, countries in Western Europe exhibit considerable differences even within one sector of the economy as to the extent of state ownership. Before the nationalization of British Leyland, state ownership of the motor industry in the UK was insignificant whereas in France Renault has long been nationalized. In West Germany and Italy the state has had virtual total domination in match production in sharp contrast with the UK and France. Tobacco manufacture is essentially a state-owned industry in France but in neither West Germany nor the UK is this the case.

The Soviet Union

In Chapter 3 we reviewed the growth of the Soviet Union under the influence of Marxist ideology. That chapter described the elements of central planning for industry in the Soviet Union and indicated some shortcomings in recent Soviet economic performance. It is now appropriate to show how in recent years Mikhail Gorbachev has been trying to make a wind of change blow through the Soviet economy. The Soviet planning system is now the subject of reform and thus provides an even less clear example of a socialist system than ever before. One of the most dramatic reforms, introduced in November 1986, allowed individuals to set up their own family businesses within the service sector. The provision of taxi hire, car repair, painting and decorating services by individuals has permitted some revival of private enterprise in the Soviet Union. A parallel reform in the same year legalized workers' co-operatives of between 5 and 50 members and allowed trading of any surplus output above that required of them by the state planning system.

The Law on the State Enterprise which became operative in 1988 encouraged factories to become 'self-financing' and less dependent on state financial support and direction. Instead of producing and selling to named buyers, some factories now have to find their own customers for output beyond that fulfilling the state's requirements. These factories will also have the opportunity of conducting trade with customers outside the Soviet Union instead of dealing only with the previous state body in charge of foreign trade.

Perestroika, the restructuring of the Soviet economy, amounts to some reduction in the power of the bureaucracy in Moscow and tries to encourage local initiative within a system which retains much central control. How the mixture of an encouraged element of capitalism will blend with a continuing centrally planned system remains to be seen.

Key Points 4.4

- **The influence of government on the economy is varied in Western European countries and is not simply related to the number of industries in public ownership.**
- **Western European economies exhibit a varied pattern of state ownership even within one sector of the economy.**
- **Recent changes in the Soviet economy are weakening the importance of central planning and commitment to Marxist ideology.**

CASE STUDY

Perestroika

Fine theories are not enough to make *perestroika* work. The real test began with the launch of Mr Gorbachev's economic reforms in the 'Law on the State Enterprise' of June 1987.

The main idea is to replace administrative whim with sound economics. Mr Gorbachev launched a frontal attack on the bureaucrats, who were seen as the saboteurs of the 1965 reforms. About half of the staff in the Moscow ministries and in the Communist Party's economic-planning bureaucracy are due to go by 1990. The remaining planners have been told to concentrate on grand strategy, not details.

Factories are to draw up their own plans, with the help of supposedly, non-binding 'control figures'. They will produce partly for obligatory 'state orders', but will eventually agree up to 70% of their output directly with customers. With these new freedoms come new responsibilities: factories are supposed to be 'self-financing', meaning that they should no longer rely on state handouts.

In foreign trade, hitherto a state monopoly tangled in red tape, reform started early. Many factories are getting permission to conduct trade for themselves. Joint ventures with Western companies, once ruled out as ideologically unsound, are now being actively encouraged.

The most promising novelty is the attempt to make *perestroika* work from the bottom up as well as from the top down. Private enterprise is being promoted, although, to spare Marx's feelings, it is called 'co-operative' business. Already there are some 50 000 co-operatives.

Mr Gorbachev wants a green revolution, too. The Soviet Union's farmers were brutally collectivized under Stalin; its farmers are only one-tenth as productive as America's. Mr Gorbachev's idea is that farmers should again become 'masters of the land', leasing land and equipment for up to 50 years. If the farmers could produce enough food to fill Russia's shops, the battle for *perestroika* would be all but won.

Another 20 years

The trouble is that the shops are far from full. The queues in front of them have got longer, not shorter. Worse, inflation is coming out into the open, fuelled by a budget deficit that has soared to about 10% of GNP (dwarfing America's, at roughly 3% of GNP). Inflation is unofficially reckoned to be 6-8% and rising. So Russians are beginning to think that *perestroika* does not work. Mr Gorbachev and his supporters are admitting that, despite all those lessons from the past, reforming Russia is proving far harder than they imagined. Why?

Part of the reason is bad luck. Just as Mr Gorbachev took over, oil prices plunged, wiping out roughly $8 billion of Russia's hard-currency earnings each year. Then came the nuclear accident at Chernobyl. Then came the earthquake in Armenia, where, according to the Soviet prime minister, Mr Nikolai Ryzhkov, rebuilding will cost the equivalent of half this year's growth in national income.

But there are many other reasons. By trying to do so much at once, Mr Gorbachev created confusion. Instead of the spectacular results the reformers unwisely promised, the economy has, if anything, got worse. That has damaged Mr Gorbachev's credibility.

Opposition to *perestroika* has been deeper than expected. It ranges from active sabotage (e.g. by the mafia that profits from black-market trading in scarce goods, and so does its best to keep the shops empty) to inertia. Awkwardly, to tackle the weaknesses of the Soviet system Mr Gorbachev has to attack some of its most popular parts. These include the egalitarian ethic and the extraordinary if shabby level of social security that the state gives Russians from cradle to grave: free housing, education and health care, and full 'employment'. Opposition has come not just from the infamous ministries, but from many ordinary people as well.

The new co-operatives are unpopular because years of communism have made people suspicious of anybody who earns a lot of money. The farm reforms have stalled because Stalin destroyed so many of the country's peasants, and becaue the ones that are left are afraid that if they take up Mr Gorbachev's leasing offer they too will one day be punished by neo-Stalinists for getting rich. In the factories, workers are being told to put in extra effort, but why should they bother? There is little to spend their roubles on in the shops.

The deepest problem with Mr Gorbachev's *perestroika,* however, is that it leaves the crucial contradictions of earlier reforms unresolved. The 60-odd ministries still have responsibility for the factories in 'their' sectors, even though these factories are supposed to have ever-more freedom. So far, the ministries have managed to keep the old planning instructions intact by using (and abusing) the 'state order' system.

Unless price-setting starts to be done by the market instead of by planners, factories will not be able to take sensible decisions on what to produce. Their supposed freedom will be a charade. The fierce debate now going on over prices is partly an argument over whether the country will be run mainly by the plan or mainly by the market.

If past reform cycles are anything to go by, this is roughly the time when Mr Gorbachev will be forced to retreat, and the reforms begin to peter out. But history need not repeat itself. The Gorbachev team knows that it will take at least another 20 years to transform Russia, and is ready for a long, hard fight. The question is whether even Mr Gorbachev has the staying-power to win it.

Source: 'Russia's Last Chance', *The Economist*, 11 Mar. 1989.

Questions

1. What are the objectives of *perestroika*?
2. The case study suggests that unforeseen events can frustrate an intended change in direction in economic policy. Explain why this has been the case in the Soviet Union.
3. Explain how there are vested interests that are opposed to *perestroika*.
4. Why does the case study argue that *perestroika* is not certain of being successful?
5. What recent developments relating to *perestroika* are you aware of?

CASE STUDY

Marx and Markets

A Labour spokesman yesterday appealed to the spirit of Karl Marx to justify the emphasis on markets in the party's current policy review.

Mr Jack Straw, the party's education spokesman, claimed in a speech at Slough that Marx would 'have supported the process of Labour's policy review, of connecting our ideas with a changing world. For this process is genuinely dialectical. It is a great pity that Marx's alleged disciples today cannot see that. They behave like born-again Christians who have read only the opening chapter of Genesis and then tell others that they know it all.'

He argued that Marxism means markets, as did clause four of Labour's constitution. 'How absurd that the flat-earthers in our movement should have suggested that coming to terms with the existence of markets represents some kind of betrayal of socialism. In today's reality Marx would have acknowledged that the key is not ownership but control.

'The critical challenge for democratic socialists is not whether markets should exist, but rather how, for whom, and by whom they should be controlled and regulated.'

Source: P. Riddell, 'Marx Means Markets, says Labour Spokesman', *Financial Times*, 2 July 1988.

Questions

1. How does Mr Straw's reported speech relate to the concept of a mixed economy?
2. What did Mr Straw mean by 'a changing world'?
3. Explain carefully the meaning of the last paragraph in the case study.
4. How can governments control markets without owning the means of production?

Exam Preparation

PRACTICAL EXERCISES

1. The data below is a scatter diagram (see Chapter 1). It plots the average growth in gross domestic product (GDP) in the period 1974–86 for 18 developed countries against the share of government spending in GDP over the period 1974–84.

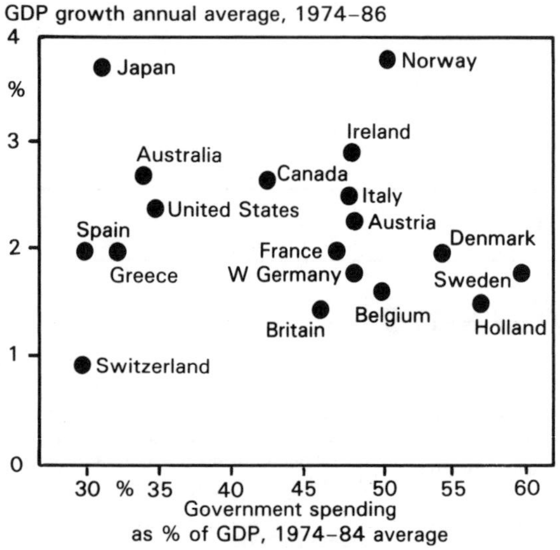

Source: *The Economist*, 7 Mar. 1987

(a) What is the nature of the relationship between the two variables?
(b) Why do you think the data on the horizontal axis is for a period of time over a decade?
(c) Can you explain the position of individual countries on the diagram?

2. General government spending in the UK in the 1980s.

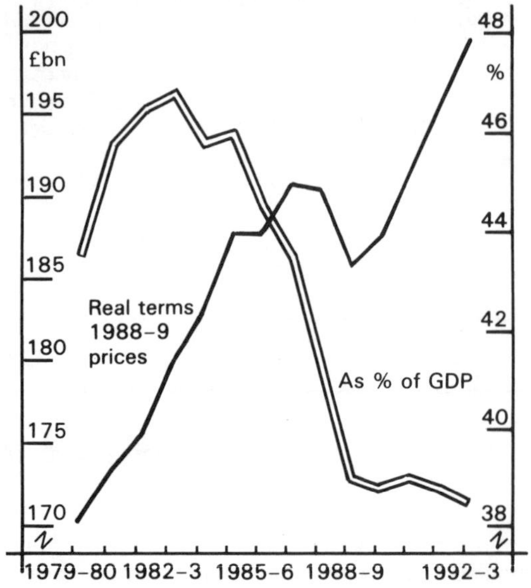

Source: *The Economist*, 18 Nov. 1989

(a) What is meant by government spending in real terms?
(b) How is it possible for government spending to rise as shown above but fall as a proportion of GDP?
(c) What do you note about the vertical scales in the graph and does this make any difference in interpreting the data?

3. General Government Expenditure in Real Terms, 1950–90 (£bn)

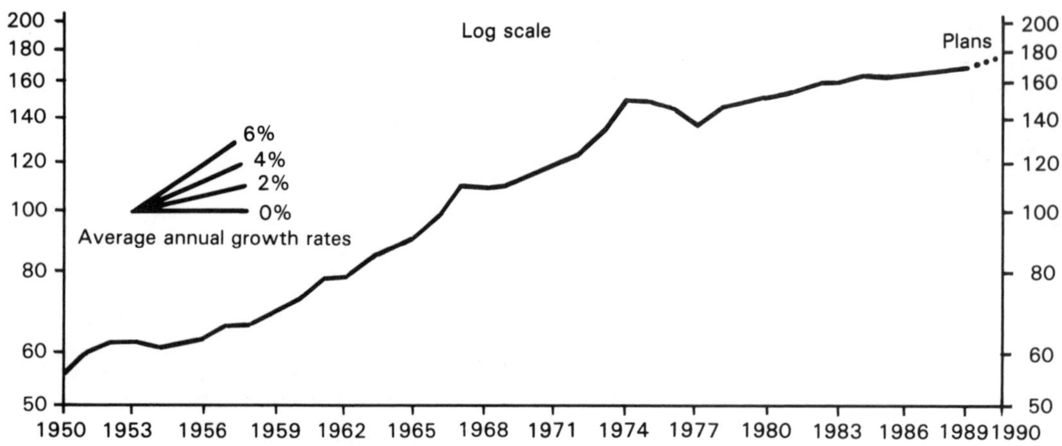

Source: *Economic Progress Report*, no. 194, Feb. 1988.

The graph is drawn on a log-scale which is why the figures in £bn do not increase in constant amounts on the vertical axis. One advantage of using a log-scale chart is its ability to handle large numbers within a small amount of space. Another advantage is that the different slopes of the trend-line show the different rate of growth per annum.

Examine the chart carefully before attempting the following questions.

(a) Why is it important that the data is expressed in real terms?

(b) What comment can you make on the rate of growth of public expenditure during the decade of the 1980s?

(c) What comment can you offer on the changing picture of public expenditure during the decade of the 1970s?

MULTIPLE CHOICE QUESTIONS

1. The main difference between a fully planned and mixed economy is the existence in the latter of both

A supply and demand situations
B commercial and industrial workers
C private and public sector
D consumers and producers

One or more of the options given in Questions 2, 3, and 4 may be correct. Select your answers by means of the code set out in the grid:

A	B	C	D
1, 2, 3 all correct	1, 2 only correct	2, 3 only correct	1 only correct

2. In mixed economies

1 both private and public sectors exist
2 government legislation modifies the operation of markets
3 the profit motive does not operate at all

3. In a mixed economy like that in the UK

1 there is political debate about the desirability of an increase in government ownership and intervention in the economy
2 at least some part of the economy is state-controlled
3 resources are allocated entirely by the free market mechanism

4. In mixed economies there is

1 debate about how much modification there should be of a free market system
2 no consistent pattern to be found in the extent to which governments influence particular industries
3 difficulty in defining precisely what constitutes the extent of government regulation of the economy

RELATED ESSAY QUESTIONS

1. Discuss the economic justification for government involvement in the provision of education and health services.

2. How are resources allocated in a free market and in a planned economy? Examine the relative merits, in terms of economic efficiency, of each method of resource allocation.

3. Discuss the view that a mixed economy is an inevitable practical compromise between a free market and a command economy.

4. Suppose you are required to assess the economic performance of alternative economic systems. What issues would be involved in your assessment?

5. Contrast the free enterprise and centrally planned approaches to solving the economic problem. Consider whether or not the growth of living standards in an economy might be significantly influenced by the type of economic system.

6. Do planned economies perform better than free market economies?

7. How are resources allocated in a free market and in a planned economy? Examine the relative merits, in terms of economic efficiency, of each method of resource allocation.

8. How does the mixed economy overcome the disadvantages of a free economy?

9. How does a pure free enterprise system try to resolve the economic problem of scarcity? Examine the problems which are likely to arise in such a system and which explain the development of a mixed economy.

10. Why do most countries choose to operate a mixed economy rather than a command or a market economy?

5 Demand and Supply

Key Points to Review

- Scarcity (1.1, 1.4)
- Increasing relative costs (1.6)
- Models (1.3, 1.8)

Questions for Preview

1 The theory of demand indicates that an inverse relationship exists between price and quantity demanded, other things being equal. Why?

2 Distinguish between (a) a change in demand and (b) a change in quantity demanded, with a given demand curve. Use graphs to aid you.

3 There is generally a direct relationship between price and quantity supplied, other things being equal. Why?

4 Why will the market-clearing (equilibrium) price be set at the point of intersection of supply and demand, and not at a higher or lower price?

The corner-stone of economic analysis is the simple demand and supply model. Understanding what demand is, what supply is, and the relationship between the two is essential for understanding virtually all economics. Demand and supply are two ways of categorizing the influences on the price of goods that you buy. This chapter is an introduction to the study of demand and supply. First, we will look at demand, then supply, and then put them together. In the case study section of this chapter, we will use demand and supply analysis to examine the market for home computers and compact discs.

Theory of Demand

The **theory of demand** can be stated succinctly as follows:

At higher prices, a lower quantity will be demanded than at lower prices, other things being equal.

Or, looked at another way:

At lower prices a higher quantity will be demanded than at higher prices, other things being equal.

The theory of demand, then, tells us that the quantity demanded of any commodity is *inversely* related to that commodity's price, other things being equal. Thus, the theory of demand states that the price and the quantity demanded move in opposite directions. Price goes up, quantity demanded goes down: price goes down, quantity demanded goes up.

Other Things being Equal

Notice that at the end of the theory of demand, there is the phrase *other things being equal** Otherwise stated, we are assuming that 'other things are held constant'. Price is not the only thing that affects purchases. There are many others, which we will look at in detail later on. One, for example, is income. If, while the price of a

*This is the **ceteris paribus** assumption where *ceteris paribus* means other things being equal or constant.

good is changing, income is also changing then we would not know whether the change in the quantity demanded was due to a change in the price or to a change in income. Therefore, we hold income constant, as well as any other factor that might affect the quantity of the product demanded.

Since we are holding all other things equal, or constant, that obviously means that we are holding the prices of all other goods constant when we state the theory of demand. Implicitly, therefore, we are looking at the price change of the good under study *relative* to all other prices. An understanding of the concept of *relative prices* is important in the study of economics.

Relative Prices

The **relative price** of any item is its price compared to the price of other goods, or relative to a (weighted) average of all other prices in the economy. The prices that you and I pay in sterling for any good or service at any point in time are called **absolute**, or nominal, prices. Consumer-buying decisions, however, depend on relative, not absolute prices. To drive this point home, let us consider the hypothetical absolute and relative prices of compact discs (CDs) and cassette tapes, which we do in Figure 5.1. We show the absolute prices of CDs and tapes in this Figure. Whereas the price of a typical CD fell in 1988, that of a cassette tape increased. Thus the relative price of CD fell in 1988 (and, conversely, the price of a tape had risen relative to a CD).

Once this distinction is made between absolute and relative price, there should be no confusion about the meaning of price (increases) during a period of generally rising prices. Someone not familiar with this distinction may contend that the theory of demand clearly does not hold because, say, the price of washing-machines went up last year by 5 per cent, but the quantity demanded did not go down at all. Assuming that other things in the economy did not change, this indeed may have been a possible refutation of the theory of demand, except for the fact that last year's prices in general may have gone up by as much as, or more than 5 per cent. It is the price of washing-machines relative to all other prices that is important for determining the relationship between price and quantity demanded.

Two Reasons Why We Observe the Theory of Demand

There are two fundamental reasons that explain why the quantity demanded of a good is inversely related to its price, other things being equal.

SUBSTITUTION EFFECT

Let us assume now that there are several goods, not exactly the same, or perhaps even very different from one another, but all serving basically the same purpose. If the price of one particular good falls, we most likely will substitute in favour of the lower-priced good and against the other similar goods we might have been purchasing. Conversely, if the price of that good rises relative to the price of the other similar goods, we will substitute in favour of them and not buy as much of the higher-priced good. Consider an example: the prices of pizzas, hamburgers, and hot dogs are all about the same. Each of us buys a certain amount (or none) of each of these three substitutable fast foods. What if the price of pizzas increases considerably, while the prices of hamburgers and hot dogs do not? What will we do? We will buy more hamburgers and hot dogs and fewer pizzas, since they are relatively more expensive, while hot dogs and hamburgers are now relatively cheaper. In effect, we will be substituting hamburgers and hot dogs for pizzas because of the relatively higher price of pizzas. Thus, you can see how the **substitution effect** affects the quantity demanded of a particular good.

REAL INCOME EFFECT

If the price of something that you buy goes up while your money income and other prices stay the same, then your ability to purchase goods in general goes down. That is to say, your effective purchasing power is reduced even though your money income has stayed the same. If you purchase ten pizzas a week at £1 a piece, your total outlay for pizzas is £10. If the price goes up by 50p, you would have to spend £15 in order

Figure 5.1
Absolute versus Relative Price. The relative price of CDs has fallen (or, conversely, the relative price of tapes has risen).

	Absolute Price (£)		*Relative price (%)*	
	1987	1988	1987	1988
CDs	11.99	10.99	184	157
Cassette tapes	6.49	6.99		

Source: British Phonographic Industry Yearbooks.

to purchase ten pizzas. If your money income and prices of other goods remained the same, it would be impossible for you to purchase ten pizzas a week at £1.50 apiece (as you used to do at the lower price) and still purchase the same quantity of all other goods and services that you were purchasing. You are poorer, and hence it is likely that you will buy less of a number of things, including the good whose price rose. The converse will also be true. When the price of one good that you are purchasing goes down without any other prices changing and without your money income changing, you will feel richer and undoubtedly will purchase a bit more of a number of goods, including the lower-priced good.

In general, the **real income effect** is usually quite small. After all, unless we consider broad categories, such as housing or food, a change in the price of *one* particular item that we purchase will have a relatively small effect on our total purchasing power (given a limited income). Thus, we expect that the substitution effect is usually more important in causing us to purchase more of goods that have become cheaper and less of goods that have become more expensive. (Read Key Points 5.1.)

Figure 5.2(a)

The Demand Schedule and Demand Curve for Wheat. Column 1 represents the price per constant-quality tonne of wheat. Column 2 represents the quantity demanded in constant-quality tonnes of wheat per year. The last column merely labels these price-quantity demanded combinations. As the price rises, the quantity demanded per year falls.

Price per tonne of constant-quality wheat	*Quantity demanded of constant-quality (million tonnes) wheat per year*	*Combination*
£50	2	A
£40	4	B
£30	6	C
£20	8	D
£10	10	E

The Demand Schedule

Let us take a hypothetical demand situation to see how the inverse relationship between the price and the quantity demanded looks. What we will do is consider the quantity of wheat demanded *per year*. Without stating the *time dimension*, we could not make any sense out of this demand relationship, because the numbers would be different if we were talking about the quantity demanded per month or the quantity demanded per decade.

In Figure 5.2(a) we show the price per constant quality tonne of wheat. The words 'constant quality' take care of the problem of varying qualities of wheat that could be sold every year. By taking an average quality, at an average price of wheat we recognize differences in the qualities of wheat purchased.

We see in Figure 5.2(a) that if the price were £10 per tonne, 10 million tonnes would be bought each year; but if the price were £50 per tonne, only 2 million tonnes would be bought each year. This reflects the theory of demand. Figure 5.2(a) is also called a **demand schedule** because it gives a schedule of alternative quantities per year at different possible prices.

The data in Figure 5.2(a) is shown as a demand curve in Figure 5.2(b) where the price per constant quality tonne is plotted on the vertical axis and the quantity measured in constant-quality tonnes per year on the horizontal axis. All we have to do is take combinations, *A, B, C, D,* and *E* from Figure 5.2(a) and plot those points in Figure 5.2(b). Now we connect the points and

Key Points 5.1

- **There is an inverse relationship between the quantity demanded of a good and its price, other things being equal.**
- **We hold constant other determinants of quantity demanded, such as income.**
- **The theory of demand holds because when the price of a good goes down: (a) we substitute in favour of it and (b) we are now richer and buy more of everything, including it.**
- **The substitution effect means the change in quantity demanded resulted from a price change of a good relative to the price of other goods.**
- **The real income effect means the change in quantity demanded resulting from a price change that gives the consumer more (or less) real income, when money income is unchanged.**

Figure 5.2(b)

We measure the quantity of wheat in millions of constant-quality tonnes per year on the horizontal axis and the price per constant-quality tonnes on the vertical axis. We then take the price–quantity combinations from Figure 5.2(a) and put them in this diagram. These points are *A, B, C, D,* and *E*. When we connect the points, we obtain a graphic representation of a demand schedule. It is downward-sloping to show the inverse relationship between quantity demanded and price.

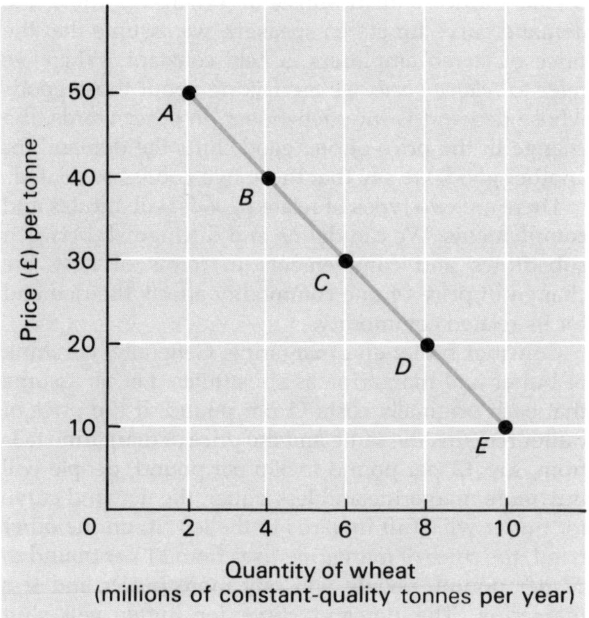

we have a **demand curve**.* It is downward-sloping (from left to right) to indicate the *inverse* relationship between the price of wheat and the quantity demanded per year.

Determinants of Demand

The demand curve in Figure 5.2(b) is drawn with other things held constant, that is, with all of the other non-price factors that determine demand held constant. There are many such determinants. The major non-price determinants are: (1) income, (2) tastes and preferences, (3) the price of related goods, (4) changes in expectations of future relative prices, (5) population (that is, market size). Other non-price determinants of demand are, for example, the season of the year for some goods and the cost of financing the purchase of some very expensive consumer items.

*Even though we call them curves for the purpose of exposition, we only draw straight lines. In many real-world situations, demand and supply 'curves' will in fact be lines that do curve. In order to connect the points in Figure 5.2(b) with a smooth line, we assume that for all prices in between the ones shown, the quantities demanded will be found along that line.

Figure 5.3

A Shift in the Demand Curve. If only the price of wheat changes, we move to a different point (co-ordinate) along a given demand curve. However, if some factor other than price changes, the only way we can show its effect is by moving the entire demand curve from *DD* to *D′D′*. We have assumed in our example that the move was precipitated by a medical discovery showing bread consumption led to a greater life expectancy. That meant that at all prices a larger quantity would be demanded than before. For example, at a price of £30 instead of 6 million tonnes per year being demanded, 10 million would be demanded. If there were a medical discovery indicating shorter life because of bread consumption, the demand curve would shift inwards to *D″D″*. At a price of £30 for example; now only 4 million tonnes per year would be consumed. Curve *D″D″* represents reduced demand.

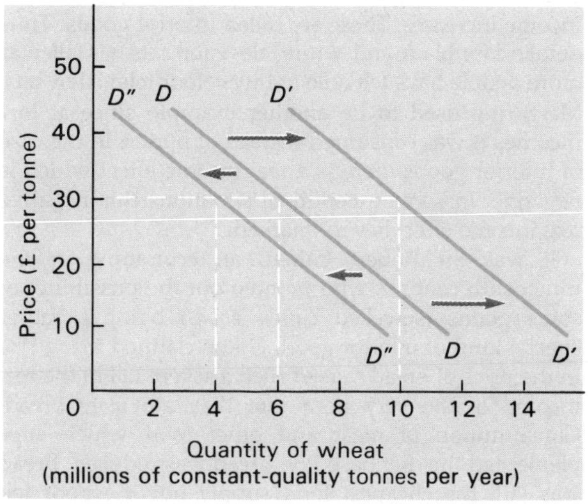

Changes in Demand

If one of the above five determinants of demand changes, then the entire demand curve shifts, either to the right or the left. Consider, for example, how we might represent a dramatic increase in the quantity of wheat demanded at all prices because of a medical discovery that, say, bread consumption increased life expectancy! The demand curve would shift outwards, or to the right, to represent an increase in demand. That is to say, there will now be an increase in the quantity demanded at each and every possible price. We do this in Figure 5.3. The demand curve has shifted from *DD* to *D′D′*. Take any price, say £30. Originally, before the great medical discovery, the quantity demanded at £30 was 6 million tonnes per year. Thus, we have witnessed a shift in the demand for wheat. We could use a similar analysis when discussing a shift inwards, or to the left, of the demand curve for wheat. This might happen, for example, in the case of a medical discovery that bread consumption actually decreased life expectancy. The demand curve would shift to *D′D′*; quantity demanded would now be less at each and every possible price.

Non-price Determinants of Demand

We mentioned that there are five major non-price determinants of demand.

INCOME

For most goods, an increased income will lead to an increase in demand. The phrase *increase in demand* always refers to a comparison between two *different* demand curves. Thus, an increase in income for most goods will lead to a rightward shift in the position of the demand curve from, say *DD* to *D'D'* in Figure 5.3. You can avoid confusion about shifts in curves by always relating an increase in demand to a rightward shift in the demand curve and a decrease in demand to a leftward shift in the demand curve. Goods for which the demand increases when income increases are called **normal goods**. Most goods are 'normal' in this sense. There are some goods for which demand *decreases* as income increases. These are called **inferior goods**. Thus demand for black-and-white television sets has fallen as more people have felt able to buy colour television sets. Margarine used to be another example since at low incomes it was consumed instead of butter. In the case of inferior goods there is a real income effect which is negative. In some exceptional situations this negative real income effect is very marked.

It was Sir Robert Giffen, an economist in the nineteenth century, who pointed out the possibility of some goods (so-called *Giffen goods*) being a rather special kind of inferior good. Giffen claimed that a rise in the price of bread caused such a severe fall in the real income of the very poor that they ate *more* bread. Consumption of meat and other food which supplemented the diet based on bread was reduced. Bread was still the cheapest food supply but the poor felt unable to spend as much money as before on other foods to augment their diet. The reverse situation also applied. When the price of bread fell the real income effect permitted a more varied diet again.

It should be noted that the terms *normal* and *inferior* are merely part of the economist's terminology; no value-judgements are associated with them.

TASTES AND PREFERENCES

A change in consumer tastes in favour of a good can shift its demand curve outwards to the right. When skateboards became the rage, the demand curve for them shifted to the right; when the rage died out, the demand curve shifted inwards to the left. Fashion changes can be related to the time of year. In the cold winter of 1982 many High Street shops in the UK rapidly sold out of Wellington boots. Brightly coloured plastic 'wellies' were so much in keen demand that many footwear shops felt obliged to put up signs 'wellies – out of stock'. But apart from the presence of ice and snow obliging people to seek waterproof footwear, the recent appearance of the Princess of Wales in green field-boots had also encouraged the shift in tastes for coloured boots. One producer in 1982 said it had already raised production by 20 per cent but ten times that amount was needed to meet demand from the retail trade. Whereas 'wellies' usually sold for about £5, field-boots cost up to £15!

PRICE OF RELATED GOODS: SUBSTITUTES AND COMPLEMENTS

Demand schedules are always drawn with the prices of all other commodities held constant. When we draw the demand curve for butter, we assume that the price of margarine is held constant. When we draw the demand curve for stereo speakers, we assume that the price of stereo amplifiers is held constant. When we refer to *related goods* we are talking about those goods whose demand is interdependent. In other words, if a change in the price of one good shifts the demand for another good, we say that those two goods are related.

There are two types of related goods; **substitutes and complements**. We can define and distinguish between substitutes and complements in terms of how the change in price of one commodity affects the demand for its related commodity.

Consider butter and margarine. Generally, we think of butter and margarine as substitutes. Let us assume that each originally costs £1 per pound. If the price of butter remains the same and the price of margarine falls from, say, £1 per pound to 50p per pound, people will buy more margarine and less butter, the demand curve for butter will shift inwards to the left. If, on the other hand, the price of margarine rises from £1 per pound to £2 per pound, people will buy more butter and less margarine. The demand curve for butter will shift outward to the right. In other words, an increase in the price of margarine leads to an increase in the demand for butter, and an increase in the price of butter will lead to an increase in the demand for margarine. Thus, for substitutes, a price change in the substitute will cause a change in the same direction in the demand for the good under study.

With complementary goods, the situation is reversed. Consider stereo speakers and stereo amplifiers. We draw the demand curve for speakers with the price of amplifiers held constant. If the price per constant-quality unit of stereo amplifiers decreases from, say, £500 to £200, that will encourage more people to purchase component stereo systems, and they will now buy more speakers, at any given price, than before. The demand curve for speakers will shift outwards to the right. If the price of amplifiers, on the other hand, increases from £200 to £500, fewer people will purchase component stereo systems. The demand curve for speakers will shift inwards to the left. In sum, a decrease in the price of amplifiers leads to an increase in the demand for speakers. An increase in the price of amplifiers leads to a decrease in the demand for speakers. Thus, for complements, a price change in a product will cause a change in the opposite direction in the demand for its complement.

The relationship between price and related goods is shown in Figure 5.4.

CHANGES IN EXPECTATIONS ABOUT FUTURE RELATIVE PRICES

Expectations about future relative prices play an important role in determining the position of a demand curve because many goods are storable. If suddenly there is an expectation of a rise in the future relative price of x, then we might predict, all other things held constant, that people will buy more now and the present demand curve will shift for *DD* to *D′D′* in Figure 5.3. If, on the other hand, there is a new expectation of a future decrease in the price of x, then people will buy less now and the present demand curve will shift instead to *D′D′* in Figure 5.3.

Note that we are talking about changes in expectations of future relative prices than *absolute* prices. If all prices have been rising at 10 per cent a year, year in and year out for 100 years, this *now fully anticipated* price rise has no effect on the position of the demand curve for a particular commodity (if the price is measured in *relative* terms on the vertical axis)* Consider, for example, what would happen to the demand curve for new motor cars if it were known that their price would rise by 10 per cent next year. If it were anticipated that the prices of all other goods would also rise by 10 per cent, then the price of new cars relative to an average of all other prices would not be any different next year from what it is this year. Thus, the demand curve for new cars this year would not increase just because of the anticipated 10 per cent price rise in absolute price.

*We assume that *all* prices have been rising, including the value of all the things that you own and the price you are paid for your labour, that is, your income.

Figure 5.5
Related Goods

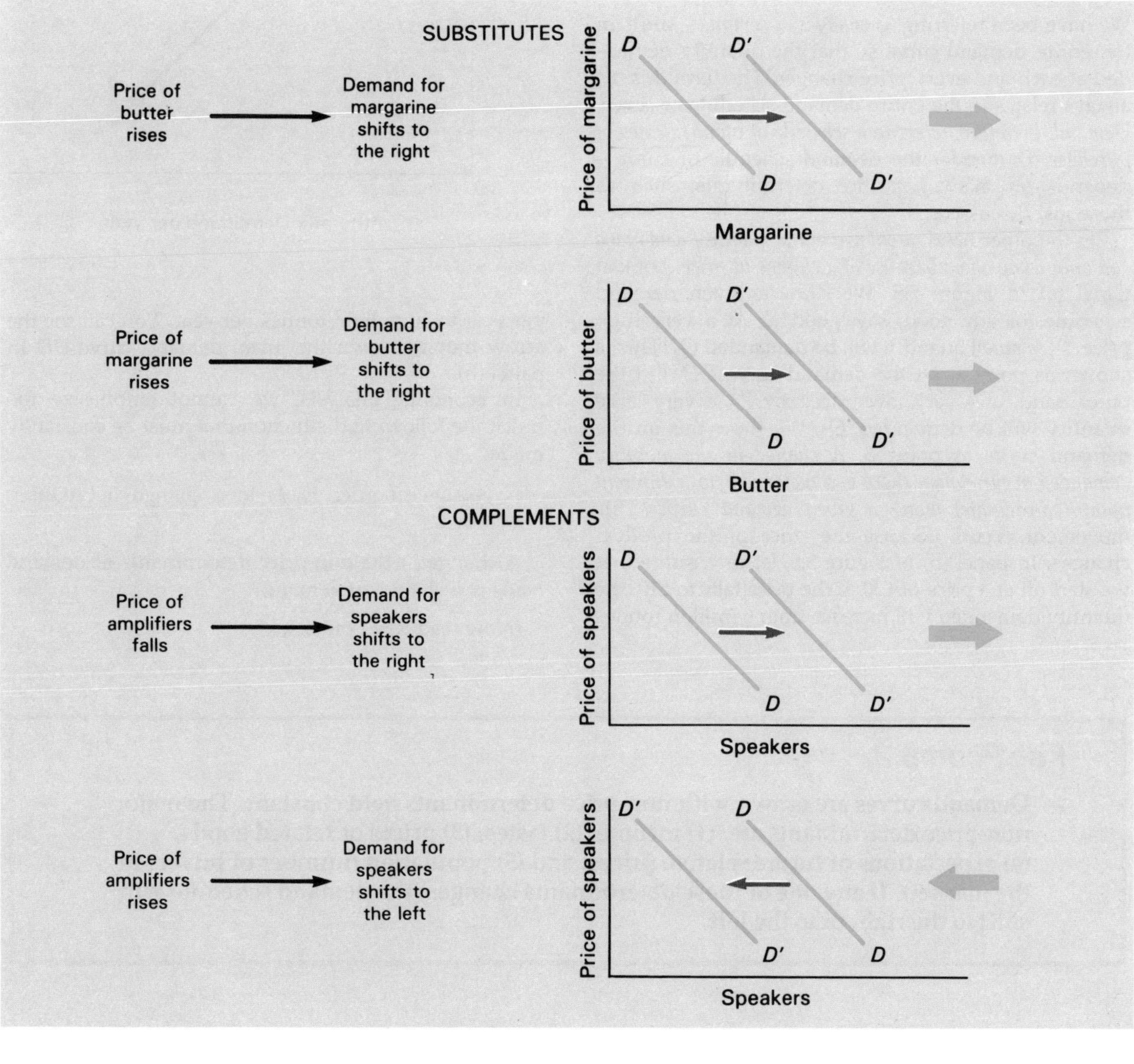

POPULATION

Often an increase in the population in an economy (holding per capita income constant) shifts the market demand outwards for most products. This is because an increase in population leads to an increase in the number of buyers in the market. Conversely, a reduction in the population will shift most demand curves inwards because of the reduction in the number of buyers in the market. An example of the impact of a change in the number of consumers in a market is the effect of birth-rates on the baby food industry. As birth-rates have recently dropped in the United Kingdom, firms dealing in baby food started to diversify. They moved into other fields because of an anticipated shift inwards in the market demand curve for their product. (Now read Key Point 5.2.)

Distinguishing between Changes in Demand and Changes in Quantity Demanded

We have been referring to *changes in demand* – shifts in the entire demand curve so that the quantity demanded at each and every price changes. The term *demand* always relates to the entire demand schedule or curve. *Demand, therefore, refers to a schedule of planned rates of purchase.* Demand – the demand schedule or curve – depends on many *non-price* determinants, such as those just discussed.

On the other hand, *a change in the quantity demanded can only come about because of a change in price.* Look at panel (a) in Figure 5.5. We draw a given demand schedule for any good, say, good X. At a very high price, P_1, a small quantity will be demanded Q_1. This is shown as point *A* on the demand curve *DD*. On the other hand, at a very low price, say P_2, a very large quantity will be demanded, Q_2. We show this on the demand curve as point *B*. *A change in the quantity demanded occurs when there is a movement to a different point (co-ordinate) along a given demand curve.* This movement occurs because the price of the product changes. In panel (b) of Figure 5.5, let us assume that we start off at a price of £30. If the price falls to £10, the quantity demanded will increase from 6 million tonnes per year to 10 million tonnes per year. You can see the arrow moving down the given demand curve *DD* in panel (b).

Figure 5.5

Movement along a Given Demand Curve. In panel (a), we show the demand curve *DD* for a hypothetical good, *X*. If price is P_1, then the quantity demanded will be Q_1; we will be at point *A*. If, on the other hand, the price is relatively low, P_2, then the quantity demanded will be relatively high, Q_2. We'll be at point *B* on *DD*. Now look at panel (b). Here we show distinctly that a change in price changes the quantity of a good demanded. It is a movement along a given demand schedule. If, in our example, the price of wheat falls from £30 a tonne to £10 a tonne, the quantity demanded will increase from 6 million tonnes per year to 10 million tonnes per year.

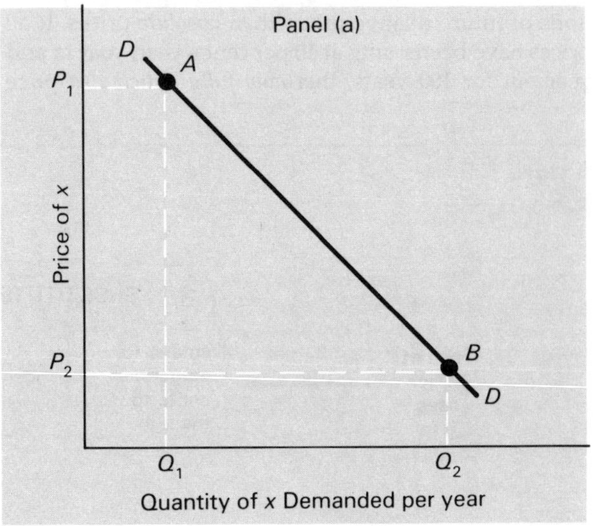

In economic analysis, we cannot emphasize too much the following distinction that must be constantly made:

A change in price leads to a change in quantity demanded.

A change in the non-price determinants of demand leads to a change in demand.

(Now read Key Points 5.3.)

Key Point 5.2

- **Demand curves are drawn with non-price determinants held constant. The major non-price determinants are: (1) income, (2) tastes, (3) prices of related goods, (4) expectations of future relative prices, and (5) population (number of buyers in the market). If any one of these determinants changes, the demand schedule will shift to the right or to the left.**

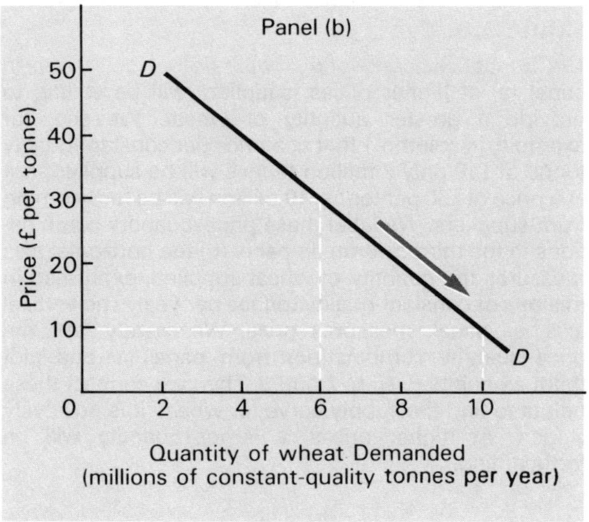

Supply

Just as there is a relationship between price and quantity demanded, so, too, is there a relationship between price and quantity supplied. This relationship is called **supply** and involves the following:

At higher prices, a larger quantity will generally be supplied than at lower prices, all other things held constant.

Or, stated otherwise:

At lower prices, a smaller quantity will generally be supplied than at higher prices, all other things held constant.

In other words, there is generally a direct relationship between quantity supplied and price. This is the opposite of the relationship we saw for demand. There, price and quantity demanded were inversely related. Here they are directly related. For supply, as the price rises, the quantity supplied rises; as the price falls, quantity supplied also falls. Producers are normally willing to produce and sell more of their product at a higher price than at a lower price, other things being constant.

Why a Direct, or Positive, Relationship?

There are a number of intuitive reasons why there is normally a direct, or positive, relationship between price and quantity supplied. These involve the incentives for increasing production facing suppliers and the law of increasing costs, discussed in Chapter 1.

INCENTIVES FOR INCREASING PRODUCTION

Consider a situation in which nothing else changes except the price per tonne of wheat obtainable in the market-place. If this occurs, farmers will find it more rewarding monetarily than it was before to spend more of their time and resources producing wheat than they used to. They may, for example, switch more of their production from barley production to wheat production because the market price of wheat has risen. The wheat farmer may even find it now profitable to add the use of more labour and machines to the production of wheat because of its higher market price.

THE THEORY OF INCREASING COSTS

In Chapter 1, we explained why the production possibilities curve is bowed outwards. The explanation basically involved the theory of increasing costs – as society takes more and more resources and applies them to the production of any specific item, the opportunity cost for each additional unit produced increases at an increasing rate. The law of increasing costs exists because resources are generally better suited for some activities than for others; and therefore, when we shift less well-suited resources to a particular production activity, more and more units of it will have to be used to get the same increase in output as we expand production.

Now apply this analysis to a wheat-farmer wishing to increase quantity of wheat supplied. That farmer will eventually find that each additional output of wheat production will involve higher and higher costs. Hence, the only way that a wheatfarmer would be induced to produce more and more wheat would be because of the lure of a higher market price that wheat

Key Points 5.3

- **A change in demand comes about only because of a change in the non-price determinants of demand.**
- **A change in the quantity demanded comes about only when there is a change in the price.**
- **A change in demand shifts the demand curve and is caused by changes in the non-price determinants of demand; a change in quantity demanded involves a movement along a *given* demand curve and is caused by a change in price.**

could fetch. For example, only if a higher market price of wheat could be fetched would a farmer be willing to pay overtime rates for workers and to pay the extra costs involved in tilling stony, less desirable land. In a sense, then, it is because of the law of increasing costs that price has to go up in order to create a situation in which the quantity supplied will also go up.*

Supply Schedule

Just as we were able to construct a demand schedule, so we can construct a **supply schedule**, which is a table relating prices to the quantity supplied at each price.

It is a set of planned production rates that depends on the price of the product. In Figure 5.6 panel (a), we show the supply schedule of wheat.

Supply Curve

We can convert the supply schedule in panel (a) of Figure 5.6 into a **supply curve**, just as we earlier created a demand curve in Figure 5.2. All we do is take the price–quantity combinations from panel (a) of Figure 5.6 and plot them in panel (b). We have labelled these combinations *F* through *J*. The curve is upward-sloping to show the normally direct relationship between price and the quantity supplied. Again, we have to remember that we are talking about quantity supplied *per year*, measured in constant-quality units. (Read Key Points 5.4.)

The Determinants of Supply

When supply curves are drawn, only the price changes, and it is assumed that other things remain constant. The other things assumed constant are: (1) the prices of resources (inputs) used to produce the product, (2) technology, (3) taxes and subsidies, (4) price expectations of producers, and (5) the prices of related goods.

*Strictly speaking, the theory of increasing costs can be used as an explanation for the generally positive relationship between quantity supplied and price only in the short run, where there is no possibility that improved production techniques resulting from the increased production will actually lower costs.

Figure 5.6

The Supply Schedule and Supply Curve for Wheat. In panel (a) at higher prices, suppliers will be willing to provide a greater quantity of wheat. We see, for example, in column 1 that at a price per constant-quality tonne of £10 only 2 million tonnes will be supplied; but at a price of £50 per tonne, 10 million will be forthcoming from suppliers. We label these price–quantity combinations in the third column. In panel (b) the horizontal axis measures the quantity of wheat supplied, expressed in millions of constant-quality tonnes per year. The vertical axis, as usual, measures price. We merely take the price–quantity combinations from panel (a) and plot them as points *F, G, H, I*, and *J*. Then we connect these points to find the supply curve for wheat. It is positively sloped. At higher prices, a larger quantity will be forthcoming.

Panel (a)

Price per constant-quality tonnes	*Quantity supplied of wheat (millions of constant-quality tonnes per year)*	*Combination*
£10	2	*F*
£20	4	*G*
£30	6	*H*
£40	8	*I*
£50	10	*J*

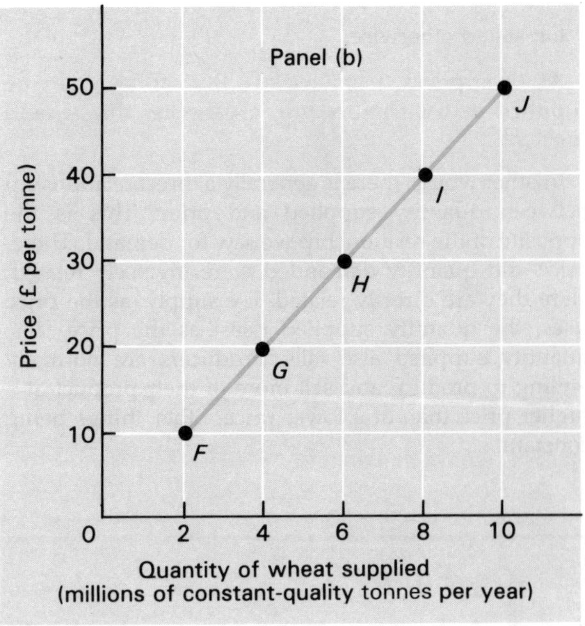

Key Points 5.4

- **There is normally a direct, or positive, relationship between price and quantity of a good supplied, other things being constant.**
- **Because of the law of increasing costs, suppliers can only be induced to incur higher additional production costs if the market price they receive for their product goes up.**

These are the major *non-price* determinants of supply. If any of them changes, there will be a shift in the supply curve.

Shifting Supply

A change in the price of the good itself will cause a movement along the supply curve. A change in the non-price determinants, however, will shift the entire curve.

Consider an example: If a new method of fertilizing and planting wheat reduces the cost per tonne of growing wheat by, say, 50 per cent, farmers will supply more wheat at all prices because their cost of so doing has fallen dramatically. Competition among farmers to produce more at each and every price will shift the supply schedule of wheat outwards to the right from *SS* to *S'S'* as we see in Figure 5.7. At a price of £30, the quantity supplied was originally 6 million tonnes per year; but now the quantity supplied (after the reduction in the costs of production) at £30 a tonne will be 9 million tonnes per year. This is similar to what has happened to the supply curve of electronic calculators and computers in recent years.

The opposite case will make the point even clearer. Suppose that a new and totally unknown disease caused a blight on wheat throughout the UK such that 60 per cent of the UK's total crop is destroyed. Users of wheat products will find a reduced supply. They – in competition with one another – will bid up its price. Ultimately, the users of wheat for wheat-based products will pay greatly increased prices. The supply curve will have shifted inwards to the left to *S″S″*. At each and every price, the quantity of wheat supplied will fall dramatically, due to the crop-destroying disease.

The Determinants in Detail

THE PRICES OF INPUTS USED TO PRODUCE THE PRODUCT

If one or more input prices fall, the supply curve will shift outwards to the right; that is, more will be supplied at each and every price. The opposite will be true if one or more inputs become more expensive. In other words, when we draw the supply curve of cars, we are holding the price of steel (and other inputs) constant.

TECHNOLOGY

Supply curves are drawn on the assumption of a given technology or 'state of the art'. When the types of production techniques available change, the supply curve will shift. For example, if a better production technique becomes available, the supply curve will shift to the right. A larger quantity will be forthcoming at each and every price because the cost of production will have fallen.

Figure 5.7

A Shift in the Supply Schedule. If only the price changes, we move along a given supply schedule. However, if for example the cost of production of wheat were to fall dramatically the supply schedule would shift rightwards from *SS* to *S'S'* so that at all prices a larger quantity would be forthcoming from suppliers. Conversely, if the cost of production rose, the supply curve would shift leftwards to *S″S″*.

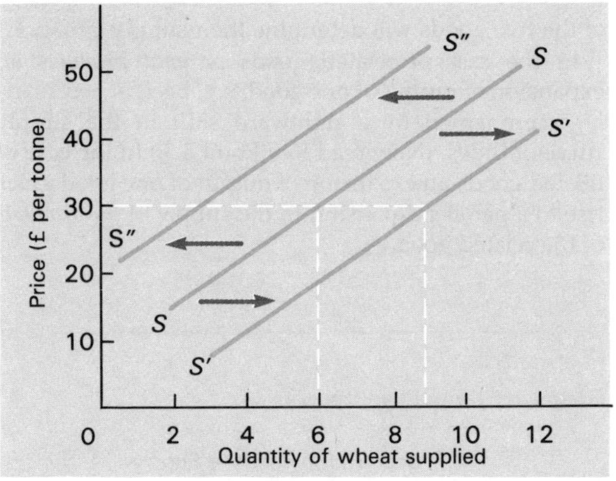

TAXES AND SUBSIDIES

Certain taxes, such as sales taxes, are effectively an addition to production costs and therefore reduce the supply. Thus, if the supply curve were *SS* in Figure 5.7, a sales tax increase would shift it is *S″S″*. A subsidy would do the opposite; it would shift the curve to *S'S'*. Every producer would get a 'gift' from the government of, say, a few pence for each unit produced.

PRICE EXPECTATIONS

A change in the expectation of a future relative price of a product can affect a producer's current willingness to supply, just as price expectations affect a consumer's current willingness to purchase. Farmers may withhold from market part of their current wheat crop if they anticipate a higher wheat price in the future. In either example, the current quantity supplied at each and every price will decrease.

The Prices of Related Goods

We saw earlier in our discussion of demand that there are two types of related goods: substitutes and complements. There is a parallel case on the supply side. Some goods are in competitive supply, meaning that one good can be quite easily produced using the same factors of production as an alternative to another good. The price relationship between two such goods will therefore have a major influence on the amounts producers are willing to supply. The relative profitability

Key Point 5.5

▶ **The supply curve is drawn with other things held constant. If non-price determinants of supply change, then the supply curve will shift. The major non-price determinants are: (1) input costs, (2) technology, (3) taxes and subsidies, (4) expectations of future relative prices, and (5) the prices of related goods.**

of the two goods will determine their supply situation.

In the case of related goods or *joint products* an expansion of output of one good, e.g. beef, is necessarily accompanied by a rightward shift in the supply curve of hides. (Now read Key Point 5.5.) In the case of related goods an expansion of output of one good gives rise to a parallel expansion in the supply of *by-products* of the related good.

Figure 5.8
Goods in Competitive Supply

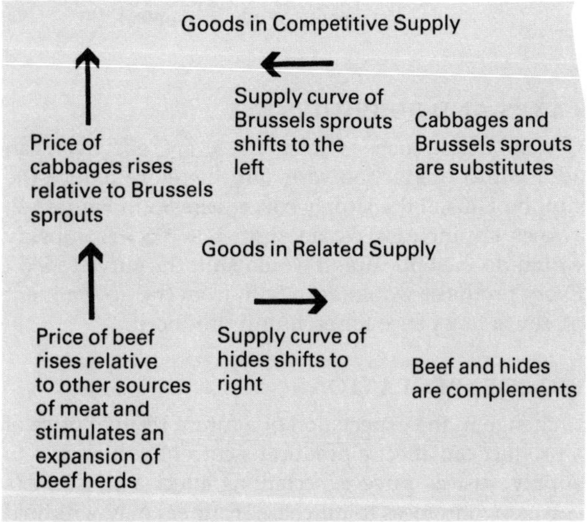

Change in Quantity Supplied and Change in Supply

We cannot overstress the importance of distinguishing between a movement along the supply curve – which occurs only when the price changes – and a shift in the supply curve, which occurs only with changes in other non-price factors. A change in price always brings about a change in quantity supplied. We move to a different co-ordinate on the existing supply curve. This is specifically called a change in quantity supplied.

But a change in technology, for example, will shift the curve such that there is a change in the quantity supplied at each and every price. This is called a change in supply. A rightward (outward) shift represents an increase in supply; a leftward (inward) shift represents a decrease in supply.

A change in price leads to a change in quantity supplied.

A change in the non-price determinants of supply leads to a change in supply.

(Read Key Point 5.6.)

Putting Demand and Supply together

In the preceding sections on supply and demand, we tried to confine each discussion only to supply or to demand. There is an interaction between the two. In this section, we will discuss how they interact and how that interaction determines the prices that prevail in our economy. So knowing, understanding how demand and supply interact is essential to understanding how prices are determined in our economy and other economies where the forces of supply and demand are allowed to work themselves out. Let us first combine the demand and supply schedules, and then we will combine the curves.

The Demand and Supply Schedules Combined

Let us place Figure 5.2(a) (the demand schedule) and panel (a) from Figure 5.6 (the supply schedule) into Figure 5.9(a). Column 1 shows the price; column 2, the

Key Point 5.6

▶ **If the price changes, we *move along* a curve – there is a change in quantity demanded and/or supplied. If something else changes, we shift a curve – there is a change in demand and/or supply.**

Figure 5.9

Putting Demand and Supply together (wheat). In panel (a) we combine Figures 5.2(a) and 5.6(a). Column 1 is the price per constant-quality tonne, column 2 is the quantity supplied, and column 3 is the quantity demanded, both on a per year basis. The difference is expressed in column 4. For the first two prices, we have a negative difference; that is, there is an excess quantity demanded (a shortage) as expressed in column 5. At the price of £40 or £50 we have a positive difference; that is, we have an excess quantity supplied (a surplus). However, at a price of £30 the quantity supplied and the quantity demanded are equal, so there is neither an excess quantity demanded nor an excess quantity supplied. We call this price the equilibrium, or market-clearing, price. In panel (b) the intersection of the supply and demand curves is at *E* where there is neither an excess quantity demanded nor an excess quantity supplied. At a price of £10 the quantity supplied will be only 2 million tonnes per year, but the quantity demanded will be 10 million. The difference is excess quantity demanded at a price of £10. There are forces that will cause the price to rise, so we will move from point *A* up the supply curve to point *E*. At the other extreme, £50 elicits a quantity supplied of 10 million, with a quantity demanded of 2 million. The difference is excess quantity supplied at a price of £50. Again, forces will cause the price to fall, so we will move down the demand and the supply curves to the equilibrium price, £30 per tonne quantity supplied, but quantity demanded would drop to 2 million, leaving a difference of (plus) 8 million, which we call an excess quantity supplied (surplus).

Panel (a)

(1) *Prices (£)*	*(2)* *Quantity supplied (tonnes per year)*	*(3)* *Quantity demanded (tonnes per year)*	*(4)* *Differences (2)–(3) (tonnes per year)*	*(5)* *Excesses*
10	2 million	10 million	−8 million	Excess quantity demanded
20	4 million	8 million	−4 million	Excess quantity demanded
30	**6 million**	**6 million**	**0**	**Market-clearing price (equilibrium)**
40	8 million	4 million	4 million	Excess quantity supplied
50	10 million	2 million	8 million	Excess quantity supplied

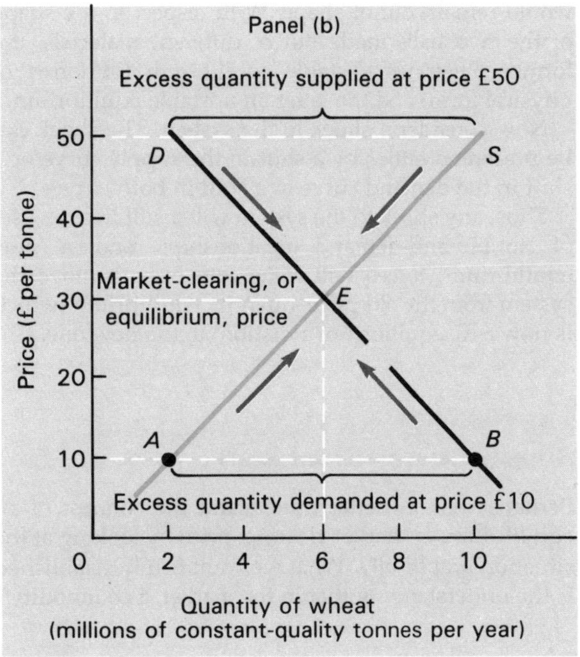

quantity supplied per year at any given price; and column 3, the quantity demanded. Column 4 is merely the difference between columns 2 and 3, or the difference between the quantity supplied and the quantity demanded. In column 5, we label those differences as either an excess quantity demanded (shortage/surplus) or an excess quantity supplied. For example, at a price of £10 there would be only 2 million tonnes supplied, but the quantity demanded would be 10 million. The difference would be a negative 8 million, which we label an excess quantity demanded (shortage). At the other end of the scale, a price of £50 per tonne would elicit a 10 million quantity supplied, but quantity demanded would drop to 2 million, leaving a difference of (plus) 8 million, which we call an excess quantity supplied (surplus).

At the price of £30 both the quantity supplied and the quantity demanded per year are 6 million tonnes of wheat. The difference then is zero. There is neither an excess quantity demanded (shortage) nor an excess quantity supplied (surplus). Hence, this price of £30 is very special. This is the **market-clearing price** since it clears the market of all excess supply or excess demand. The market-clearing price is the **equilibrium price**, or the price at which there is no tendency for change. Demanders are able to get all they want at that price; and suppliers are able to sell the amount that they want at that price.

The Concept of Equilibrium

We have used the term 'equilibrium price'. The concept of equilibrium is important in and of itself because we will frequently be referring to equilibrium situations in different markets and in different parts of the economy. **Equilibrium** in any market is defined as a situation in which the plans of buyers and the plans of sellers exactly mesh, causing the quantity supplied to equal the quantity demanded at the price in the market-place for the good. Equilibrium prevails when opposing forces are in balance. In any market, for a given supply curve and a given demand curve, the intersection gives an equilibrium price. For any given supply and demand, if price were to drift away from equilibrium – say, because of firms groping about for the 'right' price – forces would come into play to push price back to equilibrium. Such a situation is one of **stable equilibrium**. An unstable equilibrium is one in which, if there is a movement away from the equilibrium, there are forces that push price and/or quantity even further away from equilibrium (or at least do not push price and quantity back towards the equilibrium level or rate).

The difference between a stable and an unstable equilibrium can be illustrated by looking at two balls: one made of hard rubber, the other made of soft putty. If you were to squeeze the rubber ball out of shape, it would bounce back to its original form. On the other hand, if you were to squeeze the putty out of shape, it would remain out of shape. With respect to the shape of the two balls made out of different materials, the former illustrates a stable equilibrium (in terms of physical form) and the latter an unstable equilibrium.

Now consider a shock to the system. The shock can be presented either by a shift in the supply curve or a shift in the demand curve or a shift in both curves.

Thus, any shock to the system will result in a new set of supply-and-demand relationships and a new equilibrium; forces will come into play to move the system from the old price–quantity equilibrium (which is now a disequilibrium situation) to the new one.

The Demand and The Demand and Supply Curves Combined

Perhaps we can better understand the concept of an equilibrium, or market-clearing, price by looking at the situation graphically. What we want firmly established is the understanding that in the market, a commodity's price will tend towards its equilibrium, or market-clearing, price. Once that price is reached, the price will remain in effect unless either supply or demand changes.

Let us combine panel (b) in Figure 5.2 and panel (b) in Figure 5.6 into panel (b) in Figure 5.9. The only difference now is that the horizontal axis measures both the quantity supplied and the quantity demanded per year. Everything else is the same. The demand curve is labelled *DD*, the supply curve *SS*. We have labelled the intersection of the supply curve with the demand curve as *E*, for equilibrium. That corresponds to a price of £30 at which both the quantity supplied and the quantity demanded per year are 6 million. There is neither an excess quantity supplied nor an excess quantity demanded. Point *E*, the equilibrium point, always occurs at the intersection of the supply and demand curves. Now let us see why we said that this particular price is one towards which the market price will automatically tend to gravitate.

SHORTAGES

The demand and supply curves depicted in Figure 5.9 represent a situation of stable equilibrium. In other words, a non-market-clearing, or disequilibrium, price will put into play forces that cause the price to change towards the market-clearing price where equilibrium will again be sustained. Look again at panel (b) in Figure 5.9. Suppose that, instead of being at the market-clearing price of £30 per tonne, for some reason the market price is £10 per tonne. At this price, the quantity demanded exceeds the quantity supplied, the former being 10 million tonnes per year and the latter, 2 million tonnes per year. We have a situation of an excess quantity demanded or shortage at the price of £10. Demanders of wheat would find that they could not buy all that they wished at £10 per tonne. But forces will cause the price to rise: demanders will bid up the price and/or suppliers will raise the price and increase output, whether explicitly or implicitly. We would move from points *A* and *B* towards point *E*. The process would stop when the price again reached £30 per tonne.

SURPLUSES

What happens if the market price was at £50 per tonne of wheat, rather than at the market-clearing price of £30 per tonne? Clearly, the quantity supplied will exceed the quantity demanded at that price. The result will be an excess quantity supplied at £50 per tonne. This excess quantity supplied is often called a surplus. However, given *DD* and *SS*, there will be forces pushing the price back down towards £30 per tonne: suppliers will attempt to reduce their inventories by cutting prices and reducing output, and/or demanders will offer to purchase more at lower prices. The reason that suppliers will want to reduce inventories is that these will be above their optimal level; that is, there will be an excess over what each farmer believes to be the most profitable stock of wheat. After all, inventories of wheat are costly to hold. On the other hand, demanders may find out about such excess inventories of wheat and see the possibility of obtaining increased quantities of wheat at a decreased price. It induces demanders to attempt to obtain a good at a lower price, and they will therefore try to do so. If the two forces of supply and demand are unrestricted, they will bring the price back to £30 per tonne.

The point is that any disequilibrium situation automatically brings into action correcting forces that will cause a movement towards equilibrium. The market-clearing price and quantity will be stable as long as demand and supply do not change (that is, as long as the non-price determinants of demand and supply do not change). This is what occurs in a stable-equilibrium situation. And, of course, we are ignoring the possibility of restrictions in the market-place that might prevent the forces of supply and demand from changing price. (Read Key Points 5.7.)

Price Flexibility and Adjustment Speed

We have used as an illustration for our analysis a market in which prices are quite flexible. In reality, there are markets in which this is the correct analysis. There are others, however, where price flexibility may take the form of indirect adjustments such as by ways of hidden payments of quality changes. For example, the published price for an airline seat may remain the same throughout the year. None the less, the price per constant-quality unit of airline services differs, depending on how crowded the airplane is. In a sense, then, you pay a higher price for airline services during the peak holiday periods than during off-peak periods.

One must also consider the fact that markets do not get back into equilibrium immediately. There is an adjustment time that must take place. A shock to the economy in the form of a sudden rise in imported prices, a drought, a long strike, and so on will not be absorbed overnight. That means that, even in unrestricted market situations where there are no restrictions on changes in price and quantities, temporary excess quantities supplied and excess quantities demanded may appear. Our analysis simply indicates where, ultimately, the market-clearing price will be, given a demand curve and a supply curve. Nowhere in the analysis is there any indication of the speed with which a market will, for example, get a new equilibrium if there has been a shock. This caveat should be remembered as we examine changes in demand and changes in supply because of changes in their non-price determinants.

Changes in Demand and Supply

Now that we have combined both demand and supply on one graph, we can analyse the effects of changes in supply and changes in demand. In Figure 5.10 there are four panels. In panel (a), the supply curve remains stable, but demand increases from *DD* to *D'D'*. Note that the result is both an increase in the market-clearing price from *Pe* P'_e and an increase in the equilibrium quantity from Q_e to Q'_e.

In panel (b) there is a decrease in demand from *DD* to *D'D'*. This results in a decrease in both the relative price of the good and the equilibrium quantity.

Panels (c) and (d) show the effects of a shift in the supply curve while the demand curve is stable. In panel

Key Points 5.7

- **When we combine the demand and supply curves we can find the market-clearing, or equilibrium, relative price at the intersection of those two curves. The equilibrium price is one from which there is no tendency to change and towards which price will gravitate if it is higher or lower.**
- **At prices above the market-clearing price, there will be an excess quantity supplied, or a surplus.**
- **At prices below the market-clearing price, there will be an excess quantity demanded, or a shortage.**
- **Equilibrium in a market exits whenever the separate plans of buyers mesh exactly with the separate plans of sellers, so that quantity demanded equals quantity supplied at the market-clearing price.**
- **For any stable equilibrium situation, any movement of price away from the market-clearing price will put into play forces that will cause the price to gravitate towards the market-clearing price.**

(c), the supply curve has shifted rightwards – supply has increased. The relative price of the product falls; the equilibrium quantity increases. In panel (d) supply has shifted leftwards – there has been a supply decrease. The product's relative price increases; the equilibrium quantity decreases.

Figure 5.10

Shifts in Demand and in Supply. In panel (a), the supply curve is stable at *SS*. The demand curve shifts out from *DD* to *D′D′*. The equilibrium price and quantities rise from P_e Q_e to P'_e Q'_e respectively. In panel (b), again, the supply curve remains stable at *SS*. The demand curve, however, shifts inwards to the left showing a decrease in demand from *DD* to *D″D″*. Both equilibrium price and equilibrium quantity fall. In panel (c), the demand curve now remains stable at *DD*. A supply increase is shown by a movement outwards to the right of the supply curve from *SS* to *S′S′*. The equilibrium price falls from P_e to P'_e. The equilibrium quantity increases, however, from Q_e to Q'_e. In panel (d), the demand curve is stable at *DD*. Supply decreases, as shown by a leftward shift of the supply curve from *SS* to *S″S″*. The market-clearing price increases from P_e to E''_e. The equilibrium quantity falls from Q_e to Q''_e.

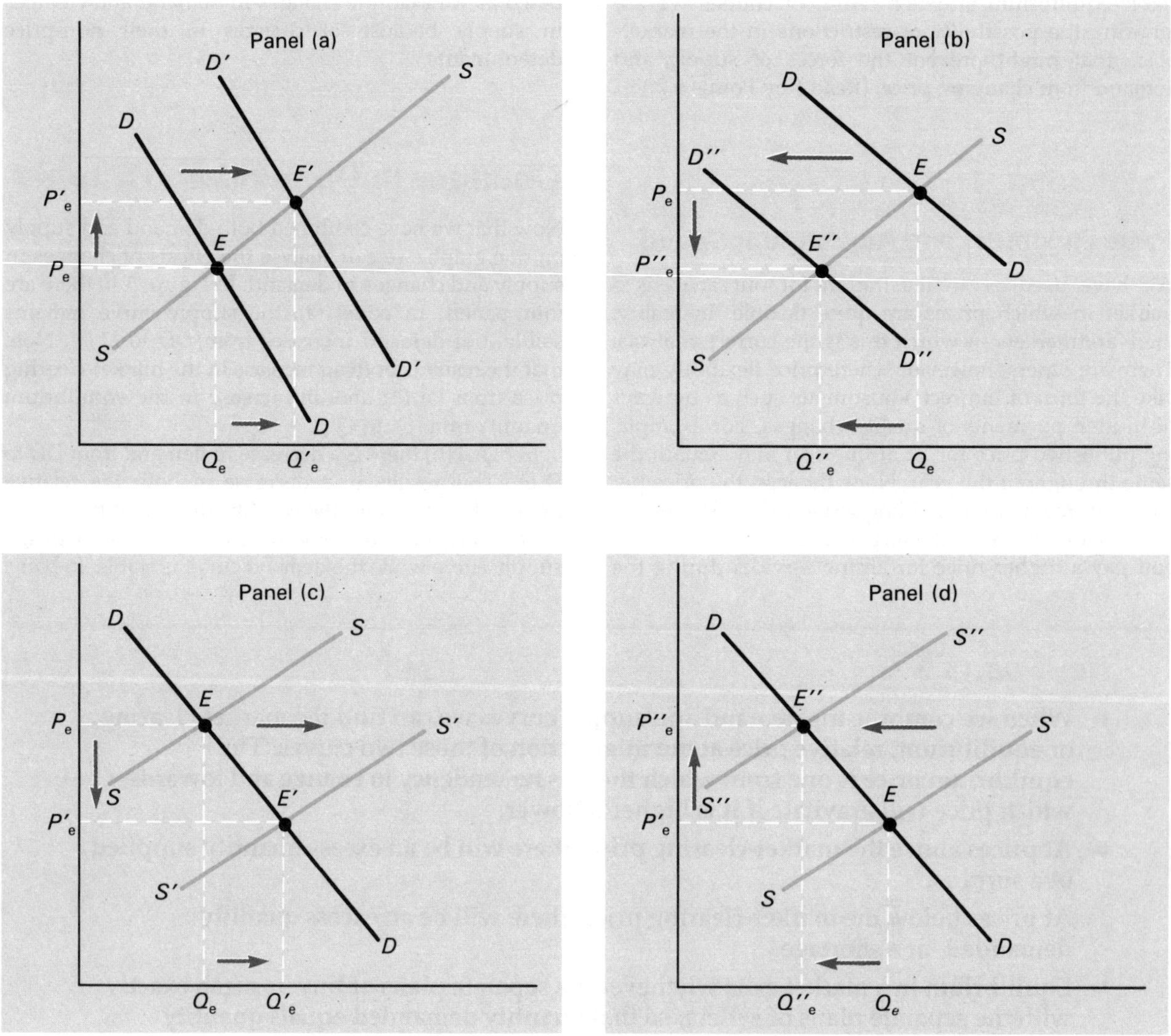

CASE STUDY

LPs and CDs

Don't throw away your old LPs. As compact discs begin to outsell vinyl for the first time, record dealers spoke yesterday of rising values for LPs.

Original albums by the Beatles, the Rolling Stones and Elvis Presley are going up in price, as are works by Prince, Jimi Hendrix and David Bowie.

It's not just rare items that are affected, such as the five early Elvis singles which sold at Christie's last year for £3 000. The most everyday Elvis albums, seen on record racks not so long ago for 20p, can command £20 in mint condition.

'All the music from the 1950s and 1960s is worth money,' Mark Hayward, owner of the London record shop Vinyl Experience, said. 'And they won't go down.'

The climb in values comes as sales of new compact discs overtake LPs. According to figures produced last week by the British Phonographic Industry, more than 8.6m CDs were bought in the three months to June, compared with 8m LPs.

Britain has been slower than the United States and Japan to take to CDs, but the medium is growing fast. Research by the HMV Shop, which has 67 stores, shows that although CDs have been around since 1983, half of all CD-users began buying their discs in the last year.

So is it farewell to the LP? Is it goodbye to the art of the album cover, to the mystery of new scratches, and the liquids that keep records clean?

'No,' said David Terrill, the HMV Shop's marketing director. 'LPs are still the main format for the majority of heavy-spending 15- to 24-year-olds. It's when CD ownership increases in this group that LPs will look like an endangered species.'

'No,' said Hayward. 'There are things people will always want on vinyl – blues, jazz, rock n' roll. It's more authentic.'

'No,' said Edward Heath, the former prime minister, who not only keeps 2 100 classical LPs in his library but also has the products of an earlier age. 'I still have my 78s, because some recordings are never issued again.'

In the United States, such concerns have not prevented the wholesale dumping of black vinyl by music-lovers transferring to CD, and some British dealers are making forays across the Atlantic to pick up what America no longer wants. 'In 10 or 15 years they'll regret this,' one said.

At the same time, the entry of Japanese buyers has helped to push up prices. David Lashmar, co-owner of Beanos of Croydon – Britain's biggest pop dealer – recently turned down £2 000 for a disc-jockey's copy of 'Please Please Me', the Beatles' first album. Had it been the plain old mono version, it would still be worth £150.

Psychedelic groups of the late 1960s, early 1970s progressive and funk, and punk/new wave of 10 years ago can also fetch three-figure sums.

Tips for good investments are: anything by major artists such as the Beatles and Stones; labels such as Chess originals (renowned for blues) or Atlantic Records; and, strangely, some CDs. Beatles CD boxed sets that sold for £49 new, but are now unobtainable, are worth £200. Promotional CDs, such as those given to journalists, can go for £100; a promo CD of Mixed Emotions, the new stones single, is already worth £25.

'I think CDs and LPs really hold their value if the artists can play their instruments,' Hayward said. 'Bros will never be worth a penny.'

Source: T. Rayment, 'Venerable Vinyls rise fast in Price Charts', *Sunday Times*, 10 Sept. 1989.

Questions

1. Identify the factors which have caused the shifts in demand for LPs.
2. Identify the factors which have caused the shift in demand for CDs.
3. How does the case study suggest that generalizations about the demand for LPs are not easily made?

CASE STUDY

Wool and Cotton

Cotton rustlers? Shortages have driven China's government to order police protection for the country's cotton crop. Around the world, limited supplies of both cotton and wool and unexpectedly high demand have sent prices rocketing. Rising consumption in the communist world is partly to blame, but demand is also increasing in the West where people are tired of sweating into polyester and acrylic.

In July 1986, cotton was at a 12-year low of 36 cents a lb; wool had slid to $4.3 a kilo from $5 three months earlier (see chart). At that price, wool was still profitable for most sheep-farmers, so the big exporters, Australia and New Zealand, were not too worried. The poorer cotton-dependent countries, like Pakistan and Sudan, were in a bind.

The cotton price was reacting to violent swings of previous years. A high price as a result of a low world crop (67.6m bales) in 1983–84 led farmers to plant enthusiastically. Good weather pushed production up to 87.4m bales in 1984–85. High stocks and another good crop in 1985-86 drove cotton prices to rock-bottom.

Wool production does not suffer such erratic movements. It has been climbing slowly through the decade. Demand, however, blipped last year, when Japan, the world's biggest importer, pulled out of the market. Japanese stocks were high, and demand for wool textiles depressed by a gloomy economy.

This year, cotton prices have risen steadily, standing at midweek at 88 cents a lb. Last year's low prices acted as a disincentive to plant, and bad weather helped shrink the world crop from 79m bales to 69m. American production, helped along by the government's production-reduction programme, was down from 13.4m bales to 9.7m in 1986–87. The Chinese government, which has seen production shrink from 28.7m bales in 1984–85 to 16.3m bales in 1986–87.

Chinese demand, however, has risen by around 30% since 1984–85. Much of that is for domestic consumption, but Chinese exports of textiles and garments to the West have also been rising fast.

Even in rich countries cotton, which looked as though it might never recover from the assault by man-made fibres, is making a come-back. American consumption declined until 1984–85, when it hit 5.5m bales, but it has now bounced back to 7.4m bales in 1986–87. Cotton's revival is due partly to last year's low prices, which encouraged textile manufacturers to increase the cotton content of their blends.

Reel price rises fleece buyers

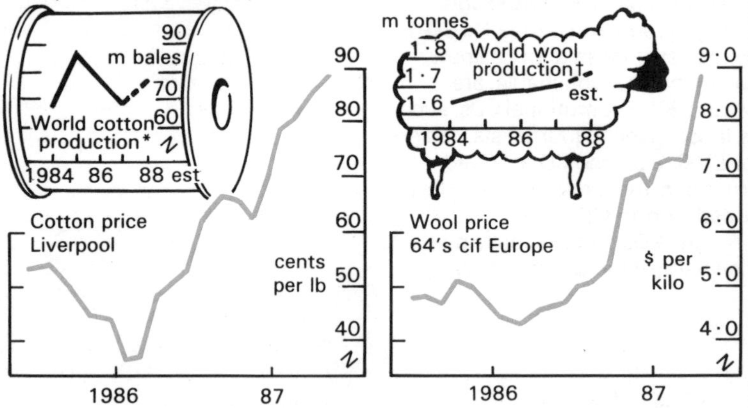

Sources: Commonwealth Secretariat: USDA Years ending *July †June

Wool is also benefiting from the move back to nature. Analysts in America say that the increase in demand has most affected the high-quality worsted markets – female executives, apparently, will not put up with synthetic suits. American consumption looks as though it will hit 150m lb this year, up from 116m in 1985. That looks less impressive when set against 1960s 410m lb.

The wool price, which has now risen to a record $8.7 a kilo, is more affected by demand from China and Russia, the world's two biggest consumers. Their appetite has grown in the past couple of years. China, especially, increased its wool consumption by 25% between 1985 and 1986. Much of that, however, was for exports of cloth and clothes to rich countries – and expansion of that business is limited by import quotas.

Wool producers are worried that current prices might cause demand to drop. Russian imports are unlikely to fall much, because too much of the country is too cold to sustain domestic production. China, however, is trying to boost production – at present it supplies only around a third of its needs. If it becomes self-sufficient – as it was in cotton from 1983 until this year – Australians and New Zealanders will suffer.

Cotton prices seem likely to stay highish during 1987, as stocks are low. But by next year the pendulum could have swung again. American cotton production in 1987–88 looks like being around 25% higher than in 1986–87. The Chinese are likely to boost output: they will not want to have to put their crop under guard next year.

Source: 'Natural Fibres: Cotton-pickin' Good', *The Economist*, 22 Aug. 1987.

Questions

1. Identify from the case study the factors that have affected the demand for (a) wool and (b) cotton.

2. Identify from the case study the factors that have affected the supply of (a) wool and (b) cotton.
3. How have changing preferences affected the demand for both wool and cotton?
4. Explain why the case study suggests that future price movements are not easy to forecast.

CASE STUDY

Housing Crisis in Cornwall

A fiercely independent streak runs through Cornish people. Cornwall County Council boasts no fewer than 28 independent councillors out of 77. So, not surprisingly, the debate raging in the county over how it should tackle its housing and development needs has taken a distinctly nationalistic turn.

Cornwall's housing problems are all too familiar. The scenic coast of north Cornwall, and picturesque harbour villages like St Mawes, have long been retirement areas. But over the last year or so the numbers have been swollen by younger people moving to take up jobs in Plymouth, just over the border in Devon.

Such migrants have often brought the gains from selling homes in the highly priced South-East and Midlands, pushing up local prices dramatically.

'Supply has dwindled, while prices have risen throughout Cornwall by up to 40 per cent in the last six months', observes Jonathan Haward of General Accident Property Services. 'A well-modernized, attractive semi-detached cottage we sold recently on the north coast in St Agnes went for £85 000. A year ago we would have expected £55 000.'

But – in a trend observable elsewhere in the country – price rises appear to have been fuelled not only by migrants, but also by the increasing prosperity of local people who are in work.

'There are a large number of people out there who can't afford to buy', says Mr Haward. 'But there are also a large number who can – first-time buyer homes have been

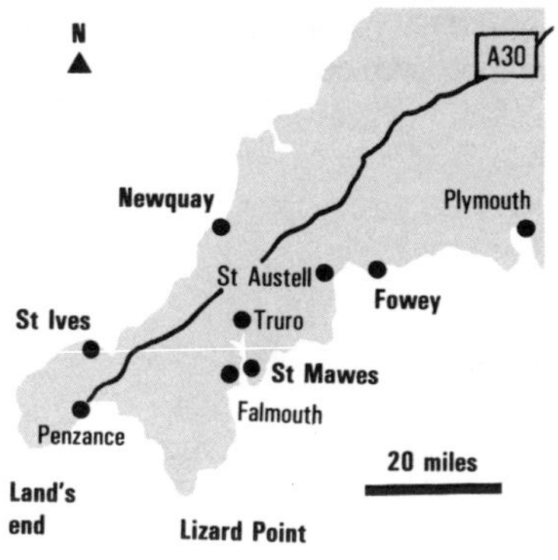

selling very strongly.' A starter house costs £45 000 in areas such as the south-east of the county and the coast; £35 000 in the less attractive industrialized areas to the west around Camborne and Redruth.

Such prices hit some people particularly hard. Tourism and associated service industries, which have replaced the traditional mining and manufacturing industries, involve primarily low-paid part-time seasonal work. As a result, Cornwall has a male unemployment rate of 11.7 per cent, two points above the national average, and average wages of around £160 a week, the lowest in the UK.

The mismatch between such purchasing power and prices has come to a head with the proposed amendment to the county's structure plan. This plan, which has to be approved by the Secretary of State, is the 'blueprint' from which six local district councils will prepare detailed proposals for where and how much development to allow.

The council originally suggested that between 1986 and 2001 around 65 000 people would move into Cornwall, and the county would need an additional 39 500 properties. This prompted an outcry, and the formation of a campaign group, the Cornwall Alternative Structure Plan (CASP). The council subsequently amended its estimate to 33 000 homes and said most of them should be in urban areas. Development in Cornwall's many designated areas of outstanding natural beauty, and in some parishes with a high percentage of second homes, it added, should favour housing which met the needs of the existing rural population.

The Department of the Environment, however, takes the line that it is impossible to define who is 'local' and that for a council to attempt to use planning to control what type of people live in a house is effectively to introduce a pass-law system.

Nevertheless, the council's approach failed to satisfy CASP, which believes that the more developers build homes, the more wealthy 'outsiders' will move into the county. 'And we don't accept the council's estimates,' says Bert Biscoe of CASP.

CASP wants a more radical approach. It wants tight control on development and the right to build the remaining 12 000 houses allowed under the structure plan allocated to a housing trust. This would sell at cost to local people, such as the estimated 8 000 on council waiting lists. On resale, owners would have to sell back to the trust for a price taking account of inflation, plus a previously agreed fixed percentage, creating a permanant pool of low-cost starter housing.

But CASP's aims are much bigger. 'Over the last 30 years the Government's policy for Cornwall has centred on improving roads and bringing more people and population into Cornwall,' says Mr Biscoe. 'It hasn't worked. The economy of Cornwall is as flaccid now as it was in the 1950s. Tourism hasn't been our saviour.

'Cornwall should formulate its own policies instead of having them imposed on us by Whitehall. We should see ourselves as an autonomous region of the European Community.' CASP wants no large-scale tourist developments such as those proposed by Peter de Savary for Land's End and the Falmouth area and argues for a shift back to manufacturing industry. Cornwall, it says, should exploit the sea as a cheap way to export goods.

It maintains the council should stop pressing for improvements to the main A30 and A38 roads into the county, asserting these will encourage imports and reduce Cornwall's self-reliance.

And it wants Cornwall to promote a negative view of itself as a retirement area. 'Many elderly who move here are unhappy and would have been better off staying in their own communities.'

Source: G. Counsell, 'Battle on the Western Front', *Independent*, 13 Aug. 1988.

Questions

1. What factors on the demand site have contributed to the rising price of private houses in Cornwall?
2. What does the case study mean when it refers to 'supply has dwindled'?
3. Why have rising house prices caused a problem in Cornwall?
4. How does the proposed method of development under a housing trust attempt to deal with this problem?

Exam Preparation

PRACTICAL EXERCISES

1. Construct a demand curve and a supply curve for electronic calculators based on the data provided in the following tables.

Price per calculator	*Quantity demanded per year (million)*
£75	3
£50	6
£35	9
£25	12
£15	15
£10	18

Price per calculator	*Quantity supplied per year (million)*
£75	18
£50	15
£35	12
£25	9
£15	6
£10	3

What is the equilibrium price? What is the equilibrium quantity at that price?

2. Give factors, other than price, that affect the demand for a good. Place each of the following events in its proper category, and state how it would shift the demand curve in question.

(a) New information is disclosed that large doses of vitamin C prevent common colds. (The demand for vitamin C.)

(b) A drop in the price of cassette recorders occurs. (The demand for LPs).

(c) A significant fall in the price of English lamb chops occurs. (The demand for mint sauce.)

3. Suppose that the demand for oranges remains constant but that a frost occurs in Florida that could potentially destroy one-third of the Florida orange crop. What will happen to the equilibrium price and quantity for oranges?

4. Examine the table below, then answer the following questions.

Price (per unit) last year	*Price (per unit) today*
Heating oil £100	£200
Natural gas £80	£320

What has happened to the absolute price of heating oil? Of natural gas? What has happened to the price of heating oil relative to the price of natural gas? What has happened to the relative price of heating oil? Will consumers, through time, change their relative expenditures? If so, how?

MULTIPLE CHOICE QUESTIONS

1. Assuming normal-sloping demand and supply curves, the effect of any tax on the price of a good in the short run, all other things remaining equal, can be shown diagrammatically by a shift of the

A demand curve to the right
B demand curve to the left
C supply curve to the right
D supply curve to the left
E demand and supply curves

2. The demand curve for a normal good will shift to the left if

A the incomes of consumers rise
B the price of the good rises
C the prices of complementary goods rise
D advertising expenditure on complementary goods increases
E taxes on the good are increased

3. In a typical demand schedule, quantity demanded

A varies directly with price
B varies proportionately with price
C is determined by the quantity offered for sale
D is independent of price
E varies inversely with price

4. In the following diagram, S_1 and D_1 represent the initial supply and demand curves for a normal commodity and X the initial equilibrium. The remaining curves represent possible shifts in the supply and demand curves.

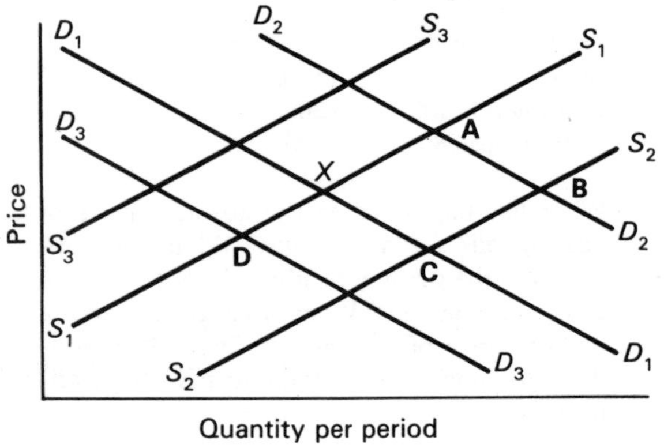

Which of the above intersection points (**A, B, C,** or **D**) represents the equilibrium point resulting from a rise in the price of a substitute commodity?

5. The diagrams show the effect of an increase in the demand for X on the demand for and price of Y. Which of the following pairs is most likely to be represented by X and Y respectively?

A Pork and pigskin
B Tea and coffee
C Potatoes and strawberries
D Houses and bricklayers
E Crude oil and petrol

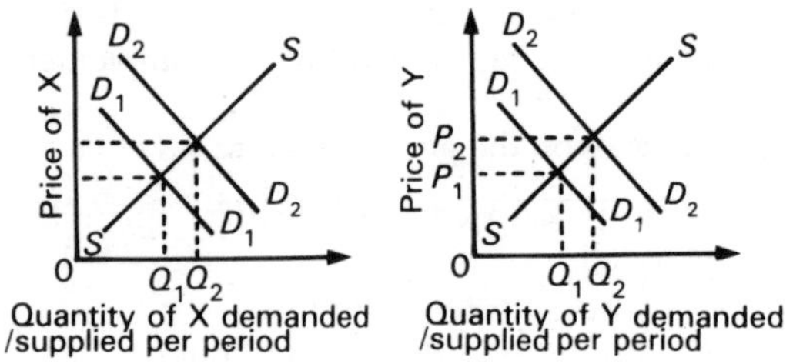

One or more of the options given in Question 7 may be correct. Select your answer by means of the code set out in the grid:

A	B	C	D
1, 2, 3 all correct	1, 2 only correct	2, 3 only correct	1 only correct

6. Cotton lint and cotton seed are produced under conditions of joint supply in proportions which cannot be altered. Other things being equal, the effect(s) of an increase in demand for cotton lint will be

1 a rise in the price of cotton seed
2 a rise in the price of cotton lint
3 an increase in the quantity supplied of cotton seed

RELATED ESSAY QUESTION

(a) What may cause changes in the demand schedule for a good?

(b) What do you believe is likely to happen to the future demand for motor cars in the UK? Justify your answer, and comment on the implications of your conclusions.

6 The Price System

Key Points to Review

- Scarcity (1.1, 1.4)
- Capitalism (2.1)
- The three key questions facing any economy: what, how, and for whom (2.2)
- Types of economy (3.1, 4.1)
- Demand (5.1)
- Supply (5.4)
- Changes in demand lead to changes in price (5.3, 5.6)
- Market-clearing price (5.7)

Questions for Preview

1 **What are the costs and benefits of specialization?**

2 **How do markets lower the transactions costs of exchange?**

3 **What is consumer sovereignty? Is consumer sovereignty worth while?**

4 **What is the difference between technical efficiency and economic efficiency?**

The model of supply and demand in Chapter 5 was a model of price determination. As such, it gave us the tools of analysis to explain the structure of relative prices within our economy. Now we need to delve into the economic system and look at it as a whole. We would like to answer questions about what determines the kinds of products that are produced and the quantities in which they are produced. In other words, how do we end up using our resources to produce motor cars instead of trains? By what mechanism was the paper, ink, and glue funnelled into the publishing industry for this very book to be published? To answer these questions, we must understand how a **price system**, or market system works, in more detail than was offered in Chapter 2. We now define a price or market system as an economic system in which (relative) prices are constantly changing to reflect changes in supply and demand for different commodities. In addition, the prices of those commodities are the *signals* to everyone within the system about what is relatively expensive and what is relatively cheap. As we shall see, it is the signalling aspect of the price system that provides the information to buyers and sellers about what should be bought and what should be produced. This chapter analyses the way in which the pure market economy works. In Chapter 4 we showed that many Western economies are not examples of this idealized economic system and so we reconsider the problems that have prompted state intervention in market economies.

Resource Allocation

Because we live in a world of scarcity, decisions must be made, whether implicitly or explicitly, about how resources shall be allocated. The problem of **resource allocation** is solved by the economic system at work in a nation. As Chapter 2 indicated, resource allocation involves answering the three questions of *what, how,* and *for whom* goods and services will be produced. Throughout this chapter, we shall show how the price system answers these three basic resource allocation questions.

1. *What and how much will be produced?* There are literally millions of different things that could be produced with society's scarce resources. Some mechanism must exist that causes some things to be produced and others to remain as either inventors' pipe-dreams or individuals' unfulfilled desires.
2. *How will it be produced?* There are many ways to produce a desired item, once the decision has been made to produce it. It is possible to use lots of unskilled labour or fewer units of skilled labour. Somehow, some way, a decision must be made as to the particular mix of inputs and the way they should be organized.
3. *For whom will it be produced?* Once a commodity is produced, who will get it? In other words, what mechanism is there to distribute commodities (and income) once they are produced?

We shall see that in a price system, literally millions of individuals are involved in solving these three fundamental questions. The interaction among the individuals within the price system is done without the use of centralized decision-making. Rather, the price system involves *de*centralized decision-making. Each decision in a price system is made by the interaction of the millions of people involved in the decision. In many parts of Western economies much of the decision-making that goes on about *what, how,* and *for whom* is carried out in markets by voluntary exchange.

Exchange Takes Place in Markets

As a society we have unlimited wants, but we must make choices among the limited alternatives available to us. When you start trading with other individuals, choices arise because you have to pick among alternative **exchanges** that you could make. Individuals in societies have been exchanging goods and services for thousands of years. For example, archaeologists tell us that during the Ice Age, hunters of mammoths in the Great Russian Steppe were trading for Mediterranean shells.

VOLUNTARY EXCHANGE

For the most part, our discussion of exchange will centre on voluntary exchanges among individuals and among nations. By necessity, prior to the undertaking of every voluntary exchange, the act of exchange itself appears to make both parties to the exchange better off. In other words, exchange is mutually beneficial or it would not be entered into. By assumption, if it were not mutually beneficial, individuals and nations would not bother exchanging.

To be sure, involuntary exchanges do occur and some are quite unpleasant for the losing parties. Involuntary exchanges occur where coercion is used to alter the behaviour of another person or nation. When individuals are robbed, they suffer exchange of goods that must be deemed involuntary. We make the assumption that only a very small part of all exchanges are involuntary and, hence, such involuntary exchanges will not affect our analysis of the price system.

The **terms of exchange** – the opportunity cost or price we pay for the desired item – are determined by the interaction of the forces underlying demand and supply. This statement, of course, relates only to an unrestricted price system. Many of the terms of exchange – the prices consumers pay – are determined by laws and regulations that are a result of the political process. Additionally, some items of exchange are determined by custom and by tradition. While custom does not play a significant role in determining prices in developed economies, in traditional societies it has been an important determinant. Customs, regulations, and laws are established by individuals acting in some type of collective manner. Thus, in a sense, all terms of exchange are determined ultimately by individuals.

In our economy, the allocation of resources takes place through voluntary exchanges in *markets.*

Markets and Information

Economists talk about markets a lot. The concept of a **market** is abstract, for it encompasses the exchange arrangements of both buyers and sellers that underlie the forces of supply and demand. In other words, demand and supply work themselves out in markets. As a general term, the word *market* refers to any arrangement or arrangements that individuals have for exchanging with one another. Economists, therefore, typically talk about product and factor markets: for example, the sugar and housing markets are examples of the former and the capital market is one of the latter types of market.

One of the major factors involved in the market is the exchange of information about such things as prices, quantities, and qualities. Indeed, markets are collectors of information that reflect the choices of consumers, producers, and the owners of resources. All this information is given by one summary statistic – the market price of goods and services. Markets with a price system also involve co-ordination without the help of a central decision-making unit. Market prices are the aids to the co-ordination of the choices of buyers and sellers. Market prices also establish a signalling system to indicate when a correct choice has been made – higher profits are made or a commodity is purchased at a 'good' price. In other words, market prices create a penalty/reward system.

Different markets have different degrees of information and speed with which that information is transmitted. The stock market in any Western economy, for example the UK, has information about the prices and quantities of stocks being bought and sold. This information is transmitted almost instantaneously throughout the country at least, if not the world. Profit-seeking entrepreneurs are constantly looking for ways to make more profits by improving on the information network within markets. That is why every market-maker can now tell you instantly the last price of any stock listed on a major stock exchange.

Why We Turn to Markets

The reason individuals turn to markets to conduct economic activities or exchanges is that markets reduce the costs of exchanging. These costs are generally called **transactions costs** because they are associated with transacting economic exchange. We can define transactions costs as all of the costs enabling exchanges to take place. Thus, they include the cost of being informed about the qualities of a particular product, its price, its availability, its durability record, its servicing facilities, its degree of safety, and so on. Consider, for example, the transactions costs in shopping for a portable microcomputer. Such costs would include phone calls or actual visits to sellers in order to learn about product features and prices. In addition to these costs, we must include the cost of negotiating the sale. The specification and execution of any sales contract is thus included, and ultimately transactions costs must include the cost of enforcing such contracts.

The transactions costs in the most highly organized markets are relatively small. Take, for example, the London Stock Exchange. It is quite easy to obtain immediate information on the price of listed shares, how many have been bought and sold in the last several hours, what the prices were the day before, and so on.

Generally, the less organized the market, the higher the transactions costs. No market can completely eliminate transactions costs, but some markets do a better job of reducing them than do others. Historically, as it has become less costly to disseminate information through technological improvements, transactions costs have fallen. (Now read Key Points 6.1.)

In a price system where there is voluntary exchange, we observe the phenomenon called **specialization**. Specialization involves working at a relatively well-defined, limited endeavour, such as accounting, selling, teaching, writing, making shoes, and so on. Most individuals in a price system specialize – they are not jacks of all trades – and they exchange the results of their specialized production activities with others who have also specialized. Just consider a typical UK household that consumes literally thousands of different commodities a year. But the members of that household who work certainly do little if anything to aid the actual production of the commodities used by the household over a year's period. The fact is that specialization leads to greater productivity, not only for each individual but for each nation. The best way to see the benefits of specialization (and then exchange) is to look at a simple numerical example.

Look at Figure 6.1. Here we show total output available for two teams of workers in a small world where they are the only ones around. At first, they do not specialize; rather, each team works 8 hours a day producing both computers and wheat. Team A can

Figure 6.1

Before Specialization. Here we show the relationship between team A's and team B's daily work-effort and the production of computers and wheat. When team A works on its own without specialization in either activity, it devotes 4 hours a day to computer production and 4 hours a day to wheat production. For its efforts, it obtains 2 computers per day and 2 tonnes of wheat per day. On the other hand, team B, again not specializing, will, during the same two 4-hour periods, produce 3 computers, but only 1 tonne of wheat. The total output of the 2 teams will be 5 computers and 3 tonnes of wheat per day.

Daily work-effort	*Team A*
4 hours	2 computers
4 hours	2 tonnes of wheat
	Team B
4 hours	3 computers
4 hours	1 tonne of wheat
Total = 5 computers, 3 tonnes of wheat per day	

After Specialization. If team A specializes in the production of wheat, it can harvest 4 tonnes of wheat for every 8 hours of work-effort. Team B, specializing in the production of computers, will produce 6 per day. Their grand total of production will be 6 computers and 4 tonnes of wheat per day, which means the benefit of specialization is increased production of 1 more computer per day and 1 more tonne of wheat per day than before they specialized.

Daily work-effort	*Team A*
8 hours	4 tonnes of wheat
	Team B
8 hours	6 computers
Total = 6 computers, 4 tonnes of wheat per day	

Key Points 6.1

- **Within a price system, supply and demand determine the prices at which exchanges shall take place.**
- **The price system is also called a market system because exchanges take place in markets where market mechanisms have reduced the costs of buyer–seller exchange.**
- **Transactions costs are all costs associated with exchange.**

produce two computers in 4 hours of work and 2 tonnes of wheat with the additional 4 hours. Team B can produce three computers in its first 4 hours of work, but only 1 tonne of wheat in its second 4 hours. The total amount that the two teams can, and choose to, produce without specialization is five computers and 3 tonnes of wheat per day.

Now look at what happens when each team specializes. We see in Figure 6.1 that after specialization, when team A spends all its time producing wheat, it can harvest 4 tonnes (since it can harvest 2 tonnes in 4 hours). Team B, on the other hand, spending all its work-day producing computers, can produce six computers per day (since it can produce three computers in just 4 hours). The total 'world' output has now increased to six computers per day and 4 tonnes of wheat per day. With the same two sets of teams using the same amount of resources, the total output of this economy has increased from five computers per day to six, and from 3 tonnes of wheat per day to 4. Obviously, the two teams would be better off (in a material sense) if they each specialized and then exchanged their products. Team A would exchange wheat for computers, and team B would do the reverse. You should note that our discussion has not dealt with the disadvantage of specialization – monotony and drudgery in one's job. But if we assume that after specialization each individual is indeed doing what he or she could do *comparatively* better than the other, then we have an appreciation of the concept of comparative advantage.

Comparative Advantage

Specialization, as outlined in the example above, rests on a very important fact: different individuals, communities, and nations are indeed different, at least when it comes to the skills of each in producing goods and services. In our simple two-team example, if these teams could do both jobs equally well, there would be no reason for specialization, since total output could not have been increased. (Go back to Figure 6.1 and make team B equally physically productive in the production of both computers and wheat, producing, say, one computer in 4 hours and 1 tonne of wheat in 4 hours, and then see what happens to our example after specialization.)

In fact, people are not uniformly talented. Even if individuals or nations had the talent to do everything better (for example, by using fewer resources, especially labour hours), they would still want to *specialize in the area of their greatest advantage*, that is, in their **comparative advantage**. To continue the example, consider the hypothetical dilemma of the managing director of a large company. Suppose that he or she can type better than any of the typists, drive a lorry better than any of the lorry-drivers, and wash windows better than any of the window-washers. That just means that the director has an **absolute advantage** in all these endeavours – he or she uses fewer labour hours for each task than anyone else in the company. However, his or her *comparative* advantage lies in managing the company, not in doing the aforementioned tasks. How is it known that that is where the comparative advantage lies? The answer is quite easy: the managing director is *paid* the most for being a managing director, not for being a typist or a lorry-driver or a window-washer for the company.

Basically, *one's comparative advantage is found by choosing that activity that has the lowest opportunity cost.* Consider the example given in Figure 6.1 before specialization. Team A in 4 hours can produce two computers or 2 tonnes of wheat. That means, the opportunity costs for two computers is 2 tonnes of wheat, so that the opportunity cost for one computer is 1 tonne of wheat. In other words, team A has to give up 1 tonne of wheat in order to produce one computer. What about team B? Since it can produce three computers in 4 hours, or 1 tonne of wheat, its opportunity cost for producing one computer is only 1 divided by 3, or ⅓ of a tonne of wheat. That is to say, the opportunity cost of team B for one computer is ⅓ of a tonne of wheat. Since one's comparative advantage is found by choosing that activity that has the lowest opportunity cost, it is clear that team B should specialize in computer production because it incurs the lowest opportunity cost. Indeed, that is what we show when the teams specialize. Team B spends all 8 hours producing computers.

Although the discussion of specialization and comparative advantage has been couched in terms of labour it applies equally well to all factors of production.

The Division of Labour

Within any given firm that includes specialized human and non-human resources, there is a **division of labour** among those resources. The most famous example of all time comes from one of the earliest and perhaps one of the most famous economists of all time. Adam Smith, who illustrated the benefits of a division of labour with this example:

> One man draws out the wire, another straightens it, a third cuts it, a fourth points, a fifth grinds it at the top for receiving the head; to make the head requires two or three distinct operations; to put it on is a peculiar business, to whiten the pins is another; it is even a trade by itself to put them into the paper.*

Making pins this way allowed ten workers without very much skill to make almost 48 000 pins 'of a middling size' in a day. One worker, toiling alone, could have made perhaps 20 pins a day; therefore, ten workers could have produced 200. Division of labour allowed for an increase in the daily output of the pin

*Adam Smith, *The Wealth of Nations* (1776), Bk. 1, Ch. 1, Everyman edn. (1964).

Key Points 6.2

- **With a given set of resources, specialization results in higher output; in other words, there are gains to specialization in terms of higher material well-being.**
- **Individuals and nations specialize in their comparative advantages in order to reap the gains of specialization.**
- **Comparative advantages are found by determining which activities have the lowest opportunity cost or, otherwise stated, which activities yield the highest return for the time and resources used.**
- **A division of labour occurs when different workers are assigned different tasks. Together, the workers produce a desired product.**

factory from 200 to 48 000! (Smith did not attribute *all* of the gain to the division of labour according to talent, but also to the use of machinery, to the fact that less time was spent shifting from task to task, and so on.)

What we are referring to here involves a division of the resource called labour into different kinds of labour. The different kinds of labour are organized in such a way as to increase the amount of output possible from the fixed resources available. We can therefore talk about an organized division of labour within a firm leading to increased output. (Now read Key Points 6.2.)

Relative Prices Revisited

We have often referred to prices as relative prices. This is even more important in understanding how the price system solves the basic allocation of resources problem. In the broad sense of the term, the relative price of a good is defined as the price of that good expressed in terms of how much of other goods must be given up to purchase a unit of the good in question. To establish relative prices, comparison with other prices must be made. Virtually all economic models, like supply and demand, relate individual behaviour to changes in relative, not absolute, prices.

Prices and Information

Relative prices are the conveyors of information in the market-place. For the buyers, the relative price of a good indicates what the individual purchaser must give up in order to obtain that good. Suppose that you are told that a loaf of bread will cost you £100 and this you regard as an incredibly high price. But then you are told that you are assumed to be earning £500 per hour? Does that £100 load of bread still sound so expensive? Is it any more expensive than, say, a price of £1 for the loaf and a wage-rate of £5 per hour? In both cases, you only have to work one-fifth of an hour to pay for the loaf of bread. It is the relative price of the loaf of bread – in this case, relative to the price of your labour – that tells you how expensive it *really* is (or what your real purchasing power is).

Now consider the relative value of the resources used to produce the bread. Its relative price will, in most cases, indicate the amount of resources given up to produce that good. Hence, when the relative price of a commodity goes up, that bit of information tells the buyer and the seller that the good is now relatively scarcer. Note that neither the producer nor the consumer has to know *why* that particular commodity has become relatively scarcer. It may not matter to you as a consumer, when allocating your budget, whether the price of petroleum has gone up *because* of a restriction on imports or *because* of a new law that requires petrol companies to install more expensive pollution-abatement equipment. The only thing that definitely matters to you is the higher relative price, for that is the basis on which you will make your decision about the quantity to purchase. The message is transmitted by the higher relative price. Of course, how you respond to the message is impossible to predict on an individual basis, for there are probably an infinite number of ways that a consumer can 'conserve' on a relatively scarcer good.

Changes in relative prices convey information on changing relative scarcity to both buyers and sellers. Of course, buyers respond differently from sellers. Sellers may see a rise in the relative price of a particular good as an opportunity to increase profits, and eventually such information may be translated into a larger amount of resources going to the production of that now relatively higher-priced good. It is in this manner that resources are allocated in a system that allows prices to convey the information about relative scarcities. In a market system prices convey the information to the individuals – both sellers and buyers – in the market-place. There is no need for a central agency to produce information or to allocate resources. This does not mean that problems will not arise and that certain economic activities could not be better handled by other than unrestricted market processes. What it does mean is that spontaneous co-ordination occurs in a decentralized price system and resource allocation requires no outside management. This is what Adam Smith meant by an invisible hand at work. (Now read Key Point 6.3.)

Key Point 6.3

- **Individuals respond to changes in *relative* prices, not absolute prices. Therefore, changes in the general price level – the average of all prices – are not central to the allocative functioning of the price system.**

Markets, Prices, and the Determination of *What* Is to be Produced

The decision about *what* is to be produced depends on the incentives generated within an economic system. Within the price system, the incentive that is foremost is *profit*: the search for higher profits causes decision-makers to produce a mix of goods whose total effective demand is the greatest relative to the scarce resources available for the production of all goods and services.

Profits

A business person seeks **profits**. We define profits as the difference between the cost of producing something and the price that it fetches in the market-place. (Remember: The only way we are strictly able to define cost is *opportunity cost* – the value of the resources in their next highest, or best, alternative use.) Another way of looking at profits is as the income generated by buying cheap and selling dear. A business person buys factors of production – land, labour, and capital – at a cost that is less than the price obtainable when the finished product is sold. This definition of profit also includes the income received by the buying of anything at a lower price than the price for which it is sold.

We take two examples to see how changes in profitability cause resources to be *re*allocated, and hence determine what is to be produced. In the previous chapters we used the market for wheat to show how demand and supply come together in a free market to determine an equilibrium price. Now let us imagine several farmers who just grow, say, carrots and potatoes. We shall now follow through the consequences of a change in one of the determinants of the demand for these goods – a change in consumer tastes.

Suppose that there is suddenly an increased and sustained demand for potatoes because it is believed that eating potatoes – whether boiled, roasted, or fried – is good for one's health. This shift in tastes would result in an outward movement in the demand curve for potatoes and their relative price rise in Figure 6.2 from P_e to P''_e. If we suppose also that carrot-eating has become less popular this is translated into an inward shift in the demand curve for carrots. The relative price of carrots falls from P_e to P'_e. Assuming now that the cost of inputs into carrot production has not changed, the lower market-clearing price will mean less profit (or maybe even losses) in growing carrots. On the other hand, assuming again that there has been no change in

Figure 6.2

Shifts in Demand Cause Prices to Change. In panel (a) we show the supply and demand for carrots. At the original equilibrium, the market-clearing relative price is P_e. When, because of a shift in tastes, the demand curve shifts leftward from *DD* to *D′D′*, the relative price, and hence profitability, of carrot-growing falls. The new market-clearing price after adjustment would become P'_e with the smaller quantity Q'_e produced. In panel (b), just the opposite has happened for potatoes. The demand curve has shifted from *DD* to *D″D″*. The market-clearing price has gone up from P_e to P''_e with the larger quantity Q''_e produced. The profitability of growing potatoes has risen. More resources will flow into potato-growing and fewer will be used in growing carrots.

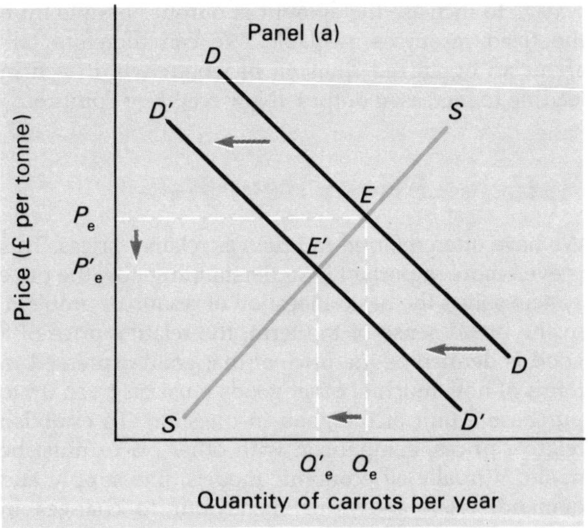

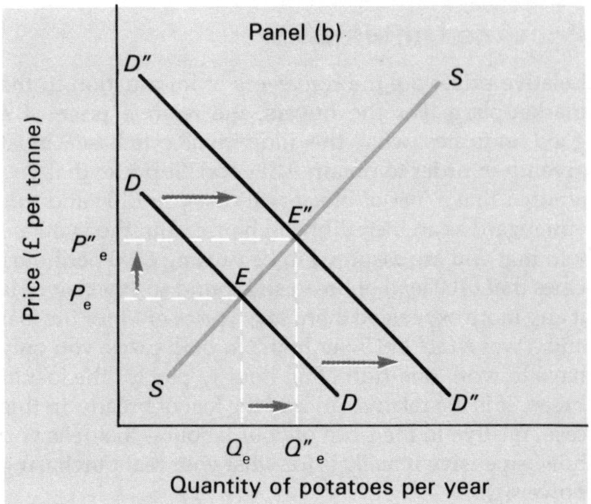

input prices, when the market-clearing price of potatoes goes up, the profits per unit will also rise. The price adjustments and ensuing changes in profitability will lead to resource reallocation. There is a profit incentive for farmers to devote more of their land and labour to growing potatoes. The incentive to minimize losses causes a cutting back on the use of these resources in carrot-growing. Thus the change in consumers' tastes results here in a response by producers to alter their production of carrots and potatoes in favour of the more profitable product – potatoes – since it is in their best interest to do so. (Read Key Point 6.4.)

Moving Resources from Lower- to Higher-valued Uses

The above examples relate to agriculture but the principle involved – resource reallocation – is generally applicable. The movement of resources in search of higher profits for businesses is simultaneously a movement of resources from lower- to higher-valued uses. When consumers no longer wanted to buy as many carrots, the demand curve shifted inwards to the left (panel (a) of Figure 6.2). Thus, carrots were no longer as valuable from a subjective point of view as they were prior to the shift in demand. Had all the resources remained in carrot-growing they would be generating a lower subjective value to consumers than they could elsewhere in the economy.

Another incentive to shift production would involve the piling up of unsold stocks of carrots. Unsold carrots due to falling orders from vegetable wholesalers and retailers provide information which encourages growers to switch resources to the production of something else.

When some of these resources were moved from carrot- to potato-growing, they were, by necessity, being moved to a use that generated a higher value to consumers. How do we know this? Because the demand curve for potatoes shifted outwards to the right. With a given supply curve, this dictated a higher relative price, which gave an indication that consumers now valued an additional unit of resources in the carrot industry more than in the past.

Note that we have stressed that consumers are the decision-makers that prompt transfers in resources. We will now examine this decision-making process more closely.

Consumer Sovereignty

The movement of resources from lower- to higher-valued uses depends crucially on consumer sovereignty. Consumer sovereignty means that the ultimate determiners of how much of what is produced are consumers, not politicians or businesses. In other words, in a world of consumer sovereignty, consumers are the decision-makers. Final production is destined to fulfil their wants and no one else's. In a pure market economy, or price system, each consumer expresses his or her desires (constrained by income) by 'voting' in the market-place with their pounds and pence. When fewer consumers were voting for carrots, this was translated into a shift leftward of the demand curve. When more consumers were expressing their votes for potatoes, this was shown by a shift rightward of the demand curve for potatoes.

The consumer voting system is, of course, not the same as a majority voting system. No firm has to receive 51 per cent of the available spending votes in order to produce a particular product. There are, for example, speciality car companies like Porsche and Alfa Romeo that receive just a few per cent of the total 'votes' for new cars in the UK each year. But they continue to exist because there is a sufficient demand to make them profitable. On the other hand, there are many products that are not produced even though they could receive 100 per cent of all of the votes by all of a small group of people who desire those goods. This is because even with 100 per cent of the votes, there would not be enough buyers for a business person to make a profit on the product. This is also another difference between political voting and money voting. In a market system you do not have to 'vote' for an entire package at one single time. Rather, you 'vote' for different parts – goods and services – of your total consumption package a little at a time. In the political arena you make your decision, at most, once a year, and sometimes only once every five years.

In sum, in a pure market economy, consumers vote with their money but it is proportional (as opposed to majority rule) voting. Manufacturers will respond and resources will be allocated proportionally to the way the total population spends its money, or votes with its income.

The Market System and Efficiency

Consumer sovereignty in a pure price system means that resources will be used as efficiently as possible. The efficient use of resources will occur because business persons in each industry are competing for the money 'votes' of consumers. Consequently, each firm (and hence the economy taken as a whole) will fully utilize its available resources and will generate maximum consumer satisfaction by fulfilling the largest

> **Key Point 6.4**
>
> ▶ **Within a market economy, businesses seek profits. In their quest for profits, they move resources out of declining industries into expanding industries.**

number of consumer desires reflected by money income spent.

There are really two parts of efficiency – **technical efficiency** and **economic efficiency**, both of which are satisfied in a pure market economy, or price system.

TECHNICAL EFFICIENCY

Technical efficiency relates to utilizing production techniques that do not waste inputs. In other words, we can assume that within the market economy businesses will never waste inputs: they will never use 10 units of capital, 10 units of labour, and 10 units of land when they could produce the same amount of output with only 8 units of capital, 7 units of labour, and 9 units of land. Technical efficiency refers to decisions within a production unit. Managers respond to the prices that are given to them from outside the firm for the resources they must use. Technical efficiency, therefore, relates to managers responding 'correctly' to the input prices facing them. The more expensive the inputs, the more incentive managers have to economize in the use of them.

ECONOMIC EFFICIENCY

This concept relates to maximizing the total subjective valuation (sometimes called utility) of our available resources. That means that resources are moved to their highest-valued uses, as evidenced by consumers' willingness to pay for the final products. As we saw above, profits signal resources to move around so that economic efficiency occurs. The forces of demand and supply guide resources to their most efficient uses. In a sense, it is the invisible-hand concept again. Individuals seeking their own self-interest end up, consciously or unconsciously, generating maximum economic value from their activities.

Economic efficiency refers to relationships outside each firm. That is to say, economic efficiency refers to market price determination within an economy. Whenever a price system is in operation, market price determination will create the 'proper' signals to market participants so that they will indeed be able to make the correct choices about resource allocation.*

Of course, an economic system can never attain economic efficiency unless within each firm or production unit technical efficiency has already been attained. That is to say, technical efficiency is implicitly a part of economic efficiency.† Usually, when discussing economic efficiency, economists assume that all profit-maximizing firms are operating technically efficiently.

How can we apply these two efficiency concepts?

1. Technical efficiency means that resources will never be wasted in producing a given output.
2. Economic efficiency means that resources will be used in their highest-valued uses.

Technical efficiency. Colour television sets will be packed to shops using the minimum amount of cardboard necessary. They will not, for example, be made 3″ thick when ⅜″ will do just as well (and also save on distribution costs because it is lighter).

Economic efficiency. Corrugated board will be used rather than oak or mahogany which have a higher-valued use today for, say, furniture. Furniture-makers will be willing to pay a lot more for that type of wood than will the makers of colour television set assemblers. (Now read Key Points 6.5.)

Organizing Production – *How* Will Goods Be Produced?

The second function of an economic system, which was mentioned at the beginning of this chapter, relates to *how* goods will be produced.

How Output Will Be Produced

The question of how output will be produced in a price system relates to the efficient use of scarce resources. Consider the possibility of using only two types of resources – capital and labour. A firm may have the following options given in Figure 6.3. It can use various combinations of labour and capital in order to produce the same amount of output. Two hypothetical combinations are given in that exhibit. The *least-cost combination* (which is technique B) will in fact be chosen, because in this manner profits will be the highest possible. If any other technique were chosen, firms would then be sacrificing *potential* profit.

*Even in a pure price system, it is possible for market prices to generate incorrect signals. We look at this problem later.

†Technical efficiency is a necessary but not a sufficient condition for economic efficiency.

Key Points 6.5

- **If consumers' sovereignty exists, proportional money voting by consumers determines the output mix. Thus, within a pure market economy, resources flow from lower- to higher-valued uses. In the process, the price system attains both technical and economic efficiency.**
- **With technological efficiency, inputs are not wasted.**
- **With economic efficiency, total subjective valuation of all resources is greatest. Resources are used in their highest-valued uses.**

Moreover, in a price system, competition will in effect *force* firms to use least-cost production techniques. Any firm that fails to employ the least costly technique will find that other firms can undercut its price. Other firms that choose the least-cost production technique will be able to offer the product at a lower price and still make a profit. The lower price at which they offer the product will induce consumers to shift sales to them from the firm with the higher prices. Inefficient firms will be forced out of business.

All this discussion assumes that technology and resources prices are held constant. But if, say, the cost of capital remained the same and the cost of labour were to decrease considerably in our example in Figure 6.3, another production technique such as A might then be less costly. Firms would shift to that production technique in order to obtain the highest profits possible.

The Distribution of Total Output

The last question that any economic system must solve is distribution – *how* is total output distributed among competing claimants? The problem of distribution of total output can be separated into two parts, one relating to the distribution of products to consumers and the other relating to the distribution of money income to individuals. It should not surprise you that the second part of this problem of distribution quickly takes us into the world of **normative economics**.

Which Consumers Get What?

In a price system the distribution of finished products to consumers is based on the consumers' ability and willingness to pay the market price for the products. If the market-clearing price of a bottle of wine is £3.50, those consumers who are able and willing to pay that price will get their wine. Those consumers who are not, will not.

Here we are talking about the *rationing* function of market-clearing prices in a price system. Rather than have a central political figure decide which consumers will get which goods, those consumers who are willing to pay the market-clearing price obtain the good. That is to say, relative prices ration the available resources, goods, and services at any point in time among those who would like to have the scarce items. If scarcity did not exist, then we would not need any system to ration available resources, goods, and services.

The Determination of Money Income

In a price system, a consumer's ability to pay for consumer products is based on size of his or her money income. That, in turn, depends on the quantities, qualities, and types of the various human and non-human resources that the individual owns and supplies to the market-place. Additionally, the prices, or payments, for those resources influence total money income. When you are selling your human resources as labour services, your money income is based on the wage-rate, or salary, that you can fetch in the labour market. If you own non-human resources – capital and land, for example – the level of interest and rents that you would be paid for your capital and land will clearly influence the size of your money income and thus your ability to buy consumer products.

What are the implications of these observations? Well, if labour services are not paid for at a common wage-rate and also not everyone has capital to invest to advantage, then we will soon face normative issues. How fair is such a system when some people have more money than others? The 'for whom' question quickly makes us stray away from the world of positive economics.

A 'perfectly performing' price system may not provide for much equality in income. That is to say, an efficient price system could still be one in which some people were starving to death. If one of the social goals in a society is to provide more income equality, then something other than the price system must be utilized. Indeed, most Western economies have a taxation system that attempts to reduce the high levels of income of the highest-income-earning individuals; and we also have a system of welfare, in which we attempt to transfer some of those revenues collected by taxes to the lowest-earning (or non-earning) members of our society.

Related to the social goal of income equality is the goal of income security. The price system may not

Figure 6.3

Production Costs for 100 Units of Product X. Technique A or B can be used to produce the same output. Obviously, B will be used because its total cost is less than A's.

		A		B	
Inputs	*Input unit price*	*Production technique A (input units)*	*Cost*	*Production technique B (input units)*	*Cost*
Labour	£10	5	£50	4	£40
Capital	£8	4	£32	5	£40
Total cost of 100 units of product X			£82		£80

guarantee income security to all. A non-market system, using government, may therefore be (and is) an alternative. For example, the provision of government-provided unemployment insurance benefits (paid by taxes) is an attempt to reduce income insecurity among the economy's participants.

This recognition of the shortcomings of a market economy concerning the distribution of goods and services prompts the need for a more general re-appraisal of the price system. What perhaps have we too readily assumed in the above analysis?

Evaluating the Price System

It is possible to evaluate the price system in terms of what it can and cannot do. When a price system alone cannot satisfy certain social goals, then government or voluntary solutions to problems need to be examined.

What the Price System Can Do

Throughout this chapter we have seen that the price system can communicate information concerning relative scarcity and opportunity costs. And, in a world in which individual preferences are self-determined (rather than programmed), individual preferences can be expressed via the purchase or non-purchase of commodities. The communication-of-information function of the price system, as we have seen, leads to efficiency.

EFFICIENCY

The price system does lead to both technical and economic efficiency. Competition among firms forces them to choose the least-cost production techniques, thus avoiding waste (technical efficiency). In the absence of restraints and imperfections in the system (to be discussed below), maximum economic value is obtained from a given set of resources at any point in time (economic efficiency). In some sense, then, the price system harnesses self-interest in order to provide society with the greatest possible output of desired goods. The price system leads to a movement of resources from lower- to relatively higher-valued uses. Thus, resources will not stay in an industry, the demand for whose product has withered away because of a change in consumer tastes.

INDIVIDUAL FREEDOM

Another aspect of the price system which can be listed as something it can do involves maximizing individual, or personal, freedom. Since the co-ordination of social organization through a price system does not require central direction or the use of force by any governmental authority, individual freedom presumably obtains. The price system allows for a type of spontaneous co-ordination that has been described as 'an invisible hand'. The price system permits, as it were, the freedoms of choice and enterprise. Individuals are free to further their self-interest. One of the contemporary champions of the price system has said that

> So long as effective freedom of exchange is maintained, the central feature of the market organization of economic activity is that it prevents one person from interfering with another in respect of most of his activities. The consumer is protected from coercion by the seller because of the presence of other sellers with whom he can deal. The seller is protected from coercion by the consumer because of other consumers to whom he can sell. The employee is protected from coercion by the employer because of other employers for whom he can work, and so on. And the market does this impersonally and without centralized authority.*

GROWTH

A price system can (and historically has) led to economic growth. Remember from Chapter 1 that we defined economic growth as an increase in the productive capacity of a nation over time (a shifting outwards to the right of the production possibilities curve). Since the price system offers a reward-and-penalty signalling system to its participants, there is an incentive to increase productivity because of the reward (profits). No centralized authority must decide which innovations should be utilized to increase productivity; rather, market participants make the decisions and those who make the correct decisions are rewarded by increased profits. Consequently, one can argue that a price system provides the setting for those who choose correctly. Moreover, because of the penalty of reduced profits, or even losses, resources do not stay in areas where consumer demand no longer exists.

What the Price System Cannot Do

The 'market' does not always work. That is to say, there are shortcomings in the way some markets operate that prevent the price system from actually attaining economic efficiency and individual freedom – as well as other social goals. And, of course, every case in which the price system cannot attain a social goal is a case in which non-market alternatives must be considered.

EXTERNALITIES

If the price system does not register all the costs and benefits associated with the production and/or consumption of commodities, then an externality arises. We define an **externality** as a cost or benefit external to an exchange. In other words, the external benefits or costs accrue to parties other than the immediate seller and buyer in a transaction. An obvious example of an external cost is the pollution of air and water. These are externalities because they result from production and consumption activities in which the parties involved do not take account of such ill effects on others. The point to be made is that whenever supply and demand

*Milton Friedman, *Capitalism and Freedom* (Chicago: University of Chicago Press, 1962).

do not fully reflect all costs and all benefits of production and consumption, the price system cannot be expected to bring about an efficient allocation of resources. Externalities are an extremely important topic in economics; we treat them in detail in Chapter 10.

PUBLIC GOODS

The price system relates to the tabulation of individual wants only. Many goods and services are not, however, financed by individuals through the market-place. Flood control programmes and national defence cannot be purchased in small amounts by households and individuals. They can be consumed only on a public, or collective, basis. The price system, then, is considered to be incapable of providing such **public goods** in optimal quantities. In instances like this the market mechanism does not work effectively. These cases are known as examples of **market failure**. (We treat them in more detail in Chapter 10.)

COMPETITION

Implicit in much of the discussion of supply and demand in Chapter 5 and of the price system in this chapter is the notion of competition, where there are many buyers and sellers of products. But even in a price system, there may be a lack of competition because of, for example, successful efforts on the part of business persons to restrict competition. Adam Smith realized that 'people of the same trade seldom meet together for fun and merriment, but the conversation ends in a conspiracy against the public, or in some contrivance to raise prices'.*

*Adam Smith, *The Wealth of Nations* (1776), Bk. I, Ch. 10, Everyman edn.

Smith's fear of conspiracies and monopolies that would hurt consumers is a fear that still is with us today. For many, this fear has taken on the form of reality, for they believe that there is little competition left in many parts of the UK economy. The price system cannot work to its fullest advantage if there are restraints on trade through monopoly. Whenever the degree of competition declines, the price system becomes less of a perfect mechanism for efficiently allocating resources.

If there is a recognition of the need to ensure a fully competitive market system then some scope for government intervention is implied. Governments may, for example, wish to restrict the willingness of large firms in particular markets to merge together and dominate them. We consider policies in the UK to make product markets more competitive in Chapter 29.

UNEQUAL INCOME DISTRIBUTION

We have already recognized that the market system may operate in a technical sense well but does so in the context of what some see as an unfair distribution of income and wealth. Government policies to redistribute income and wealth can try to 'correct' this shortcoming of the market mechanism.

FACTOR IMMOBILITY

We showed earlier in the chapter how shifts in the demand for potatoes and carrots brought about price adjustments and ensuing changes in profitability for farmers. The end result was that there would be a *reallocation of resources* and it was implicitly assumed that this process would take place readily and without difficulty. If we now broaden our horizons we can recognize that in the real world the factors of production will not, in practice, be reallocated as easily as in

Key Points 6.6

- **Within a price system competition forces producers to seek least-cost techniques of production. Competition is thus the driving-force behind the free market solution of how goods and services are to be produced.**
- **The actual distribution of goods and services is dependent on the ability and willingness of consumers to make payments for these outputs. This ability to pay will be dependent on the size of money incomes. Money incomes are unequal since there is not an even ownership of human and non-human resources.**
- **A pricing system can lead to technical and economic efficiency while permitting individual freedom within a dynamic economy. However, a price system may in practice lack strong competitive pressures to promote efficiency.**
- **A pricing system cannot, without non-market intervention, easily take care of externalities. Nor can it provide a sufficient amount of public goods. Where there are such problems in allocating resources these are instances of market failure.**
- **A pricing system can still operate in a society where income disparities are so great that government intervention (to achieve the social goal of income equality) is widely accepted as being desirable.**

this theoretical example. Labour cannot readily move from one industry to another since retraining and relocation of work are likely to be involved.

A second dimension to this problem of the less than perfect mobility of factors of production is the phenomenon of *structural change*. It is not just shifts in demand that prompt the need for resource reallocation but also the process of technological change as represented, for example, by the appearance of microprocessors and robotic equipment. Industries such as steel and motor vehicle manufacturing are undergoing major change in terms of the character of the industrial process. Can a purely market economy handle the reallocation of capital and labour without some government intervention?

Manufacturing in the UK is exposed to foreign competition both in the home market and in overseas markets, whereas some service industries like plumbing and painting by their very nature face little or no international competition at all. We must recognize that the problem of resource allocation is now more crucial than ever before due to the rapid pace of technological change and the growing competition in manufactured goods from the more advanced developing countries.

The Results of the Evaluation

The price system can, it seems, satisfy some social goals, and, at the same time, it cannot satisfy numerous others. As you might expect, therefore, the actual economic system that exists in the United Kingdom and most developed countries is a combination of the price system and a non-price system – and that is what we will examine in Chapter 8.

CASE STUDY

Mild Winter Woes

The sun may smile unseasonally, the daffodils may outdo the snowdrops, but it is a rough winter for those who depend on cold weather to help them make a living.

Ski schools in Scotland have laid off employees, winter stocks are piled high at coal merchants, glove-makers are left with thousands of unsold pairs, while fashion shops display winter coats by the rackful.

'Last winter was mild enough – which meant a lot of gloves had to be carried forward for sale this year – and now this even milder weather has struck and made things even worse,' said Mr Nigel Openshaw, chairman of Mcleod Russel Holdings whose subsidiary, Harrotts, of Aberdeen, is one of Britain's principal glove-makers.

He added: 'I have no message for the Almighty except to say if he wants to make it snow this year it's too late for glove-makers. We are big enough to ride it out but I should think many of the small independents risk going to the wall.'

The industry reports a drop of 25 per cent on normal winter sales.

Business in women's winter coats have also been hit. Fashion houses have reported an 'indifferent' winter through a combination of the weather and the return of the mini-skirt, which women are reluctant to hide beneath large coats.

At her wool shop in Tooting Market, south-west London, Mrs Carole Watson said: 'My winter yarns have not been selling as well as they should. Normally the balls just fall off the shelves, but people are coming in and asking me for summer yarns already.'

British Coal said December sales to householders were down 15 per cent and those to industry by six per cent. January would probably prove to be similar or worse.

The ski-ing industry appears to be faring worst. Mr Derek Brightman, of the Association of Ski Schools, said only 30–40 ski instructors were being employed in Aviemore, instead of 130.

Fewer waitresses, chalet maids and shop assistants had been taken on.

'The hotels are also having their troubles. If fewer people come because of the weather, then fewer people will need accommodation,' he said.

'If snow does come it will be a real struggle to cope because the staff will not be available.'

Mr Sandy Caird, who set up the Caird Sport Ski School in Aviemore 23 years ago, said about half of his guests had cancelled their holidays.

'We've had bad years, but nothing like this,' he added. There have been no complaints about the weather from rail travellers: with seasonal excuses thin on the ground British Rail has had little alternative but to run its services near enough to time.

Source: D. Graves and N. Farrell, 'Bleak Midwinter for Seasonal Workers', *Daily Telegraph*, 11 Feb. 1989.

Questions

1. The case study suggests the mild winter of 1988–9 was not the only factor affecting those producers who depend on cold weather for their livelihood. How does both the past and fashion also combine to have an effect on some industries?
2. Which types of economic activity *not* mentioned in the case study may have been adversely affected by the mild winter of 1988–9?
3. Which types of economic activity would have benefited from the mild winter of 1988–9?

CASE STUDY

Off-Court Economics

The name must have a lot to do with it: who would want to be known as a ticket tout?

Certainly the touts get a bad press – sometimes from the very newspapers which in the past couple of weeks have been raking in thousands of pounds from advertising for Wimbledon tickets in their personal columns. You must ring anonymous telephone dealers who offer 'confidentiality' and 'discretion' like the more dubious kinds of offshore financiers.

In economic terms touts offer an almost entirely beneficial service – tainted only by the damaging odour of hypocrisy and dishonesty which goes with any unregulated black market. Such operators thrive on mispricing, and fill the gaps when others make a mess of running the primary markets.

Often the mispricing is glaringly obvious, as at the Wimbledon tennis championships. Yet the touts do take risks and can get it wrong. I remember going to the Football Association *v.* Rest of the World centenary game at Wembley last August and seeing groups of disconsolate touts standing all along the Olympic Way. The market, Maradona or no, had crashed; indeed, I had been given a free ticket by a man in a pub the night before.

Such ill-judged events aside, why are tickets so badly underpriced so often? The simplest reason is that promoters find it hard to predict demand, and err on the cautious side. A second reason, however, is that there is a desire to accommodate particular groups of customers, such as the young, or poorer regular fans who could not afford the full market prices for showpiece events.

The third reason is less attractive; it is a readinesss to exercise patrongae by allocating tickets in ways which may start by rewarding deserving individuals but may end in suspicions of corruption.

Exactly why commercial promoters of overbooked shows such as *Phantom of the Opera* do not price to market I am not sure. Perhaps it is for fear of offending the regular theatregoing clientele. This certainly applies at sporting events such as Wimbledon where there is so much corporate entertainment activity. Tennis fans can be priced out of the market, while many supposedly valuable Centre Court seats are left empty for long periods because the barely interested guests are still back in the marquee eating strawberries and quaffing champagne.

In such distorted situations there may be good reasons for deciding against an open market for tickets, but there can be no sympathy for failure to take account of market forces.

It is worth recalling another Wimbledon black market phenomenon, although this time at the Plough Lane football ground rather than at the All-England Club.

When Wimbledon reached the Cup Final in 1988 the club decided to allocate tickets to regular, but non-season ticket holding, fans on the basis of vouchers handed out at the remaining home league games. Officials naively calculated that season ticket holders would not collect these vouchers because they were entitled to Wembley tickets anyway. Naturally, however, a great many season ticket holders decided that if £50 was being handed out for £10 they wanted their share. So some fans who wanted to go to Wembley went short while thousands of black market tickets sped north to Liverpool, at enormous profit.

Maybe the Wimbledon football bosses can plead lack of experience at handling excess demand. But that cannot be an excuse for the tennis authorities. They have rendered matters more complicated by conniving at the development of two distinct secondary markets in tickets.

One is the legitimate market in Centre Court tickets (2 100 out of 12 500 each day) which are the property of some 700 debenture holders. The other is the illegitimate (but not illegal) black market in tickets which are allocated to players, umpires and officials, or are sold at much below market prices via a ballot to the general public (many of whom apply for tickets without having any genuine intention of watching the tennis).

The whiff of scandal has attached itself in particular to the umpires. They receive no pay for the dubious privilege of being abused by John McEnroe, but are each allocated six double Centre Court tickets, which in aggregate could be worth well over £1 000. They are not supposed to sell them, but clearly many do.

But this year the stories of £25 face value tickets for men's finals day at Wimbledon selling for £800 have become so persistent, and the ticket touts have become such an irresistible target for cheap headline-seeking politicians, that the All-England Club may have to rethink its approach.

The laws of microeconomics dictate that wherever market forces are flouted those seedy gentlemen with bulging wallets and mobile phones will soon appear.

Source: B. Riley, 'Game, Set and Match to the Touts', *Financial Times*, 25 June 1988.

Questions

1. What does the author mean by the comment that 'the laws of microeconomics dictate that wherever market forces are flouted those seedy gentlemen with bulging wallets and mobile phones will soon appear'?
2. In what way is the activity of ticket touts in providing a secondary market a desirable activity?

3. The author points out that in the case of the All-England Lawn Tennis Club there are two distinct secondary markets in tickets. Identify these markets and then explain how ticket prices in these markets are determined.
4. What alternative pricing possibilities for tickets at Wimbledon can you suggest?

CASE STUDY

Down and Up in Copper

Last Christmas the price of copper peaked and then began to fall sharply. Many pundits reckoned the metal was about to repeat its dramatic slump of the mid-1970s and early 1980s, when it more than halved in price. The World Bank, for one, based its economic forecasts for 1988 on an average copper price of 70 cents a pound. But for the first ten months of this year the price averaged $1.10 a pound. It recently reached an all-time high of $1.54. Supply and demand in the market for copper is now so tightly matched that a relatively small shift in either could send copper prices even higher, or back into the depths.

The 1980 collapse forced mines everywhere to retrench. American mines took the most drastic action. In 1981 the annual rate of copper production in America fell by 500 000 tonnes in two weeks (to a little over 1m tonnes) following a series of mine closures. The non-communist world's production reached its bottom at 6.2m tonnes in 1982. With the price stuck at 60–70 cents a pound in the following years, copper miners concentrated on cutting costs.

Last year many mining houses (and some speculators) realized that world economic growth – and hence demand for copper – had been faster than expected. Although copper use in the mature industrialized countries remained stable, it had soared in the newly industrialized countries, whose copper consumption rose by 72% between 1979 and 1987.

Most of this increased demand was met by running down stocks rather than increasing production. Between 1984 and 1987 world stocks fell by 1.4m tonnes, according to Mr Stephen Briggs of Shearson Lehman Hutton's Metals Research Unit, while consumption in the non-communist world rose from 7.7m tonnes to 8m tonnes. The market normally feels comfortable when copper stocks are sufficient to cover eight weeks' consumption. They have not been at that level since 1985. Today stocks are so low that any threat to the supply of copper is enough to send traders into another speculative frenzy.

Supply disruptions are one thing the market has not been short of this year. Copper is unusual among base metals because a large chunk of it is mined in developing countries. Last year Peru, Zaire, and Zambia accounted for 21% of the non-communist world's copper production. All three will produce less copper this year than last. In Peru strikes have moved from being merely endemic to being continuous. Combining that with guerrilla action, natural disasters, high inflation and an actute shortage of foreign exchange, Peru's copper production is expected to fall by over 20% this year, from 392 000 tonnes last year.

Figure 6.4 World Copper Prices and Stocks

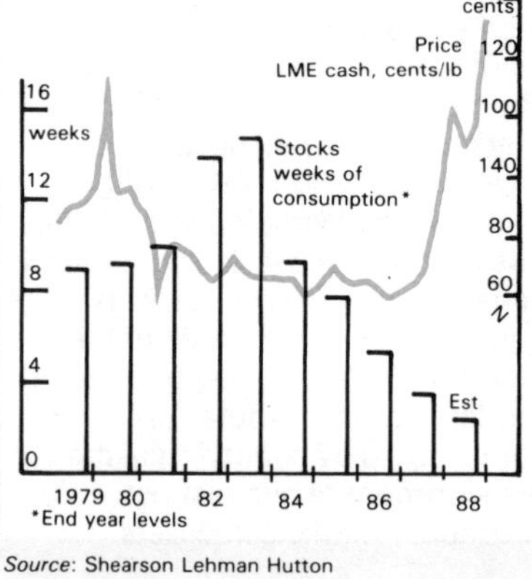

Source: Shearson Lehman Hutton

Problems afflicting Zaire and Zambia are less severe in the short term, but more fundamental. As in Peru, their copper mines are starved of the foreign exchange needed to buy spares and fuel, and the cash to pay skilled labour. There has been even less capital available to maintain the mines' infrastructure. A project begun in 1984, with the backing of the EEC, the African Development Bank, and the World Bank, attempted to rehabilitate Zambia's copper mines. It made little progress. Last year Zambia stopped paying interest to the World Bank. Mr Briggs expects Zaire and Zambia's copper outputs to fall 8% and 12% respectively this year.

The main beneficiaries of Peruvian and African difficulties have been mines in America and Chile. Next year America looks set to overtake Chile as the world's biggest copper producer as a string of new mines (and some old ones) are brought into production. Chile will probably take back the lead by the mid-1990s, when its giant Escondida mine should reach full capacity of 300 000 tonnes a year.

The one thing Chilean and American mines have in common

is that they have been planned under the most pessimistic assumptions about the copper price. The average cost of getting copper out of Escondida will be 35 cents a pound; the average cost for Phelps Dodge, America's biggest producer, is 55 cents a pound. At today's prices, these producers stand to make an operating profit of around 200%. That should leave oil companies wondering why they rushed to sell off their base-metal subsidiaries in those dark days of the early 1980s.

Source: 'Copper: Back with a Shine', *The Economist*, 12 Nov. 1988.

Questions

1. Were the factors affecting the demand for copper a greater or lesser influence on the price of copper in 1988 than factors affecting the supply side?
2. Why is the level of stocks of significance in the pricing of copper?
3. How does the case study illustrate the role of expectations in determining copper prices?
4. How does the case study illustrate the role of relative prices?

Exam Preparation

PRACTICAL EXERCISES

1. Assume that in 1980 a pint of beer cost 50p while a pint of whisky cost £5. By 1990, the respective absolute prices had risen to £1.20 and £10.80. What happened to the relative price of whisky in relation to beer? Suppose that the average of all other prices rose by 150 per cent over the same period. That is to say, in 1990 it cost £250 to buy the same goods and services that would have cost £100 in 1980. What has happened to the relative prices of beer and whisky in comparison to all other consumer goods and services?

2. List the types of transaction costs that are involved in locating and buying a home. After you have listed them, can you think of ways to economize on such transaction costs?

3. Assume that a business has found that its most profitable output occurs when it produces £172 worth of output of a particular product. It can choose from three possible techniques, A, B, and C, that will produce the desired level of output. We see the amount of inputs these techniques use along with each input price in the following table.

Price of input (per unit)	*Production techniques*		
	A *(units)*	B *(units)*	C *(units)*
£10 Land	7	4	1
£ 2 Labour	6	7	18
£15 Capital	2	6	3
£ 8 Entrepreneurship	1	3	2

(a) Which technique will the firm choose and why?
(b) What would the firm's maximum profit be?
(c) If the price of labour increase to £4 per unit, which technique will be chosen and why? What will happen to profits?

4.

Daily work effort	*Mrs Jones*
4 hours	8 jackets
4 hours	12 ties
	Mr Jones
4 hours	8 jackets
4 hours	12 ties

Total daily output = 16 jackets, 24 ties.

Given the above information, answer the following questions.
(a) Who has an absolute advantage in jacket production?
(b) Who has a comparative advantage in tie production?
(c) Will Mrs and Mr Jones specialize?
(d) If they specialize, what will total output equal?

5.

Daily work effort	*Mrs Jones*
4 hours	8 jackets
4 hours	12 ties
	Mr Jones
4 hours	4 jackets
4 hours	12 ties

Total daily output = 12 jackets, 24 ties.

Given the above information, answer the following questions.
(a) In what does Mrs Jones have an absolute advantage?
(b) In what does Mr Jones have an absolute advantage?

(c) In what does Mrs Jones have a comparative advantage?
(d) In what does Mr Jones have a comparative advantage?
(e) If they specialize according to their comparative advantages, what will total output equal?

MULTIPLE CHOICE QUESTIONS

1. Markets are important to economic exchanges because they reduce transactions costs. Transactions costs are defined as:
A the price of the product
B all the costs enabling exchanges to take place
C a market mechanism to disseminate price information
D those costs suppliers consider when determining the quantities they will put on the market.

2. The term 'relative price' refers to a price relative to:
A people's income
B people's wealth
C other prices
D what the price was in the past.

3. Use of the least-cost production technique for a given output is characteristic of:
A economic efficiency
B technical efficiency
C production possibilities
D the transformation curve.

4. Economic efficiency means that:
A least-cost methods of production are used
B resources move to their highest-valued uses via the price system
C consumer sovereignty is irrelevant in determining the outcomes of markets
D individuals and business people cannot rely on their own self-interests but must rely on the government's determination of economic decisions.

5. Opponents of the price system criticize the system for all but one of the following reasons:
A the market does not register all of the costs and benefits associated with production or consumption
B the price system is incapable of providing social goods in adequate quantities
C competition is promoted among firms which forces them to choose the least-cost production techniques
D all of the above.

RELATED ESSAY QUESTIONS

1. What are the economic strengths and weaknesses of a free market economy?

2. (a) What do you understand by the term 'economic efficiency'?
(b) Does the price mechanism allocate scarce resources efficiently? Explain your conclusions.

7 Demand and Supply Elasticity

Key Points to Review

- **Demand (5.1, 5.2)**
- **Shifts versus movements along demand curves (5.3, 5.6)**
- **Supply (5.4, 5.5)**

Questions for Preview

1. **What is price elasticity of demand?**
2. **How is total revenue related to price elasticity of demand?**
3. **What are the determinants of price elasticity of demand?**
4. **What is cross-price elasticity of demand?**
5. **What is income elasticity of demand?**
6. **What is price elasticity of supply?**

The corner-stone of microeconomic analysis is supply and demand, concepts already discussed in Chapter 5. Microeconomic analysis concerns itself with decision-making by individuals in their capacity as consumers, workers, and business persons. Our analysis of micro-economic decision-making involves an examination of how the various decisions made by individuals ultimately determine prices and quantities in the real world.

Remember from Chapter 5 that the fundamental theory of demand is that there is an inverse relationship between prices and quantity demanded, holding other things constant. If price goes up, less will be consumed or used than before. If price goes down, more will be consumed or used than before. If you are a decision-maker in a top-management position at, say, Sinclair Research, will knowing the theory of demand help you in any way to decide whether you should change the price of one of your products? The answer is obviously 'no'. You can predict the *direction* of change in quantity demanded if you raise price or lower price, but you will not be able to tell *by how much* quantity demanded will change. In August 1985 Sinclair announced a 50 per cent reduction in the price of its QL computer called Spectrum. Since its introduction Spectrum had not sold as well as anticipated. Management at Sinclair decided that it was necessary to reduce the price to induce more people to purchase it and meet competition from the new Amstrad system priced at £199. Clearly, management had to have some idea of the increase in the quantities of the QL model sold per year that would result from the 50 per cent drop in price. If potential consumers were not going to respond much to the lower price – if quantity demanded was going to remain about the same – then management at Sinclair would have made a critical business error, for the drop in price of the QL would not have been matched by much increase in quantity demanded, and the total revenues from the sale of QL would fall.

In other words, some measure of the *responsiveness* of consumers to changes in price is necessary in order to estimate the effects of changes in price. Not only management in private firms, but decision-makers within government have to have an idea of how responsive people in the real world will be to changes in price. Economists have given a special name to price-responsiveness – *price elasticity*. Elasticity is the subject of this chapter.

Price Elasticity

To begin to understand what 'elasticity' is all about, just keep in mind that it means 'responsiveness'. Here we are concerned with the price elasticity of demand and the price elasticity of supply. We wish to know the extent to which a change in the price of, say, petroleum products will cause the quantity demanded and the quantity supplied to change, other things held constant. Let us restrict our discussion at first to the demand side.

Price Elasticity of Demand

We will formally define the **price elasticity of demand,** which we will label e_d, as follows:

$$e_d = \frac{\text{percentage change in quantity demanded}}{\text{percentage change in price}}$$

What will price elasticity of demand tell us? It will tell us the relative amount by which the quantity demanded will change in response to a change in the price of a particular good.

Consider an example where a 10 per cent rise in the price of petrol leads to a reduction in quantity demanded of only 1 per cent. Putting these numbers into the formula, we find that the price elasticity of demand of oil equals the percentage change in quantity demanded divided by the percentage change in price, or,

$$e_d = \frac{-1 \text{ per cent}}{+10 \text{ per cent}} = -0.1$$

Notice that this number is pure – that is, dimensionless, a percentage divided by a percentage.*

An elasticity of -0.1 means that a 1 per cent *decrease* in the price would lead to a mere one-tenth of 1 per cent *increase* in the quantity demanded. If you were now told that the price elasticity of demand for oil was, say, -1, then you would know that a 1 per cent increase in the price of petrol would lead to a 1 per cent decrease in the quantity demanded.

Basically, the greater the numerical price elasticity of demand, the greater the demand responsiveness to relative price changes – small change in price has a great impact on quantity demanded. The smaller the numerical price elasticity of demand, the smaller the demand responsiveness to relative price changes – a large change in price has little effect on quantity demanded.

PRICE ELASTICITY OF DEMAND IS ALWAYS NEGATIVE

Remember that the theory of demand states that quantity demanded is *inversely* related to the relative price. Thus, in the preceding example, an increase in the price of oil led to a decrease in the quantity demanded. Alternatively, we could have used an example of a decrease in the relative price of oil, in which case the quantity demanded would increase a certain percentage. The point is that price elasticity of demand will always be negative. By convention, *we will ignore the negative sign in our discussion from this point on.*

RELATIVE QUANTITIES ONLY

Notice that in our elasticity formula, we talk about *percentage* changes in quantity demanded divided by percentage changes in price. We are not, therefore, interested in the absolute changes, but only in relative amounts. This means that it does not matter if we measure price changes in terms of pence, pounds, or hundreds of pounds. It also does not matter whether we measure quantity changes in, for example, ounces, grams, or pounds. The percentage change will be the same. However, if the concept of price elasticity is really quite a simple one we find that in practice the arithmetical calculation is not quite so straightforward. We now explain what the

*Miles divided by gallons gives the ratio 'miles per gallon'. But when you see a ratio without such a dimension, that means that the ratio is comparing two identical dimensions.

Key Points 7.1

- **Price elasticity is a measure of the responsiveness of the quantity demanded and supplied to a change in price.**
- **The price elasticity of demand is equal to the percentage change in quantity demanded divided by the percentage change in price.**
- **The theory of demand states that quantity demanded and price are inversely related. Therefore, the price elasticity of demand is always negative, since an increase in price will lead to a decrease in quantity demanded and a decrease in price will lead to an increase in quantity demanded.**
- **Price elasticity of demand is calculated in terms of relative percentage changes in quantity demanded and in price. Thus, we end up with a unitless, scaleless number.**

problem is confronting us and how it can be resolved. (But first read Key Points 7.1.)

Calculation of Elasticity

In order to calculate the price elasticity of demand, we have to compute percentage changes in quantity demanded and in relative price. To obtain the percentage change in quantity demanded, we can look at

$$\frac{\text{change in quantity demanded}}{\text{original quantity demanded}} \times 100 \text{ per cent}$$

To find the percentage change in price, we can look at

$$\frac{\text{change in price demanded}}{\text{original price demanded}} \times 100 \text{ per cent}$$

There is a slight problem with computation of percentage changes in this manner. We get a different answer depending on whether we move up the demand curve or down the demand curve.

Consider the hypothetical data presented in Figure 7.1 for the quantities of petrol demanded by UK consumers at various prices. For the moment we are just looking at these first four columns.

Columns 1 and 3 of Figure 7.1(a) are simply the quantity demanded and price data for the demand curve represented graphically as Figures 7.l(b) and (c). Columns 2 and 4 show changes in quantity demanded corresponding to changes in price.

Let us start with a quantity of one unit demanded at the price of £10 per unit and *move down the demand curve*. If we start at a price of £10 with 1 unit demanded, price then falls to £9. Quantity demanded increases to 2. The percentage change in price is:

[(£10 − £9)/£10] × 100 per cent, or:
(£1 ÷ £10) × 100 per cent = 10 per cent

The percentage change in quantity demanded is:

[(2 − 1)/1] × 100 per cent, or:
(1 ÷ 1) × 100 per cent = 100 per cent

Thus, price elasticity of demand is equal to:

100 per cent ÷ 10 per cent = 10

Now let us calculate the price elasticity of demand when *we move up the demand curve*. We start at a price of £9 with 2 units demanded. The price goes up to £10 and 1 unit is demanded. The percentage change in price is now equal to:

[(£10 − £9)/£9] × 100 per cent =
(£1 ÷ £9) × 100 per cent = 11.11 per cent

The percentage change in quantity demanded is:

[(2 − 1)/2] × 100 per cent, or:
(1 ÷ 2) × 100 per cent = 50 per cent

Thus, the price elasticity of demand is now equal to:

50 per cent ÷ 11.11 per cent = 4.5

Quite a difference! We show this in Figure 7.l(b).

USING AVERAGE VALUES

For the same segment of the demand curve, we get different values of price elasticity of demand because the original prices and quantities depend on whether we move up or down the demand curve. The *absolute* changes in price and quantity are the same size regardless of direction. But when moving down the demand curve, the *original* price is higher than when moving up the demand curve. When moving up the demand curve, the original quantity demanded is greater. Since a percentage change depends on the size of the original value, the percentages we calculate for price elasticity of demand will be affected by choosing a higher price and smaller quantity, or a lower price and greater quantity. One way out of this difficulty is to *take the average of the two prices and the two quantities* over the range we are considering and compare the change to the average, instead of comparing it to the price or quantity at the start of the change.

The formula for computing price elasticity of demand then becomes:

$$e_d = \frac{\text{change in quantity}}{\text{sum of quantities/2}} \times 100 \text{ per cent}$$

$$\div \frac{\text{change in price}}{\text{sum of prices/2}} \times 100 \text{ per cent}$$

We can rewrite this more simply if we do two things: (1) We can let Q_1 and Q_2 equal the two different quantities demanded before and after the price change, and P_1 and P_2 equal the two different prices; and (2) because we will be dividing a per cent by a per cent, we simply use the ratio, or the decimal form, of the per cent. Therefore,

$$e_d = \frac{\text{change in } Q}{(Q + Q_2)/2} \div \frac{\text{change in } P}{(P_1 + P_2)/2}$$

Look again at the example that showed a price elasticity of demand equal to 10 when moving from a £10 price to a £9 price, but gave an elasticity of 4.5 when moving from £9 to £10. We insert our numbers in the average formula just given, so that price elasticity of demand becomes in either case:

Figure 7.1 (a)

Numerical Calculation of Price Elasticity of Demand for Petrol Column 1 is the quantity demanded at different prices. Column 2 is the change in the quantity demanded. In other words, we merely subtract the smaller from the larger quantity. In each case, the change is 1 million gallons per day. Column 3 is the price per gallon, and column 4 is the change in the price, which happens to be £1 in each case. Columns 5 and 6 are the average quantities and prices, e.g. $(Q_1 + Q_2)/2 = (0 + 1)/2 = 0.5$ and $(P_1 + P_2)/2 = (£11 + £10)/2 = £10.5$ for the first row. Column 7 presents an approximation of the price elasticity of demand, e_d.

(1) Quantity demanded Q (millions of gallons per day)	*(2) Change in Q (millions of gallons per day)*	*(3) Price (P) (£)*	*(4) Change in P (£)*	*(5)* $\frac{Q_1 + Q_2}{2}$	*(6)* $\frac{P_1 + P_2}{2}$	*(7)* $\frac{\text{Change in } Q}{(Q_1 + Q_2)/2} \Big/ \frac{\text{Change in } P}{(P_1 + P_2)/2}$
0		11				
	1		1	0.5	10.5	1/0.5 ÷ 1/10.5 = 21
1		10				
	1		1	1.5	9.5	1/1.5 ÷ 1/9.5 = 6.333
2		9				
	1		1	2.5	8.5	1/2.5 ÷ 1/8.5 = 3.4
3		8				
	1		1	3.5	7.5	1/3.5 ÷ 1/7.5 = 2.143
4		7				
	1		1	4.5	6.5	1/4.5 ÷ 1/6.5 = 1.444
5		6				
	1		1	5.5	5.5	1/5.5 ÷ 1/5.5 = 1
6		5				
	1		1	6.5	4.5	1/6.5 ÷ 1/4.5 = 0.692
7		4				
	1		1	7.5	3.5	1/7.5 ÷ 1/3.5 = 0.467
8		3				
	1		1	8.5	2.5	1/8.5 ÷ 1/2.5 = 0.294
9		2				
	1		1	9.5	1.5	1/9.5 ÷ 1/1.5 = 0.158

Figure 7.1 (b)

Two Different Elasticities

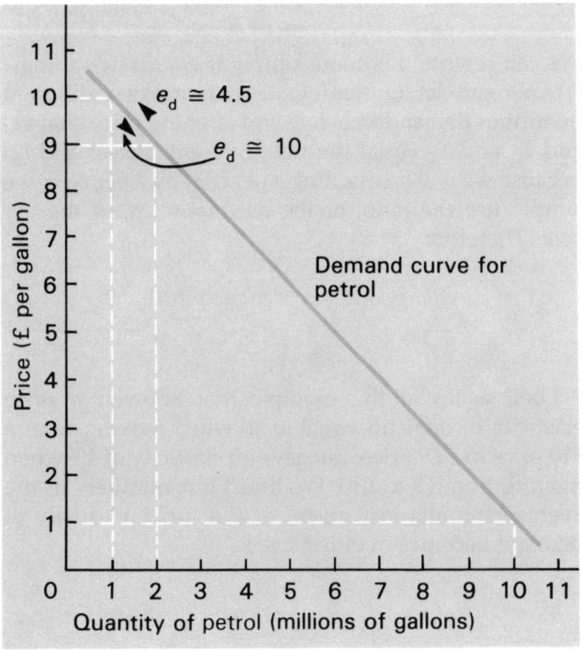

Figure 7.1 (c)

Using Average Values

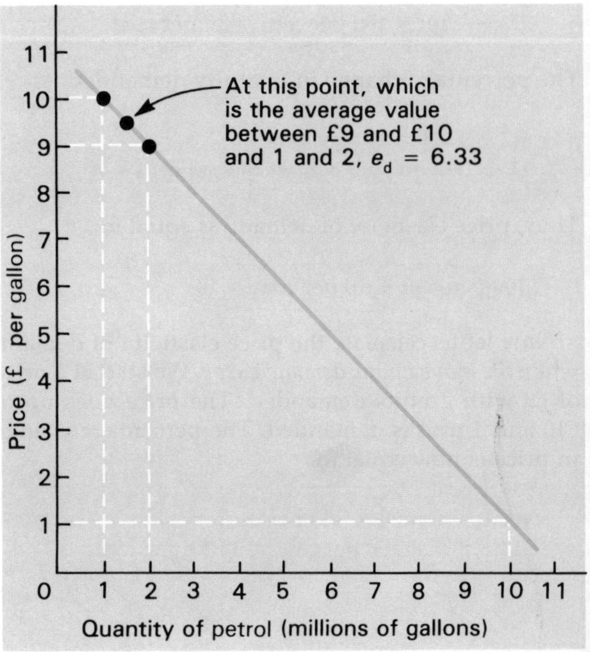

$$e_d = \left(\frac{1}{\left(\frac{1+2}{2}\right)}\right) \Bigg/ \left(\frac{1}{\left(\frac{9+10}{2}\right)}\right) = \left(\frac{1}{\left(\frac{3}{2}\right)}\right) \Bigg/ \left(\frac{1}{\left(\frac{19}{2}\right)}\right)$$

$$= \frac{2}{3} \Bigg/ \frac{2}{19} = \frac{38}{6} = 6.33$$

We show this in Figure 7.1(c).

Thus, calculating the price elasticity of demand, using the mid-point (or average) formula, yields, $e_d = 6.33$. This calculation is not affected by the direction of movement along the demand curve; that is, $e_d = 6.33$ whether we move up or down the demand curve over the range we have been considering.

If we now look again at Figure 7.1 we note that columns 5 and 6 give us the average quantities and the average prices. And finally, in the last column, a numerical example of price elasticity of demand is given.

We see that the computation of elasticity ranges from 21 down to 0.158. What does that mean? Simply that at very high prices for petrol, such as between £10 and £9 a gallon, the response to a 1 per cent decrease in price will be a 21 per cent increase in the quantity demanded. At the other extreme, at relatively low prices for petrol – say, between £2 and £1 per gallon – the elasticity of 0.158 means that a 1 per cent reduction in price will be followed by only 0.158 of a 1 per cent increase in the quantity demanded. Thus, in our example, elasticity falls as price falls.

Different Kinds of Price Elasticities

We have definitions for the varying ranges of price elasticities, depending on whether a 1 per cent change in price elicits more or less than a 1 per cent change in the quantity demanded:

1. **Price-elastic demand.** We say that a good has a price-elastic demand whenever the price elasticity of demand is greater than 1. A 1 per cent change in price causes a response greater than 1 per cent change in quantity demanded. Candidates for elastic-demand sections of our demand schedule in Figure 7.1 are obviously an e_d of 1.444 and above.
2. **Unitary price elasticity of demand.** In this situation, a 1 per cent change in price causes a response of exactly 1 per cent change in the quantity demand.
3. **Price-inelastic demand.** Here, a 1 per cent change in price causes a response of less than 1 per cent change in quantity demanded. An elasticity of 0.692 and below in the last four rows of Figure 7.1(a), represents a situation of inelastic demand. In brief, a 1 per cent change in price causes a less than 1 per cent change in quantity demanded.

Elasticity and Total Revenues

If you were in charge of the pricing decision for oil for say the Organization of Oil Exporting Countries (OPEC), how would you know when it was best to raise prices or to not raise prices? The answer depends on the effects of your pricing decision on total revenues, or total receipts, for the oil-producing countries. It is commonly thought that the way to increase total receipts is to increase price per unit. But is this always the case? Is it possible that a rise in price per unit could lead to a decrease in total revenues? The answers to these questions depend on the price elasticity of demand.

Let us look at Figure 7.2, which is a reproduction in altered form of part of Figure 7.1. In column 1, we again show the price of petrol in pounds. Column 2 lists the quantities demanded (we ignore that each value shown is actually in millions, for simplicity's sake). In column 3, we multiply column 1 by column 2 to derive total revenues; and in column 4, we copy the values of elasticity from Figure 7.1. Notice what happens to total revenues throughout the schedule. They rise steadily as the price rises from £1 to £5 per unit; then, when the price rises further to £6 per unit, total revenues remain constant at £30. At prices per unit higher than £6, total revenues actually fall as price is increased. So it is not safe to assume that a price increase is always the way to greater revenues. Indeed, if prices are above £6 per unit in this example, total revenues can only be increased by cutting prices – not by raising them.

Labelling Elasticity

The relationship between price and quantity on the demand schedule is given in columns 1 and 2 of panel (a) in Figure 7.2. In panel (c), the demand curve, *DD*, representing that schedule, is drawn. In panel (b), the total revenue curve representing the data in column 3 is drawn. Notice first the level of these curves at small quantities. The demand curve is at a maximum height, but total revenue is zero, which makes sense according to this demand schedule – at maximum price, no units will be purchased and therefore total revenue will be zero. As price is lowered, we travel down the demand curve, total revenues increase up to a price of £6 per unit, remain constant from £6 to £5 per unit, and then fall for lower unit prices. Corresponding to those three sections, demand is price-elastic, unit-elastic, and price-inelastic. Hence, we have three relationships among the three types of price elasticity and total revenues.

1. *Price-elastic demand.* A negative relationship between small changes in price and changes in total revenues. That is to say, if it lowers price, total revenues will rise when the firm faces demand that is price-elastic. And if it raises price, total revenues will fall. Consider an example: if the price of Coca-Cola were raised by 25 per cent, and the price of all other soft drinks remained constant, the

Figure 7.2

The Relationship between Price Elasticity of Demand and Total Revenues. Here we reproduce in different form, parts of Figure 7.1. In panel (a), we show the elastic, unit elastic, and inelastic sections of the demand schedule according to whether a reduction in price increases total revenues, causes them to remain constant, or causes them to decrease, respectively. In panel (b), we show graphically what happens to total revenues, and we have labelled the sections elastic, unit elastic, and inelastic, which we have also done in the accompanying demand curve shown in panel (c).

Panel (a)

(1) Price of petrol (£ per unit)	(2) Units demanded (per time period)	(3) Total revenue $TR = P \times Q$ [(1) × (2)]	(4) Elasticity $e_d = \dfrac{\text{change in } Q / [(Q_1 + Q_2)/2]}{\text{change in } P / [(P_1 + P_2)/2]}$	
11	0	0		
			21	elastic
10	1	£10		
			6.333	elastic
9	2	18		
			3.4	elastic
8	3	24		
			2.143	elastic
7	4	28		
			1.444	elastic
6	5	30		
			1	unit-elastic
5	6	30		
			0.692	inelastic
4	7	28		
			0.467	inelastic
3	8	24		
			0.294	inelastic
2	9	18		
			0.158	inelastic
1	10	10		

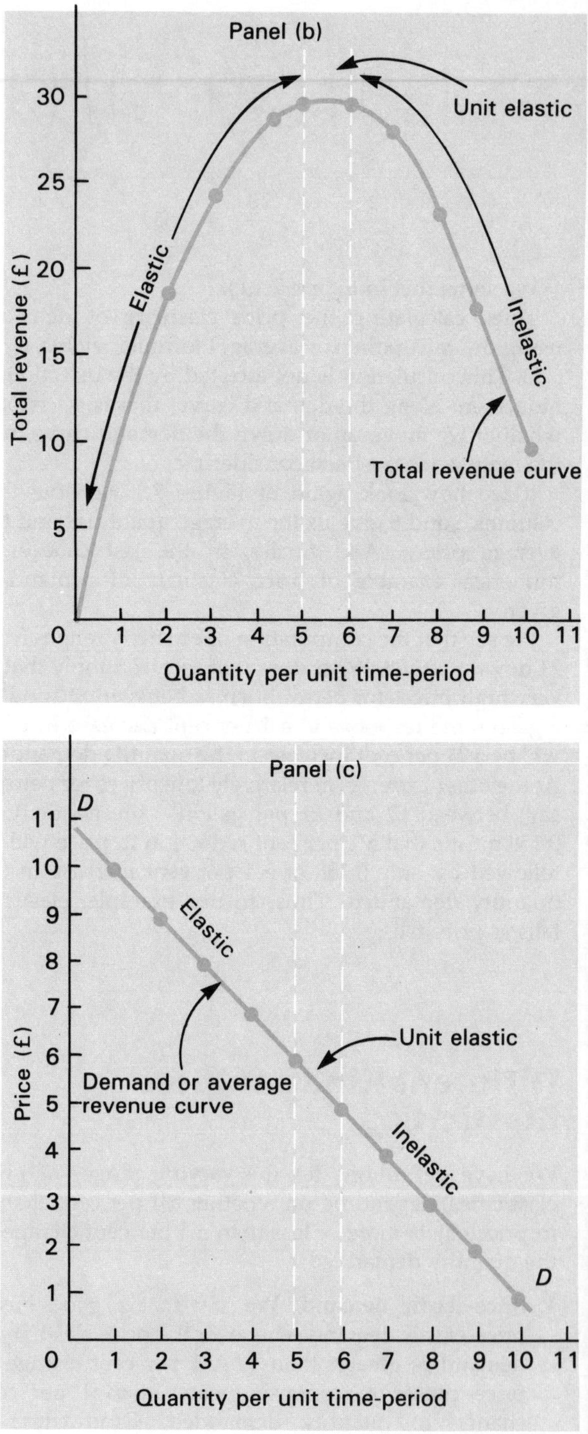

quantity demanded of Coca-Cola would probably fall dramatically. That is to say, the decrease in quantity demanded due to the increase in the price of Coca-Cola would be more than in proportion. Hence, such an increase in the price of Coca-Cola would lead, in this example, to a reduction in the total revenues of the firms that bottle Coca-Cola.

2. *Unit price-elastic demand.* Small changes in price do not change total revenues. In other words, when the firm is facing demand that is unitary price-elastic, if it increases price, total revenues will not change; if it decreases price, total revenues will not change either.
3. *Price-inelastic demand.* A positive relationship between small changes in price and total revenue. In other words, when the firm is facing demand that is price-inelastic, if it raises price, total revenues will go up; if it lowers price, total revenues will fall.

Consider an example: imagine that you are managing director of a company which has just invented a cure for the common cold that has been approved by the health authorities for sale to the public. Your company is not sure what price you should charge. It decides on a price of £1 per pill. The firm sells 20 million pills at that price over a year. You feel the price could be raised without too much effect on sales. So next year, you decide to raise the price by

25 per cent. Suppose that the number of pills sold dropped to 18 million per year. The price increase of about 25 per cent has led to approximately a 10 per cent decrease in quantity demanded. However your total revenues will have risen because of the price increase.

We can see in Figure 7.2 the areas in the demand curve that are elastic, unit elastic, and inelastic. For prices from £11 per unit to £5 per unit, as price decreases, total revenues rise from zero to £30. Clearly, demand is price-elastic. When prices change from £6 to £5, however, total revenues remain constant at £30; demand is unit elastic. Finally, when price falls from £5 to £1, total revenue decreases from £30 to £10; demand is price-inelastic. In panels (b) and (c) of Figure 7.2, we have labelled the sections of the demand curve accordingly, and we have also shown how total revenues first rise, remain constant, and then fall.

The relationship between the price elasticity of demand and total revenue brings together some important microeconomic concepts. Total revenue, as we have noted, is the product of price per unit times quantity of units sold. The theory of demand states that, along a given demand curve, price and quantity changes will move in opposite directions: one increases as the other decreases. Consequently, what happens to the product of price times quantity depends on which of the opposing changes exerts a greater force on total revenue. But this is just what price elasticity of demand is designed to measure – responsiveness of quantity to a change in price.

The relationship between price elasticity of demand and total revenue, *TR*, is summarized in Figure 7.3.

Now read Key Points 7.2.

Figure 7.3
The Relationship between Elasticity and Total Revenues

	Price Elastic Demand	Unitary Elastic Demand	Price Inelastic Demand
Price Increase	↑ × ↓ → ↓ P × Q = TR	↑ × ↓ → No Change P × Q = TR	↑ × ↓ → ↑ P × Q = TR
Price Decrease	↓ × ↑ → ↑ P × Q = TR	↓ × ↑ → No Change P × Q = TR	↓ × ↑ → ↓ P × Q = TR

Changing Price Elasticity

We have seen in the example of the demand for petrol that the price elasticity changes as we move along the demand curve. That is to say, price elasticity is high when price is high and low when price is low. (Look again at columns 3 and 7 in Figure 7.1(a).) As a general rule, along any demand curve that is a straight line, price elasticity declines as we move down that demand curve. Consider the reason why. In our example in Figure 7.1(a), the change in price was always £1 and the change in the absolute quantity demanded was always 1 million gallons per day. Remember that here we are thinking about absolute changes only. What about percentage changes? At the upper end of the demand curve, a £1 price change is in percentage terms relatively small (£1/[(£9 + £10)/2] = 10.5%) whereas the 1 million change in quantity demanded is a large percentage change of the small quantity demanded (1/[(1 + 2)/2] = 66.7%).

Thus, at the top of the demand curve, the elasticity formula will have a large numerator and a small denominator; therefore, price elasticity is relatively elastic (66.7%/10.5% = 6.33). At the lower end of the curve, the price elasticity formula will have a small numerator and a large denominator; thus, the demand curve is relatively inelastic (10.5%/66.7% = 0.158).

We can indicate the relationship between price and elasticity very concisely if we use some basic arithmetic

Key Points 7.2

- **Price elasticity of demand is related to total revenues (and total consumer expenditures).**
- **When demand is elastic, the change in price elicits a change in total revenues (and total consumer expenditures) in the opposite direction to the price change.**
- **When demand is inelastic, a change in price elicits a change in total revenues (and in consumer expenditures) in the same direction as the price change.**
- **When demand is unit elastic, a change in price elicits no change in total revenues (or in total consumer expenditures).**

manipulations. Recall that the elasticity of demand, e_d is defined as:

$$e_d = \frac{\text{percentage change in quantity demanded}}{\text{percentage change in price}}$$

$$= \frac{\dfrac{\text{change in quantity demanded}}{\text{original quantity demanded}}}{\dfrac{\text{change in price}}{\text{original price}}}$$

therefore

$$e_d = \frac{\text{change in quantity demanded}}{\text{original quantity demanded}} \times \frac{\text{original price}}{\text{change in price}}$$

$$e_d = \frac{\text{change in quantity demanded}}{\text{change in price}} \times \frac{\text{original price}}{\text{original quantity demanded}}$$

But the slope of demand curve is given as

$$\text{slope} = \frac{\text{change in price}}{\text{change in quantity demanded}}$$

so

$$e_d = \frac{1}{\text{slope}} \times \frac{\text{original price}}{\text{original quantity demanded}}$$

Note that because we assumed a linear (straight-line) demand curve, slope (and therefore 1/slope) is a constant. However, as price falls, quantity demanded rises; therefore the *ratio* of price to quantity demanded must fall. As price falls we calculate e_d by multiplying a constant (1/slope) by a decreasing ratio (price/quantity demanded); as price falls e_d falls.

Elasticity and Slope

Students often confuse elasticity and slope. As the preceding analysis clearly indicates, however, they are *not* the same. We demonstrated that along a linear demand curve (that is, a straight line that has a *constant* slope, by definition) elasticity continuously falls with price. As a matter of fact, the calculated elasticity along a downward-sloping *straight-line* demand curve goes numerically from infinity to zero as we move down the curve. We therefore must always specify the price *range* when discussing price elasticity of demand, since most goods have ranges of both elasticity and inelasticity. The only time we can be sure of the elasticity of a straight-line demand curve by looking at it is if it is either perfectly horizontal or perfectly vertical. The horizontal straight-line demand curve has infinite elasticity at every quantity (it has only one price for every quantity). The vertical demand curve has zero elasticity at every price (it has only one quantity demanded at every price). Then we know that it has infinite elasticity or zero elasticity, respectively.

Extreme Elasticities

There are two extremes in price elasticities of demand: one is total unresponsiveness, which is called a **perfectly inelastic demand** situation or zero elasticity, and the other is complete responsiveness, which is called an unlimited, infinite, or **perfectly elastic demand** situation.

We show perfect inelasticity in panel (a) of Figure 7.4. Notice that the quantity demanded per year is 8 million units, no matter what the price. Hence, for any

Figure 7.4

Two Extreme Price Elasticities. In panel (a) we show complete price unresponsiveness. The demand curve is vertical at the quantity of 8 million units per year. That means that price elasticity of demand is zero. Consumers demand 8 million units of this particular commodity no matter what the price. In panel (b) we show complete responsiveness. At a price of 30p in this example consumers will demand an unlimited quantity of the particular good in question. This is a case of infinite price elasticity of demand.

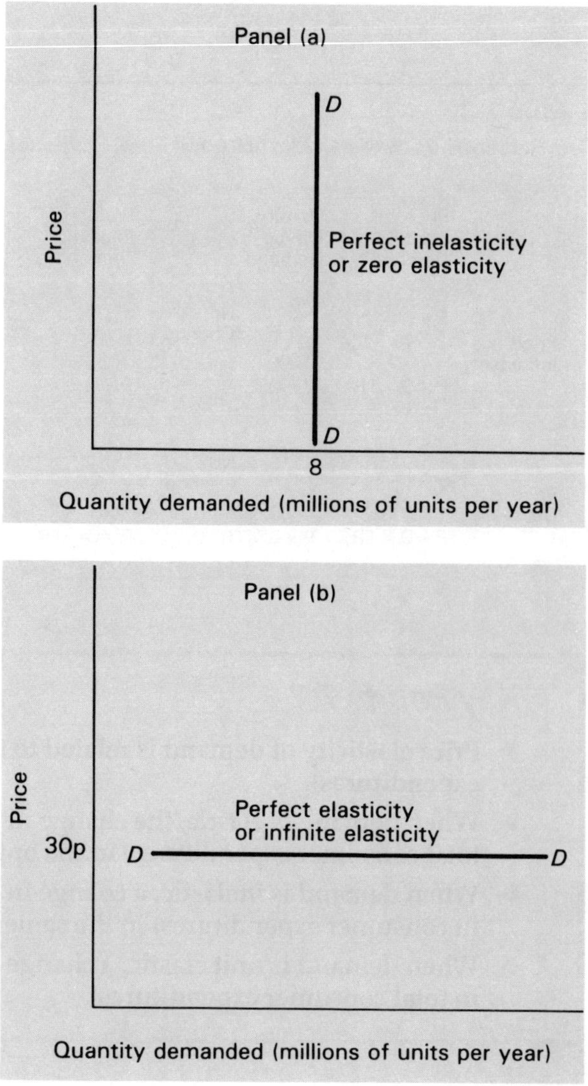

percentage price change, the quantity demanded will remain the same, and thus the change in the quantity demanded will be zero. Look at our formula for computing elasticity. If the change in the quantity demanded is zero, then the numerator is also zero, and anything divided into zero results in an answer of zero, too. Hence, perfect inelasticity.

At the opposite extreme is the situation depicted in panel (b) of Figure 7.4. Here we show that at the price of 30p, an unlimited quantity will be demanded. At a price that is only slightly above 30p, none will be demanded. In other words, there is complete, or infinite, responsiveness here, and hence we call the demand schedule in panel (b) of Figure 7.4 infinitely elastic.

Most estimated demand-schedule elasticities lie between the two extremes. For example, in Figure 7.5 we present demand elasticities for selected goods. None of them is zero, and the largest one is 3.4 – a far cry from infinity. Remember, again, that though we are leaving off the negative sign, there is an inverse relationship between price and quantity demanded and that the minus sign is implicit. Also, remember that these elasticities represent average elasticities over *given* price ranges. Different price ranges would yield different elasticity estimates for these goods.

Figure 7.5

Demand Elasticity tor Selected Items. Here we show the estimated demand elasticities for selected items. All of them are negative, although we have not shown a minus sign. For example, the price elasticity of demand for dairy produce is 0.05. That means that a 1 per cent increase in the price of dairy produce will bring about a 0.05 per cent decrease in the quantity of dairy produce demanded.

Great Britain Commodity or service	*Estimated elasticity in 1970*
Catering	2.61
Entertainment	1.40
Bread and cereals	0.22
Dairy produce	0.05

Source: A. Deaton, 'The Measurement of Income and Price Elasticities', *European Economic Review*, Vol. 6, 1975.

United States	*Long-run elasticity estimate*
Electricity	2.2
Natural gas	3.4

Source: J. Beierlein, J. Dunn, and J. McConnan Jr., 'The Demand for Electricity and Natural Gas in the Northeastern United States', *Review of Economics and Statistics*, Aug. 1981.

Constant Price Elasticity of Demand

It is possible to have a demand curve that actually curves such that price elasticity of demand is constant. We give one example in Figure 7.6.

That demand curve, *DD*, exhibits unitary elasticity at any point. We can tell this by using the total revenues approach. At a price of £8 for this product, four will be purchased for total revenues of £32. At a price of £4, the quantity demanded will be eight, for total revenues of £32 again. At £2, sixteen will be bought for total revenues of £32. A reduction in price leads to no change in total revenues; hence, price elasticity of demand is equal to 1. And this is true all along the curve because of its special curved shape. (If we extended *DD* in Figure 7.6 outwards, it would become a very flat line at the extreme ends, but, none the less, the elasticity at the extreme ends would be just the same as anywhere else on the curve.)

The way in which we found out the total revenues is an important tool that you should understand for the rest of this section. Remember the formula for total revenues:

$$\text{total revenues} = \text{price} \times \text{quantity}$$

Thus, in Figure 7.6, we measured total revenues by looking at the *rectangle* formed from the price to the demand curve to the quantity axis. The vertical side of the rectangle was always equal to the price, and the horizontal side of the rectangle was always equal to the quantity. Thus, if asked how to determine total revenue for any price–quantity combination from a demand curve, you simply form the appropriate rectangle. The *area* of that rectangle is equal to total revenues for the particular quantity under consideration. (Now read Key Points 7.3.)

Figure 7.6

Constant Price Elasticity of Demand. If the demand curve is curved in such a way that total revenues (and consumer expenditures) remain constant no matter what the price, then we have a demand curve that is everywhere unit elastic. This is what we show here.

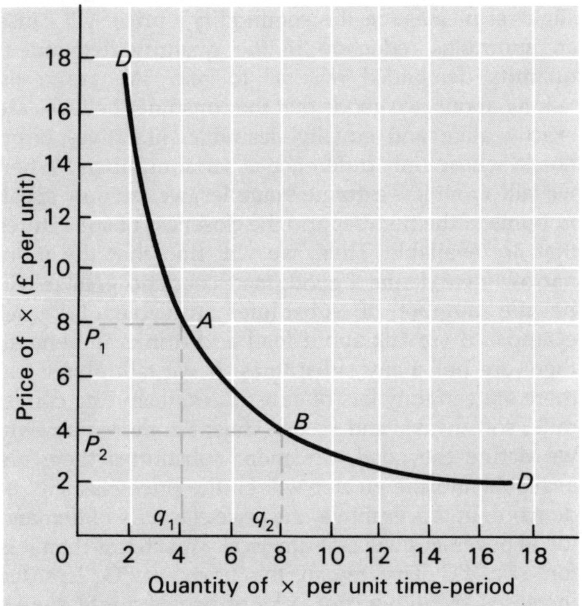

Key Points 7.3

- The price elasticity of demand changes as we move down a straight-line demand curve; it becomes relatively more inelastic.
- Price elasticity of demand cannot be determined by looking at the *slope* of a straight-line demand curve. There are two extreme exceptions:
- When a demand curve is perfectly vertical, it has zero price elasticity of demand; it is completely inelastic.
- When a demand curve is perfectly horizontal, it has completely elastic demand; its price elasticity of demand is infinite.

The Determinants of the Price Elasticity of Demand

We have learned how to calculate the price elasticity of demand. We know that it ranges numerically from zero – completely inelastic – to infinity – completely elastic. What we would like to do now is come up with a list of the *determinants* of the price elasticity of demand. The price elasticity of demand for a particular commodity at any price depends on

1. The existence and closeness of substitutes
2. The length of time allowed for adjustment to changes in the price of the commodity.

Existence of Substitutes

The closer the substitutes for a particular commodity, the greater will be its price elasticity of demand. At the limit, if there is a perfect substitute, the price elasticity of the commodity will be infinity. Thus, even the slightest increase in the commodity's price will cause an enormous reduction in the quantity demanded; quantity demanded will fall to zero. We are really talking about two goods that the consumer believes are exactly alike and equally desirable, like five-pound notes, whose only difference is serial numbers. When we talk about less extreme examples, we can only speak in terms of the number and the closeness of substitutes that are available. Thus, we will find that the more narrowly we define a good, the closer and greater will be the number of substitutes available. Take an example. If we talk about food and drinks in general, there are not many substitutes. If we talk about tea, there are certainly lots of substitutes, including coffee, milk, soft drinks, and so on. Thus, the more narrowly we define the good, the more substitutes there are available and the greater will be the price elasticity of demand. In this example, the price elasticity of demand for all beverages will be numerically much less than it is for, say, PG Tips tea. If the price of PG Tips tea increased by 20 per cent, a lot of people might switch over to another brand of tea such as Typhoo. On the other hand, if the price of all beverages went up on average by 20 per cent, certainly a smaller percentage of beverage consumers would switch over to beverage substitutes, such as food or recreation or whatever else might conceivably be considered a substitute for beverages. The availability of an alternative product for a particular commodity is, however, not the only relevant factor in determining the sensitivity of demand. In the real world consumers do not all react instantaneously to price changes and so we must recognize the importance of time.

The Time for Adjustment in Rate of Purchase

When the price of a commodity changes and that price change persists, more people will learn about it. Further, consumers will be better able to revise their consumption patterns, the longer the time they have to do so. And, in fact, the longer the time they do take, the less costly it will be for them to engage in this revision of consumption patterns. Consider a price decrease. The longer the time that the price decrease persists, the greater will be the number of new *uses* that consumers will 'discover' for the particular commodity, and the greater will be the number of new *users* of that particular commodity.

It is possible to make a very strong statement about the relationship between the price elasticity of demand and the time allowed for adjustment: *The longer any price change persists, the greater the price elasticity of demand.* Otherwise stated, price elasticity of demand is greater in the long run than in the short run.

Let us take an example. Suppose the price of electricity goes up 50 per cent. How do you adjust in the short run? You can turn the lights off more often, you can stop running the stereo as much as you used to, and so on. Otherwise, it is very difficult to cut back on your consumption of electricity. In the long run, though, you can devise methods to reduce your consumption. If your house has electric central heating you could contemplate switching to gas heating. If you are about to move house, one with gas-fired heating would have rather greater attraction than previously. The next time you move house you will have a gas-cooker installed. You may purchase fluorescent bulbs because they use less electricity. The longer you have to figure it out, the more ways you will find to cut electricity consumption. We would expect, therefore, that the short-run demand curve for electricity would be highly inelastic (in the price range around P_1), as demonstrated by D_1D_1 in Figure 7.7. However, the long-run demand curve may exhibit much more elasticity (in the neighbourhood of P_1), as demonstrated by D_3D_3. Indeed, we can think of an entire family of demand curves such as those depicted in that diagram. The short-run demand curve is for that period when there is no time for adjustment. As more time is allowed, the demand curve becomes flatter, going first to D_3D_3. Thus, *in the neighbourhood of* P_1 elasticity differs for each of these curves. It is greater for the less-steep curves (but remember, slope alone does not measure elasticity for the *entire* curve).

HOW TO DEFINE THE SHORT AND THE LONG RUN

We have mentioned the short run and we have mentioned the long run. Is the short run one week, two weeks, a month, two months? Is the long run three years, four years, five years? The answer is that there is no one answer! What we mean by the long run is that period of time necessary for consumers to make full adjustment to a given price change, all other things held constant. In the case of the demand for electricity, the long run will be however long it takes consumers to switch over to cheaper sources of heating, to buy houses that are more energy-efficient, to purchase manufactured appliances that are more energy-efficient, and so on. The long-run price elasticity of demand for electricity therefore relates to a period of at least several years. The short run – by default, as it were – is any period less than the long run.

Figure 7.7

Short-run and Long-run Price Elasticity of Demand. The longer the time allowed for adjustment the greater the price elasticity of demand. In other words for any given increase in price the longer the time allowed for adjustment, the greater the reduction in quantity demanded; and for any given decrease in price, the longer the time allowed for adjustment, the greater the increase in quantity demanded. Consider an equilibrium situation in which the market price is P_e and the quantity demanded is Q_e. Then there is a price increase to P_1. In the short run as evidenced by the demand curve D_1D_1 we move from equilibrium quantity demanded Q_e to Q_1. After more time is allowed for adjustment the demand curve rotates at original price P_e to D_2D_2. Quantity demanded falls again now to Q_2. After even more time is allowed for adjustment the demand curve rotates at price P_e to D_3D_3. At the higher price P_1 in the long run the quantity demanded falls all the way to Q_3.

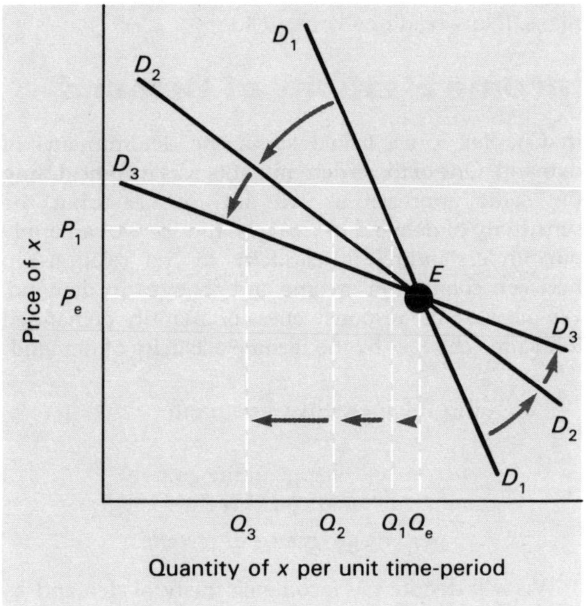

Cross-price Elasticity of Demand

We have already talked about the effect of a change in the price of one good on the quantity demanded of a related good back in Chapter 5. We defined substitutes and complements in terms of whether a reduction in the price of one caused a shift leftward or rightward, respectively, in the demand curve of the other. If the price of butter is held constant, the amount of butter demanded will certainly be influenced by the price of a close substitute like margarine. If the price of cassette players is held constant, the quantity of cassette players demanded is most likely to be affected by changes in the price of cassette recordings.

What we need to do is come up with a numerical measure of the price responsiveness of demand to the prices of related goods. This is called *cross-price elasticity of demand,* which is defined as the percentage change in the demand for one good divided by the percentage change in the price of the related good. Hence, the cross-price elasticity of demand is a measure of the responsiveness of one good's quantity demanded to changes in a related good's price.

When two goods are *substitutes,* the cross-price elasticity of demand will be *positive*. For example, when the price of margarine goes up, the quantity demanded of butter will go up too. A producer of margarine could use a numerical estimate of the cross-price elasticity of demand between butter and margarine. For example, if the price of butter went up by 10 per cent, and the margarine producer knew that the cross-price elasticity of demand was 1, he or she could estimate that the demand for margarine would also go up to 10 per cent. Plans for increasing margarine production could then be made.

When two related goods are *complements*, the cross-price elasticity of demand will be negative. To use an earlier example, when the price of cassette recordings goes up, the quantity demanded of cassette players is likely to fall. Any manufacturer of cassette players must

Key Points 7.4

- **Demand curves can be linear or non-linear. Linear demand curves have constantly changing elasticities as we move along them. Non-linear demand curves *may* be drawn with constant elasticities of any desired value. We have constructed one that exhibits unit elasticity everywhere on the curve.**
- **The determinants of price elasticity of demand are: (1) the number and closeness of substitutes and (2) the length of time allowed for adjustment to a change in prices.**
- **Cross-price elasticity of demand is the percentage change in the demand for one good divided by the percentage change in the price of the related good.**
- **For substitutes the cross-price elasticities are positive whereas for complements the cross-price elasticities are negative.**

take this into account in order to make production plans. (Now read Key Points 7.4.)

Income Elasticity of Demand

In Chapter 5, we talked about the determinants of demand. One of those determinants was income. Using the same approach as we did in measuring the sensitivity of demand to changes in price we can apply our understanding of elasticity to the relationship between changes in income and changes in demand. We measure the responsiveness of quantity demanded to income changes by the **income elasticity of demand:**

$$e_y = \text{income elasticity of demand}$$

$$= \frac{\text{percentage change in the amount of goods purchased}}{\text{percentage change in income}}$$

We will denote the income elasticity of demand by e_y.

Income elasticity of demand refers to a *horizontal shift* in the demand curve in response to changes in income (while price elasticity of demand refers to a movement *along* the curve in response to price changes). Shifts in the demand curve will obviously have major implications for business persons. Those goods whose income elasticity is positive will be ones where markets will grow as consumers have more income to spend. Conversely, goods and services whose income elasticity is negative will be ones which will experience declining markets as consumer incomes increase. Before elaborating on this important matter let us be clear how to calculate income elasticity of demand.

A simple example will demonstrate how income elasticity of demand can be computed. In Figure 7.8, we give the relevant data. The product in question is stereo records. We assume that the price of stereo records remains constant relative to other prices. In period 1, six records per month are purchased. Income per month is £200. In period 2, monthly income is increased to £300 and the quantity of records demanded per month is increased to eight. We can apply the following calculation:

$$\text{income elasticity of demand} = e_y$$

$$= \frac{(8-6)/6}{(300-200)/200} = \frac{1/3}{1/2} = 0.667$$

Hence, measured income elasticity of demand for record albums for the individual represented in this example is 0.667. Note that this holds only for the move from six records to eight records purchased per month. In the move for decreased income from £300 to £200 per month and from eight to six records per month, the calculation becomes:

$$\frac{(6-8)/8}{(200-300)/300} = \frac{2/8}{100/300} = \frac{1/4}{1/3} = 0.75$$

Thus, the measured income elasticity of demand is equal to 0.75.

To get the same income elasticity of demand over the same range of values, regardless of which direction the change (increase or decrease), we can use the same mid-point formula that we used in computing the price elasticity of demand. When doing so, we have the following:

Figure 7.8
How Income Affects Quantity of Records Demanded

Time-period	*Quantity of stereo albums demanded per month*	*Income per month*
Period 1	6	£200
Period 2	8	£300

This example involves just one product when there is a major increase in one person's income. Now let us consider the economy as a whole and how consumers alter their spending habits as they have more money available to spend. We might reasonably expect to find that spending on some goods and services is very sensitive to quite small changes in income. With yet other goods and services this income elasticity is less marked. We need something to classify the different reactions of consumers.

Different Kinds of Income Elasticity

We have the following definitions for the varying ranges of income elasticities depending on whether a 1 per cent change in income results in more or less than a 1 per cent change in the quantity demanded.

1. **Income-elastic demand.** We say that a good or service has an income elastic demand whenever the income elasticity is greater than 1. A 1 per cent change in income causes a greater than 1 per cent change in quantity demanded. In these cases we are talking about *luxury goods.*
2. **Income-inelastic demand.** Here a 1 per cent change in income causes a change of less than 1 per cent in quantity demanded. If the income inelasticity is less than 1 but above zero then this implies that the good or service is not one that is strongly sensitive to changes in consumer incomes. In other words it is a consumer *necessity*.
3. **Negative income-elasticity.** Where the income elasticity is negative then it implies that in the case of these goods, consumers are prepared to reduce their spending as they get richer. In these situations the relevant goods are *inferior goods.* In Chapter 5 we suggested that potatoes might be an example of an inferior good.

The Importance of Income Elasticity

As incomes increase and consumers adjust their patterns of spending there are important repercussions for those engaged in business activity. Figure 7.9 shows some real-world estimates of income elasticities in the UK.

Figure 7.9 points out clearly the depressing market situation facing British Coal as compared with purveyors of alcoholic drink. It also indicates that the demand for bread was declining but that in 1970 makers of sports equipment had the encouraging prospect of rising sales. So Britons appeared to wish to eat less bread and seek more healthy exercise! Households 'voted' with their money not for an increase in cigarette smoking but for more lager and 'short' drinks.

Figure 7.9 includes just one food commodity, that of bread. If we now examine the income elasticities for some other items of food we can begin to realize the implications for food processors in the UK economy (Figure 7.10). Let us have in mind the following question: do particular food markets expand or contract as households have more income to spend?

You will note that in none of these twelve groups of

Figure 7.9
Estimates for Income Elasticities of Demand in 1970

Commodity or service	*Elasticity*
Coal	−2.02
Bread	−0.49
Cigarettes and tobacco	−0.03
Beer	1.22
Catering	1.63
Recreational goods	1.98
Wines and spirits	2.59
Expenditure abroad	1.14

Source: A. Ş. Deaton, 'The Measurement of Income and Price Elasticities', *European Economic Review*, Vol. 6,1975, p. 266.

Figure 7.10
Estimates of Income Elasticities of Expenditure in 1982

Milk and cream	0.09
Cheese	0.29
Carcass meat	0.32
Fish	0.26
Fats	0.08
Sugar and preserves	−0.13
Fresh fruit	0.59
Fresh potatoes	−0.12
Fresh green vegetables	0.30
Bread	−0.04
Cakes and biscuits	0.20
Beverages	0.16

Source: Ministry of Agriculture, Fisheries and Food

foodstuffs is the income elasticity as high as 1.0 and in most cases it is closer to zero than 1.0. In three food groups it is negative. What does this mean for food processors (and indeed farmers)? It means that as households have more income available to spend they devote very little to extra food consumption. As a result food processors in most of the individual food markets do not experience steadily rising sales of food. Thus processing firms like United Biscuits cannot expect that the consumption of biscuits *in volume terms* will show any encouraging growth. So if Britons show little or no willingness to munch more biscuits as each year passes by the only course open to United Biscuits in seeking higher sales is to obtain a bigger share of the static biscuit market. By offering new varieties of biscuit in well-planned marketing campaigns United Biscuits might then prompt households to switch some of their biscuit-buying to United Biscuits brands. Rival firms would, as a result, face declining sales and lose some of their share of the market. (Now read Key Point 7.5.)

Elasticity of Supply

The **price elasticity of supply** is defined in a similar way as the price elasticity of demand. Supply elasticities are generally positive; this is because at higher

Key Point 7.5

▶ **The sensitivity of the quantity demanded to changes in income is called the income elasticity of demand. For luxury goods the income elasticity is greater than 1: for inferior goods the income elasticity is negative. The degree of income elasticity is a major determinant of how the market for a good or service is growing over time.**

prices, larger quantities will generally be forthcoming from suppliers. Our definition of the price elasticity of supply, e_s, is the following:

$$e_s = \frac{\text{percentage change in quantity supplied}}{\text{percentage change in price}}$$

We use some hypothetical data to illustrate the price elasticity of supply for petrol. This is done in Figure 7.11. Note that the price elasticity of supply remains constant and equal to 1 in this particular example. This is a special feature of any *straight-line* supply curve that passes through the origin, that is, whose intercept is zero.*

Classifying Supply Elasticities

Just as with demand, there are different types of supply elasticities. They are similar in definition.

If a 1 per cent increase in price elicits a greater than 1 per cent increase in the quantity supplied, we say that at the particular price in question on the supply schedule, *supply is elastic*.

If, on the other hand, a 1 per cent increase in price elicits a less than 1 per cent increase in the quantity supplied, we refer to that as an *inelastic supply* situation.

If the percentage change in the quantity supplied is just equal to the percentage change in the price, then we talk about *unitary elasticity of supply*.

We show in Figure 7.12 two supply schedules, SS and $S'S'$. Can you tell at a glance, without reading the caption, which one is infinitely elastic and which one is perfectly inelastic?

As you might expect, most supply schedules exhibit elasticities that are somewhere between the range of zero to infinity.

Price Elasticity of Supply and Length of Time for Adjustment

We pointed out earlier that the longer the time allowed for adjustment, the greater the price elasticity of

*If the straight-line supply curve has a vertical intercept then price elasticity of supply is greater than 1 (elastic throughout); if a straight-line supply curve intersects the horizontal axis then its price elasticity of supply is less than 1 (inelastic throughout).

Figure 7.11

Calculating the Price Elasticity of Supply for Petrol. use some hypothetical data to demonstrate how to calculate price elasticity of supply. We use the mid-point, or average, formula. Column 2 gives the change in quantity of petrol supplied derived from column 1. Column 4 gives the change in price derived from column 3. Columns 5 and 6 give the average quantity and price values. Column 7 presents the price elasticity of supply, which is constant and equal to one because the curve intercepts the origin.

(1) Quantity supplied (millions) of gallons	*(2) Change in Q (millions) of gallons*	*(3) Price (£)*	*(4) Change in P (£)*	*(5)* $\frac{Q_1 + Q_2}{2}$	*(6)* $\frac{P_1 + P_2}{2}$	*(7)* $e_s = \frac{\text{Change in Q}}{(Q_1 + Q_2)/2} \Big/ \frac{\text{Change in P}}{(P_1 + (P)/2}$
0		.00				
	2		1.0	1	0.5	(2/1) ÷ (1.0/0.5) = 1.00
2		1.00				
	2		1.0	3	1.5	(2/3) ÷ (1.0/1.5) = 1.00
4		2.00				
	2		1.0	5	2.5	(2/5) ÷ (1.0/2.5) = 1.00
6		3.00				
	2		1.0	7	3.5	(2/7) ÷ (1.0/3.5) = 1.00
8		4.00				
	2		1.0	9	4.5	(2/9) ÷ (1.0/4.5) = 1.00
10		5.00				

demand. It turns out that the same proposition applies to supply. The longer the time for adjustment, the more price-elastic is the supply curve. Consider why this is true:

1. The longer the time allowed for adjustment, the more firms are able to figure out ways to increase production in an industry.
2. The longer the time allowed, the more resources can flow into an industry through expansion of existing firms.

We therefore talk about short- and long-run price elasticities of supply. The short run is defined as the time-period during which full adjustment has not yet taken place. Thus, the long run is the time-period during which firms have been able to adjust fully to the change in price.

Figure 7.12

The Extremes in Supply Curves. Here we have drawn two extremes of supply schedules: *SS is a perfectly elastic supply curve, S′S′ is a perfectly inelastic one.* In the former an unlimited quantity will be forthcoming at the price P_1. In the latter no matter what the price the quantity supplied will be Q_1. An example of $S'S'$ might be the supply curve for fresh fish on the morning the boats arrive back in dock.

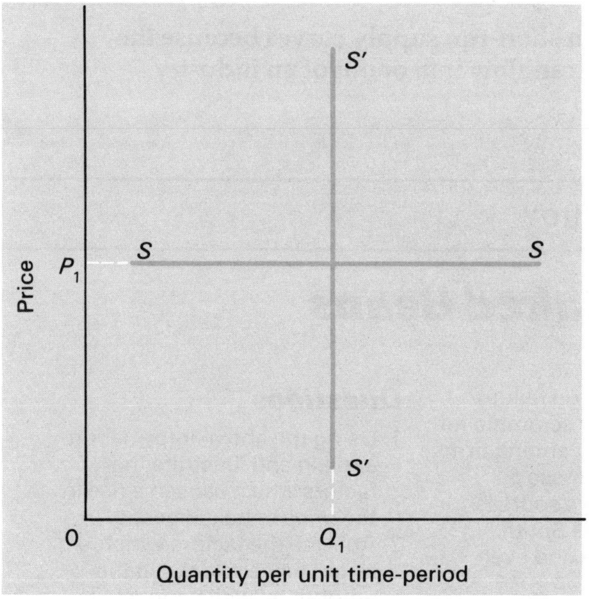

Consider an example – an increase in the price of housing. In the very short run, when there is no time allowed for adjustment, the amount of housing services offered for rent or for sale is relatively inelastic. However, as more time is allowed for adjustment, current owners of the housing stock can find ways to increase the amount of housing services they will offer for rent from given buildings. The owner of a large house can decide, for example, to have two of his or her children move into one room so that a 'new' extra bedroom can be rented out. This can also be done by the owner of a large house who decides to move into an apartment and rent each floor of the house to a family. Thus, the quantity of housing services supplied will increase. We can show a whole set of supply curves similar to the ones we generated for demand. In Figure 7.13 when nothing can be done in the short run, the supply curve is vertical, S_1S_1. As more time is allowed for adjustment, the supply curve rotates to S_2S_2 and then S_3S_3 becoming more elastic as it rotates.

REAL-WORLD ESTIMATES OF PRICE ELASTICITY OF SUPPLY

We were able to give some real-world estimates of the price elasticity of demand. In Figure 7.14 (on page 106) we give some real-world estimates of the price elasticity of supply for both the short and the long run. Notice that most short-run elasticities are considerably less than their long-run counterparts. Clearly, then, it is important to distinguish between short- and long-run price elasticities. A policy-maker who looks only at the short-run price elasticity of supply, for example, will

Figure 7.13

Short-run and Long-run Price Elasticity of Supply. The longer the time allowed for adjustment the greater the price elasticity of supply. Consider a given situation in which the price is P_e and the quantity supplied is Q_e. In the short run we hypothesize a vertical supply schedule S_1S_1. In other words we assume that suppliers are unable to do anything in the very short run even when there is a price increase. With the given price increase to P_1 therefore there will be no change in the short run in quantity supplied; it will remain at Q_e. Given some time for adjustment the supply curve will rotate at price P_e to S_2S_2. The new quantity supplied will shift out to Q_1. Finally the long-run supply curve is shown by S_3S_3. The quantity supplied again increases out to Q_2.

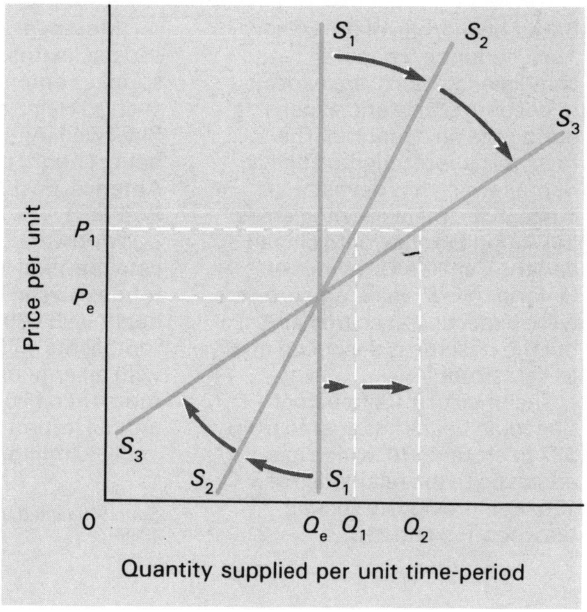

Figure 7.14

Estimated Price Elasticities of Supply of Some Commodities in the United States

Commodity	*Elasticity e_s*	
	Short run	*Long run*
Cabbage	0.36	1.20
Carrots	0.14	1.00
Cucumbers	0.29	2.20
Onions	0.34	1.00
Green peas	0.31	4.40
Tomatoes	0.16	0.90
Cauliflower	0.14	1.10
Celery	0.14	0.95

Source: M. Nerlove and W. Addison, 'Statistical Estimation of Long-run Elasticities of Supply and Demand American', *Journal of Agricultural Economics* (formerly *Journal of Farm Economics*), Vol. 40 (Nov. 1958).

incorrectly predict changes in supplies in the future, and therefore an improper policy decision might be made.

In Chapter 8 we consider how time-lags can cause considerable fluctuation in the prices of agricultural commodities and foodstuffs. Thus we will develop a dynamic model of price determination in these markets.

Key Points 7.6

- **Price elasticity of supply is given by the percentage change in quantity supplied divided by the percentage change in price.**
- **Usually, price elasticities of supply are positive – higher prices yield larger quantities supplied.**
- **Long-run supply curves are more elastic than short-run supply curves because the longer the time allowed, the more resources can flow into or out of an industry when price changes.**

CASE STUDY

The Price of Baked Beans

Baked beans, one of the UK's most enduringly popular convenience foods, are expected to become scarce and expensive during the next months. The reason is unprecedented heavy rainfall which has devastated crops in the main growing areas, the American state of Michigan and the Canadian province of Ontario. A few weeks ago growers were expecting a record harvest but the position is described now as catastrophic.

The price of a 100lb-bag of Canadian beans has soared from \$27 to around \$70, which has added 6p to the retail price of a 15oz can previously costing between 15p and 21p.

Moreover, the crop failure caused an unseemly scramble for supplies among big canning firms such as Heinz and Crosse & Blackwell. Alternative sources being sought include South America, East Africa and even Romania.

Worldwide baked bean consumption is around 800,000 tonnes a year. The British eat a healthy 80 000 tonnes, which represents 4 500 000 cans a day, with an annual retail value of more than £200 million. The annual import bill is between £20 and £30 million.

Source: adapted from *The Times*, 10 Nov 1986.

Questions

1. Using the above information, explain and illustrate the factors which caused a rise in the price of baked beans.
2. Analyse the factors which might have influenced the amount by which the retail price was raised to consumers.
3. Discuss, with reference to the information in the passage, the economic effects of the increase in the price of beans on growers.
4. Examine other posible economic effects of the increase in the price of beans.

CASE STUDY

A Decade of Change

The following table shows data relating to consumers' expenditure in the UK, 1976 to 1986, when measured at constant 1980 prices.

Figure 7.15

Category	*Expenditure in 1976 (£m)*	*in 1986 (£m)*	*% change 1976–86*	*Expenditure as % of total in 1976*	*1986*
Tobacco	4 821	3 731	−22.6	3.9	2.4
Alcoholic drinks	9 448	10 297	8.9	7.7	6.5
Food	22 159	24 174	9.0	18.0	15.4
Fuel and power	6 050	6 730	11.2	4.9	4.2
Housing	17 346	21 134	21.8	14.1	13.4
Household goods and services	9 615	11 949	24.2	7.8	7.6
Other goods and services (pharmaceuticals; toiletries; jewellery, hairdressing, etc.)	16 617	21 639	30.2	13.5	13.8
Transport and communications	19 744	28 141	42.5	16.1	18.0
Recreation and entertainment	11 117	16 604	49.3	9.1	10.6
Clothing and footwear	8 406	13 279	57.9	6.8	8.5
Total household and tourist expenditure in the UK	125 323	175 085	25.3	—	—
Less foreign expenditure by foreign tourists	−3 675	−3 967	7.9	3.0	2.5
Add Household expenditure abroad	1 400	3 374	141.0	1.1	2.1
Total household expenditure on goods and services	123 048	157 085	27.6	100	100

Source: HMSO National Accounts, 1987

Questions

1. Explain what is meant by: percentage change in consumers' expenditure, 1976–86, when measured at constant 1980 prices.
2. Select a category of expenditure which seems likely to display (i) positive and (ii) negative income elasticities of demand. Explain your answers.
3. What factors, other than a change in real income, help to explain the difference between the categories of consumers' spending during this period?
4. What impact may the changes in consumers' expenditure have had on: (i) the pattern of employment in the UK and in other countries; (ii) the sources of government tax revenue?

Exam Preparation

PRACTICAL EXERCISES

1. In Ruritania, a hypothetical country whose currency is the pound sterling (£), the three firms in the car industry together sold in 1985 12 million cars at an average price of £5 000. However, because the economy is in a depressed state the car industry is not working at full capacity and many car workers are not employed for a full working week.

The car workers' union, Vehicle and General Workers, suggest that each producer reduces his price by £200. This action, the Union argues, would result in another 2 million cars being sold while aggregate profits would be maintained at £4 000 million.

(a) Calculate the value of the elasticity of demand (correct to one decimal place) assumed by the Vehicle and General Workers Union. Comment on this value.

(b) A spokesman for the Ruritanian car industry points out that government economists have estimated that the elasticity of demand for cars is, in fact, −0.5. Assuming this estimate is accurate, what would be the impact on the car industry?

The following exercises are, strictly speaking, multiple choice questions. However, they are all numerical in content and thus very suitable for inclusion as tests of a quantitative understanding of the concept of elasticity.

2. A manufacturer produces two products, X and Y. Market prices of both products go up by the same percentage and his supply of X is increased by 100 per cent, and that of Y by 50 per cent. What can be deduced about the elasticity of supply of X and Y?

A the elasticity of X is 2, and that of Y is 1
B the elasticity of X is 1, and that of Y is ½
C the elasticity of X is between 1 and 2, and that of Y between ½ and 1
D the elasticity of X is 1, while that of Y cannot be determined
E neither of the elasticities can be determined.

3. The demand function for good A is written as follows:

$Q_D = 300 - 3P_A + 2P_B - 0.2Y$,

where Q_D is the quantity demanded of good A in millions of tonnes, where P_A is the price of good A in dollars, P_B is the price of good B in dollars, Y is the level of national income in millions of dollars.

Initially, when $P_A = 10$, $P_B = 15$, and $Y = 500$, the demand for A is 200. If Y increases to 1 000 what is the income elasticity of demand?

A $-1/10$
B $-1/5$
C $-1/2$
D -1
E -2

4. Assume that the cross-elasticity of demand for cars with respect to changes in the price of petrol is −0.5. At an average price per car of £5 000, the number of cars sold per week is 10 000. If the average price of cars remains unchanged, but the price of petrol increases from 40p to 44p per litre, the number of cars sold per week will fall to

A 5 000
B 7 000
C 8 000
D 9 000
E 9 500

5. The demand for butter is negatively related to the price of butter:

elasticity = −0.43

The demand for butter is also affected by the prices of flour, margarine, cakes, and meat. Cross-elasticities of demand for butter with respect to the prices of these goods are:

flour	−0.23
margarine	−0.10
cakes	0.59
meat	0.56

Which one of the following can be predicted from this information?

A a rise in the price of flour will lead to a rise in the demand for butter
B a fall in the price of margarine will lead to a rise in the demand for butter
C a fall in the price of cakes will lead to a rise in the demand for butter
D a fall in the price of meat will lead to a fall in the demand for butter
E a fall in the price of butter will lead to a more than proportionate rise in the demand for butter.

	1977		1982		1987	
	£m	%	£m	%	£m	%
Household expenditure on food	16 047	18.5	25 649	15.2	33 643	13.0
Expenditure on meals out	3 690	4.2	6 619	3.9	12 348	4.8
Total expenditure on food	19 737	22.7	32 268	19.1	45 991	17.8
Alcoholic drink	6 545	7.5	12 003	7.1	17 309	6.7
Total food and drink	26 282	30.2	44 271	26.3	63 300	24.5
Total consumers' expenditure	86 887	100.0	168 545	100.0	258 431	100.0

Source: *Household Food Consumption and Expenditure 1987.*

6. The table shows data on consumers' expenditure in the UK for 1977, 1982, and 1987.

(a) Why is the doubling of the amount of household expenditure on food between 1977 and 1987 not as significant as it might seem?

(b) What might explain the falling proportion of the share of household expenditure accounted for by food between 1977 and 1987?

(c) What factors might explain the amounts spent on (i) meals out of the home; (ii) alcoholic drink?

7. Study the following data on the estimated cross-price elasticities for certain foods and answer the following question.

	Elasticity with respect to the price of		
	Beef and veal	*Mutton and lamb*	*Pork*
Beef and veal	—	−0.06	0.10
Mutton and lamb	0.15	—	0.03
Pork	0.25	0.03	—
	Elasticity with respect to the price of		
	Oranges	*Apples*	*Pears*
Oranges	—	−0.03	−0.12
Apples	−0.01	—	0.05
Pears	−0.32	0.30	—
	Elasticity with respect to the price of		
	Tea	*Instant coffee*	
Tea	—	−0.09	
Instant coffee	−1.10	—	
	Elasticity with respect to the price of		
	Butter	*Margarine*	
Butter	—	−0.02	
Margarine	−0.04	—	

(*Source: Household Food Consumption and Expenditure 1987.*)

How would you interpret the above data?

MULTIPLE CHOICE QUESTIONS

1.

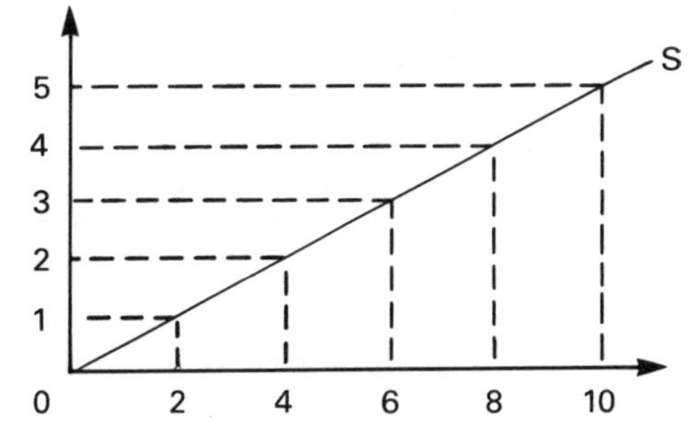

The elasticity of the supply curve shown in the above diagram is

A zero
B between zero and unity
C unity
D between unity and infinity
E infinity

†2.

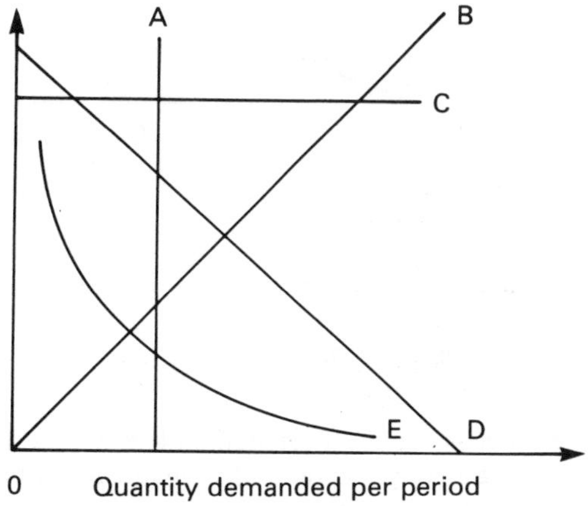

2. Which of the curves labelled **A–E** on the above diagram illustrates unitary elasticity of demand throughout its length?

3. The elasticity of a downward-sloping straight-line demand schedule is
A zero
B unity
C positive
D variable along its length
E infinity

One or more of the options given in Questions 4, 5, and 6 may be correct. Select your answer by means of the code set out in the grid:

A	B	C	D
1, 2, 3 all correct	1, 2 only correct	2, 3 only correct	1 only correct

4. In the diagram below, line 0Z represents the income/consumption curve for a particular good.

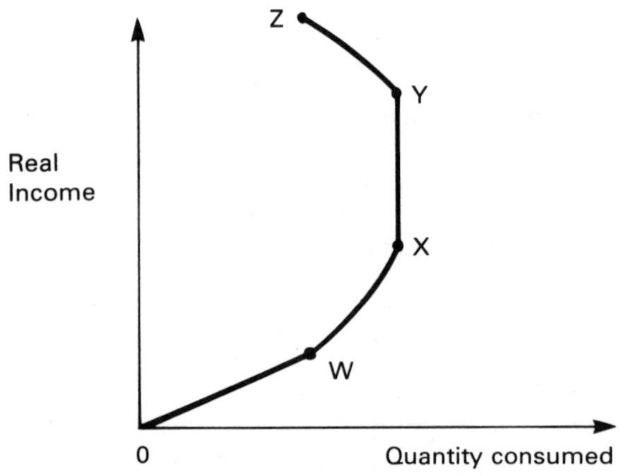

Income-elasticity of demand for the good is
1 negative from Y to Z
2 positive from 0 to W
3 unity from X to Y

5. Cross-elasticity of demand is a measure of the responsiveness of demand for commodity X to a change in the
1 price of a substitute for X
2 real income of consumers
3 price of X

6. The demand curve (above right) for a commodity is a rectangular hyperbola. It follows that

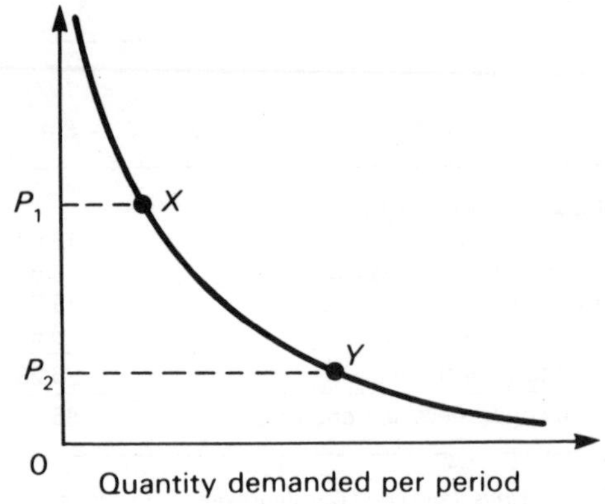

1 the price elasticity of demand is greater at X than at Y
2 a fall in price from OP_1 to OP_2 will cause a proportionate rise in the quantity demanded
3 consumer outlay on the good is the same at price OP_1 as at OP_2

RELATED ESSAY QUESTIONS

1. Describe briefly the conditions (or determinants) of demand and supply. Explain why and how price changes may occur when the conditions of demand and supply
(a) change
(b) are constant

2. Consider the effect of an increase in the price of oil on the demand for petrol, diesel, and heating oil. How might the response vary between different types of user, both in the short run and in the long run?

3. Define price elasticity of demand and outline the factors which determine its value. Show the relevance of price elasticity in analysing the effects of a rise in the price of petrol on the demand for different forms of transport.

4. **(a)** Explain why the price elasticity of demand may vary from commodity to commodity.
(b) Explain why the price elasticity of demand may vary at particular points on a given demand curve. Illustrate your answer with reference to a straight-line downward-sloping demand curve.
(c) In what circumstances might knowledge of the value of the price elasticity of demand of a commodity be useful to a decision-taker?

5. Using examples to illustrate your answer, explain why **(a)** the price of demand and **(b)** the price elasticity of supply are likely to change over time.

8 Governments and Markets

Key Points to Review

- Shifts in demand (5.3, 5.6)
- Shifts in supply (5.5, 5.6)
- Surpluses and shortages (5.7)
- Price elasticity of demand (7.1)
- Income elasticity of demand (7.5)
- Price elasticity of supply (7.6)

Questions for Preview

1 How do the concepts of price and income elasticity help explain why agriculture is the subject of government intervention?

2 How do controls on rents charged by landlords affect the market for rented accommodation?

3 Who benefits from government policies which raise the minimum level of wages that employers must pay their employees?

The pricing system answers three basic questions of resource allocation: *what* goods will be produced? *how* will they be produced? and *for whom* will they be produced? The forces of supply and demand acting through the pricing system (i.e. the market) affect the bulk of decisions that answer these three questions. But as Chapter 4 pointed out developed countries like the UK and US are not purely private market economies. In addition to market forces, there are many other forces at work that affect the allocation of resources. One of the most important of these non-market forces is government. In this chapter we will look at the impact on markets of various forms of government intervention and in doing so draw on the concepts of demand and supply elasticity explained in Chapter 7. Our aim is to show some applications of supply and demand analysis. We will firstly draw on the concepts in the previous chapters to show why agriculture in developed economies is not left to unregulated market forces. Using our theory of free market pricing we can explain why, in the absence of government intervention, the operation of forces on the demand and supply side results both in a low income and an unstable income situation for the farming community.

In the second part of this chapter we show how the concepts of price elasticity of demand and of supply are helpful in understanding the repercussions of taxes imposed by government. Of course governments need tax revenues in order to help finance a wide range of expenditure programmes. The rationale of government spending takes us firmly into the macro-field and is the subject of our first chapter in Part B.

The final part of this chapter considers the impact of government policies which control the prices that would operate in a free market. We consider specific policies which fix a maximum price level and appraise the impact in the market for rented accommodation. The labour market provides us with an illustration of another form of government intervention with the price mechanism. We study the effect of minimum wage legislation. Finally we briefly preview the problems facing governments attempting general restraints on upward price movements. But first we consider how the free market operates in the agricultural sector. Having considered in turn the demand for and supply of food we see why governments are so willing to regulate agricultural markets.

The Agricultural Problem

The Demand Side

The root cause of the problem facing the farming community is the fact that there is a limit to how much food people can eat! Adam Smith recognized this in the *Wealth of Nations:*

> The rich man consumes no more food than his poor neighbour. In quality it may be very different, and to select and prepare it may require more labour and art; but in quantity it is very nearly the same. But compare the spacious palace and great wardrobe of the one with the hovel and few rags of the other, and you will be sensible that the difference between their clothing, lodging and household furniture is almost as great in quantity as it is in the quality. The desire for food is limited in every man by the narrow capacity of the human stomach; but the desire for the convenience and ornaments of building, dress, equipage and household furniture, seems to have no limit or certain boundary.*

Even if people who are rich can 'afford' to buy huge quantities, they do not do so. We expect, therefore, that as households get richer, the percentage of their budget spent on food will fall. This occurs because the income elasticity of demand for food is less than 1. We have previously defined income elasticity of demand as follows:

$$\text{income elasticity} = \frac{\text{percentage change in amount of good purchased}}{\text{percentage change in income}}$$

If the income elasticity of demand for agricultural products is less than 1, for every 1 per cent increase in income there will be a less-than-1 per cent increase in quantity demanded, *other things being constant.* Look at Figure 8.1, where we show the income elasticity for food products in various countries. We see that income elasticity is quite low for the richer nations in the world. In fact, the richer the nation, the lower the income elasticity of demand for agricultural products. All nations seem to exhibit income elasticities for food products that are less than 1. Therefore, we predict that agriculture will be of declining importance in all nations as each becomes richer. (We are ignoring the possibility of *exports* of food becoming more and more important. If that were to happen because of increased world demand, the agricultural sector could conceivably even grow as a nation became richer.)

Figure 8.2 shows the volume of some items of food consumption in the UK. It shows that on a per capita basis consumption of seven of the fourteen categories of food products was lower in 1980 than in 1977. In some of these food products the fall in consumption was a continuation of a long-term trend, i.e. grain products (mainly bread). Clearly, changing views on what constitutes a healthy diet and many other factors besides rising incomes have affected food consumption habits in the UK but surely we can now appreciate Adam Smith's point about the 'narrow capacity of the human stomach'. As real incomes rise consumers prefer to spend their money on foreign holidays, colour televisions, and motor cars. The higher *income elasticity* values for these products compared with those for items of food indicates how society is registering its market preferences. Unhappily for farmers the slow rate of population growth in the UK does not offset the disappointing growth in demand due to rising incomes: an increase in the sheer numbers (of mouths to feed) does not counteract the basically sluggish market situation resulting from the income determinant. In 1977 the UK population was 56.19 million: three years later it had grown only to 56.33 million. In 1984 it was 56.46m and in 1987 56.93m.

The income inelasticity of demand for food means that society does not want the same number of farmers to continue in production: if numbers do remain constant their incomes relative to other groups in society must fall.

Figure 8.1

Income Elasticity for Food Products. The income elasticity of demand for food is defined as being equal to the percentage change in the quantity demanded divided by the percentage change in real income. This income elasticity is quite low for the richer nations in the world.

(a) *Data for Great Britain*

	Income elasticity
Liquid milk	−0.13
Yoghurt	0.67
Mutton and lamb	0.21
Eggs	−0.028
Fresh potatoes	−0.43
Bread	−0.18
Tea	−0.65
Instant coffee	0.28

Source: *Household Food Consumption and Expenditure*: *1987.*

(b) *Comparative data for ten countries* (all food products)

	Income elasticity
United States	0.08
Canada	0.15
Britain	0.24
Germany	0.25
France	0.25
Ireland	0.23
Italy	0.42
Greece	0.49
Spain	0.56
Portugal	0.60

Source: Charles I. Schultze, *The Distribution of Farm Subsidies*: *Who Gets the Benefits?* (Washington, DC: The Brookings Institution, 1971).

*A. Smith, *Wealth of Nations*, Bk. 1, Ch. 11, Everyman edn., 1964, pp. 1 49-50.

Figure 8.2

Food and Drink Consumption in the United Kingdom. Consumption on a per head basis was lower in 1986 as compared with 1976 in seven of the fourteen categories of foodstuffs. This decline was not just a phenomenon of recent years but part of a longer-term decline in consumption.

	kg per head per year		
	1976	*1981*	*1986*
Grain products	75.2	69.0	70.3
Sugar, honey, and glucose (sugar content)	48.7	42.6	43.6
Meat (edible weight)	55.5	55.5	55.4
Fish (edible weight)	8.3	7.2	8.0
Dairy products			
Butterfat	15.3	12.7	11.2
Solids-not-fat	18.5	18.1	18.8
Eggs and egg products (equiv. no. of eggs)	247	227	220
Oils and fats (fat content)	16.5	20.2	22.9
Potatoes and potato products (as raw equiv.)	85.0	103.4	112.4
Fruit	68.8	77.4	90.8
Vegetables (as fresh equiv.)	70.4	72.2	85.7
Pulses and nuts	4.7	4.6	5.3
Tea	3.6	3.2	2.8
Coffee and cocoa	3.0	3.3	3.2

Source: Ministry of Agriculture Fisheries and Food.

The Supply Problem

On the supply side technical progress – 'making two blades of grass grow where one grew before' – exacerbates the problems facing the farming community in developed economies. The agricultural sector has exhibited throughout history an impressive record of rising crop yields and improved productivity in livestock production due to improvements in animal husbandry. Figure 8.3 shows farming's recent record of improved productivity.

The Problem of Farm Prices

Let us now bring together both of our observations concerning the demand for and the supply of food. If the demand curve shifts horizontally only slowly over time while the supply curve shifts very perceptibly to the right due to technical progress we must surely conclude that there will be downward pressure on prices if there is an unregulated market in the pricing of agriculture. Falling prices for farm output should be the market signal for resources to move out of agriculture. But if resources do not flow out of farming then the working of the price mechanism is to that extent flawed. If the process of resource reallocation as explained in Chapter 6 does not take place then there may be grounds for governments to help *some* farmers who are receiving incomes below those in the non-farm sector of the economy.

You will note that we have just referred to the size of some farmers' *incomes*. We have seen that the interaction of supply and demand has the effect of depressing farm *prices*. Now of course for an *individual* farmer his income is the product of output times prices received per unit. Those farmers who produce little agricultural output will of course have lower incomes than those farmers whose sheer volume of production gives them much larger incomes. This simple point – that some farmers produce little output whereas other farmers are very large and account for a significant proportion of total output – in fact is the nub of 'the farm problem' in developed economies like the UK and US. Some farmers whose production is relatively small may never be able to generate enough receipts from the sale of output to be large enough to be economically viable. In

Figure 8.3

Estimated Average Yields of Crops and Livestock Products in the UK. In nearly every case a picture of increased productivity is evident.

	Unit	*Average of 1976–8*	*1983*	*1984*	*1985*	*1986*	*1987*
Wheat	tonnes/hectare	4.67	6.37	7.71	6.33	6.96	6.03
Barley	tonnes/hectare	4.03	4.65	5.59	4.95	5.22	5.02
Oats	tonnes/hectare	3.74	4.32	4.89	4.59	5.16	4.38
Potatoes	tonnes/hectare	28.10	29.87	37.03	35.84	36.04	36.70
Sugar beet	tonnes/hectare	32.67	38.30	45.90	38.28	40.35	40.00
Oil seed rape	tonnes/hectare	2.43	2.53	3.43	3.01	3.18	3.37
Peas and beans	tonnes/hectare	2.75	2.99	4.0	2.99	3.74	2.69
Dessert apples	tonnes/hectare	9.64	11.59	11.76	10.89	10.56	10.39
Culinary apples	tonnes/hectare	12.66	12.23	16.77	14.64	14.98	13.85
Pears	tonnes/hectare	8.80	12.52	11.36	12.37	11.98	9.68
Tomatoes	tonnes/hectare	136.43	155.40	171.34	186.14	191.37	186.92
Cauliflowers	tonnes/hectare	19.65	16.72	20.18	18.56	20.12	18.06
Hops	tonnes/hectare	1.39	1.51	1.55	1.37	1.20	1.29
Milk	litres/cow	4444	4967	4749	4851	4940	4850
Eggs	no./bird	240.3	258.0	256.5	258.5	258.0	262.0

Source: Ministry of Agriculture, Fisheries and Food.

Key Points 8.1

- **The income elasticity of demand is the percentage change in amount of good purchased divided by the percentage change in income. Food products consistently have an income elasticity of demand that is very much below 1. Therefore, as income goes up, the percentage of total consumer expenditures going to food falls.**
- **Agriculture in developed economies has shown remarkable technological progress.**
- **The sluggish growth in demand for food in developed economies together with the increased productivity of agriculture means that in a free market there is downward pressure on farm prices and incomes.**
- **Some farmers receive low incomes simply because they produce very little output.**

short, the low-income problem is not so much because of depressed farm prices but really the small size of farming operations. Before examining what aid government might offer farmers let us examine another aspect of farm incomes, that is their instability. (Now read Key Points 8.1.)

Unstable Incomes

The pressure on prices in an unregulated agriculture is however only part of the pricing problems facing farmers. Farmers in an unregulated market also suffer from unstable prices. Year-to-year fluctuations in weather and livestock production result in price instability – unless there is government intervention. Once more simple demand and supply theory can be used to show the effect on price of, for example, a bumper harvest and one where there is a poor crop harvest. Note that we here are using the concept of elasticity again – this time concerning price and not income elasticity of demand.

Low Price Elasticity of Demand

Not only is the income elasticity of demand for agricultural products low; so too is the price elasticity – it is relatively price inelastic. Whereas the low-income elasticity was important for explaining the long-run downward trend in the farm sector, the low-price elasticity of demand is important for understanding the high variability of farmers' incomes in the short run.

Let us consider the change in price that results from an increase in supply due to abnormally good weather conditions. In Figure 8.4 we show the supply schedule shifting from *SS* to *S′S′*. It has shifted out to the right, indicating a large increase in production. Notice that the supply schedule here is fairly vertical, indicating that the *price elasticity of supply* in the short-run period under consideration is also quite small (at *E*). After all, once farmers have planted and cultivated their crops, they can supply no more and no less – unless, of course, they decide to store or destroy the crops.

What if the demand schedule is in addition relatively elastic, such as *DD* (at *E*)? The new equilibrium price in this case will be set at the intersection of the new supply curve *S′S′* and the demand curve *DD*, or at point *E′*. The old equilibrium price was established at point *E*, or at a price of P_e'. The new price of P_e obviously lies below the old price.

What if the demand curve is relatively *less* elastic, such as *D′D′* (at *E*)? The new equilibrium price will then be established at E″, and the new equilibrium price will be P_e'', which is even lower than P_e'. We see, therefore, that when there is a given shift rightwards in the supply curve, the more price inelastic the demand for agricultural products, the greater the decline in the market price. Conversely, for any shift leftwards in the

Figure 8.4

Consequences of a Relatively Inelastic Demand. The quantity of food produced per time-period is on the horizontal axis and the price per unit on the vertical axis. Assume that the original supply curve is *SS* – relatively inelastic supply in the short run at the current price. If the demand curve facing farmers is *DD*, a shift in the supply curve from *SS* to *S′S′* due to good weather will lower the equilibrium price from P_e to P_e'. But if the demand curve is instead *D′D′*, when the supply curve shifts to *S′S′*, the new equilibrium price falls to P_e''. This accounts for the large variability in incomes of farmers in different years.

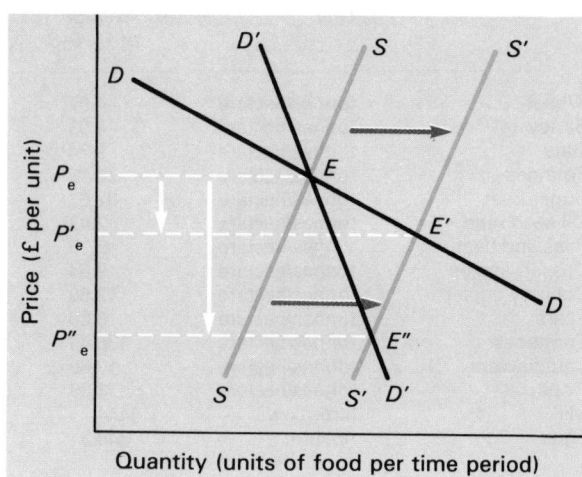

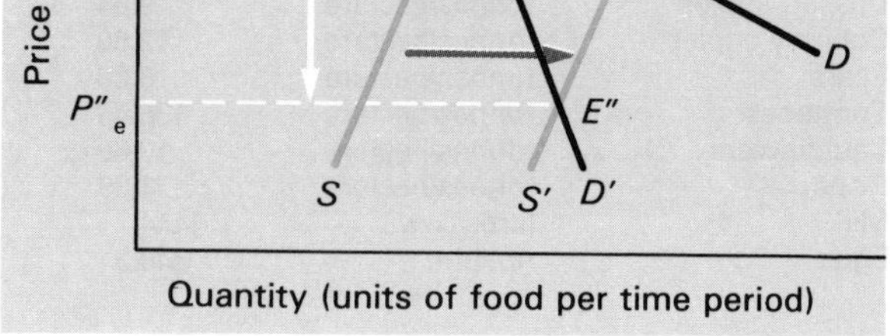

supply curve of agricultural products, the greater the price inelasticity of demand, the greater the rise in the market price of agricultural products. For example, if there is a drought, we expect prices to rise rather substantially due to the relative inelasticity of demand for food. Thus, we see that the relative price inelasticity of demand for agricultural products has also been one of the reasons that prices, and therefore farm incomes, have fluctuated more in agriculture than they have in other industries from year to year.

Figure 8.5 shows some estimates of the price elasticity of demand for certain items of household food consumption for 1987. Figure 8.6 shows the way in which total production and yields of cereal crops have varied in England and Wales over recent years.

Figure 8.5
Price Elasticity of Demand for Selected Foods

	Price elasticity
Liquid milk	−0.13
Bread	−0.25
Fruit juices	−0.65
Carcase meat	−1.17
Frozen peas	−0.75
Fresh potatoes	−0.14

Source: *Household Food Consumption and Expenditure 1987.*

The Effect on Farmers' Incomes

So far we have only demonstrated that for any given shift in the supply curve, the more price-inelastic the demand for food products, the greater will be the resultant change in the market-clearing price. Thus, when there is a bumper crop, the relatively price inelastic demand for food results in a relatively substantial drop in the market-clearing price for food products.

What, though, happens to farmers' incomes? Well, you have to go back to our discussion of the relationship between changes in price and changes in total revenues and consumer expenditures. This was discussed in Chapter 7. There we showed that any firm facing an inelastic demand would suffer a *decrease* in total revenues if it lowered price. This analysis holds for the total income in farming. Because farmers are facing a price-inelastic demand for food (that is, as a group they are undoubtedly operating in the inelastic portion of the *market* demand for food), a reduction in price – for example, from P_e to P_e'' in Figure 8.4 – will result in a reduction in total farm income.

The Cobweb

Agriculture differs from manufacturing industry due to the biological character of its form of production. Because of this the problem of price instability as just outlined is not an irregular phenomenon of this sector of the economy. Indeed we shall see that price fluctuations can take the form of fairly *regular* cycles over time. Figure 8.7 shows the ups and downs in the size of the cattle herd in the US. How can the successive expansion and contraction in the number of cattle be explained using simple price theory? We need only specify three conditions for such cyclical movements in farm output, and hence prices.

Assumption 1. There is a time-lag before an intended expansion in production actually is available for sale in market.

Assumption 2. The decision by producers to change their output is essentially taken on the basis of the current market price. Thus supplies in Year 2 are dependent on prices actually received in Year 1 rather than what is expected to be received in Year 2.

Figure 8.6
Production of Cereals in England and Wales 1984–9 ('000 tonnes)

Crop	*1984*	*1985*	*1986*	*1987*	*1988*	*1989*
Wheat	14 370	11 560	13 200	11 240	10 960	12 970
Barley total	8 490	7 780	7 720	7 160	6 750	6 030
winter	5 650	5 150	5 080	4 830	4 110	4 370
spring	2 840	2 630	2 650	2 330	2 640	1 660
Oats	395	505	365	315	375	385
Total Cereals	23 260	19 850	21 290	18 710	18 090	19 380

Cereal Yields (tonnes per hectare) in England and Wales

Wheat	7.71	6.37	6.93	5.96	6.15	6.52
Barley total	5.68	5.18	5.33	5.12	4.66	4.80
winter	6.15	5.54	5.69	5.46	5.26	5.33
spring	4.93	4.59	4.75	4.52	3.96	3.80
Oats	5.08	4.96	5.44	4.66	4.59	4.70

Source: Ministry of Agriculture, Fisheries and Food.

Assumption 3. Producers are many and they each take decisions to adjust their scale of production in isolation from each other.

The result of these three conditions is that if supplies happen to be scarce in one time-period the high level of the market-clearing price will prompt producers to begin a major expansion of production. This rise in production will in due course depress market prices which sets off a major contraction in the scale of production. Let us show how this is explained. In Figure 8.8 the fixed amount available in the short run means that the market-clearing price is OP_1. The supply curve indicates that at price OP_1 farmers would like to produce OQ_2. But they cannot do so until the next harvest (assumption 1). Suppose farmers plan to adjust output to the current market price and try to produce OQ_2 (assumption 2). If each farmer's micro-decision overlooks the consequences for total industry output – the macro-situation – then assumption 3 is fulfilled. If indeed output OQ_2 is actually harvested the market-clearing price will then be OP_2. Now the fulfilment of our assumptions will result in a contraction in production and higher prices. Note that in this example market prices move above and below the equilibrium level OP and are not stable. Depending on the nature of the supply and demand curves this instability of prices could be greater or less than as shown in Figure 8.8. (Now read Key Points 8.2.)

Can Anything Be Done to Help Farmers?

If farmers suffer from such major fluctuations in prices and hence incomes, what can be done about the problem? Is it a problem anyway?

Figure 8.7

The Ups and Downs in America's Cattle Herd. The apparent regularity of the movement in the size of the cattle herd in the US is striking. The cobweb theory helps explain this alternate expansion and contraction in cattle numbers.

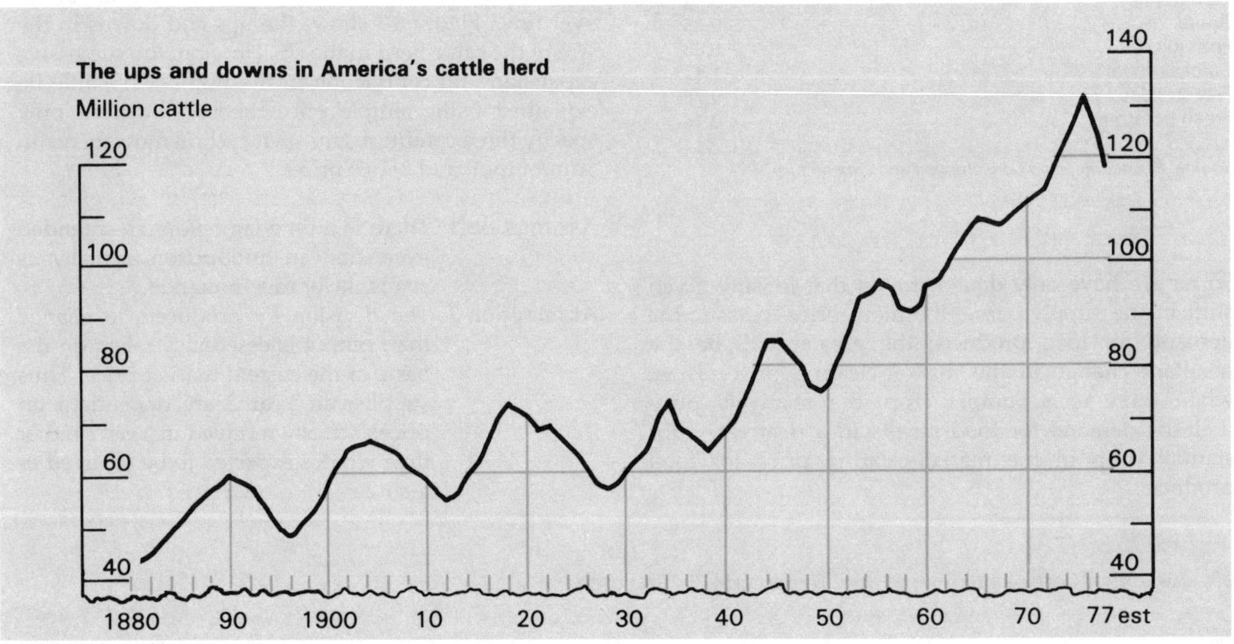

Source: 'Herd Instinct', *The Economist*, 26 Nov. 1977, p. 49.

Key Points 8.2

- **For any shift in the supply schedule, a firm facing a relatively inelastic demand curve will experience a larger fluctuation in the price of the product. It is argued that since the demand for food is relatively price-inelastic, the prices farmers receive for their products fluctuate more than in other sectors of the economy when there are shifts in supply.**
- **Farmers operate in an environment rather different from other sectors of the economy. When there are many, geographically separate decision-making units quite independent of each other and time-lags exist before planned changes in output are realized, market-clearing prices will be unstable.**

Figure 8.8

How Agricultural Prices Can Fluctuate. The market equilibrium is OP and quantity OQ but if there is a poor wheat harvest and no supplies are available from any other source it will be next year before extra supplies can be forthcoming. The fixed amount available – Q_2 – means a market, or short-run supply curve, effectively exists – the dashed line above OQ_1. The supply curve indicates that at price OP_1, farmers would like to produce OQ_2 but they cannot until the next harvest. If farmers try to produce OQ_2 and all of OQ_2 is harvested (note the assumption) then in the next year a big wheat crop will be harvested. The price will be OP_2. The price *could* oscillate around the equilibrium level OP but *never* actually at that level. A pattern can be drawn which looks like a spider's web, hence the **cobweb.**

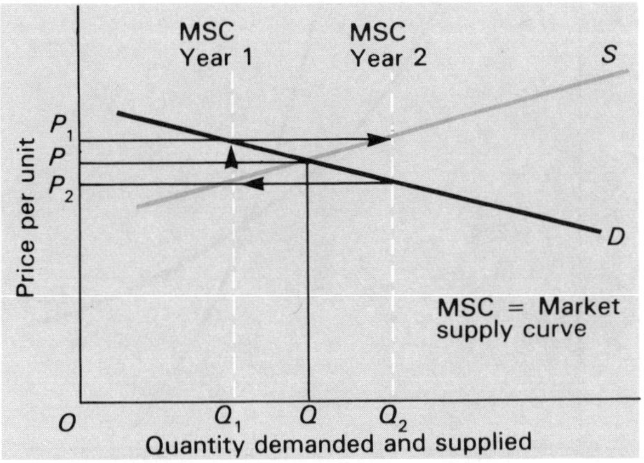

Figure 8.9

The Operation of a Buffer Stock. Buffer stock aims at maintaining the price of OP_3. If the harvest is plentiful buying QR could ensure a market price of OP_3 rather than OP_1. If the crop is poor, selling SQ would reduce the market price to OP_3 from OP_2.

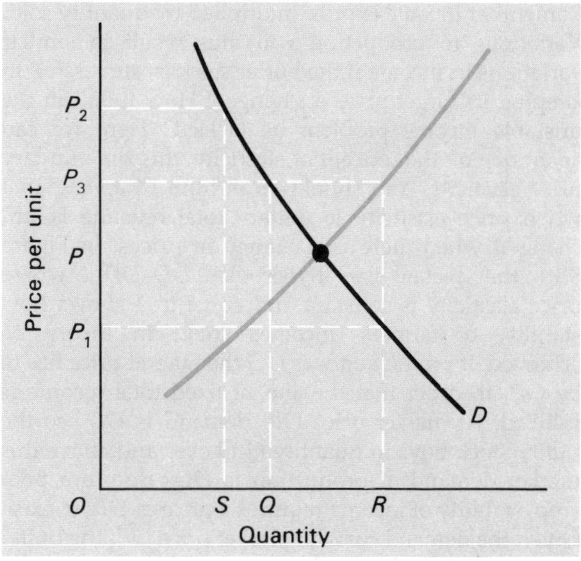

Many economists would agree that price instability in an unregulated agricultural sector results in a poorly working mechanism to effect resource reallocation. Where cobweb-type swings in production occur there is either an excessive expansion of production or an excessive reduction in production. Greater price 'stability' would avoid unnecessary changes in production and perhaps give farmers greater confidence about the future. We can recognize at once however that measures which aim at giving farmers greater price stability should not be confused with other policies that are explicitly intended to raise the incomes of farmers above free market levels. In fact the two issues tend to be difficult to separate completely from each other. We can show this in examining the **buffer stock** approach to meeting the problem of price instability.

Buffer Stocks

Price fluctuations might be minimized if an organization exists that buys in supplies in times of plentiful harvests and sells these when harvests are poor. Its purchases and sales could help to smooth out the course of market prices. In Figure 8.9 we show how such a buffer stock scheme might work.

If the buffer stock aims at maintaining the target price of OP_3 then it would buy up supplies which would otherwise result in lower market-clearing prices. In Figure 8.9 buying QR would avoid the fall in the market equilibrium price to OP_1. If, however, supplies were scarce then in the absence of intervention the market price would be OP_2. By selling SQ output at a price of OP_3 then the buffer stock organization would help to make the market price conform to its target price.

Such a scheme is assumed just to eliminate price fluctuations arising from variations in supply. If the target price is set at a level which corresponds to what the average free market price would have been for several time-periods then it should find its purchases and sales balance out. It is neither a net gainer of stocks, i.e. needs more storage capacity, nor is short of funds in order to purchase stocks when there is a bumper harvest.

Clearly those commodities that cannot be stored over time are immediately ruled out of consideration for any buffer stock scheme. But even where this problem of perishability does not exist such a scheme assumes that the target price is set at the appropriate level. If the target price turns out to have been set too high, i.e. above the actual average free market price, the buffer stock managers will find more activity in purchasing than selling. They will in fact need more physical space to store such production which has been bought in for stockpiling. The managers of a buffer stock scheme would also of course be facing the need of more financial resources. In order to keep prices stable by buying up excess supplies they might well need almost unlimited funds to carry on with the task! Perhaps you can appreciate therefore why buffer stocks while simple in concept involve tricky problems concerning their financing. Should farmers be left to finance the buffer stock or should their customers also be involved? Quite apart from their opposing viewpoints neither producers nor consumers have the perfect foresight possessed by Joseph of Old Testament times. Look up Chapter 41 in Genesis!

A buffer stock scheme may stabilize prices somewhat but does not solve the fluctuating income problem. Remember income is price multiplied by quantity sold. Variations in production will thus result in similar variations in income if the buffer stock is 'successful' in keeping its target price unchanged. How then can the unstable income problem be tackled? Here we can again deploy the concept of elasticity, this time unitary price elasticity. You should recall from Chapter 7 that when price elasticity is unitary total revenue is unchanged when there is a change in prices. In Figure 8.10 the rectangular hyperbola, DD–DD_1, where price elasticity is constant and equal to 1 shows how stability of farmers' incomes could in theory be achieved. If production was OQ the market price has to be OP_1 in order that the aim of fixed total income is fulfilled. At market price OP_1 demand is OQ_1 so the buffer stock buys in quantity Q_1Q over and above this market demand. If production is OQ_2 due to a poor crop, stability of income requires a price of OP_3 to exist. Given the demand curve at market price OP_3 the buffer stock needs to sell Q_2Q_3 from previously stored output. (Now read Key Point 8.3.)

Figure 8.10

Price and Income Stability. Demand curve DD–DD_1 shows unitary price elasticity of demand. If supplies are plentiful, i.e. OQ the required market price for income stability is OP_1 and Q_1Q needs to be purchased by the buffer stock. With a poor crop, i.e. OQ_2, the buffer stock can release some of its stocks Q_2Q_3 at the required selling price of OP_2. What relevance has price OP_4?

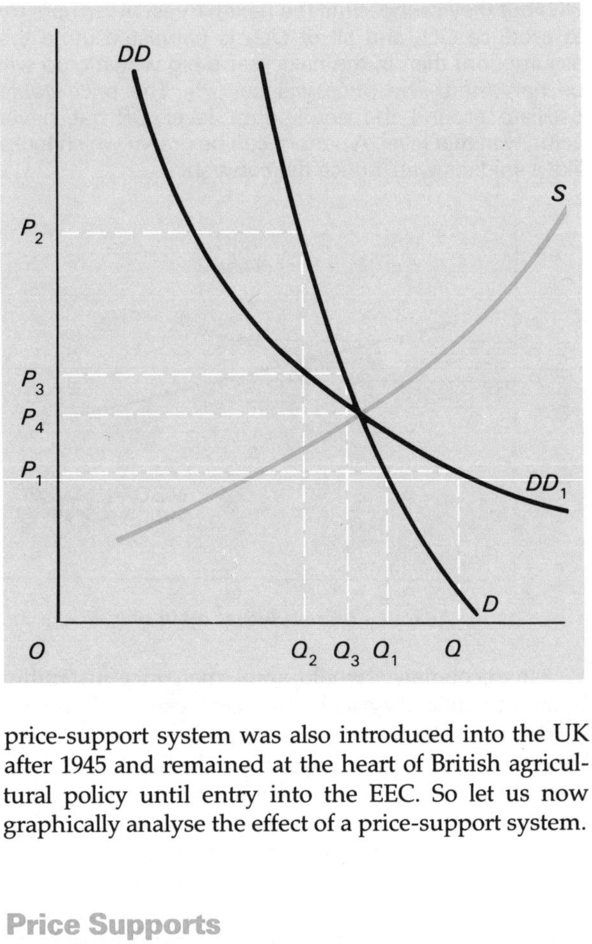

Government Policies to Help Farmers

So far we have used simple supply and demand analysis to illustrate the problem of price instability facing farmers. Let us now turn to use our understanding of price determination to show the implications of government intervention.

During the 1930s the farm sector in the United States suffered falling prices and incomes. The US government created the Federal Farm Board to begin price stabilization operations for poor farmers. The Farm Board was supposed to use the money to support the price of farm products so that farmers' incomes would not fall so much. Essentially it bought crops to keep their prices from falling. Then, when the Great Depression got into full swing, a system of **price supports** came into being. There have been some forms of price supports for wheat, feed grains, cotton, tobacco, rice, peanuts, soybeans, dairy products, and sugar. A type of price-support system was also introduced into the UK after 1945 and remained at the heart of British agricultural policy until entry into the EEC. So let us now graphically analyse the effect of a price-support system.

Price Supports

A price-support system is precisely what the name implies. Somehow the government stabilizes or fixes the price of an agricultural product so that it cannot fall below a certain level. Look at the supply and demand curves in Figure 8.11, showing the market demand and market supply of wheat. Competitive forces would yield an equilibrium price of P_e and an equilibrium quantity of Q_e per unit time-period. If the government

Key Point 8.3

- **In theory the problem of price instability facing farmers can be solved by a buffer stock buying in supplies when harvests are plentiful and selling its stocks when harvests are poor. In practice buffer stocks neither operate with ease nor solve the basic problem facing farmers which is variable incomes.**

sets the support price at P_e or below, obviously there will be no change, because the farmers can sell all they want at the market-clearing price, P_e.

Thus to achieve any help for farmers the government will set the support price above P_e – say, at P_s. At P_s the quantity demanded is only Q_d, but the quantity supplied is Q_s. That is, at the higher price, there is a smaller quantity demanded but a larger quantity supplied. The difference is the *excess quantity* supplied – *a 'surplus'*. Producers respond to higher market prices by producing more. That is why we show the supply schedule as upward sloping. At the higher prices, farmers are able to incur higher production costs and still make a profit. They will keep producing up to the point where the support price cuts the supply curve. The government guarantees to purchase everything the wheat-farmers want to sell at the price P_s. The government is therefore pledged to acquire the quantity of wheat represented by the distance between Q_s and Q_d in Figure 8.11.

The price-support system just described gives farmers the benefit of a guaranteed price and there is now not much significance in the market equilibrium – OP_e in Figure 8.11. But suppose the government wishes to allow market forces to operate more fully while still committing itself to assisting farmers? The guaranteed or target price system is one such answer. In the case of the UK a **guaranteed price** support system began after the Second World War and was at the heart of agricultural policy until British entry into the EEC. In 1973 the US government introduced a **target price** system which incorporates the same principles as the former UK policy. Let us explain how the guaranteed price system operates again with reference to a diagram.

Guaranteed prices differ from price supports in that the government guarantees that each farmer (who qualifies for inclusion in the system) will receive at least the guaranteed price. If the guaranteed price for wheat, for example, is £50 per ton, and the market-clearing price is £40 per ton, farmers may become eligible for so-called **deficiency payments** that will equal the difference between the guaranteed price of £50 and the market-clearing price of £40 times the total number of tonnes that the farmer has sold on the open market. A deficiency payment is simply another way to describe a direct subsidy paid to the farmer so the terms 'guarantee price', 'deficiency payment', and 'subsidy' are just what they seem to be. The government promised to make up the difference between the market-clearing price and the price which it deemed was appropriate that farmers should receive for their output.

Figure 8.12 shows the working of guaranteed prices in a graphic format. We have already analysed market price and the support price in Figure 8.9 where we showed that when the support price was greater than the market price, there would be an excess quantity supplied ('surplus') at the support price.

The concept of a guaranteed price is slightly different because it involves no direct purchase by government and, thus, no storage of the crop by government. In Figure 8.12 we show the market demand as *DD* and market supply as *SS*. At price P_T the quantity supplied will be equal to *QT*. At that quantity, however, consumers will only purchase it at P_c. Therefore, the subsidy to each farmer is equal to the vertical difference between P_T and P_c times the number of units that the farmer sells. We have labelled it 'per unit subsidy'. Guaranteed prices, therefore, lead to a greater use of resources, greater output, and greater consumption than in an unrestricted market. With this understanding of the effects of a guarantee system at work we need to pose the question who pays for this intervention? The funds required to pay farmers these *subsidies* obviously had to come from somewhere: using taxpayers' money meant that taxpayers were assisting consumers. In so far as rich people paid more in tax than poorer persons the farm support system in the UK was viewed by many as being socially acceptable. It was regarded as fair and enabled consumers to enjoy lower prices for food than would otherwise have been the case.

How did the price-support system affect Britain's overseas supplies of foodstuffs? We can now modify our diagram to show the effect of guaranteed prices on imports of food.

Figure 8.11

Price Supports. The quantity of wheat is measured on the horizontal axis and the price on the vertical axis. The domestic market demand and supply curves are given by *DD* and *SS*. Equilibrium is established at E with an equilibrium price of P_e and an equilibrium quantity of Q_e. However, the government steps in and sets a support price at P_s. At P_s the quantity demanded is Q_d and the quantity supplied is Q_s. The difference is the excess quantity supplied, or surplus, which the government must somehow take care of. One course of action actually adopted by the US government is to distribute surplus stocks of food to developing countries.

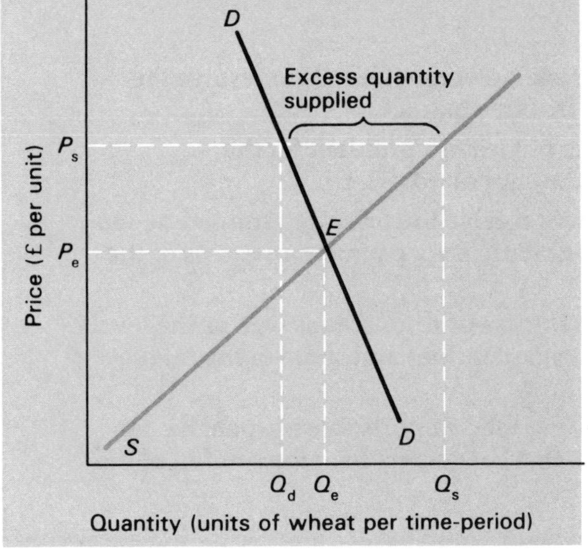

If we assume that overseas suppliers of, say, butter are willing to supply an unlimited quantity of food to the British market at a particular price then the supply curve will be perfectly elastic. If, for example, New Zealand was able to offer Great Britain butter at prices below which British farmers could not compete then the market price would be determined by the imported product.

Figure 8.13 shows that at the market price of *OW* imports of butter from New Zealand amount to *AD* and home-produced supplies to *OA*. The effect of the deficiency payment system is to raise the proportion of total supplies accounted for by home-produced supplies and diminish that of imports. The quantity of butter from New Zealand is now *BE* rather than *AD*. Thus the price-support system did not shut off supplies from abroad and deny British consumers the benefit of cheap food from countries who for geographical and climatic reasons were able to produce food at low cost. On the other hand the result of the price guarantees was to increase the degree of self-sufficiency of British food supplies.

Figure 8.12

Guaranteed Prices. We show the market demand curve, *DD*, and the market supply curve as *SS*. The intersection of *DD* and *SS* is at point E, yielding a market equilibrium price of P_e and an equilibrium quantity of Q_e. The government, however, sets the target price, P_T, above the market equilibrium price. The total market quantity produced will be Q_T. But that quantity, Q_T, can only be sold if the price, P_c is charged. Hence the market-clearing price is labelled P_c. This means that the government must pay a subsidy on each unit produced and sold of the vertical difference between P_c and P_T. This is labelled 'per unit subsidy'. Each farmer therefore receives a total subsidy of the per-unit subsidy times the number of units sold.

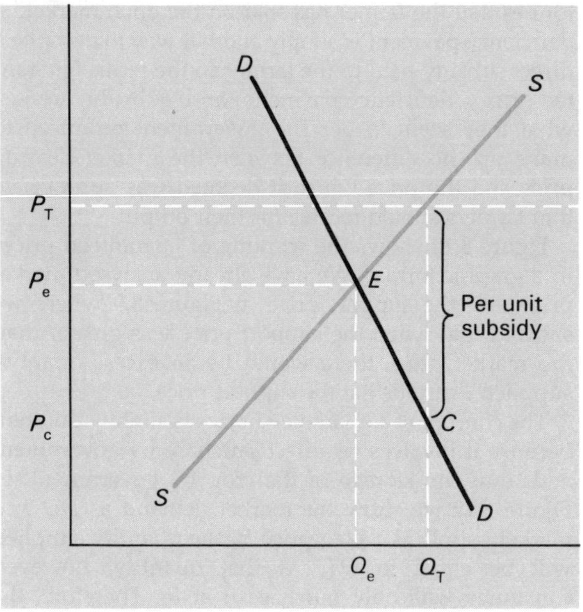

The EC System

On her entry into the European Community the UK began to move the basis of her agricultural support system over to an **import levy** system. Under this method of agricultural support the prices of imported foodstuffs are raised by levies to bring them into line with *target* prices. Figure 8.14 is a simple illustration of this system indicating how this policy results in consumers of food supporting farmers directly through high market prices. The levies on imported food are paid into a common farm fund known as FEOGA (the initials of its French title) which are partly used to subsidize the disposal of excess stocks. In so far as the EC's target prices have generally been well above world prices the cost of this method of agricultural support has been considerable. For some commodities the output of the Community's farmers has vastly exceeded consumption at the targeted price – hence the infamous butter 'mountains' and wine 'lakes'. The

Key Points 8.4

- **Governments in developed economies have tried several methods to resolve the problem of low and unstable farm incomes in a free market.**
- **Price supports can give farmers a stable price but leave a problem for the government to dispose of surplus stocks at the supported price.**
- **Guaranteed prices ensure that each farmer will receive the price determined by the government, and thus qualify for a subsidy or deficiency payment in excess of the newly determined market price.**
- **A guaranteed price system has an impact on the use of resources as well as the levels of domestically produced output, domestic consumption, and share of the market accounted for by imports.**
- **A farm-support system can be based on making food imports more expensive by imposing levies or taxes. This system means that consumers bear the burden of the policy rather than taxpayers.**

costly storage and subsequent disposal of these stockpiles has, not surprisingly, been a controversial one. Should excess butter supplies be offered at a substantial discount on world prices to the Russians? Why should low-cost suppliers like New Zealand who are non-members of the Community find their trade unfairly disrupted by the disposal of such stocks? (Now read Key Points 8.4.)

The Agricultural Problem in a Wider Context

Our brief review of farm-support programmes in the real world has illustrated how powerfully the theory of supply and demand can give us insights into present-day political issues. We can see why unregulated markets in the agricultural sector of the economy can work ineffectively. But government intervention, while trying to solve these free market weaknesses, itself brings further problems. In short we can appreciate that the interests of the farming community have posed a significant political issue for governments. But our case study of the operation of the market system has done more than just point to the implications of government intervention in the agricultural sector. You should note that we have moved the focus of our attention away from just one *closed* economy isolated from all others. Our analysis of the deficiency payments system and import levies pointed to the impact on countries other than our own. Modern economies are

Figure 8.13

The Impact of Deficiency Payments in an Open Economy. In the absence of guaranteed prices the world market price is determined by the lowest-cost supplier. If we assume that New Zealand could supply butter at a price of *OW* (the world price) then British farmers will supply *OA* at this price. Imports of butter thus dominate the UK market, being *AD*. The supply curve for both the UK and imports is thus *VYZ*. However, the effect of the guaranteed price *OG* stimulates home production and the UK share of the butter market increases from *OA* to *OB*. Imports are now *BD*. The supply curve for both the UK and imports is thus *VYPTZ*. Can you work out what the area *OGPB* means?

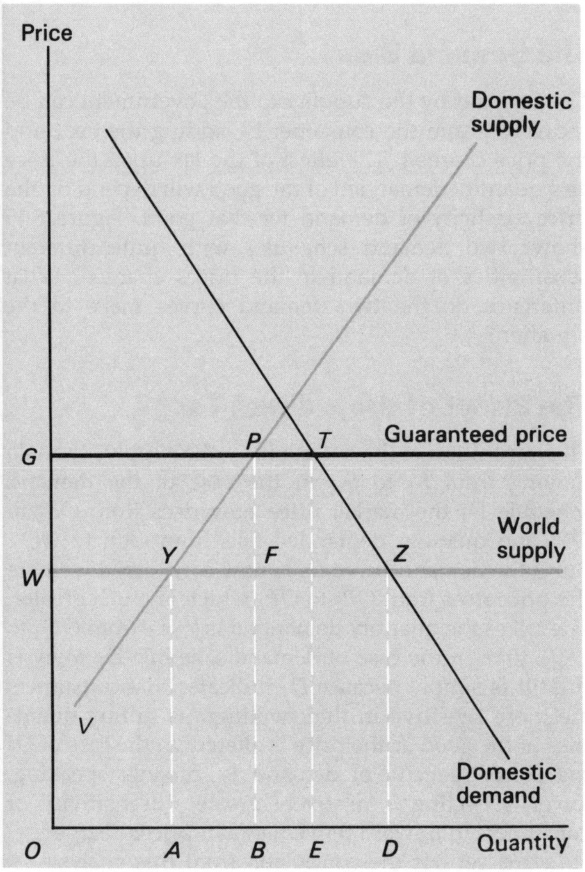

Figure 8.14

The Impact of Levies in an Open Economy. In the absence of a levy on, say, butter, the world market price is *OW* determined by the lowest-cost supplier. If we assume that New Zealand could supply butter at a price of *OW* (the world price) then British farmers will supply *OA* at this price. Imports of butter thus dominate the UK market, being *AD*. The supply curve for both the UK and imports is thus *JKM*. However, the effect of imposing. a levy *WL* stimulates home production and the UK share of the butter market increases from *OA* to *OB*. Imports are now *BC*. The new supply curve for both the UK and imports is *JKGF*. Can you work out what the area *GFEH* means?

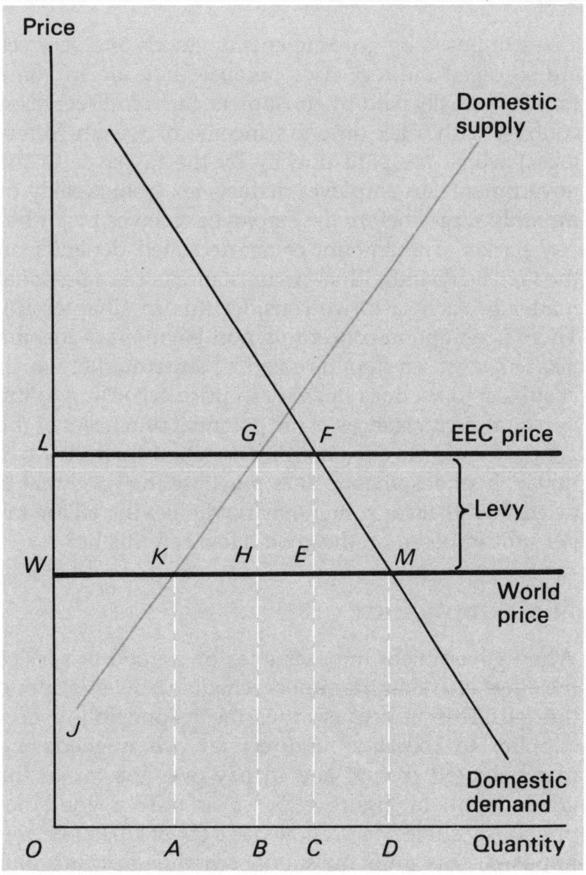

open economies, that is they are interdependent. Consumers in different countries demand goods and services from sources other than domestic suppliers. As we saw above in the case of agriculture government intervention has implications for the extent of international trade and exchange. We must therefore note the important point that government intervention in a domestic market can have an international dimension. Thus paying UK farmers more than they would receive given the existing world price means there is world resource allocation impact to be considered. We must look at the whole picture and not just the immediate and local part.

A second point to note about the case study of the agricultural sector is that it raises the important matter of how government intervention in markets is to be financed. We referred both to subsidies and levies on imports. The latter are, in effect, taxes on goods. Under the pre-1973 system the UK used tax revenues to subsidize domestic production. Where did these revenues come from? Under the current system the UK along with her EEC partners raises tax revenue by charging importers of food at the point of entry into the EEC. What we now need to do is examine in more detail how governments impose taxes on goods and services. Such taxes are known as *indirect taxes.* We shall aim to do this with the demand and supply model at the heart of the analysis.

Indirect Taxes

Taxes imposed by governments on goods and services are so-called indirect taxes because they are in some form eventually paid by consumers. Such indirect taxes contrast with a tax on one's income or wealth (direct taxes) which are paid directly by the taxpayer to the government. An employer deducts tax from weekly or monthly wages before the employee receives his or her pay packet. The amount of tax deducted depends on the taxpayer's individual circumstances. It is a personal matter in each case (we consider this in Chapter 10). There is no option concerning non-payment of income tax. However, an item on sale in a supermarket which is subject to tax does not vary in price according to the personal circumstances of the potential purchaser of the good. If someone does not buy the good then they pay no tax. Even if someone does purchase the good that is taxed then that consumer may not be paying all the tax per unit imposed on the good. How can this be?

The Supply Side

When government imposes a tax on a good or service the effect is to shift the supply schedule upwards and to the left. This is because it is the responsibility of a supplier to collect an indirect tax when goods are manufactured or sold and to pay over the tax to the government. In Figure 8.15 we assume a good not previously subject to tax now has a tax of £P_1P_3 per unit imposed. This shifts the supply schedule upwards and leftwards by an equal amount throughout the length of the original supply curve.

Figure 8.15

The Impact of Indirect Taxes. Demand schedule D_1 shows quantity demanded is more price-sensitive than is D_2. If the pre-tax price for both goods is OP_1 the price, post-tax, is OP_2 in the case of D_1 but OP_3 in the case of D_2.

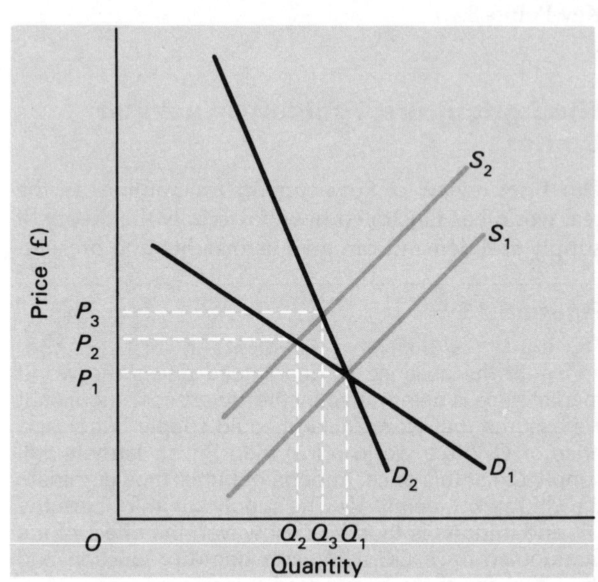

The Demand Side

The tax paid by the supplier to the government can be recovered from the consumer by adding the tax on to the price charged. The effect of the tax upon the price and quantity demanded of the good will depend on the price elasticity of demand for that good. Figure 8.15 shows two demand schedules with quite different sensitivities of demand to the prices charged. What difference do the two demand curves make to the situation?

The Effect of the Indirect Tax

The imposition of the tax results in the supply schedule moving from S_1 to S_2. In the case of the demand schedule D_1 the market price now rises from OP_1 to OP_2 and quantity demanded falls from OQ_1 to OQ_2. But if the demand curve D_2 is now considered we note the price rises from OP_1 to OP_3 which is much greater. The fall in the quantity demanded is less – from OQ_1 to OQ_3, than in the case of demand schedule D_1. Why is this? It is simply because D_1 indicates that consumers are more sensitive in their willingness to buy quantities of the good as the price is altered. In the case of D_2 the price elasticity of demand is, broadly speaking, lower, reflecting a relatively greater insensitivity of consumers to upward movements in prices charged.

Let us set out the conclusion from this analysis. A

government which wishes to raise tax revenue should impose indirect taxes on those goods the consumption of which is relatively insensitive to a tax-based increase in price. If demand for a good is highly price-elastic when the tax is imposed then the tax revenue obtained is less than where demand is less price-elastic.

Our conclusion may not seem too surprising. Thus cigarettes may seem to you to be a more obvious item to tax than say a tax on works of art. But a moment's reflection should make you realize that low price elasticity of demand for the commodity is not the only relevant aspect in selecting suitable bases for indirect taxes. Consumption of a good has to be sufficiently large for a tax to raise much revenue. Some foodstuffs as we saw in Chapter 7 have a low price elasticity of demand but taxing say butter and cheese may not be acceptable to a government. The price of basic necessities such as food has long been of political importance and thus governments have seen a more promising base for an indirect tax in the 'optional necessities' of tobacco and alcohol. Thus for many years the price charged for cigarettes, beer, wines, and spirits includes a large element of tax. These commodities need not be purchased although few citizens are total abstainers! Leaving aside the moral question of a government's revenues being at least partially dependent on the addiction of citizens to smoking and drinking, the choice of tobacco and alcoholic drinks as suitable bases for an indirect tax is quite understandable. But do smokers pay all the tax per unit that is imposed? This takes us to the matter of **tax incidence.**

Figure 8.16

The Incidence of Indirect Taxes.

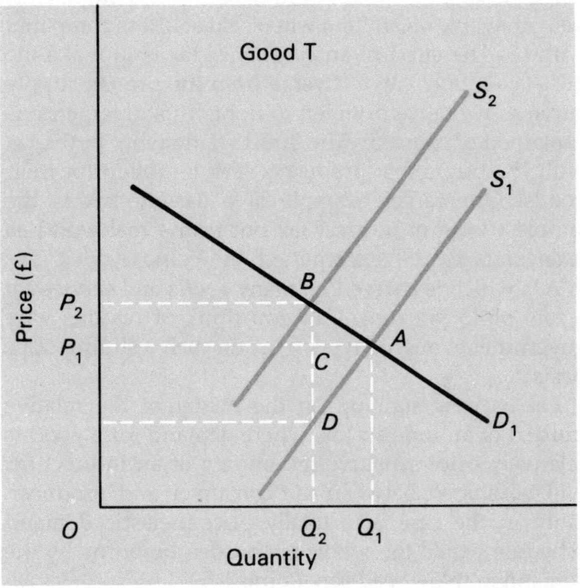

Good T		Good W	
Pre-tax price	QP_1	Pre-tax price	OP_3
Tax per unit	BD (=GI)	Tax per unit	GI
Post-tax price	OP_2	Post-tax price	OP_4
Consumer's burden	BC	Consumer's burden	GH
Supplier's burden	CD	Supplier's burden	HI

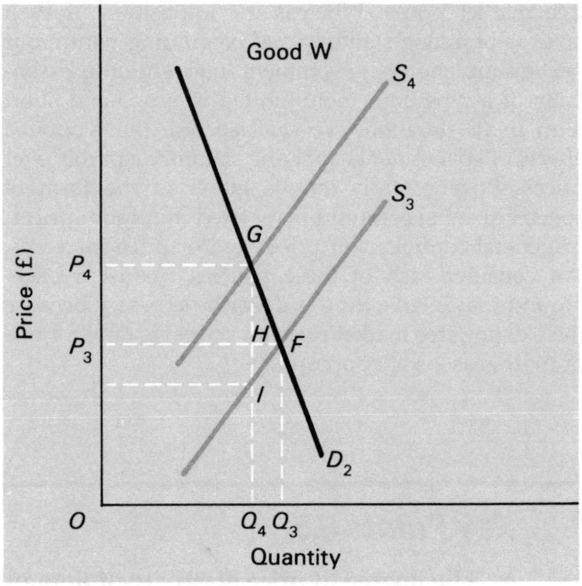

Tax Incidence

The term 'tax incidence' refers to the burden on whom a tax falls. Does it fall wholly on the consumer or does the supplier pay part of a tax?

Figure 8.16 shows the demand for two goods which have differing sensitivities of quantity demanded to prices charged. If a tax is now imposed on both goods which is of the same rate per unit what happens? In the case of good T the market price is now OP_2 rather than OP_1. The tax per unit is *BD* of which the consumer pays *BC*. In the case of good W the rise in the market price is from OP_3 to OP_4. Here the consumer pays *GH* of the same tax per unit *GI*. Clearly in the case of good T the consumer pays only a small part of the tax burden. The supplier has to bear most of the tax burden since demand is relatively price-elastic. In the case of good W the reverse happens: the supplier bears just the amount *HI* of the tax burden. The supplier is the more able to pass on the tax burden since demand for W is less sensitive than is the case with good T. The supplier of good W faces less of a difficulty in trading since his profit margin in selling good W is that much less squeezed. Both suppliers however bear some burden and face the issue whether they can somehow reduce the costs of selling these goods.

What would happen if the demand curve was perfectly inelastic rather than either of the two situations in Figure 8.16? Here you should satisfy yourself that the full impact of a flat-rate (or specific) indirect tax falls wholly on the consumer.

An *ad valorem* Tax

Our example of an indirect tax has been a flat-rate tax, such that the post-tax supply curve shifted to the left throughout its length by the same amount. If the tax varies according to the value of the item as charged by suppliers the tax is called an **ad valorem tax.** Thus a 10 per cent *ad valorem* tax would result in a higher tax being payable on an item when sold at £10 as compared with £5. The effect of an *ad valorem* tax is to make the post-tax supply curve diverge from the pre-tax supply curve as we move from left to right. This divergence is explained of course by the direct relationship of the tax with the prices that producers seek to obtain for their goods. Our earlier example of a flat-rate tax is the simplest form of indirect tax but in the real world *ad valorem* taxes are exemplified by Value Added Tax (VAT) which is charged on many goods and services at a rate of 15 per cent. Can you think of reasons why governments might favour a tax on such a sliding-scale basis?

Let us now sum up on the matter of the relative burden of an indirect tax: where demand for a good is relatively price-sensitive the burden of an indirect tax will be shared between the consumer and producer. Only in the case of a totally price-inelastic demand schedule would the whole tax burden be borne by the consumer. (Now read Key Points 8.5.)

Market Prices and Government Controls

In the final part of this chapter we move on from consideration of the impact and incidence of indirect taxes to another form of government intervention with free market prices. Whereas the imposition of such taxes is of a long-standing and continuing nature our next examination of government intervention is essentially of a type both more limited in scope and short term in its duration. We shall analyse the economic effects of governments applying statutory controls over prices. Price controls can be either in the form of specific fixed maximum prices, fixed minimum prices, or general controls over prices and/or price increases. We consider each of these policies against a background that intervention is deemed necessary because the existing free market price (or prices) is (are) for one or more reasons not appropriate.

Specific Fixed Maximum Prices

If the government fixes a maximum price in a given market below the existing market equilibrium price then that newly established price will have profound implications for the operation of that market. Why? Let us look again at the supply and demand dimensions with reference to Figure 8.17. In the UK and in several other countries rents that can be charged for property rented from landlords are subject to controls. The rationale for a maximum price to be charged is that it is necessary to keep the cost of housing as low as possible. Control of rents charged by landlords is usually one interference with the housing market: tax benefits for owner-occupiers paying for their houses with long-term loans or mortgages is yet another illustration of the social and political concern of governments with housing. Our concern here is not to query the motivation to influence the prices people have to pay for occupying either the houses they own or the property in which they are temporarily residing. But we can point out as an exercise in positive economics that Rent Acts and other policies which permit rent reductions have significant repercussions on both sides of the housing market – landlords and tenants.

In Figure 8.17 the demand for rented accommodation at the maximum rent that can be charged – price OP_1 – is OQ_3. But at this price – below an equilibrium price of OP_2 – landlords only supply OQ_1 and the distance Q_1Q_3 is unsatisfied demand at the rent OP_1. Those unable to obtain privately owned property can only try to buy a house or seek accommodation within the public sector. Landlords who are not prepared to make rented housing available at the controlled price may sell their property, leave it empty, or use it for purposes other than temporary accommodation. Whatever response the upshot is that the supply side contracts and thus a maximum rents policy really only benefits those fortunate to find and live in rented accommodation. Our analysis thus points to maximum rent policies discouraging the supply of rented private housing. In the UK we find this proposition has been borne out. Since the 1967 Rent Act the percentage of the total stock of dwellings accounted for by rented private accommodation has fallen sharply. Whereas in 1967 the figure

> ### *Key Points 8.5*
>
> - **The degree of price elasticity of demand at and around the given market price will be relevant to a government seeking to raise revenue by imposing an indirect tax.**
> - **The nature of the demand and supply schedules will affect how the incidence of an indirect tax is borne between consumers and suppliers.**
> - **Indirect taxes can be either at a flat rate per unit or where the tax per unit increases in proportion to the price charged (an *ad valorem* tax).**

was 24 per cent it fell steadily each year to 8 per cent by 1988.

Of course, maximum prices only have effects such as in Figure 8.17 if they are set below the equilibrium market price. If set at or above the equilibrium price then a maximum price will be of no consequence. You should convince yourself why this must be so: consider what the equilibrium price means.

Figure 8.17

The Market for Private Rented Accommodation. The free market equilibrium price is OP_2. A maximum price for rented property of OP_1, means demand is OQ_3 but supply available is only OQ_1.

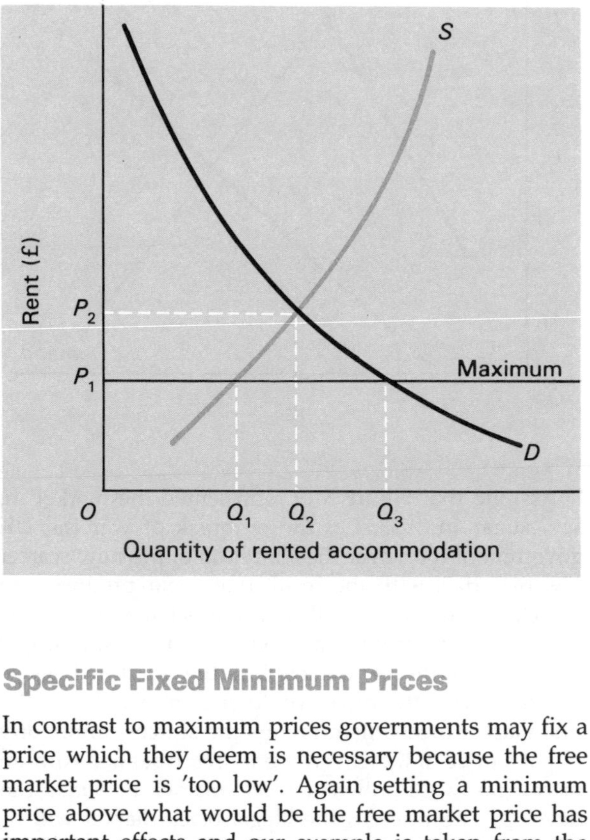

Specific Fixed Minimum Prices

In contrast to maximum prices governments may fix a price which they deem is necessary because the free market price is 'too low'. Again setting a minimum price above what would be the free market price has important effects and our example is taken from the labour market. In the UK there has been concern expressed by the government about the operation of Wage Councils which regulate minimum wage-rates. A debate has arisen between those who support such minimum rates and those critical of them. The latter argue employment would be greater if wage-rates were lower than at the regulated levels. Opponents argue that such state controls are a safety-net to prevent exploitation of workers by private employers. In the US there has been a long-running debate on the operation of minimum wage-rates. Let us see how we can understand the nature of the debate. As was pointed out earlier in this chapter, in the UK the regulation of minimum wage-rates is effected by Wage Councils. These Councils set legal minimum rates of pay for about 3 million workers employed in the manufacture of clothing and in several service sectors of the economy, such as hairdressing, laundries, catering, and retailing. Whether Wage Councils in these industries are actually desirable has recently become a political issue.

If you look at Figure 8.18 you can see that in an unrestricted labour market there will be an equilibrium wage-rate at which equal quantities of labour are demanded and supplied. What if a legal **minimum wage-rate** were set above the equilibrium wage-rate? Who benefits and who loses from the imposition of a minimum wage-rate above W? If a minimum wage W_m, which is higher than W_e, is imposed, the quantity demanded for labour is reduced to Q_D. Some of these workers may now be unemployed, but others may be employed at a lower wage elsewhere in the non-controlled sectors of the economy.

Figure 8.18

The Effect of Minimum Wages. The market-clearing wage-rate is W_e. The market-clearing quantity of employment is Q_e and is determined by the intersection of supply and demand at point E. A minimum wage equal to W_m is established. The quantity of labour demanded is reduced to Q_D; the reduction of employment from Q_e to Q_D is equal to the distance between B and A. That distance is smaller than the excess quantity of labour supplied at wage-rate W_m. The distance between B and C is the increase in the quantity of labour supplied that results from the higher minimum wage-rate.

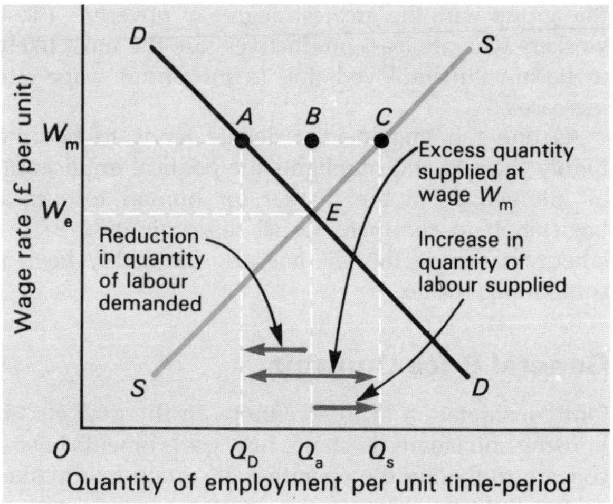

In the long run, some of the reduction in labour demanded will result from the reduction in the number of firms, and some will result from changes in the number of workers employed by each firm.

The effects of a minimum wage law depend crucially upon whether or not it is enforced. If the law is not enforced, it may have no effect whatsoever. The analysis of minimum wages is identical with the analysis of price controls. Although it is easy to analyse the effects of minimum wage legislation because the law spells out specifically which kinds of labour are covered and what exemptions are allowed, it still does not always follow that the minimum wage is effective.

Our analysis suggests that minimum wage legislation,

like price controls, benefits some but not others. In the United States a fair amount of empirical evidence has been gathered to demonstrate the unemployment effects of minimum wages on specific groups, such as teenagers. One study showed, for example, that there was a statistically significant reduction in the ratio of teenage to adult employment associated with increased minimum wage-level or coverage. The investigator estimated that a 1 per cent increase in the effective minimum wage reduces the teenage share of employment by 0.3 per cent. Teenage workers in the low-wage category clearly lose as a result of an increase in minimum wage-rates because high minimum wage-rates substantially reduce full-time employment, forcing teenagers into part-time employment or unemployment. Those teenagers who become unemployed are further disadvantaged because they have a very low probability of qualifying for unemployment benefit. Other studies suggest that only low-wage adult women appear to have gained from the minimum wage. They receive, as a group, higher wages than they would have received in the absence of the minimum wage.

Other studies have shown that minimum wage legislation weakens the economic status of those at the bottom of the distribution of earnings. The apparent redistribution of income that occurs as a result of the minimum wage appears to be from some 'have nots' to other 'have nots'. Additionally, low-wage workers who are the most skilled are the very ones who are not put out of work by increases in the minimum wage-rate. The group with the greatest degree of poverty – those workers who are least productive – are the most likely to become unemployed due to minimum wage-rate increases.

As one can imagine the debate tends to become highly charged and highlights the political implication of intervening in the market for human resources. Legislation to eliminate sexual discrimination in the labour market in the UK has also inevitably been a contentious matter.

General Price Controls

Our consideration of interventions in the markets for housing and labour illustrates how governments have a concern to modify the operation of certain free market prices. But governments also have a general concern about the pace at which *all* prices move upward. This concern is not new. In 1800 BC the ruler of Babylonia decreed that anyone caught violating his wage and price freeze would be drowned. In AD 301 the Roman Emperor Diocletian fixed the maximum price of beef, grain, eggs, and clothing and prescribed the death penalty for violators.

Moving to more recent times we should note that during the Second World War many countries imposed **price controls** on a wide range of goods and services. Such controls gave rise to the problem of their enforcement and thus control of **black markets**. We can analyse the effect of a black market by reference to the supply and demand diagram in Figure 8.19.

Figure 8.19

Black Market and Rationing. The market-clearing price is OP_1 in peacetime and OP_2 in a wartime economy. Price control at the level OP_1 means the black market price is OP_3. At the controlled price *CE* is the excess demand. Rationing distributes the available supplies *OB* (P_1C) when demand at the controlled price is *OA* (P_1E).

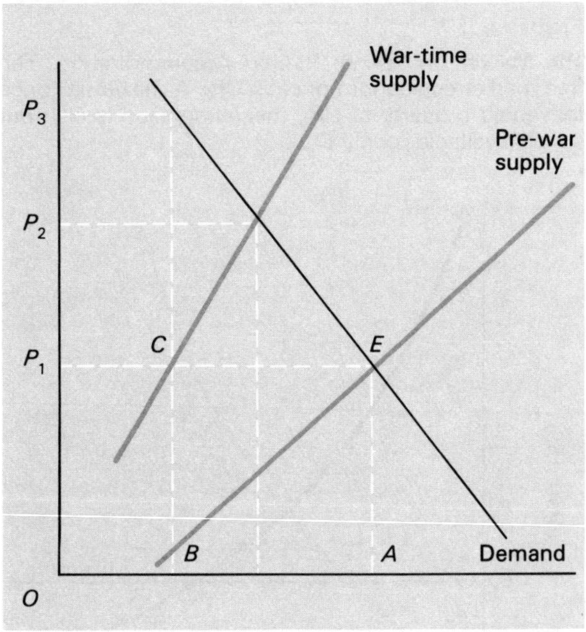

Assume that Figure 8.19 represented the market in, say, sugar in 1938. On the outbreak of war the UK government took over the allocation of the now scarcer raw materials with the result that sugar producers in the UK (in common with many other manufacturers) were unable to produce as freely as in 1938. The supply curve then shifted to the left with the result that, left to market forces, the price would rise from OP_1 to OP_2. The market mechanism rations the scarcer commodity but at a price. If the government prescribes a maximum price of say OP_1 then a black market in sugar can develop. The price in the illegal black market will be bid up to OP_3 because that is the price at which all available supplies can be sold. The distance *CE* represents the shortage at the controlled 'white market' price. If, as seems likely for social reasons, the government is unable to accept the working of the price mechanism in distributing available supplies what can it do? If it rejects a 'first-come-first-served' method by which the scarce supplies are distributed then some rationing system is necessary. What this means is that households are allocated coupons on a regular basis by which they are entitled to claim at least some sugar per week or per month. The quantities may be less than those for which many are prepared to pay. But at least the rationing system meets the objection that because there is not an equal distribution of incomes the free working of the price system is unjust in its operation. How else can it be ensured that pensioners and those on low incomes obtain some sugar and other basic foodstuffs?

Price controls thus tend to require the introduction of rationing systems. In a normal peacetime market economy neither is necessary. But that does not mean that the issue of food and other prices is not still politically important.

As we shall see in Chapter 11 the rate of movement of prices in general has been the key aspect of the Thatcher government's economic policies. But the concern is not new since nearly all post-war UK governments have resorted to policies to control the rate of price inflation. By inflation we mean a sustained and persistent rise in prices. Sometimes governments have used statutory or formal means to moderate the pace of inflation. At other times the policies used have been informal and relied on voluntary co-operation rather than legal sanctions to achieve results. Sometimes the emphasis is on controlling the rate of increase in wages in the belief that wage costs are the key element in determining prices. Yet other policies have been almost solely concerned with limiting price rises irrespective of any justification. The proper place to appraise general policies affecting the whole or greater part of the economic system is within the macro section of this book and hence is deferred till Part E. But we can from a micro-perspective emphasize the need to examine the supply and demand aspects of a rise in the price whether it be of one good or many goods. There is, as we have seen, upward pressure on the price level if the demand schedule moves to the right and/or the supply schedule shifts to the left. Artificial limits on prices prevent *market forces* from working themselves out. A kettle of boiling water cannot be controlled by fixing down the lid if there is a force of heat at work be it gas or electricity. At some point the build-up of pressure will force off the lid and have possibly serious effects. The market system adjusts to supply and demand pressures and there are dangers if the government pursues a policy of allowing only uniform rates of increases in wages and prices. Why is this? If prices cannot move according to the circumstances of particular markets then the resource allocative function of prices cannot operate properly. If relative prices get out of line then inappropriate signals are being conveyed. For example if the government has a statutory policy which permits only a flat-rate increase in wages then those who receive lower wages than the average for all workers are relatively better off. This effect may be viewed as socially desirable but there will be, by definition, a narrowing of the wage differentials between the wages for different occupations. Firms who seek people in skilled jobs cannot pay them more in order to attract them. If there is a shortage none is indicated by the wage signal in the labour market. The same difficulty arises with a statutory prices policy. In practice, governments recognize that such policies need to be flexible and allow for special circumstances. They have always learned that everyone claims to be a special case requiring relaxation from the general adherence to the norm! How many exceptions can there be before no policy is left in force?

Key Points 8.6

- **Governments tend to modify the operation of equilibrium prices for social and political reasons. Specific maximum price and minimum price controls have effects arising from the mismatch of supply and demand.**
- **A maximum price fixed below the equilibrium level results in a shortage of supply relative to quantity demanded.**
- **A minimum price above the equilibrium results in a surplus of supply relative to quantity demanded. General price controls raise the possibility of relative prices being distorted and the signalling function of the price mechanism not working effectively.**

CASE STUDY

The Desert Blooms in Saudi Arabia

Deep in the Saudi desert the giant sprinklers turn slowly round, showering the crops with precious water pumped from far beneath the ground. Hundreds of green circles, each up to 200 acres in size, stand out in lush contrast to the land around. In parts, the desert really does bloom.

It may soon begin to wither. According to Western geologists, subterranean aquifers tapped to turn the desert green are running dry. A report by the United States Department of Agriculture (USDA) says that little more than a tenth of the water used in Saudi Arabia comes from 'renewable' sources – rivers, wells replenished by rainfall, desalination plants. The rest, some 18 bilion cubic metres a year, is 'fossil' water pumped from deep aquifers which filled up thousands if not millions of years ago, before the climate of Saudi Arabia turned arid. Most of the water is used for irrigation.

Saudi Arabia's reserves of 'primary' fossil water hold about 340 billion cubic metres of extractable water. Deeper, 'secondary' reserves could yield 160 billion cubic metres more. It is unlikely that other large sources of underground water will be discovered. If water consumption continues to grow at over 10% per year, says the USDA, the aquifers could be exhausted within ten or 20 years, putting an end to most of Saudi Arabia's expensive venture in farming. In some central parts of the country water tables have already sunk to depths at which pumping is no longer economic.

Replacing underground water may not be possible, despite heady talk of piping water from the Shatt al-Arab in Iraq (as Kuwait is planning to do), from rivers in Turkey, or from the Nile (by pipe and tanker across the Red Sea). Outlandish plans to tow icebergs from the Antarctic are being reassessed. But water is unlikely to be obtained in quantities large or cheap enough to use for irrigation. Growing a single tonne of cereals using desalinated water costs an impossibly high $3 500.

It will nevertheless be politically difficult for Saudi Arabia to drop its cherished aim of reaching self-sufficiency in food. In the past decade the government has spent billions of dollars to turn thousands of acres of barren desert into productive farmland. Generous subsidies and high support prices have encouraged farmers to grow 35% of the country's food, up from only 15% five years ago. Saudi Arabia produces exportable surpluses in wheat, eggs and dairy products. But the cost of making its desert bloom makes many economists wilt.

Growing wheat in Saudi Arabia is as expensive as growing melons under glass at the north pole. This year, egged on by government support prices of $400–530 a tonne, farmers will produce over 3m tonnes of the stuff (compared with only 3 000 tonnes in 1976). With Saudi wheat consumption running at only 800 000 tonnes a year, around 2.2m tonnes of expensive wheat will be sold abroad – Russia is a big customer – or given away. The cost to the Saudi exchequer is over $1 billion. Importing the wheat from abroad would cost a mere $120m.

The government says subsidized farming has spread national wealth (though the biggest beneficiaries have been rich investors) and halted the drift from the land. But even if the government is prepared to go on pumping petrodollars into farming, the rapid depletion of water supplies means that the desert will not bloom as widely in future. The production of thirsty crops such as cereals will inevitably have to be cut back in favour of more frugal high-value crops for export. Some experts believe the precious fossil water should not be used for farming at all, but preserved for future industrial needs. Halting the profligate use of water in agriculture will not be easy. Subsidies have created a powerful lobby, which has resisted attempts to cut support prices.

Farming the desert is one of the few goals Saudi Arabia's conservative King Fahd shares with Libya's Colonel Qaddafi. For the colonel, this means pumping water in huge pipes from under the Sahara to the more fertile coastal region. The 'Great Man Made River' is expected to cost $25 billion, and thus be one of the most expensive engineering projects in the world (twice the cost of the Anglo-French Channel tunnel). It is intended to double Libya's water supply, mainly to provide irrigation for 500 000 acres of cereals and grazing for 2m sheep and 200 000 cattle.

The first stage of the project is due for completion in two years' time. It is unlikely to achieve its aim of making Libya self-sufficient in food. Like those of Saudi Arabia, the deep Saharan aquifers are non-renewable (though experts disagree fiercely on how long they are likely to last). In any event, most of the water the man-made river does eventually carry to the coast is likely to end up being used by homes and factories, leaving relatively little for farming.

Source: 'Arab Agriculture: Just add Water', *The Economist*, 15 July 1989.

Questions

1. How does the case study illustrate that agricultural production can be responsive to government intervention?
2. In what way can the concept of opportunity cost be applied in this case study?
3. What international repercussions are apparent from the Saudi government's agricultural policies?

CASE STUDY

The Economics of the Common Agricultural Policy

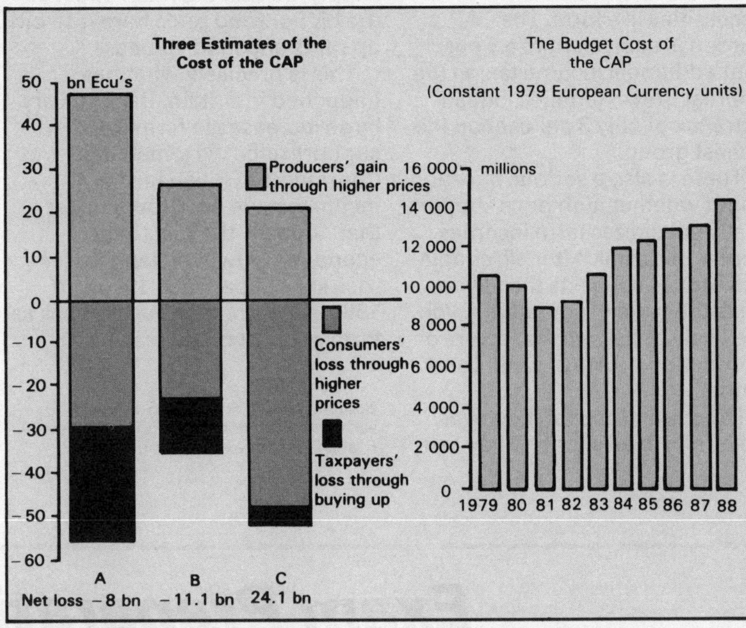

Anger is not a diplomatic emotion, but if anyone could be justifiably angry at the EEC's Brussels summit this week, it is the Prime Minister. Mrs Thatcher thought that she had wrapped up a deal at the Fontainebleau summit in 1984 at which Britain conceded an increase in the revenues available to the European Community, on condition that strict 'budgetary discipline' was applied to the Common Agricultural Policy (CAP). Rarely can a commitment have been confounded more completely.

Nearly four years on, the Community is coming back for more 'own resources' to fill its coffers, but the main reason for its problems is once again soaring expenditure on the CAP. Indeed, the average annual real rise in CAP spending before Mrs Thatcher extracted her promise was under 1 per cent. In the four years since, the average annual rise had been nearly 4 per cent.

There are always excuses, of course. The reason for the sudden surge in agricultural costs this year is the fall of the dollar, which means that the gap between EEC farm support prices and those on world markets has yawned far wider. Since large export subsidies are paid on many of the Community's food surpluses in order to persuade non-Europeans to consume them, the budget cost is going through the roof.

In reality, though, there are miserable long-term trends. When EEC production is less than consumption, these higher prices can be enforced by import levies designed to bring the price of imports up to the fixed price. That was the happy budgetary situation in the Community for many years: consumers paid the subsidy to farmers through higher prices. The tax cost of the policy was minimal.

The problem for the EEC was simply that its high food prices encouraged rapidly growing production. As production gradually exceeded consumption for commodity after commodity, so prices in EEC markets could only be supported by direct official buying of goods for storage or official subsidies for export. The consumer cost does not vanish, but the budgetary cost thus begins to rise one for one with the rise in production. Three estimates of consumer losses through higher prices, budgetary costs of support, and farmers' gains are shown in the graph. They vary in part because they refer to different years, and the gap between prices on world markets and on EC markets varies.

Put those losses into some sort of perspective: the higher prices paid by consumers are worth about 1.2 per cent of Community national income, with an additional 1 per cent of national income going in tax-payer costs. That means that a typical European family of four is paying an extra £300 a year through higher food prices, and a further £250 a year as tax-payers. About 40 per cent of all the value 'created' on European farms – itself no more than 3–4 per cent of total EEC output – comes straight from consumers and tax-payers.

If it could be demonstrated that this expenditure was in a worthy cause, it might be justified. But this monster of a policy is probably the single most ineffective piece of government intervention the entire length and breadth of Europe. It fails lamentably to achieve its own objectives, and its costs go far beyond even the direct and indirect consumer and budget costs detailed above – or the net loss once producers' gains are netted out.

The CAP particularly benefits farmers who produce a lot, and who therefore gain most from the advantage of its high, official prices. The richest quarter of farmers receive about three-quarters of the CAP's subsidy. Yet it is pressure from the three-quarters of farmers with relatively small farms, and hence small incomes, which causes farm prices to be held high.

The second inequity is that the consumer loss through high prices falls disproportionately on those with low incomes, because poor families spend a higher share of their income on necessities like food. The CAP burden is equivalent to a 6 per cent additional income tax on the poorest British families, but an extra tax of only 3 per cent on the richest group.

There is also a serious question about whether high price support really subsidizes farm incomes very much at all. After all, simple economics suggests that if you raise the price of something, you are likely to help *all* the factors of production – labour, capital and land.

Labour and capital, however, are not in fixed supply. They can be sucked in from outside the farm sector, thus gently raising the price of all labour and all capital, and employing rather more in farming that might otherwise be the case. However, land is very largely in fixed supply, so that the main effect of the higher food price here is to bid up rents and land values.

This is precisely what has happened in Britain. Despite very large increases in farm price support since we joined the Community, British farmers' incomes have not grown faster than those in the rest of the economy. However, land prices rose sixfold between 1970 and 1982 – and are now easing back as farm support is squeezed.

Sources: OECD, *Economic Studies*, no.9; author's calculations from EEC data. Note: A, B, and C are three estimates of the CAP.

Questions

1. With reference to the data in the case study explain how the impact of the CAP needs to be considered from two standpoints – the losses of both consumers and tax-payers.
2. Why is it suggested that for both farmers and consumers the benefits of the CAP are questionable?
3. Explain how the CAP has had an impact on the market for the factors of production?

Exam Preparation

PRACTICAL EXERCISES

The charts show the relationship between the world prices for butter, sugar, and cereals and that in three parts of the developed world the US, Japan, and the European Community. Study the three charts and answer the following questions.

1. Explain how the charts illustrate the way in which some developed countries protect their domestic agricultural sectors.
2. The CAP has been the subject of much critical comment. What perspective is apparent in comparing the European Community with the US and Japan in the charts?

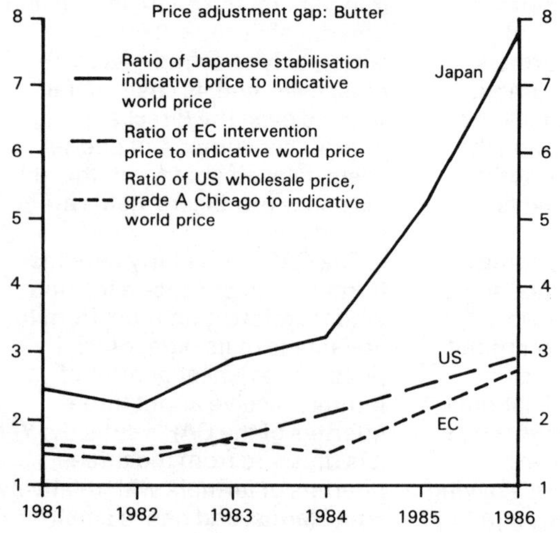

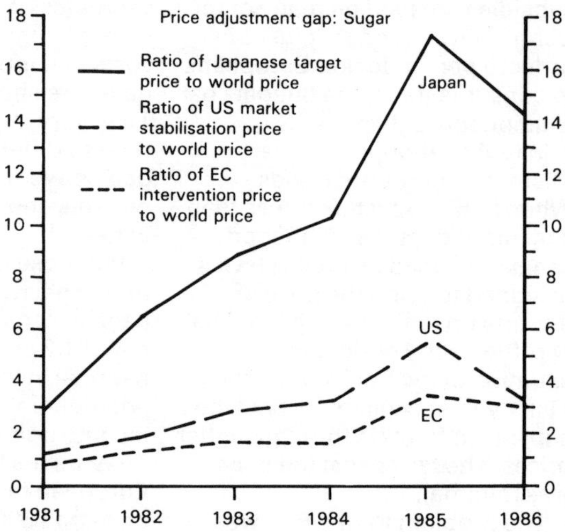

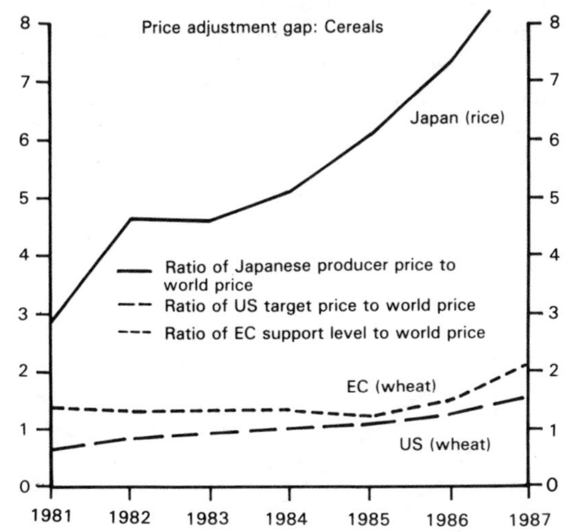

Source: The Treasury, *Economic Progress Report,* no.194, Feb 1988.

MULTIPLE CHOICE QUESTIONS

1. The diagram below illustrates the effects of a specific tax placed on a good. Which of the following represents the total tax receipts?

A RWXQ
B RWYP
C RWZQ
D QXYP
E QZYP

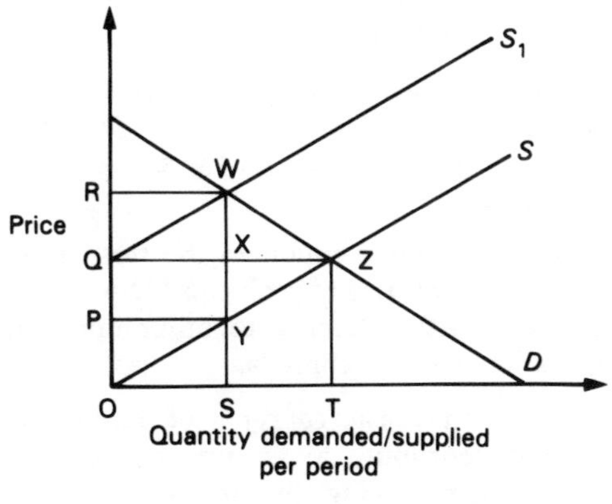

2. Economic theory predicts that controls which establish rents for housing below the equilibrium price

A will improve the quality of rented property supplied to customers
B are an effective method of dealing with excess demand for rented property
C will be effective in reducing the inflation rate
D will increase the revenue of property owners
E will reduce the quantity supplied of rented property available in the future.

3. Which diagram (**A**, **B**, **C**, or **D**) illustrates the effect on the price and sales of tobacco of an increase in the specific duty per tonne?

A

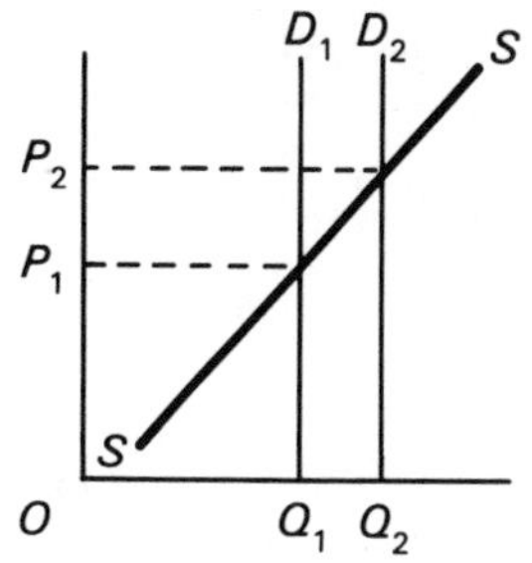

B

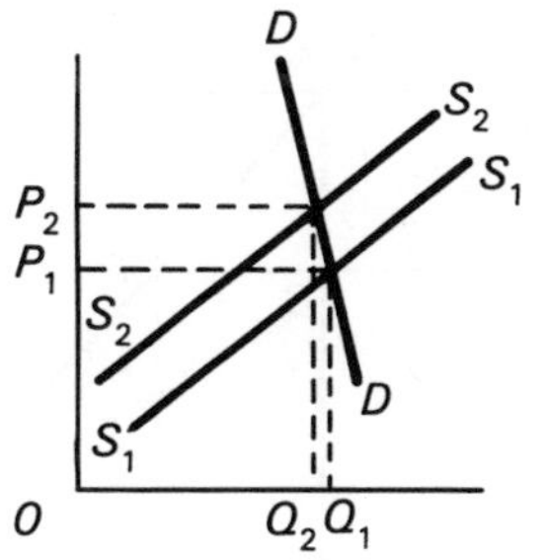

C

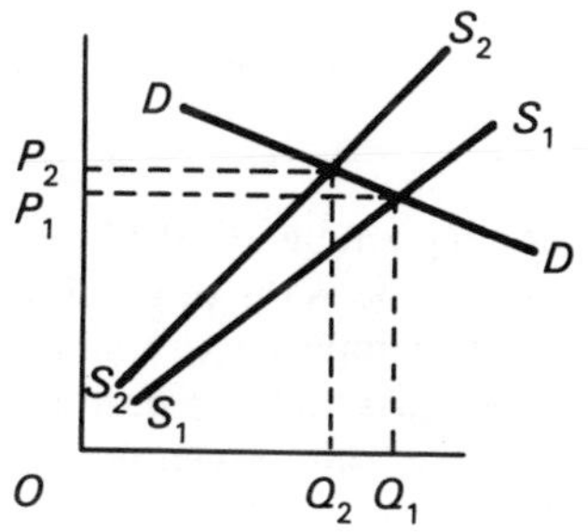

D

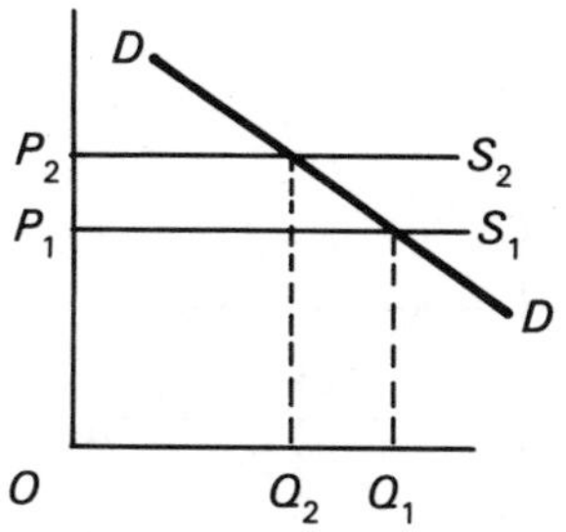

4. If a government imposes a maximum price on a commodity, then

A there will be an excess quantity supplied
B conditions for a black market will be created
C illegal price cutting will be encouraged
D stocks of the commodity will increase
E the new price will be above the equilibrium price

5. The diagram below shows the market supply and demand schedules for a particular agricultural product. The government decides to fix the price at *OM* by buying in the open market. Which area in the diagram represents the government's expenditure?
A OMNR
B RNUQ
C PMNT
D RNTQ
E NUTS

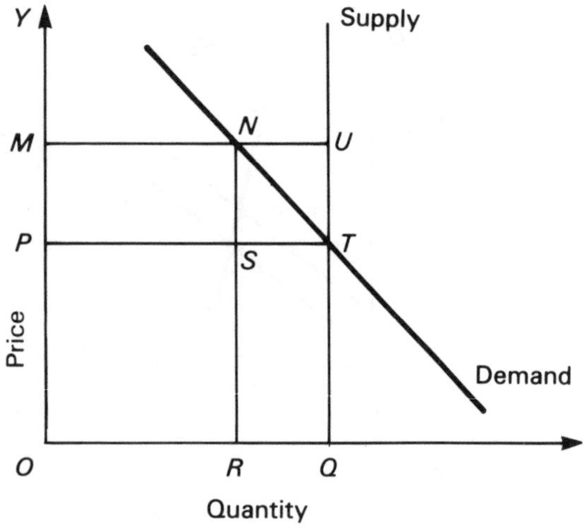

6. In the diagram below *DD* is the demand curve for good X. *SS* is the original supply curve and S_1S_1 is the supply curve after a flat-rate subsidy has been given to the producers of the good. The total subsidy given is represented by the area
A MNET
B ONRK
C MNRF
D OPWK
E MPWF

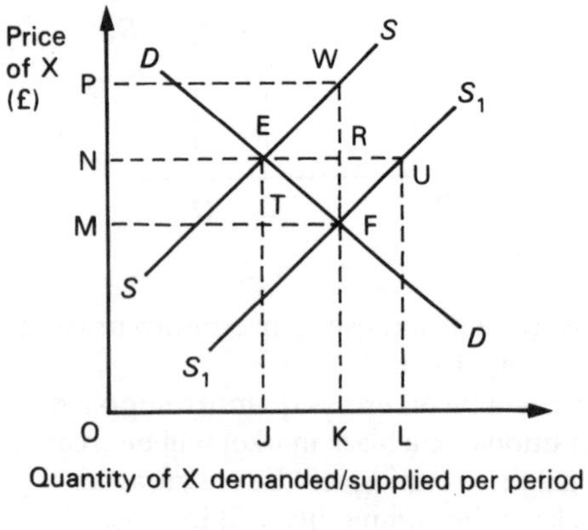

7. D_1D_1 and S_1S_1 are the original demand and supply curves for a consumer good, and the original equilibrium price is indicated by the letter X. If the government imposes an *ad valorem* tax on the good, which of the points labelled **A–E** will be the new equilibrium price?

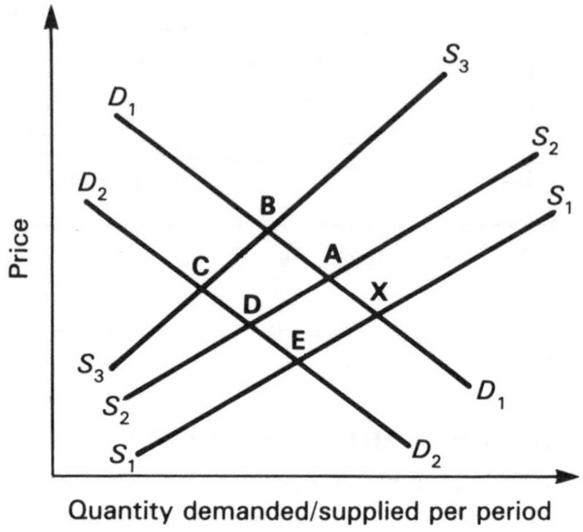

RELATED ESSAY QUESTIONS

1. Show how buffer stocks may be used to stabilize commodity prices and outline the possible effects on producers' incomes.

2. Explain fully what is meant by price elasticity of demand. How would knowledge of demand assist a government wishing to levy indirect taxes?

3. 'Government intervention in the free market inevitably gives rise to problems.' Discuss this statement with reference to minimum wage legislation and rent controls.

4. How can the basic concepts of supply and demand contribute to an understanding of the problems facing producers of primary products?

5. 'Agriculture is one of the few examples where there is a strong case for government intervention.' Discuss.

6. How do (a) rent controls and (b) tax relief on mortgages affect the market for housing?

7. What is meant by 'income elasticity of demand'? Explain the relevance of this concept to decisions taken by (a) producers of manufactured goods, (b) farmers, and (c) a government.

9 Demand and Supply in an Open Economy: International Trade and Exchange

Key Points to Review

- Opportunity cost (1.5)
- Production possibilities curve (1.5)
- Demand (5.1, 5.3)
- Supply (5.4)
- Equilibrium, surplus, shortage (5.7)
- Specialization and comparative advantage (6.2)
- Price elasticity of demand (7.1)

Questions for Preview

1 What is a foreign exchange rate?

2 What is a floating exchange rate system?

3 What is a fixed exchange rate system?

4 What is the difference between the current account and the balance of payments?

5 What are some arguments against free trade?

Thus far in this book we have noted differences between countries as to how their economic systems operate and perform. But we have not examined the interrelationships *between* countries in the sense of how international transactions take place. It is the purpose of this chapter to move on from examining markets in a domestic or internal context to analysing international markets.

When we talk about international trade, we refer to the movement of goods and services from one country to another. We must now make reference to the way in which world trade in goods, services, and financial assets is financed. How does the UK pay for its imports? How does the rest of the world pay for exports from the UK? These are questions that we will cover in this chapter. We will describe several alternative international financial systems. We will look at flexible (or floating) exchange rates and fixed exchange rates. Additionally, we will examine the measurement and the components of the balance of payments. We will follow the same approach as earlier in this book. At the outset of our analysis we assume a world where foreign exchange markets are not affected by government intervention. Then, as in Chapter 8, we will examine the nature of such intervention in international markets.

Floating, or Flexible Exchange Rates

When you decide to buy foreign products, such as French wine, you have pounds with which to pay the French wine-maker. The French wine-maker, however, would be hard pressed to pay his or her workers in pounds. The workers are French, they live in France, and they need francs to buy goods and services in that country. There must therefore be some way to exchange pounds for the francs that the wine-maker will accept. That exchange occurs in a **foreign exchange market**, which, in this case, specializes in exchanging francs and pounds. The particular exchange rate between francs and pounds that would prevail depends on the interaction of the demand for and supply of francs and pounds. In a sense, then, our analysis of the exchange rate between pounds and francs will be familiar for we explained supply and demand in Chapter 5. If it costs you 20p to buy one franc, that is the **foreign exchange rate** determined by the demand and supply of francs in the foreign exchange market. The French person going to the foreign exchange market would find that he or she needs 5 francs to buy one pound. The numbers we will use here are hypothetical. We will later show the actual exchange rate of major currencies relative to the pound. We will continue our two-country example in which the only two countries in the world are the UK and France. Now let us consider what determines the demand and supply of foreign currency in the foreign exchange market.

Our analysis will initially restrict itself to the market in foreign exchange arising from the import and export of *goods*. In the real world, exchange rates are determined, not only by the demand and supply of currency arising from international trade, but also by flows of capital. We acknowledge this important aspect of foreign exchange markets later in the chapter. (See page 138.)

The Demand and Supply of Foreign Currency

You wish to buy some Bordeaux wine. To do so, you must get French francs. You go to the foreign exchange market. Your desire to buy the French wine therefore provides a supply of pounds sterling to the foreign exchange market. In other words, your demand for French francs is equivalent to your supply of pounds in the foreign exchange market. Indeed, every transaction concerning the importation of foreign goods constitutes a supply of pounds and a demand for some foreign currency and vice versa. In this case, it constitutes a demand for French francs.

In our example, we will assume that only two goods are being traded – French wine and Shetland lamb's-wool sweaters. Thus, the UK demand for French wine creates a supply of pounds and a demand for francs in the foreign exchange market. Similarly, the French demand for Shetland sweaters creates a supply of francs and a demand for pounds in the foreign exchange market. In a **freely floating (or flexible) exchange rate** situation, the supply and demand of pounds and francs in the foreign exchange market will determine the equilibrium foreign exchange rate. The equilibrium exchange rate will tell us how many francs a pound can be exchanged for – that is, the sterling price of francs – or how many pounds (or fractions of a pound) a franc can be exchanged for – that is, the franc price of pounds.

The Equilibrium Foreign Exchange Rate

In order to determine the equilibrium foreign exchange rate, we have to find out what determines the demand and supply of foreign exchange. We will ignore for the moment any speculative aspect of buying foreign exchange; that is, we assume that there are no individuals who wish to buy francs because they think the price will go up in the future.

The idea of an exchange rate is not different from the idea of paying a certain price for something you want to buy. If you like to buy coffee, you know you have to pay, say, 35p a cup. If the price went up to £1, you would probably buy fewer cups. If the price went down to 15p, you might buy more (assuming you are a coffee-drinker). In other words, the demand curve for cups of coffee, expressed in terms of pounds, slopes downwards following the theory of demand. The demand curve for francs slopes downwards also, and we will see why.

THE DEMAND SCHEDULE FOR FRANCS

Let us think more closely about the demand schedule for francs. Let us say that it costs you 20p to purchase one franc; that is the exchange rate between pounds and francs. If tomorrow you had to pay 25p for the same franc, then the exchange rate would have changed. Looking at such an increase with respect to the franc, we would say that there has been an **appreciation** in the value of the *franc* in the foreign exchange market. But this increase in the value of the franc means that there has been a **depreciation** in the value of the *pound* in the foreign exchange market. Previously, the pound could buy 5 francs, tomorrow the pound will be able to buy only 4 francs at a price of 25p per franc. In any event, if the sterling price of francs is higher, you will probably demand fewer francs. Why? The answer lies in looking at the reason why you demand francs in the first place.

You demand francs in order to buy French wine. Your demand curve for French wine, we will assume, follows the theory of demand and is therefore downward sloping. If it costs you more pounds in order to buy the same quantity of French wine, presumably you will not buy the same quantity; your quantity demanded will be less. We say that your demand for French francs is derived from your demand for French wine. In Figure 9.1 we show the hypothetical demand schedule for French wine in the UK by a representative wine-drinker. In panel (b) we show the UK demand curve for French wine in terms of pounds.

Let us assume that the price per litre of French wine in France is 20 francs. Given that price, we can find out the number of francs required to purchase one, two, three, and four bottles of French wine. That information is given in panel (c) of Figure 9.1. One bottle requires 20 francs, four bottles require 80. Now we have a sufficient amount of information to determine the derived demand curve for French francs. If 1 franc costs 20p, a bottle of wine would cost £4 (20 francs per bottle/5 francs per pound = £4 per bottle). At £4 per bottle, our representative wine-drinker would, we see from panel (a) of Figure 9.1, demand four bottles. From panel (c), we see that 80 francs would be demanded to buy the four bottles of wine. We show this quantity demanded in panel (d). In panel (e), we draw the derived demand curve for francs. Now consider what happens if the price of francs goes up to 30p. A bottle of French wine costing 20 francs in France would now cost £6 in the UK. From panel (a), we see that at £6 per bottle, three bottles will be imported into the UK by our representative wine-drinker. From panel (c), we see that three bottles would require 60 francs to be purchased; thus, in panels (d) and (e), we see that at a price of 1 franc per 30p, the quantity demanded will be 60 francs. We do this all the way up to a price of 50p per franc. At that price, a bottle of French wine costing 20 francs in France would cost £10 in the UK, and our representative wine-drinker would import only one bottle.

DERIVED DEMAND IS DOWNWARD SLOPING

As can be expected, as the price of francs falls, the quantity demanded will rise. The only difference here from the demand analysis used in Chapter 5 is that the demand for francs is derived from the demand for a

Figure 9.1

Deriving the Demand for French Francs. In panel (a), we show the demand schedule for French wine in the UK, expressed in terms of pounds per bottle. In panel (b), we show the demand curve *DD*, which is downward sloping. In panel (c), we show the number of francs required to purchase one, two, three, and four bottles of wine. If the price per bottle of wine in France is 20 francs, we can now find the quantity of francs needed to pay for the various quantities demanded above. In panel (d), we see the derived demand for francs in the UK in order to purchase the different quantities of wine given in panel (a). The resultant demand curve *D′D′* is shown in panel (e). It is the derived demand for francs in the UK.

Panel (a)

DEMAND SCHEDULE FOR FRENCH WINE IN THE UK PER WEEK

Price per bottle	*Quantity demanded*
£10	1 bottle
£ 8	2 bottles
£ 6	3 bottles
£ 4	4 bottles

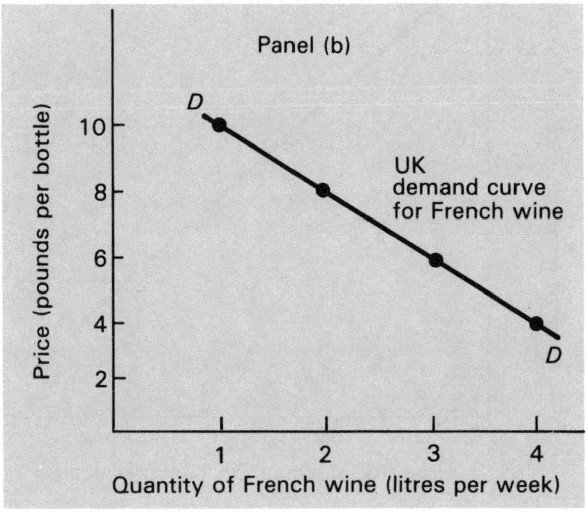

Panel (c)

Quantity demanded	*Francs required to purchase quantity demanded (at P = 20 francs per bottle)*
1 bottle	20
2 bottles	40
3 bottles	60
4 bottles	80

Panel (d)

DERIVED DEMAND SCHEDULE FOR FRANCS IN THE UK WITH WHICH TO PAY FOR IMPORTS OF WINE

Price of 1 franc	*Quantity of francs demanded per week*
50p	20
40p	40
30p	60
20p	80

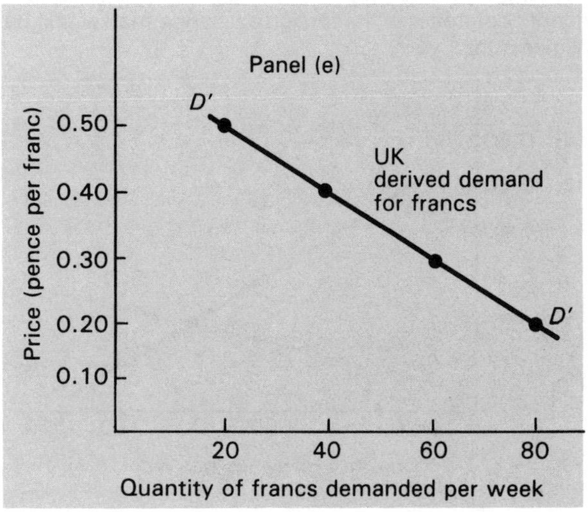

final product, French wine in our example.

THE SUPPLY OF FRENCH FRANCS

The supply of French francs is a derived supply in the sense that it is derived from a French person's demand for Shetland sweaters. We could go through an example similar to the one above to come up with a supply schedule of French francs in France. It is upward sloping. Obviously, the French need pounds in order to purchase the sweaters. If we offer more pounds for the same amount of francs, the sterling price of francs would go up. In principle, the French would be willing to supply more francs when the sterling price of francs goes up, because they can then buy more sweaters with the same quantity of francs; that is, the franc is worth more in exchange for UK goods than when the sterling price for francs was lower. Let us take an example. A sweater in the UK costs £10. If the exchange rate is 25p for one franc, the French have to come up with 40 francs (= £10 at 25p per franc) to buy a sweater. If, on the other hand, the exchange rate goes up to 50p for one franc, the French must come up with only 20 francs (= £10 at 50p per franc) to buy a sweater. At a lower price (in francs) of sweaters, they will demand a larger quantity. In other words, as the price of French francs goes up in terms of pounds, the quantity of sweaters demanded will go up, and hence the quantity of French francs supplied will go up. Therefore, the supply schedule of foreign currency (francs) will be upward sloping.

Figure 9.2

The Equilibrium Exchange Rate for Two Individuals. Here we assume that there are only two individuals – one representative British wine-drinker and one representative French purchaser of sweaters. The derived demand curve for French francs is taken from Panel (e) of Figure 9.1. The derived supply curve *SS* results from the representative French purchaser of sweaters who supplies francs to the foreign exchange market when he or she demands pounds in order to buy sweaters. The intersection of *D′D′* and *SS* is at *E*. The equilibrium exchange rate is 20p for 1 franc. The equilibrium quantity of francs in the foreign exchange market will be 80 per week.

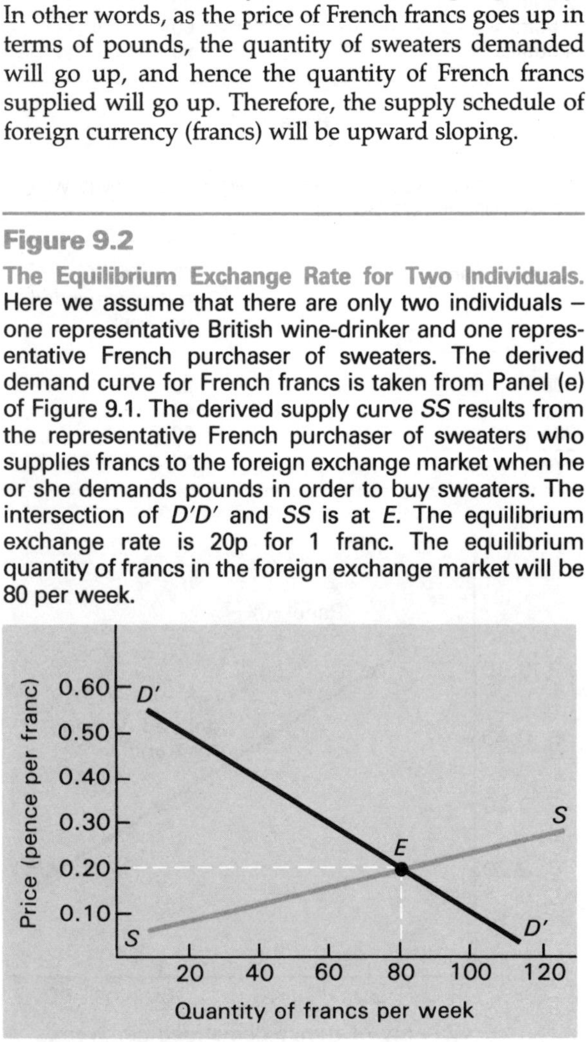

We draw an upward-sloping schedule in Figure 9.2. In our hypothetical example, assuming that there is only one wine-drinker in the UK and one demander of sweaters in France, the equilibrium exchange rate will be set at 20p per franc, or 5 francs to £1. Let us now look at the aggregate demand and supply of French francs. We take all demanders of French wine and all demanders of sweaters and put their demands and supplies of francs together into one diagram. Thus, we are showing an aggregate version of the demand and supply of French francs. The horizontal axis in Figure 9.3 represents a quantity of foreign exchange – the number of francs per year. The vertical axis represents the exchange rate – the price of foreign currency (francs) expressed in pounds (per franc). Thus, at the foreign currency price of 25p per franc, you know that it will cost you 25p to buy 1 franc. At the foreign currency price of 20p per franc, you know that it will cost you 20p to buy 1 franc. The equilibrium is again established at 20p for 1 franc. This equilibrium is not established because the British like to buy francs or because the French like to buy sterling. Rather, the equilibrium exchange rate depends upon how many sweaters the

Figure 9.3

The Aggregate Demand and Supply of French Francs. Here we have drawn the demand curve for French francs. It is a derived demand schedule – that is, a schedule derived from the demand by the British for French wine. We have drawn the supply curve of French francs, which results from the French demand for sweaters. The demand curve, *DD*, slopes downwards like most demand curves, and the supply curve, *SS*, slopes upwards. The foreign exchange price, or the sterling price of francs, in millions, is represented on the horizontal axis. If the foreign exchange rate is 25p – that is, if it takes 25p to buy 1 franc – then the British will demand 80 million francs. The equilibrium exchange rate is at the intersection of *DD* and *SS*. The equilibrium exchange rate is 20p. At this point, 100 million French francs are both demanded and supplied each year.

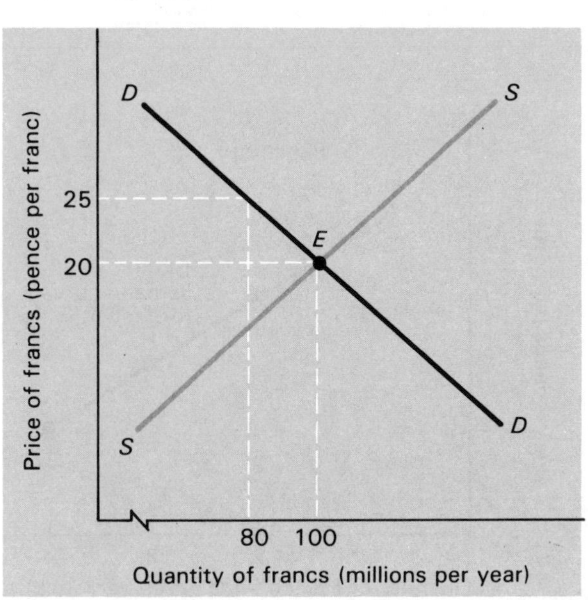

French want and how much French wine the British want (given their respective incomes, tastes, and the relative price of wine and sweaters). (Remember, however, our assumption that we have excluded from consideration the relevance of flows of capital in determining the exchange rate.)

A SHIFT IN DEMAND

Assume that a successful advertising campaign by British wine-importers has caused the British demand (schedule) for French wine to double. We now demand twice as much wine at all prices. Our demand schedule for French wine has shifted out and to the right. (Can you draw this?)

The increased demand for French wine can be translated into an increased demand for francs. Our thirst for bottles of Bordeaux wine means we will supply more pounds to the foreign exchange market while demanding more French francs to pay for the wine. Figure 9.4 presents a new demand schedule, *D′D′*, for French francs; this demand schedule is to the right and outward from the original demand schedule. If the French do not change their desire for sweaters, the supply schedule of French francs will remain stable. A new equilibrium will be established at a higher exchange rate. In our particular example, the equilibrium is established at an exchange rate of 30p. It now takes 30p to buy 1 franc, whereas it took 20p before. This is translated as an increase in the price of French wine to UK drinkers and as a decrease in the price of sweaters to the French.

Figure 9.4

A Shift in the Demand Schedule. The British experience a shift in their taste in favour of French wine. The demand schedule for French wine shifts to the right, causing the derived demand schedule for francs to shift to the right also. We have shown this shift as a movement from *DD* to *D′D′*. We have assumed that the French supply schedule of francs has remained stable – that is, their taste for sweaters has remained constant. The old equilibrium foreign exchange rate was 20p. (It cost 20p to buy one franc.) The new equilibrium exchange rate will be at the intersection of *D′D′* and *SS* – or *E′*. The new exchange rate will be higher than the old one. It will now cost 30p to buy 1 franc. The quantity of francs demanded is greater even at this higher price because the demand schedule has shifted out. The higher price of francs will be translated into a higher sterling price for French wine and a lower French franc price of sweaters.

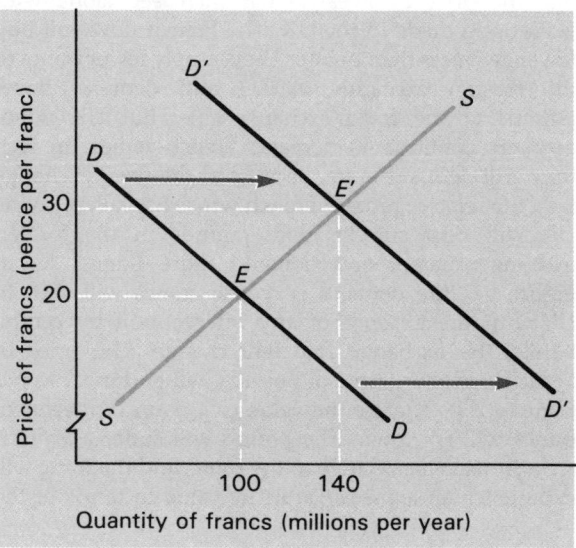

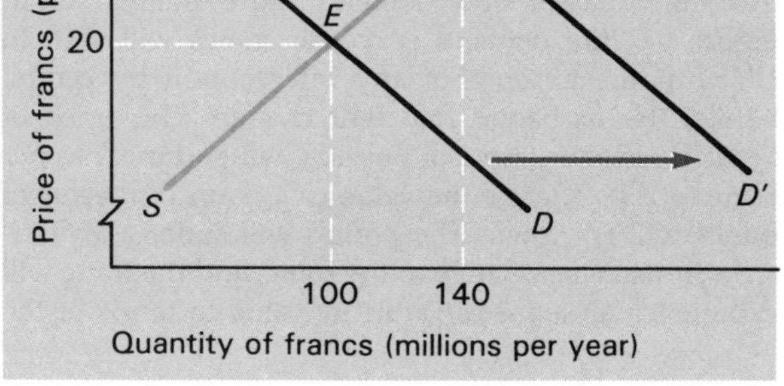

A SHIFT IN SUPPLY

In the preceding example, we assumed that the British taste for wine had shifted. Since the demand for French francs is a derived demand by the British for French wine, that caused a shift in the demand curve for francs. Now let us assume that the supply curve of French francs shifts outwards to the right. This may occur for many reasons, the most probable one being a relative rise in the French price level. For example, if the price of all French-made clothes went up 100 per cent in francs, Shetland sweaters would become relatively cheaper. That would mean that French people would want to buy more sweaters. But remember that when they want to buy more sweaters, they supply more francs to the foreign exchange market. Thus, we see in Figure 9.5 that the supply curve of French francs moves from *SS* to *S′S′*. In the absence of restrictions – that is, in a system of floating exchange rates – the new equilibrium exchange rate will be 1 franc equals 10p, or £1 equals 10 francs. The quantity of francs demanded and supplied will increase from 100 million per year to 200 million per year. We say, then, that in a free (or floating) international exchange rate system, shifts in the demand and supply of foreign currencies will cause

Figure 9.5

A Shift in the Supply of French Francs. For whatever reason, there has been a shift in the supply curve of French francs. The new equilibrium will occur at *E′*. Ten pence, rather than 20p, will now buy 1 franc. After the exchange rate adjustment, the amount of francs demanded and supplied will be 200 million per year.

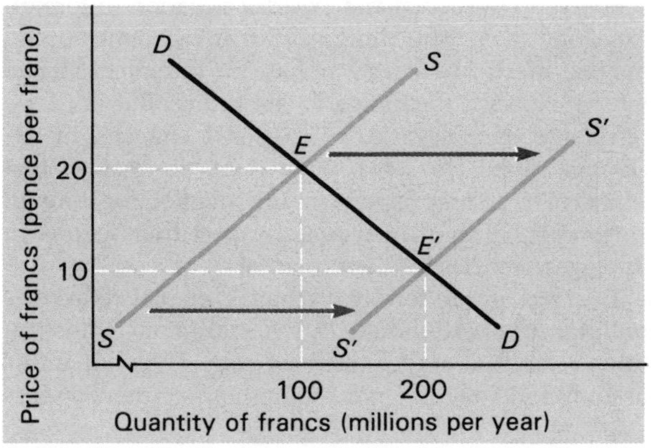

Key Points 9.1

- **The foreign exchange rate is the rate at which a unit of one country's currency can be exchanged for another's.**
- **The demand for foreign exchange is a derived demand; it is derived from the demand for foreign goods and services (and in the real world also for financial assets).**
- **The supply of foreign exchange is derived from foreigners' demands for our goods and services.**
- **In general, the demand curve of foreign exchange slopes downwards and the supply curve of foreign exchange slopes upwards. The equilibrium foreign exchange rate occurs at the intersection of the demand and supply curves.**
- **A shift in the demand for foreign goods will result in a shift in the demand for foreign exchange. The equilibrium foreign exchange rate will change**
- **A shift in the supply of foreign currency will cause a change in the equilibrium exchange rate.**

changes in the equilibrium foreign exchange rates. Those rates will remain in effect until supply and/or demand shift. (Now read Key Points 9.1.)

Capital Flows

Our analysis of how the exchange rate between Britain and France is determined has been wholly based on an interchange of goods between the two countries. But, as was noted at the beginning of the chapter, this international exchange in goods provides only one part of the demand for foreign currencies. There is a demand, not only for French wine, but also for francs, by those UK residents who travel to France for their holiday. They need francs in order to buy food (and wine!) when in France. A further demand for francs arises when, say, a UK firm wishes to acquire a firm in France, or if a UK resident wishes to buy a holiday flat in, for example, Cannes. In these cases we are referring to transactions in *financial assets*. Those involved in making decisions whether to invest abroad will be sensitive to the actual and *expected* situation in foreign exchange rates. The timing of an investment abroad may be affected by a view on how the foreign exchange rate is expected to change in the future. But once we recognize the relevance of expected changes in exchange rates, we have then come to realize that *speculation* is one aspect in the market for foreign currencies. In short, we should expect transactions in foreign currencies for their own sake.

Dealings in the foreign exchange market reflect the willingness of individuals, firms, and financial institutions to shift funds for financial gain. Thus our initial assumption that foreign exchange markets merely serve to satisfy the needs of trade in goods is now seen to be a very limited one.

Fixed Exchange Rate System

We have just described the workings of a freely floating, or flexible, exchange rate system in international finance. Now we consider a situation in which central banks intervene in order to prevent foreign exchange rates from changing. This is a system of **fixed exchange rates.** As with most systems where a price of a particular good or service is fixed, the only way that it can remain so is for the government to intervene.

Let us take our two-country example again. Suppose that the price of sweaters has increased along with everything made in the UK. The French now will buy fewer sweaters than before. They supply fewer francs to the foreign exchange market and demand fewer pounds at the fixed exchange rate. But UK wine-drinkers continue to demand French wines. In fact, they will demand more, because at the fixed exchange rate, the relative price of French wines has fallen. So the UK will now supply more pounds in the foreign exchange market and demand more francs. As in Figure 9.6, the demand curve for francs will shift to $D'D'$. In the absence of any intervention by central banks, the exchange rate will change. The price of French francs in terms of pounds will go from 20p per franc to 25p. That is, the value of a pound in terms of francs will go down. The pound will suffer a *depreciation* in its value relative to the franc, and the franc will experience an *appreciation* in its value in terms of the pound. But the UK government is committed to maintaining a fixed price of pounds in the foreign exchange market. When the French take their excess pounds and put them on to the foreign exchange markets, the UK central bank will be forced to go into the foreign exchange market and buy up those excess pounds. The Bank of England has to have foreign currency (or gold) to buy up the excess pounds. That is, it has to have a reserve of francs or gold in its coffers to buy the pounds that the French want to sell. It must supply 25 million francs per year to keep the exchange rate fixed, as seen in Figure 9.6.

The only way for the UK and other countries to support the price of the pound is to buy up excess pounds with foreign reserves – in this case, with French francs. But the UK might eventually run out of francs. It would no longer be able to stabilize the price of the pound, and a **currency crisis** would ensue. A currency crisis occurs when a country can no longer support the price of its currency in foreign exchange markets. Many such crises have occurred in the past several decades when countries have attempted to maintain a fixed exchange rate that was in disequilibrium. We will consider this matter in a later chapter but for the moment we must indicate that the world's major trading nations operated a fixed exchange rate system under the auspices of the **International Monetary Fund** (IMF) which was set up to manage the world's monetary system in 1945. We need therefore to understand how the IMF was supposed to operate. Briefly, the role of the IMF was to help member countries experiencing balance-of-payments difficulties by lending from its gold and currency holdings. These holdings arose out of the subscriptions of the members set by reference to a formula that took into account a country's importance in the world economy. After 1945 members of the IMF established fixed exchange rates for their currencies in terms of dollars and were obliged to maintain the values of their currencies in foreign exchange markets within a 1 per cent band of their declared par values. In 1970 the IMF created a new reserve asset, **Special Drawing Rights**, which countries could use to settle international payments.

Devaluation

One alternative to a currency crisis or to continuing to try to support a fixed exchange rate is to unilaterally devalue. **Devaluation** is the same thing as depreciation except that it occurs under a fixed exchange rate regime. A particular country unilaterally lowers the price of its currency in foreign exchange markets. The opposite of devaluation is **revaluation.** This occurs when, under a fixed exchange rate regime, there is pressure on a country's currency to rise in value in foreign exchange markets. Unilaterally, that country can declare that the value of its currency in foreign exchange markets is higher than it has been in the past. Revaluation is the same thing as appreciation except that it occurs under a fixed exchange rate regime.

In 1973 most of the world's major nations adopted floating exchange rates. However, central banks were still prepared to intervene in foreign exchange rates in order to counter sudden shifts in the demand for or supply of currency. Thus an intermediate system of **managed floating** was introduced. This system allows a 'pure' floating system to be modified by occasional central bank intervention in order to smooth out sharp short-run changes in exchange rates while allowing market forces to determine the prices of currencies over the long term.

The Balance of Trade and the Balance of Payments

We have talked about a flexible exchange financial system and a fixed exchange rate system. With either system, countries are concerned with their balance of payments. The **balance of payments** is a more general term used to reflect a summary of all economic

Figure 9.6

Supporting the Value of the Pound in the Foreign Exchange Market. If there is inflation in the UK, all prices go up. We assume that prices remain constant in France, so French goods become cheaper. The demand schedule for French goods shifts to the right, as does the derived demand schedule for French francs, from *DD* to *D′D′*. Without exchange rate controls, the exchange rate would rise to 25p – it would then cost 25p instead of 20p to buy a franc. The UK government, however, is committed to supporting the price of the pound. Instead of allowing the £ to equal 4 francs, the government maintains the price of a £ at 5 francs – it keeps the price at 20p per franc. But at that exchange rate there is an excess quantity demanded for francs at the fixed exchange rate of 25 million per year. The UK government must step in and supply 25 million francs from its reserves annually in order to support the £ in the foreign exchange market.

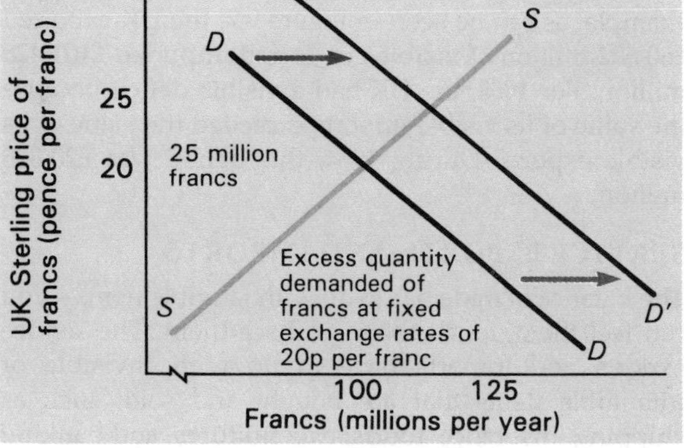

Key Points 9.2

- Fixed exchange rates are a system where countries determine that their exchange rates should not alter and central banks support the declared rates by intervening in foreign exchange markets.
- Currency crises occur when a country can no longer support the price of its currency and under a fixed exchange rate system is obliged to devalue, that is, lower the price of its currency in foreign exchange markets. When a country declares that the value of its currency is now higher than it has been it has adopted a policy of revaluation, the opposite of devaluation.
- Depreciation is the same as devaluation except that it occurs when exchange rates are floating.

transactions between two nations, usually for a period of one year. In a flexible exchange rate system, the balance of payments is always in balance because of automatic adjustments in exchange rates. But since we do not have a *truly* freely floating exchange rate system the balance of payments is an important topic in international finance.

The balance-of-payments transactions of the UK can be grouped into three categories: current account transactions, capital account transactions, and official financing transactions. We now examine these.

Current Account Transactions

During any designated period, all payments and gifts that are related to the purchase or sale of both goods and services constitute the current account in international trade. Within any current account, there are three major types of current account transactions: the exchange of visible or merchandise goods, the exchange of invisibles or services, and, third, investment earnings plus transfers.

VISIBLE TRADE TRANSACTIONS

The largest portion of any nation's balance-of-payments accounts is typically the importing and exporting of merchandise goods. During 1988, for example, as can be seen in Figure 9.7, the UK exported £80 602 million of visible goods and imported £101 428 million. For 1988, the UK had a visible deficit because the value of its visible imports exceeded the value of its visible exports. During 1984, this deficit was £20 826 million.

SERVICE EXPORTS AND IMPORTS

The balance of trade has to do with tangible items – you can feel them, touch them, and see them. The service exports and imports have to do with invisible or intangible items that are bought and sold, such as shipping, insurance, tourist expenditures, and banking services. As Figure 9.7 shows the UK enjoyed a net surplus on transactions in services in 1988 of £4 165 million.

INVESTMENT EARNINGS AND TRANSFERS

The third type of current account transactions comprises net earnings arising from overseas assets owned plus transfers of funds to and from the UK. Some of these transfers are made by private individuals but the UK's entry into the EEC has caused the relative proportion accounted for by government to increase.

BALANCING THE CURRENT ACCOUNT

The **balance on current account** is a summary statistic that takes into account the three transactions that form current account transactions. In 1988 the deficit on current account was £14 617 million. As the UK imported more visible goods than it exported and there was a net deficit on transfers, our service earnings plus overseas income did not exceed our service payments plus investments income paid to foreigners sufficiently to prevent the balance on current account being well in deficit.

Capital Account Transactions

In addition to buying and selling goods and services in the world market, it is also possible to buy and sell financial assets. There is really no difference in terms of the foreign exchange market. If, on the one hand, some people decide to buy shares in French companies, the demand for French financial assets will create a derived demand for francs and a supply of pounds. On the other hand, if the French decide they want to buy ICI shares, that demand will result in a derived demand for pounds and a supply of francs.

Capital account transactions thus comprise investment activity by private individuals, banks, companies, and publicly owned undertakings. One would expect that the wide range of persons engaged in this investment activity would vary in their motives. For some the intention is profit-seeking over the long term

Figure 9.7 (a)
Current Account of the UK Balance of Payments, 1988 (£m)

	Credits	Debits		Net difference
Visibles				
food, beverages, tobacco	5 489	9 926		−4 437
basic materials	2 134	5 452		−3 318
oil	6 018	3 231		2 787
other fuels and lubricants	242	1 476		−1 234
semi-manufacturers	24 091	27 915		−3 824
finished manufacturers	40 640	51 646		−11 006
other	1 988	1 782		206
Total goods	80 602	101 428	**Visible balance**	**−20 826**
Invisible services				
general government	520	2 353		
sea transport	3 551	4 127		
civil aviation	3 192	4 054		
travel	6 085	8 127		
financial and other services	14 583	5 105		
Total services	27 931	23 766	Services balance	4 165
Interest, profits, and dividends	55 526	49 908	balance	5 619
Transfers				
general government	2 119	5 388	balance	−3 269
private	1 657	1 963	balance	−306
Total invisibles	87 233	81 024	**Invisible balance**	**6 209**
Current total			**Current balance**	**−14 617**

Capital Account of the UK Balance of Payments, 1988 (£m)

	Credits	Debits	Net
Transactions in UK assets and liabilities			
UK external assets		−50 073	
UK external liabilities	+52 408		
UK net transactions			2 334
Balancing item			12 283

Figure 9.7 (b)
Analysis of Capital Transactions (£m)

Credits		*Debits*	
Investment in the UK by overseas residents		Investment overseas by UK residents	
direct	7 346	direct	15 219
portfolio	4 639	portfolio	9 718
Foreign currency borrowing abroad by UK banks	20 300	Foreign currency lending abroad by UK banks	14 692
Sterling borrowing abroad by UK banks	13 556	Sterling lending abroad by UK banks	4 569
Borrowing from banks abroad	3 567	Lending to banks abroad	3 035
Change in other external liabilities	3 001	Change in other external assets	81
	52 409		50 075
		Net transactions	2 334

while for others funds may be quickly moved in the light of changing conditions. Our earlier analysis of exchange rates excluded the possibility of transactions in financial assets. If we recognized the reality of such activity then participants in capital transactions may alter their behaviour in the light of anticipated movements of the exchange rate.

Earlier in this chapter we indicated that since 1973 the central banks of the world's major trading nations have been prepared to smooth out sharp short-run movements in exchange rates. They operate a managed floating system. But the extent to which these banks now intervene in foreign exchange markets is much less than in the period of fixed exchange rates until 1973. This is because under a fixed exchange rate system each country must finance any deficit or surplus arising from private-sector transactions if the fixed rates are to prevail. Thus in a fixed exchange rate system a country would either run down its foreign exchange reserves or borrow from abroad. Until 1987 when the presentation of the UK's balance of payments was changed the total change in reserves plus the amount borrowed from abroad by the Bank of England was called *official financing*. Given that the Bank of England no longer intervened in the foreign exchange market to underpin a particular exchange rate the term official financing lost much of its significance and thus the capital account in Figure 9.7 reflects this new presentation of the balance of payments. The effect of the new definition of the capital account has been to focus on transactions in UK assets and those on UK liabilities. The former relate to net purchases by domestic residents in the UK of foreign securities. Transactions in UK liabilities are net purchases by foreign residents of UK securities. Now in each of these groups of transactions sterling is either bought or sold. For UK residents to buy foreign assets they will need to sell pounds sterling to buy foreign currency: hence these transactions are recorded as minus items. For foreign residents to buy UK securities they will need to sell their own currency to buy pounds sterling. Hence in this case transactions in UK liabilities are recorded as positive items.

In the real world difficulties in identifying certain transactions result in ignorance of the precise sums crossing the foreign exchange markets. The element of unrecorded transactions is termed the *balancing item*. It is simply the difference between the overall current balance and the net transactions in UK assets and liabilities. The balance of payments must, by definition, always balance!

The Rationale of International Trade

We have now examined the ways in which trade in goods, services, and financial assets is financed with particular reference to the UK. We began with the simple example of the interchange of French wine and Shetland lamb's-wool sweaters. Having considered how the foreign exchange market exists for the buying and selling of currencies to make such an interchange possible we should now examine what is the rationale of such trade between two countries. We need to consider questions such as what are the gains from such trade? What are the costs involved? As consumers we appear to gain when we can purchase foreign products at lower prices than those made by domestic manufacturers. But what if foreign suppliers put UK firms out of business and so put some of the UK's labour force out of work? Are the gains from international trade worth the costs?

Putting Trade in Its Place

Trade among nations must somehow benefit the people of each nation by more than it costs them. World trade volume, measured in terms of exports, increased at a compound growth rate of between 5 and 8 per cent per year in the post-war period. Figure 9.8 shows that in the period after 1965 world trade expanded at a much more rapid rate than the rate of

Key Points 9.3

- **The balance of payments reflects the value of all transactions in international trade, including the trade in goods, services, transfers, and financial assets.**
- **The invisibles account presents the export and import in tangible items, i.e. services.**
- **The current account includes both goods and services and also earnings on investments abroad less payments on investments in the UK owned by foreigners, plus net government and net private transfers.**
- **The capital account includes investment flows by private individuals and the public sector. In contrast to the current account it records transactions in financial assets.**

Figure 9.8
World Trade by Volume 1960–87

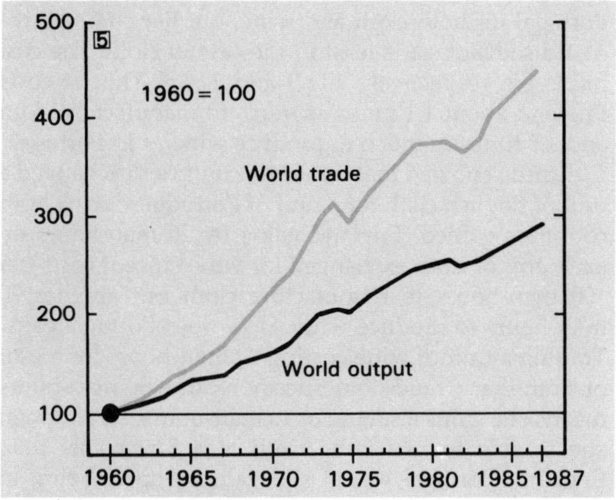

Source: *The Economist*, 26 Sept. 1987.

increase in world output. Clearly the world's trading nations showed an enthusiasm to participate in international exchange. However, in the past decade the international monetary and trading system has been subject to strain most notably due to OPEC's increase in oil prices in early 1974 and 1979. This in turn exacerbated the balance-of-payments situation of many oil-importing developing countries. Their attempts to borrow funds from banks in the US and Western Europe have subsequently given rise to problems of indebtedness. Thus after 1973 the rate of growth of international trade fell markedly reflecting the world-wide recession in world output until 1983. Rising unemployment in the US and Western Europe has strengthened the demands for restrictions on world trade. So part of the less buoyant growth in world trade since 1973 is actually explained by measures to restrict imports so that jobs are protected. These curbs on imports illustrate that international exchange does have an impact on the use of domestic resources. Where governments have restricted international trade they have judged that the costs incurred from an unrestricted exchange of goods are unacceptably high. We must therefore examine the arguments in favour of restraining the importation of goods and services from other countries.

Before we examine both the disadvantages of international exchange and its advantages we should note that international trade is of more significance to some countries than others. Figure 9.9 shows the marked

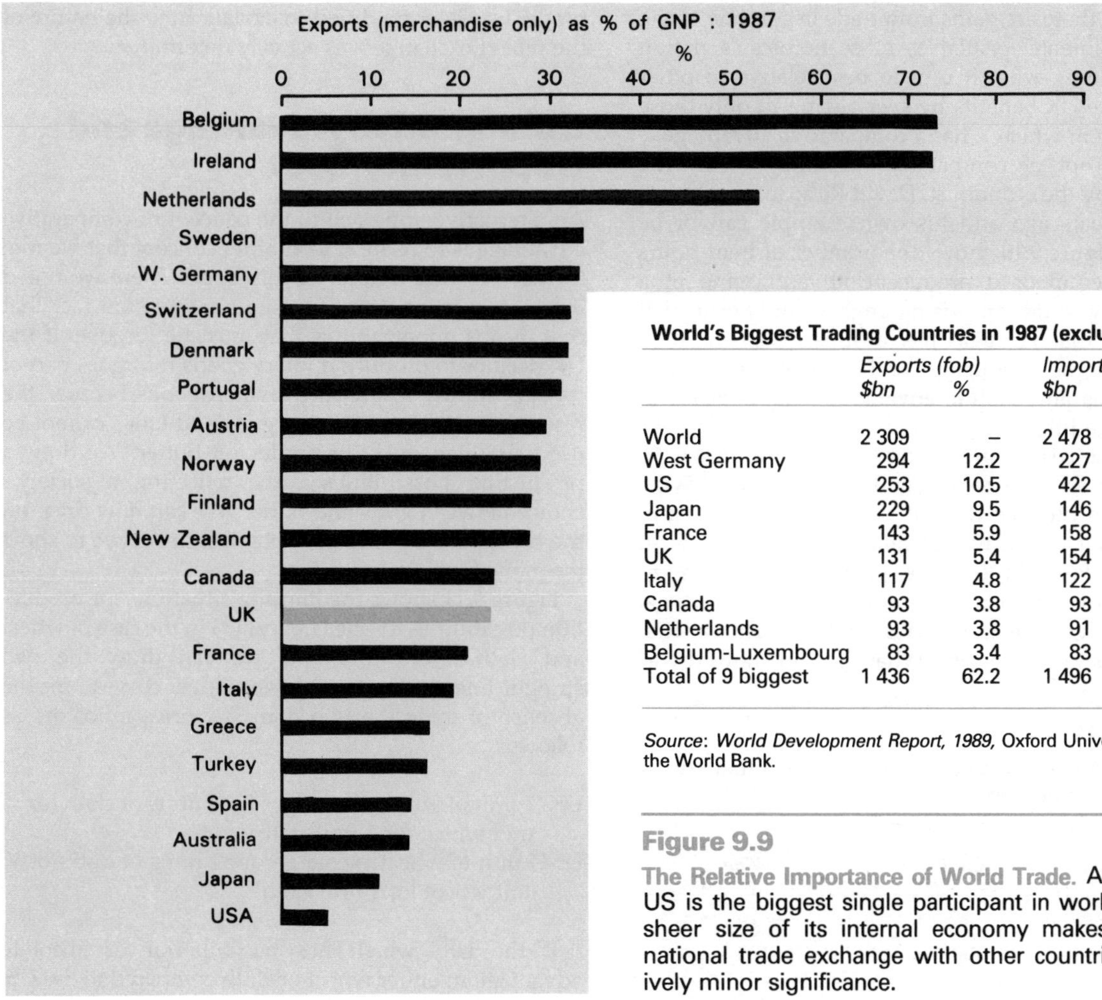

World's Biggest Trading Countries in 1987 (excluding USSR)

	Exports (fob) $bn	Exports (fob) %	Imports (cif) $bn	Imports (cif) %
World	2 309	–	2 478	–
West Germany	294	12.2	227	9.1
US	253	10.5	422	17.0
Japan	229	9.5	146	5.8
France	143	5.9	158	6.3
UK	131	5.4	154	6.2
Italy	117	4.8	122	4.9
Canada	93	3.8	93	3.7
Netherlands	93	3.8	91	3.6
Belgium-Luxembourg	83	3.4	83	3.3
Total of 9 biggest	1 436	62.2	1 496	60.3

Source: *World Development Report, 1989,* Oxford University Press for the World Bank.

Figure 9.9
The Relative Importance of World Trade. Although the US is the biggest single participant in world trade the sheer size of its internal economy makes her international trade exchange with other countries of relatively minor significance.

variation between developed countries in the proportion of gross domestic product accounted for by exports. Some countries export more than one-third of their GDPs. The United States ranks near the bottom of the list. In fact, the United States is the Western country that would suffer the least if we imagine the unlikely event of international trade ceasing to take place. In contrast the UK is a much more *open economy* or one dependent on relationships with other countries.

The pattern of the UK's trade with other countries has, historically, been an exchange of exported manufactured goods and services for imported raw materials and foodstuffs. Since the mid-1970s North Sea oil and gas has developed into a major aspect of the UK's trading position. In 1988 the UK enjoyed a balance on trade in oil of £2.7bn. Looking at the UK's trade it is reasonable to ask the following question: how did this trade pattern become established? The answer lies in the principle of comparative advantage that we explored in Chapter 6. We now re-examine that principle in an open economy context.

Comparative and Absolute Advantage

The reason there are gains from trade lies in one of the most fundamental principles of economics: a nation gains by doing what it can do best relative to other nations. The UK benefits by specializing in only those endeavours in which it has a **comparative advantage.**

The concept of comparative advantage was first explained by the economist, David Ricardo, nearly two hundred years ago and his own example cannot be bettered. Figure 9.10 shows the number of man-hours per unit required to produce cloth and wine in a two-country world comprising England and Portugal. It is evident that Portugal has a superior position to England in the production of both cloth and wine. Portugal has an **absolute advantage** over England in both commodities.

Why? The cost of producing cloth in Portugal is 90 per cent of the cost in England. In the case of wine Portugal can produce wine at two-thirds of the cost in England. But of the two commodities clearly it is in wine that Portugal has the greater or *comparative* advantage over England. But does this mean Portugal gains nothing from trade with England? This at first sight seems to be the case. What Ricardo showed was

Figure 9.10

Ricardo's Model of Comparative Cost Advantage (man-hours per unit of output)

	Cloth	*Wine*
Portugal	90	80
England	100	120

that England could *specialize* in cloth production and trade cloth exports for wine imports from Portugal to the benefit of both countries. How was this possible?

In England labour costs per unit are higher than in Portugal for both cloth and wine, but her comparative cost disadvantage is least in the case of cloth. The cost ratios are respectively 10 : 9 and 12 : 8. Thus it costs England about 1.1 times as much to manufacture cloth and 1.5 times as much to produce wine as in Portugal.

Ricardo showed that if the two countries exchanged a unit of English cloth for a unit of Portuguese wine both countries gained. England gains by 20 man-hours on each unit of cloth exchanged for wine since it costs her 100 man-hours to manufacture cloth but another 20 man-hours to produce wine. How does Portugal gain? Trading a unit of wine costing 80 man-hours for a unit of cloth that would domestically require 90 man-hours means she gains a saving of 10 man-hours. So although she is able to make the cloth at a lower cost than England, Portugal would still gain by specializing in the production of wine. Her comparative advantage is greater in wine than cloth.

Ricardo's model is, of course, a simple one. It assumes there are no transport costs incurred in shipping cloth and wine between England and Portugal. But it indicated that trade could be advantageous at a certain rate of international exchange. Ricardo's model was later modified to explain how the nature of the rate of exchange was actually determined.

Comparative Advantage and Opportunity Cost

An alternative approach to the concept of comparative advantage is to relate it to another concept that we met in the very first chapter of this book. There we noted that comparative advantage emphasizes the fact that cost means opportunities that must be forgone. If the UK decides to produce military goods it forgoes part of its opportunity to produce civilian goods because the resources used in producing guns and tanks cannot be used simultaneously in producing butter. We drew a production possibilities curve reflecting a society's choice between guns and butter. We can now draw on the concept of a production possibilities curve to show the gains from trade.

Figure 9.11 shows the limiting situations for production possibilities for the UK and US in the case of wheat and cloth. From this data we can draw the two straight-line production possibilities curves. In the absence of trade the two domestic price ratios are as follows:

UK 1 unit of wheat exchanges for 4 units of cloth (or ¼ unit wheat for 1 unit cloth)
US 1 unit of wheat exchanges for 2 units of cloth (or ½ unit wheat for 1 unit cloth)

If the UK, which has no superior or absolute advantage in either wheat or cloth compared to the US,

Figure 9.11

	Wheat	Cloth	Wheat	Cloth
UK	40	0	0	160
US	80	0	0	160

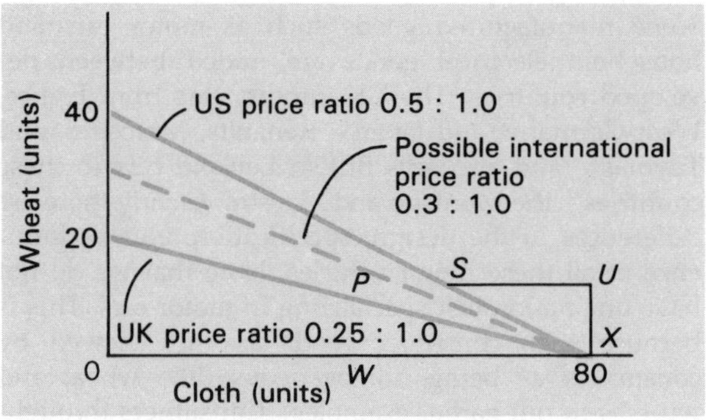

OP = pre-trade production and consumption
OX = cloth production (total specialization) if trade takes place at given international price ratio
UX = wheat imports
SU = cloth exports

Figure 9.12

Price Ratios: Can the UK and US do a deal? The solid lines indicate the pre-trade price ratios in the UK and the US. The two dashed lines indicate price relationships between wheat and cloth that would make trade between the two countries worth while.

could trade cloth on more favourable terms than one-quarter unit of wheat, she would gain. An international exchange of say 0.3 units of wheat for one unit of cloth would be advantageous to the UK. The dashed line on Figure 9.11 shows this ratio.

If the UK now produces say *OX* cloth (rather than *OW* when no trade takes place) she can purchase *UX* of wheat from the US. The UK in this case is now totally specializing in cloth and importing all her requirements of wheat. Imports of wheat of *UX* equal her cloth exports of *SU*. International exchange has enabled the UK to move outside the range of possibilities that were present before trade took place. Point *S* is beyond point *P* which was the situation before trade.

Figure 9.12 shows the price ratios before trade in the UK and US. For international exchange to be beneficial the rate of exchange must lie between the two domestic opportunity cost ratios. The UK would gain from trade if she could trade 8 units of cloth for 3 units of wheat. This would be better than the domestic price ratio of 8 units of cloth exchanging for 2 units of wheat. Likewise the US would gain from an international exchange such as 3.5 units of cloth for one of wheat. As long as the UK and US can agree on a basis of exchange both countries can gain.

Of course, as in Ricardo's model, we have assumed away the matter of transport costs. For some items these might be so high compared with the cost of the good itself that international exchange is not worth while. We have also implicitly assumed that imported goods do not face any increase in price due to the imposition of a tax or tariff. In the previous chapter we noted how international trade in foodstuffs was indeed affected by such measures. But none the less we have

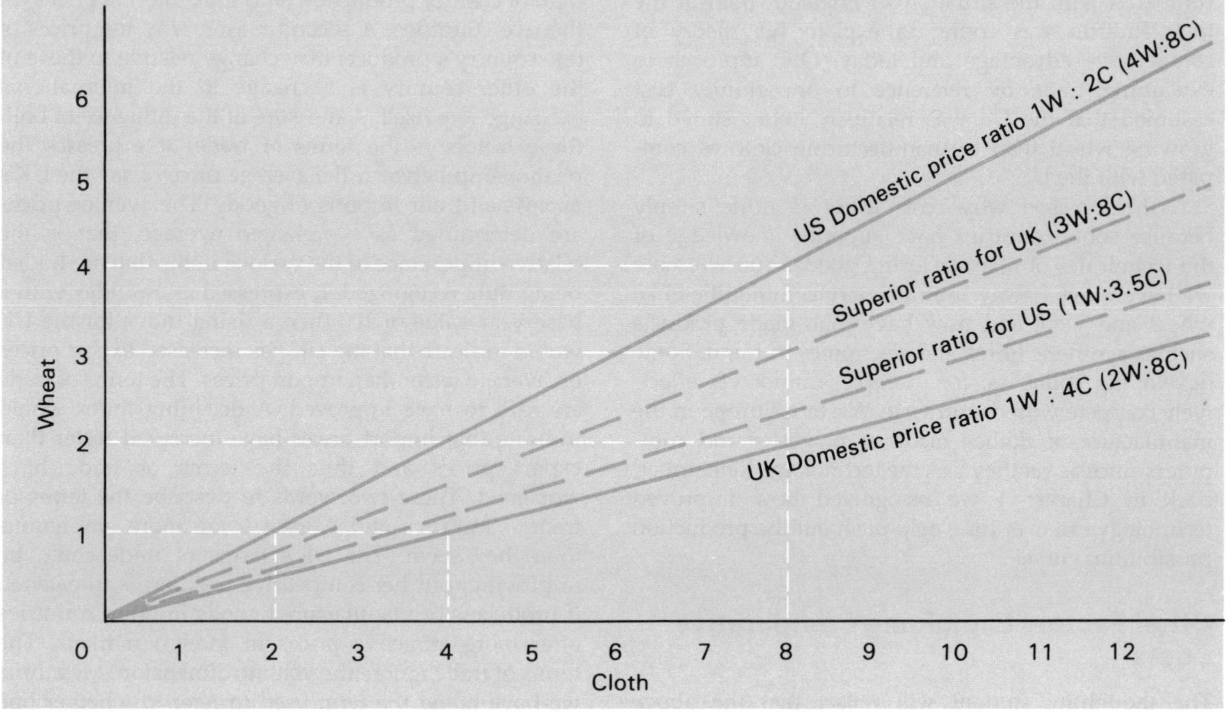

shown how, in a simple example of two countries and two products, differences in opportunity cost ratios provide the basis for countries to trade because they specialize in those commodities in which they have a comparative advantage.

You may now be thinking why comparative costs should differ between countries. The basic reason for the existence of comparative advantage – whether among individuals, companies, cities, counties, states, countries, or continents – lies in the fact that opportunity costs vary. It costs less for different parties to engage in different types of economic activities. Opportunity costs for different countries vary just as they vary for different individuals. Let us consider some of the reasons why opportunity costs and, hence, comparative advantages differ among nations.

Differing Resource Mixes

We know that different nations have different resource bases. Australia has much land relative to its population, whereas Japan has little land relative to its population. All other things being equal, one would expect countries with relatively more land to specialize in products that use more land. One expects Australia, for example, to engage in extensive sheep-raising but not Japan, because the opportunity cost of raising sheep in Japan is much higher. Since land in Japan is relatively scarce, its use carries a higher opportunity cost.

There are also differences in climates. We do not expect countries with cold, dry climates to grow bananas. Our earlier examples illustrate the natural resource and climatic differences between countries. Portugal's comparative advantage in wine is not surprising given her easier ability to grow grapes as compared with the situation in England, both at the time Ricardo was trying to explain his theory of comparative advantage and today. Our approach to explaining trade by reference to opportunity cost assumed that the US was relatively better suited to growing wheat than to manufacturing cloth as compared with the UK.

A third reason why costs differ is quite simply because some countries have superior knowledge of the techniques of manufacturing goods. You will note we have moved away from primary commodities like wheat and wool and now have man-made products such as synthetic fibres and electronics in mind. Some developing countries, for example, cannot yet effectively compete with countries in Western Europe in the manufacture of clothes made of polyester and computers since as yet they lack the technology. Remember, back in Chapter 1 we recognized how improved technology can over time help push out the production possibilities curve.

Other Factors Explaining Comparative Costs

The thoughtful student will reflect that the above reasons explaining why comparative costs can differ between countries are quite simply the inherent characteristics of a nation's factor endowment. They are supply-based aspects: Australia is a wool-producing nation since she is relatively well endowed with land, a factor of production that is essential for extensive sheep-farming. But demand conditions can also help explain why countries differ in comparative advantage. Some manufactured goods such as motor cars and household electrical goods are traded between developed countries. The UK imports cars from France, West Germany, and Japan – Renaults, Mercedes, and Toyotas – and also sells British Leyland cars to these countries – the Montego and Maestro. Clearly there are differences in the design, specification, and performance of all these motor vehicles. Note that we do not have one nation just specializing in motor cars. This is because such consumer goods are not viewed by consumers as being homogeneous (like wheat and wine as in our earlier examples). Consumers throughout the world like different types of modern consumer goods so that it is not the case that one industry is based in one country. Within an industry countries specialize in different types of goods: this trade is known as 'intra-industry trade'.

The Terms of Trade

Our earlier example of trade between the UK and US in wheat and cloth assumed that an international exchange rate between the two commodities would be established such that both countries gained from being open economies. In the real world the terms on which a country exchanges its exports for imports are, of course, measured in monetary terms – as prices. These prices alter for two reasons. First, there may be a change in the ratio of costs of production (and thus internal prices) in the two countries. A second reason why the prices of one country's products may change relative to those of the other country is a change in the international exchange rate itself. A measure of the influence of both these factors is the **terms of trade.** It expresses the relationship between the average price of say the UK's exports and our imports of goods. The average prices are determined as a weighted average, that is the relative importance of the various items that are traded being duly recognized. If expressed as an index with a base-year value of 100 then a rising index for the UK would indicate that the UK has increased export prices on average faster than import prices. The terms of trade are said to have improved. A declining index would indicate that import prices have increased faster than export prices and thus the terms of trade have worsened. These two words to describe the terms of trade – improve and worsen – are more ambiguous than they seem. The UK's terms of trade could be improving, but her competitive position is threatened if producers of manufactured goods in other countries offer more attractive prices in foreign markets. The terms of trade ignore the volume dimension. Meantime we have noted the term used to refer to whether one country is enjoying a more favourable basis of international exchange compared with the past. This picture of whether a country is relatively gaining from trade makes it appropriate to realize that trade may not benefit every country equally. What are the disadvantages of international exchange?

Advantageous Trade Will always Exist

From before the beginning of recorded history, there have been examples of trade among individuals. Since these acts of exchange have usually been voluntary, we must assume that individuals generally benefit from the trade. Individual tastes and resources vary tremendously. As a consequence, there are sufficient numbers of different opportunity costs in the world for exchange to take place constantly.

As individual entities, nations have different collective tastes and different collective resource endowments. We would expect, therefore, that there will always be potential gains to be made from trading among nations. Furthermore, the more trade there is the more specialization there can be. Specialization in turn leads to increased output and – if we measure well-being by output levels – to increased happiness. (Admittedly, we are using the term *well-being* very loosely here.) Self-sufficiency on the part of individuals undeniably means that they forgo opportunities to consume the extra output that becomes available if they are not self-sufficient. Likewise, self-sufficiency on the part of a nation will lower its consumption possibilities and therefore will lower the well-being of its inhabitants. Imagine life in your immediate locality if it was forced to become self-sufficient!

Costs of Trade

Trade does not come without cost. If one country has a comparative advantage in producing agricultural crops, other countries may not be able to succeed as sources of agricultural production. Farm-workers in these latter countries that are less efficient at agricultural production will suffer decreases in their incomes until they find other occupations or move to where alternative jobs are.

As tastes, supplies of natural resources, prices, and so on change throughout the world, different countries may find their areas of comparative advantage changing. One example of this is in the production of steel. South Korea has become increasingly competitive in steel products, and steelmakers in Western Europe are losing sales to imports. They are feeling the pinch from South Korea's ability to produce steel products at lower costs. The same competitive threat from Japan is to be found in the case of many other consumer goods exported to countries in Western Europe.

Arguments against Free Trade

There are numerous arguments against free trade but many on closer inspection turn out to be incomplete. They mainly point out the costs of trade; they do not consider the benefits or the possible alternatives for reducing costs while still reaping benefits.

Infant Industry Argument

A nation may feel that if a particular industry were allowed to develop domestically, it could eventually become efficient enough to compete effectively in the world market. Therefore, if some restrictions were placed on imports, native producers would be given the time needed to develop their efficiency to the point where they would be able to compete in the domestic market without any restrictions on imports. In terms of the concept of the supply curve, we would expect that if the protected industry truly does experience technological breakthroughs toward greater efficiency in the future, then the supply curve will shift outwards to the right so that the domestic industry can produce larger quantities at each and every price. This infant industry

Key Points 9.4

- **Countries can be better off materially if they specialize in their comparative advantage.**
- **It is important to distinguish between absolute and comparative advantage; the former refers to the ability to produce a unit of output with fewer physical units of input; the latter refers to producing that has the lowest opportunity cost for a nation.**
- **Different national will always have different comparative advantages because of differing opportunity costs due to different resource endowments, technical knowledge, and different tastes.**
- **The relationship between average export prices and average import prices is the terms of trade.**
- **Foreign trade can adversely affect certain groups in each country because of increased competition from abroad.**

argument has some merit in the short run and was used to shelter several UK industries in 1918 under the Safeguarding of Industries Act. The year is significant since the Act was a policy response to the UK's experience during the First World War. When hostilities began in 1914 the UK was dependent on German supplies in several key industrial sectors. Our dependence on a country which became a foreign enemy had highlighted the need for certain industries to be protected at least in the short term. This strand of the infant industry argument is very close to the case for protection on grounds of national security which we discuss next. However, in principle the infant industry case could be applied to industries *not* of strategic significance in a wartime economy. The general application of the infant industry case can be easily criticized. Often the protective import-restricting arrangements remain even after the infant has grown up. If other countries can still produce more cheaply, the people who benefit from this type of situation are obviously the owners of the firms (and specialized factors of production) in the industry that is still being protected from world competition. The people who lose out are the consumers, who must pay a price higher than the world price for the product in question. In any event, it is very difficult to know *beforehand* which industries will eventually survive. In other words, we cannot predict very well the specific 'infant' industries that should be protected. Note that when we talk about which industry *should be* protected, we are in the realm of normative economics. We are stating a value-judgement that comes from our hearts.

National Security

It is often argued that we should not rely on foreign sources for many of our products because in time of war these sources might well be cut off and we would have developed few, if any, substitute sources. Such an argument was part of the case for the post-war expansion of UK agriculture. The Second World War had shown the dependence of UK consumers on foreign suppliers who were thousands of miles away. The uncertain passage of ships from the Southern Hemisphere across the North Atlantic due to the threat from German U-boats appeared to underline the case for the more certain presence of home-grown foodstuffs. On the face of it the argument looked appealing. But as we noted in Chapter 8 post-war agricultural policy which offered some protection for UK farmers had an impact on the use of resources. Guaranteed prices for UK farmers had the effect of limiting the market for food imports. In so far as sales of food to the UK were restricted, there was a reduced capacity of countries like New Zealand to import items like manufactured goods. Increased UK food production certainly reduced food imports. But the overall impact on the balance of payments was not just on the flow of imported butter and lamb but also the sales of motor cars and electrical equipment to overseas buyers.

Protecting a Way of Life

Free world trade may destroy certain industries in a particular economy as comparative advantages change throughout the world. A society may wish to protect a certain group of individuals who are threatened by international competition because they believe that their particular way of life should be maintained.

Of course, there are always alternative ways to protect particular livelihoods and individual groups. For example, if a country wished to protect watchmakers, rather than restricting foreign trade, it could simply give a subsidy directly to watchmakers. This would not raise the price of watches for consumers, but it would serve as a protection of a particular way of life. Our discussion of the method of protecting UK farmers in the period 1948–73 illustrated one merit of deficiency payments over tariffs.

Stability

Many people argue that foreign trade should be restricted because it introduces an element of instability into our economic system. They point out that the vagaries of foreign trade add to the ups and downs in our own employment level. However, if we follow this argument to its logical conclusion, we would restrict trade within a country itself. After all, the vagaries of trade among particular areas of the UK sometimes cause employment in other areas. Things are sorted out over time, but workers suffer during the adjustment period. As regards the international sphere, however, people somehow change their position. They feel that adjusting to the vagaries of *international* trade costs more than adjusting to the vagaries of domestic trade. Perhaps people believe foreign trade really does not benefit us that much, and thus they argue against it, claiming that the stability of aggregate economic activity is at stake. We should note one difference between the domestic and international situations, however, that lends some truth to this argument. Labour is more mobile within a country than between countries. Immigration laws prevent workers from moving to countries where they can earn the most income. There are also many differences in language and customs that prevent workers from freely moving from country to country. Therefore, the adjustment costs to a changing international situation may in fact be higher than the adjustment costs to a changing domestic situation.

Protecting Jobs

Perhaps the most frequently used argument against free trade is that unrestrained competition from other countries will eliminate jobs at home because other countries have lower-cost labour than we do. This is indeed a compelling argument, particularly for politicians from areas that might be threatened by foreign competition. For example, a Member of Parliament from an area with textile or shoe factories would certainly be upset about the possibility of constituents losing their jobs because of competition from lower-priced cotton shirt manufacturers in Hong Kong or shoe manufacturers in Brazil and Italy. Again we note that limitations on imports may help employees in such industries but at the expense of consumers. And as we have also recognized, attempts at protecting jobs by imposing tariffs, quotas, and other restrictions on international trade lead to retaliation by our trading partners. In other words, they start imposing similar restrictions on trade with the UK. We may end up saving less productive employment at the expense of more productive employment.

Countering Foreign Subsidies and Dumping

Another strong argument against unrestricted foreign trade has to do with countering other nations' subsidies to their own producers and to dumping. When a foreign government subsidizes its producers, our competing producers claim that they cannot compete fairly with these subsidized foreigners. To the extent that such subsidies fluctuate, one can argue that unrestricted free trade will seriously disrupt domestic producers. After all, they will not know when foreign governments are going to subsidize their own producers and when they are not. Our competing industries, then, will be expanding and contracting too frequently.

Occasionally, the phenomenon called **'dumping'** takes place and is used as an argument against unrestricted trade. Dumping occurs when a producer sells its products abroad at a price below its cost of production. Although cries of dumping against foreign producers are often heard, they typically only occur when the foreign nation is in the throes of a serious recession. The foreign producer does not want to slow down its production at home because it anticipates an end to the recession and it does not want to bear large costs of financing. Therefore, it dumps its product abroad at prices below its costs. This does, in fact, disrupt foreign trade.

SOME NEWER WAYS TO RESTRICT WORLD TRADE

The late 1970s and 1980s will be known in world trade history as the era of new restrictions. Consider the following barriers to world trade that have occurred in the last few years.

France: French-language customs documents; restrictions on Japanese video-cassette recorders; delays in allowing the import of Swiss cheese.

Britain: Severe restrictions on foreign insurance firms, banks, and law firms; limits on the number of Japanese cars imported.

Japan: Excessive red tape against cosmetics produced elsewhere.

United States: 'Voluntary' limits on European steel and Japanese cars; 'buy American' rules for new bridges and roads.

These restraints on trade form a reversal to the post-war commitment by the world's trading nations to dismantle tariffs and trade restrictions. Since 1945 members of the General Agreement on Tariffs and Trade (GATT) have agreed to rounds of tariff cuts and helped stimulate the growth in world trade that we noted in Figure 9.8. Some fear that the growing number of these trade restrictions prompted by the world recession could multiply and threaten the whole basis of international exchange.

Counter-purchases: One of the newest impediments to world trade are the requirements of a *counter-purchase,* which is a set of parallel cash sales agreements in which a supplier sells a plan or product and orders unrelated products to offset the cost of the buyer. Consider the following two examples of counter-purchase requirements:

1. Canada bought $2.4 billion worth of F-18 aircraft from McDonnell Douglas, but required that McDonnell Douglas helped find customers for goods and services worth $2.9 billion.
2. Hughes Aircraft and Canada's Spar Aerospace won a $130-million space satellite contract from Brazil but had to agree to arrange to import an equal amount of products from Brazil into Canada.

Buy-back Agreements. Another impediment to world trade is a *buy-back agreement* in which, under separate agreement to the sale of a plant, the supplier agrees to purchase part of the plant's output for up to 20 years. For example, Russia made a $20-billion deal with Occidental Petroleum whereby the latter built ammonia plants and agreed to buy part of the output. China awarded a $500-million contract to a company in Italy to expand China's mines and to modernize its railroads. In return the Italian firm had to agree to buy coal from China.

Does the increase in these *non-tariff barriers* to international trade mean that the future of international trade is in jeopardy? Some believe so, but others point out that the increased restrictions in world trade have occurred mainly during periods of world-wide recession. Therefore, we might expect during periods when most countries are experiencing economic growth that such trade barriers will shrink, even if only slowly. New restraints on trade might then come back again during the next serious recession that hurts the majority of world countries.

Key Points 9.5

- **The infant industry argument against free trade contends that new industries should be allowed protection against world competition so that they can become technically efficient in the long run.**
- **The national security argument against free trade contends that we should not rely on foreign sources for crucial materials needed during time of war.**
- **Unrestricted foreign trade may allow foreign governments to subsidize exports or foreign producers to engage in dumping – selling products in other countries below their cost of production. To the extent that foreign export subsidies and dumping create more instability in domestic production, they may impair our well-being.**
- **In the 1970s and 1980s a number of new ways to restrict world trade have been instituted, such as voluntary limits on exports, counter-purchase, and buy-back agreements.**

CASE STUDY

The Foreign Currency Market in London

The Bank of England's survey of the London foreign exchange market was conducted over the twenty business days of April 1989 and coincided with similar surveys conducted in other centres around the world by other central banks. A total of 356 principals (including the Bank of England itself) and 9 brokers in foreign exchange participated in the London survey. The principals approached were mainly those banks which report regularly to the Bank of England in respect of foreign exchange exposures, although, for the first time, a number of institutions listed by the Bank under Section 43 of the Financial Services Act 1986 as market makers in foreign exchange were also included. Other institutions dealing in foreign exchange were not directly involved in the survey, although their transactions with participating principals, or through brokers, would have been reported by those institutions.

The questionnaire

Survey participants were requested to complete a questionnaire prepared by the Bank of England after consultation with representatives of the Foreign Exchange Committee of the British Bankers' Association and the Foreign Exchange and Currency Deposit Brokers' Association. For the twenty business days of the survey period, participants were asked to provide details of their gross turnover in foreign exchange, analysed by currency, type of transaction and counterparty. As in 1986, deposit business was specifically excluded from the survey. Gross turnover was defined as the absolute total value of all deals contracted, i.e. the sum of all foreign exchange transactions during the survey period without netting purchases against sales of the same currencies. Data were requested in terms of US dollar equivalents, rounded to the nearest million.

In the currency analysis, details were requested of turnover between the US dollar and each of ten specified major currencies; between the US dollar and any other currency; between sterling and the deutschmark and sterling and any other currency; between the deutschmark and the Japanese yen, the deutschmark and the Swiss franc and the deutschmark and the French franc; between the ECU and any other currency; and between any other two currencies (i.e. besides those specified).

The transactions analysis requested was broadly between business for *spot* value (i.e. for settlement no more than two business days after a deal was contracted); for *forward* value (i.e. for settlement more than two business days after dealing); in foreign currency *options* contracts (i.e. agreements which give the right to, but do not impose any obligation on, the holder of the contract to buy or sell particular foreign currencies at agreed exchange rates at agreed dates in the future); and foreign currency *futures* contracts (i.e. standardized contracts representing commitments to buy or sell fixed amounts of foreign currency at agreed exchange rates on specified dates in the future).

The results of the survey

After adjustment to allow for the double reporting of transactions between principals in the United Kingdom, the average volume of principals' gross business in London during the survey period is estimated to have been some US$187 billion per day (just over double the 1986 figure of $90 billion per day). In addition, however, brokers in London intermediated in transactions averaging the equivalent of US$12 billion per day between *principals abroad* (and not therefore included in the US$187 billion per day figure).

About 66% of participants considered the overall level of turnover during the survey period to be normal; 30% considered business below normal; and the remaining 4% thought that their figures were above average.

With an estimated daily turnover of $187 billion, London remains the world's biggest centre for foreign exchange dealing. However, larger percentage increases in turnover were revealed by the Federal Reserve Bank of New York and the Bank of Japan. The volume of foreign currency trading in New York and Tokyo increased to $129 billion and $115 billion per day respectively (compared with $58 billion and $48 billion per day in 1986). Switzerland ($57 billion per day) was the fourth largest foreign exchange centre of those which published survey results, closely followed by Singapore ($55 billion per day) and Hong Kong ($49 billion per day).

Currency Composition: International Comparisons
(Percentages of principals' overall turnover)

	London	*Tokyo*	*New York*
$/£	27	4	15
$/DM	22	10	33
$/Yen	15	72	25
$/Sw.Fc.	10	4	12
Other (including cross-currency)	26	10	15

A comparison with the results from other centres reveals that the foreign exchange market in London is more diversified than elsewhere.

In all, some twenty central banks conducted surveys of their foreign exchange markets in April, compared with only four in 1986. The surveys were broadly similar, although the details requested varied according to the particular nature of each market covered. While it would be misleading simply to aggregate the individual results to produce a figure for global turnover (because of the double counting of deals between centres), there has clearly been a substantial increase in the volume of foreign exchange activity over the last three years. The increase far exceeds published estimates of the rise in the value of world trade over the period. But, at the same time, there has also been a surge in cross-border capital flows stimulated by the deregulation of financial markets and the relaxation of exchange controls, and this must have contributed to the increase in the level of foreign exchange transactions.

Currency composition

As in 1986, the survey indicated that the bulk of principals' activity in London is in sterling/US dollar (27%) and US dollar/deutschmark (22%) transactions.

Business in the London foreign exchange market continued to be quite widely dispersed. Twenty-seven of the 356 principals participating in the survey accounted for more than 1% each of total gross turnover and, of these, ten had a share of more than 2%. These ten most active principals – seven of which were among the top ten in 1986 – held a combined overall share of some 35% (36% in 1986).

In the case of deutschmark/yen transactions, it is interesting to note that nearly 80% of the business in London is undertaken by North American and Japanese principals.

Foreign institutions accounted for 80% (78% in 1986) of principals' aggregate turnover in London. Although their share declined from 41% in 1986 to 39% in 1989, North American principals remained the major participants, followed by UK principals with 20%. EC principals (excluding the United Kingdom) generated 16% of total turnover (as in 1986), but Japanese principals (up from 7% in 1986 to 11%) and principals from 'other developed countries' (up from 10% to 13%) increased their share of the business in London. The penetration of principals from developing countries declined from 4% to 1%.

Source: 'The Market in Foreign Exchange in London', *Bank of England Quarterly Bulletin*, Nov. 1989.

Questions

1. What does the case study indicate about the relative importance of London as a centre for foreign exchange trading?
2. What reasons are given for the growth in the volume of foreign exchange activity between 1986 and 1989?
3. How does trading in foreign exchange in London differ as compared with that in other leading centres?
4. What other characteristics of the foreign exchange market in London are identified in the case study?

CASE STUDY

Tariff Protection

'In most public discussions of protection', lamented the General Agreement on Tariffs and Trade (GATT) recently, 'the right questions are seldom asked.' The discussion on the future of the Multi Fibre Arrangement (MFA) is unlikely to be an exception. Most of the debate is likely to focus on whether the UK textile industry still needs the degree of protection against imports from developing countries afforded by the MFA.

The allure of protection is that the short-term benefits for the favoured industries are highly visible and easily understood while the longer-term price paid by consumers and, even more importantly, exporters is invisible and misunderstood. The challenge for the Government is to force an answer to the question – Who pays for protection?

The burden of import duties depends on the ability of different sectors to pass on costs. Importers can usually pass on most of the burden of tariffs as higher costs for consumers. Import-competing industries whose weakness necessitated protection in the first place often act as little hindrance since they too are keen to see higher prices and profits. Goods produced domestically for home consumption are often close substitutes for imported goods and so their prices also rise. A general rise in prices feeds through into wages.

Exporters face higher wage costs and higher prices for many of their other inputs. But because they generally face prices set on world prices they are uniquely unable to pass on the cost increase. The protection tax ultimately comes home to roost with exporters.

Source: *Financial Times*, 9 May 1985.

Questions

1. What are the 'highly visible' (lines 17–18) benefits of protection of the United Kingdom textile industry?
2. What does the extract suggest about the effects of tariffs on: (i) importers; (ii) exporters?
3. What would influence 'the ability of different sectors to pass on costs' (lines 27–28)?
4. What arguments, not referred to in the extract, might be used to justify selective tariff protection?

Exam Preparation

PRACTICAL EXERCISE

Based on the following information, draw supply and demand curves for sterling to illustrate the working of the foreign exchange market:

Price of £ ($)	Demand for £ (p.a.)	Supply of £ (p.a.)
2.00	35 500	39 250
1.90	36 000	39 000
1.80	36 500	38 750
1.70	37 000	38 500
1.60	37 500	38 250
1.50	38 000	38 000
1.40	38 500	37 750
1.30	39 000	37 500
1.20	39 500	37 250
1.10	40 000	37 000
1.00	40 500	36 750

(Hint: Draw price axis from £1 = $1.00 to £1 = $2.00 and quantity axis from £34 000m to £41 000m).

What is the equilibrium exchange rate?
What would be the equilibrium exchange rate if

(a) the government cuts overseas defence spending by £500m?
(b) Arab countries wish to hold an extra £1 000m in sterling balances?
(c) American airlines buy ten new British-built aircraft, worth £100m each?
(d) a boom in the domestic economy causes firms to spend an extra £500m on stocks of imported raw materials?

MULTIPLE CHOICE QUESTIONS

1. In the diagram below, D represents the demand for the currency of country X and S represents the supply of the currency of country X (on the foreign exchange market).

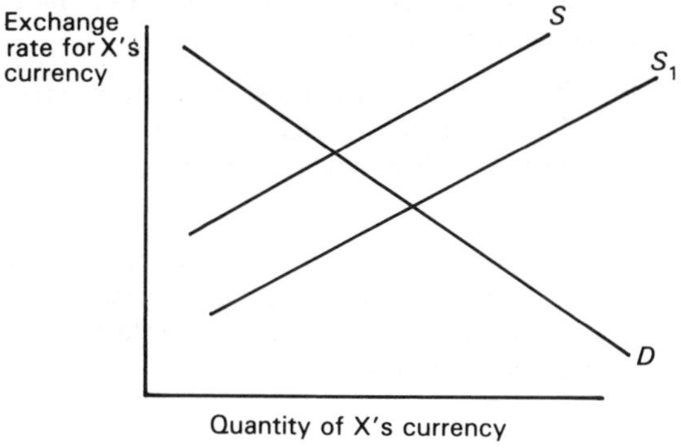

Everything else remaining the same, a shift from S to S_1 would arise if

A other countries became less willing to invest in country X
B exchange controls were imposed in country X
C country X devalued its currency
D country X increases its sales of currency on the foreign exchange market.

2. Which of the following is most likely to cause an immediate rise in the UK's gold and foreign currency reserves?

A Speculation that the Swiss franc will soon be revalued
B UK drawings from the International Monetary Fund
C A reduction in interest rates in the UK
D A rise in world primary product prices.

3. The value of the German mark (DM) changes against the pound (£) from £0.40 to £0.60. Which one of the following statements is consistent with this information?

A UK exports to Germany will now be dearer
B The pound has depreciated against the German mark
C The cost to the UK of maintaining forces in Germany will decrease
D UK imports from Germany will now be cheaper
E Germans visiting the UK will now be worse off.

4. Pre-trade demand and supply conditions for a certain product in Malaysia and Singapore are represented in the diagram.

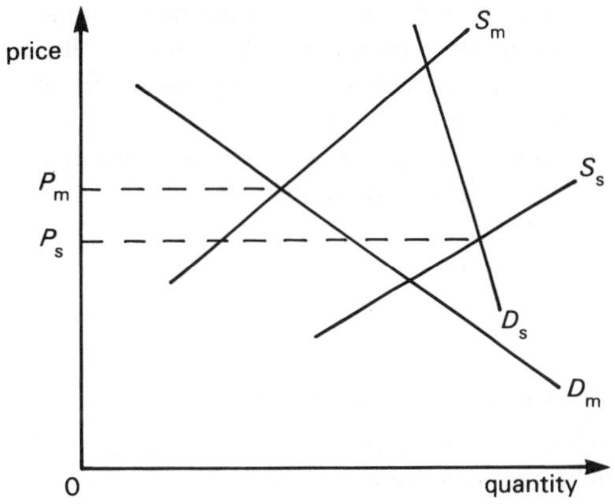

D_m and D_s represent the demand curves in Malaysia and Singapore respectively; S_s and S_m represent the supply curves.
Assuming zero transport costs, what will happen to prices in both countries after trade takes place?

A They will remain unaltered
B They will be equalized at a level between P_m and P_s
C They will be equal to P_m
D They will be equal to P_s
E They will fall below P_s.

5. Using all available resources, country X can produce 1 tonne of food or 3 tonnes of cloth, while country Y can produce ½ tonne of food or 1 tonne of cloth. Each country will benefit from trade if the price of food in terms of cloth is

A 1 tonne of food for 1 tonne of cloth
B 1 tonne of food for 1½ tonnes of cloth
C 1 tonne of food for 2 tonnes of cloth
D 1 tonne of food for 2½ tonnes of cloth.

6. The two diagrams below show production possibility curves for two countries X and Y producing both tea and linen.

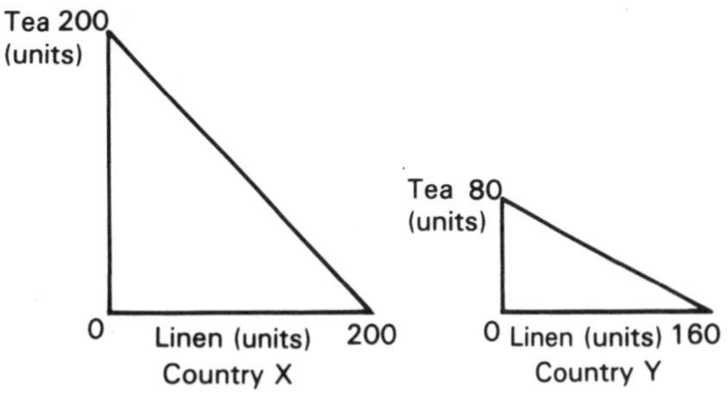

With regard to the principle of comparative advantage it can be seen that

A Neither country possesses a comparative advantage in the production of tea or linen

B Country X possesses a comparative advantage in the production of both tea and linen

C Country X possesses a comparative advantage in tea production

D Country X possesses a comparative advantage in linen production.

RELATED ESSAY QUESTIONS

1. What are the gains from international trade? Who receives them?

2. What are the main components of the overseas trade accounts? How might a country finance a persistent balance-of-trade deficit?

3. Analyse the probable economic consequences of import controls.

4. Evaluate the case for free trade. Discuss the possible effects of the current spread of trade agreements among nations.

5. (a) Explain how countries gain from specialization and international trade.
(b) Why then do countries restrict free international trade?

6. 'If the theory of comparative advantage points to the benefit of international specialization there is no basis for government interference with trade.' Discuss.

Part B

Introductory Macroeconomics

10 The Role and Size of Government

Key Points to Review

- Opportunity cost (1.5)
- Public expenditure and transfer payments (4.2)
- Market forces (5.7)
- Shifts in demand (5.3)
- Shifts in supply (5.5)
- Market failure: externalities and public goods (6.6)
- Indirect taxes (8.5)

Questions for Preview

1 What are the main economic objectives that *all* post-war governments have striven to achieve?

2 Pollution is considered to be an example of a negative externality. Why?

3 What is a public good and what examples can you think of?

4 What is the difference between a private good and a merit good?

5 What has been happening to public spending in recent years in the United Kingdom?

6 (a) What is the difference between a progressive and a regressive tax?
(b) Can you identify some specific examples of each?

The pricing system answers three basic questions of resource allocation: *what* goods will be produced? *how* will they be produced? and for *whom* will they be produced? The forces of supply and demand acting through the pricing system (that is, the market) affect the bulk of decisions that answer these three questions. But we do not live in a free-market world. In addition to market forces, there are many other forces at work that affect the allocation of resources. One of the most important of these non-market forces is government. In this chapter *first* we will look at the *role* that government plays to affect the resource allocation within the economy. Then we will look *at its size*; this will be mainly achieved by analysing government *expenditure*, as the size of government relative to the total economy is an indicator of its importance in resource allocation. Finally, we will complete the chapter by briefly looking at the related topic of taxation – as taxes also affect resource allocation.

The Role of Government in the Economy

All UK governments, regardless of political colour, provide economic functions. A significant number of these functions have arisen in order to overcome the inadequacies of the market system. **Market failure** is commonly identified by economists in many instances. Indeed any situation in which the unrestrained market system causes too few or too many resources to be allocated to a specific economic activity could be stated as an example. Consequently, it would be rather arduous to list all the specific instances of market failure that exist – but in this chapter we will deal with four of the major areas in which the market is recognized to fail. These are:

1. Market economies tend to experience severe business fluctuations.
2. The market system cannot deal effectively with the spill-over (third-party) effects of many economic activities and therefore alternative systems of allocation need to be considered.
3. Market forces cannot provide public goods and make a poor job of providing certain other goods of merit.
4. Market forces lead to an unequal distribution of income and wealth.

As already suggested the government intervenes in various ways to correct these failings. We will deal with each of these in turn before briefly considering the related problem of government failure.

Striving to achieve Economic Stability

All UK governments attempt to stabilize the economy by smoothing out the ups and downs in overall business activity. They aim to maintain full employment, keep prices steady, sustain economic growth, achieve an equilibrium on the balance of payments, prevent environmental damage, and redistribute income and welfare. UK governments have taken on the task of attempting to meet all these important objectives in order to stabilize the economy. The order of priority in which these economic objectives are attacked depends on the government in office but *all* governments ultimately desire these same objectives in their quest for economic stability.

This notion that the government should undertake actions to stabilize business activity is in historical terms a relatively new idea. In Winston Churchill's budget speech of 1929 he said: 'It is the orthodox Treasury dogma that, whatever the social and political advantages, . . . no permanent additional employment can . . . be created by state borrowing and public expenditure.' Since then, however, economic advisers and economic graduates have been appointed by governments to measure and analyse economic trends and suggest policy for their manipulation. The turning-point when governments took on responsibility for economic objectives became pronounced after the Second World War. For example, the White Paper on Employment published in May 1944 stated that the government accept 'as one of their primary aims and responsibilities the maintenance of a high and stable level of employment after the war'.

Since this statement of intent in 1944 employment policy has been an important criterion for all governments. Recently, however, it has been dropped from the number-one spot to allow a more concentrated effort on curbing inflation – which ultimately, it is hoped, will have a desirable effect on the other objectives including the reduction of unemployment. The environmental question is also becoming more important as an economic issue in the 1990s. The discussion on unemployment and inflation as key variables will be picked up again in subsequent chapters. And later on in the text the question of growth will also be discussed more fully. (Now see Key Points 10.1.)

Correcting Externalities

We now come to the second item on our list of market failures which represents a major imperfection of the price system. According to accepted criteria identified by the economist Pareto at the turn of this century, economic efficiency should describe a situation in which nobody can be made better off without making somebody else worse off. Consequently in the pure market system, competition would only generate economic efficiency when individuals are faced with the true opportunity cost of their actions. In some circumstances, the price that someone actually pays for a resource, good, or service, is higher or lower than the opportunity cost that society as a whole pays for that same resource, good, or service.

Key Points 10.1

- **The economic functions of government are largely designed to overcome recognized problems of market failure.**
- **Economic stability is a responsibility accepted by *all* post-war governments.**
- **To achieve economic stability various objectives are pursued: full employment, stable prices, equilibrium on the balance of payments, a clean environment, steady growth, and a redistribution of income and welfare.**
- **The various economic objectives identified change in their order of priority according to the government in office.**

Consider a hypothetical world where there is no government regulation against pollution. You are living in a town that so far has clean air. A steel mill moves into your town. It produces steel for which it has paid for the inputs – land, labour, capital, and entrepreneurship. The price it charges for the steel reflects, in this example, only the costs that the steel mill incurred. In the course of production, however, the mill gives off smoke – free by simply dispersing it. This is indeed taking a liberty. The steel mill does not have to pay the cost of cleaning up the smoke; rather, it is the people in the community who pay that cost in the form of dirtier clothes, dirtier cars and houses, and perhaps even more respiratory illnesses. The effect is similar to what would happen if the steel mill could take coal or oil free. There has been a spill-over effect, or an **externality**. Actually, there has been an *external cost.* Some of the costs associated with the production of the steel have *spilled over* to **third parties**, that is, parties other than the buyer and the seller of the steel. A negative spill-over is called a *negative externality* because there are costs that you and your neighbours pay – dirtier clothes and cars plus respiratory problems – even though your group is external to the market transaction between the steel mill and the buyers of steel.

Not all externalities are negative. Using a classic example, even people who *do not* receive inoculations against polio, smallpox, whooping cough, and diphtheria benefit from everyone else being inoculated, for epidemics will not break out. Thus there are benefits that are external to each individual's decision to be inoculated. We call the existence of such benefits a *positive* externality.

Attempting to Measure External Costs

Look at panel (a) in Figure 10.1. Here we show the demand curve for steel to be *DD*. The supply curve, as observed by the steel mill in your town is *SS*. That supply curve includes only those costs that the firm has to pay. The equilibrium, or market-clearing, situation will occur at a quantity of Q_e. Let us take into account the fact that there are external costs. These are the spill-over costs that you and your neighbours pay in the form of dirtier clothes, cars, houses, and increased respiratory disease due to the air pollution emitted from the steel mill. Let us include these costs in our graph. We do this to find out what the full cost of steel production really is. This is equivalent to saying that the price of some other input into steel production has increased. Remember that in Chapter 5 we showed that an increase in input prices would shift the supply curve inwards to the left. Thus, in panel (a) of Figure 10.1 the supply curve shifts from *SS* to *S′S′*. If the spill-over costs were somehow taken into acount, the equilibrium quantity would fall to Q_e' and the price would rise to P_e'. That price is implicitly being paid in full, but by two different groups of people. The lower price P_e is being explicitly paid for by the purchasers of steel and steel products. The difference between P_e' and P_e represents the cost that third parties are bearing in the form of dirtier clothes, houses, cars, and increased respiratory illnesses.

Figure 10.1

External Costs and Benefits. In panel (a) we show a situation in which the production of steel generates external costs. If the steel mill ignores pollution, at equilibrium the quantity will be Q_e, where the demand curve, *DD*, intersects the supply curve *SS*. If we include the additional cost borne by nearby residents that is caused by the steel mill's production, the supply curve would shift inward to the left to *S′S′*. This shows that the society is devoting too many resources to steel production if external costs are not taken into account, for if consumers were forced to pay a price that reflected the environmental cost of the spill-over costs the quantity demanded would fall to Q_e'. In panel (b) we show the situation in which inoculations against diseases generate external benefits to those individuals who may not be inoculated but who will benefit because epidemics will not break out. If each individual ignores the external benefit of inoculations, the market-clearing quantity will be Q_e, where *DD* intersects *SS*. If external benefits are taken into account, however, the demand curve would shift rightward to *D′D′*. The new equilibrium quantity would be Q_e' and the price would be higher, P_e'. With no corrective action, however, this society is not devoting enough resources to inoculations against contagious diseases.

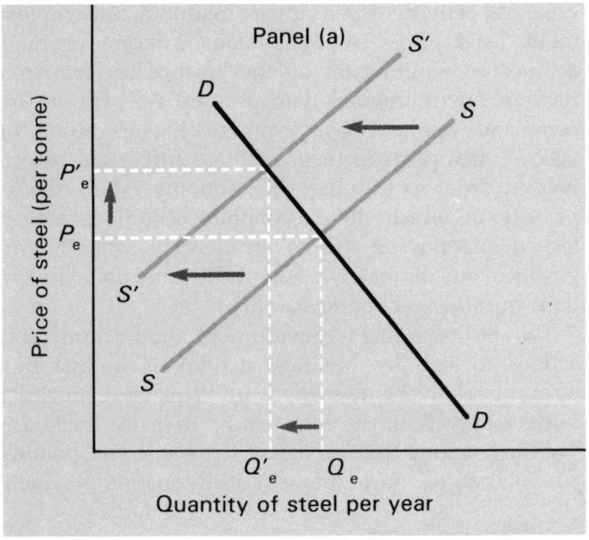

Attempting to Measure External Benefits

To demonstrate external benefits in graph form, we will use the example already mentioned concerning inoculations against various diseases. In panel (b) of Figure 10.1 we show the demand curve, without taking account of any external benefits as *DD* and the supply curve as *SS*. The equilibrium price is P_e and the equilibrium quantity is Q_e. We assume, however, that inoculations against contagious diseases generate external benefits to those individuals who may not be

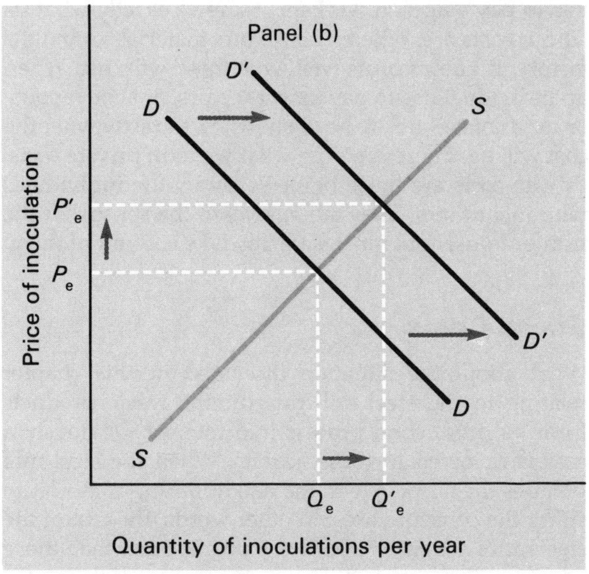

inoculated but who benefit because epidemics will not break out. If such external benefits are taken into account, the demand curve would shift out from *DD* to *D'D'*. The new equilibrium quantity would be Q_e' and the new equilibrium price would be P_e'. With no corrective action, this society is not devoting enough resources to inoculations against diseases.

SUMMARY OF EXTERNALITIES

We have seen that when there are external costs the market will tend to over-allocate resources to the production of the good in question (as these costs are not borne by the producer). In our example, too much steel was being produced. On the other hand, when there are external benefits the market forces will under-allocate resources to the production of that good or service. When there is over- or under-allocation of resources to the production of a good or service because of spill-overs, or externalities, we have cases of **market failure**.

How the Government Can Correct Negative Externalities

Since, by definition, externalities that create market failure will not be corrected by the market, we cannot expect, at least not with the examples we have given, that private individuals will prevent the over- or under-allocation of resources. The government, on the other hand, could correct externality situations in a variety of ways in all cases that warranted such action. In the case of negative externalities, at least two avenues of action are open to the government – special taxes and/or legislation.

1. *Special Taxes.* In our example of a steel mill, the externality problem originates from the fact that air as a dumping-place is costless to the firm. The government can, however, compensate for this flaw by charging a price for the use of air. In other words, the government could make the steel mill pay a tax for dumping its pollutants into the air. The government could attempt to place a tax on the steel mill, commensurate with the cost to third parties from smoke in the air. This, in effect, would be a pollution tax. There is a serious question as to how it should be assessed – at what rate and using what criteria. One way of making the mill pay for use of the air is a tax based on the mill's output of steel. After all, the more steel the mill produces, the more pollution it dumps into the air. But this way of taxing creates a problem. Besides inhibiting the production of steel, it would *not provide* an incentive for the mill to find ways to reduce the amount of pollution per unit of output. For example, let us assume that for every tonne of steel produced, ten grams of pollutants are spewed into the atmosphere. If the steel mill is taxed according to the number of tonnes of steel produced by it, it may reduce its total yearly output, but it will certainly not seek ways to reduce the number of grams of pollutants produced *per tonne* from ten down to, let us say, five. Therefore, an alternative tax system would be one based on the amount of the pollution dumped into the air rather than just a tax on output itself. Then if the steel mill came up with various methods to reduce air pollution, it would pay a lower tax.

   No matter what type of tax is used, the supply curve will move leftwards as it did in panel (a) of Figure 10.1. The ultimate effect would be to raise the price to consumers. The equilibrium quantity of steel would fall in our example. But the full cost of its production would be borne by those consuming it.
2. *Legislation.* In order to correct a negative externality, or negative spill-over, arising from steel production, the government could simply specify a maximum allowable rate of pollution. This action would require that the steel mill install pollution-abatement equipment within its facilities, or that it reduce its rate of output, or some combination of the two. In any event, the steel mill's supply curve would again shift leftwards as it did in panel (a) of Figure 10.1.

How the Government Can Correct Positive Externalities

In this section about the role of government, we have talked in terms of negative externalities and what it is possible to do about correcting them. We shall be returning to this issue later in the chapter when we will examine some specific UK government initiatives. Now, however, we shall discuss very briefly the case of positive externalities. Here the question is: What can the government do when the production of one good spills benefits over to third parties? There are several policy options facing the government: (1) financing the production of the good or producing the good itself, (2) special subsidies (negative taxes), and (3) legislation.

1. *Government Financing and Production*. If the positive externalities seem to be extremely large, the government has the option of financing the desired additional production facilities so that there will be the 'right' amount of the good produced. In the previous example of inoculations against contagious diseases, the government could finance campaigns to inoculate the population. It could even produce and operate centres for inoculation
2. *Special Subsidies*. A **subsidy** is a negative tax; it is a payment made either to a business or to a consumer when the business produces or the consumer buys a good or a service. For example, in the case of youth training, the government subsidizes everyone who is on a youth training scheme by making payments to private firms that provide the schemes. Subsidies, in this case, reduce the net price to employers, thereby causing a larger equilibrium quantity of training and a more skilled workforce for the future community.
3. *Legislation*. In the case of certain positive externalities, the government can require by law that a certain action be undertaken by individuals in the society. For example, there are regulations requiring all school-age children to be inoculated prior to entrance into schools. Some people believe that state education itself generates positive externalities. Indeed, we have regulations – laws – that require all children aged 5–16 to attend school. (See Key Points 10.2.)

A more elaborate way of accounting for both positive and negative externalities at once is via **cost-benefit analysis** and this will be dealt with after clarifying some related terms and the ideas they illustrate.

Private Costs, Social Costs, and Externalities

Private Costs

Up until this chapter we have been dealing with situations where the costs of an individual's actions are borne directly by the individual. When a business firm has to pay wages to workers, it knows exactly what its labour costs are. When it has to buy materials or build a factory, it knows quite well what these will cost. When an individual has to pay for car repairs, or shoe repairs, or for a concert ticket, he or she knows exactly what the cost will be. These costs are what we term **private costs**. Private costs are those borne solely by the individuals who incur them. They are *internal* in the sense that the firm or household must explicitly take account of them.

Social Costs

What about the situation discussed in this chapter relating to the steel mill that dumps waste products from its production process into the air? Obviously a cost is involved in these actions. When the steel mill pollutes the air people in the neighbouring community suffer the consequences. In other words, the cost of the steel mill's actions are borne by people other than those who own the steel mill. That is, the creator of the cost is not the sole bearer. The costs are not internalized by the individual or firm; they are external. When we add these *external costs* to *internal*, or private costs, we get **social costs**. Pollution problems, and, indeed all problems pertaining to the environment may be viewed as situations where social costs are greater than private costs. Since some economic agents do not pay the full social costs of their actions, but rather only the smaller private costs, their actions are socially 'unacceptable'. In such situations where there is a divergence between social and private costs, we therefore see 'too much' steel production, car-driving, and beach-littering – to pick only a few of the many examples that exist.

ENVIRONMENTAL COST: A PRIVATE OR SOCIAL BILL?

Why is the air in cities so polluted from car exhaust fumes? When drivers step into their cars, they bear only the private costs of driving. That is, they must pay for the petrol, maintenance, depreciation, and insurance on their cars. They cause, however, an additional cost – that of air pollution – which they are not forced to take into account when they make the decision to drive.

Key Points 10.2

- **Negative externalities, or negative spill-overs, lead to an over-allocation of resources to the specific economic activity. Two possible ways of correcting these spill-overs are (1) taxation or (2) government legislation.**
- **Positive externalities, or positive spill-overs, result in an under-allocation of resources to the specific activity. Three possible government corrections are: (1) financing the production of the activity, (2) subsidizing private firms or consumers to engage in the activity, or (3) legislation.**

Air pollution is a cost because it causes harm to individuals, for example, burning eyes, respiratory ailments, and dirtier clothes, cars, and buildings. The air pollution created by exhausts is a cost that, as yet, individual drivers do not bear *directly*. The social cost of driving includes all the private costs plus the costs of air pollution, which society bears. Decisions made only on the basis of private costs lead to too much driving or, alternatively, to too little money spent on the reduction of pollution for a given amount of driving.

Consider the example of lights in hotel rooms. Paying guests know that they will not pay any more on any single occasion if they leave their lights on in the hotel room. Of course, the more frequently all guests leave their lights on, the higher will be the cost of running the hotel and the higher will be the average room charge. But for the individual guest at any one point in time, there is no direct cost to being 'wasteful' with energy used for lights. In essence, lights in a hotel are a free good in the eyes of each hotel guest. We predict, therefore, that people will leave lights on more often in hotel rooms than they will in their own homes. We can look at another example and consider clean air as the scarce resource offered to car drivers free of charge. The same analysis will hold – they will use more of it than they would if they had to pay the full social costs.

Externalities Revisited

When private costs differ from social costs we have used the term *externalities* – because individual decision-makers are not internalizing *all* the costs. Rather, some of these costs remain external to the decision-making process. Remember that the full cost of using a scarce resource is borne one way or another by others who live in the society. That is, society must pay the full opportunity cost of any activity that uses scarce resources. The individual decision-maker is the firm or the customer, and external costs and benefits will *not* enter into that individual's or firm's decision-making processes.

It will help to view the problem as it is presented in Figure 10.2. Here we have the market demand curve, *DD*, for the product X and the supply curve, *SS*, for product X. As usual the supply curve includes only internal, or private, costs. The intersection of the demand and supply curves as drawn will be at price P_e and quantity Q_e. However, we will assume that the production of good X involves externalities that the private business firms did not take into account. These externalities could be air pollution, water pollution, scenery destruction, or anything of that nature.

We know that the social costs of producing X exceed the private costs. We show this by drawing supply curve *S′S′*. It is above the original supply curve, *SS*, because it includes the externalities, or the full social costs of producing the product. Now the 'correct' market equilibrium price is P_1, and the equilibrium quantity is Q_1. The inclusion of external costs in the decision-making process leads to a higher-priced product and a decline in quantity produced. We can say, therefore, that in an unrestricted situation where social costs are not being fully borne by the creators of these costs, the quantity produced is 'excessive'.

Figure 10.2

Reckoning with Full Social Costs. Here we show the demand for good X as *DD*. The supply curve, *SS* represents the summation of the costs to the firm in producing that good. These costs are internal, or private, costs; they do not include any external costs such as pollution of the air or water. If the external costs were included and added to the private costs then we would have social costs. The supply curve would shift upward to *S′S′*. In the uncorrected situation the equilibrium price would be P_e and the equilibrium quantity would be Q_e. In the corrected situation the equilibrium price would rise to P_1 and the equilibrium quantity would fall to Q_1.

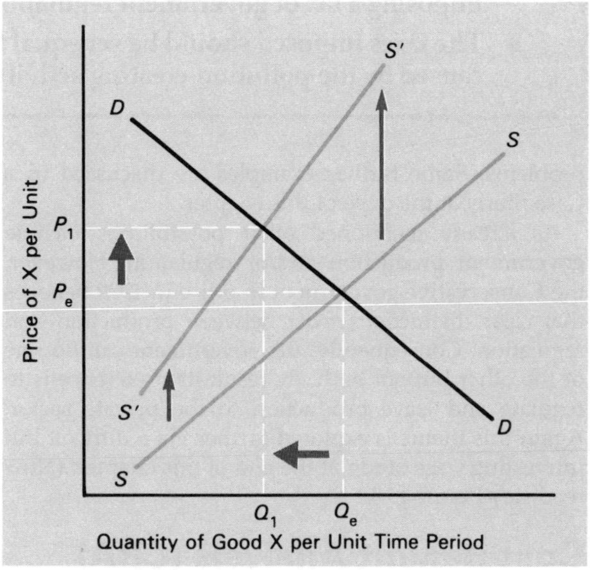

Moving towards Policies for Internalizing Externalities

We can see an easy theoretical option that presents itself as a method of reducing the amount of pollution and environmental degradation that exists. Somehow the signals in the economy must be changed so that decision-makers will take into account *all* the costs of their actions. For example, in the case of car pollution we might want to devise some method whereby motorists are taxed according to the amount of pollution they cause. To a large extent the cheaper tax imposed on users of lead-free petrol follows this theory. Indeed government policy in the UK is influenced by this theory and the price mechanism is seen as a promising possibility for solving many environmental

Key Points 10.3

- **Private costs are those explicit costs that are borne directly by consumers and producers when they engage in any resource-using activity.**
- **Social costs include private costs plus any other costs that are external to the decision-maker. For example, the social cost of driving includes all the private costs plus any pollution and congestion caused.**
- **When private costs differ from social costs, externalities exist, because individual decision-makers are not internalizing all the costs that society is bearing.**
- **When social costs exceed private costs, environmental problems may ensue, such as excessive pollution of air and water. These are problems of externalities.**
- **One way to make private costs equal social costs is to internalize the externality by imposing a tax or government regulation.**
- **The taxes imposed should be set equal to the economic damage, or externalities, caused by the pollution-creating activity.**

problems. Some further examples are discussed in a Case Study at the close of this chapter.

As already mentioned other possibilities include government production and/or regulation. However, the Conservative government in office in 1990 believes that clear distinctions exist between production and regulation. Consequently, the government can do one or the other but not both. By result its preference is to regulate and leave production to the private sector. Again this theme is explored further via a difficult but interesting Case Study at the end of this chapter. (Now read Key Points 10.3.)

Cost-Benefit Analysis (CBA)

To overcome some of the problems of resource allocation created by the market mechanism, government economists in the UK are increasingly employing an investment appraisal technique known as **cost-benefit analysis**. This method of resource allocation, popular since the 1960s, reaches the parts that most methods of resource allocation leave behind. In these analyses the external costs and benefits are considered alongside the internal (private) costs and benefits. Thus the *total* social costs and benefits are measured. The problem with this technique is that all issues need to be expressed in a common denominator for a 'total price' to be arrived at. The 'total (social) price' will incorporate internal and external costs and benefits.*

What is actually measured and how the related monetary value is identified is problematic. The externalities that are listed to a large extent rely upon normative decisions based on value-judgements. These are given monetary values based upon the principle of opportunity cost. For example, when undertaking the cost-benefit analysis of siting London's third airport, noise pollution was quantified on the principle of how much it would cost in double and treble glazing to return the houses concerned to their foregone level of silence.

Cost-benefit analysis studies have also been undertaken to assess the building of motorways, the Channel Tunnel, and the construction of the Victoria underground line in London. It may be worth your while to look at one of these examples in detail to further your understanding of the cost-benefit analysis technique. Finally, before closing this section, it should be emphasized that the technique of CBA is merely a method of *identifying* externalities; it does not automatically control them. (Now read Key Points 10.4.)

Providing Public Goods and Merit Goods

The third area which we identified in our introductory list as a market failure related to the provision of public and merit goods. In reviewing these government-provided goods and services we will, to a certain extent, revise themes that have already been raised under the heading of externalities. The benefits that people get from these particular goods depends not solely on how much they individually have, but also on how much other people have – which is part of the rationale for governments providing them.

Public Goods

In order to explain the precise nature of public goods it is appropriate to begin at the other end of the spectrum and clarify our understanding of **private goods**. Indeed, so far in this text it is these so-called private goods that we have generally discussed, for example, petrol, wheat, hamburgers, chips, wine, and manufactured commodities. These private goods are distinguished by

**Important note*: rather confusingly, some authors will employ the terms 'social' costs or benefits in the *same* way as we have used the terms 'external' costs and benefits. This confusion of terms simply represents the developmental nature of this concept in terms of exposition.

Key Points 10.4

- **Internal costs + external costs = total (social) costs.**
- **Internal benefits + external benefits = total (social) benefits.**
- **CBA involves identifying monetary values for *all* the internal and external costs and benefits of a project allowing a total (social) price to be arrived at.**
- **The problems with CBA are what to include as 'relevant' externalities and how to quantify these in monetary terms.**
- **The use of CBA in government departments is increasing.**

two basic principles, one can be termed the **principle of rivalry**. This means that if you use a private good *I cannot use it*. And conversely, if I use a private good *you cannot use it*. For example, when I use the services of a mechanic he cannot be working at the same time on your car. We compete for the mechanic's services, we are rivals for this resource, i.e. the amount of a mechanic's time is scarce. The mechanics' services are therefore priced according to our levels of demand and the available supply of their time. The other principle that characterizes a private good is **excludability**. This simply implies that anyone who does not pay for the good or service is excluded from enjoying its benefits. For example, if a road bridge is set up with a toll-gate, then the communications link that the particular bridge offers is available only to those who pay. All others are excluded by the price mechanism. Similarly, if you do not pay for an FA cup final ticket you will not be allowed into Wembley to watch the football match.

There is an entire class of goods that are not private goods. These are called **public goods**. In these cases the principles of exclusion or rivalry cannot be applied. They are non-excludable and non-rivalrous in their characteristics. That is, they can be *jointly* consumed by many individuals simultaneously without any discriminatory price system being applied. National defence, street-lighting, and protection policy are standard textbook examples of public goods.

CHARACTERISTICS OF PUBLIC GOODS

We can list therefore several distinguishing characteristics of public goods that set them apart from all other goods.*

1. *Public goods are usually indivisible*. You cannot buy or sell £5 worth of our ability to annihilate the world with bombs. Public goods cannot be produced or sold very easily in small units.
2. *Public goods can be used by increasing numbers of people at no additional cost*, e.g. once a lighthouse has been built the first and last ship to pass does so at no extra cost to the lighthouse-keeper; the opportunity cost of an extra ship benefiting from the signal is zero.
3. *Additional users of public goods do not deprive others of any of the services of the good*, e.g. if you use the beams from the lighthouse other ships do not become excluded from its illumination.
4. *It is very difficult to charge people for a public good on the basis of how much they use*. It is nearly impossible to determine how much any person uses or values national defence. It cannot be bought and sold in the market-place.

* Sometimes a distinction is made between pure public goods which have both the characteristics described above, and quasi- or near- or impure public goods, which do not. The major features of near-public goods is that they are jointly consumed.

FREE RIDERS

This last point leads us to the **free-rider problem**. It is a problem because it involves a situation in which some individuals believe that others will take on the burden of paying for public goods such as national defence. Alternatively, 'free riders' will argue that they receive no value from such government services as national defence or overseas representation and, therefore, really should not pay for it. Consider a hypothetical example: citizens will be taxed directly in proportion to how much they tell an interviewer that they value national defence for the following year. Some people will probably tell interviewers that they are unwilling to pay for national defence because they do not want any of it – it is of no value to them. Many of them would end up being free riders especially when they assume that others will pay for the desired public good anyway. We all want to be free riders when we believe that someone else will provide the commodity in question.

Look at the problem as it is represented in Figure 10.3. Here we show the different possible outcomes depending on whether you decide to pay your share of the annual national defence budget and whether others decide to pay. If everyone else pays and you pay also, the total amount of money spent on national defence would be £20 000 000 100 per year. If you do not pay, the total amount for national defence will fall only by £100 to £20 000 000 000 per year. The difference does not seem to be very much, and, expressed as a

Figure 10.3

Scoreboard for National Defence. The free rider is the one who will gladly let everyone else pay the bill. If you do not pay your share of national defence but everyone else does, there will still be £20 billion per year available for the country's defence.

	If you pay	*If you do not pay*
And if everbody else pays	£20 000 000 100/yr	£20 000 000 000/yr
And if no one else pays	£100/yr	£0.00/yr

percentage of the total defence budget, it is very small indeed. There are two other possibilities. If no one else pays and you pay, national defence spending will be only £100 per year, and then if you do not pay and no one else pays either, there will be no money spent on national defence that year.

What is a probable choice that you might make in such a situation? If you pay, either others will or they will not. If they do not, your £100 is not going to matter much; if they do, your £100 will still not matter much. Why not take a free ride? That's exactly what the free-rider problem is all about. Public goods, therefore, may be provided in too small amounts if left to the private sector.

Many products and services in our economy are public goods, e.g. the fire services, the maintenance of law and order, and overseas representation. There is a very strong case for having the government finance them. In fact even Adam Smith, the prime exponent of free-market forces, recognized that the government must provide them and in most countries today this is the case.

Merit Goods (and Demerit Goods)

Merit goods by comparison differ from country to country. What constitutes a merit good is defined by the political process according to what the government deem to be socially desirable. Once this decision has been taken those goods that are selected are made available free, or almost free, to all citizens, either by the government subsidizing the production or more commonly actually organizing the output themselves. Some examples of merit goods in the UK are: museums, ballet and the arts, health services, education, and library provision. Note that there is nothing inherent in any of these particular goods that makes them different from private goods. They *can be supplied through the market* and in some countries they actually are (e.g. medical care in America).

It is clearly a political decision, therefore, as to what constitutes a merit good, but in general terms they serve two objectives. First, they facilitate a redistribution of real income; as merit goods are largely financed out of progressive taxation – the result is that the poorer citizens get access to a standard of service that they could not otherwise afford. Secondly, by making these goods readily available to all citizens at well below the market-clearing price society can take advantage of positive externalities as individuals become better educated and healthier, and thus provide a more effective labour force and ultimately a higher standard of living for the country as a whole.

Demerit goods are the opposite of merit goods. They are goods that, through the political process, are deemed socially undesirable. Heroin, morphine, and LSD are just some examples of so-called demerit goods. The way the government exercises its role in the area of demerit goods is by taxing, regulating, or prohibiting their manufacture, sale, and use. Partly, the age restrictions imposed on juveniles purchasing alcohol and tobacco are justified by governments on the basis that these are demerit goods. (Note that there is a subtle difference between making under-age drinking illegal – a demerit good argument – and making drunken driving illegal. The latter law is based on arguments for regulating a negative externality due to its third-party effects.)

In Britain it is claimed that we have developed a 'caring society' that looks after each of us from 'the cradle to the coffin'. (Some people may well feel that we are less caring than we used to be.) In consequence more than a third of our government spending goes into the provision of these various merit goods and the regulation of demerit goods. (Now read Key Points 10.5.)

Income and Welfare Redistribution

The price (market) system will allocate nothing to those who cannot pay. Left to market forces owners of factors of production who are paid for their services will have significantly better life chances than their retired, unemployed, disabled, or under-privileged counterparts. Consequently *all* post-war governments – although with differing levels of commitment – are concerned with the distribution of income and welfare.

In general the required redistribution uses *three* systems: the *system of taxation*, especially progressive income tax which involves taxing high-income earners progressively more than the lower paid (see closing section of this chapter for more details); the *provision of merit goods* as discussed above, which makes essential services freely available to all; and *transfer payments* (defined in Chapter 4).

Transfer payments are those payments made to individuals for which no services are concurrently rendered. The main transfer payments in our system are social security, old-age pensions, and various grants.

Key Points 10.5

- **Public goods are jointly consumed. The principles of exclusion and rivalry do not apply as they do with private goods.**
- **Public goods have the following characteristics: (1) they are indivisible; (2) once they are produced, there is no opportunity cost of additional consumers using them; (3) your use of a public good does not deprive others of its simultaneous use; and (4) there is difficulty in charging consumers on the basis of use.**
- **Merit and demerit goods do not have any inherent characteristics that qualify them as such; rather, we collectively, through the political process, make judgements about which goods and services are 'good' for society and which are 'bad'.**
- **The provision of public goods and merit goods contributes to a nation's standard of living, as they accommodate positive externalities. In the UK a substantial part of government spending involves the provision of these goods.**

Some of these income-redistribution schemes are specifically means-tested to assure that only the poor benefit. Others, however, are available to all as a basic human right, regardless of financial position. In most cases the former selective payments take the form of cash benefits, whilst the latter universal provisions (often provided as merit goods) are known as 'benefits-in-kind'.

Increased expenditure on these welfare-type policies have 'knock-on' and 'knock-off' effects on the other government objectives. For example, further inflationary pressures may be generated due to increases in public expenditure and/or increased unemployment may follow as incentives to work become less attractive due to an increase in social security. In fact several of the objectives discussed within this chapter interlink and even conflict with one another. This will become more apparent when we look at policies, in Part E of the book, as often one government policy affects several government objectives, and unfortunately the results may not all be symmetrical. Indeed it is the incompatibility of the various objectives that leads to debates regarding their order of priority.

A Closing Note on Government Failure

The last point, made above, emphasizes the vulnerability of those in government. The electorate expect them continually to make correct decisions to difficult questions – yet politicians are only human and may fail occasionally. Indeed, knowing what is genuinely in the 'public's interest' is recognizably a difficult concept. To get a consensus of opinion on a topical economic issue amongst your classmates would be difficult. Similarly, Members of Parliament with their developed political values, established support groups, and often constraints of time and information will understandably find it hard always to reach the right majority decision.

Consequently, we arrive at an ironic juncture. So far throughout this chapter we have justified a role for government intervention on the basis of market failure, and we now close the section by suggesting the possibility of **government failure**. It would be a foolhardy cynic, however, who resolved this problem by claiming a situation of total failure. Often commentators on these two polar extremes of failure adopt one position or the other as correct. We would suggest that the solution lies in some kind of mix in between. (See Key Points 10.6.)

The Size and Growth of Government

When considering the role of the government in an economy its level of expenditure is a key variable for analysis. For example, in the UK around 40 per cent of the annual total expenditure is executed by the government, compared to approximately 60 per cent in Sweden and 32 per cent in the USA. In the remaining part of this chapter we will see what the government does with these resources – its expenditure. Then we will move to the other side of the balance sheet and briefly consider where it gets the revenues it spends, i.e. taxation.

In Figure 10.4 (page 166) we present a detailed breakdown of the UK's public (government) expenditure for the years 1987–92. Basically Figure 10.4 reflects many of the themes so far covered in this chapter. In fact the expenditure pattern for the various public goods, merit goods, transfer payments, and policy manœuvres that the UK government is presently involved in could be identified and calculated as separate categories. It is clear from Figure 10.4 that large increases in the health and social security areas are anticipated, while spending on energy, trade, industry, and employment will be reduced in real terms. Such observations about individual programmes provide some idea of a government's priorities, policies, and philosophy.

Key Points 10.6

- **All post-war governments in the UK are concerned with achieving some kind of 'fair' income and welfare distribution.**
- **Income redistribution is achieved through three systems: taxation, transfer payments (cash benefits), and merit goods (benefits in kind).**
- **The various economic objectives identified in this chapter are incompatible with one another and in consequence their order of priority changes according to the government in office.**
- **Market failure initially justified a role for governments. Government failure suggests a role for markets. The solution to this dilemma lies in between with some kind of mixed economy.**

Figure 10.4

Public Expenditure by Department 1987–92 (in cash terms)

	1987–8 Outturn (£bn)	*1989–90 Plans (£bn)*	*1990–1 Plans (£bn)*	*1991–2 Plans (£bn)*
Social security	46.3	51.0	55.3	58.7
Health	19.7	23.2	24.4	25.4
Defence	18.7	20.1	21.2	22.1
Education and science	17.1	19.6	20.2	20.8
Home Office and legal depts	6.5	8.0	8.4	8.6
Transport	4.5	5.4	5.5	5.7
Scotland	8.1	9.0	9.1	9.7
Wales	3.3	3.8	3.9	4.0
Northern Ireland	4.9	5.5	5.7	5.9
Employment	3.9	4.0	4.0	4.0
Trade and Industry	0.7	1.4	1.3	1.2
Arts and libraries	0.9	1.0	1.0	1.1
Energy	0.2	−0.2	−0.5	0.6
Other departments	15.9	16.9	17.9	18.4
Privatization proceeds	−5.1	−5.0	−5.0	−5.0
Reserve		3.5	7.0	10.5
Total	145.7	167.1	179.4	191.6

Source: *Autumn Statement*, Treasury 1988 and *Financial Statement and Budget Report*, Treasury 1989.

Note: In this table a summary of most government departments' expenditure is shown. However, National Debt interest payments are not included. Any differences between totals and the sum of their component parts are due to rounding.

However, a more signficant variable to discover is public spending expressed as a percentage of the total spending occurring in the country as a whole. That is, whether £145.7 bn of public spending in the year 1987–8 is a lot, or not, depends on the level of spending committed by all sectors of the economy in the same year. In formal terms we need to see public expenditure expressed as a percentage of national income (which is similar to *gross domestic expenditure*). In 1987–8 the £145.7 bn of public expenditure represented approximately 41.5 per cent of national income. By 1991–2 this proportion, it is expected, will have declined further to just under 39 per cent.

If one looks at Figure 10.4 again the final sentence of the previous paragraph may seem bewildering. You will certainly notice that in cash terms public spending in 1991–2 is the highest of all years. Yet, once inflation and the anticipated increase in national income is brought into the picture the public sector is expected to experience a reduction in size; and certainly this is the desired intention of the government. When commenting on their public spending in the Budget Report of 1989 it was explicitly stated that

> General government spending, excluding privatization proceeds, has fallen from 46¾ per cent of GDP in 1982–3 to 39½ per cent in 1988–9. The expenditure plans to 1991–2 are consistent with the Government's policy of reducing the share of national income taken by total government spending. The move to Budget surplus has reduced the burden of debt interest, and the fall in unemployment has made savings possible in the social security, employment, and training programmes. These savings, together with higher housing receipts and reduced agricultural market support, have made room for increases in priority programmes within the declining trend of total expenditure relative to national income.

The above statement is representative of the way governments have thought throughout the 1980s. Indeed the same government in their very first White Paper on public spending (in 1979) opened with the statement that 'public spending is at the heart of Britain's economic difficulties'. They believed this to be the case as they have a great respect for market forces and obviously if the public sector is cut back the market forces of the private sector may increase. In other words, the converse of reduced public expenditure is that more resources become available for the private market sector. Therefore, more decisions relating to resource allocation are being left to the province of the market and its pricing system. However, whether public expenditure will continue to be successfully cut

Key Points 10.7

- **Public spending can be analysed in two forms: in absolute terms by analysing the breakdown of total public expenditure or in terms that show government expenditure in proportion to the rest of the nation's spending, i.e. public expenditure expressed as a percentage of national income.**
- **In the UK public spending is presently around 40 per cent of our nation's national income. (In 1900 it was approximately 15 per cent, in the mid-1970s approximately 50 per cent.)**
- **The Conservative government of the 1980s wished to reduce the proportion of government spending in order to allow market forces to operate.**
- **Remember that as the role of the government decreases the role of market forces will increase.**

back through the 1990s remains to be seen. (Now see Key Points 10.7.)

Taxation

Related to public expenditure is taxation – since **taxation may be defined as the main source of income from which governments finance their spending**. Theoretically, therefore, cut-backs in public expenditure in the UK could ultimately lead to cut-backs in taxation. From the market mechanism point of view such reductions would be good, as taxes also distort market forces. This is because taxes are imposed on land, labour, capital, and interest (i.e. all factor payments) as well as most goods and services (i.e. product payments).

Categories of Taxation

In the UK it is traditional to envisage two forms of taxation: *direct* and *indirect*. **Direct taxation** is largely the tax of one's income, i.e. the tax one is billed for directly and liable to pay as a named individual. **Indirect taxation** by contrast is largely tax on spending, i.e. the tax that one may not be aware of, since it is the seller of the good or service who is liable and therefore it has an indirect nature.

Examples of Direct Taxes

All forms of income on which tax is liable fall into this category. The most obvious, and most significant example, is **income tax** (often paid through the PAYE* scheme via the employer) but there are various other forms of income and consequently various other examples, the main ones being:

Corporation tax which is paid by firms on their profits.

Capital gains tax which is paid by individuals who profit by selling a capital asset at a higher price than they originally paid.

Inheritance tax which was formerly called 'Death Duties' and should therefore be self-explanatory.

Petroleum revenue tax which is paid by firms operating in the North Sea as an extra burden for them. A kind of payment for the benefits they gain from extracting the UK natural assets.

Examples of Indirect Tax

Most taxes on spending are indirect since it is the seller of the good who is ultimately liable for the tax bill. The most obvious, and most significant, example is **Value Added Tax (VAT)** which is presently charged on most goods and services sold in the UK at a rate of 15 per cent†.

Other examples of indirect tax include the various duties obtained from specific products, for example:

oil duties which are paid on petrol, diesel, and other hydrocarbon oils.

tobacco tax which is paid on cigarettes, cigars, and pipe tobacco.

excise duties on alcohol which is paid on wines, spirits, and beers.

Each of these specific taxes is charged per unit (e.g. per pint, per gallon, per packet of twenty, per litre, or whatever) and it is not entirely clear who carries the tax burden. The seller of the products will usually strive to pass on the tax incidence to the purchaser by raising the price accordingly.

OTHER TYPES OF TAX

It may be worth recognizing that other forms of taxation also exist, which are not always collected by

* PAYE is the standard abbreviation for Pay As You Earn.

† Some essential goods and services are zero-rate.

the central government. For example, local poll taxes are the responsibility of the local authorities to assess and collect. Similarly, water rates, airport taxes, motor vehicle and TV licences are not the direct responsibility of central government but are administered by appointed public authorities acting on their behalf as revenue collectors. Finally, National Insurance contributions made by employers and employees should also be recognized as a tax, especially as both are payments which affect the demand and supply of labour.

Types of Taxation Systems

All of the taxes mentioned above can fit into one of three types of taxation system – proportional, progressive, or regressive.

Proportional Taxation

A system of **proportional taxation** means that as an individual's income goes up, so, too, do his or her taxes in exactly the same proportion. Taxpayers at all income levels end up paying the *same percentage* of their income in taxes. In other words, if the proportional tax rate were 20 per cent, an individual with an income of £10 000 would pay £2 000 in taxes while an individual making £100 000 would pay £20 000, the identical 20 per cent rate being levied on both.

Progressive Taxation

Under **progressive taxation**, as a person's income increases, the percentage of income paid in taxes increases; or to express it formally, the *marginal tax rate* is greater than the *average tax rate*. To understand this we need to examine these terms. The **marginal tax rate** is expressed as

$$\text{Marginal tax rate} = \frac{\text{change in tax}}{\text{change in income}}$$

The word *marginal* merely means incremental here.

We should compare the marginal tax rate with the **average tax rate,** which is defined as

$$\text{Average tax rate} = \frac{\text{total tax}}{\text{total income}}$$

The difference between the marginal and the average tax rate can be seen in Figure 10.5. In this example of a progressive tax system the first £100 in income is taxed at 10 per cent, the next £100 at 20 per cent, and the third £100 at 30 per cent.

Regressive Taxation

With **regressive taxation**, a smaller percentage of income is taken in taxes as income increases. The marginal rate is *below* the average rate. The following is an example of regressive taxation. Assume that the more income a family earns, the lower the percentage of its income is spent on food purchases. Now assume further that the government obtains *all* of its revenues from a 20 per cent sales tax on food purchases. Since food purchases constitute a larger proportion of total expenditure for poor people than for rich people, the percentage of total income that would be paid in food taxes under such a system would *fall* as income rose. It would be a regressive system.

The relative importance of these various taxes and how they will affect the economy will be dealt with more specifically in Chapter 31.

Figure 10.5

Progressive Tax System. The percentage of tax taken out of each additional pound earned goes up, that is, the marginal tax rate increases progressively with income. Therefore, the average tax rate is less than the marginal tax rate in a progressive tax system. Whereas, in a proportional tax system, the marginal tax rate is constant and always the same as the average tax rate.

Income	*Marginal rate*	*Tax*	*Average rate*
£100	10%	£10	$\frac{£10}{£100} = 10\%$
£200	20%	£10 + £20 = £30	$\frac{£30}{£200} = 15\%$
£300	30%	£10 + £20 + £30 = £60	$\frac{£60}{£300} = 20\%$

Key Points 10.8

- **Taxes are mainly levied by central government and enable it to finance a large part of its spending.**
- **The two main forms of tax are direct and indirect. The former are taxes on income (of which there are many forms) and the latter are taxes on spending.**
- **We can identify other forms of tax which are not necessarily administered or collected by the central government, e.g. airport taxes.**
- **We can classify tax systems into proportional, progressive, and regressive, depending on whether the marginal tax rate is the same as, greater than, or less than the average tax rate as income rises.**
- **Marginal tax rates are those applied to marginal tax brackets, defined as the spread of income over which the tax rate is constant.**

CASE STUDY

The Polluter Must Pay

Mr Nicholas Ridley, the Environment Secretary, yesterday warned that governments might be forced to impose taxes aimed at cutting the consumption of fossil fuels as part of international efforts to contain the 'greenhouse effect'.

He said that Britain in particular had remained heavily dependent on coal, despite the fact that it represented one of the most polluting of all sources of energy.

Nuclear power, he emphasized, created no 'greenhouse' gases and with proper safety controls was safe and clean.

In a letter to the Energy Secretary, Mr Cecil Parkinson, the opposition spokesman, Mr Blair, said Labour was concerned that Mr Ridley's views represented 'another piece of opportunism by the Government designed to boost nuclear power at the expense of coal . . . '

Mr Ridley suggests in his pamphlet that, apart from the possibility of imposing a carbon tax on fuels which was proportionate to the carbon dioxide they emitted, governments might have to consider strategies for halting the destruction of the rain forests and for helping less developed nations invest in non-polluting forms of energy production.

On energy conservation policy, he re-emphasized the Government's belief that the key to any programme remains one of pricing. At the same time, it had to be understood that the polluter – and ultimately his customers – had to bear the cost of pollution.

Mr Ridley emphasized, however, that there would have to be reasonable scientific evidence available before curbs were put on activities deemed environmentally harmful.

He added: 'Imposing extra cost burdens has an effect on industrial competitiveness. If we in this country unilaterally took all the action, sensible or half-baked, that we are urged to take on the flimsiest scientific evidence, we could easily price ourselves out of world markets'.

In separate remarks yesterday, Mr Ridley stressed that he felt in a better position 'to deliver the goods' if he kept his 'green' responsibilities.

Mr Ridley added: 'I think I have more clout in Cabinet when I have control of local authorities and planning.'

Source: Adapted from 'Ridley Gives Fuel Tax Warning', *Financial Times*, 9 June 1989.

Questions

1. What is meant by the 'greenhouse effect'?
2. Explain and illustrate using a supply and demand diagram
   (a) How imposing a carbon tax will affect the environment,
   (b) How much the carbon tax (in theoretical terms) should be.
3. According to the extract nuclear power creates no greenhouse gases. Identify two external costs and two external benefits that such a power source does create.
4. 'The key to any programme is pricing.' Explain how the pricing system may be used to solve a pollution problem not referred to in the extract.
5. If environmental damage is a global question, is the price system strong enough to resolve it? Explain your answer and consider alternative possibilities.

CASE STUDY

Production versus Regulation

The public interest in environmental protection is – like the public interest in fair competition or safety in the workplace – something which has to be served by regulation by bodies with no financial stake in production. And contrary to the popular misconception, it is those who believe in free-market economics who understand and practise this distinction most clearly. We have acted, often as part of the process of privatization, to establish this clear separation of functions.

Socialists by contrast have never really understood the importance of this functional split. Indeed the socialist belief in the virtue of state ownership has tended to blind them to the distinction between the producers' and the public's interest. They make a distinction between public and private ownership. We distinguish between production and regulation in the public interest. What after all is public ownership to the socialist but ownership in the public interest? With public companies under the control of government and the cosy if rather amorphous relationship which that implies between ministers and managers, and without the profit motive as the prime incentive to the producer, why should there be any need to police standards in the public sector as rigorously as in the private sector?

We all know that the practical experience of monopolistic publicly owned companies has not matched up to the ideal of public service in the public interest. The companies, and therefore the government and the public, became prey to the overriding interests of the producers who were the big public-sector unions. The lack of competition often meant poor service to the customer. Public-sector managers had to wrestle with the well-nigh insoluble conflict between their duty to meet financial targets set by government and their role as setters and enforcers of their own environmental standards. The power of the big public-sector unions in the economy and within the constitution of the Labour Party tended to mean that their interests not only took precedence over the interests of the consumer but over the best environmental practice.

Central ownership of the means of production puts two quite different functions into the hands of government – production and regulation. In all countries where the short-term interests of the producer can be served by polluting the environment, pollution is more likely to be permitted by governments where the government itself is the polluter and where it has to find the money to put things right.

Source: *Policies against Pollution: The Conservative Record and Principles,* Policy Study, no. 107, Centre for Policy Studies, London 1989.

Questions

1. How has privatization been used as a process to distinguish between the production and regulation functions? State as many examples as you can.
2. Can you think of any examples where the production and regulation functions clearly benefit by being combined?
3. (a) Explain and illustrate using a supply-and-demand diagram how government regulations imposed for environmental reasons may affect a private producer's market.
   (b) Explain without a diagram some other regulation that may be imposed by a government to affect a private producer's market.
   (c) How may the private producer avoid the regulations you have outlined in (a) or (b)?
4. An underlying theme of the issues raised in the extract relate to Market Failure versus Government Failure. Can you explain why?
5. 'Air' and 'water' are often common property owned by no one yet used by everyone. Which of the following options, in your opinion, offer governments the best chance to deter people taking liberties with their use: (a) regulation by government, (b) regulation by private agencies, (c) public ownership, (d) public production, (e) private production, (f) legal reform, (g) economic reform, (h) any other possibilities?
   Explain carefully your choice of option(s).

CASE STUDY

A Merit Good or not a Merit Good, That is the Question

. . . yet all is far from well. Any week now the Arts Minister, Richard Luce, will announce an inadequate 2 per cent increase on last year's Arts Council overall kitty of £128m. About £27m of that will go to drama; barely £7.5m to drama outside London. We live still, in the arts more than in any other sphere of public life, as two nations: London and the rest.

The mood of public expenditure stand-still and cutback has made a mockery of the Arts Council's devolutionary ambitions. Instead, the big national companies have been punished, and everyone else has been told to increase sponsorship, fix more local authority money, and generally 'wise up' to what Ian Brown, the Arts Council's drama director, calls 'different' complexities.

It is all very well for the RSC to raise £1m in sponsorship from an insurance company. But the Birmingham Rep, to take a most favoured example of an Arts Council-subsidized regional theatre, can barely raise £20 000 this year on a city sponsorship drive that yielded £50 000 two years ago.

'In the old days you beat your breast and hoped the Arts Council would listen. Now we know the Arts Council is powerless to help. And we know, too, that this Government is not interested in the arts.'

The refrain, a familiar cry of the arts lobby, might be credited to Sir Peter Hall, director of the National Theatre. In recent years he has berated the Arts Council for discarding its tetchy beggar's weeds and bowl and becoming 'a willing instrument of Government'.

In fact the speaker is Graham Murray, joint artistic director of the Royal Exchange in Manchester, an outstanding regional theatre of the last 10 years and a prime example of the 'centres of excellence' favoured in the Arts Council's controversial development manifesto of 1984, The Glory of the Garden.

That so-called 'strategy for a decade', masterminded and committed to print by Mrs Thatcher's choice of Arts Council chairman, Sir William Rees-Mogg, cleverly embraced a radical devolutionary policy, robbing the metropolitan Peters (and Trevors) in order to encourage flyaway regional Pauls, to the tune of £5.5m. £2m of this went to Drama and £2.2m to the wilting Regional Arts Associations.

Yet the Cork Report, an Arts Council-sponsored enquiry chaired by Sir Kenneth Cork, last year concluded that the effect of the strategy, in real terms, had been to restore the Leicester Haymarket and the Sheffield Crucible (two favoured clients) to 1978/9 levels of funding, while leaving most other subsidized regional theatres slightly less well off.

Source: 'Look Behind You', *Financial Times*, 31 Oct. 1987.

Questions

1. Why is art in its many guises not normally regarded as a public good?
2. Could art in its various forms be provided by the private sector? Illustrate your answer with examples.
3. Why has the provision of arts become regarded as a type of merit good? Fully explain your answer.
4. Why does the theme of devolution recur in this article?
5. The following is a list of state-funded activities:
   Natural Environment Research Council
   Sports Council
   Arts Council
   Council libraries
   Council for Small Industries in Rural Areas (COSIRA)
   National Blood Transfusion Service
   (a) In order of priority which do you think should be subject to public expenditure cuts and why?
   (b) In the second paragraph of the article funding is discussed and the closing statement suggests a move to 'different complexities'. In each of the above cases suggest alternative ways of funding the activities.
   (c) Group the above activities under one of the two following headings: Merit Good or Private Good. Briefly explain for each activity why you think the chosen heading is appropriate.
6. 'The perpetuation of culture requires state sponsorship.' Discuss.

Exam Preparation

PRACTICAL EXERCISES

1. Construct a typical supply and demand diagram. Show the initial equilibrium price and quantity. Assume that the product causes negative externalities. Adjust the diagram to compensate for that fact. How does the adjusted situation compare with the original?
2. The government is considering a road-building project, incorporating a toll-gate. The benefits, costs, and externalities arising from four possible routes are outlined in the table below (externalities have been given monetary values).

	Route A	Route B	Route C	Route D
Private benefits (£m)	125	130	100	140
Private costs (£m)	100	110	120	130
Favourable externalities (£m)	50	55	55	60
Unfavourable externalities (£m)	70	50	40	50

(a) Which of the routes (A, B, C, or D) would maximize economic welfare generally?
(b) What would be the net social gain in monetary terms from going ahead with this project.
(c) Give one example for each of the four accounting categories.

MULTIPLE CHOICE QUESTIONS

1. If a firm's private costs of production are not equal to the social costs of its production, the government could increase economic welfare by
   - **A** taxing the firm if its social costs exceed its private costs
   - **B** taxing the firm if its social costs are less than its private costs
   - **C** subsidizing the firm if its social costs exceed its private costs
   - **D** taxing other firms if social costs are less than private costs in the firm in question
   - **E** subsidizing other firms if social costs are less than private costs in the firm in question.
2. Public goods, such as street-lighting, are not supplied through the ordinary market mechanism because
   - **A** the initial capital cost would be prohibitive
   - **B** some households would not be able to afford to make their full contribution towards the cost
   - **C** the benefits would not be confined to the buyers, but would automatically be available to non-buyers
   - **D** the provision of public goods is essential, and therefore cannot be left to private initative
   - **E** monopolies would earn excess profits.

For Questions 3, 4, and 5, one or more of the options given may be correct. Select your answers by means of the code set out in the grid:

A	B	C	D
1, 2, 3 all correct	1, 2 only correct	2, 3 only correct	1 only correct

3. Because of the deficiencies of the market mechanism the state might intervene to ensure an adequate supply of
   1 public goods
   2 merit goods
   3 inferior goods.
4. In using cost-benefit analysis to assess the economic need for a Channel Tunnel, account would need to be taken of the
   1 construction costs of the tunnel
   2 effects of the tunnel on the environmental amenities at Dover
   3 effects of the tunnel on air traffic at London Airport.
5. The private-enterprise system of economic organization is criticized on the basis that in a market economy
   1 private costs do not reflect the social costs of economic activity
   2 collective consumption goods are not provided in sufficient amounts
   3 governments know what the people want.

6. A particular problem in using cost-benefit analysis to appraise public investment projects is that
   A interest rates can be unpredictable
   B social costs can differ from private costs
   C not all relevant items can be quantified
   D public investment projects can be unprofitable.

7. Which of the following forms of taxation is most regressive?
   A a progressive income tax
   B a proportional income tax
   C motor vehicle tax
   D tobacco tax.

8. Which one of the following taxes is most likely to affect the supply of labour?
   A income tax
   B a tax on corporate profits
   C death duties
   D an increase in employers' National Insurance contributions.

9. The term 'Marginal Rate of Tax' is applied to the
   A proportion of income which is paid in tax
   B amount of tax payable after allowances have been deducted
   C rate of tax paid on unearned income
   D tax paid out of an increment to income
   E rate of tax which gives the highest yield.

RELATED ESSAY QUESTIONS

1. Distinguish between public goods and merit goods. What are the arguments for and against the provision by the state of merit goods?

2. Explain the terms 'external costs' and 'external benefits'. Examine the relevance of these concepts when considering a proposal to build a nuclear power station.

3. Assess the economic arguments that the production of feature films in the UK should be subsidized by government.

4. 'Left to itself the market mechanism is incapable of allocating scarce resources in an efficient manner.' Discuss.

5. 'Reducing inequalities of income by progressive taxation penalizes initiative and enterprise.' Discuss.

6. In what sense can river pollution and traffic congestion be viewed as economic problems? Can economics make any contribution to the solution of these problems?

7. In what senses could the market system 'fail'? To what extent could your arguments be used to justify the production and distribution of goods and services by the public sector?

11 Economic Indicators: Unemployment and Inflation

Key Points to Review

- Labour as a resource (1.1)
- Excess demand (5.7)
- Relative prices (6.3)
- Price controls (8.6)

Questions for Preview

1 What is a recession?

2 What is unemployment?

3 Why is frictional unemployment not necessarily harmful?

4 What are some of the problems associated with measuring inflation?

5 Who is affected by inflation?

Sometimes the overall business climate is buoyant – few workers are unemployed, businesses are expanding, and not many firms are going bust. At other times, however, the business situation is not so good – there are many unemployed workers, businesses are cutting back in their production, and a significant number of firms are going out of business. These ups and downs in economy-wide economic activity can be called **business fluctuations** or **business cycles**.

When we talk about these fluctuations or cyclical patterns in economic activity we are suggesting that many **economic indicators** or variables are moving at once. For example: prices, employment, money supply, stocks, return on capital, savings, interest rates, balance of payments, output, exchange rates etc. These indicators are measured and presented in many ways. One readily accessible source is the free Treasury publication entitled *Economic Progress Report* (renamed *Economic Briefing* in 1990). The table presented in their Oct. 1989 issue is reproduced in Figure 11.1 with charts (from the same publication) giving a more detailed breakdown of similar information.

Of these various indicators changes in unemployment and inflation are important aspects affecting most of the other variables in one way or another. In this chapter we take a brief look at business cycles and their uses in general before tackling unemployment and inflation specifically.

Business Cycles

During most years the UK economy is growing – output, income, and employment are increasing. In other words, the trend in business and general economic activity is upward. But there are fluctuations around what we might call the 'growth-path' line. We have terms for the periods when business activity temporarily pulls us below our upward growth-path, and others for periods when business activity moves with, or in excess of, our normal growth-path. We call the former **recessions** or **depression*** and the latter **expansions** or **booms**. Think of this in terms of a growing child. The child is on a long-term growth trend in regard to body weight and height. There are however, temporary fluctuations. The child can become sick or can experience malnutrition and deviate from

*For a more accurate understanding of when to use which term see the Dictionary inclusion for 'recession'.

Figure 11.1
Economic Indicators

Published monthly		*1985*	*1986*	*1987*	*1988*	*1989*	
						July	*Aug*
Output of production industries	1985=100	100.0	102.2	105.8	109.5	109.8	—
Unemployment (adult)	million	3.04	3.11	2.82	2.30	1.79	1.75
Sterling index	1975=100	100.0	91.5	90.1	95.5	92.3	91.6
PSBR	£ billion	5.7	3.4	−23.5	−14.4	−1.4	−0.7
Interest rate: 3 months interbank	%	12.2	11.0	9.7	10.3	13.9	13.9
Volume of retail sales	1985=100	100.0	105.3	111.5	119.2	121.0	121.5
Retail Price Index	% increase over same period a year earlier	6.1	3.4	4.2	4.9	8.2	7.3
Average earnings, whole economy[1]		7½	7½	7¾	8¾	9¼	—

Published quarterly		*1985*	*1986*	*1987*	*1988*	*1989*	
						Q_1	Q_2
Balance of payments, current account	£ billion	3.20	0.07	−3.67	−14.62	−4.78	−4.91
Workforce in employment[1]	million	24.53	24.55	25.07	25.86	26.26	—
GDP (average)[2]	% increase over same period a year earlier	4.0	3.2	4.5	4.4	2.9	2.2
Total fixed investment[2]		3.9	1.9	8.8	13.1	9.8	2.2
Consumers' expenditure[2]		3.7	5.6	5.4	6.9	4.0	5.4
Exports of goods and services[2]		5.9	4.2	5.1	0.7	4.5	0.4
Imports of goods and services[2]		2.5	6.7	7.6	12.2	15.9	8.7
Productivity: whole economy[3]		2.5	2.9	3.1	1.7	1.1	—
Gross trading profits of industrial and commercial companies		19.3	−7.2	18.1	12.9	5.9	—

1. GB, millions; annual figures here are estimates for June. 2. Constant prices 1985 = 100. 3. Output per person employed.

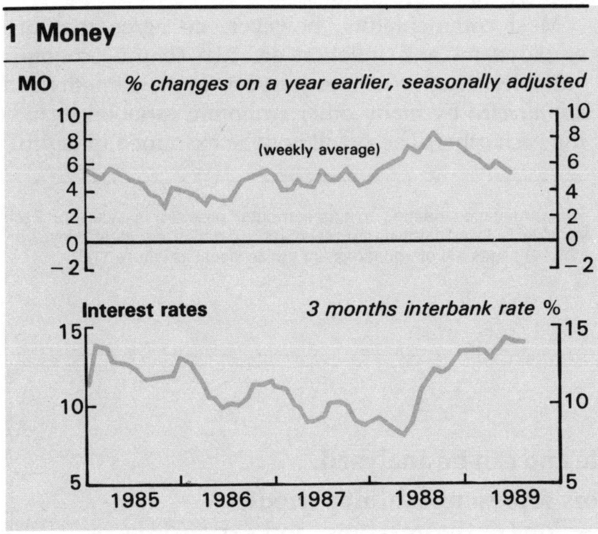

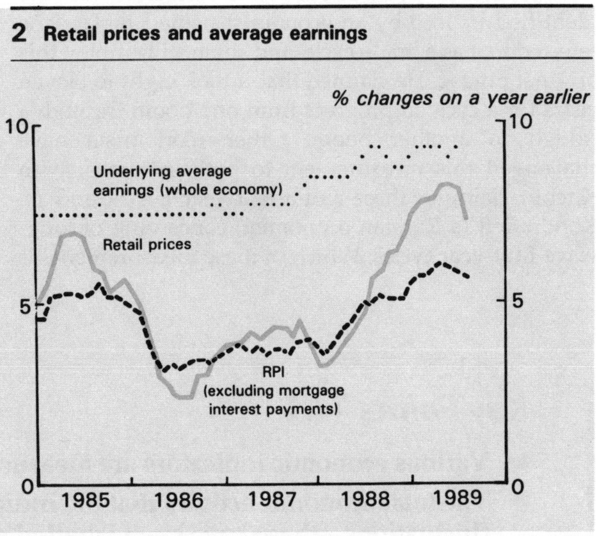

the long-term trend towards maturity. This would be the equivalent of a recession in the economy. When the child experiences growth spurts this would be equivalent to an expansion in the economy.

In Figure 11.2 we show a typical business cycle fluctuation around a smooth upward-sloping growth-line. Over the last 100 years the economy has averaged about a 1.5 per cent annual increase in the material standard of living of the average UK citizen. Alongside this overall upward trend we have experienced booms and depressions. Indeed, economists have long recognized that *left to its own devices* an economy has a

Figure 11.2

The Business Cycle. The coloured line depicts the long-term 'growth-path' around which the economic activity fluctuates – moving in some consistent pattern from expansion to recession and back again.

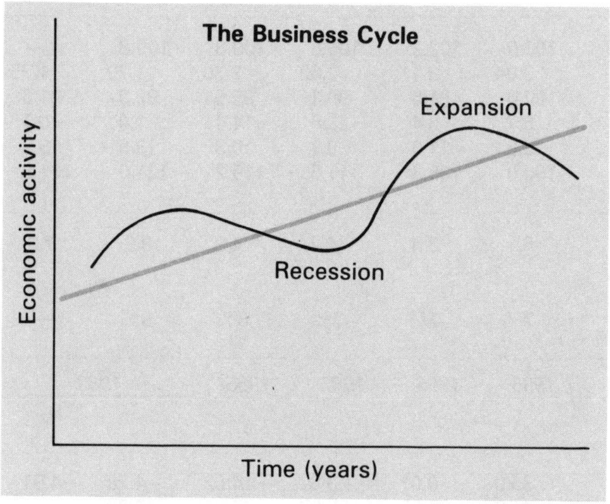

built-in cyclical pattern of its own. There are many explanations for this cycle of which the following is only one. Boom situations lead to circumstances of 'over-heating' characterized by 'shortages' of labour, capital, and stock and a consequent rising of prices. This leads into a recession characterized by falling output, and profits, rising unemployment and stocks, and a stabilizing of prices. This eventually generates a potential upswing situation to another boom.

This business cycle of boom and recession was first identified in 1860 by an economist named Juglar – he referred to it as a 'trade cycle' and some still employ this original phrase. He claimed that it took eight to eleven years for a cycle to progress from one boom through a trough to another boom. Other economists have challenged this measurement to both extremes, with Kitchin claiming three-and-a-half-year cycles and N. Kondratieff (a Russian economist) conceiving of long-wave fifty-year cycles. Which of these measurements is correct is a matter of academic debate. What is important is that cyclical economic behaviour can be perceived. Furthermore, the cyclical movement of these economic indicators interacts sufficiently to enable stabilization policies to be employed if desired, and forecasts of general economic behaviour to be attempted.

Consequently, various models of economic behaviour exist and again, whether one is more accurate than the other is arbitrary. What is important is that economic indicators can be used to make important economic forecasts.

In Figure 11.3 a dated, but simplified, Treasury model is presented in the form of a flow chart. Obviously this model has been continually revised and the conscientious student may like to reflect on which variables would need to be added to today's model. In fact, in its present computer format the Treasury list over 520 economic variables as inputs into their main program*. This model is used for estimating the effects of policy and for forecasting. Often forecasts are wrong due to false assumptions about policy changing and due to unforeseen developments (e.g. strikes), misinterpreted relationships, or faulty figures. Nevertheless forecasts do provide a guide and even the errors are useful in so far as they provide further understanding and insight into the interrelationship of the various economic variables.

The last point is important as economic forecasting is still a relatively young science – Whitehall has only been involved since the 1940s and refinements are continually being made. What is ironic, however, is that some forecasts prove to be wrong because of the way people respond (or over-respond) to the reliability of economists' predictions.

Most commentators, however, do agree that unemployment and inflation are two central economic variables. They *affect* many aspects of the economy and are *affected* by many other economic variables including each other. These will now be examined in depth.

*Documentation relating to this computer program is available. Each variable is listed with its corresponding detailed equation. However, 226(A4) pages full of equations are not as visual as Figure 11.3.

Key Points 11.1

- **Various economic indicators are measurable and can be analysed.**
- **The total economic activity that the indicators represent exhibit periodic fluctuations – these have been labelled recessions or depressions, and expansions or booms.**
- **The cyclical behaviour of the indicators leads to stabilization policies being employed and forecasts of future trends being identified.**
- **The Treasury model used for forecasting and policy evaluation is based on a computer program containing over 500 economic variables.**

Figure 11.3

Flow Chart of the Treasury Model

The direction of the arrow between the boxes represents the Treasury's interpretation of the direction of causation between variables. Those variables at the top of the page in circles are those known as **exogenous** variables, i.e. they are external to the system, determined by policy or world events. The remaining indicators in boxes are called **endogenous** variables, i.e. they are internal to the system and affect one another.

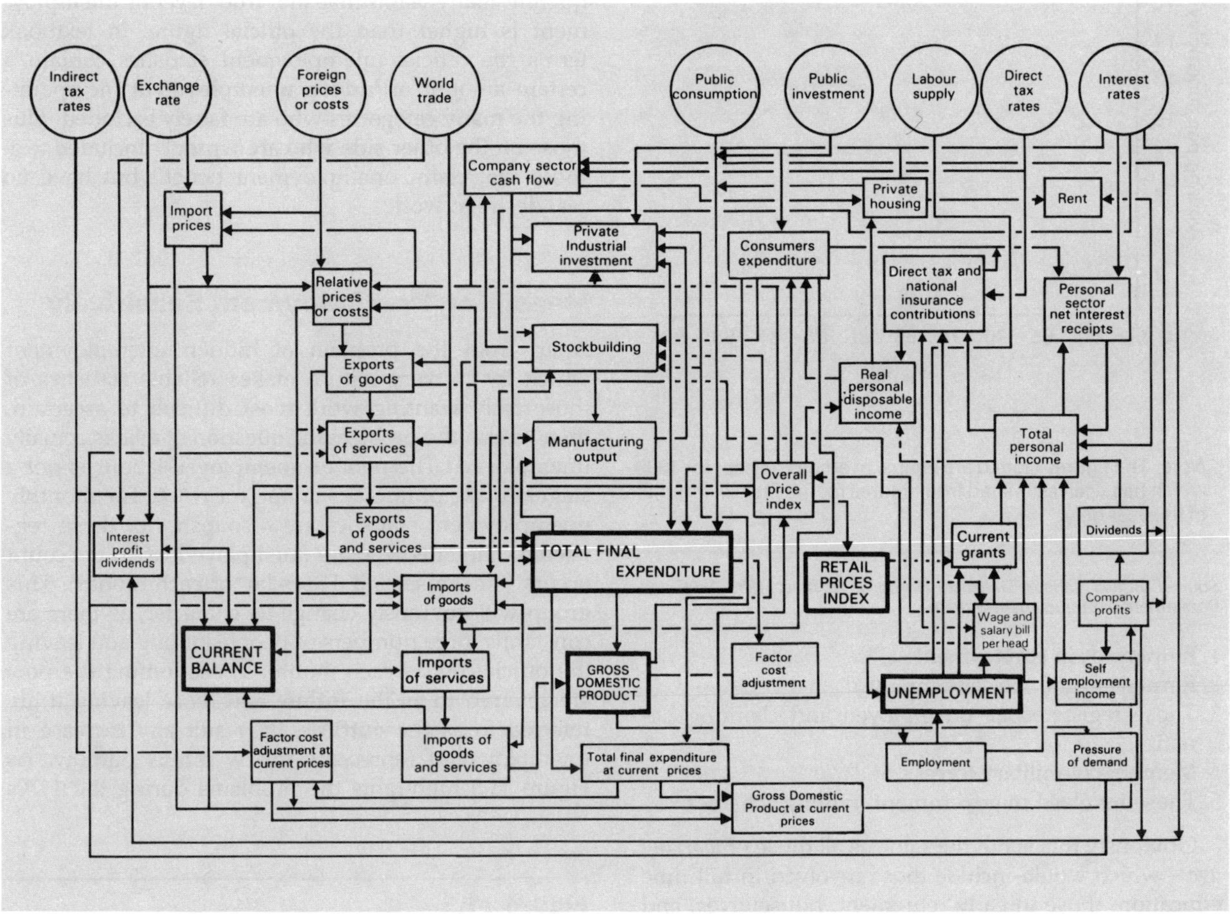

Unemployment

One of the major consequences of fluctuating business activity is the ensuing unemployment, particularly of workers, but also of other factors of production (non-human resources). Unemployment has many costs – in human suffering, in loss of dignity, in loss of output and savings – the list goes on and on. That is why policy-makers in our economy closely watch the unemployment figures published by the Department of Employment each month. Unemployment is considered to be a social evil that must be kept at an 'acceptable' level. We can see from Figure 11.4 that the rate of unemployment in the United Kingdom during the post-war period averaged around 2 per cent of the working population for most of the 1950s and 1960s and never above 3 per cent until 1971. Since then, however, the trend has been towards an increasing unemployment rate and it has become an economic and social problem of some magnitude. Remember that the 6.9 per cent unemployment rate plotted for 1989 represents nearly two million people.

The rate of unemployment is measured by dividing the total number of persons defined as unemployed by the total number of persons defined as being within the workforce. Determining who is truly unemployed and who is effectively in the labour force is no easy task.

How Official Measurements Are Defined

The workforce (working population) is presently defined by the Department of Employment as 'persons over sixteen who work for pay or gain or register themselves as "available" for such work and meanwhile claim benefit'. In less formal terms therefore the workforce includes:

.4

Unemployment Record since the 1950s

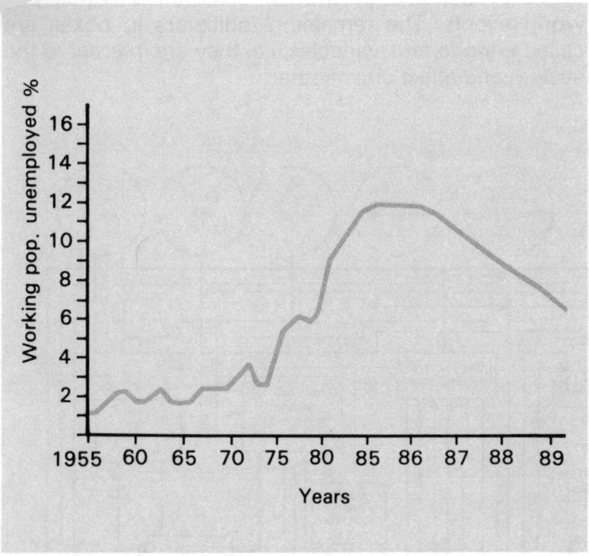

Note: The figures plotted are annual averages, except for 1989 which has been estimated from figures for the first six months of the year only.

Source: *British Labour Statistics, Historical Abstract 1886–1968* and *Department of Employment Gazette.*

1. Employees in employment
2. Employers and the self-employed
3. Those registered as unemployed and claiming benefit
4. Members of military forces
5. Those involved in government training schemes.

Obviously this is not the same as all those of *working age* – which would include those involved in full-time education, those in early retirement, housewives, and those who are seeking work but have not registered for unemployment benefit.

In numerical terms for 1987 the following figures collated from the *Department of Employment Gazette* and the *Monthly Digest of Statistics* may help clarify matters a little further:

Total population of working age	35 813 000
minus those not involved in Workforce	7 529 000
equals Workforce	28 284 000
minus Unemployed	2 905 000
equals Workforce in employment	25 379 000

Registered Unemployment

It must be recognized that to become part of the unemployment statistics in the UK one must be officially registered as a claimant at an Unemployment Benefit Office. This official measure is recognizably suspect: it excludes all those who are not eligible for benefits; it *officially excludes* all men aged over sixty who since April 1983 no longer have to sign on to claim benefit; and it also *excludes* those who register as desiring work at commercial agencies but not with the official offices as owing to marriage or similar status circumstances they are not eligible for benefit. Indeed, a labour force survey of 1988 identified some 750 000 people seeking work but not claiming benefit. Consequently many claim that the 'true' level of unemployment is higher than the official figure. In textbook terms the official unemployment statistics contain a certain amount of **hidden unemployment** incorporating the many categories who are falsely excluded, plus those on the other side who are wrongly included, e.g. those that claim unemployment benefit but have no real desire to work.

Measuring Unemployment Sensitively

Apart from the problem of hidden unemployment which by its very nature makes reliable statistics of those truly wanting work most difficult to ascertain, there is also the problematic question of *who* is actually unemployed? The pool of unemployed labour is not a stagnant lake of humans crying for work. The monthly unemployment statistics are a snapshot of those registered claimants who are unemployed when the count occurs (on the second Thursday of each month). This group will obviously change its character, as there are constantly large numbers of people joining and leaving the official books each month. Those joining the pool are referred to as the **inflow** and those leaving it are referred to as the **outflow**. By result any increase in unemployment represents inflow minus outflow. As Figure 11.5 highlights the problems during the 1970s

Figure 11.5

The Inflows and Outflows of Male Unemployment (monthly averages in thousands). It is important to remember that these figures are *monthly averages* of only those men who move into or from the official unemployment statistics.

	Inflow ('000s)	*Outflow ('000s)*
1970	248	244
1975	238	208
1978	189	197
1979	180	183
1980	217	173
1981	220	183
1982	222	214
1983	246	243
1984	248	241
1985	246	245
1986	256	255
1987	243	273
1988	196	234

Source: *Department of Employment Gazette*

and 1980s stem largely from sharp changes in outflow rather than significant changes of inflow. The corollary of this relates to how long people have to wait before leaving the unemployment pool. In formal terms the **duration** of unemployment is now longer. For example, in 1955 when unemployment was down to 1.1 per cent of the working population the average period of each case of unemployment was three and a half weeks. In 1989 the average period of unemployment is far longer – in fact over 50 per cent have been unemployed for six months or more (see Figure 11.6).

However, the idea of *average* unemployment duration no longer makes much sense, as some groups in our economy are far more vulnerable than others. For example, the old (over fifty) endure longer unemployment periods than their counterparts (see the table in Figure 11.6 for details).

Similarly one's gender, occupation, regional location, social class, and even marital status affect one's chances of unemployment. Indeed, the white, male, owner-occupier, London-based, managerial type, with two children is statistically less likely to experience unemployment than the coloured youth who is unskilled and lives in Teesside. To a large extent this is due to the way that the labour market operates which is a theme we shall explore in a Case Study in Chapter 25.

Finally, in undertaking a sensitive interpretation of unemployment statistics it is also necessary to recognize what adjustments have been made to the portrait presented. **Seasonally adjusted** is the most common and this means that the figures incorporate an adjustment to allow for those seasonal quirks which regularly cause unemployment to be particularly high or low during certain months.

Similar adjustments are made for:

(i) **School-leavers** (i.e. young persons seeking their first job).
(ii) **Adult students** (who have registered for vacation work and/or benefit).
(iii) **Temporarily stopped** (i.e. those workers who have been laid off due to bad weather or someone else's strike and are claiming benefit until they can return to work).

These three special groups are important to remember as the unemployment figures are often presented as *the number of wholly unemployed excluding the temporarily stopped, school-leavers, and adult students.* These three groups are excluded as it is felt that they do not form part of the long-term unemployed – though this may be difficult to justify in the case of present school-leavers.

Figure 11.6
Unemployment by Age and Duration

	Duration of unemployment (weeks)			*Total (= 100%) thousands*
	Up to 26	*Over 26 up to 52*	*Over 52*	
	(%)	(%)	(%)	
Males				
18-24	58	17	24	388.6
25-49	40	15	46	745.2
50 and over	27	13	60	337.1
All ages	42	15	43	1 470.9
Females				
18-24	61	18	20	207.1
25-49	50	23	27	285.3
50 and over	20	13	62	107.1
All ages	45	18	36	599.5

Source: *Department of Employment Gazette,* Jan 1989. (Totals do not sum due to rounding.)

Key Points 11.2

- **Unemployment rates in the United Kingdom during the post-war period have risen from a low of 1 to 2 per cent in the 1950 and 1960s to levels above 10 per cent in the 1980s.**
- **The working population in official terms includes: (1) employees in employment, (ii) employers and the self-employed, (iii) HM Forces, (iv) those on government training schemes, and (v) unemployed persons claiming benefit. The first four of these groups make up the employed workforce.**
- **When the outflow from the unemployment books decreases, the duration of unemployment increases and vice versa.**
- **The unemployment statistics contain certain problems and some of these are catered for by the concept of hidden unemployment.**
- **All unemployment statistics should be analysed carefully, noting if possible source, adjustments, age-categories etc.**

This section has served to highlight the sensitive nature of unemployment statistics and before closing we would like to draw your attention to Figure 11.7 which appeared in a similar format in the *Sunday Times* in 1983. Since then we have amended and updated it, as it illustrates some of the debates relating to what should or should not be included in unemployment statistics. This theme will also be raised in one of the Case Studies at the close of this chapter. (See Key Points 11.2.)

The Major Types of Unemployment

Unemployment can be categorized into four basic types: frictional, cyclical, seasonal, and structural. You may hear about these different types of unemployment, so you might want to know what they mean.

Frictional Unemployment

Of the 28 million people in the workforce more than 4 million persons will have reported themselves unemployed at one time or another during each year. What we call **frictional unemployment** is this continuous flow of individuals from job to job in and out of employment. It used to be called **'transitional unemployment'** which as the name suggests merely involves people *moving* or *changing* from one job to another. The modern phrase places the emphasis on 'time taken' to change as a result of certain frictions in the labour market. Indeed, there will always be some frictional unemployment as resources need time to be redirected within the market. To eliminate frictional unemployment completely, we would have to prevent workers from leaving their present jobs until they had already lined up other jobs at which they would start working immediately. A complete elimination of frictional unemployment would probably reduce the rate of growth of our economy. One important source of advances in productivity is the movement of workers from sectors of the economy where labour productivity and wages are low, to sectors where productivity and wages are high. The search for better job-offers is the process by which workers discover areas where their productivity is highest, that is, where they can make the most income. Frictional unemployment can, therefore, be reduced by the provision of better information services but it could never be eliminated altogether.

Cyclical Unemployment

Cyclical unemployment is related to the business cycle. In fact, cyclical unemployment is defined as unemployment associated with changes in business conditions – primarily recessions and depressions. The way to lessen cyclical unemployment would be to reduce the intensity, duration, and frequency of ups and downs of business activity. Economic policy-makers attempt, through their policies, to reduce cyclical unemployment by keeping business activity on an even keel, and these policies will be discussed in Part E, the final section of the book.

Figure 11.7

Unemployment Statistics – The Great Divide. People interpret the unemployment figures differently. Those on the left of the political chamber wish to highlight the under-counting by adding omissions, while those on the right stress the over-counting by making subtractions. Which final figures do you agree with?

Official Total: 1 960 000 (Mar. 1989)

Left-wing critics add:		*Right-wing critics subtract:*	
Unemployed over-sixties (no longer required to register)	200 000	School-leavers	100 000
Short-time working	29 000	Claimants who are not actively looking for jobs	50 000
Effect of Special Employment Measures	450 000	Job seekers with disabilities	8 000
Unregistered unemployed (Due to changes from clerical count at job centres to computer count of claimants only)	200 000	'Job changers' – out of work for four weeks or less	200 000
		'Black economy' – workers, illegally claiming benefit	160 000
Total additions	879 000	Total subtractions	518 000
Total unemployed	2 839 000	Total unemployed	1 442 000

Seasonal Unemployment

Seasonal unemployment is just that. It comes and goes with seasons of the year in which the demand for particular jobs rises and falls. For example, construction workers often can work only during the warmer months. They are seasonally unemployed during the winter. Resort workers usually can only get jobs in resorts during the summer season. They, too, become seasonally unemployed during the winter; the opposite is true for ski-resort workers. There is little we can do to reduce seasonal unemployment.

Structural Unemployment

Presumably, there have been structural changes in our economy that have caused some workers to become permanently unemployed, or at least unemployed for very long periods of time, because they cannot find jobs that use their particular skills. Structurally unemployed persons are usually those who simply cannot find *any* job they can do. **Structural unemployment** has often been associated with **technological unemployment**, that is, unemployment resulting from the increased use of labour-saving machines.

Unlike cyclical unemployment, structural unemployment is not caused by the business cycle, although the business cycle may affect it. And unlike frictional unemployment, structural unemployment is not related to the movement of workers from low-paid to high-paid jobs. Rather, structural unemployment results when the consuming public no longer wants to buy an individual's services in that location. Instead of going through retraining, that individual persists in his or her search for employment with 'obsolete' skills in a market with limited demand. Some of these people eventually will go into new industries. In most urban settings this is precisely what happens. However, in some settings this does not happen. Often people refuse to move. They wait for times to improve. The result is a permanent depression in some geographic areas due to labour immobility.*

In fact in some instances structural unemployment is very closely related to **regional unemployment** too. When an industry concentrated in one area declines as a result of changes in the pattern of demand the whole area becomes full of workers with nothing to do. To illustrate this you simply need to look at a chart showing regional unemployment (such as that in Figure 33.3) and you will notice that in those areas that have rates high above the national average, the local economy had previously been based on one industry which had undergone decline. We will return to this theme in Chapter 33.

From Unemployment Types to Policy

By categorizing unemployment in the ways above, solutions to the various problems become easier to discern. It is clear that the most serious forms of unemployment are those due to a *general* decline in demand – namely cyclical unemployment. In the post-war period advances in economic theory and policy have helped to moderate this cycle in many ways which are discussed in forthcoming chapters.

More specifically, structural, technological, or regional unemployment are often due to the decline in demand for a *specific* skill or product. These can be remedied in various ways by attempting to improve regional and occupational mobility. The policies aimed at achieving these ends are discussed in Chapter 33.

Finally, the recognition that frictional and seasonal unemployment exists alters the government's perception of what level of full employment to expect. For example, no government policy would ever aim at 100 per cent of the workforce being employed. This theme will be developed in the next section.

Defining Full Employment

As already stated full employment does not mean that everybody is employed. It is obvious that in any dynamic economy some unemployment is unavoidable. The question is, what level of unemployment is unavoidable and at what level does it become a problem?

According to Lord Beveridge's influential work *Full Employment in a Free Society* (published 1944), an unemployment rate of 3 per cent would be compatible with the aims of full employment. His figure allows 1 per cent for frictional unemployment, 1 per cent for seasonal unemployment, and 1 per cent for overseas factors. His inclusion of overseas factors is interesting as many economists ignore the interdependence of one economy's trends with another. Furthermore, Beveridge's target was effectively adhered to during the post-war period in the UK until 1971. However, other formulas of what constitutes full employment are also possible. For example, during the same period of time as we were adhering to Beveridge's criteria, the US employed a different formula. For them post-war full employment represented 96 per cent employment. Their 4 per cent unemployment was to account for frictional unemployment and the various forms of structural unemployment. Yet they, too, have been way off target since 1970.

This raises the question: what does full employment in the 1990s represent? Clearly the variables have changed. Technology has improved, more people have entered into the search for work, unemployment benefits have increased, and so on. Consequently neither Britain nor the US have come anywhere near their previous full-employment targets in the last decade. The 'correct' level needs to be redefined, but economists are hesitant to do so. The US, under political pressure, has recently suggested a target of 5½ per cent unemployment. In the UK targets of 6 per cent and higher are suggested by politicians.

*See Dictionary inclusion for **'mobility of labour'**.

Key Points 11.3

- **There are many types of unemployment including frictional, cyclical, seasonal, structural, technological, and regional.**
- **Frictional unemployment occurs because workers do not have all the information necessary about vacancies nor do employers know about all of the qualified workers to fill those vacancies. Consequently, 'job search' time must be allowed for when people wish to change jobs.**
- **Structural unemployment occurs when the demand for a commodity permanently decreases so that workers in an industry are permanently barred from the job they are used to doing.**
- **The level of frictional, seasonal, and/or structural unemployment can be used to arrive at an (arbitrary) definition of full employment.**
- **The various types of unemployment need to be identified in order to consider policy options.**

Economists themselves seem to have become disinterested in this isolated target for employment, and they are presently placing more emphasis on the concept of a **natural rate of unemployment**. This is a constantly moving rate which relates the preferable level of unemployment to that which is compatible with constant prices. It is based on the principle that every market, including labour, has an equilibrium rate. This concept will be discussed in full in Chapter 18 after inflation and related ideas have been explored. (Key Points 11.3).

Inflation

The persistent increase in most prices in the United Kingdom has affected all of us. Rising prices now seem as inevitable as death and taxes. We are constantly reminded by newspapers and magazine articles that the pound of twenty years ago is worth only 16p today. In the remainder of this chapter, we will examine what inflation is, how it is measured, and how it affects each of us in our simultaneous roles as consumers, tax-paying citizens, and income-earners.

A Definition of Inflation

At the outset, we must have a precise definition of the phenomenon called **inflation**. We will technically define it as a situation in which there is a *sustained* rise in a weighted average of all prices. An alternative definition would be a relatively *persistent* general increase in prices. Notice the emphasis on the words *sustained* and *persistent* in our definitions. A one-time increase in the (weighted) average of all prices is not, under these definitions, an inflationary phenomenon. Rather, it is just a one-off event. When the (weighted) average of all prices is rising year in and year out as it has in the United Kingdom in recent years, that is definitely inflation.

Official measurements of inflation are made monthly by the Department of Employment. They use a technique which involves buying the same 'basket' of goods and services each month, thereby enabling them to assess the purchasing power of money. In recent years to physically buy the goods (which they do not do – they merely get 'price quotations') would have required more and more money, as inflation has become a marked problem. For an historical portrait of inflation rates over the last 35 years see Figure 11.8.

Figure 11.8
Inflation Rates in the UK 1953–88

Years	*Average annual increase in prices (%)*
1953–69	3.3
1970–5	12.0
1976–9	13.5
1980–5	9.7
1985–8	4.8

Types and Causes of Inflation

There are many different explanations for inflation. Here we will hypothesize that inflation occurs either because an increase in total demand pulls up prices ('demand-pull' inflation) or because an increase in the cost of production pushes up the prices of final products ('cost-push' inflation).

Demand-pull inflation

When total demand in the economy is rising while the available output of goods is limited, **demand-pull inflation** occurs. Goods and services may be in 'short' supply either because the economy is being fully utilized or because the economy cannot grow fast enough to meet the increasing level of demand. As a result of either, the general level of prices rises. This type of inflation is often experienced as an economy approaches and reaches its full-employment level.

Consider the following possibility: total demand rises and the economy gets closer and closer to full capacity output; in fact some firms may well reach full capacity (but not all). Any further increases in demand, especially if experienced by the firms that have reached full capacity, will cause them to raise prices. Moreover, if these firms supply intermediate goods to other firms, then the increased price of these intermediate goods means that the cost of production rises for the firms using those intermediate goods. Thus, increases in demand tend to pull up prices, and hence the term *demand-pull inflation*.

Cost-push Inflation

The **cost-push inflation** theory of price increases has emerged as a popular theory. It attempts to explain why prices rise when the economy is nowhere near full employment. Cost-push inflation apparently explains 'creeping' inflation and the inflation that Britain experienced during the 1973–5 recession. There are essentially three explanations of cost-push inflation: union power, big business power, and higher raw materials prices.

UNION POWER – OR THE 'WAGE–PRICE SPIRAL'

Many people feel that unions are responsible for inflation. Their reasoning is as follows. Unions decide to demand a wage rise that is not warranted by increases in their productivity. Since the unions are so powerful, employers must give in to union demands for higher wages. When the employers have to pay these higher wages, their costs are higher. To maintain their usual profit margin, these business people raise their prices. This type of cost-push inflation seemingly can occur even when there is no excess demand for goods, and even when the economy is operating below capacity at under full employment.

The union-power argument rests on the unions having a stronghold over their particular labour markets. In terms of evaluating this argument one may resort to statistics on days lost in industrial disputes and trade union membership. As Figure 11.9 suggests both these variables have begun to show downward trends during the 1980s – and inflation has fallen. Interestingly, this is the exact opposite of the 1970s experience.

Figure 11.9

Trade Union Power 1977–87. The figures in the right-hand column represent millions of working days lost due to industrial disputes in the year concerned. During the 1960s the average number of days lost for similar reasons averaged three million. The other figures show the total number of union members at the end of each year. These increased by approximately 3 per cent a year during the 1970s (which was significantly faster than the 1960s), yet they have markedly declined during the 1980s – between 1980 and 1987 there was a 19 per cent decline.

Year	*Number of union members*	*Working days lost (millions)*
1977	12 846 000	10
1978	13 112 000	9
1979	13 289 000	29
1980	12 947 000	12
1981	12 106 000	4
1982	11 593 000	5
1983	11 236 000	4
1984	10 994 000	27
1985	10 821 000	6
1986	10 539 000	2
1987	10 475 000	4

Source: *Department of Employment Gazette*, May 1989.

BIG BUSINESS POWER, OR THE 'PRICE–WAGE SPIRAL'

The other variant of the cost-push theory is that inflation is caused when the monopoly power of big business pushes up prices. Powerful corporations are presumably able to raise their prices whenever they want to increase their profits. Each time the corporations raise prices to increase their profits, the cost of living goes up. Workers demand higher wages to make up for the loss in the standard of living, thereby giving the corporations an excuse to raise prices again, and so a vicious price–wage cycle is established.

RAW MATERIALS COST-PUSH INFLATION

Since the 1973 beginning of higher and higher prices for all forms of energy, a relatively new type of cost-push inflation has been suggested. It is raw materials cost-push inflation because the cost of raw materials seems to keep rising all the time. Coal is more expensive, so is petroleum, so is natural gas, and so are many other basic inputs into production processes.

Few economists would deny the impact of the OPEC oil prices in the early 1970s contributing to the inflationary surges experienced by most oil-importing countries in the mid-1970s. In fact it is easy to distinguish an international pattern to inflation in most developed capitalist countries. Figure 11.10 shows the marked peaks around 1975 which followed the quadrupling of oil prices in the 1973–4 period.

Figure 11.10

Inflation Rate in the UK and the Rest of OECD. From this graph it is clear that between 1968 and 1988 although the trends of inflation have been similar in most OECD countries the UK has experienced a higher than average rate of price inflation. (For a list of these countries the reader should look up OECD in the dictionary at the end of the book.) It is also notable that since 1980 both foreign and UK inflation rates have been falling.

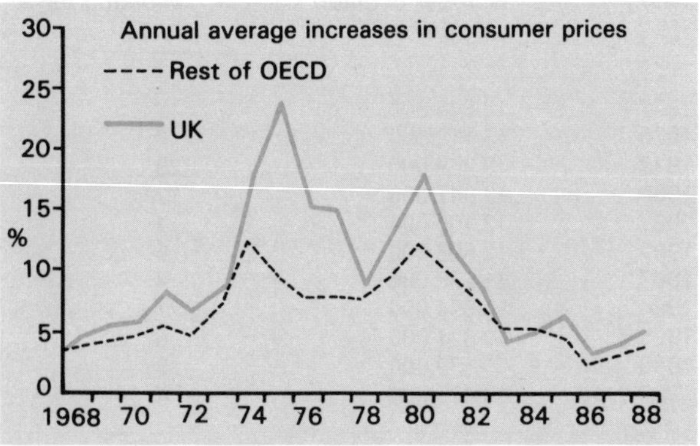

SUMMARY AND A MOVE TOWARDS POLICY

Whether it be union power, big business power, or higher prices for raw materials, the resultant increased cost of production pushed prices up; hence the term *cost-push inflation*. One solution offered as a way to stop, or at least slow down, cost-push inflation is wage and price controls. In the UK these controls have largely been employed in the form of **prices and incomes policies**. In 1965 a National Board for Prices and Incomes was established and after monitoring several policies this was abolished in 1971. From 1971 to the late 1970s the emphasis became more focused on controlling incomes directly either through government policy or public-sector wage negotiations. In all cases the policies and negotiations proved difficult to manage, and even those policies that were enforced effectively only acted as a stop-gap, temporary measure to curbing inflation. This theme will be returned to in Chapter 29. (Now read Key Points 11.4.)

Measuring Inflation

If inflation is defined as a sustained rise in the general price level, how do we come up with a measure of the rate of inflation? This is indeed a thorny problem for government statisticians. It is easy to determine how much the price of an individual commodity has risen: if last year a light bulb cost 50p and this year it costs 75p, there has been a 50 per cent rise in the price of that light bulb over a one-year period. We can express the change in the individual light bulb price in one of several ways: (i) the price has gone up 25p; (ii) the price is one-and-a-half (1.5) times as high; (iii) the price has risen by 50 per cent; (iv) by using an index number.

INDEX NUMBERS

An index number of the price rise just discussed is simply the second choice multiplied by 100, that is, the index number would be 150. All we need to do now is select a base year to compare prices.

Computing a Price Index

Of course, the problem becomes more complicated when we are dealing with a large number of goods,

Key Points 11.4

- **Inflation represents a persistent increase in prices. This has been the UK experience in the post-war period. It became a major problem in the 1970s.**
- **Demand-pull inflation occurs when the total demand for goods and services rises faster than the rate of growth of supply.**
- **Cost-push inflation is due to one or more of the following: (1) union power, (2) big business power, and/or (3) raw materials price increases.**
- **Price and incomes policies have been used to attempt the control of inflationary pressure for short periods of time.**

some of whose prices have gone up faster than others, and some may have even fallen. What we have to do is pick a representative selection, a so-called 'basket' of goods and services and compare the cost of that 'basket' of goods and services over time. When we do this, we obtain a **price index**, which is defined as the cost of our representative basket of goods today, expressed as a percentage of the cost of the same basket of goods in some starting, or base, year. In other words,

$$\text{price index} = \frac{\text{cost today of 'basket'}}{\text{cost of 'basket' in base year}} \times 100$$

A simple numerical example of a price index calculation is given in Figure 11.11. In this example there are only two goods in the basket – corn and microcomputers. The quantities in the basket remain the same between the base year 1985 and 1990. Only the prices change.

STATISTICAL WEIGHTS

So far in this section on measuring inflation we have discussed three goods: light bulbs, corn, and microcomputers. Obviously price rises in corn will affect the general public more than the price rises in light bulbs and microcomputers (especially microcomputers as these are a luxury item). To some extent this was catered for in our simple example by having a larger quantity of corn.

In official measurements, however, each item that is measured is allocated a 'statistical weight' according to its importance for the average family – this is ultimately determined by the percentage of average income that is spent on each good. Therefore, the statistical weight for food will be far higher than that for cigarettes, as changes in food prices affect everybody, whereas cigarette prices only affect smokers.

Real-world Price Indexes

A number of price indexes are used in the United Kingdom. We shall discuss the three official ones that are most commonly referred to, namely the Retail Price Index, Tax and Price Index, and Producer Price Index.

The Retail Price Index

The most often quoted of all prices indexes is the Retail Price Index (RPI). The Department of Employment uses essentially the same techniques as outlined above for this index, but of course they measure the movement of far more prices. In fact, approximately 600 goods and services are 'priced' each month in the various retail outlets up and down the country. This is administered by the 200 or so local employment offices, who end up, between them, with a total of approximately 130 000 price quotations.

These price movements are averaged out for the country as a whole by the Department of Employment. Their relative importance is then accounted for by the average price changes for each group of goods multiplied by the statistical weights. The index is then published in percentage form displaying its monthly change. Some representative figures have already been presented in Figure 11.1

Those 600 items that are chosen for measurement and the statistical weights allocated are meant to represent the *average* households, that is, those in which the main breadwinner is neither a pensioner nor a millionaire. Indeed, the Index does not attempt to measure the cost of living of the top 4 per cent in the income scale or those households which rely for the majority of their income on state pensions and benefits. In fact, separate price indexes are calculated for pensioners.

Figure 11.11

Calculating a Price Index for a Basket Containing Two Goods Only. In this simplified example, there are only two goods – corn and microcomputers. The base-year quantities and prices are given in columns (2) and (3). The cost of the 1985 basket is calculated in column (4) and totals £1 400. The 1990 prices are given in column (5). The price of the basket in 1990 is calculated in the last column and is £1 700. The price index of 1990 compared to 1985 ends up as 121.43.

(1) Commodity	*(2) 1985 basket quantity*	*(3) 1985 price per unit (£)*	*(4) Cost of basket in 1985 (£)*	*(5) 1990 price per unit (£)*	*(6) Cost of basket at 1990 prices (£)*
Corn	100 bushels	4.00	400.00	8.00	800.00
Microcomputers	2	500.00	1 000.00	450.00	900.00
Totals			1 400.00		1 700.00

$$\text{Price index} = \frac{\text{Cost of basket in 1990}}{\text{Cost of basket in base year 1985}} = \frac{1\,700.00}{1\,400.00} \times 100 = 121.43$$

The official comments on these various retail price indexes seem keen to stress that *price changes only* are being measured. This is because income tax payments, National Insurance contributions, payments to pension funds, and subscriptions to trade unions etc. are *not* included. The Retail Price Index cannot, therefore, be equally synonymous with a Cost of Living Index. To overcome this problem, to some extent, the Tax and Price Index was introduced in August 1979.

The Tax and Price Index (TPI)

This is also published monthly. It attempts to measure the changes in income before tax that Mr Average would need to maintain his purchasing power. For example, if the TPI were 120 Mr Average would need a 20 per cent increase in gross income compared to the base-year income to maintain his standard of living. To undertake this calculation the Retail Price Index is combined with changes in an employee's direct tax liability (including his National Insurance contributions).

The Tax and Price Index was launched, therefore, as a more comprehensive index. Yet non-taxpayers such as pensioners and the unemployed and those with high taxable incomes are again excluded from the calculations. Furthermore, many regard the introduction of this index as a purely political tool, as the Conservative governments in office from 1979 onwards were committed to switching from direct to indirect taxation. This inevitably played havoc with the Retail Price Index which measures prices inclusive of any indirect taxes. They hoped, therefore, to switch people's attention to the more favourable Tax and Price Index which would highlight their reduced direct tax burden. As it turned out, however, the Retail Price Index is still the one that most commentators refer to. A possible explanation for this traditional preference is that the idea of an 'average income-earner' is less relevant than the idea of 'an average shopping-basket' that everyone spends on.

The Producer Price Index

The **Producer Price Index** (PPI), formerly called the Wholesale Price Index (until August 1983), is similar to the RPI in terms of how it is calculated. The PPI measures changes in the average prices of goods sold in primary markets by producers of commodities in all stages of processing. Price quotations for about 10 000 items representative of goods purchased and manufactured by the UK industrial sector are used. This constitutes the entire 'basket' for calculating the PPI. Just as the RPI is organized into categories which are weighted according to importance, so too is the PPI.

Often journalists and economists – as well as government officials – will make note of an increase in the PPI because it represents the prices of goods in their earlier stages of production. The reasoning is that if the PPI goes up an increase in later months may well be signalled in the RPI.

The Accuracy of Price Indexes

There is continuous debate about how accurate the measured price indexes really are. Do we have an accurate view of the 'rate' of inflation? We cannot answer that question completely, but we can point out the potential biases in the two main price indexes that the government actually uses.

The Retail Price Index and the Producer Price Index allow for comparisons between years. The latter index uses base-year quantities evaluated at today's prices. Yet, is there sufficient attempt to find out if the actual quantities purchased by the average consumer change through the years? In the case of the PPI the answer is negative. The basket of goods used at the time of writing dates back to 1980. However, in the case of the RPI, the answer is more positive. Each January the statistical weights of the basket of goods and services are revised. The revision is based on information arising from the annual Family Expenditure Survey, which is undertaken by about 6 500 homes in the UK each year.

More important, perhaps, is the bias imparted to these two indexes because of improper accounting for changes in quality. For example, at the same nominal price a good is actually cheaper if its quality has been improved. Conversely, at the same nominal price a good is actually more expensive if its quality has fallen. It is difficult for government statisticians to take quality into account.

It is also difficult for government statisticians to take into account immediately the introduction of new products, such as personal home computers, compact discs, and other consumer products that may not have been widely marketed when the original basket of goods was surveyed. But as we have noted the composition of the basket measured by the RPI is, at least, adjusted annually. (The RPI will be a theme of one of the Case Studies to this chapter.) Read Key Points 11.5 before going any further.

The Effects of Inflation

Everybody complains about inflation. Just about everybody assumes that inflation is 'bad'. In order to determine how bad it is for you, you have to figure out what happens to earnings during inflation, what happens to the value of the things you own and the debts you owe. In a moment we shall examine these general effects, but first it will help if we distinguish between 'anticipated' and 'unanticipated' inflation.

We define **unanticipated inflation** as that inflation rate which comes as a surprise, as it were, to individuals in the economy – or at least to the majority of them. For example, if the inflation rate in a particular year turns out to be 10 per cent when the majority of people thought it was going to be 5 per cent, there will have been unanticipated

Key Points 11.5

- **Once we pick a 'basket' of goods, we can construct a price index which compares the cost of that basket today with the cost of the same basket in a base year.**
- **The Retail Price Index (RPI) is the most often used price index in the UK. The Producer Price Index (PPI) is the second most often mentioned. The latter gives information on changes in the weighted average of the prices of goods sold in primary markets by producers of commodities (goods sold at wholesale). Finally, there is also the new and rather underrated Tax and Price Index.**
- **All price indexes suffer from certain inaccuracies. For example, they have a hard time taking into account quality changes and the 'baskets' may not always be entirely representative of the purchases actually made.**

inflation – or an inflation greater than that which was anticipated.

Anticipated inflation is that rate of inflation that the majority of individuals believe will occur. If the rate of inflation this year turns out to be 10 per cent, and that is about what most people thought it was going to be, then we are in a situation of fully anticipated inflation. Many of the problems caused by inflation are due to the fact that it is unanticipated. For when it is anticipated, some people are able to protect themselves from its 'ravages'. With this distinction between anticipated and unanticipated inflation in mind, we can move on to see the relationship between inflation and interest rates.

Inflation Effects and Interest Rates

Let us start in a hypothetical world in which there is no inflation and no anticipated inflation. In that world, you may be able to borrow – in order to buy a house or a car – at some **nominal, or market, rate of interest** of, say, 6 per cent. If you borrow the money to purchase a house or a car and your anticipation of inflation turns out to be accurate, then you will not have been fooled, and the lender will not have been fooled either. The money you pay back in the years to come to pay the interest on that loan will be just as valuable in terms of purchasing power as the money that you borrowed.

But what about a situation in which you borrow at 6 per cent and the following year there is unanticipated inflation of, say 6 per cent? Lucky you! For you will be able to pay back the lender in pounds that are depreciating at the rate of 6 per cent a year. In effect, the **real rate of interest** that you will be paying will fall to practically zero. But of course, the lender will not be quite so happy. Consequently, if you, the lender, and everyone else now anticipate that inflation will remain at 6 per cent per year, the next time the lender offers a loan, he or she will add on a 6 per cent inflationary premium to cover the depreciation in the purchasing power of the pounds repaid by borrowers.

CREDITORS LOSE AND DEBTORS GAIN WITH UNANTICIPATED INFLATION

Now you are in a position to understand why creditors lose and debtors gain with unanticipated inflation. In the above example, unanticipated inflation caused the debtor to benefit. Why? Because the debtor was not initially charged a nominal, or market, interest rate that covered the rate of inflation that actually occurred. Why? Because the lender did not anticipate inflation correctly. The point to understand is that creditors lose and debtors gain whenever inflation rates are *underestimated* for the life of a loan. In the last several decades, there have been apparently periods in which there was considerable unanticipated inflation – as in the late 1960s, early 1970s, and the late 1970s. When we say unanticipated inflation, we mean higher-than-anticipated inflation. During those years, creditors did, on balance, lose, and debtors did, on balance gain.

In general, the elderly are net creditors because they have paid off their mortgages and have built up savings. They are hurt by unanticipated inflation. On the other hand, younger people who are borrowing a lot for homes, cars, and the like are net debtors and therefore have been beneficiaries of recent periods of unanticipated inflation.

It is, of course, possible that the rate of inflation be overestimated. When unanticipated inflation is therefore negative, creditors gain and debtors lose. Some economists argue that the abrupt drop in the rate of inflation in 1983, for example, created just such a situation.

Obviously, whenever inflation is correctly anticipated by both creditors and debtors, neither class of individuals loses (or gains).

Inflation Effects on Fixed-income Earners

Besides the transfer of wealth from creditors to debtors during periods of unanticipated inflation, there is a similar redistribution of income away from those on fixed incomes. Fixed incomes constitute student grants, old age pensions, dole money, and long-term contracts. Inevitably these payments do not cater for unanticipated inflation. Consequently, persons who are solely dependent on fixed incomes lose purchasing power during periods of inflation. Indeed, even during periods of anticipated inflation these groups are in a weak negotiating position, and for most of them the only hope is that the annual review of their situation will help them catch up.

The only exceptions to this fixed-income effect are those who have negotiated index-linked contracts. This is becoming more and more common for those who work on long-term contracts, and also for some pension schemes. Index-linking, basically links income changes to movements in the Retail Price Index, thereby overcoming problems of leaving people on totally fixed incomes as inflation increases.

Inflation Effects on Business Environment

Some economists believe that the main cost of an unanticipated inflation is the resources used to protect against inflation, and the distortions introduced as firms attempt to plan for the long run. In other words, business men have to spend time and resources to figure out ways to 'cover themselves' in case inflation is different from what it has been in the past. This may involve spending a longer time working out more complicated contracts for employment, for purchases of goods in the future, and for purchases of raw materials, or it may simply make any business decision impossible. The outcome is that business becomes more complex, expectations alter, and many firms may falter during inflationary periods. These problems are further compounded when the businesses concerned are heavily involved with imports or exports as exchange rates have to be estimated and these too are affected by inflation.

Inflation Effects on Holding Cash

Most individuals carry some cash in their wallets in the form of notes. Many individuals keep bank accounts that may average several hundred or even several thousand pounds. All of us use some form of cash and/or bank account balance because of the convenience they provide. All of us therefore lose value whenever there is inflation. That is, the purchasing power of the cash held in our wallets or bank account balances falls at the rate of inflation.

Take a simple example. Assume that you have stashed £100 away underneath your mattress. If, by the end of one year, there has been an increase in inflation of 10 per cent, the purchasing power of that £100 will be only about £90. You will have lost value equal to the 10 per cent times the amount of cash you kept on hand. In essence, then, the value of the cash we keep on hand depreciates at the rate of inflation. The only way we can avoid this type of inflationary tax, as it were, on the cash that we hold is by reducing our cash balances and purchasing valuable objects that will retain their value. Or by moving any spare cash into index-linked saving schemes.

The Effects of Disinflation

If you go back to Figure 11.8 you will notice that during the 1980s rates of inflation in the UK began to fall. A slowing down in the rate of inflation can be termed **disinflation**. Disinflation created its own problems in the 1980s, for example, with unanticipated disinflation creditors gain and debtors lose. Why? Because debtors have agreed to pay interest rates that turn out to be too high. If the nominal, or market, rate of interest for a three-year car loan is 16 per cent because the anticipated rate of inflation is say 10 per cent, any sustained reduction in the actual rate of inflation below 10 per cent will benefit those finance houses providing the

Key Points 11.6

- **Whenever inflation is greater than anticipated, creditors lose and debtors gain.**
- **Whenever the rate of inflation is less than anticipated, creditors gain and debtors lose.**
- **Individuals on fixed incomes are clearly hurt by inflation.**
- **Business men become involved in protecting themselves against unanticipated inflation. This imposes a resource cost in terms of time and often entails problems of forecasting, especially if exchange rates are involved.**
- **Holders of cash will lose during periods of inflation because the purchasing power of their cash depreciates at the rate of inflation.**
- **Disinflation is a slowing down in the rate of inflation. The unanticipated disinflation of the 1980s caused problems similar in nature to those encountered during the 1970s due to unanticipated inflation.**

funds for the car loans. Indeed, many car-buyers did find themselves saddled with relatively costly loans around the middle of the 1980s.

To summarize, the unanticipated disinflation of the mid-1980s created problems that were, in some respects, just as significant as those created by the unanticipated inflation of the early 1970s.

These problems of 'anticipation' will be dealt with further in Chapter 18 where we extend our coverage of the theories relating to expectations – and study inflation and unemployment again in a broader context. (Now read Key Points 11.6.)

CASE STUDY

Twenty-three Changes and What have you got?

The official unemployment count will be reduced by about 100 000 this autumn because a change in Government rules effectively disbars anyone under 18 from being counted as jobless.

The Department of Employment confirmed yesterday that an implication of the recent benefit changes will be to cut unemployment over a period of a few months by the number of unemployed benefit claimants at present under 18.

The change creates further questions about the integrity of the Government's sharply falling dole figures, which have been repeatedly challenged both by independent analysts and the Opposition since Mr Norman Tebbit, as Employment Secretary, first changed the post-war basis of counting unemployment in 1982. Employment officials said yesterday that the Government's 1987 manifesto promised that everybody under 18 would either have a job, a training place, or an opportunity in further education. But anyone who refused a training place would not be entitled to benefit.

School-leavers used to be counted in a special category over the summer although they were not entitled to benefit until the autumn. However, the latest change not only abolishes the summer count but also the inclusion of any unemployed under-18s from the autumn.

This is despite the fact that some school-leavers will be entitled under the Employment Act to a special transitional benefit if they cannot find an immediate training place. The official unemployment count is now entirely based on unemployed benefit claimants, unlike the pre-1982 system of counting anyone who registered as unemployed. Mr Paul Convery of the research and pressure group the Unemployment Unit said that the change would entail a 'brutal absence of choice' for many under-18s, particularly in rural areas. Despite some arrangements to ensure that the hardest cases received support, there would be youngsters who will end up relying on parents or siblings for support.

He said that the more restrictive benefit regime would be the twenty-third change to the unemployment count since the Government came to power. On the old basis of estimating unemployment, the Unemployment Unit estimates that the total would be 658 000 higher at 3 033 200. The change follows another amendment which cuts the measured unemployment rate by around 0.2 per cent. Because people undergoing training will now be counted as part of the labour force, unemployment as a percentage of the labour force falls.

Source: Christopher Huhne, 'Changes cut Under-18s from Jobless Statistics', *Guardian*, 16 July 1988.

Questions

1. Since 1979 there have been 23 changes to the method of officially counting unemployment. Name at least three of these changes.
2. Why have school-leavers always been counted in a special category?
3. 'The official unemployment count is now entirely based on unemployed benefit claimants.' Describe three other groups that you would regard as unemployed.
4. (a) Explain how the unemployment rate is calculated.
   (b) Why should the inclusion of 'people undergoing training' as part of the labour force reduce the stated unemployment rate?

CASE STUDY

Are Britain's Bosses taking the Rise?

Britain's highest paid executives awarded themselves average increases of 27 per cent last year, according to a survey by the *Guardian* of 86 of the country's top 100 companies.

The increases, which seem likely to continue this year, defy Treasury pronouncements on the need for management to set an example and keep its own salary growth to a minimum. Wages are one of the biggest factors in the control of inflation – the Government's main economic goal – and there is evidence that outstanding increases at the top levels spur larger pay demands from the workforce.

Despite the trend towards linking pay with performance, directors' income growth still shows little correlation with their companies' earnings.

The *Guardian* study shows the largest increase in salary took place at the TSB, where the earnings of the highest-paid director rose by 242 per cent. In 1987, the TSB chairman, Sir John Read, earned £116 593 but his replacement – the former chairman of the Stock Exchange, Sir Nicholas Goodison – got £398 754.

Lord Hanson, possibly the most feared corporate raider, was Britain's highest paid public company executive in 1988, earning more than £1.23 million a year, followed by Mr Tiny Rowland of Lonrho and Sir Ralph Halpern of Burton, each with around £1m.

Lord King at British Airways and Mr Cyril Stein of the betting and hotels group Ladbroke more than doubled their income between 1987 and 1988.

The heads of privatized companies have, on average, done far better than the rest of Britain's leading executives.

Mr Gordon Brown, Labour's Treasury spokesman, plans to table a clause to the Finance Bill, which will be debated in two weeks, demanding that top earners disclose more details of their pay.

Next week he will unveil a study by the Labour Research Department on the levels of take-home pay prevailing in the boardrooms of the country's biggest companies, with examples of pay rises.

Mr Brown is keen to point out the rises given to heads of privatized corporations such as British Gas, British Telecom, British Steel, British Airways and BAA, the former British airports authority.

'Those who tell us that 7 per cent rises for the workforce can't be borne are absolutely silent on increases three, four and five times as much,' he said.

'It is time for some restraint in the boardroom.'

Mr Brown said it was ironic that those executives who were urging pay restraint were the ones who tended to be paying themselves 'huge increases'.

The employers' body, the Confederation of British Industry, says it issues no guidelines to management on the level of awards to the highest earners. Big shareholding institutions have also kept quiet recently over pay rises.

Source: Lisa Buckingham and Mark Milner, 'Directors defy Treasury on Their Own Pay', *Guardian*, 1 July 1989.

Questions

1. There are many causes of inflation. Which ones do the article suggest may arise in the 1990s?
2. What is unusual about the suggestion that directors' salaries may cause inflation, and do you think it is right or wrong?
3. What other economic consequences may the structure of directors' salaries have on our economy?
4. What other statistics would you like to aid your interpretation of the above questions?
5. Does it matter if the bosses of privatized companies do particularly well? Try and identify at least four economic arguments: two for and two against.

CASE STUDY

The Retail Price Index

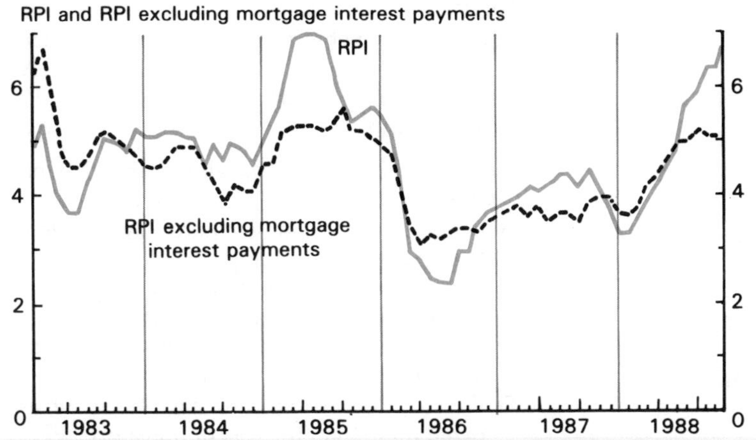

Figure 11.12

The Retail Price Index (RPI) includes mortgage interest payments as a measure of the cost of housing for owner-occupiers. This tends to make the RPI volatile because the average level of mortgage interest payments is very sensitive to changes in interest rates. In particular, it has the perverse result that when interest rates are raised to maintain downward pressure on prices, the direct effect is to increase the RPI. The RPI excluding mortgage interest payments, therefore, gives a better indication of the underlying trend of inflation.

The volatility of the RPI including mortgage interest payments is illustrated in Figure 11.12. For example, the underlying rate of inflation edged up in 1984 and 1985 but the consequent increase in interest rates led to a much larger increase in the RPI. As interest rates fell back at the beginning of 1986, the RPI inflation rate fell below its underlying trend. Similarly virtually all of the increase in the RPI since last summer is due to the increase in mortgage interest payments.

Very few countries other than the UK include mortgage interest payments in their measures of inflation. Within the European Community six countries do not include any measure of owner-occupied housing costs at all; of the remainder four include an index of imputed rents and only Ireland and the UK include mortgage interest payments. Among the other major developed nations only Canada and Australia include mortgage interest payments.

Source: The Treasury, *Economic Progress Report*, Feb. 1989.

Questions

1. The Retail Price Index is important to all those persons, agencies, institutions, or firms, whose contractual arrangements involve indexation. Think of three instances in today's economy that take advantage of being index-linked.
2. What does the Retail Price Index measure?
3. Why does the United Kingdom include mortgage interest payments in the measurements?
4. How else may interest rate movements affect the Retail Price Index?
5. 'Some measure of housing cost must be incorporated into the Retail Price Index, however imperfect.' Explain and discuss this statement.

Exam Preparation

MULTIPLE CHOICE QUESTIONS

One or more of the options given in Questions 1 and 2 may be correct. Select your answer by means of the code set out in the grid:

A	B	C	D	E
1, 2, 3 all correct	1, 2 only correct	2, 3 only correct	1 only correct	3 only correct

1. A rise in house prices can be caused by
1 a decline in house building
2 an increase in lending by building societies
3 a rise in mortgage rates

2. 'Cost-push' inflation may be caused by
1 increased prices of imported raw materials
2 exchange rate depreciation
3 wage increases unrelated to rises in productivity

3. The Tax and Prices Index will rise at a faster rate than the Retail Price Index if there is an increase in
A Value Added Tax
B income tax allowances
C specific import duties
D standard rate of income tax

4. Which group would *not* be included in the official workforce
A school-leavers on a Youth Training Scheme
B people who are overseas in the British Army
C those claiming unemployment benefit
D married women who register themselves as available for temporary work with a commercial agency
E the self-employed

5. Which one of the following policies is most likely to *reduce* the level of structural unemployment
A reduce the level of interest rates
B lower unemployment benefits
C increase the level of consumer expenditure
D increase research and development grants for technology
E increasing labour mobility

6. *Main Weights in the Retail Price Index for Country X, 1987*

Food	250
Transport and vehicles	136
Housing	119
Clothing and footwear	87
Alcoholic drink	65

It can be deduced from the above table that, on average
A people were eating more by volume than they were drinking
B family expenditure on food was rising faster than expenditure on any other category
C people placed less value on housing than on transport
D the cost of housing must have been subsidized more than the cost of transport
E families spent a smaller proportion of their income on alcoholic drink than on clothing and footwear.

RELATED ESSAY QUESTIONS

1. What economic grounds exist for government intervention in an economy? Describe and explain the forms which such intervention may take.

2. Discuss the economic argument that government should curb the power of trade unions.

3. Is it meaningful to identify different causes of inflation?

4. What are the costs and benefits of inflation? Do the benefits of inflation ever justify a government allowing inflation to continue in an economy?

5. What are the main characteristics and causes of unemployment in the UK at present? What are the costs of unemployment to the economy?

6. 'The costs incurred from the current level of unemployment in the United Kingdom are unacceptably high.' Discuss.

12 The Circular Flow of Income, Output, and Expenditure

Key Points to Review

- Factors of production (1.1)
- Money as a medium of exchange (2.3)
- Economic models (1.3, 1.8)
- Trade-off of consumer goods and capital goods (2.4)
- Equilibrium, surplus, shortage (5.7)

Questions for Preview

1 How do economists define profit?

2 Why does total income equal total output?

3 How does the existence of economy-wide saving and investment affect our simple circular flow model?

4 What happens to an economy if the total planned rate of production exceeds the total planned rate of expenditures?

We now make a distinct move into pure macroeconomics – 'the world of totals'. You have already been introduced to the basic idea that goods and services are produced by bringing together various factors of production. The **total output** (production) that arises is organized in millions of firms (owned by the public or private sector). The **total expenditure** on these goods and services emanates from millions of households (both at home and abroad). In this chapter we shall analyse the interrelationship of these various economic units (i.e. firms and households) to understand how a country arrives at a certain level of output, expenditure, and income. Therefore, we shall begin to appreciate how the behaviour of one sector of the economy directly affects another.

The ideas developed here have already been briefly encountered in Chapter 2, where the circular flow for a monetary economy was introduced. We shall now build on this model and thereby provide an important framework for our interpretation of the forthcoming chapters on understanding how to measure and manipulate economic activity.

The Simple Circular Flow

To *begin* our detailed analysis of the circular flow of income we ignore the government sector, the financial institutions sector, and the overseas sector. Technically such a model economy could be called a closed economy with no government sector. That is, it represents a simplified starting-point in which we analyse only the relationships between households and businesses. The complications of the real world will be built in later. (To appreciate the need to start with this type of economic model consider the chaos if we started by discussing all the interrelated sectors at once as illustrated in Figure 12.3.) Consider briefly Figure 12.1 therefore as our starting-point.

To make our starting model effective it is *assumed*: that households receive their income by selling the use of whatever factors of production they own, that businesses sell their entire output immediately to households, and that households spend their entire income on consumer products. These assumptions are reasonably realistic. Businesses will only make what they can sell. Production will involve buying in land, labour, capital, and enterprise, and these factor (of production) services will generate their respective income payments: rent, wages, interest, and profit.

The concept of the circular flow of income as outlined has identified three basic principles:

(i) *In every economic exchange, the seller receives exactly the same amount that the buyer spends.*
(ii) *Goods and services flow in one direction and money flows in the other.*
(iii) *There is a close relationship between income, output, and expenditure.*

These principles are laid out in their traditional format in Figure 12.1.

Figure 12.1.

The Circular Flow of Income. This diagram shows a simple economy comprised of only households and businesses. The two upper flows indicate the **product markets** wherein businesses provide *final* consumer goods and services to households (upper clockwise loop) that pay for them with money (upper anti-clockwise loop). The monetary value of these consumer goods is referred to as *total expenditure.* The two lower flows indicate the **factor markets**, wherein households exchange their factor services with businesses (lower clockwise loop) that pay for them with money (lower anti-clockwise loop). The total household receipts for services is referred to as *total income.*

Money represented in the outer loops flows anti-clockwise – from businesses to households to businesses and so on, highlighting the circular flow of income (and expenditure). Thus one man's income can be considered as another man's expenditure and vice versa.

The inner loop indicates that total output is identical to total income because for every factor involved in output there is an income: rent for the landowner, wages for the labourer, interest for the provider of capital, and profit for the entrepreneur. Again there is a circular flow involved.

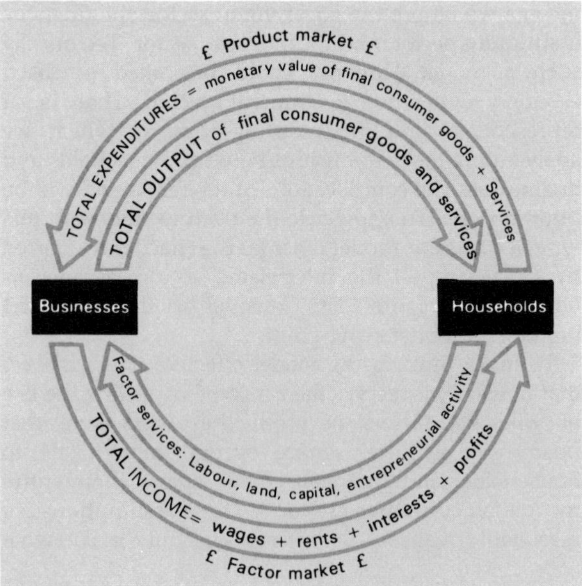

From Figure 12.1 it is possible to appreciate that the amount of economic activity in an economy can be measured in three ways:

1. By adding up the value of all the goods and services produced (in given period of time).
2. By adding up the value of all the income received (during that time-period).
3. By adding up the value of all the spending that occurred (during that period of time).

In each case the result obtained should be identical as

total income ≡ total production ≡ total expenditure.

These symmetrical identities will be discussed below.

NOTE ON PROFITS

We have indicated in Figure 12.1 that profit is a cost of production. You are probably under the impression that profits are not part of the cost of producing goods and services; but profits are indeed a part of this cost because entrepreneurs must be rewarded for providing their services, or they will not provide them. Their reward, if any, is profit. The reward – that is, the profit – is included in the cost of the factors of production. If there were no expectation of profit, entrepreneurs would not incur the risk associated with the organization of productive activities. That is why we consider profits a cost of doing business.

*Total Income ≡ Total Output ≡ Total Expenditure

On the arrow that goes from businesses to households in Figure 12.1 are the words *total income*. What would be a good definition of **total income**? If you answered 'the total of all individuals' income', you would be right. But all income is actually a payment for something, whether it be wages paid for labour services, rent paid for the use of land, interest paid for the use of capital, or profits paid to entrepreneurs. It is the amount paid to the resource suppliers. Total income, therefore, can be alternatively defined as the annual cost of producing the entire output of *final* goods and services. In other words, another method for calculating the level of economic activity would be to sum up the value of all the output generated in that year. Either way the result should be identical as all output generates income and vice versa.

Notice that we have stressed the word *final*. That is because we are referring to the actual goods and services that consumers consume. An example of a final good would be a loaf of bread. Many things went into making that loaf of bread, such as wheat and salt. The wheat and salt are not considered final goods because they are not consumed themselves, but rather used in

* The symbol ≡ means 'is identical with'. It is used to distinguish an identity from an equation. An identity is a relationship that is always equal, as a matter of definition.

the production of some other good. Remember in this chapter and in the next that income, expenditure, and output measurements relate to *final* goods and services.

On the arrow going from households to businesses are the words *total expenditure*. Now what would be your definition of **total expenditure**? Would it not involve the aggregate (total) of everything that was spent? Yes, it would. Total expenditure then can be formally defined as the total monetary value of all the *final* goods and services bought in the simple economy that we are considering. Alternatively, this spending can be regarded as total business receipts from the sale of all goods and services produced by these businesses and consumed by all households. These business receipts, of course, are the opposite side of household expenditures; when households *purchase* goods and services with money, that money becomes a business *receipt*. In every transaction, there is an expenditure and a receipt. Therefore one man's income (receipt) is another man's expenditure and vice versa. Consequently economic activity can be measured/calculated by summing up income or expenditure – the answer should be the same in either case. (See Key Points 12.1.)

The Circular Flow with Saving, and Investment

Saving

Now we wish to take account of the fact that not everything that is earned by households is spent on goods and services. Rather, households do save part of their income. **Saving** can be defined as the act of *not* consuming. Whatever is not consumed is by definition saved. Thus, the rate of saving by households in this simplified model is the difference between total income and household consumption expenditures.

Investment

When economists refer to investment, they are referring to additions to productive capacity. **Investment** may be thought of as an activity that uses resources now in such a way that they allow for greater production in the future and, hence, greater consumption in the future. When a business buys new equipment or puts up a new factory, it is investing; it is increasing its capacity to produce in the future.

The lay person's notion of investment often relates to the purchase of stocks and shares. For our purposes, such transactions simply represent the *transfer of ownership* of assets called stocks and shares. Thus, you must keep in mind the fact that investment in economics refers *only* to additions to productive capacity.

THE TWO COMPONENTS OF INVESTMENT

In our analysis we will consider the two basic components of investment. We have already mentioned the first one, which involves a firm buying equipment. This is known as a **capital good**. A capital good is simply a good that is purchased not to be consumed in its current form but to be used in order to make other goods and services. The purchase of equipment and factories – capital goods – is called **fixed investment**.

The other type of investment has to do with the change in stocks of raw materials and finished goods. Firms do not immediatley sell off all their products to consumers. Some of the final product is usually held in warehouses waiting to be sold. Firms hold stocks to meet future expected orders for their products. When a firm does increase its amount of stock of finished products it is engaging in what may be called investment in working capital. **Working capital** consists of all finished goods on hand, goods in process, and raw materials. In short, goods not yet used up in production.

The reason that we can think of a change in stock as being a type of investment is that increases one year provide for future increased consumption possibilities another year. In fact stock changes are a good indicator to business prospects.

If a firm's planned output is greater than actual sales,

Key Points 12.1

- **A closed economy is one which has no transactions with the rest of the world. In *our* rather simplified starting model there is no government or financial sector either.**
- **The simple circular flow model highlights: (a) that households sell factor services to businesses that pay for those factor services, the receipt of these payments generating total incomes: (b) that businesses sell goods and services to households that pay for them, the total output being thus absorbed by total expenditure.**
- **Total income must always equal total output which must always equal total expenditure.**
- **Economic activity can therefore be measured in three different ways.**

it will have to indulge in unplanned stock building and vice versa. This, in turn, will affect production plans in the forthcoming year.

(Finally, it may be interesting to note that the unplanned increases or decreases in stock enable the accounting identities of expenditure, output, and income to be maintained. In accounting terms what is produced is always bought if not by the households (this year) then by the businesses themselves. Conversely, when households desire more than is made in a particular year stocks are run down, disinvestment occurs. And once more, in accounting terms, the relationship between income, expenditure, and output is maintained.)

Saving and Investing Linked by Financial Institutions

What are the resources necessary for investment? And from where do they come? Basically, they come from saving that in our simplified example is provided by households. (Businesses can save, too, and thereby provide themselves with the funds necessary for investment, but for the moment we will ignore business saving.) The saving that households do each year is not directly handed over to the businesses wishing to engage in investment. Rather, the flow of saving passes through various financial institutions. These institutions include, but are not limited to, commercial banks, insurance companies, pension funds, building societies, and the stock market. In essence, households are providing funds through the financial market from which businesses obtain funds, which then become expenditures for things they invest in.

Here we an see more clearly, then, the link between saving and investment. Saving is identically equal to forgone current consumption. But since saving in our model is funnelled through financial institutions into investment, then there is a clear connection between investment and forgone current consumption.

Figure 12.2 is, therefore, a more accurate representation of the circular flow: it takes into account saving and investment.

Savings can be formally regarded as a **leakage** (sometimes termed *withdrawals*) from the circular flow. In this definition savings represent income generated by output that is *not* passed on directly in spending. It is likely as suggested in Figure 12.2 that most savings will be passed back into the system. But savings in a tin box under the bed could cause problems to the levels of economic activity. Conversely, *investment* can be regarded as an **injection**. This may be defined as an addition to the circular flow *which does not* relate to present consumer spending. An injection, therefore, could also cause changes to the level of economic activity, especially if it were funded by money from past hoardings/forgery. Theoretically, for the model economy represented in our circular flow to retain its present equilibrium the total leakage should equal the total injection. The supporting text to Figure 12.2 suggests this is the case.

Figure 12.2

The Circular Flow *with* Saving and Investment. To make the circular flow diagram more realistic, we must consider that households save. Therefore, we must represent in the diagram financial institutions (as shown by a rectangle) through which households' saving passes to businesses. Businesses use the investment funds obtained from these financial institutions to make investment expenditures on capital goods and stocks. Once businesses make these expenditures they are included as part of the monetary value of consumer and investment goods combined. This is shown by the arrow that goes from businesses to the flow line of total expenditure. In this more realistic circular flow, total output equals the monetary value of all consumer and investment goods expenditures. Of course, the actual production of investment goods also generates total income in the form of wages, rents, interest, and profit receipts to households. This is shown by the flow line on the bottom of the circular flow diagram. So once again income, expenditure, and output are still at the same level.

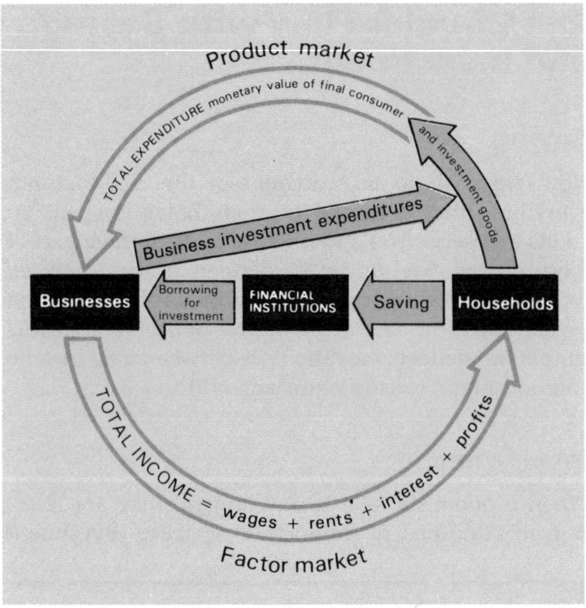

Furthermore, academic theory highlights that *actual* (realized) investment must by its very nature be equivalent to the *actual* (realized) level of saving. The former is inherently related to the latter and this relationship will be briefly identified in the following section.

The Relationship between Savings and Investments

Firstly, income (Y) can be disposed of in only two ways: by consumption (C) or by saving (S), i.e. $Y = C + S$. Secondly, income can be generated in only two areas of production (output): by producing consumer goods (C)

Key Points 12.2

- **Savings can be defined as not spending on consumer goods.**
- **Investment includes fixed investment – the purchase of plant and equipment (capital goods) and changes in the stocks of finished goods, goods in process, and raw materials.**
- **When we add saving and investment to the circular flow model, we must also include financial institutions through which the savings flow to firms which in turn make investment expenditures.**
- **When we add investment expenditures to consumption expenditures, we obtain the total demand for goods and services in the product markets.**
- **Actual investment = planned fixed capital, planned and unplanned stockbuilding.**
- **Savings can be regarded as a form of 'leakage'.**
- **Investment can be regarded as a form of 'injection'.**
- **In our model, we have assumed that households save and business firms invest. Thus, the savers and the investors are different groups of people who have different motivations.**
- **Actual savings must always equal actual investment; unplanned stock changes will cause this identity to hold.**

or producing investment goods (I), i.e. $Y = C + I$. Therefore using this standard notation one can prove that

$$Y \equiv C + I$$
$$Y - C \equiv S$$

Therefore

$$I \equiv S.$$

It may help your comprehension if you remember what was said about unplanned stockbuilding being a form of investment. (Now read Key Points 12.2.)

We have started to explore the basis of some theoretical questions relating to managing the economy. These will be raised again in Chapters 15 and 16. Meanwhile we must continue to open up our model economy and identify the remaining interrelationships.

The Circular Flow now with Government Added

Now let us introduce government to our 'picture' of circular flow. How does the government fit into this picture? To see how it fits, we must determine the flows of goods and services and the flows of income and expenditures between government and households, businesses and financial institutions.

We know certainly that there is a flow of money from households to governments in the form of taxes. We also know that households receive money from government in the form of social security payments, old-age pensions, grants, and other payments. These forms of payments are called transfer payments, which we have previously defined as those payments made from government to individuals for which no goods or services are concurrently provided in exchange. The government borrows from financial institutions to finance its deficits when its spending exceeds its revenues. In other words the government sells gilt-edged securities and similar instruments to cover its debts. When it has a surplus (when revenues exceed expenditures), it buys back some of the securities that it issued. Finally, the government adds to total expenditures when it *purchases* goods and services.

Look at Figure 12.3 on page 198. We have put government above and to the right of the financial institutions. From these financial institutions to government there is an arrow that is labelled government *net* borrowing. Net government borrowing takes account of the fact that some government departments run a surplus while others may run a deficit. The arrow going from households to government is labelled *net taxes*. It is the difference between taxes paid and transfer payments. That is why the term *net* was added.

Then there is an arrow going from the government to the consumption expenditure arrow, which leads into the product markets. This shows that government purchases of goods and services (excluding transfer payments) add to the total amount of expenditures in any one year.

Once again one can sense the process of 'injections' and 'leakages' being incorporated into the flow. For example, injections in the form of government expend-

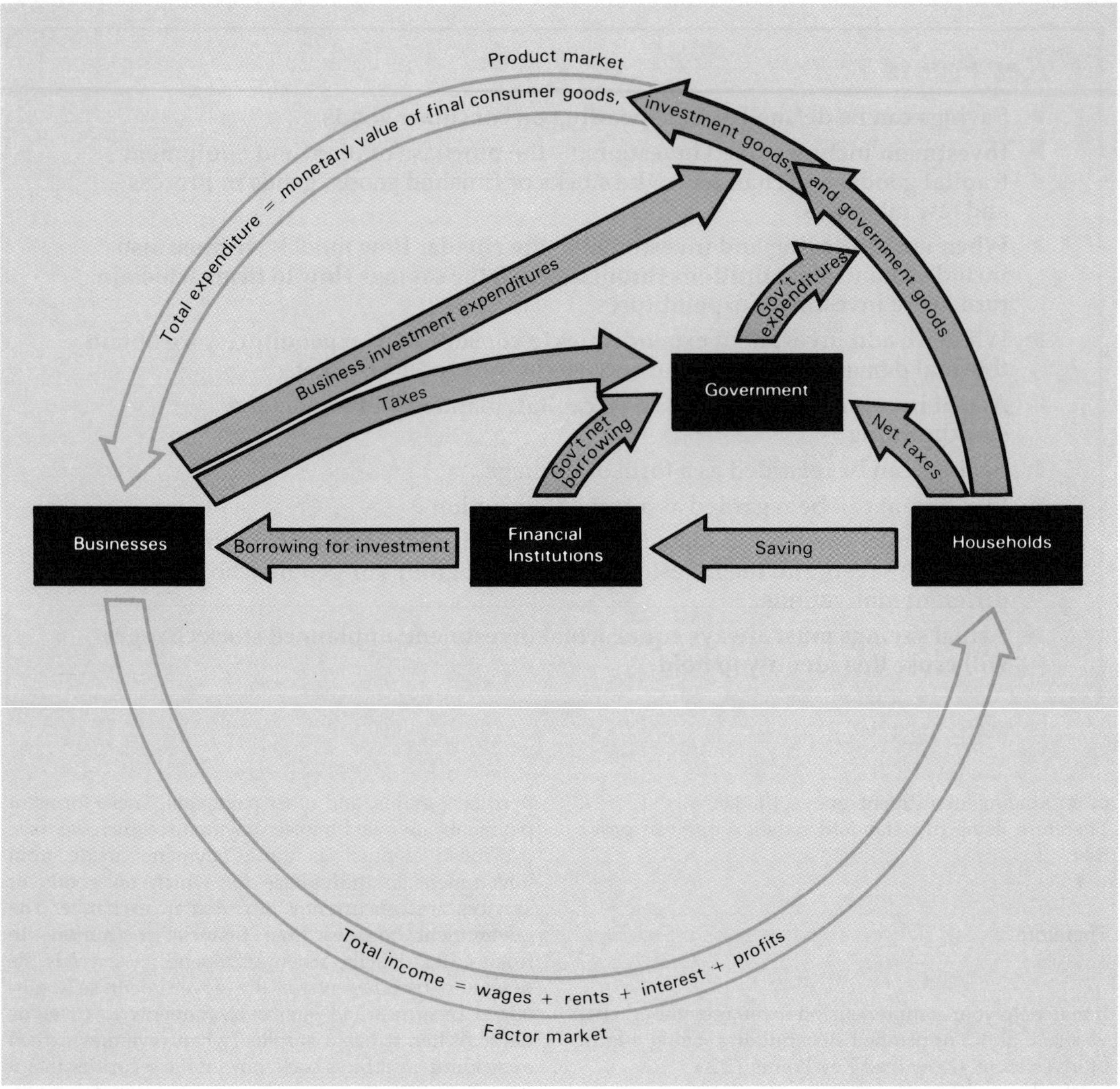

Figure 12.3

The Circular Flow of Income and Product with Government. When we add government to the picture the product market is affected (as shown by the government expenditure arrow) because governments also make expenditures on goods and services. Hence, output increases; it equals the monetary value of total consumer, investment, and government goods purchased. Of course, wages, interest, rents, and profits are generated from the production of government goods; therefore, total income increases correspondingly. The diagram also indicates that households and businesses pay net taxes to the government, and that the government may also borrow from the financial institutions. Only the money flows appear in this figure.

iture, and leakages in the form of taxation. Ideally to maintain the present level of economic activity government spending and government revenue (income) should be balanced. Government deficits and surpluses will affect the level of economic activity, unless counterbalanced by a corresponding deficit or surplus in another sector – for example, the foreign trade sector which will be briefly considered next.

The Circular Flow now with Foreign Trade

Now we will open up our model to include foreign trade. Consequently, domestic households may now spend part of their income on goods produced by businesses overseas (i.e. buy imports), while domestic businesses may now sell part of their produce to households overseas (i.e. sell exports).

Imports, therefore, constitute a leakage from our circular flow, because households spend their money abroad which in effect boosts another country's total output and total income. Conversely, exports constitute an injection into the domestic circular flow, foreign spending boosts employment of the domestic factors of production thereby increasing total output and total income. Consequently we now have a situation where the domestic total expenditure may be less or more than domestic total output.

To retain the identities of total income ≡ total expenditure ≡ total output it would be necessary to draw several hundred circular flows for all the countries involved in trade with one another. You may have the imagination to envisage this complexity – but our pages are certainly not large enough to portray the diagram. Nevertheless it is possible to conceptually understand that one country's trade deficit is its overseas partner's trade surplus. In terms of international trade, therefore, the relationship between output, expenditure, and income remains. (This will become apparent when analysing national accounts in the next chapter.)

Another complication once we enter the international trade scene is currency differences. Thus the financial institutions will be involved again. This time to exchange currencies so that the movement of goods from one country to another is possible. This in itself does not upset the domestic monetary flow. However, *speculators* in currency hoping to make a profit through fluctuating exchange rates may complicate the income–expenditure–output relationship, especially when viewed in *domestic* terms alone. It is the one-country analysis that we now wish to return to.

Equilibrium

In Chapter 5 we talked about the concept of equilibrium, that is, where supply and demand are in equilibrium. The equilibrium price, or market-clearing price, occurred at the intersection of the demand curve and the supply curve. The special feature about equilibrium is that there is no tendency for price or quantity to change once supply and demand are in equilibrium. Remember that when the market price is greater than the equilibrium price, forces start in action that push the price back down towards equilibrium. Unsold 'surpluses' are offered for sale by producers and retailers, for example, at lower prices. Producers will also reduce output. Remember also that when the price is below the equilibrium price, there is an excess quantity demanded at that price. Forces are set in motion that cause the price to go up. More-than-willing demanders bid up the price. Producers respond by increasing the quantity supplied.

Thus, the important thing to remember from equilibrium analysis is that when we are *not* in equilibrium forces will work to re-establish equilibrium. The same is true whether we are analysing equilibrium for a single product market or equilibrium for the entire economy. If the total demand for all goods and services is not equal to the total supply of all goods and services, market forces will operate so as to bring total demand and total supply back into equilibrium. In the process, total income and total output may either rise or fall. Indeed, much of this part of the text is designed to analyse the forces behind the rise and fall of total income, total output, and total expenditure.

Equilibrium is a concept that pervades all economic analysis. We have actually assumed that equilibrium prevails within the circular flow model represented in Figure 12.1. By requiring that all household earnings be spent in the product market and that all business production be offered for immediate sale, there can be no discrepancy in the basic circular flow model between the total demand and the total supply of goods and services. Thus, the basic circular flow model in Figure 12.1 accurately represents the total demand for goods and services and the total supply of goods and services, and that total demand and total supply are automatically in equilibrium. Provided we never alter this model it will continue to function at the same level for ever. Such an economy can be classed as being in **neutral equilibrium**. Neutral equilibrium means there are no pressures for change, the established set of flows will simply persist forever.

However, we then began to open up our model and introduce other sectors of the economy. Within each sector *if* the various flows of injection and leakage were equal then the flow of income around the circuit remains constant. Only when the leakages are perfectly counterbalanced by the injections could the economy be said to be in equilibrium. For example, say we have three leakages from expenditures (savings, imports, and tax) with the values of $5 + 2 + 3$ and three injections (investment, exports, and government spending) with the values of $2 + 2 + 6$. The economy would still be in equilibrium, because the total value of the injections (10) equals the total value of the leakages (10). However, as our analysis has suggested the various decisions affecting the leakages and injections of funds are carried out by different groups of individuals with different motivations. Therefore, it is unlikely that year after year leakages and injections will remain the same.

However, due to the income–output–expenditure relationship the economy will adjust to new equilibrium levels. For example, if leakages exceed injections, expenditure will be less than factor incomes. Consequently, firms will not receive sufficient revenue to cover their output costs. Stocks will accumulate and firms will cut back output and income until they equal expenditure again. A new level of equilibrium will have been established. In short, equilibrium means a 'balanced state'.

It is the character of the imbalances between leakages and injections that prompts changes in output from year to year. These changes lead to different amounts of income circulating within the economy – which represent different levels of economic activity. (All economies will tend towards an equilibrium but the equilibrium point is not necessarily the point of full employment.) Measuring these yearly changes in economic activity is the topic of the next chapter.

Conclusion

The theme that will recur in the next chapter is that total income ≡ total expenditure ≡ total output. In fact national accounts are based on these identities. The logic behind them, therefore, will be briefly restated once more before closing.

All income is generated by selling factor services. Owners of labour gain wages, the providers of land receive rent, the persons providing capital receive interest, and the entrepreneurs taking the risks gain any profits. These factors of production when combined provide output, the cost of which is identical to the payment for factor services. In fact it may help if the *prices* of final goods and services are regarded as *bundles of incomes* that have been paid out during the course of their production.

Another way of looking at the value of output is from the angle of expenditure. Indeed, you must recognize that all output is sold, even if only to the business's warehouse. Expenditure, therefore, absorbs the final goods and services either in the form of consumer goods or capital goods and sets the cycle off gain. The outcome is that total expenditure ≡ total income ≡ total output.

Key Points 12.3

- **When we add government to the circular flow we add government goods to the product market. These goods are purchased out of tax revenue from households and firms.**
- **When we incorporate foreign trade to our model the flow of income becomes complicated by import, export, and currency manœuvres.**
- **Imports represent a form of leakage. Exports represent a form of injection.**
- **All economies tend towards an equilibrium.**
- **The equilibrium point is a 'balanced state', not necessarily a point of full employment.**
- **Total expenditure ≡ total income ≡ total output. These are national accounting identities.**

CASE STUDY

Is Model Building Child's Play?

A child's model automobile or airplane looks and operates something like the real thing, but it is much smaller and much simpler, and so it is easier to manipulate and understand. Engineers for General Motors and Boeing also build models of cars and planes. While their models are far bigger and much more elaborate than a child's toy, they use them for much the same purposes: to observe the workings of these vehicles 'up close', to experiment with them in order to see how they might behave in different circumstances. From these experiments, they make educated guesses as to how the real-life version will perform. Often these guesses prove uncannily accurate, as exemplified by the success of the Boeing 747. But sometimes they are wide of the mark. The chronic mechanical problems of General Motors' Corvair prompted Ralph Nader's acclaimed book *Unsafe at Any Speed*, which helped launch the consumer movement.

Economists use models for similar purposes and with similarly mixed results. For example, when teaching at the LSE, during the 1950s and early 1960s, Professor Bill Phillips (of Curve fame) built a machine powered by pumps, controlled by valves, and comprising tanks and tubes filled with coloured water to depict the circular flow. A picture of this machine is shown in Figure 12.4

Figure 12.4 The Phillips Machine

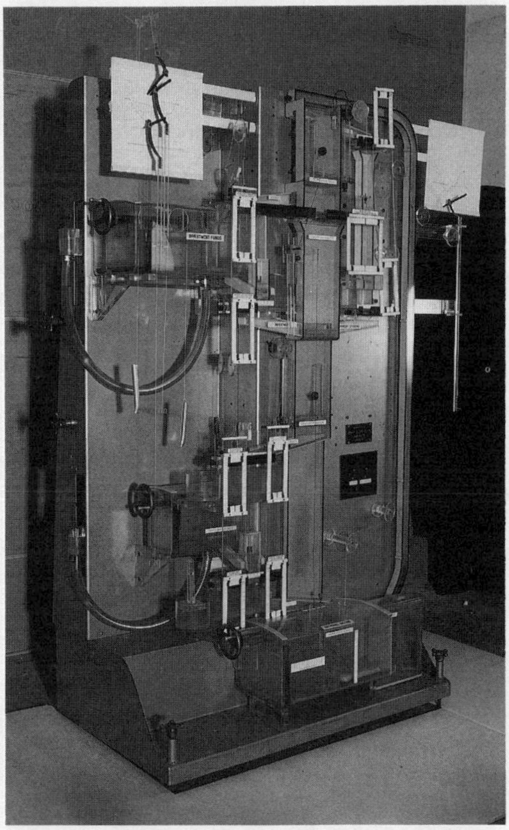

Unfortunately most economists lack Phillips's engineering background and most economic models are not like this built with metal and welding torches; most rely on pencil and paper instead. However, the format is irrelevant as all models fulfil precisely the same role. They simplify reality in order to make it understandable. They provide a starting-point. They enable us to proceed methodologically from simple beginnings to a fuller understanding of complex reality.

Source: Adapted and extended from Baumol and Blinder, *Economics Principles and Policy*, Harcourt, Brace, Jovanovich, 1986.

Questions

1. What models are you familiar with in economics? Try and state at least two examples and explain the purpose in each case.
2. What academic problems does the Phillips machine present as a means of explaining the circular flow of income?
3. What academic problems present themselves when using traditional models to explain economic ideas?
4. What are the advantages and disadvantages of using a closed-economy model for explaining the circular flow of income?
5. What other sectors need to be integrated into the closed-economy model in order to begin to study reality? Name each sector and give examples to show you understand what comprises each one.
6. The Phillips machine works on the principle of 'pumping-in' and 'syphoning-off'. These actions are meant to represent some economic activity. State examples of each of these processes.
7. 'The format of an economic model is irrelevant.' Explain and discuss.

Exam Preparation

PRACTICAL EXERCISE

1. (a) Copy Figure 12.5.
   (b) Identify the following sectors and locate them in appropriate boxes: households, businesses, government, financial institutions, and foreign trade.
   (c) Distinguish each sector's main leakage and injection in appropriate boxes remaining.

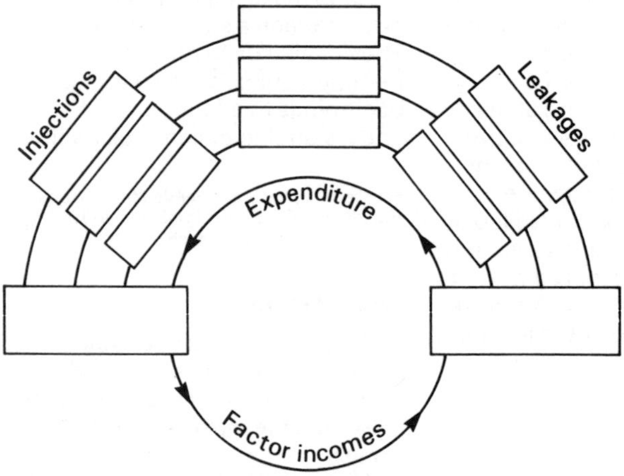

Figure 12.5 A Model of Income Flows

MULTIPLE CHOICE QUESTIONS

1. Total injections into the circular flow of income within a country during any given year consist of
   A saving + imports + tax
   B exports + government expenditure + saving
   C government expenditure + exports + consumer spending
   D investment + saving + exports − imports
   E exports + investment + government expenditure.

2. Which of the following would be correctly regarded as a withdrawal from the circular flow of a real national income?
   A a rise in consumption
   B a surplus on the balance of visible trade
   C a rise in public investment
   D a rise in private investment
   E a deficit on the balance of visible trade.

3. Which of the following sets a limit to the real output of an economy in the long run?
   A the supply of money
   B the supply of factors of production
   C the size of the government sector
   D the volume of international trade
   E the level of effective demand.

4. Which of the following represents a leakage from the circular flow of income?
   A current expenditure of nationalized industries
   B purchases of vehicles by firms
   C imports of machine tools
   D payments of rents by local authority tenants
   E interest received on capital invested abroad.

5. One or more of the three options given in Question 5 may be correct. Decide which of the responses is (are) correct. Then choose the appropriate code from the grid:

A	B	C	D	E
1, 2, 3 all correct	1, 2 only correct	2.3 only correct	1 only correct	3 only correct

Domestic economic activity could be stimulated by

1 a fall in the exchange rate
2 reduced levels of taxation
3 increased government spending.

RELATED ESSAY QUESTIONS

1. Explain the circular flow of income in an economy with government and foreign trade sectors.

2. State the conditions for the circular flow of income in an economy to be in equilibrium. Show how the equilibrium is reached.

3. (a) Distinguish between injections into and withdrawals from the circular flow of income.
   (b) Explain carefully the relationship between injections, withdrawals, and changes in the national income.

4. In a macroeconomic model, what are injections and withdrawals? Examine the consequences of changes in injections and withdrawals in an open economy.

13 Measuring Economic Activity: National Income

Key Points to Review

- Money and real values (1.3)
- Transfer payments (4.2)
- Relative prices (6.3)
- Price index (11.5)
- Effects of inflation (11.6)
- The circular flow of income (12.1)
- Actual investment (12.2)

Questions for Preview

1 **What is gross national product (GNP) and what does it measure?**

2 **What are the three approaches to measuring GNP and why do they yield identical results?**

3 **What must be added to gross domestic product (GDP) to arrive at a GNP figure?**

4 **What is the basic difference between GNP and National Income (i.e. NNP)?**

5 **How does correcting GNP for price level and population changes improve the usefulness of GNP estimates?**

Governments must know how the economy is performing in order to decide when, how, and how much stimulus or constraint should be applied. That is, policy-makers need a statistical knowledge of the nation's performance. Furthermore, a historical statistical record aids economists in testing their theories about how the economy actually works. Thus, **national income accounting** is an important topic in the study of economics. It involves attaching actual numbers to the elements of the circular flow of income, product, and expenditure that we went through in detail in Chapter 12. Consequently, it can be measured in three ways (identified in Chapter 12) by adding up each year all the expenditure, or all the income, or all the output.

For a precise idea of the magnitude of numbers involved and the areas actually measured the student can do no better than actually look at the *United Kingdom National Accounts*.* These are published annually by the Central Statistical Office (CSO) around September, and your local reference library should have a copy. For those who cannot see it at the library some extracts from this publication are included in this chapter.

*Prior to 1984 this publication was titled: *'The National Income and Expenditure Blue Book'*.

However, before becoming involved with these tables of figures we must understand what it is we are actually measuring, i.e. we must examine what gross national product involves.

Gross National Product

Gross national product (GNP) represents the total money value of the nation's annual final product, or output, produced per year. We can formally define **GNP as the total market value of all *final* goods and services produced in an economy during a year.** We are referring here to a **flow** of production. A nation produces at a certain rate, just as you receive income at a certain rate. Your income flow might be at a rate of £5 000 per year or £50 000 per year. Suppose you are told that someone earns £500. Would you consider this a good salary? There is no way you can answer that question unless you know whether the person is earning £500 per month or per week or per day. Thus, you have to specify a time-period for all flows – income received is a flow. You must contrast this with, for example, your total accumulated savings, which are a **stock** measured at a point in time, not across time. Implicit in just about everything we deal with in this chapter is a time-period – usually a year.

The Stress on *Final* Output

As we noted, GNP measures the value of *final* output. GNP ignores intermediate goods, or goods used up entirely in the production of final goods, because to include them would be to **double-count**.

We can use an example to clarify this point. Our example will involve determining the value added at each stage of production. *Value added* is the amount of value added to a product by each stage of its production. In Figure 13.1 we see the difference between total value of all sales and value added in the production of a doughnut. We also see that the sum of the values added is equal to the sale price to the final consumer. It is the 15p that is used to measure GNP, not the 32p. If we used the 32p, we would be double-counting, for we would include the total value of all of the intermediate sales that took place prior to the doughnut being sold to its final consumer. Such a double-counting would grossly exaggerate GNP if it were done for all of the goods and services sold.

Excluding Non-productive Transactions

Not only is the stress in measuring GNP on the word *final*, but it also relates to productive transactions only. Productive transactions involve some *final* purchases of *newly* produced goods or services. However, daily economic activity also involves numerous non-productive transactions. These non-productive transactions are typified by transfers of money (or the ownership of used goods). Technically these are referred to as **transfer payments** – and we shall illustrate them with four typical examples.

TRANSFER PAYMENTS

1. *Buying and selling shares.* When you purchase shares on the Stock Exchange in a public limited company, e.g. ICI or Marks & Spencer, someone else must sell them to you. In essence there is merely a transfer of ownership rights you pay to obtain a share certificate. Someone else, via the Stock Exchange, received your payment and gave up the share certificate. No productive activity is generated and consequently the bulk of the monies involved in this transaction are not included in our measurements of gross national product (only the brokerage fees for the *productive services* involved in deed transfers etc. need to be counted).

Figure 13.1

Sales Value and Value Added in Pence per Doughnut at Each Stage of Production.

Stage 1: A farmer purchases a penny's worth of fertilizer and seed that are used as factors of production in growing wheat.

Stage 2: The farmer grows the wheat, harvests it, and sells it to the miller for 2p. Thus, we see that the farmer has added 1p worth of value. That 1p represents income paid in the form of rent, wages, interest, and profit by the farmer.

Stage 3: The flour miller purchases the wheat for 2p, and adds 2p to the value added; that is, there is 2p for him as income to be paid as rent, wages, interest, and profit. He sells the ground wheat flour to a doughnut-baking company.

Stage 4: The doughnut-baking company, buys the flour for 4p and adds 6p as the value added. It then sells the doughnut to the final retailer.

Stage 5: The doughnut retailer sells fresh hot doughnuts at 15p apiece, thus creating additional value of 5p.

We see that the total value of sales resulting from the production of one doughnut was 32p, but the total value added was 15p which is exactly equal to the retail price. The total value added is equal to the sum of all income payments, including payments to rent, wages, interest, and profit.

(1) *Stage of production*	*(2)* *Value of sales (p)*		*(3)* *Value added (p)*
Stage 1 Fertilizer and seed	1		1
Stage 2 Growing wheat	2		1
Stage 3 Flour milling	4		2
Stage 4 Doughnut baking	10		6
Stage 5 Doughnut retailing	15		5
Total value of all sales	32	Total value added	15

2. *Government transfer payments.* We have already referred to transfer payments as payments for which no productive services are concurrently provided in exchange. The most obvious *government* transfer payments are social security payments, old age pensions, student grants, and interest payments on the National Debt. The recipients make no contribution to current production in return for such transfer payments (although they may have made contributions in the past in order to receive them).
3. *Private transfer payments.* Are you receiving money from your parents in order to live at school? Has a wealthy relative ever given you a gift of money? If so, you have been the recipient of a *private* transfer payment. This is merely a transfer of funds from one individual to another. As such, it does not constitute productive activity and is not included in gross national product.
4. *The transfer of used goods.* If I sell you my two-year-old car, there is no current production involved. Rather, I transfer to you the ownership of a car that was produced several years ago; in exchange, you transfer to me, say, £3 000. The original purchase price of the car was included in the GNP in the year I purchased it. To include it again when I sell it to you would be counting the value twice.

   However, if the car was bought from a second-hand car dealer, the mark-up between the price he bought it in at and the selling price would be included. The profit represents the salesman's income and is a return for a service. This final example brings us back to the central issue – gross national product calculations must incorporate payments for productive services. The car salesman will be very willing to tell you how he has improved the car before putting it out for display on his forecourt – in a way one may sense that his work has added value and is therefore part of new annual output. (Read Key Points 13.1.)

The Three Methods of Measuring GNP

GNP has been defined as the total market value of all goods and services produced in an economy during a year. Consequently, government statisticians can use one of three methods to measure its size. They can either:

1. Add up the *flow of expenditures* made on all goods and services during each year. This is known as the **expenditure approach.**
2. Add up the *flow of income* received in the same year by everybody involved in the production of these goods and services. This is known as the **income approach**.
3. Add up the specific value of the *flows of output* arising from each sector of the economy. This is known as the **output approach**.

In Britain we account *all* three methods of measurement. This is not too much of a problem, because as identified in Chapter 12 in each case the measurements should be identical. Therefore, the theory of Chapter 12 will now be revisited with the application of actual figures.

Furthermore, by analysing each of these methods of measurement, in turn, we will get an insight into the UK economy from three perspectives; according to the types of income being earned; according to the types of goods being produced; and according to the nature and purpose of our nation's expenditure.

PLAN OF ATTACK

In order that the large number of concepts and definitions involved in this section can be understood, we shall move through the calculations in three separate stages:

Firstly, by calculating GDP via each method.
Secondly, by moving from GDP to GNP figures.
Thirdly, by moving from GNP to net National Income.

Measuring GDP with the Expenditure Approach

By acquiring statistical information from a wide range of industrial enquiries, household surveys and government accounting data, the Central Statistical Office is able to produce annually tables of national expenditure.

Key Points 13.1

- **GNP is the total money value of final goods and services produced in an economy during a one-year period.**
- **GNP also represents the flow of production over a one-year period.**
- **In order to avoid double-counting, we look only at final goods and services produced or, alternatively, at value added.**
- **In measuring GNP we must exclude transfer payments, these are merely transfer of monies which do not correspond to any type of productive economic activity.**

This is laid out in its traditional format in Figure 13.2* The relevant categorizations and terminology are clarified in the following section where each numbered item in Figure 13.2 is explained.

Figure 13.2

Gross Domestic Product by the Expenditure Approach

Current market prices	*1988 (£m)*
(1) Consumers' expenditure	293 569
(2) General government final consumption	91 847
(3) Gross domestic fixed capital formation	88 751
(3) Value of physical increase in stocks and works in progress	4 371
Total domestic expenditure	478 538
(4) Exports of goods and services	108 533
Total final expenditure	587 071
(4) *less* imports of goods and services	−125 194
Gross domestic product (expenditure based)	**461 877**
Factor Cost Adjustments:	
(5) *less* taxes on expenditure	−75 029
(5) *plus* subsidies	5 883
Gross domestic product at factor cost	**392 731**
(6) Statistical discrepancy (expenditure adjustment)	2 056
Gross domestic product (average estimate)	**394 787**

Source: *United Kingdom National Accounts, 1989* (HMSO, London).

(1) Consumers' expenditure

Consumer spending falls into three categories: **durable consumer goods, non-durable consumer goods**, and **services**. Durable goods are *arbitrarily* defined as items that last more than a year; these include cars, TVs, furniture, and household appliances. Non-durable goods are all the rest, such as food, fuel, and clothes. Services are just what the name suggests: insurance, bank charges, funeral expenses, rents, and rates.

You should be aware of the fact that there are some goods and services that do not pass through the market-place. For example, food grown on the farm for household consumption by farmers' families is certainly a consumption expenditure, but it does not show up in the usual way, because it does not pass through an organized market. The £294bn spending represents therefore only official consumer spending; there will be some transactions that do not go through any official books.

(2) Government Expenditures

In addition to personal consumption expenditures, there are local and central government purchases of goods and services (these are grouped under the formal heading of *general government final consumption*). It is evident from the figures that the government sector is an important spender in our economy, and this is not at all surprising when one remembers that in Britain it provides many of our services, e.g. health, education, parks, libraries, police, and defence etc. Because many of these services are provided free or below cost they are valued in the National Accounts at their cost of provision.

(3) Investment Expenditures

Gross domestic fixed capital formation is *not* the name of a northern dance team, but is the official term for investment expenditure. In Chapter 12 we explicitly pointed out what economists mean when they say investment expenditures: it is worth repeating here because the point is so important.

First of all, investment in economics does not relate to simple *transfers* of asset ownership among individuals. Thus, if you buy a stock or a bond, that is *not* investment from the economic point of view; you have simply traded money and received in exchange a piece of paper entitling you to something. Such transfers are not investment.

Investment, therefore, relates to expenditure on our future productive capacity. It relates to newly produced goods that are carried over into the next time-period. The bulk of this £89bn worth of expenditure is therefore on items such as industrial buildings, domestic dwellings, plant, and machinery.

Apart from these items of fixed investment you will remember that we also made a reference to investment of working capital. Indeed it is important to remember that for accounting purposes businesses buy into stock any output that is not sold to the public. Consequently, we can identify a second component of investment expenditure, namely the *value of physical increases in stock*. One would expect some stock building to occur in any dynamic economy. However, in 1980, 1981, and 1982 the UK actually experienced negative values for this category as stocks were run down during the recession. To some extent stock levels are an indicator of demand for a nation's products.

(4) Overseas Expenditures

To get an accurate representation of gross domestic product, we must also include the foreign sector. That is, we must *add* to our total domestic expenditure what foreigners spend on our goods and services when they purchase export items. To get some idea of the *net* expenditures emanating from this overseas trade we must also subtract the value of imports (as these represent another country's GDP) from the value of our exports to obtain net exports for a year:

$$\text{net exports} \equiv \text{total exports} - \text{total imports}$$

In numerical terms for 1988 this would involve subtracting 125 194 from 108 533 (as indicated by (4) in

*Note: The bracketed numbers per item are the only modifications made to the table. The authors have incorporated them to support their text

Figure 13.2). Once this calculation has been accounted for we can arrive at a figure for gross domestic product at current market prices.

(5) From Market Prices to Factor Costs

The next manoeuvre is to remove the distortions caused by taxes on expenditure and subsidies. Indirect taxes, i.e. taxes on expenditure (e.g. VAT), merely increase the price of goods and services, while subsidies (e.g. the rent on certain properties) reduce market prices. Businesses are actually acting on behalf of the government when they collect VAT or claim a subsidy. Therefore, movements in expenditure taxes or subsidies move market prices for the purchasers, but the amount received by producers (other things remaining constant) will remain unaltered. In other words, the rewards to the actual factors of production remain the same, while governments move their rates of expenditure tax and/or subsidies. As our aim is to measure real economic activity, i.e. assess the productivity of our resources, it makes more sense to measure GDP at factor prices (or factor costs) and this is a common practice in National Income accounting in the UK. Thus we can arrive at another formula:

GDP at factor prices = GDP at market prices − taxes on expenditure + subsidies

Consequently, in Figure 13.2, there are several ways of looking at expenditure: particularly spending in the market-place (i.e. GDP at market prices) and spending that represents the value that the firms receive by result (i.e. GDP at factor cost).

(6) The Statistical Discrepancy

This is a kind of balancing item, and the subsequent GDP (average estimate) will make more sense if left until the next method has been explained. (Now read Key Points 13.2.)

Measuring GDP with the Income Approach

By acquiring statistical information from the Inland Revenue (who collate and organize tax returns) the CSO is able to produce annually tables of national income. This is set out in its standard format in Fig. 13.3 (page 208). The figures are expressed as factor incomes. In other words, in terms of what it costs in total to employ each factor at face value. Therefore income tax and other deductions are included.

It is interesting to note that as anticipated the final figure for GDP (average estimate) at factor cost is identical with that on the expenditure table. This is because while producing the things they sell firms incur costs which when totalled are identical to the sale price of their products. These costs are rewards (payments) to the factors of production, namely (1) wages, (2) profit, (3) rent, and (4) interest. Indeed the table may largely be summarized using these four payments and consequently the bulk of the items in the table (Figure 13.3) have been numbered (1)–(4) respectively. These numbers (along with (5) and (6)) will provide a means of cross-reference.

Key Points 13.2

- **In the UK we use three methods for measuring GNP. Namely, the expenditure approach, the income approach, and the output approach.**
- **The expenditure approach to measuring GDP requires that we add up: consumers' expenditure (C), government expenditures (G), investment expenditures (I), and net exports (NX). In general terms, therefore $GDP = C + G + I + NX$.**
- **Included in consumer expenditures are consumer durables, consumer non-durables, and services.**
- **We include government expenditures at their cost, since we do not usually have market prices at which to value government goods and services.**
- **Gross investment *excludes* transfer of asset ownership. It includes only additions to the productive capacity of a nation, plus repairs and replacements of existing capital goods, and any change in business stocks.**
- **Overseas expenditures must be incorporated into GDP. Foreigners buying exports are spending on our nation's produce and therefore these monies must be added as they represent domestic economic activity. Conversely imports must be subtracted.**
- **GDP at factor cost involves the market price distortions of indirect taxes and subsidies.**

(1) Wages

The most important category in Figure 13.3 is, of course, 'wages', including wages, salaries, and other forms of labour income. In the table, the relevant formal categories total £292 392m – this constitutes approximately 75 per cent of all income in 1988. In these figures we include: National Insurance payments (both the employees' and the employers' contributions), payments to pension schemes and union subscriptions etc., as we wish to know the factor reward before deductions.

Figure 13.3
Gross Domestic Product by the Income Approach

Current factor incomes	*1988 (£m)*
(1) Income from employment	249 775
(1) Income from self-employment	42 617
(2) Gross trading profits of companies	70 242
(2) Gross trading surplus of public corporations	7 286
(2) Gross trading surplus of general government enterprises	−70
(3) Rent	27 464
(4) Imputed charge for consumption on non-trading capital	3 408
(5) Total domestic income	400 722
less Stock appreciation	−6 116
Gross domestic product (income-based)	394 606
(6) Statistical discrepancy (income adjustment)	181
Gross domestic product (average estimate)	394 787

Source: *United Kingdom National Accounts, 1989* (HMSO, London).
Note: The numbers, in brackets (1)–(6) are the only modification made to this official table. They have been included to assist with the cross-references in the text.

(2) Profits

This category includes total gross profits *before deductions* of tax, interest payments, and allowances for depreciation. The bulk of these profits arise from companies, in the private sector, involved in finance, commerce, and industry. It is interesting to note, however, the significant surplus of public corporations, as many commentators assume that nationalized industries lose money – this is obviously not the case when the sector is taken as a whole. Similarly, general government enterprises such as passenger transport, docks and harbours etc. run on behalf of local and central government also gross up a small trading surplus when considered as a whole group.

(3) Rent

Rent includes all the receipts earned by individuals from their ownership of land and buildings, such as farms, houses, and stores.

(4) Interest

Interest payments do not equal the *sum* of all payments for the use of money capital in a year – such an inclusion would simply involve double-counting, as implied above in the section on profits. Interest is being used here to express a return on those fixed capital assets owned in a non-trading form. For example, local authority offices, the Houses of Parliament, and private houses are owned and occupied by British citizens. This ownership saves rent and generates a form of intangible service income, consequently an estimated (imputed) figure is included at this juncture.

Now we can arrive at a figure which reflects the total domestic income for the year concerned. However, you will notice that in Figure 13.3 this is still not classifiable as GDP; before we can arrive at this figure **stock appreciation** must be accounted for.

(5) Stock Appreciation

In their accounts businesses include in their profits any stocks which have gone up in value during the year due to inflation. In short, a situation where the physical volume of stock produced has not changed but its money value has. To be consistent with the other 'flows' measured, we must only take account of those incomes resulting from economic activity; therefore inflated stock values due to inflation must be estimated and subtracted, before arriving at an income-based GDP figure.

(6) Statistical Discrepancy

It may not surprise you, given the thousands of figures involved and the various estimates that have to be made, that the final GDP figure arising from each method is slightly different. As already noted the two estimates of GDP dealt with so far are built up largely from independent data, and although in *theory* the totals should be identical in *reality* they are not. Consequently an increasing prominence is given to an average figure arising from the three calculations. The difference between each independent calculation and the average figure gives a statistical discrepancy. The statistical discrepancy, therefore, acts as a kind of 'balancing item' enabling us to refer to one specific figure for GDP and not several possibilities. (Now read Key Points 13.3.)

Measuring GDP with the Output Approach

The various values for this calculation are derived from censuses of production, and statistics on the different forms of income. These enable the Central Statistical Office to produce annually a table showing the composition of final output in terms of the related income

Key Points 13.3

- **To derive GDP using the income approach, we add up all factor payments, these are wages, interest, rent, and profits.**
- **Stock appreciation is the increased value of stock due to inflation that needs to be subtracted from our measurements of economic activity.**
- **The statistical discrepancy figure is a balancing item, accounting for the data limitations. It may be formally defined as the GDP (average estimate) less the independent estimates made via expenditure or income methods.**

generated. This table is broken down into various industrial sectors to show the proportional contributions made within the UK economy. The headings used to construct this output table are presented in a standard format in Figure 13.4.

Figure 13.4
Gross Domestic Product by the Output Approach

At current factor costs by industry	*1988 (£m)*
Agriculture, forestry, and fishing	5 625
Energy and water supply	21 845
Manufacturing	93 433
Construction	25 745
Distribution, hotels, and catering; repairs	55 131
Transport and communication	28 657
Banking, finance, insurance, and business services	76 922
Ownership of dwellings	21 407
Public administration and national defence	27 023
Education and health services	35 237
Other services	25 785
TOTAL	416 810
Adjusted for financial services*	−22 204
Gross domestic product (income-based)	394 606
Statistical discrepancy (income adjustment)	181
Gross domestic product (average estimate)	**394 787**

* These are interest payments that needs to be deducted to avoid double-counting.

Source: *United Kingdom National Accounts, 1989* (HMSO, London).

Obviously the final figures will be identical to those appearing in the income and expenditure tables presented in Figures 13.2 and 13.3. This is because output is only made possible by generating rewards (income) to the factors of production involved. Correspondingly, all output is assumed to be sold (even if it is only in the form of stock building).

What is involved, therefore, is an adding-up of all the contributions to domestic output made by each producing unit in the country (*after allowing for stock appreciation*). It is important to remember, however, that the emphasis must be on the **value added** by each producing unit, otherwise some output may be counted twice. To avoid such double-counting the value of 'intermediate' products (i.e. the value of products brought in for the production process) must be subtracted from the value of the final product. This concept has already been illustrated in Figure 13.1.

Alternatively it is possible to concentrate solely on the value of *final* goods and services, as is done largely in the (public) service sector, where the value of all the input costs are totalled up to measure the final value of the output. For example, education and health services are listed in Figure 13.4 as producing £35 237m worth of output. This is simply what it costs in total to provide these services in terms of staff wages, and maintenance etc.

Having made these preparatory remarks Figure 13.4 should now be self-explanatory. (Read Key Points 13.4.)

Key Points 13.4

- **To derive GDP using the output approach, we sum up the 'value added' by each industry producing a good or service in our economy.**
- **To avoid double-counting we must *not* look at the total sales from each sector, but what has been *added* in value terms to those component products bought in (see Figure 13.1 for example).**
- **The output of some service industries is measured in terms of the value of their *final* cost.**

Moving from GDP to GNP

We have seen that GDP figures measure the total spending, income, and/or output made from *home-based resources,* and therefore exports are included. In contrast GNP (gross *national* product) figures measure the total economic activity generated by our *nation's* resources both at home and *abroad.* This may sound complex, but in national accounting terms the only calculation involved is to add to our tables a net figure for property income from abroad – in 1988 the figures were as shown in Figure 13.5.

Figure 13.5
Moving from GDP to GNP

	(£m)
Gross domestic product (average estimate)	394 787
Net property income from abroad	5 619
Gross national product (average estimate)	400 406

Source: United Kingdom National Accounts, 1989 (HMSO, London)

All we need to do now is clarify this new item and GNP will (then we hope) make sense. In addition to the movement of goods and services across frontiers explicitly accounted for within the expenditure table (see discussion of item (4) on page 206) there is the movement of interest, profit, and dividend resulting from assets owned overseas (e.g. UK oil companies have various investments in capital abroad). To arrive at a figure for *net* property income it is necessary to offset our credits from abroad against the corresponding payments made for foreign investment in the UK. The specific situation in 1988 was as follows:

	£m
Property income *from* abroad	55 526
Property income *paid* abroad	49 907
∴ Net property income from abroad =	**5 619**

Thus we have identified another important definition.

GNP = GDP + net property income from abroad.

Moving from GNP to NNP

We have used the terms *gross* national product and *gross* domestic product without really indicating what *gross* means. The dictionary defines it as 'without deductions', as opposed to 'net'. Deductions for what? you might ask. Deductions for something we call **depreciation**. In the course of a year, machines and structures wear out, become outdated, or are 'used up' as they are used in the production of national product. For example, machines need repairs, or replacement, even if firms are only going to continue production at the same rate. That is, most fixed capital depreciates. An estimate of this is subtracted from gross national product to arrive at a figure called **net national product** (NNP).

Alternatively, depreciation can be thought of as that portion of the current year's GNP that is used to replace any physical capital *consumed* in the process of production. Indeed, another term for depreciation is **capital consumption**.

Consequently, gross investment can be expressed in the following way:

gross investment = replacement investment + expansion investment.

This is a useful formula as it highlights that if we are attempting to measure a country's progress (development) we should ignore replacement investment. Consequently, in official statistics net figures are more important. This moves us towards yet another definition:

NNP = GNP – depreciation (capital consumption allowances).

To see this in numerical terms see Figure 13.6, where the 1988 data is displayed.

Obviously capital consumption does not represent an easily identifiable set of transactions, and by result it is an estimated amount arrived at using a system of accounting conventions. Depreciation does not vary greatly, therefore, from year to year as a percentage of GNP, and you will get a similar picture about what is happening to our economy by looking at either NNP or

Key Points 13.5

- **By adding property income from abroad into our accounts we can move from a GDP figure (which measures economic activity arising from *domestic* – home-based resources) to a GNP figure which measures economic activity from the broader perspective of all *national* resources both at *home* and *abroad*.**
- **Capital consumption (depreciation) represents an estimated figure to allow for the nation's fixed capital that has been 'used up' during the production process.**
- **GNP – capital consumption = NNP.**
- **NNP is officially referred to as national income.**

Figure 13.6
Moving from GNP to NNP

	£m
Gross national product (average estimate)	400 406
less **Capital consumption**	**−54 769**
Net national product at factor cost (average estimate), i.e. National Income	345 637

Source: *United Kingdom National Accounts, 1989* (HMSO, London).

GNP data. However, the final line in all official accounts is the 'net' figure. In other words, to measure a country's progress it is best to look at *net* figures, as these indicate spending, output and/or income made on behalf of 'additional' goods to a nation's economic flow. Indeed *net national product* is most commonly what economists are referring to when they talk of **national income**. (Now read Key Points 13.5.)

Uses of These National Accounts

As implied at earlier junctures in this chapter these accounts have four main uses:

1. MEASURING ECONOMIC GROWTH. As these figures are a measure of economic activity, the annual national income can be compared with previous years and an impression is thereby gained about changes in the standard of living. Indeed, economic growth rates are worked out from these accounts and this is illustrated in one of the Case Studies at the end of this chapter.
2. COMPARING COUNTRIES. Apart from comparisons across time, these national accounts also offer opportunities to make comparisons between countries in terms of development, affluence, policies, and so on. In fact, contributions to international agencies such as the IMF, Red Cross, World Bank, and the EC are often assessed as a percentage of a country's GNP.
3. GOVERNMENT PLANNING. As stated in the opening lines of this chapter, the statistical tables on expenditure, output, and income provide an important analytical tool to those economists who are involved in recommending and evaluating policies on behalf of government.
4. EVALUATION OF ECONOMIC CLIMATE. Similarly businessmen, research students, trade union representatives, and journalists involved in interpreting economic trends will find the statistical breakdowns provided in the various tables most useful for their forecasts and work in general. For example, GDP output estimates are announced quarterly during the year and are regarded as a good short-term indicator of economic prospects. The *average* GDP figures, however, are recognized as more reliable for forecasting over longer time-periods. (Now read Key Point 13.6.)

Is National Income Accounting Sufficient?

We have now completed our run-down of the different ways that the national accounts are compiled, the various totals that can be arrived at, and the main uses of these statistical presentations. What we have not yet touched on though is how reliable these figures are. Inevitably there are some limitations, and we shall deal with these next.

Once this is complete you will recognize how to interpret national income statistics and be in a position to answer questions relating to 'How sufficient national income accounting is?' This is a common theme of academic debate and often the central issue in exam questions.

Correcting National Income for Price Changes

If a video tape costs £5 this year, ten tapes will have a market value of £50. If next year they cost £10 each, the same ten tapes will have a market value of £100. There will have been no increase in the total quantity of tapes produced and sold, but the market value will have doubled. Apply this to every single good and service produced and sold in the United Kingdom and you realize that national accounts measured in 'current' values may not be a very useful indication of economic activity. After all, we are really interested in variations in the *real* output of the economy. What we have to do, then, is correct GNP for changes in general prices from year to year. This is done by converting all money values to a common base year via a price index (at present the government's base year is 1985). Consequently, two sets of figures are produced each year: *money* national income and *real* national income.

Key Point 13.6

▶ **National income accounts can be seen to have *two general* uses: (1) to make comparisons (between countries and across time) and (2) for planning and evaluation (by government, businessmen, and related parties).**

Money national income is formally referred to as **current price** or **nominal national income**, and it represents the measurements of economic activity expressed in current 'face value' terms. **Real national income**, by contrast, represents the same measurement but expressed in value terms of a specific base year. This technique of employing constant price measurements makes comparisons across time far more meaningful. For example, consider the following figures:

UK national income *1978 prices*	£130 570m
UK national income *1988 prices*	£345 637m

These figures suggest that in ten years the UK has become nearly 300 per cent richer. However, if we now account for inflation in this ten-year period and express both figures again in *constant price* terms, as follows:

1978 UK national income *1985 prices*	£243 035m
1988 UK national income *1985 prices*	£303 928m

we can see that in real terms we have only increased our economic activity from 1978 to 1988 by approximately 25 per cent.

For most purposes *real* values are more indicative of economic performance.

Per Capita GNP

Even by looking at changes in *real* national income one still may be subject to deception, especially if changes in population size have been significant. For example, if 'real' GNP over a ten-year period went up 100 per cent, you might immediately jump to the conclusion that the material well-being of the economy had increased by that amount. But what if, during the same period, population increased by 200 per cent? Then what would you say? Certainly, the amount of GNP per person, i.e. **per capita** GNP would have fallen, even though *real* GNP has risen. What we must do therefore is try and be precise by accounting for price changes and population size changes.

A significant economic variable therefore is RGNP per head (real gross national product per head). More conveniently national income per head may at times suffice. These can be calculated quite simply by the following formulas:

$$\frac{\text{RGNP}}{\text{Total Pop.}} = \text{RGNP per head.}$$

$$\frac{\text{NNP}}{\text{Total Pop.}} = \text{national income per head.}$$

With these formulas in mind one can look at population growth in the Third World and begin to sense why many of the people are starving even though their national income may increase marginally each year.

A further complication arises when income distribution is added to the picture. To appreciate this you may care to calculate UK's Money National Income per head for 1988 (taking the UK population as approximately 56m) and compare the results to *your* income in that year.

Black Economy

Another complication that the last suggested exercise brings to mind is that some student incomes will be of the 'unofficial' variety; for example, 'casual' jobs over the summer, bar work, helping in the corner shop, painting and decorating, etc. Many of these jobs are sometimes organized on a 'cash-in-hand' basis, so that the employer can avoid certain legislation and/or the employee avoids paying tax. This type of unofficial economic activity is seen as constituting an 'informal', 'hidden', or 'shadow' economy and is referred to by economists as the **black economy**.

With the general increase in unemployment and the increase in VAT many commentators feel that the black economy may be expanding relative to the 'official' economy. Indeed, the discrepancy between official recorded expenditure and declared incomes is increasing and this whole area is one of investigation. For some examples of these investigations and their findings see Figure 13.7. Also further instances are examined in a Case Study at the close of this chapter.

The existence of the black economy is not only worrying in terms of undermining national income

Figure 13.7

Estimated percentage of GDP that Escapes Official Detection in the UK

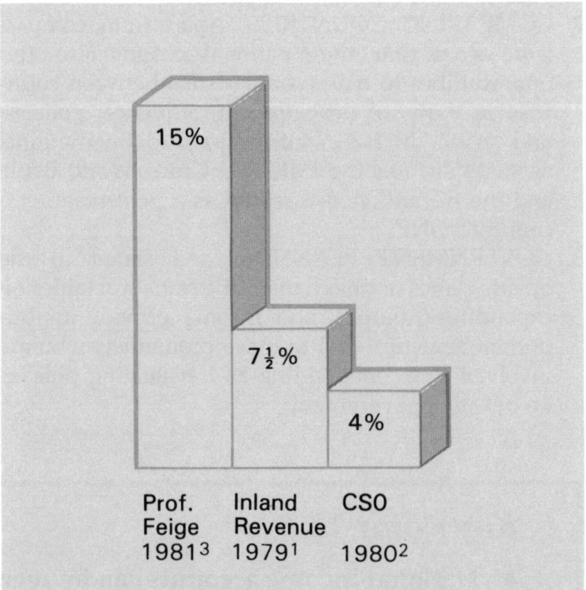

Sources: [1]Sir William Pile, Former Chairman of the Inland Revenue. [2]'A Glimpse of the Hidden Economy in the National Accounts', CSO (*Economic Trends*) 1980. [3]'The UK's Unobserved Economy', *Journal of Economic Affairs*, July 1981.

statistics but in terms of lost tax revenue. For example, the former chairman of the board of Inland Revenue estimated that the black economy may represent 7½ per cent of GDP. This would imply that a significant unofficial sector exists. In fact, if he were correct it would suggest that approximately £8 billion is being lost in tax revenue per year from these 'underground' or 'cash' activities.

Difficulties Comparing Countries' Accounts

As the last section suggests, a country's national income figures largely reflect what is recorded. In different countries official interpretations of what is eligible for recording changes according to circumstances. For example, the attempts to prohibit alcohol in the United States in the 1920s led to a large illegal bootlegging industry. This replaced a former legitimate industry, and national income figures were affected accordingly. Similarly, 'prostitutes' in those countries where they are state organized will provide an economically measurable service, whereas in other countries this will not be the case.

Not only do laws affect the figures but so does accounting convention. For example, in the US government statisticians add to their GNP figures an estimated amount for those foods which farmers have grown and their families have eaten, i.e. those foods that inevitably do not pass through a market-place. In contrast, self-sufficiency in the Third World represents a major form of existence yet these self-consumed products normally remain unrecorded for official purposes.

These problems are further compounded when there is the need to express world national income figures in a common currency, as this brings in problems of exchange rates. The $ and £ values, which are normally used for international comparisons, alter daily against other currencies. Therefore converted figures from the currency of measurement to the common currency are often suspect.

Measuring Welfare

We have presented in this chapter several measures of economic activity and obviously each measure has a different purpose. This raises the question, however, do any of them effectively measure well-being?

The critics of national accounting contend that it glorifies the materialistic society in which we live. They believe that the numbers cannot capture our true overall well-being as a nation. They point out that many forms of economic activity also produce external costs, such as pollution, noise, and accidents. These are not officially measured within national income, but they do affect welfare. Similarly, leisure, happiness, and health cannot be measured simply in terms of income, output, or expenditure.

Consequently new measures of welfare are being developed (especially in the US), and the second Case Study will explore some of these new concepts. The subsequent questions raised thereafter will help you to investigate further this difficult issue of national accounting and what it actually measures.

Key Points 13.7

- **National income is best expressed each year in a common value. At present nominal (money) national income is converted into real national income by expressing all values in 1980 prices.**
- **Ideally changes in population size should be considered to arrive at a per capita figure. For example, if you did the calculation suggested on page 212, you would have found that in 1988 UK national income per head was approximately £6172.**
- **Studies of the 'black economy' estimate the amount of 'unrecorded' or 'unofficial' economic activities that go on. These reduce the size of a country's official national income.**
- **What is officially recorded as economic activity will differ from country to country.**
- **Finally, there are the critics who contend that national income accounting is not a sufficient measure of welfare and this issue is raised in the next Case Study.**

CASE STUDY

The Scam Economy

Only a couple of months back *The Face* reported a black economy in Liverpool worth £457 million last year alone. So while it's easy to romanticize about rogues and dodgers and the uniqueness of the city, it's also plain that something's afoot . . .

So what's so special about Liverpool? The shops have concrete bollards installed in front of them so that over-stimulated late night shoppers can't reverse transit vans through the windows and make off with the goods. One crime-conscious clothing retailer installed privoting video cameras outside his premises so that they could at least get a useful mugshot of would-be asset strippers. Junior staff were amused one morning to pop the cassette into the machine and watch a hooded figure wave cheerfully at the lens before heaving a pavement slab through the frontage and getting off with a minor haul.

Next time they might consider surrounding their store with the sort of security which is giving one of the precincts in Cantril Farm the look of a Judge Dredd fantasy. Shops are protected by steel plates, reinforced glass, iron shutters and rooftop buffers while the TSB bank is as good as welded to the floor . . .

Instead of lashing out their cash on more padlocks and armed marksmen on the roof, the TSB and other banks should think seriously about investing in cheque cards bearing the owner's photograph. In Liverpool, at least, there is infinitely more cheque-related fraud against banks than there are Billy the Kid-style stick-ups. Somewhere in the back streets of the city there must be a secret laboratory in which an assembly of Tefal-headed professors conduct experiments on cheque cards; how else could anyone discover the chemistry necessary to take the signature off the card without damaging the paper strip or activating the void card underneath? This makes it perfectly easy to go on to embellish the blanched signature strip with own hand and make hay at the expense of the wicked capitalist bankers . . .

While it's difficult enough for banks and credit companies to stem fraud in Liverpool, they admit that they're as good as helpless when kids start travelling abroad for booty. Despite an increased awareness of the problem of gangs taking cheque and credit cards to the continent, shopkeepers overseas still lack the vigilance of their British counterparts.

Modern day piracy in Europe is a peculiarly Liverpudlian activity. It had a lot to do with the success of the city's two football teams and the knowledge of wealthy civilizations that accompanying journeys can bring. In 1981, after the away goals win over Bayern Munich in the semi-final of the European Cup, Liverpool supporters reluctantly showered the North Sea off Felixstowe with treasure trove. A few square yards of briny became richer than the neighbouring oilfields as Excise Men boarded the ferry to investigate reports of cash and jewellery thefts filtering back from Germany.

Many beat a hasty trail back to recoup their losses and returned to Liverpool with stories of detective-free boutiques and Swiss jewellers snoozing at their counters in the afternoon. Prosperous cities such as Antwerp, Frankfurt and Zurich have all proved popular Five Day Eurosaver destinations. The majority who avoid arrest fence their big hauls of watches and rings privately, but miscellaneous windfalls like perfume, light carat chains, Boss sweatshirts and electrical goods are sold openly on the streets, in the bars or from stalls . . .

Although shoplifters are feeling the pinch in Liverpool, rogue traders of all descriptions are laughing. Church Street, the main shopping thoroughfare, has taken on an appropriately third world demeanour with a garish array of stalls and suitcase boys selling jewellery, Reebok training shoes, boxer shorts and a range of snidies (limitations) from Givenchy aftershave to Rolex watches. The Merseyside Training Standards office held an open day last month for punters and storekeepers alike, highlighting 141 imitations which are currently doing the rounds. Opium by Yves St Laurent was not amongst them this time round. The bottle has been withdrawn and is being redesigned after consistent and costly pirating.

Smelly stuff is a big seller for the suitcase gents. Their sources are a deadly secret, but *The Face* can reveal that some racketeers are peddling something other than genuine knock-off scent. They obtain surplus or reject glass bottles from any number of factories, have passable sticky labels printed up by the ever-active lithographic community, and fill the bottles with miserable low-cost toilet water. Substances as diverse as Polycell paint stripper (blue) and glycerine and honey cough linctus are then used to tease the colour. What was all that about honour among thieves?

For proper bargains, especially in the clothing area, the city converges on Great Homer Street market in Everton. On Saturday mornings its mile-long central strip is an Aladdin's Den of consumer durables and perishables, all going for a song. Gorgeous, tanned young women will sell you baked beans, shampoo, cosmetics, chocky bars, leather boating-shoes and the ubiquitous boxer shorts. It says something for the style of the working classes that a young lad pirating Chanel t-shirts at 'Greatie' couldn't shift ten all day. When he returned to his usual stock of classic casuals the next weekend – Ocean Pacific, Next, Marc O'Polo, French Connection, Boss – trade was again hotter than July. It's difficult to prove that the goods on offer were come about with anything other than complete innocence on the part of all concerned, so the police keep a discreet watch for familiar villains while 12-year-old standoffs (lookouts) warn their masters of their whereabouts . . .

This is certainly the Liverpool you'll never see on telly. Artisans painstakingly pinpricking the serial number on to forged tax discs; amending MOT certificates with the help of baby oil; Black Boxes to stop your electricity meters going round; tiny touts selling tickets at the big football matches and stinging their faces with the Givenchy they bought with the proceeds. Money it seems, makes the city tick . . .

Source: 'The Blag Economy', *The Face*, Oct 1987.

Questions

1. *The Face* is a magazine aimed at a 16–30 age-range. It carries articles on art, fashions and music. Explain why it carried this article on the black economy.
2. The whole article has a distinct Liverpudlian bias. Explain why the people of Liverpool should be any more into the black economy than folk from other regions.
3. What examples of the black economy have you experienced or heard of?
4. Do you think you could discuss the black economy on a regional basis? Could you possibly construct a map showing areas of low and high incidence of the black economy?
5. The statistical discrepancy shown in the National Accounts does not measure the size of the black economy. Explain why this is the case.
6. Why is the black economy so hard to measure?

CASE STUDY

National Income Accounts: Measurement or Mirage?

Given the deficiencies in our national income accounts, is it possible to come up with a new measure of GNP? Ed Mishan, a former professor at the London School of Economics, would sincerely hope so. There follows an edited extract from an article of his that was published in November 1984. This will prompt some interesting questions relating to the measurement of economic growth and welfare . . .

Role of women

Let us turn first to the increased participation of women in the workforce over the last thirty years which has increased output in the private and public sectors of the economy and to that extent has increased the estimated growth in real GNP and also in per capita real income. A good part of this apparent contribution to the GNP statistics is, in an economic sense, fictitious. For while the services that women now provide for industry and commerce continue to add to the value of GNP, the concomitant reduction of services they would otherwise have provided in their homes – which on proper economic accounting would enter as a deduction from the nation's aggregate of finished goods – is ignored in the GNP computation.

Public sector versus private sector

Second, since public goods tend to be overvalued as compared with those produced by the private sector, and since the output of the public sector over the last thirty years has grown appreciably as a component of GNP, it follows that the real growth of GNP over the period will be overestimated.

Military expenditure

Third, military expenditure which is one of the largest items of public expenditure, raises another interesting question. Allowing that real military expenditure per capita has grown enormously since the turn of the century, should proper economic accounting include it as an increasing component of per capita real income?

Exploitation of irreplaceable resources

Fourth, an increasingly significant source of error arises from the global exploitation of irreplaceable resources. If the total stock of capital is taken to include not only man-made capital but also 'nature-made' capital such as fossil fuels, mineral reserves, ocean fisheries, tropical forests etc., it is entirely possible for current rates of global consumption to be reducing the stock of nature-made capital faster than it is increasing the stock of man-made capital, which implies that we are currently consuming beyond our real income – in effect, eating into the total capital we have inherited to the detriment of our future and our children's future.

Environmental considerations

A fifth factor related to the preceding one is the propensity of modern industry and its products to pollute air, soil, and water and generally to degrade the environment, which acts to reduce real income below the official figures. If, to begin with, nothing is done to curb the industrial overspill which damages the health and amenity of people, GNP is overstated to the extent of the cost of the damage that is borne – this being the value of the 'bads' that accompanies the production and distribution of the goods.

Concluding thought

If these and other deficiencies in the conventional methods of estimating changes in GNP were recognized, and allowance made for them, the real standard of living in the West as compared with that of other 'less-developed countries' would look much less impressive.

Source: E. J. Mishan, 'GNP-Measurement or Mirage', *National Westminster Bank Review*, Nov. 1984.

Questions

1. Mishan's statements imply a need for recording minuses as well as pluses to national accounts. What do you think should be taken off national accounts to arrive at a real measure of progress?
2. Professors Tobin and Nordhaus in a similar article in an American publication argue that there is also a need for *adding* activities that are not traditionally included in GNP figures. List the kind of things you think they may have in mind.
3. In the mid-1970s the Economic Development Council of Washington, DC created an entirely new measure of wealth and health, namely, the PQLI. *The Physical Quality of Life Index* bases its terms of reference on figures for life expectancy, literacy, and infant mortality. From these figures countries are rated on a scale of 1 to 100. Critically evaluate this index as a measure of welfare.
4. Suggest other indicators that may be used as measures of welfare. (It may help to look in the Lloyds Bank publication, *The British Economy in Figures.*)
5. In your own words state what the national income in its standard UK format actually measures.
6. (a) Try to design your own measure of welfare (in both social and material terms) by completing the pluses and minuses of the following table:

	Plus	Minus	
National Income	....		= Welfare

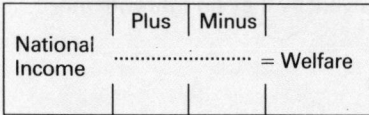

(b) What would be the main advantages and disadvantages of employing a broad measure of welfare – such as the one you have outlined.

CASE STUDY

Economic Growth: Spot the Trend

Figure 13.8

Expenditure on the Gross Domestic Product (£m, 1985 prices)

	Gross domestic product (average estimate) at market prices	*Con-sumers' expendi-ture*	*General government consumption*		*Gross domestic fixed capital formation*	*Value of physical increase in stocks and work-in-progress*	*Exports of goods and services*	*Imports of goods and services*
			Central govern-ment	*Local authorities*				
1978	320 883	186 759	41 798	26 577	54 914	2 867	85 720	76 593
1979	329 895	194 895	42 435	27 410	56 450	3 328	88 943	83 956
1980	322 668	195 060	43 690	27 272	53 416	−3 371	88 966	81 134
1981	318 527	195 173	44 108	27 074	48 298	−3 200	88 307	78 878
1982	324 045	197 051	44 421	27 318	50 915	−1 281	89 048	82 721
1983	335 593	205 484	45 281	27 912	54 476	1 357	90 971	88 116
1984	342 722	209 207	45 741	28 161	58 058	1 112	96 892	96 735
1985	355 329	217 023	45 879	28 000	60 343	615	102 639	99 165
1986	367 639	229 105	46 729	28 725	61 478	677	106 906	105 829
1987	384 996	241 382	46 819	29 527	66 894	1 051	112 355	113 905
1988	400 999	257 918	49 929	29 749	75 680	3 578	113 186	127 833

In this case study we look at some data on UK GDP (see Figure 13.8). The various items listed have been taken from Table 1.6 of the National Accounts (1989 edition).

It must be emphasized that all component items are evaluated in constant price terms. Thus one of the exercises will be to calculate some 'real' growth rates for the UK. Other uses of such data involve the analysis of past and present events and the forecasting of future ones. These issues will form the themes of the other questions.

Questions

1. Calculate the economic growth rate for the last six years. This is derived in percentage terms by taking each year separately using the following formula:

$$\frac{\text{GDP of year to be measured (e.g. 1983)} - \text{GDP of previous year (e.g. 1982)} \times 100}{\text{GDP of previous year (e.g. 1982)}}$$

2. Explain the negative values relating to stocks and works in progress that are displayed in 1980, 1981, and 1982. What do these suggest about the years of the early 1980s, and what may have caused such a change in economic pace?
3. (a) What economic climate do the figures suggest existed in the late 1980s?
   (b) What other data would help this aspect of evaluation?
4. Suggest what the UK GDP may be in the mid-1990s and give economic reasons for your estimate.
5. Calculate the statistical discrepancy for each of the last 3 years (Hint: GDP(A) – GDP(E)). What do the results imply about the accuracy of expenditure methods and what economic reasons could be stated to explain the trend that is displayed?

Exam Preparation

PRACTICAL EXERCISE

In the following four questions fill in the items that are missing to complete the formulas. Although this is a seemingly simple exercise the different definitions are important and this should help you to focus on the distinguishing features.

(i) GDP (at the market prices) = $C + I + G +$ ____.
(ii) GDP at factor cost =
(iii) GNP = GDP + ________.
(iv) NNP = GNP − ________.

MULTIPLE CHOICE QUESTIONS

1. Why are the GNP (gross national product) figures of a nation *not* considered to be accurate indicators of the welfare of its people?

A the GNP figures do not allow for depreciation
B welfare includes non-marketable goods and services enjoyed by the community
C GNP figures do not include social security benefits
D payments for social workers and doctors are made out of taxpayers' money.

2. From the following information calculate the gross national product (GNP)

	£m
Wages	= 9 000
Salaries	= 7 000
Government pensions	= 1 500
Unemployment pay and other social benefits	= 100
Rent and interest	= 1 500
Profits	= 1 500

£m
A = 18 500
B = 19 000
C = 19 500
D = 20 500

continued overleaf

3. The rate of growth of the British economy can best be seen from comparison of
A per capita gross national product at constant prices
B total volume of production
C terms of trade position
D quality of life indicators.

4. The following figures are extracted from the national income accounts of Country X for a particular year:

	£m
Consumers' expenditure	65
Fixed capital formation	20
Net addition to stocks during year	5
Government expenditure	10
Exports of goods and services	10
Imports of goods and services	12
Property income received from abroad	6
Property income paid abroad	4
Taxes on expenditure	6
Subsidies	1
Capital consumption	5

What is the value of Country X's national income (at factor cost?)
A £90 million
B £95 million
C £105 million
D £100 million

5. Which of the following would *not* give the value of the UK's gross national income?
A gross domestic product + net property income from abroad
B gross national product
C net national income + depreciation
D gross national expenditure − exports
E total factor incomes earned by UK residents.

6. A director becomes redundant as a result of a company merger. His salary in employment was £10 000 per annum. He is entitled to a redundancy payment of £5 000 (£4 000 as a lump sum and £1 000 as 10 per cent of his salary). His wife takes up employment at a wage of £1 000 per annum and his daughter increases the contribution to the family house-keeping by £500 from her earnings.

The net reduction in the contribution of the family to the measured national income in the first year of the father's redundancy is
A £5 000
B £6 500
C £7 500
D £8 500
E £9 000

RELATED ESSAY QUESTIONS

1. What insights can be gained into the performance of an economy from studying its National Income statistics?

2. Explain the words 'Gross', 'National', and 'Product' in the term 'Gross National Product'. Should GNP exclude activities not bought and sold in markets such as housework and state provision of education?

3. Explain carefully what is meant by value added and show how it is used in arriving at a figure for the national product.

4. In 1972 the gross national product of the UK was estimated to be £55.9bn. By 1982 it had risen to £228.4bn. To what extent does this increase indicate an improvement in the standard of living?

5. 'National income accounting tells us where we think we have been, around six months after we were there: it cannot show us where we are now, nor can it tell us where we are about to go.' Discuss.

6. How adequate a measure of social and material welfare are the UK National Accounts?

14 Aggregate Supply and Aggregate Demand

Key Points to Review

- Supply and demand (5.7)
- Inflation (11.4 and 11.6)
- Unemployment (11.2 and 11.3)
- Real versus nominal (13.7)

Questions for Preview

1 Why is the aggregate demand curve downward sloping?

2 Why does the aggregate supply curve have three ranges?

3 What is demand inflation?

4 Can aggregate demand–aggregate supply analysis explain changes in output and employment?

5 How is supply-side economics related to the *AS* curve?

In Chapter 5, a model of price determination using supply and demand analysis was given, but the prices that we were referring to were individual commodity prices relative to all other prices. Concern over prices at the economy-wide level is much more general, for it is a concern about why there have been continuous increases in the price level, or why there has been inflation. In Chapter 11, we found out that the UK rate of inflation has varied dramatically over time. We also found out that we have had varying periods of growing prosperity and recession, with accompanying periods of expanding employment and then unemployment.

Why, for example, was it that in 1977 the rate of inflation was 15.9 per cent but the rate of economic growth was only 2.6 per cent, whereas, in 1984 the rate of inflation was 4.6 per cent and the rate of economic growth was 2.3 per cent? We have to construct a model in our attempt to explain these variations. We will use the tools of supply and demand but with a major change: instead of looking at the price of *one* commodity, we will look at the price level (an index of general prices) and how it relates to aggregate demand and aggregate supply. The definition of the price level and how we measure changes in the price level have been given in Chapter 11. The definition of **aggregate demand** is the sum total of all *planned* expenditures in the economy. In Chapter 12, we already discussed total planned expenditures on a theoretical level in an economy that had no government and no foreign sector. In that situation, aggregate demand was equal to planned consumption expenditures by households plus planned investment expenditures by firms. **Aggregate supply** is defined as the sum total of *planned* production in the economy. Again, going back to our simplified economy in Chapter 12, total planned production consisted of consumer goods for households and investment goods for businesses.

Given the above definitions, we can now proceed to construct an aggregate demand curve and then an aggregate supply curve.

The Aggregate Demand Curve

The **aggregate demand curve**, *AD*, gives the total of all goods and services demanded at various price levels. Otherwise stated, the aggregate demand curve gives the relationship between the total amount of income, or real national output that will be purchased, and the price level. Remember from Chapter 13 that *real* national income consists of the output of final goods and services in the economy – it is everything that is produced for final use, either by firms or households. Look at Figure 14.1 On the horizontal axis is measured real national income. On the vertical axis is measured the price level. At a price level of P_1, aggregate demand will be Y_1. At a price level of P_2, aggregate demand will decrease to Y_2. The higher the price level, the lower will be the total real output demanded by the economy, and vice versa.

Figure 14.1

The Aggregate Demand Curve. On the horizontal axis we measure real national income. On the vertical axis we measure the price level. The aggregate demand curve (*AD–AD*) is downward sloping for three reasons: (1) an increase in the price level increases interest rates, which decrease the quantity demanded of interest-sensitive goods, such as cars and factories; (2) an increase in the price level reduces the real wealth of all individuals holding cash, thereby causing them to want to spend less; and (3) an increase in the UK price level causes us to buy more imports and sell fewer exports therefore reducing the demand for real output in the UK. Therefore, at price level P_1 real national income demanded will be Y_1, but when the price level increases to P_2, real national income decreases to Y_2, other things being equal.

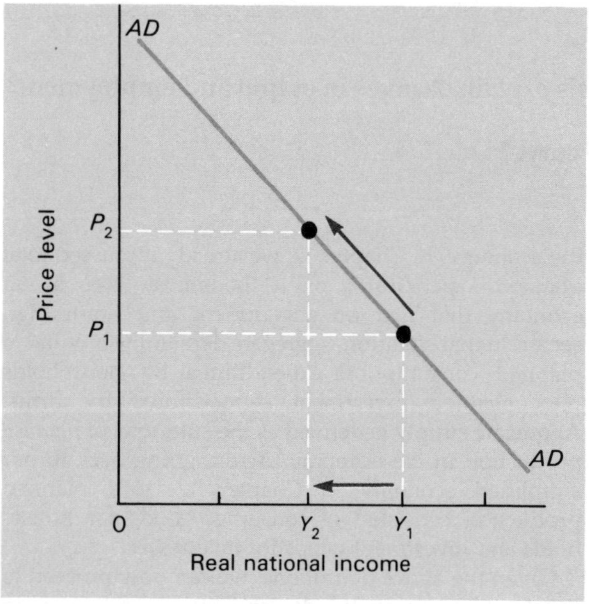

Why the Aggregate Demand Curve Slopes Down

We cannot explain the downward-sloping demand curve for all commodities in the same way as we explain the downward-sloping demand curve for individual commodities. After all, a change in the price level changes the price of all goods and services, on average. It is important to remember that demand and supply analysis *in the aggregate* is different from microeconomic analysis, despite some parallels. Because the aggregate demand curve expresses the relationship between spending and prices *in general*, we must look more deeply at the impact of changing prices on spending, to see why they are inversely related. The reasons include the following:

1. Interest rate effects
2. Wealth effects
3. Substitution of foreign-produced goods.

INTEREST RATE EFFECTS

Remember in Chapter 11, when we discussed inflation, we pointed out that one result of inflation is a rise in nominal interest rates because inflationary premia are added to all interest rates. But a rise in interest rates will reduce the quantity demanded of interest-rate-sensitive goods. These goods are those that must be financed by borrowing, such as cars, homes and new factories. Thus the link is as follows:

Price level up → Interest rates up → Quantity demanded of interest-rate-sensitive goods down → Total real income (production) falls

WEALTH EFFECTS

In Chapter 11 we saw that an increase in the price level reduces the purchasing power of cash balances (i.e. notes and coin, and bank and building society deposits). In essence, then, those individuals who hold part of their **wealth** in cash balances will find a reduction in the purchasing power of their wealth. Actually, every part of a person's wealth that is denominated in money terms only, such as government bonds with fixed interest rates, will suffer a reduction in real value when the price level increases. After all if you own a £100 bond, and the price level doubles, when you cash in that bond, the £100 will buy only half as many goods and services at the higher price level.

Consequently, whenever there is a rise in the price level, the real value of all assets denominated in money terms falls. Individuals will therefore tend to spend less. Planned purchases (real national income) will fall.

SUBSTITUTION OF FOREIGN GOODS

Any increase in the price level in the UK will make domestically produced goods relatively more expensive compared to foreign-produced goods (assuming a stable exchange rate). That means that an increase in the UK price level will cause planned purchases of domestically produced goods to fall and planned purchases of foreign-produced goods (imports) to rise because they are more competitive. It also means that foreigners will no longer want to purchase as much of UK production (i.e. exports) as before. In sum, the demand for UK domestic real output (production) will fall when the UK price level rises.

The Aggregate Supply Curve

The **aggregate supply curve** represents the relationship between real income, or output, and the price level. It would be nice to say simply that the aggregate supply curve slopes up, because the higher the price level, the more producers are willing to produce – because producers have a greater incentive and they can cover any additional costs incurred in the increased output. But remember, just as with our discussion of the aggregate demand curve, we are talking about changes in the price level – the index of the weighted average of *all* prices. Every price is allowed to vary. In order to understand the true nature of the aggregate supply curve, we have to examine three situations:

1. Large amounts of unused capacity and significant unemployment
2. Full capacity
3. Intermediate range between the two.

UNUSED CAPACITY AND SIGNIFICANT UNEMPLOYMENT

When the economy has many factories operating at less than capacity, numerous individuals unemployed, and a general underutilization of the productive capabilities of the nation, it is possible to increase output without there being any pressure on prices. In such a setting, producers can increase supply at will without having to pay higher prices for factors of production. If they need more labour, they can hire someone who was previously unemployed. They need not pay higher wages to attract people. They can put them to work with some previously idle capital equipment. In other words, per-unit costs of output will remain the same, no matter what the volume of output is, so long as significant amounts of unemployment and unused capacity remain. In these circumstances, we would expect the aggregate supply curve to be a horizontal line at the current price level. Consider that the current price level is P_1, as given on the vertical axis of Figure 14.2. The horizontal line labelled 'excess capacity' represents that part of the aggregate supply curve, *AS–AS*, that exists when there is no pressure on prices with any increase in output. Within this range, supply is perfectly elastic.

NO EXCESS CAPACITY

Now consider the other extreme situation where there is absolutely no excess capacity. In other words, the economy is at full employment. It is impossible, by definition, for any additional output to be produced. What will the shape of the aggregate supply curve look like now? Obviously, it has to be a vertical line, as shown at output rate Y_2 in Figure 14.2. It is a vertical line because there is only one thing that can happen in such a situation – the price level can rise, but no further increases in output are physically possible. Supply can be said to be perfectly inelastic.

The vertical portion of the aggregate supply curve in Figure 14.2 is also a representation of aggregate supply in the long run. That is to say, in the long run, when all prices are flexible, the potential level of real national income (total output) is independent of the price level. Rather, it depends only on the supply of resources and the economy's technology. As technology advances, and the stock of capital increases, more can be produced so the vertical line showing full capacity output willl shift gradually to the right. (This will be pursued in Chapter 34.)

Figure 14.2

The Three Ranges on the Aggregate Supply Curve. Starting out at a price level of P1 the aggregate supply curve, *AS–AS*, is a horizontal line up to quantity of real national income. It is a horizontal line up to quantity of real national income, Y_1. It is a horizontal line because there is excess capacity such that any increase in production does not raise per-unit costs. Output level Y_1–Y_2 is where some sectors experience excess capacity but others do not. In other words, bottle-necks appear as the economy moves closer and closer to maximum capacity. Those sectors experiencing near-full capacity will find that their per-unit costs are rising, and therefore the prices charged for their commodities will rise. The general price level will therefore rise as output increases from Y_1 to Y_2. This is called the intermediate range, where there is some excess capacity. At Y_2 there is no excess capacity – the economy is experiencing full employment of all its resources, and using its technology to its fullest. The only thing that can happen, therefore, is for prices to rise. Output cannot increase, by definition, past Y_2 or full capacity output.

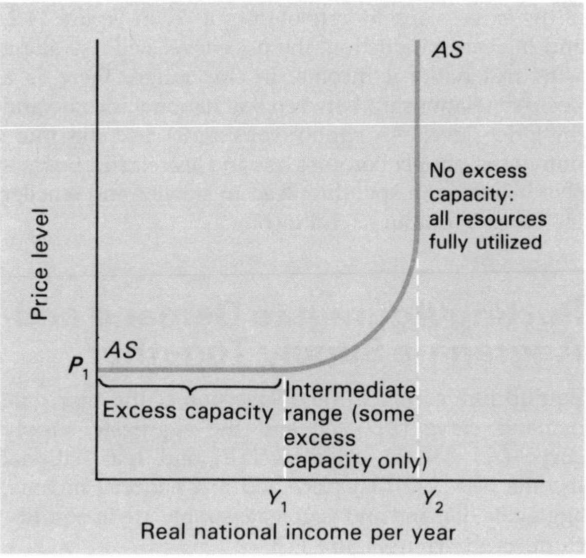

INTERMEDIATE RANGE

When there is some excess capacity in some parts of the economy, but no excess capacity in other parts of the economy, then, as production is increased, the price of some goods and services will be pushed up (but not the price of *all* goods and services).

This is the beginning of demand-pull inflation. So-called bottle-necks, or supply constraints may develop. As firms try to increase output they may experience shortages of certain inputs, most frequently, certain kinds of skilled labour. When this happens, firms can try to attract more of the scarce input by paying a higher price for it. They compete with each other for a limited supply of people with scarce skills, thus driving wage rates up. This raises their costs of production, and they then react by raising their prices whenever they can.

The intermediate range of the aggregate supply curve is, in essence, based on this bottle-neck explanation. As the aggregate supply curve starts to slope up, it will become steeper and steeper as full-capacity output is approached, because, as this happens, more and more supply constraints appear. As they appear certain prices increase. Also in this situation sellers can anyway put prices up, without losing customers. Since the price level is a weighted average of all prices, if some prices stay constant and some go up the price level will rise, too. That means that if we start at the end of the excess capacity rate of output, Y_1 in Figure 14.2, and increase production, the price level will rise along with real national income. In this range, there is a positive relationship between real national income and the price level. As supply constraints become more numerous, supply becomes less and less elastic. Successive increases in spending lead to smaller and smaller increases in output or real income.

Putting Aggregate Demand and Aggregate Supply Together

Equilibrium occurs at the intersection of the aggregate demand curve (*AD–AD*) and the aggregate supply curve (*AS–AS*), at price level P_1 and real national income of Y_1. At that price and real national income, aggregate demand and aggregate supply are in equilibrium, as shown in Figure 14.3.

Figure 14.3

Equilibrium Price Level and Output. The intersection of the aggregate demand curve, *AD–AD*, and the aggregate supply curve, *AS–AS*, generates the equilibrium price level at P_1 and the equilibrium real national income (total output) at Y_1.

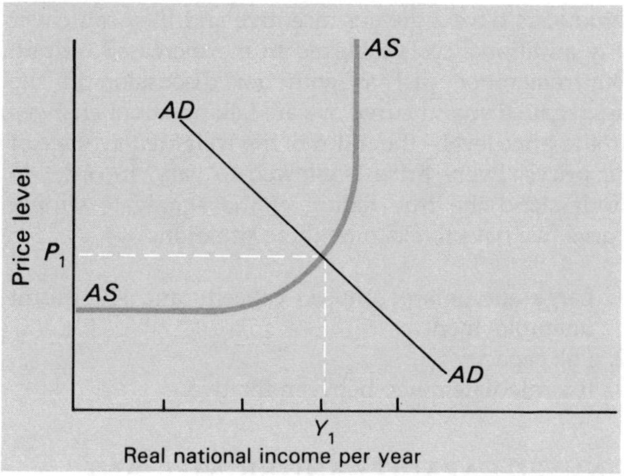

EXPLAINING INFLATION

In Chapter 11, there was a discussion of demand-pull inflation. Using shifts in the aggregate demand curve, and the aggregate supply curve shown in Figure 14.4 we can explain the phenomenon of demand inflation. Start out at price level P_0. Assume that the aggregate demand curve is AD_1–AD_1. An increase in the aggregate demand curve to AD_2–AD_2 will not alter the price level. There will be no inflation. However, as given in Figure 14.4, at any point past real national income of Y_1 per year, there will be some sectors experiencing full employment or no excess capacity. Therefore an increase in demand from AD_2–AD_2 to AD_3–AD_3 will cause the price level to increase from P_0 to P_1, and any further increase will cause an even higher price level, as firms compete for increasingly scarce resources with

Key Points 14.1

- **Aggregate demand is the sum of all planned expenditures for both consumption and investment purposes, by both the private and the public sector.**
- **Aggregate demand will fall when the price level rises, because of interest rate and wealth effects, and because of substitution of foreign for domestic goods.**
- **The aggregate supply curve shows the relationship between the price level and total output.**
- **So long as there is excess capacity, output can be increased. As more and more sectors of the economy reach full capacity, increasing output brings successively larger price increases.**
- **At full capacity, increasing aggregate demand fails to stimulate increasing output and leads only to rising prices.**

Figure 14.4

Demand-pull Inflation. The aggregate supply curve, *AS–AS*, is shown as first a horizontal line, then a positively sloped line, then a vertical line, to represent output rates with excess capacity, declining excess capacity (supply constraints), and no excess capacity. If the aggregate demand curve intersects the aggregate supply curve prior to output rate Y_1, then any increase in demand will *not lead* to a rise in the price level. Thus, a shift from AD_1 to AD_2 leaves the price level unaltered at P_0. A shift from AD_2–AD_2 to AD_3–AD_3, however, will cause the price level to increase to P_1. After output rate Y_2, any increase in demand will simply result in a higher price level, since, by definition, at full employment, no more output is physically possible. An increase in demand from AD_3–AD_3 to AD_4–AD_4 will increase the price level to P_2. Demand-pull inflation occurs any time the aggregate demand curve increases and intersects the aggregate supply curve at some output rate greater than Y_1 per year.

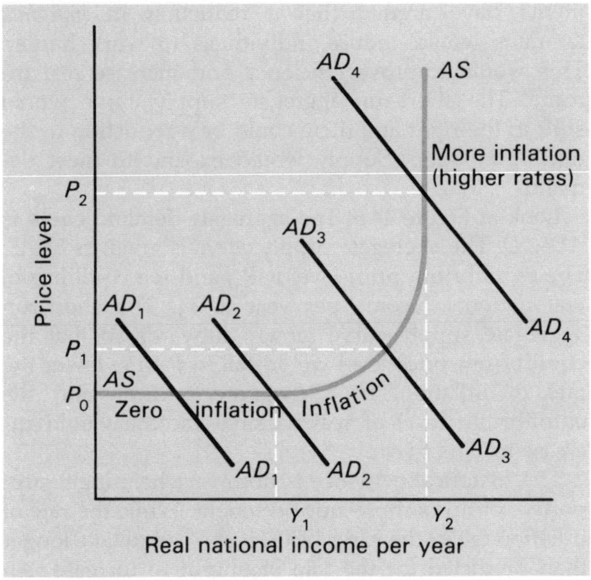

which to raise output. If the demand curve shifts to AD_4–AD_4, the price level will rise to P_2. Indeed, no output rate greater than Y_2 per year is physically possible. That means that any increase in demand after that output rate will simply result in a higher price level (inflation).

Demand inflation can be defined as any increase (rightward shift) in the aggregate demand curve after output rate Y_1.

EXPLAINING THE GREAT DEPRESSION

The Depression of the 1930s affected business everywhere, but probably most dramatically in the United States. From 1929 to 1933, real GNP fell by 29.4 per cent. Unemployment had reached 25 per cent of the civilian labour force. Prices fell by 23.6 per cent during that same period.

Aggregate supply and aggregate demand analysis can help us to understand what happened during the Great Depression. Look at Figure 14.5. Here we show an aggregate supply curve, *AS–AS*, with the three ranges discussed above. Assume that during the period 1929–33, nothing happens to shift the aggregate supply curve. In 1929, aggregate demand is AD_1–AD_1. For a variety of reasons – falling international demand for goods produced in the United States, less desired investment by firms, less desired consumption by households, and for other reasons – the aggregate demand curve decreases – shifts inwards to the left – to AD_2–AD_2. In 1929, the price level was P_1 and the real national income per year was Y_1. By 1933, the price level has fallen to P_2 and the real national income per year had fallen to Y_2. (Now read Key Points 14.1.)

Short-run versus Long-run Aggregate Supply Curves

In our discussion of the aggregate supply curve, we mentioned that the vertical portion is really equivalent to the long-run aggregate supply curve, since it indicates maximum potential output possible with given resources and given technology.

It would logically follow, then, that the horizontal and positively sloped section of the aggregate supply

Figure 14.5

Explaining the Great Depression. The supply curve for the period 1929–33, is assumed to remain stable at *AS–AS*. In 1929, the aggregate demand curve is given by AD_1–AD_1. The intersection of this aggregate demand curve and the aggregate supply curve yields an equilibrium price level of P_1 and an equilibrium output level or real national income per year of Y_1. For a variety of reasons, and, in particular, a collapse in planned investment by firms, the aggregate demand schedule decreased, that is, shifted inwards to the left to AD_2–AD_2. It intersected the aggregate supply schedule at an equilibrium price of P_2 and an equilibrium output of Y_2 per year. Prices fell, and so, too, did output.

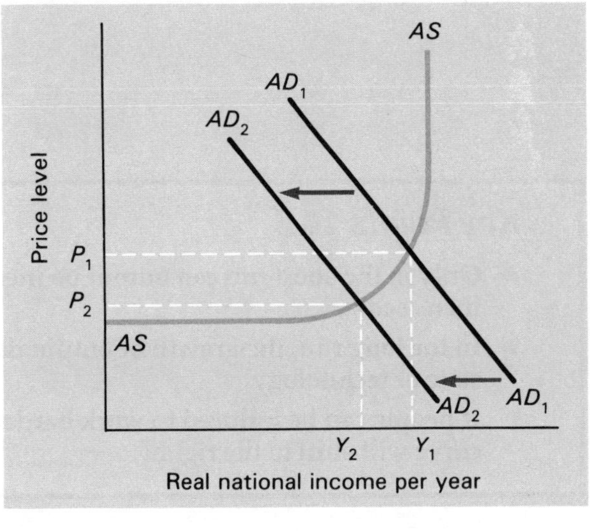

curves, as given in Figures 14.2, 14.3, 14.4, and 14.5 should properly be labelled short-run aggregate supply curves. In other words, it is only in the short run that an increase in total output in the economy is possible simply because aggregate demand has increased. If we are concerned primarily with the horizontal and positively sloped sections of the full aggregate supply curve, we can label our aggregate supply curves as short run, or *SRAS*. This will avoid any confusion with questions relating to economic growth, which properly apply only to the long-run vertical supply curve and our ability to shift it outwards over time through saving and investment as well as more efficient use of our resources.

Figure 14.6

Supply-side Economics in Theory. The equilibrium price level, P_1, and real national income, Y_1 per year, is given by the intersection of the short-run aggregate supply curve, $SRAS_{1980}$, and the aggregate demand curve. For simplicity's sake we keep the aggregate demand curve stable. A reduction in marginal tax-rates presumably was to increase incentives for workers to work harder and longer. This increase in productivity was to increase short-run aggregate supply so that $SRAS_{1984}$ would be to the right of $SRAS_{1980}$. The new equilibrium would be at an increased output of Y_2 per year, and a reduced price level, P_2. This would be an example of an aggregate supply shock with a stable aggregate demand curve.

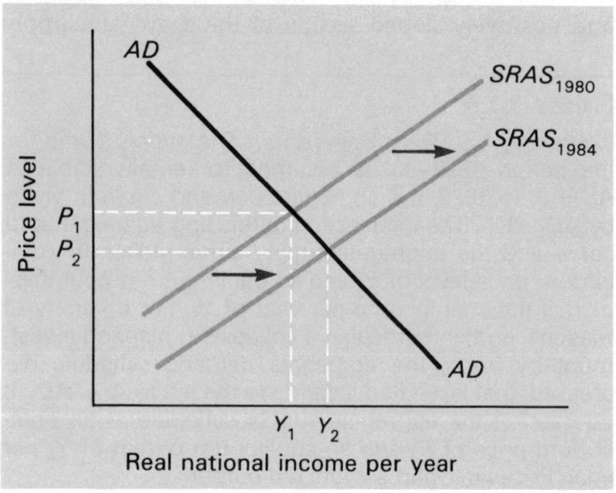

Supply-side Economics

The two examples we have already given to demonstrate the use of aggregate supply and aggregate demand related to shifts in the aggregate demand schedule. Those shifts are often called **aggregate demand shocks**. We can now look at an example in which there is an attempted shift in the short-run aggregate supply curve. This is sometimes called an **aggregate supply shock**. The example we wish to discuss concerns the government policy referred to as supply-side economics. **Supply-side economics** involves creating incentives to increase productivity. Recent governments have argued that a reduction in *marginal* tax-rates would induce individuals to work harder. This would improve efficiency and increase real income. The short-run aggregate supply curve would shift to the right and there could be a reduction in the rate of inflation. Supply would expand to meet demand.

Look at Figure 14.6. The aggregate demand curve is *AD–AD*. The aggregate supply curve is given as *SRAS*. The equilibrium price level is P_1, and the equilibrium real national income per year is Y_1. The short-run aggregate supply curve moves outwards so that the equilibrium price level would fall to P_2 (i.e. lower the rate of inflation, in a dynamic setting), and the equilibrium level of real national income would increase to Y_2 per year.

The historical evidence is not overwhelmingly supportive of this supply-side argument. While the rate of inflation fell in the early 1980s, it seemed to take longer than predicted for the rate of output to increase. An important factor in the fall in inflation was, in fact, the fall in manufacturing output which occurred during the 1980–1 recession. (Now read Key Points 14.2.)

Key Points 14.2

- **Only in the short run can output be increased simply because aggregate demand has increased.**
- **In the long run, the growth of output depends on the level of investment and the state of technology.**
- **If people can be induced to work harder or more efficiently, the aggregate supply curve will shift to the right.**

CASE STUDY

Supply Constraints, Rising Costs, and Inflation

Vacancies. One way of estimating the likely extent of supply constraints at any given time is to look at figures for vacancies. Only a proportion of vacancies which occur are notified to employment offices. But when there is a sharp increase in the number of vacancies, it does indicate that employers are having difficulty in recruiting the kind of labour they require.

Consider the increase in vacancies in 1973–4. This suggests that the economy in 1973 was at point *A* in Figure 14.7. As demand increased, and employers sought to increase output, they would be faced with a shortage of suitable labour. They would offer higher wages, costs would rise and so would prices. Any increase in aggregate demand would lead to a movement up AS_1.

Vacancies notified to employment offices (000s)

1970	188.3
1971	130.9
1972	147.3
1973	306.9
1974	297.5
1975	156.1
1976	122.0
1977	154.5
1978	210.3
1979	241.3
1980	134.2
1981	91.1
1982	113.9
1983	137.3
1984	149.8
1985	161.7
1986	188.1
1987	234.9
1988 est.	255

Source: CSO, *Economic Trends*, 1989

But, meantime, there were dramas on the international scene. OPEC countries were able to raise oil prices fourfold. This increased costs sharply – it meant that any given level of output would be produced at a higher price level. Aggregate supply shifted from AS_1 to AS_2. The new equilibrium is at *B*; a lower output is being produced at a higher price level. This is known as stagflation.

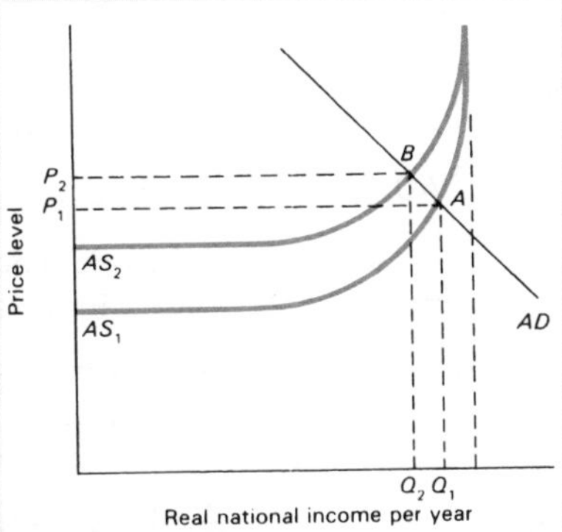

Figure 14.7

It is clear from the data that the labour market tightened again in 1979 and 1988. In both years, vacancies were rising sharply, indicating that employers were having difficulty in recruiting to some jobs. Comparing this data with Figure 11.10, we can see that these were periods of accelerating inflation. In 1988 inflation was accelerating less than in the two earlier periods. This was probably because of falling and then relatively low oil prices from 1986 onwards.

Spare Capacity. The economic recovery of the 1980s put much idle plant back to work in the main industrial economies. By 1985, data from *The Economist* gave a measure of capacity utilization almost equal to the peak level of the previous boom in 1979. The CBI's *Industrial Trends Survey* shows that from then until 1988, considerably fewer firms were reporting spare capacity. The evidence from both vacancy data and direct from firms tells the same story: between 1986 and 1988 many manufacturing firms were experiencing some difficulty in expanding output. Many were already producing the most they efficiently could, with given levels of capital investment.

It should of course be remembered that a considerable amount of industrial capacity was scrapped in the 1980–2 recession. So many firms went bankrupt that manufacturing's full-capacity output actually shrank. Plant and machinery was either sold or scrapped, and not replaced. Supply constraints in the late 1980s had therefore set in long before the economy had a chance to re-employ all or most of its workforce.

Capacity Utilization in Manufacturing

Percentage of firms answering yes to the question 'Is your present level of output below full capacity?'.

1986	Jan.	54	1988	Jan.	35
	Apr.	57		Apr.	32
	July	48		July	31
	Oct.	49		Oct.	31
1987	Jan.	50	1989	Jan.	31
	Apr.	49		Apr.	37
	July	45		July	39
	Oct.	41			

Source: CBI, *Industrial Trends Survey*.

Questions

1. Aggregate demand may change with government policy. How would decreasing aggregate demand, due to rising interest rates, affect the economy?
2. How did the 1979 oil price rise affect the UK?
3. Look at the data in Chapter 11 on inflation and unemployment. To what extent do you think accelerating inflation has been caused by excess demand? When have rising costs been a significant factor? What evidence is there of overheating in the economy in 1988?

Exam Preparation

PRACTICAL EXERCISE

1. Given the curves in the diagram below, discuss why the equilibrium price level will be at P_e and not at P_1 or P_2.

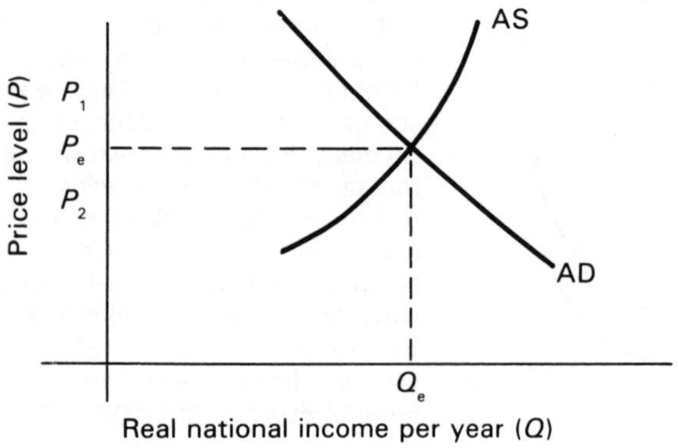

MULTIPLE CHOICE QUESTIONS

1. If aggregate demand has risen output will not increase if
- **A** productivity is rising
- **B** there are some supply constraints
- **C** the aggregate supply curve is vertical
- **D** there is underutilized capital in the economy

2. Inflation will decelerate if
- **A** aggregate demand is constant and input costs rise
- **B** aggregate demand stays constant and productivity increases
- **C** aggregate supply falls
- **D** aggregate supply is constant

RELATED ESSAY QUESTIONS

1. 'Inflation is due to excess demand.' Discuss.

2. Explain how aggregate supply can be increased (a) in the short run, and (b) in the long run.

3. Distinguish between a movement along the aggregate supply curve, and a shift of the curve to the right.

4. Is an increase in government expenditure likely to raise prices and wages rather than output and employment even in the presence of substantial unemployment and excess capacity?

5. 'The rise in the rate of inflation in 1988 was the result of over-rapid growth in the economy.' Do you agree?

15 Aggregate Demand: Consumption, Saving, and Investment

Key Points to Review

- Shift versus movement along a curve (5.6)
- Actual and planned saving and investment (12.2)
- Nominal versus real values (13.7)

Questions for Preview

1 How are saving, consumption, and income related in a closed economy with no government?

2 What are the determinants of investment?

Aggregate demand was defined as the sum total of all planned expenditures over a year's period. We found that the aggregate demand curve was downward-sloping – there is an inverse relationship between the price level and aggregate demand. In order to find the equilibrium price level and the equilibrium level of real national income per year, it was also necessary to use the aggregate supply curve. But supposing we are dealing only with that portion of the aggregate supply curve that is a horizontal line? If there are large amounts of unused productive capacity and unemployment, an increase in aggregate demand will not raise prices, and a decrease in aggregate demand will not cause firms to reduce prices. In such a situation, the equilibrium level of real national income per year is completely *demand-determined.* Thus, in order to construct a model of income determination, we need only to understand the determinants of aggregate demand. In the simple models that we have used so far, aggregate demand determinants have been limited to planned consumption expenditures on the part of households, and planned investment expenditures on the part of firms. In this chapter, we will examine what determines the rate of planned consumption expenditures and what determines the rate of planned investment expenditures.

Keynesian Economics

John Maynard Keynes, who wrote *The General Theory of Employment, Interest, and Money* suggested that many prices, and especially the price of labour (wages), are sticky downwards. Therefore, even in situations of excess capacity and large amounts of unemployment, we will not necessarily observe the price level falling. Rather, what we will observe is continuing unemployment and a reduction in the equilibrium level of real national income per year. Keynes argued that, to some extent, the lengthy duration of the Great Depression could be explained by the sticky-downward nature of prices and wages. Thus, a general economy-wide equilibrium can occur, and last for a long time, even when there is excess capacity. Keynes and his followers argued that capitalism was therefore not necessarily a self-regulating system, sustaining eternal prosperity and full employment. Keynes, at the time, was attacking the so-called classical view of the world, which argued that markets would all clear. Prices and wages would adjust; as wages fell, more people would be employed and full employment would never be far away.

Some Simplifying Assumptions

We have already assumed that prices will not rise when output rises, so for the time being, we need not concern ourselves with inflation. We will be seeing the economy in real terms. In order to simplify the income-determination model that follows, a number of other assumptions are made:

1. Firms pay no indirect taxes (for example, VAT).
2. Firms distribute all of their profits to shareholders.
3. There is no depreciation (capital consumption allowance) so that gross private domestic investment equals net investment.

4. The economy is closed, i.e. there is no foreign trade.

Given all of these simplifying assumptions, real disposable income will be equal to real national income minus taxes.

Definitions and Relationships

There are literally only two things you can do with a pound's worth of income (in the absence of taxes). You can consume it or you can save it. If you consume it, it is gone for good. However, if you save the entire pound you will be able to consume it (and perhaps more if it earns interest) at some future time. That is the distinction between **consumption** and **saving**. Consumption is the act of using income for the purchase of consumer goods. **Consumer goods** are those that are purchased by households for immediate satisfaction. Consumer goods are such things as films, food, clothing, and the like. By definition, whatever you do not consume you *save* and can consume sometime in the future.

The Difference between Stocks and Flows

It is important to distinguish between saving and savings. Saving is an action that occurs at a particular rate such as £5 a week. This rate is called a flow. It is expressed per unit of time, usually a year. Implicitly, then, when we talk about saving we talk about a flow or rate of saving. Savings, on the other hand, is a stock concept measured at a certain point or instant in time. Your current savings are the result of past saving. You may presently have savings of £1 000 that are the result of four years' saving at a rate of £250 a year. Consumption, being related to saving, is also a flow concept. You consume from after-tax income at a certain rate per week, per month, or per year.

Relating Income to Saving and Consumption

The relationship of saving, consumption, and disposable income is therefore:

$$\text{consumption} + \text{saving} \equiv \text{disposable income.}$$

This is called an 'accounting identity'. It has to hold true at every moment in time. From it we can derive the definition of saving:

$$\text{saving} \equiv \text{disposable income} - \text{consumption.}$$

Investment

Investment is also a flow concept. Investment is defined as expenditures by firms on new machines and buildings – **capital goods** – that are expected to yield a future stream of income. This we have already called *fixed investment*.* Additionally, we included in our definition *changes* in stocks. When some of current output is not sold, stocks increase. Similarly if demand exceeds current production, firms will run down stocks, to meet the demand. To the extent that stocks are run down, investment will be lower. (Now read Key Notes 5.1.)

Determinants of Planned Consumption and Planned Saving

The major determinant of planned real consumption expenditures is clearly expressed in Keynes's 1936 book. According to Keynes's General Theory, when we look at consumption, we find that:

> the fundamental psychological law, upon which we are entitled to depend with great confidence both *a priori* from our knowledge of human nature and from the detailed facts of experience, is that men are disposed, as a rule and on the average, to increase their consumption as their income increases, but not by as much as the increase in their income.

A relationship is suggested here between the planned consumption expenditures of households and their current income. This relationship is called the **consumption function**. It shows how much all households plan to consume per year with each level of real

*Fixed investment should also include expenditures by households on *new* houses. For convenience' sake, we will usually ignore this aspect of investment in this chapter.

Key Points 15.1

- **If we assume that prices will not rise as output increases, the equilibrium level of real national income is demand-determined. (The economy is on the horizontal section of the aggregate supply curve.)**
- **Saving is a flow concept, something that occurs over time. Savings, on the other hand, are a stock. They are the accumulation due to past saving.**
- **Saving equals disposable income minus consumption.**
- **Investment is a flow concept, also. It includes expenditures on new machines, buildings and equipment, new houses, and changes in the level of stocks.**

JOHN MAYNARD KEYNES

(1883–1946)

Mechanic of the Market

'The ideas of economists and political philosophers . . . are more powerful than is commonly understood . . . Practical men, who believe themselves to be quite exempt from any intellectual influences, are usually the slaves of some defunct economist. Madmen in authority, who hear voices in the air, are distilling their frenzy from some academic scribbler of a few years back.' The most important 'defunct economist' of the twentieth century is the man who penned these words – John Maynard Keynes. Over the twenty-five years following the end of the First World War, Keynes transformed the way in which economics was viewed as a discipline and as an aspect of government policy.

During the 1920s, Keynes studied European finance and wrote *The Treatise on Money* (1930), efforts on which he would later build as British representative to the 1944 Bretton Woods conference on international monetary policy. At the same time, Keynes amassed a considerable sum by speculating on the stock market, handling his transactions by telephone before getting out of bed each morning.

It was in 1936, in the midst of the Great Depression, with millions throughout Europe and the United States unemployed, that Keynes's masterwork, *The General Theory of Employment, Interest, and Money,* appeared. The market is not a self-regulating mechanism, Keynes argued. To bring the economy quickly out of depression and end high unemployment, some way of stimulating investment and capital expansion is needed; only by maintaining 'effective demand' – a desire for goods and services among people who have the money income to pay for them – can recessions be warded off. The natural entity to stimulate aggregate demand, Keynes asserted, is the government using a combination of deficit spending and regulation of tax-rates and money supply.

Just as Keynes predicted, his theories – those of an academic scribbler – were not really utilized by government policy-makers for many years after the publication of his *magnum opus.* But Keynesian economics, as it is called, has, since the 1950s, been a dominant force in government policy-making in this country and elsewhere.

Figure 15.1

Hypothetical Real Consumption and Saving Schedules. At levels of disposable income below 5 000 units, planned saving is negative. In column (4), we see the average propensity to consume, which is merely planned consumption divided by disposable income. Column (5) lists average propensity to save, which is planned saving divided by disposable income. Column (6) is the marginal propensity to consume, which shows the proportion of additional income that will be consumed, ΔC (the change in comsumption) over ΔY (the change in income). And finally, column (7) shows the portion of additional income that will be saved, or the marginal propensity to save.

Combination	*(1) Real disposable income Y_d (Units per year)*	*(2) Planned real consumption C (Units per year)*	*(3) Planned real saving $S \equiv Y_d - C$ (1) – (2) (Units per year)*	*(4) Average propensity to consume $APC \equiv C/Y_d$ (2) ÷ (1)*	*(5) Average propensity to save $APS \equiv S/Y_d$ (3) ÷ (1)*	*(6) Change in consumption $MPC \equiv \frac{\Delta C}{\Delta Y_d}$*	*(7) Change in saving $MPS \equiv \frac{\Delta S}{\Delta Y_d}$*
A	0/yr	1 000/yr	−1 000/yr	. . .	. . .	. . .	. . .
B	1 000	1 800	−800	1.80	−0.8	0.8	0.2
C	2 000	2 600	−600	1.30	−0.3	0.8	0.2
D	3 000	3 400	−400	1.133	−0.133	0.8	0.2
E	4 000	4 200	−400	1.05	−0.05	0.8	0.2
F	5 000	5 000	0	1.00	0.00	0.8	0.2
G	6 000	5 800	200	0.967	0.033	0.8	0.2
H	7 000	6 600	400	0.943	0.057	0.8	0.2
I	8 000	7 400	600	0.925	0.075	0.8	0.2
J	9 000	8 200	800	0.911	0.089	0.8	0.2
K	10 000	9 000	1 000	0.9	0.1	0.8	0.2

disposable income per year. The first three columns of Figure 15.1 show a consumption function for a hypothetical group of households.

We see from Figure 15.1 that as real disposable income goes up, planned consumption rises also, but by a smaller amount, as Keynes suggested. Planned saving also increases with disposable income. Notice, however, that below an income of 5000 units the planned saving is actually negative. The more income drops below that level, the more people dissave, either by going into debt or by drawing on past savings.

We can see the relationship between *C*, *S*, and *Y* in Figure 15.2.

Graphing the Numbers

In Figure 15.3 the vertical axis measures the level of planned consumption per year, and the horizontal axis measures the level of real disposable income per year. In Figure 15.4 the horizontal axis is again real disposable income per year, but now the vertical axis is planned saving per year. All of these are on a pounds per year basis, which emphasizes the point that we are measuring flows, not stocks.

As you can see we have taken the income–consumption and income–saving combinations in Figure 15.1. Figure 15.3 shows the consumption function and Figure 15.4 the savings function. The savings function is the complement of the consumption function because consumption plus saving always equal disposable income. What is not consumed is, by definition, saved. The difference between actual disposable income and the planned level of consumption per year must be the planned level of saving per year.

Figure 15.3 shows the consumption function intersecting, **the 45-degree line**. Along the 45-degree line, expenditure is exactly equal to income, so at point *F*, where the consumption function intersects the 45-degree line, real disposable income equals planned consumption. Point *F* is sometimes labelled the break-even income point because there is neither positive nor negative saving. This can be seen in Figure 15.4 as well. The planned annual rate of saving at a real disposable income level of 5 000 units is indeed zero.

Dissaving and Autonomous Consumption

To the left of point *F* on Figures 15.3 and 15.4 this hypothetical family engages in dissaving. The amount of saving or dissaving in Figure 15.3 can be found by measuring the vertical distance between the 45-degree line and the consumption function. This simply tells us that if real disposable income temporarily falls below 5000 units, consumption will not be cut back by the full amount of the reduction. People will instead go into debt or consume past saving in some way to compensate for the loss.

Now look at the point on the diagram where real disposable income is zero but planned consumption per year is 1000 units. This amount of planned consumption, which does not depend at all on actual disposable income, is called **autonomous consumption**. In other words, the autonomous consumption of 1000 units is *independent* of the level of disposable income. (We are, of course, assuming here that real disposable income does not equal zero year in year out.) It seems reasonable to assume that some spending continues in order to preserve life.

Figure 15.2

The Relationship between *C*, *S*, and *Y*. Here we show graphically that $C + S \equiv Y$. In panel (a) the consumption shedule is drawn. In panel (b) the saving schedule is drawn. When we add the two schedules together we get panel (c). Consumption plus saving must equal income.

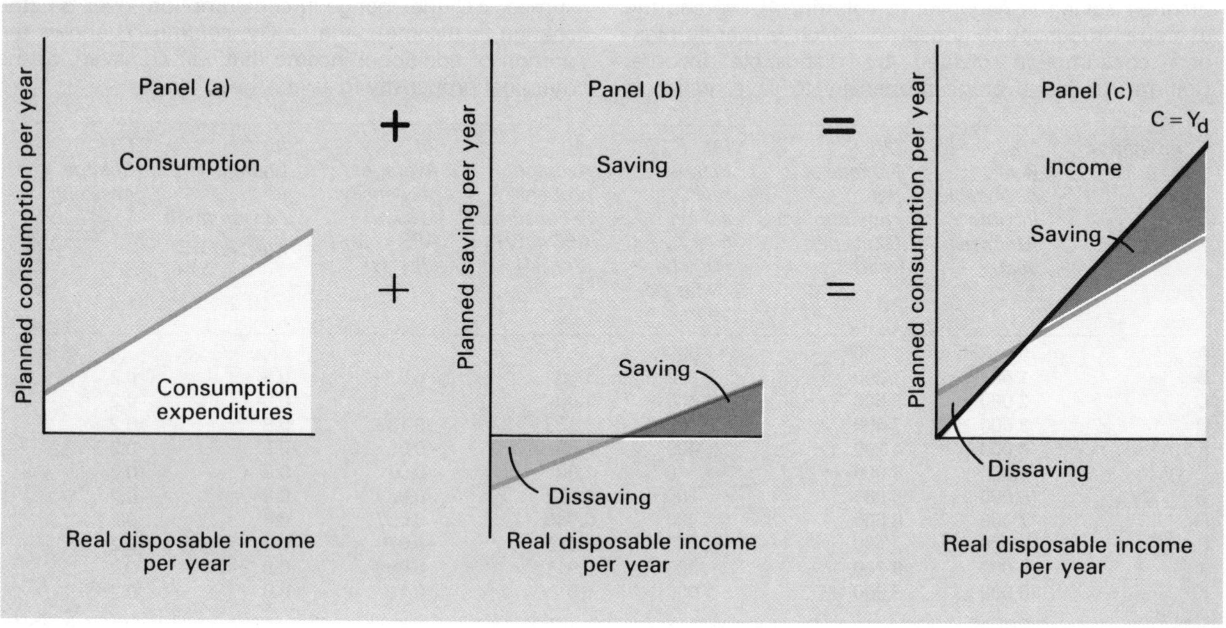

Figure 15.3

The Consumption Function. If we plot the combinations of real disposable income and planned consumption from columns (1) and (2) in Figure 15.1 we get the consumption function. Every point on the 45-degree line bisecting this diagram is equidistant from the horizontal and the vertical axes; thus, at every point on it, consumption equals real disposable income. Where the consumption function crosses the 45-degree line, we know that consumption equals real disposable income and there is zero saving. The vertical distance between the 45-degree line and the consumption function measures the rate of saving or dissaving at any given income level.

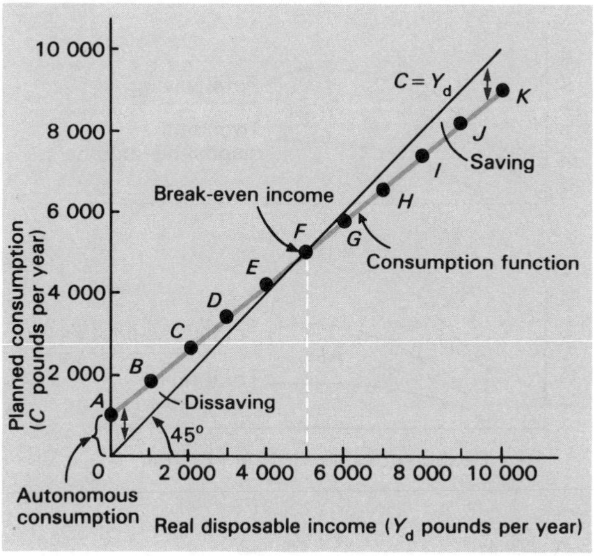

There are, of course, many possible types of autonomous expenditures. We generally take investment to be autonomous – existing independently of the model. We can assume that government expenditures are autonomous, depending as they often do on political forces.

In contrast to autonomous spending, which is independent, there is also **induced** spending. This is defined as spending which depends directly upon the level of income. Apart from their autonomous elements, saving and consumption are both induced. As incomes rise, both saving and consumption will rise too.

Average Propensity to Consume and to Save

Columns (4) and (5) of Figure 15.1 show the **average propensity to consume** (APC) and **average propensity to save** (APS). They are defined as:

$$APC \equiv \frac{\text{consumption}}{\text{real disposable income}}$$

$$APS \equiv \frac{\text{saving}}{\text{real disposable income}}$$

Figure 15.4

The Saving Function. If we plot the relationship between column (1), real disposable income, and column (3), planned saving, from Figure 15.1, we arrive at the savings function shown in this diagram. It is the complement of the consumption function presented in Figure 15.3 above.

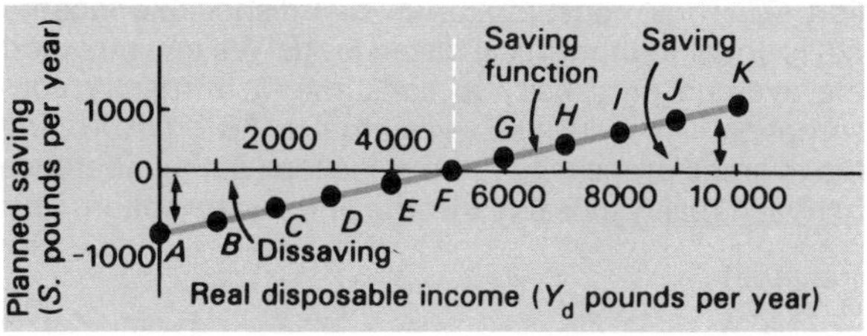

Notice that the average propensity to consume decreases as real income increases. This decrease simply means that the fraction of the family's real disposable income going to saving rises as income rises. The same fact can be found in column (5). The average propensity to save, which at first is negative, finally hits zero at an income level of 5000 and then becomes positive. In this example, it reaches a maximum value of 0.1 at income level 10000. This means the household saves 10 per cent of a 10000 income.

Marginal Propensity to Consume and to Save

Now we go the last two columns in Figure 15.1. These are labelled **marginal propensity to consume** (MPC) and **marginal propensity to save** (MPS). We have already used the term *marginal*. It means 'small change in'. The marginal propensity to consume, then, is defined as:

$$MPC \equiv \frac{\text{change in planned consumption}}{\text{change in real disposable income}} \equiv \frac{\Delta C}{\Delta Y}$$

The marginal propensity to save is defined similarly:

$$MPS \equiv \frac{\text{change in planned saving}}{\text{change in real disposable income}} \equiv \frac{\Delta S}{\Delta Y}$$

What do the MPC and the MPS tell you? They tell you the percentage of an increase or decrease in income which will go to consumption and saving. The emphasis here is on the word *change*. The marginal propensity to consume indicates how you will change your planned rate of consumption if there is a change in your disposable income. If your marginal propensity to consume is 0.8, that does not mean that you consume 80 per cent of *all* disposable income. The percentage of your disposable income that you consume is given by the average propensity to consume, or APC, which is not, at most income levels, equal to 0.8. An MPC of 0.8 means a that you will consume 80 per cent of any *increase* in your disposable income. In general, we

Figure 15.5

Marginal and Average Relationships. In panel (a), we show the relationship between the average propensity to consume (APC) and the average propensity to save (APS). Start off in panel (a) with real diposable income level equal to *OA*. This is identically equal to the horizontal distance *EB* and *DC*. Consumption at all real disposable incomes is given by the consumption function *CC*. Thus, consumption at real disposable income *OA* is equal to the vertical distance *AB*. We can now find the average propensity to consume. It is merely consumption ÷ real disposable income, or *AB* ÷ *OA*. To find the average propensity to save, we look at the difference between real disposable income and consumption. This is shown as the vertical distance *CB*, which is also equal to the vertical distance *DE*. In any event, the APS is equal to saving ÷ real disposable income or *CB* ÷ *OA*.

In panel (b), we can find the marginal propensity to consume (MPC). It is defined as the change in comsumption associated with a change in real disposable income. We show that with the change in real disposable income of *NP*, consumption will increase by *PQ*. Thus, the marginal propensity to consume is *PQ* ÷ *NP*. The marginal propensity to save is defined as the change in saving due to a change in real disposable income. In panel (c), the change in real disposable income is the horizontal distance *TU*; the change in saving is the vertical distance *UV*. Thus, MPS is equal to *UV* ÷ *TU*.

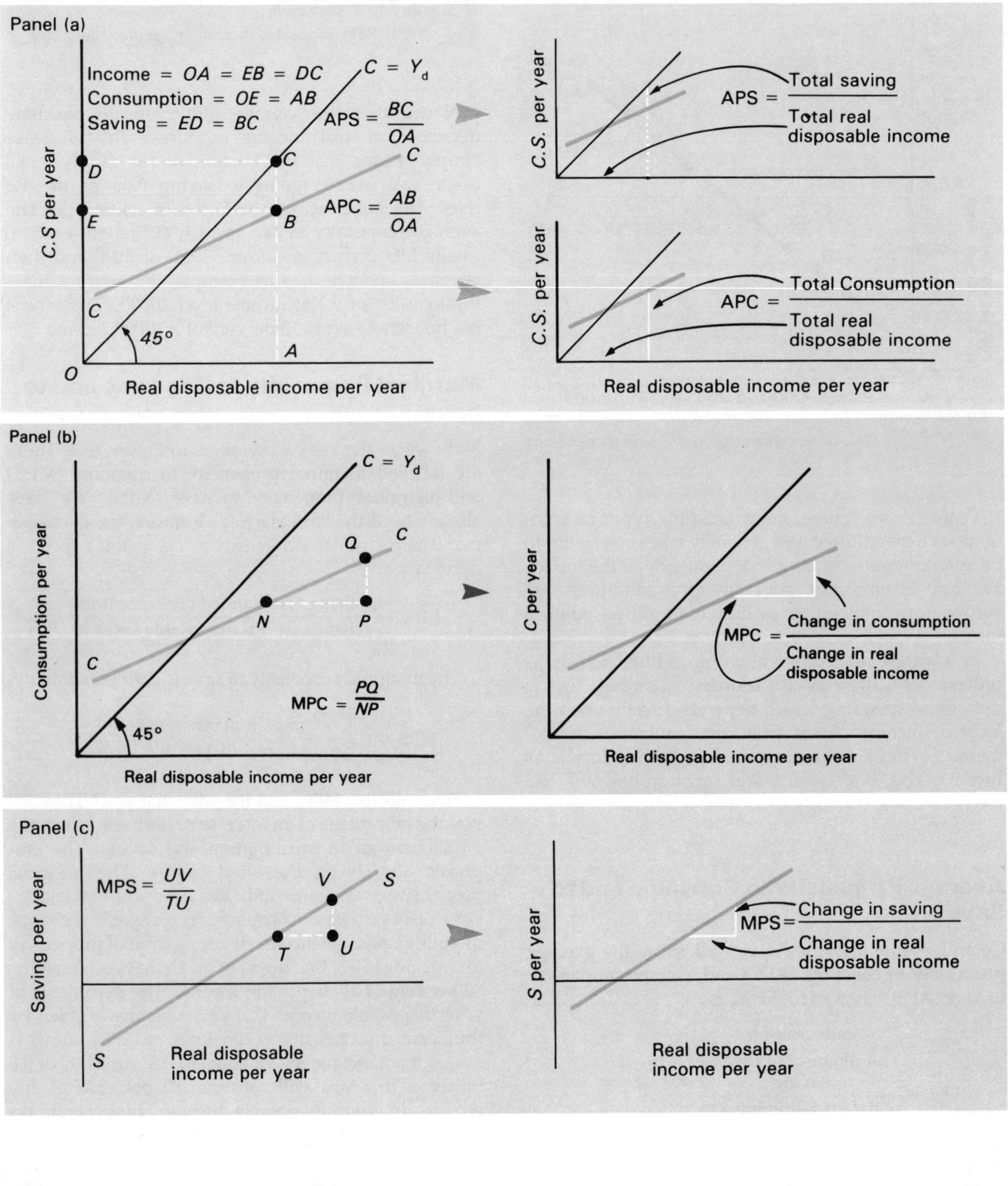

assume that the marginal propensity to consume is between zero and one. In other words, we assume that individuals increase their planned consumption by more than zero and less than 100 per cent of any increase in real disposable income that they receive.

Some Relationships

By definition, consumption plus saving must equal income. Thus, both your disposable income and the change in disposable income are either consumed or saved. The proportions of either measure must equal 1, or 100 per cent. This allows us to make the following statements:

1. APC + APS = (100 per cent of total income)

and

2. MPC + MPS = (100 per cent of the change in income)

In other words, the average propensities as well as the marginal propensities to consume and save must total 1, or 100 per cent.

We can also show some of the key relationships in the theory of income and employment in graphical terms. These are set out Figure 15.5 in panels (a), (b), and (c) which show how to measure geometrically the average and marginal propensities to consume and to save. As can be seen in panels (b) and (c), the marginal propensity to consume is equal to the slope of the consumption function, and the marginal propensity to save is equal to the slope of the saving function.

Distinguishing between a Movement and a Shift

In Chapter 5 we made a clear distintion between a *movement along* a supply or demand curve and a *shift in* either of those curves. This same distinction applies when considering the consumption or saving function. Since the saving function is the complement of the consumption function, let us simply talk in terms of movements along, or shifts in, the consumption function.

In Figure 15.6 we show the effect on consumption of a rise in real disposable income of, for example, 2500 units per year, starting from the break-even income at 5000 units per year. We move upward along the consumption function, now labelled C, from point A to point B. Planned consumption per year will increase by the marginal propensity to consume (0.8) times the increase in real disposable income, or 0.8 x 2500 units 2000 units; that is, planned consumption will rise from 5000 units to 7000 units per year. The same analysis holds for a decrease in disposable income. These represent movements along a given consumption function, CC.

How do we represent a decrease in *autonomous* consumption? In Figure 15.6 the autonomous part of planned consumption was 1000 units. If we wish to represent a decrease in the autonomous component of planned consumption, we must shift the entire consumption function downwards by the amount of this decrease. For example, a 500-units decrease in the autonomous component of consumption will shift the consumption function C down to C′. The break-even point moves from point A, or 5 000 units, to point F, or 2 500 units. If the autonomous component of consumption shifts upward, the consumption function will shift from C to C″. Another way of looking at this is to realise that an increase in the consumption function means that at *all* real disposable income levels, more will be consumed than before, and vice versa.

Shifts in the entire consumption function are similar to shifts in the demand and supply curves that we studied in Chapter 5. With a typical supply–demand relationship, a change in the price of the product brings about a movement along given demand and supply curves. Any change in a non-price determinant of demand or supply causes the curves to shift. Similarly, a change in real disposable income will cause us to move *along* a given consumption function. Any change in the non-income determinants of consumption will

Figure 15.6

Distinguishing between Movements along and Shifts in the Consumption Function. Starting at the break-even real disposable income at point *A* on line *C*, if real disposable income increases by 2500 units per year, then we will experience a movement from point *A* to point *B* along that consumption function. Planned consumption will go up by the product of marginal propensity to consume and the increase in real disposable income, or by 0.8 x 2500 units = 2000 units. Planned consumption will rise from 5000 units to 7000 units. On the other hand, if there were a 500 units per year decrease in autonomous consumption, the entire consumption function would shift from *C* to *C′*. If there were a 500 units per year increase in the autonomous component, the consumption function would shift from *C* to *C″*.

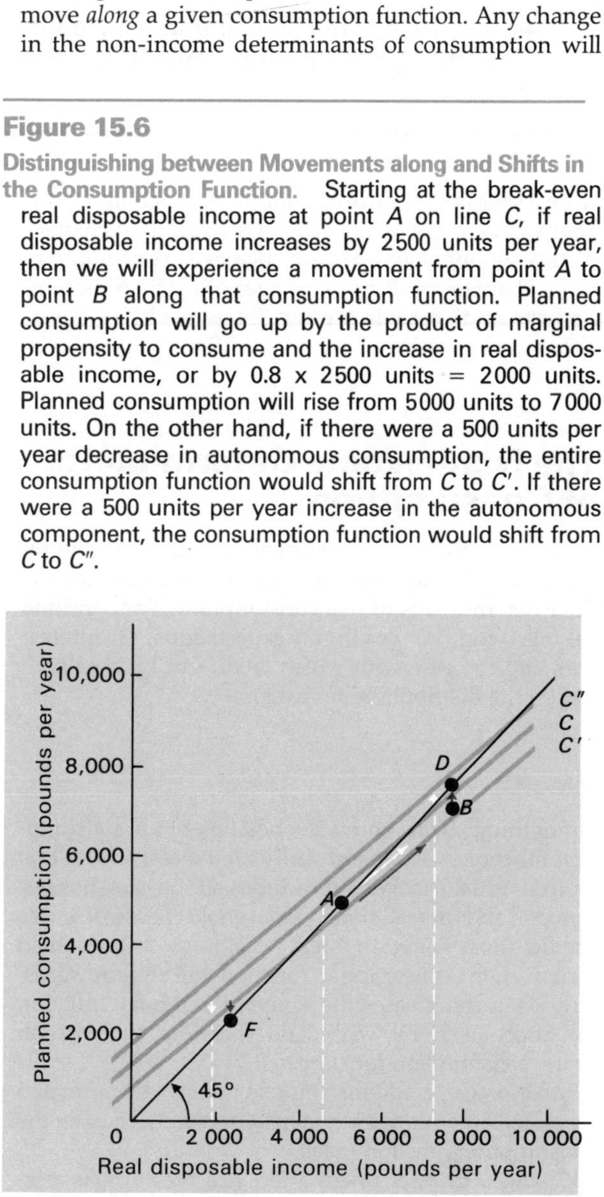

Key Points 15.2

- **The consumption function shows the relationship between planned rates of consumption and real disposable income per year. The saving function is the complement of the consumption function, since saving plus consumption must equal real disposable income.**
- **The average propensity to consume is equal to consumption divided by real disposable income.**
- **The average propensity to save is equal to saving divided by real disposable income.**
- **The marginal propensity to save is equal to the change in planned saving divided by the change in real disposable income.**
- **The marginal propensity to consume is equal to the change in planned saving divided by the change in real disposable income.**
- **APC + APS = 1, MPC + MPS = 1.**
- **Any change in real disposable income will cause the planned rate of consumption to change; this is represented by a movement along the consumption function.**

cause a *shift* in the entire consumption function. That is what we were discussing when we referred to changes in the autonomous part of planned consumption. Those changes result from changes other than those in the level of disposable income. (Now read Key Points 15.2.)

The Non-Income Determinants of Consumption

So far, the only determinant of spending in our theory of consumption has been income. There are, of course, other determinants of real consumption. They include the following: (1) wealth, (2) expectations, (3) interest rates and the ease with which credit can be obtained, and (4) the distribution of income.

Wealth

Other things being equal, the position of the consumption function will depend partly on the real wealth that an individual has. Wealth includes all the cars, houses, stereos, and bonds that a household possesses. We predict that when the real wealth of a household increases, the consumption function will shift upwards, and when it decreases the converse will hold. Inflation can affect one's real wealth and, therefore, the position of the consumption function.

Inflation can erode the value of money-denominated assets (all other things being held constant), causing the consumption function to fall.

Changes in asset prices affect real wealth, irrespective of the rate of inflation. If house prices rise much faster than the general rate of inflation, people feel richer. They may be able to remortgage their homes for a larger sum, which will give them increased spending power. The consumption function will then shift upwards.

Expectations

Particularly in the short run, expectations can influence the position of the consumption function. If households anticipate better times ahead (higher income) than currently, the consumption function may shift upwards. If they are pessimistic, it may shift downwards. The expectation of the future rate of inflation relative to today's rate of inflation may also have a bearing on planned consumption expenditures.

The Interest Rate and Credit Availability

An increase in the interest rate typically leads to a reduction in interest-sensitive purchases such as cars and houses. Most of these are financed by borrowing. Therefore, the higher the rate of interest, the more expensive it becomes to buy a car or a house. Other things being equal, an increase in the rate of interest will lead to a decrease in planned consumption expenditures at every level of real disposable income.

A credit squeeze, in which it is made harder for people to obtain loans for consumer purchases, may be associated with higher interest rates. Before they could buy durable goods, some people would have to save up, and their consumption levels will be lower than they would have been if credit had been easy.

The Distribution of Income

Income distribution becomes more unequal when some groups of the population become wealthier while others become poorer. A more equal distribution of income may result from redistributive tax and benefit systems, which tax high incomes heavily in order to pay benefits to those on low incomes. The rich will tend to have a lower marginal propensity to consume than the poor. Some of the income taken from the rich might have been saved. Practically all the income transferred to the poor will be spent on consumption. So a more equal distribution of income will, other things being equal, shift the consumption function upwards.

IS THE MPC CONSTANT?

So far we have assumed that the MPC is constant, which means that the consumption function will be a straight line. Is this reasonable? In practice, it is highly likely that the MPC will fall if income rises. Growth in the standard of living will generally cause people to save a larger proportion of increased income and consume a smaller proportion. A fall in the MPC as income rises would lead to the consumption function levelling off (rising less steeply) as income rises.

When the MPC is constant, so that the consumption function is linear, it can be stated in the form $C = a + bY$, where a is the autonomous element in consumption and b is the MPC (and the gradient of the consumption function).

Permanent-income Hypothesis

In recent years a rather different view of the consumption function has been developed. Basically, the **permanent-income hypothesis** holds that consumption doesn't depend on *current* disposable income but rather on some measure of expected, or permanent, income. The planning period may be anywhere from two to five years, or even longer, depending upon people's expectations. According to this theory, consumption will not drop drastically even if, for some reason, people's income falls below what they think their permanent income is. Conversely, consumption will not increase very much even if people's income suddenly jumps above the level they consider to be permanent. The permanent income hypothesis suggests that the level of consumption will stay fairly stable over time. (It is part of the theory underlying those views concerning inflation which stress the importance of money.)

A slightly different view of consumption has been set out in the Life-cycle Hypothesis. This shows how income varies, for most people, over the years of their lifetimes. In the early stages of their careers, most people have comparatively low earning power. They borrow heavily, to set up house and acquire assets of all kinds. In middle age they will earn more, pay off debts, and save for old age, when once again, they will have smaller incomes. Thus their consumption pattern reflects their long-run expectations of income. Short-run fluctuations in income will affect their spending less than their assessments of their lifetime spending power.

This hypothesis also implies that consumption in the aggregate will be relatively stable over time. Most people's consumption patterns will change little in response to short-lived increases or decreases in income.

The relationship between income and consumption is still subject to a good deal of uncertainty. It matters very greatly too: consumption is the biggest single component part of total expenditure. Accurate forecasting of economic trends depends on being able to predict consumption. Recent experience has underlined the difficulties. Changes in saving have brought these to the surface. (Now read Key Points 15.3.)

Determinants of the Level of Saving

Since saving is inversely related to consumption, everything which influences consumption will similarly influence saving – but in the opposite direction.

In particular, people consider interest rates, inflation rates, and expectations about the future, when taking decisions about saving. Low rates of interest give a poor return on savings held in the form of financial assets such as bank accounts, and may reduce the level of saving. Inflation, however, leads to a reduction in the value of an individual's stock of savings. If people want to keep their savings at a particular level of purchasing power (e.g. one year's income), they will have to save more for a while in order to rebuild their savings. Or they may be encouraged to save if they can buy granny

Key Points 15.3

- **The non-income determinants of consumption are wealth, expectations, interest rates and credit availability, and the distribution of income.**
- **Any change in these non-income determinants will shift the consumption function up or down.**

bonds (index-linked bonds), the value of which is linked to the rate of inflation so that they do not lose their purchasing power. Both interest rates and inflation have been found to be important in determining the level of saving in the UK in the past decade.

Expectations would seem to be important in affecting savings decisions. However, the threat of increasing unemployment has not in practice caused increased saving in the UK. The world's thriftiest people are the Japanese, who save roughly a third of their incomes. The threat of unemployment in Japan is comparatively low. Cultural factors, and habit, probably play a major part in determining the level of saving.

Determinants of Investment

Investment, you will remember, is defined as expenditure on new plant and capital equipment, and changes in stocks. Investment levels can be quite volatile, especially net investment, i.e. gross investment less depreciation or capital consumption. Figure 15.7 shows how both have fluctuated.

Figure 15.7

Trends in Gross and Net Investment. Net investment is particularly volatile. Note that these figures give absolute values. Gross investment as a percentage of GDP has grown less rapidly.

Year	*Gross investment*	*Net investment*
	(£bn, 1985 prices)	
1978	54.9	20.6
1979	56.5	21.3
1980	53.4	17.0
1981	48.3	10.7
1982	50.9	12.2
1983	53.5	13.6
1984	58.1	17.1
1985	60.3	18.5
1986	61.5	18.6
1987	66.9	23.2
1988	75.7	29.8

Source: CSO, *National Income*, Blue Book, 1989.

If we compare investment expenditures historically with consumption and saving expenditures, we find that the latter are relatively less variable over time than the former. Investment decisions are based on highly variable, subjective estimates of how the economic future looks. We just discussed the role of expectations in determining the position of the consumption function. Expectations play an even greater role in determining the position of the investment function. This could account for much of the instability of investment over time. Given this chronic instability, it is more difficult to derive a satisfactory theory of planned investment expenditures. None the less, we shall attempt to construct an investment function.

The Planned Investment Function

Consider that at any time there is a range of investment opportunities that firms can identify. These investment opportunities have rates of return ranging from zero to very high, with the number (or value) of all such projects inversely related to the rate of return. That is to say, there are certainly fewer investment opportunities with high rates of return than there are with low rates of return. Since each project is profitable only if its rate of return exceeds the opportunity cost of the investment – the rate of interest – it follows that, as the interest rate falls, planned investment spending increases, and vice versa.* There will be an increasing number of projects which yield a rate of return sufficient to cover interest charges, as interest rates fall. In other words, a fall in interest rates leads to a movement down the investment function.

A hypothetical investment schedule is given in Figure 15.8. If the rate of interest is 13 per cent, then the quantity of planned investment will be 225 million per year. Notice, by the way, that planned investment is also given on a per year basis, showing that it represents a flow, not a stock. (The stock counterpart of investment is the accumulated stock of capital in the economy.)

The rate of return on investments is sometimes called the marginal efficiency of capital (MEC), or the marginal product of capital. Keynes recognized that although interest rates and investment would be related, their relationship (i.e. the marginal efficiency of capital or the investment function) could be unstable.

Other Determinants of Investment

We saw that the consumption function could be related to the level of real disposable income. We also saw that there were other determinants that would shift the schedule up or down. The same analysis can be applied to planned investment. The rate of interest and the rate of planned investment are related. At the same time, there are many other determinants of planned investment. Increased demand in the economy would increase the rate of return. At any given interest rate more investment would take place and the MEC schedule would shift to the right. Other major influences on investment are expectations, the cost of capital equipment, innovation and technology, and the tax treatment of investment expenditure.

EXPECTATIONS

Firms estimate the future demand for their products in order to assess the likely future profitability of their investments. If higher future sales are expected, then

*Even if firms use retained earnings (corporate savings) to finance an investment, the higher the market rate of interest the greater the *opportunity cost* of using those retained earnings, which could have been earning interest, at no risk, in the bank. Thus, it does not matter in our analysis whether the firm must seek financing from external sources or can obtain such financing by using retained earnings.

more machines and bigger plants will be planned for the future. More investment will be undertaken.

Each investment undertaken will yield an income stream in the future, which is the profit from the project. This will be total revenue, less total cost. Estimating revenue means deciding the likely level of sales, at the price which the market will bear. Estimating total cost requires knowledge of the costs of all necessary inputs, and of any technological problems which are likely to arise. The resulting estimate of likely profit, for each year of the life of the investment can then be discounted (i.e. reduced by an amount corresponding to market rates of interest) in order to find its present value. If the present value of the total future income stream, yielded by the investment, is greater than the cost of the capital to be invested, then the project looks profitable enough to be viable. (Chapter 26 explains this in more detail.)

Of course there are risks involved in any investment project. One of these is the risk that unforeseen events, such as inflation, may cause costs and revenues to be less favourable than the firm's estimates suggested they might be. Technical problems may raise costs unexpectedly. Fashions may change the level of demand. The riskier the project, the greater the likelihood of profit must be before the firm goes ahead with the investment.

When firms have rosy expectations, and a high level of confidence about the prospects for their sector of the economy, the investment function will shift outwards to the right; that is, at each interest rate, more will be invested than before. If they expect the future to be grim, the investment schedule will move inwards, to the left, reflecting less desired investment at each and every interest rate.

Consider the possibility that expectations have improved dramatically. What will this do to the investment schedule? In Figure 15.9 we see that the investment schedule will shift outwards from *II* to *I'I'*. Thus, the quantity of planned investment expenditures will increase at each and every rate of interest. The rate of return on capital invested is expected to increase so that at any given interest rate, more investment will take place.

The opposite would occur if expectations took a turn downwards. The planned investment schedule would therefore shift leftwards to *I''I''*. In other words, the planned rate of investment expenditures would fall at each and every rate of interest. Chapter 16 looks in more detail at the effect of changing demand on investment.

COST OF NEW CAPITAL GOODS

If the cost of new plant and equipment suddenly were to increase (*relative* to the price at which output can be sold), firms' investment plans may change. In fact, we would expect the investment function to shift leftwards. The opposite would occur if there were an abrupt, unanticipated fall in the relative cost of capital goods. Investment goods become *relatively* cheaper, even if the price remains the same, if labour costs rise. Labour-saving investment may then increase.

INNOVATION AND TECHNOLOGY

Both improvements in current productive technology and innovations could generally be expected to shift

Figure 15.8

Planned Investment. If we plot interest rate/planned investment data, we obtain the investment function *II*. It is negatively sloped.

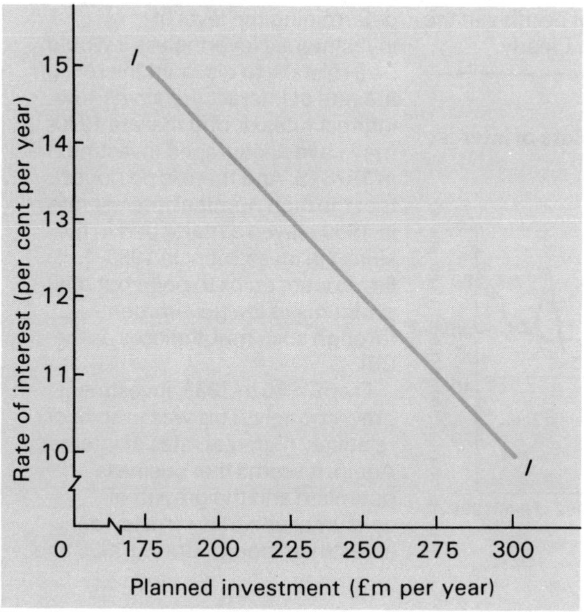

Figure 15.9

Shifts in the Planned Investment Schedule. We start off with a given investment function *II*. Consider the possibility that expectations of future profits have improved dramatically. This will shift the investment schedule to *I'I'*. If expectations change for the worse, then the investment schedule would shift to *I''I''*.

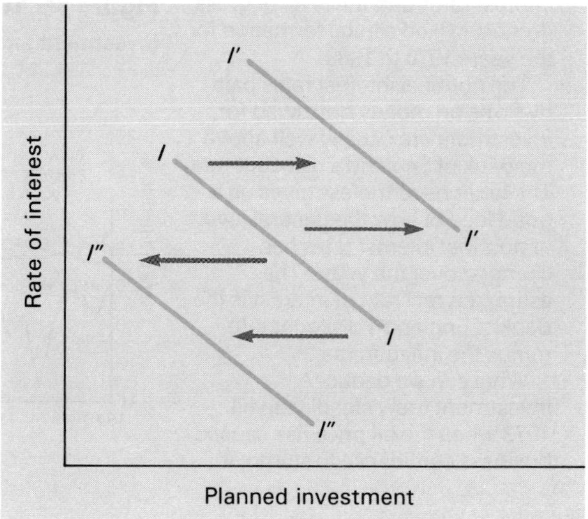

the investment function to the right, since both would stimulate a demand for additional capital goods. In other words, we would see an increase in the demand for capital goods at any given interest rate.

PROFITS TAXES

Firms estimate rates of return on investments on the basis of expected after-tax profits. If there is an increase in tax-rates on profits, other things being equal, we expect a shift in the planned investment function leftwards. If there is a decrease in tax-rates, we expect a shift rightwards.

In the UK, taxes have been designed to encourage firms to plough back profits into the business. For any given rate of interest, investment is likely to be higher if expenditure on capital reduces the tax due.

At least this is the logic. In the UK, rather low levels of profitability caused governments to give generous investment allowances in calculating corporation tax. This led to a substantial subsidy for capital investment. In the 1984 budget the system was changed in order to give more encouragement to investments generating a high rate of return, and to sectors which had not benefited under the old rules. Also, the rate of tax was reduced from 42 per cent to 35 per cent (or 30 per cent for small companies). It was also recognized that subsidizing capital investment makes little economic sense at a time when there is a large excess supply of labour. These measures may have contributed to high levels of investment in the late 1980s.

Key Points 15.4

- **Saving depends primarily on the rate of interest, the rate of inflation, and sometimes, expectations about future economic well being.**
- **Investment is related though not always closely, to interest rates.**
- **Investment is significantly affected by profits or by expectations about future profitability; by the cost (supply price) of capital; by the cost of investment relative to that of labour; and by changes in technology and profits tax.**

CASE STUDY

Are Levels of Investment Sensitive to Changes in Interest Rates, 1970–89?

Figure 15.10 shows estimated real interest rates, the average rate of discount used by the Bank of England (as a representative interest rate), and the level of gross domestic fixed capital formation for the years 1970 to 1989.

The nominal interest rates paid by firms on money borrowed for investment are usually well above the Bank of England's discount rate. The latter nevertheless gives us a good idea of how the general level of nominal interest rates has changed over the years. The estimated real rate of interest is the Bank of England's discount rate minus the inflation rate.

What can we deduce? Investment grew steadily up till 1973 when the oil price rise caused business confidence to slump. It grew again during the boomlet of 1977–9 and slumped horribly in the recession of 1980–1. Clearly

Figure 15.10

Investment and the Rate of Interest

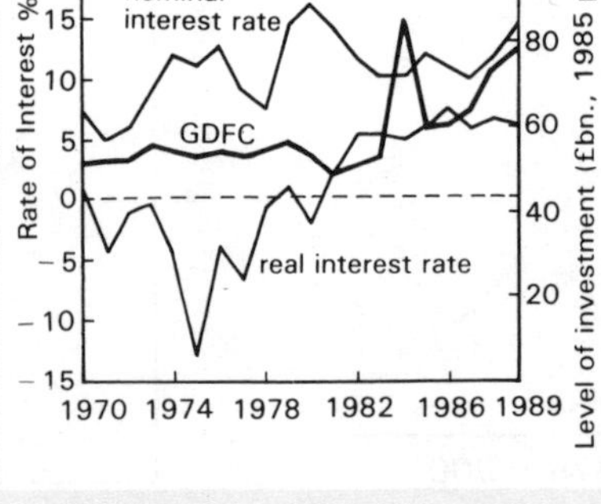

business expectations are crucial in determining the level of investment. Nevertheless it would be a mistake to discount the role of the rate of interest. *Relatively* low interest rates during the late 1970s may have encouraged investment in 1978–9. And there is no doubt that the high nominal interest rate in 1980 played a major part in the slump in investment in 1980–1. Firms were quick to point out their problems to the government through such mouthpieces as the CBI.

From 1986 to 1989, investment grew strongly. This was in spite of relatively high real rates of interest. Again, it seems that business optimism and the growth of consumer spending created an investment boom. During 1988 and

1989 investment continued to grow even though the Chancellor raised interest rates sharply. It was not until nominal interest rates had been in the 13–15 per cent range for over a year that investment really began to grow more slowly. By that time, slow growth of consumption and general business pessimism were having a strong effect.

While it is unlikely that the level of investment will respond to small changes in interest rates, either real or nominal, major and sustained changes may have a substantial effect. However, the effects of interest rates must be set alongside accompanying events. Business confidence, the level of profits, and the growth of demand are vital factors. Interest rates are just one of a range of important influences on the level of investment.

Source: CSO, *Economic Trends, 1989*, and *Treasury Progress Reports*, June 1989.

Questions

1. How has gross domestic fixed capital formation changed over the years?
2. What are the most important factors which determine how individual firms decide their investment spending?
3. When will high nominal interest rates have a serious effect on investment decisions?
4. What determines the level of real interest rates?
5. Have real interest rates had a significant effect on investment levels?

CASE STUDY

The Savings Ratio in the UK during the 1980s

The savings ratio varies considerably from year to year. There are a number of possible influences at work, often simultaneously. The level of income may influence saving in two ways. There may be a simple direct relationship. Income rises so people save more. Or, the permanent income hypothesis suggests that an increase in income which is temporary will lead to higher savings because consumption will remain stable.

These hypothetical connections between savings and income levels are not borne out by the data in Figure 15.11. There is an alternative theory of savings, which fits somewhat better. Inflation reduces the value of money. If people keep their savings in the form of money-denominated assets (i.e. bank and building society accounts, or bonds), these assets will lose some of their value as inflation takes its toll. If, for precautionary reasons, people want to hold a certain amount of purchasing power in savings, this loss of value will matter. In order to restore the value of their assets after a period of higher than usual inflation, people will have to save more than previously.

If you refer to Figure 11.10 (p. 184), we can see that inflation fell sharply in 1982, and thereafter stayed rather lower than it had been during the 1970s. This fall in inflation could mean that people felt less need to save than they had when inflation was eroding the value of their assets.

Alternatively, we can say that a low level of saving implies a high level of consumption. Figure 15.12 shows consumption data. Record levels of borrowing have provided the finance for increased levels of consumption. The rise in house

Figure 15.11

The Personal Sector Savings Ratio, 1980–9

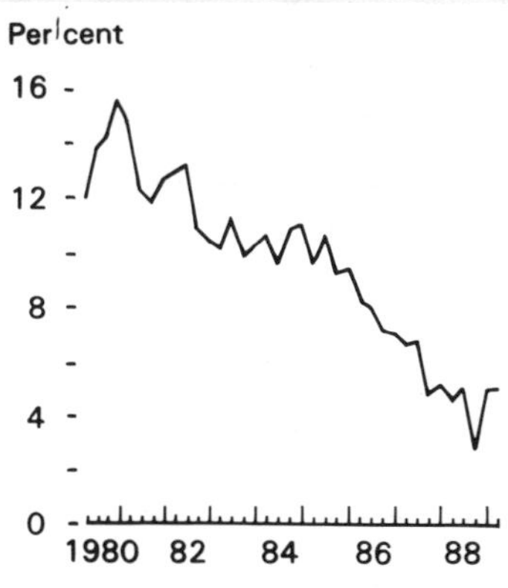

Figure 15.12

Income and consumption 1980–7 (revised)

	Marginal propensity to consume (MPC)[1]	*Average propensity to consume (APC)*[2]	*Income elasticity of consumption*[3]
1980	80.3	83.7	0.95
1981	103.3	85.4	1.23
1982	108.0	87.1	1.26
1983	91.9	87.5	1.05
1984	91.2	87.7	1.04
1985	85.2	87.5	0.97
1986	89.3	87.7	1.02
1987	98.6	88.4	1.12

1. MPC = increase in consumption/increase in personal disposable income.
2. APC = consumption/personal disposable income. (1−APC) = saving ratio.
3. Equals the annual % change in consumption/the annual % change in personal disposable income.

Source: *Lloyds Bank Bulletin*, Oct. 1988.

prices added to personal wealth and was partly responsible for consumers feeling rich enough to spend a larger percentage of their incomes on consumption.

While personal saving fell in the late 1980s, corporate saving grew. Corporate saving takes place when firms retain some of their profits, usually with a view to financing future investment. Higher than usual profits made increased corporate saving possible. It increased from a low point of 7.5 per cent of GDP in 1981 to about 12.5 per cent in 1988.

Questions

1. Is there any evidence that the level of interest rates might affect saving?
2. What effect would you expect income levels to have upon savings and consumption?
3. What major factors seem to have caused the sharp fall in saving during the 1980s?

Exam Preparation

PRACTICAL EXERCISE

1. Complete the following table

Disposable income (£)	*Consumption (£)*	*Saving (£)*
500	510	—
600	600	—
700	690	—
800	780	—
900	870	—
1 000	960	—

(a) Plot the consumption and saving schedules on graph paper.
(b) Determine the marginal propensity to consume and the marginal propensity to save.
(c) Determine the average propensity to consume and the average propensity to save for each level of income.

2. Consider the following table, then answer the questions below it.

Annual consumption (£)	*Annual income (£)*
5	0
80	100
155	200

(a) What is the APC at the annual income level £100? At £200?
(b) What happens to the APC as annual income rises?
(c) What is the MPC as annual income goes from £0 to £100? From £100 to £200?
(d) What happens to the MPC as income rises?
(e) What number is the APC approaching?
(f) What is the equation for the consumption function in this table?

3. Consider the following table, then answer the questions below it.

Annual consumption (£)	*Annual income (£)*
0	0
80	100
160	200

(a) What is the APC at annual income £100? At £200?
(b) What happens to the APC as annual income rises?
(c) What is the MPC as income rises from £0 to £100? From £100 to £200?
(d) What happens to the MPC as income rises?
(e) What is the equation for the consumption function in this table?
(f) In what way has consumption changed in this question, compared to the situation in Question 2?

MULTIPLE CHOICE QUESTIONS

1. The following data represent a consumption function for an economy

Income (£m)	*Consumption (£m)*
120	116
140	132
160	148
180	164
200	180
220	196

What is the value of the marginal propensity to consume in this economy?

A 0.00
B 0.80
C 0.90
D 0.91
E 0.98

2. If the marginal propensity to consume is rising as income rises, then the

A marginal propensity to save is rising
B marginal propensity to save is constant
C average propensity to consume is rising
D average propensity to consume is constant
E average propensity to save is rising

3. An analysis of expenditure by households at different income levels suggests that average propensity to consume (APC) is equal to the marginal propensity to consume (MPC) over low-income levels. However, at high-income levels, MPC declines with income and is less than the APC. Which one of the following describes these findings?

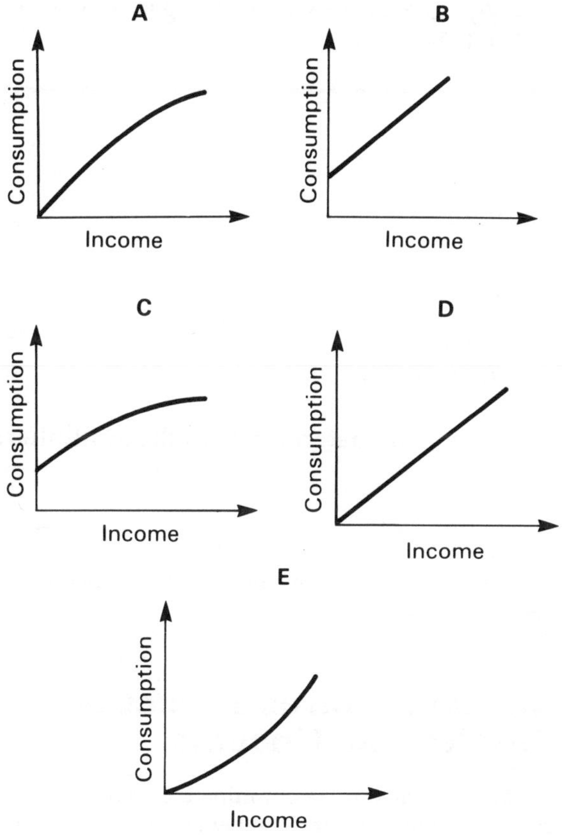

One or more of the options given in Questions 4 and 5 may be correct. Select your answer by means of the code set out in the grid.

A	B	C	D	E
1, 2, 3, all correct	1, 2 only correct	2, 3 only correct	1 only correct	3 only correct

4. Redistributing income from high- to low-income groups is likely to change aggregate consumption if

1 the average propensity to consume is constant
2 the consumption function shows a diminishing marginal propensity to consume as income rises.
3 the marginal propensity to consume of low-income groups equals unity.

5.

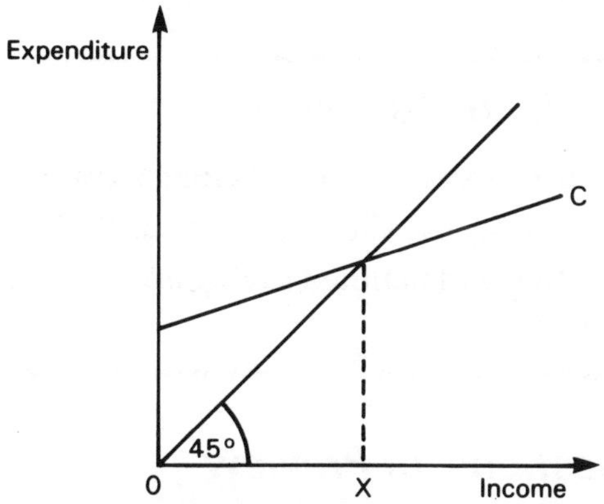

The above diagram illustrates

1 at levels of income above OX, dissaving is taking place
2 the average propensity to consume is constant
3 at income level OX the average propensity to consume is equal to unity

RELATED ESSAY QUESTIONS

1. What factors determine the level of investment in an economy? Why has the rate of investment generally been lower in the UK than in most other industrialized countries?

2. Explain the difference between consumption and investment. Discuss in which category you would place housing and education.

16 Income and Employment Determination: A Simple Model

Key Points to Review

- Shift versus movement along a curve (5.6)
- Equilibrium, shortage, surplus (5.7)
- Actual and planned saving and investment (12.2)
- National income equals national product (13.1)
- Aggregate supply and aggregate demand (14.1, 14.2)

Questions for Preview

1 What does the total *planned* expenditure curve indicate?

2 What is the interpretation of the 45-degree line?

3 Why does the equilibrium level of real national income occur at the point of intersection of the total planned expenditure curve and the 45-degree reference line?

4 What is the multiplier, how does it work, and what is the main determinant of the multiplier?

5 What is the paradox of thrift?

Why is the equilibrium level of real national income what it is? We can answer this question using a Keynesian model of income determination, subject to simplifying assumptions. The most important assumption is that the short-run aggregate supply curve is horizontal at the existing price level. The implication of this is that the equilibrium level of real national income is demand-determined. We do not have to worry about either supply constraints or changes in the price level, at least not initially.

In Chapter 12 we found that the circular flow was only in equilibrium when total planned expenditures were equal to total national output. Also, in equilibrium planned saving must equal planned investment. Whenever such was not the case, there would be unplanned changes in stocks. The unplanned changes would either cause a contraction or an expansion of the circular flow. We can now determine when the circular flow will be in equilibrium. We need to determine when aggregate (total) planned expenditure equals planned production. Since, for the moment, we are ignoring government expenditures as well as the foreign sector (net exports), our analysis involves only planned consumption expenditures and planned investment expenditures.

Consumption as a Function of Real National Income

We are interested in determining the equilibrium level of real national income. But when we examined the consumption function in the last chapter, it related planned consumption expenditures to the level of real disposable income per year. Disposable income is national income less taxes plus transfer payments.

If we assume that real disposable income is the same proportion of real national income every year, then we can substitute real national income for real disposable income in the consumption function.

The 45-degree Line

Along the **45-degree line**, planned expenditures equal real national income per year. In Figure 16.1, at the point where the consumption function intersects the

Figure 16.1

Combining Consumption and Investment. This graph is simply the consumption function with autonomous investment, *I*, added. The arrow, labelled *I*, shows by how much investment raises expenditure. The result is the consumption plus investment line, *C* + *I*, or the total planned expenditure function relating planned expenditures to different levels of real national income, under the assumption that there is no government or foreign sector.

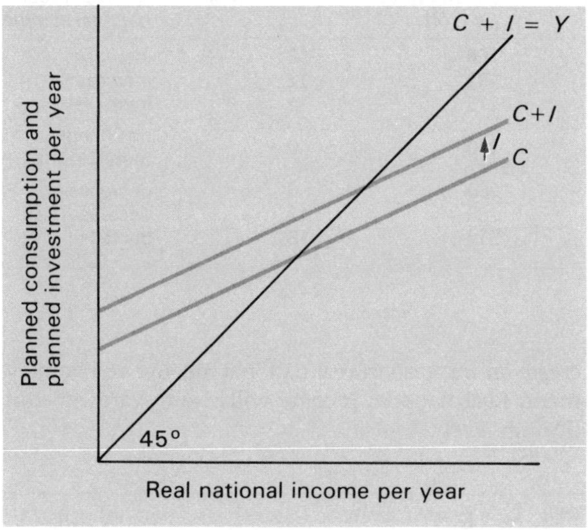

45-degree line, planned consumption expenditures will be exactly equal to real national income per year.

Adding the Investment Function

We add now the other component of private aggregate demand: investment spending (*I*). We simplify our model by considering all planned investment to be autonomous, that is, independent of income. Firms plan to invest a given, constant *amount* and will do so no matter what the level of income. How do we add this amount of investment to our consumption function? We simply add a line above the *C* line in Figure 16.1 that is higher by the vertical distance equal to the amount of autonomous investment. This distance is shown by the arrow connecting the consumption function *C* to the expenditure function, *C* + *I*.

If we ignore government expenditures and net exports (the foreign sector), the *C* + *I* line represents total planned expenditures for the economy at different levels of real national income per year. (Now read Key Points 16.1.)

Determining the Equilibrium Level of Real National Income

We continue to assume that a Keynesian short-run horizontal aggregate supply curve exists, that there is no government or foreign sector, and that investment is autonomous, and that planned consumption expenditures are determined by the level of real national income.

Assume that the consumption function has an autonomous component equal to £33 billion per year, and that the marginal propensity to consume, out of real national income, is 0.8, or four-fifths.

Using this consumption function gives us the values for consumption in column (2) of Figure 16.2 (page 244), and also the values of savings in column (3).

Planned investment in column (4) is assumed to be autonomous at a level of £15 billion per year no matter what the level of national income. Column (5) is the sum of planned consumption and planned investment. In Figure 16.3 (page 244) the horizontal axis measures real national income and the vertical axis measures consumption and investment expenditure. The consumption figures in column (2) are used to plot the consumption function *C*.

Equilibrium will occur when total planned expenditures equal total production. In Figure 16.3 total planned expenditures are given by the *C* + *I* line, which is also equivalent to aggregate demand. Total planned expenditures will equal total production, or real national income, where the *C* + *I* line intersects the 45-degree line at *E*, because points along that line are equidistant from both axes. At point *E*, there is no tendency for the equilibrium level of real national income to change. Thus at £240 billion per year, we have the equilibrium level of real national income.

Key Points 16.1

- **On all of our diagrams relating planned expenditures to real national income, we will use a 45-degree line, along which planned expenditures will be exactly equal to real national income per year.**
- **For simplicity's sake, we assume that investment is autonomous and therefore constant and unrelated to the level of real national income.**
- **When we add autonomous investment, *I*, to the consumption function, we obtain the *C* + *I* curve which represents total planned expenditures for the economy, assuming no government expenditures and no foreign sector.**

Figure 16.2

The Determination of Equilibrium Real National Income. Given that prices are constant and the short-run aggregate supply schedule is horizontal at the current price level, the equilibrium level of real national income is demand-determined only. Consequently, whenever total planned expenditures – planned consumption plus planned investment – equal real national income, equilibrium will occur. In our hypothetical example, equilibrium occurs at £240 billion per year. At this level of real national income, planned expenditures equal real national income, planned saving equals planned investment, and there are no unplanned changes in stocks.

(1) Real national income (£bn)	*(2) Planned consumption (£bn)*	*(3) Planned saving (£bn)*	*(4) Planned investment (£bn)*	*(5) Total planned expenditures (2) + (4)*	*(6) Unplanned stock changes (£bn)*	*(7) Direction of change in real national income*
150	153	−3	15	168	−18	increase
180	177	3	15	192	−12	increase
210	201	9	15	216	−6	increase
240	225	15	15	240	0	no change (equilibrium)
270	249	21	15	264	6	decrease
300	273	27	15	288	12	decrease
330	297	33	15	312	18	decrease

What about Employment?

What will be the level of employment associated with the equilibrium level of income? This figure depends on the number of employees required to produce £240 billions' worth of output annually. It may or may not be the number of people wanting work. Given a fixed amount of capital and a steady state of technology – reasonable assumptions in the short run, as it takes time to increase capital and improve technology – we can predict that an increase in output will be associated with a higher level of employment, and vice versa.

What Happens When There is Disequilibrium?

What happens if total planned expenditures exceed real national income (total planned production) or vice versa?

TOTAL PLANNED EXPENDITURES EXCEED REAL NATIONAL INCOME

If we start with a real national income at £180 billion, in Figure 16.3, we see that at this real national income level, annual planned consumption will be £177 billion. Adding planned investment of £15 billion, we get total planned expenditures of £192 billion, which exceeds real national income by £12 billion. The planned investment of firms exceeds the planned saving of households. In other words, goods and services are being bought at a faster rate than they are being produced. The result of this is seen in column (6) of Figure 16.2. Stocks are being run down at the rate of £12 billion a year, exactly the rate by which total planned expenditures exceed real national income (planned production). As a result, firms will seek to expand their production; they will take on more labour. This will create an increase in real national income and employment. Real national income will rise toward its equilibrium level.

Figure 16.3

The Equilibrium Level of Real National Income. The equilibrium level of real national income will be established at that level of real national income per year where total planned expenditures, as evidenced by the *C* + *I* line, interesect the 45-degree line, because that is where total planned expenditures will exactly equal real national income (production). In this diagram, equilibrium occurs at point *E* with an equilibrium level of real national income of £240 billion per year.

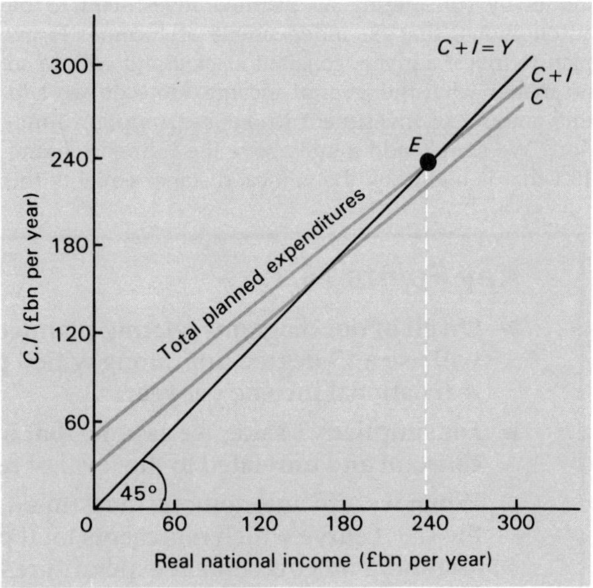

Key Points 16.2

- **The equilibrium level of real national income is at the intersection of the total planned expenditure line with the 45-degree line. At that level of real national income, planned consumption plus planned investment will equal real national income.**
- **When total planned expenditures exceed real national income, there will be unplanned decreases in stocks; the size of the circular flow of income will increase and the economy will expand.**
- **Whenever planned expenditures are less than real national income, there will be unplanned increases in stocks, the size of the circular flow will shrink – a lower equilibrium level of real national income will prevail.**
- **If we know the relationship between real national income and the required labour force, then we can determine the level of employment consistent with any given equilibrium level of real national income.**

TOTAL PLANNED EXPENDITURES ARE LESS THAN REAL NATIONAL INCOME

Now take the opposite situation. Real national income is at the £300-billion level. At that level of real national income, planned consumption is £273 billion and planned investment is still £15 billion. Total planned expenditures, $C + I$, now equal £288 billion, which is less than real national income (planned production) of £300 billion. In other words, the rate at which households plan to save exceeds the rate at which firms plan to invest. This means that firms will find their sales less than they had expected. Stocks will accumulate, as we see in column (6), at the rate of £12 billion per year. This unplanned accumulation of stocks causes firms to cut back on their production and, therefore, lay off employees. The result will be a drop in employment toward the equilibrium level, £240 billion. (Now read Key Points 16.2.)

Another Approach: Leakages and Injections

We can look at the determination of the equilibrium level of real national income using leakages and injections.

In Chapter 12, we defined **leakages** as withdrawals of potential planned expenditures from the income–expenditures stream. Leakages are saving, purchases of goods from other countries (imports), and taxes. Whenever there is a leakage, consumption necessarily falls. Leakages tend to reduce the equilibrium level of national income, unless, of course, leakages are offset by injections.

Injections are additions of potential planned expenditures to the income–expenditures stream. They add spending to the flow. Injections are investment, government spending, and foreign purchases of UK goods (exports). Injections tend to increase the equilibrium level of real national income, and they offset leakages.

To simplify, we must continue to assume that there is one leakage – saving – and one injection – investment. Chapter 17 introduces the other leakages and injections.

ATTAINING EQUILIBRIUM

When planned leakages equal planned injections, total planned expenditures will equal real national income. Equilibrium will occur because the total planned amount of non-consumption (leakages) equals the total planned amount of supplemental expenditures (injections).

GRAPHICAL ANALYSIS

In our model so far in this chapter, investment has been autonomous, that is, fixed at some level and not a function of aggregate income. In Figure 16.4 (page 246) we show real national income per year on the horizontal axis and saving and investment per year on the vertical axis. At point E, the intersection of II and SS, the equilibrium level of real national output is determined.

THE BATH-WATER THEOREM

One can visualize a bath with a specified level of water already in it. The drain is open; this is clearly a leakage. Unless there is an injection, the level of the water will fall. The injection will be water from the tap. The leakage represents saving; the injection represents investment, and the level of the bath-water represents national output (which is exactly equal to real national income).

Using the Leakages–Injections Approach

The leakages–injections approach can show us the reasons why the equilibrium level of real national income may be different from levels of real national

Figure 16.4

Leakages–Injections Approach to Equilibrium. On the horizontal axis we measure real national income per year. On the vertical axis we measure saving and investment per year. Saving constitutes a leakage. Investment constitutes an injection. Leakages equal injections where the saving schedule *SS* intersects the investment schedule *II*. This occurs at point *E*, yielding an equilibrium level of real national income per year of Y_e.

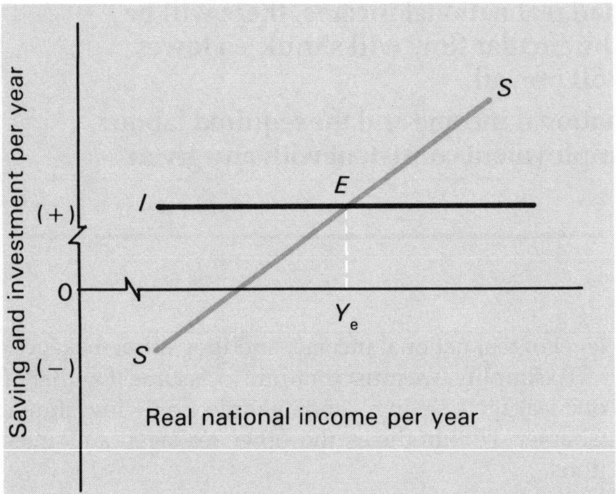

income that policy-makers might consider acceptable. Leakages in our simplified example are represented by *desired* rates of saving. Injections, on the other hand, are represented by desired rates of investment. Desired (or planned) saving and desired (or planned) investment are carried out by different parts of society and for different reasons. Basically, households save in order to provide for emergencies, retirement, and so on. Firms on the other hand invest in order to increase plant and equipment, as well as to build up stocks. Since savers and investors are often different groups of people acting for different reasons, we have no assurance that desired saving will equal desired investment at a national output and income level that results in an acceptable rate of employment. Suppose, for example, that we start off in equilibrium, where planned investment equals planned saving. Planned investment might then rise. But since investment decisions are frequently made by individuals different from those making saving decisions, there is no guarantee that *planned* saving will also rise by an equivalent amount. As another example, suppose that after starting out initially in an equilibrium where planned investment equals planned saving, savers, for whatever reason, increase their planned saving. Firms cannot be expected to automatically increase planned investment by an equal amount. Indeed the resulting loss of demand for consumer goods may make their proposals quite gloomy.

Saving and Investment: Planned versus Actual

Figure 16.5 shows planned investment as a horizontal line at £15 billion per year. Investment is constant and does not depend on the level of income.

Planned saving is represented by *SS*. It is taken directly from Figure 16.2 which shows planned saving in column (3) and real national income in column (1). The planned saving schedule is the complement of the planned consumption schedule, represented by the *C* line in Figure 16.3

Figure 16.5

Planned and Actual Rates of Saving and Investment. Only at the equilibrium level of real national income of £240 billion per year will planned saving equal actual saving, planned investment equal actual investment, and therefore planned saving equal planned investment. At higher income levels, planned investment will be less than actual investment, the difference being made up of unplanned decreases in stocks. The opposite is true for all income levels less than £240 billion per year.

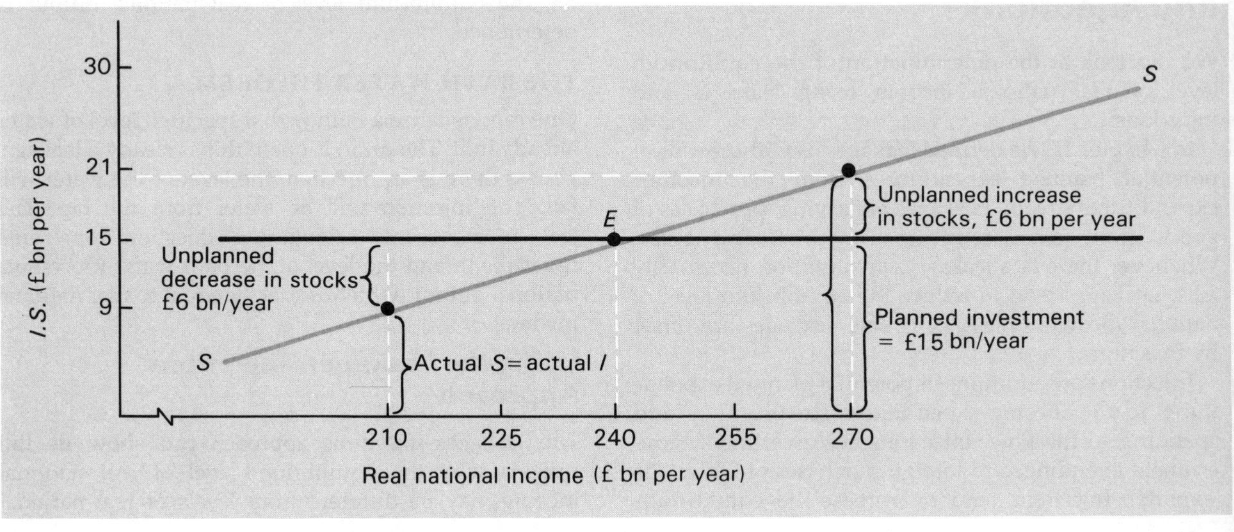

Why does equilibrium have to occur at the intersection of the planned saving and planned investment schedules? If we are at E in Figure 16.5, planned saving equals planned investment. There is no tendency for firms to alter the rate of production or level of employment, because they are neither increasing nor decreasing their stocks in an unplanned way.

However, if output is at £270 billion, planned investment is £15 billion as usual, but planned saving is £21 billion. This means that consumers will purchase less of total output than firms had anticipated. There will be an unplanned increase in stocks of £6 billion bringing actual investment into line with actual saving. But this rate of output cannot continue for long. Firms will respond to this unplanned increase in stocks by cutting back production and employment, and we will move towards a lower level of real national income.

On the other hand, if the real national income is £210 billion per year, planned investment continues annually at £15 billion; but at that output rate, planned saving is only £9 billion. This means that households and firms are purchasing more of the real national income than firms had expected. They must run down stocks below the planned level by £6 billion bringing actual investment into equality with actual saving. This situation cannot last forever either. In their attempt to increase stocks to the desired previous level, firms will increase output and employment, and real national income will rise towards its equilibrium value of £240 billion. Figure 16.5 demonstrates the necessary equality between actual saving and actual investment. Stocks adjust so that saving and investment, after the fact, are *always* equal.

Every time the saving rate planned by households differs from the investment rate planned by firms, there will be an expansion or contraction in the circular flow in the form of unplanned changes in stocks. Real national income and employment will change until there are no unplanned stock changes, that is, until we have attained the equilibrium level of real national income. (Now read Key Points 16.3, page 248.)

Figure 16.6

Changes in Equilibrium Real National Income. In panel (a) the $C + I_1$ curve intersects the 45-degree line at point E. Therefore, the equilibrium level of real national income is Y_1. This is also shown in panel (b). Leakages are shown by the saving schedule, SS; injections are shown by the autonomous investment function, I_1I_1. Those two functions intersect also at point E, giving the same equilibrium level of real national income per year of Y_1. A shift upwards in the investment schedule to I_2I_2 causes the total planned expenditures curve to shift upwards to $C + I_2$. The new equilibrium level of real national income per year is Y_2 in both panels (a) and (b). A decrease in the investment schedule to I_3I_3 causes the total planned expenditures curve to drop to $C + I_3$. The new equilibrium level of real national income per year is Y_3 in both panels (a) and (b). Notice that the change in the equilibrium level of real national income per year was greater than the change in autonomous investment.

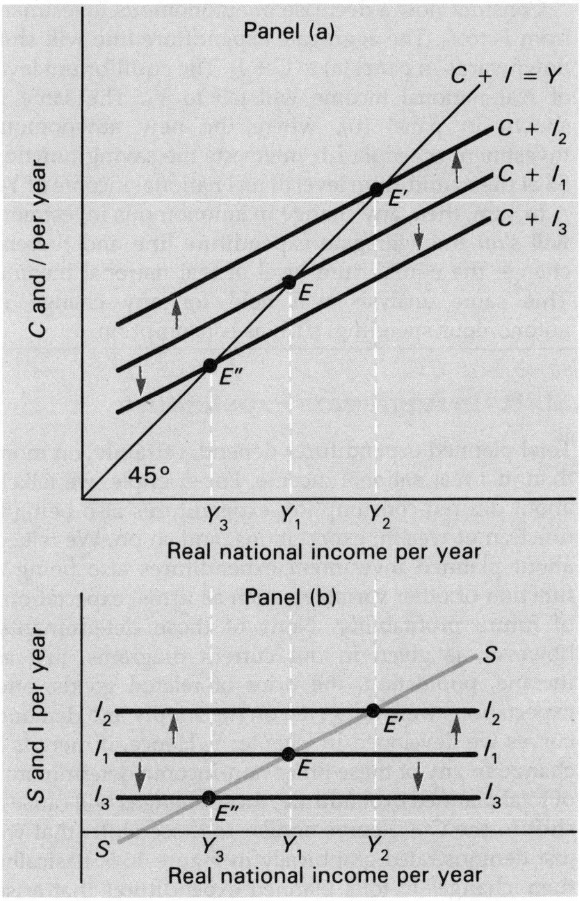

Changes in Equilibrium Real National Income and the Multiplier

The actual level of real national income is not in fact very stable. We have had long-run growth along with the ups and downs of the trade cycle. We will try now to explain *why* the equilibrium level of real national income fluctuates and *how* it fluctuates.

In our simplified model a change in autonomous investment will clearly change the equilibrium level of real national output. Figure 16.6 shows the determination of the equilibrium level of real national income per year using the two approaches previously given. In panel (a), we find that with schedule $C + I_1$, the equilibrium level of real national income will be Y_1, shown on the horizontal axis. Given the consumption function implicit in panel (a), we have its complement, the saving function, shown as SS in panel (b). Given a level of investment I_1, the equilibrium level of real national income per year is also Y_1. In panel (b), we use the leakages–injections approach. Note that the total planned expenditures in panel (a) consist of two parts – consumption and investment. Initially, investment is at I_1.

Consider an increase in autonomous investment

Key Points 16.3

- **The equilibrium level of real national income can be found where leakages equal injections, or where planned saving equals planned investment.**
- **Whenever planned saving exceeds planned investment, there will be an unplanned increase in stocks. Incomes will fall – the economy will contract.**
- **Whenever planned saving is less than planned investment, there will be an unplanned decrease in stocks. Incomes will rise – the economy will expand.**

from I_1 to I_2. This *shifts* the aggregate expenditure or demand schedule to $C + I_2$. The equilibrium level of real national income increases to Y_2 in panel (a). In panel (b), the intersection of SS with the new autonomous investment line I_2I_2, is also at that equilibrium of Y_2.

Consider now a decrease in autonomous investment from I_2 to I_3. The aggregate expenditure line will shift downwards in panel (a) to $C + I_3$. The equilibrium level of real national income will fall to Y_3. The same is shown in panel (b), where the new autonomous investment schedule I_3I_3 intersects the saving function SS at the equilibrium level of real national income of Y_3.

In sum, then, any change in autonomous investment will *shift* the aggregate expenditure line and thereby change the equilibrium level of real national income. This same analysis will hold for any change in autonomous spending, such as consumption.

Shifts in Aggregate Expenditure

Total planned expenditures depend, certainly, on more than just real national income. For example, we talked about desired consumption expenditures also being a function of wealth, expectations, and so on. We talked about planned investment expenditures also being a function of other variables, such as firms' expectations of future profitability. None of those determinants, however, is given in our current diagrams, just as income, population, the price of related goods, and expectations were not given on the supply and demand curves we developed in Chapter 5. Hence, if there is a change in any of these other non-income determinants of total planned expenditure, those changes will cause a shift in the $C + I$ curve similar to those shifts that we just demonstrated graphically in Figure 16.6. Basically, then, changes in total planned expenditures that arise from reasons other than changes in real national income are represented by shifts in the $C + I$ curve. (Now read Key Points 16.4.)

The Multiplier Effect of Changes in Autonomous Spending

In Figure 16.6, the change in investment that caused the $C + I_1$ curve to shift up and down is relatively small compared to the resulting change in the equilibrium level of national income and output. It turns out that the change in the equilibrium level of real national income will always be larger than the change in autonomous investment. In Figure 16.7 an increase in investment of £5 billion shifts the $C + I$ line upwards. The new equilibrium level of income has increased by much more than the initial increase in investment, in fact by five times that amount.

The Multiplier

What is operating here is the **multiplier** effect of changes in autonomous spending. The multiplier is the number by which a change in autonomous investment or autonomous consumption is multiplied to get the change in the equilibrium level of real national income. In other words, any increases in autonomous investment will cause a larger increase in real national income.

To get an idea of how a larger increase in income results from a given increase in investment, we can follow the progress of the increased injection around the circular flow of money. If investment rises by £5 billion, some firms are buying more plant and machinery. In doing so they increase demand for other firms'

Key Point 16.4

- **A shift in autonomous consumption or investment will cause the aggregate expenditure line to shift also. A new equilibrium level of real national income will then result.**

Figure 16.7

The Multiplier Effect. Investment, and total expenditure, rise by £5 billion. As a result real national income increases by £25 billion.

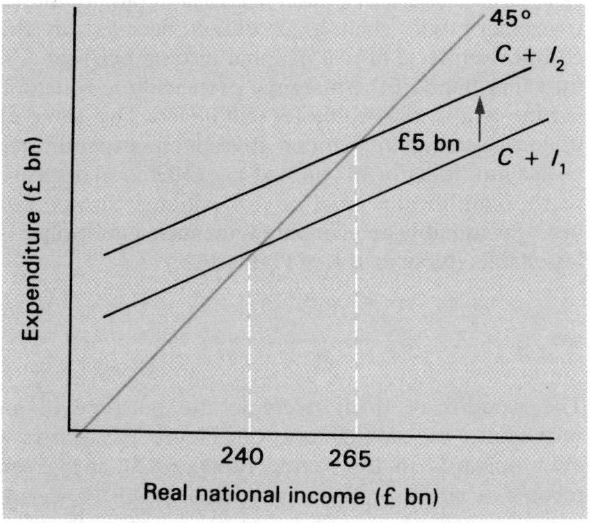

products. These other firms will need to increase their output of investment goods and to do so, will take on more labour. The new employees (assuming they were previously unemployed) will now have wages, profits will have increased, and total income will have risen by the £5 billion spent. If we assume, as before, an MPC of four-fifths and an MPS of one-fifth, we know how households will allocate their increased income: consumption will rise by £4 billion and savings by £1 billion.

This addition to consumption adds further to aggregate demand. This time, firms producing consumer goods find sales rising and stocks falling. They will increase output, take on more labour, pay more in wages, and earn more profit. Again incomes have risen and a further increase in consumption will occur. If we continue to calculate the increase in induced expenditure occurring as a result of this expansion in the economy, the general extent of the total increase in income becomes apparent. Figure 16.8 gives the figures involved.

The Multiplier Formula

It is possible to find the full extent of the multiplier effect by extending Figure 16.8 through many more rounds. In each successive round, aggregate expenditure increases by the previous increase in income, multiplied by the MPC, 0.8. See if you can work out the effect of three more rounds of the circular flow. You will find that the sum of all the successive increases in income will be five times the initial increase in investment, if the MPC is 0.8, and the MPS 0.2.

Alternatively, we can find the formula for the multiplier by comparing the original equilibrium position with the new equilibrium position, after the full multiplier effect has worked its way through the economy. First we define the multiplier:

The multiplier is the amount by which we would multiply an initial change in expenditure to find the ultimate change in income.

Stated another way, that is the ratio of the change in income to the change in expenditure which brought it about.

We can call this change in expenditure ΔI: the Greek letter Δ means 'a change in'. Similarly we call the change in income ΔY. The multiplier is therefore:

$$\Delta Y / \Delta I$$

ΔY is the difference between the initial equilibrium level of income and the ultimate equilibrium level of income, once the multiplier has fully worked through the system.

Figure 16.8

The Multiplier Effect of a £5 billion per year Increase in *I* – the Multiplier Process. We trace the effects of a £5 billion increase in investment spending on the equilibrium level of real national income. If we assume a marginal propensity to consume of 0.8, such an increase will eventually elicit £25 billion increase in the equilibrium level of real national income. Notice that with each successive round income increases, but by slightly less than before.

Round	*Increase in real national income (£m/yr)*	*Increase in planned consumption (£m/yr)*	*Increase in planned saving (£m/yr)*
1 (£5bn/yr increase in I)	5 000	4 000	1 000
2	4 000	3 200	800
3	3 200	2 560	640
4	2 560	2 048	512
5	2 048	1 638	410
.	.	.	.
.	.	.	.
.	.	.	.
All later rounds	8 192	6 554	1 638
Totals ($C + I'$)	25 000	20 000	5 000

What do we know about the equilibrium level of income? We know that planned injections and planned leakages will be equal. It follows that the size of the *increase* in planned injections must be equal to the amount by which planned leakages have increased when the new equilibrium has been reached. Stated symbolically:

$$\Delta Y \times \text{MPS} = \Delta I$$

$\Delta Y \times$ MPS is equal to the increase in savings, because the increase in savings is determined by the MPS and the increase in income.

We can now rearrange the equation to arrive at the multiplier. Dividing both sides by the MPS, we get

$$\Delta Y = \frac{\Delta I}{\text{MPS}}$$

And dividing both sides by ΔI,

$$\frac{\Delta Y}{\Delta I} = \frac{1}{\text{MPS}}$$

An alternative way of stating this uses the fact that, in a closed economy with no government,

$$\text{MPC} + \text{MPS} = 1$$

or $\text{MPS} = 1 - \text{MPC}$

Then the multiplier can be written:

$$\frac{\Delta Y}{\Delta I} = \frac{1}{1 - \text{MPC}}$$

The greater the MPS, and the lower the MPC, the lower will be the multiplier. The common sense of this is that with a high marginal propensity to save, more of any given increase in expenditure leaks away in savings, and therefore does not add to consumption demand. Equally the lower the MPS, the more any given increase in expenditure adds to consumption and therefore to demand.

If we calculate the multiplier using data on the MPC, we can use it to predict how much a given change in expenditure will affect income.

multiplier × change in expenditure = change in equilibrium level of real national income.

The multiplier, as we mentioned, works both for an increase and a decrease in expenditure. If there has been a decrease, we speak of a downward multiplier effect.

The Significance of the Multiplier

As we just stated, the larger the marginal propensity to consume, the larger the multiplier. If the marginal propensity to consume is one-half, the multiplier is two. In that case a £1 billion decrease in (autonomous) investment will elicit a £2 billion decrease in the equilibrium level of real national income per year. On the other hand, if the marginal propensity to consume is nine-tenths, the multiplier will be ten. That same £1 billion decrease in planned investment expenditures with a multiplier of 10 will lead to a £10 billion decrease in the equilibrium level of real national income per year. Presumably an economy with such a multiplier is less stable. (Now read Key Points 16.5.)

The Paradox of Thrift

The paradox of thrift refers to the outcome of an increase in the saving function. Figure 16.9 shows a shift upwards in the saving function. At any given income, a larger proportion of income will be saved, because people have decided to behave more thriftily. Any of the reasons given earlier, as to why consumption or savings might change, could account for this.

Figure 16.9

The Paradox of Thrift. With the new saving function $S'S'$, there is a new, lower, equilibrium level of income, Y_2. Here planned saving is again equal to planned investment.

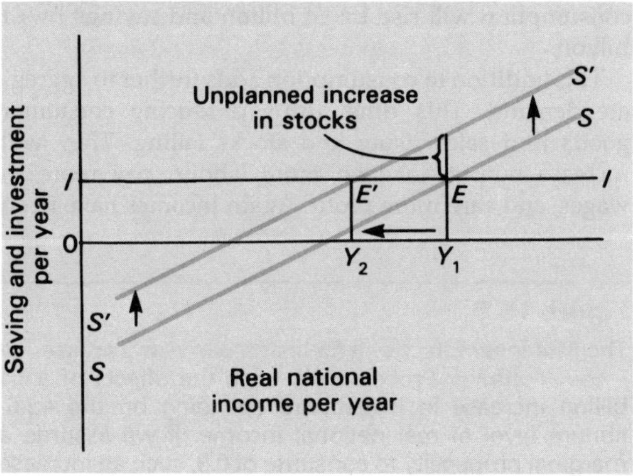

Key Points 16.5

- **Any change in autonomous expenditure causes a multiplier effect on the equilibrium level of real national income per year.**
- **The multiplier is equal to the reciprocal of the marginal propensity to save.**
- **The smaller the marginal propensity to save, the greater the multiplier. Otherwise stated, the greater the marginal propensity to consume, the larger the multiplier.**

With the initial increase in saving, planned leakages exceed planned injections. Consumption must fall; aggregate expenditure will be less than current output and firms will find that stocks are rising. They will cut production and after a time reduce employment too. So incomes will fall. But of course a fall in income means that saving will gradually fall back again – hence the paradox.

So long as planned saving exceeds planned investment, income will continue to fall because there is a leakage from the circular flow which is not balanced by injections. Incomes will cease falling once the new lower level of saving is again equal to planned investment at Y_2.

The outcome is that an intention to save more, in macroeconomic terms, leads to falling income and employment, and therefore, ultimately, to falling saving.

Is Increased Thriftiness always 'Bad'?

This argument seems to indicate that increased thriftiness on the part of individuals may end up being bad for the nation. The equilibrium level of real national income per year falls, as does the amount of saving. Whether this is bad or not depends on the general level of employment. If people are saving more because unemployment is rising and they are fearful for the future, then increased saving is bad in that it will reduce real income. But supposing unemployment is low. That which is saved is not consumed. More saving means that resources can be reallocated away from consumption and devoted to investment in new plant and equipment. Investment adds to the future productive capacity of the nation. As we will see in Chapter 34 more investment typically leads to a higher rate of economic growth. The prime example has been Japan, a country that has saved and invested at a rate nearly double that of the UK. Not surprisingly, Japan has experienced a rate of economic growth that is the envy of most of the world.

Only when there is a serious problem of less than full employment should we worry about individuals wanting to save too much.

Expansionary and Output Gaps

These are sometimes termed inflationary and deflationary gaps. It is possible that the equilibrium level of real national income per year is greater than potential output, perhaps because all the resources needed are fully employed. In Figure 16.10 we see that this has occurred. Full-capacity output is given as Y_1 per year, but the intersection of the total planned expenditures curve with the 45-degree line is at a greater level of real national income per year. There exists, at the full-employment level of real national income, therefore, an **expansionary gap.** An expansionary gap exists whenever the equilibrium level of real national income exceeds the full-capacity level of output. Clearly, an expansionary gap means that there will be pressure on the price level and that we would have to abandon our assumption of a fixed price level. The implication is that the economy would be on the upward-sloping part of the aggregate supply curve.

It is also possible for the equilibrium level of real national income per year to be less than the full-capacity level. When this occurs, we talk in terms of an **output gap**. We show an output gap in the bottom part of Figure 16.10. There the intersection of the total planned expenditures curve with the 45-degree line is at a level of real national income that is below the full-capacity level. As we will see in the next chapter, various proposed government policies can be used to fill the output gap.

Figure 16.10

Expansionary and Output Gaps. In the top diagram, at the full-capacity level of real national income per year, Y_1, total planned expenditures exceed real national income per year. There is therefore an expansionary gap. In the bottom diagram, total planned expenditures fall short of real national income at the full-capacity level of real national income. Thus there is an output gap.

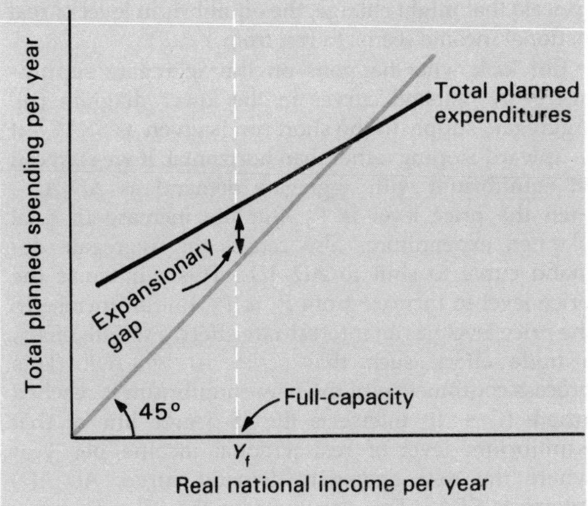

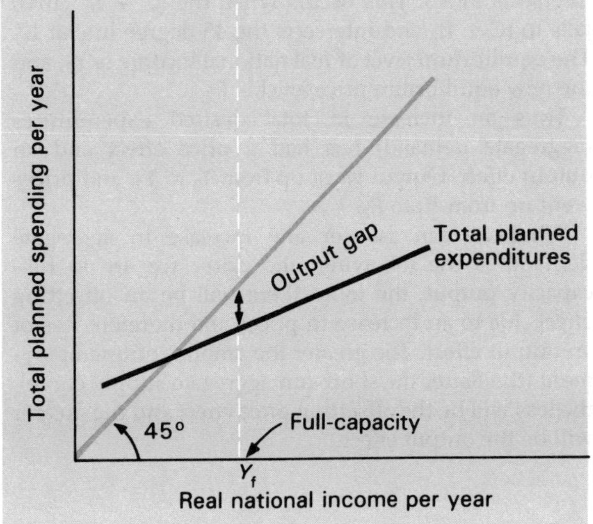

Relaxing the Assumption of a Fixed Price Level – The Determination of Output and Prices

For the moment, let us assume that we are no longer in the horizontal portion of the aggregate supply curve, but rather in the upward-sloping portion. How would an increase in aggregate demand affect the price level and real national income (total output)?

The total expenditure curve (which we have labelled $C + I$) relates total planned spending to real income, holding all other things constant. But, as real national income rises towards equilibrium following an initial rise (shift) in the $C + I$ curve, some prices will rise. This will simply cause the $C + I$ curve to then shift down, partially offsetting the initial rise in the $C + I$ curve, until a new equilibrium is reached. In other words, when prices are allowed to rise because of an increase in total desired spending (aggregate demand), there will be a feedback mechanism. Consider Figure 16.11. Initially, total planned spending (expenditures) rise from $(C + I)_1$ to $(C + I)_2$. The initial equilibrium is shown at E and it moves to E'. Ignoring other things (prices) that might change, the equilibrium level of real national income seems to rise from Y_1 to Y_2.

But look what happens on the aggregate supply–aggregate demand curves in the lower diagram (b). Aggregate supply in the short run is given as *SRAS* – it is upward-sloping rather than horizontal. If we start out in equilibrium with aggregate demand as AD_1AD_1, then the price level is P_1. But the increase in total planned expenditures also causes the aggregate demand curve to shift to AD_2AD_2. This will cause the price level to increase from P_1 to P_2. But an incrase in the price level has an interest-rate effect, a wealth effect, a trade effect, such that $(C + I)_2$ will fall. This process continues until the new equilibrium is reached where $(C + I)_3$ intersects the 45-degree line at that equilibrium level of real national income per year where the new aggregate demand curve, AD_2AD_2 intersects *SRAS*. This occurs when the $(C + I)_2$ curve falls to $(C + I)_3$ and intersects the 45-degree line at E''. The equilibrium level of real national income is Y_3, and the new equilibrium price level is P_2.

Thus an increase in total desired expenditures (aggregate demand) has had a price effect and an output effect. Output went up from Y_1 to Y_3, and prices went up from P_1 to P_2.

What we can say for any increase in aggregate demand is the following: the closer we are to full-capacity output, the more there will be an offsetting effect due to an increase in prices and therefore less of an output effect. The greater the amount of unemployment (the flatter the short-run aggregate supply curve), the less will be the offsetting price effect and the greater will be the output effect.

Figure 16.11

The Output and Price Effects of an Increase in Aggregate Demand. Assume that total desired spending is $(C + I)_1$. Assume further that short-run aggregate supply is given by *SRAS* and aggregate demand is given by AD_1AD_1. To begin with, the equilibrium level of real national income is Y_1 in both the upper and lower diagrams. The equilibrium price level is P_1. An increase in total desired expenditures to $(C + I)_2$ would give an equilibrium level of real national income of Y_2. But the increase in aggregate demand shifts the aggregate demand curve to AD_2AD_2 in the bottom part of the diagram. The equilibrium price level increases to P_2. This causes offsetting effects on total planned spending so that the total planned expenditures curve $(C + I)_2$ falls. It will keep falling until the equilibrium level of national income occurs just where aggregate demand equals short-run aggregate supply. This occurs when $(C + I)_2$ falls to $(C + I)_3$, such that the equilibrium level of national income is Y_3. The increase in aggregate demand has led to a price effect – the increase in the price level from P_1 to P_2 – and an output effect – the increase in the equilibrium level of real national income from Y_1 to Y_3. (Now read Key Points 16.6.)

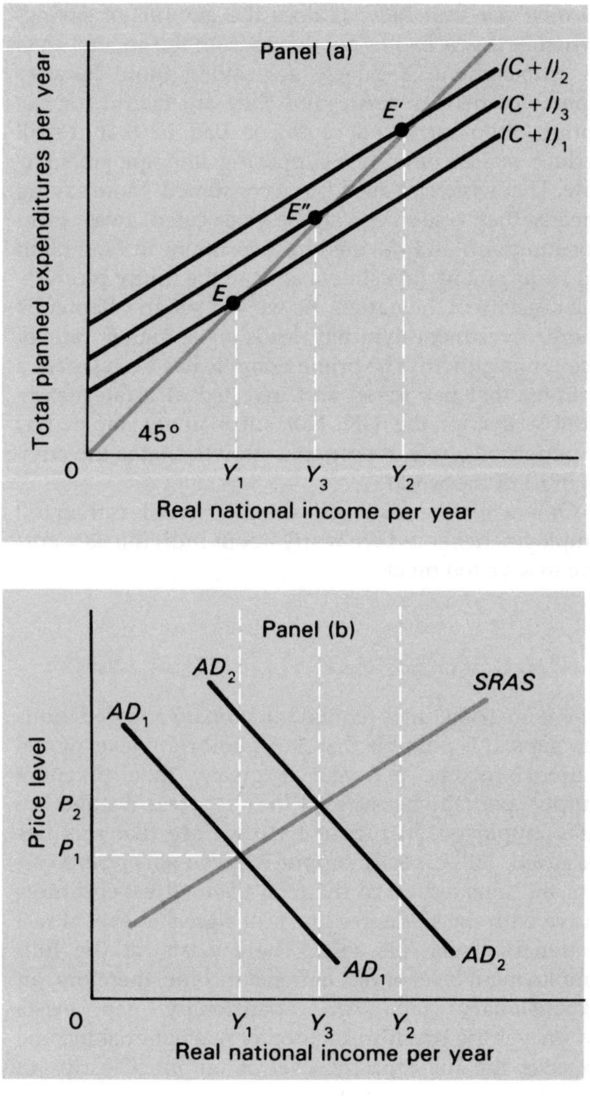

Key Points 16.6

- **The paradox of thrift shows how an increase in the saving function produces contraction in the economy and therefore a fall in the level of saving.**
- **An expansionary (or inflationary) gap exists when planned expenditure exceeds full-capacity output.**
- **An output (or deflationary) gap exists when planned expenditure is less than full-capacity output, i.e. there are unemployed resources in the economy.**
- **The closer the economy is to full capacity the more likely it is that increased expenditure leads to accelerating inflation rather than rising output.**

The Acceleration Principle

It was obvious during the nineteenth century that investment fluctuated more than output as a whole. While, for example, expenditure on food is continuous, expenditure on investment can be postponed or brought forward according to circumstance.

As sales rise, firms want to increase output. To do so they need a larger capital stock. This is known as the *acceleration principle*, or the accelerator:

The level of planned investment varies with *changes in the level* of output itself. Otherwise stated, the level of planned investment is related to the *rate of change* of output or sales.

If the capital stock – the value of the machines, equipment, and buildings – is related to the sales of a company, then we relate the *change* in sales to the *change* in capital. But the change in the capital stock – additions to or subtractions from the total amount of equipment, machines, buildings – is what we have called investment. Therefore, the change in sales is related to the *level* of investment.

We can see a simple example of the acceleration principle at work in the planned investment of A & B Heater Company. Figure 16.12 shows the relationship between the company's investment and sales. We begin by assuming that in Year 1 the firm started with just the necessary amount of capital stock, that is, machinery valued at £5 million (column (4), row Year 1).

Now, if you look at the financial data across the row for Year 1, you will see that in the first year of operation, £10 million in sales (column (2) were produced from £5 million of capital stock (shown as 'Actual stock of machines' in column (4)). We assume that the actual stock of machines in Year 1 was also equal to the required, or optimal, stock of machines in Year 1, so that there is basically a 2-to-1 relationship between sales and the value of the stock of machines necessary to produce that amount of water-heaters. This information lets us know how much to invest in new machinery to produce the expected increase in sales. For this example, we can do this by looking at the expected amount of sales and dividing that amount by 2 to find out the desired capital stock to produce those sales.

What happens when sales are expected to increase by £2 million per year, as they did in fact increase from Year 1 to Year 2? The 'Required stock of machines' (column (3)) was increased by £1 million to £6 million from £5 million.

Figure 16.12
Relationship between Investment and Sales for A & B Heater Company

(1) Year	*(2) Sales (£m)*	*(3) Required stock of machines (£m)*	*(4) Actual stock of machine (£m)*	*(5) Replacement investment (£m per year)*	*(6) Net investment in new capital (£m per year)*	*(7) = (5) + (6) Gross investment (£m per year)*
1	10	5	5	1	0	0
2	12	6	5	1	1	2
3	14	7	6	1	1	2
4	16	8	7	1	1	2
5	16	8	8	1	0	1
6	16	8	8	1	0	1
7	14	7	8	0	0	0
8	14	7	7	1	0	1
9	14	7	7	1	0	1
10	18	9	7	1	2	3
11	18	9	9	1	0	1

Depreciation

Before we proceed further, we have to consider depreciation. In this example, we assume that £1 million worth of machinery wears out every year and must be completely replaced. This means that £1 million must be spent on 'Replacement investment' (column (5)) every year just to produce the same amount of sales each year. Therefore, the A & B Heater Company will have to spend:

£1 million in *replacement investment* to take care of *depreciation* in machines and to produce the same sales as before;
and
£1 million in new machines (shown as 'Net investment in new capital' in column (6)) to produce the additional £2 million in expected sales.

The sum of those two is what we call gross investment; that is, *gross investment* equals the sum of replacement investment and net investment. In this example, for Year 2 £1 million in 'Replacement investment' (column (5)) plus £1 million in 'Net investment' (column (6)) equals £2 million in 'Gross investment' (column (7)).

Notice, the *level* of sales increases by another £2 million per year from Year 2 to Year 3 and from Year 3 to Year 4, but that 'Gross investment' (column (7)) remains constant at £2 million per year. This is a demonstration of the *acceleration principle*. Gross investment is a function of the *rate* of change of sales. If that rate of change is a constant amount, then gross investment will be a constant amount.

Now look at what happens when sales decline from £16 million a year to £14 million as they did from Year 6 to Year 7. The *required* capital stock on hand is still £8 million. In other words, there is more capital on hand than needed to produce the lower rate of sales. Furthermore, £1 million of actual machinery will wear out and need to be replaced. But since sales fell by £2 million, that means that £1 million less of machinery is needed. Thus, in this year, it is not necessary even to pay for depreciation or replacement machinery.

Therefore, we see for Year 7 that the replacement investment is, in effect, zero; the net investment is zero; and, consequently, the total gross investment is also zero. In other words, if the rate of capital formation – investment – is a function of the *rate of change* of sales, a decline in sales can lead to a zero amount of gross investment (and in some cases, to a *negative* net investment).

We can also see that small changes in sales result in large changes in planned (gross) investment. For example, from Year 1 to Year 2, sales for the A & B Heater Company went up by 20 per cent, but gross investment went up by 100 per cent. From Year 9 to Year 10, sales increased by 28.57 per cent {[(18–14) ÷ 14] × 100 per cent = 28.57 per cent}, while gross investment increased by 200 per cent {[(3 – 1) ÷ 1] × 100 per cent = 200 per cent}.

In sum, as long as the level of investment is related to the level of sales, small changes in sales may lead to magnified changes in investment. The longer the life of the capital equipment, the more marked these changes will be.

The Interaction between the Accelerator and the Multiplier

Investment is a key determinant of the equilibrium level of national income in the model that we have been using in Part B. If the rate of planned investment follows the acceleration principle, this could explain to some extent, the rather dramatic swings in business activity that we have experienced from time to time. After all, any change in investment, according to our theory, leads to a multiplier effect in which there is a multiple change in the equilibrium level of income and employment. The evidence suggests that in both the UK and the US, the accelerator, combined with the multiplier, may produce the business fluctuations that are experienced in the real world.

The accelerator and multiplier interact, affecting business as follows. We assume that the economy is moving towards full employment, national income is rising, and sales are expanding at an *increasing* rate. Because of the acceleration principle, this growth – meaning expected increases in sales – results in a relatively high level of planned investment. Furthermore, because of the multiplier, this relatively high level of planned investment provokes *even greater* increases in the equilibrium level of national income. Thus, the accelerator and the multiplier tend to reinforce each other, resulting in a strong upward movement in national income.

Eventually, however, the economy nears some level of full capacity. That is to say, since we have only a certain amount of labour, land, and other factors of production, it is impossible to continue increasing national income at the rapid rate that was experienced during the expansion phase of the business cycle. At some point, supply constraints must become a problem and growth of all of the components of the economy has to slow down. Sales will not increase forever at the same fast rate; they will begin to increase at a slower rate. This slow-down in the growth of sales means that the rate of growth of planned investment is going to turn down abruptly, just as it did, for example, when sales of the A & B Heater Company were maintained at £16 million a year. However, because of the multiplier effect, this decrease in planned investment will lead to a magnified, or multiplied, decrease in the equilibrium level of income. The reduction in the rate of growth of national income will mean a further reduction in the rate of sales growth, leading to a further reduction in gross investment, and so on. Eventually, the economy will experience a recession and the cycle will start again.

At some point, the capital stock of firms, that is, their

actual stock of machinery, buildings, and manufacturing equipment, gets into line with their reduced sales rates. This is what happened between Year 1 and Year 3 for the A & B Heater Company. When this happens, the stage is set for another upturn, another recovery, and the interaction again of the accelerator and the multiplier.

You will note that the multiplier–accelerator theory of the business cycle is one in which business cycles are self-starting and self-terminating. Each phase of the business cycle automatically leads into the next. In practice, this kind of fluctuation occurs together with changes brought about by shocks such as oil price changes.

Key Points 16.7

- **Increasing output may require investment in extra plant and machinery to create the necessary productive capacity.**
- **The accelerator shows how investment is linked to the rate of change of output.**
- **Investment will fluctuate more sharply than output.**
- **The accelerator and multiplier together help us to explain cyclical changes in output and employment.**

CASE STUDY

Investment Rollercoaster

Manufacturing output fell sharply between 1979 and 1981. High interest rates (brought in to counter inflation) reduced demand. The sharply increased flow of North Sea oil cut imports of oil. So the exchange rate rose, making exports uncompetitive. Foreign demand for UK exports fell. On all sides, manufacturing industry faced recession.

The decelerator effect on manufacturing investment between 1979 and 1982 is evident. The fall in manufacturing output was 14 per cent, but the resulting fall in investment was 40 per cent. A similar relationship holds good for all individual manufacturing industries, with the exception of food. The fall in investment was particularly heavy in metals – mainly steel – (59 per cent), chemicals (50 per cent), and mechanical engineering (49 per cent). A number of traditional industries, such as construction, transport, and distribution also had falls in investment. The falls in investment and in output were both modest in retail and wholesale distribution, and investment began to recover in 1981 in these sectors.

Since industrial investment as a whole fell by only 10 per cent, clearly some sectors must have had increases. There was a rise in energy investment, of about 10 per cent; this sector was untypical, because North Sea oil investment peaked in 1976, and was recovering from a trough in 1980. In the service industries, the big increases in investment were in business and financial services, telecommunications, and to a lesser extent in hotels and catering, with standard accelerator effects showing investment rising by a multiple of the rise in output. Investment in 'business services', which includes computer services, rose by 70 per cent in real terms, reaching £2.7bn in 1982 – about as much as in retail and wholesale distribution, nearly as much as in

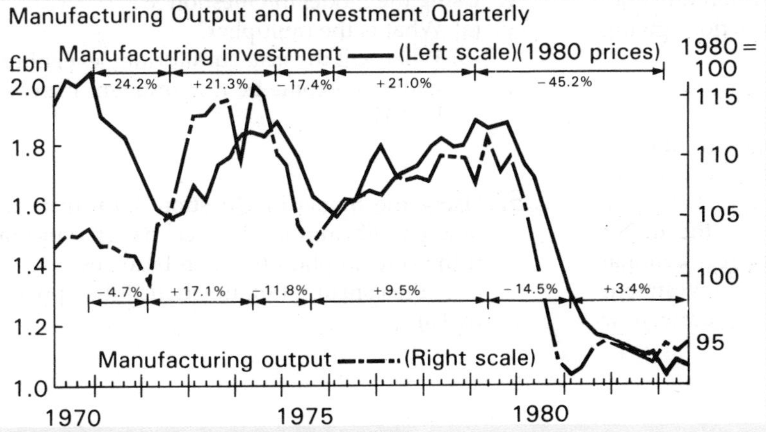

Source: Lloyds Bank Bulletin January 1984.

North Sea oil and gas, and half as much as in the whole of manufacturing industry.

Questions

1. What changes in investment took place?
2. Which industries were most affected by the fall in demand? Why do you think some sectors were much less affected than others?
3. Explain how the accelerator affected investment, 1979–82.

Exam Preparation

PRACTICAL EXERCISES

1. You are given the following information for a hypothetical economy: Assume that the marginal propensity to consume is constant at all levels of income. Further assume that investment is autonomous.

Real national income	*Consumption expenditures*	*Saving*	*Investment*
£1 000	£1 100	______	£100
2 000	2 000	______	______
3 000	______	______	______
4 000	______	______	______
5 000	______	______	______
6 000	______	______	______

APC	APS	MPC	MPS
______	______	______	______
______	______	______	______
______	______	______	______
______	______	______	______
______	______	______	______
______	______	______	______

(a) Draw a graph of the consumption function. Then add the investment function, giving you $C + I$.

(b) Right under the first diagram, draw a second diagram showing the saving and investment curves. Does the $C + I$ curve intersect the 45-degree line in the upper diagram at the same level of real national income as where saving equals investment in the lower diagram? (If not, redraw your diagrams.)

(c) What is the numerical value of the multiplier?

(d) What will happen to income if autonomous investment increases by £100?

(e) What will the equilibrium level of real national income be if autonomous consumption increases by £100?

2. Assume a closed, private economy.
(a) What is the multiplier if the MPC = ½? If the MPC = ¾? If the MPC = 9⁄10? If the MPC = 1?
(b) What happens to the multiplier as the MPC rises?
(c) In what range does the multiplier fall?

3. Consider a closed, private economy, in which
(a) $C = £30 + \frac{3}{4}Y$
(b) $I = £25$.
What will the equilibrium level of real national income (Y) be equal to in this economy? (*Hint:* In equilibrium, real national income must equal total planned expenditures, or $Y = C + I$.)

4. Using the model in Question 3:
(a) What is the multiplier?
(b) What will the *new* equilibrium level of real national income be if investment increases by £5?

5. Using the model in Question 3, calculate the new equilibrium level of real national income if the consumption function becomes $C = £35 + Y$ (the consumption function shifts upwards by £5).

MULTIPLE CHOICE QUESTIONS

For Questions 1 and 2 refer to this diagram.

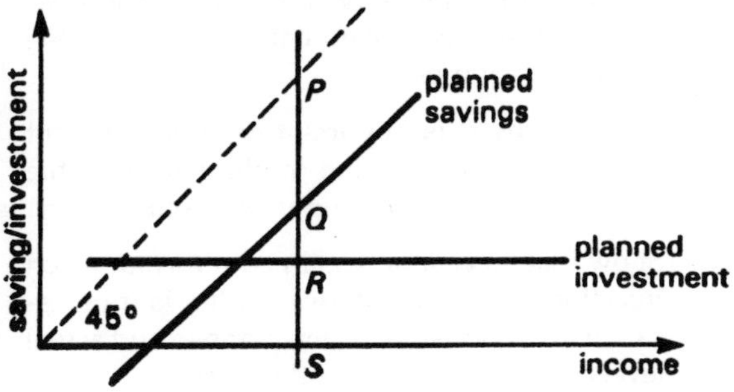

1. Which distance represents unplanned increase in stocks?
   A *PQ*
   B *PR*
   C *PS*
   D *QR*
   E *RS*

2. Which distance indicates consumption expenditure?
   A *PQ*
   B *PR*
   C *PS*
   D *QR*
   E *QS*

3. The multiplier effect of public investment is likely to be high where there is
   A a preference for foreign goods
   B a high level of stock
   C excess productive capacity in the private sector
   D heavy taxation of companies
   E a high propensity to consume

4. A new firm requires one machine for every 2 million units of consumer goods it produces each year. The machines last for four years including the year in which they are bought and then are replaced. Demand for the consumer goods is shown in the schedule.

Year	Quantity demanded (millions)
1	10
2	20
3	30
4	40
5	40
6	48

Total investment by the firm will be (in number of machines)

	Year 1	2	3	4	5	6
A	5	5	5	5	5	9
B	5	5	5	5	5	4
C	5	5	5	5	0	4
D	5	5	5	5	0	9

One or more of the options given in Questions 5, 6, and 7 may be correct. Select your answer by means of the code set out in the grid.

A	B	C	D
1, 2, 3 all correct	1, 2 only correct	2, 3 only correct	1 only correct

5. The numerical value of the multiplier is likely to rise as a result of
   1 the elimination of import quotas
   2 a reduction in the rate of direct taxation
   3 a more even distribution of income

6. Ratio of Gross Domestic Fixed Capital Formation to Gross Domestic Product, 1973–81, United Kingdom

1973	1974	1975	1976	1977
0.199	0.196	0.196	0.190	0.183
1978	**1979**	**1980**	**1981**	
0.183	0.178	0.180	0.169	

The table above indicates that, during the period from 1973 to 1981, the United Kingdom has
   1 reduced the percentage of its gross domestic product devoted to investment
   2 needed to replace capital
   3 reduced its stock of capital

7.

National income	Consumption	Planned injections
0	50	30
150	150	30
180	170	30
210	190	30
240	210	30
270	230	30
300	250	30

From the data it can be deduced that
   1 a fall in planned injections of 10 would cause the equilibrium level of income to fall by 20
   2 the average propensity to consume when income equals 150 is unity
   3 withdrawals equal planned injections at income level 240.

8. The diagram shows the equilibrium level of national income at two different levels of investment, I_1 and I_2. Which of the following ratios gives the value of the marginal propensity to save?

A $\frac{UX}{VZ}$

B $\frac{VZ}{XY}$

C $\frac{WX}{VZ}$

D $\frac{XY}{VZ}$

E $\frac{XY}{YZ}$

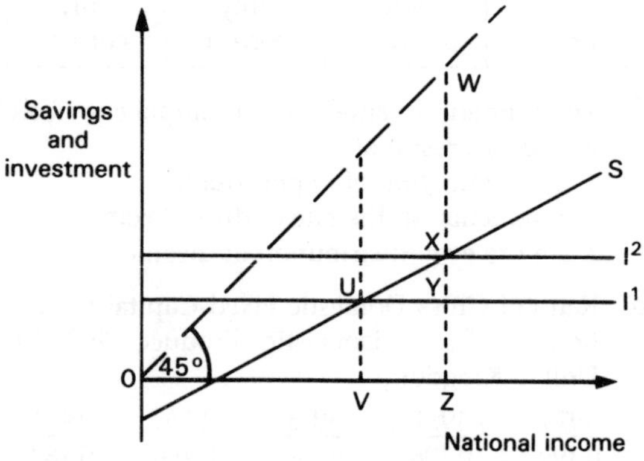

RELATED ESSAY QUESTIONS

1. Examine the effects of a rise in consumers' expenditure upon national income, investment, and savings.

2. Explain why it is important for a government to take account of the multiplier and the accelerator in determining its economic policy.

3. Show that an economy is in equilibrium when injections equal withdrawals. Why is it necessary to distinguish between planned and actual levels of injections and withdrawals?

4. (a) Distinguish between induced and autonomous investment
(b) Explain carefully the consequences, for UK GDP, of a significant increase in autonomous investment.

5. (a) Explain the relationship between the multiplier process and the consumption function.
(b) Consider the factors that might initiate a multiplier process.
(c) What reasons are there for asserting that household current income is less important as a determinant of consumption expenditure, now, than would have been the case in the 1930s when Keynes originated the concept of the consumption function?

17 Income and Employment Determination: Government and Trade

Key Points to Review

- The circular flow with a government and foreign trade (12.3)
- Equilibrium via leakages–injections (16.3)
- Multiplier effect (16.5)

Questions for Preview

1 What is fiscal policy?

2 What is an output gap, and how can fiscal policy eliminate it?

3 What is an expansionary gap, and how can fiscal policy eliminate it?

4 What are automatic stabilizers and how do they lend stability to an economy?

5 How do imports and exports affect national income?

So far we have left government out of our model of real national income determination. The tools learned already still apply when making the basic model more realistic. In this chapter, we will consider how changes in government spending and taxation will alter the equilibrium level of real national income. We will go on to examine the effects of foreign trade.

Adding Government Spending and Taxes

We now include government spending in our macroeconomic model, but we will assume that the level of government purchases is determined by political processes outside the economic system under study. In other words, we will consider G to be autonomous, just as in the last chapter we considered I, for simplicity's sake, to be autonomous.

Panel (a) in Figure 17.1 (page 260) shows the new aggregate expenditure function, $C + I + G$. Equilibrium income Y occurs where planned expenditure and real income and output are equal, that is at the intersection with the 45-degree line.

Alternatively, we can find the equilibrium level of real national income by using the leakages–injections approach. Remember that for equilibrium to occur, leakages must equal injections. In this present analysis, we have an additional injection into the system, autonomous government spending. Therefore, in panel (b) we show a new injections line that is investment plus government spending, or $I + G$. Since investment and government spending are both autonomous, or given, the $I + G$ line is horizontal. Within the model we are using, we have treated saving as induced, depending directly on the level of income. Similarly, taxes constitute a leakage and are dependent on income. They are a leakage because they reduce the level of disposable income, and therefore the level of personal consumption. They very obviously depend on income. Both direct taxes (taxes levied on income itself, such as income and profits tax) and indirect, or expenditure taxes (such as VAT and excise duties), rise with income. So we have a new leakage function, the $S + T$ line in panel (b). The equilibrium level of income is that which generates a level of savings and tax revenue which is equal to planned investment and government expenditure.

It should be noted that the level of taxes set by the government will influence saving. An increase in taxes will generally lead to both a fall in consumption *and* a fall in saving. In order to pay the higher taxes, people will save somewhat less. So a given increase in tax-rates will lead to a somewhat smaller increase in leakages.

Figure 17.1

Equilibrium Income with a Government. Aggregate expenditure is $C + I + G$. Equilibrium income is Y, the level at which expenditure is exactly equal to income and output. Panel (b) shows the injections–leakages approach, with equilibrium occurring where planned $I + G = S + T$.

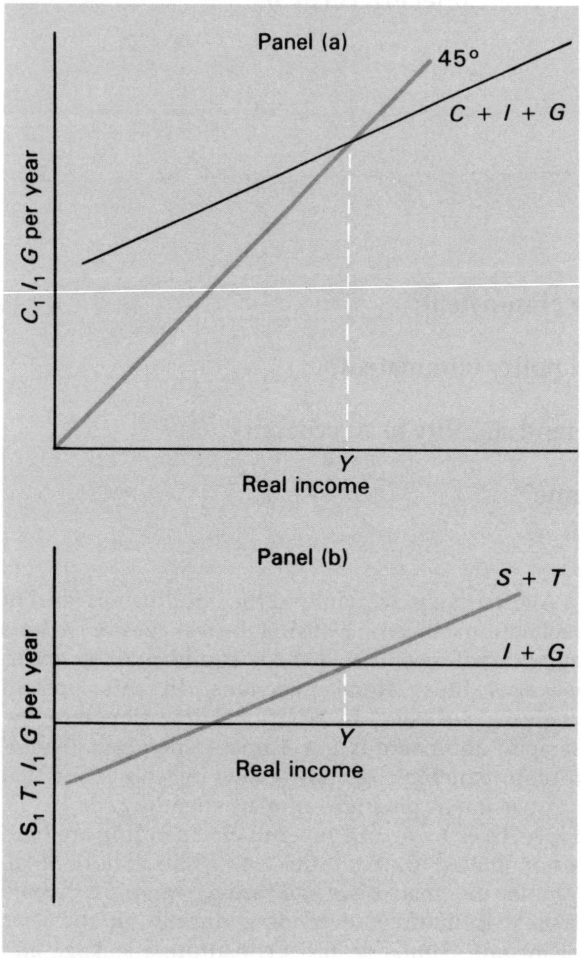

The Multiplier with a Government

Our original derivation of the multiplier was based on there being one leakage only, saving. With another leakage, taxes, the story changes. The more of any given increase in expenditure which leaks away as either saving or taxes, the smaller the multiplier.

We can of course use the original alternative formula for the multiplier, 1/(1−MPC). But this only raises the question, what is the MPC when there is the further leakage of taxes?

When households decide how much to spend on consumer goods, they examine not gross income (before tax) but disposable income (income after tax). Disposable income (Y_d) can be defined as national income less taxes:

$$Y_d = Y - T$$

Taxes will be levied at particular rates. If the marginal rate of taxation (MRT) and the average rate are both equal to 0.2, then

$$\begin{aligned} Y_d &= Y - 0.2Y \\ &= 0.8Y \end{aligned}$$

If we assume that the average and marginal propensities to consume out of disposable income are 0.9, then

$$\begin{aligned} C &= 0.9Y_d \\ &= 0.9 \times 0.8Y \\ &= 0.72Y \end{aligned}$$

Thus if the MRT is 0.2, and the MPC out of disposable income is 0.9, the MPC out of national income is 0.72. The multiplier is then 3.6. (Now read Key Points 17.1.)

Possible Discretionary Fiscal Policies

Governments can choose to vary spending or taxes, or both, in order to expand or contract aggregate expenditure.

Filling the Output Gap

Figure 17.2 shows an economy in which, initially, expenditure is insufficient to buy all of potential output. Real income, Y, can be produced by fewer people than are actually seeking work. There is some cyclical, or demand-deficiency unemployment.

If expenditure can be increased then real income and output can expand and employers will take on more labour. (The implication of there being unemployed resources is that the economy is on the horizontal section of the aggregate supply curve. Aggregate supply can expand to meet any increase in aggregate demand.)

In Figure 17.2, the increased expenditure is shown as arising from increased government expenditure. Aggregate expenditure rises from $C + I + G_1$, to $C + I + G_2$. The resulting level of real national income is Y_2. This corresponds to the level of income at which planned $I + G_2$ is equal to $S + T$ in panel (b). An alternative possibility would have been to reduce taxes. This would increase disposable income and therefore consumption. Both increasing spending and decreasing taxes serve to increase the level of the government's deficit so that injections increase in relation to leakages. Or a package of measures would be possible, perhaps

Key Points 17.1

- **Government spending is politically determined and is therefore autonomous, that is, determined outside the model.**
- **Taxes, though the rates are set by governments, depend directly on incomes, that is, they are induced.**
- **In equilibrium planned injections equal planned leakages, so $G + I = S + T$.**
- **In using the multiplier it must be remembered that its level is determined by *all* leakages.**

Figure 17.2

Reducing Unemployment with Fiscal Policy. At real income Y_1 there is substantial demand-deficiency unemployment. Increasing government expenditure from G_1 to G_2 adds to aggregate demand, causing firms to try to expand output and take on labour. The new equilibrium real income Y_2 is achieved when aggregate expenditure, $C + I + G_2$, is exactly equal to real income and output, and when $I + G_2$ (injections) equal $S + T$ (leakages).

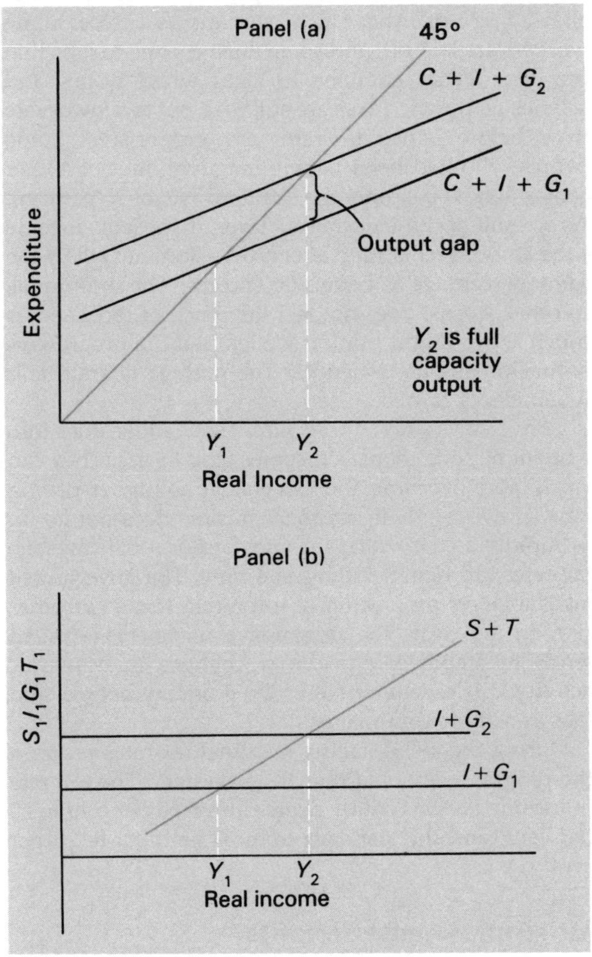

including monetary policies. All are discussed in more detail in Part E.

It should be noticed that the eventual increase in income and output is much larger than the initial increase in government spending. This is precisely what we would expect, with the multiplier at work. It means that it is important for the government to be able to predict the multiplier effect of its change in spending. Otherwise it might overdo its expansionary policy, income could increase by more than the output gap and create the reverse problem.

Reducing the Expansionary Gap

Figure 17.3 (page 262) shows an economy in which, initially, aggregate demand or expenditure exceeds output or aggregate supply. This excess demand arises because the economy is incapable of producing real income Y_1 – there simply are not enough suitable resources available to do the job. The most that can be produced – the maximum potential, or full-capacity output, of the economy – is Y_2. Supply constraints are preventing the economy from expanding and unless expenditure is reduced, prices will rise. (The economy is on the upward-sloping section of the aggregate supply curve.) This is sometimes known as *overheating*.

Figure 17.3 shows the effects of increasing taxes to reduce expenditure. The reduced disposable income causes consumption to fall, as shown in panel (a). Panel (b) shows the increase in taxes. This reduces the government's deficit, increasing leakages relative to injections. The reduced expenditure should remove the excess demand and the upward pressure on prices. An alternative would have been to reduce government spending, or some policy combination. Note again, because of the downward multiplier effect, the eventual decrease in expenditure will be greater than the initial change in spending. In this case the importance of accurate forecasting is even greater. The government needs to have good estimates not only of the multiplier but also of the extent to which a tax increase affects the level of consumption. It must know the marginal propensity to consume out of disposable income.

The Balanced Budget Multiplier

There are times when a government may wish to increase spending, and finance the increase by raising

Figure 17.3

Reducing Inflationary Pressure with Fiscal Policy. At Y_1, planned expenditures exceed full capacity output. Prices will rise due to aggregate excess demand. To reduce expenditure, taxes can be raised from T_1 to T_2. Disposable income is thus reduced and consumption falls from C_1 to C_2. There is a downward multiplier effect as expenditure falls and equilibrium real income falls from Y_1 to Y_2.

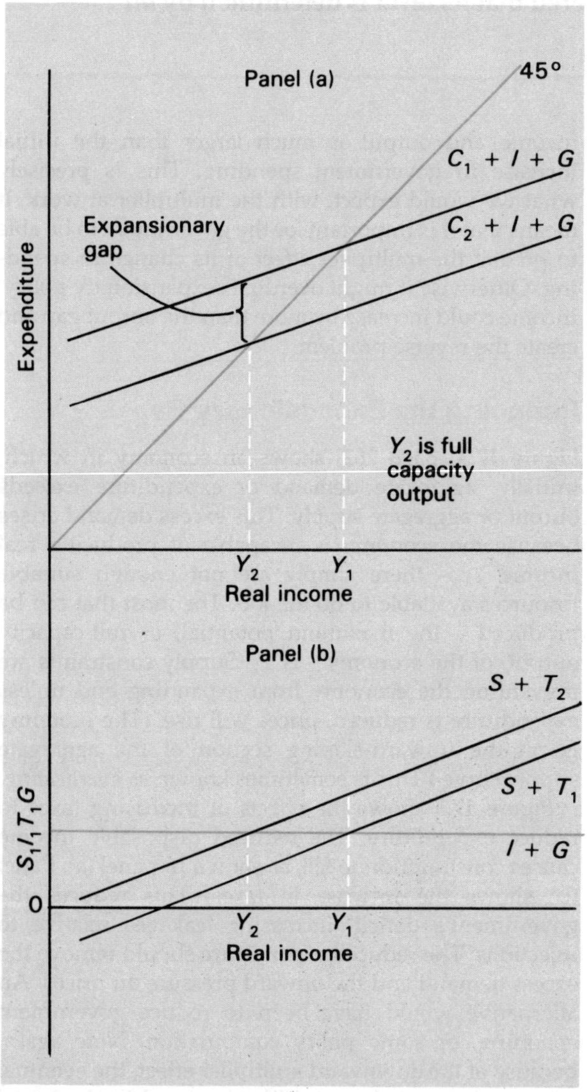

taxes to match. The increased spending is an injection into the circular flow. All of it will be spent and be subject to the multiplier effect.

The increase in taxation will reduce disposable income. This will almost certainly mean that both consumption and saving fall. But saving is a leakage. Because it diminishes somewhat the *total* increase in leakages will be less than the increase in taxes.

The net effect of this is that although both government spending and taxes have increased by an equal amount, total leakages increase by less than total injections. So the effect on the economy will be expansionary. Provided there are suitable unemployed resources available, income and output will increase.

Automatic or Built-in Stabilizers

In contrast to discretionary fiscal policy, automatic stabilizers need no new legislation in order to make them effective. The system of taxes and benefits works to counteract cylical changes in the level of expenditure automatically.

Progressive Income Taxes

As taxable income rises so does the marginal tax rate – to a maximum of 40 per cent. Thus, income tax is progressive: the higher the income, the larger the proportion of it which is paid in tax. Or we can say that as taxable income decreases, the marginal tax rate goes down. Think about this for the entire economy. Initially, personal income taxes may yield the government, say, £50 billion per year. Now suppose that, for whatever reason, business activity suddenly starts to slow down. When this happens, workers are not allowed to put in as much overtime as before. Some workers are laid off, and some must change to jobs that pay less. What happens to taxes when wages and salaries go down? Taxes are still paid but at a lower rate than before, since tax-rates are progressive. Some people who had been paying marginal rates of 40 per cent will now pay only the standard rate of 25 per cent. As a result of these decreased taxes, disposable income – the amount remaining after taxes – does not fall by the same percentage as before-tax income. The individual, in other words, does not feel the pinch of recession as much as we might think if we ignored the progressive nature of our tax schedule. The *average* tax-rate falls when less is earned.

Conversely, when the economy suddenly comes into a boom period, people's incomes tend to rise. They can work more overtime and can change to higher-paying jobs. However, their *disposable* income does not go up as rapidly as their total income, because their average tax-rates are rising at the same time. The government takes a larger proportion of income in tax, as incomes rise. In this way, the progressive income tax system tends to stabilize any abrupt changes in economic activity. Tax revenue rises as the economy booms, and falls as activity diminishes.

During the 1980s, falling marginal tax rates reduced the progressiveness of the UK tax system. The top rate of income tax was cut by degrees from 60 per cent to 40 per cent, and the standard from 30 per cent to 25 per cent.

Unemployment Benefits

Unemployment benefits work like the progressive income tax: they stabilize aggregate demand. When business activity drops, most laid-off workers automatically become eligible for unemployment benefits.

Their disposable income therefore remains positive, although less than when they were working. During boom periods, there is less unemployment and consequently fewer unemployment payments made to the labour force. Less purchasing power is being added to the economy. So government expenditure automatically offsets fluctuations in income.

The Stabilizing Impact

Progressive taxes and the benefit system reduce the impact of changes in demand on disposable income, consumption, and the equilibrium level of national income. We presented a model in which disposable income – *take-home pay* – is the main determinant of how much people desire to spend. Hence, if disposable income is not allowed to fall as much as it would otherwise during a recession, the downturn will be moderated. On the other hand, if disposable income is not allowed to rise as rapidly as it would otherwise during a boom, the boom will not get out of hand, causing prices to rise, among other things. The government automatically swings into deficit when there is a recession, and back towards surplus when the economy booms. Figure 17.4 shows this graphically.

Figure 17.4

Automatic Stabilizers. Assume that government expenditures remain constant no matter what the level of real national income. Thus they are fully autonomous and represented by *GG*. Taxes, on the other hand, vary directly with national income. Thus we see that when real national income increases from Y_0 to Y_1, taxes will exceed government expenditures as shown by the vertical distance between *GG* and the tax line, *TT*. This government budget surplus, which occurs *automatically* during expansion, could assist in offsetting possible inflationary pressures. Alternatively, when real national income falls from Y_0 to Y_2, the resultant automatic budget deficit could help offset or alleviate the recession.

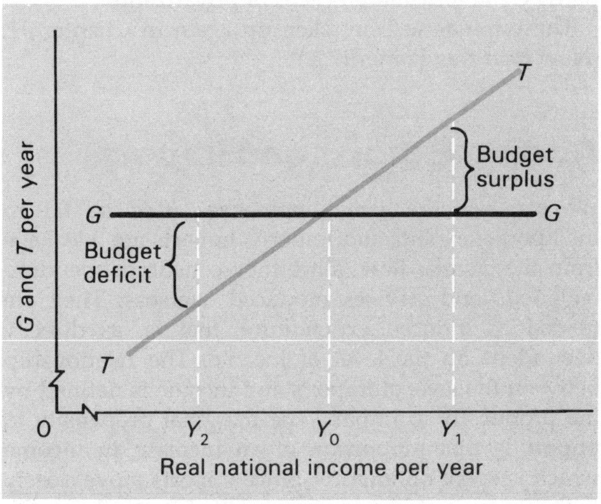

Fiscal Policy and a Full-employment Budget

We earlier discussed the government increasing expenditures, but we did not discuss how such expenditures would be financed. If we assume no increase in taxes, and if the budget is initially balanced, we can conclude that when the government spends more it ends up with a deficit. If the government is already running a deficit, it will have an even larger one. Fiscal policies have therefore been associated with **deficit spending** on the part of the government. Fiscal policy advocates point out that an increase in the deficit stimulates the economy, whereas a decrease in the deficit has the opposite effect. The government can also run a **surplus**. That is, it can take in more revenues than it spends. An increase in the government's budget surplus would have a depressing effect on the economy, just as would a decrease in government expenditures or an increase in taxes. The existence of, or an increase in, the government budget surplus presumably reduces total aggregate demand and thereby depresses economic activity.

Some economists do not like to look only at the government's *actual* deficit or surplus. They do not think it is useful to look at current levels of taxes and expenditures or the current budget deficit or surplus that results. Consider for a moment the following situation. Suppose the economy is at full employment and the government budget is in balance – no deficit and no surplus. Then the economy goes into a recession, and incomes fall. The government, however, does nothing. Spending on its part, *G*, remains the same. But since some taxes, *T*, are based on income government revenues fall. A formerly balanced budget goes into deficit, since *G* is now greater than *T*. The budget deficit should certainly not be regarded here as an active policy decision on the part of the government. It is a *result* of the recession. Therefore, economists now make calculations to determine whether *at full employment* the government budget *would be* in a deficit or a surplus position. The result is called the **full-employment government budget**. We define it as what the budget deficit or surplus would be if the economy were operating at full employment throughout the entire year.

The Budget and Fiscal Policy

Fiscal policy is set out at two annual events: the Chancellor's autumn statement, and the budget each spring. In the autumn statement, the economy is surveyed and forecasts published. In the budget, actual changes in tax-rates are decided. Underlying both, there is the policy of the government of the day, which determines what, if any, changes will be made to discretionary policies.

If policy is expansionary the government's deficit (i.e. expenditure minus tax revenue) will increase. This means that **PSBR (the public sector borrowing require-**

ment) will rise: more borrowing must take place, for the year in hand. Also, the **National Debt** will rise; this is the sum total of all outstanding government debt, past and present. However, an expansionary policy may cause real income to rise, so that tax revenues then rise. This will reduce the deficit somewhat.

If, on the other hand, policy is contractionary, taxes will be raised or maintained. Government spending will be cut. The government's deficit will fall and a surplus may develop. This surplus, or **PSDR (Public Sector Debt Repayment)** may be used to reduce the National Debt. This is what happened in the years 1987 to 1989, although government policy was less contractionary than it appeared to be because the surplus was partly created by the proceeds of privatization.

These issues will be taken up again in Chapter 31. (Now read Key Points 17.2.)

Adding Exports and Imports

We can use the same approaches used so far to incorporate exports and imports. Imports are a leakage from the circular flow, since they constitute spending on goods and services produced overseas. They are treated as induced expenditure, that is, as directly dependent on the level of income. The relationship between the level of imports and income is defined by the propensity to import. The marginal propensity to import is that proportion of an increase in income which is spent on imports. Since imports move closely with the level of income in the UK this clearly makes sense.

Exports, on the other hand, are treated as autonomous. Rather like investment, they are in fact determined by a wide range of influences which are outside the scope of the basic model. The level of aggregate demand in foreign countries with which the UK trades extensively; the exchange rate; and non-price competitiveness (factors such as design, reliability, and after-sales service) all affect the level of demand for UK exports.

As always, the equilibrium condition is that planned injections be equal to planned leakages.

$$S + T + M = I + G + X.$$

It is not necessary that any one, or all, pairs of injections and leakages be equal – only that total planned injections equal total leakages – for equilibrium to occur. The economy could be in overall equilibrium with a government deficit (G exceeding T), balanced by a private sector surplus (S exceeding I), with perhaps also a balance-of-trade surplus (X exceeding M). Or both government and trade may be in deficit, with the private sector surplus balancing both deficits. Both these situations, and many other such combinations, are consistent with overall equilibrium. (This does not mean that a balance-of-trade deficit could be ignored indefinitely.)

Figure 17.5 shows the effect of an increase in imports. Just as when any other change occurs in injections or leakages, the fall in expenditure brings about a fall in income which is larger than the initial increase in imports, because of the downward multiplier effect.

With foreign trade the expenditure function includes the net balance of exports and imports, ($X - M$), or net exports. This will be negative if imports exceed exports, creating a net leakage. Panel (a) shows how in equilibrium, planned expenditure from all sources must be equal to planned output, that is, the expenditure function must intersect with the 45-degree line. A rise in imports reduces expenditure leading income to fall from Y_1 to Y_2.

$$\text{Total expenditure} = C + I + G + (X - M)$$

Because imports are a rising function of income, low levels of income will generate a low level of imports.

Key Points 17.2

- **Fiscal policy can be used to regulate the level of expenditure in the economy.**
- **Demand-deficiency unemployment can be reduced by increasing government spending or reducing taxes.**
- **Inflationary pressures can be reduced by increasing taxes or reducing government spending.**
- **Built-in stabilizers automatically moderate changes in disposable income resulting from changes in overall business activity.**
- **Some economists make a distinction between the actual government budget and the so-called full-employment government budget, where the latter gives us what the budget deficit or surplus *would be* if the economy were operating at full employment throughout the entire year.**
- **The annual deficit, expenditure minus tax revenue, is known as PSBR.**
- **If tax revenue is greater than expenditure, there will be a surplus, or PSDR.**

Figure 17.5

The Effect of Rising Imports. As imports rise, leakages increase, expenditure on domestic output falls, and there is a downward multiplier effect on income.

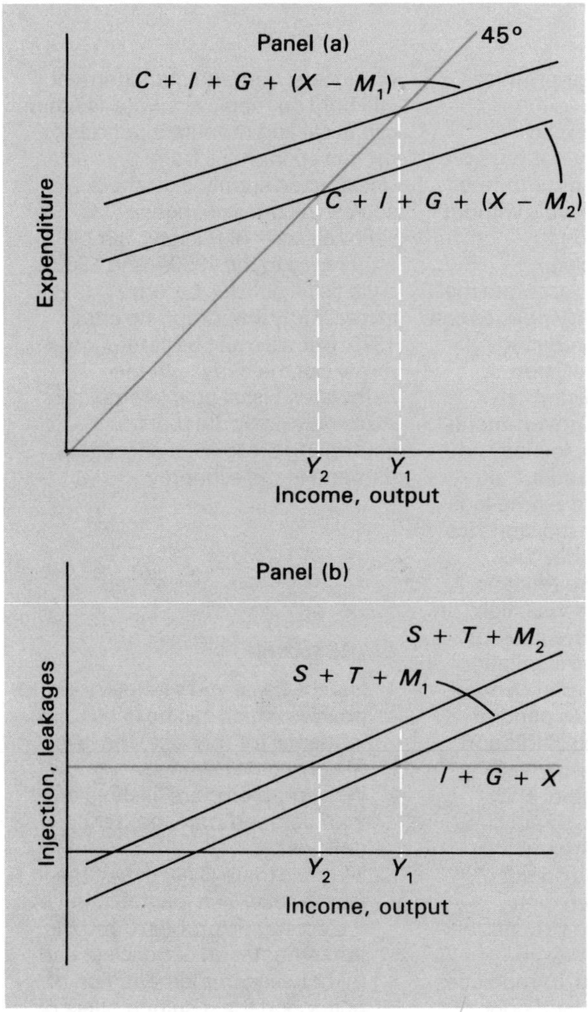

With exports autonomous, the likelihood is that when incomes are low there will be a **trade surplus**. Similarly, high levels of income generate increased imports, and probably a trade deficit. If high levels of expenditure lead to excess demand and supply constraints, it is inevitable that both firms and households find themselves unable to purchase all the goods and services they want from domestic producers. Obviously they will turn to imports to fill the gap, and a **trade deficit** will develop. This is another good reason for not allowing aggregate demand and expenditure to grow beyond aggregate supply, or the capacity of the economy to provide a growing output to meet that demand.

The Multiplier in an Open Economy

Our original formula for the multiplier

1/MPS

was based on there being a single leakage, savings. With an open economy with a government this can be amended to

1/(MPS + MRT + MPM)

where MRT is the marginal rate of taxation and MPM is the **marginal propensity to import**. (Care must be taken that these marginal rates of leakage are all expressed as a proportion of national income, as a whole, when using this formula.)

Clearly with three leakages, the multiplier will be smaller than we have tended to suggest before. An economy which has a large public sector and is very open, in that a substantial proportion of output is traded, will have a relatively small multiplier. This clearly applies to the UK. The effect of increasing expenditure on imports and the balance of trade can often be a major factor in considering future policy. Roughly 30 per cent of UK output is exported. Imports take a similar proportion of expenditure. The balance, net exports, tends to be a relatively small part of total demand.

Rising imports will tend to reduce employment in domestic firms, and rising exports to increase it. If a rising level of export demand is to be satisfied there must be suitable unemployed resources available to expand output. If there are not, rising demand will lead to rising prices rather than increased output. This is likely to reduce foreign demand for domestically produced goods anyway, as price rises erode competitiveness.

Key Points 17.3

- **Imports are induced, that is they depend directly on the level of income. They are a leakage from the circular flow.**
- **Exports are autonomous, being determined by a wide range of factors. They are an injection into the circular flow.**
- **In an open economy with a government, equilibrium requires that all planned injections equal planned leakages, $I + G + X = S + T + M$.**
- **The multiplier depends on the marginal rate of leakage.**

CASE STUDY

Keynesian Demand Management – Old Hat or Not

Initially deficit financing was Keynes's response to the 1930s depression. Whereas governments at that time were intent on policies of austerity, Keynes argued that increased spending would stimulate the economy, bringing growth and reduced unemployment.

After the Second World War these ideas became the conventional wisdom. From the end of the war until 1974 there was not a single year in which output fell. Until 1970, inflation was very seldom higher than 5 per cent, and averaged 3.3 per cent for the period 1953–69; unemployment was generally in the range of 1½ per cent to 2½ per cent and was never higher than 2.6 per cent. So it must be concluded that in certain circumstances, demand-management policies can reduce cyclical fluctuations in the economy. They can provide an economic framework which is conducive to steady growth.

Unfortunately, demand-management policies were probably oversold. In the early 1960s, Chancellors of the Exchequer said they could 'fine-tune' the economy. They would set the level of aggregate demand just so as to get the balance between unemployment, inflation, and growth exactly right. They would be able to use fiscal and monetary policies to achieve their target of aggregate demand. To be fair to the politicians, economists encouraged them to think that their promises could be made good.

There were two specific problems. It is usually not possible to achieve satisfying growth-rates and unemployment levels without a tendency for inflation to accelerate. And forecasting techniques are not so accurate that the fiscal and monetary policies can be set to produce a predicted outcome with any precision. A common failing with counter-cyclical policy is that governments take too much action, too late, and so overshoot their targets. Partly this is because there are time-lags involved. By the time the statistics have been collected they are already out of date. So reflating when unemployment was high could lead later to more inflation. And deflating, to control inflation, reduced growth and employment. It has been said that demand-management policies of this sort could make the economy less, rather than more, stable. They earned the title, *Stop-go* policies.

More generally, demand-management policies do not of themselves help much with problems which have structural causes. Monopolistic wage-bargaining processes, immobilities of labour and capital, and poor quality management, make it difficult for an economy to produce desirable products at competitive prices. So if these sorts of problems are causing supply constraints and difficulty in competing with foreign producers, demand management will hold no magic answers. Neither can fiscal and monetary policies protect economies from unexpected supply-side shocks such as oil price changes.

For all sorts of reasons, simple adherence to the 1950s- and 1960s-style fiscal policies became increasingly inappropriate after 1970. But we must be careful not to throw out the baby with the bathwater. Fiscal policy remains an extremely powerful tool for controlling the level of aggregate demand in the economy.

Questions

1. List the fiscal and monetary policies which can be used to influence (or manage) the level of aggregate demand.
2. What problems are likely to arise with demand-management policies?
3. Why are there likely to be time-lags (a) between identification of the economic problem, and the implementation of policies; and (b) between implementation of policy and the resulting effect of the policy on the economy?
4. What are the economic problems which demand management cannot help? What other policies might be needed to deal with these?

Exam Preparation

PRACTICAL EXERCISES

1. Redraw Figure 17.2 showing the effect of reduced taxes on real national income.
2. Redraw Figure 17.3 showing the effect of reducing government expenditure on real national income.
3. Study the data below, then answer the questions which follow.
The following are data for a hypothetical closed economy which initially is in short-run macroeconomic equilibrium.
   (i) The consumption function is given by the equation

   $C = 100 + 0.8\ Y_D$

   where C denotes consumption in £mn and Y_D denotes disposable after-tax income in £mn.
   (ii) All government revenue is raised by a 25 per cent proportional income tax. Hence

   $Y_D = 0.75Y$

   where Y denotes national income in £mn.
   (iii) Private investment spending = £1400mn.
   (iv) Government expenditure on goods and services = £2500mn.
   (v) National income (Y) = £10000mn.

   (a) What are the initial values of consumption, savings, and government tax revenue?
   (b) What is the relationship between the average propensity to consume and the marginal propensity to consume in this economy? How does the average propensity to consume vary as disposable income increases?
   (c) Suppose that private investment spending subsequently decreases to £1000mn. What, other things being equal, is the change in national income that is predicted by the Keynesian income–expenditure model?
   (d) If government expenditure and the tax rate remain unchanged, what is the government budget deficit or surplus at the equilibrium level of national income *following* the decrease in private investment?
   (e) Suppose the government wishes to achieve a return to the original national income of £10000mn via increasing after-tax disposable incomes by means of non-taxable cash benefits paid to households. If the consumption function is unchanged, by how much must government expenditure on cash benefits increase?

MULTIPLE CHOICE QUESTIONS

1. A deflationary policy is most likely to cause
   A a reduction in the volume of exports
   B increased monetary demand
   C a reduction in the level of taxation
   D an increase in the level of unemployment
   E a fall in the value of money.
2. Assume that investment rises by £500 million and that exports rise by £1300 million. Given that the marginal propensity to consume is ⅘, by how much will national income increase?
   A £1800 million
   B £3000 million
   C £4050 million
   D £6000 million
   E £9000 million.
3. Which of the following is likely to be deflationary?
   A index-linking of consumers' savings
   B failing to increase tax allowances in line with inflation
   C failing to balance the budget during recessions
   D funding the deficits of nationalized industries
   E reducing the external value of the currency.
4. If an open economy with government activity is in equilibrium and imports are greater than exports, which of the following *must* be true?
   A savings are greater than investment
   B investment plus government spending is greater than savings plus taxation
   C taxation is greater than government spending
   D investment plus government spending is less than savings plus taxation
   E government spending is greater than taxation.
5. A tax will have a built-in stabilizing effect if tax
   A rates automatically increase in line with inflation
   B yield increases at a faster rate than income
   C yield varies inversely with national income levels
   D yield remains constant as levels of national income change

One or more of the options given in Questions 6 and 7 may be correct. Select your answers by means of the code set out in the grid.

A	B	C	D
1, 2, 3 all correct	1, 2 only correct	2, 3 only correct	1 only correct

6. If the marginal propensity to consume home-produced goods is less than unity, then rise in the country's National Income is likely to lead to an increase in
1 savings
2 taxation revenue
3 expenditure on imports

7. A decline in government spending will not necessarily be followed by a fall in National Income if there is an increase in
1 investment
2 exports
3 taxation

RELATED ESSAY QUESTIONS

1. Discuss some of the macroeconomic consequences of a reduction in government spending.

2. (a) Given the assumption of a closed economy, explain carefully the working of the multiplier.
(b) How is the working of the multiplier affected if the economy engages in foreign trade?

3. (a) Explain the theory underlying proposals that governments should use discretionary fiscal policy to stabilize fluctuations in aggregate monetary expenditure.
(b) For what reasons has it been asserted that such policies in practice run the risk of destabilizing the economy?
(c) Explain why the actual budget deficit (or surplus) may not be a reliable indicator of discretionary changes in fiscal policy.

4. What is meant by the management of the economy?

5. Use multiplier analysis to examine the impact on employment and the balance of payments of (a) an increase in private investment, (b) an increase in the marginal propensity to consume, and (c) a devaluation of the exchange rate.

6. How can a government use fiscal policy in an attempt to change the level of aggregate demand? Examine the problems which the government might encounter in pursuing this objective.

7. Explain why, in your view, economists make such extensive use of the concept of equilibrium in formulating their theories. Discuss whether or not you regard the existence of unemployment as a sign that the national economy is in disequilibrium.

18 Income and Employment Determination: Some Alternative Views

Key Points to Review

- **Substitution and income effects (5.1)**
- **Measurement of unemployment (11.2)**
- **Measurement of inflation (11.4)**
- **Black economy (13.7)**
- **Aggregate supply and aggregate demand (14.1, 14.2)**

Questions for Preview

1 **What is supply-side economics?**

2 **What is the Laffer curve?**

3 **What is a Phillips curve?**

4 **What is the adaptive-expectations hypothesis?**

5 **What is the natural rate of unemployment?**

The income-determination models presented in the previous chapters are a good start at understanding how the macroeconomy works. But the real world presents some problems in analysis and prediction. For example, the simplified Keynesian model used throughout most of Chapter 16 assumed that demand determined the level of output, that wages and prices were inflexible, and that inflation only occurred when we hit full employment. These theoretical assumptions have all led to controversies regarding the actual determination of income and employment. Therefore, some alternative views need to be examined and these will be considered next via the concepts of:

Supply-side economics
The Phillips curve
Adaptive expectations
The natural rate of unemployment
Rational expectations

Supply-side Economics Revisited

In Chapter 14, we presented a simplified model of so-called supply-side economics. Supply-side economics involved shifting the aggregate supply curve outwards and to the right, as in Figure 14.6. We pointed out in Chapter 14 that there are two sides to fiscal policy, one of them being the effects of changes in the tax structure on the position of the aggregate supply curve. Supply-side economics is nothing more nor less than a belief in the ability to affect incentives enough to actually shift the aggregate supply curve. As an example we can follow the use of one supply-side policy, e.g. lowering marginal tax-rates. Such a policy allows the government to pursue expansionary demand-management policies – shifting the aggregate demand curve out – without suffering increased inflation, because it is simultaneously shifting the aggregate supply curve outwards. A similar supply-side economics argument is presented graphically in Figure 18.1.

Of course, supply-side economics is not new. Any attempt at increasing productivity can be labelled supply-side economics. Governments throughout the world have attempted to increase productivity by: setting up training schemes, by providing advisory services to business persons, by lowering unemployment benefit, by abolishing complex legislation relating to work and wages, by providing various tax incentives, and so on. For a more specific idea of the

Figure 18.1

Supply-side Economics. Viewed in a favourable light, the use of supply-side policies can create an increase in the equilibrium level of real national income per year without an increase in the price level. Start in equilibrium with aggregate demand as AD_1AD_1 and short-run aggregate supply as $SRAS_1$. The equilibrium price level is P_1 and the equilibrium level of real national income per year is Y_1. The government simultaneously engages in two manoeuvres: (1) expansionary fiscal policies which shift out the aggregate demand curve to AD_2AD_2, and (2) supply-side productivity-increasing policies, such as reductions in marginal tax-rates and/or training programmes, which shift out the short-run aggregate supply curve to $SRAS_2$. The new equilibrium price level remains at P_1, but the new equilibrium level of real national income per year has increased to Y_2.

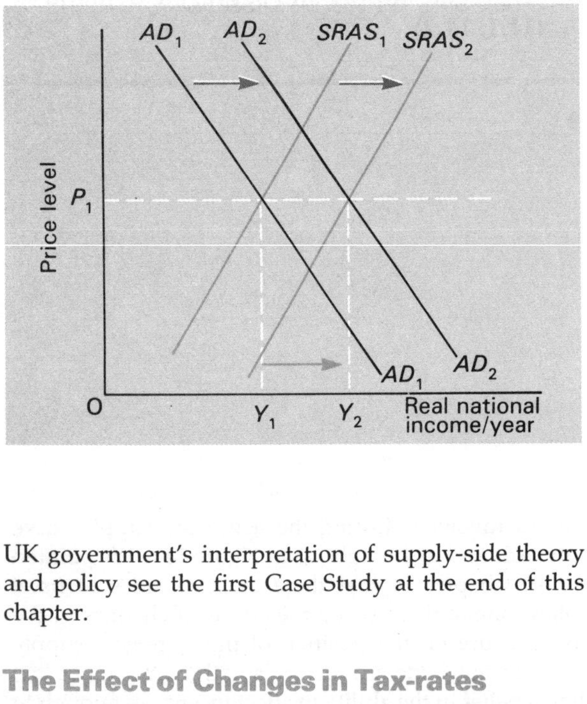

UK government's interpretation of supply-side theory and policy see the first Case Study at the end of this chapter.

The Effect of Changes in Tax-rates

Reform of tax-*rates* is central to any supply-side package. Notice the word *rates* is italicized. This is because supply-side economics deals primarily with changes in tax-*rates*, as opposed to changes in total tax revenues. The underlying assumption is that individuals, in their capacities as workers, savers, and investors, will respond to changes at the margin. What is important to the worker contemplating more or less work is the after-tax, or take-home pay (especially as there is always the choice of more or less leisure to trade this against). Similarly, what is important for the saver and the business person is the expected rate of return on their savings and investments after tax has been deducted. Therefore, the higher the marginal tax-rate, the greater the incentive to avoid paying taxes, either through legal tax avoidance, illegal tax evasion, or simply less work, less saving, and less investment. This very simple proposition dates back perhaps several thousand years. It was reborn in the 1970s as the **Laffer curve**, named after Arthur Laffer, an American economist.

The Laffer Curve

Laffer's basic argument rests on the premise that zero tax-rates would obviously produce zero tax revenues, while tax-rates of 100 per cent would also produce zero revenues, as taxpayers would cease to work (at least for money), since their incomes would be entirely taxed away. Maximum revenue would, therefore, be achieved by some rate in between. This idea is best illustrated graphically. Look at Figure 18.2. We measure tax-rates, T, on the vertical axis and tax revenues, R, on the horizontal axis. Tax-rate T_1 is the maximum rate that the government can impose before the relationship between tax-rates and revenues becomes negative, or inverse. For example, at tax-rate T_2 revenues will have dropped from R_{max} to R_2.

Figure 18.2

The Laffer Curve. The Laffer curve is a representation of the relationship between *tax-rates* and tax revenues collected. We put tax revenues on the horizontal axis and tax-rates on the vertical axis. The maximum tax revenues collectable, R_{max}, result when the tax-rate, T_1, is utilized. If the government insists on having a tax-rate of T_2 tax revenues collected fall from R_{max} to R_2. Thus, the Laffer curve policy implication is that if we believe that the real-world relationship between tax-rates and tax revenues is as depicted here, and we believe that we are above tax-rate T_1, then a reduction from current tax-rates of, say, T_2 towards tax-rate T_1 will *increase* tax revenues from R_2 to some greater amount, with the maximum reachable at R_{max}. In other words, a tax-rate reduction leads to an increase in tax revenues. The validity of this proposition rests on the empirical relationship between reductions in tax-rates and changes in the amount of work effort, investment, saving, and attempts at avoiding the payment of taxes.

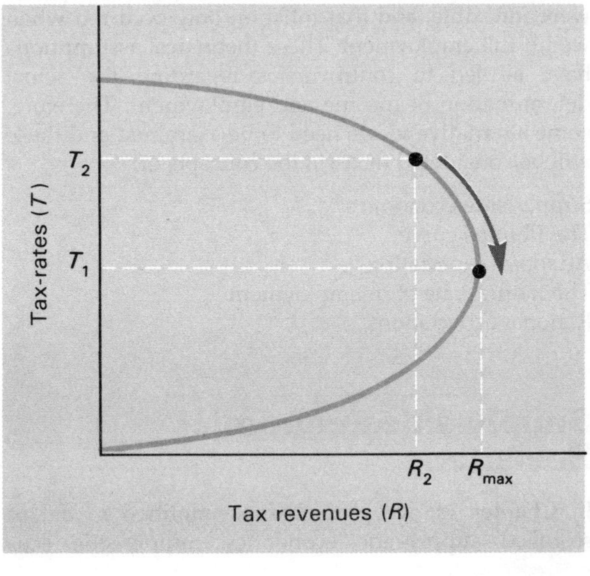

The policy implications of the Laffer curve are that if the economy is already at tax-rate T_2, a reduction in tax-rates will actually lead to an increase in tax revenues.

INCOME EFFECT OR SUBSTITUTION EFFECT?

Let us consider the supply-side effects of income tax. A change in these tax-rates could lead to both a substitution and an income effect. For example, an increase in income tax-rates reduces the opportunity cost of leisure (as workers will receive less personal disposable income for working) thereby inducing individuals – at least on the margin – to reduce their work effort and consume more leisure. The higher tax creates a disincentive effect on work while making leisure seem more attractive. This is the substitution effect. But an increase in tax-rates will also reduce spendable income and have an income effect, thereby reducing the demand for leisure and providing a greater incentive to work.

The outcome of these two effects – substitution and income – depends on which of them is stronger. Supply-side economists argue that, at least in the 1970s and 1980s, the substitution effect has dominated to the extent that increases in marginal tax-rates have caused workers to work less and decreases have caused workers to work more. This kind of reasoning has formed the basis of many income tax changes since 1979 in the UK. Indeed the basic rate of income tax in the UK was gradually cut from 33 per cent (in 1979) to 25 per cent (in 1989). Whether these reductions, however, have the desired effects is difficult to judge.

A study commissioned by the Treasury in 1987 and undertaken by Professor C. V. Brown discovered the cuts in tax did not make people work harder. Indeed, it was suggested by a way of explanation that 79 per cent of employees were restricted by the nature of their contracts from working longer hours in order to reap higher rewards. Another piece of research executed by the Institute of Fiscal Studies concluded that cuts in tax-rates are only significant as providing an incentive for married women to take jobs and/or work longer hours. To some extent this complements Brown's work as women on part-time contracts can increase their paid hours with greater ease. Whether these findings, however, are sufficient to support the general government line of the 1980s that 'lower rates of tax sharpen up incentives and stimulate enterprise' is still, to a large extent, in debate.

Criticisms of the Laffer Curve

While one cannot argue with the theoretical possibility of the existence of the Laffer curve, one can argue about where an economy is on the Laffer curve. For example, are the government correct in assuming that the UK economy has already exceeded the point at which maximum revenue would be derived (T_1)? Furthermore, can one be certain that reductions in marginal rates of taxation will stimulate the economy sufficiently to actually increase the total government tax revenue? Indeed, it is difficult to estimate how much of the underground economy will come above ground if marginal tax-rates are reduced.

Another complication is that in the UK, while direct taxes have been reduced to some extent to encourage incentives to work and invest, indirect taxes – taxes on spending – have been increased to maintain government expenditure. In some way this highlights the classic problem of lowering inflation and unemployment at the same time and this will be dealt with next. (Key Points 18.1.)

The Phillips Curve in Theory and Reality

Another important controversy that is presently debated has arisen because inflation does not only occur at full employment. In fact, some economists argue that there is a constant *trade-off* between the rate of employment and the rate of inflation. Their argument is that in order to obtain less unemployment, we have to suffer greater rates of inflation. Or, conversely, in order to reduce the rate of inflation, we have to accept more unemployment. This trade-off has been labelled the

Key Points 18.1

- **Supply-side economics deals with ways of shifting the aggregate supply curve outwards and to the right. For example, by improving the incentives to work, save, and invest.**
- **A lower marginal tax-rate is *one* way to improve the reward for working, saving, and investing.**
- **The level of impact that a change in tax-rates generates is theoretically determined by income and substitution effects – these are difficult to measure in reality.**
- **The Laffer curve shows the relationship between the tax-rates and tax revenues. According to Laffer there is a tax-rate above which tax revenues start to fall as work effort starts to fall.**

Phillips curve, named after the late Professor A. W. Phillips, who discovered that in Great Britain wages had historically risen rapidly when the unemployment rate was low and had risen more slowly when the unemployment rate was high. His empirical evidence was for the years 1861–1957.

Although Phillips's original analysis published in 1958 was in terms of *wage-rate increases* and the unemployment rate, economists have contended that the relationship also holds between *price increases* and the unemployment rate. Indeed, there does seem to be a close relationship between wage-rate changes and the Retail Price Index.

Figure 18.3 shows a hypothetical Phillips curve. With the hypothetical Phillips curve, if we are, for example, at an unemployment rate of 6 per cent and want to reduce the unemployment rate to 4 per cent, we have to accept an increase in the rate of inflation of 2 percentage points. If only the world were so simple! If it were, policy-makers could simply set a trade-off menu. Each year they could vote on whether they wanted to have less or more unemployment with concomitantly more or less inflation. Indeed, that is the way many policy-makers talked during the late 1960s and the mid-1970s.

Figure 18.3

A Hypothetical Phillips Curve. The Phillips curve shows the relationship between the unemployment rate and the rate of inflation. If we want a 3 per cent unemployment rate, we presumably have to live with 5 per cent annual inflation. If we do not want to live with 5 per cent inflation but insist on only 3 per cent, we will have to 'buy it' with more unemployment, since a 3 per cent rate of inflation is associated with a 4 per cent rate of unemployment.

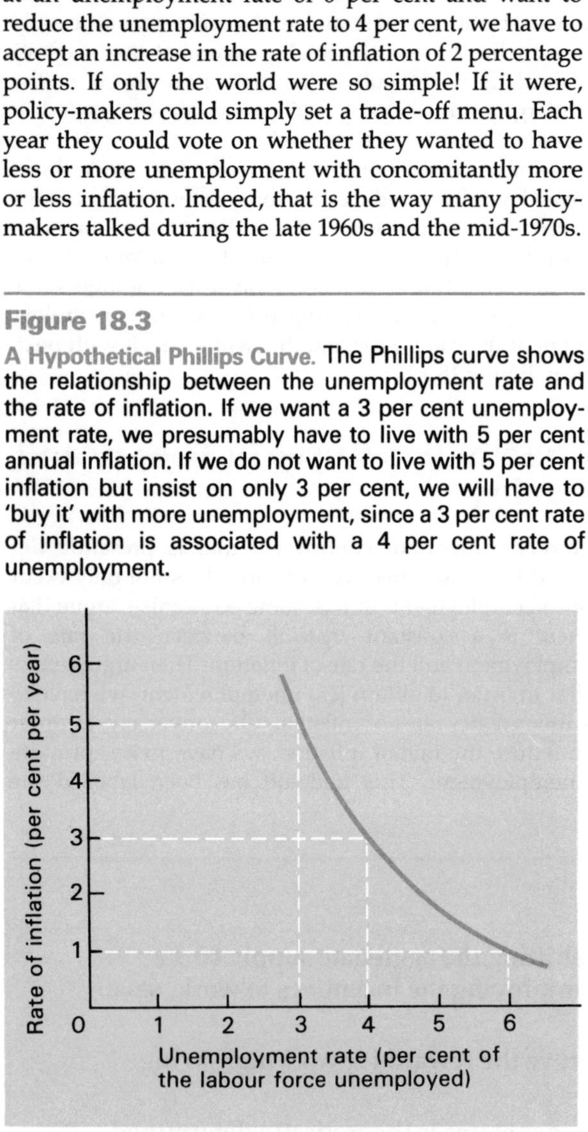

The Phillips Curve in Reality Today

In Figure 18.4 we plot the rate of inflation and the rate of unemployment that has actually occurred since Phillips's publication. Instead of there being a *negative* trade-off relationship between the rate of unemployment and the rate of inflation, in recent times there has been a *positive* one. For example, higher rates of inflation became commonly associated with higher rates of unemployment – to the extent that economists coined a special phrase to describe the situation, namely, **stagflation**. To understand why this trade-off between the rate of inflation and the rate of unemployment has diminished, we must first understand the role of expectations.

Expectations and the Phillips Curve

The hypothetical Phillips curve presented in Figure 18.3 assumes rigid expectations of future changes in the rate of inflation. Actually, the original specifications of the Phillips curve worked well for about a century in the United States and in Great Britain. Fluctuations in the rate of inflation were, to a large degree, symmetrical with unemployment, yet as time progressed this relationship changed.

With the development of increased unemployment benefit people took longer to search for work. Union strengths helped generate better wages. Employment legislation, such as minimum wages and redundancy payments, also had its effect on employment opportunities and inflationary pressure. Inflation itself became a problem, especially as its rate seems to fluctuate from year to year. Consequently, it was no longer rational for individuals to hold rigid expectations about future changes in the rate of inflation. That is changes in the expected (anticipated) rate of inflation became as important as changes in the actual rate of inflation. The new relationship between inflation and unemployment required a new explanation. This explanation developed via the accelerationist Phillips curve which complements the presentation of a natural unemploy-

Figure 18.4

The Phillips Curve Relationship in Reality 1960–88. In this diagram we plot the average annual unemployment rate against the average inflation rate for the period 1960–88. You will notice that the smooth line of the Phillips curve has been displaced by a scatter diagram. The various points no longer show the purported negative trade-off relationship.

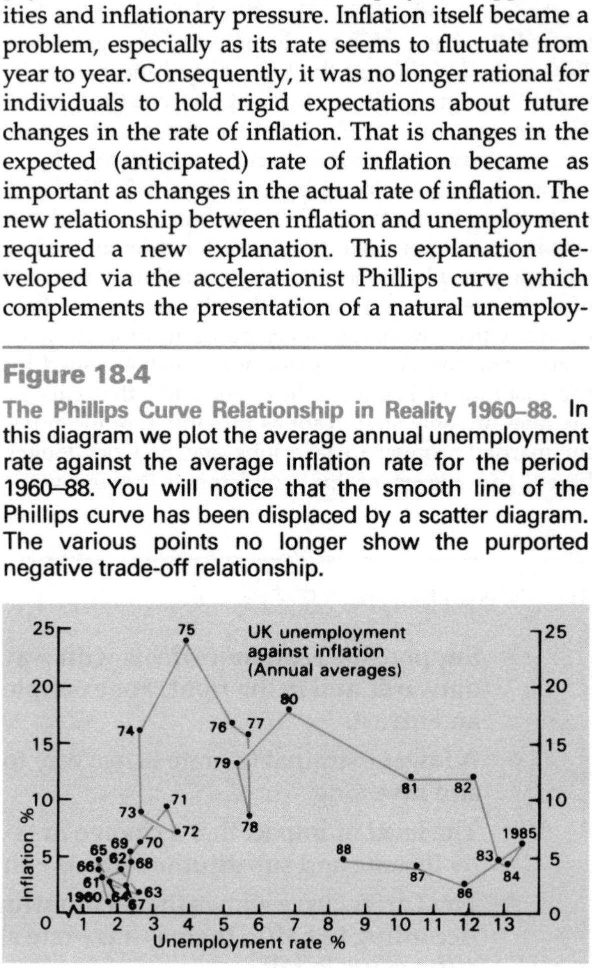

Source: The figures are taken from the *Department of Employment Gazette*.

Key Points 18.2

- **Since 1969, this country has seen simultaneous bouts of high unemployment and inflation, usually called 'stagflation'.**
- **The Phillips curve is named after A. W. Phillips who discovered that wages in Great Britain had risen rapidly when unemployment was low, and slowly when unemployment was high (during the period 1861–1957).**
- **The theoretical negative trade-off between the rate of unemployment and the rate of inflation has, in the last few decades, not been validated by the real world; rather, there seems to be a positive relationship between the rate of inflation and the rate of unemployment.**
- **Basically, the Phillips curve trade-off between the rate of inflation and the rate of unemployment only works when there is a constant relationship between the *'actual'* and *'expected'* rate of inflation.**

ment rate. Both of these more recent concepts will be explained below, after exploring the idea of expectations a little further. (Key Points 18.2.)

Adaptive Expectations

The main observation here is that workers cannot be fooled forever. Everyone can be assumed to adapt eventually to a changed situation if that adaptation is beneficial. Figuring out what the rate of inflation is going to be next year is beneficial to anybody attempting to make economic decisions, the consequences of which will carry through into the future. One way that individuals can adapt to a changing rate of inflation is by using information on past rates of inflation to make predictions about future rates of inflation. This simplistic theory of the formation of expectations has been called the **adaptive-expectations hypothesis**. It states that workers gauge what happened in the past as the best indicator of what will happen in the future. Look at Figure 18.5. Here we show, in panel (a) the actual rate of inflation. It is rising. In year 1 it is 6 per cent per annum, during the second year it is 8 per cent, during the third year it jumps to 12 per cent, and stays at 12 per cent during the fourth, fifth, and sixth years.

In the simplest adaptive-expectations model, the expected rate of inflation this year is simply whatever the rate of inflation was *last* year. This is shown in panel (b). During the second year, workers believed inflation would be 6 per cent because that is what it was the year before. During the third year they believed it would be 8 per cent (because that is what it was the year before). In this simplified adaptive-expectations model, workers are always behind in their expectation of inflation. When the rate of inflation is rising, they will always believe it is going to be less than it actually turns out to be; when the rate of inflation is falling, they will always believe it is going to be more than it actually turns out to be. Only when the rate of inflation remains constant for a period of time do expectations come into line with reality.

Figure 18.5

The Adaptive-expectations Hypothesis. According to the simplest version of the adaptive-expectations hypothesis, individuals formulate their expectation of inflation solely on what the rate of inflation was in the previous year. Consider panel (a), where we show the actual rate of inflation as being 6 per cent during year 1, 8 per cent during year 2, and 12 per cent during years 3, 4, 5, and 6. According to the simplified adapative-expectations hypothesis, in year 2 people will predict that inflation will be 6 per cent, because that is what it was in year 1. We show this in panel (b). In year 3, even though the actual rate of inflation is 12 per cent (as shown in panel (a)) the expected rate of inflation is 8 per cent (as shown in panel (b)). Finally, in year 4, the expected rate of inflation is equal to the actual rate of inflation because inflation has levelled off.

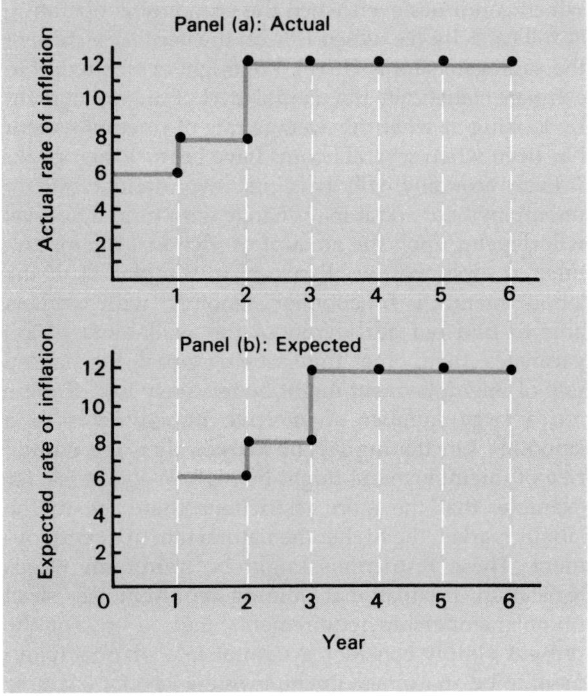

A more sophisticated model of the adaptive-expectations hypothesis will have workers forming their expectation of inflation on the basis of some combination of, say, the last three, four, or five years' rates of inflation, with more weight being given to rates of inflation in the immediately preceding years.

Adaptive Expectations and a Series of Short-run Phillips Curves

Using the adaptive-expectations hypothesis, one can posit that there still exists a series of *short-run* Phillips curves. Each short-run Phillips curve will relate to each expected rate of inflation. In order to understand the argument completely, one must first understand the concept of the natural rate of unemployment, which is typically associated with full employment.

The Natural Rate of Unemployment

The **natural rate of unemployment** is the amount of unemployment which would prevail when inflation is correctly anticipated. It would be easy, therefore, to specify an actual numerical estimate only during a phase of totally stable prices. An alternative way of presenting the natural rate of unemployment is to consider that it occurs when there is equilibrium in all product and factor markets. Consequently, the natural rate of unemployment can be regarded as the rate of unemployment that would exist in the absence of cyclical fluctuations in the economy. Obviously identifying such a theoretical rate in practice is difficult. However, we should conceptually begin to understand what the rate conveys. In the very simplest of terms, the natural rate of unemployment is that unemployment which continues even when the economy is operating at full capacity (i.e. when it is on the vertical section of the aggregate supply curve). We might even attempt to estimate statistically the natural level of unemployment by looking at what the average rate of unemployment has been when several booms have been at their peak.

Each economy will have its own natural rate of unemployment and it may change with time. The level will depend upon the amount of frictional unemployment, a topic that we discussed in Chapter 11. If the labour market is functioning smoothly, with workers able to find out quickly about the availability of job vacancies, then, other things being equal, the natural rate of unemployment might be relatively low. If there are a large number of effective impediments to a smoothly functioning labour market, then the natural rate of unemployment might be high. We surmise, for example, that the more restrictions there are in the labour market, the higher the natural rate of unemployment. These restrictions might be minimum wages legislation, occupational training requirements, strict union membership requirements, and so on. For the present simply consider a natural rate of unemployment to be an average unemployment rate for a couple of decades, and recognize that an economy may experience an actual rate that is above or below its natural rate (as shown in Figure 18.6).

Figure 18.6

A Hypothetical Presentation of the Natural Rate of Unemployment. The natural rate of unemployment is shown in the coloured line; the actual rate is the black line. We assume there has been no consistent relationship between the two; we have simply plotted the natural rate on the basis of very general principles.

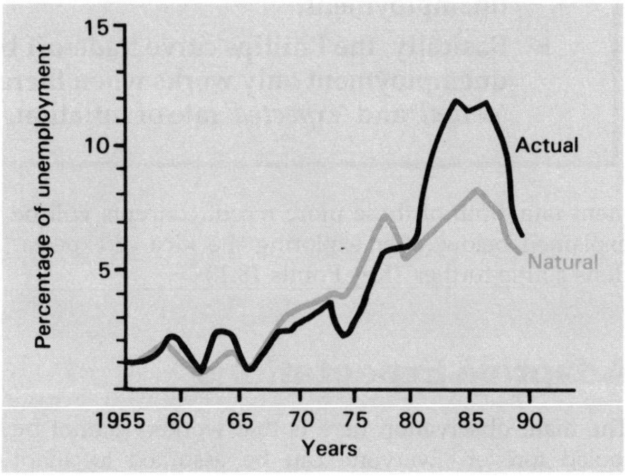

Keeping the Rate of Unemployment below Its Long-run Natural Rate

Using the adaptive-expectations hypothesis, the only way to keep the unemployment rate below its long-run natural rate is to have the *actual* rate of inflation exceed the *expected* rate. In this way workers will suffer from a 'money illusion' and believe that wage-rates are going up – making work far more worth while. But since workers adapt, in order to maintain the gap between the actual and expected rates of inflation, the rate of inflation would have continually to accelerate. What is needed to consistently increase output and reduce unemployment permanently, then, is an inflation rate that is always greater than anticipated. This can be called an **accelerationist view** of the Phillips-curve analysis.* It suggests that the only way to produce deviations from the natural rate of unemployment is to have accelerating or decelerating inflation.

GRAPHIC ANALYSIS OF THE ACCELERATIONIST VIEW

In Figure 18.7, we see two curves similar in appearance to the standard Phillips curve (thus the alternative name in the footnote.) On the horizontal axis, we measure unemployment; on the vertical axis, we measure the *actual* rate of inflation. The Phillips curves, however, are drawn for two different levels of *expected*

*Alternatively, it can be referred to as an 'expectations-augmented Phillips curve'.

rates of inflation. The left one is drawn for an expected rate of inflation of 3 per cent; the right one is drawn for an expected rate of inflation of 6 per cent. The vertical line labelled U^* represents the so-called natural rate of unemployment, which we will assume to be 5 per cent.

Those who believe in the accelerationist theory assume that the unemployment rate will eventually settle at U^* when the future inflation rate is correctly anticipated, that is, when the *actual* rate of change in prices is equal to the *expected* rate of change in prices. This would occur either at point *A*, if the actual rate of inflation were 6 per cent, or point *B*, if the actual rate of inflation were 3 per cent. Look at point *C*, however. Here the anticipated rate of inflation is 3 per cent, but the actual rate is 6 per cent. Point *C* represents 'over full' employment. Now look at point *D*. The actual rate of inflation is 3 per cent, but the anticipated rate is 6 per cent. Unemployment exceeding the natural rate thus occurs.

The accelerationist theory says that you can keep unemployment down only by increasing (creating an acceleration in) the rate of inflation. Hence, high inflation does not keep unemployment down. Only rising inflation does. If the accelerationists are correct, it does not matter much in the long run what the rate of growth of the money supply is, provided that the rate remains stable. Those who believe in the accelerationist theory believe that a continuous rate of inflation of 4 per cent per year will yield the same long-run level of unemployment as a continuous rate of change of prices of 10 per cent. The only prerequisite for this outcome is that the rate of change of prices be correctly anticipated. (Now read Key Points 18.3 on page 276.)

Figure 18.7

An Expectations-augmented Phillips Curve, showing Natural Rate of Unemployment. Here we show two Phillips curves. On the horizontal axis, the unemployment rate is measured. On the vertical axis is the rate of inflation. We assume that the 'natural' or long-run level of unemployment is at U^*, or 5 per cent of the labour force. There are two separate Phillips curves: one is for an expected rate of inflation of 6 per cent per year, and the other is for an expected rate of inflation of 3 per cent per year. If the expected rate of inflation is 6 per cent per year and the actual rate of inflation (which is measured on the vertical axis) is also 6 per cent per year, then the long-run equilibrium unemployment level will be maintained at point *A*. However, if the expected rate of inflation remains at 6 per cent per year, but the *actual* rate of inflation is only 3 per cent per year, we will find ourselves at point *D*, where there is excess unemployment – that is, unemployment over and above the normal long-run U^* of 5 per cent. Here we see that an actual rate of inflation less than the expected rate of inflation leads to unemployment. Now take the innermost curve, where the expected rate of inflation is 3 per cent. If the actual rate of inflation is also 3 per cent, then there will be no excess unemployment – that is, unemployment will be at its 'normal' long-run level of 5 per cent. We will be at point *B*. Suppose, however, that the actual rate of inflation is 6 per cent. We will find ourselves at point *C*. We will be over full employment – that is, unemployment will be less than its long-run or normal level of 5 per cent. At point *C*, individuals *underestimate* the actual rate of inflation. Contrast this with point *D*, where individuals *overestimate* the actual rate of inflation. The underestimate causes unemployment rates to fall below U^*. The overestimate causes unemployment rates to be greater than U^*.

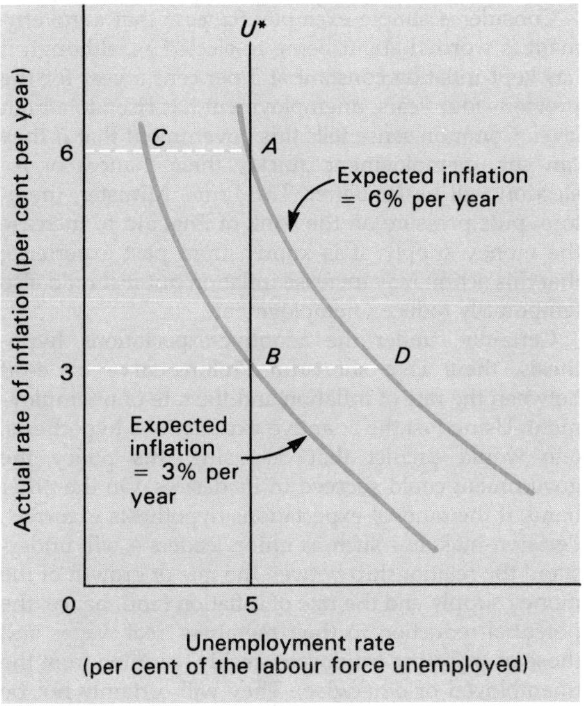

Another Modern School of Thought – Rational Expectations

Finally, it is worth looking at the criticism made by the rational-expectations school. They make the pertinent point that adaptive-expectations theorists always have workers being one step behind what is actually occurring, or what policy-makers are actually doing. This implies that workers can be fooled. No learning from experience is allowed for, which somehow strikes a false chord in the minds of this final school. Their notion is that eventually rational individuals will modify their forecasting equation to produce unbiased estimates of the rate of inflation (or whatever). Taken to its ultimate conclusion supporters of rational expectations would claim that eventually there will not even be a short-run trade-off between unemployment and inflation. (The short-run Phillips curve would thus become U^* in Figure 18.7.)

The Rational-expectations Hypothesis

The **rational-expectations hypothesis** therefore is most concerned with human behaviour; it emphasizes the

Key Points 18.3

- **The adaptive-expectations hypothesis argues that workers will make predictions of this year's rate of inflation, based on what the rate of inflation was last year, or, at most, over the previous few years.**
- **Those who believe in the accelerationist theory argue that the original Phillips-curve analysis ignores the fact that workers will eventually correctly anticipate the future inflation rate.**
- **The accelerationists believe that there are numerous short-run Phillips curves, each associated with a different expected rate of inflation.**
- **In the short run, when the rate of inflation exceeds its expected rate, workers can be fooled into accepting lower real-wage increases; hence, there is a reduction in unemployment.**
- **In the long run, once workers fully anticipate future rates of inflation, there will be no trade-off between unemployment and inflation.**
- **Only to the extent that policy-makers can keep the rate of inflation higher than what is anticipated can there be a permanent trade-off between unemployment and inflation.**

rational sifting and weighing of all available information that can be undertaken.

Rather than simply looking at what has happened in the previous year, rational individuals will form *rational expectations*. They will look at what happened in the past and combine it with their predictions of *current* government policies that they think are being pursued and *future* government policies that they think are likely to be introduced. In other words, rational expectations require a judgement about the future effects of current and future policies that are combined with lessons from whatever has happened in the past.

Consider a simple example. *Suppose* that a government is worried about being re-elected as, although it has kept inflation constant at 5 per cent a year for the previous four years, unemployment has risen to a high level. Common sense tells this government that if they can cut unemployment quickly their chances of re-election will be far better. The Prime Minister, therefore, puts pressure on the Bank of England to increase the money supply. It is known from past experience that this action may increase inflation but it should also temporarily reduce unemployment.

Certainly, under the adaptive-expectations hypothesis, there is a short-run Phillips-curve trade-off between the rate of inflation and the rate of unemployment. Using just the adaptive-expectations hypothesis, one would predict that on using this policy the government could succeed in its desires. On the other hand, if the rational-expectations hypothesis is correct, decision-makers – such as union leaders – will understand the relationship betwen the rate of growth of the money supply and the rate of inflation (and, hence, the potential reduction in their members' real wages and those of any other employees freshly recruited from the unemployed or otherwise). They will certainly not be fooled into accepting a prediction of a 5 per cent rate of inflation in the coming year, just because that is the way inflation has gone for the previous few years. They will use the information that they have about current government policy. The union leaders will demand wage increases consistent with the higher anticipated rate of inflation. The desired reduction in unemployment will not, therefore, materalize.

Now, of course, not all decision-makers will get their predictions right. It is impossible to know exactly the relationship between the rate of increase in the money supply and the rate of inflation; or, at best, it is impossible to figure out the **'time-lag'** between changes in monetary policy and changes in the rate of inflation. What the rational-expectations hypothesis suggests, however, is that workers and other decision-makers in the economy will not *consistently* and *systematically* make a forecasting error by simply basing the future on the past.

Indeed in some spheres of economics rational expectations will take on a more than proportionate significance. For example, City brokers, foreign-exchange speculators, and commodity-market dealers will depend upon their specialist, skilled, experienced, and knowledgeable judgement to move towards large profits. In the macroeconomic scene generally, however, it is debatable whether agents – managers, workers, and consumers – have the same developed level of expertise and judgement relating to government policy and the workings of an economy.

The important point from this concluding scenario is that you recognize the difficulties that economists may face when advising governments. (You can fool some people some of the time, but you can't fool all of the people all of the time.) You should certainly appreciate that *expectations* of one sort or another definitely influence economic behaviour; that time-lags compound the problems of economic analysis; and that there are no easy answers but many complex alternative possibilities. Indeed, this whole chapter has, it is hoped, opened up the supply-side of the economy generally, and thus put you in a better position to understand existing policy and the debates emanating from it.

Key Points 18.4

- **The rational-expectations hypothesis predicts that individuals will form their expectations rationally by examining all information. That means that economic agents will look not only at such things as the past rate of inflation but also at present government policies that can affect the current and future rate of inflation.**
- **The rational-expectations hypothesis simply predicts that decision-makers in the economy will *not* consistently and systematically make a forecasting error by basing the future on the past.**

CASE STUDY

The Supply-Siders

Supply-side Economics

The basic premise here is that *supply will create its own demand.* The supporters of this school believe, therefore, that it is necessary to allow the private (market) sector sufficient freedom and incentive to expand the range of goods and services that they feel it worth their while to produce. Consequently, the policies orientated towards the supply-side are aimed at making business and employment rewarding. Once supply increases, income increases (for the owners of the factors of production) and thus spending and employment, in turn, also increase.

The prime objective of any government wishing to promote these supply-determined increases in national income and employment, would be to remove the market distortions that reduce an individual's willingness to supply labour or a firm's willingness to supply goods. These policies have been at the core of the Conservative Manifesto since they came to office in May 1979. As reported in the *Economic Progress Report* of June that year their Economic Strategy is:

based on four principles: first, the strengthening of incentives, particularly through tax cuts, allowing people to keep more of their earnings in their own hands, so that hard work, ability and success are rewarded; second, greater freedom of choice by reducing the state's role and enlarging that of the individual; third, the reduction of the borrowing requirement of the public sector to a level which leaves room for the rest of the economy to prosper; and fourth through firm monetary and fiscal discipline, bringing inflation under control and ensuring those taking part in collective bargaining are obliged to live with the consequences of their actions.

The model upon which this policy is based is very different from the Keynesian presentation in most 'A'-level texts. Explanations for variations in employment and output are being made by reference to the factors which determine *Aggregate Supply* (as opposed to Aggregate Demand). The factors which can be seen to determine Aggregate Supply are: Level of profit, ease of movement into and out of markets, the level of wages, the marginal efficiency of capital, the marginal revenue product, the level of fixed costs etc. – i.e. mainly microeconomic factors. Furthermore, it is assumed that the correct level of aggregate supply will be determined by market forces and not government intervention.

The ideas outlined above date back to a French economist – Jean Baptiste Say – who lectured at the turn of the nineteenth century. (Say formulated his law of markets in 1803.) At the beginning of the 1970s Professor Lucas and T. Sargeant, both American economists, popularized these classic ideas once again. In the mid-1970s British institutions such as Liverpool University, the London Business School, and the Institute of Economic Affairs (IEA) started to add their support.

Following these academic developments governments in the USA and UK today are very much under the influence of supply-side economics. In fact, some would argue that the policies pursued by the present Conservative government should lose the title 'Monetarist' and gain the broader label 'New Classical Macroeconomics'. Indeed the various faces of monetarism that the Conservatives present all have classical roots. Supply-side economics is merely one of those roots.

Source: D. Myers, 'The Supply Siders', *Economics* (Journal of the Economic Association), Vol. XX part 4, No. 88, Winter 1984, p. 17.

Questions

1. What are the other classical roots that monetarism contains?
2. 'More detailed government intervention or greater trust in market forces.' Which policy would you promote as economic adviser to the Prime Minister?
3. Supporters of supply-side economics make frequent reference to the existence and size of the black economy. Can you explain why?
4. Supply-side policies have now been at the core of government thinking for more than a decade. How many examples can you think of that exemplify this policy in action?

CASE STUDY

Economic Sense and Political Nonsense

The unemployed in the UK become entitled to various social-security payments including: housing benefit, health benefits, family credit, and community charge rebates. Each claimant is individually assessed and subject to a means test. Consequently, to state a standard amount of entitlement is a difficult affair.

However, for purposes of illustration we shall briefly consider the financial entitlements of an unemployed single person over 25. This person could get: Unemployment Benefit of £34.70* plus income support.

The income support will provide an 80 per cent community charge rebate, free National Health Service benefits, and assistance with rent or interest payments on a mortgage for owner-occupiers.

To reduce the natural rate of unemployment these benefits could be stopped. The argument is that the unemployed person would then be obliged to find work.

Such a drastic cut in benefits would be political suicide because of the consequences that would follow. For example, a large number of people would be homeless and starving as well as unemployed. Thus 2 million (or however many unemployed there were claiming benefit) would be less likely to vote for the party who cut the benefit. Similarly the friends or relatives of the two million who were having their home and food shared would also find it unattractive to vote for the party concerned.

Questions

1. Explain and illustrate using an expectations-augmented Phillips Curve diagram, why a cut in benefit may make economic sense in terms of unemployment.
2. An alternative to reducing benefits would be to abolish all income tax. Explain why such a decision would also be economic sense and political nonsense.
3. (a) Try and find out what presently happens to those who are registered officially as unemployed but have not paid the required amount of national insurance to qualify for Unemployment Benefit.
   (b) Try and find out about two other social-security-type benefits that exist.

   (*Note*: for 3(a) and 3(b) you may find some useful leaflets at your local Post Office or Library.)
4. Identify the direct and indirect costs of employment that the Government is experiencing in the *current* year. (*Hint*: Two economists at Edinburgh University – N. Fraser and A. Sinfield – calculated the total direct exchequer costs of unemployment in 1984/5 to be approximately £20 billion – i.e. £6 600 per unemployed person.)
5. (a) Explain how an economist might advise a government to reduce unemployment.
   (b) What political advantages and disadvantages would your policies have?

---

* This is correct for April 1989 to April 1990, and as always would depend upon the correct level of National Insurance contributions having been paid during a previous period of employment.

Exam Preparation

PRACTICAL EXERCISE

1. Answer the following questions based on the graph below.
   (a) What two letters indicate zero tax revenues? How can this situation exist?
   (b) Which two related letters indicate an inefficient high tax-rate and an efficient low tax-rate? How are these points related?

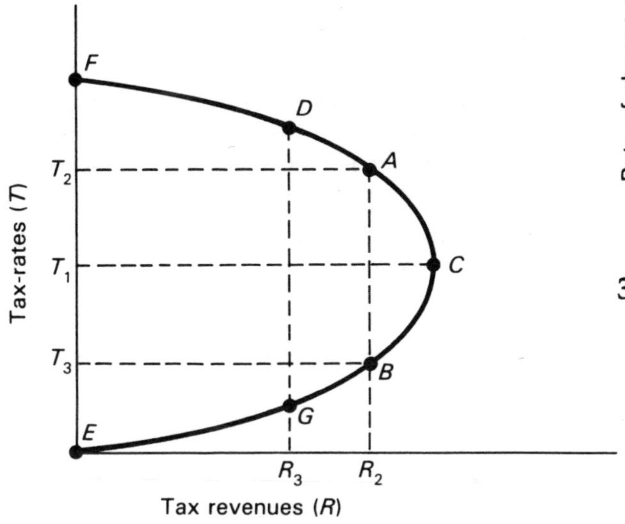

MULTIPLE CHOICE QUESTIONS

1. The term 'marginal rate of tax' is applied to the
   A proportion of income which is paid in tax
   B amount of tax payable after allowances have been deducted
   C rate of tax paid on unearned income
   D tax paid out of an increment to income
   E rate of tax which gives the highest yield.

2. Which one of the following would not constitute a supply-side policy?
   A Business start-up schemes
   B Laws reducing trade unions' power to picket and strike
   C Introduction of minimum wage legislation
   D Liberalization of the laws relating to who can provide electricity supply.

Questions 3 and 4 refer to the following diagram of the expectations-augmented Phillips curve, in which U_2 is the natural rate of unemployment, and PC_1 to PC_4 are Phillips curves associated with successively higher inflationary expectations.

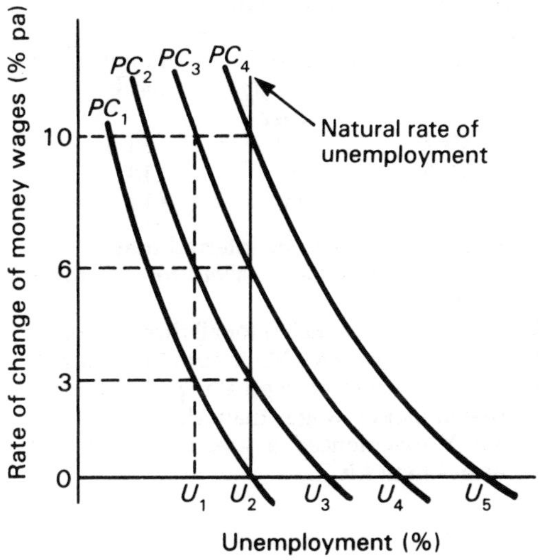

3. When there are no inflationary expectations, what will be the effect of a government attempt to reduce unemployment to U_1? One or more of the three responses given are correct. Select your answer from the code set out in the grid.
   1 in the long run, unemployment remains at U_2.
   2 the rate of change of money wages rises to 3 per cent per annum.
   3 the natural level of unemployment rises.

A	B	C	D	E
3 only	**1, 2** only	**1, 3** only	**2, 3** only	**1, 2, 3** only

4. With expectations of 3 per cent inflation, the government uses fiscal policy to reduce unemployment to U_1. Subsequently, a new government is elected which determines to eliminate wage inflation. It would be necessary, if this was to be achieved in the short run, to allow unemployment to rise to:

   A U_1 **B** U_2 **C** U_3 **D** U_4 **E** U_5.

5. Select your answer from the grid above. The natural rate of unemployment can be reduced by
   1 expansionist fiscal policy
   2 retraining schemes
   3 measures designed to reduce imperfections in the housing market.

6. The effect of an annual pay settlement on the wages of three workers in a year when retail prices rose generally by 15 per cent is illustrated in the table below.

Worker	*Initial weekly wage*	*Pay increase/ week*
Mr X	50	£8
Mr Y	80	£10
Mr Z	100	£12

From this data it may be inferred that
A money wages have fallen for all three workers
B real wages have fallen for all three workers
C real wages rose for Mr X but not for Mr Y
D Mr Z experienced a greater proportionate rise in money wages than Mr X
E Mr Y experienced a greater fall in real wages than Mr Z.

RELATED ESSAY QUESTIONS

1. Explain the term 'the natural rate of unemployment' and discuss how its level may be reduced.

2. Distinguish briefly between 'demand-side' and 'supply-side' economic policy. Should the government ignore the 'demand-side' of the economy and aim economic policy at improving 'supply-side' performance?

3. Discuss some of the macroeconomic consequences of a reduction in income tax.

4. 'The Phillips curve is no longer a useful guide to economic policy.' Discuss.

5. Compare the relative costs of unemployment and inflation to the economy. Can policy-makers choose the level of unemployment and inflation for an economy?

6. Discuss the significance of expectations in macroeconomics.

19 Money and Financial Institutions

Key Points to Review

- Opportunity cost (1.5)
- Money as a medium of exchange (2.3)
- Specialization and comparative advantage (6.2)
- Exchange rates (9.1)
- Retail Price Index (11.5)

Questions for Preview

1 What is money?

2 How is money defined in the UK?

3 Which institutions constitute the monetary sector in the UK?

4 What are the functions of the Bank of England?

5 What determines the money supply?

If someone were to ask you, 'How much money do you make?' you might answer in terms of so many pounds per week or per year. In this context, the term *money* really means income or the ability to purchase goods and services – in fact, the term is most generally used to mean income. But in this sense it is being used incorrectly. Counterfeiters 'make money'; as we shall see in this chapter, the banking system also 'makes money'. What you make is income. In this chapter and throughout the rest of the text, we will use the term *money* to mean anything which we use as a medium (means) of exchange. You use your cheque-book as a medium of exchange. The money in your building society can be regarded as a medium of exchange. Therefore, money is more than just the notes and coins that you have in your wallet or purse, or hidden in a tea-caddy. Consequently, the official money supply includes more than just **currency** – paper notes and coins.

In this chapter, we will examine the functions that money serves, the different types of money that are in existence, and the financial system generally.

The Functions of Money

There are four traditional functions of money. The one that most people are familiar with and the one that we referred to above is as a *medium of exchange*. However, money also serves as a *unit of account*, a *store of purchasing power*, and a *standard of deferred payment*.

When we say that money serves as a medium of exchange, what we mean is that sellers will accept it as a means of payment in market transactions. Without some generally accepted medium of exchange, we would have to resort to barter. In fact, before money was used, transactions took place by means of barter. *Barter* is simply a direct exchange – no intermediary good called money is used. Economic historians often suggest that the switch from barter to the use of money allowed for more rapid economic growth of the Western world, since increased specialization was then possible. It was extremely costly, that is, the transactions costs were high, to make all exchanges by barter. Imagine the difficulty you would have today if you had to exchange your labour directly for the fruits of someone else's labour. Imagine the many exchanges that would have to take place for you to get from a position where you owned, for example, 25 pairs of shoes to a position where you owned only two pairs but now also had bread, meat, a pair of jeans, and so on. The use of money facilitates exchange. Indeed, the existence of money means that individuals no longer have to hold a diverse collection of goods as an exchange inventory. Hence, more specialization can occur.

Money as a Medium of Exchange

As a **medium of exchange**, money allows individuals to specialize in any area in which they have a comparative advantage and to receive money payment for the fruits of their labour. Money can then be exchanged for the fruits of other people's labour. The usefulness of money as a medium of exchange causes more specialization. Moreover, we see that money is more important the larger the amount of trade. Thus, money would not be as important in a society of self-sufficient family units as it is in modern commercial economies.

Money as a Unit of Account

A **unit of account** is a way of placing a specific value on economic goods and services. Thus, as a unit of account, the monetary unit is used to measure the value of goods and services relative to other goods and services. It is the common denominator, or measure. It thus enables individuals to compare, easily, the relative value of goods and services. Governments use money prices to measure national income each year. A firm uses money prices to calculate profits and losses; and a typical household budgets daily its regular expenses using money prices as its unit of account.

Another way of describing money as a unit of account is to say that it is a *standard of value* that allows economic transactors to compare the relative worth of various goods and services. In short, it acts as an economic yardstick.

Money as a Store of Value

To see how money is a **store of value**, consider the following simple example. A fisherman comes into port after several days of fishing. At the going price of fish that day, he has £1 000's worth of fish. Fish are not a good store of value, because, if the fisherman keeps them too long, they will rot. If he attempts to exchange them with other tradespeople, some of the fish may rot before he can exchange the entire catch for the goods and services that he desires. On the other hand, if the fisherman sells the entire catch for money, he can store the value of his catch in the money that he receives. (Of course, he can freeze the fish, but that is costly.)

Inflation reduces the value of money. It has therefore made money into a rather poor store of value. Over time, people get used to this and look for ways of protecting themselves from inflation. They may buy houses, or equities (shares), or paintings, and hold less money. These kinds of property will appreciate: their prices will rise with inflation, though there is some risk that their prices may fall too.

Money as a Standard of Deferred Payment

The fourth function of the monetary unit is as a **standard of deferred payment**. In less technical terms this simply means that money can be used as a means of entering into agreements regarding *future* payments. This function, therefore, simultaneously involves money as a medium of exchange and a unit of account. For example, debts are typically stated in terms of a unit of account and are paid with a monetary medium of exchange. The negotiation of future payments is an essential feature of any complex society. Workers negotiate a salary for payment on completion of a job; landlords negotiate a rent that will be paid at regular intervals in the future; shareholders expect to receive a portion of their firm's profits each year, and so on.

It is interesting to note that not all countries will use their own national monetary unit to specify future payments. Often the dollar or pound is used as the unit of account as these are more acceptable as international mediums of exchange.

Liquidity

Money is an asset – something of value – that accounts for part of one's wealth. Wealth in the form of money can be exchanged later for some other asset. Although it is not the only form of wealth that can be exchanged for goods and services, it is the one most widely accepted. This attribute of money is called **liquidity**. We say that an asset is liquid when it can easily be acquired or disposed of without high costs and with relative certainty as to its value. Notes and coins are by definition the most liquid asset there is. Just compare them, for example, to a share listed on the Stock Exchange. To buy or sell that share you must call a stockbroker who will place the buy-or-sell order for you. This must be done during normal business hours. You have to pay a percentage commission to the broker. Moreover, there is a distinct possibility that you will get less for the share than you originally paid for it. This is not the case with notes and coins which can be easily converted to other asset forms.

However, when we hold notes and coins, we pay a price for this advantage of liquidity. That price is the interest yield that could have been obtained had the asset been held in another form, for example, in the form of a savings account. In other words, the cost of holding money (its opportunity cost) is measured by the alternative interest yield obtainable by holding some other asset. Notes and coins, therefore, are merely one of a whole range of assets which can represent a person's wealth. Of all the assets, however, they are certainly the most liquid.

Why Money Has Value

Today in the United Kingdom all of us accept coins, notes, and cheques in exchange for items sold, including our labour services. The question remains as to why we are willing to accept for payment some bits of paper or metal that have no *intrinsic* value. The reason is that we have a **fiduciary monetary system**. This means that the value of our currency rests upon the public's confidence that money can be exchanged for goods and services. *Fiduciary* comes from the Latin *fiducia*, which means trust or confidence. In other words, in our fiduciary monetary system, money, whether in the form of currency or cheques, is not convertible to a fixed quantity of gold, silver, or some other precious commodity. The money that people hold in their wallets, purses, or bank accounts cannot be exchanged for a specified quantity of some specified commodity. The various banknotes are just pieces of official paper that cost a fraction of their face value to produce. Similarly, coins have a value stamped on them that is normally greater than the market value of the metal in them. Regardless, currency and bank cheques are money because of their acceptability and predictability of value.

Acceptability

Bank accounts and currency are money because they are accepted in exchange for goods and services. They are accepted because people have confidence that they can later be exchanged for other goods and services. This confidence is based on the knowledge that such exchanges have occurred in the past without problems. Even during a period of relatively rapid inflation, we would still be inclined to accept money in exchange for goods and services. Why? Because it is so useful. Barter is a very costly, time-consuming alternative.

Predictability of Value

For money to have a predictable value, the relationship between the quantity of money supplied and the quantity of money demanded must not change frequently, abruptly, or in great magnitude. In this sense, the value of money is like the economic value of anything else. Supply and demand determine what it 'sells' for. What is the selling price of a pound coin? It is what one has to give up in order to 'purchase' a pound. What do you have to give up? You must give up the goods and services that you could have instead. In other words, in order to own a one-pound coin, you give up the *purchasing power* inherent in that pound. That purchasing power might be equal to a magazine or a small hamburger. The purchasing power of the pound (that is, its value) therefore varies inversely with the price level. Thus, the more rapid the rate of increase of a price index, such as the Retail Price Index, the more rapid is the decrease in the value, or purchasing power, of a pound. Money still retains its usefulness even if its value – its purchasing power – is declining year in and year out. In other words, money is still useful and accepted even during periods of inflation. Why? Because it still retains the characteristic of predictability of value. If you believe that the inflation rate is going to be around 10 per cent next year, you know that any pound you receive a year from now will have a purchasing power equal to 10 per cent less than that same pound this year. Thus, you will not refuse to use money or accept it in exchange simply because you know that its value will decline by the rate of inflation next year. (See Key Points 19.1.)

Defining and Measuring the Money Supply

Money is important. Changes in the total **money supply**, and changes in the rate at which it is growing

Key Points 19.1

- **Money is defined by its functions, which are: (1) a medium of exchange, (2) a unit of account or standard of value, (3) a store of value, and (4) as a standard of deferred payment.**
- **Since notes and coins are widely accepted in exchange for goods and services, currency is a highly liquid asset. It can be disposed of without high transactions costs and with relative certainty as to its value.**
- **The United Kingdom has a fiduciary monetary system: our money is not convertible into a fixed quantity of a commodity such as gold or silver.**
- **Money is accepted in exchange for goods and services because people have confidence that money can later be exchanged for other goods and services.**
- **Also, the reason that we continue to accept money is because it has a predictable value.**
- **The purchasing power, or value, of money is inversely related to the price level.**

affect important economic variables, such as the rate of inflation, interest rates, and employment. Although there is widespread agreement among economists that money is important they have never agreed on how to define and how to measure money. For example, the OECD published a table in 1977 showing how, at that time, its 24 members already used 23 different definitions of money supply. In the UK we have employed various definitions at different times. Today there are six alternative versions of money supply published on a regular basis (see Figure 19.1). These measures do not move in line with one another as they all measure slightly different things.

A basic difference between the definitions of money supply is that some tend towards measuring narrow money and some tend towards broad money. The **broad measures** (M4 and M4c) include various types of money on which interest is paid and therefore to some extent they indicate changes in liquidity. The **narrow measures** (M0 and M2) focus more specifically on money held primarily for transaction purposes. In other words the former stresses the role of money as a temporary store of value and the latter the role of money as a medium of exchange.

Over the years, there have been considerable changes in the way the money supply is measured. These reflect changes in the structure of the financial system, and changes in economists' and politicians' thinking about the relationships between money and the real economy. The most recent changes, in August 1989, occurred because the Abbey National Building Society changed to bank status. This meant that the money measures which include bank deposits, but not building society deposits, would have shown a very large break in the data. This would make comparisons difficult. The new measures treat similar types of deposits alike, irrespective of whether they are held in banks or building societies.

Figure 19.1

Money Supply Definitions The four main money measures are:

- M0 Narrow money. Notes and coins in circulation, plus banks' balances at the Bank of England.
- M2 Notes and coin, plus residents' sterling retail deposits with banks and building societies.
- M4 Notes and coin plus residents' sterling deposits (both sight and time) with banks and building societies.
- M4c M4 plus all foreign currency deposits held in UK banks and building societies by the UK non-bank private sector.

Source: Treasury, *Economic Progress Report*, Aug. 1989. A further measure, M5 is less frequently used. It consists of M4 plus private-sector holdings of bills, some types of National Savings deposits, and other similar assets which are slightly less liquid.

Nib (non interest-bearing) M1 is another definition, consisting of notes and coin, plus UK residents' sterling non-interest-bearing sight deposits (on which no interest is payable).

The Narrow Measures (M0 and M2)

The narrow measures consist of the following components.

1. Notes and coins
2. Bank's operational balances at the Bank of England
3. Sight deposits
4. Retail deposits

We will now examine these in order.

1. NOTES AND COINS

Notes and coins are the most liquid component of any money supply. In the UK in 1989 there were approximately £14.7bn worth of notes and coins in circulation. Taking the narrowest measure of money supply (M0) they account for approximately 99 per cent of its total. Taking a broader measure, e.g. M4, notes and coins would only account for approximately 4 per cent of the total.

2. OPERATIONAL BALANCES AT THE BANK OF ENGLAND

The remaining 1 per cent of M0 are the commercial banks' operational balances held at the Bank of England – commonly referred to as the **bankers' balances**. All commercial banks hold deposits (balances) at the Bank of England for the purposes of settling debts between themselves. (They are *also* formally obliged to hold some 'cash-ratio deposits' at the Bank of England but these cannot be withdrawn and are not included in M0.)

3. SIGHT DEPOSITS

Sight deposits in banks are those which can be withdrawn without notice. They are commonly referred to as current accounts which people can draw on by making out a cheque. These obviously represent a ready means of payment or medium of exchange and should be incorporated in any definition that wishes to measure money available for transaction purposes. About two-thirds of all sight deposits now pay a rate of interest. Interest-bearing sight deposits are bank accounts which offer normal cheque facilities, immediate access, and some interest. All sight deposits are included in M2.

4. RETAIL DEPOSITS

This is a general name for all bank accounts which can be readily used for transaction purposes. Broadly, these are all bank deposits of less than £100 000 and any building society deposits, which are withdrawable within one month. These accounts can be regarded as 'active balances' which reflect patterns of consumer spending.

The Broad Measures (M4 and M4c)

As already stated the broad measures are concerned with money in a fuller sense, not only as a medium of exchange but also as a store of value. Consequently these broader measures involve all the narrower measures, plus varying forms of interest-earning assets, that can be converted into money given some time-period. The broader measures of money incorporate the following:

5. Time deposits
6. Foreign currency bank deposits
7. Money market instruments.

5. TIME DEPOSITS

Time deposits represent all those bank accounts which require a period of notice before withdrawal. These may take several forms and for our purposes it is best to think of them as bank deposit accounts, and some building society accounts. Broadly speaking, the longer the period of notice before withdrawal, the better the interest rate is likely to be. These deposits are a major component of M4.

Certificates of deposit (CDs) provide higher rates of interest but have a fixed maturity date (though they can be sold). They are a useful type of deposit for large sums of money.

6. FOREIGN CURRENCY BANK DEPOSITS

Obviously foreign currency is not generally part of the UK money supply. But some residents of the UK do hold bank deposits in currencies other than sterling. These foreign currency deposits do represent potential stores of value, especially if speculators are hoping to make gains from fluctuating exchange rates. And these foreign currency deposits represent a medium of exchange for overseas expenditure. In consequence we have a measure of money supply that also takes these monies into account, namely M4c. Money balances, such as those discussed above, held in countries other than those of its origin, are known as **eurocurrency**.

Many large borrowers now turn to the eurocurrency markets for major loans. They will shop around for a currency in which they can get the lowest rate of interest with an acceptable exchange rate risk. So these money balances can be an important source of spending power.

7. MONEY MARKET INSTRUMENTS

In an attempt to make a full assessment of a nation's total liquidity, items classed as **'near money'** should also be incorporated in a broad definition of money supply. These items of *near money* include things such as **bank bills, Treasury bills, and local authority bills.** These bills are forms of 'paper money' as they are sold by banks (on behalf of firms), the Treasury, and local authorities at a price below their face value. The holder reaps the reward when they mature by being paid the face value. However, they may sell, or pass the bills on, to someone else before they mature. Consequently, these bills represent a claim to money as a medium of exchange and they certainly form a store of value. Thus any truly comprehensive broad measure of money supply should include these instruments. M5 includes these and other forms of 'near money' such as National Savings deposits.

From Narrow to Broad and Back Again

We have seen by now a whole series of monetary aggregates. We get the impression that money-supply definitions have evolved by simply adding more and more assets to the basic definition each time a revision is made. However, this is an entirely wrong impression. In historical terms the broader measures were defined first. M0 by comparison was introduced more recently, in June 1982. You may ask, does this shift towards a narrower measure imply that this measure is more correct? The answer is certainly No! For different purposes, different definitions are best. For example, in recent years all the money measures except M0 have grown very rapidly. From the government's point of view, M0 is the best variable to try to control. But that does not mean that it can tell us all we want to know about the growth of total spending power in the economy. For that we must look at M4.

In fact, concentrating on any one money measure makes little sense. We need to consider all of them. The pace of financial innovation during the 1980s altered all measures of money. The measure which was the main target of government monetary policy in the early 1980s, sterling M3, grew right out of control. It was duly abandoned, as a monetary target, in 1987. Now it does not appear in the statistics at all.

The truth is that data on money measures are very difficult to interpret conclusively. But we can learn a lot from the full range of measures. And it clearly makes sense to treat banks and building societies similarly, now that they undertake increasingly similar types of business.

Key Points 19.2

- **There are two basic approaches to measuring money supply – the narrow measures and the broader measures. The former give us M0 and M2, and represent the transaction balances, and the latter give us M4 and M4c and represent stores of value or liquidity.**
- **There is no one correct definition of money; each definition measures something slightly different. At present the UK regularly measures six different definitions – these are summarized in Figure 19.1.**

The British Banking Structure

So far we have looked at the functions of money and its definition. We have thus seen that a major component of the money supply is the various bank accounts that are held at the 15 000 commercial bank branches scattered throughout the UK, and the various other savings accounts organized with other financial intermediaries.

Commercial Banks

A **commercial bank** is a privately owned, profit-seeking institution. Examples include: Barclays, Lloyds, Midland, National Westminster (and its subsidiary, Coutts), and Williams & Glyn's (sometimes these six are grouped under the heading London Clearing Banks); Bank of Scotland, Clydesdale, and Royal Bank of Scotland (sometimes these three are grouped under the generic title Scottish Clearing Banks); the Co-operative Bank and the Yorkshire Bank.

Apart from accepting funds from their customers and using them to make profits, these commercial banks have other common features. They all have extensive branch networks and are major participants in the clearing system (this involves the daily settling of debts between banks that are generated by customers' cheques). In addition to all the payments made by cheque, further billions are transferred by electronic methods, for example, all those payments made by direct debit, standing order, credit cards, or electronic funds transfer.

The commercial banks are sometimes known as retail banks because they offer services to large numbers of customers, many quite small in scale. They take deposits and lend to borrowers who wish to spend on consumer or investment goods. They act as intermediaries, spreading risks by lending for a wide range of purposes. Increasingly they have become involved in mortgage business, which used to be the preserve of the building societies. The range of services they offer has been steadily increasing.

Other Financial Intermediaries

Although the commercial banks ultimately act as a link between millions of lenders and borrowers, they still have to compete with other financial intermediaries to attract their deposits. These other financial intermediaries have their own specialized functions. But recently many of them have diversified. They compete with one another in particular types of financial business. Examples of such intermediaries include: **discount houses, building societies, finance houses, the National Savings Bank, merchant banks,** and **foreign banks.** Each of their specialized areas of interest is detailed below.

Discount Houses

Here we are *not* talking of Comet, Trident, Asda, or any other household name, but an élite group of ten institutions that are unique to Britain. Their names (e.g. Gerrard & National; Seccombe, Marshall & Campion; King & Shaxson; Carter Allan) are by no means commonplace as their trading-place lies in the heart of the financial city. Their main area of interest is to act as a **financial intermediary** between the commercial banks and the Bank of England. They borrow from the commercial banks for very short periods of time (taking advantage of what is termed **'money at call'**), perhaps overnight or just for a few days, and lend to those with short-term cash-flow problems by investing in short-term bills, which may be known as **bank bills**, commercial bills, or acceptance credits. They also buy Treasury bills from the Bank of England. These bills represent 91-day loans to firms or the government respectively.

The discount houses have a unique relationship with the Bank of England. If the banks are short of cash and so withdraw their loans to discount houses, the latter can turn to the Bank of England, which will buy sufficient bills from them for them to be able to balance their books. (This gives the Bank of England a lever over interest rates: if it wants them to rise it will charge a higher rate, and the discount houses will in turn pass on the new rate to their borrowers.)

The discount houses' specialization is, therefore, interbank lending and borrowing for very short periods of time, often just overnight and rarely for longer than 91 days. The shorter the loan, the lower the interest rate.

Building Societies

Traditionally, building societies take their deposits from millions of small savers and lend to house-buyers for periods of 25 or 30 years. As financial intermediaries, they have specialized in long-term lending. However, they are increasingly offering banking services: cheque accounts, cash machines, and wide range of services which were traditionally the preserve of the banks. They are competing strongly with the banks, just as the banks have been competing for mortgage business. Both sides have diversified. Many experts now think that as far as their effect on the economy is concerned, banks and building societies are practically indistinguishable.

Finance Houses

These institutions are responsible for financing hire-purchase agreements for periods of two to three years. People usually access the funds through the retailer from whom they are buying the product. In other words, the retailer is often the agent for the finance house. However, finance houses can be approached directly and often are by firms, especially when firms wish to take advantage of their leasing facilities.

In the UK there are about 40 finance houses (e.g. Mercantile Credit, Forward Trust, United Dominions Trust, and Lombard North Central). They gain their funds largely from the financial and banking sector, and partly from the public. These funds are then lent out to those involved in hire-purchase agreements at quite high rates of interest, which reflect the risky nature of this type of lending.

The National Savings Bank

This used to be called the Post Office Savings Bank and even under its new name it is still government-run and processed through the Post Office. Thirteen per cent of all savings are presently handled through this bank. Ordinary accounts, investment accounts, savings certificates, and premium bonds are all offered to entice depositors. These deposits are then lent to the government.

The Merchant Banks

The merchant banks specialize in the affairs of large commercial and industrial companies. Indeed, one of their specialisms is issuing new shares. Thus they are sometimes called *issuing houses*. Another of their alternative titles is *accepting houses* arising out of their other specialism, namely accepting bank bills. This involves the merchant bank guaranteeing owners against loss on the bill in return for a commission calculated as a percentage of the face value of the bill.*

In summary, therefore, merchant banks are very much banks for entrepreneurs, as they organize and administer large-scale loans on behalf of companies. Interestingly, they frequently do not provide the funds themselves. Their specialism is largely service through their knowledge of the relevant markets. Merchant banks are small in size compared to the retail banks. The financial services they offer include advising and organizing take-overs and mergers. This provides some of their most profitable business.

*See Dictionary reference for bank bills.

Foreign Banks

The number of foreign banks has risen steadily in the last decade. At present there are more than 350. The majority of these are located in London, as one of their purposes is to administer the financial aspects of trade between the UK, their home country, and any other country where their interests are represented. They are therefore primarily concerned in international banking activities. London is very much a centre for such activity and these banks hold large stocks of foreign currency deposits. In fact over 80 per cent of the liabilities of these foreign banks (based in London) are held in foreign currency, worth about £500 billion in 1989. They act as a link between those who have foreign currency deposits and those who want to borrow them. To a large extent these foreign currency funds may simply be demanded for speculative purposes on the foreign exchange market. (See Key Points 19.3.)

The Central Bank

At the head of the monetary sector there is a **central bank**. Every country in the world has a central bank, and it is frequently owned and operated by government. The UK's Bank of England is one of the oldest central banks; it originated in 1694 when a number of businessmen grouped together to form a bank to raise a loan for the government. This bank-government relationship continued to develop and in 1844 the Bank was given the power to control the note issue. In 1946 it was nationalized, making it ultimately responsible to the Treasury and government for the monetary sector and the money supply.

Monetary Sector

We have just used the term monetary sector without really defining it. The monetary sector has been officially identified since 1979 as comprising two main groups of financial institutions, namely **recognized banks** and **licensed deposit-takers**.

RECOGNIZED BANKS

To be a recognized bank, a deposit-taking institution must apply to the Bank of England for recognition, and

Key Points 19.3

- **The current financial network in the UK involves many financial intermediaries competing for funds, which can then be lent out, in order to make profit.**
- **Some examples of British financial intermediaries are: commercial banks, discount houses, building societies, National Savings Bank, finance houses, merchant banks, and overseas banks.**
- **Each of these financial intermediaries tends to have a specialism to offer. Each, therefore, caters for specific market needs. But increasingly, they have diversified.**

Key Points 19.4

- **Our central bank in the UK is the Bank of England, it was set up in 1694, and formally nationalized in 1946.**
- **The Bank of England supervises and controls the monetary sector on behalf of the government.**
- **The monetary sector comprises two main groups of institutions, namely recognized banks and licensed deposit-takers. The main difference between these groups is the range of services offered, the number of years since establishment, and general financial status.**

deposit one-half per cent of its eligible liabilities in non-interest-earning accounts held at the Bank of England. Criteria that the Bank of England applies in allocating the status of recognized bank are based on an assessment of the range and depth of services offered and the reputation the institution has developed over time. This definition includes all the 'high street' commercial banks, merchant banks, and many foreign banks.

LICENSED DEPOSIT-TAKERS (LDTs)

Licensed deposit-taking institutions are the smaller, less established, financial institutions that offer a narrower range of services. Obvious examples are finance houses and some smaller foreign banks. These LDTs also have to deposit one-half per cent of their eligible liabilities in non-interest-earning accounts held at the Bank of England. (See Key Points 19.4.)

Functions of the Bank of England

Here we will set out the most important functions that the Bank* carries out for this country.

Control of the Note Issue

The Bank of England is responsible for issuing new banknotes and withdrawing old ones. It is the only note-issuing bank in England and Wales, and ultimately it could print as many notes as it liked. This is because today's currency is not backed by gold but by government securities (i.e. it is entirely fiduciary). The amount of notes in circulation at any one time, therefore, is largely dependent on public demand, for example, just before Christmas it normally reaches a peak of around £16 000 million (in various denominations). The Bank is more concerned with money supply as a whole than its specific note component.

*Whenever 'Bank' is spelt with a capital B it refers to the Bank of England.

The Bankers' Bank

Apart from the mandatory deposit of one-half per cent of their eligible liabilities that all recognized banks and LDTs must make to non-operational, non-interest-bearing accounts, all banks and licensed deposit-takers hold operational accounts at the Bank of England as well. In short the Bank of England are bankers for the whole financial community.

Of these accounts, the most important are those belonging to the clearing banks who make settlements amongst themselves after each day's clearing by drawing on their Bank of England accounts.

Finally, the Bank of England may lend money to the banks – normally via the discount houses – if times get really difficult. In this context the Bank of England is described as the *lender of last resort*. It is crucially important that the depositors have confidence in their bank's ability to meet its obligations. The banks can do this by recalling their loans to discount houses. They will then be short of funds, but will turn to the Bank of England, as we have already seen.

The Government's Bank

As we are all aware, the government collects large sums of money through taxation. The government also spends and distributes equally large sums. Consequently, the government, like any other commercial concern, needs a bank. And it does have several accounts at the Bank of England. Furthermore, when these accounts run low it is also the Bank that arranges and finances any borrowing. In fact, it is the Bank of England that administers the National Debt, making sure that holders of bonds receive their dividends and that Treasury bills are paid on maturity. (Bonds are long-term loans to the government, generally for 10 to 20 years.)

POLICY ADVICE

Additionally, like any other bank, the Bank of England will advise its customers. Thus, there is a very close relationship between the Bank of England and the government when it comes to the formulation of monetary policy. This is particularly important to maintain as it is the Bank that will ultimately have to execute any monetary policy that is required.

Control of Foreign Exchange Affairs

As agents for the government the Bank of England supervises the nation's foreign currency reserves. According to the exchange rate policies of the government the Bank will use these reserves to buy and sell currency on the foreign exchange market. This is done through the aptly named **exchange equalization account**. Until October 1990, the UK had a managed exchange rate. Although strong market forces could lead to changes in the exchange rate, the Bank of England normally had a target range. It kept the exchange rate within this range. If it started to fall below it, the Bank used its reserves of foreign exchange to buy sterling, thus defending its value. Also, it used the reserves to smooth out day-to-day fluctuations.

Now that the UK is in the European Exchange Rate Mechanism (ERM) control over the exchange rate will be stricter. As well as the Bank of England, other European central banks will intervene if market forces are pushing the exchange rate beyond its permitted range.

Supervision of the Monetary Sector

The Bank of England has a responsibility to ensure that the financial system is sound. Indeed, it administers a Deposit Protection Fund for the safeguarding of the nation's depositors, and will step in whenever a widespread banking collapse seems imminent.

The Bank takes this role responsibly by vetting all recognized banks' and LDTs' accounts at least every three months and meeting with their senior management regularly. Each institution is, therefore, judged individually and any business which is not conducted in a responsible manner could eventually lead to the Bank removing its authorization to take deposits, and this has happened in some cases.

The Bank's rules include **'prudential standards of liquidity'**. They require banks to keep adequate reserves of very liquid assets, in case of a surge in requests for withdrawals. Supervision of banks' activities is important because the Bank of England is committed to lending, as lender of last resort, to any bank which finds itself in difficulties. If it has to rescue a badly managed bank, it is immediately obvious that its supervisory efforts have failed. Irresponsible banking could ultimately allow the money stock to grow in an uncontrolled way.

Finally, if this qualitative type of control is not sufficient the Bank of England can impose certain quantitative controls. For example, they have the existing right to call in a small percentage of banks' and LDTs' eligible liabilities into **special deposit** accounts; these are then held at the Bank of England and earn a low rate of interest for as long as the Bank feels it is necessary to reduce liquidity in the system. Similar attacks on monetary-sector assets could be designed and applied if circumstances demand it, as one must remember that the Bank of England always has the power to call in government backing if necessary.

While the Bank of England supervises the monetary sector, the Financial Services Act of 1987 provides for the non-bank financial intermediaries to be supervised by other bodies, mostly under the wing of the SIB, Securities and Investment Board. The Bank of England has a strong but indirect interest in this side of financial supervision. (See Key Point 19.5.)

How Banks Work

The money supply, as given in the definition M4, was defined earlier in the chapter broadly as notes and coin, and sight and time deposits. We now look at how the Bank of England and the banks together determine the stock of money in the banking system at any one time.

Fractional Reserve Banking System

Predecessors to modern-day banks were goldsmiths and moneylenders. These individuals had the strongest vaults. Other people who had gold (and other valuables), but no means of protection, began to ask goldsmiths and moneylenders to store their gold and valuables for safe-keeping. The goldsmiths and moneylenders charged a fee for this safe-keeping service. It turned out that only a fraction of the total amount of gold and other valuables left with these guardians was ever withdrawn over any time-period. That is to say, only a small fraction of clients would ask for their deposits at any one time. Thus, to meet the requests of those clients, the vault-owners needed to keep only a relatively small fraction of the total deposits 'on reserve'.

Key Point 19.5

- **The main functions of the Bank of England are: (1) to control the issue of notes, (2) to be a bank for the financial community, (3) to be the government's bank and help advise on policy, (4) to control foreign exchange affairs, and (5) generally to supervise the whole monetary sector.**

Now, if you were a vault-owner and knew that only a certain percentage of deposits would be requested in any one time-period, you could lend the remainder out at interest and make additional income, besides the fee for the use of your vault. This is how banks grew up as part of a **fractional reserve banking system**. In other words, in such a system, reserves on hand to meet net withdrawal demands by depositors are some fraction less than 100 per cent of total deposits. Nowadays, reserves are not kept in the form of gold, but rather in the form of deposits with the Bank of England and other very liquid assets.

The Banks' Balance Sheet

In order to help us to understand how modern banks work, we should look at the summary balance sheet for UK banks (Figure 19.2).

Banks use double-entry accounting. Liabilities show deposits: they are liabilities in the sense that the bank is liable to have to make good requests for withdrawals from them. Assets show the variety of ways in which banks hold the funds deposited with them.

RESERVES

Banks must maintain a percentage of their customer deposits as **reserves**. Take a hypothetical example. If the required level of reserves, the **reserve asset ratio**, is 20 per cent and the bank has £1 billion in customer deposits, then it must hold at least £200 million as reserves. It can hold these reserves in the form of notes and coin, balances with the Bank of England, and a range of liquid assets, which can easily be turned into cash if required. These include money lent at call to the discount houses, Treasury bills (short-term loans to the government), and bank bills (short-term loans to firms, or commercial bills). If a bank has reserves in excess of £200 million then it will wish to make more loans (or advances) to customers. If it does not, then it is forgoing interest which could be earned on loans backed by the reserves in excess of £200 million. If on the other hand, the bank's reserves fall below the £200-million mark, it will have to call in some of its loans. This reduces deposits to the point where the level of reserves is again 20 per cent of total deposits.

Figure 19.2

Summary Balance Sheet for UK Banks, 30 June 1989

Liabilities	£m	*Assets*	£m
Sterling		*Sterling*	
Sight deposits	127 311	Notes and coin	2 655
Time deposits	246 209	Balances with Bank of England	1 466
CDs	42 124	Loans to discount houses	9 467
Items in transmission	10 673	Treasury bills	1 331
Capital and other funds	50 546	Local-authority bills	196
Other currencies		Other bills	9 644
Sight and time deposits	573 454	Other market loans (interbank, CDs)	125 547
CDs	82 154	Advances: UK public sector	1 887
Other	29 957	UK private sector	262 645
		Overseas	13 833
		Net lending, BoE to govt.	1 124
		Investments	21 381
		Other currencies (Mainly loans on London and overseas money markets)	685 321

Source: *BEQB*, Aug. 1989

LIQUIDITY VERSUS PROFITABILITY

Taking the assets in descending order of liquidity we come to the more profitable assets, those which earn higher interest rates. There is an inverse relationship between liquidity and profitability: the greater the liquidity, the lower the interest rate; the greater the profitability, the lower the liquidity. Advances to customers are the most profitable form of business, but the loans are not liquid because in general they will take time to be paid off.

So banks must carefully balance their need for adequate levels of reserve assets against their desire to earn profits by maximizing advances to customers. If they make too many advances, they may find themselves with insufficient liquid funds to meet their obligations when customers withdraw deposits.

The Money Supply

Over time there has been growing demand for bank loans. We observe large increases in banks' supply of money. How does this credit expansion occur?

We have already seen that making loans is profitable for banks. If customers want loans, and their banks consider them to be reasonably good risks, loans will generally be made available. But supposing the banks are short of reserve assets? In order to meet their obligations after the new loans have been made, they may require extra cash.

Their first reaction could be to withdraw their loans to discount houses (money at call). Alternatively an individual bank may be able to borrow on the interbank market. (Banks with a temporary surplus of cash will lend to banks which are short of cash.) Another possibility is to sell some bills. These are very liquid assets which can readily be sold for cash, usually to discount houses.

A bank which is expanding its lending activity may be able to meet its obligations in these ways for some while. But supposing all the banks are seeking to expand their lending activities? If they all withdraw loans from the discount houses, they in turn will be left with insufficient cash.

When this happens the discount houses turn to the Bank of England. The Bank will buy bills from them for cash. This 'relieves the shortage' as the saying is in the City. It ensures that there is always sufficient liquidity in the monetary system. The banks will always be able to meet their obligations.

Why should the Bank of England do this? There are two reasons. One is its role as 'lender of last resort'. If a bank *cannot* meet its obligations, then there would be a rapid and disastrous loss of confidence in the bank. Its customers would all rush to withdraw their deposits at once. The bank would fail, and many of its customers would go bankrupt. The economic consequences of a bank failure would be serious: bankruptcies would entail unemployment and loss of income for large numbers of people. So the Bank of England maintains sufficient liquidity to ensure that banking business continues. There is a second reason why the Bank of England will lend to the discount houses (and effectively, therefore, to the banks). If it did not, then the shortage of cash would force up interest rates. Now, sometimes, this is exactly what the Bank of England wants. If there is a need for a tighter monetary policy, higher interest rates will reduce the demand for loans, and ultimately, the level of spending in the economy. But mostly the objective is to keep interest rates fairly stable. Sharp rises in interest rates are very unpopular, with people with mortgages, people borrowing to buy consumer durables, or firms wanting to invest. This unpopularity can create political problems. So although the Bank of England *could* control the growth of bank lending (and so the money supply) by refusing to lend to the discount houses, it generally restricts itself to raising interest rates and carries on lending. It relies upon higher interest rates to reduce the *demand* for loans.

What actually happens when the discount houses borrow from the Bank of England? The discount houses borrow by *selling* Treasury and bank bills to the Bank of England, which pays for the bills with a cheque drawn on itself. When, over time, the Bank of England increases its lending in this way, the cash base of the monetary system increases. The overall effect is that the Bank of England pumps extra liquidity into the banking system by itself creating credit.

The cash base of the monetary system has already been defined as M0, or notes and coin plus banks' operational balances with the Bank of England. The result of the Bank of England's lending to the discount houses is that the discount houses have been able to pay for a bank or a Treasury bill. The previous holder of this bill now has cash and will deposit it in a bank account. The bank will place the cash in its account with the Bank of England.

M0 has increased by the amount of the Bank of England's credit creation. In other words, the cash base of the banking system, sometimes known as the **monetary base** or high-powered money, has increased. The monetary base is the foundation on which bank lending rests; it includes the banks' most liquid reserve assets. (Now read Key Points 19.6.)

The Money Multiplier

We have already seen that banks need hold only a small proportion of their total assets in the form of cash (notes and coin, and balances with the Bank of England). Consider what happens if they acquire increased deposits of cash by the means just described. Supposing they receive an extra £1 million. They might decide to keep 5 per cent of it in reserve against future withdrawals. They can then make a loan of £950 000. The borrower will spend the money on, say, machines. If the manufacturer of the machines deposits the money in the same bank, it will then have the original reserve, £50 000 *and* the new deposit of £950 000. If it keeps 5 per cent of the new deposit, £47 500 and makes a further loan of £902 500, further credit will have been created, and the process can go on for some time and many more loans.

Now it is true that when a loan is spent, the seller of the goods involved could put the money in another bank. But if the cash base is expanding for all the banks, they will all be lending more too. So the resulting increases in deposits will accumulate in all of them.

We can now make a generalization about the extent to which total deposits will increase when the banking system's reserves of cash are increased. If we assume that all banks lend as much as they are able, then the expansion of credit resulting from a given increase in the cash base will be a multiple that increases. We call this multiple the money multiplier. The following equation applies.

$$\text{maximum money multiplier} = \frac{1}{\text{cash ratio}}$$

Key Points 19.6

- **We have a fractional reserve banking system in which banks hold a percentage of deposits as reserves.**
- **The liquidity of banks' assets, and their profitability, are inversely related.**
- **When a bank's holdings of reserves increase, that bank can expand its lending.**
- **The Bank of England can increase the level of banks' reserves (the cash base of the monetary system) by buying bills from the discount houses.**
- **As banks' reserves increase they can expand their lending by a multiple of the initial increase in reserve assets. Thus the money stock increases correspondingly.**

Maintaining Confidence: Prudential Standards of Liquidity

In practice the Bank of England does not have a single cash ratio applicable to all banks. Instead it requires banks to observe prudential standards of liquidity. Banks must keep some proportion of their assets in the form of liquid reserves. The proportions, or ratios, required vary according to the type of lending involved. Riskier kinds of business require a high level of reserve assets to back them. The Bank of England monitors the performance of the banks through its supervision process.

Maintaining confidence is crucial to the efficient functioning of the banking system. As we have seen, if people lose confidence in a bank they will all want to withdraw their deposits. Since banks operate on a fractional reserve system they could not satisfy all their customers' demands at once, and the bank would crash. The Bank of England maintains confidence first by trying to ensure that banks are well managed and second by providing liquidity in the form of loans to the banking system when funds are short (the lender of last resort function).

Monetary Policy: Open-market Operations

When governments want to pursue tight monetary policies, they will seek to restrain the growth of the monetary base. To the extent that the Bank of England avoids increasing its level of lending, over time, to the discount houses, the money stock will be prevented from expanding.

If the Bank of England wants actually to restrict monetary growth, it can sell government securities, that is, engage in **open-market operations**. When it sells a **government bond**, the buyer pays with a cheque drawn on a bank account. The bank transfers the cash from the customer's account to the government's account in the Bank of England. In making this transfer, the bank must reduce its own balance with the Bank of England by the price of the bond. This reduces the level of the bank's reserve assets by a corresponding amount. If the bank has no excess reserves, it will have to reduce its lending by an amount equal to the loss of reserves times the money multiplier. This method of reducing the reserve assets available to banks can restrict the growth of credit substantially.

Key Points 19.7

- **The maximum money multiplier is the reciprocal of the reserve asset ratio.**
- **Bank of England regulations, including prudential standards of liquidity, should ensure that banks do not overlend.**
- **Monetary policy limits credit creation.**

CASE STUDY

Will there ever be a Run on the Banking System?

During the 1930s depression, many US banks failed. As an increasing number of depositors withdrew their funds, more and more banks became insolvent. They were unable to meet customers' demands for withdrawals. When a bank fails, its customers lose their money and will in many cases become bankrupt. So bank failure can have a very detrimental effect on economic activity. Hence the importance of maintaining confidence.

In 1972–3 there was a boom in property prices. Property-developers were anxious to borrow and buy property which, once bought, provided excellent security for the loan. A number of banks lent considerable amounts to property-developers. The increased demand for property generated price increases which made property deals very profitable, and so increased the demand for further loans. When the bubble burst – property was changing hands at prices in excess of its real long-term value – some banks found they had over-lent to property companies. These companies' assets were no longer saleable at prices high enough to cover the loan. So the banks which had over-lent had to be rescued by the Bank of England, with loans to tide them over.

As a result of this, the deposit insurance scheme was introduced. In future, if a bank fails, its depositors will get their money back. To some extent, the very existence of the scheme ensures that confidence in banks is maintained.

In fact, when the next bank failure occurred, with Johnson Matthey Bankers in late 1984, the Bank of England simply took the bank over completely. JMB had made too many risky loans and had become encumbered with bad debts (which would never be repaid). Suspecting bad management, the Bank of England took over rather than lend to the existing management team. Subsequent disclosures of fraud confirmed the view that the bank had been mismanaged. The key question was, why had not the Bank of England detected the mismanagement earlier, in the course of its normal supervision process?

Questions

1. Why is maintaining confidence in banks so vitally important?
2. Why do banks sometimes lend too much?
3. How can bank failures be prevented?

CASE STUDY

All Change in Britain's High Street

Deregulation, scatter-gun expansion, devilish competition, skin-thin profit margins, job losses. Sounds familiar? Right. Everything that happened during and after Big Bang* in London's wholesale securities markets is about to be replayed in Britain's retail financial markets. Banks, building societies and insurance companies are competing keenly in each other's territory. So, too, are mortgage companies, high-street stores and credit-card firms. Once again the new world will be painful for many of these firms; but consumers will gain.

Everybody, it seems wants to be everything to all men. For example, Commercial Union, an insurance company, has bought the private client bit of Quilter Goodison, a stockbroker; Lloyds Bank now owns a chain of 500 estate agents; Save & Prosper, a unit-trust group, has launched its own credit card (charging lower rates of interest than most others). Royal Life, part of the Royal Insurance group, sells unit trusts and mortgages and owns an 800-branch estate agent.

Under a new law, building societies can do more than simply finance house purchases. Most now sell insurance; several – e.g. the Halifax and the Leeds – provide unsecured personal loans and credit cards; two offer interest-bearing current accounts; the Cheltenham & Gloucester sells shares.

Britain's big high-street retailers are also muscling in. Marks and Spencer, a department-store group which already makes personal loans, unveiled an in-house unit trust this month. Burton, a clothing retailer, offers mortgages and insurance to its 2.5m cardholders; its six share shops, which nestle inside its city-centre stores, have 20 000 regular customers. The retailers apply the same policy to financial products as to clothing: they farm out production to 'manufacturers', concerning themselves with the packaging and marketing. Their advantages are both trusted brand names and friendly premises.

Competition is hottest in two areas – mortgages and the market for the public's cash deposits. Everybody is fighting for a slice of Britain's mortgage market, worth £40 billion ($68 billion) a year in new lending. Financial firms believe that once hooked with a mortgage, customers can be persuaded to buy their other services – in particular the profitable life assurance policies which are tied to most British mortgages. This explains the extraordinary £2 billion swoop,

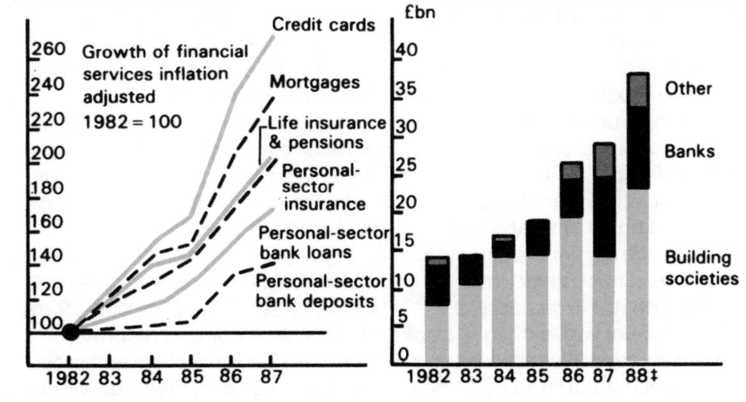

Sources: Boston Consulting Group; CSO

* The modernization of UK financial markets in 1986.

over the past two years, by banks, insurance companies and building societies on Britian's estate agents.

Estate agents have all the trimmings: they normally lounge in prime high-street premises, open longer than office-hours and are visited regularly by the public. Of Britain's 16 biggest building societies, 14 have bought chains. Estate agents are responsible for selling nearly 10% of all Britain's mortgages; Abbey National believes that in five years this will rise to 20%.

For building societies, worried by their declining share of the mortgage market, estate agents are a defensive buy. The societies have not been deterred by the public's poor perception of the probity of most estate agents. Bought-up estate agents achieve a con- version rate' of around 20% i.e. that proportion of house-buyers get their mortgage from the same firm.

Hambros, a merchant bank, has done better than most of the building societies, achieving a 40% conversion rate for its chain, Hambro Countrywide. This has been the most profitable of the new chains, making £25m last year. The merchant bank has placed financial consultants in its 500 branches, trained to sell mortgages and life assurance to house-buyers. Together with Guardian Royal Exchange, Hambros has set up a new life assurance company. Wisely, Hambros tries to sell only those few services that it thinks it can do well.

Building societies are getting into estate agency not just defensively but also to diversify. The two building societies that have tried hardest to become broad-based financial firms are Abbey National and Nationwide Anglia. Abbey reckons that to compete effectively it needs to escape the constraints of the Building Societies Act by becoming a public company; Nationwide Anglia (like the other leading societies) wants to spread without losing its mutual status.

Nationwide Anglia's expansion is aggressive. It has moved into banking with its Flexaccount, a current account with a cheque book that pays interest. Flexaccount and a similar account offered by Abbey National lose the societies money. Unlike the clearers and their more profitable high-interest accounts, these two building societies pay interest without insisting upon a minimum balance. The costs of processing the paperwork are high, since there is no limit to the number or the amount of the cheques that account holders can write. Nationwide Anglia now has over 700 000 current accounts. The society says that Flexaccount will break even at 1.2m, but points out that it is already bringing in new customers who are buying other services.

Painful though they may be for the building societies that pioneer them, interest-bearing current accounts are a time-bomb under the clearing banks. Britain's big four banks watch with horror as more and more of their customers move to Abbey National or Nationwide Anglia. The clearers know that if they do respond and slug it out with the building societies, they will suffer from their portlier costs. Building society offices are in less prestigious and cheaper sites; their managers get paid less; and while clearers still carry out many operating functions in branches – such as processing cheques and mortgages – most building societies have centralized paperwork in their head offices, leaving their branch staff more time to talk to the customers.

It costs the clearing banks about 7% in overheads to take in deposits. So provided the cost of funding in the money market is higher than 7% – it is currently about 12% – the clearers, the TSB and the Scottish banks do nicely out of their £36 billion of interest-free current account deposits. Some recent research by an investment bank, Barclays de Zoete Wedd (owned by the largest clearing bank), predicts that if these banks were to pay the 4.5% now paid by the two building societies, their pre-tax profits would slump by 30%, or £1.5 billion.

In private, some clearing bankers admit that sooner or later they will have to pay interest. Barclays Bank plans a two-pronged response. First, cut costs. Barclays will move its British banking headquarters to Coventry, services such as mortgages and unsecured loans will be centralized, and the increasing use of debit cards instead of cheques – Barclays has distributed 1.5m Connect debit cards in the past year – will reduce paperwork in branches. Open-plan designs will transform the branches.

Second, Barclays aims to provide customers with a fuller range of better products than the building societies. For instance, its new high-interest account, Capital Advantage, which demands a minimum of £10 000 and pays more than equivalent building society accounts, has attracted over £1 billion in the past ten months, 60% of it from customers who previously had no dealings with Barclays. And Barclayshare, a no-frills stockbroking service based in Watford, offers commissions on small bargains as low as £16, compared to a £25 minimum charged by most stockbrokers. Barclays keeps things cheap by buying shares through a nominee account and holding them in trust, which avoids the need to issure share certificates.

Selling is selling

Meanwhile some of the insurance companies, such as Prudential, are strongly placed to compete against banks and building societies. Their core products, such as personal pensions and the more complicated sorts of life assurance, are extremely profitable – and relatively hard for outsiders, lacking actuarial expertise, to break into. Profit margins will fall less far on these services than on more easily copied products, such as cheque accounts, mortages and credit cards. But it is only those insurers with direct sales forces who can feel confident. Certain provisions of the Financial Services Act have effectively reduced the number of independent intermediaries and so hobbled those insurance companies which depend on them for sales.

All this follow-my-leader expansion is bringing headaches to the retail markets similar to those that afflicted the wholesale financial markets after Big Bang. Building societies are finding estate agents hard to manage. For example, Nationwide Anglia initially left the firms' former partners to run the show. However, they showed less interest in the business after having cashed in their chips. So Nationwide Anglia has taken tighter control.

Some firms which looked set to become financial supermarkets have already had to retreat. Allied Dunbar, an insurance group that also sells personal pensions, mortgages, unit trusts and health insurance, admits that it became overstretched. It offered high-interest money-market accounts on the American model. But Allied Dunbar's direct sales force did not prove adept at selling such accounts, so the product was withdrawn a year ago.

'The lesson from the retailing industry is that specialists have done better than department stores,' points out Mr David Hall, head of the Boston Consulting Group's financial services division in London. 'It is hard to be a financial supermarket: in America, only Citicorp has succeeded in being all things to all people.'

Britain's clearing banks have always sold a wide range of products from all their branches. But that is now their problem. They remain more adept at making financial products than at marketing and selling them.

In an era of increasing competition, deregulation (the Building Societies Act and the single European market) and tougher supervision (the Financial Services Act), which firms will flourish? Those that invest in new technology, those that do not expand beyond markets in which they can add value, and, most important of all, those that have a clear idea of the needs of particular sorts of customers. Sounds easy, doesn't it? Yet, until now, the protection of a quasi-cartel has allowed banks to get away with uninviting branches and 'you're privileged that we have your money' current accounts. Now competition from the building societies is forcing banks to respond to what their customers want. Consumers will gain most from this high-street war. Shareholders will lose.

Source: *The Economist*, 15 Oct. 1988.

Questions

1. In what ways are financial intermediaries diversifying?
2. Why is it now possible to have a current account which pays interest?
3. In what ways might banks still have a competitive edge over building societies, and vice versa?
4. What are the implications of diversification (a) for the consumer and (b) for the holder of bank shares?
5. Which financial intermediaries seem likely to be most profitable in the future?

Exam Preparation

PRACTICAL EXERCISE

1. Arrange the following items on the proper side of the member bank's balance sheet, i.e. under Liabilities or Assets:

(a) demand deposits
(b) notes and coins
(c) time deposits
(d) balances with Bank of England
(e) advances to customers
(f) holdings of government bonds
(g) bank buildings and fixtures
(h) borrowings from other banks.

MULTIPLE CHOICE QUESTIONS

1. Lending by the monetary sector to the government is represented by one of the following:

A mortgages
B special deposits
C money at call
D Treasury bills.

2. Which one of the following is *not* a function of money?

A unit of account
B source of credit
C store of value
D medium of exchange
E standard for deferred payments.

3. If the Bank of England sells securities for £10 million on the open market, then the commercial banks

A need take no action because their assets and liabilities are both reduced by the same amount
B must reduce their existing liquid assets
C must reduce their advances by an amount dependent upon their existing liquid reserves
D can increase advances by £10 million, provided there is a sufficient demand for credit
E can increase advances by more than £10 million if their liquid assets exceed the required minimum.

4. Which one of the following is a liability of a UK commercial bank?
A loans to discount houses
B money at call
C deposit accounts of customers
D special deposits at the Bank of England
E overdrafts incurred by small traders.

5. If all banks observe a 20 per cent reserve asset ratio, by how much can the banking system increase deposits in response to a new deposit of £100?
A £100
B £200
C £400
D £500
E £2 000.

6. British commercial banks usually do all of the following *except*
A buy long-term government securities
B pay interest on some of the money deposited with them
C re-discount Treasury bills
D lend for very short periods to the money market
E subscribe to new issues of ordinary shares.

7. Which of the following activities of a London clearing bank is its largest source of income?
A making loans or overdrafts
B holding treasury bills
C holding bills of exchange
D dealing in foreign currencies
E holding investments.

RELATED ESSAY QUESTIONS

1. What factors determine the levels of advances made by commercial banks?

2. Define money and outline how its forms may vary with the level of development of an economy. Discuss why there are so many measures of the money supply in the UK.

3. Explain briefly with the aid of a numerical example, 'the money (or credit) multiplier'. Discuss the significance of the money multiplier for monetary policy.

4. (a) Explain how the commercial banking system can 'create' bank deposits.
(b) Consider how the stock of bank deposits might be affected by
(i) a sale of shares in a government-owned enterprise to the general public
(ii) an increase in the Public Sector Borrowing Requirement
(iii) a central bank sale of foreign currency to prevent depreciation in the exchange rate.

5. Why is there no unique measure of the money supply?

6. Why do all advanced economies have a central bank (such as the Bank of England)?

7. Examine the factors which might be expected to affect the amount of new loans made by commercial banks in the UK.

Part C

Product Markets

20 Consumer Choice

Key Points to Review

- Trade-offs (1.5, 1.6)
- Demand, income, and substitution effects (5.1)
- Change in demand versus change in quantity demanded (5.3)

Questions for Preview

1 What is utility?

2 What is the theory of diminishing marginal utility?

3 How does a consumer maximize his or her total utility?

4 What happens to consumer equilibrium when price changes?

5 How can the theory of diminishing marginal utility account for the law of demand?

When we first discussed the theory of demand in Chapter 5, we gave several reasons why the quantity demanded went up when the price of something went down. We pointed out that as the price of a good falls, individuals will substitute some of that good for other things. Additionally, when the price of one good in a consumer's budget goes down with all other prices remaining the same, that person's buying power will actually be greater. A person not only *feels* better off, he or she is better off. With a constant money income, when the price of one good falls, the person clearly has more real spending, or purchasing power.

The theory of demand is important and so, too, is its derivation, because it allows us to arrange the relevant variables, such as prices, incomes, and tastes, in such a way as to generate predictions about the real world.

How do we *derive* the theory of demand? We examine two explanations: first the traditional **utility analysis** and second the more comprehensive indifference curve analysis. Utility theory appears conceptually attractive on the grounds of its simplicity but it soon turns out to be rather wanting. Hence we resort to indifference curves as a more rigorous derivation of downward-sloping demand curves.

Utility Theory

When you buy something, you buy it because of the satisfaction you expect to receive from having and using it. For just about everything that you like to have, the more you have of it, the higher the level of satisfaction you receive. Another term can be used for satisfaction, namely **utility**, or want-satisfying power. This is a property that is common to all goods that are desired. However, the concept of utility is purely subjective. There is no way that you or I can measure the amount of utility that we or another consumer might be able to obtain from a particular good, for utility does not mean 'useful', 'utilitarian', or 'practical'. For this reason, there cannot be true accurate scientific assessment of the utility that someone may receive by consuming, say, a Mars bar or a packet of crisps relative to the utility that another person might receive. Thus we must recognize at the outset that the theory of utility presents us with an immediate problem of measurement.

Economists used to believe that utility could be measured. They therefore first developed utility theory in terms of units of measurable utility, to which they applied the term **util**. Thus, the first chocolate bar that you eat might yield you four utils of satisfaction; the first bag of crisps, six utils; and so on. Today, no one believes that we can actually measure utils, but the ideas forthcoming from such analysis will prove useful in our understanding of the way in which consumers choose among alternatives. Economists are not alone in using simple but inherently suspect concepts. Teachers of physics have used the concept of force. No physicist has ever seen a unit of force just as no economist has ever seen a unit of utility. But in both subject areas a rather nebulous concept has none the less proven useful for analytical purposes. Indeed we might note that even though illegal activities may be considered morally wrong by many people, they can still be analysed in terms of the utility that those activities generate for their consumers.

Total and Marginal Utility

Consider the satisfaction, or utility, that you might receive each time that you hire and watch a video-cassette on your home video. There are many video-cassettes to choose from each year and we might reasonably assume that each of them is of the same quality. Suppose you normally hire one video-cassette per week. You could, of course, hire two, three, or four per week. Presumably each time you hire another video-cassette per week you will get additional satisfaction, or utility. The question, though, that we must ask is, given that you are already hiring one per week, will the next one give you the same amount of additional utility? That additional, or incremental utility is called *marginal utility*, where *marginal* is another term for incremental, or additional. Understanding the concept of marginal is important in economics, because we make decisions at the margin. This means that at a particular point, we compare additional benefits with additional costs.

Figure 20.1

Total and Marginal Utility of Watching Video-Cassettes. If we were able to assign specific numbers to the utility derived from watching video-cassettes each week, we could then obtain a marginal utility schedule that would probably be similar in pattern to the one below. In column 1 is the quantity of video-cassettes watched per week, in column 2, the total utility from each quantity; and in column 3, the marginal utility, which is defined as the change in total utility due to a change of one unit of watching video-cassettes per week.

(1) *Quantity of video-cassettes*	*(2)* *Total utility*	*(3)* *Marginal utility (utils per week)*
0	0	
1	10	10
2	16	6
3	19	3
4	20	1
5	20	0
6	18	−2

The way to understand the concept of marginal utility is to take the specific example presented in Figure 20.1. Here we show the total and marginal utility of watching video-cassettes each week. The marginal utility is seen to be the difference between the total utility derived from a specific quantity of video-cassettes, say, Q, and the total utility derived from one more, $Q + 1$. In our example, when a person has already watched two video-cassettes in one week, and then watches another, total utility increases from 16 utils to 19. Therefore, the marginal utility (of watching one more video-cassette after having watched two already) is equal to three utils.

Graphic Analysis

We can transfer the information in Figure 20.1 on to a graph which we do in panels (a) and (b) of Figure 20.2. Total utility, which is represented in column 2 of Figure 20.1 is transferred in blocks (represented by dashed outlines) to panel (a) of Figure 20.2.

Total utility continues to rise until four video-cassettes are watched per week. This measure of utility remains at 20 utils through the fifth video-cassette, and at the sixth video-cassette per week falls to 18 utils, because we assume that at *some* quantity consumed per unit time-period, dislike sets in. If we connect the tops of the total utility blocks with a smooth line, we come up with a representation of the total utility curve associated with watching video-cassettes during a one-week period. This is shown in panel (a) of Figure 20.3.

Marginal Utility

If you look carefully at both panels (a) and (b) of Figure 20.2, the notion of marginal utility and what it is can be seen very clearly. In economics, marginal always refers to a change in the total. The marginal utility, for example, of watching three video-cassettes a week as opposed to two video-cassettes a week is the increment in total utility and is equal to three utils per day. Marginal utility is represented by the shaded portion of the blocks in panel (a) of Figure 20.2 on page 300.

We can transfer these shaded portions down to panel (b) of Figure 20.2 and come up with a graphic representation of marginal utility. When we connect the tops of these marginal utility rectangles in panel (b) of Figure 20.2 we come up with a smoothly sloping marginal utility curve. Notice that that curve hits zero when more than four video-cassettes are watched per week. At zero marginal utility, the consumer has watched all the video-cassettes that he or she wants to and does not want to watch any more. The last video-cassette watched at zero marginal utility gives the consumer no additional satisfaction, or utility.

When marginal utility becomes negative, such as it does in this example after more than four video-cassettes per week are watched, it means that the consumer is fed up with watching video-cassettes and

Key Points 20.1

- **Utility is defined as want-satisfying power; it is a property common to all desired goods and services.**
- **We artificially try to measure units of utility in utils.**
- **It is important to distinguish between total utility and marginal utility. Total utility is the total satisfaction derived from the consumption of a given quantity of a good. Marginal utility is the change in total utility due to a one-unit change in the consumption of the good.**

would require some form of compensation to watch any more. When marginal utility is negative, the additional unit consumed actually lowers total utility by becoming a 'nuisance'. (Now read Key Points 20.1.)

Figure 20.2

Total and Marginal Utility in Discrete Units In panel (a), the dashed outline indicates a total utility for each rate of viewing of video-cassettes per week. The shaded portion of each dashed box indicates a marginal utility for each video-cassette watched per week. When we transfer the shaded boxes to panel (b), we have a diagram of discrete marginal utility.

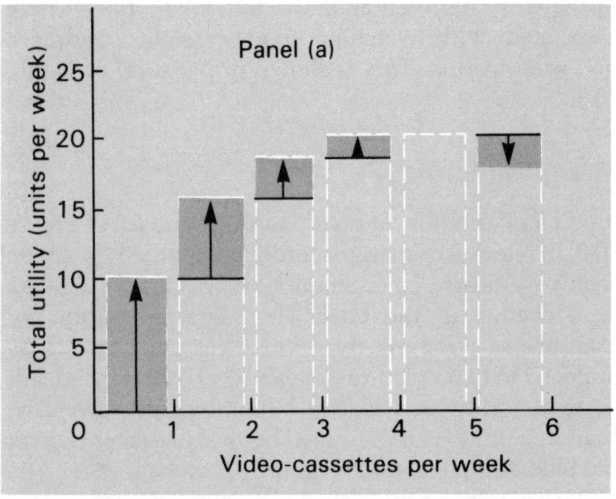

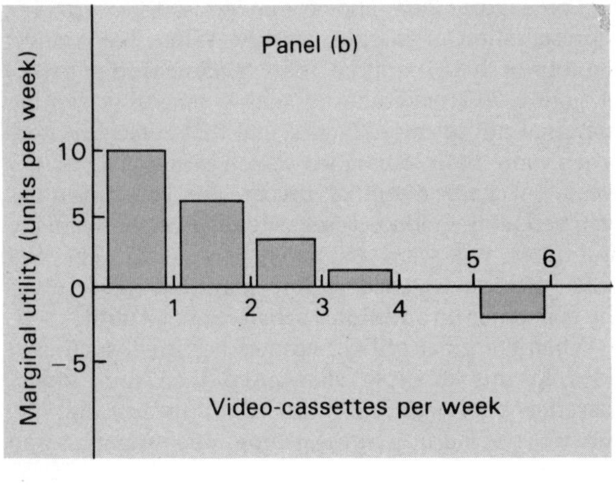

Diminishing Marginal Utility

Notice that in panel (b) of Figure 20.3, marginal utility is continuously declining. This property of marginal utility has been named **diminishing marginal utility**. There is no way we can prove diminishing marginal utility; none the less, economists and lay-persons for years have believed strongly in the assertion of diminishing marginal utility. Diminishing marginal utility has even been called a 'law'. This supposed law concerns a psychological, or subjective, utility that you receive as you consume more and more of a particular good. Stated formally, the law is:

> As an individual consumes more of the same good per unit of time, utility increases (up to a point at least). However, the extra utility added by an extra (marginal) unit of that good does not increase at a constant rate. Rather, as successive new units of the good in question are consumed, after some point that total utility will grow at a slower and slower rate. Otherwise stated, as the amount of a good consumed per unit of time increases, the marginal utility of the good tends to decrease.

Optimizing Consumption Choices

Every consumer has a limited income. Choices must be made. When a consumer has made all his or her choices about what to buy and in what quantities, and the total level of satisfaction, or utility, from that set of choices is as great as it can be, we say that the consumer has optimized his or her consumption choices. The consumer has attained an *optimum consumption* basket of goods and services.

Consider a simple example that involves two goods. The consumer has a choice between spending income on the rental of video-cassettes and the purchase of food. Suppose that the last pound spent on food yielded three utils of utility, but the last pound spent on video-cassette rentals yielded ten utils of utility. Would this consumer not increase total utility if some pounds were taken away from food consumption and allocated to videotape rentals? The answer is 'yes'. Given diminishing marginal utility, more money spent on video-cassette rentals will reduce marginal utility per last pound spent, whereas fewer pounds spent on food consumption will increase marginal utility per last pound spent. The optimum – where total utility is maximized – might occur when the satisfaction per last pound spent on both food and video-cassette rentals per week is, say, five utils.

We can put this optimum consumption situation in a clearer manner as follows: total utility of the consumer is maximized (**consumer optimum** is reached) when a fixed money income is spent on goods and services such that:

$$\frac{\text{marginal utility of } x}{\text{price of } x} = \frac{\text{marginal utility of } y \ldots}{\text{price of } y} = \frac{\text{marginal utility of } n}{\text{price of } n}$$

$x, y \ldots n$ indicate the different goods and services that the consumer might purchase.

Optimization typically refers to individual decision-making processes. When we deal with many individuals interacting in the market-place, we talk in terms of an equilibrium in the market-place. Generally speaking, equilibrium is a property of markets rather than of individual decision-making.

We can apply the theory of consumer optimum to the way in which people use their time. Every individual must make a choice among all possible uses of time. For example, the marginal utility received from the last minute used to study economics should not be radically different from the marginal utility received from the last minute used to study geography (assuming, of course, that the student is maximizing grades while faced with a time constraint). If these marginal utilities are greatly out of line, then obviously the student should change the time-mix. He or she should spend more or less time with one than the other.

Remember here that clearly we are not assuming that the student receives utility from spending time studying either economics or geography (although this is a possibility). Rather, it is the outcome of the time spent studying – higher grades and perhaps a better job in the future – that generates the utility.

Consumption decisions are summarized in the theory of demand, which you will recall from Chapter 5, states that the amount purchased is inversely related to price. We can now see why by using the theory of diminishing utility.

Decisions to purchase are made such that marginal utility of the last unit purchased and consumed is just equal to the price that had to be paid, that is, the opportunity cost for that last unit. No consumer will, when optimizing, buy ten units of a good per unit time-period when the subjective valuation placed on the tenth unit is less than the price of the tenth unit.

If we start out with the consumer optimum and then observe a price decrease, we can predict that consumers will respond to the price decrease by consuming more.

Figure 20.3

Total and Marginal Utility. If we take the total utility units from column 2 in Figure 20.1, we obtain rectangles like those presented in Figure 20.2(a). If we connect the tops of those rectangles with a smooth line, we come up with a total utility curve that peaks somewhere between four and five video-cassettes per week and then slowly declines (panel (a)). Marginal utility is represented by the increment in total utility, shown as the shaded blocks in panel (b) of Figure 20.2. When these blocks are connected by a smooth line, we obtain the marginal utility curve.

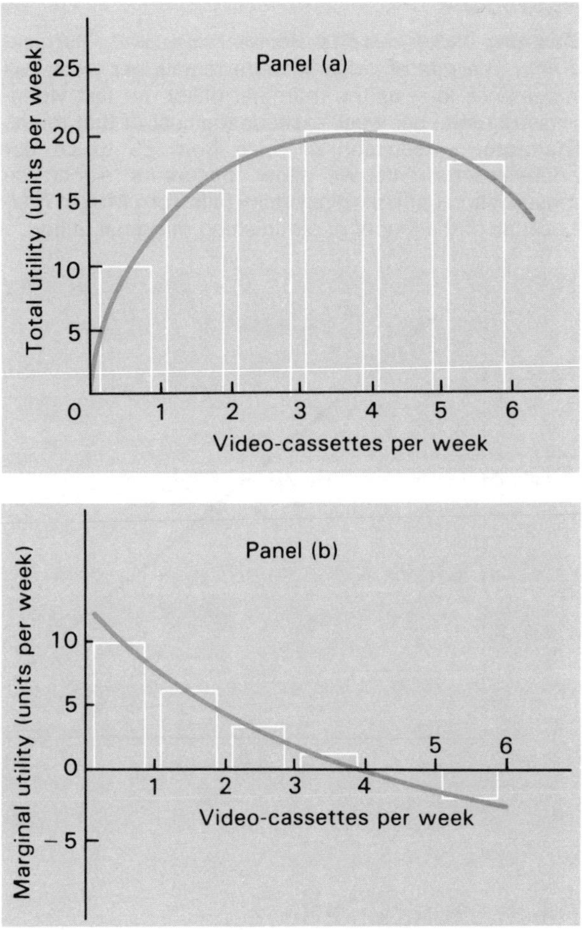

Why? Because, before the price change, the marginal utility of the last unit was about equal to the price paid for the last unit. Now with a lower price, it is possible to consume more than before. If the theory of diminishing marginal utility holds, the purchase and consumption of additional units will cause marginal utility to fall. Eventually, it will fall to equate marginal utility with the price of the final unit consumed. The limit to this increase in consumption is given by the theory of diminishing marginal utility. At some point, the marginal utility of an additional unit would be less than what the person would have to give up (price) of that additional unit.

Look at a hypothetical demand curve for video-cassette rentals per week for a typical consumer in

Figure 20.4. At a price of £5 per video-cassette rental, the marginal utility of the last video-cassette rented per week is MU_1. At a price of £4 per video-cassette rental per week, the marginal utility is represented by MU_2. Because of the theory of diminishing marginal utility, MU_2 must be less than MU_1. What has happened is that, at a lower price, the number of video-cassette rentals per week increased from two to three; marginal utility must have fallen. At a higher consumption rate, marginal utility falls down to meet the lower price for video-cassette rental per week.

Figure 20.4

Changing Video-cassette Rental Prices and Marginal Utility. The rate of video-cassette rentals per week will increase as long as the marginal utility per last video-cassette rental per week exceeds the cost of that rental. Therefore, a reduction in price from £5 to £4 per video-cassette rental will allow consumers to increase consumption until marginal utility falls from MU_1 to MU_2 (because of the theory of diminishing marginal utility).

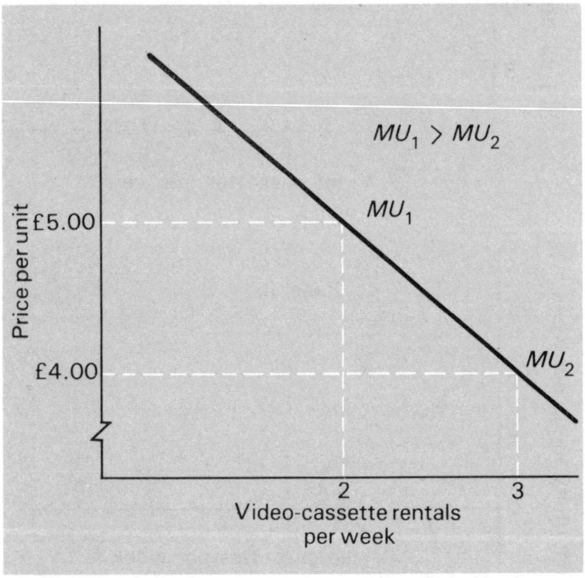

The Substitution Effect

What is happening all along, as the price of, say, video-cassette recorder rental falls, is that consumers are substituting the now relatively cheaper video-cassette rentals for other goods and services, such as restaurant meals, live concerts, and the like. We call this the *substitution effect* of a change in price of a good, because it occurs when consumers substitute in favour of relatively cheaper goods away from relatively more expensive ones.

The Income Effect

There is another reason why a reduction in price would cause an increase in the quantity demanded (or an increase in price would cause a reduction in the quantity demanded). It has to do with the ability of individuals to purchase more or less goods and services when there is a price change in one of the goods and services now being consumed. A fall in the price of any one item being purchased during, say, a week increases the purchasing power of any given amount of money income. A fall in the price of any good being consumed results in an increase in real income – the amount of goods and services that one is able to purchase. Given this increase in real income, most individuals will tend to buy more of most goods and services that they are now consuming. This increase in quantity demanded due to a price reduction, which increases real income, is called the *income effect* of a change in price. (Usually the substitution effect is more important than the income effect except for price changes of goods that constitute a fairly large part of a person's total budget.)

The Demand Curve Revisited

Linking together the theory of diminishing marginal utility and the theory of equal marginal utilities per pound gives us a negative relationship between the quantity demanded of a good or service and its price. As the relative price of video-cassette rental goes up, for example, the quantity demanded will fall; and as the relative price of video-cassette rental goes down, the quantity demanded will rise. Figure 20.4 shows this demand curve for video-cassette rentals. As the relative price of video-cassette rental falls, the consumer can maximize total utility only by purchasing more of them, and vice versa. In other words, the relationship between price and quantity desired is simply a downward-sloping demand curve. Note, though, that this downward-sloping demand curve (the theory of demand) is derived under the assumption of constant tastes and incomes. You must remember that we are keeping these important determining variables constant when we simply look at the relationship between price and quantity demanded.

Deriving the Market Demand Curve

The demand curve we have been talking about is one that relates directly to an individual. But what about a *market* demand curve, that is, the demand curve that represents the entire market for a particular good or service? How can we derive a market demand curve from the individual ones we have analysed?

Actually, deriving a market demand curve from individual demand curves is not difficult. What we have to do is add together all the individual demands horizontally (asuming that each individual's decisions are made independently of others'). We know that not all people are alike. We know, for example, that even at very low prices, certain individuals will demand no video-cassette rental whatsoever. So, to derive a demand curve for the entire market, we must add up each individual's demand. This is what we do in Figure 20.5. The figure shows explicitly that the market demand

Figure 20.5(a)

Video-cassette Rentals Demanded per Week. Individuals A, B, and C present us with the various quantities of video-cassette rentals they intend to rent at various relative prices: £2, £3, and £4. When we add quantities demanded by these individuals, we get the total or market quantity demanded at each of these various prices.

	£2	£3	£4
Individual A's quantity demanded	4	3	2
Individual B's quantity demanded	2	1	0
Individual C's quantity demanded	1	0	0
Market quantity demanded	7	4	2

Figure 20.5(b)

Deriving the Market Demand Curve. Individual A's demand curve is shown first, then individual B's and individual C's. By adding these three demand curves horizontally, we obtain the market demand curve represented by the heavily shaded line in the right-hand graph.

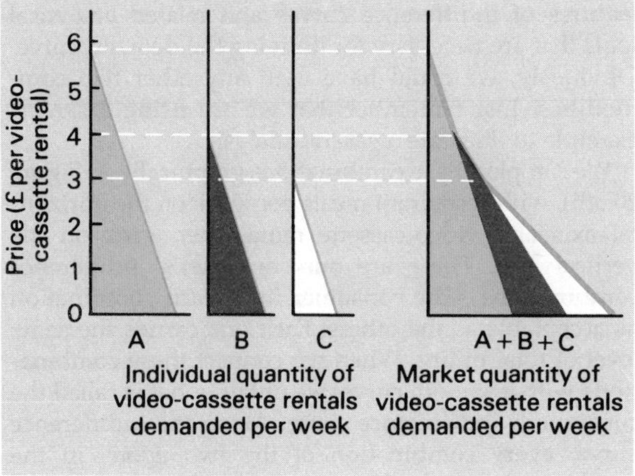

curves are fitted together to obtain the market demand curve for video-cassette rental by what we call 'horizontal addition'. Notice that the good's demand is expressed in quantity per time-period. We include a time-period to the demand analysis because we are talking about a flow through time of a demand for a specific good.

Consumer Surplus

Figure 20.5(b) provides us with the basis of an understanding with the concept of consumer surplus. It shows the market demand curve for a society of three individuals. Suppose now that the rental charge for video-cassette hire is £2. At that price the quantity demanded is seven per week. We note from Figure 20.5(a) that individual A would have been prepared to pay £4 for video hire. Presumably he considered that he would have received at least £4 of utility from viewing a video. Individual B was prepared to pay £3 for video hire and again we can presume that this reflects the utility obtained from watching a particular film. Individual C is not prepared to pay more than £2 for the rental of a video. What significance is there if this latter price is indeed that which all three members of our imaginary society actually have to pay for video rental? If the charge made to all three individuals of £2 is the same then both individuals A and B could be said to have received extra utility for which they have not had to pay. It is only individual C who actually equated his utility with the price. Thus in terms of Figure 20.5(b) the whole of the area above the horizontal line marking the price charged (£2) and below the demand curve is the measure of 'surplus' utility obtained by individuals A and B but not paid for. This area is called **consumer surplus**. The term is of relevance to us when we come to consider whether all consumers do indeed pay a common price. It might be possible for a producer to charge some individuals more than others, i.e. discriminate between them and thus transfer some of this consumer's surplus to himself. We examine this possibility in Chapter 23.

Utility Analysis — A Summary

The analysis of consumer demand using utility theory may appear abstract. That, of course, must be true every time we attempt to hypothesize anything about people's behaviour. But utility theory was developed for a very specific reason. It allowed economists to understand the importance of the factors that influence demand and the quantity demanded.

The theory of consumer choice is a theory that helps economists predict how consumers will react to changes in price, income, and so on. The goal of this analysis, as well as of any other in this text, is to allow the reader to predict what will happen when an important determining variable changes. Because we have used an example concerning consumer choice about video-cassette rentals that does not mean that the analysis stops there. It can be extended to any good or service. (Now read Key Points 20.2 on page 304.)

Indifference Curve Analysis

While the theory of diminishing marginal utility can be fairly well accepted on intuitive grounds and by introspection, if we want more elegant theorizing we can translate our discussion into graphic analyis with what are called 'indifference curves' and 'the budget constraint'. Here we discuss these terms and their relationship and demonstrate consumer equilibrium in geometric form.

Key Points 20.2

- The theory of diminishing marginal utility tells us that the extra utility added by the marginal unit of a good consumed falls.
- The consumer maximizes total utility by equating the marginal utility of the last pound (or penny) spent on one good with the marginal utility per last pound (or penny) spent on all other goods. He or she is then in consumer equilibrium.
- In order to remain in consumer equilibrium, a price decrease requires an increase in consumption; a price increase requires a decrease in consumption.
- Assuming that we can measure utility, and further assuming that the theory of diminishing marginal utility holds, the demand curve must slope down – quantity demanded and price are inversely related.

On Being Indifferent

What does it mean to be indifferent? It usually means that you don't care one way or the other about something: you are equally disposed to either of two alternatives. With this interpretation in mind, we will turn to the two choices, video-cassette rentals and restaurant meals. In Figure 20.6(a), we show several combinations of video-cassette rentals and restaurant meals per week that our representative consumer considers to be equally satisfactory. This is to say, for each combination, *A*, *B*, *C*, and *D*, this consumer will have exactly the same level of total utility.

Figure 20.6(a)

Combinations that Yield Equal Levels of Satisfaction. The combination *A, B, C, and D* represents varying combinations of video-cassette rentals and restaurant meals per week that give an equal level of satisfaction to this consumer. In other words, the consumer is indifferent about these four combinations.

Combination	*Video-cassette rentals per week*	*Restaurant meals per week*
A	1	7
B	2	4
C	3	2
D	4	1

Figure 20.6(b)

An Indifference Curve. If we plot the combinations *A, B, C,* and *D* from Figure 20.6(a), we obtain the curve *ABCD*, which is called an indifference curve.

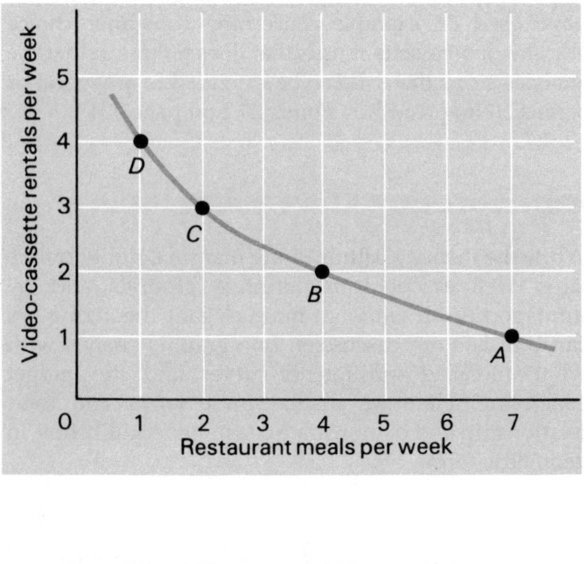

This simple numerical example that we use happens to concern video-cassette rentals and restaurant meals per week, but this example is used to illustrate general features of indifference curves and related analytical tools that are necessary for deriving the demand curve. Obviously, we could have used any other two commodities. Just remember that we are using a *specific* example to illustrate a *general* analysis.

We can plot these combinations graphically in Figure 20.6(b), with restaurant meals per week on the horizontal axis and video-cassette rentals per week on the vertical axis. These are our consumer's indifference combinations – the consumer finds each combination as acceptable as the others. Each one carries the same level of total utility. When we connect these combinations with a smooth curve, we obtain what is called the consumer's **indifference curve**. Along the indifference curve, every combination of the two goods in the equation yields exactly the same level of total utility. Every point along the indifference curve is equally desirable to the consumer; for example, four video-cassette rentals per week and one restaurant meal per week will given our representative consumer exactly the same total satisfaction as, say, two video-cassette rentals per week and four restaurant meals per week.

Properties of Indifference Curves

Indifference curves have special properties relating to their slope and shape.

INDIFFERENCE CURVES USUALLY SLOPE DOWN

The indifference curve that we showed in Figure 20.6(b) sloped down. That is to say, it had a negative slope. Consider Figure 20.7. Here we show two points,

Figure 20.7

Indifference Curves Cannot Slope up. Point *B* represents a consumption with more video-cassette rentals per week and more restaurant rentals per week than point *A*. *B* is always preferred to *A*. Therefore *A* and *B* cannot be on the same indifference curve, which is positively sloped, because an indifference curve shows *equally* preferred combinations of the two goods.

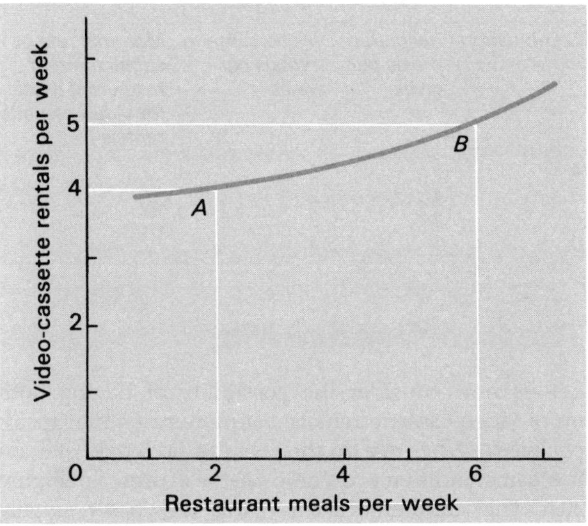

A and *B*. Point *A* represents four video-cassette rentals per week and two restaurant meals per week. Point *B* represents five video-cassette rentals per week and six restaurant meals per week. Clearly, *B* is always preferred to *A*, because *B* represents more of everything. If *B* is always preferred to *A*, then it is impossible for points *A* and *B* to be on the same indifference curve, because the definition of the indifference curve is a set of combinations of two goods that are equally preferred.

INDIFFERENCE CURVES ARE RARELY STRAIGHT LINES

The indifference curve that we have drawn in Figure 20.6(b) is special. Notice that it is curved. Why did we not draw a straight line as we have usually done for a demand curve? To find out why we do not draw straight-line indifference curves, consider the implications. We show such a straight-line indifference curve in Figure 20.8. Start at point *A*. The consumer has no restaurant meals and five video-cassette rentals per week. Now the consumer wishes to go to point *B*. He or she is willing to give up only one video-cassette rental in order to get one restaurant meal. Now let us assume that the consumer is at point *C*. That consumer is consuming one video-cassette rental and four restaurant meals per week. If the consumer wants to go to point *D*, he or she is again willing to give up one video-cassette rental in order to get one more restaurant meal per week. In other words, no matter how many video-cassettes the consumer rents, he or she is willing to give up one video-cassette rental in order to get one restaurant meal per week. That does not seem to be plausible. According to the theory of diminishing marginal utility, the more of something that a consumer has, the lower will be its marginal utility. Thus, does it not make sense to hypothesize that the more video-cassettes the consumer rents per week, the less he or she will value an additional video-cassette rental? Presumably, when the consumer has five video-cassette rentals and no restaurant meals per week, he or she should be willing to give up more than one video-cassette rental in order to get one restaurant meal. Therefore, once we accept diminishing marginal utility of video-cassette rental consumption, a straight-line indifference curve as shown in Figure 20.8 no longer seems possible. Diminishing marginal utility implies curved indifference curves like the one shown in Figure 20.6(b). In mathematical jargon, an indifference curve is convex with respect to the origin. The reason for this is the theory of diminishing marginal utility. As the individual consumes more of a particular item, the marginal utility of consuming one additional

Figure 20.8

The Implications of a Straight-line Indifference Curve. If the indifference curve is a straight line, the consumer will be willing to give up the same number of video-cassette rentals (one for one in this simple example) to get one more restaurant meal per week, whether the consumer has no restaurant meals or a lot of restaurant meals per week. For example, the consumer at point *A* has five video-cassette rentals and no restaurant meals per week. He or she is willing to give up one more video-cassette rental in order to get one more restaurant meal per week. At point *C*, for example, the consumer has only one video-cassette rental and four restaurant meals per week. Because of the straight-line indifference curve, this consumer is willing to give up the last video-cassette rental in order to get one more restaurant meal per week, even though he or she already has four.

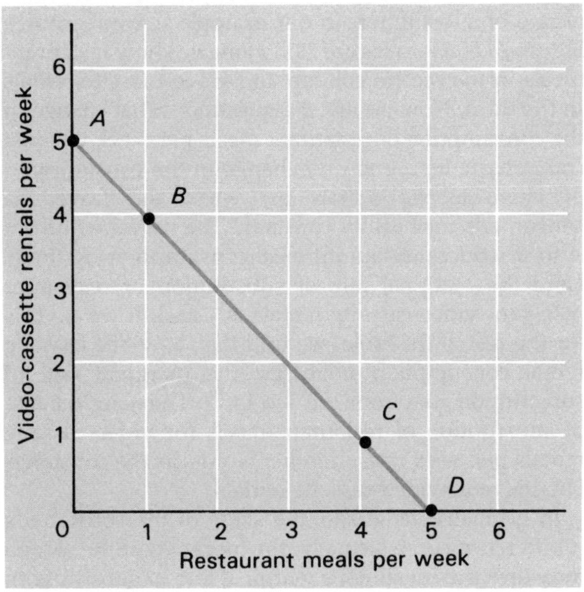

unit of that item falls, or, conversely, as the person consumes less of it, that good will have a higher marginal utility.

We can measure the marginal utility of something by the quantity of a substitute good that would leave the consumer indifferent. Let us look at this in Figure 20.6(a). Starting with combination *A*, the consumer has one video-cassette rental but with seven restaurant meals per week. To remain indifferent, the consumer would be willing to give up three restaurant meals to obtain one more video-cassette rental (as shown in combination *B*). However, to go from combination *C* to combination *D*, notice that the consumer would be willing to give up only one restaurant meal for an additional video-cassette rental per week. In other words, the quantity of the substitute considered acceptable changes as the relative scarcity of the original item changes.

Diminishing marginal utility exists throughout this set of choices and consequently the indifference curve in Figure 20.6(b) will be 'bowed in' (convex when viewed from below). If it were a straight line marginal utility would not be diminishing but constant; if it were 'bowed out' (concave when viewed from below), marginal utility would be increasing.

The Marginal Rate of Substitution

Above we discussed marginal utility in terms of the marginal rate of substitution between restaurant meals and video-cassette rentals per week. More formally, we can define the consumer's marginal rate of substitution as follows:

MRS = the change in the quantity of one good that just offsets a one-unit change in the consumption of another good, such that total well-being remains constant.

We can see numerically what happens to the marginal rate of substitution in our example if we rearrange Figure 20.6(a) into Figure 20.9. Here we show restaurant meals in the second column and video-cassette rentals in the third. Now we ask the question: What change in the consumption of restaurant meals per week will just compensate for a one-unit change in the consumption of video-cassette rentals per week and leave the consumer's total utility constant? The movement from *A* to *B* reduces restaurant meal consumption by three. Here the marginal rate of substitution of restaurant meals for video-cassette rentals is 1 to 3. If we do this for the rest of the table, we find that, as video-cassette rental consumption increases, the marginal rate of substitution goes from 1 to 3 to 1 to 1. The marginal rate of substitution of restaurant meals for video-cassette rentals per week rises, in other words, as the consumer obtains more video-cassette rentals.

In geometric language, the slope of the consumer's indifference curve (actually, the 'negative of the slope') measures the consumer's marginal rate of substitution. Notice that this marginal rate of substitution, or MRS, is purely subjective or psychological. We are not talking about financial capabilities, merely about a consumer's particular set of preferences.

Figure 20.9
Calculating the Marginal Rate of Substitution

Combination	*Restaurant meals per week*	*Video-cassette rentals per week*	*Marginal rate of substitution of restaurant meals for video-cassette rentals*
A	7	1	
			1/3
B	4	2	
			1/2
C	2	3	
			1/1
D	1	4	

The Indifference Map

Let us now consider the possibility of having both more video-cassette rentals *and* more restaurant meals per week. When we do this, we can no longer stay on the same indifference curve that we drew in Figure 20.6. That indifference curve was drawn for equally satisfying combinations of video-cassette rentals and restaurant meals per week. If the individual now has the possibility of attaining *more of both*, a new indifference curve will have to be drawn *above* and to the right of the one shown in Figure 20.6(b). Alternatively, if the individual is faced with the possibility of having *less of both* video-cassette rentals and restaurant meals per week, an indifference curve would have to be drawn *below* and to the left of the existing one in Figure 20.6(b). Thus, we can map out an entire set of indifference curves corresponding to these different possibilities. What we come up with is an indifference map.

Figure 20.10 shows several possible indifference curves. Indifference curves that are higher than others necessarily imply that more of both goods in question can be consumed. Looked at another way, if one goes from, say, indifference curve I_1 to I_2, it is possible to consume the same number of restaurant meals but be able to rent more video-cassettes per week. This is shown as a movement from point *A* to point *B* in Figure 20.10. We could do it the other way. When we move from a lower to a higher indifference curve, it is possible to rent the same number of video-cassettes and to consume more restaurant meals per week. Thus, the higher a consumer finds himself or herself on the indifference curve map, the greater that consumer's total well-being – assuming, of course, that the consumer does not become satiated.

The Budget Constraint

Our problem here is to find out how to maximize consumer satisfaction. In order to do so, we must

Figure 20.10

A Set of Indifference Curves. There are an infinite number of indifference curves that can be drawn. We show three possible ones. You should realize that a higher indifference curve represents the possibility of higher rates of consumption of both goods. Hence, a higher indifference curve is preferred to a lower one because 'more' is preferred to 'less'. Look at points *A* and *B*. Point *B* represents more video-cassette rentals than point *A*; therefore, indifference curve I_2 has to be a preferred one, since the number of restaurant meals per week is the same at points *A* and *B*.

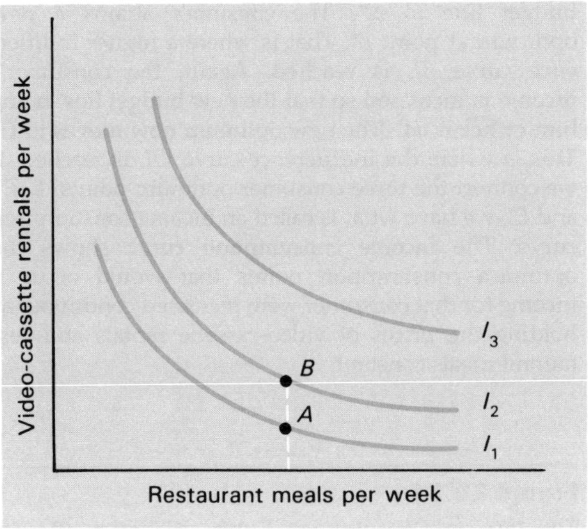

consult not only our *preferences* – given by indifference curves – but also our *opportunities* – given by our available income, called our **budget constraint**. We might want more of everything, but for any given budget constraint we have to make choices or trade-offs among possible goods. Everyone has a budget constraint; that is, everyone is faced with a limited consumption potential. How do we show this graphically? We must find the prices of the goods in question and determine the *maximum* consumption of each allowed by our consumer's budget. For example, let us assume that video-cassettes rent for £5 each and restaurant meals cost £10. Let us also assume that our representative consumer has a total budget of £30. What is the maximum number of video-cassettes the consumer can rent? Obviously, six. And the maximum number of restaurant meals per week he or she can consume? Three. So we now have, in Figure 20.11, two points on our budget line, which is sometimes called the 'consumption possibilities curve'. The first point is a *b* on the vertical axis; the second at *b'* on the horizontal axis. The line is straight because the prices do not change.

Any combination along line *bb'* is possible; and, in fact, any combination in the grey area is possible. We will assume, however, that the individual consumer completely uses up his or her available budget, and we will consider as possible only those points along *bb'*.

The Slope of the Budget Constraint

The budget constraint is a line that slopes downwards from left to right. The slope of that line has a special meaning. To see this, look carefully at the budget line in Figure 20.11. Remember from our discussion of graphs at the start of Chapter 1 that we measure a negative slope by the ratio of the fall in *Y* over the run in *X*. In this case, *Y* is video-cassette rentals per week and *X* is restaurant meals per week. In Figure 20.11, the fall in *Y* is minus two video-cassette rentals per week (a drop from four to two) for a run in *X* of one restaurant meal per week (an increase from one to two); and therefore the slope of the budget constraint is −2/1, or −2. This slope of the budget constraint represents the rate of exchange between video-cassette rentals and restaurant meals: it is the realistic rate of exchange, given their prices.

Now we are ready to determine how the consumer achieves his or her optimum consumption rate.

Consumer Optimum Revisited

Consumers, of course, will attempt to attain the highest level of total utility possible, given their budget constraint. How can this be shown graphically? We draw a set of indifference curves similar to those in Figure 20.10 and we bring in reality – the budget constraint, *bb'*. Both are drawn in Figure 20.12. Now,

Figure 20.11

The Budget Constraint. The line *bb'* represents this individual's budget constraint. Assuming that video-cassette rentals cost £10 each and restaurant meals cost £20 each and that the individual has a budget of £60, a maximum of six video-cassette rentals or three restaurant meals can be bought. These two extreme points are connected to form the budget constraint. All combinations within the shaded area are feasible.

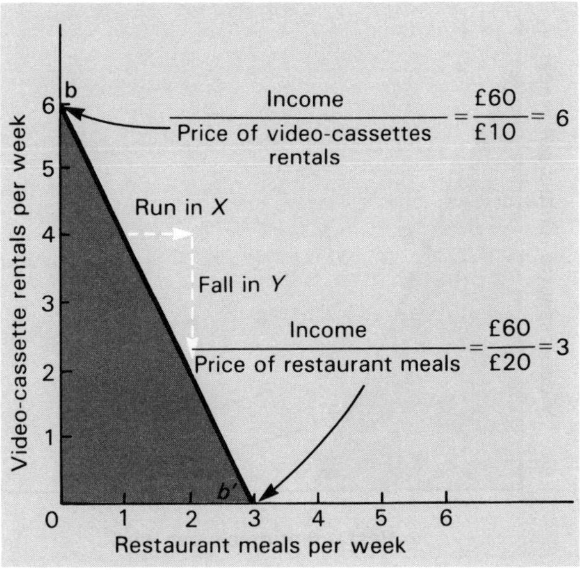

since a higher level of total satisfaction is represented by a higher indifference curve, we know that the consumer will strive to be on the highest indifference curve possible. However, the consumer cannot get to indifference curve I_3, because his or her budget will be exhausted before any combination of video-cassette rentals and restaurant meals represented on indifference curve I_3 is attained. This consumer can maximize total utility, subject to the budget constraint, only by being at point E on indifference curve I_2, because here the consumer's income is just being exhausted. Mathematically, point E is called the tangency point of the curve I_2 to the straight line bb'.

Consumer equilibrium is achieved when the marginal rate of substitution (which is subjective) is just equal to the feasible, or realistic, rate of exchange between video-cassette rentals and restaurant meals. This realistic rate is the ratio of the two prices of the goods involved. It is represented by the absolute value of the slope of the budget constraint. At point E, the point of tangency between indifference curve I_2 and budget constraint bb', the rate at which the consumer wishes to substitute video-cassette rentals for restaurant meals (the numerical value of slope of the indifference curve) is just equal to the rate at which the consumer *can* substitute video-cassette rentals for restaurant meals (the slope of the budget line).

What Happens When Income Changes?

A change in income will shift the budget constraint bb' in Figure 20.12. Consider only increases in income and no changes in price. The budget constraint will shift outwards. Each new budget line will be parallel to the original one because we are not allowing a change in the relative prices of video-cassette rentals and restaurant meals. We would now like to find out how an individual consumer responds to successive increases in income when nominal and relative prices remain constant. We do this in Figure 20.13. We start out with an income that is represented by a budget line bb'. Consumer optimum is at point E, where the consumer attains his or her highest indifference curve I, given the budget constraint bb'. Now we let money income increase. This is shown by a shift outwards in the budget line to cc'. The consumer attains a new optimum at point E'. That is where a higher indifference curve, II, is reached. Again, the consumer's income is increased so that the new budget line facing him or her is dd'. The new optimum now moves to E''. This is where the indifference curve, III, is reached. If we connect the three consumer optimum points, E, E', and E'', we have what is called an income consumption curve. The **income consumption curve** shows the optimum consumption points that would occur if income for that consumer were increased continuously, holding the prices of video-cassette rentals and restaurant meals constant.

Figure 20.12

Consumer Optimum. A consumer reaches an optimum when he or she ends up on the highest indifference curve possible, given a limited budget. This occurs at the tangency between an indifference curve and the budget constraint. In this diagram the tangency is at *E*.

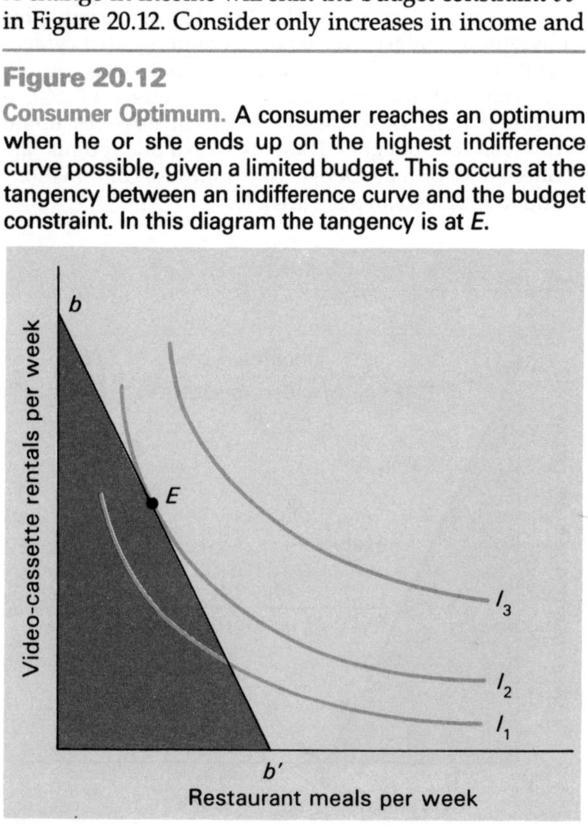

Figure 20.13

The Income Consumption Curve. We start off with income sufficient to yield budget constraint *bb'*. The highest attainable indifference curve is *I*, which is just tangent to *bb'* at *E*. Next we increase income. The budget line moves outwards to *cc'*, which is parallel to *bb'*. The new highest indifference curve is *II*, which is just tangent to *cc'* at *E'*. Finally, we increase income again, which is represented by a shift in the budget line to *dd'*. The new tangency point of the highest indifference curve, *III*, with *dd'*, is at point *E''*. When we connect these three points, we obtain the income consumption curve.

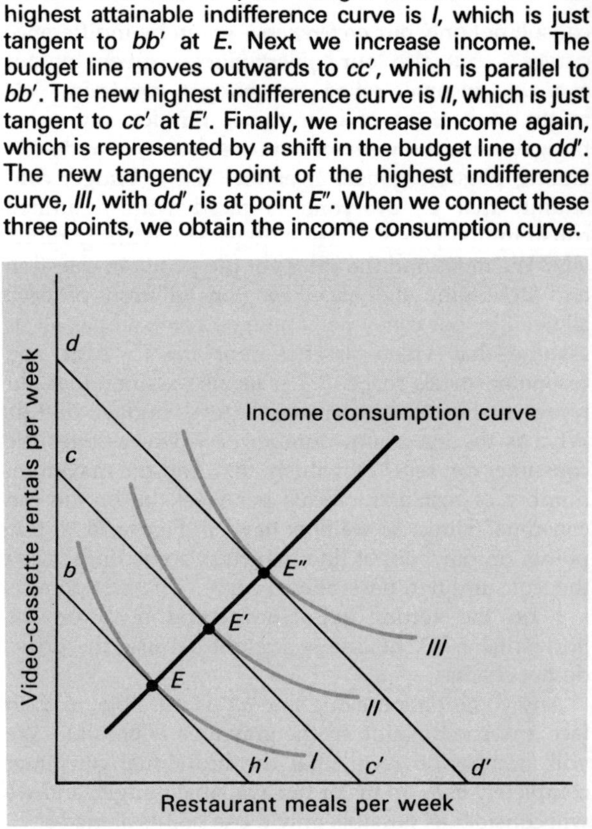

Normal and Inferior Goods

We have shown in Figure 20.13 that as income increases, the consumer purchases more of both video-cassette rentals and restaurant meals. This may not necessarily be the case. As income increases, the consumer could purchase more restaurant meals and rent fewer video-cassettes, or purchase fewer restaurant meals and rent more video-cassettes. We show these possibilities in Figure 20.14.

In Figure 20.14 panel (a), we show that as income increases, the consumption of video-cassette rentals increases, but the consumption of restaurant meals decreases. In this situation, we call video-cassette rentals a normal good and restaurant meals an inferior good. The definition of a **normal good** is one for which quantity demanded increases as income increases. The definition of an **inferior good** is one for which quantity demanded decreases as income increases. In panel (b), we show the opposite situation. As income increases, fewer video-cassettes are rented and more restaurant meals are consumed. Thus, video-cassette rentals become an inferior good and restaurant meals become a normal good.

Price—Consumption Line

In Figure 20.15 (page 310) we hold money income and the price of video-cassette rentals constant while we change the price of restaurant meals. Specifically, we keep lowering the price. As we keep lowering the price of restaurant meals, the quantity of meals that could be purchased if all income were spent on restaurant meals clearly increases; thus, the extreme points for the budget constraint keep moving outwards to the right as the price of restaurant meals falls. In other words, the budget line rotates outwards from *bb* to *bb'*.

Each time the price of restaurant meals falls, a new budget line is thus formed. There has to be a new optimum point. We find it by locating on each new budget line the highest attainable indifference curve. This is shown at points *E*, *E'*, and *E''*. We see that as price decreases for restaurant meals, the consumer purchases more and more restaurant meals per week. We call the line connecting points *E*, *E'*, and *E''* the **price–consumption curve**. It connects the tangency points of the budget constraints and indifference curves, thus showing the amounts of two goods that a consumer will buy when his or her income and the price of one commodity are held constant while the price of the remaining good changes.

Deriving the Demand Curve

We are now in a position to derive the demand curve by using difference curve analysis. In panel (a) of Figure 20.16 we show what happens when the price of restaurant meals decreases, holding the price of video-cassette rentals constant and income constant. If the

Figure 20.14

Inferior and Normal Goods. We define an inferior good as one for which the quantity demanded decreases as income increases. We define a normal good as one for which the quantity demanded increases as income increases. In panel (a) we show that as income increases, the quantity of video-cassettes rented increases, while the quantity of restaurant meals consumed decreases. In panel (a) video-cassette rentals are a normal good and restaurant meals are an inferior good. In panel (b) the quantity of video-cassettes rented decreases as the quantity of restaurant meals consumed increases. In panel (b) video-cassette rentals are an inferior good and restaurant meals are a normal good.

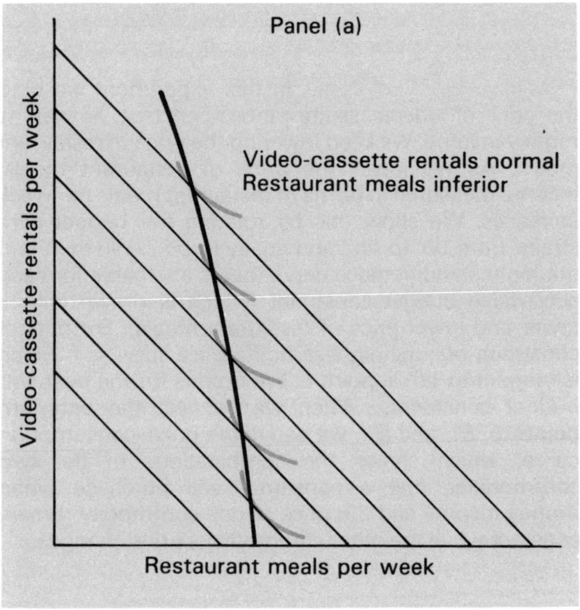

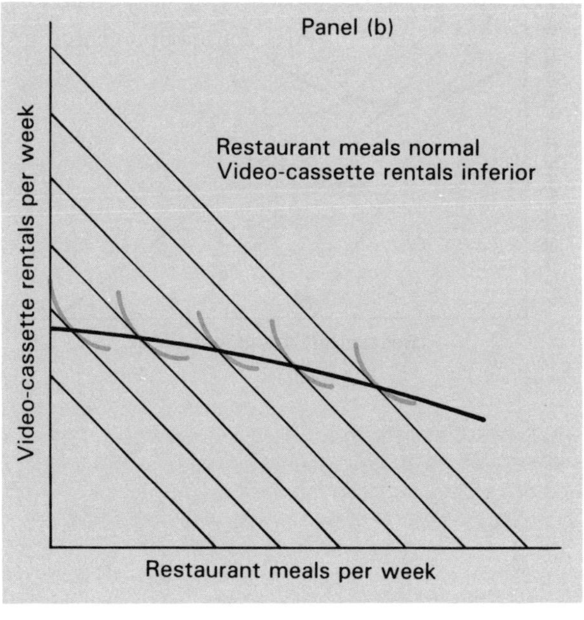

price of restaurant meals decreases, the budget line rotates from *bb′* to *bb″*. The two optimum points are given by the tangency at the highest indifference curve that just touches those two budget lines. This is at *E* and *E′*. But those two points give us two price–quantity pairs. At point *E* the price of restaurant meals is £20; the quantity demanded is two. Thus we have one point that we can transfer to panel (b) of Figure 20.16. At point *E′* we have another price–quantity pair. The price has fallen to £10. The quantity demanded has increased to five. We therefore transfer this other point to panel (b). When we connect these two points (and all the others in between), we derive the demand curve for restaurant meals; it is downward sloping.

Figure 20.15

Price–consumption Curve. In this experiment we hold the price of video-cassette rentals constant, as well as money income. We keep lowering the price of restaurant meals. As we lower the price of restaurant meals, income measured in terms of restaurant meals per week increases. We show this by rotating the budget constraint from *bb′* to *bb″* and finally to *bb‴*. We then find the highest indifference curve that is attainable for each successive budget constraint (which is drawn with a lower and lower price of restaurant meals). For budget constraint *bb′*, the highest indifference curve is *I*, which is tangent to *bb′* at point *E*. We do this for the next two budget constraints. When we connect the optimum points, *E*, *E″*, and *E‴*, we derive the price–consumption curve, which shows the combinations of the two commodities that a consumer will purchase when money income and the price of one commodity remain constant while the other commodity's price changes.

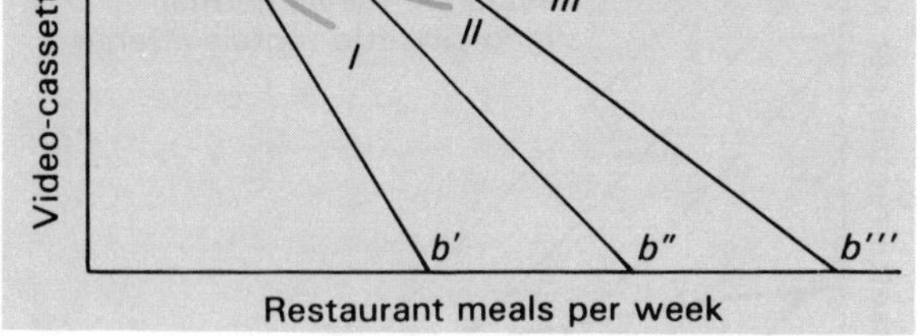

Figure 20.16

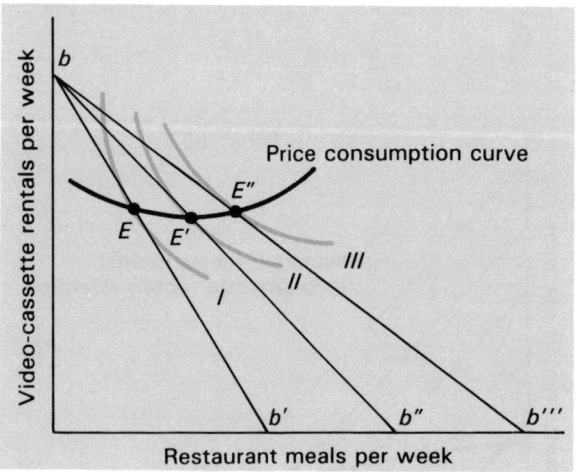

Deriving the Demand Curve. In panel (a) we show the effects of a decrease in the price of restaurant meals from £20 to £10. At a price of £20 the highest indifference curve touches the budget line *bb′* at point *E*. The quantity of restaurant meals consumed is two. We transfer this combination – the price of £20, quantity demanded two – down to panel (b). Next, we decrease the price of restaurant meals to £10. This generates a new budget line, or constraint, which is *bb″*. Consumer optimum is now at *E′*. The optimum quantity demanded of restaurant meals at a price of £10 is five. We transfer this point – the price of £10, quantity demanded five – down to panel (b). When we connect these two points, we have a demand curve, *DD*, for restaurant meals.

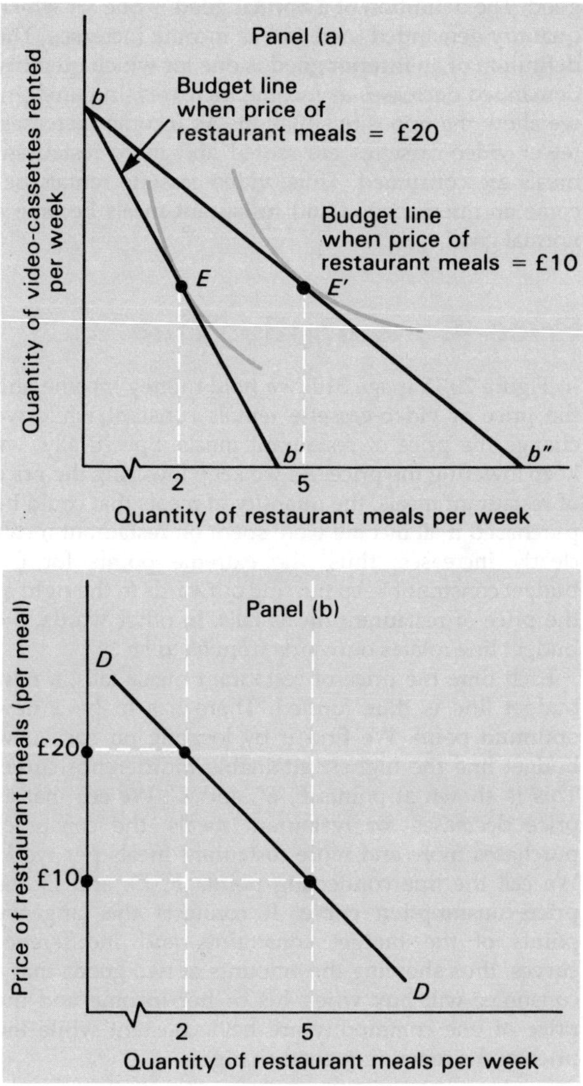

Key Points 20.3

- **An indifference curve is a set of consumption alternatives each yielding the same total amount of satisfaction.**
- **By definition an indifference curve cannot intersect with another one and each curve is usually convex with respect to the origin.**
- **Convex-shaped indifference curves reflect diminishing marginal rates of substitution between the relevant two items.**
- **Purchasers of goods and services face a budget constraint and the optimum point of consumption is reached where the slope of the budget line and the highest indifference curve possible is the same.**
- **If income changes while prices remained fixed the new series of optimum consumption points is termed 'an income consumption curve'. When consumers buy more of a good as income rises it is a normal good: if they buy less it is an inferior good.**
- **If relative prices alter but income remains unchanged the new series of optimum consumption points is termed 'a price–consumption curve'. The demand curve can be derived from the price–consumption curve.**

CASE STUDY

Why are Diamonds more Expensive than Water?

Water is essential to life. Diamonds are quite unessential to life. None the less, water is cheap relative to diamonds. In economics this is called the diamond–water paradox. For many years there was no acceptable solution to this paradox, particularly during the period when economists used to explain the value of things by the amount of labour that was required to produce them. This was called the labour theory of value. If five hours of a given quality of labour were required to produce one hat, but 10 hours were required to produce a pair of shoes, the labour theory of value would indicate that the shoes were twice as valuable as the hat. We know now that such a theory is inadequate and inaccurate. Goods that require countless hours of labour to produce will have little or no market value if few people desire to consume them.

We can use marginal utility analysis to solve the diamond–water paradox. In so doing, we must distinguish between total and marginal utility.

Total versus marginal utility

It is not the total utility of water or of diamonds that determines the price of either. To be sure, the total utility of water greatly exceeds the total utility derived from diamonds. However, in economics what determines price is what happens on the margin, and what happens on the margin is quite simple. Since we have so much water, its marginal utility (because it is diminishing) is quite small, given the total quantity that we consume. Because we have relatively few diamonds, the marginal utility of that last diamond consumed is quite high. Moreover, the price of water is the same, more or less, for everyone who buys it in a particular market situation. We find also that the price of a diamond, in another market situation, is the same for everyone who buys it. In other words, every unit must be sold for what the last (marginal), and hence least useful, unit sells for. We mean *least useful* in terms of individual subjective or psychological marginal utility.

So the diamond–water paradox is only a paradox if one confuses total utility with marginal utility. Total utility does not determine what people are willing to pay for a particular commodity. Marginal utility does.

Graphic analysis

Let us examine Figure 20.17. Here we show the demand curve for diamonds, labelled D_{diamonds} D_{diamonds}. The demand curve for water is labelled D_{water} D_{water}. We plot quantity in terms of kilograms per unit time-period on the horizontal axis. On the vertical axis is plotted price in pounds per kilogram. We use kilograms as our common unit of measurement for

Figure 20.17

The Diamond–Water Paradox. We pick kilograms as a common unit of measurement for both water and diamonds. The demand curve for water is way to the right of the demand curve for diamonds. To demonstrate that the demand for water is immense, we have put a break in the demand curve, $D_{water}D_{water}$. We have also put a break indication on the vertical axis to show that it goes much higher than indicated on this graph. Although the demand for water is much greater than the demand for diamonds, the marginal valuation of water is given by the marginal value placed on the last unit of water consumed. To find that, we must know the supply of water, which is given as *SS*. At that supply, the price of water is P_{water}. But the supply for diamonds is given by *S′S′*. At that supply, the price of diamonds is $P_{diamonds}$. The total valuation that consumers

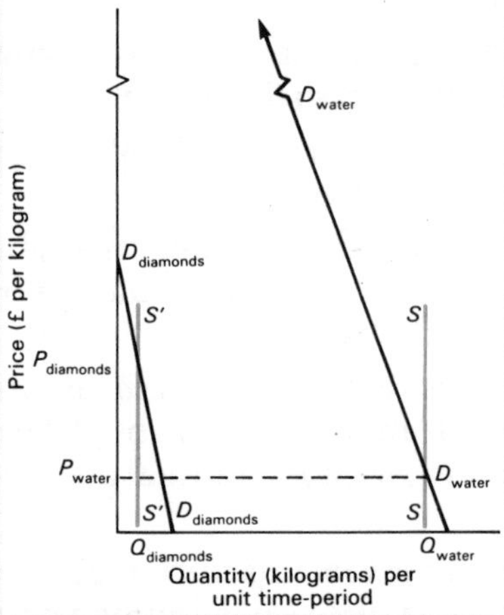

place on water is tremendous relative to the total valuation consumers place on diamonds. What is important for price determination, however, is the marginal valuation, or the marginal utility received.

water and for diamonds. We could just as well have used gallons or litres.

Notice that we have drawn the demand curve for water with a break in it to illustrate that the demand for water is many, many times the demand for diamonds. We draw the supply curve of water as *SS* at a quantity of Q_{water}. The supply curve for diamonds is given as *S′S′* at quantity $Q_{diamonds}$. Clearly, at the intersection of the supply curve of water with the demand curve of water, the price per kilogram is P_{water}. The intersection of the supply curve of diamonds with the demand curve of diamonds is at $P_{diamonds}$. Notice that $P_{diamonds}$ exceeds P_{water}. Diamonds sell at a higher price than water.

Measuring marginal valuation

If we assume that at any point along the demand curve we can infer marginal valuation of that particular quantity of the good, then we can make a determination of relative value. In other words, the point gives an indication of the consumer's monetary evaluation of the last unit consumed. The marginal valuation (marginal utility) of diamonds exceeds the marginal valuation of water. Clearly, the total value of water has got to be huge. After all, look how far over to the right the demand curve is. But price is determined by marginal utility, or marginal valuation. Since water is plentiful, as indicated by the supply curve *SS*, it intersects demand at a relatively low price.

If for some reason the supply curve of water shifted inwards to the left from *SS* in Figure 20.17, then its price could eventually far exceed the price of diamonds. In other words, what is important is relative scarcity, that is, supply relative to demand. That is how we explain the diamond–water paradox.

Questions

1. Would the analysis just presented apply to other 'necessities' such as food?
2. Why is the marginal utility of diamonds so high?
3. In the hot summers of 1989 and 1990 the supply of water in the UK became a matter of concern. How would this have affected the utility of water?

Exam Preparation

PRACTICAL EXERCISES

1. Suppose that a rational man has £10 to spend on a pub lunch. Beer costs him £2 per pint and sandwiches are £1 each.

His utility from consumption is as follows:

Beer

Pints	*Total utility*
1	30
2	55
3	75
4	90
5	100

Sandwiches

No.	*Total utility*
1	13
2	25
3	36
4	46
5	55
6	63
7	70
8	76
9	81
10	85

How should this person use his money to obtain the highest possible level of welfare?

Source: S. Charles and A. Webb, *The Economic Approach to Social Policy*, Wheatsheaf Books, 1986.

2. Suppose that you are standing in the check-out line of a supermarket. You have 5 lb of oranges and three ears of sweetcorn. Oranges cost 30p a pound; so, too, does one ear of corn. You have £2.40 to spend. You are satisfied that you have reached the highest level of satisfaction, or total utility. Your sister comes along and tries to convince you that you have to put some of the corn back and replace it with additional pounds of oranges. From what you know about utility analysis, how would you explain this disagreement?

3. In order to increase marginal utility, the consumer must decrease consumption (other things being constant). This sounds paradoxical. Why is it a correct statement, none the less?

4. Assume the Mr Warfield's marginal utility is 100 utils for the last beer he drank. If the price of beer is £1 a pint, what is Warfield's marginal utility per pound's worth of beer? What is his marginal utility per pound's worth if the price were 50p per pint? If the price were £2? How do we calculate marginal utility per pound's worth of specific commodities?

5. Consider a two-person economy in which the following table indicates each person's demand for beer.

Price per pint of beer	*Mr Smith: quantity demanded per week*	*Mr Johnson: quantity demanded per week*
£2.00	2	0
1.50	3	1
1.00	4	2
.50	5	3

(a) Construct a group demand schedule (table).
(b) Graph Mr Smith's, Mr Johnson's, and the group's demand curves.
(c) Why might Mr Smith and Mr Johnson have different demand curves for beer?

MULTIPLE CHOICE QUESTIONS

1. A downward-sloping demand curve.
- **A** has constant price elasticity throughout its length
- **B** shows the effects of increasing income of consumers
- **C** can be derived from the theory of diminishing marginal utility
- **D** shows the effects of changes in the price of substitutes
- **E** indicates the response of demand to changes in price expectations

2. Assume that a person with a fixed income spends it on only two goods, X and Y. Total utility will be maximized when the total income is distributed so that the
- **A** average utility of the last unit of X purchased equals the average utility of the last unit of Y purchased
- **B** marginal utility of the last unit of X purchased equals the marginal utility of the last unit of Y purchased
- **C** marginal utility of the last unit of X purchased divided by the price of X equals the marginal utility of the last unit of Y purchased divided by the price of Y
- **D** marginal utility of the last unit of each good purchased is equal to zero
- **E** total utility of good X is equal to the total utility of good Y.

3. A consumer's marginal utility for an economic good is greater than the price he has to pay for it. This defines
A complementary goods.
B consumer's surplus.
C comparative advantage.
D the Giffen concept.
E opportunity cost.

4. Assume that a consumer can only purchase three commodities. Satisfaction will be maximized if he purchases
A equal quantities of each commodity
B the commodity with the lowest price
C the commodity which gives the highest total utility
D the commodity which has the highest marginal utility
E sufficient quantities of each to make the ratio of price to marginal utility equal for all three commodities.

5. Consumers' surplus is
A the difference between the quantity demanded and the quantity supplied
B unsatisfied consumer demand
C unspent disposable income
D excess demand
E the difference between the aggregate amount consumers are prepared to pay and the amount they do pay.

6. In the diagram below, at output OQ consumer surplus is represented by the area
A RSQO
B PSTO
C PSQO
D RSP
E STQ.

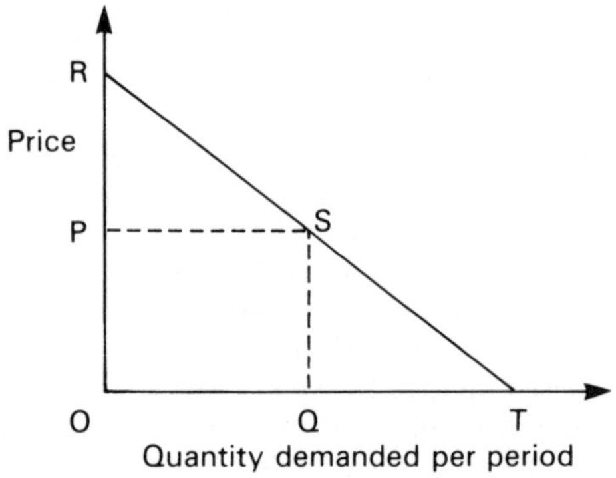

7. The market demand curve for a good slopes down from left to right primarily because
A marginal utility diminishes as consumption rises
B substitutes for the good are not available
C consumers' incomes are finite
D complementary goods are available
E price falls as supply increases.

8. The diagram below represents the market demand schedule for a product. The increase consumer surplus enjoyed as a result of a price reduction from OQ to OP is shown by the area
A PQXY
B PRZ
C PQXZ
D YXZ
E SXZT.

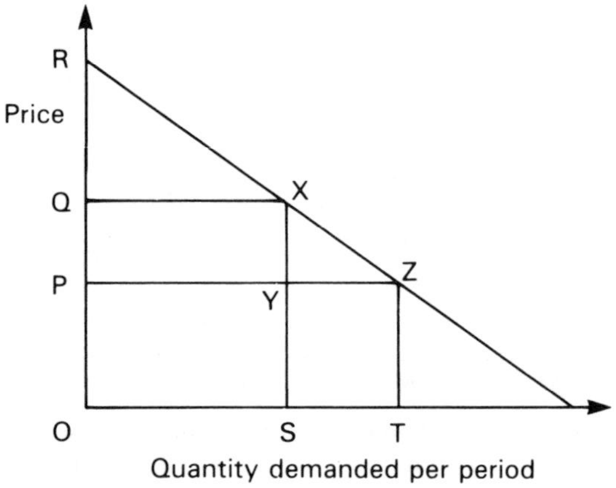

For Questions 9, 10, and 11 select your answers from the following grid:

A	B	C	D	E
1, 2, 3 all correct	1, 2 only correct	2, 3 only correct	1 only correct	3 only correct

9. A consumer maximizes his satisfaction from spending a given income when
1 he maximizes his total utility
2 the marginal utility from the last penny spent on each good is identical
3 he equalizes the ratio of the marginal utility of each good purchased to its price.

10. Assume that a consumer behaves rationally in buying 3 packets of crisps each costing 16p. This behaviour indicates that this consumer
1 obtained marginal utility from the third packet at least equal to its price
2 would have obtained greater utility from purchasing a fourth packet of crisps
3 derived a total utility from purchasing the 3 packets equal to 48p.

11. Consumer equilibrium occurs and maximum satisfaction is gained when
1 the same satisfaction is derived from the last penny spent on each commodity consumed
2 the ratio of marginal utility to price is the same for all commodities consumed
3 the total utility derived from each product is the same.

RELATED ESSAY QUESTIONS

1. Discuss and illustrate the relevance of total and marginal utility for the determination of consumer demand in the cases of water and gold.

2. Why are demand curves normally thought to be downward-sloping? Why is this not always the case?

3. Distinguish between the income and substitution effects of a price change for (a) a normal good and (b) a Giffen good.

4. (a) Explain the income and substitution effects which arise from a change in price.
(b) Does a knowledge of these help our understanding of the effects of the fall in the world price of oil in the mid-1980s?

5. (a) What assumptions about the nature of consumer tastes underlie the concept of an indifference curve?
(b) Consider whether the proposition that a decrease in the price of a good will increase the quantity demanded invariably follows from the theory of consumer choice.

6. Given the superiority of indifference analysis as a technique, what use is there for the concept of marginal utility?

7. Do you agree that the theory of consumers' behaviour rests on assumptions which are undermined by the imperfections which exist in the real world?

8. Explain the purpose of the theory of consumer behaviour and illustrate your explanation from any theory with which you are familiar. Do you think it necessary for such a theory to give a realistic explanation of spending decisions in order to be useful?

21 Businesses and Their Costs

Key Points to Review

- Opportunity cost (1.5)
- Supply (5.4)
- Resource allocation and costs (6.6)
- Indirect tax (8.5, 10.8)

Questions for Preview

1. **How does the economist's definition of profit differ from the accountant's?**
2. **What distinguishes the long run from the short run?**
3. **What is the law of diminishing returns?**
4. **Why is the average total cost (ATC) curve U-shaped?**
5. **How are the marginal cost (MC) and the average total cost (ATC) curves related?**

The last chapter dealt with a theory of the behaviour of consumers. We were looking at the behind-the-scenes elements that affected the demand side of microeconomics. But, as highlighted in Chapters 14 and 18, knowing about the demand side is not sufficient to understand how the world works; we also have to know about the supply side. Therefore we now develop a theory of how suppliers behave. We look at what is known in economics as the **theory of the firm**. How do owners of businesses react to changing taxes, changing input prices, and changing government regulations? In order to answer these questions, we have to understand the nature of production costs and revenues for each firm owner. In this chapter, we examine the nature of productivity and costs, and in the following chapters, we look at the revenue side of the picture.

Defining a Business

What is a business? Everybody knows the answer. It is the supermarket down the street, the dress shop around the corner, British Petroleum, the market stall, Marks & Spencer etc. The list will get very large indeed if we attempt to name every business in the United Kingdom. Everybody also knows that there is a difference between a corporate giant like Coca-Cola and the local dress shop. In terms of our analysis, however, we will not usually make a distinction between these types of firms, except with regard to the market power they have, that is, the extent to which they control the prices of commodities they sell.

There are legal differences, of course, among the various types of businesses, and these are briefly summarized in Figure 21.1.

The Firm

In general terms we can define a business, or **firm**, as follows:

A firm is an organization that brings together different factors of production, such as labour, land, and capital, to produce a product or service which it is hoped can be sold for a profit.

The actual size of a firm would affect its precise structure, but a common set-up would involve: entrepreneur, managers, and workers. The entrepreneur is the person who takes the chances. Because of this, the entrepreneur is the one who will get any profits that are made. The entrepreneur also decides who to hire to run the firm. Some economists maintain that the true quality of an entrepreneur becomes evident when he or she can pick good managers. Managers, in turn, are the ones who decide who should be hired and fired and how the business should generally be set up. The workers are the ones who ultimately use the machines to produce the products or services that are being sold by the firm. Workers and managers are paid contractual wages. They receive a specified amount for the specified time-period. Entrepreneurs are not paid contractual wages. They receive no specified 'reward'. Rather, they receive what is left over, if anything, after all expenses are paid. Profits are, therefore, the reward paid to the entrepreneur for taking risks.

Profit

The costs of production must include an element of profit to pay for the entrepreneur's services. If the level of profits falls in one area of activity entrepreneurs may move their resources to an industry where the returns are higher. To illustrate this behaviour economists employ a concept of **normal profit**. Normal profit may be defined as:

The minimum level of reward required to ensure that existing entrepreneurs are prepared to remain in their present area of production.

Normal profit is included in the cost of production, as it is an essential minimum reward necessary to attract the entrepreneur into economic activity. Normal profit also highlights that all resources can be employed in several ways (i.e. all resources have alternative uses). Consequently, what is meant by 'profit' in economics differs from its general meaning.

To portray the general meaning of profit the following formula could be used:

profits = total revenues − total costs

For economists an alternative formula is required:

Economic profits = total revenues *minus* total opportunity cost of all inputs used

What the economic profits formula actually involves will become clearer by looking at two areas of resource allocation and the related cost accounting calculations. The first resource is capital and the second resource is labour.

Figure 21.1
Types of Business Ownership

Type of business	*No. involved in ownership*	*Examples*	*Sources of finance*	*Liability for debts*	*Profit distribution*	*Authority and control*
Sole proprietor	1	newsagent, corner shop, butcher, baker	Bank loans and/or personal savings, HP finance, credit, etc.	Owner is fully liable for all debts incurred	Owner keeps all profits	Full control by proprietor
Partnership	2 to 20	doctors, solicitors, dentists, builders	Bank loans and/or personal savings, HP finance, mortgages, etc.	At least one partner is fully liable for all debts	Profits shared according to deed of partnership	All partners have equal power (except sleeping-partners)
Private joint-stock company	2 to ∞	small local breweries*	All the above + the issue of shares to agreed members	Limited liability for debts. Each shareholder only risks the amount put in to buy shares	Distributed between all shareholders – dividends being paid per share	Normally directed by shareholders (in proportion to the number of shares held)
Public joint-stock company	2 to ∞	ICI, Shell, banks, Sainsbury*	All the above. But the ownership of shares is open to all via the stock exchange	As for private joint-stock company. But annual general report must be available to the public and accounts publicized in the national press. (A minimum amount of share capital is another prerequisite.)		Shareholders appoint a board of directors to act on their behalf. (These directors are voted in/out at the AGM.)

Note: All the above types of business organization are owned and controlled by private individuals, that is, they form part of the private sector. In contrast government-funded and -organized firms (not detailed above) constitute the public sector.

*Since the 1980 Companies Act, a private joint-stock company must include the word 'limited' in its title, and a public joint-stock company must have the words 'public limited company' at the end of its name (this is commonly abbreviated PLC).

Opportunity Cost of Capital

Firms enter or remain in an industry if they earn, at a minimum, *a normal rate of return* (NROR), i.e. normal profit. By this term, we mean that people will not invest their wealth in a business unless they obtain a positive competitive rate of return, that is, unless their invested wealth pays off. Any business wishing to attract capital must expect to pay at least the same rate of return on the capital as all other businesses of similar risk are willing to pay. For example, if individuals can invest their wealth in almost any publishing firm and get a rate of return of 10 per cent per year, then each firm in the publishing industry must *expect* to pay 10 per cent as the normal rate of return to present and future investors. This 10 per cent is a *cost to the firm*. This cost is called the **opportunity cost of capital**. The opportunity cost of capital is the amount of income, or yield, forgone by giving up an investment in another firm. Capital will therefore not stay in firms or industries where the expected rate of return falls below its opportunity cost.

Opportunity Cost of Labour

Sole traders often grossly exaggerate their profit rates because they forget about the opportunity cost of the time that they personally spend in the business. For example, you may know people who run small grocery stores. These people, at the end of the year, will sit down and figure out what their 'profits' are. They will add up all their sales and subtract what they had to pay to other workers, what they had to pay to their suppliers, what they had to pay in taxes, and so on. The end-result they will call 'profit'. However, they will not have figured into their costs the salary that they could have made if they had worked for somebody else in a similar type of job. For somebody operating a grocery store, that salary might be equal to £6 an hour. If so, then £6 an hour is the opportunity cost of the grocery-store owner's time. In many cases, people who run their own businesses lose money in an economic sense. That is, their profits, as they calculate them, may be less than the amount of labour income they *could* have earned had they spent the same amount of time working for someone else. Take a numerical example. If an entrepreneur can earn £6 per hour, it follows that the opportunity cost of his or her time is £6 x 40 hours x 52 weeks, or £12480 per year. If this entrepreneur is making less than £12480 per year in accounting profits, he or she is actually losing money. (This does not mean that such entrepreneurs are 'stupid'. They may be willing to pay for the non-pecuniary benefits of 'being the boss'.)

We have spoken only of the opportunity cost of capital and the opportunity cost of labour, but we could have spoken in general of the opportunity cost of all inputs. Whatever the input may be, its opportunity cost must be taken into account in order to figure out true economic profits.

Another way of looking at the opportunity cost of running a business is that opportunity cost consists of all explicit (direct) and implicit (indirect) costs. Accountants are only able to take account of explicit costs, though. Therefore, accounting profit ends up being the residual after only explicit costs are subtracted from total revenues.

Accounting Profits Are not Equal to Economic Profits

You should have a good idea by now of the meaning of profits in economics.

The term *profits* in economics means the income that entrepreneurs earn, over and above their own opportunity cost of time, plus the opportunity cost of the capital they have invested in their business. Profits can be regarded as total revenues minus total costs – which is how the accountants think of them – but we must now include *all* costs.

We indicate this relationship in Figure 21.2. We are assuming that the accountants' bookkeeping costs for all factors of production except capital are correct.

Figure 21.2

Simplified View of Economic and Accounting Profit. Here we see that on the right-hand side, total revenues are equal to accounting costs plus accounting profit. That is, accounting profit is the difference between total revenues and total accounting costs. On the other hand, we see in the left-hand column that economic costs are equal to accounting costs plus a normal rate of return (NROR) or normal profit on invested capital, which is the opportunity cost of capital.

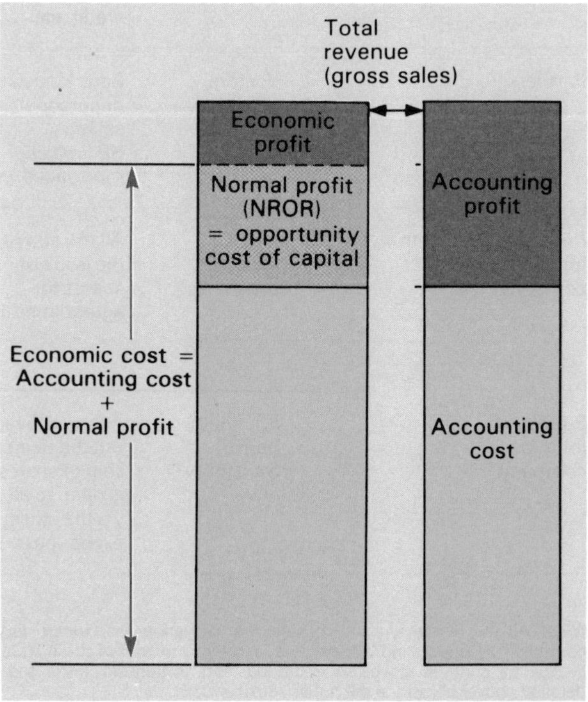

The Goal of the Firm

In most instances we will use a model that is based on maximization of profits. In other words, the firm's goal is to maximize profit; it is expected to attempt to make the positive difference between total revenues and total cost as large as it can. We use a profit-maximizing model because it allows us to analyse a firm's behaviour with respect to quantity supplied and the relationship between cost and output. Whenever this profit-maximizing model produces poor predictions, we will examine our initial assumption about profit maximization. We might have to conclude that the primary goal of *some* firms is not to maximize profits but rather to maximize sales, the number of workers, the prestige of the owners, and so on. However, we are primarily concerned with generalizations. Therefore, provided the assumption of profit maximization is correct for *most* firms, then the model will suffice as a good starting-point. (Key Points 21.1.)

The Relationship between Output and Inputs

A firm takes numerous inputs, combines them using a technological production process, and ends up with an output. There are, of course, many, many factors of production, or inputs. We classify production inputs into two broad categories (ignoring land) – labour and capital. The relationship between output and these two inputs is as follows:

output per unit time-period = some function of capital and labour inputs

Short Run versus Long Run

The time-period here is important. Throughout the rest of this chapter we will consider a 'short' time-period as opposed to a 'long' time-period. In other words, we are looking at *short-run* production relationships and *short-run* costs associated with production.

Any definition of the short run will, necessarily, be arbitrary. We cannot talk in terms of the short run being a specific time-period such as a month, or even a year. Rather, we must deal in terms of the short run having to do with the ability of the firm to alter the quantity of its inputs. For ease of understanding, we will simply define the **short run** as any time-period when there is at least one factor of production that has a fixed cost. In the **long run**, therefore, all costs are variable. That is all factors are variable.

How long is the long run? That depends on each individual industry. For McDonald's (hamburgers), the long run may be four or five months – because that is the time-period during which they can add new franchises. For British Steel the long run may be several years – because that is how long it takes to plan and build a new plant.

In most short-run analyses, the factor that has a fixed cost, or is fixed in quantity, is capital. We therefore state that in our short-run model, capital is fixed and invariable. That is not unreasonable: in a typical firm, the number of machines *in place* will not change over several months, or even over a year. After all, the input that changes the most is labour. The production relationship that we use, therefore, holds capital constant, or given, and labour is variable.

The Production Function – A Numerical Example

The relationship between physical output and the quantity of capital and labour used in the production process is sometimes called a **production function**. The term 'production function' in economics, owes its origin to production engineers for it is used to describe the technological relationship between inputs and

Key Points 21.1

- **The basic forms of private enterprise in the United Kingdom are sole trader, partnerships, private and public joint-stock companies.**
- **A firm is an organization that brings together production inputs in order to produce a good or service that can be sold for a profit.**
- **Accounting profits differ from economic profits.**
- **Economic profits are defined as total revenues minus total costs, where costs include the full opportunity cost of all the factors of production.**
- **Single-owner proprietorships often fail to consider the opportunity cost of the labour services provided by the owner.**
- **The full opportunity cost of capital invested in a business is generally not included as a cost when accounting profits are calculated. Thus, accounting profits overstate economic profits.**
- **Profit maximization is regarded as the main objective when considering a firm's behaviour.**

outputs. It depends therefore on the available technology.

Look at Figure 21.3(a). Here we show a production function relating total output in column 2 to the quantity of labour measured in worker-weeks in column 1. When there are no worker-weeks of input, there is no output. When there are five worker-weeks of input (given the capital stock), there is a total output of 50 bushels per week. (Ignore for the moment the rest of that Figure.) In Figure 21.3(b) we show this particular hypothetical production function graphically. Note, again, that it relates to the short run and that it is for an individual firm.

Figure 21.3(b) shows a total physical product curve, or the amount of physical output that is possible when we add successive units of labour while holding all other inputs constant. The graph of the production function in Figure 21.3(b) is not a straight line. In fact, it peaks at seven worker-weeks and starts to go down. To understand why such a phenomenon occurs with an individual firm in the short run, we have to analyse in detail the **law of diminishing (marginal) returns.***

Diminishing Returns

The concept of diminishing marginal returns applies to many different situations. If you put one seat-belt over your lap, a certain amount of additional safety is obtained. If you add another seat-belt, some more safety is obtained, but less than when the first belt was secured. When you add a third seat-belt, again the amount of *additional* safety obtained must be even smaller. In a similar way, Winston Churchill apparently believed that there were diminishing returns to dropping more and more bombs on German steel mills during the Second World War; extra bombs, he felt, merely moved about the wreckage from prior bombs.

The same analysis holds for firms in their use of productive inputs. When the returns from hiring more workers are diminishing, it does not necessarily mean that more workers will not be hired. In fact, workers will be hired until the returns, in terms of the *value* of the extra output produced, are equal to the additional wages that have to be paid for those workers to produce the extra output. Before we get into the decision-making process, let us demonstrate that diminishing returns can be represented graphically and can be used in our analysis of the firm.

Measuring Diminishing Returns

How do we measure diminishing returns? First, we limit the analysis to only one variable factor of production (or input). Let us say that factor is labour.

*Other names for this law are diminishing marginal productivity, diminishing marginal returns, diminishing marginal physical productivity, and the law of variable proportions.

Figure 21.3(a)

Diminishing Returns: A Hypothetical Case in Agriculture. In the first column, we measure the number of workers used per week on a given amount of land with a given amount of machinery and fertilizer and seed. In the second column, we give their total product, that is, the output that each specified number of workers can produce in terms of bushels of wheat. The last column gives the marginal product. The marginal product is the difference between the output possible with a given number of workers minus the output made possible with one less worker. For example, the marginal product of a fourth worker is 8 bushels of wheat. With four workers, 44 bushels are produced, but with three workers only 36 are produced; the difference is 8.

Input of labour (no. of worker-weeks)	*Total product (output in bushels of wheat per week)*	*Marginal physical product (in bushels of wheat per week)*
0	0	
		10
1	10	
		16
2	26	
		10
3	36	
		8
4	44	
		6
5	50	
		4
6	54	
		2
7	56	
		1
8	55	

Figure 21.3(b)

A Production Function. A production function relates outputs to inputs. We have merely taken the numbers from columns 1 and 2 of Figure 21.3(a) and presented them here.

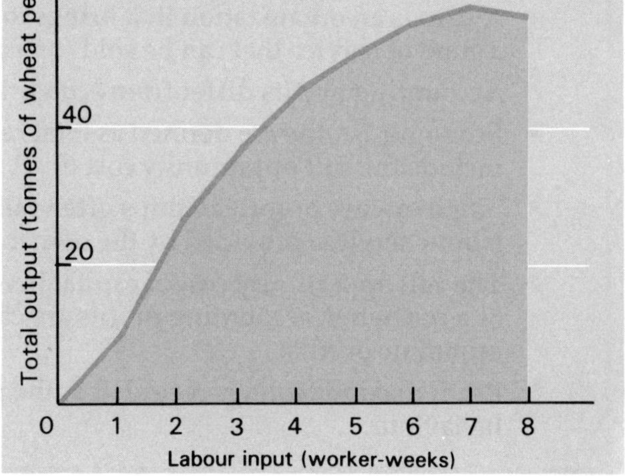

Every other factor of production, such as machines, must be held constant. Only in this way can we calculate the marginal returns from using more workers and know when we reach the point of diminishing marginal returns.

Marginal returns for productive inputs are sometimes specifically referred to as the **marginal physical product**. The marginal physical product of a worker, for example, is the change in total product that occurs when that worker joins an already existing production process. It is also the *change* in total product that occurs when that worker resigns or is laid off an already existing production process. The marginal productivity of labour therefore refers to the change in output caused by a one-unit change in the labour input.

The marginal productivity of labour may increase at the very beginning. That is, a firm starts with no workers, only machines. The firm then hires one worker, who finds it difficult to get the work started. When the firm hires more workers, however, each is able to *specialize*, and the marginal productivity of those additional workers may actually be greater than it was with the previous few workers. Therefore, at the outset increasing marginal returns are likely to be experienced. Beyond some point, however, diminishing returns must set in; each worker has (on average) fewer machines with which to work (remember, all other inputs are fixed). Eventually, the firm will become so crowded that workers will start running into one another and will become less productive. Managers will have to be hired to organize the workers.

Using these ideas, we can define the law of diminishing returns. For example consider the two following possible definitions:

> As successive equal increases in a variable factor of production, such as labour, are added to other fixed factors of production, such as capital, there will be a point beyond which the extra or marginal product that can be attributed to each additional unit of the variable factor of production will decline.

or more formally:

> As the proportion of *one* factor in a combination of factors is increased, after a point, the marginal product of that factor will diminish.

Put simply diminishing returns merely refer to a situation in which output rises less than in proportion to an increase in, say, the number of workers employed.

Figure 21.3(c)

Marginal Product – Diminishing Marginal Return. On the horizontal axis, we plot the number of workers; starting from 0 and going to 8. On the vertical axis, we plot the marginal physical product in bushels of wheat. When we go from no workers to one worker, marginal product is 10. We show this at a point between 0 and 1 worker-weeks to indicate that marginal product relates to the change in the total product as we add additional workers. When we go from one to two workers, the marginal product increases to 16. After two workers, marginal product declines. Therefore, after two workers, we are in the area of diminishing marginal physical returns. Since total product, or output, reaches its peak at seven workers, we know that after seven workers, marginal physical product is negative. In fact when we move from seven to eight workers, marginal product becomes –1 bushel. (Note, again, that we have approximated the curve by using the mid-points between the number of worker-weeks; that is why the curve peaks between 1 and 2 worker-weeks rather than exactly at 2 worker-weeks.)

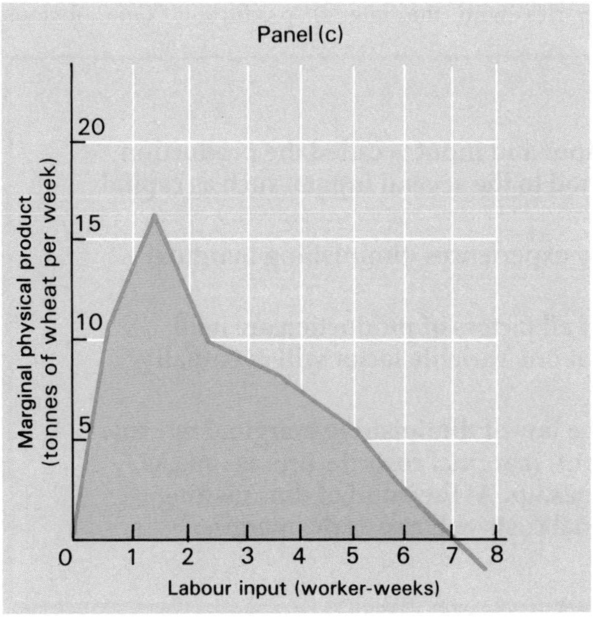

An Example

An example of the law of diminishing returns is found in agriculture. With a fixed amount of land, fertilizer, and tractors, the addition of more people eventually yields decreasing increases in output. A hypothetical set of numbers illustrating the law of diminishing marginal returns is presented in Figure 21.3(a). The numbers are presented graphically in Figure 21.3(c). Marginal productivity (returns from adding more workers) first increases, then decreases, and finally becomes negative. When one worker is hired, total output goes from 0 to 10. Thus, marginal physical product is equal to 10. When another worker is added, marginal product increases to 16. Then it begins to decrease. The point of diminishing marginal returns occurs after two workers are hired.

The Relationship between Diminishing Marginal Returns and the Theory of the Firm

If we now introduce business costs one can begin to sense the central importance of the law of diminishing returns.

For example, consider the relationship between marginal cost, i.e. the cost of an extra unit of output, and the incidence of diminishing marginal physical returns as illustrated in Figure 21.3(a). Let us assume that each unit of labour can be purchased at a constant price. Further assume that labour is the only variable input. We see that as more workers are hired, marginal physical product first rises and then falls after the point where diminishing returns are encountered. Thus, the marginal cost of *each extra unit* of output will first fall as long as marginal physical product is rising, and then it will rise as long as marginal physical product is falling. Consider specifically Figure 21.3(a). Assume that a worker is paid £100 a week. When we go from zero labour input to one unit, output increases by 10 bushels of wheat. Thus, each of those 10 bushels of wheat has a marginal cost of £10. Now the second unit of labour is hired, and it, too, costs £100. Output increases by 16. Thus, the marginal cost is £100 ÷ 16 = £6.25. We continue the experiment. We see that the next unit of labour yields only 10 additional bushels of wheat, so that marginal cost starts to rise again back to £10. The following unit of labour increases marginal physical product by only 8, so that marginal cost becomes £100 ÷ 8 = £12.50.

Marginal costs in turn affect the pattern of other costs, e.g. average variable costs and average total costs. Once these other costs have been discussed the importance of marginal cost analysis (and the above section) will become clearer. (See Key Points 21.2.)

Short-run Costs to the Firm

In the short run, a firm incurs certain types of costs. Economists label all costs incurred as **total costs**. Then we divide total costs into total fixed costs and total variable costs, which we explain below. The relationship, or identity, is, therefore:

total costs ≡ total fixed costs + total variable costs

After we have looked at the elements of total costs, we will find out how to compute average and marginal costs.

Total Fixed Costs

Let us look at a business such as the Ford Motor Company. The decision-makers in that corporate giant can look around and see big machines, thousands of parts, huge buildings, and a multitude of other pieces of plant and equipment that are in place, that have already been bought. Fords have to take account of the wear and tear of this equipment, no matter how many cars it produces. The payments on the loans taken out to buy the equipment and the rates on the land have to be paid regardless of output. All these costs are unaffected by variations in the amount of output. That is they are mainly the overhead costs. This leads us to a very straightforward definition of fixed costs:

All costs that do not vary, that is, costs that do not depend on the rate of production, are called fixed costs, or *sunk* costs.

Let us take as an example the fixed costs incurred by a manufacturer of leather handbags. This firm's total fixed costs will equal the cost of the rent on its equipment and the insurance it has to pay. We see in panel (a) of Figure 21.4 that total fixed costs per day are £10. In panel (b), these total fixed costs are represented by the horizontal line at £10 per day. They are invariant to changes in the output of handbags per day: no matter how many are produced, fixed costs will remain at £10 per day.

The difference between total costs and total fixed costs is total variable costs (total costs – total fixed costs = total variable costs).

Total Variable Costs

Total **variable costs** are those costs whose magnitude varies with the rate of production. One obvious

Key Points 21.2

- **The technological relationship between output and input is called the production function. It relates output per unit time-period to the several inputs, such as capital and labour.**
- **After some rate of output, the firm generally experiences diminishing marginal returns.**
- **The law of diminishing returns states that if all factors of production are held constant except one, equal increments in that one variable factor will eventually yield decreasing increments in output.**
- **A firm's short-run costs are a reflection of the law of diminishing marginal returns. Given any constant price of the variable input, marginal costs decline as long as marginal product of the variable resource goes up. At the point of diminishing marginal returns, the reverse occurs. Marginal costs will rise as the marginal product of the variable input declines.**

variable cost is wages paid. The more the firm produces the more labour it has to hire, the more it has to pay. There are other variable costs, though. One is materials. In the production of leather handbags, for example, leather must be bought. The more handbags that are made, the more leather must be bought. Part of the rate of depreciation (the rate of wear and tear) on machines that are used in the production process can also be considered a variable cost, if depreciation depends partly on how long and how intensively the machines are used. Total variable costs are given in column 3 of panel (a) of Figure 21.4. These are translated into the total variable cost curve in panel (b). Notice that the variable cost curve lies below the total cost curve by the vertical distance of £10. This vertical distance represents, of course, total fixed costs.

Short-run Average Cost Curves

In panel (b) of Figure 21.4, we see total costs, total variable costs, and total fixed costs. Now we want to look at average cost. The average cost concept is simply one in which we are measuring cost per unit of output. It is a matter of simple arithmetic to figure the averages of these three cost concepts. We can define them simply as follows:

$$\text{average total costs} = \frac{\text{total costs}}{\text{output}}$$

$$\text{average variable costs} = \frac{\text{total variable costs}}{\text{output}}$$

$$\text{average fixed costs} = \frac{\text{total fixed costs}}{\text{output}}$$

Figure 21.4

An Example of the Costs of Production

Panel (a)

Total output (Q/day) (1)	*Total fixed costs (TFC) (2)*	*Total variable costs (TVC) (3)*	*Total costs (TC) (4) = (2) + (3)*	*Average fixed costs (AFC) (5) = (2) ÷ (1)*	*Average variable costs (AVC) (6) = (3) ÷ (1)*	*Average total costs (ATC) (7) = (4) ÷ (1)*	*Total costs (TC) (4)*	*Marginal cost (MC) (8) = Change in (4) / Change in (1)*
0	£10.00	0	£10.00	—	—	—	£10.00	
1	10.00	£5.00	15.00	£10.00	£5.00	£15.00	£15.00	*£5.00*
2	10.00	8.00	18.00	5.00	4.00	9.00	18.00	*3.00*
3	10.00	10.00	20.00	3.33	3.33	6.67	20.00	*2.00*
4	10.00	11.00	21.00	2.50	2.75	5.25	21.00	*1.00*
5	10.00	13.00	23.00	2.00	2.60	4.60	23.00	*2.00*
6	10.00	16.00	26.00	1.67	2.67	4.33	26.00	*3.00*
7	10.00	20.00	30.00	1.43	2.86	4.28	30.00	*4.00*
8	10.00	25.00	35.00	1.25	3.13	4.38	35.00	*5.00*
9	10.00	31.00	41.00	1.11	3.44	4.56	41.00	*6.00*
10	10.00	38.00	48.00	1.00	3.80	4.80	48.00	*7.00*
11	10.00	46.00	56.00	0.91	4.18	5.09	56.00	*8.00*

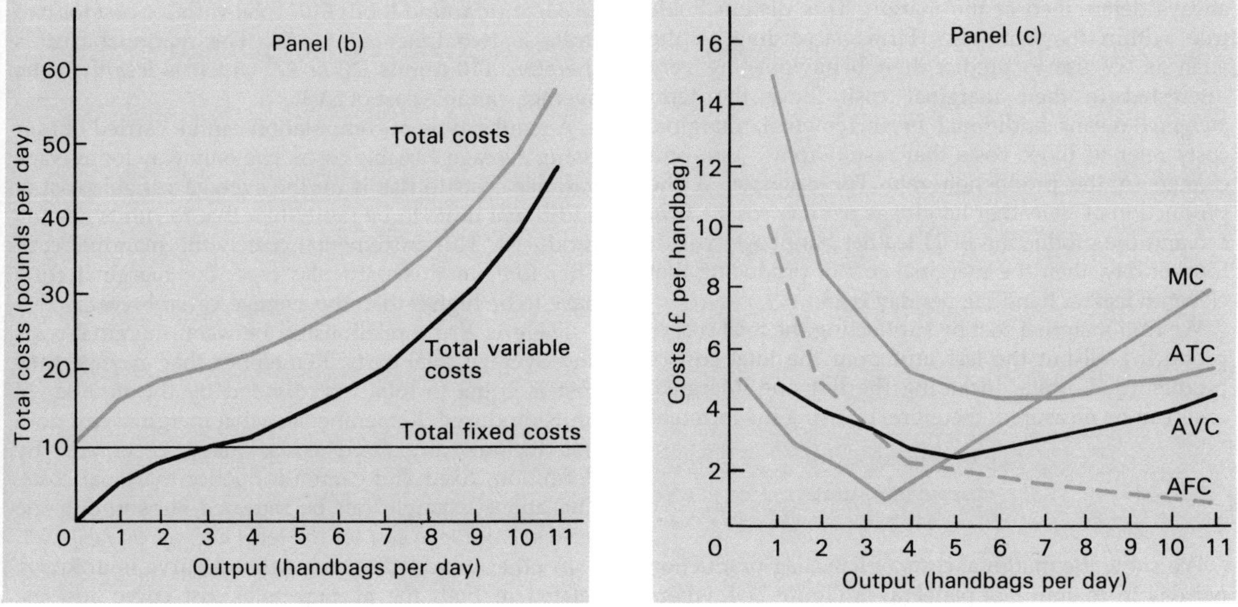

The arithmetic is done in columns 5, 6, and 7 in panel (a) of Figure 21.4, while the numerical results are translated into graphical format in panel (c). Let us see what we can observe about the three average cost curves in that graph.

AVERAGE FIXED COSTS (AFC)

Average fixed costs continue to fall throughout the output range. In fact, if we were to continue the diagram further to the right, we would find that average fixed costs would get closer and closer to the horizontal axis. That is because total fixed costs remain constant. As we divide this fixed number by a larger and larger number of units of output, the result, AFC, has to become smaller and smaller.

AVERAGE VARIABLE COSTS (AVC)

We assume a particular form of the **average variable cost** curve. The form that it takes is U-shaped: first it falls; then it starts to rise. It is certainly possible to have other shapes of the average variable cost curve.

AVERAGE TOTAL COSTS (ATC)

This curve has a shape similar to the average variable cost curve. However, it falls even more dramatically in the beginning and rises more slowly after it has reached a minimum point. It falls and then rises because **average total costs** is the summation of the average fixed cost curve and the average variable cost curve. Thus, when AFC plus AVC are both falling, it is only logical that ATC would fall, too. At some point, however, AVC starts to increase while AFC continues to fall. Once the increase in the AVC curve outweighs the decrease in the AFC curve, the ATC curve will start to increase and will develop its familiar U-shape.

Marginal Cost

We have stated repeatedly in this text that the action is always on the margin – movement in economics is always determined at the margin. This dictum holds true within the firm also. Firms, according to the analysis we use to predict their behaviour, are very interested in their **marginal cost**. Since the term *marginal* means additional or incremental, marginal costs refer to those costs that result from a one-unit change in the production rate. For example, if the production of 10 leather handbags per day costs a firm £48 and the production of 11 leather handbags costs it £56 per day, then the marginal cost of producing that eleventh leather handbag per day is £8.

We find marginal cost by subtracting the total cost of producing all but the last unit from the total cost of producing all units, including the last one. Marginal costs can be measured, therefore, by using the formula:

$$\text{marginal cost} = \frac{\text{change in total cost}}{\text{change in output}}$$

We show the marginal costs of handbag production per day in column 8 of panel (a) in Figure 21.4, where marginal cost is defined as the change in total cost divided by the change in output. In our particular example, we have changed output by one unit every time, so we can ignore the denominator in that particular formula.

This marginal cost schedule is shown graphically in panel (c) of Figure 21.4. Like average variable costs and average total costs, marginal costs first fall and then rise. It is interesting to look at the relationship between marginal costs and average costs.

The Relationship between Average and Marginal Costs

There is always a definite relationship between averages and marginals. Consider the example of ten football players with an average weight of 200 lb. An eleventh player is added. His weight is 250 lb. That represents the marginal weight. What happens now to the average weight of the team? It must increase. Thus, when the marginal player weighs more than the average, the average must increase. Likewise, if the marginal player weighs less than 200 lb, the average weight will decrease.

There is a similar relationship between average variable costs and marginal costs. When marginal costs are less than average costs, the latter are falling. Conversely, when marginal costs are greater than average costs, the latter are rising. When you think about it, the relationship is obvious. The only way for average variable costs to fall is for the extra cost of the marginal unit produced to be less than the average variable cost of all the preceding units. For example, if the average variable cost for two units of production is £4 a unit, the only way for the average variable cost of three units to fall is for the variable costs attributable to the last unit – the marginal cost – to be less than the average of the past units. In this particular case, if average variable cost falls to *£3.33 a unit*, then total variable cost for the three units would be three times £3.33, or (to round it off) £10. Total variable cost for two units is two times £4, or £8. The marginal cost is therefore £10 minus £8, or £2, which is less than the average variable cost of £3.33.

A similar type of computation can be carried out for rising average variable costs. The only way for average variable costs to rise is for the average variable cost of additional units to be more than that for units already produced. This incremental cost is the marginal cost. Therefore, in this particular case, the marginal costs have to be higher than the average variable costs.

There is also a relationship between marginal costs and average total costs. Remember that average total cost is equal to total cost divided by the number of units produced. Remember also that marginal cost does not include any fixed costs. Fixed costs are, by definition, fixed and cannot influence marginal costs. The above example can be repeated substituting the term *average total cost* for the term *average variable cost*.

In other words, the marginal cost curve is uniquely related to both the average total cost curve and the average variable cost curve because marginal cost is defined as the *change* in total cost. As we increase production, fixed costs do not change. Therefore, the average total cost curve is changing because of a change in variable costs. This means that the preceding discussion can be applied in terms of the relationship between marginal costs and average total costs. In other words, when marginal costs are less than either average total costs or average variable costs, the latter two are falling. Conversely, when marginal costs are greater than either average total costs or average variable costs, the latter two are rising. Finally, marginal costs will equal both average total costs and average variable costs at their respective minimum points. These rising and falling relationships can be seen in Figure 21.4. You can also see there that MC intersects AVC and ATC at their respective minimum points.

Finding Minimum Costs

At what rate of output of leather handbags per day does our representative firm experience the minimum average total costs? Column 7 in panel (a) of Figure 21.4 shows that the minimum average total cost is £4.28, which occurs at an output rate of seven leather handbags per day. We can find this minimum cost also by finding the point in panel (c) of Figure 21.4 at which the marginal cost curve intersects the average total cost curve. This should not be surprising. When marginal cost is below average total cost, average total cost falls. When marginal cost is above average total cost, average total cost rises. At the point where average total costs are neither falling nor rising, marginal cost must then be equal to average total cost. When we represent this graphically, the marginal cost curve will intersect the average total cost curve at its minimum.

The same analysis applies to the intersection of the marginal cost curve and the average variable cost curve. When are average variable costs at a minimum? According to panel (a) of Figure 21.4 average variable costs are at a minimum of £2.60 at an output rate of five leather handbags per day. This is exactly where the marginal cost curve intersects the average variable cost curve in panel (c) of Figure 21.4 (Key Points 21.3.)

Long-run Cost Curves

The long run, as you will remember, is defined as a time-period during which *full* adjustment can be made to any change in the economic environment. That is, *in the long run, all factors of production are variable.* For example, in the long run the firm can alter its plant size. Consequently, there may be many short-run curves as a firm develops over the years but only one long run. Long-run curves are sometimes called planning curves, and the long run may be regarded as the **planning horizon**.

We start out our analysis of long-run cost curves by considering a single firm contemplating the construction of a single plant. The firm has, let us say, three alternative plant sizes from which to choose on the planning horizon. Each particular plant size generates its own short-run average total cost curve. Now that we are talking about the difference between long- and short-run cost curves, we will label all short-run curves with an *S*; short-run average (total) costs will be labelled SAC, and all long-run average cost curves will be labelled LAC.

Look at Figure 21.5(a). Here we have shown three short-run average cost curves for three plant sizes that are successively larger. Which is the optimal plant size to build? That depends on the anticipated rate of output per unit time-period. Assume for a moment that the anticipated rate is Q_1. If plant size 1 is built, the average costs will be C_1. If plant size 2 is built, we see on SAC_2 that the average costs will be C_2, which is greater than C_1. Thus, if the anticipated rate of output is Q_1, the appropriate plant size is the one from which SAC_1 was derived.

Key Points 21.3

- **Remember the short run is that period of time during which the firm cannot alter its existing plant size.**
- **Total costs equal total fixed costs plus total variable costs.**
- **Fixed costs are those that do not vary with the rate of production; variable costs are those that do vary with the rate of production.**
- **Average total costs equal total costs divided by output, or ATC = TC ÷ Q.**
- **Average variable costs equal total variable costs divided by output, or AVC = TVC ÷ Q.**
- **Average fixed costs equal total fixed costs divided by output, or AFC = TFC ÷ Q.**
- **Marginal cost equals the change in total cost divided by the change in output.**
- **The marginal cost curve intersects the minimum point of the average total cost curve and the minimum point of the average variable cost curve.**

Note, however, that if the anticipated permanent rate of output per unit time-period goes from Q_1 to Q_2, and plant size 1 had been decided upon, average costs would be C_4. However, if plant size 2 had been decided upon, average costs would be C_3 which are clearly less than C_4.

Long-run Average Cost Curve

If we make the further assumption that during the development of a firm the entrepreneur is faced with an infinite number of choices regarding plant size then we can conceive of an infinite number of SAC curves similar to the three in Figure 21.5(a). We are not able, of course, to draw an infinite number; we have drawn quite a few, however, in Figure 21.5(b).

By drawing the envelope of these various SAC curves we find the long-run average cost curve (LAC). The long-run average cost curve, by result, represents the cheapest way to produce various levels of output, i.e. provided the entrepreneur is prepared to change the size and design of his plant. Consequently long-run average cost curves are sometimes referred to as **planning curves**.

Why the Long-run Average Cost Curve is U-Shaped

Notice that the long-run average cost curve, LAC in Figure 21.5(b) is U-shaped, similar to the U-shape of the short-run average cost curve developed previously in this chapter. The reason for the U-shape of the long-run average cost curve is not the same as that for the short-run U-shaped average cost curve. The short-run average cost curve is U-shaped because of the law of diminishing marginal returns. However, that law cannot apply to the long run, because in the long run all factors of production are variable, so there is no point of diminishing marginal returns since there is no fixed factor of production. Why, then, do we see the U-shape in the long-run average cost curve? The reasoning has to do with changes in the scale of operations. When the long-run average cost curve slopes downwards it means that average costs decrease as output increases. Whenever this happens the firm is experiencing **economies of scale**. If, on the other hand, the long-run average cost curve is sloping upwards, the firm is incurring increases in average costs as output increases. That firm is said to be experiencing **diseconomies of scale**. Finally, if long-run average costs are invariant to changes in output, the firm is experiencing **constant returns to scale**. In Figure 21.6, we show three panels (a), (b), and (c). The first one is for a firm experiencing economies of scale; the second one, constant returns to scale; and the third one, diseconomies of scale.

Reasons Why We See Economies of Scale

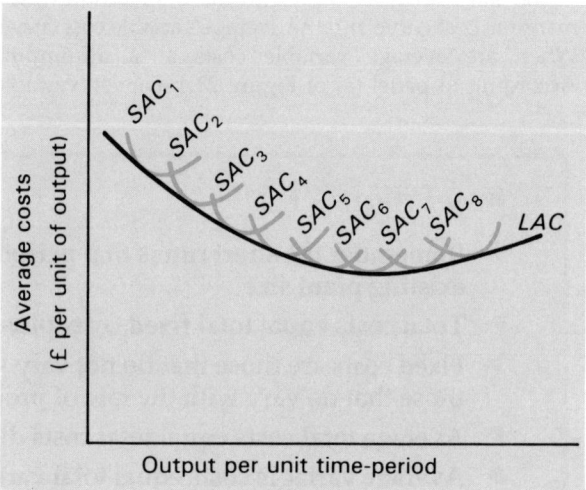

Here we list some of the reasons why a firm might be expected to experience economies of scale. Following Professor E. A. G. Robinson's approach we shall consider five possible categories.

Figure 21.5(a)

A Preferable Plant Size. If the anticipated permanent rate of output per unit time-period is Q_1, the optimal plant to build would be the one corresponding to SAC_1 because average costs are lower. However, if the rate of output increases to Q_2, it will be more profitable to have a plant size corresponding to SAC_2. Unit costs fall to C_3.

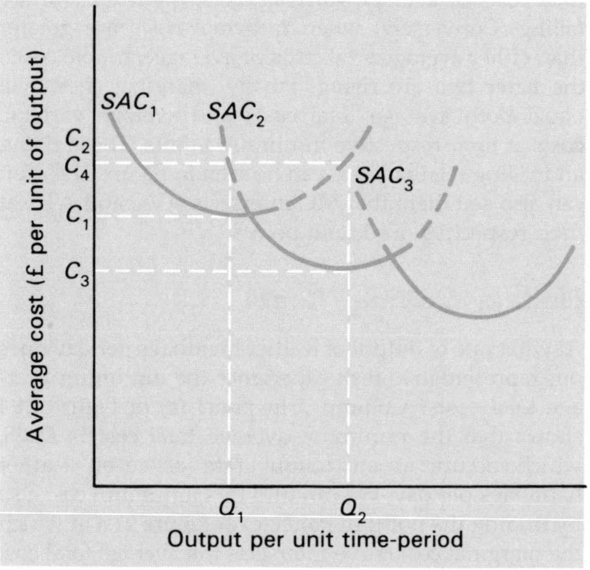

Figure 21.5(b)

Deriving the Long-run Average Cost Curve. If we draw all the possible short-run average cost curves that correspond to different plant sizes and then draw the envelope to these various curves, $SAC_1 \ldots SAC_8$, we obtain the long-run average cost curve, or the planning curve.

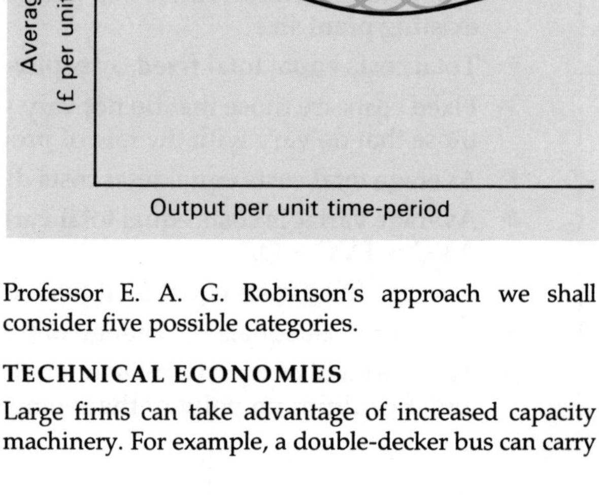

TECHNICAL ECONOMIES

Large firms can take advantage of increased capacity machinery. For example, a double-decker bus can carry

Figure 21.6

Economies of Scale, Constant Returns to Scale, and Diseconomies of Scale. Long-run average cost curves will fall when there are economies of scale, as shown in panel (a). They will be constant when the firm is experiencing constant returns to scale, as shown in panel (b). And, finally, long-run average costs will rise when the firm is experiencing diseconomies of scale, as shown in panel (c).

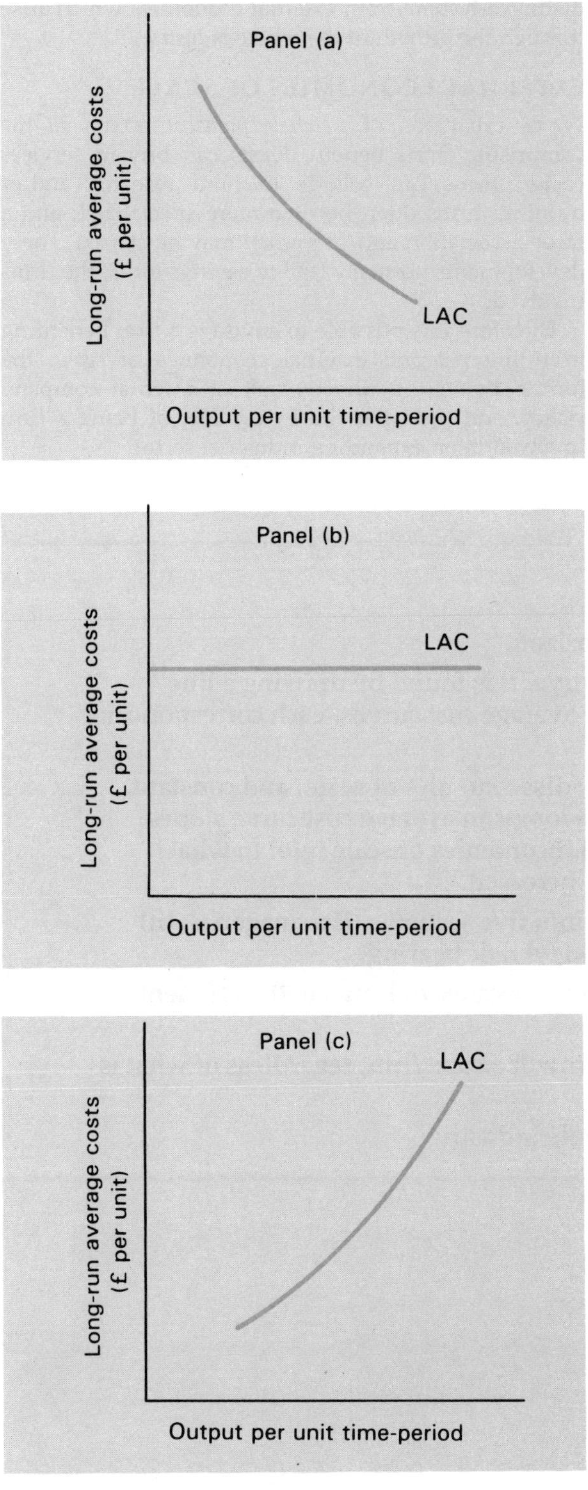

twice as many passengers as a single-decker bus. But the purchase costs and the running costs are not doubled. Similarly with boats and planes the larger the carrier the greater the saving. This economy is often linked to the principle of increased dimensions, because the volume of a sphere increases more than proportionately with its circumference. Consequently, as oil tankers and storage containers increase in size they become relatively cheaper to maintain and run. In fact a management consultancy agency once estimated that the day-to-day running costs of a 90000-tonne oil tanker was £1870 compared with £996 for a 30000-tonne oil tanker. In short, the costs were barely doubled, while the capacity was trebled.

MANAGERIAL ECONOMIES

In a small firm the manager may perform the role of cost accountant, foreman, salesman, personnel officer, stock controller etc. However, as a firm increases in size it can take advantage of specialization of labour. Each managerial role can be allocated to a specialist in that field. Furthermore, bigger firms can buy in management services and afford large in-house salaries to entice and retain the best management.

COMMERCIAL ECONOMIES

The large firm can buy its raw materials in bulk at favourable rates. Similarly, the products of the firm can be sold in bulk with reduced costs. It is only necessary to pay a salesman marginally more wages for taking an order of 5 million units compared to 5 000; packaging and administration costs are also reduced.

Large firms can also afford to advertise in the national press and on TV. This can lead to some kind of brand loyalty for larger organizations where one product of the firm leads to sales of other products with that brand name. Much of Marks & Spencer's success, for example, is owed to this type of customer loyalty.

FINANCIAL ECONOMIES

The larger the firm the greater the number of financial advantages. The larger firm can negotiate loans from banks and related institutions easily and at favourable rates. Shares may be sold on the new issue market.

RISK-BEARING ECONOMIES

All firms are subject to risk at sometime or other. However, the larger firm has distinct advantages in this area. Firstly changes in supply and/or demand can often ruin the smaller firm. The larger firm, however, can cover itself by producing a variety of products for a variety of markets. These tactics are known as 'diversification of output' and 'diversification of markets'. For illustration, list the products made by Heinz, Walls, and/or ICI and identify as many of their market outlets as possible – an exercise which should help you to appreciate what is meant by the concept of 'diversification'. Similarly, one section of a large conglomerate can lean on other parts of the company when developing or going through some irregular phase. For example, one bank branch may gain funds from another in the group. Finally, larger firms can afford to spend money on research and development. This type of expenditure can yield particularly high returns by securing footholds in tomorrow's market, whereas small firms face the risk of going out of business.

Why a Firm Might Experience Diseconomies of Scale

One of the basic reasons that the firm can expect to run into diseconomies of scale is that there are limits to the efficient functioning of management. Moreover, as more workers are hired, a more-than-proportionate increase in managers may be needed, and this could cause increased costs per unit. For example, it might be possible to hire from one to ten workers and give them each a shovel to dig ditches; however, as soon as ten workers are hired, it may also be necessary to hire an overseer to co-ordinate their ditch-digging efforts. Thus, perhaps constant returns to scale will remain until ten workers and ten shovels are employed; then decreasing returns to scale set in. As the layers of supervision grow, the costs of information and communication grow more than proportionately. Hence, the average per unit cost will start to increase.

A Final Note on Technical Terms

The economies (listed above) are all *internal* to the firm. That is to say, they do not depend on what other firms are doing or what is happening in the economy. They are formally referred to as **internal economies (or diseconomies) of scale**. This phrase is necessary to distinguish them from **external economies** which arise through the growth of the whole *industry*.

EXTERNAL ECONOMIES OF SCALE

When expansion of a *whole industry* occurs *all* the comprising firms benefit. Firms can buy in services easier; firms can collude to fund research and/or training; firms often become more specialized; and a trade association and/or journal may be started. These developments normally lead to savings for *all* the firms involved.

Therefore it is possible to envisage a firm benefiting from internal and external economies of scale; the former being the direct result of internal company policy, and the latter the by-product of being a firm involved in an expanding industrial sector.

Key Points 21.4

- **The long run is often called the planning horizon.**
- **The long-run average cost is the planning curve. It is found by drawing a line tangent to one point on a series of short-run average cost curves, each corresponding to a different plant size.**
- **The firm can experience economies of scale, diseconomies of scale, and constant returns to scale, all according to whether the long-run average cost curve slopes downwards, upwards, or is horizontal (flat). Economies of scale refer to what happens when all factors of production are increased.**
- **We can classify internal economies of scale into five sections: (i) managerial, (ii) commercial, (iii) financial, (iv) technical, and (v) risk-bearing.**
- **The firm may experience diseconomies of scale because of limits to the efficient functioning of management.**
- **Internal economies of scale arise from the growth of one firm, regardless of what is happening to other firms.**
- **External economies of scale relate to the whole industry.**

CASE STUDY

Funeral Economics

Avoiding too many puns about being a deadly topic and confirming the idea of Economics as a dismal science, a study of the costs of funerals and related issues clearly illustrates many basic economic concepts. To state just one example, funerals illustrate the theoretical extreme of perfectly inelastic demand more effectively than most other goods.

Indeed, it was partly due to their odd market characteristics that the Office of Fair Trading (OFT) investigated funeral businesses and issued a report in January 1989. This formal report was reviewed in the *Sunday Times* and some edited highlights of the article follow:

About 12 500 people were buried in Britain last week. The services, ceremonies and assorted arrangements cost their nearest and dearest some £7.3m. They also paid out a further £1.9m for flowers, urns, plots of land, entries in books of remembrance and rose bushes with bronze plaques. Did the grieving relatives get value for money, or were they taken for a funeral ride?

The code of practice agreed by the National Association of Funeral Directors states that clients should be shown leaflets explaining the basic simple funeral and all types of coffins and services provided, and 'given a written estimate of all funeral charges and disbursements'. In practice, this rarely happens.

Overall, the OFT found that less than 25 per cent of the people surveyed had seen or been given a price-list to help them choose a funeral to suit their pockets and circumstances, and 40 per cent had been given no price information *at all*. A third were never given an estimate of the total cost, and realized the true figure only when they saw the final bill.

The OFT says: 'For many this will be their first experience of death and its aftermath. Some may be too embarrassed to tell a funeral director that what he is offering seems expensive. Others may simply not take in what is said or realize what they have agreed to . . .'

'We accept the situation is not perfect', says Graham Barber, vice-president of the Funeral Directors' Association, who runs his own firm in Norwich, 'but it's not as black as it sounds. In my experience, the public's expectation of the cost is far greater. They are pleasantly surprised when it doesn't cost £1 000.'

Detailed justification for those costs is often hard to pin down. But it is possible to get close to true cost in the case of that basic item in the death business, the coffin. A retired undertaker, with 22 years' experience of death and bereavement in the East End of London, put it succinctly last week: 'A basic coffin is made of veneered chipboard and six pieces of wood. You can knock one up in a couple of hours for £50 at the most.'

But those are not the figures displayed to the grieving family. When customers walk into a funeral parlour, they are shown a brochure. The range from which they are invited to choose usually starts with the cheapest (the veneered chipboard job) at around £525, to a silk-lined oak casket that could set them back £1 250 or more. Included in this, however, just to make the comparisons more difficult, is the provision of a hearse and one mourners' car. Hidden in this package is the funeral director's fee for use of his premises and services as liaison man between the family and officialdom.

Anything else is extra and goes under the heading of disbursements, which can include: the cost of removing the body from the hospital or home, £60; the minister's fees, £25; grave diggers' fees, £45–110; crematorium, £60–90; extra cars, £60; medical certificate fees in the case of cremations, £42.40–104.

The price of a burial plot varies greatly in different parts of the country. Some church land is free, but in east London a private grave for two people will cost £500; a grave in a Jewish cemetery in Willesden runs as high as £7 000.

The cheapest way to be buried is in a common grave, with 14 others, but even for this the City of London cemetery charges £105. If a pretty little rose-bush and plaque in some serene 'garden of rest' is beginning to sound a more economical proposition, be warned: the cheapest in the City of London cemetery is £148.35 and even then you must pay half of that fee again in 10 years if you want to renew your memorial.

The average cost of a burial is currently £630 and a cremation £567, according to the OFT survey. Costs vary, however, throughout the country. Another study carried out for the Independent Order of Oddfellows, the Manchester-based friendly society, shows that the south-east is the most expensive place to die. The average interment there involves an outlay of £843, and cremation £665. A typical basic funeral, according to the Oddfellows, is now running at £736, up by a solid-looking £200 since 1986 – well above even present rates of general inflation.

It is possible and perfectly legal, if people wish, to do without the funeral director's services altogether. 'There is nothing to stop anybody making their own coffin, hiring a van and taking it to the cemetery,' said the retired undertaker. 'All you need is a box of some sort and the right papers: a death certificate and, in the case of cremation, papers signed by two doctors.'

But that possibility, even when known, does not influence many actual decisions. As the OFT reports: 'Most people do not question the need to have a ceremony or a coffin. The reason for this could well be that they feel there is no real choice. They may feel that moral, social or even legal pressures require a funeral to be organized in a particular way.'

That does not necessarily mean, however, just signing a blank cheque for whatever is on offer. There is a suggested checklist for anybody faced with this chore.

This is what the National Association of Funeral Directors recommends its members provide to clients demanding a no-frills service (but recognizes that such a limited arrangement is not always available):

- A coffin fitted and lined as is customary locally.
- Transportation of the body or delivery of a coffin.
- Care of the body prior to the funeral.
- Provision of a hearse and one car, a conductor, and bearers.
- Attending to necessary arrangements.

To supplement this the OFT recommends that:

- Consumers insist that funeral directors supply information about what arranging a funeral involves and how much it will cost. They should also make known to relatives or friends their wishes for their own funeral.
- Funeral directors should allow doctors, hospitals, and others who come into contact with the recently bereaved to keep price lists.
- Funeral directors' accounts should specify individually the charges for the coffin, hearse, and cars, and this written checklist should show what arrangements have been agreed for such items as flowers, disposal of jewellery, and charitable donations.

Source: Adapted from A. Wilson, 'Cost of dying: are we being conned into the grave?' *Sunday Times*, 28 Feb. 1989.

Average cost of a burial in Britain

Questions

1. (a) Explain, using a diagram, why the concept of perfectly inelastic demand is relevant in the case of funeral services.
   (b) Can you think of any other good or service that illustrates the theoretical concept of perfectly inelastic demand?
   (c) How does a firm faced with a nearly perfect inelastic demand schedule benefit when it comes to covering costs?
   (d) What does (c) imply for firms faced with a perfectly elastic demand schedule?
2. When it comes to funerals, it seems that market forces may not operate as effectively as they do in other sectors. A possible way of correcting the type of market failure that funeral directors benefit from would be to introduce a tax. The tax could be of two types: a unit tax per burial or a lump-sum tax per year for being licensed to bury people.
   (a) Explain and illustrate, using diagrams, the effect on some of the different costs displayed in Figure 21.4, Panel (c), of (i) a unit tax and (ii) a lump-sum tax.
   (b) Which of these two taxes, if any, would you advise a government to adopt? (How else may funeral directors be made more accountable to market forces?)
   (c) Give examples from the article that suggest funeral directors benefit from a type of market failure.
   (d) How could those involved in the funeral industry be accused of wasting resources?
3. Why do you think an Office of Fair Trading exists and which other industries might they concern themselves with?
4. (a) From the article calculate an approximate figure for the amount of burials per year and the related turnover that these burials would generate for funeral directors.
   (b) During 1988/9, Hodgson Funeral Directors had a turnover of £30m and an approximate profit of £5.3m. Do you think the number of funeral businesses will expand or contract in future years (use the concept of normal profits to start your answer)?
5. The boss of Hodgson Funeral Directors was voted the Unlisted Security Market entrepreneur of the year in 1987. Do you think the funeral industry offers much scope for entrepreneurial flair? Give examples to support your answer.
6. Explain the economic reasons why a plot in a Jewish cemetery in Willesden would be so expensive.
7. For those who own and manage graveyards the law of diminishing returns sets in quickly. Fully explain this statement using any diagram and/or examples that seem appropriate.
8. 'Surely there are certain areas where economic considerations should stop and ethical and emotional considerations take over.' Discuss this statement and conclude by stating your own opinion.

CASE STUDY

Colonel Sanders' Recipe for Success: Franchising

Franchising is a sector which has had a chequered history and uncertain image with the public but there are signs that it is now reaching maturity and stability. There are now indications that it is less exclusively associated with 'small' business. While it still offers a relatively low outlay, reduced risk for both franchisors and francisees, it is increasingly becoming the direct route to business on a substantial scale . . .

There are also indications that franchisees in many areas appear more satisfied than before. This improvement seems to have arisen not because problems of selling, staff, or financial management are less, but because franchisees are better at dealing with them.

These trends are shown in the 1988 Franchise Survey produced by Power Research Associates for the National Westminster Bank and the British Franchise Association.

The survey shows that business-format franchising is making an impact on the economy with annual sales rising by 23 per cent to £3.8 billion and significantly showing a consistent growth pattern of 33 per cent year-on-year for the past four years. Franchising now accounts for 181 500 jobs, a 31 per cent year-on-year increase since 1984.

Looking ahead to 1993, annual sales are projected to reach £9.9 billion with the annual unit sales level rising to £385000 compared with the current average of £264000. There is still some way to go to match the United States where franchisors' sales in 1987 approached £380 billion. By the year 2000, half of all retail sales, or nearly £600 billion, are expected to come from almost 2000 firms in 50 industries. Last year the Commerce Department estimated that there were more than 350000 franchise units in operation.

In the UK the growing maturity is indicated by the greater selectivity at both franchisor and franchisee level. Franchisors are applying more stringent vetting procedures before accepting franchisees, with only one in 14 applicants being appointed.

The survey also says that six out of seven franchisees say they have a satisfactory business relationship with their franchisor. It also points to the high proportion of both franchisors and franchisees – 88 per cent and 85 per cent respectively – who report no difficulty in their dealings.

The continued growth of franchised retail shops is in marked contrast with the 3 per cent annual fall in independent shops, but the survey says that franchising lends itself to a range of markets, even though service industries appear to offer greater scope than manufacturing.

Historically services to private individuals were what gave franchising its momentum but recently researchers have found indications that the main potential for sales growth lies among business customers as their value per order can be so much greater.

There has also been an increasing shift in the geographical base of franchising away from its traditional south-east home base. The north, north-west, and Yorkshire, now account for 31 per cent of all the units compared with 17 per cent in 1987.

The survey found that the average initial outlay by franchisees was £65000, an increase of 51 per cent on the previous year. About three-quarters of all franchisees borrowed money to get into business. The average borrowing was £30100, though the sample included three who had borrowed less than £5 000 and two who had borrowed more than £750000.

Franchisors considered that on average a franchisee needed two-and-a-half years to recover their initial outlay but franchisees said it took two years to start trading profitably and four years to accumulate profits to the point where initial borrowing had been covered.

Source: C. T. Woodcock, 'Overcoming a chequered history', *Guardian*, 3 Oct. 1988.

Questions

1. What is franchising? Elaborate your answer by stating some actual examples.
2. (a) When a firm is part of a franchise, do internal and external economies of scale become the same thing?
   (b) What are the disadvantages of being part of a franchise? Which of these are examples of diseconomies of scale.
3. Using a diagram(s) and two different colours, determine whether a franchise dealership is more attractive than a sole-trader with independent status operating in the same business sector (focus your answer around some of the costs identified in Figure 21.4).
4. Using the concept of average total costs, explain the final paragraph.
5. (a) What do you think the British Franchise Association does?
   (b) Would such an association be an example of an internal or external economy of scale? Explain your answer.
6. Use economic concepts to explain why the franchising arrangement has grown in popularity?

Exam Preparation

PRACTICAL EXERCISE

Data response and multiple choice questions often involve defining the various cost curves and/or their interrelationships. The following exercise, therefore, is designed to help students consolidate their understanding of these various business costs. The task is to copy and complete the 30 squares from the seven clues given.

Complete the table from the clues given below it

Output	*Total cost*	*Marginal cost*	*Average total cost*	*Average fixed cost*	*Average variable cost*	*Total variable cost*
2						
3						
4						
5						
6						

CLUES

1. Average fixed cost for 6 units of output is £9.
2. Average variable cost for 2 units of output is £30.
3. Total cost is increased by £28 when the third unit of output is added.
4. Average total cost of 4 units of output is the same as the average total cost of 3 units of output.
5. Total cost for 5 units of output is £258.
6. Total variable cost is increased by £100 when the sixth unit of output is added.
7. Total cost increases by £8 when the second unit of output is added.

Source: M. Seales, 'So you think you understand the theory of costs ...', *Economics* (Journal of the Economics Association), Vol XX, Part 4, No. 88, Winter 1984.

MULTIPLE CHOICE QUESTIONS

1. In the table below, a firm producing 'widgets' displays its short-run total costs for differing levels of output.

Quantity of widgets	*Short-run total costs (£)*
0	1000
10	1200
20	1400
30	1600
40	1800

The variable cost per unit at an output of 20 is
A £1 000
B £70
C £400
D £20
E none of the above.

2. The following table relates the total output and the total costs of a firm:

Output (units)	*Costs (£)*	*Output (units)*	*Costs (£)*
100	125	400	275
200	200	500	290
300	250		

The firm's production shows
A increasing returns throughout
B decreasing returns throughout
C increasing returns for output between 100 and 300 units and decreasing returns for output larger than 300 units
D decreasing returns for output between 100 and 300 units and increasing returns for output larger than 300 units
E constant returns throughout.

3. Each curve in the diagram below describes the different combinations of capital and labour capable of producing the level of output indicated.

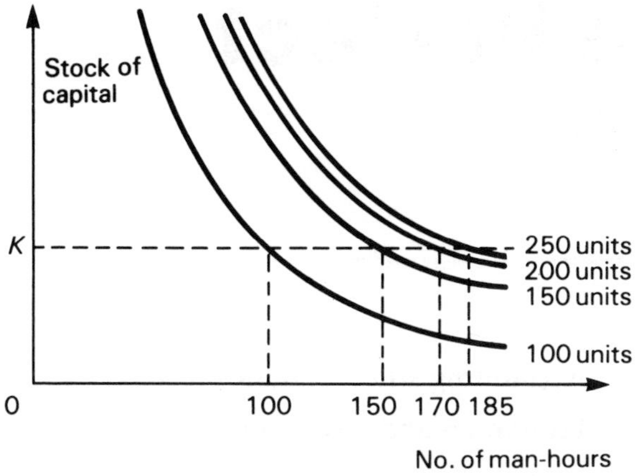

It may be deduced from the diagram that, with a fixed stock of capital, *K*, as output increases

A the average product of capital diminishes
B short-run average costs fall faster than long-run average costs
C there are diseconomies of scale
D the marginal product of labour is constant
E the marginal product of labour increases.

4. The diagram shows the relationship between the total output of a firm and the number of units of labour employed.

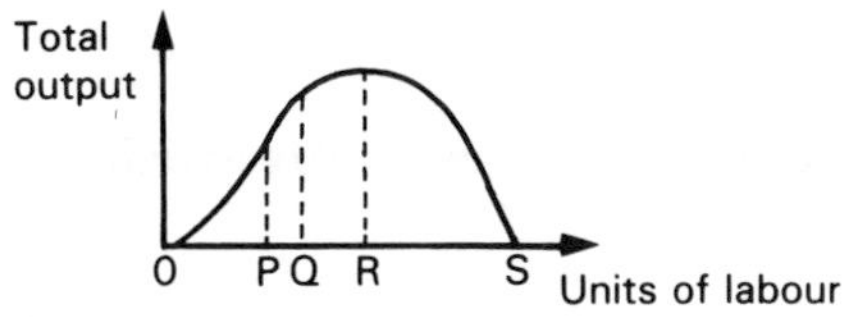

Diminishing marginal productivity of labour sets in

A from the very first unit of labour employed
B after OP units of labour are employed
C after OQ units of labour are employed
D after OR units of labour are employed
E after OS units of labour are employed.

For Questions 5 to 8 select your answer from the following grid:

A	B	C	D	E
1, 2, 3 all correct	**1, 2** only correct	**2, 3** only correct	**1** only correct	**3** only correct

5. Which of the following conditions is (are) necessary for the law of diminishing returns to apply?

1 at least one factor must be in fixed supply
2 demand must be falling
3 total production must be falling.

6. If marginal cost is lower than average total cost then it is necessarily the case that

1 average total cost is falling
2 marginal cost is falling
3 marginal revenue is less than marginal cost.

7. In the theory of costs, the term 'short run' generally refers to a period of time in which

1 some factor inputs are not variable
2 economies of scale are not attainable
3 diminishing returns eventually occur as output expands.

8.

Output (units)	*Total cost (£)*
0	100
1	150
2	180
3	280
4	460

From the above data one can conclude that

1 average fixed cost at 2 units of output equals £50
2 average variable cost at 4 units of output equals £90
3 the marginal cost of the 3rd unit of output is £180.

RELATED ESSAY QUESTIONS

1. Distinguish between internal and external economies of scale. How do economies of scale affect the number of firms in an industry?

2. Explain clearly the law of variable proportions. How does the working of this law influence a firm's cost of production?

3. What is an entrepreneur? Can governments encourage entrepreneurship?

4. Explain the distinction between diminishing returns to a variable factor and diseconomies of scale. With reference to examples, explain how diseconomies of scale might arise.

22 Pricing and Output Decisions in Perfect Competition

Key Points to Review

- Demand (5.1)
- Supply, changes in supply versus changes in quantity supplied (5.6)
- Price elasticity of demand (7.3)
- Accounting and economic profits (21.1)
- Economies and diseconomies of scale (21.4)

Questions for Preview

1 What are the characteristics of the market structure of perfect competition?

2 How much will a perfect competitor produce in the short run?

3 What is the perfectly competitive firm's short-run supply curve?

4 Can a perfectly competitive firm earn economic profits?

5 Why is a perfectly competitive market structure considered to be economically efficient?

Firms have to know not only about costs, discussed in the last chapter, but also about revenues when they make pricing and output decisions. In order to understand, for example, the relationship between output, revenues, and price, a firm has to know the structure of the market, or industry in which it is selling its product. There are various **market structures**, all dependent upon the extent to which buyers and sellers can assume that their own buying and selling decisions do not affect market price. At one extreme, when buyers and sellers indeed can correctly assume that they cannot affect market price, the market structure is one of **perfect competition** – the subject of this chapter. Whenever buyers and sellers must take into account how their individual actions affect market price, we are not in a market structure of perfect competition and have entered an *imperfectly competitive market*. We examine such markets in Chapters 23 and 24.

The Meaning of Competition

Economists use the term competion to mean two different things. In its most general sense, the term competition relates to a relatively relaxed view of the competitive process that focuses on the concept of rivalry among economic transactors. After all, in a world of scarce resources, there will be **rivalry** among sellers and among buyers. Behaviour among sellers where rivalry exists takes many forms: advertising, improvement in the quality of the product, sales promotion, development of new products, modification of old products, and so on. Rivalry among buyers also takes many forms: finding better deals, figuring out ways to take advantage of quantity discounts, offering a higher price to obtain a product that is in fixed supply, and so on. Rivalry is the real-world aspect of competition that is happening all around, because competition in the real world is a dynamic process.

The second use of the term competition is much more specific and well defined, for it relates to a particular model of market organization in which buyers and sellers do not and cannot affect the market price because there are so many of them. In this sense, competition means perfect competition. For the remainder of the chapter the term perfect competition will relate specifically to a particular market structure, the characteristics of which we will set out below.

The Characteristics of Perfect Competition as a Market Structure

In this chapter we are interested in studying how a firm acting within a perfectly competitive market structure makes decisions about how much to produce. Before we go ahead with this analysis, we want to give the characteristics of the market structure called perfect competiton. These characteristics are:

1. The product that is sold by the firms in the industry is *homogeneous*. That means that the product sold by each firm in the industry is a perfect substitute for the product sold by each other firm. In other words, buyers are able to choose from a large number of sellers of a product that the buyers believe to be the same. The product is thus not in any sense differentiated as a result of whoever is the source of supply.
2. Any firm can enter or exit the industry without serious impediments. Resources must be able to move in and out of the industry without, for example, government legislation that prevents such resource mobility to occur.
3. There must be a large number of buyers and sellers. When this is the case, no one buyer or one seller has any influence on price, and also when there are large numbers of buyers and sellers, they will be acting independently.
4. There must be the fullest information available for both buyers and sellers about market prices, product quality and cost conditions.

Now that we have defined the characteristics of a perfectly competitive *market* structure we can consider the position of an individual constituent unit. We define a **perfectly competitive firm** as follows: it is one that is such a small part of the total industry in which it operates that it cannot significantly affect the price of the product in question. Since the perfectly competitive firm is a small part of the industry, that firm has no control over the price of the product. That means that each firm in the industry is a **price-taker** – the firm takes price as given, as something that is determined *outside* the individual firm.

The price that is given to the firm is determined by the forces of market supply and market demand. That is to say, when all individual consumers' demands are added together into a market demand curve, and all the supply schedules of individual firms are added together into a market supply curve, the intersection of those two curves will give the market price, which the purely competitive or price-taking firm must accept.

This definition of a competitive firm is obviously idealized, for in one sense the individual firm has to set prices. How can we ever have a situation where firms regard prices as set by forces outside their control? The answer is that even though every firm, by definition, sets its own prices, a firm in a perfectly competitive situation will find that it will eventually have no customers at all if it sets its price above the competitive price. Let us now see what the demand curve of an individual firm in a competitive industry looks like graphically.

Single-firm Demand Curve

In Chapter 7 we talked about the characteristics of demand schedules. We pointed out that for completely elastic demand curves, if the individual firm raises the price one penny, it will lose all its business. Well, this is how we characterize the demand schedule for a purely competitive firm – it is a horizontal line at the going market price. That is, it is completely elastic (see Chapter 7). And that going market price is determined by the market forces of supply and demand. Figure 22.1 is the hypothetical market demand schedule faced by an individual leather handbag producer who sells a very, very small part of the total leather handbag production in the industry. At the market price, this

Figure 22.1

The Demand Curve for an Individual Leather Handbag Producer. We assume that the individual handbag producer is such a small part of the total market that he or she cannot influence the price. The firm accepts the price as given. At the going market price it faces a horizontal demand curve, *dd*. If it raises its price even one penny, it will sell no handbags. The firm would be foolish to lower its price below £5, because it can sell all that it can produce at a price of £5. The firm's demand curve is completely, or perfectly, elastic.

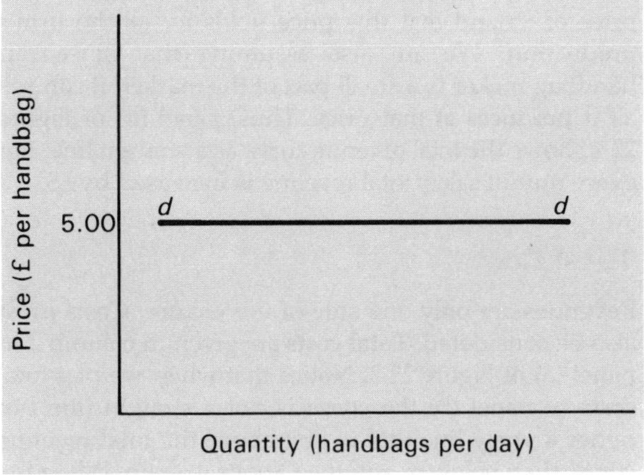

firm can sell all the output it wants. At the market price of £5 each, which is where the horizontal demand curve for the individual producer lies, people's demand for the leather handbags of that one producer is perfectly elastic. If the firm raises its price, they will buy from some other producer. We label the individual producer's demand curve *dd*, whereas the market demand curve is always labelled *DD*.

How Much Does the Perfect Competitor Produce?

As we have shown, a perfect competitor has to accept the given price of the produce. If the firm raises its price, it sells nothing. If it lowers its price, it makes less money per unit sold than it otherwise could. The firm has only one decision variable left: How much should it produce? We will apply our model of the firm to this question to come up with an answer. We shall use the *profit-maximization* model and assume that firms, whether competitive or monopolistic, will attempt to maximize their total profits, that is, the positive difference between total revenues and total costs.

Total Revenues

Every firm has to consider its **total revenues**. Total revenues are defined as the quantity sold multiplied by the price. (They are also the same as total receipts from the sale of output.) The perfect competitor must take the price as given.

Look at panel (a) of Figure 22.2. Much of the information comes from panel (a) of Figure 21.4, but we have added some essential columns for our analysis. Column 3 is the market price of £5 per handbag, which is also equal to average revenue (AR), since

$$\text{AR} = \frac{\text{TR}}{Q} = \frac{P \times Q}{Q} = P$$

Column 4 shows the total revenues, or TR, as equal to the market price, P, times the total output in sales per day, or Q. Thus, TR = $P \times Q$. We are assuming that the market supply and demand schedules intersect at a price of £5 and that this price holds for all the firm's production. We are also assuming that since our handbag maker is a small part of the market, it can sell all it produces at that price. Thus, panel (b) of Figure 22.2 shows the total revenue curve as a straight line. For every unit of sales, total revenue is increased by £5.

Total Costs

Revenues are only one side of the picture. Costs must also be considered. **Total costs** are given in column 2 in panel (a) of Figure 22.2. Notice that when we plot total costs of panel (b) the curve is not a straight line but rather a wavy line that is first above the total revenue curve, then below it, and then above it again. When the total cost curve is above the total revenue curve, the firm is experiencing losses. When it is below the total revenue curve, the firm is making profits. (When we refer to profits, we will always mean economic profits.)

Comparing Total Costs with Total Revenues

By comparing total costs with total revenues, we can figure out the number of leather handbags that the individual competitive firm should produce per day. Our analysis rests on the assumption that the firm will attempt to maximize total profits. In figure 22.2 (a) we see that total profits reach a maximum at a production rate of between seven and eight leather handbags per day. We can see this graphically in Figure 22.2 (b). The firm will maximize profits at that place on the graph where the total revenue curve exceeds the total cost curve by the greatest amount. That occurs at a rate of output and sales of either seven or eight handbags per day; this rate is called the **profit-maximizing rate of production**.

We can also find this profit-maximizing rate of production for the individual competitive firm by looking at marginal revenues and marginal costs.

Using Marginal Analysis

Marginal cost was introduced in Chapter 21. It was defined as the change in total cost due to a one-unit change in production. This leaves only **marginal revenue** to be defined.

Marginal Revenue

What amount can our individual handbag-making firm hope to receive each time it sells an additional (marginal) leather handbag? Since the firm is such a small part of the market and cannot influence the price, it must accept the price determined by the market forces of supply and demand. Therefore, the firm knows it will receive £5 for every handbag it sells in the market. So the additional revenue the firm will receive from selling one more handbag is equal to the market price of £5; marginal revenue, in this case, equals price.

Marginal revenue presents the increment in total revenues attributable to producing one additional unit of the product in question. Marginal revenue is also defined as the change in total revenue resulting from a one-unit change in output. Hence, a more formal definition of marginal revenue is:

$$\text{marginal revenue} = \frac{\text{change in total revenue}}{\text{change in output}}$$

In a perfectly competitive market, the marginal revenue curve is exactly equivalent to the price line or, in other words, to the individual firm's demand curve, since the firm can sell all of its output (production) at the market price.

Total output and sales per day (1)	*Total cost (TC) (2)*	*Market price (P) (3)*	*Total revenue (TR) (4) = (3) × (1)*	*Total profit = (TR) − (TC) (5) = (4) − (2)*	*Average total cost (ATC) (6) = (2) ÷ (1)*	*Average variable cost (AVC)* (7)*	*Marginal cost (MC) (8) = Change in (2) / Change in (1)*	*Marginal revenue (MR) (9) = Change in (4) / Change in (1)*
0	£10.00	£5.00	0	−£10.00	—	—		
1	15.00	5.00	£ 5.00	−10.00	£15.00	£5.00	£5.00	£5.00
2	18.00	5.00	0.00	−8.00	9.00	4.00	3.00	5.00
3	20.00	5.00	15.00	−5.00	6.67	3.33	2.00	5.00
4	21.00	5.00	20.00	−1.00	5.25	2.75	1.00	5.00
5	23.00	5.00	25.00	2.00	4.60	2.60	2.00	5.00
6	26.00	5.00	30.00	4.00	4.33	2.67	3.00	5.00
7	30.00	5.00	35.00	5.00	4.28	2.86	4.00	5.00
8	35.00	5.00	40.00	5.00	4.38	3.12	5.00	5.00
9	41.00	5.00	45.00	4.00	4.56	3.44	6.00	5.00
10	48.00	5.00	50.00	2.00	4.80	3.80	7.00	5.00
11	56.00	5.00	55.00	−1.00	5.09	4.18	8.00	5.00

*Taken from Figure 21.4

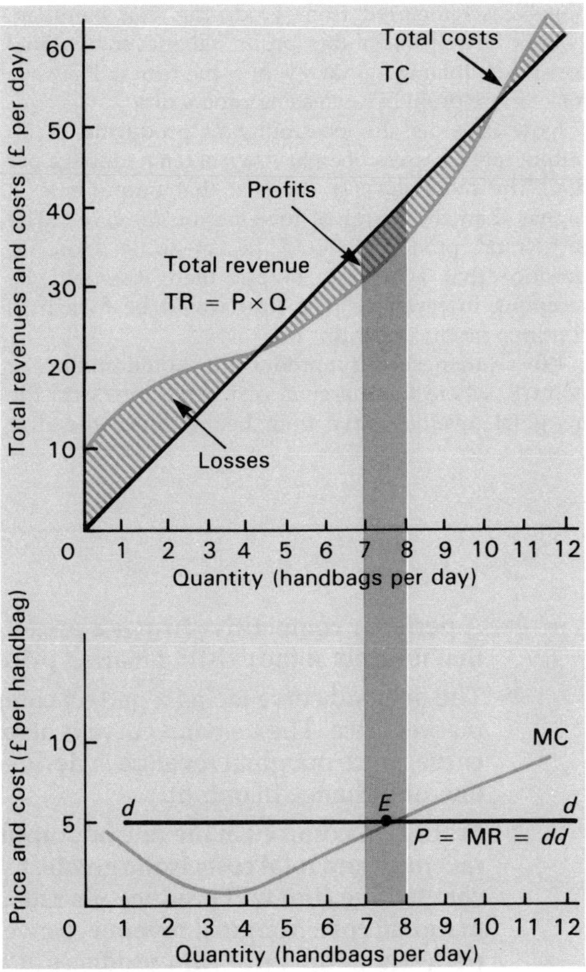

Figure 22.2 (a)

The Costs of Production and the Revenues from the Sale of Output: Finding the Profit-maximization Rate of Output and Sales. Profit maximization occurs at a rate of sales of either seven or eight handbags per day.

Figure 22.2 (b)

Finding Maximum Total Profits. Total revenues are represented by the straight line, showing that each handbag sells at £5. Total costs first exceed total revenues, then are less than total revenues, and then exceed them again. We find maximum profits where total revenues exceed total costs by the largest amount. This occurs at a rate of production and sales per day of seven or eight handbags.

Figure 22.2 (c)

Profit Maximization Using Marginal Analysis. Profit maximization occurs where marginal revenue equals marginal cost. Marginal revenue is represented by the individual firm demand curve, *dd*, which is a horizontal line at £5. The marginal cost curve is represented by MC. It intersects the marginal revenue curve at a rate of output and sales of somewhere between seven and eight handbags per day.

Thus, in Figure 22.1 the demand curve, *dd*, for the individual producer is at a price of £5 – the price line is coincident with the demand curve. But so, too, is the marginal revenue curve, for marginal revenue in this case also equals £5.

The marginal revenue curve for our competitive leather handbag producer is shown as a horizontal line at £5 in Figure 22.2 (c). Notice again that the marginal revenue curve is equal to the price line, which is equal to the individual firm's demand curve, *dd*.

When Profits Are Maximized

Now we add the marginal cost curve, MC, taken from column 8 in Figure 22.2 (a). As shown in Figure 22.2 (c), the marginal cost curve first falls and then starts to rise, eventually intersecting the marginal revenue curve and then rising above it. Notice that the numbers for both the marginal cost schedule and the marginal revenue schedule in Figure 22.2 (a) are printed *between* the figures that determine them. This indicates that we are looking at a change between one rate of output and the next.

In Figure 22.2 (c), the marginal cost curve intersects the marginal revenue (or *dd*) curve somewhere between seven and eight handbags per day. Consider a rate of production that is less than that. At a production rate of, say, six handbags per day, marginal cost is clearly below marginal revenue. That is, the marginal cost curve at an output of six is below the marginal revenue curve at that output. Since it can receive £5 per handbag, and since marginal cost is less than this marginal revenue, the firm has an incentive to increase production. In fact, it has an incentive to produce and sell until the amount of the additional revenue received from selling one more handbag just equals the additional costs incurred from producing that handbag. This is how it maximizes profit. Whenever marginal cost is less than marginal revenue, the firm will always make more profit by increasing production.

Now consider the possibility of producing at an output rate in excess of eight – say, at ten handbags per day. The marginal cost curve at that output rate is higher than the marginal revenue (of *dd*) curve. The individual producer would be spending more to produce that additional output than it would be receiving in revenues. The firm would be foolish to continue producing at this rate.

Where, then, should it produce? It should produce at point *E*, where the marginal cost curve intersects the marginal revenue curve from below. Since the firm knows it can sell all the handbags it wants at the going market price, marginal revenue from selling an additional handbag will always equal the market price. Consequently, the firm should continue production until the cost of increasing output by one more unit is just equal to the revenues obtainable from that extra unit. Profit maximization is always at the rate of output at which marginal revenue equals marginal cost. (To be strictly correct, we should add: 'and the MC curve cuts the MR curve from below'.) * For a perfectly competitive firm, this is at the intersection of the demand schedule, *dd*, and the marginal cost curve, MC. In our particular example, our profit-maximizing, perfectly competitive leather-handbag producer will produce at a rate of between seven and eight handbags a day.

Notice that this same profit-maximizing rate of output is shown in both Figure 22.2 (b), where the total revenue and total cost curves are drawn and in Figure 22.2 (c) where the marginal revenue and marginal cost curves are drawn. We can find the profit-maximizing output solution for the perfectly competitive firm by looking at either diagram. (Now read Key Points 22.1.)

Profits in the Short Run

To find what our individual, competitive leather-handbag producer is making in terms of profits in the short run, we have to add the average total cost curve to Figure 22.2 (c). We take the information from column 6 in Figure 22.2 (a) and add it to Figure 22.2 (c) to get Figure 22.3. Again, the profit-maximizing rate of output is between seven and eight handbags per day. If we have production and sales of seven handbags per day, total revenues will be £35 a day. Total costs will be £30 a day, leaving a profit of £5 a day. If the rate of output in

*The marginal cost curve, MC, also cuts the marginal revenue curve (*dd*) from above at an output rate of less than one.

Key Points 22.1

- **A perfectly competitive firm is a price-taker. It takes price as given. It can sell all that it wants at the existing market price.**
- **The demand curve facing a perfect competitor is a horizontal line at the going market price. The demand curve is also the perfect competitor's marginal revenue curve, since marginal revenue is defined as a change in total revenue due to a one-unit change in output.**
- **Profit is maximized at the rate of output where the positive difference between total revenues and total costs is the greatest. Using a marginal analysis, the perfectly competitive firm will produce at a rate of output where marginal revenue equals marginal cost. Marginal revenue, however, is equal to price. Therefore, the perfectly competitive firm produces at an output rate where marginal cost equals the price of the output.**

Figure 22.3

Measuring Total Profits. The profit-maximizing rate of output and sales is where marginal revenue equals marginal cost. Profits are the difference between total revenues and total cost. Total revenues will equal the rate of output and sales times the market price of £5. Total costs will equal the quantity produced and sold multiplied by average total cost (ATC). Profits are represented by the shaded area.

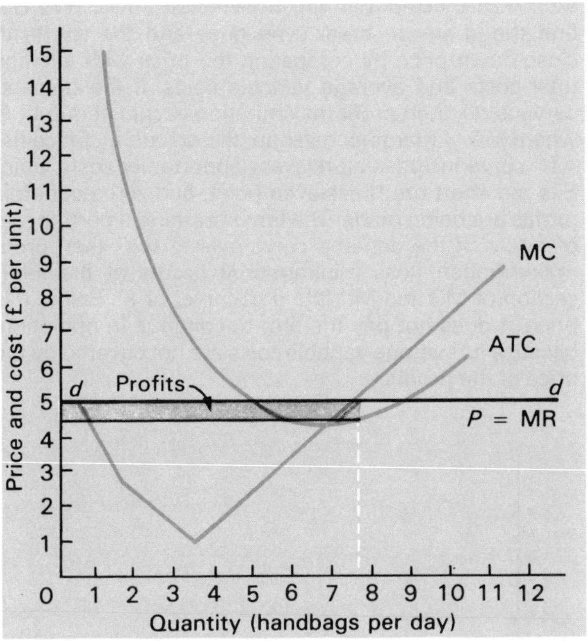

Figure 22.4

Minimizing Short-run Losses. In cases where average total costs exceed the average revenue or price, profit maximization is equivalent to loss minimization. This again occurs where marginal costs equals marginal revenue. Losses are shown in the shaded area.

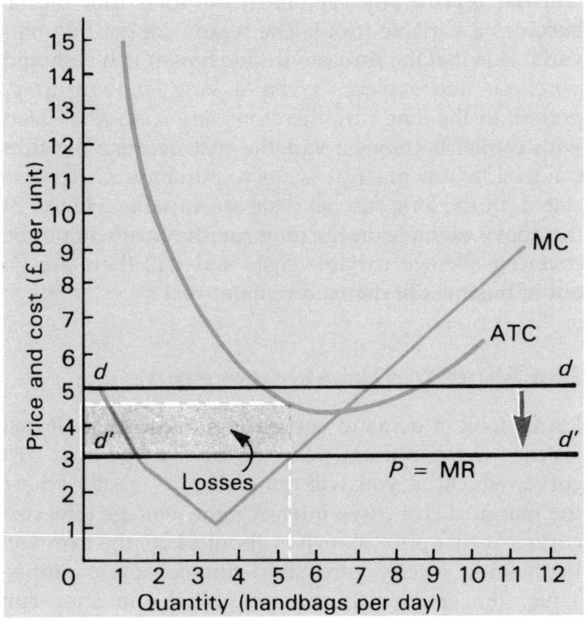

sales is eight handbags per day, total revenues will be £40 and total costs will be £35, again leaving a profit of £5 a day.

It is certainly possible, also, for the competitive firm to make short-run losses. We give an example in Figure 22.4. Here we show the firm's demand curve shifting from *dd* to *d'd'*. The going market price has fallen from £5 to £3 per handbag because of changes in market supply and/or demand conditions. The firm will always be better off by producing where marginal revenue equals marginal cost. We see in Figure 23.3 that the marginal revenue (or *d'd'*) curve intersects the marginal cost curve at an output rate of about 5½ handbags per day. The firm is clearly not making profits, because average total costs at that output rate are greater than the price of £3 per handbag. The losses are shown in the shaded area. Here, by producing where marginal revenue equals marginal cost, the firm is minimizing its losses.

Closing down in the Short Run

In Figure 22.4, the firm is making economic losses. Will it go out of business? Certainly in the long run it will, for the owners of the firm will not incur economic losses forever. But in the short run, the firm may not go out of business. So long as the loss from staying in business is less than the loss from going out of business, the firm will continue to produce. Now how can we tell when that is the case; that is, when sustaining economic losses in the short run is still worth while? We must compare the cost of staying in business (with losses) with the cost of closing down. The cost of staying in business in the short run is given by the average variable cost curve, or AVC. As long as average variable costs are covered by revenue (*P*), the firm is better off staying in business. In other words, if average unit variable costs are exceeded even a little by the price of the product, then staying in business produces something that can be applied towards covering fixed costs.

A simple example will demonstrate this situation. Let the price of a product be £8. Let average total costs equal £9 at an output of 100. In this hypothetical example, average total costs are broken up into average variable costs of £7 and average fixed costs of £2. Total revenues, then, equal £8 × 100, *i.e.* £800, and total costs equal £9 × 100, or £900. Total losses therefore equal £100. However this does not mean the firm will shut down. After all, if it does shut down, it still has fixed costs to pay. And in this case, since average fixed costs equal £2 at an output of 100, the fixed costs are £200. Thus, the firm has losses of £100 if it continues to produce, but it has losses of £200 (the fixed costs) if it shuts down. The logic is fairly straightforward: As long as the price per unit sold exceeds the average variable cost per unit produced, the firm will be paying for at least part of the opportunity cost of capital invested in the business. Although the price is below average total cost and the firm is not making a normal or competitive rate of return on its investment, at least it is making *some* return. A small rate of return on an investment is better than no rate of return at all.

If the firm continues to sustain economic losses, it will not replace any capital. In the long run, capital becomes a variable input. The reason capital becomes variable is that the firm can decide how much it should purchase and replace, given a long enough time-period. In the long run, therefore, any costs associated with capital becomes a variable cost because the firm can decide how much it wants to purchase. Otherwise stated, in the long run, all costs are variable. Hence, in the above example, in the long run the firm will not be covering average variable costs and will therefore go out of business (if demand remains at *d'd'*).

The Short-run Break-even Point

Let us look at demand curve *dd* in Figure 22.5. It just touches the minimum point of the average total cost curve, which, as you will remember, is exactly where the marginal cost curve intersects the average total cost curve. At that price, which is about £4.30, the firm will be making exactly zero short-run economic profits. Thus, that particular price is called the short-run break-even price. And point *E* is therefore called the **short-run break-even point** for a competitive firm. It is the point at which marginal revenue = marginal cost = average total cost. The break-even price is the one that yields zero short-run profits or losses.

Calculating the Closing-down Point

In order to calculate the firm's shut-down point, we must add the average variable cost (AVC) to our graph. In Figure 22.5 we have taken the AVC curve from column 7 in Figure 23.2 (a). For the moment, consider two possible demand curves, *dd* and *d'd'*, which are also the firm's respective marginal revenue curves. Therefore, if demand is *dd*, the firm will produce at *E*, where the curve intersects the marginal cost curve. If demand falls to *d'd'*, the firm will produce at *E'*. The special feature about the hypothetical demand curve *d'd'* is that it just touches the average variable cost curve at the latter's minimum point, which is where the marginal cost curve intersects it also. This price is labelled the short-run shut-down price. Why? Below this price the firm is paying out more in variable costs than it is receiving in revenues from the sale of its product. On each unit it sells, it is adding to its losses. Clearly, the way to avoid incurring these additional losses, if price falls below the closing-down point, is in fact to shut down operations. (Of course, if price falls below the short-run shut-down price, a firm may still continue in business in the short run if it decides it can afford to wait until the price moves up again, and it can profitably re-enter production.)

The intersection of the price line, the marginal cost curve, and the average variable cost is labelled *E'*. We called it the **short-run close-down point**. This point is labelled short run because, of course, in the long run, the firm will not produce below a price that yields a normal rate of return and, hence, zero economic profits.

Figure 22.5

Short-run Close-down and Break-even Prices. We can find the short-run break-even price and the short-run close-down price by comparing the price with average total costs and average variable costs. If the demand curve is *dd*, then profit maximization occurs at output *E*, where MC = marginal revenue (the *dd* curve). Since the ATC curve includes all relevant opportunity costs, point *E* is the short-run break-even point, and zero economic profits are being made. The firm is earning a normal rate of return. If the demand curve falls to *d'd'*, then profit maximization (loss minimization) occurs at the intersection of MC and MR (the *d'd'* curve) or *E'*. Below this price, it does not pay the firm to continue in operation, because its average variable costs are not covered by the price of the product.

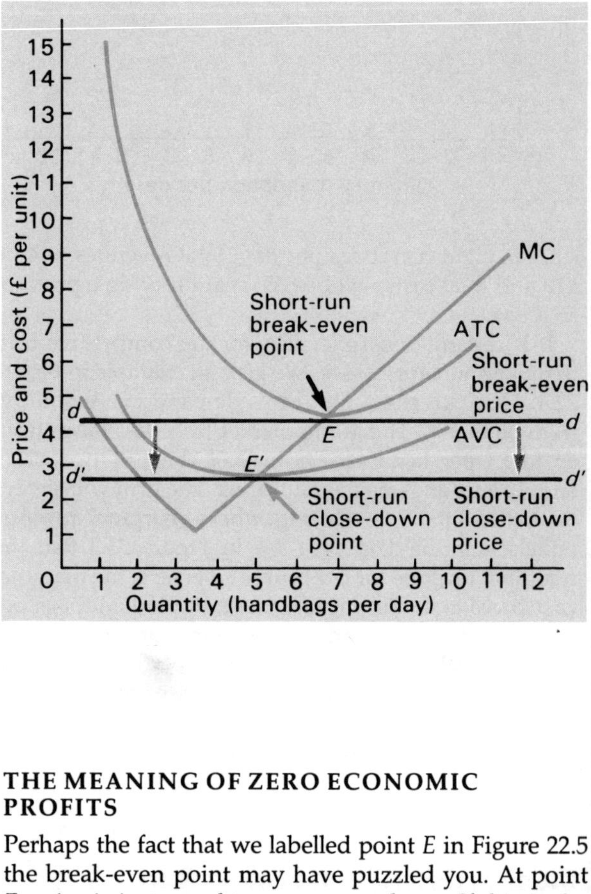

THE MEANING OF ZERO ECONOMIC PROFITS

Perhaps the fact that we labelled point *E* in Figure 22.5 the break-even point may have puzzled you. At point *E*, price is just equal to average total cost. If this is the case, why would a firm continue to produce if it were making no profits whatsoever? If we again make the distinction between accounting profits and economic profits, then at that price the firm has zero economic profits but positive accounting profits.

Accounting versus Economic Profits Revisited

Think back to the last chapter when we discussed how an accountant must total up costs. The accountant adds up all of the expenses, subtracts them from all of the revenues, and calls the result profit. What is ignored is the reward offered to investors. Those who invest in the firm, whether they be proprietors or shareholders must anticipate a rate of return that is at least as great as could be earned in similar investments of equal risk. Looking at capital alone, we know that the costs of capital is its opportunity cost. Accountants, in conforming with tax laws, do not enter the opportunity cost of most of the capital involved as a cost of doing business. (Moreover, accountants do not have an exact figure on the opportunity cost of capital; therefore, it is appropriate for them to talk in terms of profits without making the distinction that we make here.)

In our analysis, the average total cost curve includes the full opportunity cost of capital. Indeed, the average total cost curve includes the opportunity cost of *all* factors of production used in the production process.

We have defined economic profits as those profits over and above what is required to keep capital in the firm. At the short-run break-even price, economic profits are, by definition, zero. However, accounting profits at that price are not equal to zero; they are positive. Let us consider an example different from the one used in Figure 22.5. A squash-racket manufacturer sells rackets at a particular price. The owners of the firm have invested only their own capital in the business: they have borrowed no money from anyone else. Moreover, assume that they explicitly pay the full opportunity cost to all factors of production, including any managerial labour that they themselves contribute to the business. In other words, they pay themselves salaries that show up as a cost in the books, and those salaries are equal to what they could have earned in the next-best alternative occupation. At the end of the year, the owners find that after they subtract all explicit costs from total revenues, they have earned £100 000. Let us say that their investment was £1 million. Thus, the rate of return on that investment is 10 per cent per year. We will assume that this turns out to be equal to the rate of return that, on average, all other squash-racket manufacturers make in the industry.

This £100 000, or 10 per cent rate of return, is actually, then, a competitive, or normal, rate of return on invested capital in that industry or in other industries with similar risks. If the owners had only made, say £50 000, or 5 per cent on their investment, they would have been able to make higher profits by leaving the industry. Thus, we say that the 10 per cent rate of return is the opportunity cost of capital. The accountant shows it as a profit; we call it a cost. We also include the cost in the average total cost curve similar to the one shown in Figure 22.5. Thus, at the short-run break-even price, average total cost, including this opportunity cost of capital, will just equal that price. The firm will be making zero economic profits but a 10 per cent accounting rate of return.

Now we are ready to derive the firm's supply curve.

Figure 22.6

The Individual Firm's Short-run Supply Curve. The individual firm's supply curve is that portion of its marginal cost curve above the average variable cost curve.

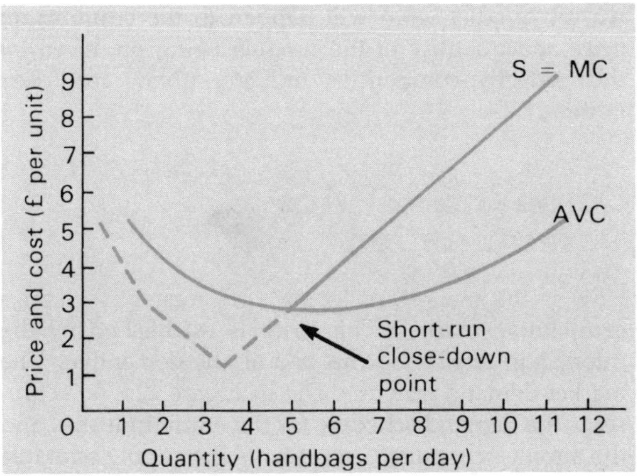

The Firm's Short-run Supply Curve

What does the supply curve for the individual firm look like? Actually, we have been looking at it all along. We know that when the price of handbags is £5, the firm will supply seven or eight handbags per day. If the price falls to £3, the firm will supply five or six handbags per day. And if the price falls below £3, the firm will shut down in the short run. Hence, in Figure 22.6 the firm's supply curve is the marginal cost curve above the short-run close-down point. This is shown as the heavily shaded part of the marginal cost curve. The definition, then, of the individual firm's supply curve in a competitive industry is its marginal cost curve equal to and above the point of intersection with the average variable cost curve.

The Industry Short-run Supply Curve

Now let us see what the market supply curve, or the supply curve for the entire industry, looks like. First what is an industry? Isn't it merely a collection of firms producing a particular product? Yes, and therefore we have a way to figure out the total supply curve of, for example, leather handbags. To do this, we merely add, for every possible price, the quantities that each firm will supply. In other words, we *horizontally* sum the individual supply curves of all the competitive firms. But the individual supply curves, as we just saw, are simply the marginal cost curves of each firm. Consider

Figure 22.7

Deriving the Industry Supply Curve. We assume there are only two firms in this industry. Marginal cost curves above average minimum variable cost are presented in panels (a) and (b) for firms A and B. We horizontally sum the two quantities supplied, q_1^a and q_2^b at price P_1. This gives us point *F*. We do the same thing for the quantities at price P_2. This gives us point *G*. When we connect those two points, we have the industry supply curve, *SS*, which is the horizontal summation of the firms' marginal cost curves above their respective average minimum costs.

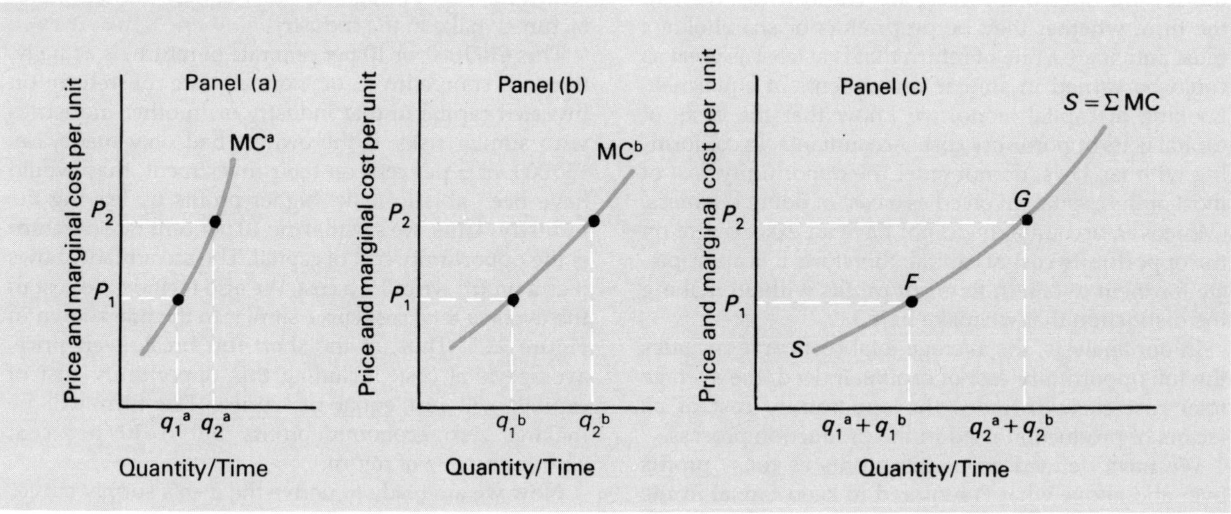

doing this for a hypothetical world in which there are only two handbag producers in the industry, firm A and firm B. These two firms' marginal cost curves are given in panels (a) and (b) of Figure 22.7. The marginal costs curves for the two separate firms are presented as MC^a in panel (a) and MC^b in panel (b). These two marginal cost curves are drawn only for prices above the minimum average variable cost for each respective firm. Hence, we are not including any of the section of the marginal cost curves below minimum average variable cost. In panel (a) for firm A at price P_1, the quantity supplied would be q_1^a. At price P_2, the quantity supplied would be q_2^a. In panel (b), we see the two different quantities corresponding to those two prices that would be supplied by firm B. Now we horizontally add for price P_1 the quantity of q_1^a and q_2^a. This gives us one point, *F*, for our **industry supply curve**, *SS*. We obtain the other point, *G*, by doing the same horizontal adding of quantities at P_2. When we connect points *F* and *G*, we obtain industry supply curve *SS*, which is also marked as Σ (the summation sign) MC, or horizontal summation of the marginal cost curves (above the respective minimum average variable cost of each firm).

Factors that Influence the Supply Curve

As you have just seen, the industry supply curve is the horizontal summation of all of the individual firms' supply curves above their respective minimum average variable cost points. That means that anything that affects the marginal cost curves of the firm will influence the industry supply curve. Therefore, the individual factors that will influence the supply function in a competitive industry can be summarized as those factors that affect the individual marginal cost curves, such as changes in factor costs – the wages paid to employees and the prices of raw materials. Changes in productivity on the part of the individual firm, taxes, and anything else that would influence the individual firm's marginal cost curves also determine the industry supply curve.

All of these are non-price determinants of supply. Since they affect the position of the marginal cost curve for the individual firm, they indeed affect the position of the industry supply curve. A change in any of the above-mentioned non-price determinants of supply will shift the market supply curve. Thus, once we are given the market demand curve in the perfectly competitive industry, if we know there has been a shift in a non-price determinant of the market supply curve, we can predict what will happen to the equilibrium price and quantity of the product being produced by the perfectly competitive industry. (Now read Key Points 22.2.)

Competitive Price Determination

How is the market, or 'going', price established in a competitive market? This price is established by the interaction of all the firms and all the demanders. The market demand schedule *DD* in Figure 22.8 (a) represents the demand schedule for the entire industry, and the supply schedule *SS* represents the supply schedule

Key Points 22.2

- **Short-run profits and losses are determined by comparing average total costs with price at the profit-maximizing rate of output. In the short run, the perfectly competitive firm can make economic profits or economic losses.**
- **The competitive firm's short-run break-even output occurs at the minimum point on its average total cost curve, which is where the marginal cost curve intersects the average total cost curve.**
- **The competitive firm's short-run shut-down output is at the minimum point on its average variable cost curve, which is also where the marginal cost curve intersects the average variable cost curve. Close-down will occur if price falls below average variable cost.**
- **The firm will continue production at a price that exceeds average variable costs even though the full opportunity cost of capital is not being met; at least some revenues are going towards paying some rate of return to capital.**
- **At the short-run break-even price, the firm is making zero economic profits, which means that it is just making a normal rate of return in that industry.**
- **The firm's short-run supply curve is that section of its marginal cost curve equal to or above minimum average variable costs.**
- **The industry short-run supply curve is a horizontal summation of the individual firms' marginal cost curves above their respective minimum average variable costs.**

for the entire industry. Price P_e is established by the forces of supply and demand at the intersection of *SS* and *DD*. Even though each individual firm has no control or effect on the price of its product in a competitive industry, the interaction of *all* the producers determines the price at which the product will be sold. We say that the price P_e and the quantity Q_e in Figure 22.8 (a) (see page 344) constitute the competitive solution to the pricing–quantity problem in that particular industry. It is the equilibrium where supplies and demanders are both maximizing. The resulting individual firm demand curve *dd* is shown in Figure 22.8 (b) at the price P_e.

The Long-run Industry Situation – Exit and Entry

In the long run, we surmise that firms in perfect competition will tend to have average total cost curves that just touch the price = marginal revenue curve, or individual demand curve *dd*. That is, in the long run in a competitive situation, firms will be making zero economic profits. How does this occur? It is through an adjustment process that depends on economic profits and losses. In Chapter 6 we referred to changes in demand and technological progress having the effect of changing prices and profits, signalling resource owners about where their resources should flow. Now we can be more precise about this process.

Exit and Entry Firms

Go back and look at Figures 22.3 and 22.4 (page 339). The existence of either profits or losses is a signal to owners of capital within and outside the industry. If the industry is characterized by firms showing economic profits as represented in Figure 22.3, this will signal to owners of capital elsewhere in the economy that they, too, should enter this industry. If, on the other hand, there are firms in the industry that are like those suffering economic losses represented in Figure 22.4, this signals resource owners outside the industry to stay out. It also signals resource owners within the industry not to reinvest and if possible to leave the industry. It is in this sense that we say that profits direct resources to their highest-valued use. Capital and labour will flow into industries where profitability is highest, and will flow out of industries where profitability is lowest. In the price system, the allocation of capital is therefore directed by relative expected rates of return on investment. It should be noted that when resources are immobile the signalling mechanism becomes ineffective.

In addition, when we say that in a competitive long-run equilibrium situation firms will be making zero economic profits, we must realize that at a particular point in time it would be pure coincidence for a firm to be making *exactly* zero economic profits. Real-world information is not as exact as the curves we use to simplify our analysis. Things change all the time

Figure 22.8 (a)

The Industry Demand and Supply Curves. The industry demand curve is a representation of the demand curve for all potential consumers. It is represented by *DD*. The industry supply curve is the horizontal summation of all those sections of the marginal cost curves of the individual firms above their respective minimum average variable cost points. We show it as *SS* and mark it as equal to ΣMC. The intersection of the demand and supply curves at *E* determines the equilibrium or market price at P_e.

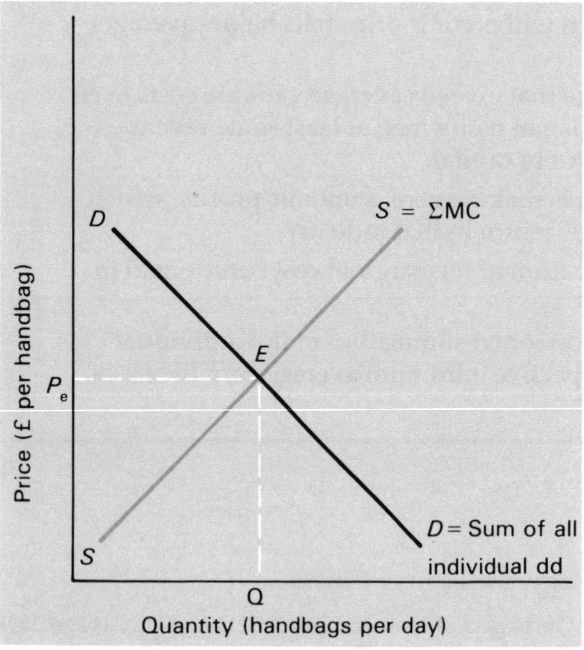

Figure 22.8 (b)

Individual Firm Demand Curve. The individual firm demand curve is set at the going market price determined in Figure 22.8 (a). That is, the demand curve facing the individual firm is a horizontal line, *dd*, at price P_e.

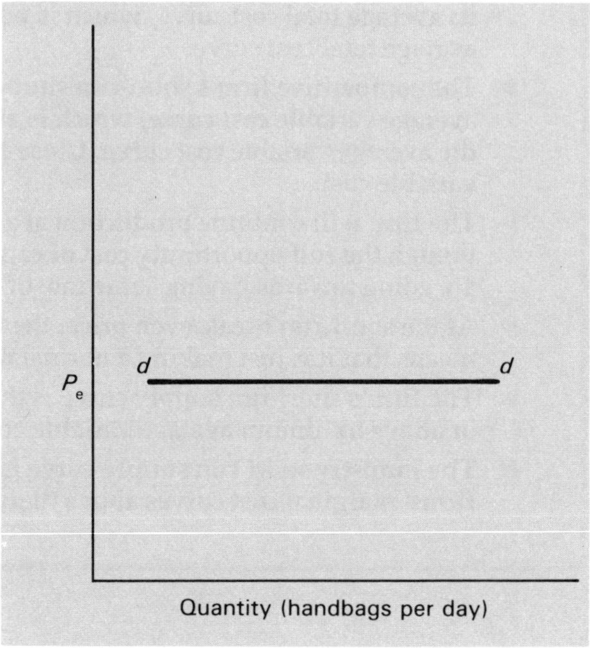

in a dynamic world, and firms, even in a very competitive situation, may, for many reasons, not be making exactly zero economic profits. Remember, in any event, that the concept of long-run zero economic profits in a competitive industry is a long-run concept. We say that their is a *tendency* towards that equilibrium position, but firms are adjusting all the time to changes in their cost curves and in their (horizontal) *dd* curve.

Long-run Supply Curves

In Figure 22.8 (a), we drew the summation of all the portions of the individual firm's marginal cost curve above each firm's respective minimum average variable costs as the upward-sloping supply curve of the entire industry. We should be aware, however, that a relative steep upward-sloping curve may only be appropriate in the short run. After all, one of the prerequisites for a competitive industry is that there be no restrictions on entry. We expect, therefore, that if the consumer demand schedule shifts out to the right (there is increased demand for the product in question), eventually more firms will enter the market so that the quantity supplied can also be expanded. In fact, each time the demand curve shifts to the right, the price can be expected to rise, other things being constant. But this means positive economic profits for the current producers. Therefore, existing firms will expand, and more producers will enter the market, thus eventually forcing the price down to its old equilibrium level, assuming costs in the industry remain constant.

Remember our definition of the long run is one in which adjustments can be made. Our definition of the **long-run industry supply curve** is a supply curve showing the relationship between quantity supplied by the entire industry at different prices after firms have been allowed to either enter or exit from the industry, depending on whether there have been positive or negative economic profits. The long-run industry supply curve is drawn under the assumption that entry and exit have been completed.

There are three possible types of long-run industry supply curves, depending on whether input costs stay constant, increase, or decrease. What is at issue here is the effect on input prices of a change in the number of firms in the industry. In the last chapter, we assumed that input prices remained constant to the firm, no matter what the firm's rate of output was. When looking at the entire industry, that assumption may not be correct if, for example, when all firms are expanding and new firms are entering, they simultaneously bid up input prices.

Constant-cost Industries

In principle, there are small enough industries that utilize such a low percentage of the total supply of inputs necessary for their production that firms can enter the industry without bidding up input prices. In such a situation we are dealing with **constant-cost industry**. Its long-run industry supply curve is therefore horizontal and is represented by S_LS_L in panel (a) of Figure 22.9.

We can work through the case in which constant costs prevail. We start out in panel (a) with demand curve *DD* and supply curve *SS*. The equilibrium price is P_e. There is a rightward shift in market demand to *D′D′*. In the short run, the supply curve remains stable. The equilibrium price rises to P_e. This generates positive economic profits for existing firms in the industry. Such economic profits induce capital to flow into the industry. The existing firms expand and/or new firms enter. The supply curve shifts out to *S′S′*. The new intersection with the new demand curve is at *E″*. The new equilibrium price is again P_e. The long-run supply curve is obtained by connecting the intersections of the corresponding pairs of demand and supply curves, *E* and *E″*. It is labelled S_LS_L and is horizontal. Its slope is zero. In a constant-cost industry, long-run supply is perfectly elastic. Any shift in demand is eventually met by an equal shift in supply, so that the long-run price is constant at P_e.

Increasing-cost Industries

In an **increasing-cost industry**, expansion by existing firms and the addition of new firms causes the price of inputs within the industry to be bid up. As costs of production rise, short-run supply curves (each firm's marginal cost curve) shift inwards to the left. The result

Figure 22.9

Constant-, Increasing-, and Decreasing-cost Industries. In panel (a), we show a situation where the demand curve shifts from *DD* to *D′D′*. Price increases from P_e to P'_e; however, in time the supply curve shifts out to *S′S′*, and the new equilibrium shifts from *E* to *E″*. The market-clearing price is, again, P_e. If we connect points such as *E* and *E″*, we come up with the long-run supply curve S_LS_L. This is a constant-cost industry. In panel (b), costs are increasing for the industry, and therefore the long-run supply curve is upward sloping; in panel (c), costs are decreasing for the industry as it expands, and therefore the long-run supply curve is downward sloping.

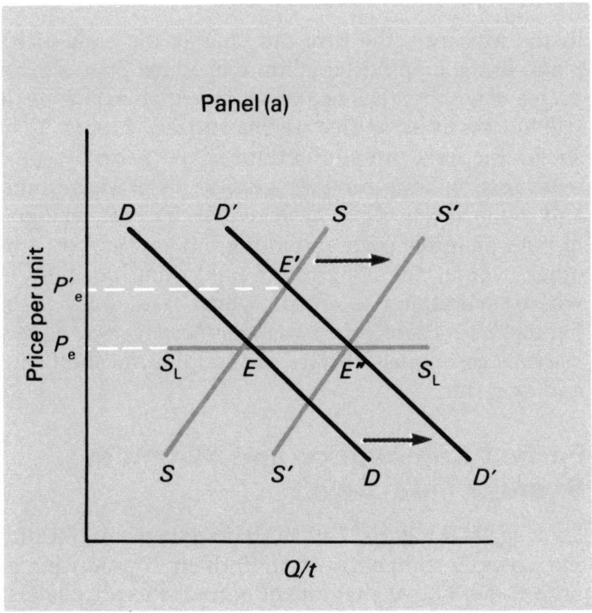

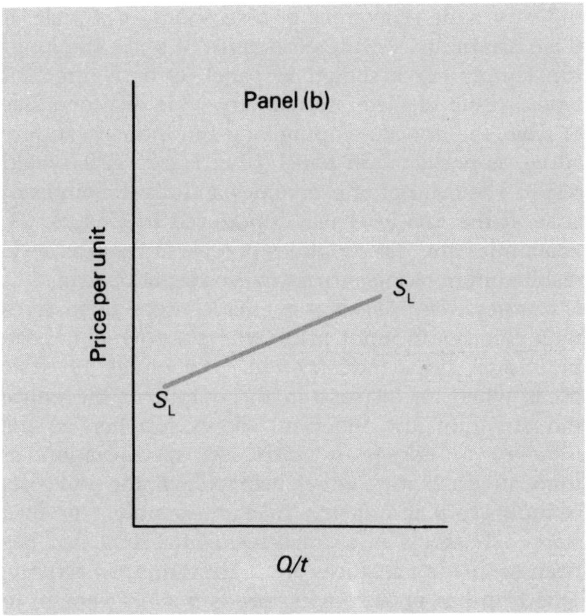

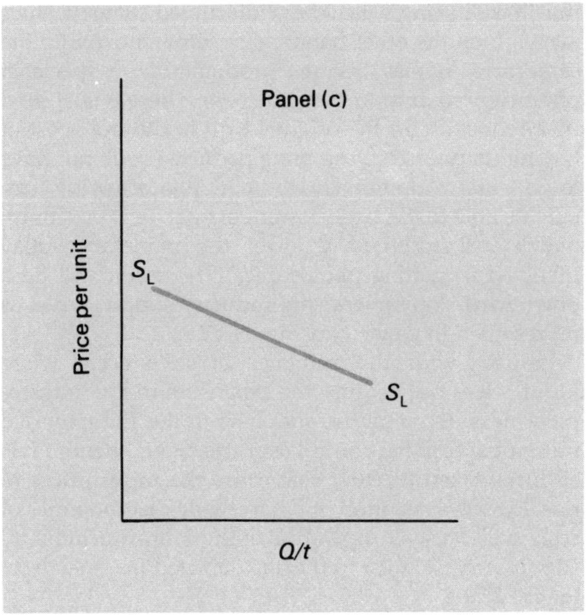

is a long-run industry supply curve that is upward-sloping and is represented by $S_L S_L$ in panel (b) of Figure 22.9.

Decreasing-cost Industries

It is possible that an expansion in the number of firms in an industry leads to a reduction in input costs. When this occurs, the long-run industry supply curve will be downward-sloping. An example is given in panel (c) of Figure 22.9. This is a **decreasing-cost industry**.

Industry-wide Economies and Diseconomies of Scale

An industry can be other than constant-cost if there are industry-wide economies or diseconomies of scale. If there are industry-wide economies of scale, the long-run supply curve shown in panel (c) of Figure 22.9 would result. If there are industry-wide diseconomies of scale, the upward-sloping long-run industry supply curve, as presented in panel (b) of Figure 22.9, would result. The concept of economies and diseconomies of scale at the *firm* level was introduced in Chapter 21. Economies and diseconomies of scale at the firm level resulted from factors *internal* to each separate firm.

Industry-wide economies of scale concern themselves with changes in input prices that are *external* to each individual firm. Industry-wide economies of scale occur when an increase in the output of the entire industry (not just one firm) allows suppliers to the industry to engage in increased specialization or innovative activities, which help to lower the unit costs of inputs to that industry. Take an example. One firm starts a business in a small residential area that has been set aside for offices and light industrial activity. This firm has photocopying needs but not enough to justify the purchase of its own equipment. The firm must take its originals to be photocopied some distance away. If, on the other hand, many firms move into the same area, it may become profitable for a specialist photocopying firm to start business. There will at least be a reduction for the original firm in the time cost of having its photocopying done because it will not have to go so far. Additionally, the new photocopying firm may be able to use large, lower-cost-per-unit machines, which will additionally lower the monetary outlay involved in getting photocopies. The result will be a downward-sloping long-run industry supply curve, as represented in panel (c) of Figure 22.9.

Industry-wide diseconomies of scale occur when input prices rise because the expansion in the industry puts pressure on all the suppliers to the industry. No individual firm has control over this phenomenon. It is all firms taken together that cause the input prices to rise. In such a situation, industry-wide diseconomies of scale will cause an upward-sloping long-run industry supply curve, similar to the one depicted in panel (b) of Figure 22.9.

Long-run Industry Response: What if Demand is Declining or Increasing?

One of the reasons we attempt to develop a model of a market structure is to predict what will happen when there are changes in the economy. Figure 22.9 can be used to predict what will happen when there are changes in a perfectly competitive industry.

In the case of increasing demand, we first need to determine whether we are dealing with a constant-, increasing-, or decreasing-cost industry. Once we have determined that, we can then tell what will happen to price as industry demand increases. The simplest case is when we are dealing with a constant-cost perfectly competitive industry. This situation is, in fact, depicted in panel (a) of Figure 22.9. An increase in industry demand leads to a larger output being sold in the long run at a constant price, P_e. If, however, we are dealing with an increasing-cost industry, increasing demand will, in the long run lead to increased production and also an increased price. Finally, if we are dealing with a decreasing-cost industry, in the long run, an increase in demand will lead to an increase in output and a *decrease* in price.

Our predictions can be made in a similar fashion if we are dealing with a declining, perfectly competitive industry – one in which market demand is falling. If we are dealing with a constant-cost perfectly competitive industry, then in the long run, output will be reduced but price will remain constant at P_e as in panel (a) of Figure 22.9. If we are dealing with an increasing-cost industry, a decline in industry demand will eventually lead to a reduction in output and a *reduction* in price. And, finally, if we are dealing with a decreasing-cost industry, a reduction in market demand will lead to a long-run reduction in output and an *increase* in price.

The Perfectly Competitive Firm in Long-run Equilibrium

In the long run, the firm can change the scale of its plant. In the long run, the firm will adjust plant size in such a way that it has no further incentive to change. It will do so until profits are maximized. Figure 22.10 shows the long-run equilibrium of the perfectly competitive firm. Long-run average costs are at a minimum and so too are short-run average costs. Price is set equal to both marginal costs and minimum average costs. In other words, the long-run equilibrium position is where 'everything is equal', which is at point E in Figure 22.10. There, *price* equals *marginal revenue* equals *marginal cost* equals *average cost* (minimum, short run, and long run).

Perfect Competition and Minimum Average Total Cost

Look again at Figure 22.10. In the long-run equilibrium, the perfectly competitive firm finds itself producing at output rate Q_e. At that rate of output, the price is just

Figure 22.10

Long-run Firm Competitive Equilibrium. In the long run, the firm operates where price equals marginal revenue equals marginal cost equals short-run minimum average cost equals long-run minimum average cost, or, where 'everything is equal'. This is given at point *E*.

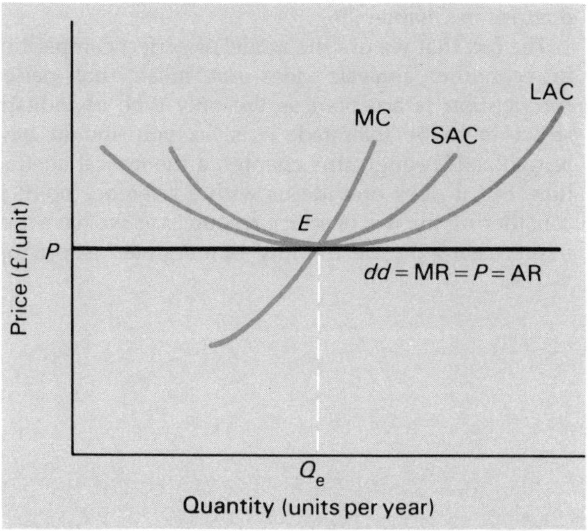

equal to the minimum long-run average cost as well as the minimum short-run average cost. In this sense, perfect competition results in no 'waste' in the production system. Goods and services are produced using the least costly combination of resources. This is an important attribute of a perfectly competitive long-run equilibrium, particularly when we wish to compare the market structure of perfect competition with other market structures that are less than perfectly competitive. We examine these other market structures in Chapters 23 and 24.

Competitive Pricing Equals Marginal Cost Pricing

In a perfectly competitive industry, each firm produces where its marginal cost curve intersects its marginal revenue (or *dd*) curve from below. Thus, perfectly competitive firms always sell their goods at a price that just equals marginal cost. For many economists, this represents a 'desirable' pricing situation because the price that consumers pay just reflects the opportunity cost to society of producing the good. In order to understand this, consider what marginal cost represents. It represents the cost of changing production by one incremental unit. Suppose a marginal cost curve shows that an increase in production from 10 000 leather handbags to 10 001 leather handbags will cost £1.50. That £1.50 represents the *opportunity cost* to society of producing one more leather handbag. Thus, the marginal cost curve gives a graphic representation of the opportunity cost of production.

The competitive firm produces up to the point where the market price just equals the marginal cost. Herein lies the element of the 'desirability' of a competitive solution. It is called **marginal cost pricing**. The competitive firm sells its product at a price that just equals the cost to society – that is, the opportunity cost – for that is what the marginal cost curve represents.

When an individual pays a price equal to the marginal cost of production, then the cost to the user of that product is equal to the scarifice or cost to society of producing that quantity of that good as opposed to more of some other good. (We are assuming that *all marginal social* costs are accounted for.) The competitive solution, then, is called *efficient*. It is efficient in the economic sense of the word. Economic efficiency means that it is impossible to increase the output of any good without lowering the total *value* of the output produced in the economy. No juggling of resources, such as labour and capital, will result in an output that is higher in value than the value of the goods and services already being produced. In an efficient situation, it is impossible to make one person better off without making someone else worse off. All resources are used in the most advantageous way possible. All goods and services are sold at their opportunity cost, and marginal cost pricing prevails throughout.

Is Perfect Competition Possible?

The analytic model presented here represents a situation that, by definition, can never be seen in reality. Perfect competition can exist only if information is also perfect. After all, the only way for a price to be uniform at every moment in time (corrected for quality changes and transportation costs) is for everybody to know what is happening everywhere at every moment in time. Obviously information is never perfect. In fact, the cost of trying to achieve perfect information would be prohibitive and therefore undesirable.

A profit-maximizing firm will produce at the point where the additional revenues obtained from producing more goods exactly cover the additional costs incurred (where marginal revenue equals marginal cost). Similarly, if we are concerned to maximize the state of market information we would never spend more than we get in return for improving information flows. We would improve information in the marketplace only up to the point where the value of doing so is equal to the marginal cost. That is certainly at a point well below *perfect* information.

A purely competitive industry has been defined as one with many sellers. To satisfy the criterion of perfect competition where each seller has *no* control whatsoever over the price of his or her product, we would have to have a tremendous number of firms. Free entry into an industry would have to be possible and firms operating with constant returns to scale production functions. However, in the real world we quickly observe that the number of firms is not large and therefore individually each firm has – at least in the short run – some control over its price. But analysing the industry in the long run, we might say that it was *tending* towards a competitive solution all the time because there were a sufficient number of firms *on the margin* attempting to increase their total sales by undercutting the other firms. Notice we said that the industry might tend towards a competitive solution at all times. That is a *dynamic* process – which is to say that it operates through time and never ends. At any time, an investigation of the particular industry would reveal that the industry was tending towards a competitive solution, but the industry would probably never reach that point.

Even if an industry is not perfectly competitive, it does not necessarily follow that steps should be taken to make it more competitive so as to ensure efficiency. After all, it is not possible to change an industry's structure from non-competitive to competitive without using resources. We will discuss some of the ways of doing this, such as legislation against restrictive business practices and regulation of non-competitive industries in Chapter 29.

The fact that we use the model of perfect competition in economic analysis does not mean that perfect competition is accepted as the only type of industry structure to be tolerated. It is, as you should have recognized through this chapter, a theoretical abstraction. But it does provide us with a reference point in considering the use of scarce resources as we have seen in discussing the 'desirability' of marginal cost pricing.

Key Points 22.3

- **The competitive price is determined by the intersection of the market demand curve with the market supply curve; the market supply curve is equal to the horizontal summation of those sections of the individual marginal cost curves above their respective minimum average variable costs.**
- **In the long run, competitive firms make zero economic profits because of entry and exit firms into and out of the industry whenever there are industry-wide economic profits or economic losses.**
- **Economic profits and losses are signals to resource owners.**
- **A constant-cost industry will have a horizontal long-run supply curve. An increasing-cost industry will have a rising long-run supply curve. A decreasing-cost industry will have a falling long-run supply curve.**
- **In the long run, a competitive firm produces where price equals marginal revenue equals marginal cost equals short-run minimum average cost equals long-run minimum average cost.**
- **Competitive pricing is essentially marginal cost pricing, and therefore the competitive solution is called efficient because marginal cost represents the social opportunity cost of producing one more unit of a good; when consumers are faced with a price equal to the full opportunity cost of the product they are buying, their purchasing decisions will lead to an efficient use of available resources.**

CASE STUDY

Lead Astray

The Snailbeach Company worked a vein of ore in West Shropshire which was once described as being one of the most productive in Europe per acre of ground. The company first took its lease on the vein in 1783 and continued to work it without interruption until 1912. It illustrates how a firm, working in a perfect market, responded to external and internal factors in an industry traditionally unstable and noted for its high-risk element. Before analysing the behaviour of the firm it is worth while to outline the essential feature of lead-mining which made for a perfect market.

Firstly, there were a large number of firms which ranged from fairly large joint-stock companies operating in Cornwall and Wales, to small partnerships of miners operating in all regions, and the further back in time one went, the smaller and more numerous became the firms. In the early years of the eighteenth century most mines worked were in effect little more than shallow holes in the ground. Enterprises of this kind were active in all the major lead-producing areas of the country – Derbyshire, the Mendips, the North Pennines, North Wales, and West Shropshire. Similar partnerships had worked tin in Cornwall from earliest times. The produce of the mines, in the form of concentrated ore, was sold at markets which were held at regular intervals in a wide number of centres. The normal method of sale was for the company or partnership to put a small sample of their ore into the market, and having inspected it buyers would then make offers for the complete lot. The price of the lead was, therefore, determined by 'the market' thus satisfying the second condition of perfect competition in that the firm had no control over the price at which its produce was sold. In times of scarcity the price of lead was high, and in times of surplus, or of demand deficiency, it fell. In consequence the price of lead exerted an enormous influence over the whole structure of the industry, determining profits, wages, and the opening up and closing down of marginal enterprises. This perfect market for lead was the framework within which the British lead-mining industry worked throughout the eighteenth and nineteenth centuries.

At the end of the Napoleonic Wars the Snailbeach Company was in a sound position. The general price increases which had occurred during that time prompted increased output which was sold at prices averaging around £12 per ton. Prices fell slightly after the wars but the continuation of industrialization and urbanization maintained a bouyant market for lead throughout the country although short price recessions accounted for many casualities among the more marginal enterprises. From the records it appears that the Snailbeach company was looking for a profit of around £2 per ton of ore, and if the price of lead increased it increased output accordingly, at the same time increasing wages. If the price of lead fell it reduced output and reduced wages.

By the 1860s improved mining techniques allowed increased output from fewer workers and profits began to rise. At the same time large deposits of lead were beginning to be exploited in Australia, Mexico, and North America, and were paying handsome returns to their shareholders. Demand also increased to such an extent that, in the early 1860s a shortage of ore occurred. These conditions were highly conducive to creating a major boom in this country and one of the results was the setting up of many 'bubble' companies, several of which worked the West Shropshire orefield. The Snailbeach Company itself was reconstituted in 1867 as a joint-stock company, though it did not become public. By the middle of the 1870s there were over fifteen companies working this orefield.

As mining techniques had improved during the eighteenth century the presence of the small partnership became less and less practical since only larger enterprises organized as joint-stock companies had sufficient funds to pay for the equipping of mines with steam-engines for drainage and crushing of ores, and to expend large sums of money on such things as sinking shafts and driving drainage adits, none of which paid immediate returns. But although the companies needed to raise large sums of money for working

Figure 22.11

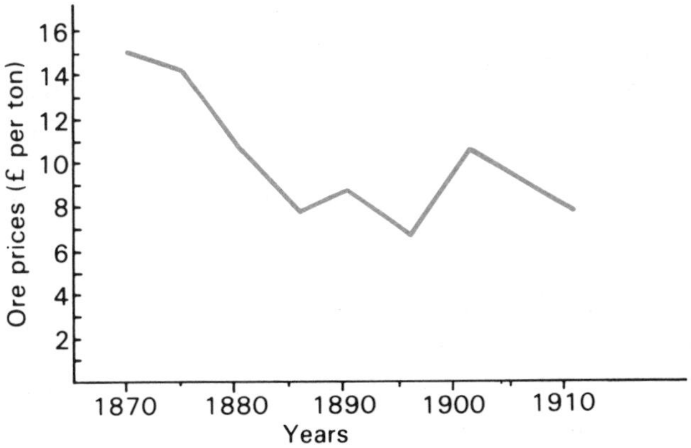

the mines, they did not create assets of an equal sum, since most of the money was spent on labour costs in making wider, deeper, and longer holes in the ground. Only a small proportion of the total capital involved in floating the company actually created physical assets – usually at the surface and consisting of pumping-engines and crushing-plant together with their housing buildings. The fixed costs of the company were very small, whereas the variable costs were high. Most of the mining companies purchased machinery either out of revenue or by drawing on capital and did not set aside sums for depreciation. Therefore, when looking for a fixed cost element which, in the long run, determined shut-down if total costs exceeded total revenue, one is hard pressed to find one. There was one cost, however, which could be regarded as fixed, and this was the cost of keeping the mine dry. If pumping stopped the mine flooded, and so we shall regard pumping costs as the main fixed cost even though it consisted of expenditure on fuels and labour.

After 1870 prices plummeted (see Figure 23.11) and by 1895 were hitting a low floor of around £7 per ton, by which time all the West Shropshire mines, with the sole exception of Snailbeach, had closed. The reason for the falling price of lead is generally held to be the increased supply into world markets from overseas sources, the success of which had originally started the boom. With falling prices it was impossible for the majority of mines to stay profitable. The reaction of the company to the falling prices is interesting in that it chose to maintain average profit rather than total profits. With falling prices it abandoned the working of all but the most productive parts of the vein where ore could still be worked at a profit. In doing this the Snailbeach Company stood out in sharp contrast to most other mining enterprises, since the normal reaction, given falling prices, was to increase output in order to maintain total revenue. However, this action, taken independently by all companies, produced in aggregate an even greater supply which depressed the price still further and forced the mines into a position of regular losses and, inevitably, closure.

The Snailbeach Company did not cease production until 1912. By 1910 the shareholders were unwilling to spend any more money with little or no chance of profits and so in 1911 the giant Cornish engine, which had kept the mines dry was stopped and the mine allowed to flood to adit level.

Source: F. Brook, 'Perfect Competition in the Lead Mining Industry – a Nineteenth-Century Case-Study', *Economics* (Journal of the Economics Association), Vol. VIII, Pt 5, no. 35, Autumn 1970, pp. 245–55.

Questions

1. Show by means of supply and demand diagram how the price of one changed in the latter part of the nineteenth century. Assume that the depression in the UK economy was reflected in the demand for lead.
2 What type of cost is critical to determining the close-down of a firm? In the case of the Snailbeach Company what is unusual about determining this cost?
3. Why would joint-stock mining firms wish to increase output as ore prices fell after 1870?
4. If the Snailbeach Company tried to maintain average profit rather than total profits how would this be shown with reference to a diagram? (Hint: the reference to average should point you towards considering average revenue and average cost.)
5 The company ceased to continue mining lead in 1912. What factors explain this situation?

Exam Preparation

MULTIPLE CHOICE QUESTIONS

1. A perfectly competitive firm finds itself in the following position:

Quantity sold	Total revenue (£)	Average variable cost (£)	Total fixed cost (£)
100	1 000	10	200

Given that the average variable cost is at its minimum the firm should

A raise its output level
B reduce its output level
C introduce an advertising campaign
D raise its selling price
E leave the industry.

2. The demand curve for the product of a firm operating under conditions of perfect competition

A is identical to the marginal revenue curve
B intersects the marginal revenue curve at the point where its marginal costs are equal to marginal revenue
C intersects the average variable cost curve at its lowest point
D is of varying elasticities in different price ranges
E is perfectly inelastic.

3.

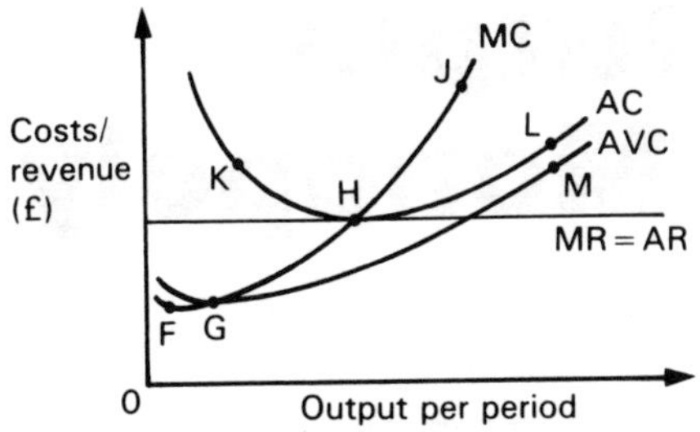

The diagram illustrates a firm operating under conditions of perfect competition. In the *short run*, the quantity of output which the firm will supply to the market at various prices is shown by the

A marginal cost curve between points H and J
B marginal cost curve between points G and J
C marginal cost curve between points F and J
D average cost curve between points K and L
E average variable cost curve between points G and M.

For Questions 4, 5, and 6 select your answers from the following grid:

A	B	C	D	E
1, 2, 3, all correct	1, 2 only correct	2, 3 only correct	1 only correct	3 only correct

4. For a firm in a long-run equilibrium position in a perfectly competitive market, the marginal cost will always be equal to the
1 market price
2 average cost at that output
3 average revenue at that output.

5. It is assumed that in a perfectly competitive market
1 the demand for each firm's product is perfectly inelastic
2 all firms produce an identical product
3 all buyers and sellers have perfect knowledge of market conditions.

6.

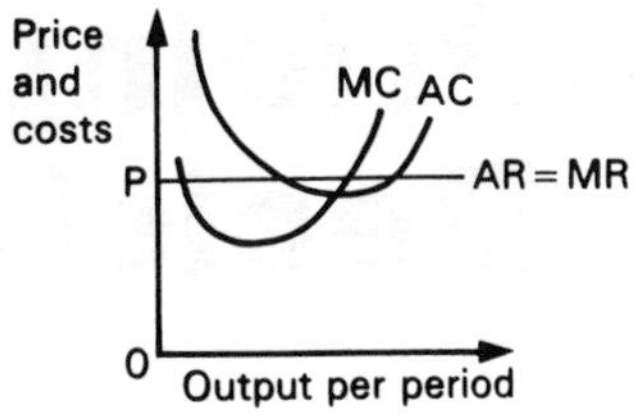

The diagram refers to a firm operating under conditions of perfect competition. Which of the following features, shown or implicit in the diagram is (are) *not* sustainable in the long run?
1 A price of OP
2 Supernormal profit
3 MR identical to AR.

RELATED ESSAY QUESTIONS

1. Construct and explain the supply curve for a perfectly competitive industry in both the short run and the long run.

2. Define, concisely, total, average, and marginal costs. Explain the relationships between the three types of cost. Should a firm cease production if it cannot cover its average costs?

3. (a) Distinguish between the short run and the long run in the theory of the firm.
(b) Explain how (i) the law of diminishing returns and (ii) diseconomies of scale affect the production costs of a firm in these two time-periods.

4. (a) Explain the meaning of the terms 'short run' and 'long run' in the theory of supply.
(b) Consider how a perfectly competitive industry might react to an increase in demand in the short run and the long run.
(c) Why is it argued that in certain circumstances an increase in demand may result in a lower long-run price in a perfectly competitive industry.

23 Pricing and Output Decisions in Monopoly

Key Points to Review

- Total revenue and elasticity (7.2)
- Perfectly elastic demand (7.3)
- The long run (21.4)
- Perfect competition (22.1)

Questions for Preview

1 **What is a monopolist, and how can a monopoly be formed?**

2 **For the monopolist, marginal revenue is less than selling price. Why?**

3 **What is the profit-maximizing rate of output for the monopolist?**

4 **What is the cost to society of monopoly?**

The world, of course, does not consist of *perfectly* competitive industries. In this chapter, we will present a model of a monopoly business and discuss how a monopolist decides what prices to charge and how much to produce. Most of the analytical tools needed here have already been introduced. In the Case Study we will look at the British plasterboard industry where a monopoly situation is now under attack.

Definition of a Monopolist

The word *monopoly or monopolist* probably brings to mind a business that takes undue advantage of the consumer, sells faulty products, gets rich, and any other bad thoughts that one can have about big business. If we are to succeed in analysing and predicting the behaviour of non-competitive firms, however, we will have to be somewhat more objective in defining a monopolist. Our definition of monopoly is one that will be as applicable to small businesses as it is to companies selling on a nation-wide basis. Thus, a **monopolist** is defined as a *single supplier* that constitutes the entire industry.

We must be careful in our definition of monopoly, for the more narrowly we define a product, the more easily we come up with a monopoly situation. Consider a small town with a single newspaper. By our definition of monopoly, the owner of the newspaper is a monopolist. He or she sells the only newspaper printed in the locality. What if we consider this product – the only local newspaper – as part of the news media industry? Do the owners of this newspaper have a monopoly in all news media? Certainly not, for they are in competition with radio, television, magazines, newspapers from nearby towns, as well as national newspapers. Thus the uniqueness about the monopolist is indeed one of degree and few monopolists are likely to face no competition at all.

As we shall see in this chapter, a seller prefers to have a monopoly rather than to face competition. In general, we think of monopoly prices as being higher than competitive prices, and of monopoly profits as being higher than competitive profits (which are, in the long run, merely equivalent to a normal rate of return). How does a firm obtain a monopoly in an industry? Basically, there must be **barriers to entry** that enable firms to receive monopoly profits in the long run. We define barriers to entry as those difficulties facing potential new competitors in an industry. What sort of difficulties might a new competitor face?

Barriers to Entry

For monopoly power to continue to exist in the long run, there has to be some way in which the market is closed to entry. Either legal means or certain aspects of the industry's technical or cost structure must somehow prevent entry. Below, we will discuss several of the barriers to entry that have allowed firms to reap monopoly profits in the long run.

Ownership of Resources without Close Substitutes

Preventing a newcomer from entering an industry is often difficult. Indeed, there are some economists who contend that no monopoly acting without government support has been able to prevent entry into the industry unless that monopoly has had the control of some 'essential' natural resource. Consider the possibility of one firm owning the entire supply of a raw material input that is essential to the production of a particular commodity. The exclusive ownership of such a vital resource serves as a barrier to entry until an alternative source of the raw material is found or an alternative technology not requiring the raw material in question is developed. A good example of control over a vital input is the Aluminium Company of America (Alcoa), a firm that prior to the Second World War controlled the world's bauxite, the essential raw material in the production of aluminium. (Such a situation is rare, though.)

Government Restrictions – Licences

In many industries it is illegal to enter without a licence provided by the government. For example, in the UK you could not operate an unlicensed postal service or radio service. In the US you cannot simply set up in business and supply electricity in competition with the existing supplier in an area. You would first have to obtain a 'certificate of convenience and public necessity' from the appropriate authority, which is usually the state's public utility commission. However, public utility commissions rarely, if ever, issue a certificate to a group of investors who want to compete directly in the same geographic area with an existing electric utility; hence, entry into the industry in a particular geographic area is prohibited, and long-run monopoly profits could conceivably be earned by the electric utility already serving the area.

It is necessary to obtain the equivalent of a certificate of convenience and public necessity in the case of the regional independent television service in the UK. The Independent Broadcasting Authority allots franchises and successful applicants to receive monopoly rights to the sale of TV advertising space in their areas for eight years. Since these franchises or licences are not granted very often, long-run monopoly profits can be earned by those firms already in the industry. Historically, TV franchises have been very profitable to own. One franchise-holder described it as 'a licence to print money'!

Another example of a licence that creates a monopoly has to do with taxi-cabs. In many major cities, it is illegal to operate a taxi-cab without first having obtained a permit to do so.

Patents

Closely related to the franchise required for entry is a patent. A patent is issued to an inventor to protect him or her from having the invention copied for a period of years. At the end of the patent period the patented invention is no longer private property but public property which anyone can copy or reproduce. Patents were first enacted in the UK as long ago as 1623 so as to encourage the process of invention by giving short-term reward for promoting scientific discovery. As one would expect patent owners jealously guard their interests and try to enforce their exclusive rights. If, in fact, the cost of enforcing a particular patent are greater than the benefits, the patent may not bestow any monopoly profits on its owner – the policing costs are then too high.

Problem in Raising Adequate Capital

Certain industries require a large initial capital investment. The firms already in the industry can, according to some economists, obtain monopoly profits in the long run because no competitors can raise the large amount of capital needed to enter the industry. This is the 'imperfect' capital market argument employed to explain long-run, relatively high rates of return in certain industries. These industries generally are ones in which large fixed costs must be incurred in order merely to start production. Their fixed costs generally are for expensive machines necessary in the production process.

Certainly, it is more difficult, at any given level of risk, to raise a larger rather than a smaller amount of capital. But a sufficiently high-risk premium can presumably be added to the anticipated rate of return from investing in the risky industry to enable a newcomer to raise the needed capital. It may be, of course, that the anticipated rate of return offered to investors in such an industry would have to be so high that it would not be profitable for an entrepreneur to undertake entry into the industry. It is not clear why such a situation is called an imperfect capital market or why it should be considered a barrier to entry any more than any other high-risk premium, but it often is.

Economies of Scale

Sometimes it is not profitable for more than one firm to exist in an industry. Such a situation may arise because of a phenomenon we have already discussed known as economies of scale. When economies of scale exist, costs increase less than proportionately to the increase

Key Points 23.1

- **A monopolist is defined as a single seller of a product or a good for which there are no close substitutes.**
- **In order to maintain a monopoly there must be barriers to entry. Barriers to entry include ownership of resources without close substitutes, large capital requirements in order to enter the industry, legally required licences, franchises, and certificates of convenience, patents, and economies of scale.**

in output. If the long-run average cost curve continues to fall as output increases then a situation of *natural monopoly* might arise. The first firm that is established is able to enjoy very low average costs per unit. If it charges a price that reflects this favourable cost situation then no rival firm can threaten its position. It is sure not to be undercut and thus is assured of being a monopolist. We examine the natural monopoly case further in Chapter 28 and how governments face up to the questions of whether such monopolies should be privately owned and left free to fix prices as the monopolists see fit. We must now examine how a monopolist determines how much output to produce and what price to charge, assuming, as in Chapter 22, that the aim is to maximize profits. (But first read Key Points 23.1.)

The Demand Curve Facing a Monopolist

How does a monopolist determine how much to produce? To answer this question let us briefly recap on the situation for the firm in perfect competition. You will recall that a competitive firm has a horizontal demand curve. That is, the competitive firm is such a small part of the market that it cannot influence the price of its product. It is a *price-taker*. Each time production is changed by one unit, total revenue changes by the going price, and price is always the same. Marginal revenue never changes: it always equals price, or average revenue. Average revenue is total revenue divided by quantity demanded, or:

$$\text{average revenue} = \frac{\text{TR}}{Q} = \frac{P \times Q}{Q} = P$$

Monopolists' Marginal Revenue

What about a monopoly firm? Since a monopoly is the entire industry, the monopoly firm faces the entire market demand curve. The market demand curve is downward sloping, just like the others that we have seen. Therefore, in order to sell more of a particular product given the industry demand curve, the monopoloy firm must lower the price. Thus,, the monopoly firm moves *down* the demand curve. If all buyers are to be charged the same price, the monopoly must lower the price on all units sold in order to sell more. It cannot just lower the price on the last unit sold in any given time-period in order to sell a larger quantity.

Imagine that you are a monopoly ferry-boat owner. Assume that you have a government-granted legal franchise, and no one else can compete with you in operating a service ferry between two islands. If you are charging, say £1 per crossing, there will be a certain quantity demanded of your services. Suppose that you are ferrying 100 people per day each way at that price. If you decide that you would like to ferry more individuals, you must lower your price to all individuals – you must move *down* the existing demand curve for ferrying services. In order to calculate the marginal revenue of your change in price, you must first calculate the total revenues you received at £1 per passenger per crossing, and then calculate the total revenues you would receive at, say, 90p per passenger per crossing.

The only way the monopolist can increase sales is by getting consumers to spend more of their incomes on the monopolist's product and less on all other products combined. Thus, the monopolist is constrained by the entire market demand curve for its product. We see this in Figure 23.1 which compares the perfect competitor's and monopolist's demand curves.

Here we see the fundamental difference between the monopolist and the firm in perfect competition. The latter does not have to worry about lowering prices to sell more. In a purely competitive situation, the competitive firm sells such a small part of the market that it can sell its entire output, whatever that may be, at the same price. The monopolist cannot. The more the monopolist wants to sell, the lower the price it has to charge on the last unit (and on *all* units put on the market for sale). Obviously, the extra revenues the monopolist receives from selling one more unit are going to be smaller than the extra revenues received from selling the next-to-last unit. The monopolist has to lower the price on the last unit to sell it because it is facing a downward-sloping demand curve. The only way to move down the demand curve is to lower the price.

Figure 23.1

Comparison of the Perfect Competitor's and the Monopolist's Demand Curves. The perfect competitor faces a horizontal demand curve *dd* in panel (a). The monopolist faces the entire industry demand curve in panel (b), and it is downward sloping.

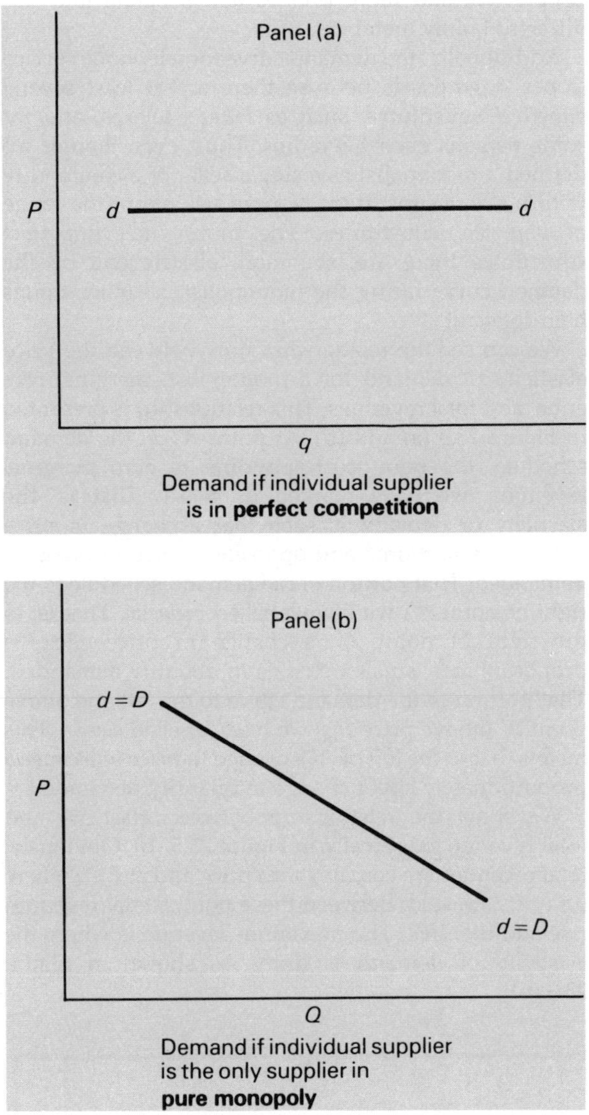

The monopolist's marginal revenue therefore is going to be falling. But it falls even more than one might think, because to sell one more unit the monopolist has to lower the price on *all* previous units, not just on the last unit produced and sold. This is because information flows freely; the monopolist will not usually be able to charge one consumer £2 and another consumer £3 on the same item. The consumer who could buy the product for £2 would buy lots of it and resell it to the one who was willing to pay £3 for a price of, say, £2.50. Unless the monopolist is successful in somehow separating *discriminating* between the different markets to prevent secondary transactions among the consumers in those markets, it will have to sell all goods at a uniform price. (We examine this possibility of discriminatory pricing later in the chapter but for the moment we assume a common price is charged to all buyers.) Therefore, when a monopolist increases production, he must charge a lower price on the last unit *and on all previous units.*

The Monopolist's Marginal Revenue is less than Price

An essential point in the above discussion is that for the monopolist marginal revenue is always less than price. To understand why, look at Figure 23.2. Here we show a unit increase in sales due to a reduction in price of, say, handbags from P_1 to P_2. After all, the only way that sales can increase, given a downward-sloping demand curve, is for price to fall. The price P_2 is the price received for the last unit. Thus, that price P_2 times the last unit sold represents what is received from the last unit sold. That would be equal to the horizontally shaded column showing the effects of a one-unit increase in sales. The area of the horizontally shaded column is one unit wide times P_2.

Figure 23.2

Marginal Revenue is always Less than Price. The only way to sell one more unit when facing a downward-sloping demand curve is to lower the price. The price received for the last unit is equal to P_2. The revenues received from selling this last unit are equal to P_2 times one unit, or the area of the horizontally shaded vertical column. However, if a single price is being charged for all units, total revenues do not go up by the amount of the area represented by that column. The price has to be reduced on all the previous OQ units that were being sold at price P_1. Thus, we must subtract the vertically lined area [the rectangle ($P_1 - P_2$) high and OQ wide] from the horizontally lined area in order to derive marginal revenue. Marginal revenue is therefore always less than price.

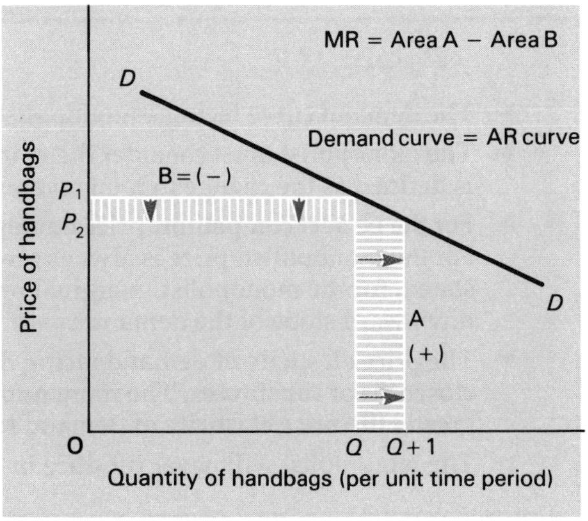

But the price times the last unit sold is not the addition of total revenues received from selling that last unit. Why? Because price was reduced on all previous units sold (*OQ*) in order to sell the larger quantity Q + 1. The reduction in price is represented by the vertical distance from P_1 to P_2 on the vertical axis. We must therefore subtract the vertically gridded row from the horizontally shaded column in order to come up with the *change* in total revenues due to a one-unit increase in sales. Clearly, the change in total revenues, i.e. marginal revenue, must be less than price, because marginal revenue is always the difference btween the two shaded areas in Figure 23.2.

Elasticity and Total Revenues

The monopolist faces a downward-sloping demand curve. That means that it cannot charge just *any* price (a common misconception) because, depending on the price charged, a different quantity will be demanded. In other words, there is a unique relationship between the price the monopolist charges and total revenues, which equal price times quantity. Thus, there is a relationship between the total revenues and the price elasticity of the demand curve. We have already discussed this relationship, but it is worth going over again briefly. The demand curve of a monopolist has varying elasticities, depending on where we are on the demand curve. Remember that a straight-line demand curve has a price elasticity of demand that goes from infinity to zero as we move down the demand curve. (Thus, it is *not* true that a monopolist faces an inelastic demand curve.)

We earlier defined a monopolist as the single seller of a specific good or service with no *close* substitutes. That does not mean, however, that the demand curve facing a monopoly is vertical, or exhibits zero-price elasticity of demand. (Indeed, as we shall see below, the profit-maximizing monopolist will *never* operate in a price range in which demand is inelastic.) After all, consumers have limited incomes and alternative wants. The downward slope of a monopolist's demand curve occurs because individuals compare the marginal satisfaction they will receive to the cost of the commodity to be purchased. Take the example of the telephone service. Assume that there is absolutely no substitute whatsoever for telephone service. The market demand curve will still slope downwards. At lower prices, people will add more phones and separate lines for different family members.

Additionally, the demand curve for telephone service slopes downwards because there are at least several *imperfect* substitutes, such as letters, telexes, and for some persons even CB radios. Thus, even though we defined a monopolist as a single seller of a commodity with no *close* substitutes, we can talk about the range of *imperfect* substitutes. The more such imperfect substitutes there are, the more elastric will be the demand curve facing the monopolist, all other things held constant.

We can see the relationship now between the price elasticity of demand for a monopolist, marginal revenue, and total revenues. This relationship is presented in Figure 23.3 (a) and (b). At point A' on the demand schedule, the point corresponding to zero marginal revenues, we have marked $e_d = -1$. That is, the elasticity of demand is such that a change in price elicits a proportional and opposite change in quantity demanded. That portion of the demand schedule to the right of point A', we have labelled *inelastic*. That is, to the right of point A', a change in price elicits a proportionately smaller change in quantity demanded. That portion of the demand curve to the left and above point A' (above price P_m) we have labelled *elastic*. This means that to the left of A' a change in price will cause a proportionately larger change in quantity demanded.

We show the relationship between elasticity and total revenue graphically in Figure 23.5 (b). Obviously, total revenues are zero at a zero price and at P_{max} where no units are sold. Between these points, total revenues rise and then fall. The maximum revenue is where the elasticity of demand is unity, as shown in Figure 23.3 (b).

Key Points 23.2

- **The demand curve facing a monopolist is downward sloping by definition.**
- **The monopolist must consider the marginal revenue curve, where marginal revenue is defined as the change in total revenues due to a one-unit change in quantity sold.**
- **For the perfect competitor, price equals marginal revenue equals average revenue. For the monopolist, price is always greater than marginal revenue. Otherwise stated, for the monopolist, marginal revenue is always less than price because of the downward slope of the demand curve.**
- **The price elasticity of demand facing the monopolist depends on the number and closeness of substitutes. The more numerous and the closer the substitutes, the greater the price elasticity of demand for the monopolist's demand curve.**
- **The monopolist will never produce in the inelastic portion of its demand curve.**

Figure 23.3 (a)

Elasticity of Demand and Total Revenues. Here we show the relationship between marginal revenue, the demand curve, and the elasticity of demand. From the point where marginal revenue equals zero – that is, point *A′* – demand is inelastic to the right and below, and elastic to the left and above. At point *A′*, demand has unitary elasticity, or equals −1. To the right, the monopolist would find that if it lowered price, the quantity demanded would increase less than proportionally. To the left of *A′* as it raised price, the quantity demanded would fall more than proportionally.

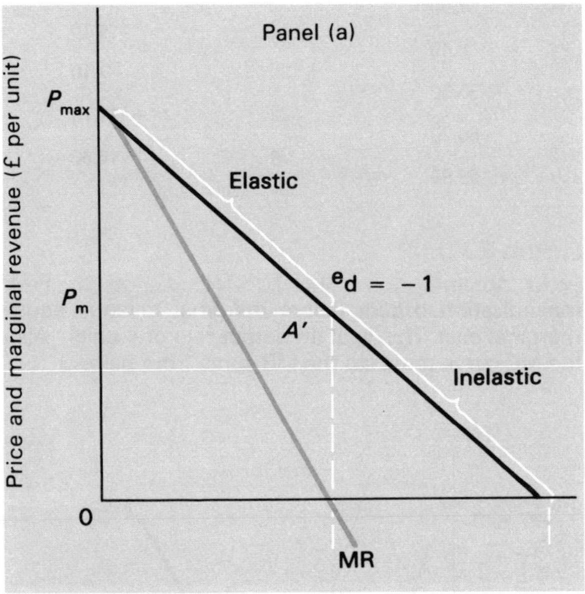

Figure 23.3 (b)

Total Revenues and the Demand Curve. Here we show the relationship between the demand curve, elasticity of demand, and total revenue. When the price is set at P_{max} in Figure 23.3 (a), the total revenues are, of course, zero. When the price is set at zero, total revenues are also zero. In between these two ends of the price possibilities scale, we will find some price that maximizes total revenues. That price happens to be where marginal revenue equals zero, or at point *A′* in Figure 23.3 (a). We have shown here that the maximum occurs at the output at which marginal revenue equals zero. If the monopolist had no variable costs at all, it would obviously want to produce at point A because that is where it would maximize its total revenues, which under *that* condition would maximize total profits.

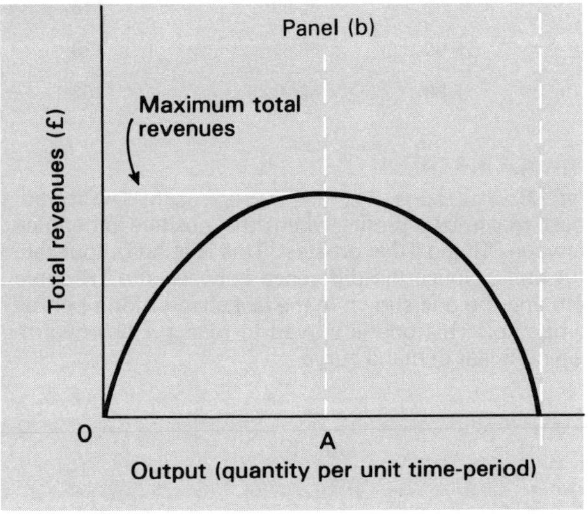

Costs and Monopoly Profit Maximization

In order to find out at what rate of output the perfect competitor would be maximizing profits, we had to add cost data. We will do the same thing now for the monopolist. We assume profit maximization is the goal of the pure monopolist, just as we assumed it was the goal of the perfect competitor. With the perfect competitor, however, we had only to decide on the profit-maximizing rate of output, because price was given. The competitor is a price-taker. For the pure monopolist, we must seek a profit-maximizing *price–output combination*. The monopolist is a *price-maker*. We can determine the profit-maximizing price–output combination in either of two ways: by looking at total revenues and total costs, or by looking at marginal revenues and marginal costs. Both approaches are given here.

Total Revenue–Total Costs Approach

We show hypothetical demand (rate of output and price per unit), revenues, costs, and so on in Figure 23.4 (a) on page 358. In column 3 we see total revenues for our hypothetical monopolist, and in column 4 we see total costs. We can transfer these two columns to Figure 23.4 (b). The only difference between this total revenue and total cost diagram (Figure 23.4 (b)) and the one we showed for a perfect competitor in the last chapter is that the total revenue line is no longer straight. Rather, it curves. For any given demand curve, in order to sell more, the monopolist must lower the price. The basic difference, therefore, between a monopolist and a perfect competitor has to do with the demand curve facing the two different types of firms. Fundamentally, the costs faced by the perfect competitor and the pure monopolist are the same. Monopoly market power is derived from facing a downward-sloping demand curve.

Profit maximization involves maximizing the positive difference between total revenues and total costs. This occurs at an output rate of about 4 units. We can also find this profit-maximizing rate of output by using the marginal revenue–marginal cost approach. The results will be the same.

Figure 23.4 (a)
Monopoly Costs, Revenues, and Profits

Rate of output	*Price per unit*	*Total revenue*	*Total costs*	*Total profit*	*Marginal cost*	*Marginal revenue*
	£	£	£	£	£	£
0	31.50	0	10	−10		
					19	29
1	29.00	29.00	29	0		
					13	23
2	26.00	52.00	42	10.00		
					11	16.70
3	22.90	68.70	53	15.70		
					12	12.30
4	20.25	81.00	65	16.00		
					14	5.50
5	17.30	86.50	79	7.50		
					17	1.10
6	14.60	87.60	96	−8.40		
					20	−7.10
7	11.50	80.50	116	−35.50		
					22	−11.70
8	8.60	68.80	138	−69.20		
					24	−16.60
9	5.80	52.20	162	−109.80		

Figure 23.4 (b)

Profit Maximization: The TR–TC Approach. The monopolist maximizes profits where the positive difference between TR and TC is greatest. This is at an output rate of 4 units. Notice the difference between the TR curve here and the one shown in the last chapter for a perfect competitor. This one is curved to reflect a downward-sloping linear demand curve.

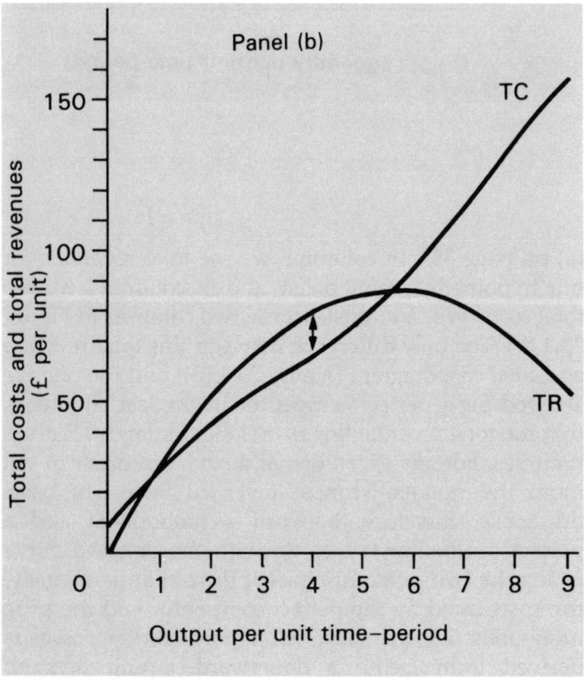

Figure 23.4 (c)

Profit Maximization: The MR–MC Approach. Profit maximization occurs where marginal revenue equals marginal cost. This is at an output rate of 4 units. (Also, the MC curve must cut the MR curve from below.)

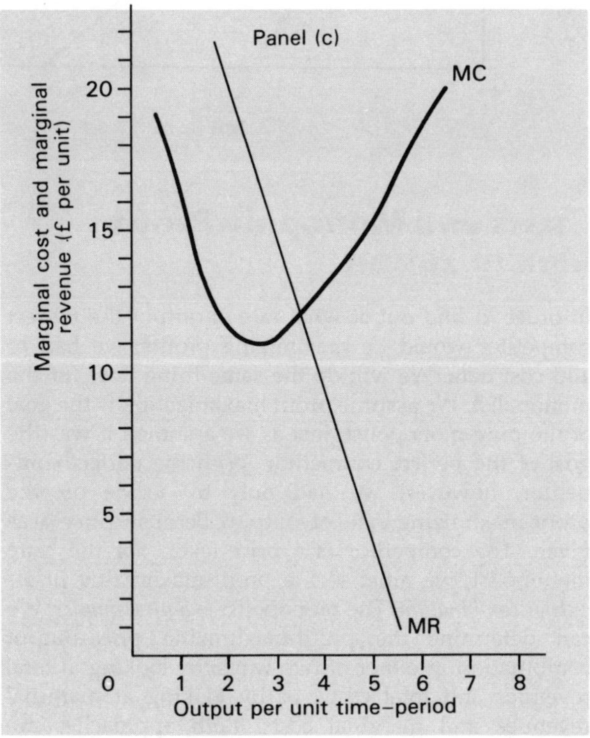

Marginal Revenue—Marginal Cost Approach

Profit maximization will also occur where marginal revenue equals marginal cost. This is as true for a monopolist as it is for a perfect competitor (but the monopolist will charge a higher price). When we transfer marginal cost to marginal revenue information from columns 6 and 7 in Figure 23.4 (a) to Figure 23.4 (c), we see that marginal revenue equals marginal cost at an output rate of about 4 units. Profit maximization occurs at the same output in Figure 23.4 (b).

If the monopolist goes past the point where marginal revenue equals marginal cost (4 units of output), marginal cost will exceed marginal revenue. That is, the incremental cost of producing any more units will exceed the incremental revenue. It would not be worth while, as was true also in perfect competiton. On the other hand, if the monopolist produces less than that, then it is not making maximum profits. Look at output rate Q_1 in Figure 23.5. Here the monopolist's marginal revenue is at *A*, but marginal cost is at *B*. Marginal revenue exceeds marginal cost on the last unit sold; the profit for that *particular* unit Q_1 is equal to the vertical difference between *A* and *B*, or the difference between marginal revenue and marginal cost. The monopolist would be foolish to stop at output rate Q_1 because if output is expanded, the marginal revenue will still exceed marginal cost and therefore total profits will rise. In fact, the profit-maximizing monopolist will continue to expand output and sales until marginal revenue equals marginal cost, which is at output rate Q_m. The monopolist will not produce at rate Q_2 because here we see that marginal costs are *C* and marginal revenues are *D*. The difference between *C* and *D* represents the reduction in total profits from producing the additional unit. Total profits will rise as the monopolist reduces its rate of output back towards Q_m.

Figure 23.5

Maximizing Profits. Here we show the monopolist's demand curve *DD*, as before and its marginal revenue curve, MR, with its marginal cost curve, MC. The monopolist will maximize profits where marginal revenue equals marginal cost; it will produce up to the point where MC equals MR and then will find the highest price at which it can sell that quantity. The profit-maximizing production rate is Q_m, and the profit-maximizing price is P_m. The monopolist would be unwise to produce at the rate Q_1, or at the rate Q_2. You should satisfy yourself why this is so with reference to points *A, B, C*, and *D*.

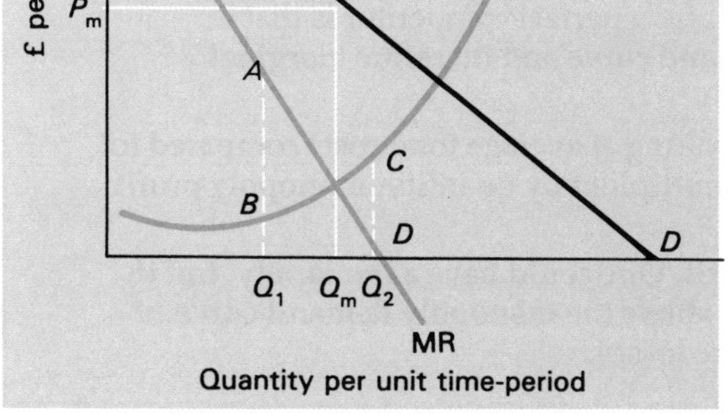

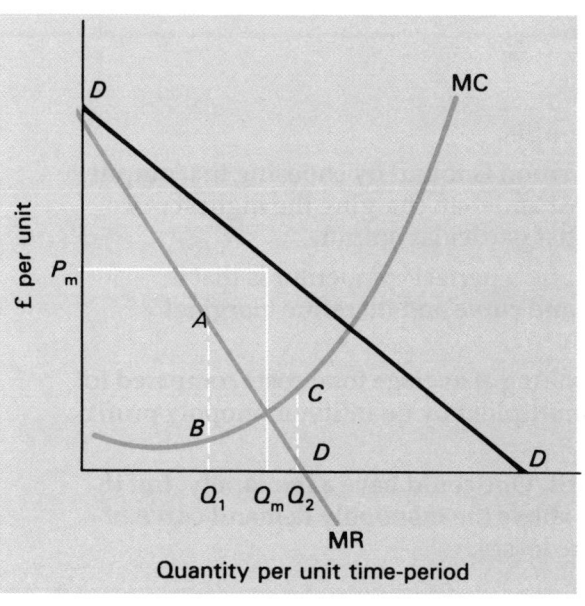

What Price to Charge for Output?

How does the monopolist set prices? We know the quantity is set at the point where marginal revenue equals marginal cost. The monopolist then finds out how much can be charged, that is, how much the market will bear for that particular quantity, Q_m in Figure 23.5. We know that the demand curve is defined as showing the *maximum* price for which a given quantity can be sold. That means that our monopolist knows that in order to sell Q_m it can only charge P_m, because that is the price at which that specific quantity, Q_m, is demanded. This price is found by drawing a vertical line from the quantity Q_m to the market demand curve. Where that line hits the market demand curve the price is determined. We find that price by drawing a horizontal line from the demand curve over the price axis; that gives us the profit-maximizing price of P_m.

In our detailed numerical example, at a profit-maximizing rate of output of 4 in Figure 23.4, the firm can charge a maximum price of £21.5 and still sell all the goods produced.

The basic procedure for finding the profit-maximizing short-run price–quantity combination for the monopolist is first to determine the profit-maximizing rate of output, either by the total revenue–total cost method or the marginal revenue–marginal cost method, and then to determine by use of the demand curve *DD* the maximum price that can be charged to sell that output.

The decision-making that a monopolist must engage in order to maximize profit is presented in tabular form in Figure 23.6.

Figure 23.6

	Production decision		
Situation	MR = MC	MR>MC	MR<MC
Decision	Stay put = profit-maximization rate of output	Increase production	Decrease production

Calculating Monopoly Profit

We have talked about the monopolist making profit, but we have yet to indicate how much profit the monopolist makes. We have actually shown total profits in column 5 of Figure 23.4 (a). We can also find total profits by adding an average total cost curve to Figure 23.4 (c). We do that in Figure 23.7. When we add the average total cost curve, we find that the profit that a monopolist makes is equal to the shaded area. Given the demand curve and a uniform pricing system, there is no way for a monopolist to make greater profits than those shown by the shaded area. The monopolist is maximizing profits where marginal cost equals marginal revenue. If the monopolist produces less than that, it will be forfeiting some profits. If the monopolist produces more than that, it will be forfeiting profits.

The same is true of a perfect competitor which produces where marginal revenues equal marginal costs because it produces at the point where the marginal cost schedule intercepts the horizontal *dd* curve. The horizontal *dd* curve represents the marginal revenue curve for the pure competitor, for the same average revenues are obtained on all the units sold. Perfect competitors maximize profits at MR = MC, as do pure monopolists. But the perfect competitor makes no true economic profits in the long run. Rather, all it makes is a normal competitive rate of return.

Figure 23.7

Monopoly Profit. We find monopoly profit by subtracting total costs from total revenues at an output rate of 4 units, which is approximately the profit-maximizing rate of output for the monopolist. Monopoly profit is given by the shaded area. This diagram is similar to Figure 23.4 (c) except that we have added the short-run average total cost curve (ATC).

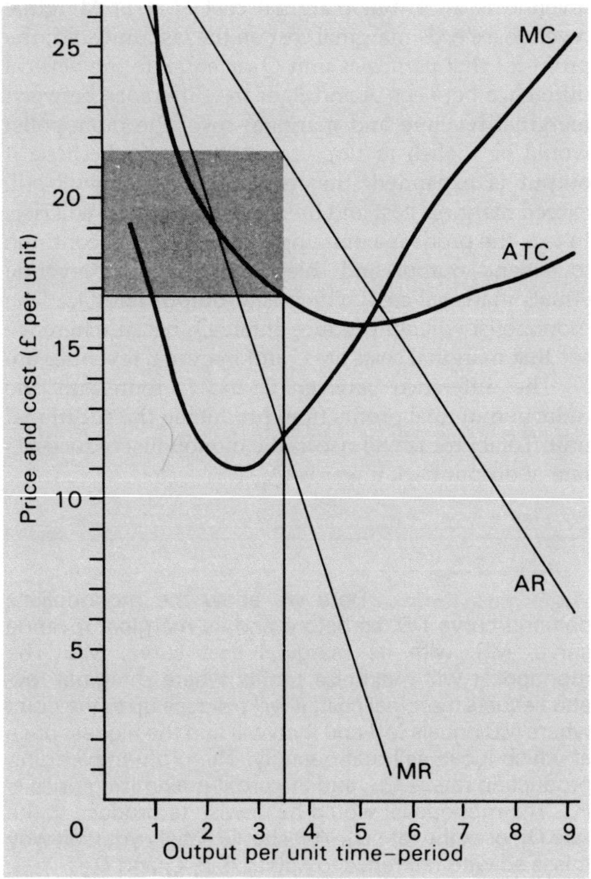

Monopoly Does not Necessarily Mean Profits

The term *monopoly* conjures up the notion of a greedy firm ripping off the public and making exorbitant profits. However, the mere existence of a monopoly does not guarantee high profits. In the United States the Penn Central railroad had a virtual monopoly in railroad service along all its routes but none the less went bankrupt as a result of competition from road transport. Numerous other monopolies have gone bankrupt, too. In the UK Rolls-Royce became bankrupt in 1971 as a result of problems in developing a new type of aero-engine. Look at Figure 23.8. Here we show the demand curve facing the monopolist as *DD* and the resultant marginal revenue curve as MR. It does not matter at what rate of output this particular monopolist operates; total costs cannot be covered. Look at the position of the average total cost curve. It lies everywhere above *DD* (the average revenue curve). Thus, there is no price–output combination that will allow the monopolist profits.

Key Points 23.3

- **We assume the monopolist will maximize profits.**
- **The profit-maximizing price–output combination is found by choosing that output where marginal revenue equals marginal cost and then charging the highest price possible as given by the demand curve for that particular output.**
- **The basic difference between a monopolist and a perfect competitor is that a monopolist faces a downward-sloping demand curve and therefore marginal revenue is less than price.**
- **Monopoly short-run profits are found by looking at average total costs compared to the price per unit. When this difference is multiplied by quantity, monopoly profit is determined.**
- **A monopoly does not necessarily mean profit. One could have a monopoly, but if the average total cost curve lies everywhere above the monopoly demand curve, it will not pay to produce because there will be losses.**

Figure 23.8

Monopolies Are not Always Profitable. The diagram depicts the situation confronting some monopolists. The average total cost curve ATC is everywhere above the average revenue or demand curve *DD*. In the short run, the monopolist will produce where MC = MR at point *E*. Output Q_m will be sold at price P_m, but cost per unit is C_1. Losses are the shaded rectabgle.

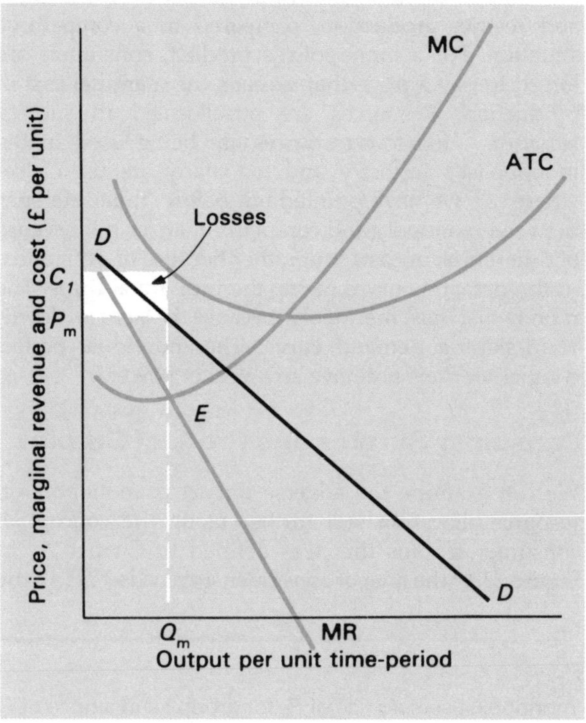

Price Discrimination

In a perfectly competitive market, each buyer is charged the same price for every unit of the particular commodity (corrected, of course, for quality differences and differential transportation charges). Since the product is homogeneous, and since we also assume full knowledge on the part of the buyers, a difference in price per constant-quality unit cannot exist. Any seller of the product who tried to charge a price higher than the going market price would find that no one would purchase from him or her. In this chapter, we have assumed up until now that the monopolist charged all consumers the same price for all units. A monopolist, however, may be able to charge different people different prices and/or different unit prices for successive units sought by a given buyer. Either one or a combination of these is called **price discrimination**. The reason a firm wishes to engage in price discrimination is that, where feasible, such a practice will lead to increased profits.

It must be made clear at the outset that charging different prices to different people and/or for different units which reflect differences in the cost of service to those particular people does not amount to price discrimination. This is **price differentiation**: differences in prices which reflect differences in marginal cost.

We can turn this around to say that a uniform price does not necessarily indicate an absence of price discrimination. If production costs vary by customer and all are charged the same price, this is also a case of price discrimination.

Necessary Conditions for Price Discrimination to Exist

There are three necessary conditions for the existence of price discrimination:

1. The firm must have some market power (i.e. it is not a price-taker).
2. The firm must be able to separate markets.
3. The buyers in the different markets must have different price elasticities of demand.

Further, it is necessary that these two or more identifiable classes of buyers can be separated at a reasonable cost. Additionally, the monopolist must be able to prevent, at least partially, reselling by those buyers who paid a low price to those buyers who would be charged a higher price. For example, charging students a lower admission price to see a film at a cinema than the price charged to non-students can be done relatively easily: the cost of checking out student IDs is not significant. Also, it is fairly easy to make sure that students do not resell their tickets to non-students. As another example, price discrimination for medical services is easy. The resale value of a coronary bypass operation is zero!

Can you think of any other examples of price discrimination? What about discos that charge females less than males? It is easy to discriminate here.

Graphic Analysis

We can see how a price-discriminating monopolist will act if there are two classes of buyers with identifiable differences in their demand curves. In panels (a) and (b) of Figure 23.9 (page 362) we see group I and group II, the two classes of buyers. To simplify, marginal cost for the monopolist is assumed to be constant. For profit to be at a maximum, we know that marginal revenue must equal marginal cost. We have a common marginal cost here, MC. We have two sets of marginal revenue curves, MR_I and MR_{II}. Thus, for profit maximization, $MR_I = MR_{II} = MC$. It is as if the goods sold to class I and II were two *different* goods having exactly the same marginal cost of production. In other words, to maximize total profits, the monopolist wants to set marginal revenue equal to marginal cost in all markets in which it is selling. If marginal revenue in market I exceeded marginal cost, profits could be increased by expanding output (lowering price) in market I. The same holds for market II. On the other hand, if marginal revenue in market I (or market II) were less than marginal cost, profit could be increased by reducing output (raising price) in market I (or II).

We show this in Figure 23.9. Group I buyers are presented in panel (a), group II buyers in panel (b). We assume for simplicity's sake that the marginal costs for servicing both classes of consumers are both equal and constant. Marginal cost equals marginal revenue for group I at quantity Q_1. The price at which the quantity can be sold is P_1. On the other hand, for buyers in group II who have a more elastic demand curve (at *any* given *P*) than buyers in group I, the intersection of marginal cost with MR_{II} is a quantity Q_{II}. The price at which this quantity is sold is P_{II}, which is lower than P_I. In other words the price-discriminating monopolist will sell that same product to the group of buyers having a relatively less elastic demand curve at a higher price than that charged to the other group of buyers having a relatively higher elasticity of demand.

The Cost to Society of Monopolies

We now consider the desirability of a monopolistic market structure as compared with a perfectly competitive industry. In Figure 23.10 we show an industry where long-run marginal costs are constant. From our analysis in Chapter 22 we know that in a perfectly competitive industry the equilibrium price would be P_c – price equals marginal cost. Now let us assume that the industry is suddenly transformed into a monopoly *and there is no change in the cost situation facing the monopolist.* The monopolist would charge a price of P_m: Output would be reduced from Q_c to Q_m. A monopolist therefore produces a smaller quantity and sells it at a higher price. This is the reason usually given when one attacks monopolists. Monopolists raise the price and restrict production, compared to a competitive situation. For a monopolist's product, consumers are forced to pay a price that exceeds the marginal cost of production. Resources are misallocated in such a situation – too few resources are being used in the monopolist's industry and too many are used elsewhere. As we have pointed out before, this difference between monopoly and competition arises not because of differences in costs, but rather because of differences in the demand curves facing the individual firms. The monopolist has monopoly because it faces a downward-sloping demand curve. The individual perfect competitor does not have any market power.

Consumer Surplus and Product Surplus

We can examine the adverse impact of monopoly on resource allocation still further using the concept of consumer surplus that was defined in Chaper 20. In Figure 23.10 the area of consumer surplus is YTP_c in the

Figure 23.9

Price Discrimination. Here the monopolist has separated buyers into those with relatively less elastic demand curves (group I) and those with relatively more elastic demand curves (group II). Profit maximization occurs when marginal revenue equals marginal cost. Therefore, our monopolist sets marginal revenue equal to marginal cost in each individual category. We find that the monopolist sets a price of P_I, for group I and a price of P_{II} for group II. Those with the relatively less elastic demand end up paying more than do those with the relatively more elastic demand for the same service. In such a situation, the monopolist earns a greater income than it would by charging a single price to all customers.

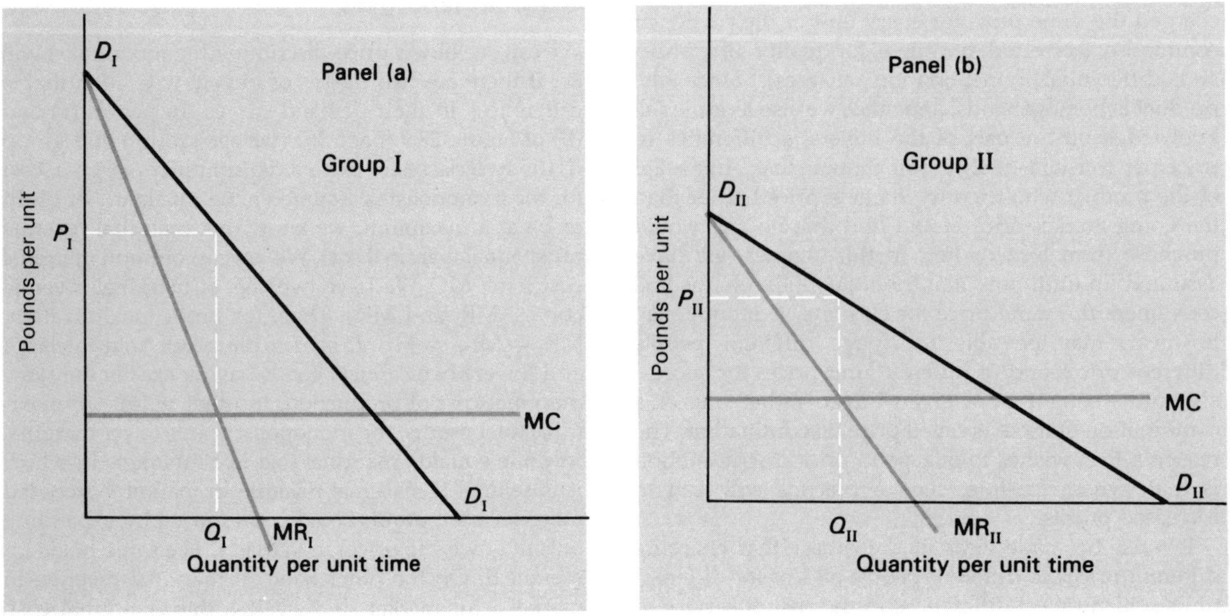

Figure 23.10

The Effects of Monopolizing an Industry. If there are constant long-run marginal costs in perfectly competitive industry then the equilibrium price would be P_c and the equilibrium quantity supplied and demanded would be Q_c. Now we assume that the industry is suddenly monopolized. We assume that the costs stay the same; the only thing that changes is that the monopolist now faces the entire downward-sloping demand curve. The monopolist will produce at the point where marginal revenue equals marginal cost. The monopolist therefore produces at Q_m and charges a price P_m. We see, then, that a monopolist charges a higher price and produces less than an industry in a competitive situation.

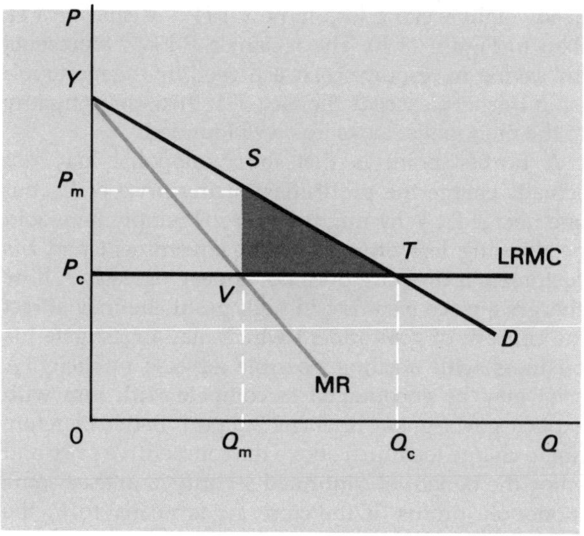

case of the perfectly competitive industry. If the industry is suddenly monopolized and there is no change in the cost situation facing the monopolist then the area under the demand curve shrinks to YSP_m. The monopolist has gained the area P_mSVP_c at the expense of consumers: this area is defined as *producer surplus*. The remaining part of the former area of consumer surplus is, of course, the triangular area *STV*. Neither consumers nor the monopolist now obtain this as a surplus: it is lost to either party. Because of this it is called the **deadweight welfare loss** arising from monopolization of the competitive industry. This very term highlights how we can build up a strong case against monopoly and a presumption in favour of competition. However, there are several other aspects that still need to be considered.

Some Other Costs of Monopoly

There are at least two additional costs in terms of resource misallocation that may occur when monopolies exist. One involves the resources used by individuals in order to obtain and maintain monopoly, and the other involves possible inefficiences within the monopoly firm.

The Resource Cost of Obtaining and Maintaining a Monopoly Firm

As we recognized earlier in this chapter some monopolies can be obtained by using the help of government in the form of restrictive licences, certificates of convenience, and the like. Individuals, in their quest for higher-than-normal rates of return, will expend resources to obtain government-bestowed monopolies. These resources can (from society's point of view) be considered wasted. As an example the Federal Communications Commission in the US has announced that it will allow only three new FM radio stations in a particular city. The *full* procedure by which an individual or a firm obtains one of the new licences is not explicitly stated in any government documents, but it certainly involves lobbying and offering hospitality to important civil servants agreeing to do public-service programmes, and the like. All of those activities of course use scarce resources. If, on the other hand, new FM licences were simply sold to the highest bidder, virtually no resources would be spent wining and dining FC officials and lobbying on behalf of potential station owners.

Efficiency Loss in Monopoly

We have assumed that all firms – whether they be perfect competitors or monopolists – will seek to minimize their costs of production. Implicit in our discussion of perfect competition was the necessity of each perfectly competitive firm to minimize costs. Because of the competitive process, if it does not minimize costs – given the large number of competitors minimizing their costs – then it will go out of business in the long run. This same argument cannot be applied directly to a monopolist. A monopolist can, in principle, not be completely minimizing the costs of production and that monopolist will not necessarily go out of business in the long run. To be sure, such non-cost-minimization will reduce monopoly profits, but bankruptcy is not the consequence as it is in a perfectly competitive firm.

The notion that costs are not minimized by effective management or that *organizational slack* occurs in monopoly has been called **X-inefficiency**. This term was used by Professor Harvey Leibenstein,* who ascribed X-inefficiency to a lack of motivational efficiency and to an inefficient market for knowledge. According to Leibenstein, X-inefficiency arises largely from losses of output due to motivational deficiency of resource owners.

> (With a given) . . . set of human inputs purchased and . . . knowledge of production techniques available to the firm, a variety of outputs are possible. If individuals can choose, to some degree the APQT bundles (Activity, Pace, Quality of

*Harvey Leibenstein, 'Allocative Efficiency versus X-Inefficiency', *American Economic Review*, Vol. 56 (June 1966), pp. 393–415).

work, Time spent) they like, they are unlikely to choose a set of bundles that will maximize the value of output.*

One of the Leibenstein's favourite examples from the field of economic development involves two identical inefficient petroleum refineries in Egypt. The introduction of a new manager at one of the refineries (the one that produced less output) apparently brought about an immediate improvement in output. After some time passed, there was a *spectacular* improvement in output. The increase in output was attributed to the new manager. In the case of the UK there is evidence that X-inefficiency exists as evidenced by the dramatic improvement in efficiency in those firms which have experienced major changes in senior management. The British Oxygen Company, while not now enjoying a monopoly in the production of gases as it once did, is a good example of how a new managing director cut out wasteful use of resources including raw materials, expense accounts, and other management fringe benefits.

The Benefits of Monopoly

Our analysis has indeed built up a critical picture of monopoly. Both from a consumer viewpoint and in general terms of resource allocation we do not end up with a favourable view of the single seller. But if you recall our analysis of the monopolization of a perfectly competitive industry we must repeat that our analysis was based on an heroic assumption. That assumption was that the monopolization of the perfectly competitive industry does not change the cost structure. Of course if monopolization results in higher marginal cost, then the cost to society is even greater. On the other hand, if monopolization results in cost savings, then the cost, if any, to society of monopolies is less than we infer from the above analysis. Indeed, we can present a hypothetical example in which monopolization leads to such a dramatic reduction in cost that society actually benefits.

Figure 23.11 shows such a possibility. If the monopolist can enjoy scale economies and thus operate on a lower short-run marginal cost curve he can produce cost savings to set against the deadweight welfare loss. The perfectly competitive price is OP_c and the monopolist charges a profit-maximizing price of OP_m. The deadweight welfare loss is now *STV* – a smaller area than in Figure 23.10. The rectangle P_cVWZ represents the saving in resource costs achieved by the monopolist. If this area exceeds the area *STV* then our antipathy to the monopolist looks less well founded.

A further point is that the monopolist may not actually charge the profit-maximizing price of P_m but one nearer P_c. Why might he do so? Simply he would be drawing less attention from government and his customers if his price does not appear 'excessive'. If he charges a price resulting in high profits he may attract the concern of government which may investigate his business with ensuing possible adverse publicity. A rival may be encouraged to compete with him with explicit government financial support. Better therefore not to charge too much above the competitive price and enjoy the benefit of continued security of at least some monopoly profits. If therefore P_m is nearer to P_c the magnitude of consumer surplus that is diverted and enjoyed by the monopolist is diminished and our case against the single seller thereby again weakened.

*Harvey Leibenstein, 'Competition and X-Inefficiency: Reply', *Journal of Political Economy*, Vol. 81 (May–June 1973), pp. 765–77.

Key Points 23.4

- **A monopolist can make higher profits if it can price discriminate. Price discrimination requires that two or more identifiable classes of buyers exist whose price elasticities of demand for the product are different, and that these two classes of buyers can be cheaply separated.**
- **Price differentiation should not be confused with price discrimination. The former occurs when there are differences in prices which reflect differences in marginal cost.**
- **The three necessary conditions for price discrimination are (1) the firm has some market power; (2) the firm must be able to separate markets; and (3) buyers in different markets have different price elasticities of demand.**
- **If we compare a perfectly competitive industry in which the cost curves are essentially the same as those facing the monopolist, then that industry's output is greater than that produced by the monopolist and also the price charged is lower.**
- **Besides raising price and restricting output, monopoly creates a situation in which resources are spent to obtain and to maintain monopoly status. Additionally, there may be organizational slack within a monopoly; this has been called X-inefficiency.**

Figure 23.11

Deadweight Welfare Loss Reconsidered. If the monopolist is able to reduce costs from SMC_c to SMC_m then resource savings can offset the deadweight welfare loss of STV. The profit-maximizing price is OP_m and output OQ_m. P_cVWZ is the area representing cost savings due to the lower SMC of the monopolist not available to the perfectly competitive firm.

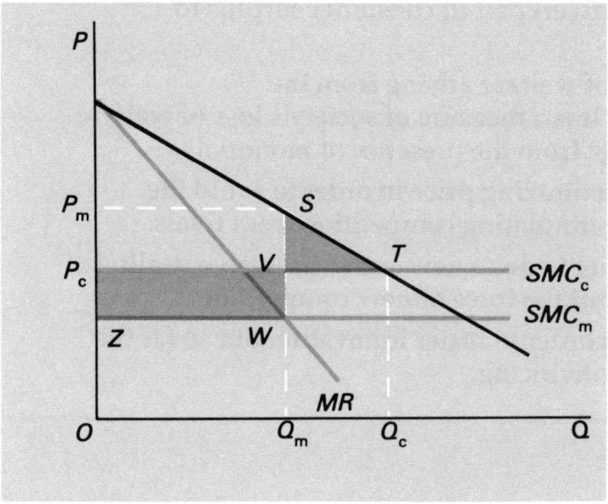

Predatory Pricing

Our discussion of what constitutes a monopoly began with reference to various difficulties facing potential new competitors. We identified several aspects of an industry's technical or cost structure that make entry into a market difficult. These structural problems – barriers to entry – now need in our present discussion of **pricing** by a monopolist to include those policies that can also deter entry.

A monopolist can make life difficult for a potential competitor by setting price at such a low level that a would-be entrant feels disinclined to persist with plans to enter this market. Where a monopoly attempts to protect its dominant position by temporarily pricing its product such that losses are incurred not only by itself but for any competitor, it is said to be practising **predatory pricing**.

This short-term form of pricing could be contemplated by the monopoly as literally a price well worth paying in order to protect its secure position. Whether society as a whole should view this anti-competitive practice with enthusiasm is quite another matter. It should not surprise you that in developed economies like the UK this abuse of a dominant market position is typically one which the authorities concerned with competition policy view critically.

How else could a monopolist protect its position? It could also make life difficult for a potential competitor by trying to deny it wholesalers who might consider distributing the product of a rival firm. **Exclusive dealing arrangements** with wholesalers such that only the monopolist's goods are handled can limit the sources of custom for a new firm. Alternatively those wholesalers and importers who wish to handle the goods of a new entrant may find they do not enjoy such favourable trading terms as other merchants who only stock the monopolist's goods. These are not just hypothetical outcomes where a monopoly situation is under attack. In 1988 BPB was fined more than £2m for alleged abuse of its monopoly situation in the British plasterboard market. We will examine this further in the Case Study at the end of this chapter.

The Process of Innovation

Our discussion of the monopolist has so far concerned the costs and prices of existing products. What about development of new products? Joseph Schumpeter, the distinguished Austrian economist, argued strongly that the process of innovation is best encouraged by monopolists who can afford to take a long-term view and finance expensive – and uncertain – research and development programmes. The security offered to the monopolist thus benefits society through the appearance of new products. The monopolist enjoys profits in the short term but sooner or later competition forces down prices and the monopolist finds his dominant position eroded away. Consider the ball-point pen. In October 1945, Milton Reynolds patented a new writing instrument, tipped with a ball-bearing instead of a nib. It cost about 80 cents to make but sold at Gimbels, the New York department store for $12.50. On the first day the pen was on sale, Gimbels sold 10 000. By March 1946, the Reynolds International Pen company had been making profits of $500 000 a month. However, by Christmas 1946, there were roughly 100 makers of ball-point pens in production, some of them selling models for as little as $2.98. Production costs had fallen below 30 cents a pen. By mid-1948, pens were selling for 39 cents, and costing 10 cents to make.

Thus the monopolist creates a new market ultimately only to see his dominance destroyed. Society can gain from the appearance of the new product and expect competitive forces to temper the monopolist charging a price well above the costs of production.

What can we offer as a comment on this dynamic case for monopoly? First, it has to be said that there is no certainty that the monopolist will innovate. As the Nobel Laureate, Lord Hicks, once put it the greatest benefit of a monopoly can be 'the quiet life'. The security of very limited competition means that there are no immediate market pressures on the monopolist to reduce costs and innovate at all: he can sit back and enjoy at least some monopoly profits. Secondly, the Schumpeterian case needs to be supported by empirical evidence. If the process of innovation is not strongly related to the sheer size of firm then the basis of arguing that only very large firms are innovators looks suspect. Current evidence indeed hardly provides one with a confident basis for viewing small firms as unwilling agents seeking technical change. Schumpeter's argument is thus relevant in considering a government policy towards monopoly and size of firm but in itself not a conclusive one that justifies a monopolistic structure. We consider the development of UK government policy towards monopoly in Chapter 29.

Key Points 23.5

- **By price discrimination, a monopolist can divert part of consumer surplus to himself and enjoy producer surplus.**
- **Deadweight welfare loss refers to the loss of welfare arising from the monopolization of a competitive industry. It is a measure of society's loss of welfare due to the misallocation of resources arising from the presence of monopoly.**
- **A monopolist may not charge the profit-maximizing price in order to avoid the disadvantage of government scrutiny and stimulating competition from rivals.**
- **A monopolist may practise predatory pricing to deter new entry. Exclusive dealing arrangements with wholesalers can also limit the force of new competition.**
- **Monopoly has been held to be desirable in order to foster innovation but so far the empirical evidence does not appear to be convincing.**

CASE STUDY

New Entry in the Plasterboard Market

Two hundred feet beneath the rich farmland of Nottinghamshire, a pair of giant diggers work round the clock to help BPB Industries preserve its dominance of the British plasterboard market.

In the 20 years since its last rival withdrew, BPB's British Gypsum subsidiary has been a monopoly supplier to the growing market for plasterboard, both as an alternative to costly wet plastering and for insulation and partitioning.

It is a monopoly that BPB has successfully defended in the face of investigation by both the monopolies and price commissions.

Now it is fighting in Brussels, after a European Court ruling last year led to a fine of more than £2m for BPB's alleged abuse of its position.

The company faces an onslaught in its home market. The trickle of imported board that has until now been BPB's only competition could soon become a torrent. Rival British plants are also being set up. Redland is pumping £50m into British manufacturing, in partnership with CSR of Australia, while Knauf, a West German group, is planning to follow the opening of its plant at Sittingbourne, Kent, with a second on Humberside.

Until recently, BPB shunned publicity, but now its chairman, Alan Turner, has decided to come out fighting.

Turner threw down the gauntlet to his new rivals and underlined his determination to preserve BPB's position with a remarkable forecast: 'Our objective is to reduce our prices by 25% in real terms over the next two years.'

Alan Brooks, his managing director of Gypsum Products, adds: 'Obviously people are going to attack what is effectively a monopoly. But we are the most efficient producer in Europe, so we are in a strong position.'

City analysts are divided over how long it will take for the dust to clear and for winners and losers to emerge from the plasterboard war. BPB argues it has been bringing its costs down in real terms for years, and still has margins to allow for further cuts.

But even after BPB has lost the 20% premium its shares once enjoyed over other building materials groups, sceptics such as Howard Seymour at Phillips and Drew remain doubtful about the company's prospects.

He says capacity in Europe will rise by 280m square metres a year by the end of 1990, but demand will increase by just 40m.

Adding more uncertainty is the likelihood that the value of BPB's natural reserves will be undermined by the arrival on the market of artificial gypsum. This is a by-product of the de-sulphurization process being installed at coal-fired power stations to combat acid rain.

But here again BPB has kept ahead of rivals. It has signed a deal with the Central Electricity Generating Board under which its plant at Sherburn will take 450 000 tonnes of artificial gypsum a year from the nearby Drax power station in North Yorkshire.

At James Capel, Malcolm Brown says price-war fears are overdone. Assuming a profit rise to £205m in 1989–90, he believes the market takes too pessimistic a view of its resilience.

Integrated mine and production complexes such as the one at East Leake in Nottinghamshire give Turner a head start in the battle.

British Gypsum's show-piece plant processes more than 15 000 tonnes of high-grade gypsum each week, turning it into plasterboard on a 350-yard long computer-controlled production line that is the most efficient in Europe.

Using diggers that scoop up several tonnes of rock in seconds, gypsum production below ground is running at seven tonnes per man hour. But even figures like these are too poor for Turner, whose drive for efficiency means that more job cuts are likely.

Turner does not see his monopoly as being critical to the drive for higher sales. New uses for plasterboards, such as soundproofing and fire prevention, means sales will rise.

BPB has had a monopoly in Britain since ICI shut its plant at Billingham, Cleveland, in 1968, but Turner says the firm has also achieved a strong position in overseas markets such as Canada, West Germany, and France where it has faced fierce competition.

Turner, is equally philosophical about the threat from Redland and Knauf, and any increase in imports by the French group Lafarge Coppée.

'People forget that most of our managers are used to a competitive situation in our overseas markets. The best defence against competition is to have well-located, low-cost plant that supplies board in the range of sizes the market wants.'

BPB will certainly lose some of its UK market share, but is well placed to hang on to its dominant position, both here and in Europe as a whole.

Source: G. David, 'We won't crack, pledges the giant of plasterboard', *Sunday Times*, 26 Feb. 1989.

Questions

1. What were the bases of BPB's dominance of the British plasterboard market?
2. What now threatens BPB's position in this market?
3. How can BPB try to maintain its leading position in this market?
4. What would you expect to happen to BPB's profits if new firms enter the plasterboard market?

Exam Preparation

PRACTICAL EXERCISES

1.

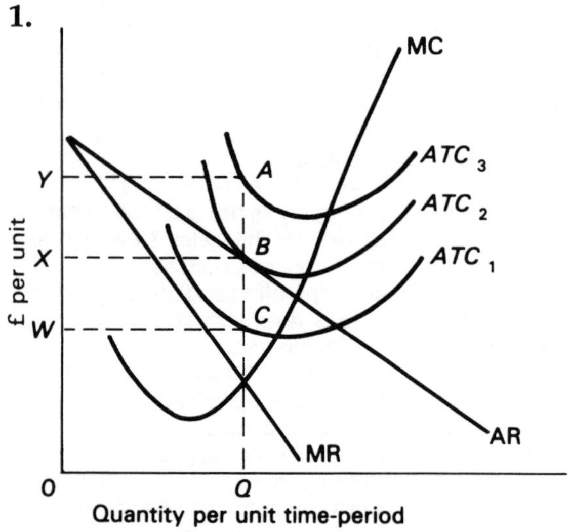

(a) Suppose the monopolist faces ATC_1. Define the rectangle that shows the monopolist's total costs at output rate *Q*. Also, define the rectangle showing total revenue. Is the monopolist showing an economic loss, a break-even (normal profit), or an economic profit situation? What is the significance of the MC=MR output?

(b) Suppose the monopolist faces ATC_2. Define the rectangle that shows the monopolist's total costs. Also, define the rectangle showing total revenue. Is the monopolist showing an economic loss, a break-even (normal profit), or an economic profit situation? What is the significance of the MC=MR output?

(c) Suppose the monopolist faces ATC_3. Define the rectangle that shows the monopolist's total costs. Also, define the rectangle showing total revenue. Is the monopolist showing an economic loss, a break-even (normal profit), or an economic profit situation? What is the significance of the MC=MR output?

2. A monopolist has separated its customers into two markets, A and B. The prices and quantities in these two markets are as follows:

Market A		*Market B*	
Price (£)	*Quantity*	*Price (£)*	*Quantity*
10	10	5	10
9	20	4.50	20
8	30	4	30
7	40	3.50	40
6	50	3	50
5	60	2.50	60
4	70	2	70
3	80	1.50	80
2	90	1	90
1	100	0.50	100

(a) What conditions are necessary for the monopolist to be able to separate the two markets in this case?

(b) (i) Plot the monopolist's demand and marginal revenue curves in markets A and B.
(ii) Assuming that the marginal cost of production is constant at £1.90, what quantity will the monopolist sell in each market if it is a profit maximizer?
(iii) What price will the monopolist charge in each market?

(c) Comment on the relationship between the price elasticity of demand and marginal revenue in market B.

(d) Assume that the monopolist now cuts its price in market A by £0.50. What is the price elasticity of demand at the new price charged?

(e) Assume that the monopolist now faces an increase in the rates payable on its premises. How will the profit-maximizing monopolist adjust the prices charged in each market?

MULTIPLE CHOICE QUESTIONS

1. A profit-maximizing monopolist will seek to produce at a level of output where

A average costs are lowest
B there is the greatest difference between marginal revenue and marginal cost
C the highest price can be obtained
D price equals marginal cost
E marginal cost equals marginal revenue.

2. Which of the points labelled **A** to **E** on the diagram below indicates the equilibrium position of a profit-maximizing monopolist?

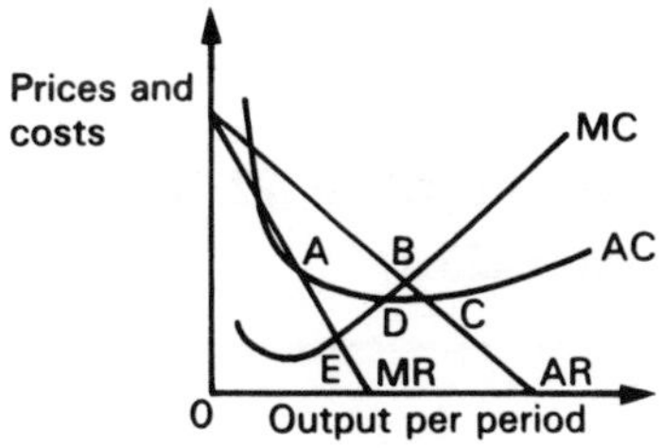

3. The diagrams below represent the operations of a price-discriminating monopolist who is able to separate the market for his product between domestic and industrial consumers. His marginal cost (MC) curve is the same in both markets.

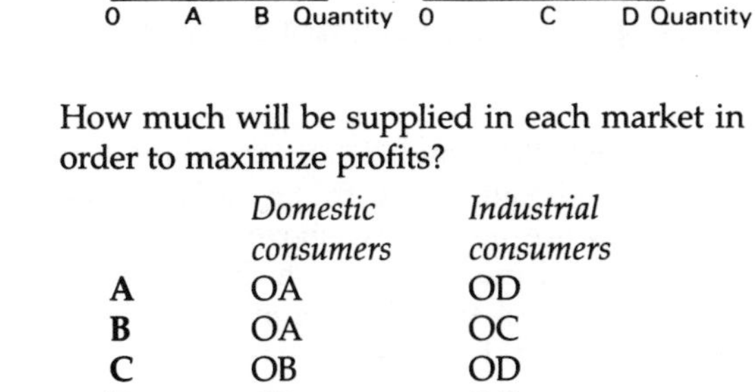

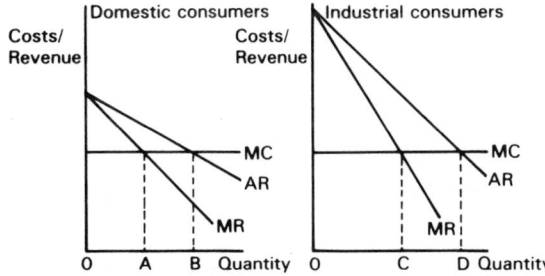

How much will be supplied in each market in order to maximize profits?

	Domestic consumers	*Industrial consumers*
A	OA	OD
B	OA	OC
C	OB	OD
D	OB	OC

4.

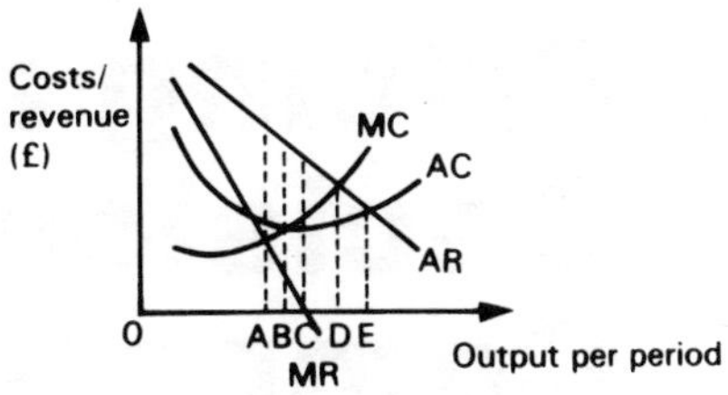

The diagram shows the cost and revenue functions of a monopolist. Around which output level will the price elasticity of demand be unity?

A OA
B OB
C OC
D OD
E OE

RELATED ESSAY QUESTIONS

1. (a) What is a monopoly?
(b) How do the price charged by a monopolist and the output produced differ from the price and output of a competitive firm? Explain your reasoning.

2. 'Too much attention is paid to the theoretical disadvantages of monopoly.' Discuss.

3. 'The uncritical acceptance of profit maximization in the theory of the firm has distorted our understanding of monopoly.' Discuss.

4. Examine the factors which might give rise to a firm being dominant in a market. Discuss *two* pricing policies which such a firm might adopt.

5. It is (a) profitable and (b) desirable for a monopoly supplier to practise price discrimination?

6. 'Under conditions of perfect competition there will be only one price charged by firms, but in the case of a single supplier there may be more than one price.' Explain this statement.

7. (a) Explain why a monopolist may be able to earn abnormal profits.
(b) Why have economists argued that monopoly leads to economic inefficiency? What qualifications would you make to this argument?

24 Pricing and Output Decisions in Monopolistic Competition and Oligopoly

Key Points to Review

- Perfect price elasticity of demand (7.3)
- Average total cost curve (21.3)
- Perfect competition (22.1)
- Monopoly (23.1)

1 What are the characteristics of the market structure of monopolistic competition?

2 How is the equilibrium price–output combination decided by the monopolistic competitor?

3 How does the monopolistic competition market structure differ from perfect competition?

4 What are the characteristics of the oligopoly market structure?

5 How do oligopolies compete?

Up to this point, we have discussed the two extremes in market structure – perfect competition and pure monopoly. In the perfectly competitive model, we assume that there are numerous firms that produce the same product and that have no influence over price: they are *price-takers*. In the pure monopoly model, we assume that the firm is a single seller of a good to the entire market: the firm is a *price-maker*. There are obviously market situations that fall between these two extremes. Indeed, almost all the UK economy is characterized by firms that are neither perfectly competitive nor purely monopolistic. After all, most firms have some control over price, that is, individually they do not face a perfectly elastic (horizontal) demand curve, but they really are not pure monopolists. In this chapter, we will look at market structures that lie in between perfect competition and monopoly. The first market structure of such an 'in-between' situation that we must look at is monopolistic competition, i.e. a situation where each seller has a small amount of market power but is in competition with a large number of others selling *almost* identical products. We then examine oligopolistic market structures where the number of competitors is small and their market power is considerable.

Monopolistic Competition – Its Origin

Back in the 1920s and 1930s, economists became increasingly dissatisfied with the polar extremes of market structure mentioned above. There seemed to have been many industries for which both the perfectly competitive model and the pure monopoly model did not apply and did not seem to yield very accurate predictions.

Theoretical and empirical research was instituted to develop some sort of middle ground. Two separately developed models of **monopolistic competition** resulted. In the US Edward Chamberlin published *The Theory of Monopolistic Competition* in 1933. In the same year, Britain's Joan Robinson published *The Economics of Imperfect Competition*. The following account is based on their important contributions to the theory of the firm.

The Characteristics of Monopolistic Competition

We define monopolistic competition as a market structure in which there are a relatively large number of producers offering similar but differentiated products. Monopolistic competition therefore has the following characteristics.

1. Significant numbers of sellers in a highly competitive market due to the freedom of entry into the industry.
2. Differentiated products.
3. The existence of advertising.

We will analyse these characteristics in turn.

Number of Firms

In a perfectly competitive situation, there is an extremely large number of firms; in pure monopoly there is only one. In monopolistic competition, there is a somewhat large number of firms, but not as many as in perfect competition.

Several important implications for monopolistically competitive industry follow.

1. Small market share. With so many firms, each firm has a relatively small share of the total market. Thus, it has only a very small amount of control over the market-clearing price.
2. Collusion is difficult. With so many firms, it is very difficult for all of them to get together to collude, that is, to set a pure monopoly price (and output!). Rigging price in a monopolistically competitive industry is virtually impossible.
3. Independence. Since there are so many firms, each one acts independently of the others. That is to say, no firm attempts to take into account the reaction of all its rival firms – that would be impossible with so many rivals. Rivals' reactions to output and price changes are largely ignored.

Product Differentiation

Perhaps the most important feature of the monopolistically competitive market is **product differentiation**. In a sense, we can say that each individual manufacturer of a product has an absolute monopoly over its own product, which is slightly differentiated from other similar products. Consider the abundance of brand names for such things as toothpaste, soap, and shampoos. Should you buy SR, or any of the numerous rival brands?

Indeed, it appears that product differentiation characterizes most markets for consumer goods in the UK. Consumers are not obliged to buy just one make of television set, toothpaste, sweatshirt or motor car. There are usually a number of similar but differentiated products from which to choose. We note that the greater the success at product differentiation, the greater the monopoly power.

REAL VERSUS ARTIFICIAL DIFFERENTIATION

Some economists like to distinguish between product differentiation that is 'real' and that which is 'artificial'. Real product differentiation involves variations in physical characteristics, such as an actual chemical difference between two brands of washing-machine detergents. Artificial product differentiation would involve no significant differences in products but different packaging materials, brand names, and advertising outlays. The above examples of 'real' and 'artificial' product differentiation, of course, represent only the tip of an iceberg. Firms can also differentiate their products on the basis of location and service provided with the products sold. Therefore in practice it is difficult to draw the line between real and artificial product differentiation.

SUBSTITUTES

However we wish to define product differentiation, the fact remains that each separate differentiated product has numerous close substitutes. This clearly has an impact on the price elasticity of demand facing the individual firm. Remember when we discussed the determination of the price elasticity of demand, we mentioned that one determinant was the availability of substitutes. The greater the number of substitutes available – other things being equal – the greater the price elasticity of demand. In other words, if the consumer has a vast array of alternatives that are just about as good as the product under study, a relatively small increase in the price of that product will lead consumers to switch to one of the many close substitutes. Thus, the ability of a firm to raise the price above the price of close substitutes is very small.

PRODUCT GROUPS

Up until now we have defined an industry as a collection of firms producing a homogeneous commodity. However, it is difficult to maintain this definition of an industry when we talk in terms of differentiated products. Each firm has a distinct product and thus in a sense constitutes an industry. But this is not a very practical approach and we can solve this problem by lumping together firms producing very closely related products. These are called product groups. Some product groups that come to mind are breakfast cereals, motor cars, toilet paper, and hand soap.

Sales Promotion – Advertising

Monopolistic competition differs from perfect competition in that in the latter there is no sales promotion. By definition, the perfect competitor is selling a product that is identical to the product that all other firms in the industry are selling.

But such is not the case for the monopolistic competitor. Since the monopolistic competitor has at least some monopoly power, advertising may result in increased profits. How much advertising should be undertaken? As much as is profitable. It should be carried to the point where the additional revenue from one more pound of advertising just equals one pound of marginal cost.

SHIFTING THE DEMAND CURVE

The goal of advertising is to shift the demand curve to the right. Advertising, it is hoped, will lead to a larger volume of business that more than covers the cost of the advertising. This is shown in Figure 24.1. In that exhibit, assume that the market-clearing price is P_1. At that price with demand curve *dd*, the quantity sold will be q_1. If, however, advertising succeeds in shifting the demand curve over to *d′d′*, then at that same price the quantity q_2 will be sold.

It is possible, on the other hand, that advertising is necessary just to keep the demand curve at *dd*. Without advertising, the demand curve might shift inwards to the left. This presumably is the case with competitive advertising. For example, cigarette manufacturers may have to expend large outlays on advertising merely to keep the share of the market they now have. If they discontinue advertising, they would lose ground to all the other companies that are engaged in heavy advertising.

Figure 24.1

Advertising's Desired Effect. The firm that advertises hopes that the advertising will shift the demand schedule for its product to the right. In other words, before advertising, the demand schedule is at *dd*; after advertising takes place, the demand schedule should shift to *d′d′*.

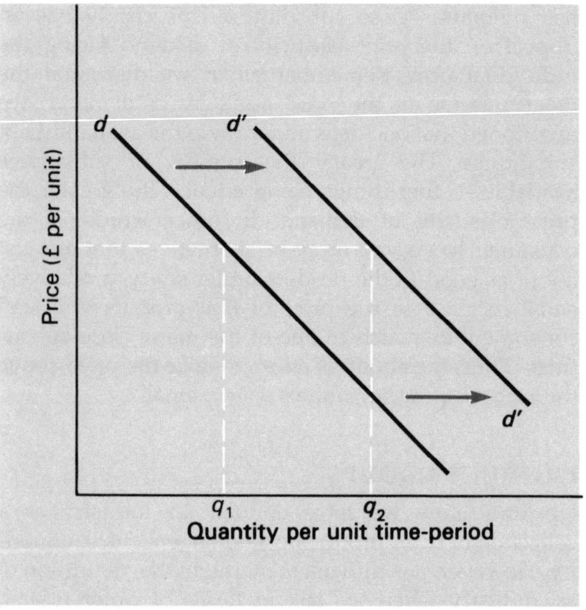

ADVERTISING AND ECONOMIES OF SCALE

An alleged reason for advertising is that the subsequent increased sales can lead to economies of scale. This is possible only if the economies of scale outweigh the advertising costs. Look at Figure 24.2. Here we find that the hypothetical average total cost curve without advertising is ATC. With advertising, it is ATC′. If production is at q_1, then without advertising average total costs will be ATC_1. If advertising campaigns shift demand and increase the profit-maximizing output to q_2, then average total costs will fall to ATC_2. The reduction in average total costs will more than outweigh the increased expenses due to advertising. If the advertising campaign were not successful and demand and production remained where they were, then the firm would stop advertising. It would not be profitable to continue. (Now read Key Points 24.1.)

Price and Output for the Monopolistic Competitor

Now that we have presented the assumptions underlying the monopolistic competition model, we can analyse the price and output behaviour of each firm in a monopolistically competitive industry. We assume in

Key Points 24.1

- **Monopolistic competition is a market structure that lies in between pure monopoly and perfect competition.**
- **A monopolistically competitive market structure has (1) a large number of sellers, (2) differentiated products, and (3) advertising.**
- **Because of the large number of firms, each has a small share of the market and collusion is difficult; firms ignore the reactions of rivals to changes in prices.**
- **The goal of advertising is to shift the demand curve outwards to the right and at the very least maintain existing market share.**
- **Proponents of advertising argue that it leads to increased sales, which allow firms to take advantage of economies of scale.**

the analysis that follows that the desired product type and quality have been chosen. Further, we assume that the budget and the type of promotional activity have already been chosen and do not change.

The Individual Firm's Demand and Cost Curves

Since the individual firm is not a perfect competitor, its demand curve is downward sloping, as is shown in panels (a), (b), and (c) of Figure 24.3. Thus, it faces a marginal revenue curve that is also downward sloping and below the demand curve. To find the profit-maximizing rate of output and the profit-maximizing price, we go to the output where the marginal cost curve intersects the marginal revenue curve from below. That gives us the profit-maximizing output rate. Then we draw a vertical line up to the demand schedule. That gives us the price that can be charged to sell exactly that quantity produced. This is what we have done in panels (a), (b), and (c) of Figure 24.3. In each of those panels, a marginal cost curve have been drawn in. It intersects the marginal revenue curve at *E*. The profit-maximizing rate of output is q_e and the profit-maximizing price is *P*.

The Short-run Equilibrium

In the short run, it is possible for a monopolistic competitor to make economic profits, that is, profits over and above the normal rate of return, or profits over and above what is necessary to keep that firm in that industry. In panel (a) of Figure 24.3, we show such a situation. The average total cost curve is drawn in below the demand curve *dd* at the profit-maximizing rate of output q_e. Economic profits are shown by the shaded rectangle in that panel.

Losses in the short run are clearly also possible. They are presented in panel (b) of Figure 24.3 (page 374). Here the average total cost curve lies everywhere above the individual firm's demand curve *dd*. The losses are marked as the shaded rectangle.

As with any market structure or any firm, in the short run it is possible to observe either economic profits or economic losses. In the long run, however, such is not the case with monopolistic competition.

Figure 24.2

Another Desired Effect of Advertising. Advertising may be able to more than pay for itself. For example, in this diagram we start out on the average total cost curve ATC at point *A* with production of q_1. Here average total costs are ATC_1. Advertising is added, and the average total cost curve shifts up to ATC′. However, if we move out to point *B*, the quantity produced will be q_2 with an average total cost of only ATC_2, which is lower than ATC_1.

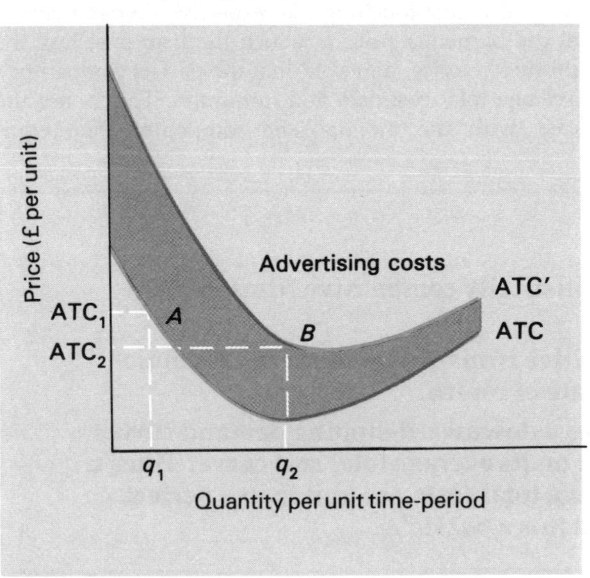

The Long Run – Economic Profits are Competed Away

The long run is where the similarity between perfect competition and monopolistic competition becomes more obvious. In the long run, since there are so many firms making substitutes for the product in question, any economic profits will be competed away. They will be competed away either through entry by new firms seeing a chance to make a higher rate of return than elsewhere, or by changes in product quality and advertising outlays by existing firms in the industry. (Profitable products will be imitated by other firms.) As for economic losses in the short run, they will disappear in the long run because those firms that suffer them will leave the industry. They will go into another business where the expected rate of return is at least normal. Thus, panels (a) and (b) of Figure 24.3 represent only short-run situations for a monopolistically competitive firm. In the long run, the average total cost curve will just touch the individual firm's demand curve *dd* at the particular price that is profit maximizing for that particular firm. This is shown in panel (c) of Figure 24.3.

A word of warning. This is an idealized, long-run equilibrium situation for each firm in the industry. That does not mean that even in the long run we will observe every single firm in a monopolistically competitive industry making *exactly* zero economic profits or *just* a normal rate of return. We live in a dynamic world. All we are saying is that if this model is correct, the rate of return will *tend* towards normal, that is, economic profits will tend towards zero.

Comparing Perfect Competition with Monopolistic Competition

If both the monopolistic competitor and the perfect competitor make zero economic profits in the long run, then how are they different? The answer lies in the fact that the demand curve facing the individual perfect

Figure 24.3

Long-run Equilibrium with Monopolistic Competition. In panel (a), we show the typical monopolistic competitor making economic profits. If that were the situation, there would be entry into the industry, forcing the demand curve facing the individual monopolistic competitor leftward. Eventually firms would find themselves in the situation depicted in panel (c), where zero economic profits are being made. At the profit-maximizing rate of output, where marginal cost equals marginal revenue, price equals average total cost. In panel (b), we show a situation where the typical firm in a monopolistically competitive industry is making economic losses. If that were the case, firms would leave the industry. The demand curve would shift outward to the right. Eventually the average industry firm would find itself in the situation depicted in panel (c).

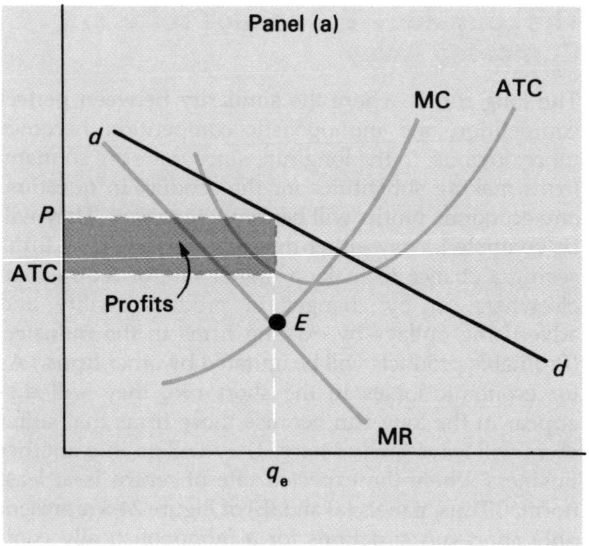

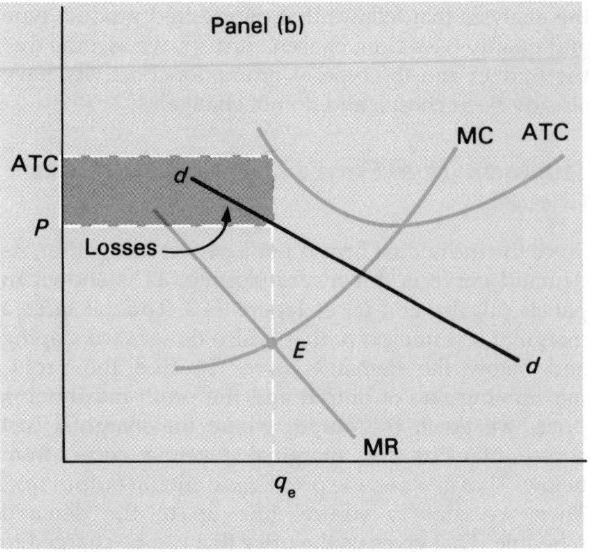

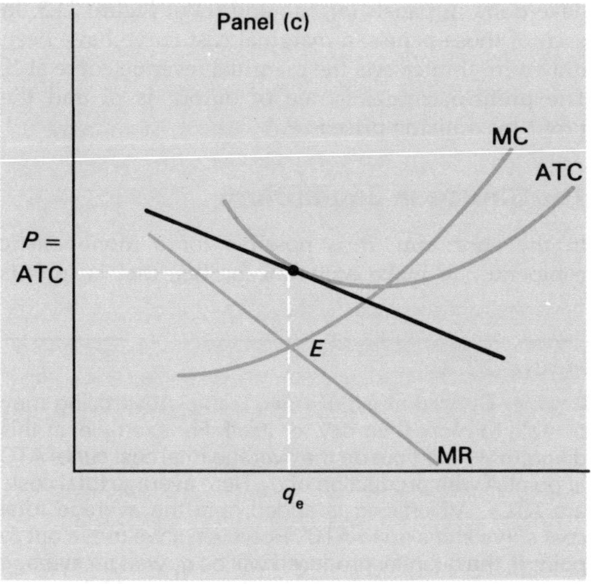

competitor is horizontal, that is, the price elasticity of demand is infinity. Such is not the case for the individual monopolistic competitor. The demand curve has *some* slope to it. This firm has some control over price; it has some market power. Price elasticity of demand is not infinite. We see the two situations in panels (a) and (b) of Figure 24.4. Both show average total costs just touching the respective demand curves at the particular price at which the firm is selling the product. Notice, however, that the perfect competitor's average total costs are at a minimum. This is not the case with the monopolistic competitor. The equi-

Key Points 24.2

- **In the short run, it is possible for monopolistically competitive firms to make economic profits or economic losses.**
- **In the long run, monopolistically competitive firms will make zero economic profits, that is, they will make a normal rate of return.**
- **Because the monopolistic competitor faces a downward-sloping demand curve, it does not produce at the minimum point on its average total cost curve. Thus, a monopolistic competitor has higher average total costs per unit than a perfect competitor would have. Some have called this a 'waste'.**

librium rate of output is to the left of the minimum point on the average total cost curve where price is greater than marginal cost. (The monopolistic competitor cannot expand output to the point of minimum costs without lowering price; and then marginal cost would exceed marginal revenue.)

It has been argued, therefore, that monopolistic competition involves waste because minimum average total costs are not achieved and price exceeds marginal cost. There are too many firms producing too little output. According to critics of monopolistic competition, society's resources are being wasted.

In his book *The Economics of Monopolistic Competition* Chamberlin had an answer to this criticism. He contended that the difference between the average cost of production for a monopolistically competitive firm in an open market and the minimum average total cost represented what he called the cost of producing 'differentness'. In other words, Chamberlin did not label this difference in cost between perfect competition and monopolistic competition necessarily a waste. In fact, he argued that it is rational for consumers to have a taste for differentiation; consumers willingly accept the resultant increased production costs in return for choice and variety of output. (Now read Key Points 24.2.)

Oligopoly – A World of Interdependence

The second form of market structure that we have yet to discuss is an important one indeed. It involves a situation where there are several large firms that dominate an entire industry. They are clearly not competitive in the sense that we have used the term; they are clearly not even monopolistically competitive. We call such a situation on **oligopoly**, which means few sellers that are interdependent.

Characteristics of Oligopoly

There are several characteristics of oligopoly that we now comment on.

SMALL NUMBER OF FIRMS

We have already mentioned that there is a small number of firms in an oligopolistic industry. Does that mean more than two but less than 100? The question is not easy to answer. Basically, though, we are interested in several firms dominating the entire industry so that these several firms really are able to set the price. By domination, we must be specific, however. We are

Figure 24.4

Comparison of the Perfect Competitor with the Monopolistic Competitor. In panel (a), the perfectly competitive firm has zero economic profits in the long run. Its long-run average total cost curve is tangent to the demand curve *dd* just at the point of intersection with the marginal cost curve. The price is set equal to marginal cost, and that price is P_1. There are zero economic profits. Also, its demand curve is just tangent to the minimum point on its average total cost curve, which means the firm is operating at its optimum rate of production. With the monopolistically competitive firm in panel (b), there are also zero economic profits in the long run, because the average total cost curve is tangent to the individual monopolistic competitor's demand curve, *d'd'*, at the output where production occurs. The price, however, is greater than marginal cost; the monopolistically competitive firm does not find itself at the minimum point on its average total cost curve. It is operating at a rate of output less than is optimal – that is, to the left of the minimum point on the ATC curve.

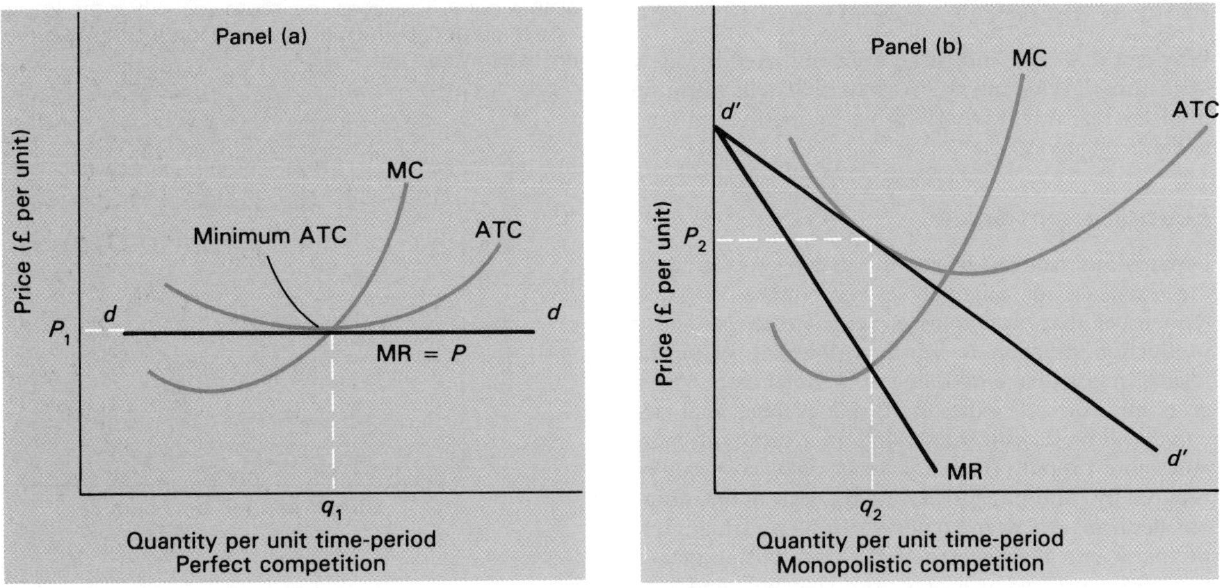

referring to the percentage of total industry output accounted for by the few top firms.

You can probably think of quite a few examples of an oligopolistic market structure. The brewing industry in the UK is dominated by six large firms. Bass Charrington, Allied Breweries, Whitbread, Grand Metropolitan, Courage, and Scottish & Newcastle together account for about three-quarters of UK beer production and own about the same number of all public house licences. In the case of the clearing banks we have already noted in Chapter 19 that the National Westminster, Barclays, Midland, and Lloyds together have the greatest number of domestic current accounts.

INTERDEPENDENCE

When there are only a few large firms dominating the industry, they cannot act independently of one another. In other words, they recognize that there is *mutual interdependence*. Each firm will react to what the other firms do in terms of output and price, as well as to changes in quality and product differentiation. To specify a complete model of oligopoly, we would have to somehow specify the manner in which an oligopolist expects his or her rivals to react. Remember, in a perfectly competitive model each firm ignores the reactions of other firms because each firm can sell all that it wants at the going market price. In the pure monopoly model, the monopolist does not have to worry about the reaction of rivals, since, by definition, there are none.

We must stress here that the mutual interdependence results from the small number of firms in the industry that produce the largest share of total industry output. In fact, we might state that in an oligopoly market structure, the firms must try to predict the reaction of rival firms. Otherwise, poor business decisions could be made that would spell lower profits.

Why Oligopoly Occurs

Why is it that some industries are dominated by a few large firms? What are the reasons that will cause an industry that might otherwise be competitive to tend towards oligopoly?

Economies of Scale

Perhaps the strongest reason that has been offered for the existence of oligopoly is economies of scale. Remember that economies of scale are defined as a production situation in which a doubling of output results in less than a doubling of the total costs. When economies of scale exist, the firm's average total cost curve will be downward sloping as it produces more and more output. That is, average total cost can be reduced by continuing to expand the scale of operation. Smaller firms will have a tendency in such a situation to be inefficient; their average total costs will be greater than those incurred by a large firm. They will tend to go out of business (or be absorbed into the larger firm, which we discuss below). Historically, in many of the industries that have become oligopolistic in the United States, it has been technical progress that has made economies of scale obtainable. For example, consider the motor-car business. When it started out, there were numerous firms in the industry. Today, in the UK and in most developed nations the number of competitors is but a fraction of those pioneering makers of motorized transport: there are three major ones.

Minimum Efficient Scale

The number of firms must be examined in light of the **minimum efficient scale** for a firm in the industry. By minimum efficient scale we mean the lowest rate of output per unit time-period at which average costs reach a minimum point for a particular firm. If you recall our discussion of costs in Chapter 21 we saw how the long-run average cost curve is determined by the nature of the returns to scale. In Figure 24.5 we show how economies of scale initially determine a declining long-run average cost curve before such economies become exhausted. When scale economies are exhausted and constant returns to scale begin the minimum efficient scale for the firm is encountered.

Minimum efficient scale is thus concerned with that rate of output where the long-run average cost of the firm flattens out. The relevant issue now is whether firms suffer a significant cost disadvantage if they are unable to sell a sufficiently large volume of output so

Figure 24.5

Minimum Efficient Scale. This long-run average cost curve reaches a minimum point at *A*. After that point, long-run average costs remain horizontal, or constant, and then, at some later rate of output, rise. Point *A* is called the minimum efficient scale for the firm because at that point it reaches minimum costs. It is the lowest rate of output at which the average long-run cost curves are minimized.

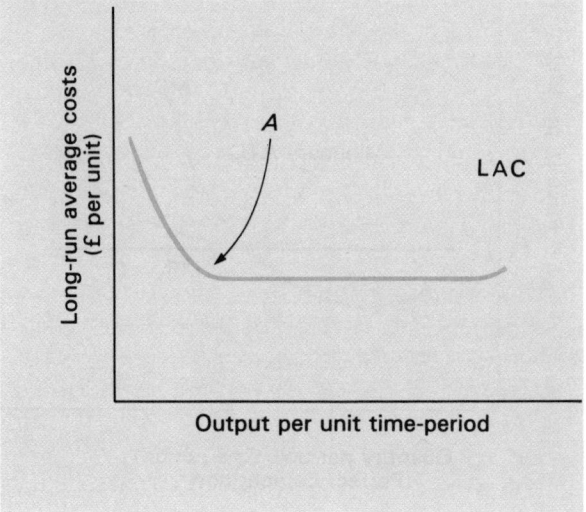

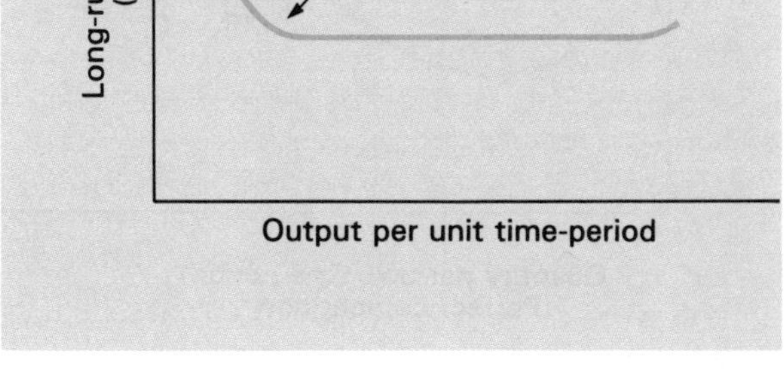

that they can enjoy all possible internal economies of scale. Empirical evidence on this is now much more extensive in the United States than in the UK. Figure 24.6 shows that in the case of products like refined sugar, aluminium semi-manufactures, and detergents we should indeed be surprised to find anything other than an oligopolistic market structure. Quite simply, scale economies explain why the number of efficient competitors will be relatively few.

Figure 24.6

Some Estimates of Minimum Efficient Scale of Plant. The data show that for some products efficient production in the supply of that product is likely to require an appreciable degree of concentration of output in few plants.

Product	*MES as a percentage of UK sales*
Flour	About 1%
Oil refining	9%
Potato crisps	About 10%
Detergent powder	10%
Refined sugar	About 20%
Cigarettes	About 21%
Sulphuric acid	26%
Ethylene	34%
Aluminium semi-manufactures	36%
Industrial diesel engines	56%
Tractors	76%

Source: *A Review of Monopolies and Mergers Policy: A Consultative Document*, Cmnd 7198, HMSO, May 1978.

Barriers to Entry

It is possible that certain barriers to entry have prevented more competition in oligopolistic industries. We defined barriers to entry in Chapter 23. They include legal barriers, such as patents, control and ownership over critical supplies, all of which can result in a pure monopoly situation existing. But there may be entry barriers of a less overwhelming kind which may result in the presence of some competitors but not as many as would create a monopolistic competitive market structure. The sort of difficulties of becoming a new entrant into an industry that we have in mind are the large sums of finance that may be required in order to set up in production, advertise heavily, and create a new brand awareness – to product differentiate – and also to build up a national distribution system.

In the 1950s Professor Joe Bain began pioneering research into the nature of entry barriers into a wide range of US manufacturing industries. The problem of capital requirements was one of the barriers that Bain tried to quantify. He found that the capital requirements barrier was the highest in cigarettes, automobiles, steel, petroleum-refining, and tractor production. However, the capital requirement difficulty was almost non-existent in flour, shoes, and meat-packing, and relatively small in canned foods and vegetables, fountain pens, and metal containers.* In Bain's view the problem of product differentiation was the most important source of entry barriers for firms contemplating entry into many consumer goods markets. From this we have something to reflect on in Chapter 29 where government policies to make markets more competitive are considered. But there is one more aspect about the creation of oligopolistic markets that has public policy implications. This is the slimming down in the number of competitors through merger activity.

Oligopoly by Merger

Another reason that explains the development of oligopolistic market structures is that a number of firms have merged. A merger is the joining of two or more firms under a single ownership or control. There are three types of merger – horizontal, vertical, and conglomerate.

HORIZONTAL MERGERS

Horizontal mergers involve firms selling a similar product. If two shoe manufacturing firms merge, that is a horizontal merger. If a group of firms all producing, say, cars merge into one, that is also a horizontal merger.

VERTICAL MERGERS

Vertical mergers occur when one firm merges with either a firm from which it purchases an input or a firm to which it sells its output. Vertical mergers occur, for example, when a shoe manufacturer purchases retail shoe outlets. (Obviously, vertical mergers do not create oligopoly as we have defined it.)

CONGLOMERATE MERGERS†

Conglomerate mergers involve the joining together of two firms which have unrelated activities. For example a tobacco firm might seek to acquire firms producing beer and foodstuffs in order to ensure that its future growth is not restricted by a decline in cigarette-smoking.

The Rationale for Mergers

We must presume that the decision by, say, the board of directors of two firms to merge is not taken lightly. There must be some rationale for the firms involved to wish to give up their independence. One would assume that the directors perceive benefits from the

* Joe S. Bain, *Barriers to New Competition* (Cambridge, Mass.: Harvard University Press, 1956).

†Also referred to as diversifying mergers, or lateral integration.

merger which outweigh any of the disadvantages involved. The wish to take advantage of scale economies by combining outputs is clearly one such potential gain from merger activity. Mergers allow companies to grow and indeed to expand in size overnight. An alternative method of company growth is for a firm to win some of the market held by its rivals. As compared with a merger, this method of growth is typically slow since it takes time to win new customers. Mergers permit a quick and more certain expansion. However, sometimes a firm is reluctant to lose its independence and is faced not with a merger option but a take-over bid from a rival. It is then a matter of persuading the shareholders of the desirability of staying independent rather than accept an attractive offer for their shares. In this case we are referring to a take-over bid, which may be contested by an unwilling recipient and the desirability of a merger keenly disputed by the two parties.

In such situations the bidding firm will be much involved in winning support from the major shareholders of its intended victim. In most companies these large shareholders are financial institutions rather than individuals. These large shareholders – pension funds, insurance companies, unit and investment trusts – thus effectively have the determination of take-over bids in their hands. In this sense they provide the **market for corporate control** of companies.

Sometimes the enthusiasm for mergers and take-overs appears to be based less on the quest to realize scale economies and more on jockeying for position by the senior management of large firms to build ever-larger companies. 'Empire-building' for its own sake and the attempt by senior managers to keep competition restricted by eliminating awkward competitors are motives for mergers that are indeed well documented. We must therefore not assume that the merger process is necessarily always in the interests of consumers. This point will be a major matter for us to consider in Chapter 29 in our review of what policies government might wish to adopt in seeking the promotion of competitive markets.

We have so far been considering the creation of oligopolies in a theoretical manner and we must now look at the actual picture of oligopolies in the UK.

Industry Concentration

We have seen that the definition of oligopoly is a situation in which a very few interdependent firms control a large part of total output in an industry. Output of the industry is *concentrated* in a few hands. How do we measure this concentration of industry output?

Concentration Ratio

The most frequent way to compute industry concentration is to determine the percentage of total sales or production accounted for by, say, the top four or top eight firms in an industry. This then gives the four- or eight-firm **concentration ratio**. An example of an industry with 25 firms is given in Figure 24.7. We account for 90 per cent of total output in the hypothetical industry which certainly describes an oligopoly situation.

Figure 24.7

Computing the Four-firm Concentration Ratio

	Annual sales (£m)	
Firm 1	150	
Firm 2	100	
Firm 3	85	= 405 (Firms 1–4)
Firm 4	70	
Firm 5–25	45	
	450	
4-firm concentration ratio	$= \frac{405}{450}$	= 90 per cent

Figure 24.8

Market Concentration by UK Manufacturing Sector Measured by Employment in 1980

Minimum list heading sectors	*No. of industries*	*Average 5-firm concentration ratio*
Vehicles, transport equipment	7	65
Extraction, metal manufacture	4	59
Food, drink, tobacco	15	58
Electrical & electronic engineering	7	57
Non-metallic mineral products	8	54
Chemicals	8	53
Textiles	9	42
Instrument engineering	4	41
Mechanical engineering	11	36
Paper, printing	3	30
Other	6	30
Leather, footwear, clothing	6	23
Timber, wooden furniture	7	21
Metal goods	5	22
	100	44

Note: Figure 24.8 shows the average five-firm concentration ratio as measured by employment using the 1980 Census of Production Minimum List Heading definition of industries. This definition of an industry is a very broad one but the data do illustrate the variation in concentration in UK manufacturing industry. Can you establish any relationship between the level of concentration and the nature of production in this table?

Source: Calculations based on Summary Tables, 1980 Census of Production by R. Clarke, *Industrial Economics* (Basil Blackwell, 1985), p. 22.

Key Points 24.3

- **Oligopoly means few sellers; an oligopoly is a market situation in which there are few interdependent sellers.**
- **An oligopolistic market structure can come about because of (1) returns to scale, (2) barriers to entry, and (3) horizontal mergers.**
- **Horizontal mergers involve firms selling a similar product.**
- **Vertical mergers involve the merging of one firm with either the supplier of an input or a firm to which it sells its output.**
- **Industry concentration can be measured by the percentage of total sales accounted for by the top four or five firms.**

UK Concentration Ratios over Time

Figure 24.8 shows the five-firm concentration ratios for various industries in 1980. But is there any way we can show or determine which industries we classify as oligopolistic? There is no definite answer. If one arbitrarily picks a five-firm concentration ratio of 52 per cent, then one could indicate that just half of the 100 industries were oligopolistic. But one would always be dealing with an arbitrary definition of what constitutes an oligopolistic industry. See in Figure 24.8 how the proportion changes if our cut-off point is raised from 52 to, say, 58 per cent.

The concept of an 'industry' is necessarily arbitrary. As a consequence, concentration ratios rise as we narrow the definition of an industry and fall as we broaden it. Thus, we must be certain that we are satisfied with the definition of the industry under study before we jump to conclusions about whether the 'industry' is truly 'too' concentrated, as evidenced by a high measured concentration ratio. (Now read Key Points 24.3.)

Oligopoly Price and Output Determination

When we analysed perfect competition, pure monopoly, and monopolistic competition, we were able explicitly to present the profit-maximizing rate of output and price combination. In each case, we were able to draw a demand curve, a marginal revenue curve, and a marginal cost curve. (For all three cases, profit maximization occurred when marginal revenue equalled marginal cost.) We cannot so easily do the same thing for oligopoly. Indeed, it is impossible for us to draw any one specific demand curve facing the oligopolist. Remember that we pointed out that each oligopolist had to take account of the reaction of other oligopolists. How can a demand curve be known or even guessed without specifying the way that the other oligopolists will react? The answer is, it cannot. In each oligopoly model, we must take account explicitly of other rivals' reactions. As you might expect, economists have come up with a multitude of oligopoly models, each one depending on a different type of reaction by rivals.

The Simplest Oligopoly Model

To begin this discussion of oligopoly on its most general level, we make six assumptions.

1. The industry has only a small number of firms. The position and shape of the long-run average cost (LAC) curve relative to the industry demand curve is such that the industry can support only a small number of efficient plants and firms.
2. The firm (and plant) LAC is upward sloping over the relevant range of outputs. The total cost curve of each firm is continuous and normal in the sense that marginal costs will always be positive and above LAC.
3. Single-plant firms are the only possibility. This would in fact be the case if there are large diseconomies at the firm level and/or the possibility of government policies precluding the operation of plants under common ownership and control.
4. Free entry. There are no barriers to entering into or exiting from the industry.
5. The firms produce similar products.
6. Profit maximization. We continue to analyse price and output determination assuming that firms strive to make the highest possible aggregate profits.

The Oligopolist's Demand Curve

Now we are faced with the difficult task of drawing the demand curve for an oligopolist. We cannot use the industry demand curve because the oligopolist is not a monopolist. We cannot use a horizontal demand curve at the market-clearing price because the oligopolist is, by definition, not a perfect competitor. We can say nothing about the demand curve of an oligopolist until we make an assumption about the interaction among oligopolists. We have to know something about the **reaction function** that we are looking at. Does each oligopolist believe that others will not react to changes in its price and/or output? If the typical oligopolist believes that they will react, we must specify the manner in which the oligopolist *expects* them to react. Remember that in a perfectly competitive model, each firm ignores the reactions of other firms because each firm can sell all that it wants at the going market price. In the pure monopoly model, the monopolist does not have to worry about the reaction of rivals, since by definition there *are* none.

Being able to ignore what other firms are doing in an industry – whether it be perfectly competitive or purely monopolistic – is therefore the key distinction to be made between those two forms of market structure and the one under study, oligopoly. We are referring here to interdependence. This interdependence lies at the heart of every oligopoly model, and thus every time a new assumption about interaction among oligopolists for a reaction function is made, a new oligopoly model is born. For this simplest of oligopoly models, we will assume the following:

Each firm expects that any change in price will be matched by all other firms in the industry.

We can see in Figure 24.9 the result of this assumption. The industry demand curve is *dd*. If the industry has only two firms of equal size, each firm will believe that its demand curve is equal to the one labelled ½*D*½*D*. This follows from our assumption that whatever price it chooses will be matched by its rivals. If we assume three equal-sized firms in the industry, each individual demand curve, as perceived by the individual oligopolist, will be ⅓*D*⅓*D*. The demand curves ½*D*½*D* and ⅓*D*⅓*D* are called **proportionate demand curves**, since they represent equal proportions of the industry.

The Equilibrium Number of Firms

We have assumed unrestricted entry and exit. Further, we assume that all firms have cost curves exactly alike. We can determine the number of firms that will be in the industry by comparing the long-run average cost curve with the firms' demand curves. This is shown in Figure 24.10. If there were one firm in the industry, other firms would be attracted because the long-run cost curve lies below the industry demand curve *DD* for a large range of outputs. If there were two firms in the industry, there would still be an incentive to enter. Finally, if three firms were in the industry, a fourth firm would not desire to enter because the LAC curve is everywhere

Figure 24.9

Proportionate Demand Curves. If each firm expects that any change in price will be matched by all other firms in the industry, and if there are two equal-sized firms in the industry, each will face a demand curve that is ½D½D. If there are three equal-sized firms in the industry, each will face a demand curve that is ⅓D⅓D.

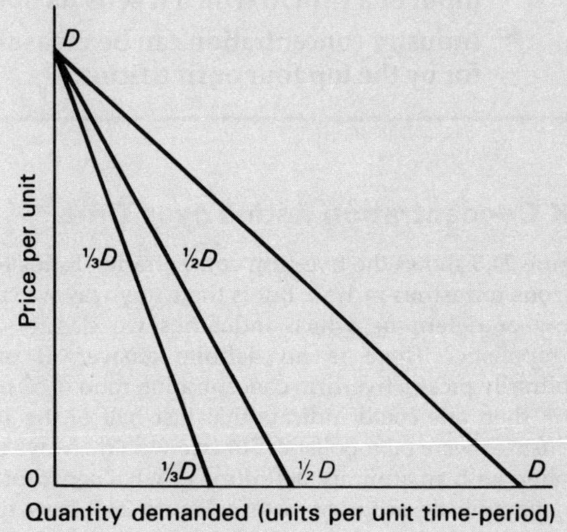

Figure 24.10

Establishing the Equilibrium Number of Firms. If the long-run average cost curve for the industry is LAC, only three firms can be supported in this industry. If a fourth enters, each will face a demand curve equal to ¼D¼D. The LAC curve is everywhere above that proportionate demand curve; all firms make losses.

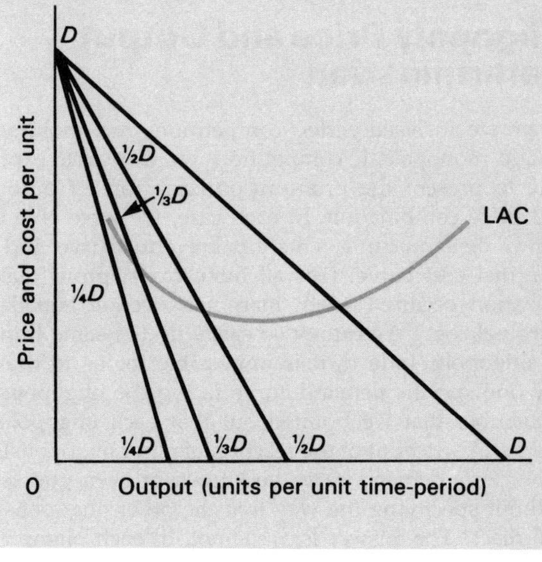

above the proportional demand curve ¼D¼D. If four firms were in the industry, by our assumptions, none could cover long-run average costs. They would all suffer economic losses.

Long-run Economic Profits

It is possible in this simple model that in the long run, economic profits will be obtained. This can be seen by transferring the proportional demand curve for an individual oligopolist when there are three firms to Figure 24.11. The demand curve facing each of the three individual firms is ⅓D⅓D. The long-run average cost curve is given as LAC, and the long-run marginal cost curve is LMC. The profit-maximizing rate of output for each individual oligopolist is at the intersection of marginal revenue and long-run marginal cost, or at a rate of output q_1. The price that the product will sell for is identically equal for each firm at P_1. Unit cost, given LAC, is C_1. Economic profits per unit time-period are equal to the shaded area in Figure 24.11.

Given the assumption in this model, this is the long-run equilibrium situation.

Price Rigidity and the Kinked Demand Curve

We can offer yet another solution to the oligopoly pricing situation. Suppose now that the decision-makers in an oligopolistic firm assume that rivals will react in the following way: they will match all price *decreases* (in order not to the 'undersold'), but not price *increases* (because they want to capture more business). The implications of this reaction function, as it were, are rigid prices and a **kinked demand curve**, which we will explain now.

In Figure 24.12 we draw a kinked demand curve, which is implicit in the assumption that oligopolists follow price decreases but not price increases. We start off at a given price of P_0 and assume that the quantity demanded at that price for this individual oligopolist is q_0. The oligopoly firm assumes that if it lowers its price, rivals will react by matching that reduction to avoid losing their respective shares of the market.

Figure 24.11

Long-run Economic Profits. We have assumed that three equal-sized firms will exist in this industry. Each faces a proportionate demand curve ⅓D⅓D. The marginal revenue curve facing each firm is MR, the output for each firm is q_1, and the price is P_1. Costs are equal to C_1 and thus each firm's profit is the shaded area.

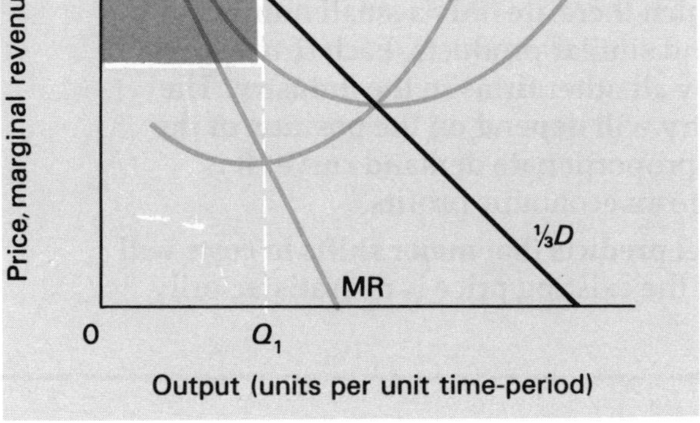

Figure 24.12

The Kinked Demand Curve. Start with the price of P_0. The quantity demanded will be q_0. Now assume that if the firm raises the price above P_0, no firm (or at least only a few firms) will follow suit. Therefore, at a price of P_0, the individual oligopolist's demand curve is relatively elastic – it will lose large amounts of business if it raises price. The demand curve is relatively flat, as shown in the portion *d* to *E*. If we were to extend it out, it would follow the broken line after point *E*. Now consider a reduction in price by the individual oligopolist. The rest of the firms will follow suit, so that a drop in price will result in very little increase in business. Demand will be relatively inelastic below price P_0, as shown by the steeper demand-curve portion from *E* to *d* as we move downwards. That demand curve, if it continued, would go up the broken line past point *E* towards the vertical axis. We can now draw marginal revenue curves for these two separately sloped demand curves. Only those portions of the two marginal revenue curves that are relevant are shown in solid black (*dA* and *B*MR). There is a discontinuous portion (AB). That is where the kink occurs in the kinked demand curve.

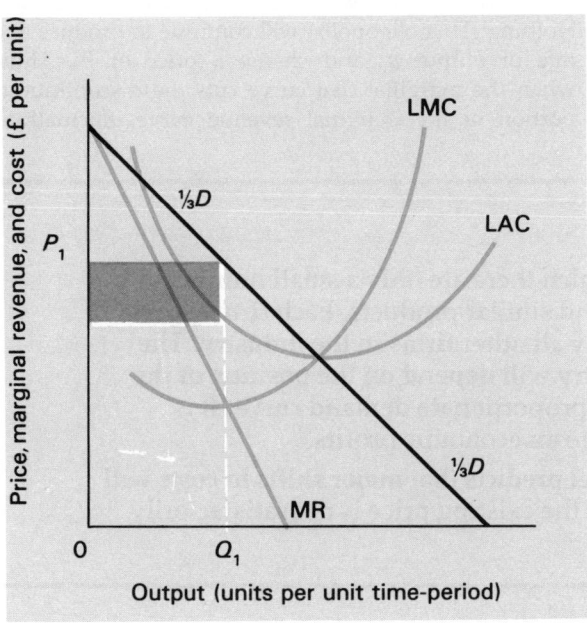

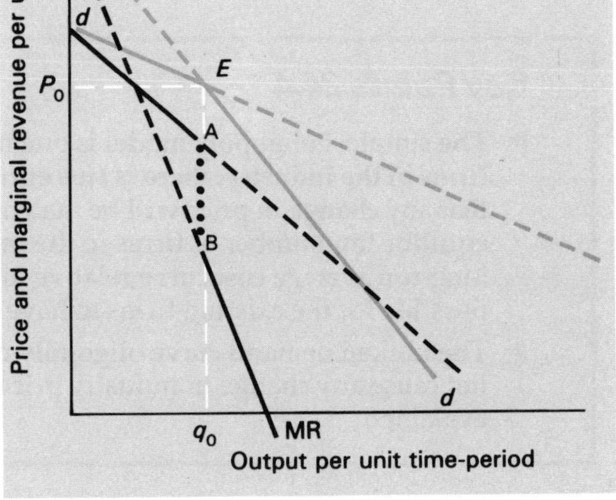

Thus, the oligopolist that lowers its price will not increase its quantity demanded greatly. The portion of its demand curve to the right of an below point *E* in Figure 24.12 is much less elastic. On the other hand, if the oligopolist increases price, no rivals will follow suit. Thus, the quantity demanded at the higher price for this oligopolist will fall off dramatically. The demand schedule to the left of and above point *E* will be relatively elastic. This is the flatter part of the curve to the left of point *E*. Consequently, the demand curve facing the oligopolist is *dd*, which has a kink at *E*.

The Marginal Revenue Curve

To draw a marginal revenue curve for the kinked demand curve in Figure 24.12, we first draw a marginal revenue curve out from the vertical axis for the elastic portion of the demand curve (from the upper *d* to a point directly below *E*). At quantity q_0, however, the demand curve abruptly changes slope and becomes steeper. The marginal revenue curve will have a discontinuous part in it that corresponds to the kink at quantity q_0 in the demand curve *dd*. To the left of that 'step', marginal revenue is relatively high. This indicates that revenues will be lost rapidly if the firm moves up (raises price) the relatively elastic portion of its demand curve. To the right of the 'step', on the other hand, marginal revenue is relatively lower. This indicates that little extra revenue can be obtained when the oligopolist moves down (lowers price) the relatively less elastic portion of the demand curve.

Price Rigidity

Over the discontinuous portion of the marginal revenue curve, the oligopolist does not react to changes in marginal cost (unless they are really large). Look, for example, at Figure 24.13. Assume that marginal cost is represented by *mc*. The profit-maximizing rate of output is q_0 which can be sold at a price of P_0. Now assume that the marginal cost curve rises to *mc'*. What will happen to the profit-maximizing rate of output? Nothing. Both quantity and price will remain the same for this oligopolist.

Figure 24.13

Changes in Cost May Not Alter the Profit-maximizing Price and Output. As long as the marginal cost curve 'intersects' the marginal revenue curve in the latter's discontinuous portion, the profit-maximizing price P_0 (and output q_0) will remain unchanged. (However, the firm's rate of profit will change.)

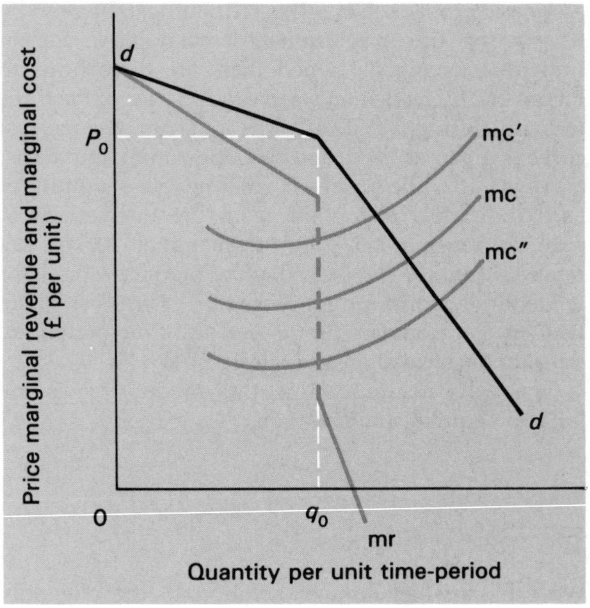

Remember that the profit-maximizing rate of output is where marginal revenue equals marginal cost. The shift in the marginal cost curve to *mc'* does not change the profit-maximizing rate of output, because *mc'* still 'cuts' the marginal revenue curve in the latter's discontinuous portion. Thus, the equality between marginal revenue and marginal cost still holds at output rate q_0 even when the marginal cost curve shifts upwards. What will happen when marginal cost falls to *mc"*? Nothing. This oligopolist will continue to produce at a rate of output q_0 and charge a price of P_0. Thus, when the marginal cost curve cuts the discontinuous portion of the marginal revenue curve, fluctuations

Key Points 24.4

- **The simplest oligopoly model is one in which there are only a small number of firms in the industry, there is free entry, and similar products. Each firm expects that any change in price will be matched by all other firms in the industry. The equilibrium number of firms in the industry will depend on the position of the long-run average cost curve relative to the proportionate demand curve. It is possible for the existing firms to have long-run economic profits.**
- **The kinked demand curve oligopoly model predicts that major shifts in costs will not cause any change in industry price but the existing price is not satisfactorily explained.**

(within limits) in marginal cost will not affect output or price, because the profit-maximizing condition MR = MC will hold. Thus, prices are seen to be rigid in oligopolistic industries if they react the way we assumed in this model.

The theory is thus an application of the revenue functions that are now familiar to us. But one of the criticisms that has been waged against the kinked demand curve is that we have no idea how the existing price, P_0, came into being. Seemingly, if every oligopolistic firm faced a kinked demand curve, it would not pay for it to change prices. The problem is that the kinked demand curve does not show us how supply and demand originally determine the going price of an oligopolist's product. (Now read Key Points 24.4.)

Collusion

Our discussion of the kinked demand curve highlighted the basic problem of the oligopolist – trying to estimate how rivals will react. In short the world of oligopoly is one of *uncertainty*. This is in contrast to the situation both in pure monopoly and in perfect competition. In the case of the former where there is only one firm the question of considering rivals does not arise. At the other end of the spectrum where the number of firms is large the decisions made by an insignificant single producer are trivial to the outcome of the whole industry. Interdependence means that oligopolists are, in a freely competing market, always unsure what will be the impact of one firm's change in market behaviour. One firm's decisions has consequences for all.

Uncertainty was seen in Chapter 16 as one basis for individuals to hold money. In a micro-context the presence of uncertainty provides managers of firms with an incentive to reduce the risks inherent in business life. How can managers in an oligopolistic market structure try to minimize the uncertainties they all face? Well they can try to agree on restraints on their independent decision-making. If they *collude* they limit their ability to use the crucial variable of price to try to gain sales from rivals.

Study of the business environment in the UK in the nineteenth century shows a 'natural' tendency for firms in concentrated industries to try to act in concert. Indeed, the operation of capitalism seems to prompt efforts by businessmen to reach either implicit or explicit agreement on prices which should be charged. This raises the very relevant issue of government policy towards such restraints on price competition and is discussed in the next chapter. For the moment we need to consider what are the possible advantages for oligopolists of engaging in **collusion**. First of all we need to define what we mean by collusion. Collusion that takes place in a **cartel** is an agreement made by a number of independent entities to co-ordinate decisions. The purpose of the cartel is that the cartel will earn monopoly profits. Thus the operation of a cartel that fixes prices takes us back to our discussion of the behaviour of a monopolist who attempts to increase total revenue by restricting output. The analysis of a profit-maximizing monopolist is the same as a cartel which seeks to maximize the joint profits of its member firms.

Duopoly

The simplest way to approach the operation of cartel pricing is to consider the case of just two firms in an industry. This situation is called **duopoly**. Suppose the two firms, Smith PLC and Jones PLC each account for half of an industry's output which is not differentiated by product and produce under identical cost conditions. These two assumptions mean the costs and revenue functions for both Smith PLC and Jones PLC are as in Figure 24.14. Profits are maximized for both firms at the level of output *OQ* and the shaded area *PRST* indicates the short-run economic profits accruing to both Smith PLC and Jones PLC. Neither firm has any incentive to charge a price other than *OP*. A cut in price by say Smith PLC would result in both firms suffering reduced profits. The interests of Smith PLC square with those of Jones PLC if the price is *OP*.

Figure 24.14

Duopoly with Identical Costs and Market Shares. The two firms, Jones and Smith are assumed to have similar costs in producing the same product and equally share the output of the industry. They each maximize profits at output *OQ* and each gains the short-run profits of *PRST*. Neither firm has any reason to undercut the other: they would both charge the common price of *OP*.

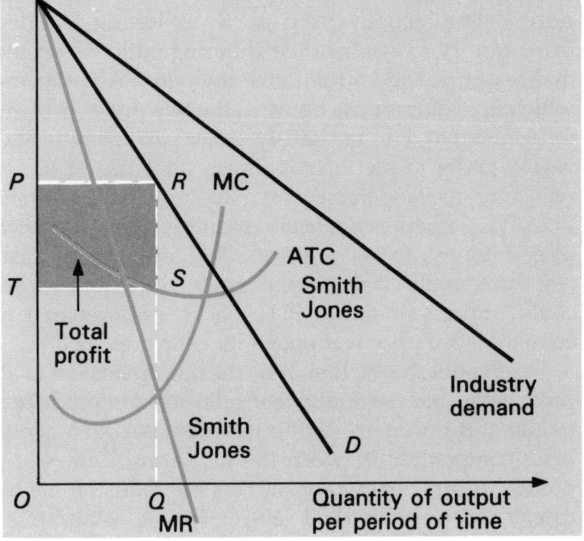

Figure 24.15

Duopoly: Costs Differ but Equal Market Shares. When one firm in a duopoly has lower costs than its rival it would wish to charge a price that differs from its competitor. Here Smith would select an output of *OW* and charge *OS* while Jones, the higher cost firm, would wish to set a higher price *OJ*. The duopolists have no common view and face a difficulty in resolving their individual outlooks.

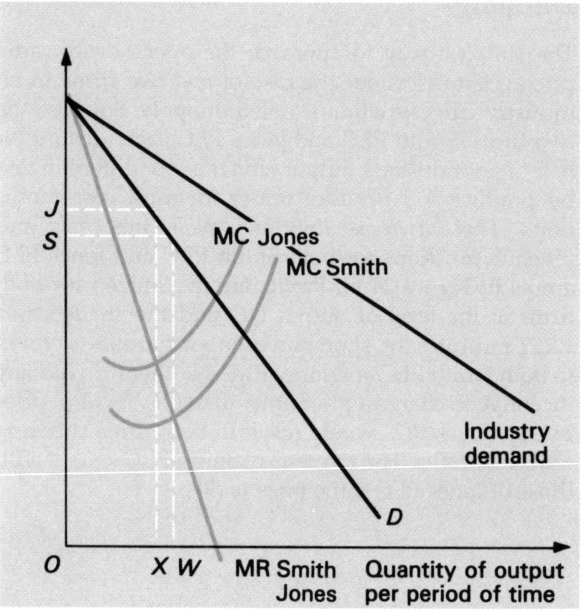

But what happens if in our duopoly model Jones PLC is now a higher-cost producer perhaps because its production facilities are older and less productive or even because of managerial inefficiency? Figure 24.15 shows that the two firms cannot sell at a price that will equate their individual interests with that of the industry as a whole. Smith PLC gains maximum profits with a price of *OS* and output *OW* but Jones PLC finds its profit-maximizing situation *OJ* and *OX*. Their interests conflict and neither firm would wish to see the price determined by its rival. By colluding the two firms can try to resolve their differing outlooks on the matter of price and output determination. An outcome which is a compromise between the two prices is likely to be one that does not satisfy either party. Smith PLC would prefer to see a compromise price nearer to *OS* reflecting its favourable cost situation. Unless Jones PLC has superior financial resources it is not well placed to try to set a price. The presence of cash resources could make a difference since Jones PLC could impress on Smith PLC that it was prepared to contemplate a price war unless its view prevailed.

This model shows, first, how the outcome is not at all predictable and, secondly, that collusion can produce a fragile and uncertain lasting interlude between active price competition between the two firms. Our model points to any temporary success in collusion being threatened by individual self-interest. A compromise price higher than *OX* leaves Smith PLC likely to concede secret price cuts to a few customers. Collusion is thus threatened since prices are undercut by a member of the price arrangement not upholding to what was agreed. Once price cuts become apparent and all parties engage in price concessions the effectiveness of the cartel is eroded until common cause is again established. Thus cartels are beset by the problem of its members being prompted to *cheat* on what they promise to uphold in common cause: self-interest clashes with the wider interest of the industry as a whole.

The recent difficulties of the oil-producing countries to agree on a common pricing policy illustrate the difficulties that face a cartel like OPEC. But at least one major oil producer has tried to provide some stability to the oil cartel and achieved some success through its relative importance in this market. This stabilizing role as performed by Saudi Arabia as a major oil-producer takes us on to yet another form of price determination within the world of oligopoly, that of price leadership.

Price Leadership

This term refers to the possibility of one firm within an oligopolistic market acting as the leader in effecting changes in prices. One firm may wish to raise its prices because its costs have risen and its profitability thus fallen. Its rivals facing common cost pressures, such as higher wages, could thus be in a similar position and content to follow suit. Thus the lead given by the first firm is one the rest of the industry is more willing to accept. As long as the leader has carefully judged the magnitude of the price rise the problem of the kinked demand curve would not then arise. The price leadership model thus describes how in an oligopolistic market virtual simultaneous changes in prices (so-called **parallel pricing**) can occur. The result appears to point to collusive behaviour but may well simply reflect how all firms await a suitable lead by one firm which acts as a *barometer* for the rest of the industry. The **barometric leader** need not be the same firm on every occasion of a change in price. On the other hand it could be the case that the largest firm in the industry is accepted as the price leader. In this case as the **dominant firm** it might be recognized as the appropriate guide for the rest of the industry. Much smaller firms may hesitate to challenge the determination of market price by the most powerful firm within the industry for fear of starting a challenge from which it may ultimately be the loser.

Limit Pricing

Our discussion has emphasized the interdependence of firms in oligopolistic markets. We can with this point in mind now reconsider one aspect of pricing that we introduced in Chapter 23. It will be recalled that there we considered the possibility of a monopolist trying to deter new entry by predatory pricing. But now we have more than one existing firm currently in the market.

Thus we need to broaden the issue of pricing to refer to several competitors all of whom share the goal of seeking to prevent yet more new competitors appearing on the scene. The concept of **limit pricing** is just such a concept. It refers to the possibility that oligopolists jointly seek to agree on a price which is the highest they can charge without prompting a new entrant to appear.

As you would expect the precise level of the limit price cannot be determined without knowledge of the difficulties that a new firm actually faces. But the higher the barriers to entry then the higher the possible level of the limit price.

Non-price Competition

By their very nature, oligopolistic firms do not exhibit active price competition. The benefits from cutting prices tend to be small given the reactions of rivals. Hence a situation where rivals keep trying to undercut one another in the battle for supremacy in the market in a so-called *price war* is unlikely to persist. The likelihood of becoming a victor is slim if costs conditions are similar. Thus price wars do erupt occasionally, but these are only temporary. Therefore, competition for an increased percentage of total sales in the market must take some other form. The alternative form is what is generally called **non-price competition**. Non-price competition cannot be neatly subdivided into categories because it takes on a large number of aspects. The only thing that we can say about non-price competition is that it is an attempt by one oligopolistic firm to attract customers by some means other than a price differential. Here we will consider only the two types of product differentiation that we have explicitly or implicitly referred to when discussing monopolistic competition.

Advertising

As we pointed out previously, the primary purpose of advertising is to shift the demand curve to the right. This allows the seller, whether it be an oligopolist, a monopolistic competitor, or a monopolist, to sell more at each and every price. Advertising may also have the effect of differentiating the product and of making the product's availability better known. A firm will advertise as a way of gaining a non-price competitive advantage over other firms. Whatever can be said about advertising, its effect on the oligopolistic firm is certainly not completely predictable.

Quality Variations

Quality differentiation results in a division of one market into a number of sub-markets. We talked earlier about differentiating product through quality variation when we discussed monopolistic competition. Now we can apply the same discussion to oligopoly. The prime example of product differentiation is the motor vehicle industry. There are specific physically definable differences between different automobile models within one single firm. A Maestro and a Montego are certainly not the same product. If we examine cars, we see that competition among oligopolistic firms creates a continuous expansion and redefinition of the different models that are sold by any one company. There is competition to create new quality classes and thereby gain a competitive edge. Being the first in the market in a new quality class has often meant higher profits. Thus oligopolists are always looking for best-selling new models. New products can promise higher sales and profits in a way that avoids the alternative risk of engaging in price competition with rivals. (Now read Key Points 24.5.)

Comparing Market Structures

Now that we have looked at perfect competition, pure monopoly, monopolistic competition, and oligopoly, we are in a position to compare the attributes of these four different market structures. We do this in summary form in Figure 24.16, where we compare the number of sellers, their ability to set price, and whether product differentiation exists.

Figure 24.16
Comparing Market Structures

Market structure	*Number of sellers*	*Unrestricted entry and exit*	*Ability to set price*	*Long-run economic profits possible*	*Product differentiation*
Perfect competition	Numerous	Yes	None	No	None
Monopolistic competition	Many	Yes	Some	No	Considerable
Oligopoly	Few	Partial	Some	Yes	Typical
Pure monopoly	One	No	Considerable	Yes	The product is unique

Key Points 24.5

- **Because the world of oligopoly is one of uncertainty there is an incentive for oligopolists to try to collude such that competition in price is at least partly eliminated.**
- **In a duopoly situation the equilibrium price and industry output could be equivalent to the pure monopoly profit-maximizing price and output combination. Differences in their cost situation makes collusion between duopolists difficult to effect.**
- **Price leadership may be one method by which oligopolists avoid the uncertainties in price determination when they do not collude. The leader may be the largest firm in an industry or simply one firm that hopes its rivals will accept its proposed change in price.**
- **Non-price competition is typical of oligopolistic market structures since if one firm tries to expand sales through price competition it is unlikely to be successful without damage to its profit situation. Advertising campaigns are the means by which oligopolists try to differentiate their products. Such expenditures highlight the new products that oligopolists strive to develop in order to win consumer support.**

CASE STUDY

Package-tour holidays

Britain's mass-travel business is a product of the British weather. In most of the past decade, its operators have concentrated on maximizing sales of minimalist fortnights of Mediterranean sun and sand (and as much sex as the holiday brochures can illustrate), all at prices well below those that other Europeans pay. Around 13m Britons now take package holidays abroad, up from 5m in 1979. But this year's sunny English summer and clouded economy for mortgage payers have caused many of those extra tourists to hesitate before booking their next Spanish beach. Early bookings for next summer are 50 per cent down on this time last year. Operators fear final bookings could be down by 20 per cent or more.

Such projections are causing near-panic in an industry that has become addicted to sharp competition for high volumes of business yielding tiny profit margins. The two big operators, Thomson and International Leisure Group (ILG), who between them sell nearly 60 per cent of foreign packages, face a choice between two strategies. If they try to keep up market share by competitive price-cutting, both could end up with overcapacity and thumping losses. If they reduce capacity and raise prices, they could compound the slump in demand, and leave the field open for new cut-price operators. Both Thomson and ILG are inclined to the second, price-raising, option. They believe the industry is at a turning-point. In future, quality will count more, quantity less. Success will demand upmarket changes in their product, their marketing and their attitude to customers.

Competing away profits

Running package holidays is a low-margin business. In 1988 the biggest operator, Thomson, made a profit of just £3.4m on a turnover of £949m, under £1 for each holiday sold. But the package-sellers require little capital of their own. The holiday-maker's advance payments see to that. Slender returns would not matter, if they could be guaranteed.

They can't be. Thomson's tiny profits of £1–10 per holiday in each year from 1984 to 1988 relied on a buoyant market which made it possible to sell over 90 per cent of holiday capacity. In the slacker climate of 1989, when package sales fell about 10 per cent, any company that breaks even will have done well. Since about half of tour operators' costs are fixed by the middle of the booking season (mainly by a commitment to buying airline seats), unbought capacity needs to be kept to near-zero. Hence the frantic last-minute discounting each late spring. If sales fall below about 80 per cent, the operator can be in deep trouble.

The obvious escape route is for operators to set brochure prices above cost. But, until recently, prices have been pared to the bone by a five-year battle for market share between Thomson Holidays and ILG's subsidiary, Intasun. Thomson realized in 1985 that Intasun was threatening its position as market leader. Its Canadian parent, the Thomson Corporation, allowed it to lose money if necessary to re-establish its grip. Within two years it had more than doubled the number of holidays sold. After buying Horizon last year, it now sells twice as much as ILG, which in turn is three times as big as the next competitor. With the market-share war over, 1990 brochure prices rose in line with inflation for the first time in five years.

Why fight to be big in an industry with knife-edge profitability? One answer lies in the profits it is supposed this can bring to a vertically integrated group from other parts of the holiday industry. The Thomson Corporation, for example, also owns Lunn Poly (the travel agent that sells many of its holidays) and Britannia Airways (the airline that carries most of its customers). Both have also now established market-leading positions.

Travel agencies yield as meagre returns as tour operating. Charter airlines tend to earn more, around £10–15 per return passenger; but they need to, to give a decent return on the much greater capital employed. A tour operator enjoys more security by owning a profitable airline, and also helps bring that airline business. When passengers are overcramming every airport, neither airline nor operator need worry much who travels how. In the mid-1980s only around 60 per cent of Thomson holidaymakers were flown with Britannia. But in harder times, vertical integration provides airlines with some guarantee of bottoms to fill their expensive seats. Today Thomson Holidays buys at least 80 per cent of the space it needs from its sister. Charter airlines with no captive market are now in trouble. That is why Davies & Newman Holdings, which owns Dan-Air, had to announce a loss of £7.7m in the first half of 1989.

Death on the High Street

Over the next year that vulnerability will spread horridly to travel agents, with or without sister tour companies. Like the tour operators three years ago, the leading travel agents are in a fight to the death for market supremacy. Like today's estate agents and stockbrokers, there are too many shops chasing too few customers in a post-boom market. The big discounts this year are therefore coming from retailers – Lunn Poly is offering buyers about half its 10 per cent cut off the price of winter holidays. Painful losses among medium-sized retailers in 1990 will bring death to some travel agencies, even if it is called rationalization.

The winners of the market-share war in the tour-operating business have always believed they would eventually be able to reap substantial spoils. Being big means buying cheap, from both airlines and hoteliers. Both Thomson and Intasun have hoped that an unassailable market position would mean profitability. So it would, if they could continue to sell close to 100 per cent of capacity without heavy discounting: after covering their fixed costs with, say, 85 per cent take-up, half of each extra holiday sold would then be profit. Alas, in the very year when the two got unassailably to the top of the dunghill, the industry has gone into slump.

How well or badly operators cope with next year's drop in demand will depend mainly on how accurately they can forecast it. Their profit or loss will depend less on their sales, as such, than on how much committed capacity remains unsold. Operators have already dumped around 10 per cent of their capacity. In the next few weeks they will be deciding how much more to shed before bookings start flowing in after Christmas. They have to finalize their own demand for airline seats by February, when bookings are still normally under half of capacity. Fewer seats may bring fewer tour sales, by reducing choice. But if, by April, Thomson and Intasun find they have not cut enough, another bloody price war could break out.

Every tour operator is quick to attribute the industry's present slump to high interest rates and hence low spending power, rather than to a crisis of confidence in the package holiday. Press reports of yobs on the costas have indeed been exaggerated. It is daft to pronounce the death of a commodity whose sales have just peaked at 60 per cent above their level of five years ago. But surveys for a consumer magazine, *Holiday Which?*, show an intriguing trend: the quality of package holidays appears to be rising slowly, but customer satisfaction is slowly falling. People who go on package holidays say they are starting to expect higher standards.

Source: 'Package-tour Operators: Spoiling their Holidays', *The Economist*, 28 Oct. 1989, pp. 37–8

Questions

1. How does the macroeconomic climate affect the nature of competition between package-tour operators in Great Britain?
2. What other factors help explain the existence of keen competition between package-tour operators?
3. Explain the meaning of the following sentence 'If sales fall below about 80 per cent, the operator can be in deep trouble'.
4. What are the key decisions that package-tour operators have to make in this market?
5. What factors affect the demand for holidays which package-tour operators have to be aware of in catering for in this particular market?

CASE STUDY

Kellogg versus the Rest

Frosties or Wheaties, Rice Krispies or Cheerios. The challenge to Kellogg being mounted by the alliance of Nestlé, the Swiss foods group, and General Mills, of the US, is going to bring a lot more snap, crackle, and pop to Europe's £1bn breakfast cereals market.

The joint venture, initiated by General Mills and agreed by Nestlé in only 11 days last month, will set up a separate company, Cereal Partners Worldwide, to market ready-to-eat cereals in the fast-growing but Kellogg-dominated markets of continental Europe.

Neither of the two new partners has any illusions about the size of the task ahead. Since it invented the cornflake in 1891, Kellogg has spread its ready-to-eat cereals from its base in Battle Creek, Michigan, across the breakfast tables of 50 countries around the world. It commands the international market it has largely created, with some 40 per cent of global sales, mainly in the US, Canada, Britain and Australia.

Consumption of both hot and cold cereals has reached the highest levels in those 'Anglo-Saxon' markets. It has been stimulated in the past decade by a number of trends, identified by Euromonitor, the UK market researcher.

- Increased demand for convenience foods. Large breakfasts cooked at home have become less common due to the increase in working women and smaller households. Instant cereals are also more frequently seen as a snack to be eaten at any time of day.
- Health concerns. Many cereals can be marketed on a health platform without needing expensive reformulations, Euromonitor says, 'Mueslis, bran and wheat germ cereals, products with added vitamins and dried fruit, and most recently, oat cereals have enjoyed the most rapid growth during the 1980s.'
- Demographic factors. The ageing of the population is encouraging the shift to high-fibre cereals, and the children of the baby-boom generation are presenting another opportunity to expand the market.
- Supermarket growth. The increasing dominance of supermarkets in food retailing has allowed full ranges of cereal products to be displayed. More than 70 per cent of sales in the US and UK are through supermarkets.

Even in the most mature markets, growth has been impressive. Sales rose from $3.9bn to $6.1bn in the US between 1983 and 1988, and from £440m to £726m in the UK.

Throughout this period, Kellogg has never lost the grip it secured as the pioneer of the industry. Its operations remain tightly focused, with cereals accounting for 90 per cent of sales. The original Cornflakes brand – still the largest worldwide though slowly declining – has been supported by a constant flow of new products such as Fruit 'N' Fibre, Nutri-Grain, Raisin Splitz and Toppas.

Kellogg today has a range of 48 different products – wheat, rice, oats, and corn, flaked and puffed, sugared and unsweetened, mixed with nuts and fruit, flavoured with chocolate or raisin purée.

It backs them with heavy media advertising. In the US last year, Kellogg spent around $550m on advertising. In the UK, it was the third largest advertiser, spending £45m, nearly three-quarters of the total for breakfast cereals.

Competitors have found such production and marketing strengths daunting. In Britain, where the average person spoons down more than 7kg of cereals a year, the most successful challengers have been the retailers, whose own-label brands have captured 22 per cent of sales against Kellogg's 42 per cent. But even that competition has been fading slightly under the impact of Kellogg's assiduous brand marketing.

Weetabix, a private company, has taken a 14 per cent share with its eponymous biscuit, and with Alpen, the first heavily marketed muesli. Ranks Hovis McDougall, whose Viota subsidiary produces own-label cereals, acquired Nabisco's Shredded Wheat in 1988 for £80m to become the fourth largest player. Quaker Oats of the US and Allied-Lyons, the makers of Ready Brek, dominate the hot cereals corner of the market – but it is a small corner.

In general, Kellogg's competitors in the UK, as elsewhere, have found it difficult staying in the race. In Australia's A$355m (£175m) market, its 43.5 per cent share is double that of its nearest rival, Nabisco.

But Nestlé and General Mills may have chosen the right moment to launch their challenge. In the US this year, Kellogg appears to have stumbled. After years of successfully anticipating the changing demands of consumers, it underestimated both the strength and suddenness of the craze for oat bran which swept the US after reports that it helped reduce blood cholesterol levels.

Kellogg apparently dismissed it as a passing fad, gambled instead on a new sweet cereal, and saw the oat-based Cheerios – from its main competitor, General Mills – sweep up the list of best-selling brands followed by other rival oat products. More marketing initiatives flopped. Kellogg had set its sights on a 50 per cent market share by 1992; instead it saw it fall from 42 per cent to 39. General Mills increased its share to 27 per cent – and, in the view of some analysts, has the impetus to lift it over 30 per cent in the next two years.

Such problems at home must have encouraged Nestlé and General Mills in their bid to test

Kellogg's hold on newer, developing markets. Craig Shulstad, director of media and financial relations at General Mills, says: 'We see breakfast cereals as a significant growth market in continental Europe... We shall focus on Europe first but it is our intention to move out from there worldwide.'

By the end of the century, Mr Shulstad estimates retail sales of cereals in Europe will have quadrupled to the present $6bn level of the US.

The UK – which the partners will bypass – at present accounts for nearly three-quarters of Europe's sales. Throughout Europe, no nation eats anything like the amount of breakfast cereals downed by the British. Some industry analysts think that the joint venture's hopes for growth outside the UK may be too optimistic.

Bernard Casal, head of Nestlé food products, is confident that the combined clout of the new joint venture will soon make its presence felt elsewhere.

'I believe we can produce and market our cereal range as a pan-European brand from Gibraltar to the North Cape,' he says. 'I believe we can grow that way very efficiently. And we are prepared to invest for the long term rather than chase short-term profits.'

Source: Adapted from P. Rawstorne, 'The coming battle of the breakfast table,' *Financial Times*, 21 December, 1989.

Questions

1. What characterizes the competitive process in the market for breakfast cereals?
2. What factors have affected consumption habits during the past decade?
3. What benefits would a joint venture provide for the partners involved?
4. Explain the meaning of the following sentence: 'We are prepared to invest for the long term rather than chase short-term profits'.
5. What difficulties might be expected to face a firm that seeks growing sales of breakfast cereals in several different countries?

Exam Preparation

PRACTICAL EXERCISES

1. The term 'minimum efficient scale' refers to the output level at which there are no further economies of scale. Thus the average cost curve becomes horizontal rather than continuing to fall. The table below gives some estimates of the minimum efficient scale of output of plants in ten different industries both in the USA and in the UK. Thus it is estimated that in the cement industry an efficient plant would account for 1.7 per cent of the total market for cement in the US and 6.1 per cent of the cement market in the UK. Column 3 shows that if a cement plant operated at just one-third of the optimum size then its costs of production would be 26 per cent higher than one operating at the most efficient size.

   Study the data in the table on the right and answer the questions (a) to (d).

   (a) Compare the effects on average costs in the following industries when they are operating at one-third MES; cement; steel; shoes.

   (b) What is the significance of this data for producers in the cement, steel, and shoe industries?

   (c) With reference to column 2, discuss the implications for the maximum number of plants operating efficiently in the following industries: steel; glass bottles; refrigerators; ball-bearings.

   (d) Examine the data for petroleum-refining, paints, cigarettes, and shoes and make out a case for restrictions on mergers in these industries.

   (e) Examine the possible benefits of operating on a large scale in *one* of the industries in the above table.

Minimum Efficient Scale (MES) for selected industries in the UK and USA

Industry	*(1) MES as % of US market*	*(2) MES as % of UK market*	*(3) % increase in average costs at ⅓ MES*
Cement	1.7	6.1	26.0
Steel	2.6	15.4	11.0
Glass bottles	1.5	9.0	11.0
Ball-bearings	1.4	4.4	8.0
Fabrics	0.2	1.8	7.6
Refrigerators	14.1	83.3	6.5
Petroleum refining	1.9	11.6	4.8
Paints	1.4	10.2	4.4
Cigarettes	6.5	30.3	2.2
Shoes	0.2	0.6	1.5

Source: F. M. Scherer *et al.*, *The Economics of Multiplant Operation* (Harvard University Press, 1975).

2. The following passage is adapted from an article by Antony Thorncroft entitled *How Companies Fix Prices.*

Pricing in practice is exceptionally far removed from the view of traditional economic theory on how companies fix their prices. According to traditional economic theory, price is determined at the level of output at which marginal revenue equals marginal cost. But a recent survey by Industrial Market Research, into how 220 manufacturing companies fix their prices, suggests otherwise. Many prices are 'cost-plus' prices, arrived at by taking a view on the average costs of producing a particular output and then adding a profit margin. Only a third of companies investigate the acceptability of their prices before fixing them. Few companies make use of price in their advertising; they see price as important rather than as vital in overall marketing strategy. As the report says: 'Price is seen as a handicap that has to be carried in the competition stakes while the race itself is won or lost on the basis of quality, applicational engineering or reputation.' Companies increase prices when costs go up, but rarely reduce them if costs ever fall. Price changes are not seen as a means of expanding market share and seldom are scientific methods used to assess the impact of pricing decisions. Hardly any of the firms investigated tested prices.

(a) (i) Explain the statement: 'According to traditional economic theory, price is determined at the level of output at which marginal revenue equals marginal cost.' (lines 3–6)

(ii) Suggest reasons why firms may adopt 'cost-plus' pricing. (line 10)

(iii) If prices are usually determined on a cost-plus basis, has the traditional theory of the firm any relevance?

(b) Why may firms use methods of competition other than price changes in order to expand their market share?

MULTIPLE CHOICE QUESTIONS

1. Conglomerate mergers are most likely to be embarked upon by a firm wishing to

A retain its share of the market for its main product
B gain control of its raw material supplies
C eliminate overseas competitors
D diversify and extend its range of products
E reduce its dependence on supplies of skilled labour.

2. Oligopoly is best described as a market situation where

A there is a large number of competing firms with similar products
B there is a large number of competing firms whose products differ slightly
C there is a small number of competing firms
D there are only two competing firms
E the market is dominated by one firm only.

3. The diagram represents the market for an economics textbook. The author is paid a royalty by the publisher that is a fixed percentage of the publisher's total sales revenue. At what published price (**A** to **E**) would the author maximize his royalties?

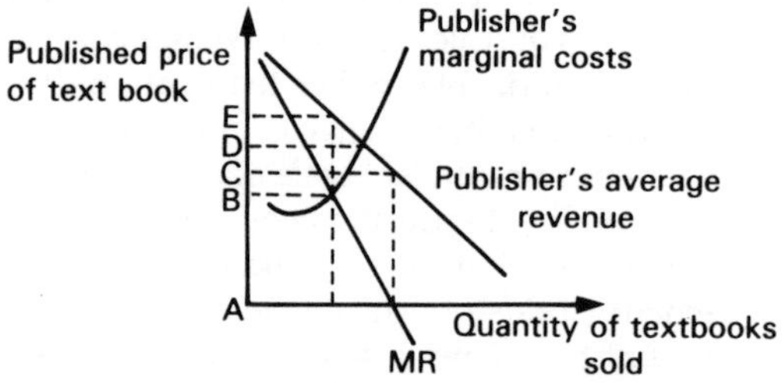

4. In industry X, the four largest firms produce 50 per cent of the industry's total output. In industry Y, the four largest firms produce 70 per cent of the industry's output. It can be concluded from the information that

A firms are larger in industry Y than in industry X
B there are more economies of scale in industry Y than in industry X
C the concentration ratio is higher in industry Y than in industry X
D small firms have more chance of survival in industry X than in industry Y.

5. The diagram depicts an oligopolist's average and marginal revenue curves when production is at output OX.

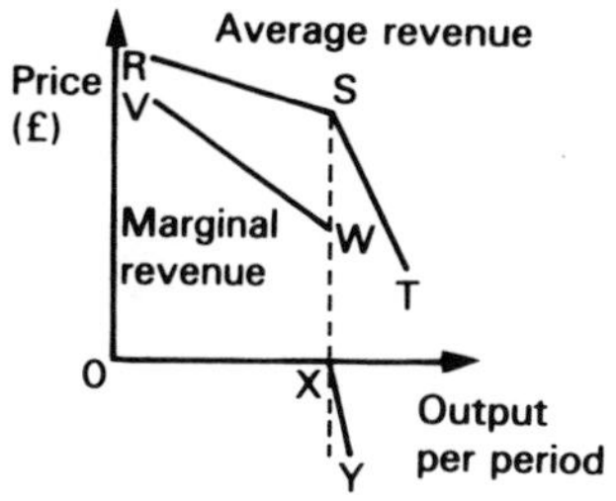

Which of the following would represent the demand curve if the oligopolist cut his price and his competitors were to do the same?

A RS
B ST
C VW
D WX
E XY

RELATED ESSAY QUESTIONS

1. Explain the differences between oligopoly and monopolistic competition. Why do some industries tend towards oligopoly and some towards monopolistic competition?

2. 'The only realistic theories of the firm are to be found under the heading of oligopoly.' Discuss.

3. Examine the main differences in the determination of price and output in conditions of monopoly and oligopoly.

4. 'Barriers to entry determine the long-run level of profits in an industry.' Discuss this statement and, where possible, illustrate your argument with examples drawn from UK industries.

5. 'Oligopoly involves interdependence in a way unlike any other market structure.' Explain this statement and discuss its implications.

6. (a) Describe some of the ways in which the size of firms in an industry can be measured.
(b) Discuss why firms may want to merge, and outline the main types of merger.
(c) Is an increase in industrial concentration necessarily undesirable for the economy?

7. In what circumstances will there be relatively stable prices in an oligopolistic market?

8. Do imperfections of competition lead to an undesirably large number of product varieties, wasteful use of resources, and excessively high prices?

9. What types of market structure might give rise to the following, and why?
(a) low prices
(b) high profits
(c) advertising

10. What is meant by barriers to entry into an industry? What implications do they have for the profits earned by firms and the use of efficient methods of production?

11. Contrast price and output determination in perfect competition and monopolistic competition in both (i) the short run and (ii) the long run.

12. Why do firms merge? Has recent United Kingdom experience shown that mergers are in the public interest?

Part D

Factor Markets

25 Demand and Supply in the Labour Market

Key Points to Review

- Substitution and income effect (5.1)
- Determinants of elasticity (7.4)
- Law of diminishing returns (21.2)
- Profit maximization (22.1)
- Monopolist's demand, marginal revenue less than price (23.2)

Questions for Preview

1 In hiring labour, what general rule will be followed by employers who wish to maximize profits?

2 What is the profit-maximizing rate of employment for (a) a perfectly competitive firm? and (b) an imperfectly competitive firm?

3 What is the shape of the supply of labour curve?

4 How is an industry wage-rate determined?

5 What effect do trade unions have on wages?

6 In what ways is the labour market imperfect?

How much people are paid, and the extent to which their labour resources are used, are crucial issues in economics because they determine who is rich and who is poor. These factors determine what percentage of national income goes to wages and what percentage goes to interest, profits, and dividends.

Before analysing the distribution of income, we try to predict the amount of a particular input that firms will demand and the price they will pay for it. We assume that there is only one variable factor of production: labour, and that all other factors of production are fixed; in other words, the firm has a fixed number of machines but can hire or fire workers.

A firm's demand for inputs can be studied in much the same manner as we studied the demand for output in different types of market situations. Our analysis will always end with the conclusion: a firm will hire employees up to the point where it is not profitable to hire any more. It will hire employees to the point where the marginal benefit of hiring a worker will just equal the marginal cost. We will start our analysis under the assumption that the market for input factors is perfectly competitive, and that the output market is perfectly competitive, also. This provides a bench-mark against which to compare other situations where labour markets and/or product markets are not perfectly competitive.

A Competitive Market

Let us take as our example a prerecorded-tape manufacturing firm that is in competition with many companies selling the same kind of product. Assume that the labour hired by our tape-manufacturing firm needs no special skills. The firm sells its product in a perfectly competitive market and also buys its variable input – labour – in a perfectly competitive market. The firm can influence neither the price of its product nor the price that it must pay for its variable input; it can purchase all the labour it wants at the going market wage without affecting that wage. The 'going' wage is established by

Figure 25.1(a)

(1) Labour input	(2) Total physical product (per week) ≡ TPP	(3) Marginal physical product ≡ MPP	(4) Price of tape (P = £2.50) × Marginal physical product ≡ MRP (£ per additional worker)	(5) Wage-rate (£ per week) Marginal factor cost ≡ MFC ≡ change in total costs / change in labour
6	822			
		118	295	£200
7	1 000			
		111	277.50	£200
8	1 111			
		104	260	£200
9	1 215			
		97	242.50	£200
10	1 312			
		90	225	£200
11	1 402			
		83	207.50	£200
12	1 485			
		76	190	£200
13	1 561			

the forces of supply and demand in the labour market. The total labour demand is the sum of all the individual firms' demands.

Marginal Physical Product

Look at Figure 25.1(a). In column 1, we show the number of worker-weeks that the firm can hire. In column 2, we show total physical product (TPP) per week. In other words, column 2 shows the units of total *physical* production, or real output that different quantities of the labour input will generate in a week's time. In column 3, we show the additional output gained when a tape-manufacturing company adds additional workers to its existing capital capacity. You will notice that the third column, **marginal physical product (MPP),** represents the extra (additional) output attributed to employing additional units of the variable input factor, which in this case is labour. Thus, if this firm adds a seventh worker, the marginal physical product is 118. You will recall that the law of diminishing marginal returns predicts that additional units of a variable factor will, after some point, cause the marginal physical product to decline, other things being equal.

Why Does Marginal Physical Product Decline?

If our tape-manufacturing firm wants to add one more worker to an assembly line, it has to crowd all the existing workers a little closer together because it does not increase its capital stock (the assembly line equipment) at the same time that it increases the workforce. Therefore, as we add more workers, each one has a smaller and smaller fraction of the available capital stock with which to work. If one worker uses one machine, adding another worker will not normally double the output, because the machine can run only so fast for so many hours per day.

Figure 25.1(b)

Marginal Revenue Product Curve. The employer hires workers up to the point where the marginal revenue product equals the wage-rate. In our case it is 12 worker-weeks. If the employer hired only 11 worker-weeks, potential profit represented by triangle *A* would be lost. If 13 worker-weeks are hired, profit is reduced by an amount shown in triangle *B*. *E* is the equilibrium at the intersection of demand and supply, or the point where the MRP equals the going wage.

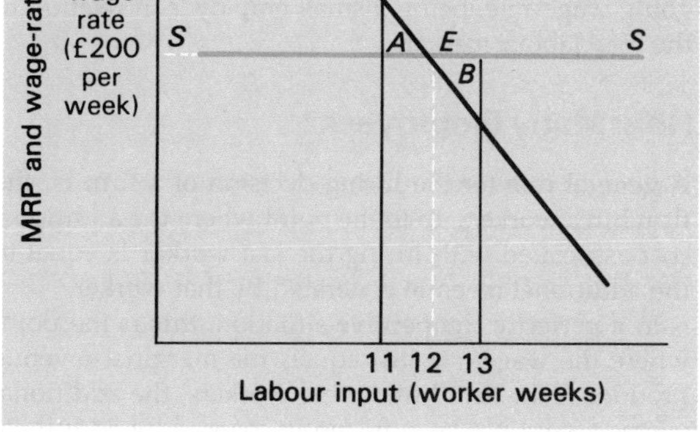

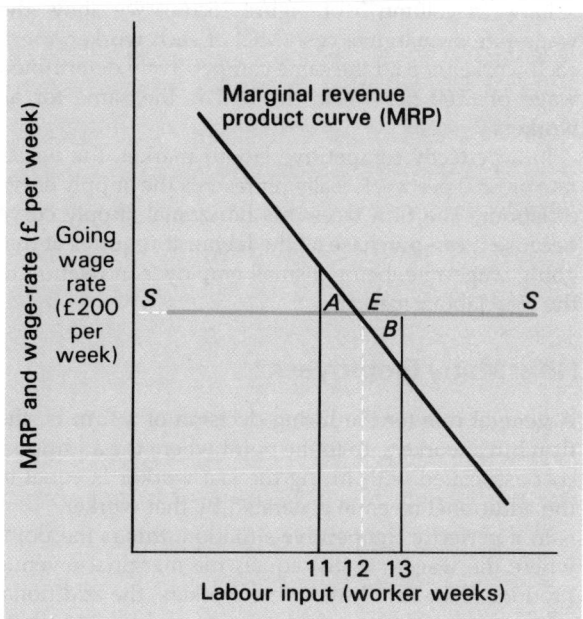

ALL WORKERS PAID SAME WAGE

What additional information do we need to determine the number of workers to be employed? Since we have assumed that labour is employed in a competitive market, then every worker we employ is paid the same wage-rate. Figure 25.1(b) assumes that this wage-rate is £200 per week.

In addition, we need to know the price of the product. Since we have assumed perfect competition, the hypothetical market equilibrium price established in Figure 25.1 is £2.50. Our firm will employ workers up to the point where the marginal revenue, or benefit, of hiring a worker will equal the additional (marginal) cost.

The marginal cost of workers is the extra cost we incur in employing that factor of production. We recall that

$$\text{marginal cost} = \frac{\text{change in total cost}}{\text{change in amount of resource used}}$$

In our example, one additional worker can be hired at a constant cost of £200 per week.

Marginal Revenue Product

We now need to translate the physical product into a money value. This is done by multiplying the MPP by the market price of tapes. If the seventh worker's MPP is 118, and the market price is £2.50 per tape, then the **marginal revenue product** is £295 (118 × £2.50). The marginal revenue product is shown in column 4 Figure 25.1(a). *We call the individual worker's contribution to total revenues the marginal revenue product or MRP.*

Now in column 5 of Figure 25.1(a), we show the wage-rate or marginal cost (MC) of each worker. Since each worker is paid the same competitively determined wage of £200 per week, the MC is the same for all workers.

In a perfectly competitive labour market, the wage-rate of £200 per week really represents the supply curve of labour. The firm faces this horizontal supply curve because it can purchase all the labour it requires at that going wage-rate, being a small employer in relation to the total labour market.

How Many Employees?

A general rule for the hiring decision of a firm is: the firm hires workers up to the point where the additional cost associated with hiring the last worker is equal to the additional revenue generated by that worker.

In a perfectly competitive situation, this is the point where the wage-rate just equals the marginal revenue product. If the firm hired more workers, the additional wages would not be sufficiently covered by additional increases in total revenue. If the firm hired fewer workers, it would be forfeiting the contributions that those workers could make to total profits.

Therefore, referring to columns 4 and 5 in Figure 25.1(a), we see that this firm would certainly employ the seventh worker, because the MRP is £295 while the MC is only £200. The firm would continue to employ workers up to the point where MC = MRP because as workers are added, they contribute more to revenue than to cost.

We can also use Figure 25.1(b) to find how many workers our firm should hire. The horizontal supply curve, *ss*, intersects the marginal revenue product curve at 12 worker-weeks. At the intersection *E*, the wage-rate is equal to the marginal revenue product. This MRP curve is also a *factor demand curve,* assuming only one variable factor of production and perfect competition in both the factor and product markets, because it shows how much labour employers want at each level of wages. The firm in our example would not hire the thirteenth worker who will only add £190 to revenue but £200 to cost. If the firm were to hire the thirteenth worker, its net income would be reduced by £10 (shown by triangle B). If the firm hired only 11 workers it would be forgoing £7.50 of revenue over and above the cost of a twelfth worker (shown by triangle A).

Derived Demand

This demand curve is *derived,* that is, it shows a **derived demand**, because the tape firm does not want to purchase the services of workers simply for the services themselves. Factors of production are rented or purchased not because they give satisfaction but because they can be used to produce products that can be sold at a profit. This is different from a consumer's desire to buy a product.

The MRP curve, because it is derived, will shift

Figure 25.2

Demand for Labour, a Derived Demand. The demand for labour is a derived demand – derived from the demand for the final product being produced. Therefore, the marginal revenue product curve will shift whenever the price of the product changes.

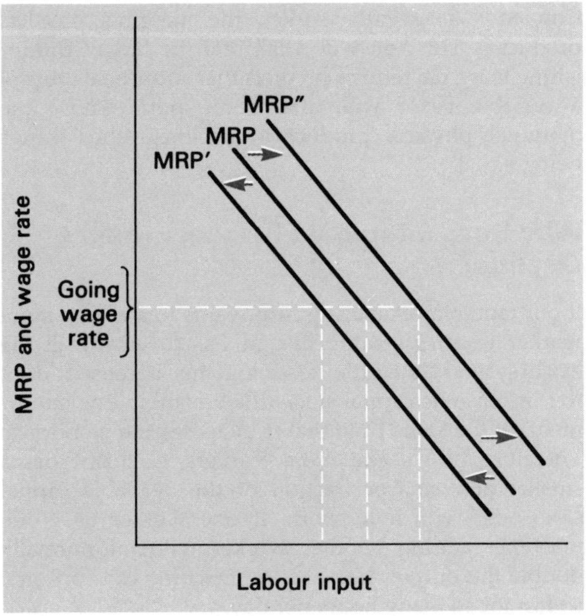

whenever there is a change in the demand for and price of the final product. If, for example, the demand for tapes goes down, the price will go down, and the marginal revenue product curve will shift inwards to the left, to MRP′ in Figure 25.2. If demand for, and the price of, tapes go up, the MRP curve will shift outwards to the right, since MRP = MPP × price of product. If output and price fall, so, too, does the demand for labour; at the same going wage-rate, the firm will require fewer workers. Conversely, if output and price rise, the demand for labour will also rise, and the firm will want to hire more workers at each and every possible wage-rate. Hence wages will generally be higher in industries with growing demand than in industries with declining demand. Growing demand may be associated with a rise in the relative price of a substitute, with rising incomes, with shifts in tastes and fashions, or with a fall in the price of a complement. Changing technology may be an integral part of the picture.

Equally, a change in productivity (output per worker) can change MRP. If marginal physical product rises, e.g. because of more efficient management or technology, MPP × price, or MRP, will be higher for any given quantity of labour. In other words the MRP curve will have shifted to the right. (Now read Key Points 25.1.)

Determinants of Demand Elasticity for Inputs

Just as we were able to discuss the price elasticity of demand for different commodities in Chapter 7, we can discuss the price elasticity of demand for labour. The price elasticity of demand for labour is the percentage change in quantity demanded divided by the percentage change in the price of labour (the wage-rate). When this ratio is less than 1, it is considered inelastic; when it is 1, unitary; and when it is greater than 1, elastic.

There are four principal determinants of the price elasticity of demand for an input:

1. The easier it is for a particular input to be substituted for by other inputs, the more price elastic the demand for that variable input will be.
2. The greater the price elasticity of demand for the final product, the greater the price elasticity of demand for the variable input.
3. The smaller the proportion of total costs accounted for by a particular variable input, the lower its price elasticity of demand.
4. The price elasticity of demand for a variable input will be greater in the long run than in the short run.

Substitute Factors

If it is technically possible to substitute capital for labour, an increase in real wages will probably lead to an increase in labour-saving capital investment; more capital-intensive methods of production will be adopted. So an increase in wages may lead to a more than proportional decrease in quantity demanded: the demand for labour is price-elastic. Equally if the price of capital falls, wage costs rise relatively and the outcome will be similar. In some situations no substitution of capital is possible and demand for labour will be inelastic. Another way of stating the case is to relate the availability of substitute factors to their elasticity of supply. If the supply of substitute factors is elastic, it will be possible to increase the use made of them.

Key Points 25.1

- **The change in total output due to a one-unit change in one variable input, holding all other inputs constant, is called the marginal physical product, or MPP.**
- **When we multiply marginal physical product by the price per unit of output, we obtain the marginal revenue product, or MRP. MRP, defined as P × MPP, applies *only* to perfect competition where a firm sells all output at a constant price per unit.**
- **A (perfectly) competitive firm will hire workers up to the point where the additional cost of hiring one more worker is equal to the additional revenues generated. For the individual firm, therefore, its MRP curve is also its demand for labour curve.**
- **The demand for labour is a derived demand, derived from the demand for final output. Therefore, if the price of final output changes, this will cause a shift in the MRP curve.**
- **If demand for the product is growing, it will sell at a relatively high price, and the wages of those producing it will tend to be above average. This will be evident in a growing industry.**
- **If demand for the product is declining, its price may be falling relatively, MRP will fall and wages in that industry will tend to be low.**

Final Product Price-Elasticity

The second determinant of factor demand elasticity is the price elasticity of demand for the final product. We have already seen that the demand for an input is a *derived* demand. Since it is derived from the demand for the final output, we would expect the elasticity of the derived demand to mirror the elasticity of the demand for the final product, other things being equal.

Assume the elasticity of demand for electricity is very low. If the wages of skilled workers in the electricity industry are forced up by a strong union, the companies will pass on part of the increase in costs to customers in the form of higher prices. But since the elasticity of demand for electricity is relatively low, customers will not reduce by very much the quantity of electricity demanded. The electricity companies will lay off very few workers. The low elasticity of demand for the final product leads to a low elasticity of demand for the factors of production. The converse is also true. If firms cannot pass on increased costs to the consumer, because quantity demanded would fall sharply if they did, they will be unable to pay higher wages without a substantial cut in employment.

Proportion of Total Input Costs

The third elasticity determinant is the proportion of total costs accounted for by the input under study. This determinant merely points out that if a factor of production accounts for only a very small part of the total cost of the product, any given price change will not affect total costs by much. Take the example of electricity as an input of manufacturing. On the average, the cost of electricity accounts for about 1 per cent of the total cost of manufactured goods. If electricity accounts for exactly 1 per cent and prices now double, only 1 per cent more would be added to total costs. Hence, demand for electricity will not fall by very much. This may explain the relative amount of power that a union has in raising wage-rates. If the labour input constitutes a very small percentage of the total cost of producing a commodity, then an increase in wages will not add very much to total cost. In such situations, unions will be able to get their members higher wage-rates than they would when labour input constitutes a significantly greater percentage of total production costs.

Length of Time Allowed for Adjustment

The fourth determinant concerns the difference between the short run and the long run. The long run is usually defined as the time-period during which people adjust easily to a change in their business environment. The more time there is for adjustment, the more elastic both the supply and the demand curves will be. This assertion holds for *input* demand curves as well. The longer the time allowed for adjustment to take place, the more responsive firms will be to a change in the price of a factor of production. Particularly in the long run, firms can reorganize their production process to minimize the use of a factor of production that has become more expensive relative to other factors of production.

Consider one implication of this fourth determinant of the price elasticity of demand of an input. A union, for example, could succeed in raising workers' wage-rates – the price of the labour input – considerably above what they are without immediately experiencing a substantial cut-back in employment. The short-run price elasticity of demand for labour might be relatively small. If, however, time is allowed for adjustment, the union may find that the large increase in wage-rates will result in significant cut-backs in employment, that is, in the quantity of the labour input demanded, as firms invest in more labour-saving capital. (Now read Key Points 25.2.)

The Supply of Labour

Having developed the demand curve for labour in a particular industry, let us turn to the labour supply curve. By adding supply to the analysis, we can come up with the equilibrium wage-rate that workers earn in

Key Points 25.2

The determinants of input price elasticity of demand are:

- **The easier it is to substitute other inputs for the input under study, the more price-elastic will be that input's demand.**
- **The greater the price elasticity of demand for the final product, the greater the price elasticity of demand for the variable input.**
- **The smaller the proportion of total costs accounted for by the variable input under study, the lower its price elasticity of demand.**
- **The greater the time allowed for adjustment, the greater the price elasticity of demand for an input.**

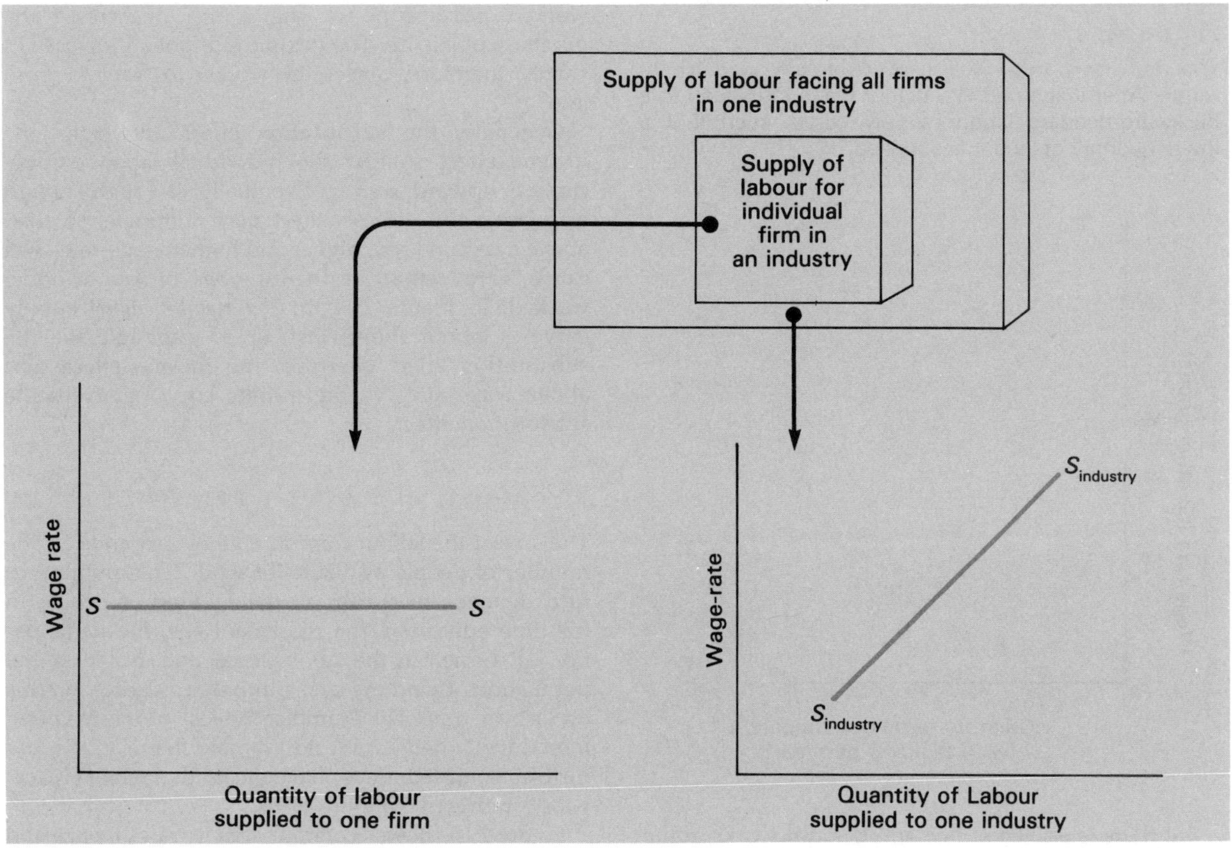

Figure 25.3

Two Supply Curves of Labour. The individual firm that represents a very small part of the total market faces a horizontal supply curve of labour at the going wage-rate. This firm's supply curve of labour is represented by *ss* on the left-hand side of the diagram. The industry, on the other hand, faces an upward-sloping supply curve, similar to the one labelled $S_{Industry}$ $S_{Industry}$ on the right-hand side of this diagram.

an industry. We can think in terms of a supply curve for labour that is upward sloping in a particular industry. At higher wage-rates, more workers will want to enter that particular industry – in our example, tape manufacturing. The individual firm, however, does not face the entire *market* supply curve. Rather, in a perfectly competitive case, the individual firm is such a small part of the market that it can hire all the workers that it wants at the going wage-rate. We say, therefore, that the industry faces an upward-sloping supply curve but that the individual *firm* faces a horizontal supply curve for labour. Figure 25.3 shows the difference.

The market supply curve of labour is simply the summation of the individual supply curves of labour. We do, however, assume that we are only operating in that range where the individual supply curve of labour is upward sloping. That is why we show the industry supply curve to be only upward sloping.

THE LABOUR/LEISURE CHOICE AND THE INDIVIDUAL LABOUR SUPPLY CURVE

All work involves an opportunity cost – the highest-valued alternative non-work choice. As such, analysing the individual decision about how much to work is similar to analysing the consumer's decision about what to buy in the product market. In essence, the individual is choosing between leisure (not working) and the consumption of commodities that can be bought in the market-place (because that is what one can do with the income earned from working). A decision to increase the consumption of purchased commodities is, by necessity, a decision to reduce the consumption of leisure.

In order for an individual to make a decision, that individual must know the opportunity cost of leisure. That opportunity cost is best represented by the wages that could have been earned (after taxes). Assume that the worker can make, after taxes, £4 an hour. A decision to work four hours less, therefore, represents a decision not to be able to consume £16 worth of purchased commodities.

Consider, then, the effect of an increase in wages. The worker is given an incentive to work more because leisure has become more expensive. Therefore, the worker substitutes in favour of work and against leisure. This is called the *substitution effect* of an increase in wages. Looking only at the substitution effect, any increase in wages will cause the worker to want to work longer hours.

Figure 25.4

The Individual's Backward-bending Labour Supply Curve. After wage-rate W_1, higher wage-rates lead to a backward-bending labour supply curve, such that a lower quantity of labour is supplied.

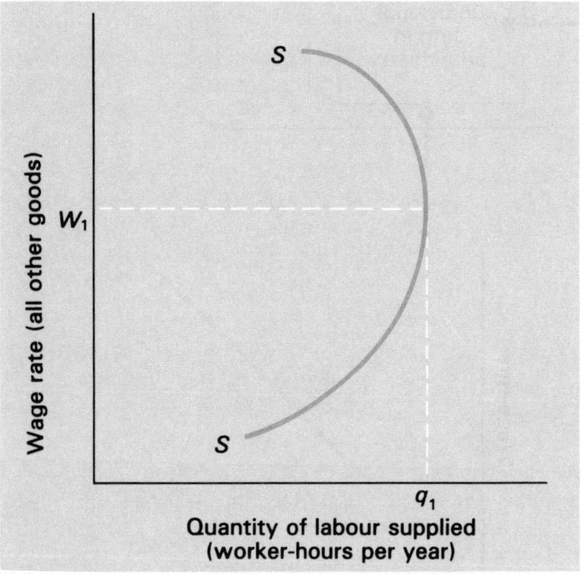

But there is also an *income effect,* and it works in the opposite direction. A higher wage-rate means that, for any given number of hours worked, the worker has a greater income. With a greater income, the worker will tend to purchase more of everything, including leisure. Thus, a wage increase has an income effect that causes the worker to want to reduce the number of hours worked because he or she wants to increase the purchase of leisure. The income effect of an increase in wages, therefore, causes the worker to want to work less.

Generally, the substitution effect outweighs the income effect so that the individual labour supply curve is upward sloping. Eventually, at a high enough wage-rate, the income effect may dominate, so that, above a certain level, higher and higher wage-rates will cause a reduction in the number of labour-hours worked. In Figure 25.4 this *backward-bending* supply curve of labour shows that, up to wage-rate W_1, the substitution effect overrides the income effect, and above wage-rate W_1, the income effect overrides the substitution effect.

The Supply of Labour in Practice

The size of the labour force as a whole depends on the number of people available for work. This number in turn depends primarily on the number of people in full-time education, the retirement age, the participation of women in the labour force, and, not least, the population of working age. Quite sharp changes in this occur over time. For example, the loss of many young men during the First World War and the relatively low birth-rate subsequently, have meant that relatively few people retired during the 1980s.

Figure 25.5 shows economic activity rates by age and sex, that is, the proportion of the population in each age group which is available for work. The increasing participation of women in the labour force during the 1970s has levelled off during the 1980s. Earlier retirement is reducing activity rates for older members of the labour force.

Figure 25.5

Civilian Labour Force Economic Activity Rates: by Age and Sex in Great Britain (percentages).

	16–19	*20–24*	*25–44*	*45–59*	*60–64*	*65+*	*All aged 16 or over*
Males							
1971	69.4	87.7	95.4	94.8	82.9	19.2	80.5
1979	73.0	86.7	95.7	93.8	73.0	10.3	77.5
1984*	73.5	85.0	94.5	89.6	57.3	8.4	74.5
1988	77.1	86.1	94.4	87.8	55.0	8.0	74.2
2000†	77.7	84.0	94.1	87.7	53.9	4.4	73.0
	16–19	*20–24*	*25–44*	*45–54*	*55–59*	*60+*	*All aged 16 or over*
Females							
1971	65.0	60.2	52.4	62.0	50.9	12.4	43.9
1979	72.0	67.7	61.7	67.0	53.8	7.4	47.4
1984*	69.4	70.2	65.9	69.5	51.8	7.8	49.0
1988	72.9	71.5	70.9	70.5	52.8	6.6	51.1
2000†	76.9	74.8	79.0	70.4	53.6	6.1	54.5

*At this time definitions of the labour force changed slightly to include slightly fewer than before.
†Projections

Source: Department of Employment

The Elasticity of Supply of Labour

In practice wage-rates can depend very crucially on the elasticity of supply of labour. In some circumstances a relatively small increase in wages will provide a substantial incentive and will attract many extra employees. In other circumstances an increase in supply will not be forthcoming unless a large pay increase is offered. Supply is then inelastic. The supply curve will slope steeply upwards from left to right.

There is a special case in which supply is perfectly inelastic. The reward to labour is then said to be demand determined. Figure 25.6 shows how wages may rise or fall depending solely on the level of demand.

When the supply of a particular kind of labour is inelastic because there is some form of restriction upon it, **economic rent** is earned. Economic rent is that part of earnings which is in excess of what could be earned in an alternative occupation. This opportunity cost, of working in any given occupation, is what could be earned elsewhere, and is known as **transfer earnings.** Thus:

Economic rent=Total earnings−Transfer earnings

A typical situation in which economic rent is earned occurs when the supply of labour is inelastic in the short-to-medium run because there is a long training period needed to generate the skills for the job. Equally, if supply can be restricted by unions or professional associations, economic rents can be earned. The supply of doctors, barristers, and some crafts skills can be restricted by both factors. Economic rent is usually highest of all for people whose characteristics are unique, as in the case of pop stars, comedians, sports personalities, and other unique performers.

In general, both geographical and occupational immobility can restrict the supply of labour to particular occupations. For example, there may easily be shortages of computer repair specialists in the Thames Valley. House prices are high, deterring suitable workers from moving into the area. It takes time to train an increased supply of workers with the necessary skills. Substantially higher incomes may be needed to attract additional labour with these scarce skills. Differentials between wages in different areas, and between wages in different occupations (generating a similar marginal product) will persist so long as geographical and occupational immobilities prevent the labour market from adjusting to employers' demands.

Figure 25.6

Perfectly Inelastic Supply of Labour. If supply is perfectly inelastic, it has no effect on wages, which are determined solely by the level of demand.

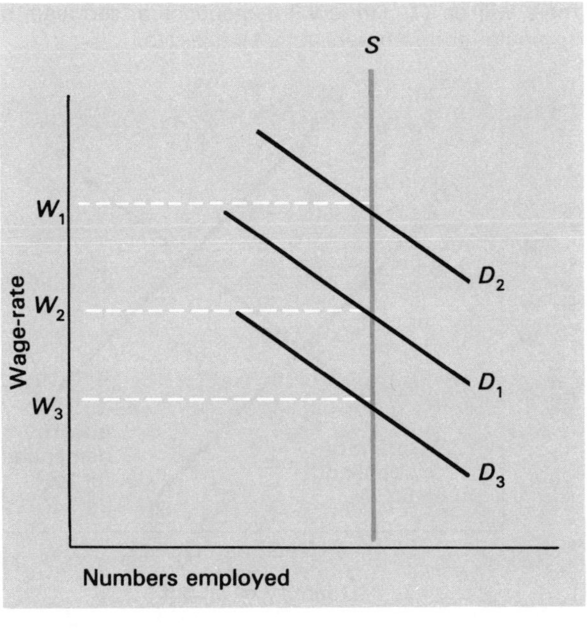

Wage-rate Determination

Going back to the tape industry, we put down the demand curve for labour in that industry as *DD* in Figure 25.7 (page 402), and the supply curve of labour is shown as *SS*. When we put supply and demand of labour in the tape industry together on one graph, we find that the equilibrium wage-rate of £200 a week is established at the intersection of the two curves. The quantity of workers both supplied and demanded at that rate is Q_1. If for some reason the wage-rate fell to £150 a week, we would find in our hypothetical example that there was an excess quantity of workers demanded at that wage-rate. Conversely, if the wage-rate rose to £250 a week, there would be an excess quantity of workers supplied at that wage-rate.

Shifts in the Supply and Demand of Labour

Just as we discussed shifts in the supply curve and the demand curve for various products in Chapter 5, we can discuss the effects of a shift in supply and/or demand in labour markets.

Reasons for Shifts in the Labour Demand Curve

These include:

1. The demand for final products shifts.
2. The price of a related factor of production changes (a substitute or a complement).
3. Labour becomes more or less productive.

If any one of these determinants of the position of the demand curve for labour changes, then the demand curve for labour will shift.

Figure 25.7

The Equilibrium Wage-rate and the Tape Industry. The intersection of demand and supply curves is at point *E*, giving an equilibrium wage-rate of £200 per week and an equilibrium quantity of labour demanded of Q_1. At a price above £200 per week there will be an excess quantity of workers supplied. At a price below £200 per week there will be an excess quantity of workers demanded.

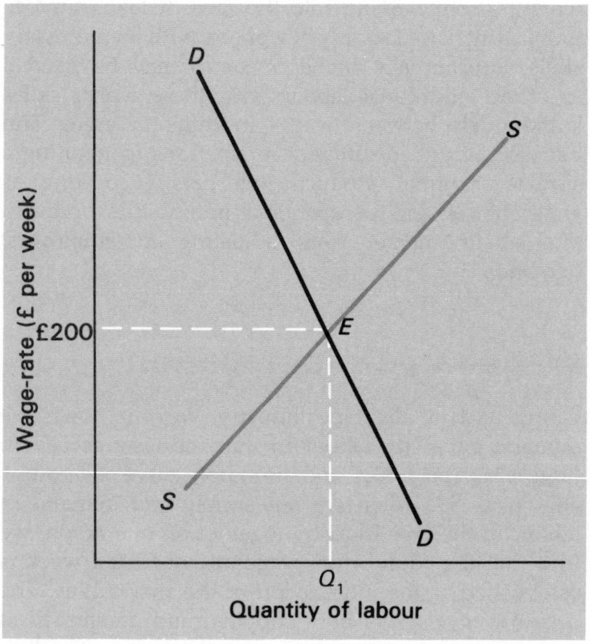

Determinants of the Supply Curve of Labour

There are several reasons why the supply curve of labour in a particular industry will shift. They include:

1. The alternative wage-rate offered in other industries changes.
2. Non-monetary aspects of the particular occupation change.

Consider the first reason for a shift in the supply curve of labour. If wage-rates for factory workers in the prerecorded-tape industry remain constant, but wage-rates for factory workers in the laser compact disc industry go up by 50 per cent, the supply curve of factory workers in the prerecorded-tape industry will shift inwards to the left.

If working conditions in the prerecorded-tape industry improve markedly because of some new production technique, then the supply curve of labour in the prerecorded-tape industry will shift outwards to the right. The converse will be true if working conditions deteriorate.

Shifts in Demand and the Problem of Labour Market Shortages

Labour markets do not adjust instantaneously. When there is an increase in demand, wage-rates do not change immediately. Consider Figure 25.8. Here we show the supply curve of computer programmers as *SS*. The demand curve is *DD*. The wage rate is W_1, and the equilibrium quantity of programmers is Q_1.

Consider that a big break-through has occurred in the computer industry so that 50 per cent more businesses want computers and, therefore, more computer programmers. The demand curve shifts outward to *D′D′*. There would be no shortage if the wage-rate increased to W_2, because at W_2 the new demand curve intercepts the stable supply curve at *E′*. The equilibrium quantity of computer programmers would be Q_2.

But the wage-rate does not rise instantaneously to its equilibrium rate. It moves gradually, and during this period of transition, shortages do indeed exist at the lower-than-equilibrium wage-rates. Take, for example, the wage-rate W_3. These organizations desiring to hire computer programmers during this period will experience what they call a 'shortage'. They will not be able to hire all the computer programmers they want *at the going wage-rate*. A shortage of this sort can take many

Figure 25.8

Adjustments to Increases in Demand for Computer Programmers. We start out in equilibrium at point *E*, where the wage-rate is W_1 and the quantity of employment of computer programmers is Q_1. Assume demand increases to *D′D′*. The new market-clearing equilibrium occurs at point *E′*. The wage-rate would be W_2, and the amount of employment of computer programmers would be Q_2. However, because of lags in adjustment, the wage-rate at first only rises to W_3. At that wage-rate, the quanitity demanded of computer programmers will be Q_3, but the quantity supplied of computer programmers will be Q_4. Firms will experience a 'shortage' of computer programmers at that wage-rate.

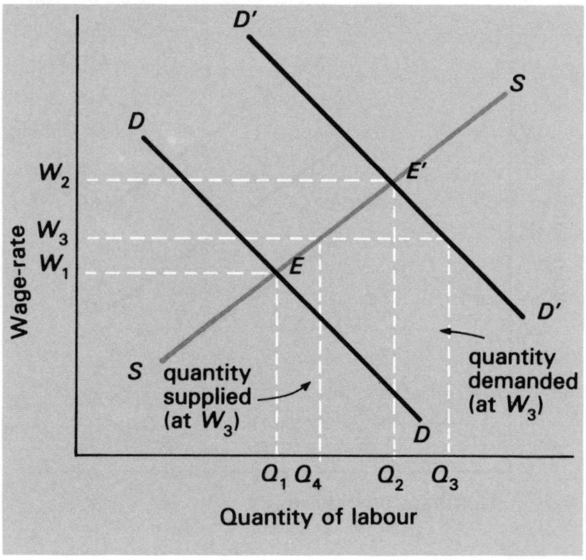

Key Points 25.3

- **The individual competitive firm faces a horizontal supply curve – it can buy all the labour it wants at the going market wage-rate.**
- **The industry supply curve of labour is upward sloping.**
- **Each individual faces a labour/leisure choice. The individual may have a backward-bending labour supply curve.**
- **When we put on the same diagram an industry-wide supply curve for labour and an industry-wide demand curve for labour, we obtain the equilibrium wage-rate in that industry.**
- **The supply of labour is affected by the population, and the age of entering and leaving the labour force.**
- **When the supply of labour is inelastic, a part of earnings is termed economic rent, being that part which is in excess of transfer earnings (the opportunity cost of earnings in an alternative occupation).**
- **The labour demand curve can shift because (1) the demand for final product shifts, (2) the price of a related (substitute or complementary) factor of production changes, or (3) labour changes in its productivity.**
- **The supply curve of labour will shift if the alternative wage-rate offered in other industries changes and if the non-monetary aspects of the job change.**
- **Abrupt changes in demand in a particular industry may lead to temporary 'shortages' as wage-rates move gradually to their long-run equilibrium level.**

years to be eliminated when the demand curve continues to shift to the right faster than the wage-rate and people adjust. (Now read Key Points 25.3.)

Monopoly in the Product Market

We now continue our assumption that the firm purchases its factors of production in a perfectly competitive factor market, but assume that the firm sells its product in an *imperfectly competitive* output market. In other words, we are considering an output market structure of monopoly, oligopoly, or monopolistic competition. In all such cases, the firm faces a downward-sloping demand curve for its product. Throughout the rest of this chapter, we will simply refer to a monopoly output situation for ease of analysis. The analysis does, certainly, hold for all industry structures that are less-than-perfectly competitive. The fact that the firm faces a downward-sloping demand curve for its product means that if it wants to sell more of its product it has to reduce the price, *not only on the last unit, but on all preceding units. The marginal revenue received from selling an additional unit is continuously falling as the firm attempts to sell more and more.*

The Monopolist's Input Demand Curve

Now, in considering the demand for an input, we must account for the facts that (1) the marginal *physical* product falls because of the law of diminishing returns as more workers are added, *and* (2) the price (and marginal revenue) received for the product sold also falls as more is produced and sold. That is, for the monopolist firm, we have to account for *both* the diminishing marginal physical product, *and* the diminishing marginal revenue. In other words, marginal revenue is always less than price for the monopolist. The marginal revenue curve is always below the downward-sloping demand curve.

How Many Employees?

For the monopolist, marginal revenue product (MRP) will tend to fall off more sharply as sales increase. Nervertheless the profit-maximizing output continues to be that at which the MRP is equal to the going wage. That is, the monopolist stops hiring when the wage-rate is equal to the marginal revenue product, since additional workers add more to cost than to revenue. (It stops hiring when MR = MC.) But since marginal revenue may diminish sharply, both output and employment may be lower under monopoly than they would be in a competitive industry.

Cost Minimization

How can the firm minimize its total costs for a given output? Assume you are an entrepreneur attempting to minimize costs. Consider a hypothetical situation in which if you spend £1 more on labour, you would get, say, twenty more units of output, but if you spend £1 more on machines, you would get only ten more units of output. What would you want to do in such a situation? Most likely, you would wish to hire more workers or sell off some of your machines for you are not getting as much output per last pound spent on labour. In other words, you would want to employ relative amounts of every factor of production so that the marginal products per last pound spent on each are equal.

To minimize total costs for a particular rate of production, the firm will hire factors of production up to the point where the marginal physical product per last pound spent on each factor of production is equalized, or:

$$\frac{\text{marginal physical product of labour}}{\text{price of labour}} = \frac{\text{marginal physical product of machines}}{\text{price of machines}} = \frac{\text{marginal physical product of land}}{\text{price of land}}$$

All we are saying here is that the profit-maximizing firm will always use *all* resources in *such combinations* that cost will be minimized for any given output rate. We are referring here to what is commonly called the *least-cost combination of resources.* (Now read Key Points 25.4.)

An Imperfect Labour Market

So far, we have assumed that employers compete to hire workers. We also have assumed that workers are actively competing in the sale of their labour services to employers. There are at least two situations in which these assumptions must be altered. The first one involves restraints on the competition among workers arising from trade union activities. Then we look at restraint among employers in their bidding for workers.

Trade Union Power and the Labour Movement

The concept of **unions** goes back at least as far as the Middle Ages when guilds were formed. By the twelfth century, Western European guilds were of two broad types: merchant and craft. The medieval craft guilds were the original occupational associations, formed by the artisans in a particular field.

Modern trade unions use their bargaining power to influence wage-rates, working conditions and, often, the actual production arrangements. The majority of unions are relatively small: only nine are larger than 250 000, although they account for 55 per cent of all union members. **Craft unions** include workers with similar skills from many industries, such as the electricians' union (EETPU). General unions attract a wide range of occupations, mainly from the semi-skilled and unskilled groups. The Transport and General Workers Union (TGWU) is one of these. **Industrial unions** cover all or most of the employees in one industry, such as the Iron and Steel Trades Federation (ISTF). White-collar unions restrict membership to professional, administrative, and clerical occupations. MSF (Manufacturing, Science and Finance) exists for supervisory and managerial staff in industry. This type of union membership has tended to grow in recent years; most other unions face falling membership except where they have amalgamated. Increasing unemployment caused union membership to fall during the 1980s.

Unions and Collective Bargaining

Unions can be looked at as setters of minimum wages. Through collective bargaining, unions establish minimum wages below which no individual worker can offer his or her services. Collective bargaining is collective in the sense that the union leaders bargain for all workers in the bargaining unit. Typically, collective bargaining contracts between management and the union apply also to non-union members who are employed by the firm or the industry.

While it is still true to say that the strike is an important source of union power, its use has greatly

Key Points 25.4

- **When a firm sells its output in a monopoly market, it must take account of marginal revenue, which is less than price.**
- **As under perfect competition, the profit-maximizing combination of factors will occur when each factor is hired up to the point where its MRP is equal to its unit price.**
- **In order to minimize total costs for a given output, the profit-maximizing firm will hire each factor of production up to the point where the marginal physical product per last pound spent on each factor is equal to the marginal physical product per last pound spent on each of the other factors of production.**

Figure 25.9

Industrial Disputes – Working Days Lost (UK)

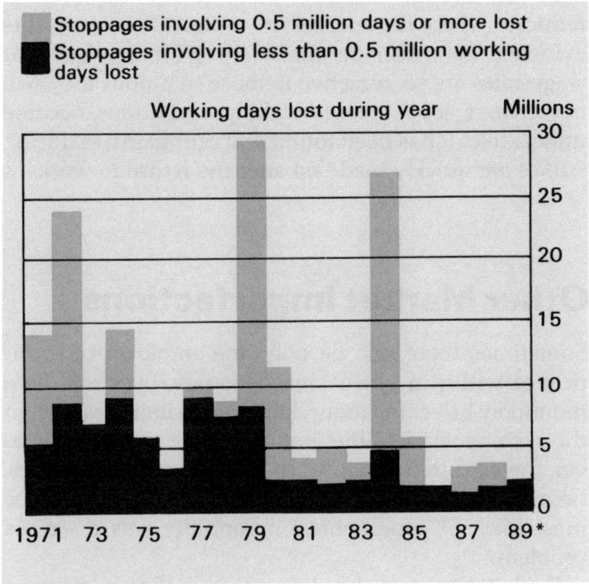

* Data for first six months only

Source: CSO, *Social Trends*, 1990

diminished during the 1980s (apart from the miners' strike of 1984–5). Figure 25.9 shows the days lost through strike action in recent years.

Closed Shops

Quite a few management–labour contracts contain a provision requiring all workers to join the same union. This is a closed shop. It gives the union greater bargaining power but it also may suit the employer, who is saved the necessity of negotiating with a number of unions.

Negotiated Wage-rates

We have already pointed out that unions can be looked at as setters of minimum wages. In many situations, any wage-rate set higher than a competitive market-clearing wage-rate will reduce total employment in that market. This can be seen in Figure 25.10. We have a competitive market for labour. The market demand curve is *DD* and the market supply curve is *SS*. The market-clearing wage-rate will be W_1; the equilibrium quantity of labour will be Q_e. If the union establishes by collective bargaining a minimum wage-rate that exceeds W_1, there will be an excess quantity of labour supplied (assuming no change in the demand schedule). For example, if the minimum wage established by collective bargaining is W_2, the quantity supplied would be Q'_e; the quantity demanded would be Q_d. The difference is the excess quantity supplied, or 'surplus'. The union which establishes a wage-rate above the market-clearing price may try to ration available jobs among the excessive number of workers who wish to work in unionized industries. In order to reduce the excess quantity supplied, the union may lengthen the apprenticeship period for new entrants to the trade. There is a trade-off here that must be faced by any union.

Figure 25.10

Union Wage Rates. If demand for labour is *DD* and supply is *SS*, the equilibrium wage-rate is W_1 and the number employed Q_e. If the union negotiates higher wages, W_2, demand for labour will be Q_d and supply will be Q_e'. There will be an excess supply of labour equal to $Q'_e - Q_d$.

Restricting Supply Over Time. As demand increased, that is, as the demand schedule shifted out to *D′D′* from *DD*, the union restricted membership to its original level of Q_e. The new supply curve is *SS′*, which intersects *D′D′* at *E′*, or at a wage-rate of W_3. Without the union, equilibrium would be at *E″* with a wage-rate of W_2 and employment of Q'_e.

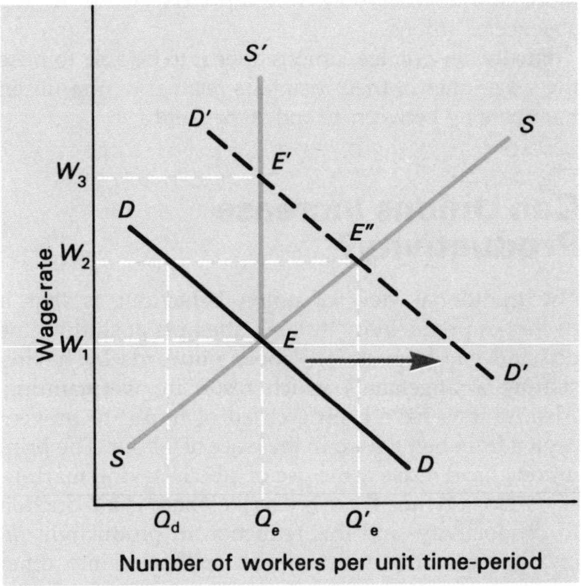

Limiting Entry over Time

Unions may limit the size of their membership to the size of their employed work force when the union was first organized. No workers are put out of work at the time the union is formed. If demand for labour in the industry increases, these original members receive larger wage increases than otherwise would be the case. We see this in Figure 25.10. If the supply of labour can be restricted from then on, these higher wages will continue to be paid.

Have Unions Raised Wages?

Unions are able to raise the wages of their members if they are successful in limiting the supply of labour in a particular industry. They are also able to raise wages above what wages would otherwise be to the extent that they can shift the demand for labour outwards to the right. This can be done through overmanning agreements, which include a specified number of workers for any given job, e.g. requiring a pilot, co-pilot, and engineer in the cockpit of a jet aeroplane, even if an engineer is not required on short flights. Economists have done a great deal of research to determine the actual increase in union wages relative to non-union wages. They have found that, in certain industries, such as construction, and in certain occupations, such as pilots in commercial airlines, the union wage differential can be as high as 50 per cent or more. This is to say, unions have, in some industries and occupations, been able to win wage-rates 50 per cent or more above what they would otherwise be in the absence of unions.

Finally, on average, unions appear to be able to raise the wage-rates of their members relative to non-union members by between 10 and 20 per cent.

Can Unions Increase Productivity?

The traditional view of union behaviour is that it decreases productivity through attempts at shifting the demand curve for union labour outwards by having staffing arrangements which result in overmanning. Also, unions have been accused of trying to prevent capital from being used in the place of labour. The print unions have resisted the use of labour-saving machinery. Also, anytime there is a strike, there is a reduction in productivity, and this reduction in productivity in one sector of the economy can spill over into other sectors.

Recently, this traditional view against unions has been countered by a view that unions can actually increase productivity. Some economists contend that unions act as a collective voice for their members. In the absence of a collective voice, any dissatisfied worker simply remains at his job and works in a disgruntled manner. But unions, as a collective voice, can listen to worker grievances on an individual basis and then apply pressure on the employer to change working conditions. The individual worker does not run the risk of being singled out by the employer and harassed. Also, the individual worker does not have to spend his or her time in trying to convince the employer that some change in the working arrangement should be made. Given that unions provide this collective voice, worker turnover in unionized industries should be less, and this should contribute to productivity. Indeed, there is strong evidence that worker turnover is reduced when unions are in place. Of course, this evidence may also be consistent with the fact that wage-rates are so attractive to those in unions they will not change jobs unless working conditions become unbearable. It has been found that output losses during strikes are quickly made up after the return to work.

Other Market Imperfections

Sometimes there will be only one employer of significance within a given area. This employer will be a monopoly buyer of labour, known as a **monopsonist**. In these circumstances the employer may well be able to get the required amount of labour for lower wages, because employees have no alternative. This would be most likely if geographical immobility was a serious problem.

Exploitation may be defined as paying a resource less than its value. By one definition, labour exploitation would be equal to the difference between the wage-rate and the marginal revenue product of labour.

It will be possible for exploitation to occur if employers have more market power than employees, that is where employers have a degree of monopsony while employees are competing to obtain work. Exploitation allows a larger proportion of total revenue to accrue as profit while a smaller proportion of revenue accrues to labour.

Sometimes a monopsony can be created by an **employers' association**. While there may be many employers, they can agree to negotiate as a unified association, all paying the same wage-rate. **Bilateral monopoly** exists in the labour market when a single employer or employers' association negotiates with a single union which covers all the employees in the industry. An example of this could be seen when British Coal faced the National Union of Mineworkers. (The establishment of the Union of Democratic Mineworkers has altered this.)

Wage councils set wages nationally for low-paid, poorly unionized sectors such as catering. Effectively, they set a minimum wage for the occupations they cover.

Key Points 25.5

- **Unions negotiate minimum wage-rates, and working conditions.**
- **Union activity can lead to higher wages but may lead also to fewer jobs being available.**
- **On average, unions appear to raise wage-rates for their members relative to non-union members by between 10 and 20 per cent.**
- **Some economists believe that unions can increase productivity by acting as a collective voice for their members, thereby freeing members from the task of spending their time trying to convince their employers that some change in their working arrangements should be made. Unions may reduce employee turnover, thus adding to productivity also.**
- **Exploitation may occur if there is a monopsony, or a single employer (buyer of labour).**
- **Bilateral monopoly exists when a single employer deals with a single union, so that there is one buyer and one seller.**

CASE STUDY

Sticky Labour Markets?

Competitive markets usually clear, in the sense that the price changes until it reaches an equilibrium in which there is neither excess supply nor excess demand. In theory, wage-rates are free to find their own level in the market-place. In practice since human beings are sometimes slow to react to stimuli, even financial ones, there may be time-lags before markets adjust to new situations. For example, a shortage of high-technology skills may lead to high rates of pay being offered. But because training takes time, it may take some while for the skill shortage to diminish. In the long run, however, we would expect freely functioning markets to clear so that excess supply and excess demand are eliminated.

What is the evidence? First, we must remember that the labour market is not one, but many markets, for different types of labour in different places. Then we can look at the signs of excess supply: large numbers of unemployed people.

Simultaneously we can see excess demand – unfilled vacancies where employers are seeking people with scarce skills. The culprit here is easily spotted: it is geographical and occupational immobility of labour. These prevent a free flow of labour to employers who require it.

For all labour markets to clear, it would be necessary for wages sometimes to fall. Among other things, J. M. Keynes pointed out that money wages are inflexible (sticky) downwards – there is a ratchet effect. This would make for inflexible labour markets, slow to adjust to employers' changing needs.

Questions

1. Define the terms occupational and geographical immobility.
2. What other imperfections can you identify that exist in the labour market?
3. Explain, and illustrate with a supply-and-demand diagram, how increased training will affect wage-rates in the long run.
4. Identify three ways in which the government may help the labour market to function more efficiently.
5. What sectors have excess demand for labour now? Give evidence to support your answer.

CASE STUDY

1992 and the Labour Market

What effect will the advent of 1992 have on Europe's labour market? The usual answers concentrate on one issue: whether growing economic and cultural integration will increase the mobility of workers among EC countries. The consequences of 1992 for labour markets run deeper, however.

Three main factors affect the power of workers to raise wages. Two relate to the labour market itself: the extent to which workers are unionized; and whether they are sheltered (e.g. by the cost of hiring, training and firing) from 'underbidding' by other workers.

Two economists, Mr David Begg and Mr Charles Wyplosz, argue that the key to labour-market power is the third factor: the extent to which a firm is sheltered from competition. In a perfectly competitive market any attempt by one firm's workers to raise wages would simply put that company out of business. But the less competitive the market for its products, the bigger the 'rents' to be divided between the firm and its workers – and the easier to pass on higher wages as higher prices.

The rents available to workers in uncompetitive markets can be substantial. Take Europe's airlines, where regulations control fare-setting and the maximum share of capacity that can be offered by each country's carriers. In addition, bilateral agreements allow carriers to collaborate on scheduling and to pool revenues.

After years of timid liberalization, EC transport ministers agreed on 5 December that, from January 1993, capacity-sharing arrangements will be abandoned and access to European routes made freer, while cut-price fares will be less easily blocked by member governments. What are the likely consequences of such a comprehensive deregulation package?

Figure 25.11 compares the labour costs and productivity of eight American airlines (American, Continental, Delta, Eastern, Pan Am, TWA, United and USAir) with those of six European airlines. In Britain (where Margaret Thatcher's government has scrapped many airline regulations), labour costs of pilots and co-pilots are lower than in America; costs of other cockpit staff are one-fifth higher, while those of cabin crew are one-third lower. But continental European airlines have far higher costs: cockpit staff are paid an average of 2.6 times as much as their American counterparts, cabin crew 1.6 times as much.

Figure 25.11
Airline labour costs and productivity

(Average per employee, 1987)	*Labour costs ($'000)* Pilots/ co-pilots	Other cockpit staff	Cabin crew	Productivity*
Eight US majors	**92**	**40**	**28**	**1.6**
BA/BCal (Britain)	65	48	19	1.1
Lufthansa (W Germany)	na	130	40	0.8
SAS (Scandinavia)	na	103	41	0.6
UTA (France)	164	119	45	0.8
Alitalia (Italy)	na	93	59	0.7
Iberia (Spain)	109	80	37	0.7

*Revenue passenger-kilometres
Source: McGowan and Seabright

This does not reflect higher productivity, as Figure 25.11 shows. Measured in terms of 'revenue passenger kilometres per employee', the American airlines average 1.6m, a figure only approached by the now-merged BA/BCal's 1.1m. Continental European airlines average just 0.7m. And inefficiency is rife: European carriers have, on average, 2.9 times as many ticketing and other non-flight staff as flight staff, compared with America's average of 1.7. All this suggests that the higher labour costs of European airlines reflect rents spawned by lack of competition.

By breaking down frontier barriers and reducing (or standardizing) regulation, 1992 aims to make Europe's product markets more competitive. Liberalizing Europe's airlines could benefit consumers by $1½–2 billion a year.

Losing the wage war

Unions are a mechanism that workers use to try to get a share of economic rents. How will Europe's unions respond to increasing pressure on rents, and hence on wages? One way might be to try to reorganize on a pan-European basis in those industries which become more competitive after 1992. Differing cultures, languages and political sentiments will make that difficult, however, as will less widespread union membership.

The advent of the single market may also change the structure of Europe's wage-bargaining. In a country with highly centralized bargaining, unions are powerful enough to affect wages. But, because of their large size relative to the whole economy, they have to take into account the effect of their actions on overall employment and inflation. In a highly decentralized economy, unions are too weak to affect wage levels.

Those intermediate positions, where unions are big enough to influence wages but too small to care about their effect on the whole economy, tend to be more harmful. In the 1980s Britain, France, and Italy have fallen into this intermediate category, between highly decentralized America, Japan, and Switzerland and highly centralized Denmark, Belgium, Holland, and West Germany.

By boosting the size and

competitiveness of European firms' product markets, 1992 will make wage-bargaining less centralized in most European countries. In countries that already have centralized wage-bargaining, this change could be bad: it will move them towards the harmful intermediate position. For those countries already in the intermediate position, it will be beneficial, moving them closer to the fully competitive extreme.

More competitive product-markets will mean lower wages and feebler unions. That will benefit consumers, but some workers will initially lose their jobs. To compensate them, the European Commission has called for a big increase in EC regional funds. An alternative solution is an EC-wide minimum unemployment benefit, which could be topped up by governments, and which would automatically help 1992's victims. But could Mrs Thatcher accept what she would undoubtedly see as a further erosion of Britain's national sovereignty?

Source: Adapted from *The Economist*, 9 Dec. 1989.

Questions

1. To what extent do labour costs differ between airlines?
2. What reason does the article give as to why labour costs differ?
3. What factors (other than those mentioned in the article) might have some bearing on airline rates of pay?
4. What effect have uncompetitive markets had on airline rates of pay?
5. What effect is expected if stronger competition develops between European airlines?

CASE STUDY

Pay Deals and Productivity at Ford

The outcome of the strike ballot at Ford, due to be announced today, may depend as much on the 31 800 manual workers' attitude to changes in work practice as their stance on pay.

The proposals in the present two-year pay offer are the company's third assault on the traditional production-line method of working at Ford. They mark the latest in a series of attempts to lift the productivity of the company's UK plants to that of their European counterparts.

What, then, would the proposed changes mean for working patterns? And what has been the effect of those implemented since 1985?

The changes are designed to erode traditional demarcation-lines separating production from maintenance workers, unskilled work from skilled work and eventually, blue collar workers from white collar workers.

They challenge the traditional method of Ford production by which efficiency was assured by production workers carrying out distinctive, repetitive tasks, and plants being serviced by a series of separately qualified maintenance workers.

The current offer affects 9 800 line workers and 5 000 maintenance workers. The company says it will pay line workers an allowance of 3 per cent of their basic rates, on top of the 10.2 per cent available to all workers in the first year of the deal, on condition that they agree to 'ongoing changes in working practices'.

The initiative is similar to one in 1985 which paid a 2 per cent allowance in exchange for concessions including agreement to 'seek and repair'. Under this a worker was required to make sure there were no obvious defects in his job or the one preceding it. He had to either rectify or draw attention to any problems. In addition, in common with other production workers, line workers were required to clean up their work stations.

Ford has indicated that the next phase of line-work productivity improvements, which it wants negotiated locally, are unlikely to be onerous. Although some line workers are concerned that the company has not spelt out exactly what it wants – and may vote against the offer as a result – the strongest resistance to working practice changes, and payments associated with them, comes from skilled workers.

The skilled workers believe they have borne the brunt of the changes already agreed and this has happened at a time when their status and pay differentials with unskilled workers have suffered. When the 1985 pay agreement made provision for the reduction in the number of job classifications in Ford plants from 550 to 52, the

Figure 25.12

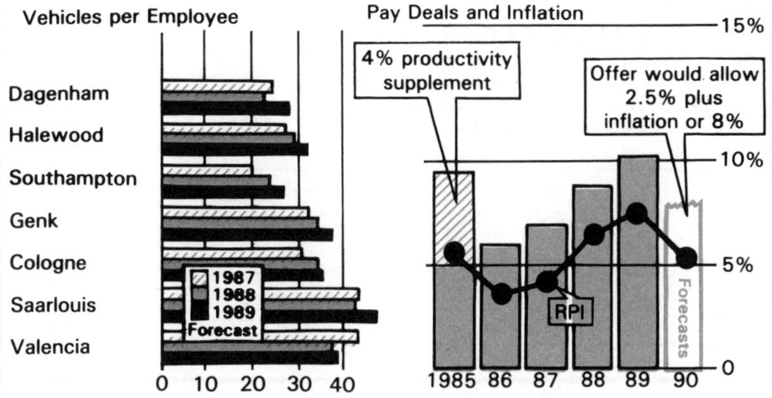

skilled grades were reduced from more than 40 to two: electricians and mechanical technicians.

Under the new system the company required craftsmen to be more interchangeable, so that, say, an electrician replacing a faulty motor would slacken bolts without calling for a mechanical fitter, or a tool maker would do installation work.

The 1987 agreement envisaged skilled workers in some instances joining in groups of 10 or 12 mainly unskilled workers which were being set up as part of the company's move to introduce greater group working under group leaders who would eventually replace the old function of foremen.

In group working, leaders recruited from the shopfloor, are responsible for ensuring quality, arranging breaks and organizing maintenance. Part of the aim of groups is to improve job flexibility.

In the latest proposed deal the company is back again, this time offering to pay allowances of 5 per cent to skilled workers who agree to join integrated manufacturing teams of skilled and semi-skilled workers which will be responsible for the maintenance and operation of a specific segment of the manufacturing process.

Ford says it has achieved largely what it wanted from the last agreement, even though deals had to be negotiated at plant level to ensure implementation. It will not say how far it is towards achieving its goal of cutting several hundred jobs which it hoped would be possible as a result of cutting out the tier of management made possible by the introduction of group leaders.

There is no doubt that productivity is growing rapidly in the company's UK plants. Dagenham employees are thought to have increased their output between 1987 and 1989 from 24 to 28 cars each a year and Halewood from 27 to 32.

But then Ford's continental Europe plants are improving too – and from a higher base.

During the pay negotiations, union leaders have constantly stressed that they are not opposed to working-practice changes. They have, however, argued that the payments for specific workers, linked to changes in working practices, are divisive and that the company should have kept to a commitment made by both sides two years ago to go ahead with plans to implement a new pay structure this year.

Craftsmen should, perhaps, be expected to be pleased by the offer. After all, as well as the 10.2 per cent basic increase they could be eligible for 5 per cent extra for joining integrated manufacturing teams. (Some electricians will be entitled to a further 5 per cent for undergoing training courses.)

Many craftsmen are likely to vote against the deal because they believe they could lose shift payments and are opposed to the company's next step outlined in the deal: to enter negotiations on the development of a single craft function combining electrical and mechanical skills.

Source: Michael Smith, *Financial Times*, 24 Jan. 1990.

Questions

1. Why did Ford want to increase productivity?
2. Use an MRP diagram to show how increased productivity can make it possible to pay higher wages.
3. Show how the proposed measures could reduce costs of production.
4. What information does the data give as to Ford UK's competitiveness?
5. Why were Ford workers suspicious of the deal?

Exam Preparation

PRACTICAL EXERCISES

1.

Quantity of labour	*Total product per week*	*MPP*	*MRP*
1	250	____	____
2	450	____	____
3	600	____	____
4	700	____	____
5	750	____	____
6	750	____	____

Assume the product (left) sells for £2 per unit.

(a) Use the information above to derive a demand curve for labour.

(b) What is the most that this firm would be willing to pay each worker if five workers were hired?

(c) If the going salary for the quality of labour is £200 per week, how many workers would be hired?

2. Below are some production function data for a firm in which the only variable input is capital; the labour input is fixed. First fill in the other columns. What quantity of capital will the firm use if the price of capital is £90 per machine-week? If the price of capital is £300 per machine-week, what quantity of capital will the firm use?

Explain.

Quantity of capital (machine-weeks)	*Total product (units/week)*	*Marginal product of capital (units/week)*	*Product price (£/unit)*	*MRP (£/week)*
0	0	____	£10	____
1	25	____	10	____
2	45	____	10	____
3	60	____	10	____
4	70	____	10	____
5	75	____	10	____

3. The graph below indicates the supply and demand for labour in the construction industry.

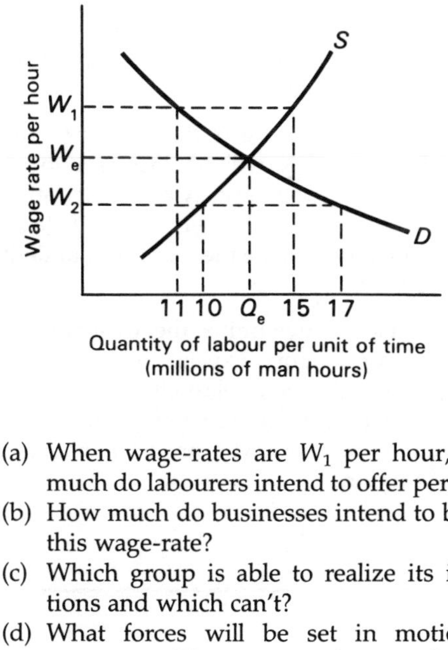

(a) When wage-rates are W_1 per hour, how much do labourers intend to offer per unit?
(b) How much do businesses intend to buy at this wage-rate?
(c) Which group is able to realize its intentions and which can't?
(d) What forces will be set in motion at wage-rate W_1, given a free market for labour?

4. Using the graph in Question 3 above, answer the following questions.

(a) At wage-rate W_2, how many labour-hours do labourers intend to offer?
(b) At W_2, how many labour-hours do businesses intend to purchase?
(c) Which group can realize its intentions and which can't?
(d) What forces will be set in motion at W_2, if a free market for labour exists in this industry?
(e) What will the equilibrium wage-rate be?

5. Some people argue that the extraordinary earnings of entertainment and sports 'superstars' are not pure economic rents at all, but merely the cost of ensuring that a steady stream of would-be stars and starlets continues to flow into the sports and entertainment fields. Outline the argument.

MULTIPLE CHOICE QUESTIONS

1. The marginal productivity theory of wages maintains that
A the amount of labour employed determines its wage
B the value of labour depends upon its marginal productivity
C productivity can be the result and not the cause of wages
D marginal changes in wage levels have little effect on employment.

2. The elasticity of demand for a factor of production will be high when
A it is difficult to substitute some other factor for it in production
B the cost of a factor is a small part of total cost
C the factor is highly specific to the production of the final product
D the elasticity of demand for the final product is high.

3. An employer who pays a flat-rate wage to all her employees was previously employing 100 workers at a rate of £30 per day. She now has to raise the wage by 50p per day in order to attract one additional worker. Given that all other costs remain constant, the marginal cost of labour per day in this case is
A 50p
B £30.50
C £50.50
D £80.50
E £3 080.50

For Question 4 select your answer from the following grid:

A	B	C	D	E
1, 2, 3, all correct	1, 2 only correct	2, 3 only correct	1 only correct	3 only correct

4. The elasticity of demand for a factor of production is likely to be low where the
   1 price elasticity of demand for the final product is low
   2 factor accounts for a small proportion of total costs
   3 factor has no alternative uses.

5. 'Economic rent' is
   A an alternative term for 'transfer earnings'
   B a rent allowing reasonable incomes to landlords
   C income in excess of a factor's supply price
   D characteristic of perfectly competitive conditions
   E reduced when supply is inelastic.

6. A trade union wishes to increase the wages of its members in a given industry without causing unemployment among them. Which of the following would weaken the union's bargaining position?
   A The labour force is highly skilled
   B Employers have no central bargaining organization
   C There is a low degree of elasticity of substitution of alternative factors of production
   D The price elasticity of demand for the workers' product is high
   E Wages form a low proportion of total production costs.

RELATED ESSAY QUESTIONS

1. Explain the income differentials between hospital cleaning staff and accountants.
2. How are factor earnings related to productivity?
3. Distinguish between economic rent and transfer earnings. With reference to examples, explain what determines the economic rent earned by factors of production.
4. Give examples of low-paid workers in Britain and suggest reasons why they are low paid. Would a national minimum wage improve the position of the low paid in Britain?
5. (a) What factors affect the ability of trade unions to increase the real wages of their members relative to other groups?
   (b) In what sense, if any, could it be argued that trade unions protect workers from 'exploitation' by employers?
6. Outline the theory of relative pay determination in a freely competitive market. How far is it possible to explain salary differentials within the teaching profession and between teaching and other professions in terms of labour supply and demand analysis?
7. It has been suggested that the incentive to work in the UK will be increased by (a) a reduction in social security payments, and (b) a reduction in the higher rates of taxation. Explain and evaluate the reasoning underlying these views.
8. What factors determine the elasticity of demand for labour? Explain how you would expect the degree of elasticity to affect (a) the wage level and (b) the employment level of a group of workers who are all members of a trade union.

26 Rent, Interest, and Profits

Key Points to Review

- Trade-off between consumer and capital goods (1.7)
- Profit as a resource allocator (6.4)
- Elasticity of supply (7.6)
- Credit creation (19.6)
- Accounting versus economic profits (21.1)

Questions for Preview

1 What is rent?

2 What is interest?

3 What is the economic function of interest rates?

4 What is the economic function of profits?

We have talked about four factors of production – labour, land, capital, and entrepreneurship. So far in Part D, we have discussed only the demand and supply of labour and the factor payments to labour – wages and salaries. The other three factors of production and their respective factor payments – rent, interest, and profits – are also important. In this chapter, we will look at the determination of each of these factor payments.

Rent

Land, in general, is in completely *inelastic* supply. Thus, the supply curve for land is a vertical line. That is to say, no matter what the prevailing market price for land, the quantity supplied will remain the same. The term rent has been associated with the payment for the use of land, for land seems to be the best example of a resource that is in fixed supply. When, indeed, no matter what the price, the quantity and quality of a resource will remain at their current levels, then we say there is **pure economic rent**. (Chapter 25 examined this in relation to labour.) We define pure economic rent as that price paid to, in this case, land (or any other productive factor) that is in completely inelastic supply.

Does Economic Rent Have an Allocative Function?

In a price system, changes in prices usually cause people to change their behaviour. If the price of petroleum products goes up relative to other prices, suppliers are induced to supply more, and consumers are induced to consume less. Does economic rent have a similar allocative function? Some economists would answer yes, and others would answer no. Those who do not believe economic rent serves an allocative function point out that, by definition, it is associated with unique properties of a resource that cannot be changed. If an exceptionally productive tract of land exists, does this property's high economic rent mean that somehow additional tracts with the same high productivity will come into being? The answer is no. After all, if economic rent exists, it means that it is attributed to a factor's qualities that cannot be altered in the long run. Therefore, by definition, if economic rent is being earned, it cannot serve an allocative function.

Those who believe that economic rent does serve an allocative function indicate that it serves the purpose of regulating the use of society's resources, particularly its natural resources that are fixed in supply. In a competitive market-place, economic rent serves as a guide by rationing the available supply to the most efficient use.

Since the value of bare, urban land has nothing to do with the talents or effort of the owner, but with the presence of other people, some have argued that the pure economic rent of land should be taxed.

Quasi-Rent

A **quasi-rent** is defined as a payment over and above what is necessary to keep a factor of production in existence *in the short run* in its current quantity and quality. In the long run, if the quasi-rent is inadequate, the factor of production will be allowed to depreciate and not be replaced. Consider a factory that has a fixed amount of plant and machinery. Assume that nothing can be done with the capital equipment; it can be used only to continue producing the same product. In the short run, it is possible for the owners of that fixed capital not to be paid very much at all. In the long run, however, if those owners of fixed capital are not paid at least a normal rate of return for their investment, they will keep the equipment running until it wears out, but will not then replace it.

Economic Rents to Other Factors of Production

This analysis is equally applicable to any other factor of production that is fixed in supply. Economic rents accrue to individuals possessing scarce natural talents. It is defined as any payment over and above what is necessary to maintain a factor of production in its current activity. Natural talents that human beings possess will be more significant in some occupations than in others. They seem to be particularly important in athletics, acting, music, and other entertainment endeavours. In some cases, pure economic rents can explain a great part of the difference between the extraordinary earnings of highly successful musicians, for example, and the average musician. (Now read Key Points 26.1.)

Interest

Interest is the price paid for the use of capital. Capital is the factor of production that is typically considered man-made. Capital exists because individuals, as a group, have been willing in the past to forgo consumption – to save. Those resources not consumed were usually used by firms for investment purposes, which added to our stock of capital. The production of capital goods occurs in our society because of the existence of credit markets, where borrowing and lending take place.

Owners of capital, whether directly or indirectly, obtain income in the form of interest. They receive a specific interest rate. Thus, we can look at the interest rate as either the rate earned on capital invested or the cost of borrowing – the two sides of the credit market. For the moment, we will look only at the cost of borrowing.

Interest and Credit

When you obtain credit, you actually obtain money to have command over resources today. We can say, then, that interest is the payment for current rather than future command over resources. Thus, interest is the payment for obtaining credit. If you borrow £100 from me, you have command over £100 worth of goods and services today. I no longer have that command. You promise to pay me back £100 plus interest at some future date. The interest that you pay is usually expressed as a percentage of the total loan calculated on an annual basis. Thus, if at the end of one year, you pay me back £110, the annual interest is £10 ÷ £100, or 10 per cent. When you go out into the market-place to obtain credit, you will find that the interest rate charged differs greatly. A loan to buy a house (a mortgage) may cost you 10–15 per cent annual interest. An instalment loan to buy a car may cost you 15–25 per cent annual interest. The government, when it wishes to obtain credit (by selling bonds) may have to pay

Key Points 26.1

- **Pure economic rent is defined as any payment to a factor of production that is completely inelastic in supply.**
- **Pure economic rent is a payment to a resource over and above what is necessary to keep that resource in existence at its current level in the long run.**
- **Economic rent serves an allocative function by guiding available supply to the most efficient use.**
- **A quasi-rent is that payment over and above what is necessary to keep a resource in its current quality and quantity in the short run, but not sufficient to do so in the long run.**
- **Factors of production other than land can earn pure economic rents if their supply is completely price-inelastic.**

10–13 per cent annual interest. Variations in the rate of annual interest that must be paid for credit depend on the following factors.

LENGTH OF LOAN

In some (but not all) cases, the longer the loan will be outstanding, other things being equal, the greater will be the interest rate charged.

RISK

The greater the risk of non-repayment of the loan, other things being equal, the greater the interest rate charged. Risk is assessed on the basis of the credit-worthiness of the borrower. It is also assessed on the basis of whether the borrower provides collateral for the loan. Collateral consists of any asset that will automatically become the property of the lender should the borrower fail to comply with the loan agreement. Typically, when you borrow to purchase a car, the car itself is collateral for the loan. Should you default on payments to the lending institution, it can, in most cases, repossess the car, sell it, and pay off the loan that way. The more and the better the collateral offered for a loan, the lower the rate of interest charged, other things being equal.

ADMINISTRATIVE CHARGES

It takes resources to set up a loan. Papers have to be filled out and filed, credit references have to be checked and so on. It turns out that the larger the amount of the loan, the smaller will be the administrative charges as a percentage of the total loan. Therefore, we would predict that, other things being equal, the larger the loan, the lower the interest rate.

Loans are taken out both by consumers and by firms. It is useful for us to separate the motives underlying the demand for loans by these two groups of individuals. We therefore will treat consumption loans and investment loans separately. But before we do that, we will examine the relationship between interest rates and present value – or how to relate the value of future sums of money to the present.

In the discussion that follows, it will be assumed that there is no inflation; that is, that there is no consistent increase in general prices.

The Interest Rate, the Present, the Future, and Present Values

Interest rates are used to link the present with the future. After all, if you have to pay £110 at the end of the year when you borrow £100, that 10 per cent interest rate gives you a measure of the price of things one year from now compared to the price of things today. If you want to have things today, you have to pay the 10 per cent interest rate in order to have purchasing power.

Turned around somewhat, the question could be put this way: What is the present value (the value today) of £110 that you could receive one year from now? That depends on the market rate of interest, or the rate of interest you could earn in a bank account. To make the arithmetic simple, let us assume that the rate of interest (also called the **rate of discount**) is 10 per cent. Now you can figure out the **present value**, as it were, of £110 to be received one year from now. You figure it out by asking the question, 'How much money must I put aside today at the market rate of interest of 10 per cent to receive £110 one year from now?' Mathematically we represent this question by the following:

$$(1 + 0.10)P_1 = £110$$

where P_1 is the sum that you must set aside now.

Let us solve this simple equation to obtain P_1:

$$P_1 = £110 \div 1.10 = £100.$$

That is to say, £100 will accumulate to £110 at the end of one year with a market rate of interest of 10 per cent. Thus, the present value of £110 one year from now, using a rate of interest of 10 per cent, is £100. The formula for present value of any sums to be received one year from now thus becomes:

$$P_1 = \frac{A_1}{(1 + i)}$$

where

P_1 = present value of a sum one year hence
A_1 = future sum of money paid or received one year hence
i = market rate of interest.

The same method can be used to calculate the present value of income expected in the more distant future. We call this **discounting**. It enables firms to assess the present value of the income they are likely to receive from an investment project. This helps them in deciding whether a given capital expenditure is likely to be worth while.

What Determines Interest Rates?

The overall level of interest rates in the economy is determined by the supply of loanable funds and the demand for loanable funds. Let us first look at the supply and then the demand.

THE SUPPLY OF CREDIT, OR LOANABLE FUNDS

The supply of loanable funds depends on individuals' willingness to save. To induce people to save more, one must offer a higher rate of interest. Thus, we expect that the supply curve of loanable funds will be upward sloping. At higher rates of interest, savers will be willing to offer more current consumption to borrowers, other things being equal.

The supply of credit will also depend on how much credit banks can create, and therefore on the Bank of England's operation of monetary policy. (This is dealt with in more detail in Chapters 19 and 30.)

THE DEMAND FOR LOANABLE FUNDS

There are three major sources of the demand for loanable funds:

1. Households that want funds for the purchase of services, non-durable goods, and consumer durables, such as cars and houses.
2. Firms that want funds for investments.
3. Governments that want to cover their deficits – the excess of government spending over tax revenues, or PSBR.

THE CONSUMER DEMAND FOR LOANABLE FUNDS

On average, consumers prefer earlier consumption to later consumption. By borrowing, consumers can spread out purchases more evenly during their lifetimes. Consider that sometimes individual household income falls below the average income level expected over, say, the next few years. Individuals will go to the credit market to borrow whenever they perceive a temporary dip in their current income – assuming they expect their income to go back to normal later on.

The demand by consumers for loanable funds will be inversely related to the cost of borrowing – the rate of interest. Why? For the same reason that all demand curves slope down: a higher rate of interest means a higher cost of borrowing, and a higher cost of borrowing must be weighed against alternative uses of limited income. At higher costs of borrowing, consumers will forgo current consumption.

FIRMS' DEMAND FOR LOANABLE FUNDS

Firms demand loanable funds to make investments in new plant and machinery, new production techniques, research and development, new types of organizations, and any other type of investment that they believe will increase productivity. Any time a business believes that, by making an investment in its production process, it can increase revenues (net of other costs) by more than the cost of capital (the rate of interest on loanable funds), it will borrow and invest. Firms compare the interest rate that they must pay in the loanable funds market with the rate of return, or profit that they think they can earn by investing. This comparison helps them to decide whether to invest.

At higher interest rates, fewer investment projects will make economic sense to firms – the cost of capital will exceed the rate of return on the capital investment. Conversely, at lower rates of interest, more investment projects will be undertaken because the cost of capital will be less than the expected rate of return to the capital investment. (We can relate this to the planned investment function in Chapter 15. J. M. Keynes called the rate of return on capital the 'marginal efficiency of capital'.)

The demand for loanable funds by households, firms, and the government, and the supply of loanable funds, interact to produce an equilibrium interest rate. (In practice there are, as we have seen, a number of interest rates for loans of different duration and for different purposes.) Funds are traded, that is to say, lenders lend, and borrowers borrow, on the capital or money markets. This consists of a wide range of financial intermediaries, including banks, building societies, insurance companies and pension funds, discount houses, merchant banks and finance houses. These institutions aim to provide a very wide range of loans for borrowers with different needs and similarly varied ways of saving for potential lenders. They will compete to offer their customers the most favourable terms and interest rates. This is one market which will clear all the time. Interest rates are flexible and the institutions can lend to one another on a short-term basis should there be excess supply of or demand for their funds. The theory relating to the supply of and demand for money is examined in Chapter 30.

Real versus Nominal Interest Rates

Up to now, we have assumed that there is no inflation. In a world of inflation – a consistent rise in all prices – **nominal**, or market, **interest rates** will be higher than they would be in a world with no inflation. Basically, market rates of interest eventually rise to take account of the anticipated rate of inflation. If, for example, there is no inflation and no inflation expected, the market rate of interest might be, say, 5 per cent for mortgages. If the rate of inflation goes to 10 per cent a year and stays there, then everybody will anticipate that inflation rate. The market, or nominal, rate of interest will rise to 15 per cent to take account of the anticipated rate of inflation. We generally say that the real rate of interest is equal to the nominal rate of interest, minus the rate of inflation. When loans are made in terms of a fixed sum of money, the purchasing power of that money declines if there is inflation so that the lender is repaid a smaller amount of real purchasing power. The higher nominal interest payments compensate for this. In short, you can expect to see high nominal rates of interest in periods of high and/or rising inflation rates. **Real rates of interest** may not necessarily be high, though. We must correct the nominal rates of interest for inflation, before determining whether real interest rates are, in fact, higher than normal.

The Allocative Role of Interest

Interest is a price that allocates funds (credit) to consumers and to firms. Within the business sector, interest allocates funds to different firms and therefore to different investment projects. Those investment, or capital, projects whose rates of return are higher than the market rate of interest in the credit market will be undertaken, given an unrestricted market for loanable funds. For example, if the expected rate of return on the purchase of a new factory in some industry is 20 per cent and loanable funds can be acquired for 15 per cent, then the investment project may take place. If, on the other hand, that same project had only an expected rate of return of 9 per cent, it would not be undertaken. In sum, the interest rate allocates loanable funds to those

Key Points 26.2

- **Interest is the price paid for the use of capital. It is also the cost of obtaining credit.**
- **In the credit market, the rate of interest paid depends on, among other things, the length of the loan, the risk, and the administrative charges.**
- **In order to express a future sum of money (or income stream) in terms of today's pounds, we must discount the future sum back to the present by using the appropriate discount rate. The result is the present value.**
- **The interest rate is determined by the interaction of the supply of credit, or loanable funds, and the demand for credit, or loanable funds.**
- **The demand for loanable funds comes from households, firms, and governments.**
- **Nominal, or market, interest rates adjust to take account of inflation. Therefore, during periods of high anticipated inflation, nominal, or market, interest rates will be historically high. Real interest rates, on the other hand, may not, because they are defined as the nominal interest rate minus the anticipated rate of inflation.**

industries where resources will be the most productive.

It is important to realize that the interest rate performs the function of allocating money capital – loanable funds – but that what this ultimately does is allocate real physical capital to various firms for investment projects. Often, non-economists view the movement of loanable funds (credit) simply as something that has to do with 'money' and not with the 'real' world of machines and factories. (Now read Key Points 26.2.)

Profits

In Chapter 1, we called entrepreneurship, or entrepreneurial talent, the fourth factor of production. Profit is the reward that this factor earns. You may recall that entrepreneurship involves engagement in the risk of starting new businesses. In a sense, then, nothing can be produced without an input of entrepreneurial skills.

We cannot easily talk about the demand and supply of entrepreneurship. For one thing, we have no way to quantify entrepreneurship. What measure should we use? First we will point out what profit is *not*. Then we will examine the sources of true, or economic, profit. Finally, we will look at the functions of profits in a market system.

Distinguishing yet again between Economic Profits and Business, or Accounting Profits

In Chapter 21 we saw a distinction between economic and accounting profit. The accountant calculates profit for a business as the difference between total explicit revenues and total explicit costs. Consider an extreme example. You are given a large farm as part of your inheritance. All the land, fertilizer, seed, machinery, and tools are fully paid for. You take over the farm and work on it diligently with half a dozen labourers. At the end of the year you sell the output for, say, £200 000. Your accountant then subtracts your *explicit* expenses.

The difference is called profit, but it is not economic profit because no accounting was taken of the implicit (as opposed to the explicit) costs of using the land, seed, tools, and machinery. The only explicit cost that was considered was the labourers' wages. As long as the land could be rented out, the seed could be sold, and the tools and machinery could be leased, there was an opportunity cost of using them. To derive the economic profits that you might have earned last year from the farm, you must subtract from total revenues the full opportunity cost of all factors of production used (which will include both implicit and explicit costs).

As a summary, then, accounting profits' main use is the definition of taxable income and, as such, includes returns to both owner's labour and capital. Economic profit, on the other hand, represents a return over and above the opportunity cost of all resources (including a normal profit to the owner's entrepreneurial abilities and labour).

When viewed in this light, it is possible for economic profit to be negative, even if accounting profits are positive. Using the farming case again, what if the opportunity cost of using all the resources turned out to be £220 000? Then you would have suffered economic losses.

In sum, the accountant's definition and the economist's definition of profits usually do not coincide. Economic profits are a residual. They are whatever remains after *all* economic, or opportunity, costs are taken into account.

Is Economic Profit a Payment for Managerial Skill?

It is often argued that profit is a payment for 'managing' a business venture well. Clearly, better managed firms will earn higher rewards than poorly managed ones, but *profit* cannot be called the reward for good management, because managerial skill is a *service* available on the market. Any entrepreneur can hire a manager, in other words. Better managers, typically, earn higher salaries than poorer ones. The good entrepreneur who apparently earns high profits because of his or her good management is only earning an *imputed salary*, in effect, what he or she could have earned *elsewhere* by managing *someone else's* business.

Economic profit, strictly speaking, cannot be called the reward for managerial skill. For the firm which prospers owing to good management, payment for management is a cost of production rather than profit.

Is Economic Profit a Payment for Taking Risk?

Unlike a manager who might be employed by the owner, the person owning the enterprise takes the *risk* that the enterprise may fail. It is often argued, therefore, that profits are the reward for bearing such risks. After all, if the business fails, it is the owner who suffers a reduction in net worth. However, many risks can be reduced by purchasing an *insurance policy*. Small and big businesses alike may purchase strike insurance, crop failure insurance, and so on.

So What Is Profit?

Profit is a residual. But it does not arise accidentally; it is a consequence of the unique capabilities of the firm's owner. It rewards the taking of risks which cannot be spread by insurance. It can be explained in other ways too.

Exploitation

The classical economists' view of profit was indistinguishable from what we would now call interest. This is because their concern was not for individual markets and individual factor prices, but rather for the *share of national income* earned by various *social classes*.

Karl Marx (see pen portrait on page 36, Chapter Three) argued that the source of profits was **exploitation**. His definition of exploitation was phrased quite carefully, and was different from our normal use of the word. As he used the word, firms actually 'exploited' workers by paying them precisely what their labour was *worth*.

Marx based his entire argument upon the **labour theory of value** – a theory accepted by all the classical economists – which stated that the force underlying the value of all goods was the amount of labour needed to produce them. This amount included 'direct' labour – the actual amount of work expended by a labourer of average skill – and 'indirect' labour – the labour-value of the portion of the *tools* used in producing the commodity.

Marx put forward his exploitation thesis by asking: if the value of any commodity is measured by the direct and indirect labour-time needed to produce it, what can the value of *labour-time* itself be? He answered that it must be *subsistence*, the amount of goods and services needed to enable a worker and his family to keep body and soul together. This is what it cost, in other words, for society itself to 'produce' one worker. Therefore, when the worker earned subsistence, he or she was earning a 'fair wage', because the labour power provided by the worker was priced in a fashion similar to that of all other commodities.

Marx was restating (albeit in a highly potent, political fashion) what all the classical economists believed: owners of firms earned profit because they could legitimately claim anything 'left over' after all costs of production had been paid. But Marx went further. Even though the source of profit was 'exploitation', in that workers produce goods of much higher value than the price of their subsistence, by the rules of the game of capitalism itself, 'exploitation' was a perfectly *fair* wage. When workers 'sold their labour power', as Marx put it, if they earned subsistence they received the *full* value of the service they provided. This argument led to Marx's conclusion that a complete revolutionary change in, rather than reform of, the capitalist system was in the best interest of the working class.

Restrictions on Entry

We pointed out in Chapter 23 that monopoly profits – a special form of economic profits – are possible when there are barriers to entry. Monopoly profits due to entry restrictions are often called monopoly rents by economists. Entry restrictions exist in many industries, including taxis, cable television franchises, prescription drugs and spectacles, and numerous others. Basically, monopoly profits are capitalized into the value of the business that owns the particular right to have the monopoly.

Innovation

A number of economists have maintained that economic profits are created by innovations, which is defined as the creation of a new organizational strategy, new marketing strategy, or a new product. The innovator creates new economic profit opportunities by his or her innovations. The successful innovator obtains a temporary monopoly position, allowing him or her to have temporary economic profits. When other firms catch up, those temporary economic profits disappear. In order to encourage innovation this temporary advantage may be extended by granting patents, which prevent copying of the innovation for a certain length of time.

The Function of Economic Profit

In a market economy, the expectation of profits induces firms to discover new products, new production techniques, and new marketing techniques – literally all the new ways to make higher profits. Profits in this sense spur innovation and investment.

Additionally, as we pointed out in Chapter 6, profits cause resources to move from lower-valued to higher-valued uses. Prices and sales are dictated by the consumer. If the demand curve is close to the origin, then there will be few sales and few, if any, profits. The lack of profits therefore means that there is insufficient demand to cover the opportunity cost of production. In the quest for higher profits, firms will take resources out of areas where either accounting losses or lower-than-normal rates of return are being made and put them into areas where there is an expectation of higher profits. The profit incentive is an inducement for an industry to expand when demand and supply conditions warrant it. The existence of economic losses, on the other hand, indicates that resources in the particular industry are not as valued as they might be elsewhere. These resources therefore move out of that industry or, at a minimum, no further resources are invested in it. Therefore, resources follow the firm's quest for higher profits. They allocate resources, guiding them towards production of the goods and services which consumers most want. (Now read Key Points 26.3.)

Key Points 26.3

- **Profit is the reward to entrepreneurial talent, the fourth factor of production.**
- **It is necessary to distinguish between accounting profits and economic profits.**
- **Accounting profits are measured by the difference between total revenues and all explicit costs.**
- **Economic profits are measured by the difference between total revenues and the total of all opportunity costs of all factors of production.**
- **There are numerous theories of why profits exist. These include the notions that profits are (1) a reward to risk-taking, (2) a result of disequilibrium in the market-place, and (3) a result of imperfect competition.**
- **The function of profits in a market economy is to allocate scarce resources. Resources can be expected to flow to where profits are highest.**

CASE STUDY

The Determination of Land Prices

The simplest models of land-price determination have always emphasized the importance of supply inelasticity. At the limit we can argue that the total quantity of land available is fixed. If this is the case land prices will be entirely demand-determined.

Thus, in Figure 26.1, if demand is d_1d_1, the market clearing price will be p_1. If demand increases to d_2d_2, then price increases to p_2 but quantity remains unchanged. Similarly, if demand reduces to d_3d_3, price falls to p_3 but there is no effect on quantity.

This raises two questions: what determines demand and can land really be regarded as being in fixed supply? With respect to demand, most land is not wanted for its own sake but rather is a derived demand based on the value of the output arising from that land. So in the case of agriculture, the maximum that people will be prepared to pay for a given piece of land will be the discounted value of the most suitable crop less the other costs of production, including normal profit. Similarly, for housing the developer estimates the expected price that can be obtained for the dwellings to be built less the costs of building, including profit. The residual determines the maximum

Figure 26.1

The Demand for Land

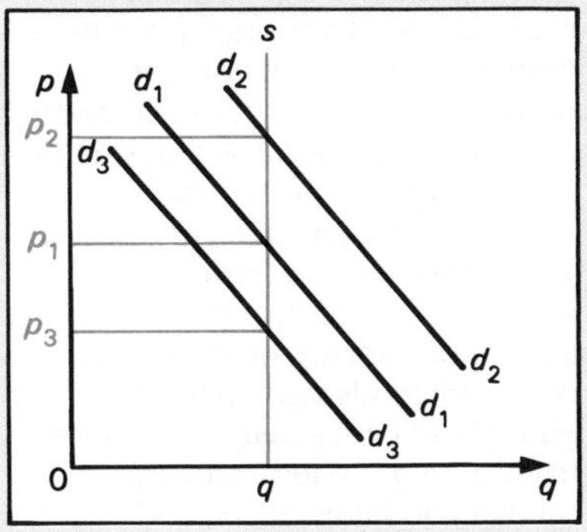

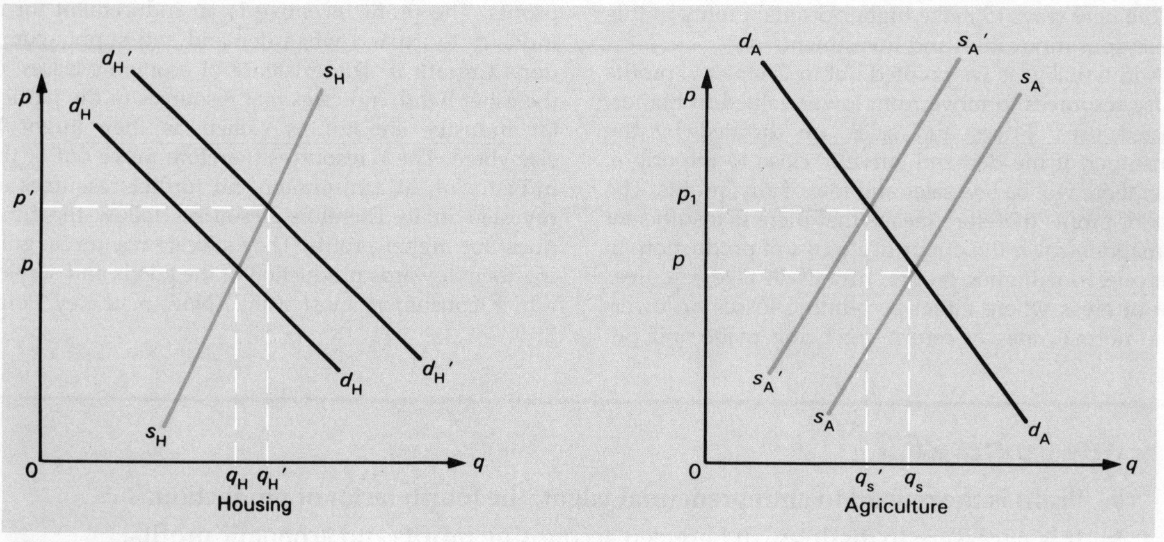

Figure 26.2
Land in Different Markets

that the developer will be prepared to pay for the land. Different users will bid different prices on the basis of relative profitability – and the most profitable use will win.

It is clear, therefore, that while the total land available may be fixed, the amount supplied to any particular use is not. In particular, different parcels of land have different attributes so their productivity varies between uses. The most important attributes which determine this productivity are:

- the type and quality of soil which will affect both its capacity in different types of agricultural production and its suitability for construction;
- other physical attributes such as height, gradient, drainage, etc., which similarly affect output and construction costs;
- environmental aspects which affect the desirability of the land in different uses; and
- accessibility, because all uses involve transport costs which will vary with location. Where the land is used for production, the costs of bringing together factors and sending out final products must be taken into account; where for housing, the financial, time and other costs of getting to work and other non-residential activities are relevant.

How much different groups – house purchasers, commerce, manufacturing, agricultural, etc. – will be prepared to pay for particular parcels of land will vary depending upon the extent of demand and these attributes. In a free market, landowners will offer their land to the highest bidder and uses will therefore be allocated to different parcels of land on the basis of their productivity. The supply curve in each sector will be upward sloping both because of the different attributes and because there are costs involved in transferring land from one use to another – but it will not be infinitely inelastic.

For example, if the demand for housing land increases, some land will be transferred from other less profitable uses, thus expanding the supply of housing land. In Figure 26.2 we assume that the only alternative use is agriculture. As demand for housing land goes up from d_H to $d_H{}'$ – e.g. because incomes are increasing and with them the quantity of housing demanded – land is attracted away from the agricultural sector until the price per unit (p') is the same in both markets. The price of housing land increases, but so does the supply of that land. In the agricultural sector, on the other hand, prices also go up but the quantity of land available declines from q_s to $q_s{}'$. Thus under free-market conditions increased demand for land in one sector affects all other sectors as land is transferred to more productive uses.

Further, although the total supply of land can be regarded as fixed, the quantity actually in use is likely to be very much less than this total because of these varying attributes and the differential costs of bringing land into production (e.g. drainage, provision of infrastructure, etc.). For some types and location of land there may be no profitable use at all. As demand for land increases it will become worth while to bring more land into use – so the elasticity of supply of land, even in total, is not zero. Rather, the supply curve reflects the fact that there are increasing marginal costs as land that is less and less suitable for production is brought into use.

One final point to remember at this stage is that, as land becomes relatively more expensive, there will be an incentive on the part of consumers to substitute other factors of production and so use the land more intensively. In the agricultural sector this has led to rapidly increasing yields and forecasts that, given world demand, a great deal of marginal land will no longer be required for agricultural purposes. In the housing sector, densities have increased and the types of dwelling being built have changed. As a result a given quantity of land produces more housing units – and housing costs are kept down.

Source: C. E. M. Whitehead, *Economic Review*, May 1988

Questions

1. What determines the productivity of land?
2. What determines the price of land in any given use?
3. To what extent is land for housing fixed in supply?
4. What recent developments have affected (a) the demand for and (b) the supply of land? What effect have these had on the allocation of resources?
5. Does the idea of economic rent still apply in the market for land?
6. Using supply and demand diagrams explain how the residential and office property markets interrelate, within a locality that you know.

CASE STUDY

Finding Finance for Investment

When a firm wants to invest, it can seek funds either internally, or externally, or both. **Internal finance** is generated from the firm's own savings. This is known as corporate saving, or retained profit, or sometimes as depreciation allowances. Its purpose is to provide for the replacement of productive capacity. Typically a profitable firm saves for several years, during which it will seek to obtain the best interest rate it can on its surplus funds. (It may obtain a CD or some other high-interest-yielding asset.) When it has accumulated assets, it will try to identify the most profitable investment project open to it. This may be a replacement of existing productive capacity, perhaps with more technically advanced machinery. Or it may add to existing capacity: this would be expansion, or net investment. The more profitable the firm is, the more profit it can retain for future investment, and the more likely it is to have dynamic plans for the future. In general, firms may often be more willing to take risks if they have substantial retained profits. They do not have to justify the use of internal funds to their bankers and so may undertake riskier projects. On average, during the 1980s, perhaps half of total finance for expansion typically came from internal finance.

In addition to internal finance, the firm may seek **external finance**. This may come from a number of sources, all of which are part of the capital or money markets. **Debt finance** involves borrowing fixed amounts on which a predetermined rate of interest is paid. **Equity finance** involves issuing shares in the company; the returns will be not interest but dividends, a share of the profit which will vary from year to year depending on the performance of the company.

Debt finance

Companies can borrow either short or long term. Much the most important source of short-term finance or working capital is the bank overdraft. The advantage of this is that interest is payable only on the amount outstanding; the disadvantage is that the company must regularly review its position with the bank, and may have to pay more for the loan when interest rates rise. An alternative source of short-term finance is the commercial bill. This is a promise to pay a stated sum on a certain date, usually three months hence. There is a market in commercial bills, which are *discounted*, i.e. bought for less than their face value. (See Chapter 19.)

Long-term loan finance may involve the issue of corporate bonds or debentures. These allow the firm to borrow at a fixed rate of interest; repayment at maturity may be twenty years hence. The company then has an assured source of finance which may be linked to the life of its capital equipment. However, it must be able to offer reasonable security to lenders, and of course the interest must be paid irrespective of whether the firm is making profits. The other sources of long-term loans are banks and finance houses. Such loans would normally be tied to the life of a particular investment project, so that both interest and repayments are paid from the income generated by the investment. Such loans may extend over five to ten years.

Equity finance

When people buy equities, or shares in a company, they buy, literally, an entitlement to a share of the future profits of the company. When a firm needs more capital, it will make a **new issue** of shares through a merchant bank acting as an issuing house. The latter will advertise the new issue; alternatively, the company may offer a **rights issue** to existing shareholders. This gives each one the right to buy a certain number of the new shares usually in proportion to their existing holdings. A rights issue is cheaper than a new issue; the latter is likely to be used only if large amounts of capital are being sought.

From the company's viewpoint, the attraction of equity finance is that the buyer shares the risks. In a bad year little or no dividend need be paid. From the shareholders' viewpoint, precisely *because* they have carried the risk, they can expect to get a higher rate of return over the long run than they would from a fixed interest loan. Also they may make capital gains. Inflation erodes the value of assets denominated in money terms, so that the lender loses some of the real value of the loan, and the interest paid. Meanwhile, profits will tend to be at least stable in the long term, or perhaps will grow. In money terms the value of the share will grow, provided the firm is healthy. If the firm is very profitable then, of course, the share price will rise further. So inflation may increase the attractions of equities as assets, provided business confidence does not suffer.

At the same time, inflation can lead to high nominal interest rates and this can cause firms with extensive loan finance to have difficulty in meeting interest payments. They will have a **cash flow problem**. This can further enhance the attractiveness of using equity finance for investment.

Markets

When we speak of the capital market, we refer to the market in funds for investment, that is, for loans and new issues, both of which provide long-term finance. When we speak of the money market, we refer to the market in short-term funds, lent by selling commercial and Treasury bills and by other similar means, through banks and discount houses. The **Stock Exchange** is separate and has particular functions: it allows the *exchange* of stocks (bonds and equities), that is, the transfer of ownership of stocks from one body to another. It does not lead to the creation of *new* loans or equities. Just to confuse you though the Stock Exchange does handle new issues of government bonds; they are issued through the primary dealers on the Stock Exchange who have been accepted as such by the Bank of England.

These very many ways of lending and borrowing money, of putting money productively to work mean that there are many different rates of return to be had, depending on the circumstances. Blue chip companies can be relied upon to pay dividends. Firms seeking venture capital are going to be adventurous with your capital, probably in an area of high technology. They will pay little in dividends, but may provide substantial capital growth (i.e. the share price will go up) if the companies themselves grow rapidly. The government will pay relatively low rates of interest, but is very safe – hence, gilts. Other sorts of loans will have interest rates falling between the extremes, but higher for longer loans and vice versa.

Banks which are buying shares in the stockbroking firms which trade on the Stock Exchange will become **financial conglomerates**. They will be offering many different kinds of financial products through their different departments.

Questions

1. Why do interest rates vary at any given time?
2. In what circumstances will firms seek external finance?
3. What factors will savers take into account when deciding how to invest their funds?

Exam Preparation

PRACTICAL EXERCISE

1. 'All revenues obtained by the Italian government from Renaissance art museums are pure economic rent.' Is this statement true or false, and why?

MULTIPLE CHOICE QUESTIONS

1. A man earns £100 per week. The next most highly remunerative job available to him would carry a wage of £95 per week. The £95 is known as his
   A economic rent
   B quasi-rent
   C rent of ability
   D transfer earnings
   E transfer payments

2. If the demand for a factor in absolutely inelastic supply were to increase, then the
   A transfer earnings would fall
   B transfer earnings would rise
   C economic rent would fall
   D economic rent would rise
   E quasi-rent would fall

For Question 3 select your answer from the following grid:

A	B	C	D	E
1, 2, 3, all correct	1, 2 only correct	2, 3 only correct	1 only correct	3 only correct

3. Quasi-rent is a payment, received by a factor of production, which
   1 is in excess of that required to keep the factor in its current use
   2 arises because of short-term shortages of that factor
   3 is eliminated when a government introduces a rent freeze.

RELATED ESSAY QUESTIONS

1. How do enterprise and capital differ as factors of production? How might the supply of entrepreneurs be increased?

2. What is the essential role of the Stock Exchange in the workings of the financial system?

3. (a) In what circumstances could a factor of production be described as earning economic rent?
   (b) Explain why a distinction is sometimes drawn between rent and quasi-rent.
   (c) Consider the argument for regulations controlling the prices of factors of production which earn economic rent.

4. Distinguish between transfer earnings and economic rent. Discuss the contention that economic rent may be earned by any factor of production.

5. What is the role of profit in a free enterprise system? To what extent does profit perform this role in a mixed economy?

6. Are profits the reward for a useful service?

27 How Income is Distributed

Key Points to Review

- Positive versus normative economics (1.9)
- Marginal revenue product (25.1)
- The elasticity of supply of labour (25.3)

Questions for Preview

1 How are factor and product markets related?

2 How does structural change affect the labour market?

3 Is marginal productivity an important influence on income distribution?

4 What other factors influence wages?

5 How equal is the distribution of income in the UK?

We know that there are many rich and many poor people, and some of us think we know why. The real reasons are more complex than most of us care to admit. In this chapter we will present some of the more obvious reasons why in the UK the **distribution of income** is uneven. And we will examine the relationship between factor and product markets.

The Functional Distribution of Income

Income accrues to factors of production in return for their services. Figure 27.1 shows the share of total income arising from labour, capital, and property respectively, that is, wages, profit, and rent. 1981 illustrates an exceptionally bad year for profits. Worldwide recession and government counter-inflation policies combined to reduce company profits substantially: they had been running at around 18 per cent of total income. Since 1983 the share of profits has risen as economic growth increased. And high levels of unemployment have made it possible for employers to hire some kinds of labour (mainly unskilled) at relatively low rates of pay.

Factor and Product Markets

So far, we have kept factor and product markets separate. We examined supply of and demand for products in Part A. To some extent supply-and-demand analysis is applicable to labour and capital markets, which appeared in Chapters 25 and 26. We call this **partial equilibrium analysis**. The meaning of partial equilibrium analysis can best be expressed by a particular qualifying statement that we have tacked on to most of our 'laws' and theories. That particular statement is: 'other things being equal'. In partial equilibrium analysis, it is assumed that, aside from whatever else we are analysing, almost everything else is held constant. In essence, partial equilibrium analysis allows us to focus on a single market and view it in isolation. For analytical purposes, the market is viewed as independent and self-contained. That is, it is independent of all other markets.

General Equilibrium Analysis

General equilibrium analysis regards all sectors as important. General equilibrium analysis recognizes the important fact that everything depends on everything else. It takes account of the interrelationships among

Figure 27.1
Factor Incomes

	1978 (£m)	%	1981 (£m)	%	1988 (£m)	%
Income from employment	98 843	74.0	149 573	75.8	249 775	73.0
Income from self-employment	13 539		19 937		42 617	
Gross trading profits of companies (private sector)	22 382	18.4	27 295	15.8	70 242	19.3
Gross trading surplus of public corporations (public sector)	5 393		7 821		7 286	
Gross trading surplus of government enterprises	216		236		–70	
Rent	10 036	6.6	16 365	7.3	27 464	6.9
Total Domestic income*	151 854		223 561		264 157	

*Includes some capital consumption and stock appreciation. *Source*: CSO, *Blue Book, 1989*, Table 1.3

prices and quantities of various goods and services. It is a more precise analysis than partial equilibrium analysis, but also a more difficult one to undertake. Just as partial equilibrium analysis does not require that *all* other things be held constant, general equilibrium analysis does not permit *all* other things to vary. There is a limit to how many markets can be taken into account in any analysis. That limit is reached either by the cerebral limits of the economist doing the analysis or by the capacity of the computer that he or she is utilizing. When economists talk of general equilibrium analysis in dealing with practical problems, they are taking account of *several markets* and the relationships among them. If the goal of the economist is to predict what will happen when the economic environment changes, his or her choice of general equilibrium analysis depends on (1) the question being asked, and (2) the degree to which the answer will change if several markets are *not* considered. One would want to use general equilibrium analysis when analysing the effects of, say, a new law requiring the producers of steel to pay a 300 per cent tax on the value of all steel produced. There would be important interrelationships among the steel industry, the car industry, and the labour markets involved in both industries, as well as effects on and from a multitude of other industries in the economy.

Let us now look at the simplest general equilibrium model. We will go back to the world of guns and butter discussed in Chapter 1.

THE CIRCULAR FLOW IN A TWO-GOOD WORLD

Assume that there are only two goods available – guns and butter. Nothing else is produced, nothing else is consumed. All income is spent on either guns or butter. Thus, there are two industries. We show the circular flow of income and product in Figure 27.2 (page 426). We have broken the factor markets and the product markets into two industries – guns and butter. We have also assumed that there is only one factor of production – labour. (Of course, there have to be others, but we want to make the model simple to show the interrelationships involved.) Let us start off in equilibrium in both labour markets and both product markets. The equilibrium prices and quantities of guns and butter are P_G, P_B, Q_G and Q_B, respectively. The equilibrium wage-rates and quantities of labour are W_G, W_B, L_G, and L_B, respectively.

Now, to show how the interrelationships work, we will assume an increase in the demand for guns. This is shown by a shift in the demand schedule in the product market from D_GD_G to $D'_GD'_G$. The short-run equilibrium price, given the supply curve of S_GS_G, will rise from P_G to P'_G. This means that firms in this industry will be making higher than normal profits. (We assume they were in equilibrium before; thus, they were making normal profits, or a competitive rate of return.) That is why output expands to Q'_G.

THE LABOUR MARKET

There is one way for firms in the guns industry to expand, however. More resources must be obtained. Considering labour alone, the demand curve for labour in the gun industry must shift from d_Gd_G to $d'_Gd'_G$. It will shift outwards to the right because, as you will remember, the demand for labour is a derived demand. Now that output (guns) can be sold at a higher price (P'_G), the marginal revenue product curve shifts outwards to the right, and so too does the demand curve for labour in the gun industry. The only way the industry can attract more workers is for the wage-rate to increase. That is why we show an upward-sloping labour supply curve of s_Gs_G. The wage-rate rises to W'_G.

Figure 27.2

A Simplified General Equilibrium Model: Guns and Butter. In this world we have just two products, guns and butter. We have a simplified circular flow diagram in which firms purchase resources in the labour market and sell goods and services in the product market. Households sell factor services to the labour market and receive national income as factor payments. Households purchase goods and services in the product market and make consumer expenditures. We assume that there is a shift in tastes in favour of guns. In the diagrams below we use lower-case *d*'s and *s*'s for the demand and supply curves in the labour markets and upper case *D*'s and *S*'s for the demand and supply curves in the product markets. The demand curve for guns shifts out to $D'_G D'_G$. The price increases to P'_G. This causes the derived demand curve for labour in the gun industry to shift outwards to $d'_G d'_G$ Wage-rates in the gun industry increase to W'_G. Concurrently, the demand curve for butter shifts inwards to $D'_B D'_B$. The price of butter falls to P'_B. The derived demand for labour in the butter industry decreases to $d'_B d'_B$. Wage-rates fall in the butter industry to W'_B. In the long run, further shifts occur. Labour and resources flow into the gun industry so that the supply curve shifts outwards. The supply curve in the butter industry shifts inwards. Prices move to P''_G in the gun industry and to P''_B in the butter industry. Workers move into the gun industry so that its supply curve of labour shifts outwards. The supply curve of labour shifts inwards in the butter industry. The equilibrium wage-rate in the gun industry goes to W''_G. The equilibrium wage-rate in the butter industry goes to W''_B. There are further adjustments that then take place, which we do not show.

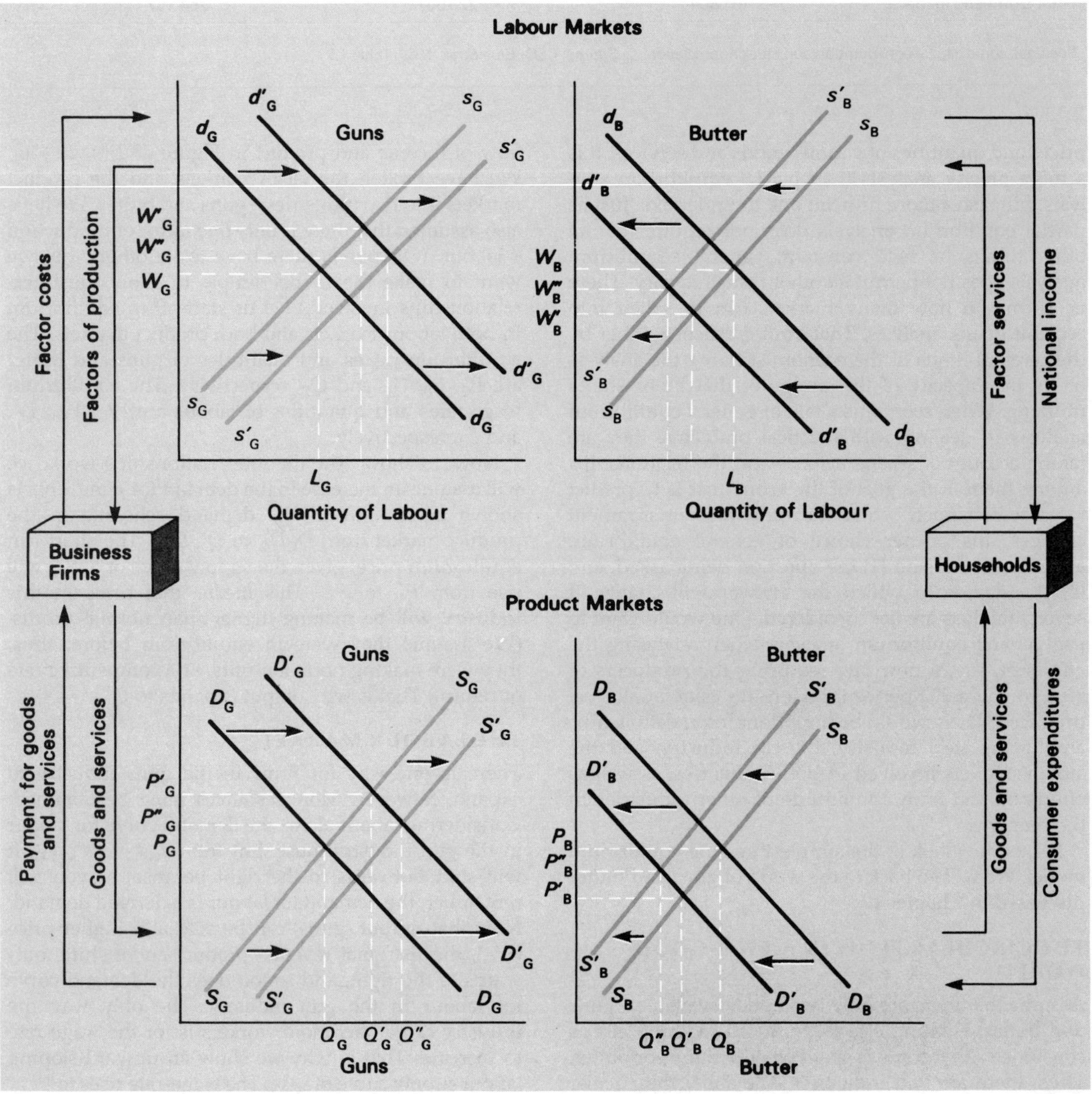

WHAT ABOUT THE BUTTER INDUSTRY?

The opposite short-run adjustments will occur in the butter industry. The product demand curve will shift leftwards from D_BD_B to $D'_BD'_B$. This is so because we are living in a two-good, full-employment world. The only way for the population to demand and consume more guns is to reduce its demand and consume less butter. Given the supply curve S_BS_B, the short-run equilibrium price will fall in the butter industry to P'_B. Looking at the labour market, since the demand for labour is a derived demand, the demand curve will shift leftwards from d_Bd_B to $d'_Bd'_B$. The market-clearing wage-rate will fall to W'_B, and labour will leave the butter industry and enter the gun industry.

General Equilibrium in the Long Run

What we have done is trace the short-run adjustments to a shift in demand in favour of guns and away from butter. This is only a short-run situation because at the new equilibrium, economic profits are being made in the gun industry while economic losses are being made in the butter industry. Resources will flow out of the butter industry into the gun industry. That is to say, firms may go out of business in the butter industry; they or others will quickly see a place to make higher profits and move into the gun industry even before bankruptcy threatens. Thus, the supply curve in the gun industry will shift outwards from S_GS_G to $S'_GS'_G$. Simultaneously, the supply curve will shift inwards in the butter industry. A new long-run equilibrium price will prevail in both industries. It will fall in the long run from P'_G to P''_G in the gun industry. In the butter industry, it will rise from P'_B to P''_B.

There will be long-run adjustments also taking place in the resource markets. Workers will shift out of the butter industry and into the gun industry. The supply curve in the former will shift leftwards while simultaneously the supply curve in the latter will shift rightwards. The new equilibrium wage-rate in the long run will fall slightly in the gun labour market from W'_G to W''_G. It will simultaneously rise in the butter labour market to W''_B.

FURTHER ADJUSTMENTS

The process does not end there, for the demand curve for labour in both markets will have to shift again. Remember, the demand for labour is a derived demand. When the price of guns and the price of butter change again to P''_G and P''_B, this will cause the marginal revenue product to change also. We do not show these further changes, but they will continue with the demand and supply curves shifting until the long-run equilibrium is established in both the labour markets and the product markets. If we were to consider the possibility of other markets existing, that is, a world in which there were more than two goods, we would also take into account shifts in the demand for other goods due to a change in the price of guns and of butter. We would then have to find out what would happen to the resources used in other industries. A true general equilibrium analysis would take account of every relevant market.

A Short Digression: Perfect Competition and Economic Efficiency

Underlying this description is a perfectly competitive economy. It turns out that the perfectly competitive price system has a very special quality. There is a correspondence between an efficient allocation of resources and the results of the allocation from a perfectly competitive price system. Indeed, this correspondence is exact. Every perfectly competitive allocation in long-run equilibrium yields an economically efficient allocation of resources. The definition of economic efficiency is a situation in which the economy is deriving maximum economic value from the economy's given resources. Once we have attained a position of economic efficiency, it is impossible to make any person better off without making another person worse off. Costs are kept to a minimum and each pound spent on inputs yields output of equal value.

THE MEANING OF A PERFECTLY COMPETITIVE PRICE SYSTEM

Let us be specific about what we mean by a perfectly competitive price system. In such a system, each good has an equilibrium price that is established by the interaction of supply and demand. The equilibrium price clears each market; the quantities demanded and supplied of each good are equal.

Consumers take the price of the goods and services they buy as given. Subject to their budget constraints, they adjust their behaviour to maximize satisfaction, or utility. Firms, of which there are a large number, each operate to maximize profits. Under these conditions, three things happen:

1. Profit-maximizing competitive firms produce at an output rate at which price equals marginal cost. Price reflects the worth to consumers, because they are willing to pay the price of a product. Marginal cost reflects the social opportunity cost of the resources needed in production. Thus, when price is set equal to marginal cost, the extra value placed on goods and services by consumers is just equal to the extra social opportunity cost of producing those goods and services. We say, then, that the optimal output of each commodity gets produced.
2. Perfect competition results in each good or service being produced at minimum long-run average total cost. Thus, there is no 'waste' in the system. Goods and services are produced using the least costly combinations of resources. Specifically, for each industry, the last pound spent on each factor input generates the same marginal physical product. Additionally, perfect competition results in every

factor of production being paid its marginal revenue product (MRP).

3. Consumers will choose in competitive markets so that the distribution of output will maximize consumer satisfaction, or utility. That is to say, each consumer will buy goods and services in such amounts that the last pound spent on each good or service yields the same amount of extra satisfaction, or marginal utility.

The Real World: Market Failure and Structural Change

We have explained the relationship between factor and product markets in terms of perfect competition. This approach is useful in two ways. First, it shows us how resources are reallocated *across many markets* when changes in demand take place. And second, it reminds us that keeping markets competitive whenever possible can help to promote an efficient allocation of resources. However, the real world is full of instances of market failure. These are situations in which market forces either cannot work freely, or cannot respond to all the economic forces at work.

For example, it is clear that any kind of change in demand will require changes in the structure, or composition, of output. We call this process **structural change**. Resources must move out of lines of production which face lower demand (and losses), and into production of goods and services for which demand is growing. Because human beings often find change difficult and disruptive, structural change can be a painful process. In particular, if resources are not very mobile, it may produce **structural unemployment**. People who are made redundant from declining industries may lack the skills needed by growing industries, or may live far away from them. The market fails to ensure an easy reallocation of resources. They may be unemployed for some time, especially if the declining industry is a localized one such as shipbuilding: heavy unemployment will then persist. Similarly, capital must move also, in the long run.

When capital equipment wears out, it will not be replaced unless it has been making a profit. Instead, the owners of the capital will seek to reinvest in a more profitable enterprise. So we see whole factories closing down altogether, and new ones opening up.

Because the demand for labour is *derived* from the demand for the product, structural change is a major source of income differentials. Firms in growing industries will pay more to attract the labour they need. So pay in the electrical and electronics industries is usually higher than it is in the textile trade. Electronics firms are often located in places with relatively low unemployment (e.g. the Thames Valley) and may have difficulty in recruiting all the labour they need. They will have to pay well to attract and to keep people with scarce skills. A textile firm in Bolton which has been laying off its employees will pay less well. Some of them may be without work years after they were made redundant. Their skills are abundant in relation to the demand for them, and their market power is therefore very limited. (Now read Key Points 27.1.)

Marginal Productivity Theory

When trying to determine how many workers a firm would hire, we had to construct a marginal revenue product curve. We found that as more workers were hired, the MRP fell due to diminishing marginal returns. If the forces of supply and demand established a certain wage-rate, workers would be hired until marginal revenue product was equal to the going wage-rate. Then the hiring would stop. This analysis suggests what *all* workers can expect to be paid in the labour market. *They can each expect to be paid the value of their marginal product* or MRP, assuming, of course, that there are low-cost information flows and that the labour and product markets are competitive.

We have already seen that rising demand for a

Key Points 27.1

- **The functional distribution of income describes the shares of total income forming rewards to land, labour, and capital.**
- **Partial equilibrium analysis is one that does not take account of interrelationships among markets.**
- **General equilibrium analysis attempts to take into account the interrelationships among different markets.**
- **A change in the demand for one good will elicit changes in the demand for another good and also cause changes in the corresponding factor markets.**
- **It is possible to show that there is a correspondence between perfect competition and economic efficiency.**
- **Changing patterns of demand lead to structural change in the composition of output, and to differentials in incomes between different industries.**

product will result in higher prices, and therefore increasing MRP. Other things being equal, wages will rise as MRP rises.

Rising demand may occur for a number of reasons. Improved competitiveness with substitutes, whether of price or non-price factors, will increase demand. Rising incomes will be important for products with high income elasticity of demand. Falling demand will be associated with the development of efficient production of a substitute abroad, or of new substitutes. Shifting tastes and fashions can work both ways.

Process of Competition

In most situations, the marginal productivity theory gives us a rough idea of what workers will be paid. In a competitive situation, with mobility of labour resources (at least on the margin), workers who are being paid less than their MRP will be bid away to better employment opportunities. This process will continue until each worker is paid his or her MRP. In general, employers will not want to keep workers if their wage-rates are greater than their MRPs. In such a situation, it would pay an entrepreneur to fire or lay off those workers who are being paid more than the worth of their contribution to total output.

Full Adjustment is Never Obtained

Individuals are not always paid their MRPs. This can be because we do not live in a world of perfect information, or in a world with perfectly competitive input and output markets. Employers cannot always seek out the most productive employees available. It takes resources to research the past records of potential employees, their training, their education, and their abilities. You may know musicians, artists, photographers, singers, and other talented people who are being paid much less than well-known, publicized 'stars'. But this does not mean that marginal productivity theory is invalid. It merely indicates that information is costly. Furthermore, we must distinguish carefully between the *market* evaluations of an individual worker's worth and *subjective* evaluations. You may subjectively believe that the output of a particular artist is extremely valuable. Unfortunately for the artist and perhaps for your sense of fairness, few other people may share your subjective evaluation. Therefore, the artist is unable to sell his or her work very easily or at very high prices. Finally, the marginal productivity theory of wages applies in the large, that is, on average. It will not necessarily explain every single case.

Bearing in mind that it is sometimes very difficult to determine what an employee's contribution to production actually is, we would expect to find many cases where the connection between pay and product is not obvious.

If we accept marginal productivity theory, then we have a way to find out how people can, in fact, earn higher incomes. If they can manage to increase their marginal physical product, they can expect to be paid more. Some of the determinants of marginal product are innate intelligence, education, experience, and training. Most of these are means by which marginal product can be increased.

INNATE ABILITIES AND ATTRIBUTES

These factors are obviously the easiest to explain and the hardest to acquire if you do not possess them. Innate abilities and attributes can be very strong, if not overwhelming, determinants of a person's potential productivity. Strength, good looks, co-ordination, mental alertness, and so on are all facets of non-acquired human capital and, thus, have some bearing on one's ability to earn income.

EDUCATION AND TRAINING

Education is usually placed under the heading of 'investment in human capital', a topic we will discuss later. For the moment, suffice it to say that education improves one's productivity by increasing the human capital one has available for use in the labour market. Education usually allows an individual to be more versatile in the things he or she can do. On-the-job training can be as important as basic education in increasing productivity.

EXPERIENCE

Additional experience at particular tasks is another way to increase one's productivity. Experience can be linked to the well-known *learning curve* that occurs when the same task is done over and over. Take an example of a person going to work on an assembly line at Ford Motor Company. At first, he or she is able to screw on only three bolts every two minutes. Then the worker becomes more adept and can screw on four bolts in the same time plus insert a rubber guard on the bumper. After a few more weeks, even another task can be added. Hence, we would expect experience to lead to higher rates of productivity. And we would expect people with more experience to be paid more than those with less experience. More experience, however, does not guarantee a higher wage-rate. The *demand* for one's services must also exist. Spending a long time to become a first-rate archer in modern society would probably add very little to the income of the person who becomes an archer. As another example, a more experienced pianist in a society uninterested in music may earn the same as an inexperienced pianist, for they both may earn virtually nothing at all, since there is little demand for their talents. Experience only has value if the output is demanded by society.

CAPITAL INVESTMENT

The more capital people have to work with, the higher will be their productivity. A better machine will enable its operator to increase marginal physical product. In the long run, increases in real wages come from the increase in marginal revenue product resulting from this improved productivity.

Problems with Marginal Productivity Theory

Marginal productivity theory can help us to understand *why* some differentials in wages exist and persist. It does not imply that people *should* be paid any particular wage. It may, in fact, lead to some people being paid very poorly indeed. But this is not all. A weakness of the theory is that, for many people, it is very difficult to determine what their marginal physical product is. How would we evaluate the productivity of a railway signalman, a restaurant cleaner, or a primary-school teacher?

It is vitally important to consider both whatever marginal productivity theory can tell us, *and* all other relevant features of the labour market, including the market imperfections which exist. Immobilities, restrictions on supply, monopoly buyers and sellers of labour, and special conditions relating to individual occupations and localities, are all important.

DISCRIMINATION

It is possible – and, indeed, quite obvious to most – that discrimination affects the distribution of income. Certain groups in our society do not receive wage-rates comparable to those received by other groups, even when we correct for productivity. Some argue that all of these differences are due to discrimination against, for example, non-whites and women. We cannot simply accept *all* differences in income as due to discrimination, though. What we need to do is discover why differences in income across groups exist, and then determine if explanations other than discrimination in the labour market can explain at least some of those differences in incomes. That part of income differences across groups that is not explained is what we can rightfully call the result of discrimination.

Which People Have the High-paying Jobs?

White males, on average, occupy jobs in the highest-paying occupations more than non-white males and all females. As for the lowest-paying jobs, they are dominated by females, white and non-white, and by non-white males. Clearly, the distribution of groups across occupations is one of the major reasons why there are income differentials among whites and non-whites and males and females.

Some argue that this uneven distribution of jobs among groups is the result of past and current discrimination in the job market. In any society where white males dominate management positions, if there is racial and sexual prejudice, then white males will tend to hire white males, rather than non-white males or females.

Other Determinants of Income Differences

There are a multitude of determinants of income differences. They have to do with age, talent, education, productivity, and the like.

The Age–Earnings Cycle

Within every class of income-earners, there seem to be regular cycles of earning behaviour. Most people earn more when they are middle-aged than when they are younger or older. This is called the **age–earnings cycle**. Every occupation has its own age–earnings cycle, and every individual will probably experience some variation from the average.

When individuals start working at a young age, they typically have no work-related experience. Their ability to produce is lower than that of more experienced workers. That is, their productivity is lower. As they become older, they attain more training and more experience. Their productivity rises, and they are therefore paid more. Moreover, they start to work longer hours, in general. At the age of forty-five or fifty, the productivity of individual workers usually peaks. So, too, do the number of hours per week that are worked. After this peak in the age–earnings cycle, the detrimental effects of ageing usually outweigh any increases in training or experience.

Trade Unions

Sometimes employers pay good wages because of market forces. Trade unions may then appear to be quite successful while in fact making relatively little difference. There are some circumstances, however, in which unions can be successful in raising wages, irrespective of market forces. Where large numbers of employees work on one site, it is easy for unions to recruit and communicate with their members. It will be easy to organize industrial action and this will give the union extra muscle. Similarly, if the production process is highly integrated, so that a large number of people contribute in varied and specialized ways, strike action by a very few people can disrupt production. In the car industry, where production involves many people contributing parts for and working on an assembly line, quite small groups of people can halt production if they withdraw their labour. This sort of union power is much reduced by the threat of unemployment.

Inelastic Demand for the Product

When wage costs are rising, the firm can pass the cost on to the consumer in the form of higher prices for the product. If demand is inelastic then consumers will continue to buy the product despite the higher price. If on the other hand demand is elastic, people will switch to a cheaper substitute or do without the product altogether. So the firm cannot raise prices without facing a substantial drop in demand, and will therefore try to avoid paying higher wages.

Restricted Supply of Labour

In Chapter 25 we considered various reasons why the supply of labour may be inelastic. Whenever labour is scarce in relation to the demand for it, wages will tend to rise. Supply may be kept scarce by shortages of training facilities (reflecting occupational immobility) or by entry restrictions (as with barristers, reflecting some monopoly power) or by individuals' unique qualities.

When particular skills are in scarce supply, there are said to be **supply constraints**. (Now read Key Points 27.2.)

Investment in Human Capital

Investment in human capital is just like investment in any other thing. If you invest in a building, you expect to receive a rate of return on your investment. You expect to receive some reward for not consuming all your income today. The same is true for investment in human capital. If you invest in yourself by going to college, rather than going to work after school and earning more money, you presumably will be rewarded in the future by a higher income and/or a more interesting job.

On average, the rate of return to investment in human capital is similar to the rate of return to investment in other areas. The main cost of education is the income forgone, or the opportunity cost, through not working. The extra income earned over a lifetime is almost always more than enough to compensate for this.

Technology, Jobs, and Wages

Increasing capital investment, using better technology, and investment in human capital, are processes which go hand in hand. They all increase labour productivity and, together, they are the source of long-run economic growth. All three can be seen to lead to increasing wages.

But there are other factors which make the connections complex. For example, in agriculture there has been an enormous amount of capital-spending on machines, and much technical progress in seeds, fertilizers, and production methods. What has happened to employment? Many jobs have been lost, and agricultural work is still very poorly paid compared to the rest of the economy.

In order to understand this, we must allow for the nature of demand for the product, and of the supply of labour. The demand for food products grows slowly, if at all. Food has a low income elasticity of demand – most of us in the UK already eat more than enough; higher incomes mean only modest increases in demand for some more expensive foods. So improved technology in agriculture leads to the substitution of capital for labour rather than to expansion of production. The labour needs of the industry then diminish; at any given wage there will be excess supply of labour. Agricultural workers are widely separated geographically and therefore have a weak union structure. They live on the job and are geographically rather immobile. So inevitably their wages have remained low in spite of massive increases in productivity. Farm workers have moved into other occupations but not fast enough to create conditions of scarcity for themselves.

Figure 27.3 shows how different the effects of investment, technical progress, and education may be. If demand for the product is static or slow-growing,

Key Points 27.2

- **There are numerous determinants of income differences.**
- **If we accept the marginal productivity theory of wages, workers can expect to be paid their marginal revenue product. Note, however, that full adjustment is never obtained, so that some workers may be paid more or less than their marginal revenue product. The marginal productivity theory does not necessarily explain every single individual case.**
- **Marginal revenue product rises when the price of the product rises.**
- **Marginal productivity depends on: (1) innate abilities and attributes, (2) education, (3) experience and training, (4) capital invested per employee.**
- **Wages and salaries may be greatly affected by factors other than marginal productivity, such as labour market imperfections.**
- **Most people follow an age–earnings cycle in which they earn relatively small incomes when they first start working, increase their incomes until about age fifty, then slowly experience a decrease in their real incomes.**
- **Trade unions may be able to influence wages.**

then employers' labour needs will be progressively reduced and wages will probably stay low. If on the other hand the fall in costs and prices leads to a growing market, then the industry may expand rapidly and create new jobs. This is what happens whenever a new product is created, using modern technology to mass produce and develop a large market. Televisions, calculators, and VCRs all followed this path. In the initial period of expansion, the wages paid to attract labour to the new line of production may be above average. In the long run the wages paid will depend partly on whether the skills needed are still scarce.

Wealth and Income are not the Same

So far we have looked at income distribution primarily as a matter of differentials in earnings, the return to labour. Individuals also receive a return for the ownership of land. We have called this rent. Individuals receive income as a return to the ownership of capital. We have called this interest. And, finally, entrepreneurs receive economic profits as a return to entrepreneurial ability, again a form of human wealth. Income is a flow received year in and year out. It is the flow received from wealth, which is a stock of both human and non-human capital.

Therefore, the discussion of the distribution of income is not the same thing as a discussion of the distribution of wealth. A complete concept of wealth would include tangible objects, such as buildings, machinery, land, cars, and houses – non-human wealth – as well as people who have skills, knowledge, initiative, talents, and so on – human wealth. The total of *human* and non-human wealth gives us our nation's capital stock. (Note that the terms *wealth* and *capital* are often used *only* with reference to non-human wealth.) The capital stock refers to anything that can generate utility to individuals in the future. A fresh ripe tomato is not part of our capital stock. It has to be eaten before it turns rotten, and after it is eaten it can no longer generate satisfaction.

Stocks and Flows – a Digression

The wealth that you have is a **stock**. (Note here that we are not talking just about stock in a company, shares of which are sold on, say, the Stock Exchange.) Lots of other things are stocks, too, such as a building that you might own. Stocks are defined independently of time,

Figure 27.3
The Effect of Technology, and Investment on the Labour Market

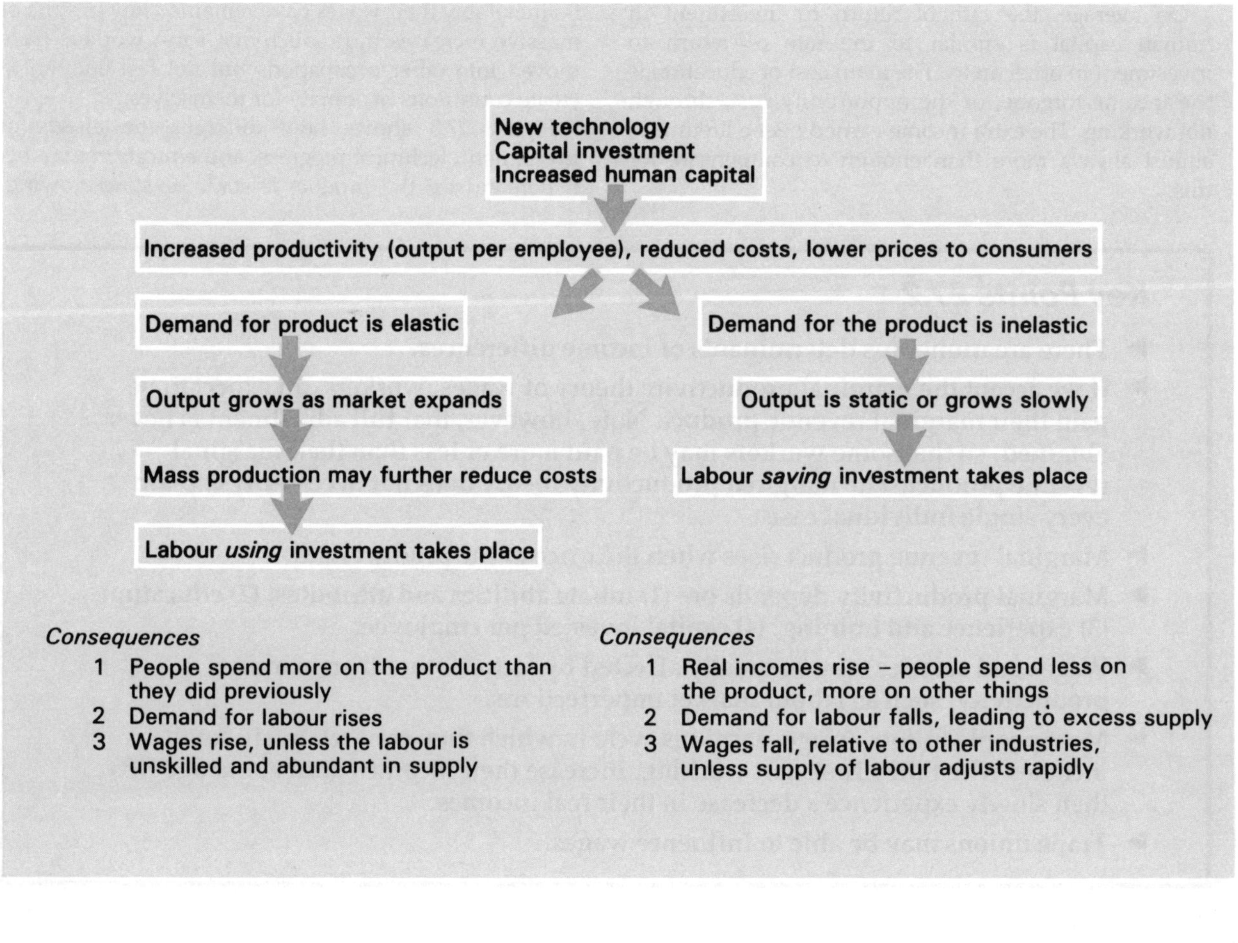
New technology
Capital investment
Increased human capital
Increased productivity (output per employee), reduced costs, lower prices to consumers
Demand for product is elastic
Demand for the product is inelastic
Output grows as market expands
Output is static or grows slowly
Mass production may further reduce costs
Labour *saving* investment takes place
Labour *using* investment takes place
Consequences
1 People spend more on the product than they did previously
2 Demand for labour rises
3 Wages rise, unless the labour is unskilled and abundant in supply
Consequences
1 Real incomes rise – people spend less on the product, more on other things
2 Demand for labour falls, leading to excess supply
3 Wages fall, relative to other industries, unless supply of labour adjusts rapidly

although they are assessed at a point in time. A car dealer can have a stock of cars that may be worth £50 000. A timber company may have five acres of trees worth £10 000; this is a stock of trees.

On the other hand, the income you make is a flow. Remember, a **flow** is a stream of things through time. It is a certain number of things per time-period. You receive so many pounds per month or so many pounds per year. The number of cars that a car dealer sells per week is a flow; the number of cars he has is a stock. Flows, in other words, are defined as occurring over a given *period* of time; stocks are defined at a *point* in time.

If you want to add to your stock of wealth or capital, you must save. That is, you must not consume part of your income. The act of saving is a flow that makes your stock of wealth larger. You should not confuse the act of saving with how much you have in savings. 'Savings' is a stock concept akin to wealth, as we have defined it.

People build up their wealth positions by saving. Savings can be held as cash (not such a good idea if there is inflation), or put into stocks, bonds, businesses, precious metals, or consumer durable goods. The purchase of a house, for example, adds to one's accumulated savings, or wealth.

What Determines Differences in Wealth

Each of us either *inherits* a certain amount of wealth, or otherwise has some of our parents' generation's wealth transferred to us in some form. Some people, for example, inherit a home or large estate consisting of stocks and bonds, cash, diamonds, and other assets. Some people inherit a small amount – perhaps just a

Figure 27.4

Redistribution of Income through Taxes and Benefits, all Households (UK), 1986. A quintile is one-fifth of the sample. One-fifth of the population surveyed had almost no income of their own and relied on benefits. They include many retired people and some young families. The total effect of taxes and benefits is progressive.

	Quintile groups of households ranked by original income					*All house-holds*
	Bottom fifth	*Next fifth*	*Middle fifth*	*Next fifth*	*Top fifth*	
Average per household (£ per year)						
Earnings of main earner	10	1 420	5 980	9 400	16 050	6 570
Earnings of others in the household	–	80	710	2 760	6 720	2 050
Occupational pensions, annuities	50	770	720	480	620	530
Investment income	50	400	480	430	1 180	510
Other income	10	130	130	110	220	120
Total original income	130	2 800	8 030	13 180	24 790	9 790
+ Benefits in cash						
Contributory	1 750	1 880	740	380	270	1 000
Non-contributory	1 620	840	510	490	410	780
Gross income	3 500	5 520	9 280	14 060	25 470	11 570
– Income tax and NIC[1]	–10	330	1 490	2 710	5 650	2 030
Disposable income	3 510	5 200	7 790	11 350	19 820	9 530
– Indirect taxes	880	1 540	2 280	2 900	4 250	2 370
+ Benefits in kind						
Education	370	450	650	850	850	630
National Health Service	910	870	730	710	720	790
Travel subsidies	50	60	50	50	100	60
Housing subsidy	130	80	50	30	20	60
Welfare foods	50	40	30	20	20	30
Final income	4 130	5 150	7 020	10 120	17 260	8 740
Average per household (numbers)						
Adults	1.4	1.7	1.9	2.2	2.6	2.0
Children	0.4	0.4	0.7	0.8	0.7	0.6
Economically active people[2]	–	0.6	1.2	1.8	2.2	1.2
Retired people	0.8	0.8	0.3	0.1	0.1	0.4
Number of households in sample	1 435	1 436	1 436	1 435	1 436	7 178

1 Employees' national insurance contributions.
2 Comprising employees, the self-employed, and others not in employment but who were seeking or intending to seek work, but excluding those away from work for more than 1 year.

Source: CSO, *Social Trends*, 1990.

parental contribution to a university grant. And it may be a negative amount – if, for example, we have to support our parents in their old age or take over their debts when they die.

No matter what its initial size, you can only add to your wealth by saving: you must set your flow of spending at a level lower than your flow of after-tax income.

Do the rich get richer 'automatically'? A favourite saying is that the 'rich get richer and the poor get poorer'. This is not a very accurate or well-thought-out theory of wealth differences. In fact, the classical economists such as Thomas Malthus, David Ricardo, Adam Smith, and Karl Marx were satisfied that this simple theory was an explanation not only of wealth distribution but also of income distribution. They believed that wealth 'bred' more wealth, and therefore, once one's endowment was established, so was one's income. After all, income – as we pointed out before – is simply the 'return' to wealth. In particular, rent is the return to land and interest is the return to ownership of capital. Clearly, people who own more land and more capital will receive more rent and more interest than those who own no land or no capital. The children of wealthy parents, in other words, are far more likely – all other things being equal – to have an increase in their stock of wealth and hence have higher incomes, than are the children of poor parents.

This simple classical theory is outmoded in any modern democratic society, according to many economists. Wealth, as we pointed out before, includes non-tangible assets, such as people's skills, knowledge, initiative, and talents. The stock of society's human wealth is important in determining income differences. From this point of view, entrepreneurs receive profits as a return to their endowment of entrepreneurial ability, workers receive wage and salary income from their endowment of ability to work.

The Distribution and Redistribution of Income in the UK

Figure 27.4 shows how earnings are distributed in the UK. Earnings consist of wages and salaries and exclude all 'unearned income', that is income from profits, interest, and rent. Neither does wealth in any form appear here. Average earnings are given for each fifth, or quintile of the population, from the poorest to the richest fifth.

Also shown are the taxes and benefits which redistribute income. Taken together with earnings, these give figures for disposable income – the average amounts which families in each quintile have to spend. Three-fifths of the families surveyed have below-average disposable incomes. Most of the poorest fifth have no economically active family member: they are retired, unemployed or disabled, or caring for the young or the sick. On average, the richest fifth have two economically active family members.

As far as earnings are concerned, a fair amount of redistribution takes place. Because wealth has never been redistributed very effectively or systematically (in spite of death duties), the distribution of total income is much more uneven.

Key Points 27.3

- **Capital is invested in human beings as they develop skills and knowledge through education and training.**
- **The effect of improvements in technology on wages and employment depends partly on demand for the product and the supply of labour to produce it.**
- **Wealth is not the same thing as income. Wealth is a stock concept, such as your accumulated savings at a point in time.**
- **Stocks must be distinguished from flows; flows are measured over time. You have a flow of saving, which might be so many pounds per month that you put into your savings account.**
- **Earnings undergo some redistribution through the tax and benefit system of the UK.**

CASE STUDY

Poverty in Britain: a Growing Problem?

Figure 27.5

Official estimates of numbers of persons (including children) on a low income in Great Britain 1972–85.

	Below SB level	On or below SB	Less than 140% SB
End of year estimates (millions)			
1972	1.8	5.9	–
1973	1.6	5.4	–
1974	1.4	5.1	–
1975	1.8	5.6	12.5
1976	2.3	6.4	14.9
1977	2.0	6.2	14.0
Annual averages (millions)			
1977	1.9	6.0	13.0
1979	2.1	6.1	11.6
1981	2.6	7.5	14.6
1983	2.8	8.9	16.4
1985	2.4	9.4	15.4

Source: House of Commons Social Services Committee, Fourth Report, *Families on Low Income: Low Income Statistics,* Session 1987–88, HC 565, July 1988.

Notes: SB: Supplementary benefit level (i.e. Income Support). The figures are derived from the annual *Family Expenditure Survey* which uses a relatively small sample and is subject to sampling error. The figures relate only to people living in private households, excluding for example those living in institutions. Owing to a slight change in the basis of the estimates, the figures before and after 1977 are not strictly comparable. Figures for that year are given on both bases.

It is often said that the poor are always with us, although the validity of this statement varies from one period to another. The 600 000 people below the official poverty line in the mid-1950s had doubled by 1960 and had quadrupled by the mid-1980s.

Part of this increase can be explained by changes in the levels of supplementary benefits. As the minister responsible explained: 'The government does not consider that a simple poverty line can be drawn . . . To define poverty or deprivation in households by reference to supplementary benefit levels has the paradoxical result that improvements in supplementary benefit increase the numbers counted as poor or deprived' (House of Commons, Official Report, Hansard, 13 Nov. 1979).

This explanation of the increase in measured poverty since 1979 was, however, rejected by the House of Commons Social Services Committee (1988) which pointed out that, although there had been some increase in the value of supplementary benefit when compared with price rises, it had gone up rather less than earnings.

Explaining the growth of poverty

How is this increase in poverty to be explained? There seem to be three different sets of factors: demographic, economic, and policy-related. Demographic factors are those which are due to changes in the size and make-up of the population. For instance, people are tending to live longer nowadays, so that the number of people in the population aged over 65 increased from 5.5 million to 8.5 million between 1951 and 1986. Since most of these were retired and dependent on state pensions, many would automatically find themselves living on a low income. A second important demographic trend has been the growth in the number of families where there is only one parent. By the mid-1980s 13 per cent of dependent children were living in single-parent families, compared with only 8 per cent in 1972. Many such families have to depend on social security, especially when the children are young, because of the lack of opportunity for the parent to take up paid employment. In more general terms, there has been an increasing tendency for people to set up their own households, rather than to share a household with their parents (when young) or their children (when old). People on a low income are therefore less sheltered from poverty than when they are able to share the income of other members of the family.

While such demographic factors are important in helping to explain long-term trends, they offer little explanation for the recent very sharp rise in the numbers in poverty. Population changes take decades to show their effects rather than years. Economic factors are more important in understanding shorter-term changes in the scale of the problem. Unemployment rose steeply from the mid-1970s onwards, pushing more people on to a low income. In part this was due to a growth in the number of people looking for work, although it also reflected the effects of the economic recession at home and abroad.

The unemployment rate in the United Kingdom rarely exceeded 1.5 per cent of the workforce during the 1950s; even in the 1960s it never went above 2.6 per cent. The 1970s saw a rapid increase in the size of the problem. Registered unemployment stood at only 3 per cent in 1970, but by the mid-1970s it had doubled to 6 per cent and by the mid-1980s it had almost doubled again, to 11 per cent. Changes in the pattern of employment were almost as important as changes in its overall level. Older manufacturing industries, which had previously provided relatively well-paid, full-time jobs (mainly) for men, were now on the decline. In their place most of the new jobs created were in the service sector, employing mainly women on a part-time basis.

Partly associated with this downward trend in employment and the change in the pattern of jobs was the upward trend in the numbers earning low wages. The economic recession of the early 1980s exerted a powerful downward pressure, especially on the wages of the low-paid who tended to be most vulnerable to losing their jobs altogether. By the late 1980s, almost ten million adult workers were earning less than the Council of Europe 'decency threshold', an increase of two million over a period of ten years.

It is the breakdown of the assumption of full employment and adequate wage levels that led to the growth of poverty from the 1960s onwards. Increasing numbers of people found themselves without a job and having to depend on a social security system that was never intended to cope with unemployment on a scale such as that witnessed in the 1930s. Many of those who were in work found that their wages, even with child benefit, were insufficient to allow them to make ends meet. Yet they were excluded from claiming social security benefits. Even when the social security system was extended, on a piecemeal basis, to the 'working poor' through family income supplement and housing benefits, this was insufficient to prevent many low-paid families falling below the poverty line. The result was that social security was unable to offset the effects of the demographic and economic changes noted above. Despite the Welfare State, poverty was on the increase.

Who are the poor?

The composition of the poor is changing. Whereas for most of the period since the war pensioners were the most visible group amongst the poor, that is no longer the case. There has been a shift in the burden of poverty away from pensioners to people below pension age. Between 1979 and 1985 the numbers of pensioners living on or below the poverty line fell from 3.1 million to 2.8 million, a fall of 8 per cent. Over the same period the numbers of people below pension age living on or below the poverty line rose from 3 million to 6.5 million, a rise of 120 per cent.

More than half a million – nearly four in ten of all those with incomes below the supplementary benefit level – were in households with at least one full-time wage-earner. As we noted above, the social security system, when it was set up after the war, made no provision for this group. The assumption was that wages would be sufficient to keep all but the largest families above the poverty line. So those with an income from full-time work have always been excluded from being able to claim supplementary benefit which might at least have brought them up to the poverty line.

Almost as many people are rendered poor as a result of unemployment. This group accounted for 510 000 people, or 34 per cent of those living on an income below the supplementary benefit level. The steepest rises in poverty in recent years have been amongst the unemployed – over three and a half times as many unemployed people were living on or below the poverty line in 1985 as in 1979.

Source: C. Pond, 'Poverty in Britain', in *Developments in Economics* ed. G. B. J. Atkinson (Causeway Press).

Figure 27.6

People under pension age living in, or on the margins of, poverty in 1985 – by economic status of head of household

Numbers (thousands) and percentage of total numbers in each income group

	Unemployed		*Full time work*		*Sick & disabled*		*Others*	
	Nos.	*%*	*Nos.*	*%*	*Nos.*	*%*	*Nos.*	*%*
Below SB	510	34	560	38	60	4	340	23
On and below SB level	3 530	53	560	8	380	5	2 080	31
Up to 140% of SB	3 750	38	2 900	29	650	6	2 550	25

Source: DHSS

Note: SB = Supplementary benefit; others = single parents, full-time students, full-time workers temporarily away from work, and carers.

Questions

1. To what extent have benefit levels kept pace with growth in real incomes generally?
2. In 1979 the government decided to publish figures for the number of people with low incomes only every two years, instead of annually. In 1988, official calculation of the figures ceased altogether. What reasons might underlie this decision?
3. Identify the three demographic reasons why more people are living on or below the benefit level.
4. There are two other major reasons for the rising number of people on low incomes. Explain the economic background to these trends.
5. Are these problems inevitable?

CASE STUDY

Food, Technology, and Jobs

The introduction of new technology on production and packaging lines in the food and drink industry has not caused large job losses but has allowed large productivity gains with staff numbers static, says a government-funded study.

The study of the use of technology in 10 plants by the Policy Studies Institute shows automation has not had the feared effect of de-skilling jobs either for process workers or for skilled craft workers.

The survey for the National Economic Development Council finds some jobs were lost among unskilled and semi-skilled production workers, with a comparatively small rise in jobs among skilled staff and technicians.

It concludes that 'new technology allows often dramatic increases in productivity without either huge reduction in jobs or substantial gain. So far, new technology has not been a destroyer of jobs on the massive scale once feared.'

Unions and workers were reported by managers to have welcomed proposals for investment in new technology because they felt it safeguarded jobs in the long-term. There were no instances of substantial resistance.

New technology was one of the main factors promoting flexible skills within plants because of the need to minimize downtime (idle periods) and for maintenance staff to be able to work on electro-mechanical equipment.

However, many production workers simply acquired a basic knowledge of fairly low-level tasks outside their main area of expertise.

Most workers did not feel that automation had de-skilled their jobs. Skill demands on craftsmen were felt to have risen and there was some evidence of increased skills among operations staff where flexibility was involved.

The job losses because of automation had commonly been softened by the 'relatively painless' method of losing people by natural wastage and voluntary redundancy.

The study says the use of micro-electronics in process applications allowed companies 'to achieve often spectacular gains in productivity and consistency or output without sizeable increases in employment'.

Source: *Financial Times*, 2 Mar. 1990 and NEDO.

Questions

1. What changes has new technology brought about in food processing?

2(a). What is the reason given for the low level of job losses?

(b). What *other* reasons can you think of why *in this case* job losses were not caused?

3. What advantages might the new technology have for (a) consumers and (b) employees in the industry?

Exam Preparation

MULTIPLE CHOICE QUESTIONS

For Question 1 select your answer from the following grid:

A	B	C	D
1, 2, 3 all correct	1, 2 only correct	2, 3 only correct	1 only correct

1. The table below is reproduced from a report by the Diamond Commission on the distribution of income and wealth.

Most wealthy (% of adult population)	*% of total wealth owned*	
	1971	*1977*
5	51.8	46.4
10	65.1	61.1
25	86.5	83.9
50	97.2	95.0

From the data it is evident that from 1971 to 1977

1 a slightly more equal distribution of wealth occurred
2 the wealthiest 10% became poorer
3 incomes became more evenly distributed.

2. Which of the following statements is *untrue* in the UK?

A wealth is more equally distributed than income
B inheritance leads to major differences in income
C government expenditures tend to lead to a more equal distribution of income
D a larger proportion of gross national product constitutes returns to labour than to land or capital.

3. The government imposes a minimum wage upon a particular industry above the level of the lowest-paid workers. Which of the following conditions is *most* likely to minimize redundancies?

A The supply of labour is inelastic.
B The demand for labour is elastic.
C The demand for the final product is elastic.
D The original wage of the lowest-paid workers was below their marginal revenue productivity.
E Capital and labour can be easily substituted.

4. The diagram below represents two different earnings profiles.

The diagram shows that
1 lifetime earnings of graduates are higher
2 the earnings of graduates are less over the ten years after the compulsory school leaving age
3 the opportunity cost of university education is represented by the shaded area Z.

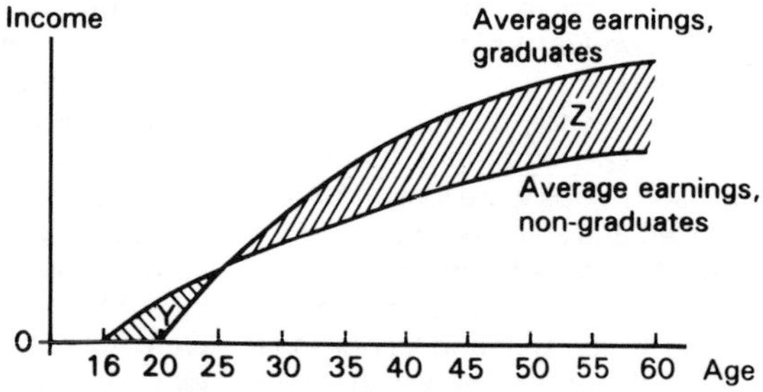

RELATED ESSAY QUESTIONS

1. Assess the ways by which the UK's tax and benefit system could be used to reduce inequalities in the distribution of income.

2. How does economic theory account for differences in wages? Discuss briefly whether the theory adequately accounts for the differences between male and female wages.

3. Discuss the economic argument that government should curb the power of trade unions.

4. 'Although wage differentials have an economic, purpose, differences in income may have none.' Discuss.

5. How might knowledge of the average and marginal productivities of a factor of production be useful to an entrepreneur?

6. Britain's top-paid city executive earns more than £2.5 million a year . . . up to 250 times higher than that of an average schoolteacher . . . Economics textbooks are packed with rationales for big pay differentials (*Financial Times*, 9 Oct. 1987, M. Prowse, 'Why the City pays too Much'). Outline an economic theory of pay differentials, and explain whether or not you feel it gives a satisfactory explanation of the example quoted.

Part E

Economic Policies and Issues

28 Nationalized Industries and Privatization

Key Points to Review

- Nationalization (4.3)
- Public goods (10.5)
- Merit goods (10.5)
- Externalities (10.2)
- Cost-benefit analysis (10.4)
- Average costs and marginal costs (21.3)
- Internal economies of scale (21.4)
- Diseconomies of scale (21.4)

Questions for Preview

1 What are the distinguishing features of goods produced by nationalized industries?

2 Which industries are *presently* nationalized in the UK?

3 What is a natural monopoly and how could one arise?

4 What does privatization mean and which industries have undergone this process?

5 What arguments have been put forward to support privatization?

In Chapter 10 we explained that due to certain characteristics some goods were best provided by the government – these goods were called 'Public Goods' or 'Merit Goods'. We now turn our attention to another type of good produced and administered on behalf of the government, namely goods produced by **nationalized industries.** (See Chapter 4 for a discussion of Nationalization.) The distinguishing feature of these goods is that they are 'private-type goods' but produced by the government sector and charged for through the market mechanism.

Examples of such goods and services in the UK include: railways, coal, and the Post Office. The proportion of output arising from nationalized industries differs from country to country and across time. In France, for example, the tobacco and the match industry are existing nationalized industries. In Sweden, distilling is nationalized. In the past the UK's list has included the British Sugar Corporation, Thomas Cook, Rolls-Royce and Jaguar Cars.

Industries come under national ownership for various political and economic reasons. The arguments for include: they are responsible for a lot of employment, their existence is central to the rest of the economy, they need financial help, they offer government control over the economy, they increase efficiency, they encourage industrial democracy, and they enable the government to accommodate externalities.

Obviously each of these arguments could be challenged and it is feasible and possible that many public-sector assets could be privately owned and controlled (as they are largely in the US). This explains why the list of nationalized industries varies across time and between countries. Indeed in Britain between 1979 and 1989 over 20 major state-owned businesses were transferred to the private sector. This process, known as privatization, will be dealt with towards the close of this chapter. First of all, we begin our overview by looking at why nationalized industries exist and their importance in the UK.

Nationalized Industries in the UK: The Arguments For

In total there were ten remaining nationalized industries in the UK at the end of 1989. In the previous decade their significance had declined. Their contribution to the share of national output had fallen from approximately 9 to 5 per cent, their share of investment in total fixed capital had halved from 12 to 6 per cent, and employment in these industries had diminished by similar proportions from 8 to 4 per cent of the total workforce. Regardless of this decline in magnitude the nationalized industries are still of considerable importance to the economy. For example, in terms of growth the 800 000 employees concerned increased their individual productivity by an average of 4.1 per cent per annum (from 1979 to 1989) compared to 2.2 per cent for the economy as a whole.

A close analysis of the previous statistics should highlight that the nationalized industries have always been more than proportionately capital intensive. Consequently very few entrepreneurs in the private sectors could meet the capital cost of setting up. Indeed, it is the distinctive cost structure that has led economists to develop the **natural monopoly** argument as an underlying reason for certain industries to be nationalized. This argument will be explored first.

The Natural Monopoly Argument

In many industries a tremendous amount of capital is required to produce a product or service. Think about how much money you would require to start a railway system or national postal network. Once you have started, however, the *marginal cost* of providing the service is relatively small. Thus, in industries where large capital requirements are needed just to get started, average fixed costs fall dramatically with higher and higher production rates. That is, the average total cost curve would be downward sloping throughout a very large range of production rates.

In Figure 28.1, we have drawn a downward-sloping long-run average total cost curve (LAC) for a railway. (A long-run cost curve is one that relates to a time-span long enough for all inputs, including all fixed costs, to be freely variable.) When we explained the relationship between marginal costs and average costs we pointed out that when average costs are falling, marginal costs are less than average costs; and when average costs are rising, marginal costs are greater than average costs. We can apply the same analysis to the long run. Thus, when long-run average total costs are falling, the long-run marginal cost curve (LMC) is below the average total cost curve. In our example, long-run average costs are falling over such a large range of production rates (relative to demand) that we would expect that only one firm could survive in such an industry. That firm would be the natural monopolist. It would be the first one to take advantage of the

Figure 28.1

The Cost Curves that Might Lead to a Natural Monopoly. Here we show the long-run average cost curve falling over a very large range of track mileage. The long-run marginal cost curve is, of course, below the average cost curve when the average cost curve is falling. A natural monopoly might arise in this situation. The first firm to establish the low-unit cost capacity would be able to take advantage of the lower average total cost curve. This firm would drive out all rivals by charging a lower price than the others could sustain at their higher average costs.

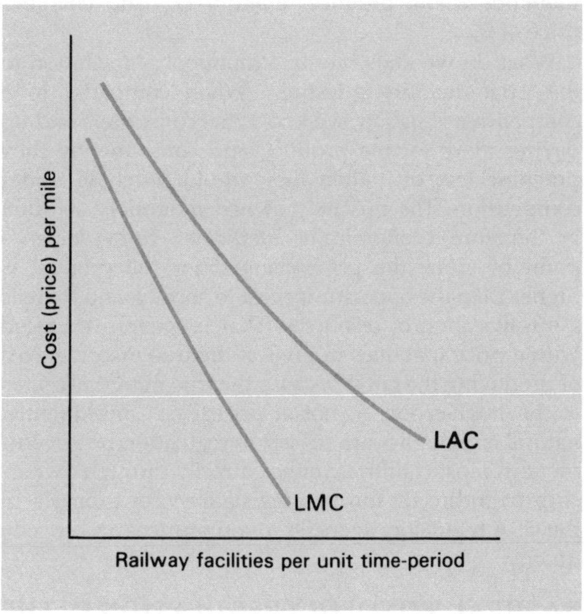

Figure 28.2

Profit Maximization. The profit-maximizing natural monopolist here would produce at the point where marginal cost equals marginal revenue, that is, at point *A*, which gives the quantity production Q_m. The price charged would be P_m.

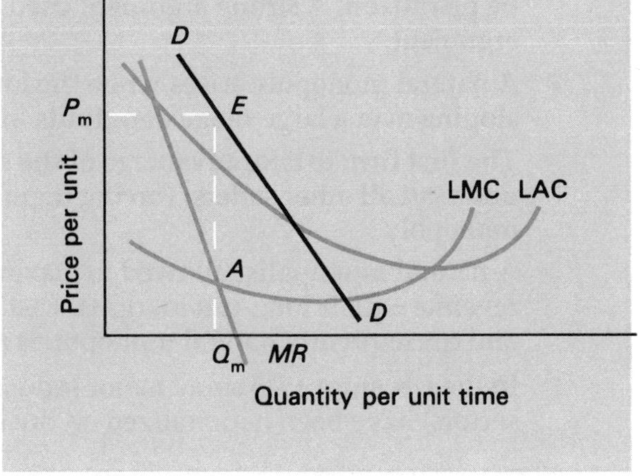

decreasing average costs, that is, it would construct the large-scale facilities first. As its average total cost curve fell, it would lower prices and get increasingly larger shares of the market. Once that firm had driven all other firms out of the industry, it would set its price to maximize profits. Let us see what this price would be.

A profit-maximizing monopolist will set the output rate where marginal revenue is equal to marginal cost. Let us draw in the market demand curve, *DD*, and the marginal revenue curve, *MR*, in Figure 28.2 The intersection of the marginal revenue curve and the marginal cost curve is at point *A*. The monopolist therefore would produce quantity Q_m and charge a price of P_m.

What do we know about a monopolist's solution to the price-quantity question? When compared to a competitive situation, we know that consumers end up paying more for the product, and consequently they purchase less of it than they would purchase under competition. The privately owned monopoly solution is therefore economically inefficient from society's point of view; the price charged for the product is higher than the opportunity cost to society, and there is a misallocation of resources. That is, people are faced with a price that does not reflect the true marginal cost of producing the good because the true marginal cost is at the intersection *A*, not at price P_m. Consequently, natural monopolies are subject to regulation by government in most countries; either directly through ownership or indirectly through legislation. For example in the USA regulatory agencies monitor prices and specify quality.

NATURAL MONOPOLY REGULATION IN THE UK

In the UK regulation has involved the transformation of private monopoly into *public* monopoly by nationalization. The Labour government of 1945–50 *started* this process by taking into public ownership a number of industries. In each case it was felt that the natural monopoly argument was applicable. The industries that were nationalized *first* were largely in the energy and transport sectors, i.e. electricity, gas, coal, road transport, and railways. There was, however, considerable debate at the time (and to some extent this still continues) as to how far the natural monopoly argument was applicable. For example, it is debatable whether in these industries the technical characteristics of production point to single producers only. It is possible that the market is so large that *some* form of competitive production may be envisaged as the privatization process has highlighted. While contemplating these issues of debate relating to the number of *producers* in each industry, one final point should be raised, namely *distribution*.

The distribution aspect of gas, electricity, and water provides a further impetus to the natural monopoly argument. The supply channels required for such services – pipes – certainly suggest that one common network is most desirable for all users. A system of competing services would involve the road being opened up for a lot of time to access pipes for maintenance work etc. (Now read Key Points 28.1.)

The Price Arguments

If we take for the moment as given the desirability of, say, the railway industry being nationalized, we still have to consider how those appointed to manage its affairs are to fix the price to be charged. Let us assume that the government decides to make the natural monopolist produce as in a perfectly competitive situation. Where is that perfect competitive solution in Figure 28.3? It is at the intersection of the long-run marginal cost curve and the demand curve, i.e. point *A*. However, given the different character of a natural

Key Points 28.1

- **A nationalized industry is a state-owned and administered corporation, producing goods for the public and charging the consumer for the product.**
- **There is no agreed national policy whether nationalized industries should remain or be privatized. A strong argument used in their favour is the natural monopoly argument.**
- **A natural monopoly arises when the long-run average cost curve is downward sloping over a large range of outputs in relation to industry demand.**
- **The first firm to take advantage of the declining long-run average cost curve can undercut all other sellers, forcing them out of business, thereby obtaining natural monopoly.**
- **A natural monopolist allowed to maximize profit will set quantity where marginal revenue equals long-run marginal cost. At this point prices and profits are very high and consequently natural monopolies are often state-regulated.**
- **In the UK since 1945 some major industries (especially in the energy and transport sectors) have been nationalized on the basis of being natural monopolies.**

Figure 28.3

Regulating Natural Monopolies – Marginal Cost Pricing. If the government attempted to regulate natural monopolies so that a competitive situation would prevail, it would make the nationalized industry set production at the point where the marginal cost curve intersects the demand schedule, because the marginal cost schedule would be the competitive supply schedule. The quantity produced would be Q_1 and the price would be P_1. However, average costs at Q_1 are equal to P_2. Losses would ensue, equal to the shaded area. It would therefore be self-defeating for the government to force a natural monopolist to produce at a competitive solution without subsidizing some of its costs.

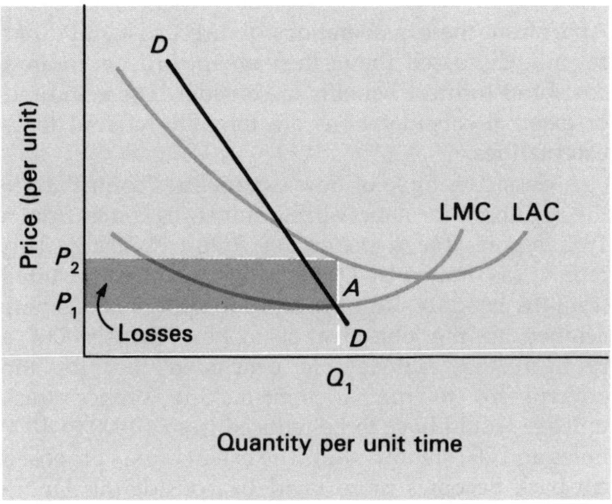

monopolist's costs at this point it cannot make a profit. Indeed it makes a loss equal to the shaded area of Figure 28.3.

SUBSIDIZATION

How do we get out of such a dilemma? There are several possible answers. The first is to have the nationalized industry price at marginal cost and then subsidize production. That is, the government could give the industry a subsidy that will allow it to break even (including a normal rate of return on investment). The subsidy per unit of output in this particular case would have to be equal to the difference between P_2 and P_1; it would have to match the industry's per unit losses. The government would have to pay an amount $(P_2 - P_1)$ on every unit produced and sold to keep output at this level.

Marginal cost pricing thus involves the issue of how desirable it is to use taxpayers' money to finance subsidies in public enterprises.

PRICE DISCRIMINATION

Another possible solution is to allow the monopoly in public ownership to **price discriminate.** This means it could charge different prices to different customers who have different elasticities of demand for the product. The state-owned undertaking would charge a lower price to those who have very elastic demands and a higher price to those who have relatively less elastic demands. Essentially, then, the demanders with relatively less elastic curves would allow the public body to recover sufficient revenues to cover fixed costs. You might say that those with less elastic demands would be subsidizing those with more elastic demands. (This would still be a misallocation of resources.)

As mentioned in previous chapters, *any* monopolist can earn higher profits if it can discriminate among the demanders of the product. Assume the monopolist is not discriminating but instead is charging everyone the same price. Now assume the monopolist begins to discriminate. First, the monopolist raises the price to less elastic demanders and lowers the price to more elastic demanders. When the price to less elastic demanders is raised, the total revenue received from them will rise because the fall in the quantity demanded is proportionately smaller than the increase in price. When the price to more elastic demanders is lowered, total revenues from them will rise also. The increase in the quantity demanded will be proportionately greater than the decrease in price. The monopolist therefore improves profits in both areas, and total revenues rise.

As to the *desirability* of price discrimination, the economist can only point out that it is 'unfair' that those with less elastic demands are forced to pay more than those with more elastic demands, i.e. problems of equity arise. Regardless of this observation it is commonplace for many nationalized industries in the UK to price discriminate. For example, British Rail discriminates against businessmen and in favour of other customers (especially students and OAPs) by lowering prices (often in the form of special offers) in between the rush hours.

TWO-PART TARIFF

Another solution adopted by the gas and electric industries in the UK is the principle of two-tier pricing system. Firstly, the user pays a fixed sum for access to the service and, secondly, a price per unit consumed. The fixed sum (standing charge) is intended to cover the fixed costs of production and distribution and the marginal charges are intended to cover the variable costs which alter with the amount provided. Supporters of nationalized industries would argue that the standing charges will be lower if you only have to cover the fixed costs of a single, government-organized industry.

VARYING TARIFF RATES

Nationalized industries can use a form of price discrimination that favours their bigger customers. This is based on a principle which may be called **declining block pricing** – a name derived from its graphic presentation. Look at Figure 28.4. If the nationalized industry concerned wanted to sell the quantity Q_3, it could do so by charging the same price of P_3 to everyone for each unit purchased. Its total revenues

Figure 28.4

Declining Block Pricing. Nationalized industries often use declining block pricing in which separate 'blocks' of the service or product can be purchased at declining prices. If the industry charges a uniform price of P_3, its revenues will be OP_3CQ_3. If, however, it charges a price of P_1 for the first Q_1 of units used, and then P_2 for the next 'block' used up to quantity Q_2, and then price P_3 for the next 'block'up to Q_3, its total revenues will equal $OP_1AQ_1 + Q_1DBQ_2 + Q_2ECQ_3 = OP_1ADBECQ_3$.

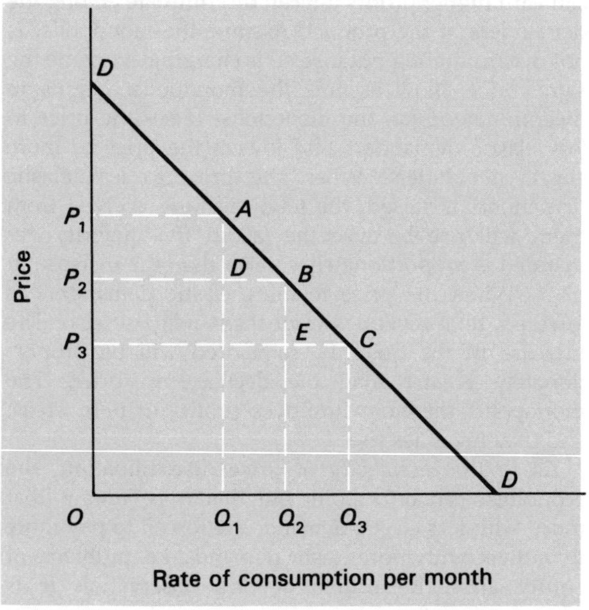

would be represented by the rectangle OP_3CQ_3. However, if it engages in declining block pricing or price discrimination, it might charge P_1 for the first Q_1 of units sold per month. It could charge P_2 for those units sold between Q_1 and Q_2. And then finally it could charge P_3 for the units sold between Q_2 and Q_3. The revenues it would receive would be the sum of the areas of the rectangles OP_1AQ_1 plus Q_1DBQ_2 plus Q_2ECQ_3, or $OP_1ADBECQ_3$. The sum of these three areas of the rectangles exceeds the area of the rectangle given by uniform pricing of P_3 times the quantity sold, Q_3.

Whether varying tariff rates are more effectively administered by a centralized monopoly is again debatable. But at least nationalized industries have the capacity to offer a range of varying prices that ultimately stem from the principles of economies of scale. These economies of scale were discussed in Chapter 21 and provide another argument in favour of nationalized industries. (Now read Key Points 28.2.)

The Externalities Argument

Apart from the considerations of direct cost and direct revenue discussed above, there are the broader indirect costs and indirect benefits to consider. These indirect or external considerations are formally referred to as **externalities**.

A classic example of how externalities contribute to the argument for nationalized industries comes from a 1963 report, *The Reshaping of British Railways*. This report was drafted by Dr Beeching, who was recruited from the board of directors of ICI to apply his business acumen to the objective of making British Rail a profit-making service. He concluded that for the government to run a profit-making service track mileage would have to be reduced from 17 000 to 8 000 miles and 700 stations shut. The extent of this proposed cut-back becomes more vivid by considering Figure 28.5.

Beeching had used as his criteria the potential direct costs and potential direct revenues of running each part of the network – those lines that would not pay went on to his list for axing.

His proposals were *not* fully acted on (in fact today there are approximately 11 000 miles of track) as the government also had to consider the *external* costs and benefits of doing so. For example, if the proposed reductions were fully carried out social hardship would have followed: certain areas and their populations would have become remote (see Figure 28.5 for exact areas); there would have been more road congestion, a

Key Points 28.2

- **If the nationalized industry is forced to set a price equal to long-run marginal cost, the industry will sustain losses. One way to compensate for the losses is to introduce a government subsidy.**
- **Another way for the nationalized industry to avoid losses is for it to be allowed to price discriminate.**
- **A two-part tariff system provides a way of covering the high fixed costs by a standing charge and adding a unit charge for consumption thereafter.**
- **Price discrimination can take the form of varying tariffs in which successive blocks are sold to buyers at lower and lower rates. This principle illustrates the economies of scale.**

Figure 28.5
Making British Rail a Profit-making Service

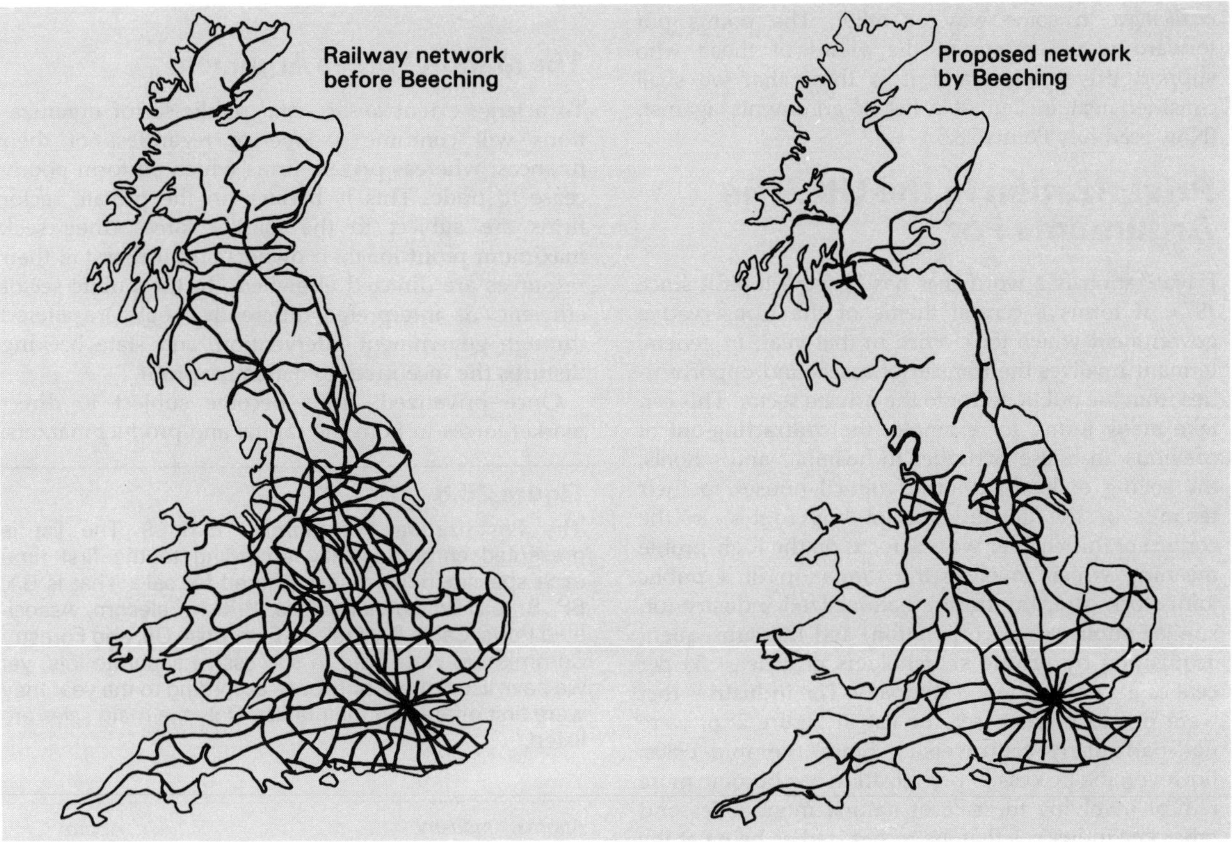

loss of local jobs, and a waste of social capital if people were forced to move because of a reduction in transport facilities.

Some key industries are seen to be best run by the government, as they can employ broader terms of reference when appraising investment. Indeed, most nationalized industries since the 1970s have been subject to the broader cost–benefit analysis criteria when decisions have been made regarding investment and disinvestment. For example, Rolls-Royce and British Leyland were nationalized in 1971 and 1976 respectively as 'lame ducks'. They may have been financially bankrupt, but in terms of being important employers to local communities, potential 'flag ships' for British exporters, and big traders with other firms involved in British manufacturing, they could not be allowed to collapse, as their external benefits outweighed their private costs. After a phase of state sponsorship both these firms were restructured and returned to private enterprise.

Similarly when making out a case for wishing to nationalize the 'commanding heights' of the economy the Labour government can do so largely on the grounds of social virtue, or more formally by analysing externalities.

MOVING TOWARDS ARGUMENTS AGAINST

In these last three sections we have tried to show that if the state does nationalize industries there are major issues to be resolved concerning the definition of a natural monopoly, the structure of prices charged, and the evaluation of investment programmes. All these

Key Points 28.3

- **Externalities involve accounting for the *indirect* costs and benefits of projects. When these are considered the value to the community as a whole is brought into the picture. For example, some loss-making railway lines are economically justifiable.**
- **The arguments *against* nationalized industries are equally numerous, and these will be considered next via the arguments for privatization.**

aspects are largely affected by value-judgements and although we have tried to discuss the issues in economic terms, political values do cloud these policies. In fact each argument *for* nationalization can be *challenged* in some way or other. The points put forward would represent the views of those who support privatization and it is these that we shall consider next in lieu of a list of arguments against. (Now read Key Points 28.3.)

Privatization in the UK: The Arguments For

Privatization is a word that has become topical since 1979; it forms a central theme of the Conservative government which took office in that year. In general terms it involves the transfer of assets and opportunities from the public sector to the private sector. This can take many forms, for example: the **contracting-out** of previous 'in-house' activities in hospitals and schools, the selling of local-authority council houses to their tenants, or the **deregulation** of bus routes. In the context of this chapter we will focus on the high-profile meaning which involves the formation of a public joint-stock company from a nationalized industry (or, similar public-sector corporation) and the subsequent acquisition by private shareholders of at least 50 per cent of the newly formed company. The industries that were privatized first (see the list in Figure 28.6) were not particularly controversial. Since the mid-1980s, however, the process of privatization has become more radical involving the sale of natural monopolies and other key industries that are recognized as being at the 'commanding height' of an economy (see Figure 28.6 for details). During the early 1990s it is intended to continue this process with the privatization of electricity and coal.

Obviously such a large transfer of activities from the public to private sector has several consequences. For example, in the decade from 1979 to 1989 privatization involved the sale of over 15bn shares, raising in the region of £25bn for the British government and transferring the responsibility of one million jobs from the public to the private sector. Furthermore, out of this privatization process developed a host of related commercial activities for the merchant bankers that administer the flotations and for the advertising agents that promote it. Indeed, the UK has established a significant set of invisible earnings, as privatizations across the world have taken advantage of the City's expertise – and paid the London institutions handsomely for their services. In fact in a newsletter *Privatization International* published early in 1989 it was reported that the UK merchant banks had handled a total of 90 privatizations in 21 countries. The banks provided expertise relating to the feasibility of the privatization, the form it should take, the price, and state of the market.

Privatization, therefore, is no longer solely a British phenomenon. It has been adopted by many countries of different political persuasions and varying stages of economic development – these international aspects will be explored further in a Case Study at the close of this chapter. Meanwhile we must overview the general arguments for.

The Market Forces Argument

To a large extent *unsuccessful* public-sector organizations will continue to operate regardless of their finances; whereas private firms which perform poorly cease to trade. This is because in the private sector firms are subject to the market forces, they seek maximum profit for their owners and if they fail their resources are directed elsewhere. In the public sector efficiency is interpreted differently, goals are altered through government intervention, and state backing disturbs the incentives to maximize profit.

Once privatized, firms become subject to direct market forces in both the capital and product markets.

Figure 28.6

The Privatization Programme: 1979–89. The list is presented chronologically according to the first time each specific industry was offered for sale. That is BA, BP, Britoil, British Aerospace, British Telecom, Associated Ports, Cable & Wireless, Enterprise Oil, and Forestry Commission were sold in successive separate lots, yet we have listed them only once according to the year they were first offered on the market. Only the main sales are listed.

Approx. year	*Industry*	*Approx total raised from all sales (£m)*
1979	British Petroleum	3 845
	ICL	37
	Ferranti	55
	Fairey	22
1981	British Aerospace	390
	British Sugar	43
	Cable & Wireless	1 021
	Amersham International	64
1982	National Freight Corporation	7
	Britoil	1 053
1983	Associated British Ports	97
	Forestry Commission	127
	British Rail Hotels	45
1984	British Telecom	3 900
	Enterprise Oil	380
	Sealink	66
	Jaguar Cars	297
1986	TSB	1 300
	British Gas	5 434
1987	Unipart	31
	Rolls-Royce	1 028
	Royal Ordnance Factories	187
	British Airways	854
	British Airports Authority	1 225
1988	British Steel	1 139
	National Bus Co. (Subsidiaries)	36
1989	Water Authorities	5 000

Source: HM Treasury, Jan. 1989 (CM 621) and various newspaper articles.

Within the product market suppliers would have to become sensitive to price to gain consumers' preferences; this may entail altering quality, lowering costs, adapting quickly to changes in taste etc. Within the capital market firms would become accountable to shareholders. If these shareholders became disappointed with their returns on investment, they would be hesitant to purchase any further shares when the firm attempted to raise capital for new projects. Shareholders clearly have alternative investment opportunities. Indeed, to a large extent the commercial world of finance is far more concerned with profits and repayments than the open purse of the government treasury, which in the final resort will always honour any debts generated. As some reviewers on this topic have neatly put it: 'the government as banker is a softer touch than a commercial bank'.*

The important objective is to expose the public sector to market forces on the basis that competition increases efficiency. For example, in the USA, where electricity is generated by competing companies, research shows that costs are generally less than where electricity is generated in a monopoly situation.

The PSBR Argument

The PSBR is an important indicator for any monetarist government, for example, the Conservative government from 1979 onwards. It is important to them that their annual targets for PSBR should not be exceeded and ultimately the overall size of the PSBR should be reduced and ideally transferred into a PSDR†.

By selling off assets the government obviously gains a short-term boost to revenue. For example, the 1979–89 sales list in Figure 28.6 represents an income of at least £27bn. Obviously this has diverted needs to raise funds through gilt sales, to print money, or increase tax. In fact some opponents of privatization scornfully regard the policy as a short-sighted process which entails selling off 'the family silver' to cover present financial embarrassments. However, a standard response to this kind of argument is that in the long term the transfer of nationalized industries to the private sector will reduce government responsibilities which should facilitate a fall in the tax burden. Finally, some claim that a reduction in the PSBR may stimulate private investments which had previously been 'crowded out' by government borrowing.

The Diseconomies Argument

To paraphrase the famous economist Lord Hicks: the best thing about monopoly is a quiet life. This statement is even more apt when the monopoly concerned is a nationalized industry. There is no pressure from competitors, there is no pressure to reap rewards and in the case of the nationalized industries there are numerous government White Papers and administrative machinery behind which the management can hide. As the Financial Secretary to the Treasury stated in November 1983, 'The protection from competition granted by statutory monopoly powers and the availability of government financial support in times of troubles enabled inefficiencies to persist.' It can be argued, therefore, that making public enterprise cost-effective entails opening it up to competition, making it accountable to market criteria, and generally providing a freer framework; even to the extent that where competition is deemed impractical a regulated private natural monopoly would be regarded as preferable. Franchising, decentralizing, and commercializing are in effect key concerns of the privatization process. Thus the transfer of state monopolies into private-sector monopolies has occurred in some instances.

This ironic development has been accompanied by the establishment of new regulatory agencies whenever necessary. For example, the privatization of British Telecom and British Gas included the creation of their related regulatory agencies OFTEL and OFGAS. These industry-specific offices of fair trading monitor consumer affairs and pricing policies. Similar 'watchdog' agencies have now been set up for water and electricity.

The Share-Ownership Argument

Phrases such as 'popular capitalism' and 'a share-owning democracy' have become important tags associated with the privatization process in the UK. These ideological aspects of wider share-ownership are of significant importance to the government; sponsored surveys by the Treasury on a regular basis to investigate the distribution of share ownership epitomize this importance. Based on the findings of these surveys privatization could be deemed a success. The 1988 survey shows 9m people in the UK (i.e. 20.5 per cent of the adult population) own shares. This compares with an estimated 3m people in 1979 (i.e. 7 per cent of the adult population). Of this threefold increase a significant number hold shares in privatized companies (i.e. 13 per cent of all adults – approximately 6m people) and more than half of this number own the shares of privatized companies only. Interestingly 1.5m shareholders own shares in the company for which they work.

The economic significance of these statistics, in quantitative terms, can be made to look impressive. The total number of UK shareholders is now similar to the number of trade union members. In fact the former is increasing whilst the latter is declining. Workers owning shares of the company for which they work can be seen potentially to improve industrial relations. The 'enterprise culture' can be characterized as thriving. In qualitative terms, however, it is worth recognizing that approximately half of the UK shareholders own shares in only one company, and many of these holdings are worth under £1 000. The contentious nature of this data will be investigated further in a Case Study at the close of the chapter.

---

* Kay and Silberston, *Midland Bank Review*, Spring 1984

† PSDR stands for Public Sector Debt Repayment and will be dealt with in Chapter 31.

Key Points 28.4

- **Privatization is a policy of the Conservative government which involves the transfer of assets from the public sector to the private sector.**
- **A case for privatization can be made by respecting market forces. Once privatized, firms are directly affected by market forces in both the capital and product markets and consequently they should become more efficient.**
- **The PSBR argument for privatization is based on the need to balance the government books, ultimately reduce the annual government borrowing, and 'crowd in' private investment.**
- **The diseconomies argument follows the line that monopoly power is not necessarily efficient, especially if that monopoly is centralized.**
- **The share-ownership argument relies on the idea of an 'enterprise culture' where managers and employers have greater freedom and better motivation. Share ownership has increased threefold since 1979 and 1½ million people own shares in the company for which they work.**

CASE STUDY

Forty Years Can Make a Lot of Difference

NATIONALIZATION versus PRIVATIZATION

'Amalgamation under public ownership will bring great economies in operation and make it possible to modernise production methods . . . Public ownership . . . will lower charges, prevent competitive waste, open the way for co-ordinated research and development . . . **Only if public ownership replaces private monopoly can industry become efficient**'

LABOUR PARTY MANIFESTO 1945

'Privatization is bringing about a fundamental change in the operation and efficiency of key sections of the UK economy. Its success . . . is self-evident . . . Privatization liberates managers and employees and allows them to reach their full potential . . . **Privatization increases productive efficiency whether or not a monopoly is involved**'

FINANCIAL SECRETARY TO THE TREASURY 1985

Questions

1. What was nationalized after the 1945 Labour manifesto statement?
2. What has been privatized since (in keeping with the tone of the 1985 statement)?
3. Both statements refer to 'efficiency' – what do economists mean by this term?
4. What types of inefficiency may affect a public corporation?
5. What economic arguments complicate the two statements?

CASE STUDY

An Assessment of Privatization

Over the decade since 1979, the Treasury estimates that the number of shareholders has risen from 3m to 9m, or one in five of the adult population. This is a whole new political constituency of property-owners, as the Tories' election mailshots to people who brought privatized shares showed. (The economic significance of this spreading ownership is another matter: the shareholdings are so small that the proportion of shares owned by institutions like pension funds and life assurance companies has continued to rise despite the enormous increase in the number of shareholders. On one estimate, the institutions own more than three-quarters of all equities quoted on the London Stock Exchange.)

Meanwhile, the remaining utilities are on the slipway. Water and electricity are already being advertised on prime-time television, a sure sign that their prices will be sufficiently attractive to ensure that Fred and Alice make a small but gratifying profit by speculating on the issues (unless a crash intervenes). The coal industry is possible, and the railways could go too. By the end of this parliament, the momentum of privatization will have dismantled Morrison's legacy of nationalized industries brick by crumbling brick.

The trend is also catching on internationally, although an IMF study argues that it is not quite as popular overseas as ministers' public relations sometimes suggests. Apart from Britain, only France has had an extensive privatization programme although even there the proceeds are equivalent to just one year's sales in Britain. The Japanese are selling Nippon Telegraph and Telephone, and there have been privatizations in Chile, Malaysia, Niger, and Turkey. However, sales in Germany and Italy have been little more than tidying-up operations.

The irony though, is that the British drive to privatize still looks more like a felicitous accident than a carefully designed scheme to revive the economy. A major reason for the acceleration of asset sales under Nigel Lawson's chancellorship since 1983 was the happy side-effect of reducing the Public Sector Borrowing Requirement – the budget deficit caused by spending more than revenue. This released the Treasury from an uncomfortable hook by allowing a more expansionary budgetary policy than would otherwise have occurred. By curious accounting convention, asset sales count as negative public spending. In other words, the more you sell, the more you reduce public spending (and therefore borrowing). At a time when the government and the markets were making a fetish of borrowing limits, asset sales allowed higher public spending or lower taxes than would otherwise have been the case. They were one way the Treasury could wriggle out of its highly restrictive borrowing limits at a time of record unemployment.

The criticism that the government was 'selling the family silver', in Harold Macmillan's splendidly emotive phrase, was always wide of the mark. Indeed, it is very hard to see in economic theory why there should be any difference to the government if it finances its deficit by getting cash in exchange for issuing bonds – promises to pay interest in the future – or if it finances its deficit by selling assets – which are entitlements to a stream of income in the future. If the capital markets are working efficiently, it should be impossible to tell which is the better course of action to take . . .

The real economic arguments about privatization should revolve around whether the companies work better in the private or in the public sector. The public claims about the relative economic efficiency of privately owned companies, or the benefits of rolling back the frontiers of the state, are not as clear-cut as ministers like to argue. The more the theorists write about the subject, the clearer it becomes that the simple idea that many of the former nationalized industries could operate independently of government scrutiny is so much eyewash. The real choice is between actually owning the business, and regulating them tightly. The government is simply not going to be able to wash its hands of most of the privatized industries.

The key determinant of whether the government can take its hands off the tiller is whether the companies are operating in a competitive market. If they are, then it can safely let the management get on with it. Companies like Jaguar or Amersham International must perform, or they lose market share, sales and profits. If they do not perform, there are plenty of companies big enough to make a takeover bid. Even the threat of takeover may encourage the management. Like most ordinary joint-stock companies, they face competitive pressure in the markets for their products, for their inputs and for their capital.

With this type of company, theory suggests that the switch from public to private ownership makes more sense. Any conflict between social and private objectives is likely to be smaller in competitive markets than in monopoly ones. A competitive market means that the price of goods and service will be fairly set to reflect demand and supply, which ensures that resources are efficiently allocated. Private ownership may in turn encourage another type of efficiency: internal or X-efficiency, which is the more efficient production of a given good or service for fewer inputs of labour, land, and capital. The private owner, or his or her manager, has more incentive to save costs than a public-sector manager who will receive no extra reward if he or she does.

The sensible response of policy is to introduce as much competition as possible into the market, either by splitting up corporations or encouraging new competitors. Yet the government, until its recent proposals on electricity, has been very slow to recognize the case for competition as opposed to a change in ownership. British Gas was left intact, and BT has had to contend only with Mercury. A much more sensible solution might have been to split the industry up, as the Americans did with AT&T. If competition is not introduced, or if it cannot be introduced because the industry is effectively a natural monopoly like the water business, then the government choice is between public ownership and regulated private ownership. That is where we are with the existing privatizations, and where we will be later with water.

The impact on the economy will take time to assess, but it is not going to be easy to do so. Productivity changes may be one proxy for internal efficiency. The evidence so far is that different rates of productivity growth in the public-sector companies bear little relationship to whether the company is on the slipway to privatization. Matthew Bishop and John Kay conclude that 'gains in British Coal and British Steel (where privatization has not been in prospect until recently) and the electricity supply industry have matched those in British Gas and the poorest performance since 1983 comes from the flagship of privatization, British Telecom'. However, a conclusive study would have to compare similar industries in the public and private sector.

Another measure is profitability. There has been a large difference between the profits as a percentage of the replacement cost of capital – the rate of return – between the public and private sectors. In 1985, for example, industrial and commercial companies earned 21.3 per cent against 2.6 per cent for public corporations. But the closing of the profits gap with private business is not necessarily a good indicator of increased efficiency, since it may come about due to more vigorous exploitation of monopoly power to levy high prices. There are, as a Lloyds Bank report makes clear, plenty of loopholes in British Telecom's regulation and pricing rules.

Nor will it be enough to see whether the prices charged to consumers have risen more slowly than before. One danger of a regulated regime is that the company 'captures' the regulators so that they become ineffective; however, there is also the opposite danger that excessively strict regulation of output prices – or the fear of excessively strict future regulation – leads to under-investment in plant and equipment. This, indeed, was one of the original reasons proposed for utility nationalization: the rate of return required by the private owners in assessing investment possibilities was perceived to be higher than the social one. (This argument is used by the Labour Party to justify the renationalization of British Telecom, which will not lay two-way information technology cables to every household.) Willy-nilly, the government or its agencies are going to have to be involved in the decisions of those privatized companies which continue to enjoy a monopoly.

There is, though, not much doubt that Britain's public corporations performed poorly through the 1970s. The profits gap was too large to be explained by the nationalized industries' pursuit of social objectives (for example, British Rail subsidizing commuter services to avoid city congestion). Productivity growth was also low, and the rate of return on capital abysmal. A sharp change in regime was certainly called for, and even the preparation for private ownership seems to have produced substantial results. It may be that big and bureaucratic corporations, like economies in some Schumpeterian or Mancur Olson view of the world, benefit from occasionally being shaken by the scruff of the neck. Fifty years on, renationalization may be needed to put them all on their toes.

Indeed, it is a further irony, given the political mileage which the government seeks to make from privatization, that many of the original nationalizations were pushed through not by an ideologically motivated socialist government but by the Tory government and Tory municipalities in the 1930s. A recurrent problem in electricity supply, for example, was that the regulation which the authorities rightly thought was necessary to stop an abuse of a local monopoly in turn led to under-investment in generating assets. There may simply be a certain range of industries, largely effective natural monopolies, which need the discipline of being periodically shuttle-cocked between the public and the private sector.

Source: Adapted from *'Private Waters' Marxism Today* Nov. 1989.

Questions

1. What is a natural monopoly?
2. Explain and discuss 'X-efficiency' using a production possibility curve.
3. The extract originally appeared in *Marxism Today*. Identify the economic arguments made against privatization that may reflect a Marxist bias. Hint: It may be useful to refer back to parts of Chapter 3.
4. Identify some arguments from the extract in favour of privatization.
5. What other arguments for and against privatization are you aware of?

CASE STUDY

To be Public or Private? That is the Question

Figure 28.7

A: Public Assets in OECD Countries: For Sale

Austria	Graz-Koflacher Eisenbahn und Bergbau GmbH; Fepla-Hirsch GmbH; Futurit Werk AG; OMV
Britain	British Airports Authority; British Airways; Royal Ordance; Rolls-Royce; Shorts; Unipart
Canada	Donohue (Quebec); Eldorado Nuclear; Teleglobe
France	AGF; CGCT; Paribas; TF1
Netherlands	KLM
Italy	Alfa Romeo; Alitalia; Banco Nazionale del Lavoro
Japan	Japan Airlines; Japan National Railways; Japan Tobacco Corporation
Spain	Iberia
Turkey	Sömerbank; Turkish Cement Corporation; Turkish Fertilizer Corporation
USA	Conrail; Continental Illinois; assorted government loans
W.Germany	Deutsche Pfandbriefanstalt; Deutsche Siedlungs und Landesrentenbank; Deutsche Verkehrskreditbank; IVG; Volkswagen

B: Public Assets in OECD Countries: Sold

Austria	Bayou Steel Company
Britain	Associated British Ports; Amersham International; British Aerospace; British Gas; British Petroleum;* British Rail Hotels; British Sugar Corporation; British Telecom;* Britoil; Cable & Wireless; council houses; Enterprise Oil; Inmos; International Aeradio; Jaguar; land; National Bus Company; North Sea oil licences; Sealink; some other bits and pieces
Canada	Cambior (Quebec); Canadair; Canadian Arsenals; Canada Development Corporation;* de Havilland; Nanisivik Mines; Northern Transportation; Pacific Western Airlines (Alberta); Quebecair (Quebec); Urban Transport Development Corporation (Ontario)
Denmark	Kryolitselskabet*
France	Elf-Aquitaine;* St Gobain*
Italy	Aeritalia;* Selenia; Sirti*
Japan	Nippon Telegraph & Telephone*
Spain	GESA; ENTURSA; SEAT; Secoinsa; SKF; Textil Tarazona; Viajes Marsans
Turkey	Bosporus bridge; Keban dam
W.Germany	Veba; Viag*

* Government still holds some ordinary shares

Source: OECD, reprinted in *The Economist*, 20 Dec. 1986.

C: Public Ownership in Various OECD Countries, 1989

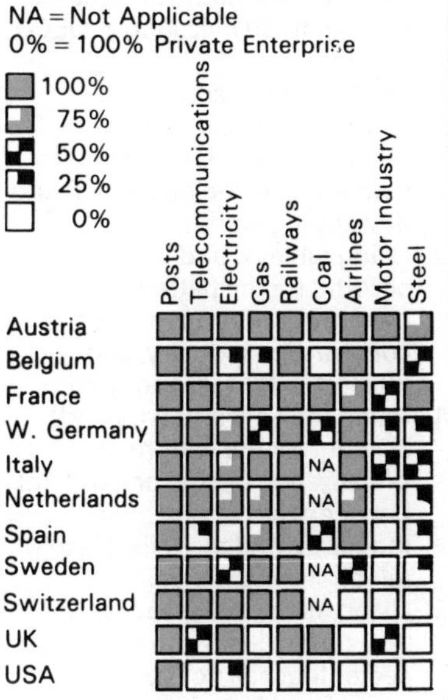

Source: Adpated from R. Pennant-Rea and B. Emmot, *The Pocket Economist*, 1987.

D: Public Ownership in Various Developing Economies, 1989

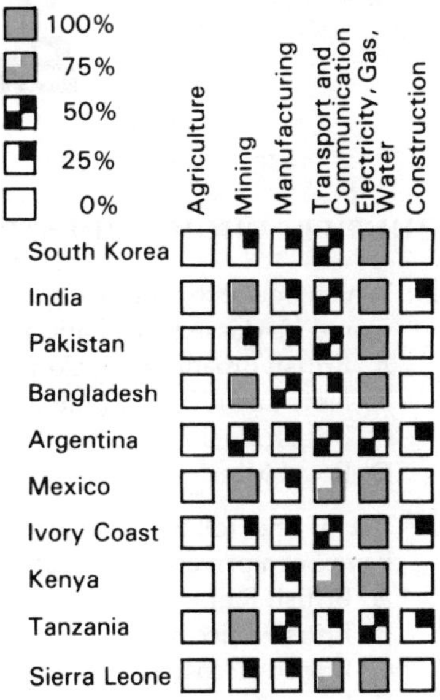

Source: Adapted from World Bank, *World Development Report, 1983*

The tables in Figure 28.7 show some international comparisons of public and private enterprise. These have been gathered from various sources and should enable you to consider the following questions.

Questions

1. Study tables A and B and identify three common features relating to privatization in OECD countries.
2. Study tables C and D and identify common features relating to the extent of public ownership in the developed and developing world.
3. Using tables C and D again, account for the pattern of public ownership portrayed in (i) the construction industry, and (ii) electricity, gas, and water.
4. Using tables A and B try and account for the pattern of privatization (actual or pending) between the car and airline industries and the railways and telephone industries.
5. Using all the tables in Figure 28.7 try to identify an industrial sector that has not yet been considered for privatization. Explain your answer as fully as possible.
6. What economic relationships do you sense may exist between state ownership and different stages of economic development? Try and use the tables in Figure 28.7 to provide evidence for your answers.
7. In an article* entitled *'Privatization in Developing Countries'*, J. Aylen makes the point that 'state enterprise is not only widespread . . . it is also diverse in character'. Taking two extremes, Pohang Steel Company (POSCO) in South Korea and the Steel Authority of India (SAIL) have little in common apart from the fact they both make steel and are both publicly owned. The South Korean firm is highly entrepreneurial, technically up-to-date, and arguably the world's lowest-cost integrated steel producer. The Steel Authority of India has outdated plant, is slow to commission new projects, is heavily protected from imports, and has a labour productivity per worker perhaps a tenth that of its South Korean rival. A significant part of the overmanning at SAIL is due to a superstructure of administrators absent at POSCO. These polar cases of commercial success and bureaucratic excess typify two different patterns of state enterprise. We call these the 'market model' (POSCO) and the 'bureaucratic model' (SAIL).
   (a) List the features that you think may characterize each of these models.
   (b) What common features do these two models share?
   (c) Can you draw an analogy from the private sector that would make the same point as the author is making with the public sector.
   (d) What important point(s) does this extract and exercise contribute to the privatization/nationalization debate.
8. Although tables C and D have already been modified since their orginal presentations, the data continues to change. What changes could you make to tables C and D to bring them more up-to-date?

Lloyds Bank Review, Jan. 1987.

Exam Preparation

MULTIPLE CHOICE QUESTIONS

1. Which one of the following public corporations would be classed as a nationalized industry?
A British Broadcasting Corporation
B New Town Development Corporation
C British Coal
D Royal Mint

2. All of the following nationalized industries have been privatized except one. Which is it?
A British Rail
B British Telecom
C British Aerospace
D Jaguar Cars

3. In order to use its resources efficiently, a city's passenger transport undertaking should charge
A higher fares during peak periods because much of the equipment needed for peak-period travel is idle for the rest of the day
B lower fares during peak periods to keep down travel costs for the maximum number of people
C higher fares during off-peak periods because the cost per passenger is higher during these periods
D the same fares throughout the day to avoid distorting people's preferences between peak and off-peak travel
E lower fares in the evening during non-working hours when demand is likely to be more inelastic

For Questions 4 and 5 select your answers from the following grid:

A	B	C	D
1, 2, 3 all correct	1, 2 only correct	2, 3 only correct	1 only correct

4. The cost and revenue curves shown below are those of a firm producing a uniform product for sale to industrial and household customers. If the firm sells an output Q_1 at a price of P_1 to industrial customers, and an output Q_2 at a price of P_2 to household customers, it can be deduced that

1 the household customers are subsidizing the industrial customers
2 price discrimination is taking place
3 the firm is maximizing profits

5. Because of spare capacity at certain times of the day, a nationalized railway may offer lower fares to customers travelling off-peak compared with the fares charged to rush-hour passengers.
This is an illustration of

1 price discrimination
2 two-part tariff
3 externalities

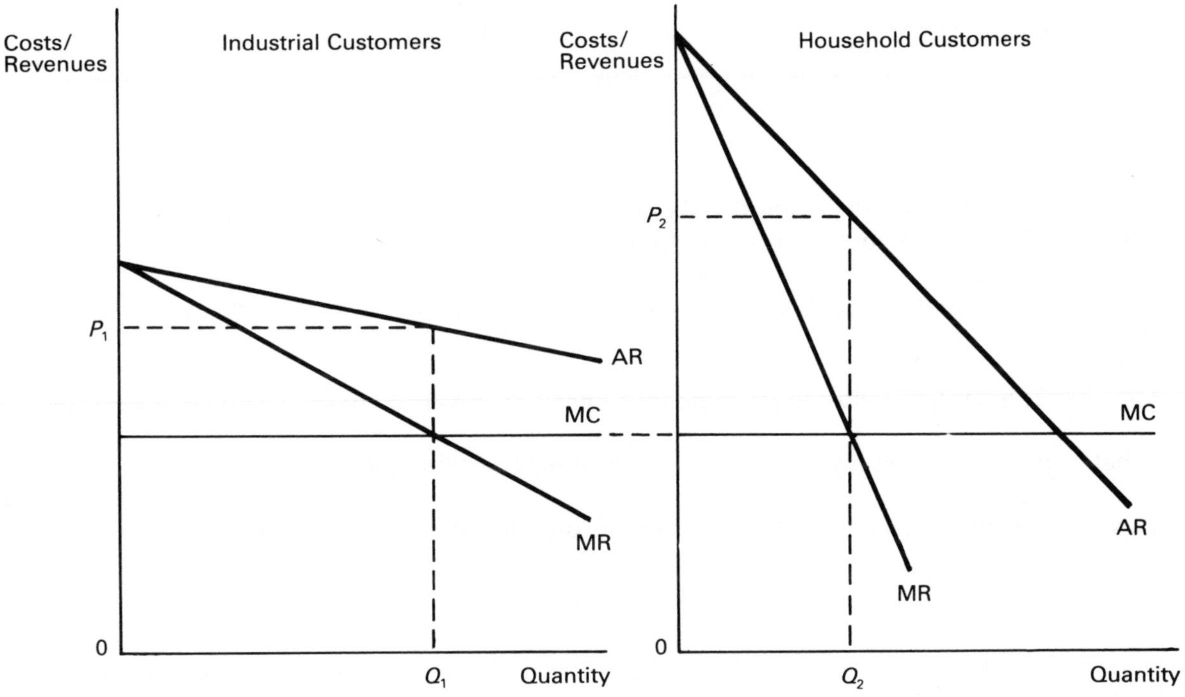

RELATED ESSAY QUESTIONS

1. Explain what is meant by marginal cost pricing and discuss the problems involved in employing it in the nationalized industries.

2. 'Privatization without competition cannot increase efficiency or improve resource allocation.' Explain and discuss.

3. Briefly distinguish between privatization and deregulation. Discuss the advantages and disadvantages of deregulation for the UK economy.

4. 'Privatization may have short-term benefits but in the long-run it will reduce economic welfare.' Discuss.

5. Outline briefly the factors which can cause a market economy to fail to achieve an optimum allocation of resources. To what extent is the government's programme of privatization likely to improve the efficiency of resource allocation.

6. 'Privatization of the production and distribution of goods and services is possible in all cases except public goods.' Discuss.

7. What theoretical arguments would you use to justify a policy of the privatization of state-owned activities?

29 Competition Policy

Key Points to Review

- Competition and a pricing system (6.6)
- Economies of scale (21.4)
- Barriers to entry (23.1)
- Price descrimination (23.4)
- Mergers (24.3)
- Collusion (24.5)

Questions for Preview

1 Why would you expect the strength of competitive pressures in a market economy to be influenced by the macroeconomic situation?

2 Why might the government regard a keenly competitive economy as not being a desirable objective?

3 How can competition between firms be influenced by government policy on takeover bids?

2 What is government policy on firms which dominate certain markets?

2 How can governments influence the nature of competition in an open economy?

In the previous chapter we considered the provision of goods and services by the government. We saw that in the case of the UK the post-war Labour government effected the transformation of several private monopolies into public monopolies. Since 1979 the Thatcher government has begun to return these nationalized industries to the private sector through its privatization policies. Our focus now is to review what have been the policies of successive UK governments towards those firms that have continued to operate within the private sector. Thus we are now concerned with those policies which represent the attempt by government to prevent the creation of monopolies and also the fostering of keen competition between firms. We shall see that the British approach to devising competition policies has been essentially cautious in espousing any of the virtues associated with the competition ethic. We showed in Chapter 6 that competition is the driving force in a capitalist economy. But while competition may be 'a good thing' governments in the UK have not exhibited a consistent and enthusiastic acceptance of such a viewpoint. To see why this has been the case we need very briefly to consider the course of the economy in the UK during the past century.

The Historical Perspective

In Chapter 24 it was suggested that the operation of capitalism seems to prompt efforts by businessmen to seek relief from the rigours of a competitive market economy by establishing agreement on prices to be charged. Why should businessmen behave in this way? It is explained by the wish to reduce the risks inherent in business life. If businessmen agree not to undercut one another's prices then the possibility of business failure for some firms is considerably reduced. It should not surprise you to learn that the fear of business failure becomes greater when the macro-state of the economy is relatively depressed and firms find themselves operating well below full capacity. In such times firms see a real danger of prices being cut dramatically as each tries to boost sales at the expense of competitors. Competition is thus seen as a process which results in many more losers than winners: in short, in the death of business.

When we look at the state of competition in the UK economy in the early years of the present century we find that most sections of manufacturing industry were characterized by explicit arrangements to restrict competition and control prices. Firms in an industry would often seek to fix prices by discussion in national organizations called **trade associations**. Domestic firms found their common cause a matter of increasing relevance as they faced growing competition in the UK market from imports.

What was the attitude of government to the attempts by businessmen to restrain the degree of rivalry between themselves? Before showing the changing course of government policy we could usefully note Adam Smith's own view on the matter. In Chapter 6 we referred to his now much-quoted observation that businessmen were keen in meetings together to uphold their own interests rather than those of consumers (see p. 85). Another of Smith's comments which has been less well reported reads as follows:

> It is impossible indeed to prevent such meetings, by any law which either could be executed, or would be consistent with liberty and justice. But though the law cannot hinder people of the same trade from sometimes assembling together, it ought to do nothing to facilitate such assemblies, much less to render them necessary.*

This view overlooks the political pressures from business interests on the need for behaviour to be co-operative rather than competitive when the economy is in difficulty. The 1920s and 1930s provided an environment for co-operative behaviour to be regarded as not just acceptable but even desirable. We thus find that the response of the Lloyd George coalition government in 1920 to this matter began the cautious approach that has characterized the spirit of British competition policy. Price-fixing arrangements were recognized as having the *potential* for firms to charge excessive prices to the detriment of consumers. But the situation was not so clear-cut that such practices should be *prohibited* by legislation. What was required was a review of the particular situation in individual industries. Thirty industries were investigated by the Board of Trade in 1920 and 1921 as the basis for establishing whether the interests of consumers were *in practice* being adversely affected. But this concern for consumers quickly evaporated during the 1920s and 1930s as the three major political parties showed increased disenchantment with the desirability of stimulating greater competition. Competition was now seen as a hindrance to the development of strong national concerns capable of meeting foreign competition. Mergers were thus encouraged such that 'wasteful competition' could be eliminated and firms achieve economies of scale while the macro-environment was so depressing.

Thus we see that by 1939 there was very little emphasis in government policy towards industry placed on the desirability of competitive rivalry. This muted enthusiasm for competitive free enterprise contrasted strongly with the explicit presumption in favour of competition which characterized policy in the United States. Let us now see how the UK's post-war legislation concerning competition has continued to reflect an uncertain commitment to the cause of a competitive economy.

The 1948 Monopolies and Restrictive Practices (Inquiry and Control) Act

This Act did not condemn either monopoly or price-fixing outright. Instead a case-by-case approach was adopted such that each situation could be judged on its merits. Monopoly was presumed neither good nor bad and it was up to the newly created Monopolies and Restrictive Practices Commission to investigate particular situations and make a judgement in accordance with some vague expression of 'the public interest'. The Commission was not able to begin an investigation unless at least one-third of the supply of goods was supplied by one person or by two or more persons who restricted competition by agreement (thus including the restrictive activity of trade associations). The Commission consisted mainly of part-time lay persons and they could consider only situations referred to then by the Board of Trade. Action on a report by the Monopolies Commission was left in the hands of the government.

The Act was thus a modest statement on the desirability of a competitive economy. Members of the Commission found the terms of 'the public interest' capable of uncertain interpretation and even a cursory examination of section 14 of the 1948 Act shows why this was so. The public interest was defined as the need to achieve:

1. the production, treatment, and distribution by the most efficient and economical means of goods of such types and qualities, in such volume and at such prices as will best meet the requirements of home and overseas markets;
2. the organization of industry and trade in such a way that their efficiency is progressively increased and new enterprises encouraged;
3. the fullest use and best distribution of men, materials, and industrial capacity in the United Kingdom; and
4. the development of technical improvements and the expansion of existing markets and the opening up of new markets.

As one member of the Commission, the late Professor G. C. Allen, put it 'The guidance given by the Act consisted of a string of platitudes which the Commission found valueless and it was left for the members

*A. Smith, *Wealth of Nations*. Bk. 1, Ch. X, Pt II, Everyman edn., p. 233.

themselves to reach their own conclusions by reference to the assumptions, principles or prejudices which their training and experience caused them to apply to economic affairs.'* The Commission worked slowly and between 1948 and 1956 produced just seventeen reports. But these reports did none the less present a clear picture of how widespread were the restrictions on competition throughout British industry. Firms typically agreed common prices for goods sold whether to wholesalers, retailers, or in contracts supposedly subject to secret tendering. Private courts punished individual members of agreements who infringed the rules of the trade.

In a general report on Collective Discrimination published in 1955 the Commission assembled evidence on a variety of restrictive practices and declared itself satisfied that all of them adversely affected the public interest. The Conservative government responded with its 1956 Restrictive Trade Practices Act.

The 1956 Restrictive Trade Practices Act

This Act had three elements to it. On restrictive practices the Act obliged firms to register their agreements with a Registrar of Restrictive Trading Agreements. These registered agreements were to be made open to public inspection and presumed contrary to the public interest unless the parties involved could satisfy otherwise before the Restrictive Practices Court. Thus the legislation represented a much clearer statement in favour of competition than the Monopolies Commission. The Act affected the whole industry and not merely those parts selected for inquiry. There was a precise government commitment against the desirability of price-fixing. The unwillingness to take action by government on Monopolies Commission reports now contrasted with the precise requirement of the Registrar to refer every price agreement to the Court. The judgement of the Court was binding on the respondents if contempt proceedings were to be avoided.

The new Act became the more effective because of the macro-state of the UK economy. The level of unemployment rose in each year between 1955 and 1959 and thus the more competitive climate ushered in by the Act was reinforced by a less buoyant market for many consumer goods. Firms found themselves working at lower levels of capacity than in the recent past. Hitherto many sections of UK industry had enjoyed a sellers' market as the economy recovered from wartime. Where there was excess capacity the price-fixing arrangements had disguised its influence on price levels. Now businessmen not only had to learn how to price their products but to begin doing so in a more difficult trading environment. The result was predictable – in many manufacturing industries there was a marked downward trend in prices charged. In this respect it has generally been accepted that within a few years of its implementation the 1956 Act was successful in its attack on price-fixing agreements between firms.

A second aspect of the 1956 Act was its prohibition of the collective enforcement of resale price maintenance by the withholding of supplies by a group of manufacturers. This made it no longer possible for a uniform stance to be taken by several manufacturers against a retailer who wished to trade on terms other than those laid down by his suppliers. But the 1956 Act did not have a dramatic impact on the manufacturer–retailer relationship since individual suppliers were able to take action in the courts against traders not maintaining their specified trading terms. The ending of individual retail price maintenance was not brought about till 1964. The Resale Prices Act adopted the same approach as the 1956 Act with the practice of minimum resale prices being prohibited subject to exemptions on specific grounds. As with restrictive practices the Restrictive Practices Court was given the task of hearing applications by manufacturers to continue a form of competitive behaviour now generally deemed unacceptable. Once more the Court began to set a precedent in its early cases on resale price maintenance as with price-fixing which left very few manufacturers expecting to make a successful defence. Thus by the end of the 1960s there was little doubt that two aspects of competition policy had become effective by virtue of the fact that legislation expressed a clear presumption in favour of free competition. Price-fixing and uniform retail prices were no longer seen as desirable practices. In respect of price agreements firms had been given till the end of 1957 to register their existing agreements and the first full case in the Court was not heard until October 1958. Few trade associations chose to take their agreements to the Court when the evidence was clear that the chances of a successful defence were slim. Thus although over 4 000 agreements have now been registered under the Act the vast majority have been voluntarily abandoned and not the subject of a Court case. In respect of resale price maintenance there have been very few cases before the Court and only books and medicines have provided the supporters of fixed trading terms the satisfaction of a costly legal appraisal that survived a Court hearing.

The 1956 Act had yet a third element – the restricting of the Monopolies and Restrictive Practices Commission. Given the creation of the Restrictive Practices Court the Commission was now confined to investigation of monopoly situations and thus appropriately lost two words in its title. But the hesitant nature of UK policy towards large firms continued to manifest itself. The new Commission was reduced to a maximum membership of ten persons and it was no longer able to function in separate panels on particular investigations as it had done since 1953. The Commission may have been viewed in 1956 critically in some quarters as simultaneously 'prosecutor, judge and jury' but at least it was not so actively at work that it troubled many of Britain's major firms. Any revival in the significance of the Commission had to await the development of UK policy towards the acquisition of one firm by another.

*G. C. Allen, *Monopoly and Restrictive Practices* (1968), p. 66.

Figure 29.1

The Principal Provisions of the Fair Trading Act 1973

The Act provides for the creation of an Office of Director-General of Fair Trading ('The Director')

Responsibilities

(i) To keep under review 'with a view to becoming aware of and ascertaining the circumstances relating to':
  (a) consumer trade practices which may adversely affect the economic interests of consumers,
  (b) commercial activities relating to monopoly situations of uncompetitive practices.

(ii) To give information and assistance to Secretary of State about these matters and make recommendations to him for action.

(iii) To keep himself appraised of actual or prospective mergers which may qualify for investigation and advise Secretary of State about them.

(iv) Empowered to make references to CPAC and limited powers to make monopoly references to MMC.

(v) Empowered to take action to curb conduct which is unfair to consumers and detrimental to their interests – by seeking written assurance or taking proceedings before Restrictive Practices Court.

(vi) Empowered to require information to be provided to assist him in deciding whether to make a monopoly reference.

(vii) Advise Ministers on reports of the MMC and to negotiate (at request of Minister) the securing of undertakings and keep the carrying out of them under review.

Relationships with aspects of competition policy

RESTRICTIVE PRACTICES	*MONOPOLIES AND MERGERS*	*CONSUMER PROTECTION*
(a) Functions of Registrar of Restrictive Trade Agreements transferred to Director	(a) Monopolies Commission renamed Monopolies and Mergers Commission (MMC)	(a) Provides for the appointment of a Consumer Protection Advisory Committee (CPAC)
(b) Empowers Secretary of State to require the registration of certain agreements (including information agreements) between suppliers of services other than professional services (Cf 1965 Act)	(b) Definition of monopoly reduced from a market share of one-third to one-quarter	(b) CPAC may receive references from the Secretary of State or the Director to report on whether particular consumer trade practices adversely affect the economic interests of consumers (excluding professional services referrable to MMC)
(c) Agreements relating to recommendation of resale prices and patent and design pooling made registrable	(c) Monopoly, but not merger, references may be made by Director (subject to veto) as well as Secretary of State	
	(d) National corporations may be referred but only by Secretary of State and appropriate Minister jointly	
	(e) Restrictive labour practices made referrable	

Source: M. C. Fleming, *The Fair Trading Act 1973*, Loughborough Paper in Recent Developments in Economic Policy and Thought, Loughborough University, 1974, p. 2.

The 1965 Monopolies and Mergers Act

Policy on mergers effectively began in 1965 in the wake of a takeover bid by Imperial Chemical Industries for Courtaulds. The Labour government found itself with no explicit means to declare its position on such a merger. Its solution was to make use of an existing body, the Monopolies Commission, as the appropriate forum where the desirability of a change in the structure of an industry could be examined. The Board of Trade was now able under the Monopolies and Mergers Act to refer a merger proposal to the Commission if the market share of the two firms satisfied the one-third share of the market or if the value of assets taken over exceeded £5m. The Labour government had equipped itself with this new power but neither intended automatic referral to the Commission nor any presumption of hostility to a proposed merger. A Mergers Panel consisting of civil servants was created to advise the appropriate government minister. The Commission, once referred a merger case, had to operate with some speed and normally report back within six months. Its remit was simply whether the proposed merger was against 'the public interest'. Inevitably this same vague principle which had given the Commission such an uncertain orientation back in 1948 was to prove the basis of growing criticism in its handling of merger cases after 1965. Before examining these criticisms we first appraise the many provisions of legislation introduced in 1973.

The 1973 Fair Trading Act

This Act brought about changes not only in the administration of competition policy but also its substance. The newly created office of Director-General of Fair Trading assumed the functions of the Registrar of Restrictive Trading Agreements but with much wider responsibilities. It was charged with keeping under review both commercial activities relating to monopoly situations or uncompetitive practices and also trade practices which might adversely affect the interests of consumers. The Director-General was thus now formally given the task of advising the Secretary of State about all these matters as a continuing brief. Figure 29.1 summarizes the main aspects of the 1973 Act. Of particular significance was the new legal definition of monopoly – the criterion reduced to one-quarter market share – and the broader interpretation of the market as compared with the 1948 Act. The Fair Trading Act made it now possible to refer monopolies of a local character to the Monopolies and Mergers Commission (MMC) rather than those relating to the UK as a whole. Furthermore the monopoly situation of the nationalized industries and other statutory trading bodies were now brought within the scope of the Act. But apart from these extensions of the work of the MMC the Act spelt out a much clearer orientation for the members of that body. Section 84 now made the promotion of competition a key aspect of its approach to particular investigations. If you compare the following criteria with section 14 of the 1948 Act (see above) you will note the new emphasis on the process of competition as a means of securing economic efficiency.

> . . . the Commission shall take into account all matters which appear to them in the particular circumstances to be relevant and, among other things, shall have regard to the desirability:
>
> (a) of maintaining and promoting effective competition between persons supplying goods and services in the United Kingdom;
> (b) of promoting the interests of consumers, purchasers, and other users of goods and services in the United Kingdom in respect of the prices charged for them and in respect of their quality and the variety of goods and services supplied;
> (c) of promoting, through competition, the reduction of costs and the development and use of new techniques and new products, and of facilitating the entry of new competitors into existing markets;
> (d) of maintaining and promoting the balanced distribution of industry and employment in the United Kingdom; and
> (e) of maintaining and promoting competitive activity in markets outside the United Kingdom on the part of producers of goods, and of suppliers of goods and services, in the United Kingdom.

The 1973 Act thus represented a more confident belief in the virtues of competition than had been the case in the immediate post-war years. Legislation seven years later actually included the word in its title – the 1980 Competition Act.

The 1980 Competition Act

This Act tried to deal with business behaviour which might amount to an *anti-competitive practice*. Responsibility for supervising the investigation of such practices was given to the Director-General of Fair Trading. Figure 29.2 summarizes the procedures laid down in the Act for investigating those courses of business conduct pursued by a person which

> of itself or when taken together with a course of conduct pursued by persons associated with him, has or is intended or is likely to have the effect of restricting, distorting or preventing competition in connection with the production, supply or acquisition of goods in the United Kingdom or any part of it or the supply or securing of services in the United Kingdom or any part of it.

You should note that Figure 29.2 provided for the circumstances of each anti-competitive practice to be examined thus continuing the case-by-case approach of the Monopolies Commission. But you must be wondering *what* practices might in specific instances constitute an anti-competitive practice? The Office of Fair Trading has identified three instances concerning the pricing of goods and six practices relating to their distribution and these are briefly explained in Figure 29.3.

The provisions of the 1980 Act were not to apply in the case of small firms (those with an annual turnover of less than £5m and which have less than a 25 per cent share of a relevant market). Also specifically exempted from the Act were sectors such as international shipping and civil aviation (where governments have long agreed to regulation of prices and services).

Two further aspects of the 1980 Act illustrate how the public sector was now seen as appropriate for inclusion within legislation concerned with the promotion of competition and efficiency. The Act empowered the Secretary of State for Trade to refer to the MMC questions about the efficiency and costs of, the service provided by, and possible abuse of a monopoly situation by nationalized industries. It also empowered the Secretary of State to direct the Director General of

Figure 29.2

The investigation of Anti-competitive Practices under the 1980 Competition Act

OFT gets complaint, makes inquiries, and investigates whether a particular course of conduct amounts to an anti-competitive practice and then informs

↙ ↓ ↘

Secretary of State for Trade | Company | Public

If such a practice is identified in the OFT investigation in a study lasting three months the OFT then

↓

Seeks negotiation of voluntary undertakings

or

If not negotiated, then the OFT refers the matter to the Monopolies and Mergers Commission for its investigation (lasting up to nine months)

↓

If then the MMC reports that the practice is against public interest

↓

then the firm must either voluntarily abandon the practice or anticipate an

↓

Order from Trade Secretary prohibiting the practice.

Fair Trading to investigate questions about prices of major public concern, either because they are of general economic importance or because consumers are significantly affected. This provision reflected the political concern with the cost of living. This aspect of the 1980 Act provides an appropriate point to indicate that it was not the first time that UK governments have shown their sensitivity to the rate of increase in prices. As a major electoral issue several post-war governments have been prepared if not to take action on prices at least keen to exhibit a willingness to allow a statutory body *other than the MMC* to make a public inquiry into a particular industry. This concern of government with prices was noted in Chapter 10 where we indicated that wage and price controls have been seen as a method of slowing down cost–push inflation.

The Macro-Dimension

As inflationary pressures became more acute in the 1960s governments looked for means other than monetary and fiscal policies to try to contain the upward movement of prices. They perceived that investigation

Figure 29.3

Forms of Competitive Conduct that Might Constitute an Anti-competitive Practice

(a) *Pricing Policy*

Falling into this category would be:

Price discrimination – the practice of selling goods or services, where there are no cost differences, to distinct and separate groups of customers these groups being charged varying prices according to their degree of sensitivity to price levels. Some variants of price discrimination take the form of differential rates of discount or rebate from list prices perhaps in return for loyalty or exclusive supply arrangements. An important variant arises where a purchaser's buying power enables him to insist that suppliers grant him advantageous terms, so artificially enhancing his ability to compete on price in the market in which he sells;

Predatory pricing – which is usually defined as the practice of temporarily selling at prices below cost, with the intention of driving a competitor from the market, so that in the future prices may be raised and enhanced profits extracted;

Vertical price squeezing – which can arise when a vertically integrated firm controls the total supply of an input which is essential to the production requirements of its subsidiary and also its competitors. The input price can be raised and the downstream output price reduced, so that the profits of competitors are squeezed, possibly with a view to driving them from the market.

(b) *Distribution Policy*

There are a number of practices which might serve to restrict, distort, or prevent competition, either at manufacturing or distribution level. These include:

Tie-in-sales – a stipulation that a buyer must purchase part or all of his requirements of a second (tied) product from the supplier of a first (tying) product.

Full-line forcing – which requires a buyer to purchase quantities of each item in a product range in order to be able to buy any of them.

Rental-only contracts – which restrict customers to rental or lease terms only and which can be anti-competitive where there are no alternative methods of acquiring those goods;

Exclusive supply – whereby a seller supplies only one buyer in a certain geographical area, which limits competition between that buyer and his competitors;

Selective distribution – which is the practice of choosing as sales outlets only those which satisfy specific qualitative or quantitative criteria;

Exclusive purchase – which arises when a distributor contracts to stock only the products of one manufacturer, possibly in return for an exclusive supply arrangement.

Source: Office of Fair Trading, 1980.

Key Points 29.1

- **UK competition policy has developed from a concern with monopoly (the 1948 Act) to restraints on price competition (the 1956 Act) and only in the late 1960s to takeover bids (the 1965 Act).**
- **UK policy has been essentially pragmatic rather than doctrinaire. The approach has essentially been to consider individual cases on their merits.**

of an industry by a specialist agency offered the possibility of breaking any mechanistic adjustment by firms in determining final product prices whenever they incurred higher labour or raw materials costs. Governments did not accept that manufacturers were necessarily entitled to pass on all higher costs to consumers. Were competitive pressures really strong enough to force at least some containment of costs by increased efficiency? Did parallel pricing by firms amount to a situation where market pressures in some industries were not strong enough to help restrain the upward movement in prices? Investigation of the nature of competition in some major industries by an impartial body like the MMC would not only ascertain the facts but provide the government with evidence that it was 'doing something' tangible to try to achieve some measure of price stability. Obviously the concern with prices assisted the calls for wage restraint being made to the trade union movement. We recognize at once then that single-industry and single-firm inquiries represent a piecemeal micro-approach to the broad goal of macroeconomic policy. But that is not to imply that individual industry inquiries are necessarily insignificant in their ultimate impact. A body that has to examine industries immediately enters a politically charged world. Neither management nor trade unions are likely to welcome the full glare of publicity brought upon them.

The Labour government's chosen body to implement its prices and incomes policy between 1965 and 1970 was the National Board for Prices and Incomes (NBPI). In several of its reports the NBPI claimed that competitive pressures were weak and also that the competitive process could not always be relied upon to ensure that production was carried out by the most efficient means. The problem that faced the NBPI like the long-established MMC was its lack of teeth – to see put into immediate effect such remedies as it deemed appropriate in particular cases. Its whole working was set in a political context with its subjects for inquiry not determined by itself but by the government of the day. To this extent its references were seen as being *too* politically motivated.

The Conservative government in 1970 soon abolished the NPBI and preferred to resort to the MMC to handle inquiries where it seemed to have reservations about the strength of competition in particular industries. Like its predecessor the political dimension was not absent as the new government had to contend with the escalation in world commodity prices in 1973–4. The Heath government set up a Prices Commission as an explicit price control body. Large firms were required to pre-notify intentions to increase prices and which could only be permissible under the rules laid down in a Price Code. The work of this Commission under the chairmanship of Lord Cockfield was essentially supervision of an accountancy exercise affecting all firms that fell within its scope. However, the Cockfield Commission was also asked under the provisions of the 1973 Counter-Inflation Act to make such examinations of industries as directed by the Secretary of State. This meant that the Cockfield Commission was asked to undertake studies of the nature of competition in those areas of the UK economy where presumably the government felt unsure about the extent of competitive pressures. The Commission was in effect a surrogate MMC but the attraction to government was its speedy reporting on the nature of pricing without reference to 'the public interest' or the need at the outset to establish whether monopoly conditions existed.

As raw material prices stabilized after 1974 the need for the strait-jacket to constrain firms in their pricing of final goods disappeared. However, the Callaghan government sought to reach accord with the trade unions on incomes policy. This meant that although cost-related controls might no longer be necessary, pre-notification of proposed price increases would serve as the tangible element in government prices policy in support of an understanding on wages. But the 1977 Price Commission Act went further than just requiring firms to continue notifying the new Price Commission under Mr Charles Williams of intended price rises. It gave the Williams Commission *discretion* to select particular companies for investigation. These investigations had to be made in a very short space of time – no more than three months. It had a positive role of 'promoting competition' (1977 Act, section 2) and improving efficiency ('the desirability of encouraging reductions in costs by improvements in the use of resources'). The work of the new Commission was thus firmly placed within the context of competition policy but operating independently from the existing instruments of this policy (the OFT and MMC). The PC was thus now being asked to make single-firm studies and, unlike either the NBPI or MMC, able to select its own cases for investigations.

In fact, the PC made forty-four investigations of notifications of price increases during its lifetime. It also continued to undertake two of the sectoral studies begun by its predecessor of the same name. These studies continued under the terms of the 1977 Act and some nineteen examination reports were undertaken at the request of the newly established Ministry for Prices and Consumer Protection. Thus within a very short period of time the PC issued no less than sixty-five reports. Its rapid rate of working sharply contrasted with the lengthy nature of MMC inquiries. Yet both the PC and MMC were agents of competition policy. The inevitable question arose: was there justification for two separate bodies if each was trying to bring about more competitive markets? Certainly the two agencies had different procedures and philosophy but any enthusiasm by the Labour government for a merger of the MMC and PC had come to nothing by the time of the 1979 General Election. In abolishing the PC the new Conservative government was anxious not to be seen as unconcerned about the nature of competition. Its remedy in the 1980 Competition Act for the demise of the PC was the concept of anti-competitive practices which we discussed earlier. Our task now must be to review how competition policy has operated since 1980. We shall see that the subject is still politically contentious.

Competition Policies: An Assessment

Our review of the development of competition policy has attempted to show that Labour and Conservative governments in the post-war period have each introduced legislation concerned with the structure of markets and forms of business behaviour. The whole subject-matter appears to be continually debated to establish whether the nature of policy is appropriate to current conditions. In fact this is not just surmise but the very truth of the matter. Competition policy has indeed been the subject of continual review during the last forty years. The question that now needs to be faced is whether the whole panoply of laws since 1948 really amounts to a clear statement by government on the desirability and benefits of competition. Several observers feel that the present stance of competition policy suffers from an ambivalent view of the benefits of competitive markets. The 'every case to be judged on its merits' means that no clear picture is offered of those forms of business behaviour that are regarded as unacceptable. The 'rules of the game' are held to be still too vague to amount to an explicit policy *for* competitive markets. Consequently some have argued that rather than rely on the OFT for redress for those persons who feel aggrieved by forms of anti-competitive conduct we should adopt a more judicial approach. Rather than OFT official action there should be encouragement for *private* actions such that the business community is deterred from participating in behaviour such as predatory pricing. The US approach which incorporates criminal penalties and payment of damages amounting to three times the alleged loss (the so-called 'triple damages concept') may be thought too extreme for adoption on this side of the Atlantic but it reflects a view that the aim of competition policy is to stop unfair trading practices in the first place. The UK approach is rather to provide a means whereby problems that do arise can be resolved. Perhaps a change to a 'privatization' in the enforcement of competition would be desirable. Why has such a viewpoint arisen? It seems to have its root in part at least in reservations over the role of the MMC.

In its monopoly inquiries the MMC has not attracted as much critical attention when compared with its judgements on takeover bids. One exception was its recommendation in March 1989 that two-thirds of the retail outlets of the big six national brewing firms should be sold, along with the ending of all subsidized loans to secure exclusive dealing arrangements. These strong recommendations proved too radical for the government to accept, and compulsory divestment by the brewers was absent from the government's modified plans to increase competition in the industry. But most other studies by the MMC in the private sector have prompted little political reaction, and indeed the study of monopoly situations by the MMC in recent years has been marked by those within the public sector or newly privatized. Studies of British Coal and British Gas amount to an efficiency audit of both existing and former public corporations.

In contrast, in its work on takeovers the MMC typically enters a much more politically charged atmosphere. Mere referral to the MMC has prompted some

Key Points 29.2

- **In times of escalating inflation there is a tendency for governments to create an agency to help restrain rising prices both directly and indirectly as an element in support of an incomes policy. The NBPI and both the 1973–7 and 1977–9 Price Commissions were all given scope to make micro-studies as part of macroeconomic policies.**
- **These non-specialist agencies of competition policy have made many studies of the nature of competition policy but hitherto have not survived during the life of a Conservative government.**

bidders to abandon plans to continue with an acquisition. In the period between 1965 and 1968 thirty-three mergers were abandoned during the inquiries made by the MMC out of 107 referrals. Of the remaining referrals the MMC broadly found as many to be takeover situations against the public interest as those not against it.

It has been argued by some for several years that mergers policy is misdirected. These critics hold that rather than establish whether a merger between two firms would not be against the public interest the MMC should explicitly seek for benefits that might follow from a change in market structure. In other words it should apply an explicit weighing-up of the benefits and costs arising from a change in the status quo. Our discussion of consumer surplus in Chapter 23 in appraising the desirability of monopoly is a formal expression of such a neutral approach to mergers.

Of course the MMC can in the meantime apply itself only to those merger situations referred to it by the government. Although as Figure 29.1 shows the Secretary of State for Trade and Industry receives advice from the OFT whether to refer a merger to the MMC, the ultimate decision rests with the Minister. Inevitably acceptance or rejection of the OFT's advice exposes a Minister to keen political debate.

The bid by Nestlé for Rowntrees in 1988 (see Case Study below) was not referred to the MMC and provoked a major debate on the desirability of such a large British firm passing into foreign ownership without any scrutiny of the implications arising from the takeover. However, in the same year a bid by Goodman Fielder Wattie, based in Australia, for Ranks Hovis McDougall was referred to the MMC. Businessmen argue that mergers policy is unclear and there is no predictability in decisions to refer mergers to the MMC.

As regards restrictive practices critics feel the ostensible success of the 1956 Act flatters the true position on the enforcement of competitive markets. When firms have defied rulings in the Restrictive Practices Court they have not been heavily fined. This inevitably puts into doubt what deterrence there is when the penalties are far from being penal. Extensive price-fixing and collusive-tendering arrangements have come to light in industries as varied as bread-making, photo-copying equipment, concrete pipes, road black-top materials, and telephone cables. Not surprisingly Sir Gordon Borrie, the Director-General of Fair Trading, has sought tougher sanctions and favoured the EEC approach which prohibits anti-competitive practices. At present only trade between the UK and the rest of the EEC is governed by the Common Market's rules.

In a White Paper published in July 1989 the government proposed to strengthen current legislation by making price-fixing cartels illegal and applying the sanction of fines up to 10 per cent of turnover of large firms found in contempt of the new law. This proposal effectively brought UK anti-competitive legislation more into line with the rest of the European Community. The proposed new legislation also intends to include a wide range of professions – barristers, solicitors, doctors, nurses, opticians, accountants, architects, and teachers – within its scope.

Of those case where suppliers were once successful in defending a restrictive agreement only two now survive. One of these is the Net Book Agreement which allows publishers to fix the retail price of books. Even here its continued existence is not assured as some booksellers wish to have freedom to price books as they see fit (see the Case Study below). In 1987 the price-fixing arrangements of the Cement Makers' Federation were abandoned mainly as a result of growing competition from foreign suppliers (see Case Study below).

As indicated above it is now the professions which are facing keen scrutiny of their regulations on competitive pricing. The recent demise of the trading arrangements between brokers and jobbers on the Stock Exchange illustrates this particularly well.

In 1979 the OFT referred the rules of the Stock Exchange to the Restrictive Practices Court. An agreement was reached between the government and the Stock Exchange in July 1983 whereby special legislation was introduced to exempt the Stock Exchange from the 1956 Act and end the impending court case. As part of the 'deal' the Stock Exchange agreed to give up its minimum commission scales. It was soon realized that increased competition would undermine the traditional separation of functions by brokers and jobbers (single-capacity trading) and plans made to allow dual-capacity trading as from 27 October 1986. Without doubt the court case set in train the possibility of more competitive financial markets. So ultimately one might argue the thrust of the 1956 Act prevailed. This application of the 1956 Act to the service sector of the economy may well, in due course, come to be seen as a major milestone in the evolution of competition policy. But there are other services which have experienced more competitive trading conditions. The two Thatcher administrations have taken the view that in certain professions a more competitive environment was desirable. The monopoly of solicitors in house conveyancing and that of opticians in selling spectacles has been challenged. The committed enthusiast of unfettered competition may, however, point to other areas of the economy where restraints on competition have government backing. For example, imports of cars from Japan are subject to understandings with Nissan, Toyota, and Mazda. Competition for UK textile manufactures is restrained by the Multi-Fibre Agreement. Competition between airline operators in Western Europe has been limited by price-fixing, revenue-sharing, and agreements on capacity. And what about a sector of the economy where there is an import tariff which sometimes reaches 100 per cent and the government agrees to buy all the produce this industry cannot sell abroad at a price well above free market levels? Yes, agriculture. Consider why these deviations from competitive markets are accepted by governments!

The European Dimension

Competition policy is clearly very relevant to the creation of a European internal market. It is not logical for competition policy to be administered mainly by national governments. Takeover bids that involve companies in separate countries should be considered on a consistent basis. An integrated market is only meaningful if in all countries the rules relating to competitive behaviour and state support for industry are reasonably similar. The 1957 Treaty of Rome gave the European Commission some power to vet mergers as a supplement to national legislation, but for many years this supranational element of competition policy was not actively pursued. Other aspects of European Community competition policy have been more prominent. In 1989 23 chemical companies were fined £92m for operating a price-fixing cartel in the European market for PVC and low-density polythene.

In Chapter 23 the Case Study on plasterboard referred to BPB being fined over £2m for alleged abuse of its market power to stop imported plasterboard from Spain being sold in the UK. But as the single European market in 1992 looms still closer the European Commission has been seeking to persuade Community members to give it an EC basis of merger-control regulations. There seems no doubt that future cross-border mergers between the largest of Europe's companies will now involve more attention in Brussels than in the relevant capital cities.

Key Points 29.3

- **The pragmatic style of UK competition policy has given rise to criticism that it is too uncertain in operation and still lacks a positive commitment to the virtues of competition.**
- **The professions have increasingly become the subject of government attempts to foster greater competition but agriculture and some areas of manufacturing industry continue to receive protection from overseas competition.**
- **In the European Community policy towards competition and takeover bids now involves the European Commission, in Brussels, as well as the relevant authorities in member states.**

CASE STUDY

Are Books Different?

Culture is threatened by commercialism. That was the basic message in Michael Schmidt's trenchant defence of the Net Book Agreement in the *Sunday Correspondent* two weeks ago and his condemnation of Dillons's efforts to break free. [The Net Book Agreement ensures that book retailers are not allowed to reduce prices below those set by publishers.]

Mr Schmidt accepts the NBA may be a retailing anachronism but argues it should be retained because books are 'privileged merchandise'. Its disappearance would 'hit particularly small independent booksellers'; squeeze the 'margins that spell the difference between survival and extinction'; result in bookshops giving pride of place to the objectives of 'stock turnover per shelf foot and turnover per employee' rather than holding comprehensive stock; and threaten the 'vulnerable infrastructure of literary publishing'.

I dispute this graphic portrayal of doom and destruction. If Mr Schmidt's arguments were correct, Dillons would be acting in an irrational manner that would quickly bring our commercial ruin.

Dillons is a specialist stockholding bookseller. The typical new Dillons store stocks 60 000 titles, roughly four times as many as the average bookshop. If we believed the success of our campaign to end the NBA would lead to reduced margins and cuts in the number of titles stocked, we would literally have been mad to have invested so heavily in large stockholding bookshops.

The infrastructure of literary publishing may or may not be as vulnerable as Mr Schmidt fears. Our central contention is that in the absence of the NBA, that vulnerability would reduce further. Dillons and other bookshops would have the freedom to use price discounting selectively as a marketing tool to widen the market.

The expansion of the market, through developing the habit of book-buying beyond the relatively restricted social groups that comprise a bookshop's regular customers, is Dillons's central mission. The abolition of the NBA is simply a tactic in this battle. Our retail experience and market research confirm that if customers can be attracted by our marketing efforts into our bookshops, they will not only buy one of the limited number of titles we are promoting. Many will find their way to the poetry department and browse among the literary backlist. The result will be that more books of all types will be bought, in increased numbers.

Many critics of Dillons's stance on the NBA misunderstand this. We are not in the business with the aim of starting price wars or setting up discount stores in every High Street. We are simply seeking to put bookselling on a par with other retail trades so we can market the attractions of buying books by comparison with a whole variety of other mind-expanding, leisure-consuming experiences that the public is offered. The literary world needs to have more confidence and optimism in the merits of its basic product.

I would not dispute Mr Schmidt's arguments that books should be regarded as 'privileged merchandise'. The trouble, however, with the way books have traditionally been marketed is that it has kept them for too long as merchandise for the privileged.

What I find most objectionable is the supposition that while Dillons is pushing its commercial interest in pressing for the end of the NBA, booksellers who disagree are speaking for the public interest.

Our sympathizers include publishers large and small, literary and popular. Some would dearly like to get around the constraints of the NBA by making some of their new books 'non-net', thus allowing Dillons to discount titles, for example, of leading literary fiction. The trouble is no publisher wants to be seen to be first.

What holds many publishers back is W. H. Smith. Publishers fear, whether justified or not, that the wrath of Smiths will fall on the head of any publisher who breaks ranks, evidencing itself in an unwillingness to give normal prominence to that publisher's titles or in a flood of returned books (for which the publisher would be obliged to reimburse W. H. Smith).

These fears are the common currency of gossip in the book trade. A large book chain which stocks a narrow range and disproportionately derives its income from bestsellers clearly has the most to lose from discounting. It is not surprising that suspicions are aroused that it will use its muscle to maintain its short-term profit margins. If W. H. Smith feels these fears and suspicions unfairly represent its position, it should make clear its intentions not to treat publishers in the way I have described.

This cannot hold for ever, as many of our sympathizers in publishing now realize. The NBA is an organized hypocrisy. Like the regimes of Eastern Europe, once the will to sustain it has gone, it will collapse.

Source: Adapted from T. Maher, 'Merchandise for the privileged', *Sunday Correspondent*, 3 Dec 1989, p. 51.

Questions

1. Explain the argument that some bookshops wish 'to use price-discounting selectively as a marketing-tool to widen the market'.
2. Why do other bookshops and some publishers fear the consequences of price competition among booksellers?
3. Why does the author suggest that publishers are not wholeheated in their support for the NBA but do not wish to be seen as breaking up that agreement?

CASE STUDY

The Price of Chocolate

Mergers as Threat to Competition

Sir, The price at which Nestlé is bidding for Rowntree represents a spectacular increase over what a well-informed Stock Exchange had thought Rowntree was worth. There has been no indication that it is previously unexpected cost savings that could justify the size of the bid premium. But of course, if the bid succeeds, any threat that Rowntree's further advance into European markets might have been to Nestlé's existing profit margins in those markets would be removed.

If that is the main factor, then we have a notable instance of how much an existing incumbent is willing to pay in order to protect his market against potential competition.

You report (May 11) both the Trade and Industry Minister and the Agriculture Minister as referring to the implications for mergers policy of the creation of the single European market. Alas, they seem to be drawing the wrong conclusion. For the benefits that are claimed to follow from this increase in market size depend on there actually being a sustained increase in effective competition, as the removal of artificial barriers allows small and medium-sized firms to challenge the existing incumbents.

If the journey towards 1992 begins with a series of international – or indeed domestic – horizontal mergers between the companies already dominant in each domestic market, then the terminus will surely not be more competition, but less.

If effective competition is to survive, can decisions about the long-term structure of industry be left to a willingness to pay which largely reflects the desire to foreclose markets, and to defend market power? Who will be providing the effective competition, when only the world-megacorps are left?

Yours faithfully,
A. Sutherland,
Trinity College, Cambridge.

Implications of Rowntree Bids

Sir, In your issue of May 26 you give the text of Lord Young's statement explaining his reasons for not referring the bid to the Monopolies and Mergers Commission:

> . . . the main consideration is the effect of the merger on competition. Neither of these proposals raises competition issues which justify a reference. Nestlé and Suchard have only 3 per cent and 2 per cent, respectively, of the UK chocolate market.

That may be valid so far as *existing* competition is concerned, but it does not take account of the future, of *potential* competition.

Nestlé and Suchard are apparently each prepared to pay over £2 billion to acquire the Rowntree brands. If each were unable to acquire those Rowntree brands, each would be forced to build up its own, competing brands. Even if each spent only one half of what each is prepared to pay for Rowntree, that would be an enormous stimulus to competition in the chocolate market and so benefit consumers.

One is forced to the conclusion that our present merger policy is deficient, if it does not permit investigation of possible future competition.

J. P. Cunningham,
London

Source: Letters in *The Times*, 16 May 1988, and 7 June 1988.

Questions

1. How do the two authors emphasize the role of time in respect of a company making a takeover bid?
2. How do the authors view the relationship between mergers and the state of effective competition?
3. How do the authors view the state of mergers policy in the light of the creation of the single European market?

CASE STUDY

A Cartel: Is It Cemented Together?

One of the oldest cartels in the country has been disbanded leaving British cement manufacturers to fight it out. Blue Circle Industries (the market leader with 56.5 per cent of the market share), Rugby Portland Cement and Rio Tinto Zinc will now be able to charge variable prices throughout the country. This was a reluctant decision on the part of the cartel.

The common price agreement has been in existence since 1934, the firms maintaining that it was in the public interest for cement prices to be fixed countrywide. However, faced with a declining market after the construction industry peak in 1973, the major cement manufacturers were vulnerable. Thus, while gross domestic product rose by 16 per cent over the period 1973–85, output of the construction industry fell by 15 per cent. By the late 1970s our excess capacity in Britain was accompanied by a surplus in the rest of the world. The British market became a perfect target for importers.

Another development has been the growth in the use of substitute materials or extenders. Blast furnace slag and pulverized fuel ash are the two materials which can be blended successfully with ordinary Portland cement without impairing its cementatious properties.

Source: Adapted from A. Jackson, 'Cement splits to face the frost of competition'; *The Times*, 13 Feb. 1987.

Questions

1. Define the term 'cartel'.
2. Why should the author suggest that the abandonment of the cement cartel was 'a reluctant decision' of UK cement manufacturers?
3. How might the cement manufacturers have argued that the cartel was in the public interest?
4. Using appropriate diagram(s), analyse the factors which caused cement manufacturers to become 'vulnerable' after 1973.

Exam Preparation

PRACTICAL EXERCISES

1. Figure 29.3 identifies nine forms of competitive conduct that might constitute an anti-competitive practice. Three of these were noted in earlier chapters. Which are these three practices?

2. *The Fixing of European Air Fares*

When distances are drawn in proportion to airline fares, the world map has a peculiar shape. The English Channel becomes almost as wide as the Atlantic. Travellers cannot understand why it may cost them the same to fly from London to Rome as it does from London to Boston, which is four times the distance. How does this come about?

It is because in today's airline industry there are two different systems of establishing air fares. The first is by free competition. On transatlantic routes, British Airways would not dare charge more than Trans-World Airlines or Pan American. As it is, they have to try to compete with Virgin Atlantic who charge 20 per cent less. The same system applies to charter holiday flights, where rival travel firms hire aircraft to fly tourists to and from holiday destinations. The air fare has to be kept low to make the holiday package competitive.

The second system governs European 'scheduled' fares which, unlike transatlantic and charter fares, are not so subject to *competitive forces* and passengers have little choice but to pay the fares asked. In this world of expensive travel the fares are fixed in collusion by two airlines, usually state-owned, which have to run regularly scheduled flights on routes given to them by the governments concerned. The fares have to be identical, and often they share out the revenue.

Who pays these European scheduled fares? Thousands of British people, for example, fly to do business in Europe every day. The *cartel airlines* have been happy to exploit this captive business market. The alternative, which would involve enticing a wider range of passengers by lower fares, is less attractive because it is financially risky.

Source: Adapted from an article by Lord Bethel, *Sunday Express Magazine*, March 1986.

(a) Explain the meaning of the following phrases *as used in the passage:*
   (i) competitive forces;
   (ii) cartel airlines.

(b) Outline those factors which an airline may need to consider when deciding its fares on a transatlantic route.

(c) Why are airlines able to charge relatively low fares for charter holiday flights?

(d) Suggest *two* reasons why state-owned airlines might seek to maintain high fares on European routes.

(e) Explain why business travellers on European scheduled flights may be considered as 'captive'.

(f) In what ways may air travellers benefit or suffer if European scheduled air travel were to operate under free competition?

RELATED ESSAY QUESTIONS

1. (a) In what circumstances may some form of monopoly be inevitable?
(b) Why should such a monopoly be regulated by a government?
(c) Describe and comment on the methods of regulation which may be adopted.

2. Chiplin and Wright *(The Logic of Mergers)* describe current UK mergers policy as 'benign' and imply that it is unsystematic.
(a) What evidence is assembled by the authors in support of these conclusions?
(b) What changes in criteria and procedure would, in their view, make mergers policy more effective?

3. 'The central purpose of competition policy is to promote industrial efficiency through the identification and control of monopolies, cartels, and other potential abuses of market power' (C. J. M. Hardie). Discuss.

30 Money, Monetary Policy, and Inflation

Key Points to Review

- Exchange rates (9.1)
- Inflation (11.4)
- Multiplier effect (16.5)
- Expansionary and output gaps (16.6)
- The natural rate of unemployment (18.3)
- Rational expectations (18.4)
- Functions of money (19.1)
- Definitions of money (19.2)
- Supply of money (19.6)

Questions for Preview

1. What is the demand for money and how is it related to the interest rate?
2. Why is the price of bonds* inversely related to the interest rate?
3. What is monetary policy and what are the monetary policy tools of the Bank of England?
4. How do the supply and demand for money determine the interest rate?
5. What is a monetarist?

There is a market for money just as there is a market for goods and services. There is a demand for money – for a number of different purposes. There is a supply of money. The Bank of England's monetary policy seeks to control aggregate monetary demand in the economy. The objectives of policy are to achieve a high level of employment without undue inflation, and to maintain external balance. Monetary policy can be carried out using a range of tools. These can be seen as influencing either the supply of, or the demand for, money. In the main they use interest rate control as a means to an end. We look first at the theory of money, and then at the practicalities of monetary policy. Since banking systems were somewhat deregulated world-wide, during the 1980s, controlling the *supply* of money (i.e. banks' willingness to lend it) has become more difficult. So the Bank of England has used interest rates to control the *demand* for money.

*See dictionary for clarification.

The Demand for Money

Why do people hold money instead of alternative assets, such as bonds, stocks, and durable goods? J. M. Keynes distinguished three different reasons why we hold money.

1. ***Transactions demand.*** Households and firms hold a certain amount of money because of its usefulness as a generally acceptable medium of exchange. Holding money facilitates economic exchanges. With money we can buy products and financial assets quickly when and where we want. The transactions demand for money relates to the fact that our receipts of money income do not match our expenditures. For example, throughout a year you may get paid on the first of each month but spend your income at a relatively even rate throughout the entire month.
2. ***Precautionary demand.*** A certain amount of money holdings are desired by households and firms in order to meet unplanned emergencies. The trans-

actions demand for money relates to planned expenditures. Precautionary demand relates to unplanned expenditures, such as unexpected illness, unemployment, and so on. People like to hold a certain amount of their wealth in the form of very liquid assets, that is, assets denominated in money terms, such as bank balances and building society deposits.

3. ***Speculative demand.*** The *nominal* value (in money terms) of money is fixed. That is not true for a share in a company or for a bond, a house, or a painting. Thus, compared with other assets that a household could own, there is more safety in holding money because its nominal value does not change. People particularly wish to hold money as an alternative to other assets when the market prices of other assets are falling or when they anticipate that the value of non-money assets such as shares will fall in the future.

The Price of Holding Money

Money, you will remember, is the most liquid of all assets. Clearly though, we pay a price for holding money. The price we pay is the *opportunity cost* involved. What is the opportunity cost? It is the interest that we could have earned on an alternative income-earning asset, such as a bond, a stock or a building society account. Therefore, we state that:

The opportunity cost of *holding* money, or cash, is the interest income forgone.

Figure 30.1
Liquidity Preference

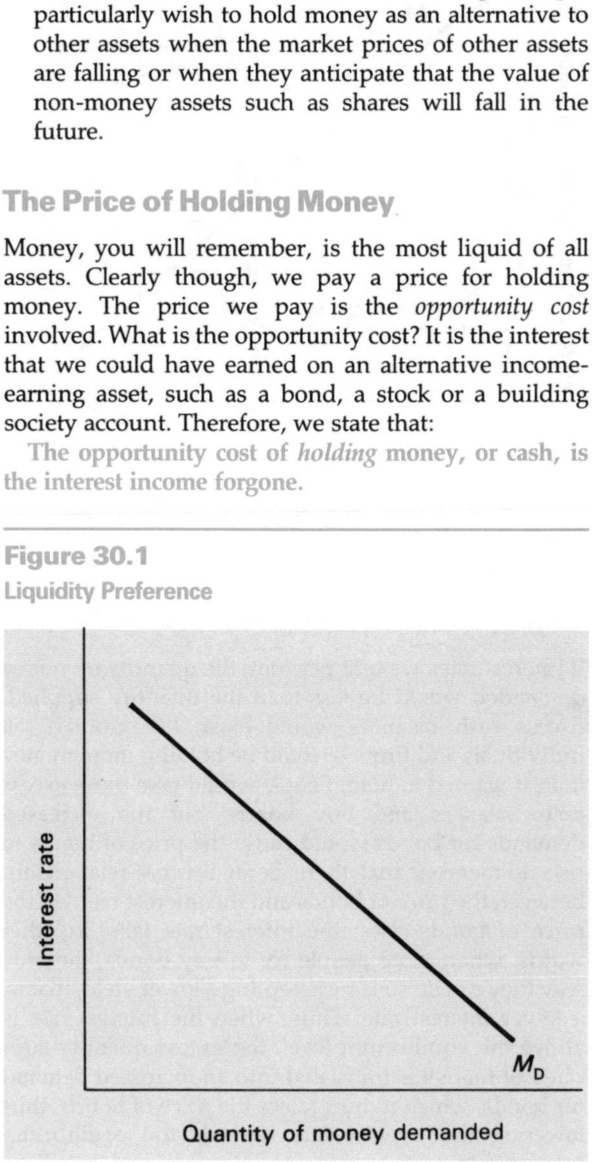

If you keep £100 in currency under a pillow for one year, what is the cost of holding that currency? If the best alternative asset you could have purchased with the £100 was an asset that yielded 5 per cent after taxes, then you forfeited £5. Would you think differently about keeping that £100 in currency under your pillow if an alternative asset could yield you a 20 per cent after-tax rate of return? Perhaps you might. You might then decide to put that £100 in an income-earning asset instead of keeping it as part of your wealth in the form of currency under your pillow. We can surmise, therefore, that the higher the cost of holding money, the lower the quantity of money people wish to hold. In other words, there is an inverse relationship between the quantity of money demanded and the cost of holding it, which is the interest rate that you could earn on alternative assets. Money provides the services of liquidity. The higher the opportunity cost of liquidity, the less you will buy. In other words, the higher the alternative interest rate you could earn on money, the less money you will want to hold.

The Money Demand Schedule – Liquidity Preference

Figure 30.1 shows a hypothetical money demand curve where the 'price' of holding money is the interest rate. The higher the interest rate, the lower the quantity of money demanded holding everything else constant. The money demand curve is downward sloping; Keynes called it the **liquidity preference function,** because it shows the nation's preference for complete, or perfect, liquidity in the form of money.

THE ALTERNATIVE TO HOLDING MONEY

In the most simplified model, the alternative to holding money is basically financial assets such as bonds. Thus, for a given liquidity preference function, if the interest rate rises, a smaller quantity of money will be demanded, but a larger quantity of other financial assets will be desired. That means that as the interest rate rises, individuals attempt to purchase bonds with some of their money holdings. In other words, they substitute income-earning (or higher income-earning) financial assets for part of the money that they are holding, either in their transactions accounts or as paper currency. Alternatively, for any given liquidity preference function (demand-for-money function), if the interest rate in the economy falls, a larger quantity of money will be demanded. Individuals will attempt to sell off some of the income-earning financial assets that they own in order to have more cash. They will attempt to substitute cash for some of the bonds and stocks they own.

THE PRICE OF BONDS AND THE INTEREST RATE

Consider the case in which individuals, for whatever reason, feel that they have more money (cash holdings) than they need – there is an excess supply of money. They attempt to replace some of their money holdings with, say, bonds. Thus, the decreased excess supply of money leads to an increased quantity of bonds demanded. What will this do to the price of *already existing* bonds? It will cause their price to rise. But this price rise for already existing bonds can only mean one thing – the interest yield in those old bonds will *fall*. How can this be, you might ask, for is not the interest on a bond fixed? The answer is 'yes'. The value of interest payments on a bond are fixed, but the actual *yield* (or rate of return) on a bond is not. Consider a simple example. You have just purchased a £1 000 bond that promises to pay you £100 a year for twenty years. That means that your interest yield is £100 ÷ £1 000, which equals 10 per cent per year. Now let us say that everyone suddenly demands more bonds, so that the price of all bonds goes up. You find that you can now sell the old bond that you have for £2 000. It still pays £100 a year as before, but what has happened to the effective interest yield on that bond received by the buyer of the bond? It has fallen for it is now £100 per year ÷ £2 000 which equals 5 per cent per year. The important point to be understood is:

The market price of existing bonds (and all fixed-income assets) is inversely related to the rate of interest prevailing in the economy.

To drive this point home, look at another example taken from the other side of the picture. Assume that the average yield on bonds is 5 per cent. You decide to purchase a bond. You buy a bond that will pay you £50 a year. You will be willing to pay £1 000 for it because £50 ÷ £1 000 = 5 per cent. Suppose you purchase the bond. Next year something happens in the economy. For whatever reason, you can go out and obtain bonds that have effective yields of 10 per cent. That is to say, the prevailing interest rate in the economy is now 10 per cent. What has happened to the market price of the old bond that you owned – the one you purchased last year? It will have fallen. If you try to sell it for £1 000, you will discover that no one will buy it from you. Why should they, for they can obtain £50 a year from someone else by paying only £500? Indeed, unless you offer your bond for sale at a price of £500, no buyers will be forthcoming. Hence, an increase in the prevailing interest rate in the economy has caused the market value of your old bond to fall. Once again, existing bond prices are inversely related to the prevailing interest rate in the economy.

Adding the Money Supply: The Theory

At any given time there is a specific stock of money in the economy. Figure 30.2 shows the quantity of money fixed at the level M_S. This implies that the *supply* of money is completely insensitive to the interest rate. It is assumed to be determined solely by the banking system and the Bank of England. With this supply schedule and a demand schedule (the liquidity preference function), we should be able to find an equilibrium point. It is at the intersection of the supply schedule and the demand schedule, or point *E*. At point *E*, the equilibrium interest rate happens to be 10 per cent per year. This is the interest rate that equates the quantity of money demanded with the quantity of money supplied.

Figure 30.2

Putting together the Demand and Supply of Money. The demand schedule, M_DM_D, is downward sloping; the supply schedule is not only upward sloping, it is vertical at some given quantity of money supplied by the monetary authorities. The equilibrium rate of interest is at 10 per cent. An interest rate of 9 per cent could not prevail for very long, because the quantity of money demanded would exceed the quantity supplied. If people desired more money, they would have to sell bonds. But when they sell bonds, they must lower their price.

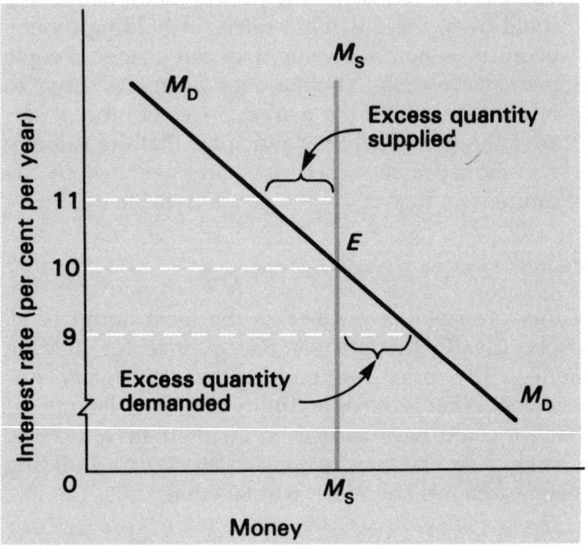

Excess Quantity Supplied

If interest rates were 11 per cent, the quantity of money demanded would be less than the quantity supplied. Excess cash balances would exist; the group – all individuals and firms – would be holding more money than it wanted to hold. People would take those excess cash balances and buy bonds, but the increased demands for bonds would cause the price of bonds to rise. Remember that there is an inverse relationship between the price of bonds and the interest rate. As the price of bonds rises, the interest rate falls. In other words, when more people try to buy bonds, the only way they can do so is by accepting a lower yield, that is, a lower interest rate. Thus, when the interest rate is above the equilibrium level, the excess quantity supplied of money is translated into an increased demand for bonds, which in turn raises the price of bonds, thus lowering the interest rate towards the equilibrium interest rate.

Excess Quantity Demanded

If the interest rate were lower than 10 per cent (the equilibrium rate) there would be an excess quantity demanded for money. People would sell their bonds in

Key Points 30.1

- **Money is an asset that is desired because of the services of liquidity that it provides.**
- **The opportunity cost of holding money is the interest forgone.**
- **The demand for money function, or liquidity preference function, is therefore inversely related to the rate of interest.**
- **The alternative to money as an asset is considered here to be other financial assets only, such as bonds.**
- **There is an inverse relationship between the prevailing rate of interest in the economy and the market price of old (existing) bonds.**
- **The intersection of the demand-for-money function and the supply-of-money function generates the equilibrium rate of interest.**

an attempt to make up the deficiency between actual cash balances and desired cash balances. As people reduce their demand for bonds, the price of bonds falls, that is, the interest rate rises. Another way of looking at it is that since the demand for bonds has fallen, the only way people can be induced to hold them is by offering them higher yields, that is, higher interest rates. Hence, when the interest rate is below the equilibrium level, there is an excess demand for money that translates into a decreased demand for bonds; this causes the price of bonds to fall and the interest rate to rise until equilibrium is reached in the economy. (Now read Key Points 30.1.)

Adding Monetary Policy to the Keynesian Model

The interaction of the demand for money with the supply of money determines the interest rate. Changes in the rate of interest will change the rate of planned investment. In Chapter 15, we drew the planned investment schedule as a downward-sloping curve, with the interest rate on the vertical axis and planned investment on the horizontal axis. Figure 30.3 shows a similar planned investment schedule in panel (b). The lower the rate of interest, the greater the quantity of planned investment.

Panel (a) of Figure 30.3 (page 472) shows the demand and supply of money. Assume that the equilibrium rate of interest, r_1, is established by the intersection of the money supply schedule M_S and the money demand schedule M_DM_D. Remember that the money supply in our simplified model is given by the monetary authorities. At interest rate r_1, we can see in panel (b) that the quantity of planned investment per year will be I_1. This quantity of investment will yield – given the consumption function and government expenditures – the total planned expenditures curve labelled $C + I_1 + G$ in panel (c). It intersects the 45-degree line where total planned expenditures are identically equal to real national income (why?) at real national income per year of Y_1.

Now consider expansionary monetary policy. The Bank of England may increase the flow of base money by buying bonds or bills. If banks increase their lending, there is a rightward movement in the money supply curve from M_S to M'_S in panel (a). The increased money supply creates an excess supply of money. The demand for bonds increases thereby driving up their prices and lowering their yields. The equilibrium rate of interest will fall to r_2, as shown in panel (a), for at this interest rate, the quantity of money demanded and the quantity of money supplied is now equal again.

But at interest rate r_2 in panel (b), we see that there is an increase in the quantity of planned investment per year. That increase is shown by the horizontal arrow moving from I_1 to I_2.

The investment component of the total planned expenditures curve, $C + I_1 + G$ in panel (c) will now have to move upwards by the full amount of the increase in planned investment. This upward movement is shown by the vertical arrow. The new total planned investment curve becomes $C + I_2 + G$. The equilibrium level of real national income per year will increase from Y_1 to Y_2. Note, as always, this change in the equilibrium level of real national income per year is greater than the change in planned investment. This is because there is a multiplier at work – the investment multiplier.

The effects of a contractionary monetary policy can be shown in a similar way. The money supply schedule would shift to the left, causing the equilibrium rate of interest to rise. This would cause a decrease in total planned expenditures and a decrease in the equilibrium level of real national income per year.

The Keynesian Transmission Mechanism

We are assuming that there is a specific transmission mechanism by which changes in the money supply bring about changes in the equilibrium level of real national income. Specifically, the money transmission mechanism involves changes in the interest rate, which

Figure 30.3

Adding Monetary Policy to the Keynesian Model. If the money stock is increased for M_S to M'_S there will be an excess supply of money. Demand for bonds will increase, the interest rate will fall, investment will be stimulated, aggregate expenditure increases and income will rise by an amount determined by the multiplier.

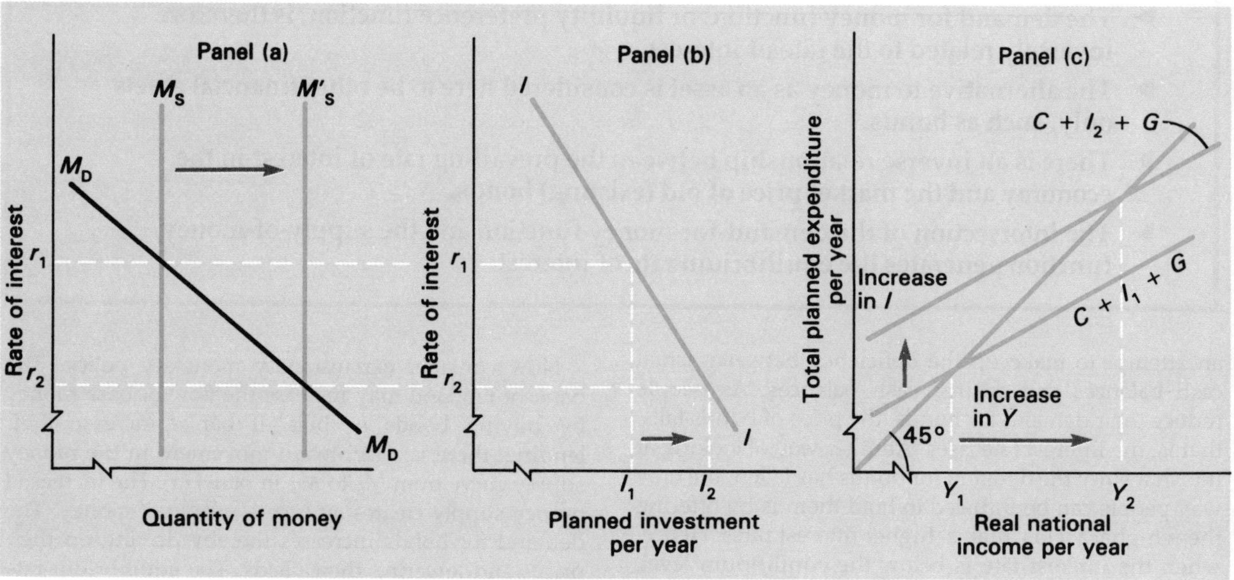

cause a change in investment, which causes a change in income and employment. This transmission mechanism is shown in Figure 30.4.

The overall effect of a change in monetary policy will be somewhat offset by feedback effects. Rising incomes increase the transactions demand for money, shifting the demand for money function rightwards. This will tend to raise interest rates, reversing the original trend, but only by a limited amount. (Now read Key Points 30.2.)

Alternatives to Keynesian Monetary Theory

The monetary theory presented so far in this chapter is Keynesian in origin. The Keynesian view of monetary theory stresses that the monetary authority (the Bank of England) should target interest rates. When interest rates are changed the demand for funds for investment will change and, hence, so will total planned expend-

Key Points 30.2

- **Expansionary monetary policy involves the open-market purchase of government securities, thereby increasing banks' reserves and credit creation.**
- **An *excess* quantity of money supplied leads to an attempted shift (at the then prevailing interest rate) away from money in favour of bonds, thereby driving up bond prices and lowering interest rates.**
- **The decrease in interest rates increases the quantity of investment spending, leading to a multiple expansion in output, income, and employment.**
- **A decrease in the money supply leads to an excess quantity of money demanded, which leads to increased sales of bonds, lowering their prices and thereby increasing interest rates. The increase in interest rates reduces the quantity of investment spending, leading to a multiple contraction in output, income, and employment.**

Figure 30.4
The Keynesian Money Transmission Mechanism

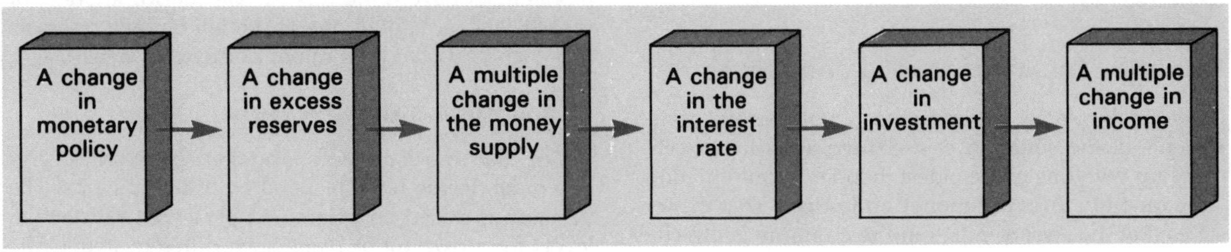

itures. For many years, monetary theory generally was not held in high regard. Some economists believed that, even though changes in the money supply would affect interest rates, the planned investment schedule was such that the resulting changes in interest rates would have little effect on the quantity of planned investment. In other words, they believed that planned investment was relatively insensitive, or unresponsive, to interest-rate changes. Consequently, many of their policy recommendations were concentrated on the fiscal side – changes in government spending and/or in taxation.

The view that money *does* matter in influencing the equilibrium level of real national income and the rate of inflation has its origins in the theories which preceded Keynes's work. The idea that changes in the money supply result in changes in the price level was a fundamental tenet of classical economic reasoning. In fact, this relationship is one of the oldest known in the history of economic thought. We can look at the link between money and prices by means of the **equation of exchange** formally developed by an American economist, Irving Fisher, at Yale University in the early 1900s (also known as the Fisher equation).

The Equation of Exchange

Banknotes that you have in your wallet, purse, or bank account are eventually spent and in the process change hands. It is difficult to see how fast each individual five-pound note is spent, but we can compute an average velocity of the number of times that five-pound notes generally change hands to purchase final goods or services during the year. We call this the **velocity of circulation**, which is designated V. The velocity of circulation is defined as the average number of times per year that the nation's stock of money is spent on purchasing the economy's annual flow of output (or its GNP).

If we let M stand for the total money supply, then our formula for the velocity of circulation is:

$$V = \frac{\text{GNP}}{M}$$

Let us take an example. In 1983 GNP was approximately £260bn and the money supply (£M3) was approximately £100bn. The velocity of circulation, V, therefore equalled £260bn divided by £100bn, or 2.6. In other words, each pound changed hands an average 2.6 times that year.

TRANSPOSING THE EQUATION

Let us multiply both sides of the equation by M. This gives us:

$$MV \equiv \text{GNP}$$

Now let us break down GNP into its separate components – quantities and prices. We will let P stand for the average price of final products produced during the year in question. We let Q stand for the physical, or real, quantities of final outputs. Thus, the value of final output is price times quantity, or GNP = $P \times Q$. Now the equation can be rewritten as:

$$MV \equiv PQ^*$$

In fact, this is the standard notation and form in which the equation of exchange is presented.

Consider a simple numerical example in which we consider a one-commodity economy. In this economy, the total money supply, M, is £100. The quantity of output, Q is 50 units of a good. The average price of this output is £10 per unit. Thus, using the equation of exchange we have:

$$\begin{aligned} MV &= PQ \\ £100V &= £10 \times 50 \\ £100V &= £500 \\ V &= 5 \end{aligned}$$

Therefore, each pound is spent an average of five times a year.

EQUATION OF EXCHANGE IS AN IDENTITY

The equation of exchange is an identity. It is true by definition. It is what we call an *accounting identity*, which tells us that the total amount of money *spent* on final output, MV, *is equal to the total amount of money received* for final product, PQ. Thus, we can look at a given flow of money from either the buyers' or the

*Sometimes Q for quantity is represented by T for transactions.

producers' side of the picture. The value of goods purchased is equal to the value of goods sold. This is true by definition.

Quantity Theory of Money and Prices

If we make some assumptions about certain components of the equation of exchange, we can actually come up with one of the oldest theories about inflation – the **quantity theory of money and prices.** That theory states that the level of prices in the economy is directly proportional to the quantity of money in circulation per unit of output. To state this theory in symbols, we divide both sides of the equation of exchange by Q. Thus $MV = PQ$ becomes:

$$P = M \times \left(\frac{V}{Q}\right)$$

To derive the quantity theory of money and prices, we now have to make an assumption. If we assume that both V and Q are fairly constant, then as M increases or decreases, so, too, does P, and at the same rate. In fact, classical economists believed that V was constant because it was determined by the long-run money-holding habits of firms and households, which seemed to them to be fairly stable. Q was also assumed fairly constant because of their prediction that the economy tended towards full employment. Given that V and Q are constant one could predict therefore that a 10 per cent increase in M would cause a 10 per cent increase in P.

The Empirical Evidence

Evidence for the quantity theory of money and prices seems relatively favourable if we look at fairly long periods of time. For example, the inflation that occurred in England during 1750–1800 was probably due to the rapid expansion of banks and the resultant increase in money supply during that period. The inflation of the 1970s is similarly explained as a possible by-product of the money-supply expansions caused by deficit financing by governments striving to maintain full employment. Thus it may be said that M and P are correlated – but they are certainly *not* proportional to the extent that if M is doubled P will rise twofold.

Modern Monetarism

During the 1960s, some economists began again to think that the quantity of money has a major part to play in the determination of price levels. Professor Milton Friedman at the University of Chicago and others at that time started research on the relationship between changes in the rate of growth of the money supply and changes in macroeconomic variables such as national income and the price level. Not surprisingly, Friedman and his followers took on the name of **monetarists**. The monetarists have stressed the need for monetary targets. To understand why monetarists have placed so much stress on monetary targets, we must look at an expanded demand-for-money equation that includes more than simply the interest rate. The monetarists have done this by considering money, or cash balances, as only one of the wide range of assets that each of us can hold in our portfolio of wealth.

The Choice among Assets

Given that everyone faces a budget constraint, everyone must decide how to spend on different items. The decision is based on prices and perceived satisfaction levels from owning or using such different items. The demand for money, or cash balances, can be treated simply as the demand for one particular alternative way of holding one's wealth. People can opt to hold larger cash balances by giving up the purchase of other assets such as bonds, houses, cars, or compact-disc players. We acquire cash balances by *not spending* part of our income, that is, by holding part of our income in the bank or in notes and coin.

Modern Monetarist Demand-for-Money Function

The modern monetarist demand-for-money function shows that the demand for money depends on the following:

1. *Nominal income,* because that represents your budget constraint, or how much you have to spend, per time-period, on all items, including liquidity or cash balances.
2. *The rate of return on alternative assets,* such as bonds.
3. *The expected rate of inflation,* because as the price level goes up, the purchasing power of the pound goes down. The rate of inflation can be thought of as the rate of depreciation of your cash balances. The faster they depreciate, the more expensive they are to hold.

The modern monetarist view of the demand for money includes more than the simplified Keynesian liquidity-preference function given in this chapter. In other words, it includes more than 'the' interest rate. Additionally, the modern monetarist demand-for-money function includes the rate of return on all alternative assets. So it is inconsistent with the transmission mechanism outlined for the Keynesian model. In the Keynesian model, when households and firms found themselves with an excess quantity of money, their only alternative asset was bonds. If the money supply increased, there would be an increased demand for bonds, thus driving up the bond prices and lowering interest rates. So planned investment increased, and there was a multiplier effect on the equilibrium level of real national income.

Modern monetarists do not deny the validity of this indirect transmission mechanism for monetary policy. Rather, they indicate that it is too narrow. Indeed, post-Keynesian economists agree that the traditional simplified Keynesian view of the transmission mechanism is too narrow.

MILTON FRIEDMAN

ECONOMIST, FORMERLY OF THE UNIVERSITY OF CHICAGO

The Iconoclast as Institution

Milton Friedman is America's leading conservative economist. A controversial figure, he has seen his views embraced by the libertarian right and dismissed as nonsense by Keynesian liberals; by the left, he has been damned for his opposition to social welfare programmes and for his advisory role to the Chilean authorities during the years of military dictatorship in Chile. For many years an outsider to the Keynesian orthodoxy, Friedman, who won the Nobel Prize in 1976 for his monetary theories, has gained so much influence among economists in recent years that he threatens to become a prominent part of the status quo himself.

Friedman's standing among contemporary economists derives primarily from his advocacy of the modern quantity theory of money and prices, of what has come to be known as *monetarism* – the doctrine that the one crucial ingredient shaping short-run economic fluctuations is change in the amount of money in circulation. The key to a healthy and non-inflationary economy, Friedman has argued persistently over the last three decades, is a constant rate of growth in the money supply. Monetary authorities, Friedman says, instead of tightening money during booms and loosening money during recessions (which is ineffective because of the time-lags), should simply increase the supply of money at a steady rate of between 3 and 5 per cent per year.

Friedman's work shows quite impressively that, rather than being ineffective, monetary policy *caused* the Great Depression. He pointed out that the money supply was reduced dramatically at the hands of the Fed (the US Central Bank) during that period; that reason, and that reason alone, caused a serious recession to descend into the greatest depression the US has ever had. Friedman, like most monetarists, believes that the macroeconomy is intrinsically stable – if left alone by the prying hand of government.

His philosophy carries over into all areas of government intervention. He has pointed out time and again the unintended, negative effects of government intervention in the economy. His solution to many of society's ills is a more competitive private marketplace, rather than increased government regulation, intervention, and spending.

A More Generalized Transmission Mechanism

Money is one asset of a possible range, or portfolio, of assets. If there is an increase in the supply of money, individuals will not simply increase their demand for bonds. Rather, they will increase their demand for bonds, equities, consumer durables, gold, diamonds, silver, and any other alternative asset. That means that an increase in the money supply, rather than simply increasing the demand for bonds, reducing the interest rate, and thereby increasing planned investment, will increase the demand for a wide variety of assets including consumer and investment goods.

Basically, the increase in the money supply means that the supply of money is greater than the demand for money, and there is a monetary disequilibrium. This excess supply of money causes individuals to attempt to reduce their money balances. In the aggregate, this causes desired expenditures to rise. As in the Keynesian model, this increase in total planned expenditures can initially be satisfied by reducing stocks, but eventually the drop in inventories will cause firms to increase production (or to raise prices). The equilibrium level of national income will increase, probably with a time-lag of one to two years.

Equilibrium in the aggregate will occur when the demand for money again equals the supply of money. Since the monetarist's demand-for-money function also has income as a component, as national income rises, the demand for money also increases. Equilibrium is re-established when the demand for money increases sufficiently to equilibrate the supply and demand for money.

So the transmission mechanism that the monetarists use sees an increase in the money supply causing increased spending not just on bonds but on property, equities, and consumer goods. This increased spending causes aggregate demand to increase directly, and it also means that an increase in the money supply will be felt relatively quickly throughout the entire economy. Contrast this transmission mechanism with the simplified Keynesian one, where the increase in the money supply is felt in the bond market and then in the investment market.

Key Points 30.3

- **The equation of exchange states that expenditures by one person will equal income receipts by another. In its simplest form, the money supply times velocity (*MV*) equals national income (GNP).**
- **Viewed as an accounting identity the equation of exchange is always correct, since the amount of money spent on final output must be equal to the total amount of money received for final output.**
- **If we assume that *V* (the velocity of circulation) and *Q* (output) are fairly constant, then any change in the money supply (*M*) will change the price level (*P*) by the same proportion.**
- **Monetarists are those economists who believe that changes in the rate of growth of the money supply determine, to a large extent, changes in numerous macroeconomic variables such as the equilibrium level of national income and the price level.**
- **A modern monetarist demand-for-money equation includes nominal income, the rate of return on alternative assets (including, but not limited to, bonds), and the expected rate of inflation.**
- **The monetarist transmission mechanism shows that a change in the money supply would change the demand for a variety of assets and thereby be felt as a change in aggregate demand throughout the economy. The simplified Keynesian monetary transmission mechanism has monetary policy directly affecting only the bond market and the investment market.**

The Implications: What Actually Happens?

We have examined two different theories about how money affects the economy. In fact, the outcome of a change in the money stock depends crucially on whether *real* income *can* increase. In Chapter 14 we examined the effect of changes in aggregate demand on the price level. We saw that if there were spare capacity in the economy – under-utilized labour and capital – then output could increase with little or no increase in the price level. But if the economy is already producing at or near its full-capacity output, then increasing demand will lead to rising prices rather than rising output.

In Chapter 16 we examined the Keynesian approach to expansion in the economy. It was pointed out that the simple Keynesian model assumes that output can be expanded, i.e. that the economy is on the horizontal section of the aggregate supply curve. So a Keynesian view would be that given some unemployed resources, increased spending would lead to increased output and employment.

A crucial factor in the monetarist view of the world is that it sees little scope for such expansion. Generally speaking, unemployment is seen as having its roots in structural problems rather than in the deficiency of aggregate demand. This view suggests that the economy is functioning on the upward-sloping section of the aggregate supply curve. Increasing aggregate demand will lead mainly to rising prices and not, except possibly in the short run, to rising output. In the long run, monetarists believe, output can grow only slowly as the capacity of the economy grows through capital investment and improved technology. The economy will, after a short period of expansion, revert to the level of output associated with the natural rate of unemployment. This is the level of unemployment determined by rigidities in the labour market, such as immobilities and inflexible wages. (This was explained alongside the discussion of the Phillips Curve in Chapter 18.) Monetary expansion will increase aggregate demand and induce firms to increase output. But at or below the natural rate of unemployment, firms will encounter supply constraints. Efforts to recruit labour with scarce skills, in order to expand, will lead to rising wages as firms try to attract employees. The increased demand will end in rising price levels rather than in increased output.

Of course if unemployment were to be *above* the natural rate at the outset, then resources would be available for at least some increase in output. So the effect of changes in the money stock on the real economy depends on the nature of the unemployed workforce at the time. In other words, it all depends whether the economy is on the horizontal or the upward-sloping section of the aggregate supply curve.

A part of the argument that output will not increase when the money stock is expanding involves the permanent-income hypothesis (referred to in Chapter 15). Short-run increases in money income will not lead to significant increases in consumption, because consumption depends on expectations about income over the long run rather than the short run. The permanent-income hypothesis was developed by Friedman and contrasts with the more short-run view of consumption contained in the Keynesian model.

Whichever theory provides the clearest insights at any particular time, it is clear that the way in which changes in the money stock affect the economy will be much influenced by the availability of underutilized resources and the flexibility of the labour market. If the resources needed to expand output are scarce, then an increase in the money stock will, after a time, lead to a rise in prices.

Figure 30.5
Velocities (GNP ÷ Money Stock)

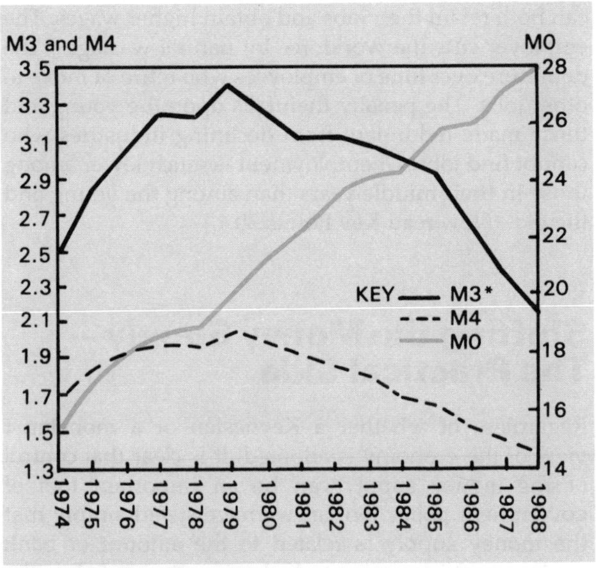

Source: Bank of England, 1989.
*M3 was the main measure of broad money until 1987.

ARE V AND Q REASONABLY STABLE?

A further issue relevant to the Keynesian monetarist debate concerns the behaviour of velocity of circulation and of Q, the number of transactions. In a recession, the latter falls. In a boom, it rises. While there will be a long-run trend underlying the short-run fluctuations, these fluctuations can be quite marked.

The close, inevitable, connection between money and prices depends on the velocity of circulation being fairly stable. Data measuring the velocity of circulation must be treated with caution. However, the data in Figure 30.5 do suggest that velocity has slowed significantly during the 1980s.

A Tight Monetary Policy

So far we have been concerned with the effect of an increase in the money stock. What happens if the government imposes a monetary squeeze?

Let us suppose that there is inflation. Rising prices are increasing transactions' demand for money. In Figure 30.6 panel (a), the demand for money function shifts to the right. The government seeks to hold the money stock constant and as a result, interest rates rise. Investment is discouraged (panel (b)) and there is a downward multiplier effect on real income and employment (panel (c)).

This is a Keynesian approach. The monetarist approach, beginning with an excess demand for money, foresees falling demand for a wide range of assets including investment and consumer goods. Irrespective of the approach, it is clear that firms will experience decreased demand for their output, stocks will pile up, and unemployment will rise.

Most frequently, tight monetary policies are introduced in response to inflation. Just how is this very sad

Figure 30.6
A Monetary Squeeze

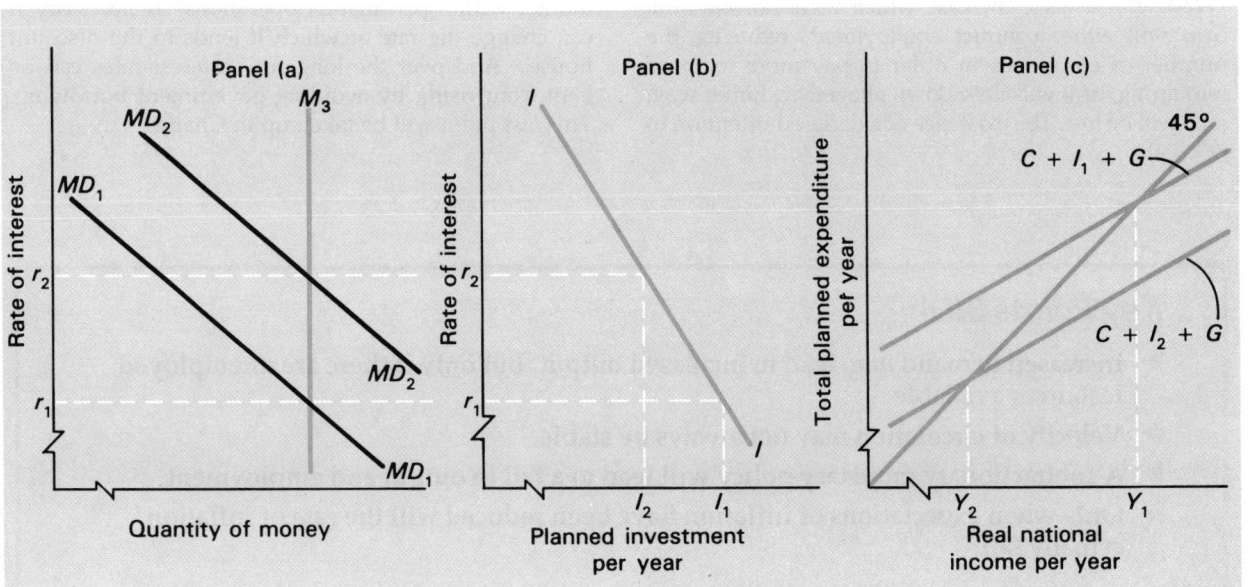

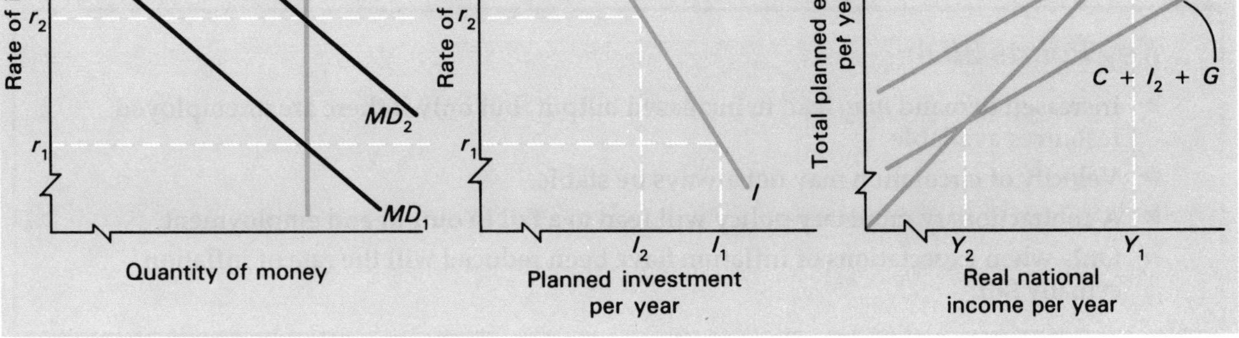

fall in output and employment going to reduce the rate at which prices are increasing?

First, the tight monetary policy will reduce any excess demand in the economy. In the simple, aggregate demand–aggregate supply approach developed in Chapter 14, the policy shifts the aggregate demand function to the left, reducing overheating and relieving supply constraints in the economy. But the policy goes beyond this. A component part of inflation is a continuing series of wage increases throughout the economy. As unemployment increases, trade unions become much more wary of negotiating large wage increases. They will do so only if they feel confident that existing employees will not lose their jobs. In 1981–2 inflation fell sharply, partly because many firms were close to bankruptcy. Further wage increases would have brought even more job losses.

Keynesians and monetarists would agree that contractionary policy operates through this effect on output and employment. They would disagree as to how much unemployment is needed to reduce inflation by a given amount.

The Keynesian approach observes that labour markets are not very flexible. Wages seldom fall in real terms. Many people are able to negotiate wage increases, even in hard times, because *their* jobs are not seriously threatened. So output and employment might fall far before expectations of future inflation were much reduced. The experience of 1980–2 when unemployment almost doubled should be considered.

The monetarist approach is more hopeful. It hinges upon the idea of rational expectations, outlined in Chapter 18. Its influence could be distinctly heard behind Mrs Thatcher's speeches about firmness in handling the economy. The argument goes like this. If those who negotiate wage bargains (both unions and employers) know from experience that the government intends to control credit creation firmly, then they will know also that employers will not be able to borrow from the banks to pay inflationary wage increases. Faced with a wage increase which it cannot pay, the firm will either contract employment, reducing the number of employees in order to pay more to those remaining, or it will close down altogether. Either way, jobs will be lost. The existence of a declared intention to exert strict monetary control will therefore be sufficient to deter unions from demanding excessive wages.

If unions get the message quickly, then output need not fall very much. Do unions get the message in the UK? The trouble is, not everyone is vulnerable. Consumers will continue to buy many products even if prices rise and incomes fall. Producers of these are not seriously threatened by falling aggregate demand and the employers in these sectors may continue to increase wages and pass on the cost to the consumer.

According to the theory, employers even then need not pay higher wages if there is an adequate supply of unemployed labour willing to work for less. In practice, union-negotiated minimum wage rates and closed shops ensure that the unemployed do not get the chance to work for less. Quite often, existing employees can both retain their jobs and obtain higher wages. The employer cuts the workforce by natural wastage – the departure over time of employees who retire or move to other jobs. The penalty then falls upon the young and those made redundant from declining industries who cannot find jobs. Unemployment is much lower among those in their middle years than among the young and the old. (Now read Key Points 30.4.)

Shifting the Money Supply – The Practical Side

Regardless of whether a Keynesian or a monetarist view of the economy is adopted, it is clear that control of the money supply can be an important tool of government policy. So far, we have stated simply that the money supply is related to the amount of bank lending, which will itself be constrained by the monetary policies of the Bank of England.

In recent years the Bank of England has pursued its monetary policy primarily through controlling interest rates. On a day-to-day basis it intervenes in the money market with 'open-market operations'. If necessary it can change the rate at which it lends to the discount houses. And over the long run, interest rates can be kept from rising by avoiding government borrowing. This last point will be taken up in Chapter 31.

Key Points 30.4

- **Increased demand *may* lead to increased output, but only if there are unemployed resources available.**
- **Velocity of circulation may not always be stable.**
- **A contractionary monetary policy will lead to a fall in output and employment.**
- **Only when expectations of inflation have been reduced will the rate of inflation actually fall.**

Open-market Operations

The Bank of England sells both short- and long-term government debt, Treasury bills and bonds respectively. When it sells debt the immediate effect is that the buyer pays for it with a cheque drawn on a bank account. In order to make good the payment, that bank will make a transfer from its account with the Bank of England, to the government account. Since the bank's account with the Bank of England is its most liquid reserve asset (other than notes and coin), its reserves have now been reduced. But the bank must still keep adequate reserve assets, so that it may be able to meet customers' requests for withdrawals. The effect of reducing the bank's reserves is to force it to reduce its lending proportionately.

In general, reducing banks' reserves in this way leaves them short of cash. They may have to borrow to make good that day's requests for withdrawals. When they seek to borrow (probably on the inter-bank market), they will be competing for scarce funds and the result will be to drive up interest rates. So the Bank of England, by selling bonds and bills, can exert upward pressure on interest rates.

If, conversely, the Bank of England wants interest rates to fall, it can buy bonds and bills. It will pay for them with cheques drawn on itself. The sellers will deposit these cheques in their bank accounts. Their banks' balances with the Bank of England will increase, giving the banks larger holdings of liquid reserve assets. These can form the basis for increased bank lending. Generally speaking, the Bank of England maintains a level of intervention in the money market such that it both buys and sells bills continuously. Most of the time it will seek to keep interest rates stable: it will buy enough bills, so that the banks do not become short of cash and do not bid up interest rates.

There are times when open-market operations do not give the Bank of England sufficient control over interest rates and the money market. This is likely to occur when the Bank wants to raise interest rates. It can then announce a higher **rate of discount**, or intervention rate. This means that when the Bank of England buys bills it will pay less for them, i.e. charge a higher interest rate: it refuses to discount them at the old rate. This method has been used several times in recent years to steady the market when it has become nervous and unstable.

During the mid- to late-1980s, extensive changes in the banking system made control of the monetary aggregates difficult. The emphasis shifted entirely on to controlling interest rates. By making borrowing expensive, the Bank of England effectively controls the demand for money, rather than its supply.

Monetary Policy in Recent Years

The rapid inflation of the mid-1970s prompted much rethinking of policy. In 1976 the UK found itself with 15 per cent inflation and a massive deficit in the balance of trade, which forced the then Labour government to seek a loan from the IMF. The IMF requires its borrowers to conform to its policy prescriptions. (In fairness, governments are often glad to have an outside body which can be blamed for the necessity of introducing unpopular policies.) In this case the IMF required tighter monetary policy, in effect upgrading its importance as a tool of economic policy. Specifically, monetary targets were introduced for M1 and M3. These were rolling targets: that is, they were revised every six months and applied to the year ahead. They were part of a package of measures, including fiscal and incomes policies, designed to reduce aggregate monetary demand.

When the Conservatives came to power in 1979, it was their declared intention to control inflation with a much stricter monetary policy. Monetary targets were revised downwards, and interest rates raised. Several different trends became apparent. In spite of tighter monetary policies, M3 behaved rather badly. It did not begin to grow within its target range until 1982.

Nevertheless the economy behaved as if policy were very contractionary. Cuts in many areas of government expenditure reduced demand. High interest rates attracted a capital inflow, and this together with the arrival of North Sea oil, pushed up the exchange rate. This made exports dearer and imports cheaper – UK manufacturers faced a serious loss of competitiveness. The combined effect of high interest rates, falling demand, and loss of competitiveness pushed the economy into the sharpest recession since the 1930s.

As unemployment rose, wage bargains moderated. No one wanted his/her pay rise to end in the employer's bankruptcy: the chances of getting another job were not good. By the end of 1982 inflation was down to 5 per cent. Monetarism was seen to have worked, but the cost was high. Twelve per cent of the workforce was unemployed and manufacturing output was 14 per cent below its 1979 level.

THE RECOVERY, 1982–6

Monetary growth during the recovery continued apace. The institutional changes which have made it so difficult to measure the money stock – new kinds of bank loans, the greater freedom of banks, and building societies to compete – contributed to a big expansion in lending. M3 (the then broad money measure) grew on average at 17 per cent. M0, introduced in 1982, grew on average at about 5 per cent.

The monetary targets for M3 began to look very silly. Despite being revised upward, they were still overshot. Less and less was heard of them. Instead the Chancellor said he would monitor all the monetary aggregates, including the exchange rate. In time, the government and the Bank of England decided that M0 was the best variable to target.

In general, interest rates were kept lower as the economy slowly recovered. The exchange rate fell, bringing greater competitiveness. Productivity rose as redundancies continued. Unemployment continued to rise until 1986 (partly because the labour force was growing).

THE BOOM 1986–8

Helped by low oil prices, output and standards of living rose fast. As before the broad money aggregates grew at an unprecedented rate. Unemployment fell. The Chancellor was confident that aggregate supply would grow fast enough to meet the fast-growing aggregate demand. Interest rates were mostly below 10 per cent. The Stock Market crash of October 1987 brought fears of a slump. Worldwide, governments reduced interest rates to forestall the drop in demand. (The **wealth effect** – the consequence of people's assets having lost value – would be expected to reduce spending). In the event this did not happen.

By spring 1988 it was clear that the UK economy was overheating. Skill shortages were developing. Inflation was accelerating. Consumers were turning to imports to obtain the extra goods which the UK could not produce fast enough. Mr Lawson raised interest rates sharply.

TIGHT MONETARY POLICY ONCE MORE

The experience of the years 1988–90 again suggests that the response to tightening monetary policy is both slow and uncertain. The increases in interest rates in the summer of 1988 did slow down spending, but only a little. During the calendar year 1989 total real expenditure grew by 4.5 per cent: considerably more than the growth of output. Earnings grew by 9 per cent, compared to a rate of inflation of 7.5 per cent. It is clear that there are time-lags in the response of the economy to policy.

What Have We Learned?

Despite all the rhetoric, the government's monetary policy was at times during the 1980s quite flexible. In the mid-1980s the money stock expanded sharply. At no time did the Bank of England exert really strict control over monetary growth, even allowing for the fact that some of the growth was more apparent than real. Stricter control of the money stock would have required higher, and more sharply fluctuating, interest rates. These are politically unpopular with both investors and people with mortgages.

On the other hand interest rates were several times used to exert downward pressure on the demand for credit, and caused considerable difficulties for borrowers. Furthermore, interest rates were often kept high to maintain the exchange rate. A high exchange rate can be an important component part of monetary policy. Firstly, when the exchange rate is high imports are cheaper. These lower prices feed directly into the RPI, to the extent that we import finished goods. Imported inputs will be cheaper too, and may help to keep prices of UK manufactures down. But low import prices have another strong influence. They make domestically produced products less competitive. They put great pressure on firms to cut costs, to keep prices down, and to resist large wage claims.

This external effect of high interest rates is now seen by the Bank of England and the Conservative government to be central to the fight against inflation.

At the time of writing, the government is seeking to control inflation with high interest rates. This contrasts with the early 1980s, when fiscal policy was a major part of the package, and even more with the mid-1970s, when the government used fiscal and monetary measures and an incomes policy (direct controls on the growth of wages). You should now assess for yourself the extent to which experience since this was written has differed. In particular consider what has been the effect of entering the European Exchange Rate Mechanism on the government's approach.

Key Points 30.5

- **The emphasis of UK monetary policy is upon the control of interest rates.**
- **Open-market operations reduce the liquid reserves of the banks and make them contract the growth of lending.**
- **The Bank of England's intervention rate, or rate of discount, can be altered by the Bank's refusing to buy bills except at the new rate.**
- **If necessary the Bank of England can announce a higher rate of discount.**
- **Monetary targets became increasingly difficult to maintain during the 1980s because of major changes in the banking system.**
- **The government responded to the overheating of the economy in 1988 with sharp increases in interest rates.**
- **The exchange rate and monetary policy are closely related. A tight monetary policy will tend to keep the exchange rate higher than it would otherwise be.**

CASE STUDY

Who Would Be Chancellor?

Figure 30.7
Money supply

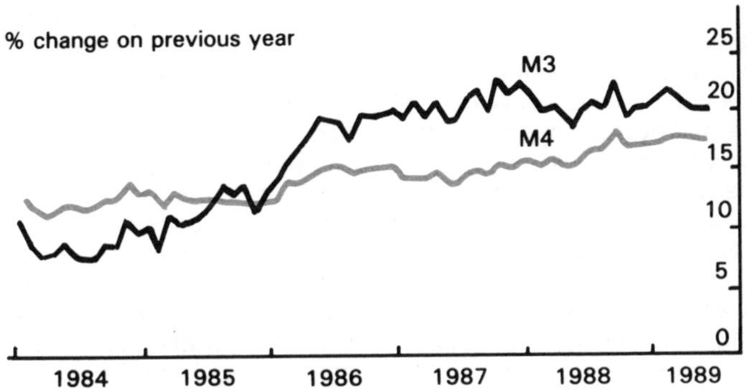

Sources: Shearson Lehman Hutton, Bank of England

M3 (né sterling M3) was initially the centrepiece of the government's 'medium-term financial strategy'. By controlling M3 the government believed it could control money-GDP – and hence inflation. Mr Lawson dropped M3 as a target in 1986 because its relationship with money-GDP seemed to have collapsed as a result of financial deregulation. In 1980–1, for example, sterling-M3 misled the government into pursuing an unintentionally tight policy and causing a deeper recession than it would have wished.

After a series of flirtations, sometimes with several measures of money at the same time, the government began a more lasting affair with M0 – the narrowest measure, which consists mainly of notes and coins. M0 is probably a good indicator of current inflationary pressure, but it has few friends in the City. It tends to mirror changes in demand, instead of giving advance warning of them: individuals and companies adjust their holdings of cash to changes in income and spending, not vice versa.

There are some, like Mr Tim Congdon, economics adviser to a discount house, Gerrard & National, who would like broad-money targets to be brought back from the dead. He was one of the few economists to sound the alarm about rapid monetary growth in 1986. He was right – monetary policy was too loose. But broad-money had cried wolf so often: M3 had been accelerating since 1984, with no apparent ill effects.

Mr Congdon's preferred target today is M4 (a broader measure still, which includes building-society deposits). It has a steadier link with money-GDP than does M3 – but it failed to reveal a strong monetary expansion in 1986 (see Figure 30.7). The fact is that the relationship between broad money and money-GDP is too unstable to be much use by itself in guiding policy.

Mr Congdon reckons that if inflation is to be reduced to below 5 per cent, the target for M4 should be 9–13 per cent over the next 12 months. In the past year it has risen by more than 18 per cent. How would Mr Congdon bring it back within target? His answer is higher interest rates and a policy of 'overfunding', which in present circumstances means buying in fewer gilts (government bonds) than the government ought to in view of its budget surplus. Overfunding, in effect, replaces bank deposits (that is, money) in the financial assets of Britain's private sector with government bonds (which are not money).

Higher interest rates have two drawbacks. The first is that most sorts of broad money earn interest: higher interest rates may tend to reduce money by discouraging bank lending, but equally they tend to increase it by making bank deposits a better investment. The second is that Mr Lawson may prefer not to be lynched.

Overfunding has its disadvantages too. Since it raises long-term interest rates relative to short-term rates, it tends to discourage investment more than consumer spending.

Since the aim of monetary policy is to reduce the growth of money-GDP, why not target it directly? The snag, says the Treasury, is that money-GDP is published only quarterly and after a delay of about 11 weeks. Even so, by December 1987 the Treasury should have been on red alert. It then knew that the growth in money-GDP had accelerated to more than 10 per cent by the third quarter of 1987. If the government had been targeting money-GDP it would have tightened policy at least six months earlier. But even this might have been too late.

Source: adapted from 'Is Monetarism Back From the Dead', *The Economist*, 10 June 1989.

Questions

1. What problems has the government had with monetary targets?
2. Why is M0 not an ideal measure of monetary growth?
3. What are the advantages and disadvantages of using M4 as a monetary target?
4. What policies are suggested to deal with excessive monetary growth?
5. What disadvantages do these policies have?

CASE STUDY

The Bank of England View, August 1989 to February 1990

*Read both extracts from the *Bank of England Quarterly Bulletin (BEQB)* before considering the questions.

Inflation may have reached its peak . . .

The upward trend in inflation which has been evident since the beginning of 1988 continued in the first half of the year, with the twelve-month rate of increase rising from 7.5 per cent in January to 8.3 per cent in May and June. The gap between the all-items RPI and that of the RPI excluding mortgage interest payments has widened as a result of the increase in mortgage interest payments over the past year; on the latter measure inflation in the year to June was 5.9 per cent.

Monetary tightening at home is having continuing effects . . .

It is now well over a year since monetary policy in the United Kingdom began to be tightened. It was expected that the effect on the economy would take time to emerge in full, with some asset prices and forms of expenditure affected before others, while the prices of most goods and services would react only to a slackening of demand. Developments so far have been consistent with those expectations. However, the economy is now seen to have been expanding more rapidly, and with greater inflationary implications, when policy was first tightened than appeared at the time; only in this sense has progress been disappointing. While the balance of evidence is strongly that adjustment to last year's tightening is by no means yet complete, the mechanism is working as expected.

The housing market was the first to react to policy tightening, most noticeably in the South-East, where high house prices and heavy mortgage borrowing had made borrowers most exposed to interest rate increases; and where prices have begun to fall. Prices in the North continue to rise but at a more subdued rate.

So far this year spending on household durables – most likely to be affected by the slowdown in the housing market – has been at a quarterly level almost 5 per cent below the peak reached last year. Private sales of motor vehicles have, on the whole, proved relatively resilient. Spending on non-durables has been erratic, with the only source of persistent strength coming from 'other services', which includes international travel.

Industrial investment in the first quarter was surprisingly flat. Industrial companies can no longer rely on widening profit margins to finance investment as in recent years. Collectively they have recently moved into financial deficit and borrowed heavily from the banks. Capital expenditure has been trimmed in previous periods when economic growth generally has slowed.

The labour market remains tight . . .

So far, as would be expected, slower growth in the economy has not had very marked effects in the labour market. Manufacturing employment, however, has resumed its decline in recent months, and the rate of fall of unemployment is not as great as it was. Growth in underlying earnings has not advanced further and the earlier acceleration was less than might have been expected on the basis of similar periods of high-demand pressure in the past. Settlements, however, continue to rise, notably in services, where they have been running recently at about the rate of retail price inflation. The rash of industrial disputes reflects both pressure for, and resistance to, higher settlements, following the acceleration of prices.

Earnings have grown at broadly similar rates in different sectors and have not reflected differences in growth of productivity. In manufacturing, where productivity has continued to grow rapidly, unit wage costs are rising at around 3 per cent per annum.

With a period of slower economic growth in prospect, for a time below the potential growth of the economy, underlying inflation should fall, with reduced profit margins providing the earlier contribution, followed in the next pay round by the further consequences of an easing in labour market pressures. Slower domestic demand will also help to reduce the current account deficit, but again, slowly.

So far private-sector confidence seems remarkably robust but expenditures might be adjusted more rapidly, bringing about a faster reduction in inflation (and the current account deficit), at a greater immediate cost in terms of output and employment.

Source: *BEQB*, Aug. 1989.

Conditions in the labour market may be easing slightly but remain tight . . .

There are now increasing signs that the fall in output growth is having some effect on the labour market, though this has so far taken the form of a slowing in the rates at which unemployment is falling and employment is rising. Labour market conditions therefore remain tight overall. Unemployment continued to fall in the fourth quarter of last year, reaching 1.6m, or 5.8 per cent of the workforce, by the end of the year. Since peaking in July 1986, recorded unemployment has now fallen by about 1.5m to reach its lowest level for nine years. There has been a perceptible moderation in the rate of decline, however; over the last six months the monthly fall in unemployment has averaged 29 000, which compares with 48 000 in the corresponding period a year earlier.

Figure 30.8

Unit Wage Costs Rising (percentage changes on a year earlier)

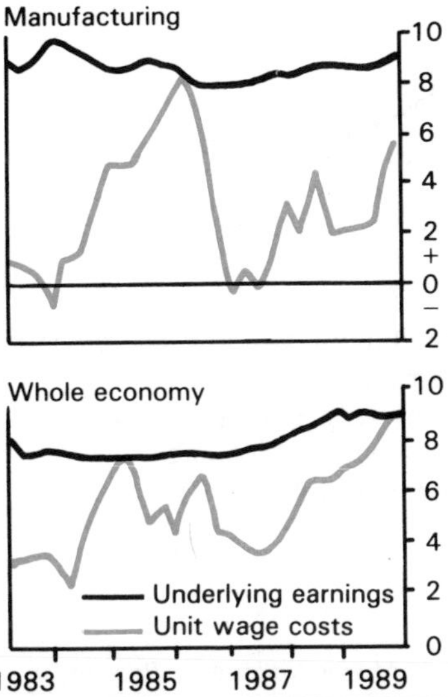

Although the labour market may be easing, the rate of earnings growth continues to rise in response to its earlier tightness. Underlying average earnings in the whole economy grew by 9.25 per cent in the year to November. The strongest upward pressure on wage settlements during last year came from the rise in the rate of inflation. According to the CBI, over half of all firms in the private sector cited the cost of living as a very important upward influence on settlements during the 1988–9 pay round. The need to recruit and retain labour in tight labour market conditions also had a major influence. About one-third of manufacturing firms and just under a half of private service sector firms reported this factor as an important upward pressure on settlements. This reinforces the message from the CBI industrial trends survey which indicates that, while shortages of skilled labour declined in importance as a constraint on output in 1989, they remained significant throughout the year.

With a fall in the rate of productivity growth in manufacturing to an annual rate of around 3 per cent at the end of last year, unit wage costs in manufacturing accelerated and by November were almost 6 per cent higher than a year earlier. Given the strains already evident in company finances, this is unlikely to prove sustainable. Unless earnings growth moderates, the implications of the slowdown in the economy for employment may become increasingly serious as employers seek to contain labour costs by shedding labour.

Inflation

Inflation, as measured by the twelve-month rise in the all-items RPI, stood at 7.6 per cent in the fourth quarter, significantly lower than in the second quarter when a peak of 8.2 per cent was recorded.

Over the coming months the inflation rate is likely to remain fairly volatile. The dropping out of higher mortgage interest rates at the beginning of 1989 will have the effect of putting some downward pressure on the all-items inflation rate while the switch from rates to the community charge may increase it.

Source: *BEQB*, Feb. 1990.

Figure 30.9

Inflation in the UK (percentage changes on a year earlier)

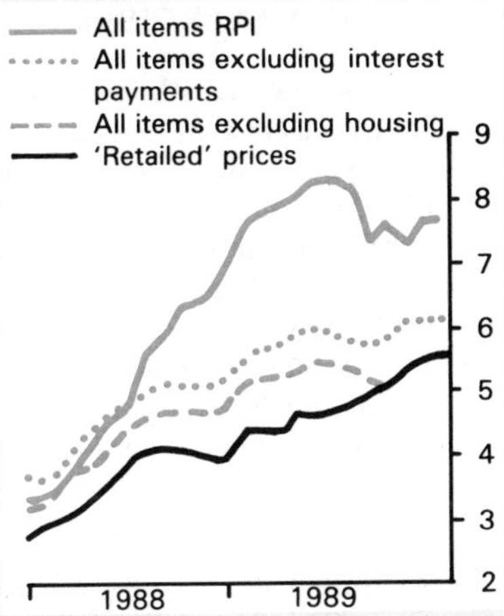

Questions

(Read all the questions before trying to answer)

1. How did the Bank of England think counter-inflation policy was working in August 1989?
2. What was the relationship between the rate of inflation, the rate of economic growth, and the condition of the labour market?
3. What differences do you note between the Bank's assessment in August 1989 and six months later?
4. To what extent are the rate of earnings growth and changes in unemployment related?
5. On the evidence here, do you think that wage increases adjust quickly to changes in monetary policy?
6. Are time-lags an important feature of the adjustment process?

Exam Preparation

PRACTICAL EXERCISES

1. (a) Assume that a bond promises to the holder £1 000 per year for ever. If the interest rate is 10 per cent, what is the bond worth now?
(b) Continue (a) above: what happens to the value of the bond if interest rates rise to 20 per cent? Fall to 5 per cent?
(c) Suppose there were an indestructible machine expected to generate £2 000 per year in revenues but costing £1 000 per year to maintain – for ever. How would that machine be priced relative to the bond described above in (a)?

2. Assume that M = £300 billion, P = £1.72, and Q = 900 billion units. What is the velocity of circulation?

MULTIPLE CHOICE QUESTIONS

1. All of the following measures would tend to reduce the rate of increase of the money supply *except*
A an increase in the rate of interest on gilts
B an increase in the value of Premium Bond prizes
C a reduction in the Public Sector Borrowing Requirement
D the sale of long-term government bonds to the banking sector
E the sale of Treasury bills to the discount houses

2. If undated government bonds originally sold for £1 000 with a nominal interest rate of 3%, and their price has since fallen to £200, their yield is now
A 3%
B 9%
C 15%
D 18%
E 25%

For Questions 3, 4, 5, and 6 select your answers from the following grid:

A	B	C	D	E
1, 2, 3 all correct	1, 2 only correct	2, 3 only correct	1 only correct	3 only correct

3. Which of the following motives affect(s) the demand for money which J. M. Keynes termed 'liquidity preference'?
1 transactions motive
2 precautionary motive
3 speculative motive

4. In the diagram below, the curve shows the aggregate demand for money.

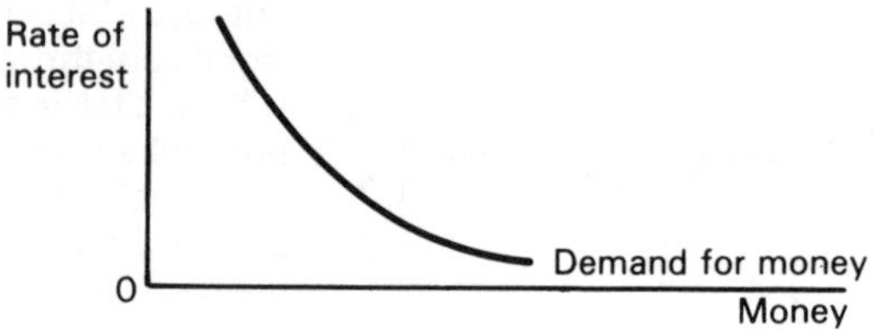

Which of the following would cause the curve to move to the right?
1 An increase in the general price level
2 An increase in national income
3 A fall in the rate of interest

5.

Year	*Money stock (£bn)*	*Money National Income (£bn)*	*Price Index (Year 1 = 100)*
1	40	120	100
2	45	140	120
3	50	160	140
4	55	180	160

From the above data relating to an economy it can be inferred that, between Year 1 and Year 4,
1 real National Income fell
2 the velocity of circulation was constant
3 the rate of inflation was constant

6. A rise in the supply of money will usually, other things remaining equal,
1 decrease the market rate of interest
2 raise the market price of financial assets
3 reduce the holdings of speculative money balances

RELATED ESSAY QUESTIONS

1. 'Monetarism in the UK has been a signal failure.' Would you agree?

2. (a) Distinguish between the money market and the long-term capital market.
(b) Describe and explain the influence of the Bank of England in each of these markets.

3. What methods are used to control the money supply? How successful have they been?

4. Outline briefly the main differences between Keynesian and monetarist approaches to monetary policy. In 1986 the money supply (sterling M3) grew by about 18 per cent whereas price inflation was about 3 per cent. What are the implications of this for government policy to control inflation?

5. (a) How does economic theory explain the determination of interest rates?
(b) Account for the present level of interest rates in the UK.

6. What problems face the Bank of England in attempting to control the supply of money?

7. 'Inflation is entirely a monetary phenomenon that can only be overcome by effective control of the money supply.' Discuss.

31 Fiscal Policy

Key Points to Review

- The objectives of government policy (10.1, 10.6)
- Using taxes to correct externalities (10.2)
- Government expenditure (10.7)
- Taxation (10.8)
- Fiscal policy in the Keynesian model (17.1, 17.2)

Questions for Preview

1 What are the objectives of fiscal policy?

2 How are taxes levied?

3 What are PSBR and PSDR?

4 How does fiscal policy affect interest rates and expenditure in the economy as a whole?

5 How does fiscal policy interact with monetary policy?

6 How does fiscal policy affect resource allocation?

7 What controversial issues have arisen in relation to fiscal policy?

Fiscal policy means the use of taxation and expenditure to achieve political ends. These ends are many and varied. A range of them was identified in Chapter 10. One of these – the achievement of economic objectives and stability – can be further broken down into three categories. These are influencing the allocation of resources, redistributing income and wealth, and macroeconomic control of the economy.

The government has a substantial effect on the allocation of resources towards consumption, investment, and exports. It achieves this partly through the operation of the tax system: taxes reduce disposable income and therefore personal consumption. This may affect both the pattern and the level of investment. Further, discriminatory taxes on firms affect the profitability, and therefore the level, of investment. Also, because fiscal policy affects aggregate demand, it influences the levels of imports and, indirectly, of exports.

In seeking to *control the economy*, the government will try to promote economic growth, stable prices, low levels of unemployment and will try to avoid balance-of-trade deficits. It will usually be difficult to achieve all these at once but governments act according to their priorities at any given time.

Expansionary fiscal policies will promote economic growth and high levels of employment. They may lead to inflation accelerating. They may well lead to increases in imports. Further, the buoyant home market may deter firms from exporting, which demands more effort than home sales. So expansion may produce an external deficit. Contractionary policies reduce inflation, but also growth and employment. However, imports will fall, and firms will turn to export markets to maintain sales. So the balance of trade will improve, and a current account surplus may develop.

In a quite different way, the government influences the *allocation of resources* on a microeconomic level. By taxing some products and subsidizing others a particular consumption pattern is promoted. In the UK economy, owner occupation of houses is subsidized while alcohol, tobacco, and petrol are taxed.

Fiscal policy can be used to *redistribute income and wealth*. Progressive income taxes raise funds which can provide benefits for those who are badly off. Capital gains tax and inheritance tax reduce somewhat the value of individuals' holdings of wealth.

Different governments have different approaches to fiscal policy. During the 1980s fiscal policy became steadily less and less important as a macroeconomic policy tool. Nevertheless the major shift from public deficit to public surplus had a significant effect on the economy. Rather less redistribution of income took place. This had an effect on the overall distribution of income and wealth.

Significant changes took place in the way resources were allocated. Privatization, changes in the composition of public spending, and tax changes, all contributed.

Raising Revenue – Taxation

Tax revenues are needed for a range of purposes. They must, first, raise revenue simply to finance expenditure. But they may also be used to redistribute income and wealth, to affect consumption patterns, and to influence the level of aggregate demand. Obviously taxes which raise substantial revenue will also be effective in reducing aggregate demand.

Each tax has its own role to play in meeting government objectives. The composition of tax revenue has important effects on the economy. Figure 31.1 shows the relative contributions of each kind of tax to total tax revenue.

Figure 31.1
UK Tax Revenue 1988

	Revenue (£bn)	*% of total revenue*
Direct taxes		
Income tax	43.7	26.2
Corporation tax	15.8	9.5
National Insurance	31.7	19.0
Total	91.2	54.7
Property taxes		
Rates	18.4	11.0
Inheritance tax	1.1	0.7
Capital gains tax	3.7	2.2
Total	23.2	13.9
Expenditure taxes		
Excise taxes (alcohol, tobacco, betting, petrol)	20.4	12.2
VAT	28.7	17.2
Customs duties, etc.	1.6	1.0
Total	50.7	30.4
Revenue from North Sea oil	*1.5*	*0.9*
Total	116.6	100.0

Source: *UK National Accounts, 1989.*

Direct Taxes

These are levied directly on incomes and profits. *Income tax* is progressive in two respects. The personal allowances are tax free. Subsequent income is taxed at the standard rate of 25 per cent, up to a limit of £20 700 (in financial year 1990–1). Beyond that, additional tax is payable at a marginal rate of 40 per cent. So tax as a proportion of income rises as income rises. Income tax applies not only to wages and salaries but also to unearned income from interest, profits, and rent. It is therefore important as a revenue raiser, as a means of redistributing income, and as a means of reducing aggregate demand. It is the progressive nature of income tax which makes it effective as an automatic stabilizer, reducing demand when incomes are high and may exceed output, and increasing demand when incomes are low and unemployment is an increasing problem.

Corporation Tax is levied on firms' profits at a rate of 35 per cent; generally it contributes only a small amount to total tax revenue. In the past it was levied with allowances for investment so as to subsidize capital investment. This was inadvisable at a time of high unemployment and the present arrangements no longer encourage investments with low rates of return.

National Insurance Charges (NICs) include both the employers' and employees' contributions. Up to an income level of £14 800 contributions rise with income. (Very low incomes are exempt.) Above that level, contributions are constant. The employees' contributions are not unlike an income tax although they are less progressive. It should be remembered that an increase in income will be subject to both increased tax and increased NIC. So the marginal rate of taxation at some income levels is about 35 per cent. The employer's contribution, by contrast, is in effect a pay-roll tax. It raises the cost of employing labour. Recent changes in the rates at which it is levied attempt to modify its impact so that employers are encouraged to take on more low-paid labour and reduce unemployment. The main function of NICs is to raise revenue for the payment of benefits.

Property Taxes

Rates have contributed substantially to local authority revenue. (The other major component is the Rate Support Grant paid by central government.) Since they are levied on property, their impact varies. The *Community charge*, replaced rates for households from April 1990. Set at a fixed amount, within each area, for all able-bodied adults, its precise impact will be unclear for some time. It is known that it will be more expensive than rates to collect. People dependent on benefits will pay 20 per cent of the flat rate. It is intended to increase the accountability of local government.

Inheritance tax will continue to be levied on the estates of the richer deceased. *Capital transfer tax* – which was levied on gifts made during a person's lifetime – was abolished in the 1986 budget. It had led to problems in keeping businesses intact over time. This does mean that gifts are once again a means of avoiding death duties. These taxes are (or were) aimed at redistributing wealth by reducing the amount of wealth concentrated in the hands of a few individuals.

Capital gains tax is levied on the increase in the value of property. This means that owners of shares which show substantial capital growth must pay tax on the capital gain when they come to sell the shares.

Expenditure Taxes

Excise taxes are generally levied at a flat rate – so many pence per item. **Value added tax (VAT)**, in contrast, takes 15 per cent of value added at each stage of production. The value added is the revenue from sales minus the cost of inputs other than land, labour, and capital. It is the value added *by* the factors of production.

In principle, expenditure taxes tend to be more regressive than income taxes. They are seen mainly as revenue raisers. They also serve to reduce consumption of harmful goods such as tobacco and alcohol, and of goods which are potentially scarce in the long run, such as petrol. In practice, because VAT is not levied on food for home preparation, fuel, housing, public transport, and printed matter, it is not very regressive in its impact.

North Sea Oil Revenue

This includes petroleum revenue tax (PRT), royalties, and licence fees. Falling oil prices have reduced these revenues although some of this reduction can be claimed back if the excise duty on petrol is raised.

The Composition of Tax Revenue

The balance between direct and indirect taxation can be varied to suit circumstances. While income tax must always be the most effective tax for redistributive purposes, it is evaded (illegally) and avoided (legally) in a number of ways, thus losing some of its usefulness. Expenditure taxes tend to be more regressive because poorer individuals spend a higher proportion of their incomes than do richer individuals. They can be expensive to collect, but are harder to avoid than direct taxes.

During the 1970s, with VAT at 8 per cent, the UK was deriving more revenue than now from direct taxes. Other European countries relied more heavily on indirect taxes. The Conservative government shifted the balance markedly in 1979, reducing income taxes and raising VAT. It had many reasons, giving as the primary reason improving the incentive to work. The reduced income redistribution which resulted from the change was in line with Conservative political philosophy of encouraging people to take care of themselves.

If tax evasion and avoidance become more of a problem a further shift towards expenditure taxes might be considered advisable. (Now read Key Points 31.1.)

Revenue and Expenditure

To the extent that government expenditure exceeds revenue, there must be borrowing. The annual amount needed to cover the difference between spending and tax revenue (the deficit) is the **public sector borrowing requirement (PSBR).** The accumulated past debt – the sum total of all government debt outstanding – is the **National Debt**. Borrowing may be financed by selling Treasury bills (for short-term borrowing), or bonds (for long-term borrowing).

When revenues exceed expenditure, there is a surplus known as the **public sector debt repayment**. The surplus funds can be used to buy back bonds, reducing the size of the National Debt.

Whether the government is in surplus or deficit depends upon a number of factors. One is the state of the trade cycle; another, interest rates.

The Trade Cycle

During the boom phase of the trade cycle, high incomes generate large tax revenues. Unemployment is low so benefits are less costly. Automatically, the government's finances move towards surplus. Conversely in a slump, benefits rise, tax revenues fall, and a deficit is likely to develop (or get larger). Discretionary fiscal policy can be used similarly: taxes can be reduced and government expenditure increased if there are resources in the economy which are unemployed because of a deficiency of demand. Other things being equal, PSBR would grow if incomes were falling or stagnating and diminish if incomes were rising. If there

Key Points 31.1

- **Taxation is used to raise revenue, to redistribute income and wealth, and to control the level of aggregate demand, and to influence the allocation of resources.**
- **Taxes may be levied by indirect and direct methods and the balance between the two can be varied according to circumstances.**
- **In 1979 there was a shift towards greater emphasis on expenditure taxes in the UK.**

is a PSDR, it will shrink when incomes fall and grow if they rise.

Interest Rates

To finance a PSBR the Bank of England will want to sell government bonds. To induce the public to buy them, attractive interest rates must be paid. The government can obtain finance relatively cheaply because it can guarantee repayment, based on its right to tax. (Bonds are often known as gilts – they are as good as gold.) But the more finance it needs, the higher the rate of interest on bonds must be.

If there is a deficit, the government may need to borrow on a large scale. It will compete for funds in the money markets with private borrowers contemplating investment projects. If high interest rates are available on government bonds, the returns to private investment will need to compare favourably, or few people will be prepared to invest. So it is possible for government borrowing to make private investment more expensive. Governments never want to discourage investment. An urge to keep interest rates down for this reason can cause governments to cut PSBR.

A surplus, which can be used to buy back government bonds, should in theory help to keep interest rates down. It will reduce the burden of future interest payments and should lead to taxes being lower than would otherwise have been possible. Conservative governments tend to see this as a higher priority than other parties would. They welcome it as a way of reducing the scope of the public sector.

Financing a Deficit: the Options

We have seen that the size of a deficit may have some effect on interest rates. Financing it affects monetary growth in other ways also. To see this we must examine the ways in which a PSBR can be funded.

We have identified two ways of financing a PSBR: the sale of bonds and bills. **Treasury bills** raise finance for three months. They can be used to make good the weekly shortfall between spending and revenue. They are very liquid reserve assets to the banks which are the main providers of bill finance. **Bonds** raise long-term funds from a wide range of sources such as individuals, and from financial institutions such as pension funds. There are two other sources of finance. A major source is **National Savings** (non-marketable debt). For the government, this is very favourable because it pays relatively low interest rates and the funds are cheap and reliable. For savers, funds kept in National Savings are very liquid and convenient. A fourth source of finance is the Bank of England. By itself holding bonds, the Bank can create credit. One way in which it may do this is by **expanding the note issue**. It holds bonds as backing for the note issue. (Where notes are the *liabilities* of the Bank of England, bonds are the corresponding *assets*.) The Bank of England may hold more bonds, making a loan to the government which it then spends. The note issue is increased, the recipients of the government spending place the funds in their bank accounts, and banks' balances with the Bank of England rise. This is base, or high-powered, money and will allow banks to create extra credit by a multiple of the original increase in their liquid reserves.

So increasing government borrowing by this method would lead to expansion of the money stock through credit creation. What of the other sources of finance? The sale of Treasury bills has a similar effect. A Treasury bill bought by a bank gives the government funds to spend. The recipients deposit those funds in their banks. The bank has less cash, but still has the bill, which is a very liquid asset. Overall its reserve asset position is unchanged except that it now has, in addition, the increased deposits resulting from the government's spending. So it can create more credit. Borrowing from the Bank of England, and increasing the issue of Treasury bills, are together known as monetary finance.

The other forms of government borrowing have a very different effect. National Savings involve a straight transfer to the government from the small saver. No banks, and no credit creation, are involved. Bonds sold to people, and institutions other than banks, similarly involve no credit creation. (Remember open-market operations? The sale of bonds reduced banks' balances

Key Points 31.2

- **The PSBR covers the government's deficit. It is the amount which the government must borrow in any given year to cover the difference between expenditure and tax revenue.**
- **PSBR will tend to rise in a recession and fall in a boom because of automatic stabilizers; discretionary policy may also be used in the same way.**
- **A large PSBR may require higher interest rates.**
- **Unless it is financed by bond sales or National Savings, government borrowing may increase the inflation rate.**
- **If tax revenue exceeds government expenditure there will be a surplus or PSDR.**

with the Bank of England. But in this case, the increased government spending will lead recipients to deposit an equal amount with their banks, so there is no change at all in the banks' reserve asset position.)

In conclusion, a government with a tight monetary policy will finance a deficit from a combination of National Savings and bond sales. The former tend to stay fairly constant over time so any increase in PSBR means more bonds must be sold. If this means raising interest rates, the government may prefer to avoid increasing its deficit. (Now read Key Points 31.2.)

The Shift to Surplus

Because unemployment rose in the early 1980s, there was a big increase in government spending on benefits. So PSBR stayed fairly high. Eventually, however, the PSBR began to fall. Cuts in spending on housing and other local-government responsibilities helped. Council house sales brought in revenue. Privatization increased receipts substantially. Rising incomes increased revenue from both direct and indirect taxes.

Figure 31.2 shows how the deficit swung into surplus, and the size of the contribution from privatization.

It should be noted that deficits and surpluses are not easy to predict, and can be surprises. They are the difference between two very large numbers. Revenue depends on income levels and will change as do incomes. Spending depends on changes in the economy: if unemployment changes, social security payments change. Neither can always be predicted precisely.

Figure 31.2
Deficit and Surplus

Year	*PSBR (−)/PSDR (+) (£ bn)*	*% of GDP*	*Privatization proceeds (£ bn)*
1977	−5.5	3.8	–
1978	−8.2	4.9	–
1979	−12.6	6.4	0.37
1980	−11.8	5.1	0.40
1981	−10.5	4.1	0.49
1982	−4.9	1.8	0.49
1983	−11.6	3.8	1.14
1984	−10.3	3.2	2.13
1985	−5.7	2.1	2.70
1986	−3.4	0.6	4.42
1987	+3.5	0.4	4.10
1988	+14.4	3.6	7.0
1989 (est.)	+13	–	–

Source: *CSO Economic Trends,* 1989; A. Griffiths and S. Wall, *Applied Economics,* 1989; and Treasury: *Economic Progress Report,* Feb. 1990.

The 1980s Experience

Traditionally fiscal policy has been used to control aggregate demand. With the advent of monetarism, however, fiscal policy (in the macroeconomic sense) became subordinate to monetary policy. The argument is that fiscal expansion can do little to create employment, but will lead to inflation. This inflation must be controlled by a tight monetary policy, which must be supported by fiscal contraction, and in particular by minimizing government borrowing.

This fitted neatly with the Conservative government's objective of reducing the scale of the public sector. As soon as inflation became less threatening in the mid-1980s, the government sought to cut income tax rates, partly in order to create incentives to work. This too reduces the role of fiscal macroeconomic policy. If taxes must be kept down to preserve incentives then the option of raising taxes to curb excess demand no longer exists.

Taxes are still important both as a means of raising revenue and as a means of influencing the allocation of resources. Examples of the latter include the reduction in taxes on unleaded petrol, and the reduction of National Insurance charges on low-paid workers (designed to encourage the creation of more jobs by making labour cheaper to employ).

It should be remembered that a wide range of fiscal policy options continues to exist, even if they are not all in use at the present time. Furthermore not all fiscal policies are widely advertised. Governments can cut tax *rates* while tax *revenues* are rising because incomes are rising. And government spending is still a significant percentage of GDP. (Now read Key Points 31.3.)

Some Fiscal Policy Issues

Over the years a number of aspects of fiscal policy have become controversial. One controversy surrounds **tax expenditures**. These occur when a tax-free allowance is given for some particular reason. Mortgage interest and

Key Points 31.3

- **The UK government swung into budget surplus in 1987.**
- **Fiscal policy has in recent years been used mainly as a complement to monetary policy.**
- **Fiscal policies can be used to achieve microeconomic objectives.**

Figure 31.3
National Debt as a Proportion of GDP

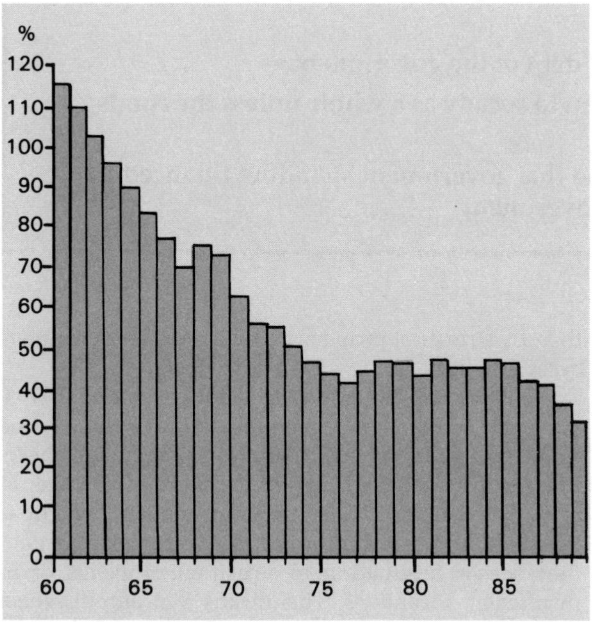

Source: *BEQB*, 1984 and 1989.

pension contributions are both subject to tax relief, and there are now some tax benefits for people buying shares. Tax expenditures are controversial in that they are not recorded in government spending totals, but they do considerably reduce tax revenues and are of great benefit to the recipients. (This issue is taken up in a Case Study on page 496.)

An Old Debate: Is the National Debt a Burden?

It is true that the National Debt grew continuously until 1987. However, the total National Debt is not what we should look at to analyse the burden of the debt. Figure 31.3 shows that in relation to GDP the National Debt has been falling steadily. One reason for this is that the government borrows in money terms. If it sells a bond it borrows, say, £100. If the bond matures twenty years later the holder is still repaid £100. But by then inflation has reduced the real value of the repayment to very much less. As a borrower the government gains from inflation. The lenders lose.

It is possible that more borrowing in the future could increase the interest burden. It should be remembered that this would not be a *national* burden, however. It involves transfer payments from one group of people (taxpayers) to another (holders of government bonds). If, on the other hand, bonds are sold abroad, then interest payments are made to foreigners, and are an outflow of funds on the invisibles account of the balance of payments. Whether or not increased borrowing makes sense depends partly, therefore, on what sort of spending it will finance. If it is spent on investment it should yield an income in the future which will cover the interest and repayment of the debt. The investment could be in plant and machinery, or in infrastructure – roads, say – or in education, which is investment in human capital and makes people more productive.

A More Recent Debate: Does Government Spending Crowd Out Private-Sector Investment?

If there is a limited supply of credit, and the government offers higher interest rates, it will be able to borrow more. On the other hand, private-sector demanders of credit may respond to higher interest rates by demanding a smaller quantity of credit. Then higher interest rates ultimately result in the government obtaining a greater amount of the total credit supplied than previously. Hence the government borrowing has 'crowded out' private borrowing. The reduced growth rate of private investment leads, via the multiplier, to a reduced growth in income, output, and employment. Offsetting this is a *greater* growth of government spending and, via the multiplier, an increased growth in output, income, and employment. The net effect is to *reduce* the expansionary effect of any government spending. The crowding-out effect is shown in Figure 31.4.

Awareness of the crowding-out effect dates back to Adam Smith. Keynes was also concerned with crowding out, as we see in his *General Theory of Employment, Interest and Money*.

If, for example, a Government employs 100 000 additional men on public works, and if the multiplier . . . is 4, it is not safe to assume that aggregate employment will increase by 400 000. For the new policy may have *adverse reactions on investment* in other directions . . . The method of financing the policy and the increased working cash, required by the increased

Figure 31.4
Crowding Out

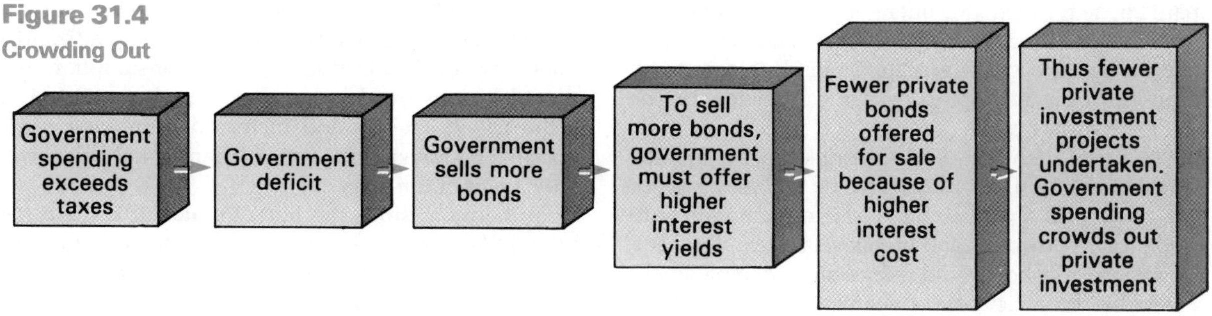

Key Points 31.4

- **Tax expenditures are tax-free allowances which reduce total tax paid, and are significant.**
- **The National Debt is the accumulated total debt of the government.**
- **Interest on the National Debt is not a burden to society as a whole unless the funds were borrowed abroad.**
- **Critics of expansionary fiscal policy contend that government spending financed by deficits leads to a crowding out of private investment.**

employment and the associated rise of prices, may have the effect of increasing the rate of interest and so *retarding investment in other directions.*

It should be pointed out that increased government borrowing does not always require higher interest rates. Increased government spending may occur at a time when private investment is low anyway, because of gloomy business expectations. The evidence that crowding out actually happens is rather scanty. (Now read Key Points 31.4.)

Has Government Borrowing Been Inflationary?

Chapter 17 showed how Keynesian fiscal policies developed. Until the late 1960s, counter-cyclical fiscal policies were quite successful in stabilizing economies. Then unemployment began to rise. The standard Keynesian response would have been to increase aggregate demand by increasing government spending, reducing taxes, and perhaps using expansionary monetary policies as well.

But from the start of the 1970s inflation began to accelerate and remained a major threat. In these circumstances expansionary fiscal policy can lead to accelerating inflation rather than increased output and employment. The crucial question is whether there is underutilized capacity in the economy or whether supply constraints will prevent output from growing further. If there is spare capacity then the unemployment is at least partly due to demand deficiency and expansionary policies may be effective. The implication is that the economy is operating on the horizontal section of the aggregate supply curve. If there is no spare capacity, then the unemployment is rooted in structural problems and immobilities, and will not be reduced by increased aggregate demand: the economy is on the upward-sloping or vertical section of the aggregate supply curve.

While not denying that unemployment can be structural in origin, Keynesians would still see a role for fiscal policy in maintaining a stable economy with good growth prospects and high levels of employment. Expansionary policy would reduce any unemployment caused by the deficiency of aggregate demand rather than by structural problems. This is known as counter-cyclical policy.

Monetarists have drawn different conclusions. They have observed that governments have had some difficulty in forecasting changes accurately and therefore in producing the right amount of change in aggregate demand. They see cyclical unemployment as transient and short-term in nature. Unemployment they see as originating in structural problems or in insufficient incentives. This means that output *cannot* increase rapidly to meet increased aggregate demand and that fiscal expansion will therefore lead to accelerating inflation. So the monetarist policy prescription is the **fixed throttle**: aggregate monetary demand should be allowed to grow at the same rate as productive capacity. So demand would grow exactly in line with the long-run trend in output. Alongside these views on fiscal policy, monetarists hold that control of inflation makes restrictive monetary policy essential. The net effect of this is to downgrade the importance of fiscal policy: it becomes an important buttress to the prevailing monetary policy. It is not used in its own right but as part of an overall package.

This approach calls for unemployment to be dealt with by means of microeconomic measures rather than by expanding aggregate demand. These policies seek to make labour more mobile, to improve information, and to increase generally the efficiency with which the labour market functions. These policies are examined in Chapter 33.

Clearly, if the economy is close to full-capacity output, increased government spending or tax cuts can lead to excess demand, overheating, supply constraints, and accelerating inflation. However, fiscal policies have tended to be tight since 1976. In spite of the tax cuts of 1987 and 1988, overall there was a fiscal surplus developing, albeit one owing much to privatization. These tax cuts did lead to increased consumption, but the subsequent overheating owed much to other factors – the fall in savings and increased borrowing made possible by house price appreciation. Fiscal policy was only a part of the story.

Furthermore since the mid- to late-1970s there has been little recourse to monetary finance (i.e. funding the deficit by selling treasury bills and increasing the note issue). Figure 31.5 shows that most government

Figure 31.5

Composition of the Sterling National Debt

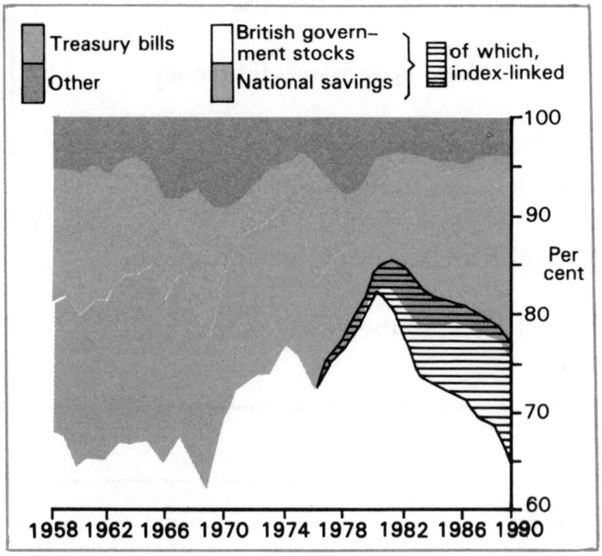

Source: *BEQB*, 1989.

debt is covered by bond sales or National Savings, which do not add to the money stock.

Can Expansionary Policy Create Jobs?

As we have seen, the Keynesian view would be that if there are unemployed labour and capital in the economy, fiscal expansion could lead to increasing output without accelerating inflation.

The monetarist view is that the economy is usually quite close to full-capacity output, and unemployment is predominantly structural. Fiscal expansion creates inflation, not jobs. Unemployment must be tackled by policies to make the labour market more flexible.

The conclusion depends upon the nature of the labour market and to some extent upon your political view.

Do Taxes Act as a Disincentive to Work?

It has been strongly felt by politicians that tax cuts create an incentive to work harder. The evidence for this is rather sketchy. A study in the US found that there was some evidence of a rise in incentives when top tax rates were cut from 60 to 45 per cent.

Cutting the top UK income tax rate to 40 per cent may not have reduced tax revenue by much. When marginal rates are lower people have less incentive to avoid tax (legally) or evade tax (illegally). So a larger share of higher incomes has been taxed.

At the other end of the scale, there is strong evidence that low-paid workers and unemployed people face disincentives. A low-paid worker who gets an increase in income may find that tax payments together with lost benefits (which are usually means-tested) take most or all of their increased income. Unemployed people with families may be little better off in work. The long-term unemployed are especially vulnerable. Recent changes in the way benefits are calculated have reduced this disincentive but not eliminated it. Perhaps a million or more families are affected to some degree by very high effective marginal tax rates.

How Have Contractionary Policies Worked?

When fiscal and monetary policies reduce aggregate monetary demand they cut the demand for many firms' products. These firms will begin to make losses. They may contract, making some of their workforce redundant, or they may close, reducing employment still further. If they face rising costs of production they will be unable to pass them on in the form of higher prices, because if they did sales would fall further.

In this situation, with unemployment rising, demands for higher wages will be somewhat reduced. Trade unions will know that higher wages will create more losses and thus contract the number of jobs further. Wage settlements will be gradually reduced. In theory the knowledge that tight fiscal and monetary policies will be introduced and adhered to could induce unions to accept lower wage settlements. In practice unions must advance the interests of their working members, and unemployment may rise substantially before they are pressured into accepting less. So while contractionary policy does reduce inflation, it may do so at quite a high cost in terms of lost output and employment. Also, inflation may have responded favourably to other influences, such as falling commodity or oil prices. This seems to have been a major factor in keeping inflation low during 1986. (Now read Key Points 31.5 on page 394.)

Key Points 31.5

- **If the economy is close to full-capacity output, fiscal expansion can cause excess demand and accelerating inflation.**
- **Keynesians think fiscal expansion can create jobs if there is demand-deficiency unemployment.**
- **Monetarists think fiscal expansion will always lead to inflation.**
- **In practice, government deficits have mostly been financed in non-inflationary ways.**
- **Taxes can sometimes act as a disincentive especially for people on low incomes or benefits.**
- **Tight fiscal and monetary policies can reduce inflation but the loss of output and employment may be substantial.**

CASE STUDY

Why is Public Spending so Hard to Control?

Figure 31.6
Public Spending, 1980–93 at 1990–1 prices (£bn)

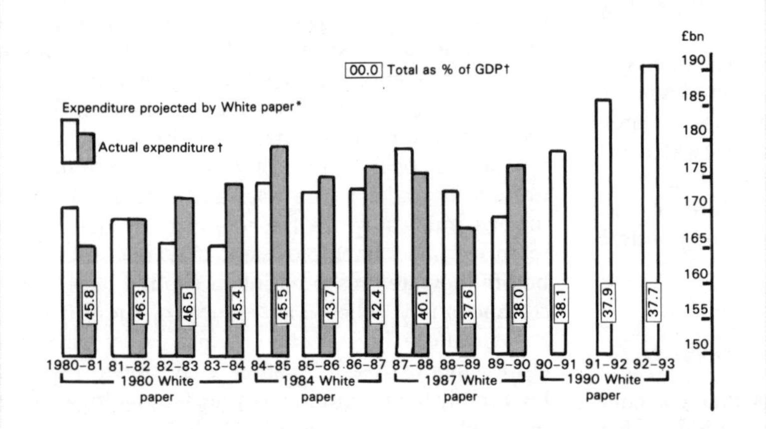

*'Planning total' †Includes debt interest and other adjustments not in 'planning total'

Thatcherism in the 1980s meant more public spending. Mrs Thatcher or her successors are unlikely to reverse that trend in the present decade.

In March 1980 the recently elected government of Mrs Thatcher presented its first detailed plans to cut public expenditure. Its aim was relatively modest – to reduce spending by about 3 per cent in real terms over four years – but marked a clear change in direction from the outgoing Labour government, which had been planning annual rises of around 2 per cent.

In practice, the first four years of the 1980s saw not a fall but a rise in public spending – by just over 6 per cent in real terms. Over the rest of the decade expenditure repeatedly rose and fell without showing any clear trend. But the government's plans for the first three years of the 1990s, published on 30 January 1990, show that spending is expected to rise by 8 per cent by 1992–3.

What has gone wrong? In terms of reducing the relative burden of public expenditure on taxpayers, arguably nothing. By stemming the growth in its expenditure during the late 1980s, when the economy was growing quickly, the government cut spending substantially as a proportion of GDP – from 46 to around 38 per cent.

That achievement was impressive in international terms: of the other six leading industrial economies, only Canada and West Germany have significantly reduced the public-spending share below its all-time peak, both by much less than Britain. Only two of the big seven, the Americans and the Japanese, now spend less of their income publicly than the British. In 1980 the Canadians and Italians did too; in 1970 so did the

French and Germans.

Nevertheless, the failure to stem the rise in the absolute volume of public expenditure is a bitter disappointment to the keenest Thatcherites. The happy combination in the late 1980s of falling tax rates and rising public-sector surpluses may prove an aberration – destroyed in the 1990s by slower growth, the end of windfall revenues from privatization, and the growing burden of supporting the elderly.

Why, then, did public spending not fall as planned? Partly because reducing the size and scope of the state has not drastically cut its cost. There has been little change in the number of people employed directly by central and local government – about one-sixth of the workforce. Their pay grew by 17 per cent in real terms during the 1980s, according to new estimates by the Public Finance Foundation. But private-sector pay grew faster – by 29 per cent. In the 1990s, when labour scarcities develop public-sector workers will be pressing to catch up.

The number of people working for nationalized industries halved between 1980 and 1987. The £3bn being paid to them via subsidies in 1980 had by 1987 been cut to £300m; in 1988 state industries for the first time showed a surplus. But that surplus lasted only one year, and the remaining state firms are expected to run up annual deficits of £1.5bn in 1991–3.

Most trimming of public-spending programmes has been at the margin. Only housing has been slashed, by 67 per cent between 1979–80 and 1989–90. That saved £7bn; about half as much was devoted to a 53 per cent rise in spending on law and order. But the overwhelming influence on the public expenditure total comes from four big programmes – social security, health, education, and defence – which between them cost £123bn, 70 per cent of all spending.

Social Security

Welfare benefits are by far the biggest item of government spending costing over £50bn – and one of the hardest to control. Over the government's first five years in office they grew 30 per cent in real terms, fuelled by rising unemployment. After 1987 the total declined slightly, as unemployment fell. But the one big reform of the 1980s, the 1986 Social Security Act, did little to control the overall level. The social security budget is still determined largely by demographic and economic trends rather than government decisions.

In the next three years those trends will again lead to a sharp increase – estimated at 12.5 per cent in real terms, or an extra £6.6bn in today's prices. Nearly half the rise will go to pensioners; their numbers will increase by only 1 per cent, but their benefits will rise 10 per cent.

Figure 31.7

Social security

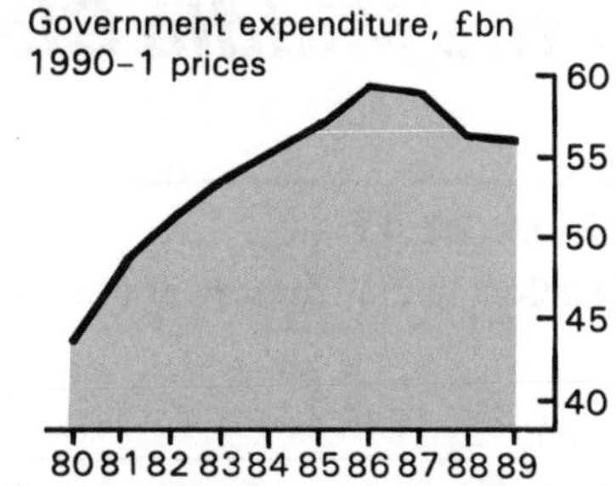

Source: White Paper. Years beg. April

Health

Ministers have a ready answer to critics who say they neglect the National Health Service: real spending on it rose by more than 30 per cent in the 1980s. Certainly the health needs of an ageing population have risen too, as have the costs of modern medicine; there is no neutral way of measuring whether spending has kept pace. Hospitals treated 23 per cent more in-patients and 16 per cent more out-patients in 1988 than a decade before.

A 9 per cent real rise in health spending projected for the next three years will go disproportionately to family-practitioner services.

Figure 31.8

Health

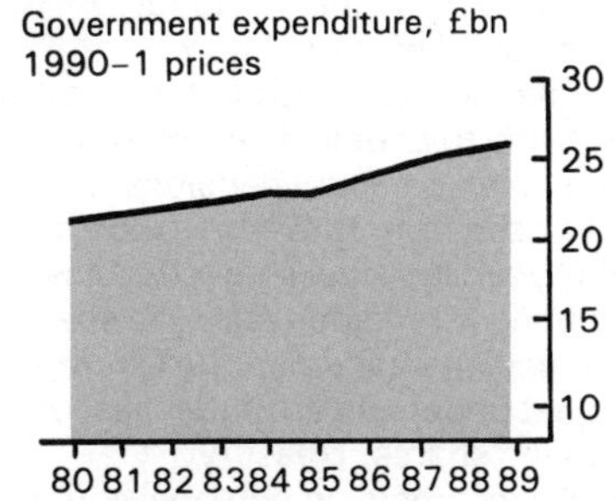

Source: White Paper. Years beg. April

Education

Demand for schooling dropped during the 1980s with the declining number of children; the supply of schools and teachers dropped by less. Today the state supports one teacher for every 17 pupils, compared to one for every 19 in 1980. The training demands imposed by the national curriculum will make it difficult to go back to the higher ratio.

In the 1990s when pupil numbers rise the education budget will rise. Spending on polytechnics and universities will grow by 7.5 per cent in real terms by 1992–3. Student numbers are forecast to rise 10 per cent by 1992, stabilize until 1995, and then grow again.

Figure 31.9

Education and science

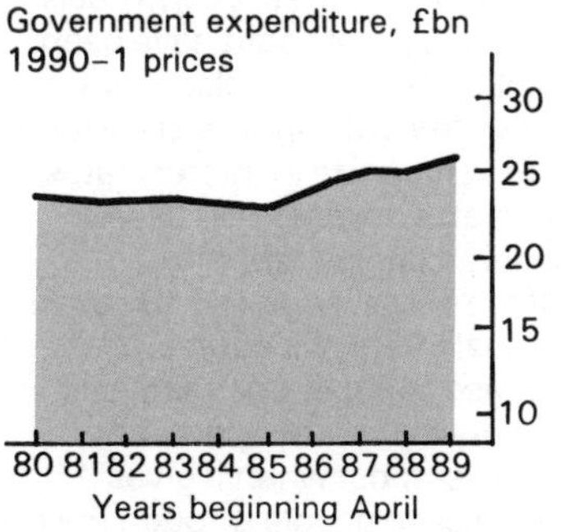

Source: White Paper.

Defence

Britain's replacement of its Polaris submarines with Trident is already causing a switch from conventional to nuclear forces; ministers are not inclined to jump too quickly on a bandwagon that might cut troops further. But by next summer the prime minister might be looking for a grand gesture which could be incorporated into the last pre-election spending round. Fewer guns, more butter might well fit the bill.

Source: *The Economist*, 3 Feb. 1990.

Figure 31.10

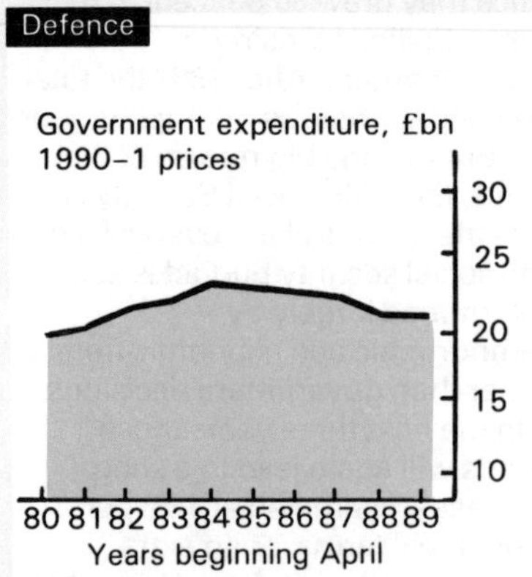

Source: White Paper.

Questions

1. How did public expenditure change during the 1980s?
2. What trends are expected in the 1990s?
3. Identify general reasons why spending may rise.
4. Identify reasons for increased spending within individual departments. Why have spending cuts proved so difficult to implement?

CASE STUDY

The Growing Cost of Propping up a Welfare State for the Middle Class

The government takes pride in its tough attitude towards public spending. Yet there is a vast area in its domain where it has presided over very sharp increases with scant public debate.

The only item which receives some public scrutiny is mortgage interest relief. This rose by a cool 27 per cent to £7bn last year. That is real money that could have been spent on something else. It was easily a record and was occasioned by the sharp rise in interest rates, on what is now a broad base of owner-occupied property.

If the Treasury gives £1bn to, say, the coal industry it counts as an increase in public spending and appears in the main part of the document; but when it gives subsidies to people through the tax system it counts as a reduction in revenue.

Subsidies to pension funds (including employers' and employees' contributions and lump-sum payments) now gobble up £10bn a year.

But the tax subsidies to watch are the new ones which the government has gone out of its way to encourage and which (because they are open-ended) could become the mortgage interest relief of the future.

Figure 31.11

The Cost to the Treasury of Mortgage Interest Relief (at current prices)

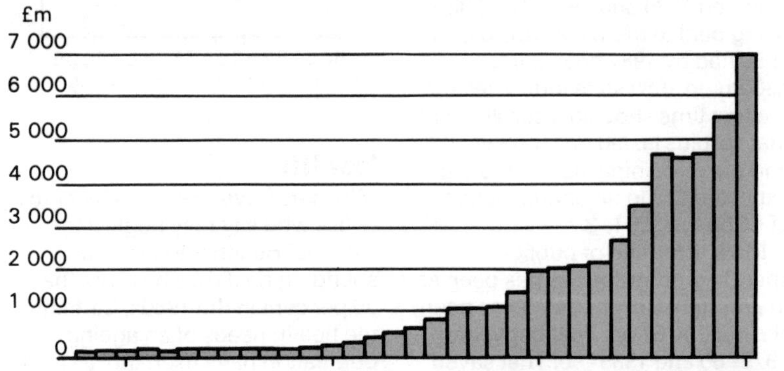

Source: Inland Revenue

The most dramatic of these is the subsidy to people who take out their own personal pensions. This has risen from nowhere to £800m this year. It is now so big that it is limiting Mr Major's ability to spend money in other areas. Just starting to get underway are subsidies for buying shares. Treasury disbursements on personal equity plans, employee profit-sharing, and the business expansion scheme came to a comparatively modest £100m in 1989–90, but with plenty of scope for improvement.

This area could grow and grow. Some City analysts reckon the tax perks available for buying shares will be more financially attractive than mortgage interest relief during the 1990s when share prices may outperform a stagnating housing market.

The interesting point about these subsidies is that if they were abolished then income taxes could be reduced very substantially. People who didn't know better might think that the existence of these subsidies would be a gold-mine of opportunity for someone like Mrs Thatcher, who wants to reduce the overall burden of taxation. After all, she has been very active in removing subsidies from the poor, from the unemployed, and from industry in the public and private sectors.

But instead of reducing them she is actually moving strongly in the other direction, to the extent that the cost of them is beginning to hamper her tax-cutting ambitions. Even at this late stage she is reported to be trying to persuade the Treasury to *increase* mortgage interest relief in next month's budget to assuage the people she lured into home ownership only to knock them on the head with high interest rates.

It is all a question of priorities. All the billions which the Treasury shells out on shares and homes (and, soon, private health for old people) is money which is available to be spent on education, training, science, or industrial investment, all of which have been, or are about to be, squeezed.

There is little immediate political return from giving more money for science or training or even education, but there is from the warm glow of people making effortless money.

Or, there was until recently. It is now clear that the huge increase in the value of people's homes has helped to wreck the government's counter-inflationary policy. People borrowed on the security of inflated house values to buy consumer goods (mainly imported) and when interest rates were raised to try to douse demand this fuelled inflation further as wage-bargainers sought to recoup the increased cost of interest rates.

These tax subsidies go, almost by definition, to people who are better off. The poor don't own their own houses and can't afford personal equity plans or private health care.

Mortgage interest relief has become such a deeply ingrained part of our culture that it is very difficult for any party to pledge to abolish it. They fear they simply won't get back into office if they do because the majority of voters will deem themselves to be 'losers', even though they would be beneficiaries of the tax cuts which abolition could finance.

Future historians may look back critically at a nation which gave more importance to feathering its own financial nest than laying down the seed-corn for future prosperity. If you don't feed the industrial geese, they won't deliver the nest-eggs for tomorrow.

Source: *Guardian*, 14 Feb. 1990.

Questions

1. What is meant by the term 'tax expenditures'?
2. Estimate the total cost of tax expenditures in 1989–90.
3. By how much could total expenditure rise if tax expenditures were abolished?
4. What are the most important types of tax expenditure?
5. What effect do tax expenditures have on the distribution of income and wealth?
6. Why would abolition be difficult?
7. What are the arguments for abolition of tax expenditures?

Exam Preparation

MULTIPLE CHOICE QUESTIONS

1. Which of the following methods of financing an increase in the public-sector borrowing requirement will lead to an increase in the money supply?

A sales of securities to the overseas sector
B a sale of securities to the non-bank private sector
C sales of Treasury bills that are purchased by the banking system
D sales of securities to the banking system.

2. Which of the following is the most accurate description of the National Debt?

A The annual gap between government expenditure and tax revenue
B The amount of money owed by the United Kingdom to the IMF
C The net accumulation of UK balance-of-payments deficits
D The net accumulation of UK budget deficits
E The total amount of outstanding UK foreign debt

3. Which of the following measures would be inflationary?

A The sale by the Bank of England of securities on the open market
B The ending of existing restrictions on consumer credit
C A rise in direct taxes
D A decrease in the amount of money in circulation

E A call for Special Deposits from the commercial banks

4. According to monetarists, public-sector investment 'crowds out' private-sector investment as a result of a rise in
A the money supply
B interest rates
C aggregate demand
D liquidity preference

For questions 5 and 6 select your answers from the following grid.

A	B	C	D	E
1, 2, 3 all correct	1, 2 only correct	2, 3 only correct	1 only correct	3 only correct

5. In the Keynesian theory of liquidity preference, the transactions demand for money is affected by the
1 level of national income
2 price of bonds
3 rate of interest

6. A fall in the PSBR is likely to occur, other things remaining the same, when
1 the interest rate on gilt-edged securities rises
2 the level of unemployment falls
3 zero rating of value added tax on commodities is abolished

RELATED ESSAY QUESTIONS

1. Distinguish between fiscal and monetary policy. Discuss the role of fiscal policy in the management of the economy by a 'monetarist' government.

2. Discuss the relative merits of direct and indirect taxes. Evaluate the economic implications of a reduction of the basic rate of personal taxation.

3. What is meant by the management of the economy?

4. Discuss some of the macroeconomic consequences of a reduction in the PSBR.

5. Explain the difference between automatic and discretionary fiscal policies. What problems can arise in the operation of discretionary fiscal policies?

6. Why does the PSBR have implications for the Bank of England's ability to control the money supply?

7. Define the term 'budget deficit' and explain how such deficits may arise. Discuss the possible effects on the international economy of a large budget deficit such as that experienced by the USA in recent years.

32 Economic Policy in an Open Economy

Key Points to Review

- Exchange rates (9.1, 9.2)
- The balance of payments (9.3)
- Trade barriers (9.5)
- Imports and exports in the circular flow (17.3)
- Price elasticities (7.1)

Questions for Preview

1 How do changing patterns of trade affect the economy?

2 What effect do capital movements have?

3 How do exchange rate changes affect the trade balance?

4 Why did the world shift to floating exchange rates, and then back to managed rates?

5 How can governments deal with trade deficits?

Over the years, almost all economies have become more open. They export and import more. Small countries tend to be the most open of all, larger countries less so, since it is rather easier for them to be more self-sufficient.

Increasing openness has resulted from increasing exploitation of comparative advantage. As countries develop, they discover new and competitive ways of exploiting their resources. Exports expand. The income they earn can be spent on more imports. The developed countries which already produce many and diverse products, will innovate, produce new products and trade more manufactures with each other, as individual firms develop a comparative advantage in the design, or the attractiveness, of their products.

Figure 32.1 shows that just under one-third of UK economic activity is devoted to exporting, and about the same proportion of total expenditure is on imports.

Changing Trade: The Effect on the Domestic Economy

Changing patterns of demand and supply imply changes in the structure of output. When competitive sources of imports are newly available, competing domestic industries face falling demand. Two kinds of adjustment are possible. As the domestic industry declines, its revenues fall (relatively if not absolutely) and wages and profits in the industry will be less attractive. The resources employed in the industry (both labour and capital) will have an incentive to move to more lucrative uses. (This process was examined earlier in Chapter 27.)

Meantime, somewhere in the economy, alternative opportunities will be opening up: there may be growing demands for a new product, or a product being produced with a new, cheaper technology, or a product which can be exported to meet growing demand abroad, or (if incomes are rising) for a product with high income elasticity of demand. So structural change takes place and resources are reallocated.

An alternative adjustment route may take place through exchange rate changes. Rising imports will increase the supply of sterling. This will depress the exchange rate. The price of imports will rise; the price of exports will fall (or they will become more profitable). New opportunities to make competitive exports will open up and unemployed resources will be attracted into exporting industries.

Figure 32.1
Imports, Exports, the Trade Balance, and GDP (£bn)

Year	*Exports*	*Imports*	*Current balance**	*GDP*
1978	47.5	45.6	+0.9	149.1
1979	54.9	54.4	−0.6	172.8
1980	62.8	57.8	+2.8	200.5
1981	67.6	60.7	+6.6	218.2
1982	72.9	68.1	+4.6	237.8
1983	80.4	77.9	+3.8	260.4
1984	92.2	93.0	+1.9	279.4
1985	102.6	99.2	+3.2	305.9
1986	98.4	101.6	0	324.0
1987	107.1	112.3	−3.7	355.6
1988	108.5	125.2	−14.6	394.8

*Includes adjustments.
Source: CSO, *Pink Book, 1989*.

Figure 32.2
Appreciation. As less oil was imported, fewer pounds were supplied to the foreign exchange market as less foreign currency was needed. The supply curve of the £ shifted leftwards and the new equilibrium exchange rate was higher.

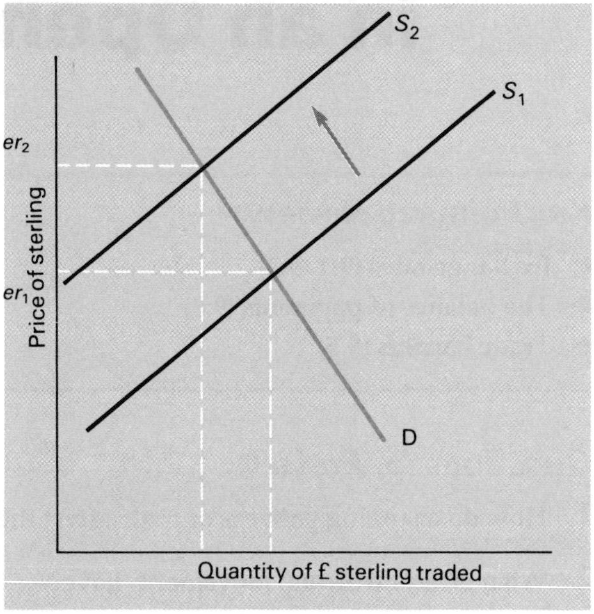

The increase in trade which takes place in this way leads to lower production costs, worldwide, and is a potent source of economic growth.

Structural change is not costless. In the short run both labour and capital are immobile. There may be a long transition period when industries decline in painful ways.

Changing Trade: The Effect on the Exchange Rate and the Balance of Payments

If trade patterns shift, a change in the exchange rate acts to restore equilibrium on the balance of payments. Take the case of North Sea oil. As oil became available from 1978 onwards, less imported oil was needed. The amount of sterling supplied to the foreign exchange market (in order to buy foreign currency) fell. The supply curve of sterling shifted leftwards. The exchange rate appreciated. Figure 32.2 shows this.

What was happening meanwhile to the balance of payments? When less oil was imported, the balance of trade swung into surplus. The subsequent rise in the exchange rate made imports cheaper and exports dearer. Exports (other than of oil and especially of manufactures) fell. Imports rose. The short-term balance-of-trade surplus (disequilibrium), resulting from the reduced oil imports, was eliminated and equilibrium restored.

From time to time a much longer-run trend also is discernible. During this century, the countries which compete with the UK in manufacturing production have grown in numbers and efficiency. For some products – cars and televisions, for example – they have reduced (though not eliminated) the UK's comparative advantage. Over the years, therefore, UK imports have often risen faster than exports. There has been a tendency towards a balance-of-trade deficit.

Figure 32.3 shows that there are shifts in both supply of and demand for sterling. Fewer exports mean reduced demand for sterling to pay for them. More imports mean an increased supply of sterling needed to pay for the foreign currencies to buy the imports. Figure 32.3 shows how the exchange rate depreciates. This depreciation now makes imports dearer and exports cheaper. (Try it: if £1 = $1.50, a £5 000 car sells for $7 500 in the US. If £1 = $1, the car now sells for $5 000: it has become a much better bargain and is more competitive in relation to other countries' cars.) Exports will sell better. There will be fewer imports: the domestic product will be better able to compete on the home market. The balance of trade will improve: the deficit will be gradually eliminated over a period of one to two years.

These kinds of exchange rate changes are a response to changes in trade patterns and help to prevent long-run balance-of-payments disequilibrium (surplus or deficit). Note that if the exchange rate is to be fixed at a certain parity market forces will operate, but be countered by central bank action.

The Effect of Capital Movements

International **capital movements** happen for two possible reasons. There may be profitable opportunities to invest in productive capacity, e.g. by setting up a factory abroad. This is direct investment. Ford Dagenham is an overseas investment of the US Ford

Figure 32.3

Depreciation. As more imports are demanded the supply of sterling shifts rightwards: at any given exchange rate more sterling will be supplied to pay for foreign currency. As fewer exports are demanded the demand for sterling shifts leftwards. The new equilibrium exchange rate will have depreciated.

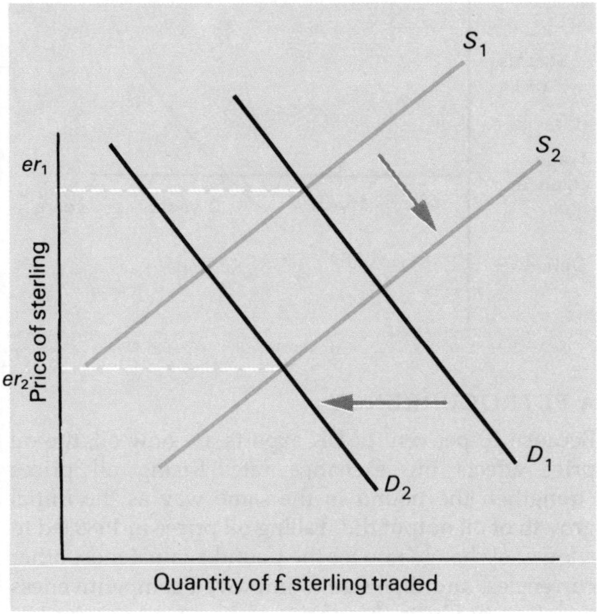

parent company. Such investments are long-term in nature. The other reason for capital movements is interest rate differentials. Funds available for a short time will be placed in bank accounts in the currency which earns the highest interest rate. So if one country raises its interest rate it can expect a capital inflow of what are sometimes called footloose funds, or hot money. These flows may be speculative in nature.

How will capital movements affect exchange rates? If a UK bank decides to buy dollars, the supply of sterling rises. This will depress the price of sterling. Other things being equal, sterling will depreciate. The effect will be reversed if there is a capital inflow.

The Role of the Bank of England

In Chapter 19, we saw how the Bank of England uses the Exchange Equalization Account to intervene in the foreign exchange market. It irons out day-to-day fluctuations in exchange rates, and keeps the rates within a target range. It cannot resist a major market movement, perhaps with a panic leading to a run on the pound. But it can defend the exchange rate against market forces to a considerable extent, provided it has sufficient foreign currency reserves.

How will domestic monetary policy affect all this? If interest rates are being kept high in order to constrain the growth of expenditure, a capital inflow will be attracted. The exchange rate will tend to rise. Imports will become cheaper. Exports lose competitiveness. Spending on domestically produced goods and services will be further reduced. Excess demand will be prevented, but the trade balance (exports minus imports) will probably worsen.

Alternatively, the logic may be quite different. Interest rates might be kept high to ensure the exchange rate is kept stable. A consequence of that would be a contraction of the domestic economy. In an open economy, domestic, trade, and exchange rate policy are very closely linked. To the extent that the UK intends to keep the exchange rate fixed, adjustment must take place via interest rate and other domestic policies. (Now read Key Points 32.1.)

The Effect of the Exchange Rate on Trade

We have looked at how trade affects the exchange rate. But the links are two-way. Supposing there are exchange rate changes, not so much in response to shifting trade patterns as to large capital movements.

A major banking and financial centre such as the UK can experience very large capital inflows and outflows, and in recent years capital movements have been the major influence on the sterling exchange rate. A large capital inflow shifts the demand for sterling to the right. Other things being equal the exchange rate will appreciate. Domestic producers will lose competitiveness; imports will increase and exports decrease. A balance-of-trade deficit will develop. Capital movements can produce an exchange rate at which firms have difficulty in competing. Connect this up with a conclusion we drew just now about monetary policy: a high interest rate, a capital inflow (or less outflow perhaps), a high exchange rate. Tight monetary policy may have its dampening effect on the economy

Key Points 32.1

- **Economies have tended to become more open with time.**
- **Changing patterns of trade lead to change in the structure of output.**
- **Changing patterns of trade lead to exchange rate changes, as do capital movements.**
- **Trade and exchange rate changes affect the domestic economy and interact with interest rate changes.**

through its influence on the exchange rate. Higher imports mean more leakage. Lower exports mean less injection. The economy will contract.

PRICE ELASTICITIES

When working out the likely effect of an exchange rate change, remember that the exchange rate determines prices of traded goods, and the response to price changes is determined by elasticities. The demand for most UK exports (other than oil) is fairly elastic. Foreigners can go somewhere else on holiday and buy their aircraft engines from Pratt and Whitney instead of Rolls-Royce. UK exports often have good substitutes. So depreciation and improved competitiveness can lead to substantially increased exports of such products.

Looking at imports, the picture is rather different. Where there are good domestic substitutes, i.e. demand is elastic, as with cars, depreciation will encourage falling imports. For products such as iron ore or coffee, demand is rather inelastic because there is no domestic substitute. (Also, for raw materials, they form only a small part of total production costs.) Depreciation will make little difference to the level of imports of raw materials and food products. It will have more effect on imports of manufactures as these compete with UK products.

ELASTICITIES IN THE SHORT RUN

What will happen *immediately* after an exchange rate depreciation? Initially, many importers and exporters will have contracts to fulfil. It will take time for foreigners to discover that UK exports are now more competitive. So in the short-run the elasticity of demand for exports will be much lower than in the long-run. Similarly, it may take time to find alternative domestic supplies to replace imports. Demand for imports will be inelastic in the short-run.

Even if the demand for more exports exists, supply may not. Depreciation will make exports increasingly profitable but if producers actually do not increase output, more cannot be sold. In other words, supply constraints would prevent depreciation from leading to increased production for exports and for home consumption. The chances of output for export increasing are much greater in the long than in the short run, because supply will become more elastic as adjustments take place over time.

This phenomenon is known as **the J-curve effect**. Figure 32.4 shows why.

Figure 32.4

The J-curve. A depreciation will lead at first to the trade balance worsening. In time (12–24 months) it will usually improve. After an appreciation a reverse (upside down) J-curve may be observed.

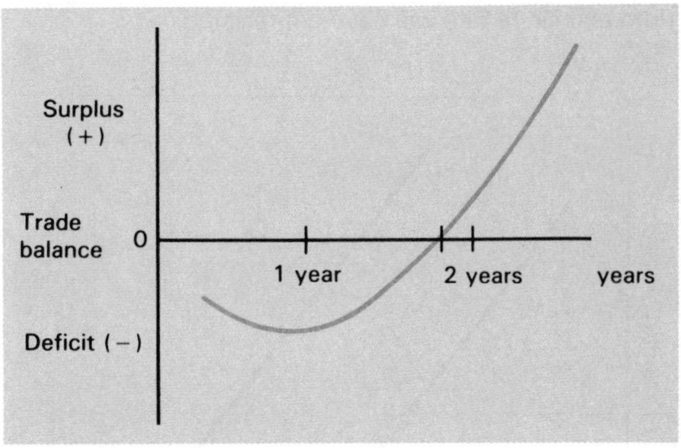

A PETROCURRENCY

Because 10 per cent of UK exports are now oil, the oil price affects the exchange rate. Rising oil prices strengthen the pound in the same way as the initial growth of oil output did. Falling oil prices in 1986 led to a lower exchange rate for the pound against most other currencies, and therefore to improved competitiveness for other products. It remains to be seen how the UK economy will adjust to oil price changes within the ERM. (See Key Points 32.2.)

Important International Institutions

So far we have been looking at the background to policy: the links between trade, the domestic economy, and the exchange rate. We cannot discuss policies without being aware of the international institutions too.

The International Monetary Fund

We saw in Chapter 9 how the IMF presided over the system of fixed exchange rates from 1945 to 1971. The IMF has its head office in Washington, USA, and has 130 member states. Its original brief was to provide international finance to maintain exchange rate stabil-

Key Points 32.2

- **The effect of exchange rate changes on the trade balance will depend upon price elasticities of demand and supply.**
- **A depreciation may initially cause the trade balance to worsen, but eventually it will usually improve.**

ity. Primarily, it was intended to assist member countries by lending to them in times of deficit from its holdings of gold and currencies. These are accumulated from subscriptions by members in relation to their *quotas*. Each member's quota was set according to a formula that took into account its importance in the world economy.

This arrangement, set up by J. M. Keynes after the Second World War, was known as the Bretton Woods system. Eventually it gave way to a system of floating exchange rates, and this changed the IMF's role somewhat. In time it became clear that floating exchange rates would not eliminate payments surpluses and deficits. So IMF loans have continued to be needed to help with short-term deficits. An IMF loan can prevent destabilizing lurches in exchange rates, allowing countries time to make necessary adjustments.

Nowadays all IMF loans are made to developing or East European countries. The developed countries generally survive deficits by means of loans between their own central banks. (The large US trade deficit has been financed largely by Japanese lending.)

IMF loans are not freely given. They are lent *on condition* that certain policies are followed. Sometimes these policies are very unpopular in borrowing countries. They may be required to devalue their currencies, raise taxes, and cut government spending. The borrower government may need to blame the IMF for the tough policies.

The IMF has an important role as a co-ordinator. It provides a framework for international discussion. It undertakes surveillance: it observes member governments' policies and tries to ensure that they are not inconsistent with other member countries' policies. All countries cannot have trade surpluses and surplus countries can be encouraged to help deficit countries by reducing the surplus.

At the present time, interest on IMF loans is paid in full by the borrower. Developing countries could be helped in the future by lending at concessional (i.e. lower) interest rates.

The World Bank

The other international organization set up at Bretton Woods in 1945 was the **International Bank for Reconstruction and Development**, informally referred to as the World Bank. As its official title suggests its funds were meant to promote the development of countries' economies, especially those in the Developing World (see Chapter 35). Projects such as dams, roads, and power-stations have been undertaken, as well as monies being provided for certain kinds of private enterprise. In addition, the World Bank provides extensive technical assistance. It gives advice on all aspects of economic and development policy. Increasingly, the work of the World Bank and the IMF are integrated.

In general, the World Bank's funds are borrowed on commercial terms on the world's major capital markets (London, New York, and Tokyo, etc.). They are lent at market rates of interest to the borrowers. They are not really aid, since the projects they finance must pay their way. What the World Bank can do is to make finance available to bodies which would not have access to ordinary bank loans – they may lack contacts or be considered too risky.

For purposes where commercial borrowing is impossible (e.g. for health-care facilities for poor people), the World Bank has its soft loan agency, the International Development Association (IDA). This is financed by member countries' subscriptions (similar to the IMF's quota system). Money can be given in grant form, or lent at concessional rates of interest (i.e. lower than commercial rates). This is known as multilateral aid: it comes from many countries via an international body.

The Group of Seven

The seven countries involved are the USA, West Germany, Japan, UK, France, Italy, and Canada – collectively known as G7. They meet sometimes at the same time as the IMF, to discuss regularly matters of mutual economic interest. If Italy and Canada aren't included, its G5.

These meetings have come about because it is now recognized that nations are interdependent. Economic policies in any one major country will have repercussions in its trading partner countries. Different countries' economic policies may conflict with one another. For example, the persistent twin deficits in the US during the 1980s – deficits in both the trade balance and the public sector – created an unstable situation. The G5 made two agreements to deal with this: the Plaza Accord in 1985 and the Louvre Accord in 1987. Their central banks undertook to co-operate to reduce the dollar's exchange rates, to help reduce the trade deficit. Since then Japan has been encouraged to allow the yen to appreciate and to import more.

G5 and G7 provide an opportunity for collaborative discussion when economic issues affect a number of countries and co-operative action is needed. (Now read Key Points 32.3.)

Some Major Policy Issues: Exchange Rates

A vital issue concerns the nature of the exchange rate regime. Broadly, we need to consider three alternatives – although there are all kinds of fine gradations possible between them. Fixed exchange rates imply stable parities: that is, exchange rates will be maintained over time by means of central bank intervention. Floating rates respond to market forces, without any intervention (other than that required to iron out day-to-day fluctuations). A managed exchange rate implies that there will be considerable central bank

Key Points 32.3

- **The IMF exists primarily to help countries deal with balance-of-payments deficits. It provides a forum for international discussion.**
- **The World Bank lends on commercial terms for major projects in developing countries.**
- **G5 and G7 allow for possible co-operation in economic policy matters for interdependent countries.**

influence but also a strong element of market forces in the determination of the exchange rate. The exact balance between the two will depend on exchange rate policy at any given time.

FIXED EXCHANGE RATES

The Bretton Woods system which served well until 1971 was based on the dollar, which was in turn based on a fixed value in terms of gold. It was stable in that the dollar provided a fixed point, and other currencies' values were defined in terms of the dollar. Central bank intervention ensured that the rate stayed fixed. It was also flexible. If a fundamental balance-of-payments deficit developed, devaluations (or for a surplus, revaluations) could be negotiated within the IMF framework, for all countries other than the USA. When this happened to the UK in the mid-1960s, devaluation was agreed in 1967, and by 1969 (after a standard J-curve effect) the current account was in surplus.

WHY DID FIXED EXCHANGE RATES BREAK DOWN?

Up to the late 1960s, most developed countries had similar, fairly low inflation rates. After that time, inflation rates started to diverge. A country with inflation which is faster than that of its trading partners will lose competitiveness. To maintain it, it will need a lower exchange rate. Its currency loses value both externally and internally. It cannot very well keep its exchange rates fixed. If inflation is fast and variable, frequent devaluations are needed and the point of fixed exchange rates, stability, is lost.

Secondly, the USA itself developed a huge current-account deficit. It needed to regain competitiveness. It couldn't devalue. In 1971 there was a major currency realignment in which most other countries revalued against the dollar. Even this did not restore stability, and during the course of 1972 most major currencies were floated with only a minimum of management from their central banks.

Probably also, shifting trade patterns meant more pressure for flexibility in exchange rates. Further, the growth of trade meant more finance was needed, and a system with gold at its heart meant that funds would ultimately be restricted in supply.

If these forces had not finished off fixed exchange rates, then the massive oil price rises of 1974 certainly would have.

This is not just ancient history. It is important to remember *why* fixed exchange rates ceased to work well. As the world shifts gradually away from floating rates in the search for greater stability, we should remember what problems fixed rates can bring.

Floating Exchange Rates

The great advantage which floating rates have (in theory) is that they allow the balance of payments to adjust automatically to change. If imports grow faster than exports, the supply of currency grows, there is exchange rate **depreciation**, imports become dearer and exports cheaper. The country becomes more competitive. After a time-lag, imports will fall and exports will rise. The current-account deficit will be automatically eliminated. The reverse process occurs if there is a current-account surplus.

The big problem with floating rates is, of course, instability. Traders cannot predict the price at which they will be doing business in the future. Risks are greater and some deals may, as a result, not take place. Economic activity in inhibited. Forward markets develop, in which currency can be bought forward (as opposed to spot), i.e. a contract is made to exchange currencies at a fixed, agreed price on a certain future date. These reduce the risks somewhat.

A second problem is the link between the exchange rate and inflation. A depreciating exchange rate makes imports dearer. If, as in the UK, 30 per cent of total expenditure is on imports, the impact of depreciation on the RPI is considerable. A counter-inflation policy can be much hampered by depreciation.

Managed Exchange Rates

A managed exchange rate allows the government to have an exchange rate policy, without having to defend its currency if market forces build up strongly. It means that exchange rate policy can be linked to domestic monetary policy. It is possible to keep the exchange rate strong in order to prevent rising import prices. Cheap imports can be used to force domestic producers to cut costs and resist wage claims. Equally, if depreciation is judged to be beneficial, it can just be allowed to happen.

Floating exchange rates have not, in fact, eliminated current-account surpluses and deficits. This weakens the case for a floating exchange rate policy and makes management of the exchange rate more likely.

HOW MUCH INTERVENTION HAS THERE BEEN?

We can get an idea of the level of intervention by looking at the data for foreign currency reserves. If they fall, it is clear that the Bank of England has been buying sterling to maintain its value, and vice versa. If they stay constant, no intervention has taken place except on a day-to-day basis. Figure 32.5 gives the reserves and, for comparison, the sterling exchange rate index over the same period. If reserves fell *and* so did the exchange rate, then the Bank of England was only partially successful in maintaining its value – perhaps purposely so.

During late 1989 the large current deficit brought considerable selling of sterling, some depreciation, and intervention to prevent further depreciation. (See the Case Study at the end of this chapter.)

Figure 32.5
Reserves, the Exchange Rate, and Interest Rates

Year	*Drawings on (+) or additions to (−), official reserves (£m)*	*Sterling exchange rate index, 1985 = 100*	*Nominal interest rate (base rate)*
1980	−291	122.6	16.0
1981	2419	126.5	12.0
1982	1421	113.7	12.0
1983	607	105.3	10.0
1984	908	100.6	9.5
1985	−1758	100.0	12.0
1986	−2891	91.6	11.0
1987	−12012	90.1	9.5
1988	−2761	95.8	11.0
1989 est.	—	—	13.0

Source: CSO, *Economic Trends, 1989*, and *Financial Statistics, May 1989.*

A Cross between Fixed and Floating Rates: The ERM

Until recently the Exchange Rate Mechanism (ERM) of the European Monetary System included all long-standing EC members except the UK. Why?

The ERM keeps European exchange rates fixed in terms of each other, allowing fluctuations within a narrow band. If market forces start to push a currency outside that band, the government concerned initially adjusts its domestic policy. If this proves inadequate, central banks and the European Monetary Co-operation Fund ensure that funds are available for intervention in the foreign exchange markets. If all else fails, a realignment of currency values takes place. The system is dominated by the West German Bundesbank, by virtue of its long-standing commitment to counter inflation.

In October 1990, the then Chancellor, John Major finally persuaded Mrs Thatcher to let the UK enter the ERM. There will now need to be much closer collaboration with the Bundesbank. There will be some loss of independence in monetary and exchange rate policy. There may be a problem if oil prices change. Sterling is a petro-currency, strongly affected by oil prices. A major change would probably entail realignment of the exchange rate. Perhaps most importantly, if we continue to have relatively high inflation rates we may be constantly imposing contractionary policies in order to keep sterling stable.

On the credit side, ERM membership will mean more stability, less fear of depreciation, and therefore less need to keep interest rates high in order to prevent a run on the pound.

It remains to be seen how fast the new Chancellor, Norman Lamont can reduce interest rates. (Now read Key Points 32.4.)

Dealing with a Payments Deficit

A current-account deficit may be purely short term. Imports and exports fluctuate month by month, and imports could exceed exports for some months or even years before it came to be seen as a serious problem.

Key Points 32.4

- **Fixed exchange rates worked well until 1971, under the Bretton Woods System.**
- **Changing inflation rates brought a shift to floating exchange rates.**
- **Floating exchange rates are less stable than fixed rates but allow easier adjustment to balance-of-payments problems.**
- **Increasingly, exchange rates are managed by central banks.**
- **Exchange rate policy and monetary policy are closely linked.**
- **The UK became a member of the ERM in October 1990.**

But a persistent deficit, sometimes known as a fundamental balance-of-payments disequilibrium, reflects a real imbalance somewhere in the system. There must be some serious difficulty in maintaining competitiveness. A number of policy responses are possible.

A Short-run Deficit

Quite often, a current-account deficit can be balanced by a surplus on capital account. This could mean that foreign investment in the UK (e.g. in the North Sea oil-fields) is larger than usual and the inflow of currency can be offset against the outflow of payments for imports. More likely, the capital inflow will reflect short-term lending, mainly by banks. In 1988, when there was a current deficit of £14.6bn, foreign currency lending to the UK was also £14.6bn, net of loans flowing abroad. Foreign currency loans, mainly from banks, financed the extra imports. Provided interest rates are high enough to attract lending on the scale required, this kind of short-run finance will plug the gap. So initially, raising interest rates may be an appropriate policy response.

A Long-run Deficit

Foreign creditors will lend for quite a while to a country with a current-account deficit and an attractive interest rate. But eventually they will begin to suspect that the debtor country does not have the ability to repay. At this point they may panic, and sell currency before it is too late. If many people panic there will be a currency crisis, a run on the pound, and a very sharp depreciation will take place over the space of just a few days.

Of course this may be exactly what is needed to restore competitiveness. Depending on the exchange rate regime, we use different language to describe the situation. Under fixed rates, market forces may be such that the central bank can no longer defend the currency and the fixed exchange rate will be devalued. Alternatively, the exchange rate may be maintained by the central bank at its high level, but reserves will fall sharply. Loans may be arranged through official financing, usually from friendly central banks in other countries. These loans will, it is hoped, restore confidence in the currency and allow time for other measures to work.

Under a floating exchange rate, there will be a depreciation.

Expenditure-switching Policies

Expenditure-switching policies work by shifting expenditure away from foreign-produced goods, towards domestically produced goods.

Let us assume that a depreciation has taken place. Imports are dearer, so demand will fall and spending on foreign goods will decrease. There will be increased demand for domestically produced substitutes. Export prices will fall and demand and sales will rise. Expenditure switching takes place.

There is another way of bringing about expenditure switching. Tariffs, quotas, and other import controls make imports dearer. They protect domestic producers. To the extent that imports are reduced and demand turns towards domestic products, there is expenditure switching. (These policies were dealt with fully in Chapter 9.)

Expenditure-reducing Policies

Imports generally depend on the level of income, and they tend to have a high income elasticity of demand. **Expenditure-reducing policies** (tax increases, government expenditure cuts, high interest rates) reduce income and aggregate demand. They lead to falling imports. They also lead to falling demand for domestic output. Faced with falling sales, firms which can export will pursue export markets with increased vigour. Contractionary policies reduce spending and in so doing lead to an improvement in a current-account deficit.

The only problem is that expenditure-reducing policies are not popular. They reduce incomes. They tend to inhibit economic growth. Unemployment may rise.

Policy Packages

Single policies usually work less well than combinations. Supposing a depreciation takes place. There is increased aggregate demand and expansion follows. What happens if the economy is close to full-capacity output? There will be excess demand, overheating, and accelerating inflation. The recently gained competitiveness will be lost.

Conclusion: If depreciation or devaluation are accompanied by expenditure-reducing policies, the increase in foreign demand will be offset by a decrease in domestic demand. Excess demand can be avoided.

Or supposing there is an exchange rate target (or a fixed rate). Depreciation is felt to be impossible. Expenditure reducing has to be relied upon, with all its unpopularity. The necessarily high interest rate will probably secure enough foreign loans to provide a temporary breathing-space. Other useful policies might be export subsidies. Import controls are possible, though they may greatly restrict economic growth in the long run. If they ever come back into fashion, incomes policies are another possibility; they would aim to prevent further cost increases through wage inflation.

Recent Experience

Figures 32.1 and 32.5 together tell most of the story. During the early 1980s there was no problem. North Sea oil, and recession, created a massive current

Figure 32.6

(a) The oil and non-oil balances (£bn)

Year	*Net exports of oil*	*Non-oil exports*	*Non-oil imports*	*Non-oil balance*
1978	−2.0	45.2	41.3	+3.9
1979	−0.7	50.8	49.6	+1.2
1980	0.3	56.7	52.0	+4.7
1981	3.1	58.6	54.7	+3.9
1982	4.6	62.3	62.0	+0.3
1983	7.0	67.9	72.4	−4.5
1984	6.9	77.4	85.1	−7.7
1985	8.1	86.5	91.2	−4.7
1986	4.1	90.3	97.4	−7.1
1987	4.2	98.6	108.1	−9.5
1988	2.8	102.5	122.0	−17.5

(b) Volume indices, 1985 = 100

Year	*Exports of non-oil goods*	*Exports of services*	*Imports of non-oil goods*	*Imports of services*
1978	88.8	96.8	68.5	82.2
1979	88.8	98.5	77.2	89.9
1980	90.3	95.3	74.9	94.6
1981	86.7	95.2	73.7	96.3
1982	87.8	90.3	79.2	98.4
1983	88.2	91.8	87.7	97.1
1984	94.9	93.3	96.5	100.3
1985	100	100	100	100
1986	104.0	104.8	106.7	105.0
1987	111.2	110.5	115.5	116.3
1988	114.8	108.9	131.9	126.3

Source: CSO, *Pink Book, 1989*.

surplus, which gradually subsided. In 1986 oil prices fell. In spite of the resulting fall in the exchange rate, which increased competitiveness, a large current deficit developed, becoming very intractable. High levels of consumer spending in 1987–9 sucked in imports and created a buoyant market for domestic output, reducing the incentive to export. Government policy dictated high interest rates (which allowed large-scale foreign currency borrowing from the banks), and a modest depreciation of the exchange rate (in late 1989). What has been the outcome? Has the current deficit fallen? Or has something else happened which changed our whole view of the situation? Time will tell and *you* will have the answer.

Figure 32.6 shows how the current account breaks down into the oil balance and the **non-oil balance**. Oil plays a large part in setting the exchange rate. The current balance is determined by the response of exporters and importers of non-oil products to the exchange rate. Before drawing totally gloomy conclusions, look at the volume indices for non-oil goods exports: they have grown by 29 per cent over the decade. But imports have grown more.

The Effect of the EC on Policy

In examining policy in an open economy for the UK, we must not overlook the EC angle.

The European Communities consisted initially of France, West Germany, Italy, Belgium, The Netherlands, and Luxembourg. They combined in the 1950s with the objective of creating freer trade between themselves. Together they created a single Common External Tariff (CET), giving them a unified trade policy with respect to the rest of the world. The UK, Denmark, and Eire joined in 1973. Since then, Greece, Spain, and Portugal have joined.

The objective is to promote trade within the community by reducing trade barriers and harmonizing regulations. Potentially this process can cut costs through increased specialization and increased competition. The possible gains over the long-run are large.

The EC has had two major effects on UK economic policy. One is that as a member, the UK no longer decides its trade policy alone, but is a party to collective decisions made in Brussels. For example, the UK participates in the Uruguay Round negotiations of GATT as a member country of the EC delegation. (These negotiations, begun in 1987, are aimed at reducing trade barriers worldwide.)

The other major area of impact has been through the CAP (Common Agricultural Policy). This sets agreed prices on agricultural products and protects farmers from cheap imports by means of a variable levy, equal to the difference between the world price and the CAP price. Prices have usually been quite high, and agricultural output within the EC has grown steadily, helped by technological change. The result has been that imports of agricultural products are now much reduced. (Chapter 8 looked at this issue.)

It is important to study the EC and its implications but the pace of change means that anything in a textbook will be out of date before it is printed. Newspapers, periodicals, and *Lloyds Bank Bulletins* make better sources on this topic. (Now read Key Points 32.5 on page 508.)

Key Points 32.5

- A short-run current-account deficit may be financed by borrowing foreign currency, usually from banks.
- A persistent deficit may require expenditure-switching policies, or expenditure-reducing policies, or a combination of the two.
- Expenditure-switching can be achieved by exchange rate depreciation or by import controls.
- Expenditure-reducing policies reduce income by increasing taxes or interest rates, or cutting government expenditure, or all of these.
- During the 1980s the UK's non-oil current balance has deteriorated.
- The EC exists to increase specialization and competition within member countries and by so doing to promote economic growth.

CASE STUDY

Bank of England Poised to Prop Up the Pound

The Bank of England is braced to mount a further major support operation to prop up the pound this morning as the government tries to head off pressure for another rise in the cost of borrowing.

The performance of sterling will be the focus of both political and City attention after last week's sharp fall, triggered by Tuesday's announcement of a £2 000m August trade deficit.

Financial markets were pressing for a rise in bank base-lending rates on Friday, whilst Labour's economic spokesmen have made it clear they will target the government's interest rate dilemma at their party's conference this week.

Bank of England officials were monitoring the pound's performance in the Far Eastern markets overnight and will be anxiously watching to see if investors begin selling sterling in Europe this morning.

The main test, however, is likely to come later in the week, when the Germans and Japanese may raise their domestic interest rates, which could put further pressure on the pound.

The problem for the Chancellor, Nigel Lawson, is that an increase in base rates from the 14 per cent level set in May would almost certainly force building societies to increase the cost of home loans. Mortgage rates are currently about the 13.5 per cent to 13.75 per cent level.

But if the Bank of England is unable to head off the selling pressure on sterling on the foreign exchanges, Mr Lawson will have to raise rates or abandon an important part of his anti-inflation strategy by allowing the pound to fall.

The Bank's determination to support the pound was doubly underlined on Friday. First it continued to buy pounds on the foreign exchanges – helped by the Bundesbank, the US Federal Reserve and the Bank of Japan – and it clearly signalled to the money markets it was not prepared

Figure 32.7

How Britain's Interest Rate Compares

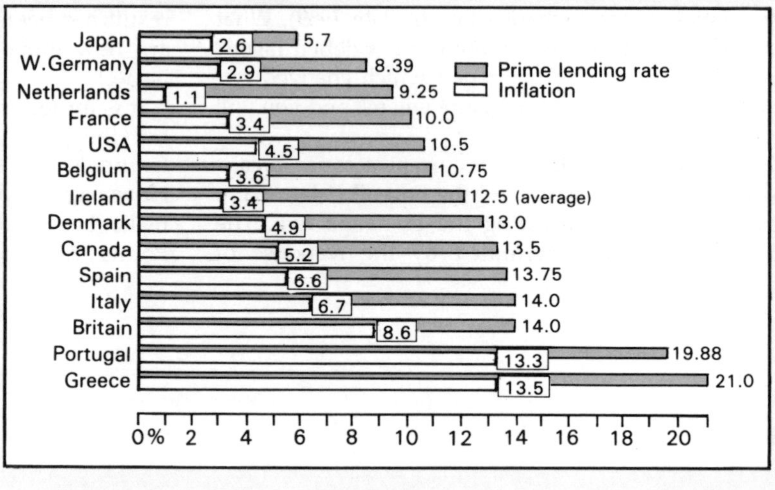

Source: Mark Milner, *Guardian*, 2 Oct. 1989.

to sanction an increase in interest rates.

Though that eased the immediate pressure, money market rates remained well above the current 14 per cent base rate level – indicating that City expectations of a rise have not been dampened.

Some reports suggest the Bank may have spent some $800m in its latest campaign to prevent the pound from falling too far. Figures showing the movement in Britain's foreign exchange reserves in September are due to be published tomorrow. They may, however, prove a less than reliable guide to the full extent of the Bank's foreign exchange intervention since the announcement of the August trade deficit.

They will, for example, include some sales of dollars as part of the co-ordinated campaign to push the dollar down by the Group of Seven biggest industrialized countries, but they will not take in the amount the Bank spent on Thursday and Friday last week to ease pressure on the pound.

Some analysts argue a rise in base rates is not inevitable, though the risk remains high. They say a rise in West German interest rates is now so widely expected that it will have little impact if, and when, it arrives.

They also point out that there are no major UK economic statistics due out until the latest inflation figures due 13 October, the last day of the Conservative party conference.

Shadow chancellor, John Smith said yesterday a Labour government would use credit controls in preference to high interest rates in the battle against inflation. He also disclosed he would soon be visiting European capitals to discuss the conditions for Britain's entry into the European exchange rate mechanism.

Source: Mark Milner, *Guardian*, 2 Oct. 1989.

Drop in Reserves is Less than Expected

Britain's gold and foreign currency reserves fell by $931m in November, an indication that the Bank of England intervened less to support the pound last month than it did in October, when reserves fell by a record $2.9bn.

The decline in underlying reserves to $38.8bn announced by the Treasury yesterday was smaller than City expectations. The average analysts' forecast had been for a decline of $1.5bn.

The figures led to speculation that Mr John Major, the Chancellor, may be taking a more benign approach to sterling's devaluation than his predecessor, Mr Nigel Lawson.

Figure 32.8
UK Official Reserves

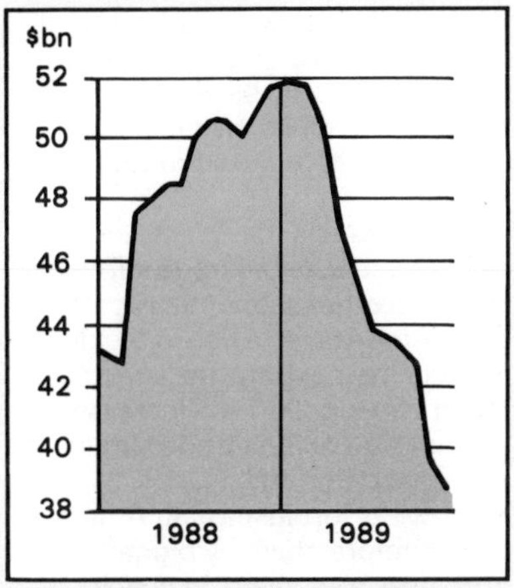

During November, the pound fell 4 per cent on the Bank of England's trade weighted index and nearly 6 per cent against the D-Mark. In that time Mr Major declined to raise bank base rates to bolster the currency and Bank intervention was relatively light.

Sterling has been under pressure on the currency markets in the past month because of domestic political upheavals, concern about Britain's economic outlook and growing doubts over the Government's willingness to raise interest rates to stabilize the currency. The strength of the D-Mark, buoyed by political change in East Germany, has exacerbated the pound's weakness. The figures will be regarded by some City analysts as further proof that Mr Major has adopted the policy favoured by the Prime Minister of letting the pound find its own level on the foreign exchange markets.

Source: Patrick Harverson, *Financial Times*, 5 Dec. 1989.

Questions

1. Explain why the trade figures led to a sharp fall in the exchange rate.
2. Why would rising interest rates in West Germany and Japan create problems in the UK?
3. Why would allowing the pound to fall mean that Lawson was abandoning an important part of his anti-inflation strategy?
4. What is the evidence as to the extent of Bank of England intervention in the foreign exchange market?
5. How might (a) credit controls, or (b) joining the ERM alter the situation?
6. What were the main sources of instability in the exchange rate, present at the time?

CASE STUDY

US Deficits

A reduction in America's current-account deficit is needed for world economic stability. But how can the burden of adjustment best be shared among its trading partners?

America's current-account deficit fell from a peak of $154bn in 1987 to $135bn last year. This year the improvement seems to have stalled, and on present policies the deficit looks set to grow next year. A recent study* by Mr Bill Cline, of the Institute for International Economics in Washington, forecasts that on unchanged policies and real exchange rates, America's deficit will top $150bn again by 1992.

The solution to America's deficit is no secret: some combination of a cut in the budget deficit and a further fall in the dollar will do the trick. Some question the need for a further drop in the dollar, given that the 40 per cent trade-weighted decline since 1985 has made little dent in the deficit. Mr Cline's answer is that the previous decline in the dollar has prevented the current-account deficit exploding: if the dollar had stayed as high as it was in 1985, the deficit might now be $400bn.

Mr Cline's model suggests that each 1 per cent real devaluation of the dollar improves America's current account by $9bn. But for devaluation to work it must be accompanied by a cut in the budget deficit. Otherwise, increased demand for exports quickly bumps up against capacity constraints, boosting inflation.

The dangers of America continuing to run an external deficit of $100bn or more have been much discussed. But little attention has been given to the implications of a reduction in America's current-account deficit for its trade partners. Here Mr Cline discovers a big snag: the cost of solving America's deficit could be bigger external imbalances elsewhere, especially in Britain, and between West Germany and other European countries.

Even if, as in the base case (i.e. assuming no change in current policy), America's deficit continues to grow, the impact on its trade partners varies widely. Japan's surplus is expected to rise as is West Germany's. In contrast, the current-account deficits of France, Italy, Britain, Canada and many other industrial economies are forecast to deteriorate. Britain's current-account deficit is forecast to leap to $76bn by 1992, from $26bn last year and only $3bn in 1987.

Mr Cline's model suggests that if the dollar depreciated by 10 per cent uniformly against all currencies, economies which already have trade deficits would face a disproportionately large share of the burden of adjustment. The surpluses of West Germany and Japan would be virtually unchanged, while the deficits of France and Italy would roughly double.

The reason is that West Germany and Japan have big trade surpluses with industrial economies apart from America, so a rise in the dollar price of their exports (as a result of the cheaper dollar) will increase the dollar value of their trade surpluses with these countries. Their narrowing surpluses with America are therefore offset by bigger surpluses elsewhere. In deficit countries, on the other hand, declining surpluses with America are compounded by bigger deficits with West Germany and Japan. Countries with widening deficits might resort to greater protectionism. America's trade deficit would be shrinking, but protectionist pressures might continue to mount there too because the deficit with Japan would still loom large.

The implication of all this is that if global current-account imbalances are to be smoothly unwound, exchange rate changes must be concentrated on those economies with the biggest surpluses. Mr Cline wants a drop in the dollar's real trade-weighted exchange rate of 10 per cent from its late 1987 level – rather more, therefore, from today's stronger level – but with the biggest decline against the yen and the D-mark. He reckons that both must appreciate by more than 30 per cent from current levels to around ¥102 and DM1.33 by the end of 1989. The currencies of other surplus European countries, such as Holland and Switzerland, should rise by the same amount as the D-mark; but deficit countries such as France and Italy need appreciations against the dollar of only 15 per cent from today's levels.

Awkwardly, this would imply a massive EMS realignment – including, for example, a 17 per cent rise in the D-mark against the French franc. It is hard to see how the EMS could withstand such a shake-up.

Britain, whose current-account deficit as a proportion of GNP is bigger than America's, is the only economy for which Mr Cline prescribes no appreciation against

Figure 32.9

Current-account Balance ($bn)

		1992 forecasts	
	1987	*Base case*	*Cline package*
USA	−153.9	−153.2	−48.4
Japan	86.6	136.4	63.4
West Germany	45.2	84.8	15.7
France	−1.5	−6.7	0.4
UK	−3.4	−76.1	−22.5
Italy	−0.7	−20.9	−6.3
Canada	−6.3	−11.8	−14.2
Other industrial	−6.2	−22.9	−83.1
Taiwan	18.0	−1.6	−9.3
South Korea – Singapore – Hong Kong	11.0	−6.9	−27.5
Argentina	−3.7	−3.5	−2.3
Brazil	1.2	15.5	19.1
Mexico	3.9	3.9	5.0
Other Latin America	−9.1	−8.3	−2.0
OPEC	−5.0	−34.8	−34.9
Other Africa	−4.7	−20.5	−10.2

*American Trade Adjustment: The Global Impact. By William Cline. IIE paper no. 26.

the dollar. This implies the unlikely rate for sterling against the D-mark of DM2.30, compared with DM3.18 currently. Don't hold your breath. For the moment the British government is sticking to its firm exchange-rate policy. History suggests that the effects of a sterling devaluation on that scale would largely be offset by higher inflation.

Feeding these currency changes into Mr Cline's model – along with the elimination of America's budget deficit over four years – suggests that America's current-account deficit would fall to $48bn in 1992. This should stabilize the ratio of net foreign debt to GNP, and pose no financing problems.

The biggest improvement in America's bilateral trade-balance between 1987 and 1992 would be with Japan. The bilateral deficit would halve from $57bn to $30bn. Japan's total current-account surplus is also forecast to shrink. This should help to reduce the pressure for protectionist measures against Japan. West Germany's bilateral trade surplus with America would actually increase, but its total current-account surplus would fall as its surplus with other European economies narrowed. The balances of France, Italy, and Britain would all improve.

In theory Mr Cline offers a neat solution. But how on earth could such exchange-rate movements be agreed, let alone put into practice? Expect external imbalances, no matter what happens in America, to persist for some time.

Questions

1. Assuming the USA succeeds in cutting its current-account deficit, what problems are anticipated for its trading partners?
2. Why would depreciation of the dollar leave Japan's and West Germany's surpluses virtually unchanged?
3. What major danger could result from continuing, persistent, trade deficits? Why is this outcome undesirable?
4. What alternative approach does Mr Cline suggest?
5. What advantages does this approach have?
6. Why is Mr Cline's solution difficult to bring about?

Exam Preparation

MULTIPLE CHOICE QUESTIONS

1. Given that the initial balance of trade is zero, which of the following combinations of elasticities is most likely to create a positive balance of trade following a devaluation in the home country?

A The elasticity of demand for imports is 1.2 and that for exports is 0.6.
B The elasticity of demand for imports is 0.6 and that for exports is 1.2.
C The elasticities of demand for both imports and exports are less than unity.
D The elasticities of demand for both imports and exports are equal to unity.
E The sum of the elasticities of demand for imports and exports is greater than 2.

For Questions 2, 3, and 4 select your answers from the following grid:

A	B	C	D	E
1, 2, 3 all correct	1, 2 only correct	2, 3 only correct	1 only correct	3 only correct

2. The International Monetary Fund uses the funds at its disposal to

1 help countries in temporary balance-of-payments deficit
2 give development aid to underdeveloped countries of the Third World
3 assist national governments with a budget deficit

3. In the short-run, a depreciation of the sterling exchange rate could be expected to

1 increase the competitiveness of UK exports
2 increase the price of imports into the UK
3 improve the UK's terms of trade

4. Other things being equal and assuming that the UK is a net oil exporter and that the demand for UK oil overseas is inelastic, a substantial reduction in the world price of oil would tend to

1 cause the value of sterling to fall
2 worsen the UK's balance of payments
3 lead to a fall in UK tax revenue

RELATED ESSAY QUESTIONS

1. Explain what is meant by fixed, flexible, and managed foreign exchange systems. Discuss the advantages and disadvantages of these systems from the point of view of both the UK and the world economy.
2. Will a depreciation of the exchange rate necessarily improve the balance of trade of an economy?
3. (a) What may cause a rise in the external value of a country's currency?
   (b) What may be the likely economic consequences of such a rise for your country?
4. 'If unit labour costs rise faster at home than abroad, the exchange rate will have to fall.'
   'A sudden outflow of capital will trigger depreciation.'
   'A large rise in the domestic money supply will raise prices by inducing depreciation of the exchange rate.'
   Explain and assess these statements.
5. 'Rapid rises and rapid falls in the pound's exchange rate have been equally damaging to the UK economy.' To what extent does recent experience support this view?
6. Does the UK benefit from a rise or a fall in North Sea oil prices?
7. 'There is no case for reducing the rate of inflation in the UK below the average rates prevailing in other advanced countries.' Discuss.

33 Industrial Policy

Key Points to Review

- External benefit (i.e. positive externalities) (10.2, 10.4)
- Taxation (10.8, 31.1)
- Structural and regional unemployment (11.3)
- Economies of scale (21.4)
- Entrepreneurship (1.1, 26.3)

Questions for Preview

1 What is the aim of industrial policies and what examples can you cite?

2 What does the immobility of labour mean?

3 Why are training policy and regional policy so difficult to evaluate?

4 Why are the concepts of *enterprise* and *competition* essential for the success of research and development policy and small firms policy?

5 What constitutes an 'enterprise culture'?

In the last five chapters we have generally discussed fiscal, monetary, and exchange rate policies, alongside the specific chapters on privatization and competition policy. Consequently, some readers may feel that industrial-type policies have been adequately covered. To some extent such a view would be justified.

However, the **Department of Trade and Industry (DTI)** along with the **Training Agency** execute a significant amount of policy aimed at changing the nature and structure of industry in the UK. For example, in the period 1989–90 the DTI spent approximately £1.5bn, while the Training Agency spent nearly double (£2.9bn). Furthermore, these expenditures relate to a period when much government policy emphasized a need to achieve greater competition and enterprise. This emphasis in effect reduces government costs in terms of related programmes as obviously, from a government perspective, the process of freeing markets is cheaper than intervening. Much of the industrial policy of the late 1980s and 1990s relates, therefore, to improving market performance by removing various barriers to entry. These barriers may formally be referred to as **structural rigidities**.

Structural rigidities are obstacles that hinder the efficiency of many markets. Examples of such rigidities include: excessive taxes, an insufficient supply of trained labour, subsidies, wages that are above the equilibrium level due to union activity, minimum-wage legislation, and excessive social security payments.

In very general terms, therefore, industrial policy during the 1980s has shifted from emphasizing intervention and a related 'culture of dependency' to the freeing of market forces and policies promoting an **enterprise culture**.

An enterprise culture is dependent on profit, freedom, competitiveness, liberalization, deregulation, incentives, ownership, and decentralization. Implicitly, these features will recur as we review the industrial policy emanating mainly from the two government agencies mentioned above. Indeed, the Department of Trade and Industry is often referred to by its nickname

Figure 33.1

The Assisted Areas of Great Britain. The areas shown were designated by the Department of Trade and Industry on 29 November 1984 as eligible for regional grants to encourage industrial development. Alongside these general areas, are 25 named *enterprise zones* (e.g. Dudley, Corby, Isle of Dogs, Hartlepool, Wakefield, and Speke). These encourage industrial development largely through local and administrative incentives, e.g. easier planning permission and no rates. The enterprise zones began in the early 1980s and are administered by the Department of the Environment. Generally they are areas that need to become more attractive, as they contain large areas of derelict land.

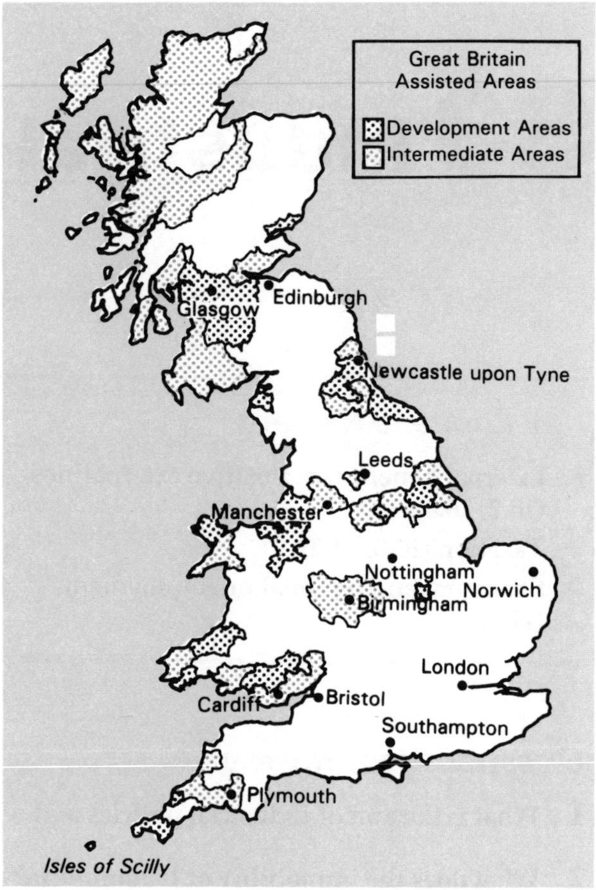

'the Department for Enterprise'.

For organizational purposes we shall review four specific areas, namely: Regional Policy, Training Policy, Research and Development Policy, and Small Firms Policy. By studying these categories in chronological order some insight will be gained into the confused understanding of the relationships that exist between industrial performance and the role of the state. It is certainly a matter of some controversy and consequently policies that have already been tried and tested may be revived.

Regional Policy

Regional policy dates back to 1934. In 1934 the *Special Areas Act* was passed, which identified certain depressed areas as being in need of incentives to promote industrial diversification. Consequently, certain areas today can actually offer firms financial assistance to entice them to develop within their locality. These areas, designated as **assisted areas**, were last revised in 1984 and are identified in Figure 33.1. In the period between this first piece of legislation in 1934 and the most recent in 1988 regional policy experienced its heyday. That is, the 1960s and 1970s were very much a period of regional policies.

The decline in emphasis since is epitomized by the 1988 legislation which involved the abolition of the automatic (mandatory) Regional Development Grant and the creation of a more limited discretionary system.

Figure 33.2

Regional Selective Assistance Industrial Grants

	1988–9 outturn	*1989–90 estimated outturn*
Number of offers	1 261	1 150
Value of offers (£m)	121	100
Related projects costs (£m)	1 604	950
Number of associated jobs:		
New	25 187	24 995
Safeguarded	7 658	8 331
Payments (£m)*	106	113

* The payment figures cover claims paid during the year and do not relate to the other data which are for offers made during the year. The assistance is paid in instalments, usually 2 or 3.

Source: *The Government's Expenditure Plans, 1990–1993*, HM Treasury, Jan. 1990.

What is Regional Policy?

Regional Selective Assistance (RSA) grants are available to firms in those areas outlined in Figure 33.1. They are provided for projects which maintain or create employment. The monies paid out in grants relate mainly to capital expenditure. To gain some idea of this scheme see Figure 33.2.

Alongside RSA payments are Regional Enterprise Grants (REG) which are payable to small firms (i.e. those with fewer than 25 employees) that wish to invest in those regions designated as development areas (see Figure 33.1). These grants totalled an estimated £5.5m in 1989–90.

Regional Policy clearly represents a small and declining percentage of industrial expenditure. For example, in 1984 regional policies cost the government approximately £500m. In 1987–8 they totalled less than £400m. By 1992–3 RSA and REG are planned to cost no more than £200m.

Why Regional Policy Developed

If one looks at Figure 33.1 the areas for assistance all have something in common. In the main they represent areas where shipbuilding, textiles, heavy engineering, or coalmining previously took place. These so-called staple industries were important **localized industries** during the UK economy's industrial heydey. A localized industry is one that dominates a whole geographical area, that is, few alternative industries exist in the locality. When a localized industry declines, therefore, so does the regional economy of a whole area. In consequence, the areas designated as areas for assistance also tend to have higher levels of unemployment than the national average (see Figure 33.3).

Furthermore, people tend to stay where they have their social roots. As economists would express it people tend to be **geographically immobile**. Put simply 'Of all baggage human baggage is the most difficult to move'. Consequently the idea of moving work to people becomes an attractive possibility.

Does Regional Policy Work?

Regional policy of one sort or another has been experienced for over fifty years. Yet it is still difficult to evaluate as an effective policy tool. In common with most economic policy there is the problem of not knowing what would have happened without the policy.

Official comments in a government White Paper ('Regional Industrial Development') published in 1983 suggested that the regional policy enforced since 1960 had resulted in there being half a million more jobs in the assisted areas than otherwise would have existed. This is a dubious estimate but it is official! Research carried out since has produced slightly higher estimates. For example, Moore, Rhodes, and Tyler (in 1986) suggested that over 780 000 jobs were created in the assisted areas during 1960–81 and 600 000 of these were still in existence in 1981.

Other commentators look at the figures for regional unemployment, such as those in Figure 33.3 and they recognize, as you can, that those areas that traditionally had higher rates of unemployment than the national average still have them. But again you cannot be sure what kind of statistical portrait would exist if this policy had never been adopted.

What does seem to be agreed, however, is that this policy is not as cost-effective as some of its alternatives. If the official estimate that half a million jobs were created between 1960 and 1983 is correct, it means that each job has cost approximately £40 000 to create. Official research by B. Moore, I. Rhodes, and P. Tyler in the early 1980s put the average cost at approximately £35 000 per job created. Towards the end of the 1980s economists have been estimating costs as high as £50 000 per job created. What complicates these evaluations is the unknown indirect effects, which would generate a regional multiplier and thus reduce the actual costs per job.

Figure 33.3

Regional Unemployment Rates (%). The figures below show the various regions monitored. We have chosen data relating to the years 1933, 1966, 1975, and 1990. Each of these had been purposely selected to enable the years 1966 and 1975 (major phases of regional policy) to be studied alongside data reflecting the situation before and after. The regional categorizations and processes of recording unemployment have changed since 1933 so comparisons are not perfect. Regardless, patterns are evident, e.g. unemployment tends to be consistently above the national average in the northern and western areas (i.e. the first five regions listed) and always well below the national average in the South-east, South-west and East Midlands.

	*1933**	*1966†*	*1975†*	*1990**
Northern Ireland	28.9	5.3	7.9	14.2
Scotland	30.2	2.7	5.2	8.8
North		2.5	6.9	9.0
North-west	25.7	1.4	5.3	7.9
Wales	37.8	2.8	5.6	7.2
West Midlands	20.2	0.8	4.1	6.1
Yorkshire and Humberside		1.1	4.0	7.1
South-west	19.6	1.7	4.7	4.5
East Midlands	20.2	1.0	3.6	5.2
South-east	17.0	0.9	2.8	3.8
United Kingdom	23.4	1.4	4.1	6.0

*Figures relate to January of that year.
†Figures relate to annual averages.

Source: *Department of Employment Gazette* and *Historical Abstract of Labour Statistics.*

Whatever the correct estimate regional policy seems an expensive option. It favours capital projects and often benefits firms that would locate regardless of financial incentives. Consequently, the opportunity cost of employing regional policy is high and alternatives have taken priority. (Now read Key Points 33.1.)

Training Policy

Training policies in the UK began to take off as regional policy waned. Initially, in the mid-1970s, the Manpower Services Commission (MSC) was established to co-ordinate a national training programme. In September 1988 this was superseded by the Training Agency. Like its counterpart the Training Agency operates within the Department of Employment.

The Training Agency's tasks are identified in the December 1988 White Paper entitled *Employment for the 1990s* as being:

- to encourage employers to develop the skills and experience of their employees of all ages;
- to provide and encourage appropriate training for young people when they have full-time education;
- to help the long-term unemployed acquire the skills and experience that will help them find regular employment;

Key Points 33.1

- **Industrial policy is concerned with affecting the structure and performance of industry and labour within specific sectors of the economy using tools such as: competition policy, macro-policies, regional policy, training policy, research and development policy, and small-firms policy.**
- **Much industrial policy of the 1980s and 1990s relates to improving market performance by reducing structural rigidities.**
- **Regional policy dates back to 1934 and since then a range of incentives to encourage firms to develop in certain areas has been on offer.**
- **The range of incentives available depends upon geographical location and the areas presently designated for assistance are shown in Figure 33.1.**
- **Research suggests that regional policy may not be as cost-effective as its alternative policy options. Consequently, its usage is being reduced.**

• to help the education system become more relevant to working life and more responsive to changing demands and opportunities in the labour market;
• to ensure that the distinctive needs of the self-employed and small firms for training, counselling, and other support are met.

In brief, the Training Agency, on behalf of the nation, co-ordinates the activities of employers, the education service, training providers, and trade unions in an effort to overcome skill shortages and thereby reduce unemployment.

What Is Training Policy?

The Training Agency organizes a range of programmes. The most important of these in terms of expenditure and throughput are: the Youth Training Scheme, Employment Training, the Enterprise Allowance Scheme, and the Technical and Vocational Educational Initiative. These are briefly outlined below.

YOUTH TRAINING SCHEME

The Youth Training Scheme (YTS) was introduced in April 1983 and has trained over two million young people since at a cost of over £1bn per year. Its aim is to provide all 16–18-year-olds who do not go directly to employment or stay in education, with training and work experience. Those on a typical two-year programme will be given at least 20 weeks off-the-job training (e.g. at the local technical college) to complement their work experience and wherever possible vocational qualifications will be obtained. Through this scheme the government aims to prepare school-leavers for work in such a way that Britain's future labour force will be more flexible and adaptable. Subsequently, this should have beneficial implications for the workings of the labour market. In 1988–9 64 per cent of the 370 000 YTS-leavers gained full-time employment (41 per cent of these had gained some kind of recognized qualification) and 14 per cent became registered as unemployed.

EMPLOYMENT TRAINING

The Employment Training Scheme (ET) was launched in September 1988 and in its first year provided training for 400 000 at a cost of £1.4bn. The aim, according to its promotional slogan, is to 'train the workers without jobs, to do the jobs without workers'. The various programmes are targeted at adults who have been unemployed for six months or longer. Initially, individuals on the scheme have an interview to identify their training needs and agree a personal action plan. The unemployed are then allocated to training agents (employers mainly from the public sector and voluntary groups) who provide a small allowance to supplement the unemployment benefit, whilst trainees receive a mix of off-the-job training and work experience. The objectives of this scheme are to provide the long-term unemployed with the skills they need to obtain and keep jobs, and to guarantee some kind of training opportunity to reconcile the problem of skill shortages.

At the outset the scheme has faced some problems. Most importantly, the first recruits have not had the success rate of their YTS counterparts in securing full-time jobs after completing their training. Secondly, the trade unions have complained about the quality of the training and the lack of permanent jobs available thereafter. Consequently, ET has begun with very high drop-out rates. Regardless of these teething problems Employment Training continues. The target for 1990–1 is to provide training to 450 000 adults (with an average of 215 000 at any one time) at a cost of £1.2bn.

THE ENTERPRISE ALLOWANCE SCHEME

The Enterprise Allowance Scheme (EAS) was launched in 1983. It is designed to help the unemployed to start their own business. They are paid a flat-rate sum (presently £40 per week) for 52 weeks and are offered a programme of training. More than 450 000 people have joined the scheme since it started and many of these had previously been unemployed for over a year. More coverage to this scheme is given on page 521 in the section relating to small-firms policy.

TECHNICAL AND VOCATIONAL EDUCATION INITIATIVE

The Technical and Vocational Education initiative, or TVEI as it is commonly referred to, should be more familiar to readers of this book since every school curriculum in Britain has been affected by this programme since 1987. The basic aim of TVEI is to ensure that the education of 14–18-year-olds prepared school students for the demands of working life in a rapidly changing society. The strategies employed to achieve this end are numerous and subtle and some case study material at the close of this chapter will involve further reflection on this initiative. What is interesting, however, is that large amounts of Training Agency funds are now subsidizing the Department of Education and Science. In the year 1989–90 a total of approximately £240m was spent on TVEI and related educational initiatives, and this was planned to increase to approximately £287m by 1992–3. These figures represent roughly 10 per cent of the Training Agency's annual budget.

SUMMARY

The total expenditure and throughput involved in these programmes is summarized in Figures 34.4 and 34.5. It is evident that the government's responsibility for training has not diminished – in fact the trends of the 1980s suggest quite the reverse. This may seem an odd development for a government that came to power with the specific objective of rolling back the state. Recognizing this ironic development, it is proposed that government training schemes in the future will be administered by local Training Enterprise Councils (TECs). It is envisaged that there will be approximately 80 of these based in areas with a working population of 250 000 each having an average budget of £20m. They will be encouraged to supplement the funding they receive from the government by raising money from local employers and other sources. Further consideration of these will be incorporated in a Case Study at the close of this chapter.

Figure 33.4

Employment and Training Measures, 1977–89

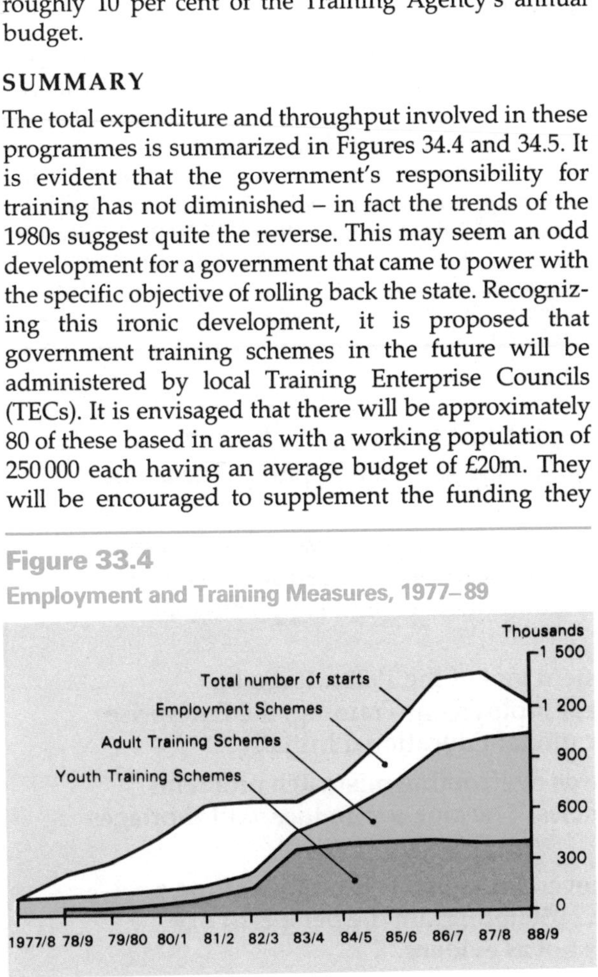

Source: *Social Trends 1990.*

Figure 33.5

Department of Employment Spending on Training and Education Programmes (£m in 1989–90 constant prices)

	Training and Education Support	*Education Initiatives*	*Training for unemployed adults*	*Youth Training Scheme*	*Training for the employed*
1981–2	–	–	690	631	–
1982–3	–	–	739	803	–
1983–4	–	10	928	1 074	–
1984–5	–	33	1 071	1 095	–
1985–6	–	128	1 190	1 080	–
1986–7	–	218	1 673	1 136	–
1987–8	–	197	1 711	1 224	–
1988–9	107	215	1 461	1 134	–
1989–90	89	239	1 338	1 118	54

Source: Training Agency, 1990.

Why Training Policy Developed

Not only is labour geographically immobile, but it is also said to be **occupationally immobile**. That is, people find it difficult to transfer from one job area to another. Yet this is necessary in a dynamic economy. Many government White Papers of the past have highlighted how our problems of unemployment during the 1970s coexisted alongside large numbers of job vacancies. This seemingly odd situation was largely due to the unemployed having the wrong skills and partly due to them lacking information. It was these problems of *mismatch* between vacancies and unemployed labour that largely provided the impetus for training-type policies.

Since then there has been a slight shift in emphasis. If an economy is to be dynamic in a single European market it must meet the training standards of its competitors and be more enthusiastic about overcoming skill shortages. As a result economic commentary has become increasingly conscious of overseas attitudes to training and more aware of the relationships between training and productivity. Detailed comparative studies (carried out by A. Daly in 1984) suggest that an up-grading of 1 per cent of the labour force from unskilled to skilled would raise productivity by 2 per cent. Similar research by D. Worwick highlighted that lower-skilled workforces require more supervisory labour in the form of quality control and general management.

This shift in emphasis has been furthered by the separation of information services, via job centres, and training. Both are now separate functions of the Department of Employment.

The outcome was that during the 1980s state-sponsored training increased (this is supported by the data in Figures 33.4 and 33.5).

Does Training Policy Work?

In numerical terms the various Training Agency schemes seem to have a high take-up rate. To provide just one statistical snapshot – over one million people benefited from Training Agency grants during the year 1988–9. Of this total approximately 400 000 were involved in some form of training at any one time. These numbers represent a great reduction in the unemployment figures and in consequence some criticize the policies as merely being a *cosmetic device*. This phrase is self-explanatory, in so far as the schemes certainly put a prettier face on the unemployment statistics. It is not only the trade unions that advance this argument. Even the Bank of England, in a discussion paper published during 1989, acknowledged that much of the decline in unemployment since the mid-1980s has been as a result of training schemes rather than a growth in jobs.

However, the key question is, how many people effectively benefit from their training experiences. A regular survey carried out on YTS-leavers suggest that since 1986 over 60 per cent have left the scheme for some kind of employment. The Enterprise Allowance Scheme has also produced more than 50 per cent success rate for those who wanted to start their own business. The stumbling-block with these evaluations is the same as with regional policy, namely you never know what the employment situation would have been for these people (and all the others on the schemes) had the training not existed.

Other research contains less promising findings. We are still suffering from shortages of skilled personnel in certain areas. For example, a survey carried out by the CBI in 1986 showed that 19 per cent of manufacturers expected shortages of skilled labour to affect their output. A follow-up survey one year later claimed that 34 per cent of manufacturers were concerned about skill shortages and these were not just shortages of high-level skills. Apparently in some parts of the country shortages of all types of labour were developing. Furthermore, our vocational education is still deemed to be a poor comparison to the American, German, and Japanese equivalents.

In terms of cost-effectiveness, however, Training Agency expenditure (and its predecessor the MSC) seems to provide value for money. In a research paper published in 1985 G. Davies and D. Metcalf estimated the annual cost per job created by training-type measures to be £2 050 (in 1984–5 prices). When put into a broader context this cost is particularly impressive since unemployment benefits and other social security payments would have been saved and some taxation payments would be collected. Indeed according to data in Case Study question to Chapter 18 the cost to the government of an unemployed person is £6 600 (in 1984–5 prices).

Finally, figures such as these never fully account for the various indirect costs and indirect benefits that should form an important part of any evaluation concerned with training and/or unemployment. (Now read Key Points 33.2.)

Research and Development Policy

Research and development – R & D – involves exploring and inventing new product areas. This, by its very nature, is a dodgy affair. Those involved have to take the risk of investing time and money, but can never be sure that the expensive resources used will produce anything. Furthermore, when a product is developed there is little to stop others benefiting from the research; that is, the external benefits often exceed the private benefits.

Key Points 33.2

- **The Manpower Services Commission was established in the mid-1970s (1974) to administer training-type policies. This was superseded by the Training Agency in 1988.**
- **The Training Agency's main aims are concerned with: helping the school-leaver and the long-term unemployed by providing training, assisting the education system to become more responsive to the needs of the labour market, and supporting the self-employed and their small firms.**
- **Training policy represents a major government tool of the 1980s. It can be exemplified by the Youth Training Scheme, Employment Training, the Enterprise Allowance Scheme, and Technical and Vocational Educational Initiative.**
- **Training policies are basically geared towards overcoming mismatch problems between unemployed labour and job vacancies. The aim is to reduce skill shortages and make labour more mobile.**
- **Training policy is difficult to evaluate for several reasons. For example, from a simple cost perspective it seems effective (£2 050/job); from the perspective of reducing skill shortages the effectiveness is not as evident.**

As detailed in Chapter 10, whenever externalities relating to growth and welfare cannot be absorbed by the market mechanism, the government may step in. R & D is an example of such intervention and the UK government, as most others in the OECD group, are committed to expenditure in this area.

In the UK approximately 2½ per cent of our annual GDP is spent on R & D and slightly less than one-half of this is met by the government. To appreciate how this compares with other nations, Figure 33.6 shows some approximate statistics gathered by the OECD. It is interesting to note that the UK devoted roughly the same percentage of GDP to R & D in 1963 as it does now. Since 1963, however, GDP has increased significantly – especially in Japan and Germany. Consequently, in absolute terms we have slipped from second place in the R & D expenditure league. We now trail behind Japan, Germany, Sweden, and the USA in the amounts spent per year on R & D. Moreover, approximately 50 per cent of the UK (and USA) government-funded R & D goes towards defence-related programmes, and inevitably defence R & D crowds out other R & D work and does not necessarily lead to any commercial application.

What is Research and Development Policy?

Once again there is no simple single answer to cover this section. R & D policy involves a range of government incentives and has been subject to various institutional support.

The institutional support dates back to 1948 when the **National Research and Development Corporation (NRDC)** was established. This Corporation was intended to encourage technical progress through the allocation of funds for the development of new products that were in the public's interest. In 1981 the NRDC was merged with another government institution, the **National Enterprise Board (NEB)**. The NEB had been a type of state-holding company established in the mid-1970s. The Board had gained some experience with modern technological firms striving to gain a foothold in the market.

Figure 33.6

Statistics relating to Research and Development in Seven Major Countries 1987–8

	Approx. expenditure on R & D as a % of GDP	*Approx. % of R & D financed by government*
UK	2.4	38
Japan	2.9	22
Sweden	2.8	34
West Germany	2.8	33
Italy	1.3	55
France	2.3	53
USA	2.7	51

Source: OECD, *Science and Technology Indicators* (1989)

The merger of NRDC and NEB in 1981 formed the BTG – the **British Technology Group (BTG)**. The Group's main objective is to orchestrate joint ventures, involving new technology, between the private and public sectors. In journalistic terms BTG is in the business of technology transfer. This involves linking the academic research-orientated world with the commercial profit-orientated sector. This is achieved through joint projects and licences. The outcome is that the British Technology Group is self-financing. In fact its commercial viability may well be formalized through some form of privatization in the near future.

A similar collaborative type of venture, but in a more specialized area, is the 'Alvey directorate'. This agency was established in the early 1980s specifically to fund and co-ordinate the work of researchers from university and industry involved in fifth-generation computers. The government has spent over £500m on this project.

These institutional agencies promoting collaboration have set a trend. Government expenditure on R & D is now channelled through various schemes linking government departments, research projects, and industry. Moreover, the benefits of collaboration are not solely confined to this country and a European project known as 'Eureka' is also presently being funded. This project seeks to encourage industry-led collaboration between European firms sharing interests in advanced technology. Some financial assistance is provided by the respective national government. In 1988 there were 160 Eureka projects of which Britain participated in 57.

The government is, therefore, increasingly acting as a catalyst to get industry and research organizations to work together. Alongside this development run three kinds of incentive: tax concessions allowable against R & D expenditure, the provision of laws regarding 'Patents', and some direct financial incentives from the government. The outcome of this policy is that government expenditure on R & D is undergoing some decline, whilst business expenditure on this activity is increasing. According to OECD data the UK in 1987 spent £11146m on R & D and £6339m of this was accounted for by private business. The decade of the 1980s has clearly experienced a switch in emphasis: explicit support to single companies has given way to a greater emphasis on recognizing the importance of creating an economic environment where companies have the financial room and confidence to develop R & D programmes along with other like-minded enterprising firms.

Does Research and Development Policy Work?

It seems that in the UK we lack a long-run philosophy behind R & D: governments change, institutions come and go, and shifts in emphasis from the public to the private sector are experienced. By result, we have a reputation as a nation of innovating but not effectively developing our products. Recent data published by the OECD confirm this reputation.

The OECD since 1988 has begun to collate data specifically relating to the international trade of patents, know-how, designs, inventions, and associated technical services – a so-called 'Technological Balance of Payments'. According to data for 1986 the UK is one of four countries out of the group of 24 that has a technological balance-of-payments surplus.* This is shown in Figure 33.8 which forms the core of a Case Study at the close of this chapter.

It would seem, therefore, that one of the problems facing the UK is that for effective research and development to occur a longer time-horizon may be necessary. In short, the UK lacks co-ordinated, stable R & D policy. This seems particularly salient when one considers the approaches overseas. France, for example, indulges in **indicative planning** in which the government discusses and co-ordinates the direction of the economy over a number of years. The Japanese, similarly, have recognized that R & D policy can be employed as a means of winning strategic advantages in certain international markets. In fact, the aforementioned Alvey directorate arose as a response to Japanese government funding for computing.

These overseas strategies present a planned solution to R & D problems. A UK government could adopt such an approach. The present government, however, prefers to place a trust in enterprise and competition as the forces that underpin the research and development process. It is not, therefore, solely a matter of increasing expenditure to improve research and development. Managerial attitudes, organization, confidence in the future stability of markets, and rates of return on capital are equally important.

Alternatively, there may be some way of developing a British R & D strategy by creating a closer link between the policies offered here and those outlined elsewhere in this chapter. For example, R & D and training expenditure are more potent in combination than either of them can be separately. This idea of integration will be furthered in the final section. (Read Key Points 33.3 next.)

*The others in surplus are: USA, Denmark, and Sweden.

Small-Firms Policy

The current emphasis on policy for small firms is not confined to Britain. A whole range of policies to encourage and support the development of small firms is in force througout Europe, America, and Canada. These policies are popular as they encourage enterprise, which many governments presently regard as central to reviving flagging economies.

Apart from specific policies, a whole range of institutions has developed to support, advise, and represent the small firm in all sectors of the economy. To take only British examples there exists: the CBI Small Business Unit, the National Federation of Self-employed and Small Businesses, the Small Firms Service administered by the Department of Trade and Industry, the Association of Independent Businesses; and even a parliamentary minister responsible for small firms.

Therefore, although policy for small firms represents the most recent emphasis of UK industrial policy, it is by no means the least important. Apart from being an integral part of many of the policies discussed so far in this chapter, there were over 100 specific measures implemented during the 1980s that influenced the development of the small-firm sector. In the next section we shall review *some* of them. But before that we should look at what is actually meant by a small firm.

The most widely accepted definition of a small firm

Key Points 33.3

- **R & D involves exploring and inventing new product areas, including those involved with defence.**
- **Most governments, including the UK, are committed to providing assistance for R & D, since one successful development may have many external benefits.**
- **The British Technology Group is an important organization responsible for developing new technologies. It was formed in 1981 by merging the NEB and NRDC. It is at the forefront of 'technology transfer'.**
- **Various collaborative projects exist. These bring industry, research organizations, and government departments into a R & D team. The Alvey directorate and Eureka are two examples of collaborative ventures.**
- **Government incentives are provided in the form of financial assistance, tax concessions, research grants, and patent law.**
- **In many ways R & D policy is still developing. Recent government expenditure has identified themes for collaboration. The present emphasis is for grants to provide businesses with the correct environment to fund and undertake their own R & D.**

is: **one which has a small share of the market, is owned and managed by the same individuals or group of individuals, has a small number of employees, and is legally independent (i.e. it does not form part of a larger enterprise).**

To express this definition in precise statistical terms is far more complex. For example, there has been a wide margin between the definitions used to describe a small firm in The Netherlands and the USA – in the former it had less than 50 employees and in the latter less than 1 000! Aspects of definition vary within countries too; some focus on turnover, some on the value of capital employed, and so on. Indeed the Bolton Committee when undertaking their research on small firms in the UK used seven different definitions to survey the various industrial sectors that they studied.* Choosing a specific, universal, statistical statement of 'small' is clearly an unresolvable academic difficulty. What we notionally mean by the small firm is, however, easier to grasp and for our purposes the previous highlighted paragraph will suffice.

What Is Small-Firms Policy?

Much of the small-firms policy introduced since 1979 has involved tax benefits and incentives aimed to reward enterprise and encourage the development of small businesses. For example, since the 1984 Budget there has been a lower rate of Corporation Tax for small firms. In 1990 those firms whose annual rate of profits did not exceed £200 000 paid 25 per cent Corporation Tax compared to a 35 per cent rate for larger firms.

Another group of measures has been aimed at removing the administrative 'red tape' that seems to complicate the life of so many small firms. For example, the 1980 Employment Act provided for the *exemption* of small firms from requirements relating to industrial tribunals, maternity reinstatement, and unfair dismissal procedures. These have been extended since the mid-1980s to include simple planning procedures, building regulations, and auditing requirements.

Three specific financial schemes have also been created directly to encourage small businesses. First, and most importantly is the Enterprise Allowance Scheme (EAS) which we outlined on page 517. This scheme costs the government about £200m per year to fund. It is, however, considered to be money well spent, as it allows the budding, yet unemployed, entrepreneur to have the opportunity of running his/her own business. It is estimated that for every 100 supported by the EAS 56 are still in business after three years and that these firms are providing an additional 84 people with full-time employment.

The Loans Guarantee Scheme, as its name suggests, involves the government acting as a guarantor for bank loans to small firms. By 1989 over 22 000 small businesses had taken advantage of this scheme and had raised in excess of £750m. This scheme creates jobs both directly and indirectly and, therefore, even though some bankruptcy debts have to be repaid by the government, it is still assumed worth while. One study estimates that this scheme had created some 44 500 jobs at an average cost of £2 200 per job.

Thirdly, there is the Business Expansion Scheme. This scheme provides tax relief on money invested in businesses. It is expected, therefore, to encourage the supply of venture capital. Indeed, between 1983 and 1987 £577m was raised under this scheme from 80 000 investors. All of these schemes enable the potential small businessman to overcome some of the barriers to entry that exist in markets.

Finally, reference should be made to those provisions that help overcome the barriers to growth. Since the late 1980s an increasing emphasis has been placed on advice and counselling. The aim is for the small firm to have access to external expertise. The government will cover at least half of the costs involved and the firm will receive a 5–15 day consultancy. A small firm is thereby encouraged to take support on matters relating to design, marketing, finance, planning, and quality control.

All of these policy measures and others are summarized in Figure 33.7 on page 522. The intention of this chart is to emphasize the range of specific incentives available and to highlight some of the interrelationships between this section and the other policy areas discussed in this chapter.

Does Small-Firms Policy Work?

The problem, outlined above, of finding an appropriate statistical definition for small firms makes it difficult to assess the effectiveness of policy. Most commentators, however, tend to look at VAT data as firms with turnovers in excess of a certain threshold (£25 400 in 1990) must register themselves for this tax whilst others look at the numbers of self-employed. Both these statistical series have to be used cautiously as an assessment of small-firm growth – but both suggest some remarkable increases.

The number of businesses registered for VAT increased by 285 000 (i.e. 22 per cent) between 1979 and the end of 1988. Over the same time-horizon the numbers of self-employed rose from just under 2m to 3m (i.e. 60 per cent). Not only is this an enormous increase but it represents a major change in behaviour. The number of self-employed had actually fallen by 7 per cent between 1973 and 1979. The main growth areas were transport, motor trades, finance, construction, and services.

Following this data it is assumed that most of the growth in the number of firms has been represented by small firms. Indeed it is estimated by government sources that at the beginning of 1990 small firms accounted for approximately 25 per cent of employment and 20 per cent of the GNP.

How far this growth in small-firm sector is a result of the policy manœuvres outlined above is a matter of

**Report of the Committee of Inquiry on Small Firms* (HMSO, 1971), often referred to as the Bolton Committee after the name of its chairman.

Figure 33.7

Examples of Policies to Promote Small Firms

Direct financial assistance	Business Expansion Scheme Loan Guarantee Scheme Enterprise Allowance Scheme
Indirect financial assistance	Raising VAT threshold Reducing Corporation Tax liability
Premises & planning	Government factory building with an emphasis on small premises Enterprise Zones Simplified planning procedures and building regulations
Red tape & business burdens	Reducing form-filling Relaxing Health and Safety requirements (under consideration) Relaxing Employment Protection (under consideration)
Provision of advice	Establishment of Counselling Services Enterprise Agencies (Trusts)
Education & training	Youth Enterprise Business in schools Start-up training Business Growth training TVEI
Regional assistance	Regional Enterprise Grants Counselling Services (two-thirds of costs met by government)
Research & development	Small Firms Merit Awards for Research and Technology (SMART)

Source: Adapted and extended, Storey *et al.*, *The Performance of Small Firms* (1987).

some debate. As already suggested in other industrial-policy sections it is difficult to assess what the situation would have been in the absence of policy. (For example, the economy's management during the 1980s would have affected businesses whatever their size.) The recurring methodological issue has not, however, been ignored in the case of small-firm policy evaluation.

A concept known as *deadweight* has in fact been created to aid the discussion. 'Deadweight' involves decisions that would have been made irrespective of policy. For example, a study carried out in 1984 suggested that 50 per cent of the firms formed under the Enterprise Allowance Scheme would have formed anyway – regardless of the scheme. The Department of Employment estimates that 'deadweight' is as high as 44 per cent in the financial schemes geared towards the development of small firms.

A further methodological issue that has been considered in relation to small-firm policy is *displacement*. Displacement relates to the indirect effects that new firms cause to existing firms. For example, a policy designed to assist unemployed people to set up business as hairdressers may be highly successful in achieving its aim. But the hairdressing market is already highly competitive and total demand is constant. Consequently existing businesses may find themselves forced out by the new firm, especially if that newcomer is benefiting from some form of government subsidy. Displacement is a recognized problem – its measurement, however, is difficult. The Department of Employment estimates that the 'displacement' effect resulting from small-firm policy may be as high as 50 per cent. 'Displacement' is probably counterbalanced in some instances by the positive indirect effect that new firms also create employment. The new firm will place demands on other firms for their services and products, and employment opportunities in these neighbouring sectors will improve.

Any evaluation, therefore, of small-firms policy would not be complete until *all* the costs and benefits had been assessed. Such a cost-benefit exercise is clearly complex. Many measurements problems would have to be faced and very few have tackled this question to date.

Furthermore, there is still a lot of debate whether

Key Points 33.4

- **Policy aimed at encouraging and supporting small firms has been popular with most governments in Europe, America, and Canada since 1980.**
- **In the UK small-firms policy has taken three main forms: (1) changes to the tax systems; (2) changes to the administrative 'red-tape' requirements, and (3) several financial incentives made available through various schemes. Examples of these policies are summarized in Figure 33.7.**
- **There is a consensus that the small-business sector has increased in size during the 1980s.**
- **In evaluating small-firms policy several measurement problems are incurred, e.g. deadweight, displacement, and the actual definition of what constitutes a small firm.**
- **Whether the revival in the small-firms sector is sufficient to get the whole economy moving again is the subject of much academic and political debate.**

solutions to our industrial problems actually lie in the innovating and personalized small-firms sector or whether a full economic revival can only come from the large-firm sector where economies of scale will enable them to break into national and international markets. In brief, there seems to be some controversy over the question of whether 'big' or 'small' firms are more beneficial to an economy.

The Political Dimension

An answer to the closing question could partly reconcile the divide between the Conservative and Labour parties, and avoid continual further changes to industrial policy. At present, Conservative strategy seems to rely heavily on the market mechanism, encouraging the independence of firms and a favourable environment for private initiatives. Labour, on the other hand, when in office, have tended towards large-scale organizations and intervention into the market mechanisms. In consequence, no long-term co-ordinated industrial policy has ever been effectively developed. (See Key Points 33.4.)

CASE STUDY

A Technological Balance of Payments

Figure 33.8

Technological Balance of Payments (1986). Each nation's figures represent its own national currency in millions.

	Receipts	*Payments*	*Balance*
USA	19 701	7 007	+
Japan	224 078	260 577	–
Germany	1 981	4 159	–
France	7 888	9 486	–
UK	668	619	+
Italy	326 438	1 056 350	–

Note: The figures displayed represent monies paid or received for the use of patents, licences, trademarks, designs, inventions, know-how, and closely associated technical services.

Source: OECD, *Science and Technology Indicators* (1989).

Questions

1. Define in your own words what a technological balance of payments involves.
2. Give two actual examples of the type of expenditure represented by this data.
3. (a) Calculate the actual balances involved for each state.
   (b) Convert all balances to a common currency.
4. Given the UK R & D record, how could the UK surplus be explained?
5. Account for Germany's large deficit.
6. If the UK government gave allowances of 150 per cent against tax for private-sector spending on R & D, how would this affect the technological balance of payments? (Explain your answer.)

CASE STUDY

The Austrians

The Austrian economists (such as Hayek, Schumpeter, and Kirzner) assert that actual economies consisting of real-world firms and industries are never in equilibrium (that is, never at a state of rest). Instead, economies are characterized by ignorance and uncertainty, which leads to continuous change and continuous market disequilibrium. Ignorance and uncertainty create opportunities for profits and it is the entrepreneur's task to discover these profitable opportunities. To the Austrians, competition means continuous rivalry with entrepreneurs searching for opportunities to make money before anyone else – all of which occurs in a world of ignorance and uncertainty where there is no such thing as perfect information and knowledge. To the Austrians, trial-

and-error price adjustments, and trial-and-error advertising and product variations are simply a *search and discovery process* – they are methods of trying to obtain market information in situations where knowledge is imperfect and costly to acquire. But conventional theory regards these actions by a businessman as evidence that he possesses some monopoly power. In other words, the competitive process which we witness in the high street is alien to the model of a perfectly competitive equilibrium. In the high street, the trial-and-error price cuts made by businessmen are simply examples of the way they try to gain information on their profit-maximizing price (they are searching for profits).

The public policy implications of the Austrian approach concern two major issues in particular. In the first place, they concern the role of *profits*. At any given moment, profits may seem to be monopolistic resulting from output restrictions – the monopoly problem. Austrians, however, regard high profits as temporary since rival entrepreneurs will be attracted into the relatively profitable activity. Austrians believe therefore that any public policy which minimizes the rewards of entrepreneurship will reduce future entrepreneurial effort with adverse effects on the competitive process.

Secondly, they concern *industrial organization*. Austrians believe that policy-makers should avoid making statements either about the most efficient form of industrial organization or about the wastes of advertising, product differentiation, and duplication. Austrians claim that no one has sufficient knowledge and competence to judge which form of market structure is the most efficient for meeting tomorrow's consumer needs (given that some of today's sunrise industries will almost certainly prove to be tomorrow's dinosaurs and smokestack industries). Entrepreneurs do not have perfect foresight, but they do have a greater motivation than politicians and bureaucrats to meet new and unexpected consumer demands – namely their desire to seek out profitable opportunities.

Source: Adapted, *Understanding the UK Economy*, ed. P. Curwen (1990).

Questions

1. The Austrian School influenced government policies in the UK during the 1980s and early 1990s. Explain and elaborate, using examples from industrial policy.
2. The Austrians would be concerned with highlighting 'Government Failure'. What do you think this means (see Chapter 10 for help if necessary)?
3. French and Japanese industrial policy has not been as influenced by the Austrian School as the UK. Give evidence that supports and explains this statement (page 520 might help).
4. Assume the arguments the Austrians would make to proposals to increase each of the following:
   (a) Research and development policy
   (b) Training policy
   (c) Small-firms policy
   (d) Regional policy
   (e) Competition policy
   (f) Privatization
5. Identify at least two policy issues that an economic adviser, influenced by the Austrian School, would recognize as important for the improvement of industrial performance.
6. List some arguments against the Austrian School of thought.

CASE STUDY

Where Do Skills Come From?

The prospect of a Europe dominated by 80m Germans – most of them well educated and well trained – is once more concentrating the minds of British ministers on one of the country's weakest public services: education. Ministers rightly calculate that the system's chief defect is not the lack of cash for universities or the poor pay of primary-school teachers – though dons and teachers still grumble loudly – but the unusually high drop-out rate among 16-year-olds. In Britain 60 per cent of children abandon full-time education at 16, compared with only 10 per cent in West Germany and America and 4 per cent in Japan.

On 27 March 1990 the departments of education and employment jointly announced their solution: training credits or 'vouchers'. In ten pilot areas 16-year-olds who leave school will be offered a voucher, worth about £1 000, which they will be able to set against part-time courses of their choice. Employers will be expected to provide jobs at market wages and give young people time off for study. Training and Enterprise Councils (TECs) – employer-led bodies financed partly by the government and partly by business – will provide and certify training at local level.

This solution merely side-steps the greatest weakness of British education: its obsession with selecting the best at the expense of all the rest. This characteristic, the main source of unflattering comparisons with Germany, has endured for well over a century, surviving even the ballyhoo over comprehensive reforms in the 1960s. Less promising children are screened out early, and the education system thrives on a homogenized curriculum with little relevance to the personal interests and vocational needs of the mass of 16-year-olds. Most leave school as soon as the law allows – bored, alienated, and utterly lacking in skills.

The unsurprising consequence is a chronic shortage of skilled labour. The proportion of British companies expecting skill shortages to constrain their output is rising fast, from 2½ per cent in 1982 to about 20 per cent this year. This is a national handicap, in an international race where countries increasingly compete not on brawn or raw materials but on the ingenuity and flexibility of their workers. With fewer youngsters coming on the job market, Britain has less scope than ever to waste them through bad schooling.

Will vouchers succeed where past reforms have failed? Almost certainly not. As the number of teenagers declines between now and 1994, so their pay will rise. Why bother with training credits, when jobs beckon today with ready cash and a drink after work? As for the TECs, most will offer only narrow training: hair-dressing for aspirant hair-dressers, brick-laying for would-be brickies. Yet the market needs broader skills, basic but easily adaptable. And Britain's businessmen, now charged with running the TECs, have never shown much enthusiasm for training their own workers.

Instead, the voucher scheme will make the already messy world of post-16 education messier still. Employers complain of an alphabet soup of acronyms, some denoting different qualifications, others describing squabbling organizations. The TECs will add to current confusions – and, to make matters worse, each will be responsible for awarding certificates and policing standards in its locality.

A better answer would be to build on the existing education system. The government ought to be improving what it already offers 17- and 18-year-olds, not erecting a new and ramshackle employer-led arrangement. The most effective – as well as the simplest – way to do this would be a diversified curriculum, geared to differences in ability and aptitude, and leading to tailor-made qualifications.

A minority of adolescents could study a predominantly academic syllabus – although this ought to be broader than the current sixth-form curriculum, with its constricting A-levels. Others could follow a different kind of course: broadly based and vocationally flavoured, with some instruction in core academic subjects (notably mathematics) and a generous amount of work-experience. Such a restructuring would not be cheap. But if Britain continues to leave the mass of its 16- to 18-year-olds poorly educated, it will be trapped between high-skill economies such as Germany and low-wage economies such as Portugal or the newly liberated countries of Eastern Europe. If Britain cannot afford education, it cannot afford a modern economy.

Source: 'Teach don't train', *The Economist*, 31 Mar. 1990.

Figure 33.9

Fourth- and Fifth-Year Attitudes to School

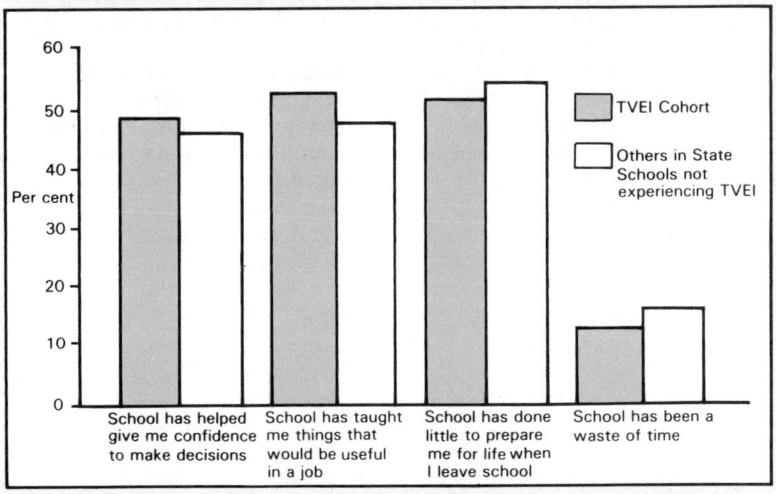

The above data relate to a survey carried out in 1986. One thousand TVEI students aged 16 were compared to their contemporaries in other schools who had not been involved in any TVEI work.

Source: Youth Cohort Study of England and Wales Cohort 3

Questions

1. According to *The Economist* most leave school 'bored, alienated, and utterly lacking in skills'. How does this compare with your experience and that of your friends?
2. Why are there fewer youngsters joining the job market?
3. (a) What do you understand TECs to be.
   (b) What are their purpose?
   (c) Where is the closest TEC to your locality, who comprises its members, and what is known of its work?
4. Identify in order of priority which of the following schemes you would consider to be most effective in overcoming skill shortages:
   (a) a broader sixth-form curriculum
   (b) a training voucher system
   (c) Training Enterprise Councils
   Explain the order of your choices.
5. (a) How far should TVEI remedy the problems outlined in the final paragraph?
   (b) How do your experiences compare to each of the four tabulated in Figure 33.9?
6. A recent study estimates that British firms devote 0.15 per cent of their turnover to training (compared with 1 to 2 per cent in Japan, West Germany, and France).

(a) Why do firms spend so little on training?
(b) Why does the UK spend less than our overseas competitors?

7. Should training be the concern of education, the Department of Employment, the employer, or the individual? Justify your answer.

8. How would you suggest that the UK training problems may be remedied?

CASE STUDY

Small-Firms Policy – An Academic's View

A healthy industrial economy will have a mixture of large, medium, and small firms. Although any judgement as to the appropriate proportions will be very subjective, the fact that the UK has a smaller proportion of small firms than other industrial countries and that there have been certain identifiable tax advantages to large firms does suggest that we might aim to enlarge that proportion.

Turning to the effects that an increase in the proportion of small firms might have on the economy, our discussion of investment and innovation suggests that the extent of both activities depends to a fairly large extent on the nature of the industry rather than the size of firm. Neither the overall level, nor (for investment) its variability, will be much affected by small shifts in the proportion. However, certain types of innovation are sensitive to firm size, so that any substantial incentives to one size at the expense of the other might well be harmful.

There are, of course, many other factors which would enter into any consideration of policy. *(1) What would happen to the extent of competition; (2) the level of union power; (3) the degree of inflationary pressure within the economy? (4) What would be the effect on the level and mixture of training and experience acquired by the workforce? (5) Would the encouragement of small firms lead to greater job satisfaction or more opportunities for exploitation?* Unfortunately, we do not have the space to discuss these issues here, but must move on to consider whether the government has any power to influence the size of the small-firm sector.

The fact that other countries have appreciably large small-firm sectors does suggest the possibility of change, but these larger sectors probably reflect long-established attitudes and institutions, and it is likely that any attempt to produce a *rapid* shift will both be unsuccessful and do a great deal of harm. The government has very little direct influence over attitudes, and is limited to the indirect effect which shorter-term financial encouragement of small firms might eventually have.

Source: R. Allard, 'The importance and position of small firms', *Economic Review*, Nov. 1983.

Questions

1. In the third paragraph of the extract we have italicized some questions that the author raises, and we have numbered them (1) – (5). Take each point in turn and consider: What would happen if more small firms did develop?
2. Identify at least two beneficial (positive) indirect effects that small firms may create.
3. Does the author of the extract think the government policy for small firms will be successful or not?
4. This article was originally written in 1983. Which statements suggest that circumstances have changed since?

Exam Preparation

MULTIPLE CHOICE QUESTIONS

For Questions 1 and 2 select your answers from the following grid:

A	B	C	D	E
1, 2, 3 all correct	1, 2 only correct	2, 3 only correct	1 only correct	3 only correct

1. The 'natural' rate of unemployment can be reduced by
1 expansionist fiscal policies
2 retraining schemes
3 measures designed to reduce imperfections in the labour market

2. The free-market approach to solving the problem of less prosperous regions assumes that
1 labour is geographically mobile
2 wage differentials would reflect regional prosperity
3 capital would be allocated among regions according to the return it yields

3. Which of the following comes closest to being a merit good:
A Training
B Research and development
C Enterprise Zones
D The Small Firms Loans Guarantee Scheme
E Enterprise Allowance Schemes

4. The opportunity cost to society of running a government-funded training policy is:
A the money spent on the schemes
B the regional policy and R & D policy that could otherwise have been used had the training policy option not been adopted
C the cost of government borrowing needed to finance the schemes
D the goods and services that could otherwise have been produced by the people on the training schemes had the policy not been running.

5. Which of the following is an example of occupational mobility of labour?
A professional footballers transferring from one football club to another
B miners moving from South Wales to Lancashire
C men taking part-time jobs in addition to their normal employment

*(Choices **D** + **E** in next column.)*

D men retraining as plumbers after some years in shipbuilding
E married women returning to their old jobs after maternity leave

RELATED ESSAY QUESTIONS

1. Discuss the arguments for and against the free-market approach to regional economic imbalance.

2. Examine the problems of measuring the costs and benefits of government training schemes.

3. Discuss the ways and means by which discriminatory government policy might affect small-business enterprise.

4. Briefly describe the chief characteristics of industrial policy in recent years. Discuss whether, in your opinion, experience supports the view that less direct government intervention is desirable or that more is required.

5. 'UK industrial policy is designed to enable markets to work more efficiently.' Discuss.

6. (a) How do enterprise and capital differ as factors of production?
(b) How might the supply of entrepreneurs be increased?

7. Explain briefly what is meant by
(a) the mobility of labour and
(b) the mobility of capital.
Examine the relevance of the mobility of factors of production to the problem of regional imbalance.

8. Why is it necessary for government to seek to regulate the economy?

9. Discuss the possible effects of advances in information technology on the efficiency of the economy. Consider how such changes are likely to affect the structure of employment in the UK.

10. What is meant by enterprise and entrepreneurship in economics? And what factors are likely to govern their supply? In your opinion, are government and other schemes to increase the supply of enterprise in the economy likely to be successful?

34 Economic Growth

Key Points to Review

- Factors of production and scarcity (1.1, 1.4)
- Production possibilities curve (1.5, 1.6)
- Trade-off of present and future consumption (1.7)
- Retail Price Index (11.5)
- Savings and investment (12.2)
- GNP (13.1)
- Is national income accounting sufficient? (13.7)
- The law of diminishing returns (21.2)
- X-inefficiency (23.4)
- Human capital (27.3)
- Regional policies and training policies (33.1, 33.2)
- Research and development policies (33.3)

Questions for Preview

1 What is economic growth?

2 What does economic growth measure?

3 What are some of the ways your family could experience economic growth?

4 What are the determinants of economic growth?

5 What government policies may affect the level of economic growth?

Growth is a controversial topic. The business community typically sees economic growth as a means to continuing prosperity. Certain sectors of society see economic growth in this country as the only way that the poor and disadvantaged will ever attain higher standards of living. In direct contrast other sectors of society want economic growth to stop. They argue that we in the UK with only a very small percentage of the world's population use 'too much' of the world's resources. Growth is, therefore, a topic of academic and political debate; and in the Case Studies at the end of this chapter we will return to this opening theme and encourage you to consider whether economic growth is a desirable or undesirable target.

What Is the Meaning of Economic Growth?

As this is the penultimate chapter in the book, most of you probably have a general idea of what the term *economic growth* means. When a nation grows, its citizens are in some ways better off, at least in terms of material well-being. A general definition of **economic growth** might read as follows:

Economic growth is the increase in an economy's level of real output over time.

Generally, economic growth is measured by the *rate of change* of some measure of output. In this nation, and in most other countries today, the most commonly used measure of economic output is gross national product (GNP). In discussing the rate of change of actual output, we have to correct GNP for changes in prices through the use of a price index.

When we do, we get what is called *real* GNP, as discussed and illustrated in Chapter 13. Hence a more formal measure of economic growth may be defined as the rate of change in real GNP over time.

For example, from 1985 to 1988 in the UK, the average annual rate of growth of nominal GNP (i.e. uncorrected for price changes) was 10.4 per cent. During that period, the average annual rate of inflation was 4.6 per cent. Therefore the approximate average annual increase in *real* GNP was 10.4 per cent minus 4.6 per cent, or 5.8 per cent.*

Correcting for Population Growth

The above measure might be misleading if, for example, the population is growing rapidly at the same time that real GNP is growing. An alternative and perhaps more appropriate definition of economic growth is in terms of per capita output; defined as the total production of goods and services in one-year period *divided* by the population. The self-explanatory mathematical formula for this calculation has already been presented and discussed in the section headed 'per capita GNP' in Chapter 13. We can therefore move to yet another definition, the fullest and official measure, namely:

Economic growth is the increase in per capita real output; it is officially measured by the percentage rate of changes in *real* GNP *per head* of the population from one time-period to another – normally a year.

Problems of Definition

Nothing is stated in the above definitions about the *distribution* of output and income. A nation might grow very rapidly in terms of increases in total or even per capita real output, while at the same time the nation's poor people remain poor or become even poorer.

Nothing has been said about changes in the leisure time available to the nation. In one sense, 'real' standards of living can improve without there being any positive economic growth as measured by increases in real per capita output.

Similarly, nothing in the above definitions of economic growth relates to the spiritual, cultural, and environmental quality aspects of the 'good' life.

All these themes have already been reviewed in Chapter 13, explicitly, when we discussed the question 'Is National Income Accounting Sufficient'? and implicitly, when we considered the Case Study entitled

*This is only an approximate figure based on the general principle used for converting nominal (money) GNP into real GNP.

Figure 34.1

The OECD Growth League for 1989 and 1990. shows approximate growth rates in the twenty-four OECD countries based on their national accounts. They should be regarded as broad approximations only, since they are the official statistics of governments and omit the varying rates of growth of unrecorded economies, which are substantial in some countries. Nevertheless, they do indicate marked differences. The average figure for 1989 was 3.6 per cent, whilst the forecasted average for 1990 is 2.9 per cent.

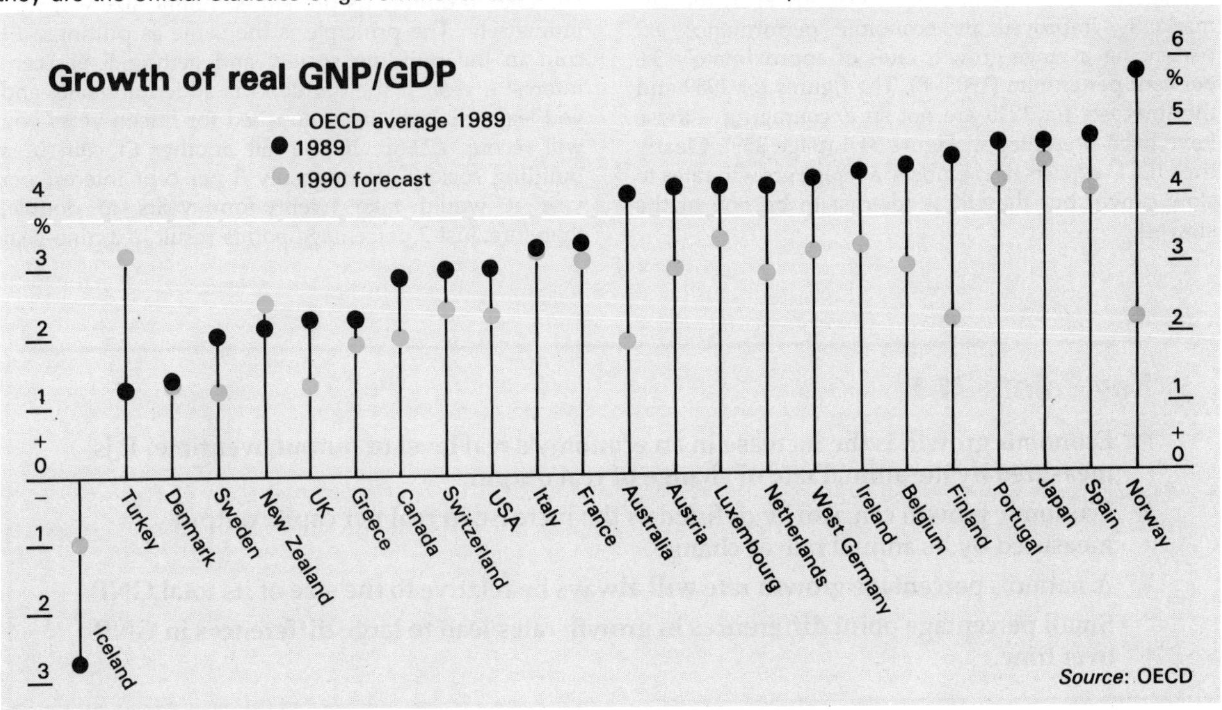

Source: Adapted from *The Economist*, 6 January 1990.

Figure 34.2

From the income per head column (given the similarity in population size) it is possible to ascertain that the UK is a slightly more developed nation in 1987. However, if these growth trends persist the UK will soon be overtaken in the rate of economic activity by Italy – this is suggested by the shorter doubling-time in the final column.

	Population (mid-1987)	*Income per hd. in 1987 ($)*	*Average yearly growth rate 1965–87 (%)*	*Doubling-time (if existing growth rate is maintained)*
United Kingdom	56.9m	10 420	1.7	42 years
Italy	57.4m	10 350	2.7	27 years

Source: World Bank: *World Development Report*, 1989

'National Income Accounts: Measurements or Mirage'.

Students of economics, therefore, recognize that no measure of economic growth is perfect. Yet, the measures that we do have allow us to make comparisons across countries and through time, and if used judiciously, can provide important insights. In sum, GNP may be a defective measure of well-being, but it is a serviceable measure of economic activity.

The UK Growth Record

Economists often arrange the countries of the world in a kind of 'league table' each year. During the 1970s and early 1980s the UK was consistently one of the worst performers within these growth leagues. For example, the UK experienced an average annual growth of 1 per cent of GDP from 1973 to 1983, compared to an OECD average of 2.1 per cent. Since 1985, however, the UK markedly improved its economic performance experiencing average growth rates of approximately 3.8 per cent per annum (1985–8). The figures for 1989 and the forecasts for 1990 are not so encouraging – these have been presented in Figure 34.1 (page 259). Clearly the OECD expects its members' average growth rates to slow down, but the UK is forecast to be one of the slowest.

The Importance of Growth Rates

The question arises, therefore, of how important these percentage point differences are. The answer is twofold.

Firstly, you must always ask the question, 'percentage of what'? Any developed country's growth rates in percentage terms will traditionally be lower than a developing country. In the developed country you are thinking along the lines of a 3½ per cent increase on £400 000m, while in a developing nation one is considering a percentage increase of a far smaller total. It is like comparing a 5 per cent increase of £100 to a 5 per cent increase of £1bn – even the innumerate will recognize that the latter is far larger.

The second problem is slightly more complex since it relates to compounded rates of growth. If a nation consistently has a low or high rate of growth the time it will take to double its present economic size will vary immensely. The principle is the same as putting a £1 coin in the building society and getting 5 per cent interest a year. If the dividend is added annually and you leave the amount untouched for fifteen years you will recoup £2.08p. If one left another £1 coin in a building society offering only 3 per cent interest per year it would take twenty-four years to double, therefore, just 2 percentage points result in a nine-year

Key Points 34.1

- **Economic growth is the increase in an economy's real level of output over time. It is measured by the annual rate of change of real output.**
- **Economic growth can also be defined as the increase in real per capita output measured by its annual rate of change.**
- **A nation's percentage growth rate will always be relative to the size of its total GNP.**
- **Small percentage point differences in growth rates lead to large differences in GNP over time.**

difference in 'doubling-time'. These concepts are illustrated in a more international setting in Figure 34.2. Italy has been chosen because it is similar in population size to Britain. (Read Key Points 34.1.)

Growth and the Production Possibilities Curve

We can graphically show economic growth by using the production possibilities curve presented in Chapter 1. Figure 34.3 shows the production possibilities curve for 1990. On the horizontal axis is measured the output of agricultural goods, and on the vertical axis, manufactured goods. If there is economic growth between 1990 and 1995 then the production possibilities curve will shift to the right (or outwards). The distance that it shifts represents the amount of economic growth, that is, the increase in the productive capacity of the nation.

Figure 34.3

Economic Growth. If there is growth between 1990 and 1995 then the production possibilities curve for the entire economy will shift outwards from the line labelled 1990 to the outer curve labelled 1995. The distance that it shifts represents an increase in the productive capacity of the nation.

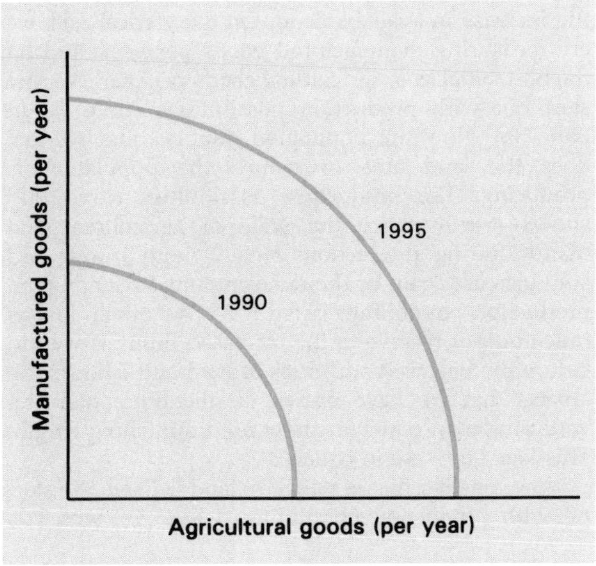

Potential and Actual Output

Remember that the production possibilities curve represents the maximum rate of output that *can* be achieved with the nation's available resources. It is possible for resources to be underutilized. The production possibilities curve could shift outwards, but the actual utilization of resources might be less than the maximum use represented by the curve. Look at Figure 34.4. Here we show the production possibilities curve for 1990 shifting out as it did in Figure 34.3. We start at point *A*, but find that by the year 1995 we have ended up on point *B* because of underutilization of actual resources in 1995. It is even possible for the economy to have a decrease in actual output if we move inwards to point *C*. Thus, in a sense, the production possibilities curve for 1995 is a representation of maximum **potential output** which is defined as the level of output that a nation could attain if it were operating on the production possibilities curve. **Actual output** will therefore never exceed potential output but it may be smaller. In the long run, it may be changes in potential output that determine government and business planning, but in the short run it is changes in actual output that are important.

Figure 34.4

Potential versus Actual Output. The production possibilities curve may shift out from 1990 without necessarily ending up on the new potential production possibilities curve for 1995. For example, if we start out at position *A*, we may only progress to point *B*. The 'actual' output rate symbolized by *B* represents an underutilization of resources. We are not producing at our maximum potential rate. Indeed, one could even envisage a situation developing where the economy moves inwards towards *C*: this would represent an 'actual' growth rate well below potential.

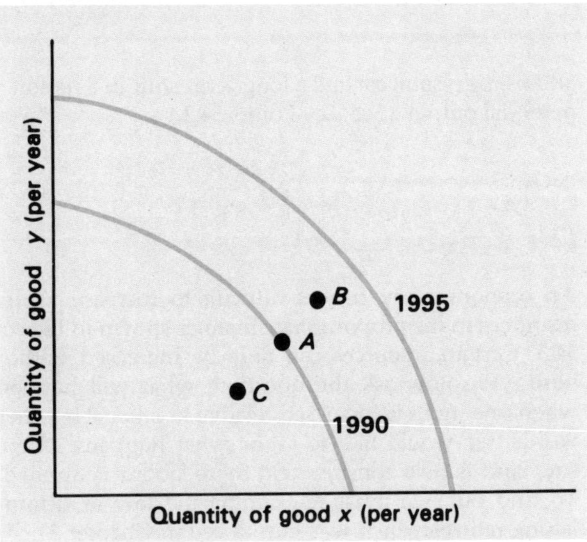

Let us develop this concept of potential output a stage further. Potential output can be increased by enlarging productive capacity which is a long-run process. In contrast, therefore, economic growth achieved by simply utilizing existing spare capacity should be recognized as qualitatively and quantitively different – and certainly more short-term in nature. This latter type of growth can be regarded as a kind of *recovery* phase. Economic growth built on a recovery basis only will ultimately lead to full-capacity use of the existing resources. A distinction, therefore, needs to be drawn between a shorter-term recovery phase (based

Key Points 34.2

- **Growth is shown by an outward movement in the production possibilities curve for the entire economy.**
- **Economists make a distinction between potential and actual growth rates. The former represents maximum efficiency with resources and provides a target; the latter represents resource utilization in practice, and illustrates the outcome.**
- **Growth can be achieved in two forms: (1) through increased productive capacity, and (2) by utilizing existing capital equipment more fully. The former should lead to long-term growth, the latter simply represents short-term recovery.**

on *existing* resources) and a long-term shift in a nation's potential output. (See Key Points 34.2.)

Growth and the Law of Diminishing Returns

An economy may find it difficult to increase all its resources in the proportionate manner shown in Figure 34.3. Certain resources can only be increased within limits. We now ask the question: what will happen when one input is increased relative to others? In other words, we would like to know what happens when, say, land is held constant and more labour is applied. To find out, we must re-examine the **law of diminishing returns** which was introduced in Chapter 21.

A common-sense notion of this law is that beyond some level of output, successive increases in one input – holding all other inputs constant – will generate smaller increases in output. In order for the law of diminishing returns to operate, we must assume that only *one* input is allowed to vary. All others are held constant. This gives us a formal definition of the law of diminishing returns:

As successive, equal amounts of one input, such as labour, are added to other inputs which are fixed (such as land and technology), beyond some output the resulting increases in output will diminish in size.

In other words, total output may continue to increase as we add, say, more and more labour to a fixed amount of land, but the *rate of increase* in output will fall after some point. In Chapter 21 when we discussed this we talked in terms of an average and marginal product – remember? (If not it may be worth re-reading that section before continuing any further.)

An Example: Illustrating the Law of Diminishing Returns

Consider two possible situations: one in which there is a balanced increase in all production inputs including land, the other in which land is fixed. In panel (a) of Figure 34.5 we show the probable effects of balanced growth: there is a population increase that just matches the increase in available land. On the vertical axis, we are measuring manufactured goods per year; and on the horizontal axis, agricultural goods per year. We first start out with production possibilities curve *PP* in panel (a). Now the population doubles, and so, too, does the land area on which the population is producing. The production possibilities curve *P′P′* shows exactly twice the scale of agricultural and manufacturing production. Finally, both labour and land increase again by the same amount. We end up on production possibilities curve *P″P″*. We obtain just as much output relative to the increased input as we did before the balanced additions of land and labour. The arrows that we have drawn on the horizontal and vertical axes in panel (a) show no diminishing length. This is *not* the case in panel (b).

Now consider that in panel (b) land is fixed. We start off with production possibilities curve *ZZ*, which is

Key Points 34.3

- **The law of diminishing returns tells us that as successive equal amounts of one variable input are added to the other *fixed* inputs, the resulting increases in output will diminish in size.**
- **The law of diminishing returns can be portrayed by comparing the outward movement in the production possibilities curve when all factors of production are increased in a balanced manner and when, say, land is fixed. With land fixed, the same increase in the variable inputs leads to a smaller and smaller outward shift in the production possibilities curve.**

Figure 34.5

The Law of Diminishing Marginal Returns. In panel (a), we show balanced growth where population (labour) and land are increased at equal rates. In panel (b), we show a situation where only labour is increased while land is held fixed. In panel (a), proportional increments in labour and land result in proportional increments in potential output, as shown by the increase in the production possibilities curve from *PP* to *P′P′* to *P″P″*. The arrows on the axes labelled 1, 2, and 3 do not diminish in size. In panel (b) they do, however. As we add equal increments of labour, the production possibilities curve shifts out by smaller and smaller amounts. Thus, the arrows 1, 2, and 3 get smaller and smaller in length. In panel (b), we have shown the effects of diminishing marginal returns to labour when land is held constant. As more workers are added, each labourer has less land on which to work. (Of course, technological development may dramatically increase agricultural productivity, making substantial outward shifts in the schedule possible.)

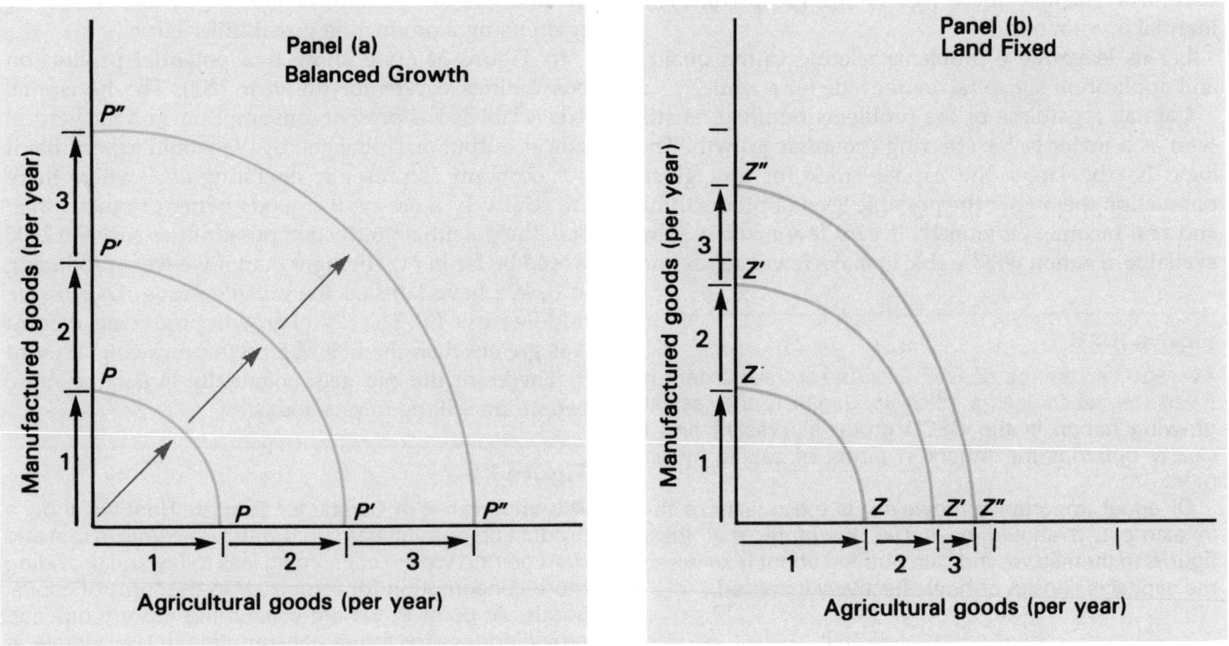

exactly of the same dimensions as *PP* in panel (a). This time, however, *land is held constant*, while the population doubles. Each worker therefore has less land to work than under the balanced-growth situation depicted in panel (a). Production possibilities curve *Z′Z′* results. It is below production possibilities curve *P′P′* in panel (a). Finally, we add another equal amount of labour, *still holding land fixed*. The new extra output is even lower than the output produced before. This can be seen by the diminishing lengths of the arrows on the vertical and horizontal axes in panel (b). What has happened in panel (b) resulted from diminishing marginal returns. In other words, equal increments in labour (holding land fixed) resulted in diminishing increments in output. (Read Key Points 34.3.)

Factors Determining Economic Growth

Potential economic growth is largely determined by the factors of production that a nation has at its command. Actual growth, however, is determined by how effectively these factors are developed and combined.

Natural Resources and Economic Growth

A large amount of natural resources is not sufficient to guarantee economic growth. A number of less-developed countries are fantastically rich in natural resources. However, they have not been overly successful in exploiting these resources. Natural resources must be converted to useful forms. For example, in the USA, the Indians had many natural resources available to them, but they were unable to increase their standard of living or experience economic growth.

People must devise the methods to convert natural resources into usable forms. Countries with similar natural resources vary in their ability to do this.

In short, abundant natural resources are not sufficient in themselves. People are necessary to develop resources into useful things. Less-developed nations require this type of human resource before they are able to exploit the natural resources they possess.

Capital Accumulation and Economic Growth

It is often asserted that a necessary prerequisite for economic development is a large capital stock –

machines and other durable goods – that can be used to aid in the production of consumption goods and capital goods in the future. It is true that developed countries do have large capital stocks per capita. For example, in Figure 34.6 we present a bar chart showing the amounts of fixed capital investment (i.e. plant, machinery, and buildings) that various OECD countries undertook on average between 1982 and 1986. These figures provide some indication of production potential; however, they say nothing about how wisely the capital investment is chosen or how effectively it is used. For example these figures include private residential investment.

Let us leave these problems relating to the quality and application of capital on one side for a while.

Capital, regardless of the problems outlined, is still seen as a major factor affecting economic growth. The logic is: the larger the capital stock for any given population the higher the possible level of productivity and real income. Obviously, if very few machines are available, a nation will be able to make fewer goods and services and therefore income will be lower. Conversely more machines will mean more income can be generated. Therefore, the larger the capital stock, the larger the income pie.

BUT HOW DOES CAPITAL STOCK GROW?

It grows by people making the decision not to consume all their income today. The more saving by households and the more investment by firms there is, as a percentage of total income, the larger will be the capital stock, and therefore, the higher will be possible future income. We can perhaps demonstrate this decision by again using a production possibilities curve.

In Figure 34.7 we show two potential production possibilities curves for the year 2000. The horizontal axis is labelled as present consumption, and the vertical axis as output of capital goods. We would expect that if our economy is presently operating at *A* where there are relatively more capital goods being produced than at *B*, the potential production possibilities curve in 2000 would be farther to the right than if we were producing at *B*. We have labelled the outside curve *AA* and the middle curve *BB*. The rate of growth producing at point *A* is greater than the rate of growth producing at point *B*. Therefore the pie gets potentially larger the more people are willing to save today.

Figure 34.6

Average Percentage of GDP Devoted to Investment in Fixed Capital for Years 1982–86. Japan is the fastest-growing nation in the OECD group at present and it clearly outstrips the others in terms of capital investment.

Of equal importance, however, is the quality of this investment. It should be noted, therefore, that these figures in themselves indicate nothing about how wisely the capital is chosen or how effectively it is used.

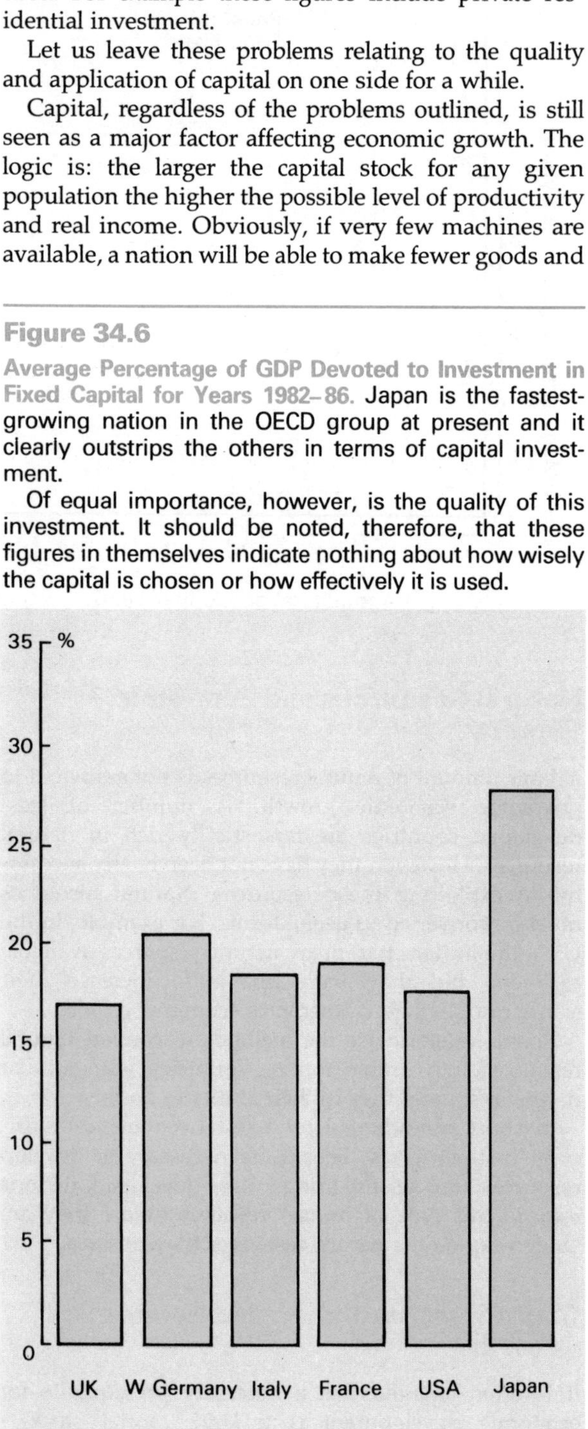

Source: OECD, 1988.

Figure 34.7

The Importance of Capital for Growth. Here we show a production possibilities curve with two points in it, *A* and *B*. At point *A* we are consuming less today and providing more consumption for tomorrow in the form of capital goods. At point *B*, we are consuming more today and providing less for future consumption. If we operate at point *A*, we may end up on a production possibilities curve of *AA* in year 2000. However, if we are at point *B*, we may end up at a production possibilities curve of only *BB* in year 2000. In other words, there will be less growth during the next decade if we consume more goods today instead of saving and investing in capital goods that provide for more future consumption.

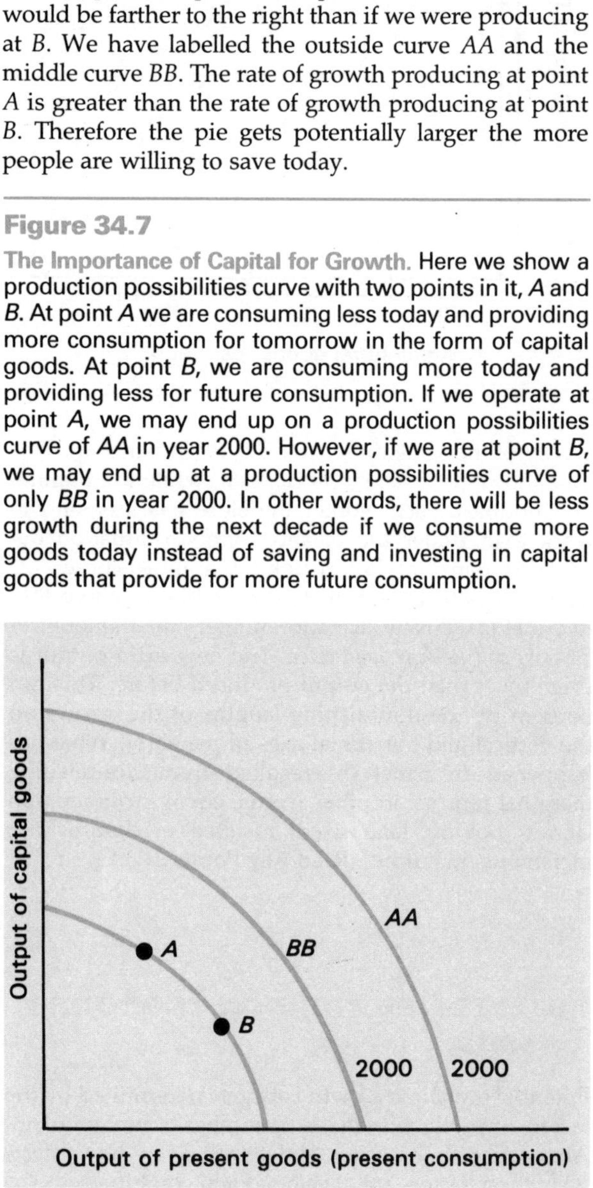

Key Points 34.4

- **Natural resources are not sufficient to guarantee economic growth; many countries without a large natural resource base have had relatively high growth rates.**
- **Capital accumulation is a possible determinant of growth. The more capital goods we produce today, the higher our potential growth, other things being equal.**
- **There is a trade-off between present goods and future (capital) goods.**
- **Technological progress allows a nation to produce greater output with a given amount of labour and capital.**
- **Technological progress and the accumulation of human and material capital determine, to a large extent, the rate of economic growth.**

Technological Progress and Economic Growth

When technological progress takes place, it is possible to obtain more output from the same amount of inputs as before. Technological progress or change results in outward shifts in the production possibilities curve. Thus, technological progress determines, at least in part, a nation's rate of economic growth. The ability of a nation to effect and sustain technological change depends on:

1. the scientific capabilities of the population,
2. the quality and size of the nation's educational and training system, and
3. the percentage of income that goes into basic research and development each year.

Technological progress does not occur only in the industrial sector of developed nations. In the less-developed countries, technological change has involved the use of improved pesticides, higher-yielding hybrid seeds, and improved irrigation techniques. Much of the technological change that first occurred in the developed countries has been transferred to the less-developed countries, thereby allowing them to increase their rate of growth. Consider the example of the invention and widespread use of 'miracle' rice, which has caused a 'green' revolution in less-developed countries. Miracle rice, although requiring more fertilizer, has much greater yields per acre planted than any other previously existing strain of rice. The innovation and use of miracle rice has increased the actual output for the limited capital and skilled labour available to less-developed countries.

We can tentatively conclude, therefore, that technological progress, along with the *associated* accumulation of human and physical capital, is important in determining a nation's economic rate of growth. (Now read Key Points 34.4.)

Can We Tell which Factor Is Most Important?

Is it possible to find out which factor is most important in determining a nation's economic growth rate? This is indeed difficult to answer. One way to simplify the problem, though, is to talk in terms of two determinants of economic growth that can be measured – at least in theory:

1. growth of capital stock, and
2. growth of the labour force.

Now if we assume that these two determinants alone will account for all the economic growth that is sustained, it seems relatively straightforward to find out the numerical importance of the factors. The researcher simply estimates the average annual rate of growth in capital and labour.

But the task is not really so easy. Certainly we can measure the value of the number of machines that are put in place and the number of workers that have entered the labour force. But what about the *quality* of the capital we use? And the *quality* of the labour force? Part of the growth in our capital stock and labour force has to do with quality improvement. 'One unit' of a machine today is certainly of a higher quality than the 'same' machine of a hundred years ago. Similarly, the average worker today has much better training and a higher educational attainment level than the worker a hundred years ago. Thus we can say that to a large extent the measurement of the growth in capital and in labour does not take into account the growth in the *quality* of these two factors.

No Growth Theory

Because of the quality/quantity dilemma outlined above, it is most difficult to identify which factor – labour or capital – is the more important contributor to the growth process.

Furthermore, other factors – such as natural resources and technological progress – also need to be brought into the formula. But these two factors *also* have inherent problems of measurement.

Consequently, economists in the 1990s can still not agree on the relative importance of the factors that contribute to economic growth. To paraphrase R. Lipsey from his famous textbook *Positive Economics*: of all economic variables growth is the most difficult to control. (Now read Key Points 34.5.)

Key Points 34.5

- **Capital, labour, natural resources, and technological progress all contribute to economic growth. But it is most difficult to identify which is most significant, largely due to problems of measurement.**
- **When considering changes in capital and labour there is a problem distinguishing between quantity and quality aspects. (The same is true of measuring technological progress and natural resources.)**
- **There is no accepted growth theory yet developed.**

Policies to Promote Growth

Because economists cannot agree on one growth theory, it follows that when governments wish to promote economic growth their advisers have no unanimous policy package to follow. All that exists are several possibilities, *some** of which are outlined below.

Promote Savings

The logic is straightforward: capital is recognized as a key determinant of growth and capital accumulation can depend on the level of savings. If resources are fully utilized increased investment may require reduced consumption. Therefore, increased investment, or capital accumulation, would require increased savings. Why? Quite simply because savings can be defined as *non*-consumption, in the short term, and investment can be defined as the creation of future productive capacity in the long term. Only if individuals are willing *not* to consume everything will businesses be able to obtain resources for their investment activities.

Consequently, we could potentially increase the rate of growth in the United Kingdom drastically if we somehow increased the saving rate of the population, and this additional saving led to the additional production of capital goods.

The classic example is Japan where the impressive growth has often been attributed to their high rates of saving. It is a fact that Japan's savings rate during the 1960s, 1970s, and 1980s has clearly outstripped that of the UK and its average annual rate of real growth was more than double that of the UK for the years 1965–90. Japan now has a far higher income per capita than the UK, and if its rate of growth continues unabated it is destined to become the richest country within the next thirty years.

In an attempt to follow this trend the UK and other European states have been changing legislation, tax, and stamp duty to encourage a wider ownership of shares and the habit of saving.

This trend was epitomized by the UK budget of 1990 which was headlined as a 'Budget for Savers'. It incorporated measures designed to increase SAYE† schemes, Personal Equity Plans (PEPs), and special savings accounts that had the incentive of being tax-exempt. The latter were nicknamed TESSA (Tax Exempt Special Savings Account) and were aimed at the small saver wishing to make a gain over a five-year period.

Whether these schemes will have the desired effect of reviving a 'culture of thrift' is not clear at the time of writing, and even more complex to identify will be whether the saved funds will have the desired knock-on effects on productive capital investment. These problems of analysis are compounded further by the development of the world capital market – this will be a theme of one Case Study at the end of this chapter.

*You should be able to identify others, especially if you have read the 33 preceding chapters!

†Save As You Earn.

Promote Mobility

Economic growth implies change and development. Therefore, factors of production will need to be reallocated from industrial sectors that are declining into those that are expanding. However, restrictive practices, such as union-enforced manning levels, prevent some of this reallocation taking place in the UK. Added to this are the universal problems that people are hesitant to uproot themselves or change jobs mid-career. Consequently immobility may cause growth to slow down.

Equally, measures designed to improve mobility may encourage faster growth. Such measures may involve legislation against unions. Alternatively, incentives, such as those discussed in Chapter 33, may be offered to entice labour and capital to be more mobile. These incentives were dealt with under the headings of regional and manpower policies, and may well be worth revisiting at this juncture, in order to glean some relevant sample policy options.

Promote Education and Training

Spending on education and training is regarded by economists as investment in **human capital**, and through this term it can be seen as complementary to, and just as important as, investment in physical capital. Investment in physical capital involves putting time and money into machinery; investment in human capital involves putting time and money into labour.

We need specialized labour to operate and develop specialized machinery for we live in a capital-intensive society.

Levels of investment in human capital must, therefore, be maintained and/or increased for economic growth to continue. Consequently, we could tabulate the expenditure on education and training from one country to another and assess its importance in the growth process. However, such figures are complicated by the fact that expenditure on education and training is carried out by both the public and private sectors. Furthermore, as with physical capital, how does one measure its effectiveness, especially as the benefits of education and training are often only realized in the long run?

At present the UK government is trying to make the educational process more vocational. It is shifting funds to science and technology subjects and placing an increased emphasis on business training – in this way it is hoped that the quality of our human capital will improve. But only time will tell.

Promote Research and Development

So far in this section we have recognized that investment can be put into human capital or physical capital. We can now complete this by introducing **R & D capital**. R & D capital is the money used for research and development, or to use other words, for invention and innovation. Clearly, such break-throughs would play an important part in the growth process. Consequently, the government engages in funding and undertaking a considerable amount of R & D through research grants and joint projects with business. R & D spending is also allowable against tax. These initiatives have already been reviewed in Chapter 33 in some detail and will not be repeated here.

As with all investments in capital the returns can only be measured in the future. Any analysis of R & D investment expenditure is further complicated by the fact that some of it results in no commercial developments. Consequently, economists are still uncertain about the precise importance of R & D policies to the growth process, and this a question that academics are currently studying.

Promote the Supply Side

Supply-side ideas have been at the centre of government thinking since 1979, the aim being to increase the incentives for businessmen and labour to supply their goods and services. This philosophy is based on a trust in market forces. The ways to achieve this are seen to stem from personal initiative and enterprise. Consequently, supply-side theorists place a huge emphasis on free-market forces. As a result government intervention, and specific structural rigidities, especially in the labour market, have been reduced. Many of these have already been examined in Chapter 18.

The aim is that more efficient use will be made of resources. You may remember that we reviewed Leibenstein's x-inefficiency in Chapter 23. Obviously the converse of this concept may occur where output increases due to a more effective use of inputs. This may be prompted by reining back union power, by increasing the forces of competition, and so on. And research does suggest that total factor productivity has improved in the UK during the 1980s.

A specific example of a supply-side effect is presented in Figure 34.8, where productivity in public-sector-type industries is examined. It is evident that productivity growth in these industries increased after 1983. This is when the privatization and deregulation programme began. It is noticeable that performance has improved whether the industry had been privatized or not, e.g. British Gas and British Rail respectively. This suggests that a more commercial approach to management and the emphasis on competition has improved performance throughout the public and private sectors.

Figure 34.8
Total Factor Productivity in Eight UK Industries

	Annual rate of increase (%)	
	1979–83	*1983–8*
BAA	0·0	2·8
British Coal*	0·6	4·6
British Gas	−0·2	6·2
British Rail	−0·4	2·7
British Steel	8·4	12·4
British Telecom	2·0	2·5
Electricity supply	−1·6	4·0
Post Office	3·6	3·3
Average	*1·6*	*4·8*

*Adjusted for effects of 1984–5 coalminers' strike.
Source: Bishop & Kay, 'Towards a skill revolution', CBI, 1989.

These supply-side policies work, therefore, by squeezing out inefficiences. There is a limit, however, to further and further productivity gains of this nature. The more gains achieved the harder it becomes to increase productivity further. Long-term growth requires not so much a change in the efficiency with which existing inputs are used as a change in the quality of inputs themselves. (Now read Key Point 34.6.)

A CLOSING NOTE

Finally, it must be remembered that growth is only one government economic objective. Therefore, spending, legislation, and/or tax cuts to promote growth may cause conflict with the other economic objectives. Consequently, planning and the stage of development are also crucial considerations. These aspects should be a little clearer to the student after the final chapter has been read, and some reflection on the contents of the completed text undertaken.

Key Point 34.6

▶ **Several government policies can be envisaged to promote economic growth. There is no agreed policy package. Possible examples include: (1) promoting savings, (2) promoting mobility, (3) promoting education and training, (4) promoting research and development, and (5) promoting the supply side of the economy.**

CASE STUDY

Into the 1990s: 'Industrial Renaissance' or 'Deindustrialization'

During the late 1970s and early 1980s Britain was seen to be undergoing a process of deindustrialization. This was defined and accounted for by economists in many ways. In very general terms the definitions seemed to focus on a decline in the industrial (manufacturing) sector as measured by a loss of employment or output. Sometimes these measures were expressed in absolute terms, whilst others focused on the decline in terms of a percentage share in manufacturing employment and/or output.

Explanations for this process ranged through a number of causes. At one extreme was the argument that deindustrialization is an inevitable accompaniment of economic development and growth: the natural development of a post-industrial society. Whilst at the other extreme concern focused on the increasing size of Britain's government sector: the non-market, service-dominant, sector was seen to be 'crowding out' the manufacturing activities of the market sector.

Towards the end of the 1980s, however, the emphasis shifted. An article in America's *Fortune* magazine in January 1987 set the ball rolling by coining the idea of 'Britain's industrial renaissance'. Foreign observers were clearly struck by Britain's new surge in productivity. Many of the features of our recovery are displayed in the data in Figure 34.9. The British press followed up these themes; remarking on the British efforts to catch and match the best in the world. But reservations were also in store.

As Christopher Smallwood in the

Figure 34.9
Productivity Up . . . Labour Costs Down . . . and Britain Is Tops

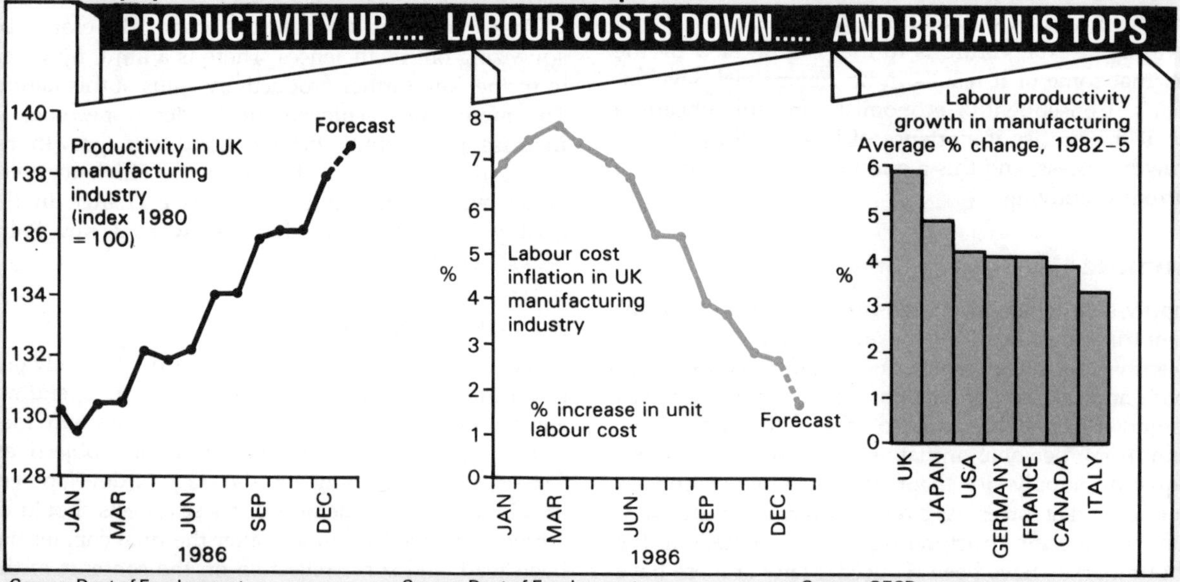

Source: Dept of Employment
Forecast: Credit Suisse First Boston

Source: Dept of Employment
Forecast: Credit Suisse First Boston

Source: OECD

Sunday Times (May 1988) remarked: 'Companies heading for the wall in the early years of this decade have saved themselves by laying workers off on a scale hitherto undreamed of.' This produced spectacular productivity gains, which were widely expected to peter out as de-manning came to an end.

In the event, de-manning led to a continuing and dynamic improvement in productivity. Partly, this was because high unemployment and the new trade union laws transformed industrial relations. The combination of more determined management, once more in control, and a more flexible workforce opened the way to the adoption of the best techniques already in use abroad but which had been blocked in Britain for years . . .

To its own surprise, Britain has found itself in a process of rapid productivity growth which has continued to accelerate. There is, however, a limit to what can be achieved by an unremitting drive to make operations leaner and fitter. If Britain is finally to close the gap with West Germany, it has to invest adequately in capital stock that is as productive as Germany's, and the workforce must be as skilled as Germany's. There are worries on both scores.

Through the years of high growth, investment has been disappointing.

Much of the increase in demand has been met by raising the degree of utilization of the existing capital stock. It is now at its highest on record and bottlenecks are appearing, particularly in industries such as chemicals and motor vehicles which are important for the trade balance.

Companies are at last starting to authorize capital expenditure on a significant scale, and manufacturing investment is expected to rise by 11 per cent this year. But it is a race against time to bring the new capacity on stream before excess demand produces a new bout of inflationary pressure, forcing the authorities to rein back growth.

An even more fundamental constraint on Britain's expansion is the growing skills crisis. A recent CBI survey reported that the number of manufacturers expecting shortages of skilled labour to affect output rose from 19 per cent in 1986 to 34 per cent in 1987, and fears of a shortage continue to grow.

The most dispiriting aspect of the current economic scene is the lack of evidence that companies have begun to face, or in many cases even to recognize, the paramount need to increase the supply of skills if we are to go on expanding strongly and close the gap with our Continental neighbours.

Overwhelmingly, industry's response to skill shortages has been to resort to overtime and to use temporary workers. Companies have also 'poached' from other firms by bidding up pay.

In many respects, Britain's industry has got its act together extraordinarily well, as *Fortune*'s article recognizes. It is leaner, fitter and more dynamic. The achievements are formidable.

But the harsh truth is that unless we now make a different type of effort – a major national effort to tackle the problem of our under-skilled workforce – and approach it with the degree of determination which enabled us to overcome our traditional problems of overmanning and bad labour relations, Britain's industrial renaissance could still founder, leaving the West German-style levels of efficiency and production still tantalizingly out of reach.

Source: Extended and adapted from 'Fresh skills needed to keep it booming,' *Sunday Times*, 8 May 1988.

Questions

1. Explain the meaning of the phrase 'Britain's industrial renaissance'.
2. Define labour productivity.
3. If Britain was seen to be experiencing deindustrialization during the 1990s would it be more easily recognized in terms of employment or output? Explain your answer.
4. Identify four causes of deindustrialization.
5. What is meant by 'the growing skills crisis', and how do you think this could be solved in Britain?
6. (a) Explain why so much press coverage is given to Britain's industrial performance.
   (b) Try and identify manufacturing performance in the 1990s.
   (c) Are we still experiencing a renaissance?
7. Explain and discuss using a production possibilities curve how the manufacturing sector may affect the UK's economic growth record.
8. Production is becoming a global affair. More and more multinational corporations are taking the place of national firms. How does this world development affect the deindustrialization/renaissance debate? (Give examples to illustrate your answer.)
9. Outline the trends shown by the charts in Figure 34.9 and describe what other information you need for a full evaluation of these charts.

CASE STUDY

Economic Growth and the Environment: Incompatible Objectives?

It would perhaps be frivolous to claim that concern for the environment is beginning to become a craze like pop music or the mini-skirt. Nevertheless some strange statements are being made and passing unchallenged. I am as keen as the next man to see the ozone layer repaired, our countryside preserved, our water purified and our streets cleansed of filth and litter. But we must not lose our sense of proportion, and demand what is impossible.

British society makes a living by producing goods and services. This way of life is coming increasingly under attack and is depicted as materialistic, squalid and dirty. It might be nobler to be a nation of soldiers like ancient Sparta and more spiritually elevating to be a land full of monks like Tibet, but our national genius has not taken us in these environmentally friendly directions.

We became a great power because of our ability to invent and our skill at manufacturing and marketing our inventions. We have lost our great-power status along with much of our industry and our marketing expertise. But we are stuck with our heritage. For nearly 200 years that has not been intimately linked to green fields, however much we would like to think that it has.

Evolution and foreign competition has driven us out of some of our environmentally unappealing industries. This is the age of the information explosion where the computer dominates. The work of the majority has become cleaner and Britain as a country of smokestacks is a fading memory. All of this can be welcomed, providing we do not forget some relevant facts.

We have an underclass that is not sufficiently prosperous to enjoy the luxury of being fanatical about the environment. Its work, when it can find any, is arduous, unpleasant and poorly remunerated. It does many of the dirty jobs the rest of us don't want. When the labour of the day is done, it goes home to seedy accommodation in mean streets to eat junk food in overcrowded and uninviting rooms.

One has to have a pretty thick skin to tell these hapless millions that those of us living in comfort are starting to have serious doubts about whether we want economic growth, if it is going to disturb the amenity and pleasure of our lives. That we cannot countenance having houses built anywhere near us that might increase the housing pool and so free some marginally better homes for the underclass. That we want the polluting industries, in which they are able to find a few jobs sweeping up and cleaning latrines, shut down, thus consigning them to the dole.

'Oh but we don't want anything like that,' say the anti-growth environmentalists. 'These people should be paid a generous minimum wage if they work and a basic income if they don't.' But a high minimum wage would destroy hundreds of thousands of existing jobs and how 'basic' would be the basic income? Remember British society would have eschewed economic growth and would be trying the experiment of paying for social improvement out of a static or falling revenue.

I notice a tendency to wish the underclass away. If it is mentioned, one is told, snappishly, it ought not to be there. Surely a civilized, modern society can dredge up from somewhere a few hundred billion pounds to eliminate poverty at a stroke? No government has ever managed that trick and I do not recall hearing one that thought it could combat poverty without increasing national wealth.

The underclass will not be the only group who will suffer if our environmental anxieties become manic. Those of us who live in pleasant homes, overlooking green fields, ought never to forget that our tranquillity is built upon the ceaseless, noisy activity of a busy society going about its industrial and commercial business.

Everybody needs a little illusion in their lives. It does good, rather than harm, providing that we recognize it for what it is. The majority have not suddenly been transformed into country squires. Nearly everything most of us possess would be at risk if we neglected the national economy. The beauty and contentment we seek is, and has to be, underpinned by the sweat, dirt and striving of the working world.

I would not attempt to deny that the wealth-creating process has an inclination to ignore, or underestimate, the damage it does to the environment. It is a sign of greater knowledge and maturity that more of us now recognize the perils of unregulated growth. But we need the kind of regulation that safeguards the environment without severely inhibiting economic activity.

It is not all that difficult to be an environmental moderate and the only reason it seems so is because of pressure groups, which are not content with half a loaf. It ought to be possible to establish rational priorities in environmental protection and to judge whether the economic price being paid for rapid improvement is excessive.

To take a simple example, it is inexcusable that any local authority should not swiftly clear its streets of litter. That is one of the first duties of local government and ranks above the needs of more grandiose projects. It will cost money, which will have to be raised from the local population. But it is money well spent and it is better to resolve to spend it, rather than hope that more prosecutions, fines and propaganda will get rid of the problem.

By destroying wildlife it is possible to put its habitat to commercially profitable use. But that is another area where the bias should be towards the environment.

Public and private transport poses a more difficult equation to balance. Motorways and new roads do destroy part of the countryside, or open spaces in towns. But unless we prohibit people from using cars we have to construct them. I think the projected road-building programme is too large and some of the money might be better spent on improving public transport.

We have to build new houses. By all means let us site them carefully, but if we do not put them up, we shall find that some of our industry will depart for Belgium and France after 1992. Industry needs workers, who must have houses to live in.

Though so-called 'green taxes' have a role in discouraging polluters, we must not recklessly impose taxation that will be passed on to the consumer and worsen inflation. We cannot improve the environment by taxing industry out of business.

The two great fallacies about the relationship between work and the environment are that we can have a neutral tax system that leaves everything to the free market, or that we can save the planet by destroying the market. Common sense decrees that we take a middle way.

Source: adapted from B. Walden, 'Why heads in the ozone need feet on the ground', *Sunday Times*, 15 Oct. 1989.

Questions

1. Using some kind of graphic analysis explain and account for the trade-offs that may exist between economic growth and environmental decay.
2. Outline the arguments that may be put forward by
   (a) those who favour economic growth,
   (b) those who would support the anti-growth lobby.
3. The author implies that some sectors of society may bear the costs of growth more than others. In rank order identify the sectors that may bear these costs.
4. Is the environmental problem an economic issue? Explain your answer as fully as possible.
5. John Maynard Keynes wrote an article in the late 1920s entitled: 'Economic possibilities for our grandchildren'. In this he concluded that around the year 2000 the economic problem may be solved.
   (a) What do you think Keynes was referring to?
   (b) Would the author of this extract agree with Keynes?
   (c) Would you agree with Keynes?
6. The author concludes with the statement: 'Common sense decrees that we take a middle way.'
   (a) Explain, with examples, how you interpret this statement.
   (b) How would you suggest the dilemma between growth and the environment may best be resolved?
   (c) Is the market appropriate for dealing with environmental problems?

CASE STUDY

A Capital Mystery

Figure 34.10
Savings – Investment Correlations

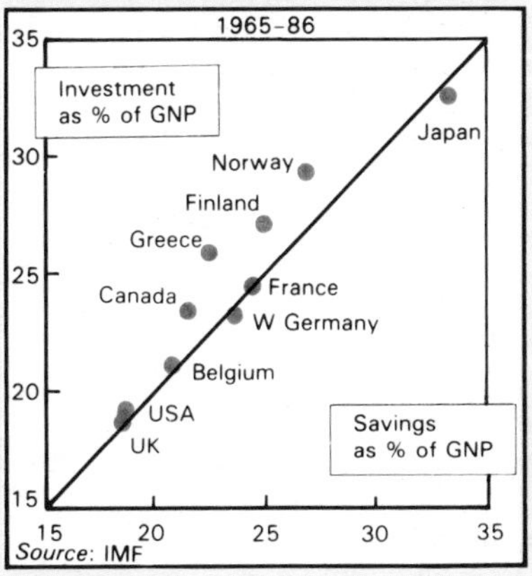

Source: IMF

Every reader of the financial press has been told a thousand times that the world's once-separate financial markets have merged to form a single pool of capital. In that case, my dear Watson, why does the world economy behave as though they hadn't?

Suppose the world had a truly integrated market for capital. Savings would flow into this international pool and the money needed by investors would flow out, with little if any regard for national boundaries. If, in any one country, profitable investment opportunities exceeded the savings available to finance them, the extra funds could be drawn from the pool. Equally, if the country saved more than it could profitably invest, the surplus would flow through the pool to be profitably used elsewhere.

At first glance, this seems to fit the facts. Japan saves more than it invests; its surplus savings flow to the rest of the world, and especially to America, which invests more than it saves. That is the integrated capital market at work. Studies of interest rates (suitably adjusted for inflation, exchange rate changes, and so on) also suggest that the various national markets have merged into one.

Now look closer, the idea of a single capital market does not really fit the facts at all. Savings rates ought to differ from country to country according to social preferences (among other things); investment rates ought to differ according to the opportunities for making money. There should, it seems, be no connection between the two. Savings and investment should be uncorrelated. Plot countries in a diagram, with investment on one axis and savings on the other, and you should see a more or less random scatter.

Look at Figure 34.10. The savings and investment rates are highly correlated. To put this another way, savings–investments gaps (that is, current account imbalances) are smaller than they should be. This suggests not a single worldwide capital market, but many self-contained markets.

Source: adapted from *The Economist*, 7 Oct. 1989.

Questions

1. Explain fully what is meant by the phrase 'an integrated market for capital'.
2. Distinguish between the economic meaning of savings and investment.
3. What correlations can you identify from the data in Figure 34.10, that may suggest relationships between savings, investment, and economic growth?
4. How can Canada, Finland, Greece, and Norway be recorded as investing more than they save?
5. What economic mechanisms may prevent a random scatter diagram from occurring?
6. State three problems related to gathering and plotting data such as that presented in Figure 34.10.
7. How may inflation influence the savings–investment–growth relationship?

Exam Preparation

PRACTICAL EXERCISES

1. List as many costs of economic growth as you can.

2. List as many benefits of economic growth as you can.

3. Using supply and demand curves, show how it is possible for a nation to consume more of a resource over time even though the resource is becoming relatively scarcer.

MULTIPLE CHOICE QUESTIONS

For Questions 1, 2, 3, and 4 select your answers from the following grid:

A	B	C	D
1, 2, 3 all correct	1, 2 only correct	2, 3 only correct	1 only correct

1. To calculate the economic growth of a country as measured by changes in the *real* level of National Income, information is required on
1 social security payments
2 the retail price index
3 the GNP less capital consumption

2. A country may NOT wish to maximize economic growth if this leads to
1 a reduction in its non-renewable resources
2 a greater inequality of incomes
3 social costs greatly exceeding private costs

3. Which of the following influence(s) real income per head?
1 the size of the population
2 capital investment
3 technological development.

4. The diagram below represents the production-possibility boundaries for an economy for the years 1965 and 1985. The X represents the position achieved in the economy for each of those years. The diagram shows that when comparing 1965 with 1985 the economy experienced

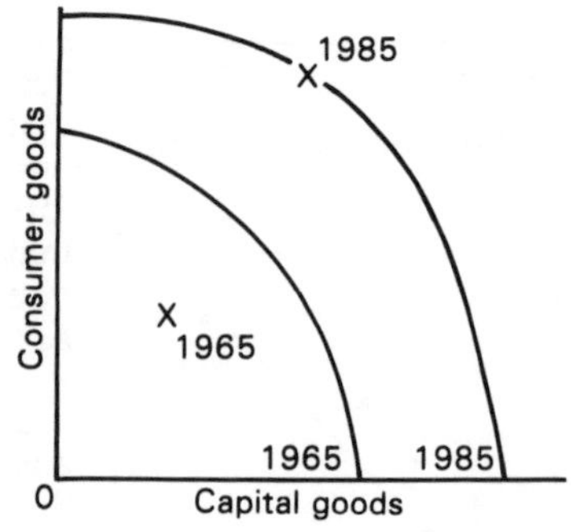

1 a growth in output
2 increasingly efficient use of factors of production
3 an increase in the general level of prices.

5. The diagram below shows two production-possibility curves.

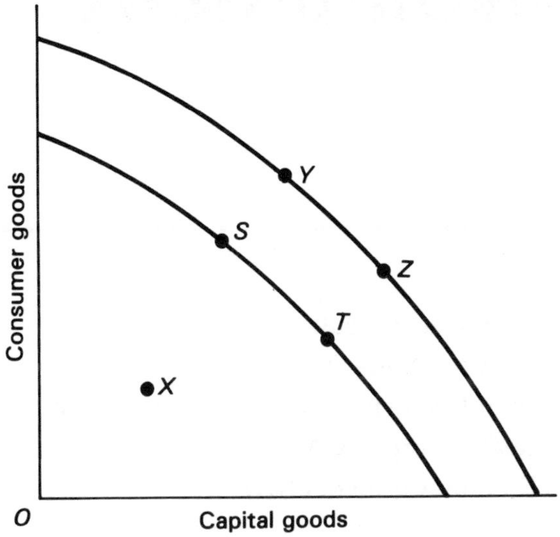

Which movement depicts an increase in the utilization of existing productive capacity?
A *X* to *T*
B *S* to *T*
C *S* to *Y*
D *S* to *Z*
E *T* to *Y*

6. Economic growth is most effectively defined as:
A an increase in money GDP
B an increase in real GDP
C an increase in both material welfare and social welfare
D an increase in real GNP per head.

RELATED ESSAY QUESTIONS

1. Do the costs of economic growth outweigh the benefits?

2. What are the major determinants of economic growth? To what extent is a policy for growth incompatible with other macroeconomic policy objectives?

3. Explore the nature of the relationship between the level of investment and national income.

4. Discuss the factors which might explain the difference in relative rates of growth among the industrialized nations.

5. Discuss the main causes of Britain's economic growth in recent years. Is growth necessary, or desirable, in your opinion?

6. (a) What is a country's Gross National Product?
(b) Analyse and comment on the factors which may cause an increase in a country's real Gross National Product.

7. 'Increase in people's welfare can be measured by increases in the economic growth rate.' Discuss this statement with reference to one country only.

8. What factors are likely to increase the level of 'labour productivity' in an economy? Would rapid growth in labour productivity solve the UK's economic and social problems?

9. Discuss the possible effects of advances in information technology on the efficiency of the economy. Consider how such changes are likely to affect the structure of employment in the UK.

10. 'The pursuit of different macroeconomic objectives illustrates the concept of opportunity cost.' Discuss with reference to at least three objectives.

35 Economic Development

Key Points to Review

- Factors of production (1.1)
- Capital goods and future consumption (1.7)
- Specialization and comparative advantage (6.2, 9.4)
- Price elasticities (7.1, 7.6)
- Income elasticity of demand (7.5)
- Buffer stocks (8.3)
- Terms of trade (9.4)
- Infant industry case for protection (9.5)
- Real per capita GNP (13.7)
- Economic growth (34.1)

Questions for Preview

1 What is a less-developed country (LDC)?

2 Do LDCs all face similar problems in trying to attain fast economic growth?

3 To what extent can LDCs rely on international trade in order to spur economic growth?

4 How can developed nations assist LDCs?

The previous chapter discussed economic growth with reference to countries like the UK. When we examine the same topic in relation to those countries in the world that are not yet developed, we enter the study of economic development. It is hard for us in the UK to realize that what we consider a low level of income in the UK exceeds the average income in a good part of the world. In fact, many of the world's people live at or close to subsistence: just enough to eat for survival. Developed nations encounter problems associated with being relatively rich such as obesity, urban sprawl, and pollution. The **less-developed countries**, or LDCs, are grappling with abject poverty and squalor; in short, with mere existence. The tragic pictures that we have seen of hunger and starvation in Ethiopia have vividly illustrated this contrast with the relative affluence of life in developed nations. Can governments do more to assist countries like Ethiopia? Before considering this we must first examine the nature of developing countries and consider why some countries are more developed than others.

Defining a Developing Country

There are a number of ways to classify nations by level of economic development. The 'three worlds' classification scheme has gained relatively wide acceptance. The **First World** is the highly industrialized, non-communist Western European nations, plus the United States, Australia, Canada, New Zealand, and Japan. The **Second World** includes the nations of Eastern Europe, the Soviet Union, and the People's Republic of China (PRC). The **Third World** is the term given to identify remaining countries, i.e. in Africa, Asia, and Latin America. But this classification of the globe has as much a political dimension to it as economic. A more basic distinction has been made between mainly developed countries situated in the Northern Hemisphere – 'the North' – and the vast majority of countries which are less developed and are located below the Equator – 'the South'. The rich North–poor South distinction is necessarily a crude one but still begs the question: what is the definition by which a country is deemed developed rather than developing?

Economists have traditionally used a cut-off point in GNP data to make this distinction. The precise figure used is of course quite an arbitrary one. In 1989 the World Bank defined forty-two low-income developing countries as those with a per capita income of less than \$480 in 1987. Fifty-three countries with a per capita income of \$400 or more constituted middle-income developing economies.

A fundamental question in looking at different countries is how can we compare the GNP of India measured in rupees with that of a developed country like the UK measured in pounds sterling? We do need a common unit of measurement. Translating all the GNP data into one country's currency seems to solve this problem. As we have just seen, the World Bank uses dollars as this common currency. Thus India's GNP in terms of dollars is measured as follows

$$\frac{\text{India's GNP per capita in rupees}}{\text{India's exchange rate between rupees and dollars}} = \text{India's GNP per capita in terms of dollars.}$$

The calculation implies that the foreign exchange rate is an international barometer of the cost of living. But a few moments' reflection should make you realize that the exchange rate is determined by the goods and services that are the subject of international exchange. Some items of consumer spending do not enter into world trade, e.g. going to a disco, getting a haircut. Thus our GNP data expressed in dollars (or pounds sterling) present an imperfect picture of the actual cost of living throughout the world. To try and surmount this problem economists have tried to see the differing cost of a common basket of goods and services purchased in various countries. This has revealed that the cost of living in many so-called developing countries can be high relative to countries like the UK, France, and West Germany. Figure 35.1 presents one such international comparison. Of the sixteen capital cities where the costs of living exceeded that of London nine were to be found in countries outside Western Europe, Japan, North America, and Australia.

We must appreciate that GNP per capita data are thus suggestive of the standards of living rather than precise pictures of differences in the welfare of the world's peoples.

Fortunately we find that other approaches to the

Figure 35.1

The Cost of Living in 33 Capital Cities. The chart shows the cost of buying a common basket of 126 goods and services and rents in each country weighted by consumer spending in 1985. London is taken as the point of reference with an index of 100. Thus the cost of living in Abu Dhabi was more than twice that in London. Can you suggest a reason why life in Lagos was surprisingly so expensive?

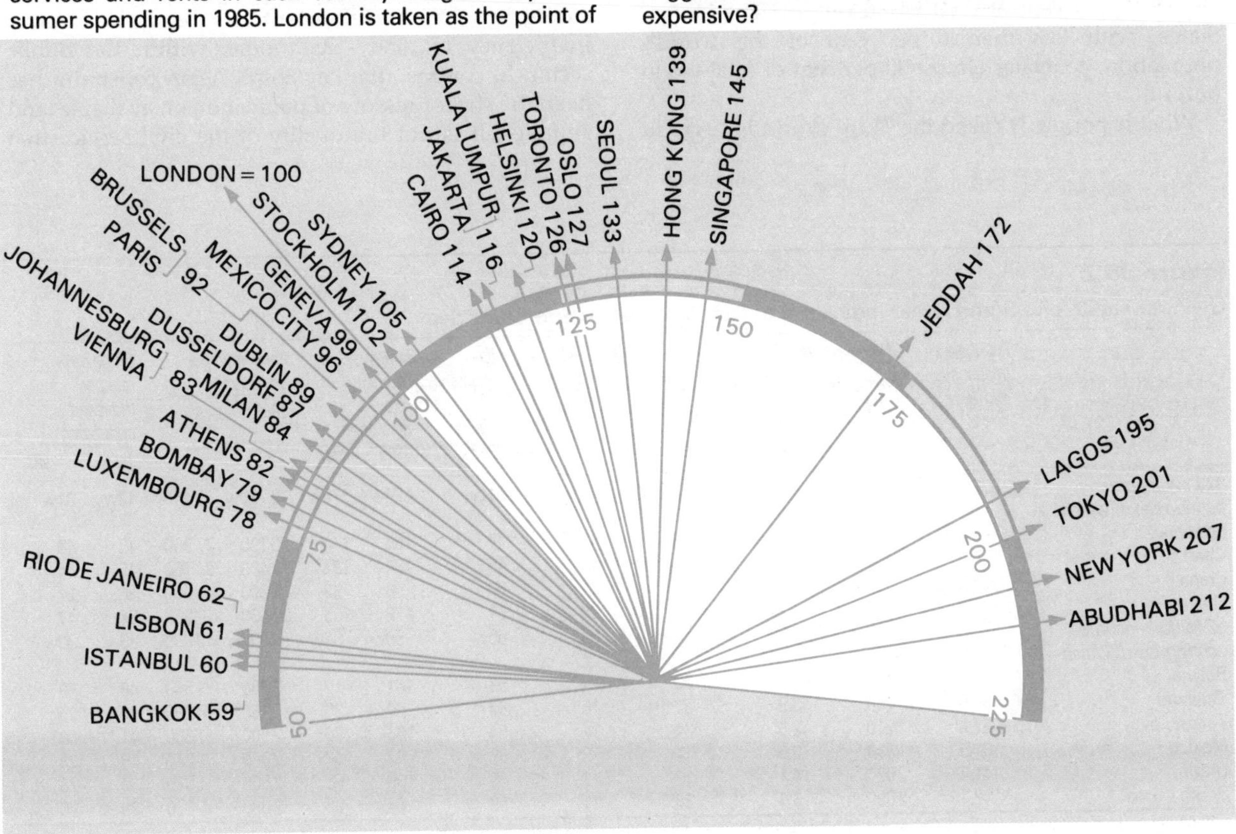

Source: Union Bank of Switzerland survey, *The Economist*, 21 Sep. 1985, p. 107.

definition of development do not really conflict with the broad message of GNP statistics. If we resort to so-called **non-monetary indicators** there is a sufficient correlation between these and GNP data. In Figure 35.2 we see that as we move up through levels of GNP per capita life expectancy as at birth tends to increase. We find that countries with a low level of GNP per capita suffer from high infant mortality, tend to have low levels of literacy, and typically have a high proportion of their people involved in the primary sector of the economy, that is, engaged in agriculture, forestry, and fishing. Indeed, it is by using some of these alternative measures of development that the **least-developed countries** have come to be defined. In 1971 the UN identified those countries with severe long-term constraints on development using three criteria:

(a) GDP per capita of $100 or less in 1970,
(b) a share of manufacturing in GDP of 10 per cent or less, and
(c) a literacy rate of 20 per cent or less of the population aged 15 years or older.

This definition identified twenty-four countries in 1971.

This consideration of the poverty of some countries in the world underlines the harsh fact of global inequality. When we look at the amount of world output accounted for by developed countries, the inequality is even more striking. The industrialized market economies (the First World) have less than 18 per cent of world population, but none the less generate almost 65 per cent of total world output. The United States, with less than 6 per cent of the world's population, generates almost 30 per cent of total world output!

What is popularly called the Third World is larger in terms of the number of countries than the First World and the Second World combined. But the concept of the Third World is rather vague, because it masks the marked variation *within* it. It lumps together countries that are very different not only in economic terms, but also in cultural, political, racial, and ethnic terms. A look again at Figure 35.1 points to oil as one important determinant of the differences within the Third World. A number of geographic regions and social classes within the Third World have living standards that are closer to Western Europe than to those of other Third World countries. Consider the oil states, for example. Those countries are normally classified as Third World countries, yet the total output per person in the United Arab Emirates in 1987 was $15 830. The output per person in Kuwait was over $14 600. These figures can be compared with $10 420 for the UK, $18 530 for the USA, and $21 330 for Switzerland!

Some LDCs are developing so rapidly that they have come to be termed **newly industrializing countries (NICs)**. Such countries as Mexico, Brazil, South Korea, and Malaysia are now seen as providing increasingly stiff competition for firms in the manufacturing sectors of the older industrialized countries of Western Europe.

One can identify rather different problems in each of the three continents of Latin America, Africa, and South Asia. In Latin America many economists see the unequal distribution of land as a major problem, frustrating the growth of agriculture. While many African countries face major pressing problems in feeding their populations a longer-established constraint on their development has been the relative inefficiency of many institutions within the public sector. In contrast, the key South Asian constraint has been the sheer pressure of population on available land supplies. It is not the quality of the civil service that

Figure 35.2

GNP per capita and Some Other Indicators of Development in Ten Countries

	Population (millions) mid-1987	*GNP per capita*		*Percentage of GDP in agriculture*		*Life-expectancy at birth (years) 1987*	*Infant mortality rate (age under 1)*		*Population per physician*		*Crude birth-rate per thousand population*	
		Dollars in 1987	*Average annual growth rate (per cent) 1965–87*	*1965*	*1987*		*1965*	*1987*	*1965*	*1984*	*1965*	*1987*
42 Low-income economies of which	2 822.9	290w	3.1w	43w	31w	61w	124w	76w	9 790w	5 410w	42w	31w
Ethiopia	44.8	130	0.1	58	42	47	166	154	70 190	77 360	43	48
Chad	5.3	150	−2.0	42	43	46	184	132	72 480	38 360	45	44
China	1 068.5	290	5.2	39	31	69	90	32	1 600	1 000	38	21
Nigeria	106.6	370	1.1	54	30	51	179	105	29 530	7 980	51	47
52 Middle-income economies of which	1 038.5	1 810w	2.5w	20w	n.c.	65w	99w	56w	4 030w	2 390w	38w	30w
Bolivia	6.7	580	−0.5	23	24	53	161	110	3 300	1 540	46	43
Thailand	53.6	850	3.9	32	16	64	90	39	7 160	6 290	41	25
Turkey	52.6	1 210	2.6	34	17	64	165	76	2 900	1 380	41	30
Mexico	81.9	1 830	2.5	14	9	69	82	47	2 080	1 240	45	29
Brazil	141.4	2 020	4.1	19	11	65	105	63	2 500	1 080	39	28
South Korea	42.1	2 690	6.4	38	11	69	64	25	2 680	1 170	36	20

Notes: *w* = a weighted average n.c. = not calculated.
Source: World Bank, *World Development Report 1989*, Oxford University Press, Tables 1, 27, 28, and 32.

Key Points 35.1

- **Any definition of a less-developed country (LDC) is arbitrary. Typically, a cut-off point in terms of per capita income of around $480 helps us define an LDC.**
- **LDCs can also be defined in terms of so-called non-monetary indicators such as their levels of literacy, education, infant mortality, and life expectancy. In virtually all LDCs, these socioeconomic indicators are quite different from what they are in the developed countries.**
- **LDCs differ among themselves almost as much as the differences between them and the countries in the First World.**

raises worries but the whole balance of resources. (Now read Key Points 35.1.)

Geographical Theories of Economic Development

One of the earliest and most simplistic theories of growth concerns geographical location. This might also be called the North–South theory of economic development. According to this theory, nations that are in the colder climates will be more developed than nations in the warmer climates. Most LDCs are between the Tropics of Cancer and Capricorn. This fact offers a robust challenge to the North–South theory of development. One might more convincingly argue an 'equator' theory of development, namely, that countries closer to the equator will develop more slowly than countries farther away from the equator. Basically, though, geographical theories of development cannot be used to predict development with a high degree of accuracy. If the North–South theory had any relevance or validity, it should apply also to the past. If does not. Some of the first civilizations were in the hot southern regions of the world. Look at the Mayas in Central America and all the great civilizations in the Mediterranean area and the Near East. The Germans and the Saxons were far behind the Greeks in development, even though the Greeks enjoyed a warmer climate. As a final example, consider that in AD 1100, the Near East was highly developed relative to the West. By the beginning of the Industrial Revolution, this was clearly no longer true.

This assessment, however, is in danger of playing down the significance of climatic factors that can hamper development of countries within the tropics. We must at least recognize the problem of agriculture in many LDCs arising from the quality of its soils, the variability of the rainfall, and the multiplicity of pests and diseases. The tropical climate is an important parameter in the development of many LDCs. This point has relevance to our consideration of the nature of the development process which now follows.

Factors in the Development Process

In Chapter 34 we considered the role of natural resources, capital accumulation, and technical progress in determining economic growth. Although our context was then the developed nations such as the UK you should find it helpful to read that review again as much of the analysis is of universal application. We will, however, briefly recap on our earlier conclusions.

We argued that the presence of large natural resources is certainly helpful but not vital for successful economic development. The fastest growing LDCs in the past two decades have been Singapore, Taiwan, South Korea, and Hong Kong. None of these countries is blessed with oil fields.

In any event, it is difficult to find a strong correlation between the natural resources of a nation and its stage of development. Japan has virtually no crude oil and must import most of the natural resources that it uses as inputs into its industrial production. Brazil has huge amounts of natural resources, including fertile soil and abundant minerals. Yet Brazil has a lower per capita income than Japan. Only when we include the human element of natural resources can we say that natural resources determine economic development. This comment takes us neatly into the issue of capital accumulation. Capital is important in both the physical and human sense. Indeed, recent research by the World Bank has pointed to the importance of human development. The Bank now believes better education, nutrition, and family planning can promote development as effectively as capital investment in physical plant.

In the early post-war period the World Bank was keen to help finance the extension of the infrastructure – investment in power, irrigation, and transport. This meant lending funds which were used to buy bricks and mortar and items of capital equipment. Such items are, of course, a means to an end – the improvement in human welfare. By 1980 the World Bank's review of the empirical evidence pointed to the significance of improved health, nutrition, and education as not only another means of bringing about economic development but as being desirable *in themselves*. The World

Bank's research points to education, as measured by literacy and primary school attendance, as the main factor linked to the level of human development. In its World Development Report it showed how in one study that educated farmers – defined as those with at least four years of primary education – tended to produce up to 13 per cent more than farmers who had not attended school at all. Expenditure on human capital – better education, health, and nutrition – tends to reduce birth-rates and reduce infant mortality. Thus we find a virtuous circle of self-supporting improvements in human welfare rather than the vicious circle of illiteracy, malnutrition, ill-health, high birth-rates, and low life expectancy for babies. Figure 35.3 identifies the relationships between the various dimensions of human capital and their limits with levels of income per head.

Figure 35.3

The Dimensions of Human Capital. The chart depicts the interrelated nature of health, education, fertility, and nutrition and their impact on income levels.

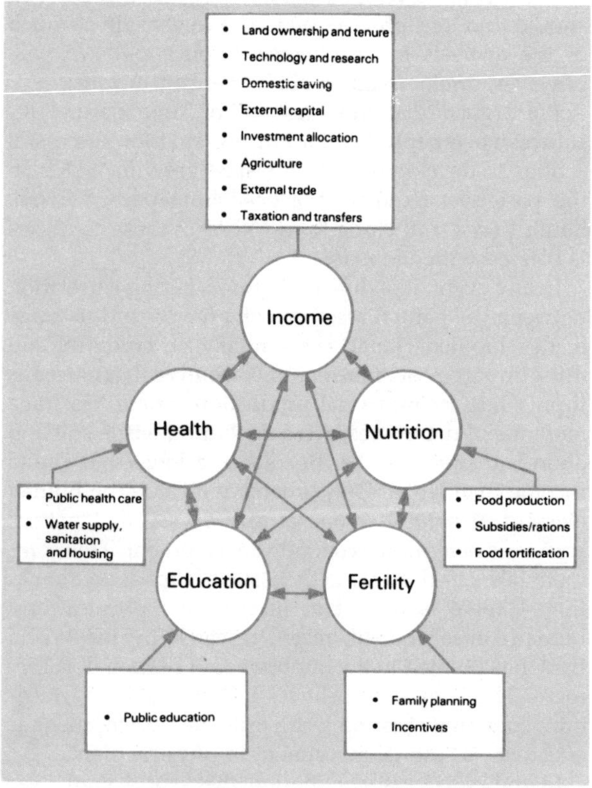

Source: World Bank, *World Development Report*, 1980, p. 69.

When we considered technology in Chapter 34 we noted that there has long been a transfer of technology from the developed world to LDCs. The benefits of this international process have not always been self-evident. The London-based Intermediate Technology has recently illustrated this with a sombre story. Ten years ago when the last dreadful famine gripped the Horn of Africa, 40 000 nomads were airlifted from their barren land and set down in a fertile plain in Somalia. They were provided with new brick-built homes and the most sophisticated farming machinery that money could buy. Today ten years on, their 'model' village is deserted. Half the nomads slipped quietly away into the bush to go back to their old way of life. The rest built their traditional stick huts and began to farm the land using the methods of their ancestors. In a vast four-acre compound, row upon row of tractors, bulldozers, and combine harvesters lie idle, corroded with rust. A workshop the size of an aircraft hangar has barely been used since the day it was built.

This spectacular white elephant cost millions. Whatever went wrong? These people who have always lived by the simplest means were suddenly faced with technology that was too complicated and too alien for them to accept. The gap between their knowledge and Western technology was simply too great for them to make use of the 'help' that was offered.

Capital-intensive technology may be, in a technical sense, 'efficient' but LDCs may have as much if not more concern with employment as output. With rapidly growing populations there is an understandable concern with the provision of jobs. The introduction of a highly automated factory producing plastic sandals in one African country, for example, put 7 000 leather shoemakers out of work. It reduced the incomes of the makers of leather, glue, thread, fabric linings, tacks, dressings, polishes, hand tools, wooden lasts, and carton boxes.

The 7 000 shoemakers were replaced by forty injection-moulding machine-operators. Dependence switched to manufacturers of plastic machinery and PVC grains abroad, because the local industry could not meet the new technological demands.

Our earlier example of the capital-intensive 'solution' in Somalia shows how it is important to match the needs and skills of people with appropriate technology. (Now read Key Points 35.2.)

How Developed Nations Influence LDCs: International Trade

In Chapter 9 we noted the gains from international trade if countries specialize in the production of goods in which they enjoy a comparative advantage. Given their relative abundance of land this would point to LDCs being exporters of primary products exchanged for manufactures and capital equipment. Indeed, many of today's independent countries were sources of raw materials and foodstuffs back in colonial days. But in the 1980s these countries which are now able to determine their own economic policy have reservations about the wisdom of specializing on primary production. They have a basis for hesitating to rely on international exchange to spur economic development. Why is this?

Key Points 35.2

- **Many LDCs are to be found within the equatorial belt of the globe. While any deterministic view of the environment seems misplaced we can recognize certain problems of economic development in this part of the world.**
- **Natural resources are helpful but not critical for economic development.**
- **Health, nutrition, and education expenditures are now considered to be important means of bringing about economic advance.**
- **Capital-intensive technologies may well permit a growth in output but do little to meet the need of LDCs to find jobs for their growing populations.**

Export Dependence

Several LDCs rely on a single commodity for more than half their export earnings. This marked dependence requires broadly stable market conditions for such reliance on one commodity not to cause problems. If for whatever reason export earnings fluctuate then the whole economy is affected. Why should there be fluctuations in these earnings?

Price-Inelastic Supply and Demand

A key problem is that, because both supply and demand are insensitive with respect to price, commodity prices fluctuate much more than in the case of manufactured goods. In Chapter 8 we saw that this prompted efforts by governments to try to stabilize agricultural prices in developed economies. We shall thus need, later in this chapter, to reconsider how LDCs can try to stabilize the prices of tea, coffee, and copper on the world's commodity markets.

Technological Progress

A further problem facing some commodity producers is that scientific advance has promoted the development of synthetic substitutes for natural products. In 1970 consumption of natural rubber was already about 2.2m tonnes less than half the consumption of synthetic rubber at 4.6m tonnes. High prices for products like rubber and copper prompt a search in the West for more stable sources of raw materials which tends not to be reversible in any subsequent decline in price of the natural product. Sisal is another example of a natural product that has faced the problem of a synthetic substitute. Furthermore, technological progress in the broadest sense is reducing the volume of metals used. Goods like radios and computers have become smaller and use less materials per unit weight than before. Another example is foodstuffs which are now packed in lighter and thinner cans than a decade or so ago. This has meant some reduction in the demand for tin.

Income Elasticities of Demand

In Chapter 8 we pointed out that the income elasticity of demand for foodstuffs is typically below unity. This means that the growth in demand for foodstuffs shows very little significant growth as time goes by. Indeed, in a country like the US it has reached virtual saturation point. The concern over obesity in Western Europe is encouraging the demand for 'healthy' foods which are often based on synthetic sources. This situation is hardly encouraging for the sugar-cane producers in the Third World! Furthermore, the growth in the market due to population increases in the developed economies also does not provide any sales expansion in commodity markets in terms of sheer volume.

We noted in Chapter 9 that the recession in world output after 1973 had been accompanied by a marked fall in the rate of growth of international trade. The sluggish state of manufacturing industry in the West has inevitably had an adverse impact on LDC supplies of industrial raw materials and fuels.

Increased Supply

We noted in Chapter 34 how the adoption of 'miracle' rice has in part contributed to an improved agricultural situation in some LDCs. However, while the enhancement of food supplies at home has been welcome the greater availability of output on world markets has reinforced the downward pressure on commodity prices.

Declining Terms of Trade

We defined the relationship between a country's average export prices in relation to its average import prices as the terms of trade in Chapter 9. In the case of LDCs the dramatic oil price increases of 1973 pushed down the terms of trade of all oil importers, both LDCs and developed countries. However, the boom in commodity prices partially offset this adverse effect for the LDCs such that they did not need to sell abroad to pay for their import requirements. However, the second OPEC oil increase in 1979 hit the LDCs harder than the developed countries. More expensive oil coincided with collapsing commodity prices and left the LDCs with a worsening terms of trade situation.

Given all these depressing factors at work it should not surprise you that LDCs have for many years sought to stabilize world commodity prices. They have seen

international commodity agreements (ICAs) as a means of effecting this objective. While these are simple in concept they have proved difficult to implement. ICAs are in essence the buffer stock schemes that we examined in Chapter 8 on a world scale. ICAs require agreement between producing countries and importers: the interests of the producers and importers conflict in determining what price the buffer stock should try to maintain by support buying. If it is decided that the buffer stock should try to set a price which proves to be above the long-run free market price level it needs unlimited funds to keep up the regulated price (as the Tin Agreement found in 1985). In 1989 the International Coffee Agreement collapsed because of the differing interests of producing and consuming countries. The International Cocoa Agreement had previously failed. Was the aim of such agreements to stabilize prices around the long-term market trend or to raise returns to growers as a form of aid to producing countries? When commodity prices rise sharply as in 1973 consuming countries have a keen interest in 'stability', but when they are declining they have little incentive to accept regulated market prices.

OPEC's early success in 1973 appeared to promise the cartel as a model to be emulated by other commodity producers until closer examination of the market in oil pointed to the conclusion that it was a rather untypical product. The price elasticity of demand and supply, product homogeneity, and the religious ties between its producers suggest that oil is much the most promising candidate for cartelization. Ambitious plans in the mid-1970s for an integrated programme of buffer stocks for a wide range of commodities financed from a common fund have failed to get beyond the discussion stage. They have thus not achieved the goal of what LDCs see as being needed – a **new international economic order (NEIO)**, that is, a recasting of the whole basis of international exchange between rich and poor countries. (Now read Key Points 35.3.)

The Stages of Development

If we look at the development of modern nations we find that they go through three stages. First, there is the agricultural stage when most of the population is involved in agriculture. Then there is the manufacturing stage when much of the population becomes involved in the industrialized sector of the economy. And, finally, there is a shift towards services which is what is happening in the UK; the so-called tertiary or service sector of the economy is growing by leaps and bounds, whereas the manufacturing sector (and its percentage employment) is declining in relative importance.

Putting the situation another way we could say that one characteristic of many developed countries is their high degree of industrialization, although there are clearly exceptions – Hong Kong and New Zealand, for example. In general, nations with relatively high standards of living are more industrialized than countries with low standards of living. Perhaps it is not too surprising that LDCs have taken this to mean that industrialization can be equated with economic development. The policy prescription seems obvious: so-called backward nations in which a large percentage of total resources are devoted to agricultural pursuits should attempt to obtain higher living standards by industrializing. But the reason why there is a declining agricultural sector and increased industrialization in economies that are experiencing ever higher levels of GNP per capita is to be found in our discussion of elasticity back in Chapter 8. We noted that the income elasticity of demand for food declines as nations get beyond the stage where the basic needs of life are satisfied. The income elasticity of demand for manufactured goods and services promises a growing market for consumer goods and personal services. Thus as incomes grow there is a market signal indicated to farmers and manufacturers. For an LDC to build factories as it were ahead of demand is to confuse the direction of causation. If the agricultural sector is successfully satisfying the basic needs of food of an LDC there is a basis for it to contribute effectively to successful economic development *through its ultimate relative decline in the economy*. The proposition that agriculture can be neglected as industrialization takes a poor LDC into rapid economic development has unhappily been shown to be fallacious thinking. Neglect of agriculture has been a pretty sure recipe for economic stagnation. The data in Figure 35.4 while not necessarily providing conclusive evidence points to the critical importance of a healthy agricultural sector if a significant rate of economic growth is to be enjoyed.

Key Points 35.3

- **As a broad generalization there are some discouraging aspects relating to the demand for and supply of commodities which make international trade appear an uncertain influence on LDCs.**
- **The terms of trade have in recent years moved against the LDCs.**
- **International commodity agreements have been neither easy to arrange nor free from troubles where they have been introduced.**

Figure 35.4

Growth of Agriculture and GDP in the 1970s. The data show that out of 17 countries whose GDP grew by less than 3 per cent a year in the 1970s 11 had growth rates of agriculture that were less than 1 per cent. How do you explain the situation of countries in the top left column?

Agricultural growth	*GDP growth*		
	Above 5%	*3–5%*	*Below 3%*
Above 3%	Cameroon China Colombia Dominican Rep. Guatemala Indonesia Ivory Coast Kenya Korea, Rep. of Malawi Malaysia Paraguay Philippines Thailand Tunisia Turkey Yemen Arab Rep.	Bolivia Burma Mali Somalia Tanzania	Liberia Nicaragua Senegal
1–3%	Costa Rica Ecuador Egypt Lesotho	Bangladesh Central African Rep. El Salvador Haiti Honduras India Pakistan Sri Lanka Sudan Upper Volta (Burkina)	Burundi Sierra Leone Zaire
Below 1%	Morocco Nigeria	Togo	Angola Chad Congo Rep. Ethiopia Ghana Madagascar Mauritania Mozambique Nepal Niger Uganda

Source: *The Economist*, 2 Feb. 1985, p. 95.

Industrialization through Import Substitution

The worries of today's LDCs concerning world trade as an engine of growth are not new. Latin American countries such as Brazil found the 1930s Depression had a devastating impact on their export earnings. When a country experiences a fall in revenues by one-half it is not surprising that it will not contemplate exposing itself to the dangers a second time. Thus countries such as Brazil, Chile, and Argentina resolved to become less dependent on demand for their coffee, copper, and beef and built up manufacturing industries behind high tariff walls. Imported consumer goods were thus made uncompetitive and domestic manufacture given a basis to encourage through the process of **import substitution**. The rationale was not only understandable given the situation of the 1930s but could draw support from the **infant industry** case for temporary protection that we noted in Chapter 9. The problem in practice has come to be that the growth of the infants has not always been healthy. Behind high tariffs and imports quotas the pressures to become efficient are weak. The opportunity costs incurred in terms of resource use have in some cases been enormous. Thus, on the one hand, we can appreciate that the Ricardian theory of comparative advantage that we saw in Chapter 9 is set in a static context. It follows that LDCs may reject its message on the grounds that they wish to *develop* a comparative advantage and not just accept that they are forever condemned just to be purveyors of fuels and foodstuffs and never participants in manufacturing or services. But, on the other hand, grossly inefficient production of manufactured goods involves a misallocation of *today's* resources which cannot be easily discounted. As it happens, inward-looking import substitution is no longer fashionable as it was in the early post-war years. The evidence points to gains being reaped by LDCs who positively seek out markets for manufactured goods on which they can enjoy the benefit of relatively low labour costs. During the last two decades the structure of LDC export trade has been changing with the importance of primary products falling. Manufactures now provide the dynamic element in LDC exports. The only cloud on the horizon is something we indicated in Chapter 9 – the growing trend towards protectionist policies in developed economies! The LDCs do seem bedevilled with problems on the international front.

Can Aid Help?

The developed economies can also assist LDCs in the form of finance from their government, i.e. aid. This, as its name implies, is help that rich countries can bring to poor countries so as to augment their sparse sources of domestic finance. However, despite the call for rich nations within UNCTAD to make contributions equal to 0.7 per cent of their GNP few countries within the OEDC have consistently met this target as Figure 35.5 (on page 552) shows. They have felt able to plead balance-of-payments reasons as justifying an inability to contribute more generously. In truth Western governments have seen aid programmes as an easy area to effect economies when they have sought cuts in public expenditure programmes. If we try to examine the rationale of official development assistance, to give aid its proper name, we find that the case for it is not everywhere taken for granted merely because it is called aid. Critics, notably Professor Peter Bauer, have argued that aid cannot really promote development because it is given to *governments*. Because the flow of funds is put too much into a political arena, they see aid as strengthening the position of governments whose policies in the past have rarely been directed towards the lot of the poorest peoples in LDCs. Furthermore, they argue that aid weakens the need for self-reliance

Key Points 35.4

- **LDCs can turn both to governments in the developed world and also commercial banks for external funds in order to assist their development efforts. Both forms of finance have given rise to difficulties.**
- **Official aid is a form of external finance from donor governments to recipient governments. Critics argue this means certain types of project are favoured and these are held to be not always the best choice that could be made using overseas finance.**
- **Borrowing from banks in the 1970s gave rise to a sudden indebtedness in some upper-middle-income developing countries.**

and the need to tackle internal problems without relying on the easy option of external help. Even those who feel that the critics overstate their case concede that in LDCs there have been pressures for aid to be directed towards *urban-biased* projects which arguably have been of marginal significance in many LDCs. Professor Michael Lipton has argued that the possibility of rural-based projects has been relatively ignored by Western donors. As a result the supporters of aid have not had the opportunity of pointing to as many success stories as they would have wished to underpin their case.

The fact is that, within LDCs, there has been bias towards large, urban-based prestige investments. Adam Smith noted this more than two centuries ago:

> The proud minister of an ostentatious court may frequently take pleasure in executing a work of splendour and magnificence, such as a great highway . . . But to execute a great number of little works [that] . . . have nothing to recommend them but their extreme utility, is a business which appears in every respect too mean and paltry to merit the attention of so great a magistrate. Such works are almost always entirely neglected.*

Whatever the benefits that aid may have brought about in particular cases this aspect of external finance has been rather overshadowed by another source of finance from developed countries. Major problems of indebtedness have arisen due to LDCs having resorted to borrowing from banks in USA and Western Europe in order to finance their current account deficits. The rise

*A. Smith, *An Enquiry into the Nature and Causes of the Wealth of Nations*, Bk. V, ch. 1 (Everyman edn., p. 217).

Figure 35.5

The Aid Programme of the Developed Countries in 1989. Few of the seventeen members of the OECD donated aid in 1989 that amounted to 0.7 per cent of their GNP.

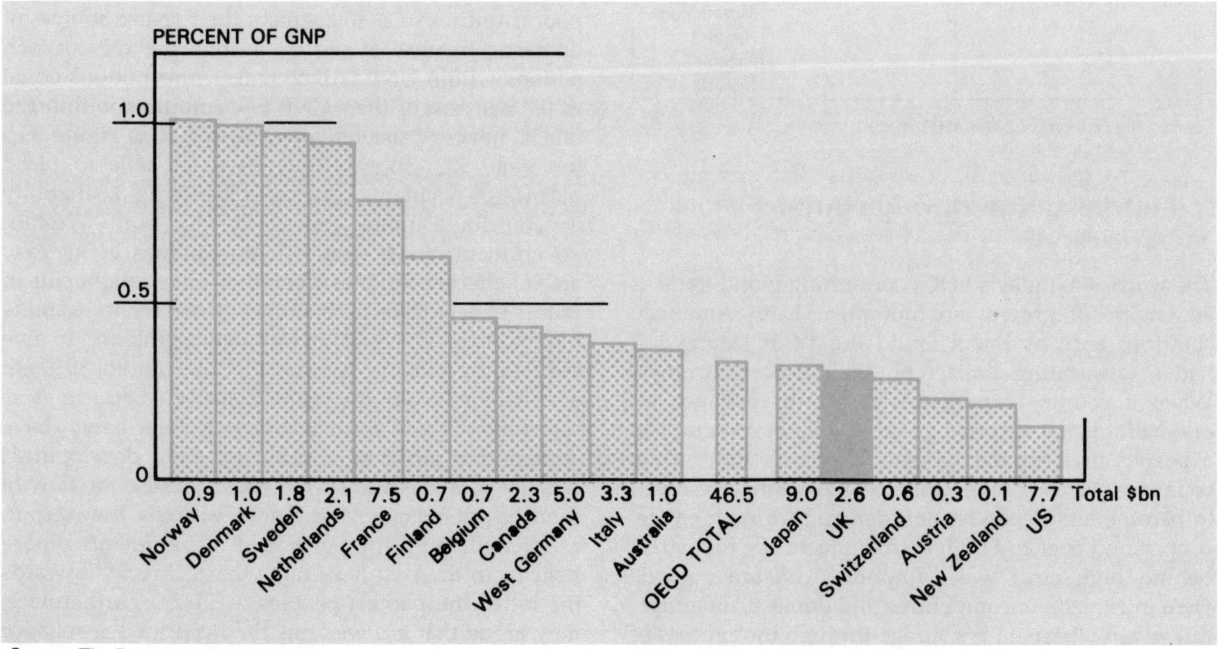

Source: *The Economist*, 30 June 1990

in oil prices in both 1973 and 1979 caused the balance-of-payments situation in LDCs to worsen. The higher real cost of loans from Western banks still further increased the share of LDC export revenues needed to service their debts. The result was that the total external debt of non-oil LDCs rose sharply from less than $200bn in 1973 to $670bn in 1983. Five countries – Mexico, Brazil, Argentina, South Korea, and Venezuela – accounted for nearly one-half of this total. The risk of one LDC defaulting on its debts is still a very real one but lenders have so far tried to accommodate those countries in obvious difficulties by extending the time by which existing loans should be repaid. But perhaps more dramatic is the way in which in the 1980s developing countries as a whole moved from being a net recipient of funds from the developed world to being a net provider. How did this come about? It has happened because new lending by commercial banks to developing countries fell sharply but interest charges on old loans rose sharply. As a result between 1982 and 1989 the developing countries (primarily those in Latin America) transferred about $240bn to the rich countries because debt repayments and interest charges exceeded new loans. Even with official aid flows included the overall flow of finance was negative for the developing countries. It is not surprising that the IMF and World Bank (see Chapter 32) have become much involved in seeking to help particular developing countries deal with increasingly difficult economic situations. The Case Study on Zambia illustrates this.

Development Strategy

The forgoing has suggested that the enthusiasm for industrialization in LDCs has waned in recent years. We have also tried earlier in this chapter to show that economists now believe that human capital is an important element in explaining economic progress.

The shift in thinking is illustrated by the changing character of the lending by the World Bank. Whereas in the financial year 1967 lending on infrastructure projects relating to transportation, power, and communications accounted for 54 per cent of its total lending, by 1977 the figure had fallen to 30 per cent. Agriculture received a much-enhanced share – up from 7 per cent to 32 per cent. Lending for industry increased from 11 per cent to 21 per cent.

We saw earlier in this chapter that the World Bank now regards spending on education, health care, and nutrition as desirable not only as a means to achieve economic growth but as desirable in itself. This view indicates how economists are now aware of the relevance of objectives of policy other than maximization of the growth rate. Until quite recently most economists took the view that in a rapidly growing economy the benefits of faster growth would ultimately *'trickle down'* throughout all sections of society. Thus economic growth would in due course provide a solution to any problems of unemployment and disparities in income distribution. This optimistic view is no longer as popular as it once was.

Brazil grew impressively in the twenty-one years of military rule, becoming the eighth largest economy in the Western world. But its rapid economic development left many sections gaining little or no benefit from this very creditable achievement. In August 1985 the Brazilian Minister of Planning Senhor João Sayad declared:

> 'We must humanize development. At least 40 per cent of the country's economically active population of 40 million received no benefit whatsoever.' Senhor Sayad acknowledged that after four years of recession, many poor families are simply not getting enough to eat. Senhor Sayad agreed that urgent measures to alleviate poverty are imperative. A respected economist, with a PhD from Yale, he said:
>
> 'If you tell an economist that someone is starving, he will tell you that you must first eliminate the public deficit and then take measures to promote employment. The problem is that by then the person is dead.'*

This view illustrates the increased attention which economists have given to the real meaning of economic development. As the late Dudley Seers once put it the critical questions in an LDC are:

> What has been happening to poverty? What has been happening to unemployment? What has been happening to inequality? If all three of these have declined from high levels then beyond doubt this has been a period of development for the country concerned. If one or two of these central problems have been growing worse, and especially if all three have, it would be strange to call the result 'development' even if per capita income doubled.†

In order to try to realize faster growth LDCs have in recent years lost their enthusiasm for the detailed type of planning once favoured, as we saw in Chapter 3, by the Soviet Union.

*Reported in *The Times*, 24 Aug. 1985.

†D. Seers, 'The meaning of development', Eleventh World Conference of the Society for International Development, New Delhi (1969), p. 3.

Key Points 35.5

- **The post-war enthusiasm for development via import substitution has faded as LDCs have come to find that neglect of agriculture is an almost certain recipe for stagnation.**
- **The conventional wisdom in the mid-1980s was that LDCs needed to give greater attention to the operation of market forces and place less reliance on planning.**

CASE STUDY

Zambia: An Economy in Trouble

Zambia won its independence from British rule in 1963. Known until then as Northern Rhodesia, Zambia has since independence, been ruled continuously by one man. Mr Kenneth Kaunda has arranged to be re-elected as president of Zambia six times.

On its northern border with Zaire lies a belt of copper which the country has been mining since the 1920s. At independence, Zambia inherited what was then black Africa's largest industrial base. Between 1965 and 1980 Zambia's GNP rose by only 1.8 per cent a year; in the 1980s, Zambia's economy actually contracted, at an average rate of 1.1 per cent a year.

Taking *population growth* into account, the figures look worse. The population has been growing at roughly 3½ per cent a year. So living standards during the 1980s for Zambians have crashed. Between 1977 and 1987, GNP per Zambian fell 47 per cent in nominal dollar terms.

In the 1970s the price of oil soared; the price of *copper* twice peaked and then crashed. The metal accounts for over 90 per cent of Zambia's export earnings, which reached $1.3bn in 1974. In 1986 Zambia's exports were worth less than half that (in nominal terms). The result was a crippling shortage of foreign exchange. The volume of imports fell by 30 per cent between 1975 and 1980. That was followed by another fall of two-thirds over the next five years.

Zambia's Errors

The Zambian government's response to the first copper-price crash was to print money to cover its *budget deficit*. In 1971 half the government's revenue came from the copper mines. Attempts to encourage farming (which had been neglected for years) by increasing producer prices had little effect, thanks to the inefficient, government-controlled marketing system. Subsidies for town-dwellers, intended to offset the rise in food prices, increased the deficit.

The government resorted to borrowing to cover this ever-widening gap in its finances. Its external *debt* rose from $623m in 1970 to $6.4bn by 1987. By the mid-1980s Zambia had a debt-to-exports ratio half as big again as Brazil's.

As the country fell deeper into debt, gross domestic *investment* dropped from an average of 25 per cent of GNP between 1965 and 1980 to 11 per cent in 1987. To fill this gap, the government took on an ever greater role in the economy: according to the World Bank, state-owned enterprises accounted for three-quarters of investment by the mid-1980s.

The effect of dwindling investment and greater government control is easy to see in the copper industry. The mines have to cope with persistent shortages of spare parts, fuel and explosives; management is often incompetent or corrupt or both. Output peaked at 720 000 tonnes in 1969. The target for the year to March 1989 is 500 000 tonnes, but mining analysts say Zambia will be lucky to produce more than 400 000 tonnes. That shortfall, with copper prices now back at near-record highs, will cost Zambia $300m in lost exports.

Zambia arranged its first loan from the International Monetary Fund in 1973. After 1976 it had 11 more in succession. But it was not until 1985 that the IMF could persuade Zambia's government of the need for drastic changes in economic policy. In October that year, an orthodox IMF programme was adopted.

The government promised to remove price controls and subsidies, to freeze the wages of civil servants, and to raise interest rates so that they gave a positive return on capital (after taking inflation into account). But the core of the plan was a *devaluation* of the kwacha. This was needed to reduce imports and increase earnings from copper exports. The IMF swallowed its dislike of dual exchange rates; it accepted the government's plan to keep the official (overvalued) rate for its own dealings, and to hold weekly auctions at which firms with government-approved plans could bid for foreign currency. At the first auction the kwacha fell 55 per cent, to five to the dollar.

The government found it hard to cope with the side-effects of this devaluation while pressing on with other parts of the adjustment programme. In December 1986, 15 people died in riots after the government announced it would stop subsidizing 'breakfast meal', a staple of the Zambian diet. The subsidy stayed. The shortage of foreign exchange forced the government to reduce the frequency and size of its foreign-currency auctions. As a result the auctions were no longer regarded as a reliable source of hard currency.

By May 1987 the kwacha had fallen to 21 to the dollar, and the government decided enough was enough. It angrily severed relations with the IMF. The Zambians said that the adjustment programme had been designed at a desk in Washington and failed to take into account its impact on the urban poor. (With 48 per cent of its population living in towns, Zambia is one of black Africa's most urbanized countries.) Besides, the country had not received enough foreign exchange to enable the plan to work. The IMF replied that the plan had not been given time.

After May 1987 the government revalued the kwacha at eight to the dollar. It also reimposed controls on prices and interest rates and set a ceiling on debt-service payments at 10 per cent of exports.

The results were disastrous. A report prepared by the Commission for Development Planning in June 1988 concluded, in excessively moderate language, that the government's independent policies had 'not succeeded in tackling the problems of inflation, the government's budget deficit, the scarcity of essential commodities and the worsening levels of unemployment'.

After decades of neglect, agriculture and the *rural infrastructure* need massive investment. As much as a third of 1988's bumper harvest is thought to have been spoilt by rain as it waited to be transported by a government-controlled monopoly. The government tried to get private-sector trucks to do the job instead, but few owners wanted to risk their only assets on Zambia's appalling rural roads.

Zambia is now ineligible to borrow from the World Bank or the IMF. (It owes the Fund more than SDR600m, or $800m, in arrears.) Most of the big aid donors will refuse to help until Zambia has regained IMF approval. The future looks grim. Known *copper reserves* will be exhausted within 20 years. The population is heavily infected with AIDS. The only growing parts of the economy are crime and the black market.

Concern for the poor, bolstered by the fear of more riots, persuaded Mr Kaunda to abandon the task of economic reform in Zambia. Yet Zambia's economic plight has led to a sharp increase in nutrition-related child mortality. A survey carried out by UNICEF in 1987 found that over a quarter of the 433 children admitted to Lusaka's teaching hospital during one week died; of these deaths 60 per cent were linked to malnutrition. Only the lucky ones get into hospital.

According to the World Bank, 48 per cent of Zambians lack access to a secure supply of *food* in a normal year. (That is a remarkably bad figure, by any standards: even war-torn, famine-prone Ethiopia is lower, at 46 per cent.) In theory, the Zambian poor could be insulated from the pain of economic reform with measures such as ration shops, food stamps and food-for-work schemes. In 1987 the World Bank carried out a study of how such schemes might work, but the Zambian government honestly admitted that it lacked the administrative capacity to put the reforms into practice.

Source: adapted from Schools Brief, 'Zambia the slow, Malawi the poor', *The Economist*, 18 Feb. 1989, pp. 96–7.

Questions

1. Explain the effects of a devaluation of the kwacha in Zambia in 1985.
2. What is the impact of an overvalued foreign exchange rate on the agricultural sector?
3. What explains the poor state of agriculture in Zambia?
4. To what extent do you consider that Zambia's economic situation is of her own making?

CASE STUDY

The Developing World as Viewed in Washington

The World Bank has lent money to 137 countries. It approved another $14bn in loans in the year to 30 June and had an enviable financial record: a best-ever profit of $1.1bn; an average rate of return of 18 per cent on projects it finances; no bad debts; and a triple-A rating for its bonds. But the bank is not just another financial institution. It is an international development agency. The bank's early lending was biased by the belief of its member nations that industrialization was the key to development. Its confidence in this approach faltered as it became obvious that inadequate investment in farming – and, especially, such disincentives as artificially low prices for farm products – caused the worst misery of all. In consequence, the bank became more involved in agriculture. Its encouragement of India's green revolution, converting the world's begging bowl into a grain exporter, ranks as one of its greatest achievements.

The bank's experience in agriculture gave rise to two strands of thought about lending. One stressed the need for human development and the relief of

Figure 35.6
New Loans Approved by Sector

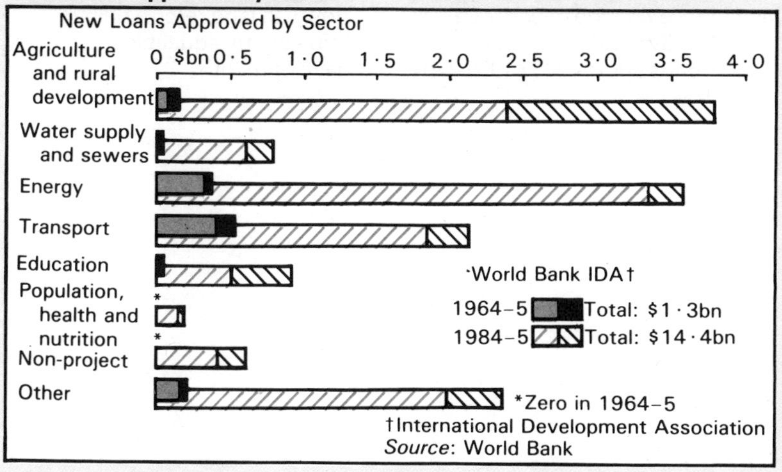

Source: World Bank, 1985.

poverty as ends in themselves. The other was that it is nigh impossible to have good projects where there is bad internal economic policy.

The first strand is seen in the work of the International Development Association, the bank's soft-loan branch. The IDA's borrowers must be short of credit and must also be poor (they do not qualify if they have a GNP of more than $790 a head; indeed, about 90 per cent of the loans go to countries with a GNP per capita of below $400). It is also seen in the recent emphasis on Africa, for which a special fund has been established and over $1bn contributed.

The second strand of thought about bad policies, combined with recent macroeconomic calamities, has led to closer bank involvement in borrowers' economic policies and to 'structural adjustment' loans to help changes in policy – generally towards freer markets. The authors give a snapshot of this continuing process. They exuberantly recommend market solutions to the problems of agriculture. At least, they would like to see the monopoly of state marketing boards ended; at best, they would prefer to see such boards abolished altogether (an idea that many World Bank officials applaud in private).

Much of their advice centres on the problems of running a mixed economy. The bank praises the *contrat plan* used in some French-influenced countries (e.g. Senegal) where public enterprises are made more publicly accountable. In Senegal, public enterprises have to agree with the government about their aims, and about how much they will spend and how many people they will employ to achieve them; they are then given more autonomy in deciding how best to fulfil their objectives within their limited resources. A main theme in the study is the harm done by cost overruns, said (ambiguously) to average 35 per cent on World Bank projects.

When foreign exchange is made available to poor countries, they often substitute scarce capital for abundant labour. There are many examples of these 'inappropriate technologies', e.g. replacing navvies by bulldozers that require skilled maintenance engineers and imported spare parts. Worry about this bias for foreign technology is one reason why the bank now finances some local costs – a paradoxical, but sensible, decision.

The bank is its own best critic. Project evaluation absorbed 59 man-years of staff time last year. This helps uncover harmful side-effects of development programmes. A new dam in Ghana was found to have caused a large increase in the number of children suffering from bilharzia, and a dam in Sudan increased the number of children suffering from malaria. These are brave admissions. Resist any temptation to sneer at such embarrassments to the bank. To change things, and to experiment, is to risk failure.

There are many squabbles about priorities. Third-world governments spend much more on education than on health, and the bank laments the lack of basic health services. Yet the bank, being a lending rather than a granting agency, also finds it hard to balance the aims of long-term development and of relieving the misery of these who are alive and poor now.

The loans approved in 1984–5 by the bank for population, health and nutrition projects were little more than a twentieth in value of those approved for energy or for agriculture, and less than a quarter of those approved for education. This may reflect demand rather than supply; and the pattern of lending has changed enormously since 1965 (see chart), but some bank officials think it necessary to justify health projects on the grounds that 'health facilitates development'.

In so far as the authors support land reform – a subject to which they devote two rather grudging paragraphs – they do so as a foundation for long-term economic growth. Many of its critics say it is equally important that land redistribution of the right kind could in many countries give immediate relief to the very poor. Equitable development, the bank's self-adopted goal, is not the same thing at all as the direct attack on poverty.

Source: 'The World Bank's development priority', *The Economist*, 14 Sept. 1985, p. 73.

Questions

1. What does the Case Study mean by the words 'the need for human development and the relief of poverty as ends in themselves'?
2. Why has the World Bank come to believe that the growth of agriculture is critical in the development process?
3. What differences are there in making loans to agriculture as compared with loans for energy?
4. How can land reform help to bring about 'equitable development'?

CASE STUDY

The World in Perspective

Figure 35.7 gives data on population and GNP per capita for various parts of the world.

Figure 35.7

Country/region	*Population in 1985 (millions)*	*GNP per capita in 1985 ($)*
All low-income economies ($400 or less)	2 439	270
China and India	1 805	290
Other low-income economies	634	200
All middle-income economies ($401 or more)	1 242	1 290
Total	3 681	
Developing countries where exports of manufactures account for more than 30% of total exports	2 098	520
Developing countries where oil accounts for more than 30% of total exports	523	1 060
Developing countries with severe debt servicing difficulties	554	1 410
Sub-Saharan Africa	418	400
Saudi Arabia, Libya, Kuwait, and the United Arab Emirates	18	9 800
Other developing countries	70	–
Total	3 681	610
Industrial market economies	737	11 810
USSR and Eastern European countries	362	(No estimate)

Source: adapted from *World Development Report, 1987*, OUP.

Questions

1. Comment on the distribution of the world's income and population as shown in the table.
2. In 1985 the UK's estimated per capita GNP was $8 460 whilst that of Ethiopia was $110. What reservations would you have about concluding that the standard of living in the UK was therefore more than seventy times greater than in Ethiopia?
3. Examine the rates of growth between 1965 and 1986 for the different parts of the world. Explain why these growth rates differ.
4. Consider the projected growth rates for the period 1986–95. What are the implications of these data for living standards?

Figure 35.8 gives data on economic growth for the period 1965–86 and alternative projections for 1986–95 under two assumptions about the policies adopted by both industrial and developing countries. All growth rates for developing countries are based on a sample of ninety countries.

Figure 35.8
(average annual percentage change)

Country/region	*Growth of GDP per capita*			*Projected growth rates 1986–95*	
	1965–73	*1973–80*	*1980–6*	*Optimistic*	*Pessimistic*
All developing countries	3.9	3.2	1.5	3.9	2.0
All low-income economies	2.9	2.5	5.4	4.8	2.8
All middle-income economies	4.4	3.3	−0.3	3.2	1.4
Exporters of manufactures	4.8	4.1	4.3	5.3	2.7
Oil exporters	4.3	3.2	−1.8	1.9	1.1
Highly indebted countries	4.2	2.9	−1.8	3.1	1.2
Sub-Saharan Africa	3.6	0.3	−3.4	0.7	0.0
Industrial market economies	3.7	2.1	1.6	3.9	2.0

Source: adapted from *World Development Report, 1987*, OUP.

Exam Preparation

PRACTICAL EXERCISES

The following exercises relate to the data in Figure 35.2 on page 546.

1. (a) Plot the data for GNP per capita in 1987 on the horizontal axis and life-expectancy at birth in 1987 on the vertical axis. What is the nature of the relationship?
(b) Plot the data for the same countries of population per physician in 1984. What is the nature of the relationship in this case?
(c) Plot the data for the same countries of the crude birth-rate in 1987. What is the nature of the relationship in this case?

2. In how many low-income countries was the average annual growth rate between 1965 and 1987 a negative one?

3. Why are the figures for population per physician in 1984 lower than in 1965?

4. What factors explain the lower figures for infant mortality rates in 1987 compared with 1965?

5. Suggest four non-monetary indicators other than those in Figure 35.2 which might provide a basis for distinguishing between the low-income, middle-income, and industrial market economies? State in each case whether these would be directly or inversely related to GNP per capita.

RELATED ESSAY QUESTIONS

1. What role do international economic organizations play in improving the economies of developing countries?

2. Describe the problems, both in their domestic economies and in international trade, that may hinder the economic progress of less-developed countries.

3. How would you distinguish between the terms 'economic growth' and 'economic development'? Compare the possible effects of a policy of population control with either investment in manufacturing, or improvements in agriculture on the standard of living in a less-developed economy.

4. How can developed economies best assist the less-developed countries?

5. 'Economic growth in less-developed countries may be assisted by receiving aid from more-developed countries and by increasing opportunities for trade.'
(a) Describe the ways in which aid can be given and trade encouraged.
(b) What problems may arise from the various countries concerned as a result of this assistance?

Dictionary

absolute advantage The ability to produce a good or service at an 'absolutely' lower cost, usually (but not necessarily) measured in hours of work required to produce the good.

absolute or nominal prices The prices that we observe today in terms of today's pounds. Also called nominal or current prices.

accelerationist view A view, or theory, of inflation that holds that since workers adapt to changing inflation rates, inflation can only reduce unemployment temporarily, the result being that the rate of inflation will tend to accelerate as policy-makers continue to attempt to reduce the unemployment rate by creating more inflation.

accelerator The level of investment depends upon the *rate of growth of demand.* A given percentage change in demand may require a larger percentage change in investment. The accelerator shows by how much the rate of growth of investment exceeds the rate of growth of demand (and of output).

accounting profit The difference between total revenues and total explicit costs.

adaptive-expectations hypothesis A theory of behaviour which states that people's expectations of the future rate of inflation are formed primarily on the basis of what the rate of inflation has been in the immediate past.

***ad valorem* tax** A duty on a good that increases in relation to the price charged by producers.

aggregate demand All planned expenditures for the entire economy summed together.

aggregate demand curve Planned purchase rates for all goods and services in the economy at various price levels.

aggregate demand shock Any shock that causes the aggregate demand curve to shift inwards or outwards.

aggregates Total amounts or quantities: aggregate demand, for example, relates to the total quantity demanded within a nation.

aggregate supply All planned production for the entire economy summed together.

aggregate supply curve The relationship between planned rates of total production for the entire economy and the price level.

aggregate supply shock Any shock that causes the aggregate supply curve to shift inwards or outwards.

anticipated inflation That inflation rate which individuals believe will occur, and when it does, we are in a situation of fully anticipated inflation.

appreciation The increasing of the value of a domestic currency in terms of other currencies. This occurs in a freely floating exchange market when the quantity demanded for the domestic currency exceeds the quantity supplied at the current price. In a fixed exchange rate market, appreciation cannot occur spontaneously; it must be done officially. Then it is called *revaluation.*

asset Anything of value that is owned. Customers' deposits create assets in that the bank holds sums of money which it can use until customers withdraw them.

assisted areas These are geographical areas that have been designated by government as needing industrial development; hence they are assisted by having government incentives available to firms (see Figure 33.1 for actual locations and further details).

automatic, or built-in, stabilizers Built-in stabilizers do not require initiation and action on the part of the government. Examples are the progressive income tax system and unemployment benefits both of which have built into the system the ability to modify changes in disposable income caused by the change in overall business activity.

autonomous consumption That part of consumption that is independent of, or does not depend on, the level of disposable income. Changes in autonomous consumption shift the consumption function.

average fixed costs Total fixed costs divided by the number of units produced.

average propensity to consume (APC) Consumption divided by disposable income for any given level of income. The proportion of total disposable income that is consumed.

average propensity to save (APS) Saving divided by disposable income. The proportion of total disposable income that is saved.

average tax rate The total tax payment divided by total income. It is the proportion of total income paid in taxes.

average total costs Total costs divided by the number of units produced.

average variable costs Total variable costs divided by the number of units produced.

balance of payments A summary of transactions concerning visible goods and invisibles – services, investment earnings, and transfers – (the current account) and financial assets (the capital account). Movements of the official reserves and other official flows comprise total official financing. This figure represents the sum requiring official financing arising from both current and capital transactions.

balance of trade The difference between the value of visible exports and the value of visible imports. Thus a country can be in surplus or in deficit on its visible transactions with one or all countries.

bank bills A bill which will be honoured at a stated date in the future (usually 91 days). This helps with cash flow as the seller (often an exporter) is effectively giving a period of 'grace' before payment. A distinguishing feature of these bills is that they may be passed on for cash to another party (at a rate slightly below face value) before the pay due date. The final holder of the bill will then present it for payment on maturity.

Similar bills may be drawn up by commercial organizations, local authorities, and the Treasury to help with cash flow problems. It may be simpler to regard all these 'bills' as post-dated cheques which may be redeemed for cash at a slight loss before the pay date if necessary.

bankers' balances The balances, or deposits, that commercial banks keep with the central bank (i.e. Bank of England).

bankruptcy The situation when a business entity is unable to meet its debts.

barometric price leader A price increase announced by one firm is quickly followed by rivals. The leader may or may not be the same firm on each occasion of a price increase.

barriers to entry Barriers that make it either impossible or difficult for firms to enter an existing industry and offer competition to existing producers or suppliers. Some barriers include government restrictions and legislation.

barter A system of exchange in which goods or services are exchanged for goods or services without the use of money.

base year The year which is chosen as the point of reference for comparison (e.g. of prices) in other years.

bilateral monopoly A situation in which the market consists of a single buyer and a single seller.

birth-rate The number of births per 1000 people in the population per year.

black economy The unofficial economic activity that cannot be precisely measured because it fails to go through official accounts.

black market A situation where the official 'white' market price is controlled but buyers are prepared to pay a price which reflects the relative scarcity of the good. Black markets usually exist only in a wartime economy when the availability of civilian goods is curtailed.

bonds The government issues bonds in order to raise long-term finance (typically for 20 years). (Private companies may issue corporate bonds.) Government bonds are known as gilts because they are 'as good as gold' – there is no risk of default.

British Technology Group (BTG) The name of the organization formed in 1981 by combining the National Enterprise Board and the National Research Development Corporation. The BTG's primary function is to promote the development and commercialization of inventions arising in the UK.

broad measures Methods of measuring the money supply by looking at money as a medium of exchange and a temporary store of value. These measures provide a guide to the amount of liquidity in an economy.

budget constraint The resource constraint imposed on households and firms at any point in time. It represents the set of opportunities facing each decision-maker.

buffer stock An organization, whether owned and run by a group of producers or financed by the government, that attempts to smooth out fluctuations in prices by the purchase and sale of stocks.

building societies A group of financial institutions that specialize in providing long-term loans for house purchase (i.e. mortgages).

business fluctuations The ups and downs in overall business activity, as evidenced by changes in national income, employment, and prices.

buy-back agreement A commitment to purchase all or part of a plant's output for a specified amount of time in order for the plant to be sold.

capital All manufactured resources, including buildings, equipment, machines, and improvements to land.

capital consumption *See* **depreciation** which is another name for the same concept.

capital gains The positive difference between the purchase price and the sale price of an asset.

capital goods Goods that are used in the production of other goods. Examples include cranes, factories, and foundries. Consumers do not directly consume capital goods.

capitalism An economic system in which individuals privately own productive resources; these individuals can use the resources in whatever manner they choose, subject to common protective legal restrictions.

capital movements The flow of funds across international boundaries, for investment in plant and machinery, or in response to interest changes, or expectations of interest rate changes.

cartel The most explicit means by which oligopolists effect collusion. A cartel is an association of independent entities that attempts to determine output, sales, and prices such that cartel members can secure monopoly profits. Members of a cartel invariably face a conflict between self-interest and the common cause of all producers.

central bank A banker's bank, usually an official institution that also serves as each country's Treasury's bank. Central banks supervise commercial banks.

certificate of deposit (CD) A time deposit with a fixed maturity date offered by banks and other financial institutions.

***ceteris paribus* assumption** The assumption that all other things are held equal, or constant, except those under study.

circular flow model A model of the flows of resources, goods, and services, as well as money, receipts, and payments for them in the economy.

clearing system A mutually agreed system shared by commercial banks in the UK. It refers to the process by which the debts between these banks, generated by their customers' cheques, are settled each day.

closed economy An economic system that has no transactions with any other economy.

closed shop A business enterprise in which an employee must belong to the union before he or she can be employed. That employee must remain in the union after he or she becomes employed.

cobweb A dynamic model which tries to explain why cyclical fluctuations in output and prices can occur such as in the agricultural sector.

collective bargaining Bargaining between management of a company or of a group of companies and management of a union or a group of unions for the purpose of setting a mutually agreeable contract on wages, fringe benefits, and working conditions for *all* employees in the union(s). Different from *individual* bargaining, where each employee strikes a bargain with his or her employee individually.

collusion Price determination by oligopolists which is co-ordinated and aims to avoid the danger of price wars breaking out.

command economic system A system in which the government controls the factors of production and makes all decisions about their use and about the distribution of income. The political character of such a government is indeterminate.

commercial bank This is a privately owned profit-seeking institution, sometimes referred to as a *joint stock bank* to highlight the fact that it has shareholders. Most high street banks, such as National Westminster and Barclays etc. are commercial banks.

commercial bills *See* **bank bills.**

communism In its purest form, an economic system in which the state has disappeared and in which individuals contribute to the economy according to their productivity and are given income according to their need.

community charge (poll tax) A flat-rate tax payable by all able-bodied adults to finance local authority spending, in place of rates (property taxes).

comparative advantage An advantage arising out of relative efficiency, which follows from scarcity of resources. Comparative advantage is the advantage measured in terms of other goods that could be produced, not in terms of factor inputs. If a country has a comparative advantage in one good, it must have comparative *disadvantage* in another. As long as the opportunity cost of doing the same job differs for different people or different countries, each will have a comparative advantage in something.

competition Rivalry among buyers and sellers of outputs, or among buyers and sellers of inputs (i.e. factors of production).

complement Two goods are considered complements if a change in the price of one causes an opposite shift in the demand for the other. For example, if the price of tennis rackets goes up, the demand for tennis balls will fall; if the price of tennis rackets goes down, the demand for tennis balls will increase.

concentration ratio The percentage of all sales contributed by the leading four or leading eight firms in an industry; sometimes called the industry-concentration ratio.

conglomerate A firm which has interests in several, and very different markets.

constant-cost industry An industry whose total output can be increased without an increase in per-unit costs; an industry whose long-run supply curve is horizontal.

constant prices Sterling expressed in terms of real

purchasing power, using a particular year as the base or standard of comparison.

constant returns to scale A situation in which the long-run average cost curve of a firm remains flat, or horizontal, as output increases.

consumer optimum A choice of a basket of goods and services that maximizes the level of satisfaction for each consumer.

consumer (or consumption) goods Goods that are used directly by consumers to generate satisfaction. To be contrasted with capital goods.

consumer sovereignty The concept of the consumer as the one who, by his or her spending, ultimately determines which goods and services will be produced in the economy. In principle, competition among producers causes them to adjust their production to the changing desires of consumers.

consumer surplus The difference between the amount that a consumer is willing to pay for a commodity and the amount that is actually paid. This surplus utility which is not paid for is measured by the area above the price charged and below the demand schedule.

consumption That which is spent on new goods and services out of a household's current income. Whatever is not consumed is saved. Consumption includes buying food, going to the cinema, going to a concert, and so on.

consumption function The relationship between the amount consumed and disposable income. A consumption function tells us how much people plan to consume out of various disposable income levels.

consumption goods Goods that are bought by households to use up, such as films, food, and clothing.

contracting-out When this term is used in the context of privatization it refers to the transference of publicly provided activities to private contractors.

contractionary policy (or deflation) The use of tax increases and expenditure cuts to reduce inflationary pressure, or overheating, in the economy, or to reduce a balance-of-trade deficit.

cost-benefit analysis (CBA) This is a way of appraising an investment proposal. It is normally undertaken by government departments, since it involves adding the indirect (external) costs and benefits to the conventional direct costs and benefits (revenue). This is done by estimating monetary values for aspects such as health, time, leisure, and pollution.

cost-push inflation Rising prices caused by rising production costs, union wage negotiations, or bosses seeking more profits.

counter-cyclical policy The use of fiscal and monetary policy to offset booms and slumps by contractionary and expansionary policies respectively.

counter-purchase An agreement to buy an offsetting amount of unrelated products to counter the cost of buying a particular product; for example, country *X* can sell to country *Y* an airplane costing £1m only if country *X* agreed to purchase £1m worth of some other products in return.

craft unions Labour unions composed of workers who engage in a particular trade or skill, such as baking, carpentry, or plumbing.

cross-price elasticity of demand The percentage change in the demand for one good divided by the percentage change in the price of a related good. Cross-price elasticity of demand is a measure of the responsiveness of one good's quantity demanded to changes in a related good's price.

cross-section data Empirical observations about one or more variables gathered at a particular point in time.

crowding out The expansion of public sector expenditure which reduces private sector spending.

CSO The recognized abbreviation for the Central Statistical Office. This office is responsible for the government's statistical services.

currency Notes and coins – often simply referred to as 'cash'.

currency crisis A situation in the international money market that occurs when a country no longer has the foreign exchange resources to support the price of its currency. A currency crisis brings forced devaluation under a fixed exchange rate system.

cyclical unemployment Unemployment resulting from business recessions that occur when total demand is insufficient to create full employment.

deadweight welfare loss A measure of the reduction in consumer surplus arising from monopolization of a competitive industry which may be partially or even wholly offset by resource savings accruing to the monopolist.

death-rate The number of deaths per 1000 people in the population per year.

declining block pricing A system of price discrimination in which consumers are charged different prices per unit of electricity for each 'block' of electricity that they buy. The per-unit price for the first block is higher than the per-unit price for the second block, which is higher than the per-unit price for the third block.

decreasing-cost industry An industry in which an increase in output leads to a reduction in per-unit costs, such that the long-run industry supply curve is downward sloping.

deficiency payment A payment made to qualified farmers for any difference between the target price for their product and the market price that they actually received; a direct subsidy paid to farmers.

deficit spending Government spending that is in excess of government tax revenues.

demand curve A graphic representation of the demand schedule. A negatively sloped line showing the inverse relationship between the price and the quantity demanded.

demand-pull inflation Inflation caused by total demand exceeding the current supply. This is a particular problem when the economy is at full employment.

demand schedule A set of pairs of numbers showing various possible prices and the quantities demanded at each price. This is a schedule showing the rate of planned purchase per time-period at different prices of the good.

demerit good The opposite of a merit good; one which the political process had decided is socially undesirable.

Department of Trade and Industry A multi-faceted government department whose prime aim is to encourage wealth creation through a competitive and open economy. It is often referred to by its nickname 'the department for enterprise'.

dependent variable A variable whose value changes according to changes in the value of one or more independent variables.

depreciation (capital) Reduction in the value of capital goods over a one-year period due to physical wear and tear and also to obsolescence.

depreciation (currency) A lessening of the value of a domestic currency in terms of foreign currencies. Depreciation occurs in a freely floating foreign exchange market when there is an excess supplied of the domestic currency. In a fixed exchange rate market, depreciation can occur if the government allows it.

deregulation Often used in the context of privatization to describe the opening up of State monopolies to competition from other suppliers.

derived demand Input factor demand derived from demand for the final product being produced.

devaluation The same as depreciation except that it occurs officially under a regime of fixed exchange rates.

diminishing marginal utility The smaller increase in total utility from the consumption of a good or service as more is consumed.

direct relationship A relationship between two variables that is direct, or positive, such that an increase in one is associated with an increase in the other, and a decrease in one is associated with a decrease in the other.

direct tax Tax liability targeted at one person on the basis of income.

discount houses A small group of specialized institutions which borrow for very short periods of time from the banks (*see* **'money at call'**) and invest in 'bills' (*see* **bank bills**) and other short-term assets. The discount houses are therefore specialists in the movement of short-term funds between financial institutions. Indeed, they often act as a middle-man between the Bank of England and commercial banks.

discounting The method by which the present value of a sum or a stream of sums is obtained.

discount rate (intervention rate) The interest rate at which the Bank of England discounts bills (intervenes in the discount market).

discretionary fiscal policy Government policy with respect to taxes or spending, or both, that involves a deliberate change legislated by Parliament for the purpose of altering the equilibrium level of real national income.

diseconomies of scale When increases in output lead to increases in long-run average costs.

disinflation A term coined in the early 1980s to describe the process that saw high rates of inflation begin to reduce.

distribution of income The way income is distributed among the population. For example, a perfectly equal distribution of income would result in the lowest 20 per cent of income-earners receiving 20 per cent of national income and the top 20 per cent also receiving 20 per cent of national income. The middle 60 per cent of income-earners would receive 60 per cent of national income.

division of labour The segregation of a resource into different specific tasks; for example, one car worker puts on bumpers, another doors, and so on.

dominant price leader The leading firm in an industry which is the first to change prices. A smaller firm may be content either to let the larger firm judge when prices need to be adjusted, or feel the kinked demand curve situation could apply if it led an increase in prices.

dumping The export of products at a price below their cost of production.

duopoly A market structure in which there are only two sellers of a commodity and thus the matter of interdependence is critical for price determination.

durable consumer goods Goods used by consumers that have a life-span of more than one year; that is, goods that endure and can give utility over a longer period of time.

economic efficiency The use of resources that generate the highest possible value of output as determined in the market economy by consumers.

economic goods Any good or service that is scarce.

economic growth Defined either as the increase in an economy's real level of output over time or as the increase in the economy's real per capita level of output over time. Economic growth is therefore measured by the rate of change of real output or real per capita output.

economic profit The difference between total revenues and the opportunity cost of all factors of production.

economic rent That part of earnings which is in excess of transfer earnings. Economic rent will be earned when the supply of a particular skill or personality is restricted, i.e. inelastic.

economics A social science studying human behaviour, and, in particular, the way in which individuals and societies choose among the alternative uses of scarce resources to satisfy wants.

economic system The institutional means through which resources are used to satisfy human wants.

economies of scale When increases in output lead to decreases in long-run average costs.

electronic funds transfer system A system whereby bank account balances, credits, and debts are all done via electronic signals rather than through the use of paper memos.

employers' association A group of employers who negotiate wages jointly with trade unions.

enterprise culture This is a relatively new idea which has been popularized since Margaret Thatcher took office in 1979. It is used to describe a hard-working, efficient society driven forward by the profit motive, in freely competitive markets, towards greater amounts of wealth.

entrepreneurship The fourth factor of production involving human resources that perform the functions of raising capital, organizing, managing, assembling other factors of production, and making basic business policy-decisions. The entrepreneur is a risk-taker.

equation of exchange The number of monetary units multiplied by the number of times each unit is spent on final goods and services is identical to the prices multiplied by output (or national income). Formally written as $M \times V = P \times Q$.

equilibrium A situation in which the plans of buyers and sellers exactly coincide so that there is neither excess supply nor excess demand.

eurocurrency Currency deposits held in banks outside their country of origin, e.g. eurodollars are US dollar deposits held in banks outside the US (often, but not necessarily, in Europe).

exchange The act of trading, usually done on a voluntary basis, in which both parties to the trade are subjectively better off.

exchange equilization account An account held and managed by the Bank of England on behalf of the government. It is used to prevent undesirable fluctuations to the sterling exchange rate.

exchange rate target The Bank of England may set a target range for the exchange rate. Maintaining this may promote stability in the economy more effectively than adherence to a monetary target, which may be subject to change for other reasons than the growth of the money supply.

excise duties on alcohol *See* **tax.**

excludability *See* **principle of exclusion.**

exclusive purchase A distributor contracts to stock only the products of one manufacturer, possibly in return for an exclusive supply arrangement.

exclusive supply A seller supplies only one buyer in a certain geographical area, which limits competition between that buyer and his competitors.

expansion A business fluctuation in which overall business activity is rising at a more rapid rate than previously, or at a more rapid rate than the overall historical trend for the nation. This is sometimes referred to as a 'boom'.

expansionary gap Exists whenever the equilibrium level of real national income exceeds the full-capacity level of real national income; the positive difference between total desired spending and the full-capacity level of real national income.

expansionary policy (or reflation) The use of tax cuts and increased government spending (perhaps along with an easy monetary policy) to increase aggregate demand and promote increased economic growth and employment.

expenditure approach A way of computing national income by adding up the values of all spending at current market prices on final goods and services.

expenditure-reducing policies Contractionary macroeconomic policies designed to reduce incomes and so reduce spending on imports and on goods which could be exported.

expenditure-switching policies Policies which lead to a fall in spending on imports and a rise in spending on domestically produced goods for both the export and the domestic markets.

exploitation Paying a resource less than its value (MRP).

externality A cost or benefit external to an exchange. In other words, the external benefits or costs accrue to parties other than the immediate seller and buyer in a transaction.

factor markets In the factor market, households are the sellers; they sell resources such as labour, land, capital, and entrepreneurial ability. Businesses are the buyers in factor markets; business expenditures represent receipts or, more simply, income for households (see Figure 12.1).

fiduciary monetary system A system in which currency is issued by the government, and its value is based uniquely on the public's *faith* that the currency represents command over goods and services.

finance houses A group of financial institutions that specialize in providing funds for hire-purchase agreements.

financial intermediaries Those financial institutions that link up groups of borrowers, e.g. commercial banks.

financial markets Those markets through which saving passes before it goes either to governments or to business firms for investment purposes. Included are insurance companies, commercial banks, and pension plans.

firm An organization that brings together different factors of production, such as labour, land, and capital, to produce a product or service that can be sold for a profit. A firm is usually made up of an entrepreneur, managers, and workers.

First World The industrialized non-communist countries of Western Europe plus the United States, Australia, New Zealand, Canada, and Japan.

five-year plans Economic plans set up by the central government in a country that plots the future course of its economic development. The first five-year plan was devised in Russia by Stalin after Lenin's death.

fixed costs The costs that do not vary with output. Fixed costs include such things as rent on a building and the price of machinery. These costs are fixed for a certain period of time; in the long run they are variable.

fixed exchange rates A system of exchange rates that requires government intervention to fix the value of each nation's currency in terms of every other nation's currency.

fixed investment Purchases, made by business, of newly produced producer durables, or capital goods, such as production machinery and office equipment.

fixed throttle Controlled growth of aggregate monetary demand at a constant rate, equal to the long-run growth of productive capacity.

flow Activities that occur over time. For example, income is a flow that occurs per week, per month, or per year. Consumption is also a flow, as is production.

foreign banks The name given to banks whose country of origin is overseas. These banks tend to specialize in foreign currency business and are often located in London.

foreign exchange market The market for buying and selling foreign currencies.

foreign exchange rate The price of foreign currency in terms of domestic currency, or vice versa. For example, if the foreign exchange rate for francs is 25p this means that it takes 25p to buy one franc. An alternative way of stating the exchange rate is that the value of the pound is four francs. It takes four francs to buy one pound.

45-degree line The line along which planned expenditures equal real national income or output per year; a line that bisects the total planned expenditures real national income quadrant.

fractional reserve banking system A system of banking whereby banks keep only a fraction of their deposits on reserve.

free enterprise A system in which private business firms are able to obtain resources, to organize those resources, and to sell the finished product in any way they choose.

free good Any good or service that is available in quantities larger than are desired at a zero price.

freely floating (or flexible) exchange rates Exchange rates that are allowed to fluctuate in the open market in response to changes in supply and demand. Sometimes called free exchange rates or floating exchange rates.

free-rider problem A problem associated with public goods in which individuals presume that others will pay for the public goods, so that individually they can escape paying for their production without a reduction in production occurring.

frictional unemployment Unemployment associated with frictions in the system that may occur because of the imperfect job market information that exists.

full-employment government budget An indication of what the government budget deficit or surplus would be if the economy were operating at full employment throughout the year.

full-line forcing This requires a buyer to purchase quantities of each item in a product range in order to be able to buy any of them.

general equilibrium analysis Economic analysis that takes account of the interrelationships among markets; to be contrasted with partial equilibrium analysis, which does not.

geographically immobile *See* **mobility of labour**.

GNP deflator A price index that measures the changes in prices of all goods and services produced by the economy.

government failure This term has developed along with the emphasis on microeconomics to highlight how government policy may not necessarily improve economic efficiency.

gross domestic investment The creation of capital goods, such as factories and machines, that can yield production and hence consumption in the future. Also included in this definition are changes in business stocks and repairs made to machines or buildings. In sum, it is investment before depreciation.

gross domestic product (GDP) The most common measurement of a nation's income generated from resources within its own boundaries: the value of its output of goods and services.

gross national product (GNP) Another measurement of the wealth of a country. It represents the total output of goods and services produced by the country in a year, plus the value of *net property income from abroad.*

guaranteed (or target) price A price set by the government for specific agricultural products. If market-clearing prices fall below target prices, a 'deficiency' payment equal to the difference between the market price and the target price is given to each farmer who qualifies.

horizontal merger The joining of firms that are producing or selling a similar product.

human capital Investment which has taken place in education and training which enhance the productivity of the individual.

import levy A tax imposed on a good when landed at a port or other point of entry into a country.

import substitution The process by which many LDCs have begun to industrialize, i.e. attempt to manufacture consumer goods rather than resort to foreign supplies to meet domestic demand.

income approach A way of measuring national income by adding up all factor rewards, namely, wages, interest, rent, and profits.

income consumption curve The set of optimum consumption points that would occur if income were successfully increased, nominal and relative prices remaining constant.

income-elastic demand A given change in income will result in a larger percentage change in quantity demanded in the same direction.

income elasticity of demand The percentage change in the quantity demanded divided by the percentage change in money income; the responsiveness of the quantity demanded to changes in income.

income-inelastic demand A given change in income will result in a less than proportionate change in demand in the same direction.

increasing-cost industry An industry in which an increase in industry output is accompanied by an increase in per-unit costs, such that the long-run industry supply curve is upward sloping.

independent variable A variable whose value can change freely.

indexing Linking a specific nominal sum to the rate of inflation; for example, under some schemes pensions can be indexed so they increase at the rate of inflation.

indicative planning A system which involves the government setting up general targets for the major sectors of the economy to assist the private sector in their decision-taking. This form of planning is used effectively in France.

indifference curve A curve composed of the set of consumption alternatives each yielding the same total amount of satisfaction.

indirect tax The tax imposed on spending. In this case the seller has ultimate responsibility to pay.

induced spending A variable which depends on the level of income is said to be induced.

industrial unions Labour unions that consist of workers from a particular industry, such as car or steel manufacturing.

infant industry argument An argument in support of tariffs: tariffs should be imposed to protect (from import competition) an industry that is trying to get started. The presumption is that after the industry becomes established and technologically efficient, the tariff can be removed.

inferior good A good of which the consumer purchases less as income increases.

inflation A sustained rise in prices, formally measured by the Retail Price Index.

inheritance tax *See* **tax.**

injections Supplementary expenditures not originating in the household sector; can include investment, government purchases, and exports.

institutions The laws of the nation as well as the habits, ethics, mores, folkways, and customs of the citizens of that nation.

interest The payment for current rather than future command over resources; the cost of obtaining credit. Also, the return paid to owners of capital.

International Bank for Reconstruction and Development More commonly referred to as the 'World Bank'. An institution which is based in Washington and co-ordinates investment funds on behalf of developing countries.

International Monetary Fund (IMF) An institution set up to manage the international monetary system. It came out of the Bretton Woods Conference in 1944, which established more or less fixed exchange rates in the world.

inverse relationship A relationship that is inverse, or negative, such that an increase in one variable is associated with a decrease in the other, and a decrease in one variable is associated with an increase in the other.

investment The spending by businesses on things like machines and buildings, which can be used to produce goods and services in the future. The investment part of total income is that portion which will be used in the process of producing goods in the future.

J-curve This refers to the way in which the trade balance may initially worsen after an exchange rate depreciation.

joint-stock company A legal entity owned by stockholders. The stockholders are liable only for the amount of money they have invested in the company. These firms are sometimes referred to as *corporations.*

kinked demand curve A model of pricing in an oligopolistic market structure where rivals follow one firm's decision to make a price decrease but not a price increase. The demand curve is thus bent or kinked and the associated marginal revenue curve has a discontinuous part in it.

labour The human resource involving productive contributions of persons who work, which involve both thinking and doing.

labour theory of value A theory that the value of all commodities is equal to the value of the labour used in producing them.

Laffer curve A graphical representation of the relationship between tax rates and total tax revenues raised by taxation.

laissez-faire The viewpoint that government should not intervene in a detailed way in the business life of a country other than remove legal restraints on trade. Adam Smith's *Wealth of Nations* represents this doctrine.

land The natural resources that are available without alteration or effort on the part of labour. Land as a resource includes only original fertility and mineral deposits, topography, climate, water, and natural vegetation.

law of diminishing (marginal) returns After some point, successive increases in a variable factor of production, such as labour, added to fixed factors of production, will result in less than a proportional increase in output.

law of increasing relative costs This law is an economic principle that states that the opportunity cost of additional units of a good generally increases as society attempts to produce more of that good.

leakages Those parts of national income not used for consumption, e.g. net taxes, saving, and imports.

least developed countries The poorest of the LDCs defined with reference to three indicators of the state of development.

less developed countries (LDCs) Those countries that are in the process of development and that have not yet reached an arbitrary per capita living standard which in 1983 the World Bank defined as $400.

liability Anything that is owned. Customers' deposits create a liability in that the bank must be prepared to repay the customer at any time.

licensed deposit-takers (LDTs) Institutions permitted (licensed) by the Bank of England to take deposits from the public.

limit pricing The determination of a price charged lower than a profit-maximizing price, which seeks to deter the entry of new firms.

liquidity A characteristic of any asset; it describes the degree to which the asset can be acquired or disposed of without much danger of any intervening loss in nominal value and with small transaction costs. Money is the most liquid asset.

liquidity preference function An inverse relationship between the opportunity cost of holding money (interest receipts forgone) and the quantity of money demanded – otherwise called the demand for money function.

local authority bills *See* **bank bills**.

localized industry This is when one industry dominates a whole geographical area, i.e. it is dominant in one locality.

long run That time-period in which all factors of production can be varied.

long-run average cost curve This represents the cheapest way to produce various levels of output given existing technology and current resource prices. It is derived by joining the minimum point of various SAC curves.

long-run industry supply curve A market supply curve showing the relationship between price and quantities forthcoming after firms have been allowed the time to enter or exit from an industry, depending on whether there have been positive or negative economic profits.

macroeconomics The study of economy-wide phenomena, such as unemployment and inflation.

managed float A freely floating exchange system that involves governments stepping in to stabilize the value of their currencies. To be contrasted with a 'clean' float, where there is no government intervention in the foreign exchange market.

marginal cost (MC) The change in total costs due to a one-unit increase in the variable input. The cost of using more of a factor of production.

marginal cost pricing A system of pricing in which the price charged is equal to the opportunity cost to society of producing one more unit of the good or service in question. The opportunity cost is the marginal cost to society.

marginal physical product (MPP) The output that the addition of one more worker produces. The marginal physical product of the worker is equal to the change in total output that can be accounted for by hiring the worker, holding all other factors of production constant.

marginal propensity to consume (MPC) The ratio of the change in consumption to the change in disposable income. A 0.8 marginal propensity to consume tells us that an additional £100 earned will lead to an additional £80 consumed.

marginal propensity to import The proportion of an increase in income which is spent on imports.

marginal propensity to save (MPS) The ratio of the change in saving to the change in disposable income. A 0.2 marginal propensity to save indicates that out of an additional £100 earned £20 will be saved. Whatever is not saved is consumed. The marginal propensity to save plus the marginal propensity to consume must always equal 1, by definition (if taxes are ignored).

marginal revenue (MR) The change in total revenues resulting from a change in output and sale of one unit of the product in question.

marginal revenue product (MRP) The marginal physical product (MPP) times the price at which the product can be sold in a competitive market.

marginal tax rate The change in the tax payment divided by the change in income, or the percentage of additional pounds that must be paid in taxes. The marginal tax rate is applied to the last tax bracket of taxable income.

market An abstract concept concerning all the arrangements that individuals have for exchanging with one another. Thus, we can speak of the labour market, the car market, and the credit market.

market-clearing (or equilibrium) price The price that clears the market where there is no excess quantity demanded or supplied. The price at which the demand curve intersects the supply curve.

market economic system A system in which individuals own the factors of production and decide individually how to use them; a system with completely decentralized economic decision-making.

market economy An economy in which prices are used to signal firms and households about the value of individual resources. It is also called the price system, or one using the price mechanism.

market failure A situation in which an unfettered market leads to either an under- or over-allocation of resources to a specific economic activity. Externalities are cases of market failure.

market for corporate control The situation that arises in a contested takeover bid when one company, in seeking to acquire another, is involved in the crucial task of winning the support of a majority of the shareholders of the takeover target.

market structures The characteristics of a market which determine the interrelationships between participants in that market. Decision-making in any given market will depend on whether buyers and sellers can assume that they can or cannot affect market price. Thus the type of market structure is determined by the number of buyers and sellers and the ease of entry into (and exit from) a market.

market supply curve The locus of points showing the minimum prices at which given quantities will be forthcoming; also called the short-run industry supply curve.

medium of exchange Money is anything that is generally accepted for the buying and selling of goods and services. Money, therefore, acts as a means (medium) of payment (exchange).

merchant banks The name given to a small group of banks whose specialisms involve raising money for companies and advising on portfolio management.

merit good A good that has been deemed socially desirable via the political process.

microeconomics The study of the economic behaviour of households and firms and how prices of goods and services are determined.

minimum efficient scale The lowest rate of output per unit time-period at which average costs reach a minimum point.

minimum wage legislation Laws which regulate the lowest rates of pay for various occupations that can be paid by employers.

mixed economy An economic system in which the decision about how resources should be used is made partly by the private sector and partly by the government.

mobility of labour The ease with which labour can be transferred from one type of employment to another. Mobility of labour can thus be considered in terms of geographical or occupational mobility. The converse concept *immobility of labour* is often employed by economists.

models, or **theories** Simplified representations of the real world used to make predictions or to better understand the real world.

monetarists Individuals who believe that changes in the money supply are important in the determination of the equilibrium level of nominal national income. Monetarists place money in a more important role in their national income determination model than do Keynesians.

monetary base The notes and coin in circulation and banks' balances with the Bank of England. Also known as M0 or high-powered money.

money at call Very short-term lending by commercial banks, ranging from an overnight loan to one that lasts for 14 days. The discount houses are the principal borrowers of these funds.

money multiplier The reciprocal of the reserve asset ratio, assuming no leakages into currency and no excess reserves. It gives the amount by which credit expands as a result of a given increase in the monetary base.

money supply A generic term used to denote the amount of 'money' in circulation. There are numerous specific definitions of the money supply. See Figure 19.1 for details of each definition.

monopolist The single supplier that comprises the entire industry.

monopolistic competition A market situation where a large number of firms produce similar but not identical products. There is relatively easy entry into the industry.

monopsonist A single buyer.

multiplier The ratio of the change in the equilibrium level of real national income to the change in expenditures which brought it about; that number by which a change in investment or autonomous consumption, for example, is multiplied to get the change in the equilibrium level of real national income.

narrow measures Methods of measuring the money supply by looking at money predominantly as a medium of exchange.

National Debt The accumulated govenment debt, the total outstanding.

National Enterprise Board (NEB) *See* **British Technology Group.**

National Income The value of the flow of goods and services becoming available to a nation during a given period of time (usually one year).

national income accounting A measurement system used to estimate national income and its components. This is one approach to measuring an economy's aggregate performance.

nationalization The taking into public ownership of part or all of economic activity in a key sector of the economy.

nationalized industries Examples of these vary from time to time and country to country. Basically they involve the government owning and running an industry, the products of which are sold through the market and priced accordingly.

National Research and Development Corporation *See* **British Technology Group.**

National Savings Bank A public sector institution that offers banking-type facilities over post-office counters.

natural monopoly A monopoly that arises from the peculiar production characteristics in the industry. Usually a natural monopoly arises when production of the service or product requires extremely large capital investments such that only one firm can profitably be supported by consumers. A natural monopoly arises when there are large economies of scale relative to the industry demand, and one firm can produce at a lower cost than can be achieved by multiple firms.

natural rate of unemployment That rate of unemployment which would prevail when inflation is anticipated correctly, year in and year out.

near monies Assets that are almost money. They have a high degree of liquidity; they can be easily converted into money without loss in value. Deposit accounts held in building societies and Treasury bills are examples.

negative income elasticity A given rise in income will result in a fall in the quantity demanded.

net investment Gross investment minus an estimate of the wear and tear on the existing capital stock. Net investment therefore measures the change in our capital stock over a one-year period.

net national product (NNP) GNP minus depreciation.

new international economic order A proposed international institution to be sponsored by the United Nations that would basically attempt to stabilize raw materials prices and increase the amount of foreign aid given by industrialized nations to LDCs.

newly industrializing countries (NICs) Those upper-middle-income developing countries such as Mexico and South Korea that have developed rapidly over the past decade and are now increasingly significant exporters of consumer goods.

nominal rate of interest The market rate of interest that is expressed in terms of today's pounds.

nominal values The values of variables such as GNP and investment expressed in current pounds. Also called money values. Otherwise stated, measurement in terms of actual market prices at which goods are sold.

non-durable consumer goods Goods used by consumers that are used up within a year.

non-monetary indicators Measures of the state of development such as the number of persons who are literate and average life expectancy. Such measures avoid the problems of using GNP data in making international comparisons.

non-oil balance Imports minus exports excluding oil.

non-price competition The means by which firms strive to increase sales and increase market share other than by undercutting rivals. Instead of lowering prices and competing by price, firms resort to advertising campaigns, encourage new product development, and regard sales as being sensitive to effective marketing.

non-tariff barriers Restraints on international trade other than import duties.

normal goods Goods for which demand increases as income increases. Most goods that we deal with are normal.

normal profit The normal rate of return to investment; otherwise known as the opportunity cost of capital.

normative economics Analysis involving value judgements about economic policies; relates to whether things are good or bad. A statement of *what ought to be*.

number line A line that can be divided into line segments of equal length, each associated with a number.

occupationally immobile *See* **mobility of labour.**

OECD The Organization for Economic Co-operation and Development. This could be regarded as a club comprising all the capitalist countries as members who discuss together economic issues of mutual interest. In fact the OECD has 24 member countries, namely, Australia, Austria, Belgium, Canada, Denmark, Finland, France, West Germany, Greece, Iceland, Ireland, Italy, Japan, Luxembourg, The Netherlands, New Zealand, Norway, Portugal, Spain, Sweden, Switzerland, Turkey, the United Kingdom, and the United States. The organization's offices are based in Paris and it produces various economic publications each year.

oil duties *See* **tax.**

oligopoly A market situation where there are very few sellers. Each seller knows that the other sellers will react to its changes in prices and quantities.

open economy An economy that is in some way dependent on one or more other economies. Goods are traded and international exchange takes place.

open-market operations The buying and selling of government securities (e.g. bonds) in the open market by the Bank of England.

opportunity cost The highest-valued alternative that must be sacrificed to attain something or satisfy a want.

opportunity cost of capital The normal rate of return or the amount that must be paid to an investor to induce her or him to invest in a business. Economists consider this a cost of production and it is included in our cost examples.

organization The co-ordination of individuals, each doing different things in the furtherance of a common end.

origin The intersection of the y axis with the x axis in a graph.

output approach A way of measuring national income by adding up the value of the output produced by each specific sector of the economy. (The emphasis is on 'value added'. See Figure 13.1.)

output gap Exists whenever the equilibrium level of real national output is less than the full-capacity level; the negative difference between total desired expenditures and the full-capacity level of real national income.

paradox of thrift An increased desire to save (an increase in the MPS) will lead to a reduction in the equilibrium level of saving.

parallel pricing The simultaneous changes in prices in an oligopolistic market situation which is explained by collusion or barometric price leadership.

partial equilibrium analysis A way of analysing a market in isolation without taking account of the interrelationships among markets.

partnership A business entity involving two or more individuals who join together for business purposes. In most instances, each partner is liable for the debts of the business to such an extent that he or she can lose his or her personal wealth if the business becomes bankrupt.

perfect competition A market structure in which the decisions of buyers and sellers have no effect on market price.

perfectly competitive firm A firm that is such a small part of the total industry picture that it cannot affect the price of the product it sells.

perfectly elastic supply A supply curve characterized by a reduction in quantity supplied to zero when there is the slightest decrease in price.

perfectly inelastic supply The characteristic of a supply curve for which quantity supplied remains constant, no matter what happens to price.

perfectly price-elastic demand A demand curve that has the characteristic that even the slightest increase in price will lead to a zero quantity demanded.

perfectly price-inelastic demand A demand curve that exhibits zero responsiveness in changes in price, i.e. no matter what the price is, the quantity demanded remains the same.

permanent-income hypothesis A theory of the consumption function that states that people's desire to spend is a function of their permanent or long-run expected income rather than of their current disposable income.

petroleum revenue tax *See* **tax.**

Phillips curve A curve showing the relationship between unemployment and changes in wages or prices. The Phillips curve gives the trade-off between unemployment and inflation.

planning curve Another name for the long-run average cost curve.

planning horizon Another name for long-run cost curves. All inputs are variable during the planning period.

poll tax *See* **community charge.**

positive economics Analysis that is strictly limited to making either purely descriptive statements or scientific predictions; for example, if *A, then b.* A statement of *what is.* Positive statements can be checked against the evidence.

potential output The maximum level of output achievable if the economy were operating on its production possibilities curve.

predatory pricing The practice of temporarily selling at prices below cost with the intention of driving a competitor from the market, so that in the future prices may be raised and enhanced profits extracted.

present value The value of the future amount expressed in today's pounds; the most that someone would pay today to receive a certain sum at some point in the future.

price–consumption curve The set of consumer optimum combinations of two goods that the consumer would choose as the relative price of the goods changes, while money income remains constant.

price control Government regulation of free market prices such that a legal maximum price is specified.

price differentiation A situation in which price differences for similar products reflect only differences in marginal cost in providing those commodities to different groups of buyers.

price discrimination This is a system of pricing often employed by nationalized industries and other monopolists; it involves charging different prices to different customers who have different elasticities of demand for the product.

price-elastic demand A characteristic of a demand curve in which a given percentage change in price will result in a larger percentage change in quantity demanded, in the opposite direction. Total revenues and price are inversely related in the elastic portion of the demand curve.

price elasticity of demand The responsiveness of the quantity demanded for a commodity to changes in its price per unit. The price elasticity of demand is defined as the percentage change in quantity demanded divided by the percentage change in price.

price elasticity of supply The responsiveness of quantity supplied of a commodity to a change in its price. Price elasticity of supply is defined as the percentage change in quantity supplied divided by the percentage change in price.

price index The cost of today's basket of goods expressed as a percentage of the cost of the same basket during a base year.

price-inelastic demand A characteristic of a demand curve in which a given change in price will result in a less than proportionate change in the quantity demanded, in the opposite direction. Total revenue and price are directly related in the inelastic region of the demand curve.

price mechanism Prices are used as a signalling system between firms and households concerning the use of resources. Where the price mechanism operates there is a market economy.

prices and incomes policies Policies emanating from the government which restrict the increase of prices and incomes, the intention being to promote price stability.

price supports Minimum prices set by the government. To be effective, price supports must be coupled with a mechanism to rid the market of 'surplus' production that arises whenever the supported price is greater than the market-clearing price.

price system An economic system in which (relative) prices are constantly changing to reflect changes in supply and demand for different commodities. The prices of those commodities are signals to everyone within the system about what is relatively expensive and what is relatively cheap.

price-taker Another definition of a competitive firm. A price-taker is a firm that must take the price of its product as given. The firm cannot influence its price.

principle of exclusion This simply means that anyone who does not pay will not be allowed to benefit from consuming a particular good or service – they will be left out.

principle of rivalry Stated briefly, when I use a private good, my use prevents the possibility of your use. You and I cannot eat the *same* apple simultaneously.

private costs Those costs incurred by individuals when they engage in using scarce resources. For example, the private cost of running a car is equal to the petrol, oil, insurance, maintenance, and depreciation costs. Also called explicit costs.

private goods Goods that can only be consumed by one individual at a time. Private goods are subject to the principles of exclusion and rivalry.

privatization In very general terms this involves the transfer of assets from the public sector to the private sector.

producer price index A statistical measure of a weighted average of prices of those commodities that firms purchase from other firms.

product differentiation When consumers perceive there are differences in the characteristics of products which are alternatives to each other. Product differentiation thus gives producers some freedom in price determination.

production function The relationship between inputs and output. A production function is a technological, not an economic, relationship.

production possibilities curve A curve representing all possible combinations of total output that could be produced assuming (a) a fixed amount of productive resources and (b) efficient use of those resources.

product markets Transactions, where households buy goods, occur in the product markets, that is where households are the buyers and businesses are the sellers of consumer goods (see Figure 12.1).

profit The income generated by selling something for a higher price than was paid for it. In production, the income generated is the difference between total revenues received from consumers who purchase the goods and the total cost of producing those goods.

profit-maximizing rate of production That rate of production which maximizes total profits, or the difference between total revenues and total costs; also, that rate of production at which marginal revenue equals marginal cost.

progressive taxation A tax system in which, as one earns more income, a higher percentage of the additional pounds is taxed. Put formally, the marginal tax rate exceeds the average tax rate as income rises.

proportional taxation A tax system in which, as the individual's income goes up, the tax bill goes up in exactly the same proportion. Also called a *flat-rate tax*.

proportionate demand curve A demand curve that represents the arithmetic portion of an entire industry that an individual firm faces when it sells its product.

prudential standards of liquidity The various reserve asset ratios which banks must observe for various types of lending, in line with the Bank of England's supervision requirements.

public goods Goods for which the principles of exclusion and rivalry do not apply; they can be jointly consumed by many individuals simultaneously, at no additional cost, and with no reduction in the quality or quantity of the provision concerned.

public sector The simplest (but rather misleading) definition is to include all forms of public expenditure by all types of government.

public sector borrowing requirement The difference between government expenditure and tax revenue, which must be financed by borrowing.

public sector debt repayment The amount by which government revenue, from tax and other sources, exceeds government expenditure in any one year.

pure economic rent The payment to any resource that is in completely inelastic supply. The payment to any resource over and above transfer earnings.

quantity theory of money and prices The theory that changes in the price level are directly related to changes in the money supply. The quantity theory is based on the equation of exchange.

quasi-rent A payment over and above what is necessary to keep a factor of production in existence in its same quality in the short run, but not in the long run.

rate of discount The rate of interest used to discount future income streams back to present value.

rational-expectations hypothesis A hypothesis or theory stating that individuals combine the effects of past policy changes on important economic variables with their own judgement about the future effects of current and future policy changes.

rationing A distribution of restricted supplies by the government which is based on some objective criteria (such as numbers per household) at a time when quantity demanded exceeds quantity supplied. Rationing tries to effect a fair distribution of the limited supplies of basic necessities such as foodstuffs in a wartime economy.

reaction function The manner in which one oligopolist reacts to a change in price (or output or quality) of another oligopolist.

real income effect The change in people's purchasing power that occurs when, other things held constant, the price of one good that they purchased changes. When that price goes up, real income, or purchasing power, falls; and when that price goes down, real income, or purchasing power, increases.

real rate of interest The rate of interest obtained by subtracting the rate of inflation from the nominal rate of interest.

real values Measurement of economic values after adjustments have been made for changes in prices between years.

recession A period of time during which the rate of growth of business activity is consistently less than its long-term trend, or is negative. This may also be referred to as an economic depression if it is unduly prolonged as in the 1930s.

recognized banks The generic title given to those institutions recognized as banks by the Bank of England.

regional policy Government grants and incentives made available to firms moving into certain designated areas. Previously these designated areas were referred to as 'areas for expansion'; now they are referred to as 'assisted areas'.

regressive taxation A tax system in which, as more pounds are earned, the percentage of tax paid on them falls. The marginal tax rate is less than the average tax rate as income rises.

relative price The price of a commodity expressed in terms of the price of another commodity or the average price of all other commodities.

rental-only contracts This restricts customers to rental or lease terms only and which can be anticompetitive where there are no alternative methods of acquiring those goods.

R & D capital This represents the monies invested into research and development, with the aim of inventing and exploring new products/areas.

reserve asset ratio The percentage of total assets that banks must hold in liquid form.

reserve assets Liquid assets and cash which can be used to make good customers' requests for withdrawals from the bank.

resource allocation The assignment of resources to specific uses. More specifically, it means determining what will be produced, how it will be produced, who will produce it, and for whom it will be produced.

resources Inputs used in the production of the goods and services that we desire. Also called factors of production.

Retail Price Index A statistical measure of a weighted average of prices of a specified set of goods and services purchased by representative families.

revaluation The opposite of devaluation.

rivalry A basic definition of competition in which individual economic agents attempt to improve their relative position in a market by advertising, marketing, developing new products, seeking improved deals, and so on.

saving The act of not consuming all one's current income. Whatever is not consumed out of spendable income is, by definition, saved. *Saving* is an action measured over time, whereas *savings* are an existing accumulation resulting from the act of saving in the past. We usually talk about how much we save out of our pay cheque every week or every month.

scarcity A reference to the fact that at any point in time there exists only a finite amount of resources – human and non-human. Scarcity of resources therefore means that nature does not freely provide as much of everything as people want.

scatter diagram A diagram, or graph, showing the points that represent observations of the dependent and independent variables. These points are scattered throughout the *xy* quandrant.

seasonal unemployment Unemployment due to seasonality in demand or in the supply of a particular good or service.

Second World The communist nations of Eastern Europe plus the Soviet Union and the People's Republic of China. This concept was always rather unsatisfactory and is perhaps increasingly inappropriate.

selective distribution The practice of choosing as sales outlets only those which satisfy specific qualitative or quantitative criteria.

services Things purchased by consumers that do not have physical characteristics. Examples of services are those obtained from doctors, lawyers, dentists, repair personnel, house-cleaners, educators, retailers, and wholesalers.

shortage Another term for an excess quantity demanded or insufficient quantity supplied. The difference between the quantity demanded and the quantity supplied at a specific price below the market-clearing price.

short run That time-period in which a firm cannot alter its current size of plant.

short-run break-even price The price where a firm's total revenues equal its total costs. In economics the break-even price is where the firm is just making a normal rate of return.

short-run close-down price The price where the profit-maximizing price just covers average variable costs. This occurs just below the intersection of the marginal cost curve and the average variable cost curve.

short-run industry supply curve The locus of points showing the minimum prices at which given quantities will be forthcoming; also called the market supply curve.

sight deposits Those bank accounts that allow the customer immediate access to his or her funds. Often called 'current accounts'.

slope The change in the *y* value divided by the corresponding change in the *x* value of a curve; can be thought of as the 'pitch' of the curve.

social costs The full cost that society bears when a resource-using action occurs. For example, the social cost of driving a car is equal to all of the private costs plus any additional cost that society bears, including air pollution and traffic congestion. (Some authors use this term to simply imply external costs. See footnote on p. 162.)

socialism An economic system in which the state owns the major share of productive resources except for labour. Also, socialism usually involves a greater redistribution of income than would be the case with a purely capitalist system.

sole proprietorship A business owned by only one person.

special deposits Interest-earning accounts that are not active; held at the Bank of England on behalf of the commercial banks. The Bank of England can request these funds when it wishes to curb liquidity, but has not done so since 1980. Nevertheless, it has the right to do so.

special drawing rights (SDRs) A reserve asset created by the International Monetary Fund that countries can use to settle international payments.

specialization The division of productive activities among persons and regions so that no one individual or one area is totally self-sufficient. An individual may specialize, for example, in law, medicine, or car production. A nation may specialize in the production of coffee, computers, or cameras.

stable equilibrium A situation in which, if there is a shock that disturbs the prevailing equilibrium between the forces of supply and demand, there will normally be self-corrective forces that automatically cause the disequilibrium eventually to become an equilibrium situation.

stagflation A period of simultaneous high unemployment and rising prices. In other words, a period of both economic stagnation and inflation.

standard of deferred payment A quality of an asset that makes it desirable for use as a means of settling debts maturing in the future; an essential prerequisite of money.

stock The quantity of something at a point in time. A bank account at a point in time is a stock. Stocks are defined independently of time although they are assessed at a point in time; different from a flow. Savings are a stock, as is wealth.

stock appreciation This represents the increased value of stock due to inflation.

stocks (inventories) Inasmuch as stocks of goods can be sold in the future, they too are classed as investment. They may consist of unused inputs, kept by the firm for use in future production, or unsold products.

store of value The ability of an item to hold value over time; a necessary quality of money.

structural change A change in the composition of output which necessitates reallocation of resources.

structural rigidities These are obstacles within markets which prevent a swift response to changing forces of supply and demand. They are more prevalent in some markets than others, for example trade union activity affects the dynamics of the labour market.

structural unemployment Unemployment resulting from fundamental changes in the structure of the economy.

subsidies Negative taxes; payments to producers or consumers of a good or service. For example, farmers often get subsidies for producing wheat, corn, or milk.

substitute Two goods are considered substitutes when a change in the price of one causes a shift in demand for the other in the same direction as the price changes. For example, if the price of butter goes up, the demand for margarine will rise; if the price of butter goes down, the demand for margarine will decrease.

substitution effect The tendency of people to substitute in favour of cheaper commodities and away from more expensive commodities.

supply The relationship between the price and the quantity supplied (other things being equal) which is usually a direct one.

supply constraints If it is not possible, or if it is very costly, to increase quantity supplied, supply constraints are said to exist.

supply curve The graphic representation of the supply schedule; a line showing the supply schedule, which slopes upwards (has a positive slope).

supply schedule A set of numbers showing prices and the quantity supplied at those various prices; a schedule showing the rate of planned production at each relative price for a specified time-period, usually one year.

supply-side economics This generally applies to attempts at creating incentives for individuals and firms to increase productivity; relates to discussions of what causes the aggregate supply curve to shift.

surplus (microeconomic) Another name for an excess quantity supplied or insufficient quantity demanded. The difference between the quantity supplied and the quantity demanded at a price above the market-clearing price.

surplus (macroeconomic) The excess of tax revenue, over and above government spending.

tax The compulsory transfer of funds from individuals and businesses to the government. These transfers may be levied on oil, tobacco, alcohol, petroleum or inheritance – to name just a few of the specific taxes that exist.

tax bracket A specified interval of income to which a specific and unique marginal tax rate is applied. For example, a tax bracket may exist between £15 000 and £19 999.

tax expenditures Allowances made so that certain sorts of spending (*e.g.* mortgage interest) are deducted from taxable income.

tax incidence The distribution of tax burdens among various groups in society.

technical efficiency The utilization of the cheapest production technique for any given output rate; no inputs are wilfully wasted.

technological unemployment Unemployment caused by technological changes reducing the demand for labour in some specific tasks.

terms of exchange The terms under which the trading takes place. Usually the terms of exchange are given by the price at which a good is traded.

terms of trade The relationship between the weighted average price of exports and the weighted average price of imports. Expressed as an index based on 100 in the base year, the terms of trade have become more favourable if the index rises and have worsened if the index falls.

theory of demand Quantity demanded and price are inversely related – more is bought at a lower price, less at a higher price (other things being equal).

theory of the firm A theory of how suppliers of commodities behave – how they make choices – in the face of changing constraints.

third parties Parties who are external to negotiations and activities between buyers and sellers. If you agree to buy a car with no brakes and then run me over, I am a third party to the deal struck between you and the seller of the car, and my suffering is the negative externality.

Third World The less developed countries (LDCs).

tie-in sales A stipulation that a buyer must purchase part or all of his requirements of a second (tied) product from the supplier of a first (tying) product.

time deposits Savings account balances and certificates of deposit held in commercial banks and building societies. The bank or building society can require, say, 30 days' notice of your intent to withdraw from your deposit account, but often this time requirement is waived.

time-series data Empirical observations about the value of one or more economic variables taken at different periods over time.

tobacco tax *See* **tax.**

total costs All the costs of a firm combined, including rent, payments to workers, interst on borrowed money, and so on.

total expenditure The total monetary value of all the final goods and services bought in an economy during the year.

total income The total amount earned by the nation's resources (factors). National income, therefore, includes wages, rent, interest payments, and profits that are received, respectively, by workers, landowners, capital owners, and entrepreneurs.

total output The total value of all the final goods and services produced in the economy during the year.

total revenues The price per unit times the total quantity sold.

trade association An organization of firms within an industry that undertakes activities on behalf of its members. In the UK trade associations developed in the nineteenth century to reduce the intensity of competition between members but since 1956 are now involved in public relations activities and the dissemination of statistics concerning the relevant trade.

trade deficit When imports exceed exports there is a trade deficit, when vice versa, a surplus.

trade-off A term relating to opportunity cost. In order to get a desired economic good, it is necessary to trade off some other desired economic good whenever we are in a world of scarcity. A trade-off involves a sacrifice, then, that must be made in order to obtain something.

trade unions Organizations of workers that usually seek to secure economic improvements for their members.

Training Agency The Training Agency is responsible for co-ordinating the UK's training and vocational education programmes. It operates as an agency within the employment department and is largely concerned with minimizing the level of unemployment. Until May 1988 this agency was known as the MSC (Manpower Services Commission).

Training and Enterprise Councils (TECs) These are employer-led groups responsible for the management of training and enterprise schemes in local areas. In other words they replace the functions of the Training Agency area offices. They are funded by subsidies from the Department of Employment. The first of these TECs began business in 1990. By the year 2000 it is estimated that approximately 80 such councils will exist in England and Wales.

transactions costs All of the costs associated with exchanging, including the informational costs of finding out price and quality, service record, durability, etc., of a product, plus the cost of contracting and enforcing that contract.

transfer earnings The amount which an employee could earn in an alternative occupation.

transfer payments Money payments made by governments to individuals for which no services or goods are concurrently rendered. Examples are social security payments and student grants.

transmission mechanism The way in which changes in the money stock affect income, output, and prices.

Treasury bill A means of borrowing by the government for a short period of time (usually 91 days).

two-part tariff This is a way of pricing employed by industries such as telephone, gas, electricity, and water, where a composite charge is made comprising a 'standing charge' to cover the fixed costs of providing the service and a 'unit charge' to cover the variable costs of supplying each additional unit thereafter.

unanticipated inflation Inflation whose rate comes as a surprise to an individual. Unanticipated inflation can be either at a higher or lower rate than anticipated.

unitary price elasticity of demand A property of the demand curve, where the quantity demanded changes exactly in proportion to the change in price. Total revenue is invariant to price changes in the unit elastic portion of the demand curve.

unit of account A measure by which prices and values are expressed; the common denominator of the price system, and a central quality of money.

util An artificial unit by which utility is measured.

utility The want-satisfying power that a good or service possesses.

utility analysis The analysis of consumer decision-making based on utility maximization.

value added The value of an industry's sales, minus the value of intermediate goods (e.g. raw materials and parts) purchased for use in production.

value-added tax (VAT) A tax assessed on the value added by each producing unit. In other words, it is the total sale price of output *minus* the cost of raw materials and intermediate goods purchased from other firms.

variable costs Those costs that vary with the rate of production. They include wages paid to workers, the costs of materials, and so on.

velocity of circulation The average number of times per year each pound is spent on final goods and services. It is equal to GNP divided by the money stock.

vertical merger The joining of a firm with another that either sells an input or buys an output.

vertical price squeezing When a vertically integrated firm controls the total supply of an input which is essential to the production requirements of its subsidiary and also its competitors, the input price can be raised and the downstream output price reduced, so that the profits of competitors are squeezed, possibly with a view to driving them from the market.

wage councils Bodies set up by the government to determine pay in occupations with little union organization and relatively low pay, e.g. retailing.

wealth That which has value; usually, the difference between what a person owns (assets) and what a person owes (liabilities).

wealth effect When a fall in the money value of assets leads to a lower level of personal wealth, consumer spending may fall.

working capital Investment into working capital involves changes in the stocks of finished goods and goods in process; as well as changes in the raw materials that businesses keep on hand. Whenever stocks are decreasing, investment is negative; whenever they are increasing, investment is positive.

working population Those who are employed, self-employed, claiming benefit, or in the Forces.

***x*-axis** The horizontal axis in a graph.

***x*-inefficiency** Organizational slack within a firm that results in costs per unit being higher than would be the case if strong competitive pressures exist. Since a monopolist faces weak competition *x*-inefficiency is held to be associated with this form of market structure, particularly a monopoly.

***y*-axis** The vertical axis in a graph.

Answers

Answers to Practical Exercises

Chapter 1

1. (a) See graph

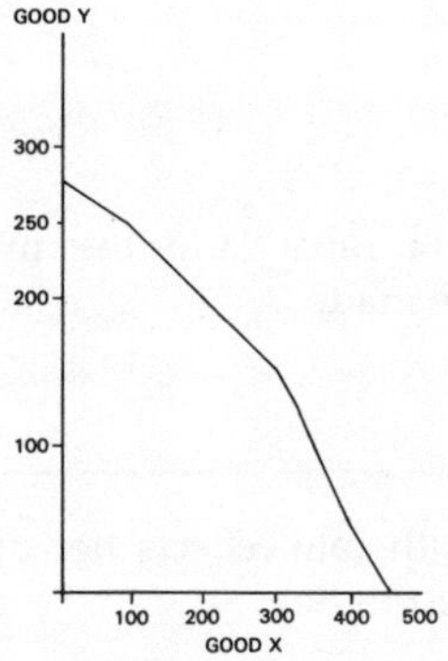

(b) In the case of both good X and good Y the addition of 100 extra workers to an initial workforce of 100 workers at first leads to a rise in total production but later additions lead to a modest increase in total output.

The changes in output per 100 extra workers once 100 are employed are:

X	*Y*
60	40
70	45
70	50
70	40
50	35
40	25
30	15

(c) The production possibility curve would move outwards to the right. Thus a new set of combinations of output of X and Y would now be possible.

(d) In the second year there is a reduction in the output of consumer goods. This would be regarded as a fall in the living standards of this economy but there is every prospect of the economy growing more rapidly in the future as a result of the enhanced productive potential arising from the greater use of resources for investment. Thus living standards in the longer term might be higher than if present consumption levels are maintained at the expense of investment.

2. Few (if any) students find they have unlimited resources and thus their task is to make limited funds stretch as far as possible over many potential claims on these slender resources. Students have to buy books and stationery whilst also requiring funds for various other expenditures such as toiletries and cosmetics, records, bus fares and other expenses. Holiday work can provide some income to meet these expenditures. For parents the many costs of running a household add up to a total to be budgeted for out of the income of one or more breadwinners. If unforeseen expenses stretch the income available then some expenditures may need to be delayed or even postponed such as a family holiday or replacing a three piece suite of furniture. Local government in the UK is mainly financed by funds from the central government but here the opportunity cost principle still applies. Funds will not allow local authorities to achieve all their aspirations in the provision of social facilities such as libraries, museums, recreation facilities and social services. Help for the elderly, the handicapped and families in difficulty is never as much as they would wish to provide. For central government the use of taxpayers money on defence necessarily constrains the amount that can be spent on schools and health provision. The opportunity cost principle not only applies to people and governments but also to companies, charities, clubs, and societies. All these institutions have, to varying degrees to budget expenditures in the light of anticipated income or revenues. Priorities have to be chosen and some activities, whilst thought desirable, are not capable of being pursued as quickly given budget constraints.

Chapter 2

1. Private property, free enterprise and choice, self-interest, competition, a price system, limited role for government.

2. Consumer sovereignty might not exist because (a) there is insufficient information about characteristics and qualities of consumer products in the market-place; (b) there is an overwhelming amount of fraud and misrepresentation, so that consumers cannot find out about the qualities of consumer products; or (c) there is insufficient competition among firms in the economy to provide the desired assortment of goods and services. Consumer sovereignty relates to the output mix in the economy being determined by consumer spending votes. Consumer choice, on the other hand, relates to the freedom to choose among the goods and services that can be produced in the economy. It is possible to have a situation where consumer sovereignty exists but little consumer choice does because of, for example, government restrictions on the manufacture and sale of certain products. The drug industry might be a case in point. Consumers conceivably could be sovereign in that their spending votes for various drugs would determine what was produced. They do not, however, have complete choice because the government restricts which drugs can be purchased without prescription. Furthermore, the government controls which drugs can be sold even with a prescription.

Chapter 3

1. Steel (and coal and coke), glass, tyres (and rubber), plastics, railways (and steel!). Moreover, decisions on resource allocations concerning labour and other inputs for each of *these* (and the many other) industries must be made.

Chapter 4

1. (a) There is no obvious pattern to the data evident from a quick visual examination of the chart. The eighteen countries do not exhibit any tendency either to bunch together or show a consistent relationship between the proportion of GDP accounted for by government spending and the record of economic growth.

   (b) The ten year period allows for any 'freak' years not to distort the data. Thus for each of the 18 countries the proportion of GNP accounted for by government spending is a truly representative one, that does not present a false picture of the degree of state involvement, which might be the case due to any sudden change (up or down) over a one or two years period.

   (c) The highest percentage figure for government spending is that in Sweden, a country where a succession of socialist governments has led to an extensive programme of state welfare benefits and government intervention in its economy. The Swiss government is at the other extreme but both Norway and Denmark share something of the Swedish style of extensive state intervention. As regards the vertical axis Japan's relatively rapid growth rate in the period 1974-86 reflects her successful development of many consumer goods industries, the products of which have been exported to the Western European countries in the chart. Norway's growth rate reflects her development of oil in the North Sea.

2. (a) It is government spending expressed not in terms of the actual sums spent in the year as depicted in the chart but those sums recalculated to reflect the rise in prices. Thus over a period of time there is a picture of money expenditures which are 'like with like'. The chart can thus show whether there is literally a real rise or fall in the amount spent by government in the period 1979–80 to 1992–93.

   (b) Government spending is but one element of GDP. It is thus possible for GDP to rise faster than government spending and as a result the latter is a smaller proportion of the whole economy.

   (c) The two vertical axes are not shown with a base or zero line. This means that the rise in real government spending over the period shown is somewhat exaggerated and the falling proportion of GDP accounted for by government spending is also shown more vividly than it would be if the base line were shown.

3. (a) The 40 year period is a long one and the value of money has fallen considerably during it. There is thus a need to take account of the changing purchasing power of the pound in charting government expenditure over four decades.

   (b) The average annual growth rate in the early years of the decade was about 2 per cent, markedly below that in the earlier part of the period on the chart. Whilst the new government after 1979 clearly constrained the growth of public expenditure it is nonetheless clear that an upward course in the data is still apparent.

(c) The growth in public expenditure was rapid in the early 1970s – around 5 per cent – but it then fell back later in the decade when cuts in spending evidently occurred. The reasons are not explained here but the chart provides a picture of a then Labour government making a major change in the direction of its economic policy. After 1977 an upward growth in government spending was resumed.

Chapter 5

1. The equilibrium price is £30. The quantity supplied and demanded is about 10.5 million calculators per year.

2. (a) The demand curve for vitamin C will shift outwards to the right because the product has taken on a desirable new quality. (b) The demand curve for LPs will shift inwards to the left because the substitute good – tapes – are now a lower-cost alternative (change in the price of a substitute). (c) The demand curve for mint sauce will shift outwards to the right because the price of a complementary good – lamb chops – has decreased.

3. As the diagram indicates, demand does not change, supply decreases, the equilibrium price of oranges rises, and the equilibrium quantity falls.

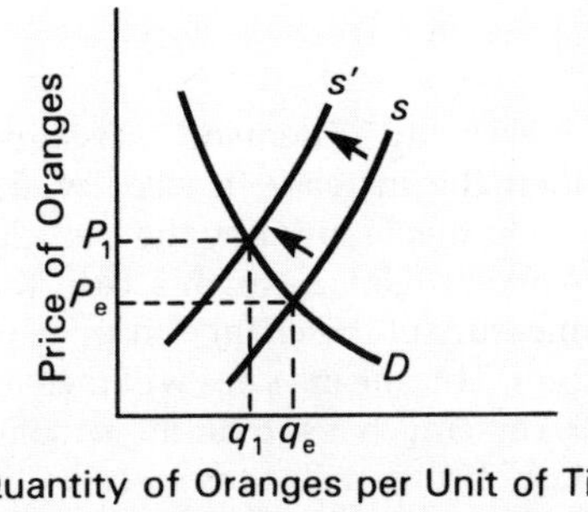

4. The *absolute* price of heating oil has doubled, while the price of natural gas has quadrupled. The *relative* price of heating oil has decreased; that of natural gas has increased. Consumers will start buying more heating oil and less natural gas.

Chapter 6

1. The relative price of whisky in relation to beer has fallen from 10 beers per bottle to 9 beers per bottle. Although the absolute prices of beer and whisky rose, the relative prices of both commodities fell in relation to all other goods and services, because neither rose by as much as 150 per cent.

2. Transactions costs are the costs of engaging in a transfer of goods over and above the sale price of the goods. In the purchase of a home, some of these costs are the costs of petrol and travel during the search; the opportunity cost of the time of the buyers who are searching; the fees that must be paid for checking the validity of the title; the fees paid to the estate agent, if one is used; the fees paid to a solicitor to draw up the contract; the costs of securing a loan, if the house is to be mortgaged, including the costs of searching for the most attractive credit terms; the costs of moving family and furniture into a new home and community; the costs of adapting or remodelling the house to your tastes; and the costs of disposing of the residence being given up for the new location. Each of these costs, and others that you may think of, may present possibilities of economizing. Organizing the search effort, hiring an estate agent to do the searching, finding a solicitor who handles legal matters at reduced rates, buying a new house that can be built to your own specifications, contributing more or less of your own capital to defray credit costs – all are potential ways of reducing transactions costs.

3. (a) The firm will choose technique C because it incurs the lowest cost of the three methods at the prices given, £107, as opposed to £120 for A and £168 for B. (b) The firm's maximum profit will be £65. (c) If labour increases to £4 per unit, technique A becomes the most profitable, because its cost increases to only £132, less than the £143 that C now costs. Therefore A would be chosen. Profits would drop to £40.

4. Neither has an absolute advantage; therefore neither has a comparative advantage. As a consequence, total output would not change if specialization occurred.

5. Mrs Jones has an absolute advantage in jacket production, as she can produce twice as many as can Mr Jones. Mr Jones does not have an absolute advantage in anything; he is less productive than Mrs Jones at jacket production and equally productive at tie production. Mrs Jones has a comparative advantage in the production of jackets; she is twice as productive as Mr Jones in jacket production and equally productive in the production of ties. Mr Jones has a comparative advantage in the production of ties; he is just as productive in tie production and only half as productive in jacket production. If Mrs Jones specializes in jackets and Mr Jones specializes in ties, total production equals 16 jackets and 24 ties; tie output remains the same but jacket production increases from 12 to 16.

Chapter 7

1. (a) The price elasticity of demand using the arc elasticity formula is −3.77.

$$\left(\frac{2}{13} \div \frac{200}{4900}\right)$$

(b) If the price elasticity of demand is assumed to be −0.5 then the increase in sales would be much less than that assured by the Vehicle and General Workers' Union. In this case the arc elasticity measure of the change in price (£200) is 4.0 per cent. This means sales will increase by just 240 000 cars, much less than the situation in (a). The car firms will thus receive lower revenues and, unless costs fall significantly, lower profits.

2. E

3. C

4. E

5. D

6. (a) The data is in current terms and if it was shown in real terms then any impression that households are spending a higher proportion of their income on food would not be evident.

(b) The data shows a modest shift to eating out of the home after 1982 which could be explained by an economy where household incomes were rising strongly enough for people to feel able to afford to pay for meals cooked for them.

The chapter indicated that in a growing economy consumers find an ever increasing list of possible expenditures which can be made once the basic needs of food, clothing and shelter are met in a developed economy. Only so much food can be eaten!

(c) Rising real household incomes as indicated in (b). Unemployment and labour unrest in manufacturing industry could be expected to influence the ability of households to eat out of the home. The changing availability of out of home places to eat could also be expected to influence the amounts spent i.e. pubs serving food, the development of fast food outlets and the growing number of motorway restaurants and snack bars.

7. All the four groups of foods contain items which, one would think, were to a considerable extent substitutes for each other. On this basis one would expect the cross price elasticities to be positive in sign. In fact of the 16 elasticities only 7 are actually positive. It thus seems on the basis of this data that consumers in the UK do not readily substitute lamb for beef, oranges for apples, tea for coffee or margarine for butter. There would appear to be sufficiently strong preferences for some of these foods for some consumers not to be very ready to shift their purchases of meat, fruit, drink and fats.

Chapter 8

1. In the case of the three commodities there are three ratios comparing the world price with that in the US, Japan and the EC during the 1980s. In all three of the commodities government intervention has the effect of protecting farmers by raising prices received above what is the world price. Whilst the world price may be a somewhat arbitrary level in a world of widespread protectionism the charts show strong evidence that in the case of butter and sugar farmers in all three parts of the world do not face the competitive threat of a world price. The divergence between the world price for cereals and maintained prices in both the US and EC is less marked than in the case of butter and sugar.

2. For all three commodities Japan's protectionism contrasts strongly with that in the US and EC. Also apart from the brief period of 1985–86 in the case of sugar the degree of protectionism has grown in contrast with that in either the US or EC. The degree of divergence between the world price and the maintained price for sugar in Japan has been notably high.

Chapter 9

1. See graph below. The equilibrium exchange rate is £1=$1.50.

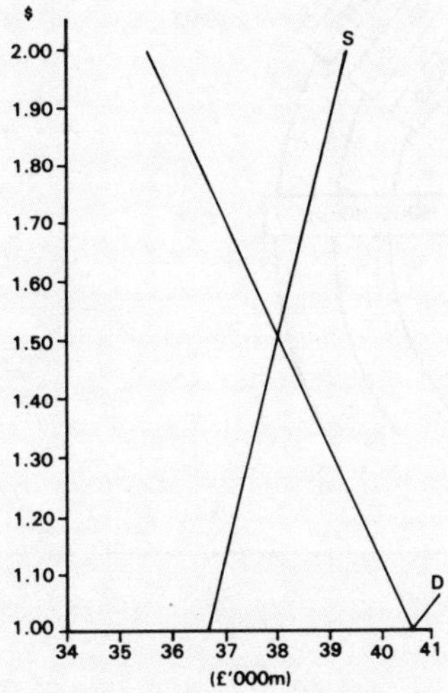

(a) The new rate will now be $1.565 as the supply of £ curve shifts to the left.

(b) Demand for sterling rises by £1000m. The new rate is £1=$1.635.

(c) As in (b).

(d) New exchange rate is $1.435.

Chapter 10

1. When the external costs are added to the supply curve the total (private plus public) costs of production are above the private supply schedule. Consequently an efficient allocation of resources would see reduced quantity to Q_2 and price raised to P_2.

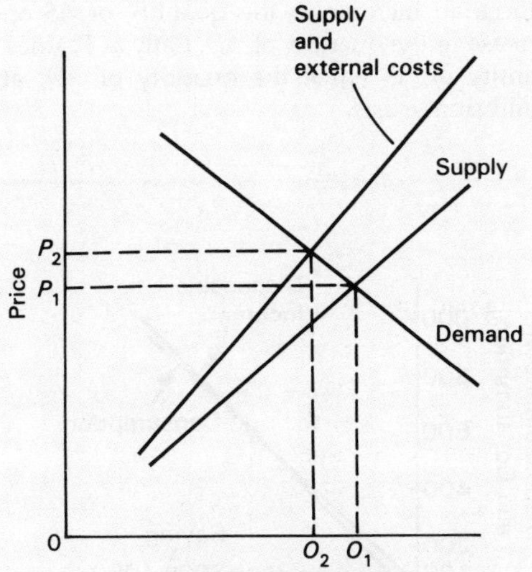

2. (a) B.

(b) £25m.

(c) In consecutive order: toll gate money, road building cost, reduced travelling time, noise and air pollution. (These are just examples – other possibilities exist in each case for question 2c.)

Chapter 12

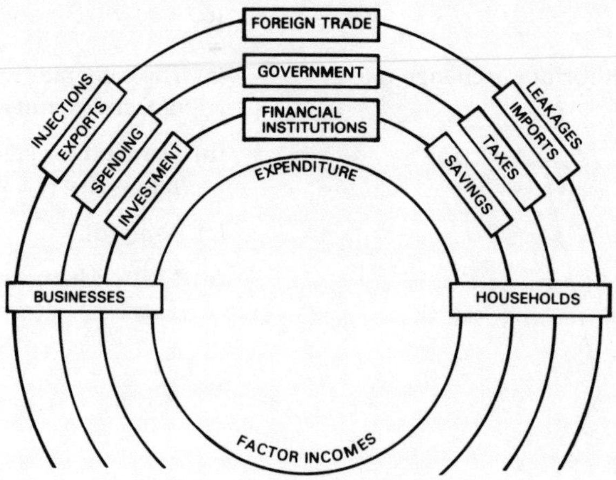

Chapter 13

i GDP (at Market Prices) = C + *I* + *G* + *NX (Net Exports)*

ii GDP (at Factor Cost) = C + *I* + *G* + *NX* – *Indirect Taxes* + *Subsidies*

iii GNP = GDP + Net Property Income from abroad

iv NNP = GNP – Capital Consumption

Chapter 14

1. At P_1 the quantity of *AS* exceeds the quantity of *AD*; therefore, a surplus of real national income (output) exists. At that price level, suppliers are willing to produce more than buyers want to purchase; in this surplus situation, producers find their stocks rising involuntarily and they find it profitable to reduce prices and output. At P_2 the quantity of *AD* exceeds the quantity of *AS* and a shortage exists. At that price level, buyers want more than producers are willing to produce, and buyers, competing for goods and services, will bid the price level upwards. A higher price level induces an increase in the quantity of *AS* and a decrease in the quantity of *AD*. Only at P_e does the quantity of *AS* equal the quantity of *AD*; at P_e equilibrium exists.

Chapter 15

1.

Disposable income	*Consumption*	*Saving*
£500	*£510*	–£10
600	*600*	0
700	*690*	10
800	*780*	20
900	*870*	30
1000	*960*	40

(a) See graph.

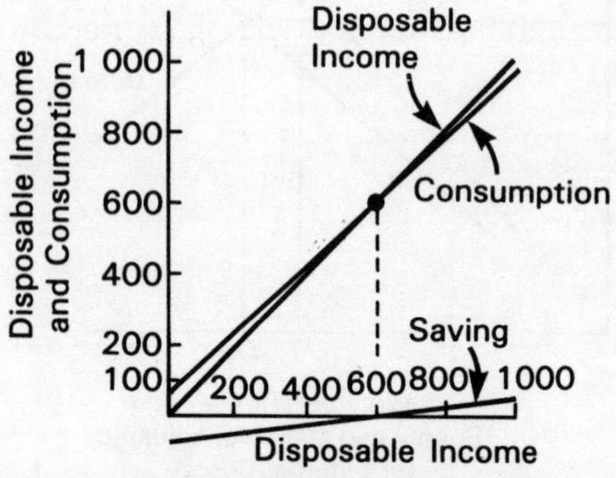

Graph of Disposable Income Consumption and Saving

(b) The marginal propensity to consume is 0.9; the marginal propensity to save is 0.1.

(c)

Disposable income	*Average propensity to consume*	*Average propensity to save*
£500	1.0200	−0.0200
600	1.0000	0
700	0.9857	0.0142
800	0.9750	0.0250
900	0.9667	0.0333
1000	0.9600	0.0400

2. (a) 80 ÷ 100 = 0.8; 155 ÷ 200 = 0.775; (b) it falls; (c) (80 − 5) ÷ (100 − 0) = 0.75; (155 − 80) ÷ (200 − 100) = 75 ÷ 100 = 0.75; (d) remains constant; (e) the APC is always falling and approaches the MPC, or 0.75; (f) $C = 5 + 0.75Y$.

3. (a) 80 ÷ 100 = 0.8; 160 ÷ 200 = 0.8; (b) remains constant at 0.8; (c) (80−0) ÷ (100 − 0) = 0.8; (160 − 80) ÷ (200 − 100) = 0.8; (d) remains constant at 0.8 (e) $C = 0 + 0.8Y$; (f) there is no autonomous element in consumption, i.e. no dis-saving at low levels of income.

Chapter 16

1.

National income	*Consumption expenditure*	*Saving*	*Investment*
£1000	£1100	−100	£100
2000	2000	0	100
3000	2900	100	100
4000	3800	200	100
5000	4700	300	100
6000	5600	400	100

APC	*APS*	*MPC*	*MPS*
1.1	−0.1	0.9	0.1
1.0	0	0.9	0.1
0.967	0.033	0.9	0.1
0.950	0.050	0.9	0.1
0.940	0.060	0.9	0.1
0.933	0.067	0.9	0.1

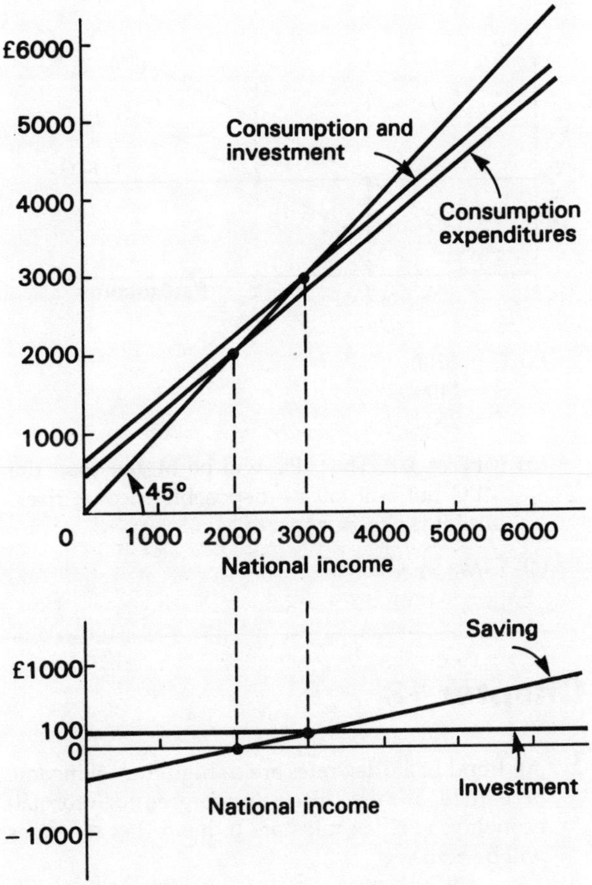

(a) See graph.

(b) See graph.

(c) The value of the multiplier is 10.

(d) Equilibrium income will rise by £1000.

(e) Equilibrium income will again rise by £1000 to £4000.

2. (a) 2, 4, 10, infinity: an increase in aggregate demand would lead to an infinite expansion in income; (b) it rises; (c) 0 to infinity.

3. Aggregate supply ≡ $Y = C + I$ ≡ *aggregate demand*

$$Y = (30 + \tfrac{3}{4}Y) + 25$$
$$Y = 55 + \tfrac{3}{4}Y$$
$$\tfrac{1}{4}Y = 55$$
$$Y = £220.$$

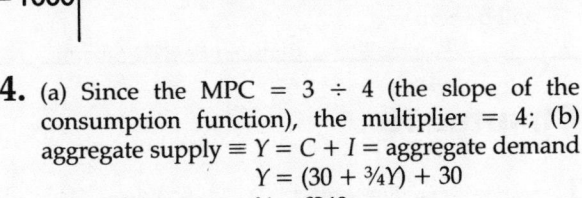

4. (a) Since the MPC = 3 ÷ 4 (the slope of the consumption function), the multiplier = 4; (b) aggregate supply ≡ $Y = C + I$ ≡ aggregate demand

$$Y = (30 + \tfrac{3}{4}Y) + 30$$
$$Y = £240.$$

5. Aggregate supply ≡ $Y = C + I$ in equilibrium; therefore, $Y = (35 + \tfrac{3}{4}Y) + 25$

$$Y = 240.$$

Chapter 17

1.

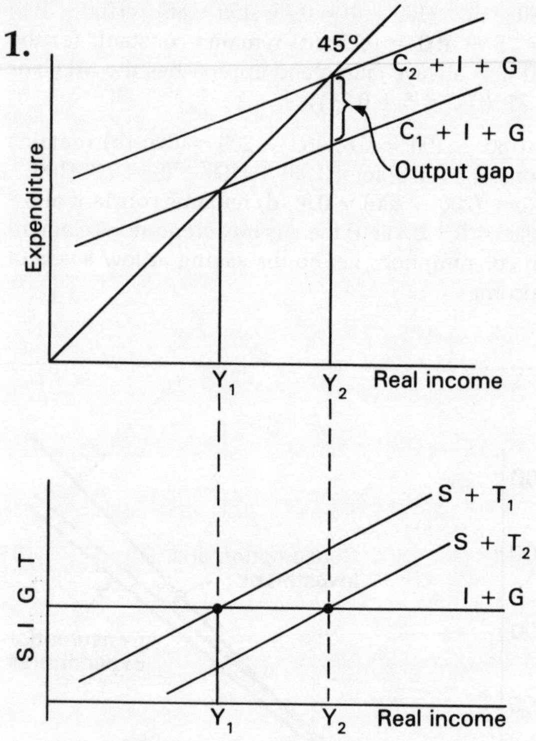

2.

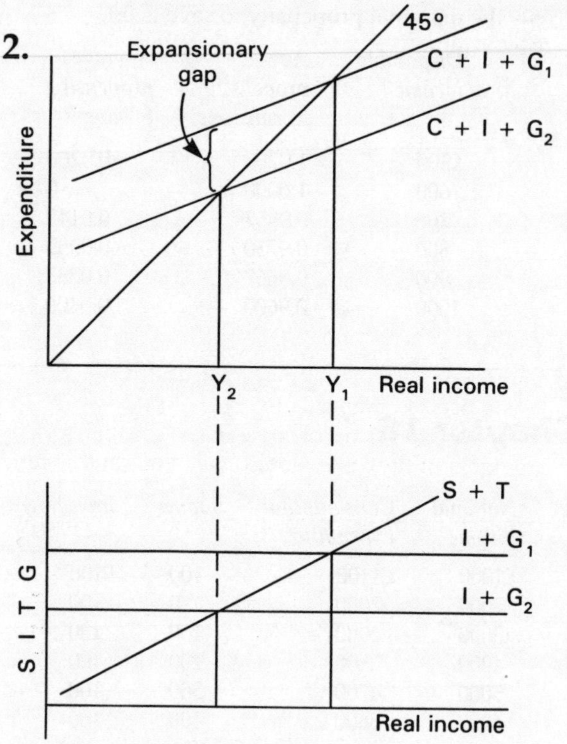

3. (a) C = 6100
S = 1400
T = 2500

(b) MPC = 0.8. The APC will be higher than the MPC but will fall as disposable income rises, until it is almost equal to MPC.

(c) *Y* falls by £1000m.

(d) Budget deficit = £250m.

(e) This means raising G by an amount equivalent to the fall in I. However it is unlikely that the consumption function will remain unchanged, if the benefits are paid mainly to people with relatively low incomes.

Chapter 18

1. (a) *F* and *E*; at *F* tax rates are so high that all income is earned in the black (underground/informal) economy; at *E* tax rates are 0, hence tax revenues will be zero.

(b) *A* and *B*; they both generate the same amount of tax revenue.

Chapter 19

1.

Liabilities	*Assets*
(a) demand deposits	(b) notes and coin
(c) time deposits	(d) deposits with the Bank of England
(h) borrowing from other banks	(e) advances to customers
	(f) holdings of bonds
	(g) buildings and fixtures

Chapter 20

Introductory Exercises

1. Total utility is maximized when buying three pints of beer and four sandwiches.
Note the

$$\frac{\text{marginal utility of beer}}{\text{price of beer}} = \frac{\text{Marginal utility of sandwiches}}{\text{price of sandwiches}}$$

2. For you, the marginal utility of the fifth pound of oranges is equal to the marginal utility of the third ear of corn. Apparently, your sister's tastes differ from yours – for her, the marginal utilities are not equal. For her, corn's marginal utility is too low, while that of oranges is too high – that is why she wants you to get rid of some of the corn (raising its marginal utility). She would have you do this until marginal utilities, for her, were equal. If you follow her suggestions, you will end up with a market basket which maximizes *her* utility subject to the constraint of *your* income. Is it any wonder that shopping from someone else's list is a frustrating task?

3. The statement is correct because of the law of diminishing marginal utility. As more is consumed, the additional unit leads to a smaller increase in total utility than the previous unit did. Therefore, in order to increase marginal utility, consumption must be decreased.

4. 100; 200; 50; divide marginal ability by price per unit.

5. (a) Group Demand Schedule

Price per hamburger	*Quantity demanded per unit of time*
£2.00	2
1.50	4
1.00	6
.50	8

(b) See graph.

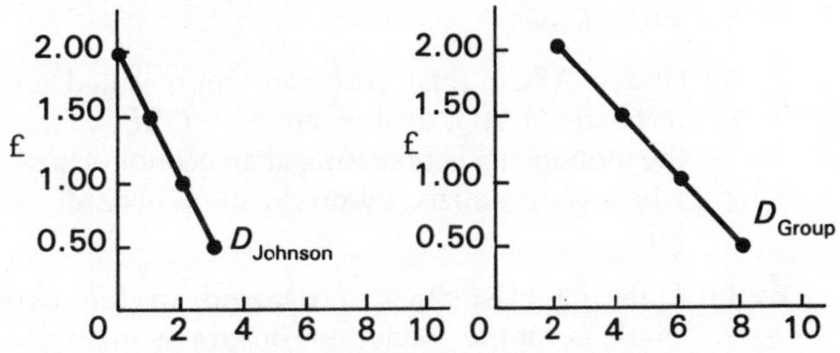

Mr Johnson's demand for hamburgers | **Group demand for hamburgers**

(c) They might have different incomes, tastes for hamburgers (marginal utility schedules), and wealth.

Chapter 21

Output	*Total cost*	*Marginal cost*	*Average total cost*	*Average fixed cost*	*Average variable cost*	*Total variable cost*
		8				
2	114		57	27	30	60
		28				
3	142		47.3	18	29.3	88
		47.2				
4	189.2		47.3	13.5	33.8	135.2
		68.8				
5	258		51.6	10.8	40.8	204
		100				
6	358		59.7	9	50.7	304

Chapter 23

1. (a) The rectangle that shows total costs under ATC_1 is *OWCQ*. Total revenue is shown by *OXBQ*. This monopolist is in an economic profit situation. MC = MR is the output at which profit – the difference between total cost and total revenue – is maximized.

(b) With ATC_2, the rectangle showing total costs is *OXBQ*. The same rectangle, *OXBQ*, gives total revenue. This monopolist is breaking even. MC = MR shows the only quantity that does not cause losses.

(c) Under ATC_3, total costs are represented by rectangle *OYAQ*, total revenue by *OXBQ*. Here the monopolist is operating at an economic loss, which is minimized by producing where MC = MR.

2. (a) Differing elasticities of demand in the two markets, for the goods and consumers unable to buy the goods in both markets.

(b) (i) See graphs
(ii) Market A Output = 45 units
Market B Output = 36 units
(iii) Market A Price = £6.50
Market B Price = £3.70

(c) The average revenue curve is downward-sloping and the accompanying marginal revenue (MR) curve slopes down more steeply, intersecting the horizontal axis at 55 units. The positive section of the MR curve relates to that part of the demand curve where price elasticity of demand is greater than one – elastic – while that relating to the negative section of the MR curve relates to the inelastic portion of the demand curve. Where MR is zero then the price elasticity is unitary.

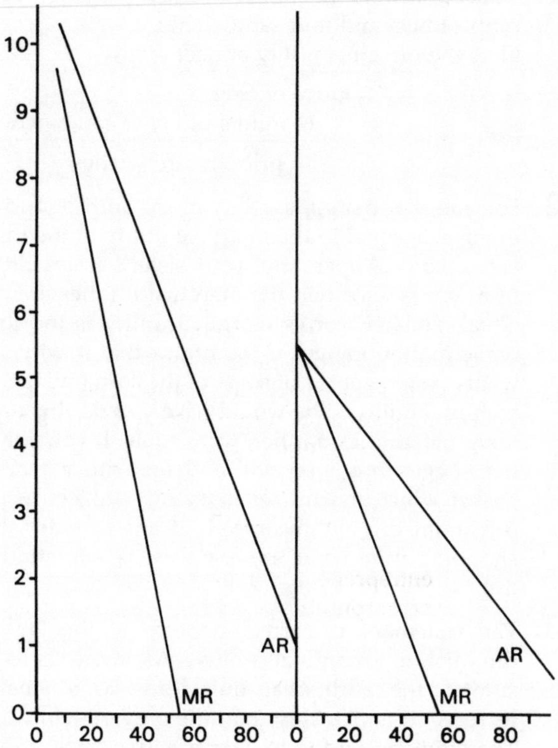

(d) Price in Market A falls from £6.50 to £6.00. Quantity demand rises from 45 to 50 units. If the arc elasticity calculation is used this means

$$\frac{5}{47.5} \div \frac{0.50}{6.25} = 1.3$$

(e) Since the MC curve is unaffected by the change in a fixed cost then the monopolist will not adjust the price charged.

Chapter 24

1. (a) Costs rise significantly – 26% if a cement plant is operated at one-third capacity as compared with the most efficient one. In the case of steel the cost disadvantage of a sub-optimum plant is less marked – 11% as compared with 26%. Scale economies are virtually non-existent in the shoe industry and thus no competitive disadvantage arises for small scale producers in this industry.

(b) Whereas in the case of cement scale economies are apparent but less obviously so in the case of the steel industry, they are not significant in the shoe industry. Hence one would expect fewer firms in the cement industry than in the case of shoes. One would expect few high cost cement plants to be able to compete with lower cost plants unless transport conditions give protection or local monopoly conditions prevail. Easy entry conditions in the case of shoes suggest that profitability is likely to be below that earned by cement producers.

(c) The number of MES plants that would satisfy the UK market are roughly as follows:

Steel	7
Glass bottles	11
Refrigerators	2
Ball bearings	22

There is no consistent relationship with the situation in the USA. The impact of distribution costs varying within the ten industries depicted partly explains this. The data points to costs per unit declining slowly as the output of refrigerators increases. This industry is interesting since long run average costs are falling but sub-optimum sized plants do not face a severe handicap, given the modest higher cost position they face.

(d) Petroleum – 9 efficient plants could satisfy the market; 10 in the case of paints; 4 in cigarettes, and 167 in shoes. Thus, in three cases there is some suggestion that an oligopolistic market will prevail.

However, there is little penalty for the sub-optimal plant in terms of costs and thus the argument that scale economies are highly important in these cases simply does not get empirical support. Thus, a sceptical standpoint for mergers is not an unreasonable one for the government to pursue.

2. (a) (i) The statement is one that is explained in detail on p336 in Chapter 22. The principle is that to achieve maximum profitability an entrepreneur will not produce an extra unit of output if the addition to total cost is greater than the addition to total revenue.

(ii) It is not easy in the real world to determine the profit maximizing point of output. Data on both the cost and revenue sides may not permit a precise determination of the profit maximizing price to be calculated. Furthermore both considerations of taking a longer term view of pricing and customer reaction may disincline a producer from attempting to secure the maximum possible level of profits in the short term. A 'cost-plus' pricing system is a flexible solution to the problem.

(iii) The traditional theory points to one outcome and can serve as a model to contrast with alternative outcomes. The contrast between price and output determination in the perfectly competitive model and other market situations provides the economist with a view on the problem of efficient resource allocation in the real world.

(b) Non-price competition avoids the 'open' and risky alternative of using price as the key marketing variable. In a price war no firm can expect to be comfortable about its long term prospects. Advertising, sales promotion and effective marketing can not only help boost market share but allow demand for a firm's goods to become less price sensitive. Thus a new demand curve arising from advertising, as in Figure 24.1, may also rotate clockwise and provide a firm with a greater number of customers committed to the product's characteristics rather than its price.

Chapter 25

1.

Quantity of Labour	*Total product per week*	*MPP*	*MRP*
1	250	250	£500
2	450	200	400
3	600	150	300
4	700	100	200
5	750	50	100
6	750	0	0

(a) Demand for schedule for labour:

Weekly wage	*Labourers demanded per week*
£500	1
400	2
300	3
200	4
100	5

(b) If five workers were hired, the firm would be willing to pay no more than £100 for each one.

(c) At £200 per week, four labourers would be hired.

2.

Quantity of capital (machine weeks)	*Marginal product of capital (units/week)*	*MRP (£/week)*
0		
	£25	£250
1		
	20	200
2		
	15	150
3		
	10	100
4		
	5	50
5		

The firm will use 4 units of capital if the price is £90 per machine week. At £300 per machine week the firm will cease to operate: it cannot cover fixed costs at any level of output.

3. (a) 15 million man-hours per unit of time; (b) 10 million per unit of time; (c) buyers can get all the labour they want at W_1; labourers cannot sell all they want to sell at W_1; (d) since a surplus of labour exists, the unemployed will offer to work for less and industry wage rates will fall toward W_e.

4. (a) 11 million man-hours per unit of time; (b) 17 million man-hours per unit of time; (c) sellers of labour are working as much as they care to at W_2, but buyers of labour cannot get all they want at that rate; (d) since a shortage of labourers exists, buyers of labour will compete for labour and drive wage rates up towards W_e; (e) W_e, since neither a surplus nor a shortage exists at that wage rate.

5. We already know that any payment above that which is required to keep a resource in its current use is an economic rent. It must follow, then, that there is some economic rent going to the superstars if they are receiving more than their next best opportunity would provide. To make the argument in this question, it is necessary to draw on the distinction between short-run and long-run supply and demand. Human beings are not eternally durable. They grow old and step aside for more popular and more productive younger talent. It is possible that younger talent in the entertainment field is not attracted by 'scale' wages that are paid to the majority who never reach stardom. Rather it is the *chance* of making the astronomical salary that draws great talent. Without this possibility, potential actors and athletes would seek other employment. Even as they continue to work at mediocre scale wages, young performers may be deriving non-money income because they are building and investing in their own talent and they are buying the opportunity to be available when stardom calls. Thus, although the high salaries may be more than is necessary to keep current talent performing (their short-run supply curve is inelastic), such prizes may be needed to attract future talent (their long-run supply curve is elastic).

Chapter 26

1. The statement is false. Although there may be a substantial portion of rent in the revenues from these museums, we would have to assume that the museums are absolutely costless to keep in their current use in order to make the statement that *all* revenues are economic rent. The most obvious expenses of keeping the museums operating are the costs of maintenance: cleaning, lighting, and other overhead costs. But these may be minor compared to the opportunity cost involved in keeping the museum *as a museum*. The buildings might make ideal government office buildings. They may be on land that would be extremely valuable if sold on the real estate market. If there are any such alternative uses, the value of these uses must be subtracted from the current revenues in order to arrive at the true level of pure economic rent. Forgoing these alternative opportunities is as much a cost of operating the museum as is the monthly utility bill.

Chapter 29

1. Two pricing policies – price discrimination and predatory pricing were both discussed in Chapter 23. One practice relating to distribution – exclusive dealing – was also discussed with reference to the British plasterboard market.

2. (a) (i) The presence of alternatives in a market place such that a customer has the option of seeking the lowest possible price from a supplier freely competing with rivals.

   (ii) The situation where all suppliers agree the terms on which they will charge customers.

   (b) Reputation for service in the eyes of customers. The time of year may prompt attention to seasonal discounts from a standard fare.

   (c) The prospect of a keen demand for holiday travel ensures full loads can be carried and thus average costs per passenger are reduced as compared with planes not carrying a full complement of passengers.

   (d) The fear of being under-cut is not a worry so high fares can be charged without this concern being present. Profits on the European routes can help subsidize other less profitable routes.

   (e) Businessmen need regular services between European cities to conduct their business. The cost of travel is met by their companies and they are able to bear the cost incurred.

   (f) Keen competition might be expected to reduce fares and also prompt airlines to improve their marketing to attract customers. On the other hand competition may in due course lead to withdrawal of services if an airline judges operating a service is no longer very attractive in terms of profitability.

Chapter 30

1. (a) £10000

(b) Value falls to £5000 then rises to £20000. The rate of return of the machine is £1000, i.e. the same as the interest payable on the bond. So both would have the same value at any market rate of interest.

2. $V = \frac{P \times Q}{M} = 5.16.$

Chapter 34

1. The costs that are associated with economic growth, e.g. noise and air pollution, congestion and a decline in the 'quality of life' (the stresses and strains of a society where the pace of life is hectic).

2. The benefits of economic growth, e.g. an increased standard of living in material terms and also increased leisure time. Minimization of the problem of labour unemployment.

3. A resource becoming relatively scarce is a resource for which the supply curve is shifting back, or to the left (see graph). On the supply and demand diagram, such a shift is represented by the movement of supply from S_1 to S_2 to S_3. The amount consumed can still increase if the demand is increasing more rapidly than supply is decreasing. The shifts between curves D_1, D_2, D_3 are greater than the corresponding shifts in supply. Thus the quantity produced has increased from Q_1 to Q_3 and the market price has risen more than proportionately.

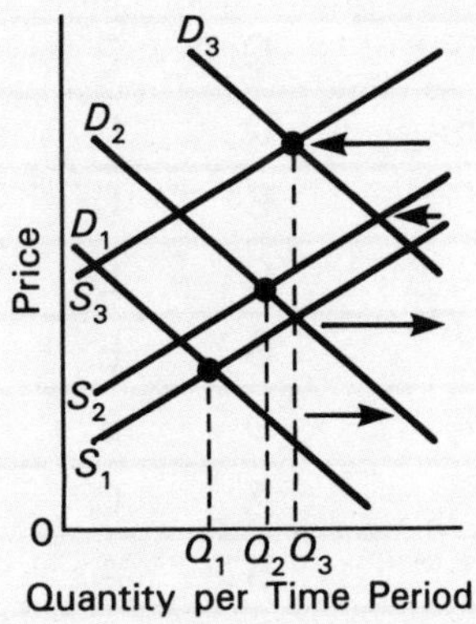

Changing Supply and Demand for an Increasingly Scarce Resource

Chapter 35

1. (a) The relationship is not a wholly clear-cut positive one. Life expectancy in China is high relative to other low income economies.

(b) Again China is an exception to the relationship between GNP and population per physician in the low income group. The differing population sizes in the middle income countries partly explains the inconsistent pattern amongst these six countries.

(c) Again China is the notable exception to the predictable inverse relationship.

2. One country – Chad. Ethiopia also barely achieved any economic growth in the period.

3. Improved medical facilities such that the average physician now served fewer patients in 1984 as compared with 1965.

4. Mothers and babies typically enjoyed better medical care and nutrition in 1987 as compared with 1965.

5. Such indicators as calorie supply per capita, energy consumption per head, the number of motor vehicles per 1000 population, and the number of telephones per 1000 population could be used as measures of the state of development. All of these would be examples where a direct relationship with the level of GNP exist. The number of persons per 1000 population unable to read and write and average family size are two indicators that would have an inverse relationship with the level of GNP.

Answers to Multiple Choice Questions

The answers that have been provided for multiple choice questions set by examination Boards are entirely the responsibility of the authors of this book; answers have been neither provided nor approved by the Boards concerned.

Chapter	Question number 1	2	3	4	5	6	7	8	9	10	11
1	C	B	A	B	B	C	B				
2	B	C	D	D							
3	B	A	D	D	C	A					
4	C	B	B	A							
5	D	C	E	A	E	C					
6	B	C	B	B	C						
7	C	E	D	B	D	C					
8	B	E	B	B	B	E	B				
9	D	B	B	B	D	C					
10	A	C	B	A	B	C	C	A	D		
11	B	A	D	D	E	E					
12	E	E	B	C	A						
13	B	B	A	A	D	E					
14	C	B									
15	B	C	A	C	E						
16	D	A	E	A	C	B	A	D			
17	D	E	B	B	B	A	B				
18	D	C	B	D	D	C					
19	D	B	C	C	D	C	A				
20	C	C	B	E	E	D	A	C	A	D	B
21	D	A	E	B	D	D	A	B			
22	E	A	B	A	C	B					
23	E	E	B	C							
24	D	C	C	C	B						
25	B	D	D	B	C	D					
26	D	D	D								
27	D	A	D	B							
28	C	A	A	C	D						
30	E	C	A	B	D	B					
31	C	D	B	B	D	C					
32	E	D	B	A							
33	C	A	A	B	D						
34	C	A	A	B	A	D					

Index

Index entries are arranged alphabetically in letter-by-letter order (spaces between words being ignored); 'accelerationist view' therefore comes before 'acceleration principle'.

Numbers are arranged as though spelled out, '45-degree line' being treated as 'forty-five . . .'.

References to dictionary pages bear the suffix D, and those to footnotes are indicated by n.